IIT-JEE
SOLVED PAPERS
(JEE Main & Advanced)

Mathematics

2020-2002

✓ *Includes Latest Question Papers with Solutions*

Contents

Edition : 2021

Price : ₹549

ISBN : 978-93-90278-57-2

OSWAL PUBLISHERS

Head Office : 1/12, Sahitya Kunj, M.G. Road Agra-282 002
Phone : (0562) 2527771-4, 7534077222
E-mail : contact@oswalpublishers.com, sales@oswalpublishers.com
Website : www.oswalpublishers.com

The cover of this book has been designed using resources from Freepik.com

Preface

We feel immense pleasure in introducing the first edition of IIT JEE Solved Papers for JEE aspirants. This edition strictly adheres to the latest syllabus prescribed by the National Testing Agency (NTA), New Delhi.

The book has been carefully designed so as to be useful for JEE aspirants. The solutions have been fully explained so that each reader can acquire the relevant knowledge as per their requirements.

Special features of the book include:

- a number of solved question papers, conducted in previous years, are incorporated for practice to enhance the ability of a student to understand the concept clearly and develop the skills to answer accurately.

- last 19 years' (Main & Advanced) questions, i.e. from 2020-2002.

- questions arranged 'Chapter-wise' for students to prepare the section that requires more attention.

- simple and lucid question-solving method for the students to prepare perfectly.

All endeavors have been made to make this book student-friendly by simplifying the graphs and tables.

In spite of our best efforts, the possibilities of some errors of omission cannot be ruled out. Constructive suggestions will be appreciated and thankfully acknowledged.

–Publisher

HOW TO HANDLE YOUR ENTRANCES AND BOARDS LIKE A PRO

Entrance tests and board exams have always been a worrisome affair for the students, for they have always posed a tough task before them. Getting your preparation right is important as these tests can be a Launchpad for your career.

It becomes difficult to balance between the highly competitive entrance exams like NEET, IIT-JEE, and board exams. This raises the performance pressure and anxiety among students. Hence, it is essential to have a proper plan and execute it effectively.

Valuable tips to prepare well for the entrances and boards:

» **Understanding the basic concepts** : You should always follow the right CBSE solutions/ICSE Solution books to prepare for 10th or 12th board exams as they can help you to identify these areas easily.

» **Optimising your Preparation** : IIT-JEE is a highly competitive entrance exam which is taken to get admissions into specialisations like engineering in the IIT colleges of India. Oswal textbooks and question banks for IIT-JEE completely corresponds with the prescribed NCERT syllabus. You can use these as a reference and prepare well for both the entrance test as well as the main board exams.

» **Simplifying and Prioritising** : Always utilise your time efficiently as these exams are very important for your career. By referring to IIT-JEE books and other subject books, you can prioritise the topics that are important. This will help you prepare in a hassle-free manner.

» **Studying and Revising** : Revising the same chapters can be monotonous but having a quick glance at Oswal IIT-JEE exam books will surely boost your preparation. Divide the syllabus in an organised manner and finish the complete course at a normal pace, leaving adequate time to revise as well.

» **Mock Analysis** : In order to use time optimally, try to do the mock analysis for self-assessment regarding your preparation. Practising mock tests saves your time and efforts from being wasted on chapters that don't need too much attention.

» **Wise Planning and Taking a Break** : Preparing for both entrance and board exams can be quite frustrating at times. So, don't forget to set aside some time for relaxation by taking small breaks, a short nap, having your favourite snack, meditating or going for a walk.

Sets, Relations and Functions

⌕ QUESTIONS

1. If the function $f(x)=\begin{cases} k_1(x-\pi)^2 -1, & x \le \pi \\ k_2 \cos x, & x > \pi \end{cases}$ is twice differentiable, then the ordered pair (k_1, k_2) is equal to sets : **[2020, Main]**

(a) $\left(\dfrac{1}{2}, 1\right)$　　　　(b) $(1, 1)$

(c) $\left(\dfrac{1}{2}, -1\right)$　　　　(d) $(1, 0)$

2. The negation of the Boolean expression $x \leftrightarrow \sim y$ is equivalent to : **[2020, Main]**

(a) $(\sim x \wedge y) \vee (\sim x \wedge \sim y)$　　(b) $(x \wedge \sim y) \vee (\sim x \wedge y)$

(c) $(x \wedge y) \vee (\sim x \wedge \sim y)$　　(d) $(x \wedge y) \wedge (\sim x \vee \sim y)$

3. A survey shows that 73% of the persons working in an office like coffee, whereas 65% like tea. If x denotes the percentage of them, who like both coffee and tea,then x cannot be : **[2020, Main]**

(a) 63　　　　(b) 38

(c) 54　　　　(d) 36

4. If the minimum and the maximum values of the function $f: \left[\dfrac{\pi}{4}, \dfrac{\pi}{2}\right] \to R$, defined by :

$$f(\theta) = \begin{vmatrix} -\sin^2 \theta & -1-\sin^2 \theta & 1 \\ -\cos^2 \theta & -1-\cos^2 \theta & 1 \\ 12 & 10 & -2 \end{vmatrix}$$

are m and M respectively, then the ordered pair (m, M) is equal to : **[2020, Main]**

(a) $(0, 4)$　　　　(b) $(-4, 4)$

(c) $(0, 2\sqrt{2})$　　　　(d) $(-4, 0)$

5. Let $f(x) = x \cdot \left[\dfrac{x}{2}\right]$, for $-10 < x < 10$, where $[t]$ denotes the greatest integer function. Then the number of points of discontinuity of f is equal to .... **[2020, Main]**

6. The negation of the Boolean expression $p \vee (\sim p \wedge q)$ is equivalent to : **[2020, Main]**

(a) $\sim p \vee \sim q$　　　　(b) $\sim p \vee q$

(c) $\sim p \wedge \sim q$　　　　(d) $p \wedge \sim q$

7. The position of a moving car at time t is given by $f(t) = at^2 + bt + c, t > 0$, where a, b and c are real numbers greater than 1. Then the average speed of the car over the time interval $[t_1, t_2]$ is attained at the point : **[2020, Main]**

(a) $a(t_2 - t_1) + b$　　　　(b) $(t_2 - t_1)/2$

(c) $2a(t_1 + t_2) + b$　　　　(d) $(t_1 + t_2)/2$

8. Set A has m elements and Set B has n elements. If the total number of subsets of A is 112 more than the total number of subsets of B, then the value of $m.n$ is .... **[2020, Main]**

9. Let $f: R \to R$ be defined as

$$f(x) = \begin{cases} x^5 \sin\left(\dfrac{1}{x}\right) + 5x^2, & x < 0 \\ 0, & x = 0 \\ x^5 \cos\left(\dfrac{1}{x}\right) + \lambda x^2, & x > 0 \end{cases}$$

The value of λ for which $f''(0)$ exists is .... **[2020, Main]**

10. The set of all real values of λ for which the function $f(x) = (1 - \cos^2 x).(\lambda + \sin x), x \in \left(-\dfrac{\pi}{2}, \dfrac{\pi}{2}\right)$, has exactly one maxima and exactly one minima is : **[2020, Main]**

(a) $\left(-\dfrac{1}{2}, \dfrac{1}{2}\right) - \{0\}$　　(b) $\left(-\dfrac{1}{2}, \dfrac{1}{2}\right)$

(c) $\left(-\dfrac{3}{2}, \dfrac{3}{2}\right)$　　(d) $\left(-\dfrac{3}{2}, \dfrac{3}{2}\right) - \{0\}$

11. Consider the statement : "For an integer n, if $n^3 - 1$ is even, then n is odd." The contrapositive statement of this statement is : **[2020, Main]**

(a) For an integer n, if $n^3 - 1$ is not even, then n is not odd

(b) For an integer n, if n is even, then $n^3 - 1$ is odd

(c) For an integer n, if n is odd, then $n^3 - 1$ is even

(d) For an integer n, if n is even, then $n^3 - 1$ is even

12. For a suitably chosen real constant a, let a function, $f : R - \{- a\} \to R$ be defined by $f(x) = \dfrac{a - x}{a + x}$. Further suppose that for any real number $x \neq - a$ and $f(x) \neq - a$, $(fof)(x) = x$. Then $f\left(-\dfrac{1}{2}\right)$ is equal to : **[2020, Main]**

(a) $\dfrac{1}{3}$

(b) 3

(c) $- 3$

(d) $-\dfrac{1}{3}$

13. Given the following two statements :

$(S_1) : (q \vee p) \to (p \leftrightarrow \sim q)$ is a tautology.

$(S_2) : \sim q \wedge (\sim p \leftrightarrow q)$ is a fallacy.

Then : **[2020, Main]**

(a) only (S_1) is correct

(b) both (S_1) and (S_2) are correct

(c) both (S_1) and (S_2) are not correct

(d) only (S_2) is correct

14. A survey shows that 63% of the people in a city read newspaper A whereas 76% read newspaper B. If $x\%$ of the people read both the newspapers, then a possible value of x can be : **[2020, Main]**

(a) 65

(b) 37

(c) 29

(d) 55

15. Let f be a twice differentiable funcion on $(1, 6)$. If $f(2) = 8$, $f'(2) = 5$, $f'(x) \geq 1$ and $f''(x) \geq 4$, for all $x \in (1, 6)$, then : **[2020, Main]**

(a) $f(5) \leq 10$

(b) $f'(5) + f''(5) \leq 20$

(c) $f(5) + f'(5) \geq 28$

(d) $f(5) + f(5) \leq 26$

16. Let $\overset{50}{\underset{i=1}{\cup}} X_i = \overset{n}{\underset{i=1}{\cup}} Y_i = T$, where each X_i contains 10 elements and each Y_i contains 5 elements. If each element of the set T is an element of exactly 20 of sets X_i's and exactly 6 of sets Y_i's, then n is equal to : **[2020, Main]**

(a) 45

(b) 15

(c) 50

(d) 30

17. Consider the two sets :

$A = \{m \in R :$ both the roots of $x^2 - (m + 1)x + m + 4 = 0$ are real$\}$ and $B = [- 3, 5)$.

Which of the following is not true ? **[2020, Main]**

(a) $A - B = \{- \infty, - 3) \cup (5, \infty)$

(b) $A \cap B = \{- 3\}$

(c) $B - A = (- 3, 5)$

(d) $A \cup B = R$

18. The function, $f(x) = (3x - 7)x^{2/3}$, $x \in R$, is increasing for all x lying in : **[2020, Main]**

(a) $(- \infty, 0) \cup \left(\dfrac{3}{7}, \infty\right)$

(b) $(- \infty, 0) \cup \left(\dfrac{14}{15}, \infty\right)$

(c) $\left(- \infty, \dfrac{14}{15}\right)$

(d) $\left(- \infty, - \dfrac{14}{15}\right) \cup (0, \infty)$

19. The proposition $p \to (p \wedge \sim q)$ is equivalent to : **[2020, Main]**

(a) $(\sim p) \vee q$

(b) q

(c) $(\sim p) \wedge q$

(d) $(\sim p) \vee (\sim q)$

20. The statement $[p \to (q \to p)] \to [p \to (p \vee q)]$ is : **[2020, Main]**

(a) a contradiction

(b) equivalent to $(p \wedge q) \vee (\sim q)$

(c) a tautology

(d) equivalent to $(p \vee q) \wedge (\sim p)$

21. Let $A = \{a, b, c\}$ and $B = \{1, 2, 3, 4\}$. Then the number of elements in the set $C = \{f : A \to B \mid 2 \in f(A)$ and f is not one-one is $\dots\dots\dots\dots$. **[2020, Main]**

22. If the function $f : R \to R$ is defined by $f(x) = \mid x \mid (x - \sin x)$, then which of the following statement is TRUE ? **[2020, Advanced]**

(a) f is one-one, but NOT onto

(b) f is onto, but NOT one-one

(c) f is BOTH one-one and onto

(d) f is NEITHER one-one NOR onto

23. Consider all rectangles lying in the region

$$\left\{(x, y) \in R \times R : 0 \leq x \leq \dfrac{\pi}{2} \text{ and } 0 \leq y \leq 2 \sin (2x)\right\}$$

and having one side on the x-axis. The area of the rectangle which has the maximum perimeter among all such rectangles is : **[2020, Advanced]**

(a) $\dfrac{3\pi}{2}$

(b) π

(c) $\dfrac{\pi}{2\sqrt{3}}$

(d) $\dfrac{\pi\sqrt{3}}{2}$

24. Let $f : [0, 2] \to R$ be the function defined by

$$f(x) = [3 - \sin (2\pi x)] \sin \left(\pi x - \dfrac{\pi}{4}\right) - \sin \left(3\pi x + \dfrac{\pi}{4}\right)$$

If $\alpha, \beta \in [0, 2]$ are such that $\{x \in [0, 2] : f(x) \geq 0\} = [\alpha, \beta]$, then the value of $\beta - \alpha$ is $\dots\dots\dots\dots$. **[2020, Advanced]**

25. Let the functions : $(- 1, 1) \to R$ and $g : (- 1, 1) \to (- 1, 1)$ be defined by

$$f(x) = |2x - 1| + |2x + 1| \text{ and } g(x) = x - [x],$$

where $[x]$ denotes the greatest integer less than or equal to x. Let $fo : (- 1, 1) \to R$ be the comosite function defined by $(fog)(x) = f(g(x))$. Suppose c

is the number of points in the interval $(-1, 1)$ at which fog is NOT continuous and suppose d is the number of points in the interval $(-1, 1)$ at which fog is NOT differentiable. Then the value of $c + d$ is .... **[2020, Advanced]**

26. Let b be a non-zero real number. Suppose $f : R \to R$ is a differentiable function such that $(0) = 1$. If the derivative f' of f satisfies the equation

$$f'(x) = \frac{f(x)}{b^2 + x^2}$$ for all $x \in R$, then which of the

following statements is/are TRUE ?

[2020, Advanced]

(a) If $b > 0$, then f is an increasing function
(b) If $b < 0$, then f is a decreasing function
(c) $(x)\,(-x) = 1$ for all $x \in R$
(d) $(x) - f(-x)$ for all $x \in R$

27. Let the function $f : [0, 1] \to R$ be defined by $f(x) =$

$\dfrac{4^x}{4^x + 2} \cdot$ Then the value of

$$f\left(\frac{1}{40}\right) + f\left(\frac{2}{40}\right) + f\left(\frac{3}{40}\right) + \ldots + f\left(\frac{39}{40}\right) - f\left(\frac{1}{2}\right)$$

is .... **[2020, Advanced]**

28. Let $f : R \to R$ be a function which satisfies $f(x + y) = f(x) + f(y)\,\forall x, y \in R$. IF $f(l) = 2$ and $g(n) = \displaystyle\sum_{k=1}^{(n-1)} f(k)$ $n \in N$ then the value of n, for which

$g(n) = 20$, is : **[2020, Main]**

(a) 5   (b) 9

(c) 20   (d) 4

29. Let $f : (-1, \infty) \to R$ be defined by $f(0) = 1$ and

$fx) = \dfrac{1}{x}\, \log_e (1 + x)$, $x \neq 0$. Then the function f :

[2020, Main]

(a) decreases in $(-1, \infty)$
(b) decreases in $(-1, 0)$ and increases in $(0, \infty)$
(c) increases in $(-1, \infty)$
(d) increases in $(-1, 0)$ and decreases in $(0, \infty)$

30. Which of the following is a tautology ?

[2020, Main]

(a) $(\sim p) \wedge (p \vee q) \to q$
(b) $(q \to p) \vee \sim (p \to q)$
(c) $(p \to q) \wedge (q \to p)$
(d) $(\sim q) \vee (p \wedge q) \to q$

31. Let EC denote the complement of an event E. Let E_1, E_2 and E_3 be any pairwise independent events with $P(E_1) > 0$ and $P(E_1 \cap E_2 \cap E_3) = 0$. Then $P(E_2^C \cap E_3^C / E_1)$ is equal to : **[2020, Main]**

(a) $P(E_3^C) - P(E_2)$ (b) $P(E_2^C) + P(E_3)$

(c) $P(E_3^C) - P(E_2^C)$ (d) $P(E_3) - P(E_2^C)$

32. Let R_1 and R_2 be two relations defined as follows :
$$R_1 = \{(a, b) \in R^2 : a^2 + b^2 \in Q\} \text{ and}$$
$$R_2 = \{(a, b) \in R^2 : a^2 + b^2 \notin Q\},$$
Where Q is the net of all rational numbers. Then : **[2020, Main]**

(a) R_2 is transitive but R_1 is not transitive
(b) R_1 is transitive but R_2 is not transitive
(c) R_1 and R_2 are both transitive
(d) Neither R_1 nor R_2 is transitive

33. Suppose $f(x)$ is a polynomial of degree four, having critical points at $-1, 0, 1$. If $T = \{x \in R \mid f(x) = f(0)\}$, then the sum of squares of all the elements of T is : **[2020, Main]**

(a) 6   (b) 8

(c) 4   (d) 2

34. The set of all real values of λ for which the quadratic equations,
$(\lambda^2 + 1)x^2, 4\lambda x + 2 = 0$ always have exactly one root in the interval $(0, 1)$ is : **[2020, Main]**

(a) $(-3, -1)$ (b) $(1, 3]$

(c) $(0, 2)$ (d) $(2, 4]$

35. Let p, q, r be three statements such that the truth value of $(p \wedge q) \to (\sim q \vee r)$ is F. Then the truth values of p, q, r are respectively : **[2020, Main]**

(a) T, F, T   (b) F, T, F
(c) T, T, F   (d) T, T, T

36. If a function $f(x)$ defined by

$$f(x) = \begin{cases} ae^x + e^{-x}, & -1 \le x < 1 \\ cx^2, & 1 \le x \le 3 \\ ax^2 + 2cx, & 3 < x \le 4 \end{cases}$$

be continuous for some $a, b, c \in R$ and $f'(0) + f(2) = e$, then the value of a is : **[2020, Main]**

(a) $\dfrac{e}{e^2 - 3e - 13}$ (b) $\dfrac{e}{e^2 + 3e + 13}$

(c) $\dfrac{1}{e^2 - 3e + 13}$ (d) $\dfrac{e}{e^2 - 3e + 13}$

37. The contrapositive of the statement" If I reach the station in time, then I will catch the train" is :

[2020, Main]

(a) If I will catch the train, then I reach the station in time.

(b) If I do not reach the station in time, then I will not catch the train.

(c) If I will not catch the train, then I do not reach the station in time.

(d) If I do not reach the station in time, then I will catch the train.

38. If $R = \{(x, y) : x, y \in Z, x^2 + 3y^2 \leq 8\}$ is a relation on the set of integers Z, then the domain of R^{-1} is : **[2020, Main]**

(a) $\{-2, -1, 1, 2\}$ **(b)** $\{-1, 0, 1\}$

(c) $\{-2, -1, 0, 1, 2\}$ **(d)** $\{0, 1\}$

39. The domain of the function $f(x) = \sin^{-1}\left(\dfrac{|x|+5}{x^2+1}\right)$

is $(-\infty, -a] \cup [a, \infty)$. Then a is equal to : **[2020, Main]**

(a) $\dfrac{1+\sqrt{17}}{2}$ **(b)** $\dfrac{\sqrt{17}-1}{2}$

(c) $\dfrac{\sqrt{17}}{2}+1$ **(d)** $\dfrac{\sqrt{17}}{2}$

40. If $g(x) = x^2 + x - 1$ and $(gof)(x) = 4x^2 - 10x + 5$, then $f\left(\dfrac{5}{4}\right)$ is equal to : **[2020, Main]**

(a) $\dfrac{3}{2}$ **(b)** $-\dfrac{1}{2}$

(c) $-\dfrac{3}{2}$ **(d)** $\dfrac{1}{2}$

41. Let $X = \{n \in N : 1 \leq n \leq 50\}$. If $A = \{n \in X : n$ is a multiple of 2$\}$ and $B = \{n \in X : n$ is a multiple of 7$\}$. then the number of elements in the smallest subset of X containing both A and B is .... **[2020, Main]**

42. The inverse function of $f(x) = \dfrac{8^{2x} - 8^{-2x}}{8^{2x} + 8^{-2x}}$, $x \in$ $(-1, 1)$, is : **[2020, Main]**

(a) $\dfrac{1}{4}(\log_8 e)\log_e\left(\dfrac{1-x}{1+x}\right)$

(b) $\dfrac{1}{4}\log_e\left(\dfrac{1-x}{1+x}\right)$

(c) $\dfrac{1}{4}(\log_8 e)\log_e\left(\dfrac{1+x}{1-x}\right)$

(d) $\dfrac{1}{4}\log_e\left(\dfrac{1+x}{1-x}\right)$

43. Let S be the set of all functions $f : [0, 1] \to R$, which are continuous on $[0, 1]$ and differentiable on $(0, 1)$. Then for every f in S, there exists a $c \in$ $(0, 1)$, depending on f, such that **[2020, Main]**

(a) $|f(c) - f(1)| < (1 - c)|f'(c)|$

(b) $|f(c) - f(1)| < |f'(c)|$

(c) $|f(c) + f(1)| < (1 + c)\,|f'(c)|$

(d) $\dfrac{f(1) - f(c)}{1 - c} = f'(c)$

44. Let $f : (1, 3) \to R$ be a function defined by $f(x) = \dfrac{x[x]}{1+x^2}$, where $[x]$ denotes the greatest integer $\leq x$. Then the range of f is : **[2020, Main]**

(a) $\left(\dfrac{3}{5}, \dfrac{4}{5}\right)$

(b) $\left(\dfrac{2}{5}, \dfrac{3}{5}\right] \cup \left(\dfrac{3}{4}, \dfrac{4}{5}\right)$

(c) $\left(\dfrac{2}{5}, \dfrac{4}{5}\right]$

(d) $\left(\dfrac{2}{5}, \dfrac{1}{2}\right] \cup \left(\dfrac{3}{5}, \dfrac{4}{5}\right)$

45. If $A = \{x \in R : |x| < 2\}$ and $B = \{x \in R : |x - 2| \geq 3\}$; then : **[2020, Main]**

(a) $A \cup B = R - (2, 5)$ **(b)** $A \cap B = (-2, -1)$

(c) $B - A = R - (-2, 5)$ **(d)** $A - B = [-1, 2)$

46. Let S be the set of all real roots of the equation, $3^x(3^x - 1) + 2 = |3^x - 1| + |3^x - 2|$. Then S : **[2020, Main]**

(a) is an empty set.

(b) contains at least four elements.

(c) contains exactly two elements

(d) is a singleton.

47. Let f and g be differentiable functions on R such that fog is the identify function. If for some a, $b \in R$, $g'(a) = 5$ and $g(a) = b$, then $f'(b)$ is equal to : **[2020, Main]**

(a) $\dfrac{2}{5}$ **(b)** 1

(c) $\dfrac{1}{5}$ **(d)** 5

48. Let $f(x) = x^2$, $x \in R$. For any $A \subseteq R$, define $g(A) = \{x \in R : f(x) \in A\}$. If $S = [0, 4]$, then which one of the following statements is not true ? **[2019, Advanced]**

(a) $g(f(S)) \neq S$ **(b)** $f(g(S)) = S$

(c) $g(f(S)) = g(S)$ **(d)** $f(g(S)) \neq f(S)$

49. Let $f(x) = \log_e(\sin x)$, $(0 < x < \pi)$ and $g(x) = \sin^{-1}(e^{-x})$, $(x \geq 0)$. If α is positive real number such that $a = (fog)'(\alpha)$ and $b = (fog)(\alpha)$, then : **[2019, Advanced]**

(a) $a\alpha^2 + b\alpha + a = 0$ **(b)** $a\alpha^2 - b\alpha - a = 1$

(c) $a\alpha^2 - b\alpha - a = 0$ **(d)** $a\alpha^2 + b\alpha - a = -2a^2$

50. The domain of the definition of the function

$$f(x) = \frac{1}{4 - x^2} + \log_{10}(x^3 - x) \text{ is :}$$

[2019, Advanced]

(a) $(-1, 0) \cup (1, 2) \cup (3, \infty)$

(b) $(-2, -1) \cup (-1, 0) \cup (2, \infty)$

(c) $(-1, 0) \cup (1, 2) \cup (2, \infty)$

(d) $(1, 2) \cup (2\ \infty)$

51. Two newspapers A and B are published in a city. It is known that 25% of the city population reads A and 20% reads B while 8% reads both A and B. Further, 30% of those who read A but not B look into advertisements and 40% of those who read B but not A also look into advertisements, while 50% of those who read both A and B look into advertisements. Then the percentage of the population who look into advertisements is :

[2019, Advanced]

(a) 13.9   **(b)** 12.8

(c) 13   **(d)** 13.5

52. If $f(x) = \log_e\left(\dfrac{1-x}{1+x}\right), |x| < 1,$ then $f\left(\dfrac{2x}{1+x^2}\right)$ is

equal to :   **[2019, Advanced]**

(a) $2f(x)$ **(b)** $2f(x^2)$

(c) $(f(x))^2$ **(d)** $-2f(x)$

53. Let $f(x) = a^x\ (a > 0)$ be written as $f(x) = f_1(x) + f_2(x)$, where $f_1(x)$ is an even function and $f_2(x)$ is an odd function. Then $f_1(x + y) + f_1(x - y)$ equals :

[2019, Advanced]

(a) $2f_1(x) f_1(y)$ **(b)** $2f_1(x + y) f_1(x - y)$

(c) $2f_1(x) f_2(y)$ **(d)** $2f_1(x + y) f_2(x - y)$

54. For $x \in \left(0, \dfrac{3}{2}\right)$, let $f(x) = \sqrt{x}, g(x) = \tan x$ and

$h(x) = \dfrac{1 - x^2}{1 + x^2}$. If $\phi(x) = ((h \circ f) \circ g)(x)$, then $\phi\left(\dfrac{\pi}{3}\right)$

is equal to :   **[2019, Advanced]**

(a) $\tan\dfrac{\pi}{12}$ **(b)** $\tan\dfrac{11\pi}{12}$

(c) $\tan\dfrac{7\pi}{12}$ **(d)** $\tan\dfrac{5\pi}{12}$

55. Let S be the set of all $\alpha \in R$ such that the equation, $\cos 2x + \alpha \sin x = 2\alpha - 7$ has a solution. Then S is equal to :   **[2019, Advanced]**

(a) R   **(b)** $[1, 4]$

(c) $[3, 7]$ **(d)** $[2, 6]$

56. Let A, B and C be sets such that $\phi \neq A \cap B \subseteq C$. Then which of the following statement is not true ?   **[2019, Advanced]**

(a) $B \cap C \neq \phi$

(b) If $(A - B) \subseteq C$, then $A \subseteq C$

(c) $(C \cup A) \cap (C \cup B) = C$

(d) If $(A - C) \subseteq B$, then $A \subseteq B$

57. Let $f(x) = \sin(\pi \cos x)$ and $g(x) = \cos(2\pi \sin x)$ be two functions defined for $x > 0$. Define the following sets whose elements are written in the increasing order :   **[2019, Advanced]**

$X = \{x : f(x) = 0\}$, $Y = \{x : f'(x) = 0\}$,

$Z = \{x : g(x) = 0\}$, $W = \{x : g'(x) = 0\}$,

List−I contains the sets X, Y, Z and W. **List−II** contains some information regarding these sets.

List−I	List−II
(I) X	**(P)** $\supseteq \left\{\dfrac{\pi}{2}, \dfrac{3\pi}{2}, 4\pi, 7\pi\right\}$
(II) Y	**(Q)** an arithmetic progression
(III) Z	**(R)** Not an arithmetic progression
(IV) W	**(S)** $\supseteq \left\{\dfrac{\pi}{6}, \dfrac{7\pi}{6}, \dfrac{13\pi}{6}\right\}$
	(T) $\supseteq \left\{\dfrac{\pi}{3}, \dfrac{2\pi}{3}, \pi\right\}$
	(U) $\supseteq \left\{\dfrac{\pi}{6}, \dfrac{3\pi}{4}\right\}$

Which of the following is the only correct combination ?   **[2019, Advanced]**

(a) (I), (P), (R)   **(b)** (II), (Q), (T)

(c) (I), (Q), (U)   **(d)** (II), (R), (S)

58. Let $f(x) = \sin(\pi \cos x)$ and $g(x) = \cos(2\pi \sin x)$ be two functions defined for $x > 0$. Define the following sets whose elements are written in the increasing order :   **[2019, Advanced]**

$X = \{x : f(x) = 0\}$, $Y = \{x : f'(x) = 0\}$,

$Z = \{x : g(x) = 0\}$, $W = \{x : g'(x) = 0\}$,

List−I contains the sets X, Y, Z and W. **List−II** contains some information regarding these sets.

List−I	List−II
(I) X	**(P)** $\supseteq \left\{\dfrac{\pi}{2}, \dfrac{3\pi}{2}, 4\pi, 7\pi\right\}$
(II) Y	**(Q)** an arithmetic progression
(III) Z	**(R)** NOT an arithmetic progression
(IV) W	**(S)** $\supseteq \left\{\dfrac{\pi}{6}, \dfrac{7\pi}{6}, \dfrac{13\pi}{6}\right\}$
	(T) $\supseteq \left\{\dfrac{\pi}{3}, \dfrac{2\pi}{3}, \pi\right\}$

Which of the following is the only correct combination ? **[2019, Advanced]**

(a) (III), (R), (U)
(b) (IV), (P), (R), (S)
(c) (III), (P), (Q), (U)
(d) (IV), (Q), (T)

59. Let N denote the set of all natural numbers. Define two binary relations on N as

$R_1 = (x, y) \in N \times N : 2x + y = 10\}$ and

$R_2 = \{(x, y) \in N \times N : x + 2y = 10\}$.

Then : **[2018, Main]**

(a) Range of R_1 is {2, 4, 8}.
(b) Range of R_2 is {1, 2, 3, 4}.
(c) Both R_1 and R_2 are symmetric relations.
(d) Both R_1 and R_2 are transitive relations.

60. Consider the following two binary relations on the set A = {a, b, c} :

$R_1 = \{(c, a), (b, b), (a, c), (c, c), (b, c), (a, a)\}$ and
$R_2 = \{(a, b), (b, a), (c, c), (c, a), (a, a), (b, b), (a, c)\}$

Then : **[2018, Main]**

(a) both R_1 and R_2 are not symmetric.
(b) R_1 is not symmetric but it is transitive
(c) R_2 is symmetric but it is not transitive
(d) both R_1 and R_2 are transitive.

61. Let $S = \{(\lambda, \mu) \in R \times R : f(t) = (|\lambda| e^{|t|} - \mu) . \sin(2|t|)$, $t \in R$, is a differentiable function}.

Then S is a subset of : **[2018, Main]**

(a) $R \times [0, \infty)$
(b) $[0, \infty) \times R$
(c) $R \times (-\infty, 0)$
(d) $(-\infty, 0) \times R$

62. Let X be the set consisting of the first 2018 terms of the arithmetic progression 1, 6, 11, ..., and Y be the set consisting of the first 2018 terms of the arithmetic progression 9, 16, 23, ... Then, the number of elements in the set $X \cup Y$ is ....

[2018, Advanced]

63. Let $f(x) = 2^{10} . x + 1$ and $g(x) = 3^{10} . x - 1$. If $(fog)(x) = x$, then x is equal to : **[2017, Main]**

(a) $\dfrac{3^{10} - 1}{3^{10} - 2^{-10}}$
(b) $\dfrac{2^{10} - 1}{2^{10} - 3^{-10}}$

(c) $\dfrac{1 - 3^{-10}}{2^{10} - 3^{-10}}$
(d) $\dfrac{1 - 2^{-10}}{3^{10} - 2^{-10}}$

64. If

$$S = \left\{x \in [0, 2\pi] : \begin{vmatrix} 0 & \cos x & -\sin x \\ \sin x & 0 & \cos x \\ \cos x & \sin x & 0 \end{vmatrix} = 0\right\},$$

then $\displaystyle\sum_{x \in S} \tan\left(\dfrac{\pi}{3} + x\right)$ is equal to : **[2017, Main]**

(a) $4 + 2\sqrt{3}$
(b) $-2 + \sqrt{3}$
(c) $-2 - \sqrt{3}$
(d) $-4 - 2\sqrt{3}$

65. The functon $f : N \to N$ defined by $f(x) = x - 5\left\{\dfrac{x}{5}\right\}$, where N is the set of natural numbers and [x] denotes the greatest integeer less than or equal to x, is : **[2017, Main]**

(a) one-one and onto.
(b) one-one but not onto.
(c) onto but not one-one.
(d) neither one-one nor onto.

66. Let $f : R \to R, g : R \to R$ and $h : R \to R$ be differentiable functions such that $f(x) = x^3 + 3x + 2$, $g(f(x)) = x$ and $h(g(g(x))) = x$ for all $x \in R$. Then

[2016, Advanced]

(a) $g'(2) = \dfrac{1}{15}$
(b) $h'(1) = 666$
(c) $h(0) = 16$
(d) $h(g(3)) = 36$

67. For $x \in R, x \neq 0, x \neq 1$, let $f_0(x) = \dfrac{1}{1-x}$ and $f_{n+1}(x) = f_0(f_n(x))$, $n = 0, 1, 2, ...$ Then the value of $f_{100}(3) + f_1\left(\dfrac{2}{3}\right) + f_2\left(\dfrac{3}{2}\right)$ is equal :

[2016, Main]

(a) $\dfrac{8}{3}$
(b) $\dfrac{5}{3}$
(c) $\dfrac{4}{3}$
(d) $\dfrac{1}{3}$

68. If the two roots of the equation, $(a - 1)(x^4 + x^2 + 1) + (a + 1)(x^2 + x + 1)^2 = 0$ are real and distinct, then the set of all values of 'a' is : **[2015, Main]**

(a) $\left(-\dfrac{1}{2}, 0\right)$
(b) $(-\infty, -2) \cup (2, \infty)$
(c) $\left(-\dfrac{1}{2}, 0\right) \cup \left(0, \dfrac{1}{2}\right)$
(d) $\left(0, \dfrac{1}{2}\right)$

69. Let $f(x) = \sin\left(\dfrac{\pi}{6}\sin\left(\dfrac{\pi}{2}\sin x\right)\right)$ for all $x \in R$ and $g(x) = \dfrac{\pi}{2}\sin x$ for all $x \in R$. Let $(f \circ g)(x)$ denote $f(g(x))$ and $(g \circ f)(x)$ denote $g(f(x))$. Then which of the following is (are) true? **[2015, Advanced]**

(a) Range of f is $\left[-\dfrac{1}{2}, \dfrac{1}{2}\right]$

(b) Range of fog is $\left[-\dfrac{1}{2}, \dfrac{1}{2}\right]$

(c) $\lim\limits_{x \to 0} \dfrac{f(x)}{g(x)} = \dfrac{\pi}{6}$

(d) There is an $x \in R$ such that $(gof)(x) = 1$

70. If $X = \{4^n - 3n - 1 : n \in N\}$ and $Y = \{9(n-1) : n \in N\}$, where N is the set of natural numbers, then $X \cup Y$ is equal to : **[2014, Main]**

(a) X   **(b)** Y

(c) N   **(d)** Y − X

71. If $a \in R$ and the equation
$$-3(x - [x])^2 + 2(x - [x]) + a^2 = 0$$
(where $[x]$ denotes the greatest integer $\leq x$) has no integral solution, then all possible values of a lie in the interval : **[2014, Main]**

(a) $(-2, -1)$ **(b)** $(-\infty, -2) \cup (2, \infty)$

(c) $(-1, 0) \cup (0, 1)$ **(d)** $(1, 2)$

72. Let $f_k(x) = \dfrac{1}{k}(\sin^k x + \cos^k x)$ where $x \in R$ and $k > 1$

Then $f_4(x) - f_6(x)$ equals : **[2014, Main]**

(a) $\dfrac{1}{4}$ **(b)** $\dfrac{1}{12}$

(c) $\dfrac{1}{6}$ **(d)** $\dfrac{1}{3}$

73. A relation on the set $A = \{x : |x| < 3, x \in Z\}$, where Z is the set of integer is defined by $R = \{(x, y) : y = |x|, x \neq -1\}$. Then the number of elements in the power set of R is : **[2014, Main]**

(a) 32   **(b)** 16

(c) 8   **(d)** 64

74. Let $f : R \to R$ be defined by $f(x) = \dfrac{|x| - 1}{|x| + 1}$ then f

is : **[2014, Main]**

(a) both one-one and onto

(b) one-one but not onto

(c) onto but not one-one

(d) neither one-one nor onto.

75. Let f be an odd function defined on the set of real numbers such that for $x \geq 0$,
$$f(x) = 3 \sin x + 4 \cos x$$

Then $f(x)$ at $x = -\dfrac{11\pi}{6}$ is equal to : **[2014, Main]**

(a) $\dfrac{3}{2} + 2\sqrt{3}$ **(b)** $-\dfrac{3}{2} + 2\sqrt{3}$

(c) $\dfrac{3}{2} - 2\sqrt{3}$ **(d)** $-\dfrac{3}{2} - 2\sqrt{3}$

76. Let P be the relation defined on the set of all real numbers such that
$$P = \{(a, b) : \sec^2 a - \tan^2 b = 1\}. \text{ Then P is :}$$
[2014, Main]

(a) reflexive and symmetric but not transitive.

(b) reflexive and transitive but not symmetric.

(c) symmetric and transitivie but not reflexive.

(d) an equivalence relation.

77. If A and B are two events such that $P(A \cup B) = P(A \cap B)$, then the incorrect statement amongst the following statements is :

[2014, Main]

(a) A and B are equally likely

(b) $P(A \cap B') = 0$

(c) $P(A' \cap B) = 0$

(d) $P(A) + P(B) = 1$

78. A set S contains 7 element. A non-empty subset A of S and an element x of S are chosen at random. "Then the probability that $x \in A$ is : **[2014, Main]**

(a) $\dfrac{1}{2}$ **(b)** $\dfrac{64}{127}$

(c) $\dfrac{63}{128}$ **(d)** $\dfrac{31}{128}$

79. Let $f : [0, 4\pi] \to [0, \pi]$ be defined by $f(x) = \cos^{-1}(\cos x)$. The number of points $x \in [0, 4\pi]$ satisfying the equation **[2014, Advanced]**
$$f(x) = \dfrac{10 - x}{10}$$

80. Let $f(x) = x \sin \pi x$, $x > 0$. Then for all natural numbers n, $f'(x)$ vanishes at : **[2013, Advanced]**

(a) a unique point in the interval $\left(n, n + \dfrac{1}{2}\right)$

(b) a unique point in the interval $\left(n + \dfrac{1}{2}, n + 1\right)$

(c) a unique point in the interval $(n, n + 1)$

(d) two points in the interval $(n, n + 1)$

81. The function $f : [0, 3] \to [1, 29]$, defined by $f(x) = 2x^3 - 15x^2 + 36x + 1$, is **[2012, Advanced]**

(a) one-one and onto

(b) onto but not one-one

(c) one-one but not onto

(d) neither one-one nor onto

82. Let $f(x) = x^2$ and $g(x) = \sin x$ for all $x \in R$. Then the set of all x satisfying $(fogogof)(x) = (gogof)(x)$, where $(f \circ g)(x) = f(g(x))$, is **[2011, Advanced]**

(a) $\pm \sqrt{n\pi}$, $n \in \{0, 1, 2, ...\}$

(b) $\pm \sqrt{n\pi}$, $n \in \{1, 2, ...\}$

(c) $\dfrac{\pi}{2} + 2n\pi$, $n \in \{... -2, -1, 0, 1, 2, ...\}$

(d) $2n\pi$, $n \in \{....., -2, -1, 0, 1, 2, ...\}$

83. Let $S = \{1, 2, 3, 4\}$. The total number of unordered pairs of disjoint subsets of S is equal to :

[2010, Advanced]

(a) 25

(b) 34

(c) 42

(d) 41

84. Let f be a real-valued function defined on the interval $(-1, 1)$ such that $e^{-x} f(x) = 2 + \int_0^x \sqrt{t^4 + 1}$ dt, for all $x \in (-1, 1)$, and let f^{-1} be the inverse function of f.

Then $(f-1)(2)$ is equal to : **[2010, Advanced]**

(a) 1

(b) $\dfrac{1}{3}$

(c) $\dfrac{1}{2}$

(d) $\dfrac{1}{e}$

85. If r, s, t are prime numbers and p, q are the positive integers such that the LCM of p, q is $r^2 t^4 s^2$, then the number of ordered pair (p, q) is: **[2006, Main]**

(a) 252

(b) 254

(c) 225

(d) 224

86. If $f(x)$ is a twice differentiable function and given that $f(1) = 1, f(2) = 4, f(3) = 9$, then :

[2005, Main]

(a) $f''(x) = 2$, for $\forall\, x \in (1, 3)$

(b) $f''(x) = f'(x) = 5$ for some $x \in (2, 3)$

(c) $f''(x) = 3, \forall\, x \in (2, 3)$

(d) $f''(x) = 2$, for some $x \in (1, 3)$

87. If the function $f(x)$ and $g(x)$ are defined on $R \to R$ such that

$$f(x) = \begin{cases} 0, & x \in \text{rational} \\ x, & x \in \text{irrational} \end{cases},$$

$$g(x) = \begin{cases} 0, & x \in \text{irrational} \\ x, & x \in \text{rational} \end{cases}, \text{ then } (f-g)(x) \text{ is :}$$

[2005, Main]

(a) one-one and onto

(b) neither one-one nor onto

(c) one-one but not onto

(d) onto but not one-one

88. If P(x) is a polynomial of degree less than or equal to 2 and S is the set of all such polynomials so that P$(a) = 1$, P$(0) = 0$ and P$'(x) > 0 \ \forall\, x \in [0, 1]$, then : **[2005, Main]**

(a) $S = \phi$

(b) $S = \{(1-a)x^2 + ax \quad 0 < a < 2$

(c) $(1-a)x^2 + ax \ a \in (0, \infty)$

(d) $S = \{(1-a)x^2 + ax \quad 0 < a < 1$

89. If $f(x) = \sin x + \cos x, g(x) = x^2 - 1$, then $g(f(x))$ is invertible in the domain : **[2004, Main]**

(a) $\left[0, \dfrac{\pi}{2}\right]$

(b) $\left[-\dfrac{\pi}{4}, \dfrac{\pi}{4}\right]$

(c) $\left[-\dfrac{\pi}{2}, \dfrac{\pi}{2}\right]$

(d) $[0, \pi]$

90. Domain of definition of the function $f(x) = \sqrt{\sin^{-1}(2x) + \dfrac{\pi}{6}}$ for real valued x, is :

[2004, Main]

(a) $\left[-\dfrac{1}{4}, \dfrac{1}{2}\right]$

(b) $\left[-\dfrac{1}{2}, \dfrac{1}{2}\right]$

(c) $\left(-\dfrac{1}{2}, \dfrac{1}{9}\right)$

(d) $\left[-\dfrac{1}{4}, \dfrac{1}{4}\right]$

91. Range of the function $f(x) = \dfrac{x^2 + x + 2}{x^2 + x + 1}; x \in R$ is :

[2003, Main]

(a) $(1, \infty)$

(b) $(1, 11/7)$

(c) $(1, 7/3]$

(d) $(1, 7/5]$

92. Suppose $f(x) = (x + 1)^2$ for $x \geq -1$. If $g(x)$ is the function whose graph is the reflection of the graph of $f(x)$ with respect to the line $y = x$, then $g(x)$ equals : **[2002, Main]**

(a) $-\sqrt{x} - 1, x \geq 0$

(b) $\dfrac{1}{(x+1)^2}, x > -1$

(c) $\sqrt{x+1}, x > -1$

(d) $\sqrt{x} - 1, x \geq 0$

93. Let function $f : R \to R$ be defined by $f(x) = 2x + \sin x$ for $x \in R$. then f is : **[2002, Main]**

(a) one-to-one and onto

(b) one-to-one but NOT onto

(c) onto but NOT one-to-one

(d) neither one-to-one nor onto

94. The set of all real numbers x for which $x^2 - |x + 2| + x > 0$ is : **[2002, Main]**

(a) $(-\infty, -2) \cup (2, \infty)$

(b) $(-\infty, -\sqrt{2}) \cup (\sqrt{2}, \infty)$

(c) $(-\infty, -1) \cup (1, \infty)$

(d) $(\sqrt{2}, \infty)$

ANSWER KEY

1. (a)	**2.** (c)	**3.** (d)	**4.** (d)	**5.** (8)	**6.** (c)	**7.** (d)	**8.** (28)	**9.** (5)	**10.** (d)
11. (b)	**12.** (b)	**13.** (c)	**14.** (c)	**15.** (c)	**16.** (d)	**17.** (d)	**18.** (b)	**19.** (a)	**20.** (c)
21. (19)	**22.** (c)	**23.** (c)	**24.** (1)	**25.** (4)	**26.** (a)	**27.** (19)	**28.** (a)	**29.** (a)	**30.** (a)
31. (a)	**32.** (d)	**33.** (c)	**34.** (b)	**35.** (c)	**36.** (d)	**37.** (c)	**38.** (b)	**39.** (a)	**40.** (b)
41. (29.00)	**42.** (c)	**43.** (a)	**44.** (d)	**45.** (c)	**46.** (d)	**47.** (c)	**48.** (c)	**49.** (b)	**50.** (c)
51. (a)	**52.** (a)	**53.** (a)	**54.** (b)	**55.** (d)	**56.** (d)	**57.** (c)	**58.** (b)	**59.** (b)	**60.** (c)
61. (a)	**62.** (3748)	**63.** (d)	**64.** (d)	**65.** (d)	**66.** (b,c)	**67.** (b)	**68.** (c)	**69.** (a,b,c)	**70.** (b)
71. (c)	**72.** (b)	**73.** (b)	**74.** (d)	**75.** (c)	**76.** (d)	**77.** (a)	**78.** (b)	**79.** (3)	**80.** (b,c)
81. (b)	**82.** (a)	**83.** (d)	**84.** (b)	**85.** (c)	**86.** (d)	**87.** (a)	**88.** (b)	**89.** (b)	**90.** (a)
91. (c)	**92.** (d)	**93.** (a)	**94.** (b)						

ANSWERS WITH EXPLANATIONS

1. **Correct Response :** (a)

   $f(x)$ is continuous and differentiable

   $$f(\pi^-) = f(\pi) = f(\pi^+)$$
   $$-1 = -k_2$$
   $$k_2 = 1$$
   $$f'(x) = \begin{cases} 2k_1(x-\pi); & x \le \pi \\ -k_2 \sin x; & x > \pi \end{cases}$$
   $$f'(\pi^-) = f(\pi+)$$
   $$0 = 0$$

   so, differentiable at $x = 0$

   $$f''(x) = \begin{cases} 2k_1 & ; x \le \pi \\ -k_2 \cos x; & x > \pi \end{cases}$$
   $$f''(\pi^-) = f''(\pi^+)$$
   $$2k_1 = k_2$$
   $$k_1 = \frac{1}{2}$$
   $$(k_1, k_2) = \left(\frac{1}{2}, 1\right)$$

2. **Correct Response :** (c)

   $$p \leftrightarrow q \equiv (p \to q) \wedge (q \to p)$$
   $$x \leftrightarrow \sim y \equiv (x \to \sim y) \wedge (\sim y \to x)$$
   $$\because \quad (p \to q \equiv \sim p \vee q)$$
   $$x \leftrightarrow \sim y \equiv (\sim x \vee \sim y) \wedge (y \vee x)$$
   $$\sim (x \leftrightarrow \sim y) \equiv (x \wedge y) \vee (\sim x \wedge \sim y).$$

3. **Correct Response :** (d)

   $C \to$ person like coffee

   $T \to$ person like Tea

   $$n(C) = 73$$
   $$n(T) = 65$$
   $$n(C \cup T) \le 100$$

   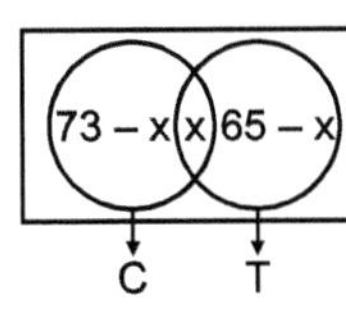

   $$n(C) + n(T) - n(C \cap T) \le 100$$
   $$73 + 65 - x \le 100$$
   $$x \ge 38$$
   $$73 - x \ge 0 \Rightarrow x \le 73$$
   $$65 - x \ge 0 \Rightarrow x \le 65$$
   $$38 \le x \le 65.$$

4. **Correct Response :** (d)

   $$C_3 \to C_3 - (C_1 - C_2)$$
   $$f(\theta) = \begin{vmatrix} -\sin^2\theta & -1-\sin^2\theta & 0 \\ -\cos^2\theta & -1-\cos^2\theta & 0 \\ 12 & 10 & -4 \end{vmatrix}$$
   $$= -4[(1 + \cos^2\theta)\sin^2\theta - \cos^2\theta(1 + \sin^2\theta)]$$
   $$= -4[\sin^2\theta + \sin^2\theta\cos^2\theta - \cos^2\theta$$
   $$- \cos^2\theta\sin^2\theta]$$
   $$= -4[\cos^2\theta - \sin^2\theta]$$
   $$f(\theta) = 4\cos 2\theta$$
   $$\theta \in \left[\frac{\pi}{4}, \frac{\pi}{2}\right]$$
   $$2\theta \in \left[\frac{\pi}{2}, \pi\right]$$
   $$f(\theta) \in [-4, 0]$$
   $$(m, M) = (-4, 0).$$

5. **Correct Response :** (8)

   $$x \in (-10, 10)$$
   $$\frac{x}{2} \in (-5, 5)\ 9 \text{ integers}$$

   check continuity at $x = 0$

   $$\left. \begin{array}{l} f(0) = 0 \\ f(0)^+ = 0 \\ f(0)^- = 0 \end{array} \right\} \text{continuous at } x = 0$$

function will be discontinuous when

$$\frac{x}{2} = \pm 4, \pm 3, \pm 2, \pm 1$$

8 points of discontinuity.

6. **Correct Response :** (c)

Negation of $p \vee (\sim p \wedge q)$

$$p \vee (\sim p \wedge q) = (p \vee \sim p) \wedge (p \vee q)$$
$$= (T) \wedge (p \vee q)$$
$$= (p \vee q)$$

Now negation of $(p \vee q)$ is

$$\sim (p \vee q) = \sim p \wedge \sim q$$

7. **Correct Response :** (d)

$$\frac{f(t_2) - f(t_1)}{t_2 - t_1} = 2at + b$$

$$\frac{a(t_2^2 - t_1^2) + b(t_2 - t_1)}{t_2 - t_1} = 2at + b$$

$$\Rightarrow \quad a(t_2 + t_1) + b = 2at + b$$

$$\Rightarrow \quad t = \frac{t_1 + t_2}{2}$$

8. **Correct Response :** (28)

$$2^m - 2^n = 112$$
$$\Rightarrow \quad 2^n (2^{m-n} - 1) = 2^4 (2^3 - 1)$$
$$n = 4$$
$$m - n = 3$$
$$m = 3 + 4 = 7$$
$$m = 7, n = 4$$
$$(2^7 - 2^4 = 112)$$
$$m \times n = 7 \times 4 = 28$$

9. **Correct Response :** (5)

$$f(x) = x^5 . \sin \frac{1}{x} + 5x^2 \qquad \text{if } x < 0$$

$$f(x) = 0 \qquad \text{if } x = 0$$

$$f(x) = x^5 . \cos \frac{1}{x} + \lambda x^2 \quad \text{if } x > 0$$

LHD of $f'(x)$ at $x = 0$ is 10

RHD of $f'(x)$ at $x = 0$ is 2λ

if $f''(0)$ exists then

$$2\lambda = 10$$
$$\Rightarrow \quad \lambda = 5.$$

10. **Correct Response :** (d)

$$f(x) = (1 - \cos^2 x) (\lambda + \sin x)$$

$$x \in \left(\frac{-\pi}{2}, \frac{\pi}{2} \right)$$

$$f(x) = \lambda \sin^2 x + \sin^3 x$$
$$f'(x) = 2\lambda \sin x \cos x + 3 \sin^2 x \cos x$$
$$f'(x) = \sin x \cos x (2\lambda + 3 \sin x)$$

$$\sin x = 0, \frac{-2\lambda}{3}, \ (\lambda \neq 0)$$

for exactly one maxima & minima

$$\frac{-2\lambda}{3} \in (-1, 1) \Rightarrow \lambda \in \left(\frac{-3}{2}, \frac{3}{2} \right)$$

$$\lambda \in \left(\frac{-3}{2}, \frac{3}{2} \right) - \{0\}$$

11. **Correct Response :** (b)

P : $n^3 - 1$ is even q : n is odd

Contrapositive of $(p \to q)$ is $\sim q \to \sim p$

For an integer n, if n is even then $(n^3 - 1)$ is odd.

12. **Correct Response :** (b)

$$f(x) = \frac{a - x}{a + x}$$

$$x \in R - \{-a\} \to R$$

$$f[f(x)] = \frac{a - f(x)}{a + f(x)} = \frac{a - \left(\frac{a-x}{a+x} \right)}{a + \left(\frac{a-x}{a+x} \right)}$$

$$f[f(x)] = \frac{(a^2 - a) + x(a + 1)}{(a^2 + a) + x(a - 1)} = x$$

$$\Rightarrow (a^2 - a) + x(a + 1) = (a^2 + a)x + x^2(a - 1)$$
$$\Rightarrow a(a - 1) + x(1 - a^2) - x^2(a - 1) = 0$$
$$\Rightarrow \qquad a = 1$$

$$f(x) = \frac{1 - x}{1 + x},$$

$$f\left(\frac{-1}{2} \right) = \frac{1 + \frac{1}{2}}{1 - \frac{1}{2}} = 3$$

13. **Correct Response :** (c)

Let TV(r) denotes truth value of a statement r.

Now, if $\quad$ TV(p) = TV(q) = T

$\Rightarrow \qquad$ TV(S_1) = F

Also, if $\quad$ TV(p) = T & TV(q) = F

$\Rightarrow \qquad$ TV(S_2) = T.

14. **Correct Response :** (c)

$$n(A) = 63\%$$
$$n(B) = 76\%$$
$$n(A \cap B) = x\%$$
$$n(A \cup B) = n(A) + n(B) - n(A \cap B)$$
$$= 63 + 76 - x$$
$$n(B) \leq n(A \cup B) \leq n(U)$$
$$\Rightarrow \quad 76 \leq 76 + 63 - x \leq 100$$
$$\Rightarrow \quad -63 \leq -x \leq -39$$
$$\Rightarrow \quad 63 \geq x \geq 39.$$

15. Correct Response : (c)

$f(2) = 8, f'(2) = 5, f'(x) \geq 1, f''(x) \geq 4, \forall\ x \in (1, 6)$

$$f''(x) = \frac{f'(5) - f'(2)}{5 - 2} \geq 4$$

$\Rightarrow \qquad f'(5) \geq 17 \qquad\qquad\qquad …(1)$

$$f'(x) = \frac{f(5) - f(2)}{5 - 2} \geq 1 \Rightarrow f(5) \geq 11 \quad …(2)$$

$f'(5) + f(5) \geq 28.$

16. Correct Response : (d)

$$n(X_i) = 10. \overset{50}{\underset{i=1}{\cup}} X_i = T$$

$\Rightarrow \qquad n(T) = 500$

Each element of T belongs to exactly 20 elements

of $X_i \Rightarrow \dfrac{500}{20} = 25$ distinct elements so

$$\frac{5n}{6} = 25 \Rightarrow n = 30.$$

17. Correct Response : (d)

$$A : D \geq 0$$

$\Rightarrow \qquad (m + 1)^2 - 4(m + 4) \geq 0$

$\Rightarrow \quad m^2 + 2m + 1 - 4m - 16 \geq 0$

$\Rightarrow \qquad m^2 - 2m - 15 \geq 0$

$\Rightarrow \qquad (m - 5)\,(m + 3) \geq 0$

$\Rightarrow \qquad m \in (-\infty, -3] \cup [5, \infty)$

$\therefore \qquad A = (-\infty, -3] \cup [5, \infty)$

$\qquad\qquad B = [-3, 5)$

$\qquad A - B = (-\infty, -3) \cup [5, \infty)$

$\qquad A \cap B = \{-3\}$

$\qquad B - A = (-3, 5)$

$\qquad A \cup B = R.$

18. Correct Response : (b)

$\qquad f(x) = (3x - 7)x^{2/3}$

$\Rightarrow \qquad f(x) = 3x^{5/3} - 7x^{2/3}$

$\Rightarrow \qquad f'(x) = 5x^{2/3} - \dfrac{14}{3x^{1/3}}$

$$= \frac{15x - 14}{3x^{1/3}} > 0$$

$$\overset{+}{\underset{0}{\quad}} \quad \overset{-}{\quad} \quad \overset{+}{\underset{\frac{14}{15}}{\quad}}$$

$\therefore \qquad f'(x) > 0\ \forall\ x \in (-\infty, 0) \cup \left(\dfrac{14}{15}, \infty\right)$

19. Correct Response : (a)

$p \to\ \sim (p \wedge \sim q) =\ \sim p\ \vee \sim (p \wedge \sim q)$

$\qquad\qquad\qquad = \sim p\ \vee \sim p \vee q$

$\qquad\qquad\qquad = \sim (p \wedge q) \vee q$

$\qquad\qquad\qquad = \sim p \vee q.$

20. Correct Response : (c)

p	q	$q \to p$	$p \to$ $(q \to p)$	$p \vee q$	$p \to$ $p \vee q$	$[p \to (q \to p)] \to [p \to (p \vee q)]$
T	T	T	T	T	T	T
T	F	T	T	T	T	T
F	T	F	T	T	T	T
F	F	T	T	F	T	T

21. Correct Response : (19)

$C = \{f : A \to B \mid 2 \in f(A)$ and f is not one-one$\}$

Case-I : If $f(x) = 2\ \forall\ x \in A$ then number of function $= 1$

Case-II : If $f(x) = 2$ for exactly two elements then total number of many-one function $= {}^3C_2\ {}^3C_1 = 9.$

Case-III : If $f(x) = 2$ for exactly one element then total number of many-one functions $= {}^3C_1\ {}^3C_1 = 9.$

$$\text{Total} = 19.$$

22. Correct Response : (c)

$f(x)$ is a non-periodic, continuous and odd function

$$f(x) = \begin{cases} - x^2 + x \sin x, & x < 0 \\ x^2 - x \sin x, & x \geq 0 \end{cases}$$

$$f(-\infty) = \lim_{x \to -\infty} (-x^2)\left(1 - \frac{\sin x}{x}\right) = -\infty$$

$$f(\infty) = \lim_{x \to \infty} x^2 \left(1 - \frac{\sin x}{x}\right) = \infty$$

$\Rightarrow \quad$ Range of $f(x) = R$

$\Rightarrow f(x)$ is an onto function. $\qquad\qquad …(1)$

$$f'(x) = \begin{cases} - 2x + \sin x + x \cos x, & x < 0 \\ 2x - \sin x - x \cos x, & x \geq 0 \end{cases}$$

For $(0, \infty)$

$\qquad f'(x) = (x - \sin x) + x(1 - \cos x)$

$\qquad\qquad$ always + ve   always +ve

$\qquad\qquad\qquad$ or 0 $\qquad$ or 0

$\Rightarrow \qquad f'(x) > 0$

$\Rightarrow \qquad f'(x) \geq 0, \forall\ x \in (-\infty, \infty)$

equality at $x = 0$

$\Rightarrow f(x)$ is one-one function. $\qquad\qquad …(2)$

From (1) & (2), $f(x)$ is both one-one & onto.

23. Correct Response : (c)

$$\text{Perimeter} = 2(2\alpha + 2 \cos 2\alpha)$$

$$P = 4(\alpha + \cos 2\alpha)$$

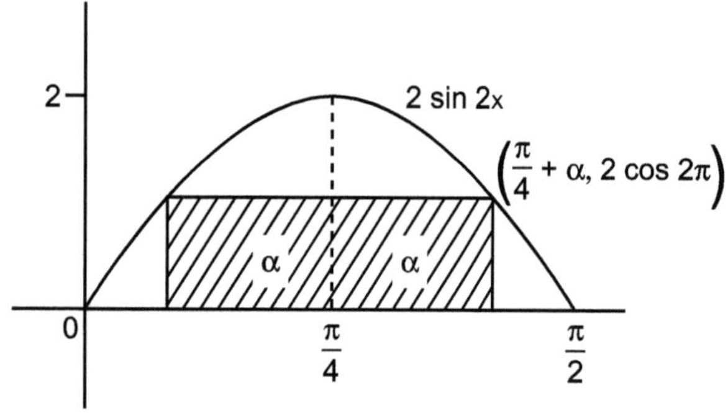

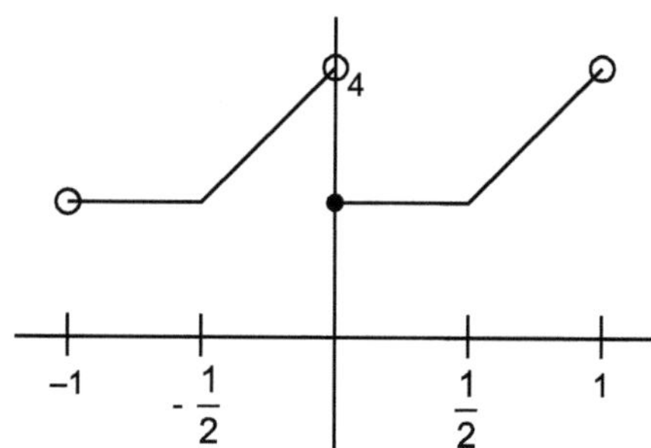

$$f[g(x)] = |2\{x\} - 1| + |2\{x\} + 1|$$

$$= \begin{cases} 2 & \{x\} \le 1/2 \\ 4\{x\} & \{x\} > 1/2 \end{cases}$$

$$\frac{dP}{d\alpha} = 4(1 - 2\sin 2\alpha) = 0$$

$$\sin 2\alpha = \frac{1}{2}$$

$$2\alpha = \frac{\pi}{6}, \frac{5\pi}{6}$$

$$\frac{d^2P}{d\alpha^2} = -4\cos 2\alpha$$

for maxima $\qquad \alpha = \dfrac{\pi}{12}$

$$\text{Area} = (2\alpha)(2\cos 2\alpha)$$

$$= \frac{\pi}{6} \times 2 \times \frac{\sqrt{3}}{2} = \frac{\pi}{2\sqrt{3}}.$$

24. Correct Response : (1)

Let $\quad \pi x - \dfrac{\pi}{4} = \theta \in \left[\dfrac{-\pi}{4}, \dfrac{7\pi}{4}\right]$

So, $\left(3 - \sin\left(\dfrac{\pi}{2} + 2\theta\right)\right)\sin\theta \ge \sin(\pi + 3\theta)$

$\Rightarrow \qquad (3 - \cos 2\theta)\sin\theta \ge -\sin 3\theta$

$\qquad\qquad (\because \sin 3\theta = 3\sin\theta - 4\sin^3\theta)$

$\Rightarrow \sin\theta [3 - 4\sin^2\theta + 3 - \cos 2\theta] \ge 0$

$\Rightarrow \sin\theta [6 - 2(1 - \cos 2\theta) - \cos 2\theta] \ge 0$

$\Rightarrow \quad \sin\theta (4 + \cos 2\theta) \ge 0$

$\Rightarrow \qquad\qquad \sin\theta \ge 0$

$\Rightarrow \qquad\qquad \theta \in [0, \pi]$

$\Rightarrow \qquad\qquad 0 \le \pi x - \dfrac{\pi}{4} \le \pi$

$\Rightarrow \qquad\qquad \dfrac{\pi}{4} \le \pi x \le \dfrac{5\pi}{4}$

$\Rightarrow \qquad\qquad x \in \left[\dfrac{1}{4}, \dfrac{5}{4}\right]$

$\Rightarrow \qquad\qquad \alpha = \dfrac{1}{4}, \beta = \dfrac{5}{4}$

$\Rightarrow \qquad\qquad \beta - \alpha = 1.$

25. Correct Response : (4)

$$f(x) = |2x - 1| + |2x + 1|$$

$$g(x) = \{x\} = x - \{x\}$$

discontinuous at $x = 0 \Rightarrow c = 1$

Now differential at $x = -\dfrac{1}{2}, 0, \dfrac{1}{2}$

$\Rightarrow \qquad\qquad d = 3$

$\therefore \qquad\qquad c + d = 4.$

26. Correct Response : (a)

$$f'(x) = \frac{f(x)}{b^2 + x^2}$$

$$\int \frac{f'(x)}{f(x)}\, dx = \int \frac{dx}{x^2 + b^2}$$

$\Rightarrow \qquad \ln|f(x)| = \dfrac{1}{b}\tan^{-1}\left(\dfrac{x}{b}\right) + c$

Now $\qquad f(0) = 1$

$\therefore \qquad\qquad c = 0$

$\therefore \qquad |f(x)| = e^{\frac{1}{b}\tan^{-1}\left(\frac{x}{b}\right)}$

$\Rightarrow \qquad f(x) = \pm e^{\frac{1}{b}\tan^{-1}\left(\frac{x}{b}\right)}$

since $\qquad f(0) = 1$

$\therefore \qquad f(x) = e^{\frac{1}{b}\tan^{-1}\left(\frac{x}{b}\right)}$

$x \to -x$

$$f(-x) = e^{-\frac{1}{b}\tan^{-1}\left(\frac{x}{b}\right)}$$

$\therefore \quad f(x).f(-x) = e^0 = 1$ (option c)

and for $\qquad b > 0$

$$f(x) = e^{\frac{1}{b}\tan^{-1}\left(\frac{x}{b}\right)}$$

$\Rightarrow f(x)$ is increasing for all $x \in R$ (option a).

27. Correct Response : (19)

$$f(x) + f(1-x) = \frac{4^x}{4^x + 2} + \frac{4^{1-x}}{4^{1-x} + 2}$$

$$= \frac{4^x}{4^x + 2} + \frac{4/4^x}{\dfrac{4}{4^x} + 2}$$

$$= \frac{4^x}{4^x+2} + \frac{4}{4+2.4^x}$$

$$= \frac{4^x}{4^x+2} + \frac{2}{2+4^x}$$

$$= 1$$

so,

$$f\left(\frac{1}{40}\right)+f\left(\frac{2}{40}\right)+f\left(\frac{3}{40}\right)+\ldots+f\left(\frac{39}{40}\right)-f\left(\frac{1}{2}\right)$$

$$= \underbrace{1+1+1+\ldots+1}_{19\ \text{times}}+f\left(\frac{1}{2}\right)-f\left(\frac{1}{2}\right)$$

$$= 19+f\left(\frac{1}{2}\right)-f\left(\frac{1}{2}\right) = 19.$$

28. Correct Response : (a)

$$f(x+y) = f(x)+f(y)$$
$$\Rightarrow \quad f(n) = nf(1)$$
$$f(n) = 2n$$
$$g(n) = \sum_{k=1}^{n-1} 2n = 2\left(\frac{(n-1)n}{2}\right)$$
$$= n(n-1)$$
$$g(n) = 20 \Rightarrow n(n-1) = 20$$
$$n = 5$$

29. Correct Response : (a)

$$f(x) = \frac{\dfrac{x}{1+x}-ln(l+x)}{x^2}$$

$$= \frac{x-(1+x)ln(l+x)}{x^2(l+x)}$$

Suppose $h(x) = x - (1 + x)\,l\,n(1 + x)$

$\Rightarrow h'(x) = 1 - l\,n(1 + x) - 1 = -l\,n(1 + x)$

$h'(x) > 0,\ \forall\ x \in (-1, 0)$

$h'(x) < 0,\ \forall\ x \in (0, \infty)$

$h(0) = 0 \Rightarrow h'(x) < 0\ \forall\ x \in (-1, \infty)$

$\Rightarrow f(x) < 0\ \forall\ x \in (-1, \infty)$

$\Rightarrow f(x)$ is a decreasing function for all $x \in (-1, \infty)$

30. Correct Response : (a)

Option (a) is

$\sim p \wedge (p \vee q) \to q$

$\equiv (\sim p \wedge p) \vee (\sim p \wedge q) \to q$

$\equiv CV(\sim p \wedge q) \to q$

$\equiv (\sim p \wedge q) \to q$

$\equiv \sim(\sim p \wedge q) \vee q$

$\equiv (p \vee \sim q) \vee q$

$\equiv (p \vee q) \vee (\sim q \vee q)$

$\equiv (p \vee q) \vee t$

so $\sim p \wedge (p \vee q) \to q$ is a tautology.

31. Correct Response : (a)

Given E_1, E_2, E_3 are pairwise independent events

so $P(E_1 \cap E_2) = P(E_1).P(E_2)$

and $P(E_2 \cap E_3) = P(E_2).P(E_3)$

and $P(E_3 \cap E_1) = P(E_3).P(E_1)$

& $P(E_1 \cap E_2 \cap E_3) = 0$

Now $P\left(\dfrac{\overline{E}_2 \cap \overline{E}_3}{E_1}\right) = \dfrac{P[E_1 \cap (\overline{E}_2 \cap \overline{E}_3)]}{P(E_1)}$

$$= \frac{P(E_1)-[P(E_1 \cap E_2)+P(E_1 \cap E_3)-P(E_1 \cap E_2 \cap E_3)]}{P(E_1)}$$

$$= \frac{P(E_1)-P(E_1).P(E_2)-P(E_1)P(E_3)-0}{P(E_1)}$$

$= 1 - P(E_2) - P(E_3)$

$= [1 - P(E_3)] - P(E_2)$

$= P(E_3^C) - P(E_2)$

32. Correct Response : (d)

Let $a^2 + b^2 \in Q$ and $b^2 + c^2 \in Q$

e.g. $a = 2+\sqrt{3}$ and $b = 2-\sqrt{3}$

$a^2 + b^2 = 14 \in Q$

Let $c = (1+2\sqrt{3})$

$$b^2 + c^2 = 20 \in Q$$

But $a^2 + c^2 = (2+\sqrt{3})^2 + (1+2\sqrt{3})^2 \notin Q$

for R_2 Let $a^2 = 1$, $b^2 = \sqrt{3}$ and $c^2 = 2$

$a^2 + b^2 \notin Q$ and $b^2 + c^2 \notin Q$

But $a^2 + c^2 \in Q$

33. Correct Response : (c)

$$f'(x) = x(x+1)(x-1) = x^3 - x$$
$$\int d\,f(x) = \int x^3 - x\,dx$$
$$f(x) = \frac{x^4}{4} - \frac{x^2}{2} + C$$
$$f(x) = f(0)$$
$$\frac{x^4}{4} - \frac{x^2}{2} + C = C$$
$$\frac{x^4}{4} - \frac{x^2}{2} = 0$$
$$x^2(x^2 - 2) = 0$$
$$x = 0, 0, \sqrt{2}, -\sqrt{2}$$
$$x_1^2 + x_2^2 + x_3^2 = 0+2+2 = 4$$

34. Correct Response : (b)

If exactly one root in (0, 1) then

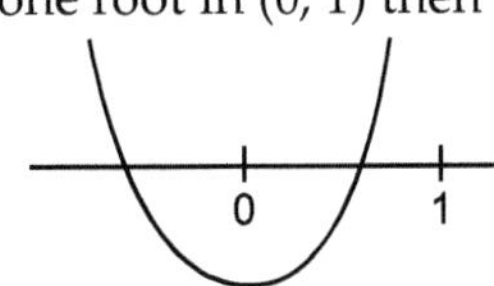

$$\Rightarrow \qquad f(0).f(1) < 0$$
$$\Rightarrow \qquad 2(\lambda^2 - 4\lambda + 3) < 0$$
$$\Rightarrow \qquad 1 < \lambda < 3$$
$$\Rightarrow \qquad (\lambda - 1)(\lambda - 3) < 0$$

Now for $\lambda = 1$, $\ 2x^2 - 4x + 2 = 0$

$(x - 1)^2 = 0, x = 1, 1$

So both roots doesn't lie between (0, 1)

$\therefore \lambda \neq 1$

Again for $\lambda = 3$
$$10x^2 - 12x + 2 = 0$$
$$\Rightarrow \qquad x = 1, \frac{1}{5}$$

so if one root is 1 then second root lie between (0, 1) so $\lambda = 3$ is correct.

$\therefore \lambda \in (1, 3]$.

35. Correct Response : (c)

$(p \wedge q) \rightarrow (\sim q \vee r) = \text{false}$

when $(p \wedge q) = T$

and $(\sim q \vee r) = F$

So $(p \wedge q) = T$ is possible when $p = q = \text{true}$

$\therefore \sim q = \text{False} \ (q = \text{true})$

So $(\sim q \vee r) = \text{False}$ is possible if r is false

$\therefore p = T, q = T, r = F$

36. Correct Response : (d)

$$f(x) = \begin{cases} ae^x + e^{-x}, & -1 \leq x < 1 \\ cx^2, & 1 \leq x \leq 3 \\ ax^2 + 2cx, & 3 < x \leq 4 \end{cases}$$

$$\underset{x \to 1^-}{\text{Lim}}\, f(x) = \underset{x \to 1^+}{\text{Lim}}\, f(x)$$

$$\Rightarrow \quad ae + be^{-1} = c \Rightarrow b = ce - ae^2 \qquad ....(1)$$

For continuity at $x = 3$

$$\underset{x \to 3^-}{\text{Lim}}\, f(x) = \underset{x \to 3^+}{\text{Lim}}\, f(x)$$

$$\Rightarrow \qquad 9c = 9a + 6c$$
$$\Rightarrow \qquad c = 3a \qquad ...(2)$$

$$f'(0) + f'(2) = e$$

$(ae^x - be^x)_{x=0} - (2cx)_{x=2} = e$

$$\Rightarrow \qquad a - b + 4c = e \qquad ...(3)$$

From (1), (2) and (3)

$\ \ a - 3ae + ae^2 + 12a = e$

$$\Rightarrow \quad a(e^2 + 13 - 3e) = e$$

$$\Rightarrow \qquad a = \frac{e}{e^2 - 3e + 13}$$

37. Correct Response : (c)

Let p denotes statement

p : I reach the station in time.

q : I will catch the train.

Contrapositive of $p \rightarrow q$

is $\sim q \rightarrow \sim p$

$\sim q \rightarrow \sim p$: I will not catch the train, then I do not reach the station in time.

38. Correct Response : (b)

$R = \{(x, y) : x, y \in z, x^2 + 3y^2 \leq 8\}$

For domain of R^{-1}

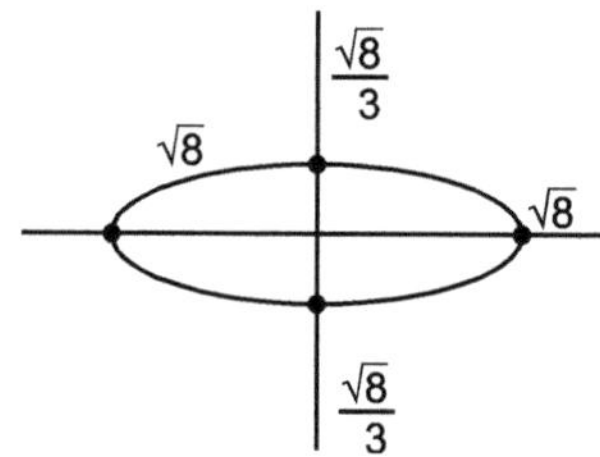

Collection of all integral of y's

For $x = 0, 3y^2 \leq 8$

$\Rightarrow y \in \{-1, 0, 1\}$

39. Correct Response : (a)

$$f(x) = \sin\left(\frac{|x| + 5}{x^2 + 1}\right)$$

For domain :

$$-1 \leq \frac{|x| + 5}{x^2 + 1} \leq 1$$

Since $|x| + 5$ & $x^2 + 1$ is always positive

So $\dfrac{|x| + 5}{x^2 + 1} \geq 0 \ \forall \ x \in R$

So for domain :

$$\frac{|x| + 5}{x^2 + 1} \leq 1$$

$$\Rightarrow \qquad |x| + 5 \leq x^2 + 1$$
$$\Rightarrow \qquad 0 \leq x^2 - |x| - 4$$

$$\Rightarrow 0 \leq \left(|x| - \frac{1 + \sqrt{17}}{2}\right)\left(|x| - \frac{1 - \sqrt{17}}{2}\right)$$

$$\Rightarrow |x| \geq \frac{1 + \sqrt{17}}{2} \ \text{or} \ |x| \leq \frac{1 - \sqrt{17}}{2} \quad \text{(Rejected)}$$

$$\Rightarrow x \in \left(-\infty, -\frac{1 + \sqrt{17}}{2}\right] \cup \left[\frac{1 + \sqrt{17}}{2}, \infty\right)$$

So, $\qquad a = \dfrac{1 + \sqrt{17}}{2}$

40. Correct Response : (b)

Explanation :

$$g(x) = x^2 + x - 1$$
$$g(f(x)) = 4x^2 - 10x + 5$$
$$= (2 - 2x)^2 + (2 - 2x) - 1$$
$$\Rightarrow \qquad f(x) = 2 - 2x$$

$$f\left(\frac{5}{4}\right) = \frac{-1}{2}$$

41. Correct Response : (29.00)

Explanation :

$$n(A) = 25$$
$$n(B) = 7$$
$$n(A \cap B) = 3$$
$$n(A \cup B) = 25 + 7 - 3 = 29$$

42. Correct Response : (c)

Explanation :

$$f(x) = \frac{8^{4x} - 1}{8^{4x} + 1} = 1 - \frac{2}{8^{4x} + 1}$$

so, $\quad 8^{4x+1} = \dfrac{2}{1-y} \Rightarrow 8^{4x} = \dfrac{1-y}{1-y}$

$\Rightarrow \qquad x = \ell n \left(\dfrac{1+y}{1-y} \right) \times \dfrac{1}{4\ell n 8} = f^{-1}(y)$

Hence, $\quad f^{-1}(x) = \dfrac{1}{4} (\log_8 e) \log e \left(\dfrac{1+x}{1-x} \right)$

43. Correct Response : (a)

Explanation :

Bonus option (1), (2), (3) are incorrect for $f(x) =$ constant and option (4) is incorrect $\dfrac{f(1) - f(c)}{1 - c} =$

$f'(a)$ where $c < a < 1$ (use LMVT)

Also for $f(x) = x^2$ option (4) is incorrect.

44. Correct Response : (d)

Explanation :

$$f(x) = \begin{cases} \dfrac{x}{x^2 + 1} & ; \quad x \in (1, 2) \\[3mm] \dfrac{2x}{x^2 + 1} & ; \quad x \in [2, 3) \end{cases}$$

$f(x)$ is decreasing function

$\therefore \ f(x) \in \left(\dfrac{2}{5}, \dfrac{1}{2} \right) \cup \left(\dfrac{3}{5}, \dfrac{4}{5} \right]$

45. Correct Response : (c)

$A : \in (-2, 2); \ B : x (-\infty - 1] \cup [5, \infty]$

$\Rightarrow \qquad B - A = R - (-2, 5)$

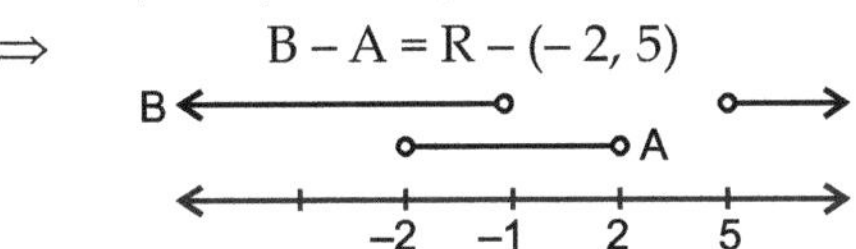

Bonus option (1).

46. Correct Response : (d)

Explanation :

Let $3^x = t ; t > 0$

$$t(t - 1) + 2 = |t - 1| + |t - 2|$$
$$t^2 - t + 2 = |t - 1| + |t - 2|$$

Case-I : $t < 1$

$$t^2 - t + 2 = 1 - t + 2 - t$$
$$t^2 + 2 = 3 - t$$
$$t^2 + t - 1 = 0$$

$$t = \frac{-1 \pm \sqrt{5}}{2}$$

$t = \dfrac{\sqrt{5} - 1}{2}$ is only acceptable

Case-II : $1 \le t < 2$

$$t^2 - t + 2 = t - 1 + 2 - t$$
$$t^2 - t + 1 = 0$$

$D < 0$ no real solution

Case-III : $t \ge 2$

$$t^2 - t + 2 = t - 1 + t - 2$$
$$t^2 - 3t - 5 = 0 \Rightarrow D < 0 \text{ no real solution}$$

47. Correct Response : (c)

Explanation :

$$f(g(x)) = x$$
$$f'(g(x)) \, g'(x) = 1$$

put $x = a$

$\Rightarrow \qquad f'(b) \, g'(a) = 1$

$$f'(b) = \frac{1}{5}$$

48. Correct Response : (c)

Explanation :

$$f(S) = S^2$$

$\Rightarrow \qquad 0 \le f(S) \le 16 \qquad \qquad ...(i)$

$$g(S) = \{x : x \in R, x^2 \in S\}$$
$$= \{x : x^2 \in [0, 4]\}$$

$\Rightarrow \qquad -2 \le g(S) \le 2 \qquad \qquad ...(ii)$

Equation (i) implies

$$g(f(S)) = \{x \in R : f(x) \in f(S)\}$$
$$= \{x : x^2 \in [0, 16]\}$$
$$= \{x \in R : -4 \le x \le 4\}$$

$\Rightarrow \qquad -4 \le g(f(S)) \le 4 \qquad \qquad ...(iii)$

Equation (ii) implies

$$0 \le (g(S))^2 \le 4$$
$$f(g(S)) = (g(S))^2$$

$\Rightarrow \qquad 0 \le f(g(S)) \le 4 \qquad \qquad ...(iv)$

Equation (i) and (iv) implies option (b) is correct.

Equation (iv) and $S \in [0, 4]$ implies option (a) is correct.

Equations (iii) and (ii) implies option (d) is incorrect.

Equations (iii) and $S \in [0, 4]$ implies option (c) is incorrect.

49. Correct Response : (b)

Explanation :

$$f(g(x)) = In (\sin (\sin^{-1} (e^{-x}))$$
$$= In (e^{-x})$$
$$= -x$$

$\Rightarrow \qquad (f(g(x)))' = -1$

Now,

$$f(g(\alpha)) = -\alpha$$
$$= b$$

And $f(g(x))'$ at $x = \alpha$ is $-1 =$ i.e., $a = -1$
So,

$$a\alpha^2 - b\alpha - a = -\alpha^2 - (-\alpha)\alpha + 1$$
$$= 1$$

50. Correct Response : (c)

Explanation :

Given function is

$$f(x) = \frac{1}{x^2 - 4} + In\,(x^3 - x)$$

For domain $x^2 - 4 \neq 0$ therefore, $x \in R - \{-2, 2\}$.
Now, $x^3 - x > 0$

$$\Rightarrow x(x - 1)\,(x + 1) > 0$$

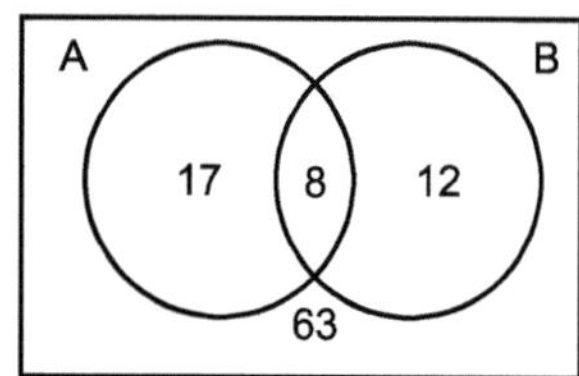

$$\Rightarrow x \in (-1, 0) \cup (1, \infty)$$

Required domain is $x \in (-1, 0) \cup (1, 2) \cup (2, \infty)$.

51. Correct Response : (a)

Explanation :

Let the total number of persons be 100.
Then, according to the given information,
25 read A, 20 read B, 8 read both A and B.
40% of $A^C \cap B \Rightarrow 4.8$ look into advertisements.
30% of $A \cap B^C \Rightarrow 5.1$ look into advertisements.
50% of $A \cap B \Rightarrow 4$ look into advertisements.
Total number of persons who look into advertisements is 13.9 or 13.9%.

52. Correct Response : (a)

Explanation :

$$f(x) = In\left(\frac{1-x}{1+x}\right),\ |\,x\,| < 1$$

$$f\left(\frac{2x}{1+x^2}\right) = In\left(\frac{1 - \dfrac{2x}{1+x^2}}{1 + \dfrac{2x}{1+x^2}}\right)$$

$$= In\left(\frac{1 + x^2 - 2x}{1 + x^2 + 2x}\right)$$

$$= In\left(\left(\frac{1-x}{1+x}\right)^2\right)$$

$$= 2\,In\left(\frac{1-x}{1+x}\right)$$

$$= 2\,f(x)$$

53. Correct Response : (a)

Explanation :

Given,

$$f(x) = a^x$$

$$f(x) = \frac{a^x + a^{-x} + a^x - a^{-x}}{2}$$

So,

$$f_1(x) = \left(\frac{a^x + a^{-x}}{2}\right)$$

and,

$$f_2(x) = \left(\frac{a^x - a^{-x}}{2}\right)$$

$$f_1\,(x + y) + f_1(x - y)$$

$$= \frac{1}{2}\left[a^{x+y} + \frac{1}{a^{x+y}} + a^{x-y} + \frac{1}{a^{x-y}}\right]$$

$$= \frac{1}{2}\left[a^x \cdot a^y + \frac{1}{a^x \cdot a^y} + \frac{a^x}{a^y} + \frac{a^y}{a^x}\right]$$

$$= \frac{1}{2}(a^x + a^{-x})\,(a^y + a^{-y})$$

$$= 2f_1(x)\,f_1(y)$$

54. Correct Response : (b)

Explanation :

The relation $\phi(x)$ is given by,

$$\phi(x) = (ho(fog))\,(x)$$

$$= h\left(\sqrt{\tan x}\right)$$

$$= \frac{1 - \tan x}{1 + \tan x}$$

$$= \tan\left(\frac{\pi}{4} - x\right)$$

The value of $\phi\left(\dfrac{\pi}{3}\right)$ is,

$$\phi\left(\frac{\pi}{3}\right) = \tan\left(\frac{\pi}{4} - \frac{\pi}{3}\right)$$

$$= \tan\left(\frac{-\pi}{12}\right)$$

$$= \tan\left(\frac{11\pi}{12}\right)$$

55. Correct Response : (d)

Explanation :

It is given that,

$$\cos 2x + \alpha \sin x = 2\alpha - 7$$
$$1 - 2\sin^2 x + \alpha \sin x = 2\alpha - 7$$
$$2\sin^2 x - \alpha \sin x + (2\alpha - 8) = 0$$

The value of $\sin\,(x)$ is,

$$\sin x = \frac{-\alpha \pm \sqrt{\alpha^2 - 8\,(2\alpha - 8)}}{4}$$

$$= \frac{-\alpha \pm \sqrt{\alpha^2 - 16\alpha + 64}}{4}$$

$$= \frac{\alpha \pm (\alpha - 8)}{4}$$

$$= \frac{2\alpha - 8}{4}, 2$$

Since, the value of sin x lies in the range of $(-1, 1)$, so the value of 2 is not possible.

The value of α is given by,

$$-1 \le \frac{\alpha - 4}{2} \le 1$$

$$-2 \le \alpha - 4 \le 2$$

$$2 \le \alpha \le 6$$

56. Correct Response : (d)

Explanation :

$$A = \{1, 2, 3, 4\}$$
$$B = \{3, 4, 5, 6\}$$
$$C = \{1, 2, 3, 4, 7, 8\}$$

Here $\quad A \cap B = \{3, 4\} \subseteq C$

$$A - C = \phi \subseteq B$$

But, $\qquad A \nsubseteq B$, Not true

57. Correct Response : (c)

Explanation :

The given function is,

$$f(x) = \sin(\pi \cos x)$$

Solve the above function,

$$f(x) = 0$$
$$\sin(\pi \cos x) = 0$$
$$\pi \cos x = n\pi$$
$$\cos x = n$$

Solve further as,

$$\cos x = -1, 0, 1$$

$$X = \left\{ n\pi, 2(n+1)\frac{\pi}{2} \right\}$$

$$= \left\{ n\frac{\pi}{2}, n \in I \right\}$$

The derivative of the given function is as shown,

$$f'(x) = 0$$
$$\cos(\pi \cos x)(-\pi \sin x) = 0$$
$$\pi \cos x = (2n+1)\frac{\pi}{2}$$
$$\cos x = n + \frac{1}{2}$$

Solve further as,

$$\cos x = \pm \frac{1}{2} \text{ or } x = n\pi.$$

Therefore,

$$Y = \left\{ 2n\pi \pm \frac{\pi}{3}, 2n\pi \pm \frac{2\pi}{3}, n\pi, n \in I \right\}$$

$$= \left\{ \ldots\ldots -\frac{2\pi}{3}, -\frac{\pi}{3}, 0, \frac{\pi}{3}, \frac{2\pi}{3}, \pi, \frac{4\pi}{3}, \ldots\ldots \right\}$$

which is an arithmetic progression.

58. Correct Response : (b)

Explanation :

The given function is,

$$g(x) = \cos(2\pi \sin x)$$

Solve the above function,

$$g(x) = 0$$
$$\cos(2\pi \sin x) = 0$$
$$2\pi \sin x = (2n+1)\frac{\pi}{2}$$
$$\sin x = \frac{(2n+1)}{4}$$

Solve further as,

$$\sin x = \pm \frac{1}{4}, \pm \frac{3}{4}$$

$$Z = \left\{ n\pi \pm \sin^{-1}\frac{1}{4}, n\pi \pm \sin^{-1}\frac{3}{4}, n\pi, n \in I \right\}$$

The derivative of the given function is as shown,

$$g'(x) = 0$$
$$-\sin(2\pi \sin x)(2\pi \cos x) = 0$$
$$2\pi \sin x = n\pi$$
$$\sin x = \frac{n}{2}$$

Solve further as,

$$\sin x = 0, \pm \frac{1}{2} \pm 1 \text{ or } x = (2n+1)\frac{\pi}{2}.$$

Therefore,

$$W = \left\{ n\pi, (2n+1)\frac{\pi}{2}, n\pi \pm \frac{\pi}{6}, n \in I \right\}.$$

59. Correct Response : (b)

Explanation :

Natural number which satisfy the equations for R_1 and R_2 is $2x + y = 10$ and $x + 2y = 10$ respectively.

$$R_1 = \{(1, 8), (2, 6), (3, 4), (4, 2)\}$$
$$R_2 = \{(8, 1), (6, 2), (4, 3), (2, 4)\}$$

Thus, the range of R_1 and R_2 is the value of the y coordinates *i.e.*,

Range of $R_1 = \{8, 6, 4, 2,\}$

Range of $R_2 = \{1, 2, 3, 4,\}$

60. Correct Response : (c)

Explanation :

The two binary relations are,

$$R_1 = \{(c, a), (b, b), (a, c), (c, c), (b, c), (a, a)\}$$
$$R_2 = \{(a, b), (b, a), (c, c), (c, a), (a, a), (b, b), (a, c)\}$$

The relation R_1 is not symmetric.

For relation R_1,

$$(c, a) \in R_1 \text{ and } (b, c) \in R_1.$$

But,

$$(b, a) \in R_2 \text{ and } (b, a) \notin R_1.$$

Thus, R_1 is not transitive.

The relation R_2 is symmetric.

For relation R_2,

$$(b, a) \in R_2 \text{ and } (a, c) \in R_2.$$

But

$$(b, c) \in R_1 \text{ and } (b, c) \notin R_2.$$

Thus, R_2 is not transitive.

Therefore, relation R_2 is symmetric but it is not transitive.

61. Correct Response : (a)

Explanation :

Let, $S = \{(\lambda, \mu) \in R \times R\}$

And

$$f(t) = (|\lambda| e^{|t|} - \mu) \sin 2|t|$$

The right hand derivative is,

$$\text{RHD} = \lim_{h \to 0} \frac{f(0+h) - 0}{h}$$

$$= \lim_{h \to 0} \frac{\left(|\lambda| e^{|h|} - \mu\right) \sin 2|h|}{h}$$

$$= 2 \lim_{h \to 0} \left(|\lambda| e^{h} - \mu\right) \left(\frac{\sin h}{h}\right) (\cos h)$$

$$= 0$$

The left hand derivative is,

$$\text{LHD} = \lim_{h \to 0} \frac{f(0-h) - 0}{-h}$$

$$= \lim_{h \to 0} \frac{\left(|\lambda| e^{|-h|} - \mu\right) \sin 2|-h|}{-h}$$

$$= 2 \lim_{h \to 0} \left(|\lambda| e^{h} - \mu\right) \left(\frac{\sin h}{-h}\right) (\cos h)$$

$$= 2\left(|\lambda| e^{h} - \mu\right)(-1)(1)$$

For differentiable function,

$$\text{LHD} = \text{RHD}$$

$$|\lambda| e^{h} = \mu$$

This gives the following condition,

$$\mu \geq 0$$

Here,

$$\lambda \in R$$

Therefore, S is a subset of $R \times [0, \infty)$.

62. Correct Response : (3748)

Explanation :

The given sets are,

$$X = \{1, 6, 11, \dots\dots 10086\}$$
$$Y = \{9, 16, 23, \dots\dots 14128\}$$

The intersection of set X and set Y is,

$$X \cap Y = \{16, 51, 86 \dots\dots\}$$

The number of elements in the set $X \cap Y$ is,

$$16 + (m - 1)\, 35 \leq 10086$$
$$m \leq 288.71$$
$$m = 288$$

The number of elements in the set $X \cup Y$ is,

$$m\,(X \cup Y) = m(X) + m\,(Y) - m\,(X \cap Y)$$
$$= 2018 + 2018 - 288$$
$$= 3748$$

63. Correct Response : (d)

Explanation :

The composition of f and g is,

$$fog\,(x) = f(g(x))$$

Then,

$$f(3^{10}\, x - 1) = 2^{10}\,(3^{10}\, x - 1) + 1$$
$$2^{10}\,(3^{10}\, x - 1) + 1 = x$$
$$2^{10} \cdot 3^{10}\, x - 2^{10} + 1 = x$$

Rearrange the above equation :

$$2^{10} . 3^{10} x - x = 2^{10} - 1$$
$$x(2^{10} . 3^{10} - 1) = 2^{10} - 1$$

$$x = \frac{2^{10} - 1}{2^{.10}\, 3^{10} - 1}$$

$$x = \frac{1 - 2^{-10}}{3^{10} - 2^{-10}}$$

64. Correct Response : (d)

Expalnation :

According to given question :

$$S = \left\{ x \in [0, 2\pi] : \begin{vmatrix} 0 & \cos x & -\sin x \\ \sin x & 0 & \cos x \\ \cos x & \sin x & 0 \end{vmatrix} = 0 \right\}$$

$$\cos^3 x - \sin^3 x = 0$$
$$\tan^3 x = 1$$
$$x = \tan^{-1}(1)$$

The relation of x is,

$$x \in \left\{ \frac{\pi}{4}, \frac{5\pi}{4} \right\}$$

Then,

$$\sum_{x \in S} \tan\left(\frac{\pi}{3} + x\right) = \sum_{x \in S} \frac{\tan \dfrac{\pi}{3} + \tan x}{1 - \tan \dfrac{\pi}{3} \tan x}$$

$$= \sum_{x \in S} \frac{1 + \tan \dfrac{\pi}{3}}{1 - \tan \dfrac{\pi}{3}}$$

There are only two value of set. Hence, the sum is given as :

$$S = 2 \times \frac{\sqrt{3} + 1}{1 - \sqrt{3} \times 1}$$

$$= 2 \times \frac{\sqrt{3} + 1}{1 - \sqrt{3}} \times \frac{1 + \sqrt{3}}{1 + \sqrt{3}}$$

$$= -4 - 2\sqrt{3}$$

65. Correct Response : (d)

Explanation :

$$f(x) = x - 5\left[\frac{x}{5}\right]$$

Substitute the values of random natural numbers for x.

$$f(1) = 1 - 5\left[\frac{1}{5}\right]$$

$$= 1$$

$$f(6) = 6 - 5\left[\frac{6}{5}\right]$$

$$= 1$$

Thus, it is a many to one function.
Substitute $x = 10$ in the given function.

$$f(10) = 10 - 5\left[\frac{10}{5}\right]$$

$$= 0$$

This is not in co domain, therefore, it is a many one and into function.

66. Correct Response : (b, c)

Explanation :

Given differential functions are,

$$f(x) = x^3 + 3x + 2$$

$$g(f(x)) = x$$

And, $\qquad h(g(g(x))) = x$

Differentiate the function $f(x)$ with respect to x,

$$f'(x) = 3x^2 + 3$$

$$> 0 \ \forall x$$

The function $f(x)$ is invertible.

Therefore,

$$g(f(x)) = x$$

$$f(x) = g^{-1}(x)$$

$$f^{-1}(x) = g(x)$$

Since,

$$g(f(x)) = x$$

$$g'(f(x)) f'(x) = 1$$

Substitute $x = 0$ in the above function,

$$g'(f(0)) f'(0) = 1$$

$$g'(2) \times 3 = 1 \qquad [\because f(0) = 2]$$

$$g'(2) = \frac{1}{3}$$

Also, $\qquad h(g(g(x))) = x \qquad \qquad ...(1)$

Differentiate with respect to x,

$$h'(g(g(x))) \, g'(g(x)) \, g'(x) = 1$$

Substitute $x = 236$ in the above equation.

$$h'(g(g(236))) \, g'(g(236)) \, g'(236) = 1$$

$$h'(1) \, g'(6) \, g'(236) = 1$$

$$\left[\begin{array}{c} g'(f(1)) = \dfrac{1}{3(1)^2 + 3} \\[2mm] g'(6) = \dfrac{1}{6} \end{array} \right]$$

$$h'(1) \times \frac{1}{6} \times \frac{1}{111} = 1$$

$$h'(1) = 666$$

Similarly, substitute $x = 16$ in equation (1).

$$h(g(g(16))) = 16$$

$$h(0) = 16$$

For $x = 38$,

$$h(g(3)) = 38$$

67. Correct Response : (b)

Explanation :

The given function at $n = 0$ is,

$$f_0(x) = \frac{1}{1 - x}$$

And also at $(n + 1)$ the expression of the function is,

$$f_{n+1}(x) = f_0(f_n(x))$$

Now, substitute $n = 0$ in above function $f_{n+1}(x)$,

$$f_{0+1}(x) = f_0(f_0(x))$$

$$f_1(x) = f_0(f_0(x))$$

Substitute the given value in the function,

$$f_1(x) = \frac{1}{1 - f_0(x)} ; f_0(x) \neq 1$$

$$= \frac{1}{1 - \dfrac{1}{1 - x}} ; x \neq 0$$

$$= \frac{1 - x}{-x}$$

$$= 1 - \frac{1}{x}$$

Again, substitute $n = 1$ in above function $f_{n+1}(x)$,

$$f_{1+1}(x) = f_0(f_1(x))$$

$$f_2(x) = f_0(f_1(x))$$

Substitute the value in function $f_2(x)$.

$$f_2(x) = f_0(f_1(x))$$

$$= \frac{1}{1-f_1(x)}; f_1(x) \neq 1$$

$$= \frac{1}{1+\dfrac{1-x}{x}}$$

$$= x$$

Similarly substitute the value $n = 2, 3, 4, \ldots$ in the function $f_{n+1}(x)$.

$$f_3(x) = f_0(x)$$
$$f_4(x) = f_1(x)$$
$$f_{100}(x) = f_1(x)$$

Therefore, the required value is,

$$f_{100}(3) + f_1\left(\frac{2}{3}\right) + f_2\left(\frac{3}{2}\right) = f_1(3) + f_1\left(\frac{2}{3}\right) + f_2\left(\frac{3}{2}\right)$$

Substitute the values in the above expression,

$$= \left(1 - \frac{1}{3}\right) + \left(1 - \frac{3}{2}\right) + \left(\frac{3}{2}\right)$$

$$= \frac{5}{3}$$

Hence, the required value is equal to $\dfrac{5}{3}$.

68. Correct Response : (c)

Explanation :

The given equation is,

$$(a-1)(x^4 + x^2 + 1) + (a+1)(x^2 + x + 1)^2 = 0$$
$$(a-1)(x^2 - x + 1) + (a+1)(x^2 + x + 1) = 0$$
$$ax^2 + x + a = 0$$

For the roots to be real and distinct,

$$D > 0$$
$$(1)^2 - (4 \times a \times a) > 0$$

Further, simplify the above expression,

$$1 - 4a^2 > 0$$
$$4a^2 < 1$$
$$a^2 < \frac{1}{4} \qquad [a \neq 0]$$

$$a \in \left(-\frac{1}{2}, 0\right) \cup \left(0, \frac{1}{2}\right)$$

69. Correct Response : (a, b, c)

Explanation :

The given function is,

$$f(x) = \sin\left(\frac{\pi}{6}\sin\left(\frac{\pi}{2}\sin x\right)\right)$$

Known relation,

$$-1 \leq \sin x \leq 1 \qquad [\text{as } x \in R]$$

$$-\frac{\pi}{2} \leq \frac{\pi}{2}\sin x \leq \frac{\pi}{2}$$

$$-1 \leq \sin\left(\frac{\pi}{2}\sin x\right) \leq 1$$

Simplify the relation,

$$-\frac{\pi}{6} \leq \frac{\pi}{6}\sin\left(\frac{\pi}{2}\sin x\right) \leq \frac{\pi}{6}$$

$$\sin\left(-\frac{\pi}{6}\right) \leq \sin\left(\frac{\pi}{6}\sin\left(\frac{\pi}{2}\sin x\right)\right) \leq \sin\left(\frac{\pi}{6}\right)$$

$$\frac{-1}{2} \leq \sin\left(\frac{\pi}{6}\sin\left(\frac{\pi}{2}\sin x\right)\right) \leq \frac{1}{2}$$

Hence, the required range is $\left[-\dfrac{1}{2}, \dfrac{1}{2}\right]$.

Hence, option (a) is correct.

The block diagram for the function $f \circ g(x)$ is,

Range of $g(x) = \left(-\dfrac{\pi}{2}, \dfrac{\pi}{2}\right) \cap$ domain of $f(x) = R$

$$\text{Common} = \left(-\frac{\pi}{2}, \frac{\pi}{2}\right)$$

Range of $f \circ g(x)$ = range of $f(x)$ when input $\left(-\dfrac{\pi}{2}, \dfrac{\pi}{2}\right)$

Hence, option (b) is correct.

Solve the value for the option (c),

$$\lim_{x \to 0} \frac{\sin\left(\frac{\pi}{6}\sin\left(\frac{\pi}{2}\sin x\right)\right)}{\left(\frac{\pi}{2}\sin x\right)}$$

$$= \lim_{x \to 0} \left(\frac{\sin\left(\frac{\pi}{6}\sin\left(\frac{\pi}{2}\sin x\right)\right)}{\frac{\pi}{6}\sin\left(\frac{\pi}{2}\sin x\right)}\right) \frac{\frac{\pi}{6}\sin\left(\frac{\pi}{2}\sin x\right)}{\left(\frac{\pi}{2}\sin x\right)}$$

$$= \lim_{x \to 0} \frac{\pi}{6}(1)$$

$$= \frac{\pi}{6}$$

Hence, option (c) is correct.

The block diagram representation for the function $g \circ f(x)$.

Range of $f(x) = \left[-\dfrac{1}{2}, \dfrac{1}{2}\right]$

$$gof(x) = \dfrac{\pi}{2}\sin f(x)$$

$$= \dfrac{\pi}{2}\sin\underbrace{\left(\sin\left(\dfrac{\pi}{6}\sin\left(\dfrac{\pi}{2}\sin x\right)\right)\right)}_{\frac{1}{2}\,to\,\frac{1}{2}}$$

$$= 1$$

$$\sin\left(-\dfrac{1}{2}\,to\,\dfrac{1}{2}\right) = \dfrac{2}{\pi}$$

$$\approx 0.6379 \qquad \text{(not possible)}$$

$$\dfrac{1}{2} \approx 28.5°$$

Hence, option (d) is not correct.

70. Correct Response : (b)

Explanation :

The given function is,

$X = \{4^n - 3n - 1 : n \in N\}$

Simplify the above function.

$X = \{4^n - 3n - 1 : n \in N\}$

$X = \{(1 + 3)^n - 3n - 1: n \in N\}\ [(1 + x)^n = {}^n C_0 x^0$
$\qquad\qquad\qquad\qquad + {}^n C_1 x + ... + {}^n C_n x]$

$X = 3^2\{({}^n C_2 + {}^n C_3 \times 3 + ... + 3^{n-2}) : n \in N\}$

The above function is divisible by 9.

$$Y = \{9(n - 1) : n \in N\}$$

The above function is also divisible by 9.

So,

$$X \subseteq Y$$

Above $\qquad X \cup Y = Y$

71. Correct Response : (c)

Explanation :

Consider the given equation,

$-3(x - [x])^2 + 2(x - [x]) + a^2 = 0 \quad (\because [x] = x - \{x\})$
$\qquad\quad 3\{x\}^2 - 2\{x\} - a^2 = 0$

Since $a \neq 0$. So,

$$3\left(\{x\}^2 - \dfrac{2}{3}\{x\}\right) = a^2$$

Add and subtract with $\dfrac{1}{3}$ in the above expression,

$$a^2 = 3\left(\{x\}^2 - \dfrac{2}{3}\{x\}\right) + \left(\dfrac{1}{3}\right) - \left(\dfrac{1}{3}\right)$$

$$a^2 = 3\left(\{x\}^2 - \dfrac{2}{3}\{x\} + \left(\dfrac{1}{3}\right)^2\right) - \left(\dfrac{1}{3}\right)$$

$$= 3\left(\{x\} - \dfrac{1}{3}\right)^2 - \dfrac{1}{3}$$

Apply the relation,

$$0 \leq \{x\} < 1$$

$$\dfrac{-1}{3} \leq \{x\} - \dfrac{1}{3} < \dfrac{2}{3}$$

$$0 \leq 3\left(\{x\} - \dfrac{1}{3}\right)^2 < \dfrac{4}{3}$$

$$\dfrac{-1}{3} \leq 3\left(\{x\} - \dfrac{1}{3}\right)^2 - \dfrac{1}{3} < 1$$

For non-integral solution :

$$0 < a^2 < 1$$

$$\Rightarrow \qquad a \in (-1, 0) \cup (0, 1)$$

72. Correct Response : (b)

Explanation :

The given expression is,

$$f_k(x) = \dfrac{1}{k}\left(\sin^k x + \cos^k x\right)$$

Simplify the given expression by substituting the value of k,

$$f_4(x) - f_6(x)$$

$$= \dfrac{1}{4}\left(\sin^4 x + \cos^4 x\right) - \dfrac{1}{6}\left(\sin^6 x + \cos^6 x\right)$$

$$= \dfrac{1}{4}\left(1 - 2\sin^2 x\cos^2 x\right) - \dfrac{1}{6}\left(1 - 3\sin^2 x\cos^2 x\right)$$

$$= \dfrac{3\left(1 - 2\sin^2 x\cos^2 x\right) - 2\left(1 - 3\sin^2 x\cos^2 x\right)}{12}$$

Further, simplify the above expression,

$$f_4(x) - f_6(x) = \dfrac{3 - 2}{12}$$

$$= \dfrac{1}{12}$$

73. Correct Response : (b)

Explanation :

For $|x| < 3$, the set A is,

$\qquad A = \{-2, -1, 0, 1, 2\}$

For $y = |x|$ and $x \neq -1$, the set R is, z

$\qquad R = \{(-2, 2)\ (0, 0)\ (1, 1)\ (1, 2)\}$

The power set of R is,

$\qquad 2^4 = 16$

74. Correct Response : (d)

Explanation :

The given function is,

$$f(x) = \dfrac{|x| - 1}{|x| + 1}$$

$$= \begin{cases} \dfrac{x - 1}{x + 1}, & x \geq 0 \\[2mm] \dfrac{-x - 1}{-x + 1}, & x < 0 \end{cases}$$

Check the function for one-one,

The given function is one-one if,

Assume, $\qquad f(a) = f(b)$

Shows, $\qquad a = b$

Now, $\qquad f(a) = f(b)$

$$\frac{|a|-1}{|a|+1} = \frac{|b|-1}{|b|+1}$$

$$|a||b| - |b| + |a| - 1 = |a||b| + |b| - |a| - 1$$

$$|a| = |b|$$

Here at $a \geq 0$, and $b < 0$,

$$a \neq b$$

Hence, the given function is not one–one.

Check the function for onto,

The given function is onto if,

$$f(x) = y$$

Now, $\qquad f(x) = \dfrac{|x|-1}{|x|+1}$

$$y(|x| + 1) = |x| - 1$$

$$|x| = -\frac{(y+1)}{(y-1)}$$

For $x < 0$, $\qquad x = \dfrac{(y+1)}{(y-1)}$

Therefore, $\qquad f\left(\dfrac{y+1}{y-1}\right) = \dfrac{\dfrac{y+1}{y-1}-1}{\dfrac{y+1}{y-1}+1}$

$$= \frac{\dfrac{y+1-y+1}{y-1}}{\dfrac{y+1+y-1}{y-1}}$$

$$= \frac{2}{2y}$$

$$= \frac{1}{y}$$

Here, $\qquad f(x) \neq y$

Hence, the given function is not onto.

Hence, it is clear that f is neither one-one nor onto.

75. Correct Response : (c)

Explanation :

The function f is an odd function,

$$f(-x) = -f(x)$$

The value of the function $f(x)$ at $-\dfrac{11\pi}{6}$

$$f\left(-\frac{11\pi}{6}\right) = -\left[3\sin\left(+\frac{11\pi}{6}\right) + 4\cos\left(+\frac{11\pi}{6}\right)\right]$$

$$= -\left[3\sin\left(2\pi - \frac{\pi}{6}\right) + 4\cos\left(2\pi - \frac{\pi}{6}\right)\right]$$

$$= \left[+3\sin\left(\frac{\pi}{6}\right) - 4\cos\left(\frac{\pi}{6}\right)\right]$$

$$= \frac{3}{2} - 2\sqrt{3}$$

76. Correct Response : (d)

Explanation :

The given expression is reflexive :

$$\sec^2 a - \tan^2 b = 1 \quad \forall x \in \mathrm{R}$$

For symmetric :

$$\sec^2 a - \tan^2 b = 1$$

$$\sec^2 b - \tan^2 a = 1 \qquad \ldots(1)$$

To prove;

$$\sec^2 b - \tan^2 a = 1 + \tan^2 b - (\sec^2 a - 1)$$

$$= 1 + \tan^2 b + 1 - \sec^2 a$$

$$= 2 - (\sec^2 a - \tan^2 b)$$

$$= 1$$

It is clear from the equation (1), the function is symmetric.

For transitive :

$$\sec^2 a - \tan^2 b = 1 \qquad \ldots(2)$$

$$\sec^2 b - \tan^2 c = 1 \qquad \ldots(3)$$

To prove : $\sec^2 a - \tan^2 c = 1$

Proof : L.H.S.

$$\sec^2 a - \tan^2 c = 1 + \tan^2 b + 1 - \sec^2 b$$

$$= 1$$

The point P is reflexive, symmetric and transitive.

Hence, the given relation is an equivalence relation.

77. Correct Response : (a)

Explanation :

Draw the Venn diagram for the given events,

$$P(A \cup B) = P(A \cap B)$$

A $\qquad$ B

Hence, from the Venn diagram observation, the incorrect option is (a).

78. Correct Response : (b)

Explanation :

Total number of the empty subsets,

$$N = 2^7 - 1$$

$$= 127$$

Consider $x \in S$ present in A.

The number of A contain x,

$$X = 2^6$$

$$= 64$$

The probability that $X \in A$,

$$P = \frac{X}{N}$$

$$= \frac{64}{127}$$

79. Correct Response : (3)

Explanation :

The function is given by,

$$f(x) = \cos^{-1}(\cos x)$$

The equation is given by,

$$f(x) = \frac{10 - x}{10}$$

The graph of the function as shown below,

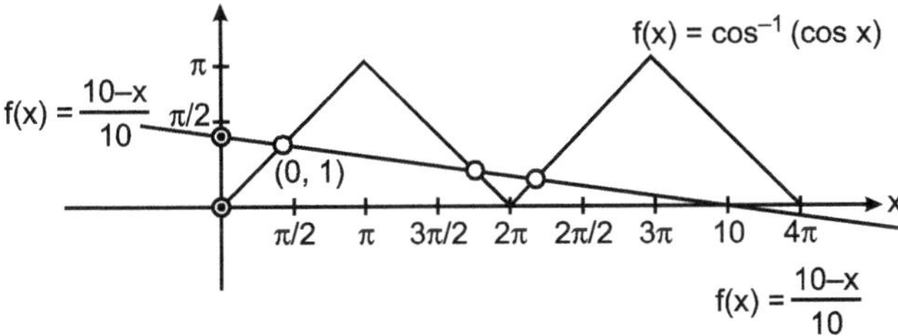

From the above figure, it is clear that the function $f(x) = \cos^{-1}(\cos x)$ and $f(x) = \dfrac{10 - x}{10}$ intersect at three distinct points so that the number of solution is 3.

80. Correct Response : (b, c)

Explanation :

Let, the given function is,

$$f(x) = x \sin \pi x$$

Differentiate above function,

$$f'(x) = \sin \pi x + \pi x \cos \pi x$$
$$0 = \sin \pi x + \pi x \cos \pi x$$
$$\sin \pi x = -\pi x \cos \pi x$$
$$\tan \pi x = -\pi x$$

Solve further,

$$\pi x \in \left(\frac{2n+1}{2}\pi, (n+1)\pi\right)$$

$$\pi x \in \left(n + \frac{1}{2}, n+1\right) \text{ or } x \in (n, n+1)$$

81. Correct Response : (b)

Explanation :

The given function is,

$$f(x) = 2x^3 - 15x^2 + 36x + 1$$

Differentiate with respect to x,

$$f'(x) = 6x^2 - 30x + 36$$
$$= 6(x^2 - 5x + 6)$$
$$= 6(x - 3)(x - 2)$$

The figure shows the domain.

The function has local maxima in a domain and it is many-one.

The value of function at $x = 0$ is,

$$f(0) = 2(0)^3 - 15(0)^2 + 36(0) + 1$$
$$= 1$$

The value of function at $x = 2$ is,

$$f(2) = 2(2)^3 - 15(2)^2 + 36(2) + 1$$
$$= 29$$

The value of function at $x = 3$ is,

$$f(3) = 2(3)^3 - 15(3)^2 + 36(3) + 1$$
$$= 28$$

The range of the function is [1, 29].

Therefore, the function $f(x)$ is onto but not one – one.

82. Correct Response : (a)

Explanation :

Let, the given functions are $f(x) = x^2$ and $g(x) = \sin x$.

Solve the given equation.

$$f\big(g(g(f(x)))\big) = g\big(g(f(x))\big)$$

$$(\sin(\sin x^2))^2 = \sin(\sin x^2)$$

$$\sin(\sin x^2)[\sin(\sin x^2) - 1] = 0$$

Now, solve for first factor.

$$\sin(\sin x^2) = 1$$

$$\sin x^2 = 2n\pi + \frac{\pi}{2}$$

For $n = 0$,

$$\sin x^2 = \frac{\pi}{2}$$

The above value is not possible.

Solve for other factor.

$$\sin(\sin x^2) = 0$$
$$\sin x^2 = n\pi$$

For $n = 0$,

$$\sin x^2 = 0$$
$$x^2 = n\pi$$
$$x = \pm\sqrt{n\pi}$$

Therefore, $n \in \{0, 1, 2, ...\}$.

83. Correct Response : (d)

Explanation :

Apply the formula to find the total number of unordered pair of disjoint subset,

$$\text{Total number} = \frac{3^n + 1}{2}$$

$$= \frac{3^4 + 1}{2}$$

$$= \frac{81 + 1}{2}$$

$$= 41$$

84. Correct Response : (b)

Explanation :

Differentiate the given expression with respect to x,

$$\frac{d}{dx}e^{-x}f(x) = \frac{d}{dx}\left(2+\int_0^x \sqrt{t^4+1}\,dt\right)$$

$$e^{-x}\left(f'(x)-f(x)\right) = \sqrt{x^4+1}$$

$$f'(x) = f(x)+\sqrt{x^4+1}\,e^x$$

The function f^{-1} is the inverse function of f so,

$$f^{-1'}\left(f(x)\right)\left(f'(x)\right) = 1$$

$$f^{-1'}\left(f(x)\right) = \frac{1}{\left(f'(x)\right)}$$

$$= \frac{1}{f(x)+\sqrt{x^4+1}\times e^x}$$

The value of $f(x)$ is equal to 2 at $x = 0$ from the given expression.

Substitute (2) for $f(x)$ in the above equation.

$$f^{-1'}(2) = \frac{1}{2+\sqrt{0^4+1}\times e^0}$$

$$= \frac{1}{3}$$

85. Correct Response : (c)

Explanation :

The number of ordered pair (p, q) is calculated as,

$(2 \times 3 - 1)(2 \times 5 - 1)(2 \times 3 - 1) = (5)(9)(5)$

$$= 225$$

86. Correct Response : (d)

Explanation :

Let, function be $g(x) = f(x) - x^2$.

The value of function at $x = 1$ is,

$$g(1) = f(1) - 1$$

$$= 1 - 1$$

$$= 0$$

The value of function at $x = 2$ is,

$$g(2) = f(2) - 4$$

$$= 4 - 4$$

$$= 0$$

The value of function at $x = 3$ is,

$$g(3) = f(3) - 9$$

$$= 9 - 9$$

$$= 0$$

So, $g(x)$ has 3 real roots. Also, $g'(x)$ has two real roots and $g''(x)$ has one real root.

Differentiate $g(x) = f(x) - x^2$.

$$g'(x) = f'(x) - 2x$$

$$g''(x) = f''(x) - 2$$

$$0 = f''(x) - 2$$

$$f''(x) = 2$$

Therefore, $f''(x) = 2$ for some $x \in (1, 3)$.

87. Correct Response : (a)

Explanation :

Let, function be $h(x) = f(x) - g(x)$

$$h(x) = \begin{cases} x, & x \in \text{irrational} \\ x, & x \in \text{rational} \end{cases}$$

Therefore, $h(x)$ is one - one and onto.

88. Correct Response : (b)

Explanation :

Let, polynomial of degree 2 be $P(x) = ax^2 + bx + c$.

The value of polynomial at $x = 0$ is,

$$P(0) = a(0)^2 + b(0) + c$$

$$c = 0$$

The value of polynomial at $x = 1$ is,

$$P(1) = a(1)^2 + b(1) + 0$$

$$a + b = 1$$

Differentiate the polynomial with respect to x.

$$P'(x) = 2ax + b$$

$$= 2(1 - b)x + b > 0$$

Therefore, $b \in (0, 2)$ and $S = \{(1 - a)x^2 + ax,\ 0 < a < 2\}$.

89. Correct Response : (b)

Explanation :

Solve the composite function.

$$g\left(f(x)\right) = g\left(\sin x + \cos x\right)$$

$$= (\sin x + \cos x)^2 - 1$$

$$= \sin^2 x + \cos^2 x + 2\sin x \cos x - 1$$

$$= \sin 2x$$

It is known that $\sin x$ is invertible or bijective if

$$x \in \left[-\frac{\pi}{2}, \frac{\pi}{2}\right].$$

Therefore, $g\left(f(x)\right)$ is bijective if $x \in \left[-\frac{\pi}{4}, \frac{\pi}{4}\right]$.

90. Correct Response : (a)

Explanation :

The domain of given function is,

$$\sin^{-1}(2x) + \frac{\pi}{6} \geq 0$$

$$\sin^{-1}(2x) \geq -\frac{\pi}{6}$$

$$-\sin\frac{\pi}{6} \leq 2x \leq 1$$

$$-\frac{1}{4} \leq x \leq \frac{1}{2}$$

Therefore, domain is $\left[-\frac{1}{4}, \frac{1}{2}\right]$.

91. Correct Response : (c)

Explanation :

Let, the function is,

$$f(x) = y = \frac{x^2 + x + 2}{x^2 + x + 1}$$

Simplify the equation.

$$x^2 y + xy + y = x^2 + x + 2$$

$$(1 - y) x^2 + (1 - y) x + 2 - y = 0$$

Discriminant of quadratic equation is,

$$D \geq 0$$

$$(1 - y)^2 - 4 (1 - y)(2 - y) \geq 0$$

$$- 3y^2 + 10y - 7 \geq 0$$

Therefore, the range of the function is $\left(1, \dfrac{7}{3}\right]$.

92. Correct Response : (d)

Explanation :

The function $g(x)$ is the inverse of function $f(x)$. The inverse of function $f(x) = (x + 1)^2$ is,

$$x = (y + 1)^2$$

$$\sqrt{x} = y + 1$$

$$y = \sqrt{x} - 1$$

Therefore, $\qquad g(x) = \sqrt{x} - 1, x > 0$

93. Correct Response : (a)

Explanation :

Differentiate given function with respect to x.

$$f'(x) = 2 + \cos x > 0$$

As, $x \to \infty$ then $f(x) \to \infty$. Also as $x \to -\infty$ then

$$f(x) \to -\infty.$$

Therefore, f is one - one and onto.

94. Correct Response : (b)

Explanation :

If $x \geq -2$, then the set of possible values of x is,

$$x^2 - x - 2 + x > 0$$

$$x^2 > 2$$

$$x \in \left(-\infty, -\sqrt{2}\right) \cup \left(\sqrt{2}, \infty\right)$$

For $x \geq -2$, $x \in \left[-2, -\sqrt{2}\right) \cup \left(\sqrt{2}, \infty\right)$.

If $x < -2$, then set of possible values of x is,

$$x^2 + x + 2 + x > 0$$

$$x^2 + 2x + 2 > 0$$

$$x \in (-\infty, \infty)$$

Hence, $x \in \left(-\infty, -\sqrt{2}\right) \cup \left(\sqrt{2}, \infty\right)$.

●●

21

Complex Numbers and Quadratic Equations

⌨ QUESTIONS

1. If the four complex numbers z, $\bar{z}$, $\bar{z} - 2\,\mathrm{Re}(\bar{z})$ and $z - 2\mathrm{Re}(z)$ represent the vertices of a square of side 4 units in the Argand plane, then $|z|$ is equal to : **[2020, Main]**

(a) 4
(b) 2
(c) $4\sqrt{2}$
(d) $2\sqrt{2}$

2. The region represented by $\{z = x + iy \in \mathbb{C} : |z| - \mathrm{Re}\,(z) \le 1\}$ is also given by the inequality : **[2020, Main]**

(a) $y^2 \ge x + 1$
(b) $y^2 \ge 2(x + 1)$
(c) $y^2 \le x + \dfrac{1}{2}$
(d) $y^2 \le 2\left(x + \dfrac{1}{2}\right)$

3. Let $z = x + iy$ be a non-zero complex number such that $z^2 = i|z|^2$, where $i = \sqrt{-1}$, then z lies on the : **[2020, Main]**

(a) imaginary axis
(b) real axis
(c) line, $y = x$
(d) line, $y = -x$

4. Let $u = \dfrac{2z + i}{z - ki}$, $z = x + iy$ and $k > 0$. If the curve represented by $\mathrm{Re}(u) + \mathrm{Im}(u) = 1$ intersects the y-axis at the points P and Q where PQ = 5, then the value of k is : **[2020, Main]**

(a) 3/2
(b) 4
(c) 2
(d) 1/2

5. If a and b are real numbers such that $(2 + \alpha)^4 = a + b\alpha$, where $\alpha = \dfrac{-1 + i\sqrt{3}}{2}$, then $a + b$ is equal to : **[2020, Main]**

(a) 57
(b) 33
(c) 24
(d) 9

6. If $\left(\dfrac{1+i}{1-i}\right)^{\frac{m}{2}} = \left(\dfrac{1+i}{i-1}\right)^{\frac{n}{3}} = 1$, $(m, n \in \mathbb{N})$ then the greatest common divisor of the least values of m and n is .... **[2020, Main]**

7. The value of $\left(\dfrac{-1 + i\sqrt{3}}{1 - i}\right)^{30}$ is :

(a) $2^{15}\, i$
(b) -2^{15}
(c) $-2^{15}\, i$
(d) 6^5

8. Let S be the set of all complex numbers z satisfying $|z^2 + z + 1| = 1$. Then which of the following statements is/are TRUE ? **[2020, Advanced]**

(a) $\left| z + \dfrac{1}{2} \right| \le \dfrac{1}{2}$ for all $z \in S$
(b) $|z| \le 2$ for all $z \in S$
(c) $\left| z + \dfrac{1}{2} \right| \ge \dfrac{1}{2}$ for all $z \in S$
(d) The set S has exactly four elements

9. For a complex number z, let $\mathrm{Re}(z)$ denote the real part of z. Let S be the set of all complex numbers z satisfying $z^4 - |z|^4 = 4iz^2$, where $i = \sqrt{-1}$. Then the minimum possible value of $|z_1 - z_2|^2$, where $z_1, z_2 \in S$ with $\mathrm{Re}(z_1) > 0$ and $\mathrm{Re}(z_2) < 0$, is .... **[2020, Advanced]**

10. The imaginary part of $(3 + 2\sqrt{-54})^{1/2} - (3 - 2\sqrt{-54})^{1/2}$ can be : **[2020, Main]**

(a) $-2\sqrt{6}$
(b) 6
(c) $\sqrt{6}$
(d) $-\sqrt{6}$

11. If z_1, z_2 are complex numbers such that $\mathrm{Re}(z_1) = |z_1 - 1|$, $\mathrm{Re}(z_2) = |z_2 - 1|$ and $\arg(z_1 - z_2) = \dfrac{\pi}{6}$, then $\mathrm{Im}(z_1 + z_2)$ is equal to : **[2020, Main]**

(a) $\dfrac{\sqrt{3}}{2}$
(b) $\dfrac{2}{\sqrt{3}}$
(c) $\dfrac{1}{\sqrt{3}}$
(d) $2\sqrt{3}$

12. The value of $\left(\dfrac{1 + \sin\dfrac{2\pi}{9} + i\cos\dfrac{2\pi}{9}}{1 + \sin\dfrac{2\pi}{9} - i\cos\dfrac{2\pi}{9}}\right)^3$ is : **[2020, Main]**

(a) $\dfrac{1}{2}(\sqrt{3} - i)$
(b) $-\dfrac{1}{2}(\sqrt{3} - i)$
(c) $-\dfrac{1}{2}(1 - i\sqrt{3})$
(d) $\dfrac{1}{2}(1 - i\sqrt{3})$

13. If $\text{Re}\left(\dfrac{z-1}{2z+i}\right) = 1$, where $z = x + iy$, then the point $\{(x, y)$ lies on a : **[2020, Main]**

    (a) circle whose centre is at $\left(-\dfrac{1}{2}, -\dfrac{3}{2}\right)$

    (b) circle whose diameter is $\dfrac{\sqrt{5}}{2}$

    (c) straight line whose slope is $\dfrac{3}{2}$

    (d) straight line whose slope is $-\dfrac{2}{3}$

14. Let α and β be the roots of the equation $x^2 - x - 1 = 0$. If $p_k = (\alpha)^k + (\beta)^k, k \geq 1$, then which one of the following statements is not true ? **[2020, Main]**

    (a) $(p_1 + p_2 + p_3 + p_4 + p_5) = 26$

    (b) $p_5 = 11$

    (c) $p_3 = p_5 - p_4$

    (d) $p_5 = p_2 \cdot p_3$

15. If $\dfrac{3 + i\sin\theta}{4 - i\cos\theta}, \ \theta \in [0, 2\pi]$, is a real number, then an argument of $\sin\theta + i\cos\theta$ is : **[2020, Main]**

    (a) $-\tan^{-1}\left(\dfrac{3}{4}\right)$

    (b) $\tan^{-1}\left(\dfrac{4}{3}\right)$

    (c) $\pi - \tan^{-1}\left(\dfrac{4}{3}\right)$

    (d) $\pi - \tan^{-1}\left(\dfrac{3}{4}\right)$

16. If the equation, $x^2 + bx + 45 = 0 \ (b \in R)$ has conjugate complex roots and they satisfy $|z + 1| = 2\sqrt{10}$, then : **[2020, Main]**

    (a) $b^2 - b = 42$

    (b) $b^2 + b = 12$

    (c) $b^2 + b = 72$

    (d) $b^2 - b = 30$

17. Let $\alpha = \dfrac{-1 + i\sqrt{3}}{2}$. If $a = (1 + \alpha)\sum\limits_{k=0}^{100} a^{2k}$ and $b = \sum\limits_{k=0}^{100} \alpha^{3k}$, then a and b are the roots of the quadratic equation : **[2020, Main]**

    (a) $x^2 - 102x + 101 = 0$

    (b) $x^2 + 101x + 100 = 0$

    (b) $x^2 - 101x + 100 = 0$

    (c) $x^2 + 102x + 101 = 0$

18. Let z be complex number such that $\left|\dfrac{z - i}{z + 2i}\right| = 1$ and $|z| = \dfrac{5}{2}$. Then the value of $|z + 3i|$ is :

    [2020, Main]

    (a) $\sqrt{10}$

    (b) $2\sqrt{3}$

    (c) $\dfrac{7}{2}$

    (d) $\dfrac{15}{4}$

19. The number of real roots of the equation. $e^{4x} + e^{3x} - 4e^{2x} + e^x + 1 = 0$ is : **[2020, Main]**

    (a) 4

    (b) 2

    (c) 3

    (d) 1

20. Let $a, b \in r, a \neq 0$ be such that the equation $ax^2 - 2bx + 5 = 0$ has a repeated root α, which is also a root of the equation, $x^2 - 2bx - 10 = 0$. If β is the other root of this equation, then $\alpha^2 + \beta^2$ is equal to : **[2020, Main]**

    (a) 26

    (b) 25

    (c) 28

    (d) 24

21. If z be a complex number satisfying $|\text{Re}(z)| + |\text{Im}(z)| = 4$, then $|z|$ cannot be : **[2020, Main]**

    (a) $\sqrt{\dfrac{17}{2}}$

    (b) $\sqrt{10}$

    (c) $\sqrt{8}$

    (d) $\sqrt{7}$

22. Let α and β be two real roots of the equation $(k + 1)\tan^2 x - \sqrt{2} \cdot \lambda \tan x = (1 - k)$, where $k \, (\neq -1)$ and λ are real numbers. If $\tan^2(\alpha + \beta) = 50$, then a value of λ is : **[2020, Main]**

    (a) 5

    (b) 10

    (c) $5\sqrt{2}$

    (d) $10\sqrt{2}$

23. The least positive value of 'a' for which the equation $2x^2 + (a - 10)x + \dfrac{33}{2} = 2a$ has real roots is.................. **[2020, Main]**

24. If $a > 0$ and $z = \dfrac{(1 + i)}{a - i}$, has magnitude $\sqrt{\dfrac{2}{5}}$, then $\bar{z}$ is equal to : **[2019, Main]**

    (a) $-\dfrac{1}{5} - \dfrac{3}{5}i$

    (b) $-\dfrac{3}{5} - \dfrac{1}{5}i$

    (c) $\dfrac{1}{5} - \dfrac{3}{5}i$

    (d) $-\dfrac{1}{5} + \dfrac{3}{5}i$

25. If α and β are the roots of the quadratic equation, $x^2 + x\sin\theta - 2\sin\theta = 0, \ \theta \in \left(0, \dfrac{\pi}{2}\right)$, then $\dfrac{\alpha^{12} + \beta^{12}}{(\alpha^{-12} + \beta^{-12}) \cdot (\alpha - \beta)^{24}}$ is equal to : **[2019, Main]**

    (a) $\dfrac{2^{12}}{(\sin\theta - 4)^{12}}$

    (b) $\dfrac{2^{12}}{(\sin\theta + 18)^{12}}$

    (c) $\dfrac{2^{12}}{(\sin\theta - 8)^{6}}$

    (d) $\dfrac{2^{6}}{(\sin\theta + 8)^{12}}$

26. The number of real roots of the equation $5 + |2^x - 1| = 2^x(2^x - 2)$ is : **[2019, Main]**

    (a) 3

    (b) 2

    (c) 4

    (d) 1

27. If z and w are two complex numbers such that $|zw| = 1$ and $\arg(z) - \arg(w) = \dfrac{\pi}{2}$, **[2019, Main]**

(a) $\bar{z}w = i$

(b) $z\bar{w} = \dfrac{-1+i}{\sqrt{2}}$

(c) $\bar{z}w = -i$

(d) $z\bar{w} = \dfrac{1-i}{\sqrt{2}}$

28. If m is chosen in the quadratic equation $(m^2 + 1) x^2 - 3x + (m^2 + 1)^2 = 0$ such that the sum of its roots is greatest, then the absolute difference of the cubes of its roots is : **[2019, Main]**

(a) $10\sqrt{5}$

(b) $8\sqrt{3}$

(c) $8\sqrt{5}$

(d) $4\sqrt{3}$

29. Let $z \in C$ be such that $|z| < 1$. If $\omega = \dfrac{5+3z}{5(1-z)}$, **[2019, Main]**

(a) $5\,\mathrm{Re}(\omega) > 4$

(b) $4\,\mathrm{Im}(\omega) = 5$

(c) $5\,\mathrm{Re}(\omega) > 1$

(d) $5\,\mathrm{Im}(\omega) < 1$

30. Let $p, q \in R$. If $2 - \sqrt{3}$ is a root of the quadratic equation, $x^2 + 9x + q = 0$, then : **[2019, Main]**

(a) $p^2 - 4q + 12 = 0$

(b) $q^2 - 4p - 16 = 0$

(c) $q^2 + 4p + 14 = 0$

(d) $p^2 - 4q - 12 = 0$

31. If α and β be the roots of the equation $x^2 - 2x + 2 = 0$, then the least value of n for which $\left(\dfrac{\alpha}{\beta}\right)^n = 1$ is : **[2019, Main]**

(a) 2

(b) 5

(c) 4

(d) 3

32. The sum of the solution of the equation $|\sqrt{x} - 2| + \sqrt{x}(\sqrt{x} - 4) + 2 = 0$, $(x > 0)$ is equal to : **[2019, Main]**

(a) 9

(b) 12

(c) 4

(d) 10

33. If $z = \dfrac{\sqrt{3}}{2} + \dfrac{i}{2}\,(i = \sqrt{-1})$, then $(1 + iz + z^5 + iz^8)^9$ is equal to : **[2019, Main]**

(a) 0

(b) 1

(c) $(-1 + 2i)^9$

(d) -1

34. The number of integral values of m for which the equation $(1 + m^2) x^2 - 2(1 + 3m) x + (1 + 8m) = 0$ has no real root is : **[2019, Main]**

(a) 1

(b) 2

(c) infinitely many

(d) 3

35. The number of solutions of the equation $1 + \sin^4 x = \cos^2 3x$, $x \in \left[-\dfrac{5\pi}{2}, \dfrac{5\pi}{2}\right]$ is : **[2019, Main]**

(a) 3

(b) 5

(c) 7

(d) 4

36. The equation $|z - i| = |z - 1|$, $i = \sqrt{-1}$, represents :

(a) a circle of radius $\dfrac{1}{2}$. **[2019, Main]**

(b) the line through the origin with slope 1.

(c) a circle of radius 1.

(d) the line through the origin with slope -1.

37. Let $z \in C$ with $\mathrm{Im}(z) = 10$ and it satisfies $\dfrac{2z - n}{2z + n} = 2i - 1$ for some natural number n. Then : **[2019, Main]**

(a) $n = 20$ and $\mathrm{Re}(z) = -10$

(b) $n = 40$ and $\mathrm{Re}(z) = 10$

(c) $n = 40$ and $\mathrm{Re}(z) = -10$

(d) $n = 20$ and $\mathrm{Re}(z) = 10$

38. Let S be the set of all complex numbers z satisfying $|z - 2 + i| \geq \sqrt{5}$. If the complex number z_0 is such that $\dfrac{1}{|z_0 - 1|}$ is the maximum of the set $\left\{\dfrac{1}{|z - 1|} : z \in S\right\}$, then the principal argument of $\dfrac{4 - z_0 - \bar{z}_0}{z_0 - \bar{z}_0 + 2i}$ is **[2019, Advanced]**

(a) $-\dfrac{\pi}{2}$

(b) $\dfrac{\pi}{4}$

(c) $\dfrac{\pi}{2}$

(d) $\dfrac{3\pi}{4}$

39. Let α and β be the roots of $x^2 - x - 1 = 0$, with $\alpha > \beta$. For all positive integers n, define

$$a_n = \dfrac{\alpha^n - \beta^n}{\alpha - \beta}, \quad n \geq 2,$$

$$b_1 = 1 \text{ and } b_n = a_{n-1} + a_{n+1}, \quad n \geq 2.$$

Then which of the following options is / are correct ? **[2019, Advanced]**

(a) $a_1 + a_2 + a_3 + \ldots + a_n = a_{n+2} - 1$ for all $n \geq 1$

(b) $\displaystyle\sum_{n=1}^{\infty} \dfrac{a_n}{10^n} = \dfrac{10}{89}$

(c) $b_n = \alpha^n + \beta^n$ for all $n \geq 1$

(d) $\displaystyle\sum_{n=1}^{\infty} \dfrac{b_n}{10^n} = \dfrac{8}{89}$

40. Let $\omega \neq 1$ be a cube root of unity. Then the minimum of the set $\{|a + b\omega + c\omega^2|^2 : a, b, c \text{ distinct non-zero integers}\}$ equal to .... **[2019, Advanced]**

41. If $\lambda \in R$ is such that the sum of the cubes of the roots of the equation, $x^2 + (2 - \lambda)x + (10 - \lambda) = 0$ is minimum, then the magnitude of the difference of the roots of this equation is : **[2018, Main]**

(a) $4\sqrt{2}$ (b) $2\sqrt{5}$

(c) $2\sqrt{7}$ (d) 20

42. The set all $\alpha \in R$, for which $\omega = \dfrac{1 + (1 - 8\alpha)z}{1 - z}$ is a purely imaginary number for all $z \in C$ satisfying $|z| = 1$ and $\text{Re } z \neq 1$ is : **[2018, Main]**

(a) an empty set   (b) $\{0\}$

(c) $\left\{0, \dfrac{1}{4}, -\dfrac{1}{4}\right\}$ (d) equal to R

43. If tan A and tan B are the roots of the quadratic equation, $3x^2 - 10x - 25 = 0$, then the value of $3 \sin^2 (A + B) - 10 \sin (A + B) \cdot \cos (A + B) - 25 \cos^2 (A + B)$ is : **[2018, Main]**

(a) -10 (b) 10

(c) -25 (d) 25

44. Let p, q and r be real numbers ($p \neq q$, $r \neq 0$), such that the roots of the equation $\dfrac{1}{x+p} + \dfrac{1}{x+q} = \dfrac{1}{r}$ are equal in magnitude but opposite in sign, then the sum of squares of these roots is equal to : **[2018, Main]**

(a) $\dfrac{p^2 + q^2}{2}$ (b) $p^2 + q^2$

(c) $2(p^2 + q^2)$ (d) $p^2 + q^2 + r^2$

45. The least positive integer n for which $\left(\dfrac{1 + i\sqrt{3}}{1 - i\sqrt{3}}\right)^n = 1$ is : **[2018, Main]**

(a) 2   (b) 3

(c) 5   (d) 6

46. Let $S = \{x \in R : x \geq 0 \text{ and } 2\left|\sqrt{x} - 3\right| + \sqrt{x}(\sqrt{x} - 6) + 6 = 0\}$. Then S : **[2018, Main]**

(a) is an empty set.

(b) contains exactly one element.

(c) contains exactly two elements.

(d) contains exactly four elements.

47. If $\alpha, \beta \in C$ are the distinct roots, of the equation $x^2 - x + 1 = 0$, then $\alpha^{101} + \beta^{107}$ is equal to : **[2018, Main]**

(a) -1 (b) 0

(c) 1   (d) 2

48. The sum of all the real values of x satisfying the equation $2^{(x-1)(x^2 + 5x - 50)} = 1$ is : **[2018, Main]**

(a) 16   (b) 14

(c) -4 (d) -5

49. The equation $\text{Im}\left(\dfrac{iz - 2}{z - i}\right) + 1 = 0$, $z \in C$, $z \neq i$ represents a part of a circle having radius equal to : **[2018, Main]**

(a) 2   (b) 1

(c) $\dfrac{3}{4}$ (d) $\dfrac{1}{2}$

50. Let $p(x)$ be a quadratic polynomial such that $p(0) = 1$. If $p(x)$ leaves remainder 4 when divided by $x - 1$ and it leaves remainder 6 when divided by $x + 1$; then : **[2018, Main]**

(a) $p(2) = 11$ (b) $p(2) = 19$

(c) $p(-2) = 19$ (d) $p(-2) = 11$

51. Let $z \in C$, the set of complex numbers. Then the equation, $2|z + 3i| - |z - i| = 0$ represents : **[2018, Main]**

(a) a circle with radius $= \dfrac{8}{3}$.

(b) a circle with diameter $\dfrac{10}{3}$.

(c) an ellipse with length of major axis $\dfrac{16}{3}$.

(d) an ellipse with length of minor axis $\dfrac{16}{9}$.

52. Let ω be a complex number such that $2\omega + 1 = z$ where $z = \sqrt{-3}$. If

$$\begin{vmatrix} 1 & 1 & 1 \\ 1 & -\omega^2 - 1 & \omega^2 \\ 1 & \omega^2 & \omega^7 \end{vmatrix} = 3k,$$

then k is equal to : **[2017, Main]**

(a) z (b) -1

(c) 1   (d) $-z$

53. Let a, b, x and y be real numbers such that $a - b = 1$ and $y \neq 0$. If the complex number $z = x + iy$ satisfies $\text{Im}\left(\dfrac{az + b}{z + 1}\right) = y$, then which of the following is (are) possible value (s) of x? **[2017, Advanced]**

(a) $-1 + \sqrt{1 - y^2}$ (b) $-1 - \sqrt{1 - y^2}$

(c) $1 + \sqrt{1 + y^2}$ (d) $1 - \sqrt{1 + y^2}$

54. If x is a solution of the equation, $\sqrt{2x + 1} - \sqrt{2x - 1} = 1$, $\left(x \geq \dfrac{1}{2}\right)$, then $\sqrt{4x^2 - 1}$ is equal to : **[2016, Main]**

(a) $\dfrac{3}{4}$ (b) $\dfrac{1}{2}$

(c) 2   (d) $2\sqrt{2}$

55. Let $z = 1 + ai$ be a complex number, $a > 0$, such that z^3 is a real number. Then the sum $1 + z + z^2 + \dots + z^{11}$ is equal to : **[2016, Main]**

(a) $-1250\sqrt{3}\,i$ (b) $1250\sqrt{3}\,i$

(c) $1365\sqrt{3}\,i$ (d) $-1365\sqrt{3}\,i$

56. The point represented by $2 + i$ in the Argand plane moves 1 unit eastwards, then 2 units northwards and finally from there $2\sqrt{2}$ units in the south-westwards direction. Then its new position in the Argand plane is at the point represented by : **[2016, Main]**

(a) $2 + 2i$ (b) $1 + i$

(c) $-1 - i$ (d) $-2 - 2i$

57. If the equations $x^2 + bx - 1 = 0$ and $x^2 + x + b = 0$ have a common root different from -1, then $|b|$ is equal to : **[2016, Main]**

(a) $\sqrt{2}$ (b) 2

(c) 3   (d) $\sqrt{3}$

58. A value of θ for which $\dfrac{2 + 3i\sin\theta}{1 - 2i\sin\theta}$ is purely imaginary, is **[2016, Main]**

(a) $\dfrac{\pi}{3}$ (b) $\dfrac{\pi}{6}$

(c) $\sin^{-1}\left(\dfrac{\sqrt{3}}{4}\right)$ (d) $\sin^{-1}\left(\dfrac{1}{\sqrt{3}}\right)$

59. Let $-\dfrac{\pi}{6} < \theta < -\dfrac{\pi}{12}$. Suppose α_1 and β_1 are the roots of the equation $x^2 - 2x\sec\theta + 1$ and α_2 and β_2 are the roots of the equation $x^2 + 2x\tan\theta - 1 = 0$. If $\alpha_1 > \beta_1$ and $\alpha_2 > \beta_2$, then $\alpha_1 + \beta_2$ equals **[2016, Main]**

(a) $2(\sec\theta - \tan\theta)$ (b) $2\sec\theta$

(c) $-2\tan\theta$ (d) 0

60. The least value of $\alpha \in R$ for which $4ax^2 + \dfrac{1}{x} \geq 1$, for all $x > 0$, is **[2016, Advanced]**

(a) $\dfrac{1}{64}$ (b) $\dfrac{1}{32}$

(c) $\dfrac{1}{27}$ (d) $\dfrac{1}{25}$

61. The sum of all real values of x satisfying the equation $(x^2 - 5x + 5)^{x^2 + 4x - 60} = 1$ is : **[2016, Main]**

(a) 3   (b) -4

(c) 6   (d) 5

62. A complex number z is said to be unimodular if $|z| = 1$. Supoose z_1 and z_2 are complex numbers such that $\dfrac{z_1 - 2z_2}{2 - z_1\bar{z_2}}$ is unimodular and z_2 is not unimodular. Then the point z_1 lies on a : **[2015, Main]**

(a) straight line parallel to x-axis.

(b) straight line parallel to y-axis.

(c) circle of radius 2

(d) circle of radius $\sqrt{2}$

63. Let α and β be the roots of equation $x^2 - 6x - 2 = 0$. If $a_n = \alpha^n - \beta^n$, for $n \geq 1$, then the value of $\dfrac{a_{10} - 2a_8}{2a_9}$ is equal to : **[2015, Main]**

(a) 6   (b) -6

(c) 3   (d) -3

64. For any integer k, let $\alpha_k = \cos\left(\dfrac{k\pi}{7}\right) + i\sin\left(\dfrac{k\pi}{7}\right)$, where $i = \sqrt{-1}$. The value of the expression
$$\dfrac{\displaystyle\sum_{k=1}^{12}\left|\alpha_{k+1} - \alpha_k\right|}{\displaystyle\sum_{k=1}^{3}\left|\alpha_{4k-1} - \alpha_{4k-2}\right|}$$
is : **[2015, Main]**

65. If in a regular polygon the number of diagonals is 54, then the number of sides of this polygon is : **[2015, Main]**

(a) 10   (b) 12

(c) 9   (d) 6

66. Let S be the set of all non-zero real numbers such that the quadratic equation $\alpha x^2 - x + \alpha = 0$ has two distinct real roots x_1 and x_2 satisfying the inequality $|x_1 - x_2| < 1$. Which of the following intervals is (are) a subset(s) of S? **[2015, Advanced]**

(a) $\left(\dfrac{-1}{2}, \dfrac{-1}{\sqrt{5}}\right)$ (b) $\left(\dfrac{-1}{\sqrt{5}}, 0\right)$

(c) $\left(0, \dfrac{1}{\sqrt{5}}\right)$ (d) $\left(\dfrac{1}{\sqrt{5}}, \dfrac{1}{2}\right)$

67. Let $z \neq -i$ be any complex number such that $\dfrac{z - i}{z + i}$ is a purely imaginary number. Then $z + \dfrac{1}{z}$ is : **[2014, Main]**

(a) 0

(b) any non-zero real number other that 1.

(c) any non-zero real number

(d) a purely imaginary number.

68. The sum of the roots of the equation,

$x^2 + |2x - 3| - 4 = 0$, is : **[2014, Main]**

(a) 2   (b) -2

(c) $\sqrt{2}$ (d) $-\sqrt{2}$

69. For all complex numbers z of the form $1 + i\alpha$, $\alpha \in R$, if $z^2 = x + iy$, then : **[2014 Main]**

(a) $y^2 - 4x + 2 = 0$ (b) $y^2 + 4x - 4 = 0$

(c) $y^2 - 4x + 4 = 0$ (d) $y^2 + 4x + 2 = 0$.

70. Let α and β be the roots of equation $px^2 + qx + r = 0$, $p \neq 0$. If p, q, r are in A. P. and $\dfrac{1}{\alpha} + \dfrac{1}{\beta} = 4$, then the value of $|\alpha - \beta|$ is : **[2014 Main]**

(a) $\dfrac{\sqrt{34}}{9}$ (b) $\dfrac{2\sqrt{13}}{9}$

(c) $\dfrac{\sqrt{61}}{9}$ (d) $\dfrac{2\sqrt{17}}{9}$

71. If $x = -1$ and $x = 2$ are extreme points of $f(x) = \alpha \log |x| + \beta x^2 + x$ then : **[2014, Main]**

(a) $\alpha = 2, \beta = -\dfrac{1}{2}$ (b) $\alpha = 2, \beta = \dfrac{1}{2}$

(c) $\alpha = -6, \beta = \dfrac{1}{2}$ (d) $\alpha = -6, \beta = -\dfrac{1}{2}$

72. If z_1, z_2 and $z_3 z_4$ are 2 pairs of complex conjugate number, the $\pi \arg\left(\dfrac{z_1}{z_4}\right) + \arg\left(\dfrac{z_2}{z_3}\right)$ equals :

[2014, Main]

(a) 0   (b) $\dfrac{\pi}{2}$

(c) $\dfrac{3\pi}{2}$ (d) π

73. If α and β are roots of the equation,

$x^2 - 4\sqrt{2}\,kx + 2e^{4 \ in \ k} - 1 = 0$ for some k, and $\alpha^2 + \beta^2 = 66$, then $\alpha^3 + \beta^3$ is equal to : **[2014, Main]**

(a) $248\sqrt{2}$

(b) $280\sqrt{2}$

(c) $-32\sqrt{2}$

(d) $-280\sqrt{2}$

74. $z_k = \cos\left(\dfrac{2k\pi}{10}\right) + i \sin\left(\dfrac{2k\pi}{10}\right)$ $k = 1, 2, ..., 9.$

List I	**List II**
P. For each z_k there exists a z_j such that $z_k \cdot z_j$	**(1)** True
Q. There exists a $k \in \{1, 2, ..., 9\}$ $z_1 \cdot z = z_k$ has no solution z in the set of complex numbers.	**(2)** False

R. $\dfrac{|1 - z_1||1 - z_2|...|1 - z_9|}{10}$ equals   **(3)** 1

S. $1 - \sum_{k=1}^{9} \cos\left(\dfrac{2k\pi}{10}\right)$ equals   **(4)** 2

	P	Q	R	S
(a)	1	2	4	3
(b)	2	1	3	4
(c)	1	2	3	4
(d)	2	1	4	3

[2014, Advanced]

75. The quadratic equation $p(x) = 0$ with real coefficients has purey imaginary roots. Then the equation

$$p(p(x)) = 0$$ **[2014 Advanced]**

(a) only purely imaginary roots

(b) all real roots

(c) two real and two purely imaginary roots

(d) neither real nor purely imaginary roots

76. If equations $ax^2 + bx + c = 0$, $(a, b, c \in R, a \neq 0)$ and $2x^2 + 3x + 4 = 0$ have a common root, then $a : b : c$ equals : **[2014, Main]**

(a) $1 : 2 : 3$ (b) $2 : 3 : 4$

(c) $4 : 3 : 2$ (d) $3 : 2 : 1$

77. If $\dfrac{1}{\sqrt{\alpha}}$ and $\dfrac{1}{\sqrt{\beta}}$ are the roots of the equation,

$ax^2 + bx + 1 = 0$ $(a \neq 0, a, b \in R)$, then the equation, $x(x + b^3) + (a^3 - 3abx) = 0$ has roots : **[2014, Main]**

(a) $\alpha^{3/2}$ and $\beta^{3/2}$ (b) $\alpha\beta^{1/2}$ and $\alpha^{1/2}\beta$

(c) $\sqrt{\alpha\beta}$ and $\alpha\beta$ (d) $\alpha^{-\frac{3}{2}}$ and $\beta^{-\frac{2}{2}}$

78. Let $\omega = \dfrac{\sqrt{3} + i}{2}$ and $P = \{\omega^n : n = 1, 2, 3, ...\}$. Further $H_1 = \left\{z \in C : \operatorname{Re} z > \dfrac{1}{2}\right\}$ and $H_2 = \left\{z \in C : \operatorname{Re} z > \dfrac{-1}{2}\right\}$, where C is the set of all complex numbers. If $z_1 \in P \cap H_1$, $z_2 \in P \cap H_2$ and O represents the origin, then $\angle z_1 O z_2 =$ **[2013 Advanced]**

(a) $\dfrac{\pi}{2}$ (b) $\dfrac{\pi}{6}$

(c) $\dfrac{2\pi}{3}$ (d) $\dfrac{5\pi}{6}$

79. Let complex numbers α and $\dfrac{1}{\alpha}$ lie on circles $(x - x_0)^2 + (y - y_0)^2 = r^2$ and $(x - x_0)^2 + (y - y_0)^2 = 4r^2$, respectively. If $z_0 = x_0 + iy_0$ satisfies the equation $2|z_0|^2 = r^2 + 2$, then $|\alpha| =$

[2013, Advanced]

(a) $\dfrac{1}{\sqrt{2}}$ (b) $\dfrac{1}{2}$

(c) $\dfrac{1}{\sqrt{7}}$ (d) $\dfrac{1}{3}$

80. Let ω be a complex cube root of unity with $\omega \neq 1$ and $P = [p_{ij}]$ be a $n \times n$ matrix with $P_{ij} = \omega^{i+j}$. Then $P^2 \neq 0$, when $n =$ **[2013, Advanced]**

(a) 57   (b) 55

(c) 58   (d) 56

Paragraph for Q. No. 81 and 82

Let $S - S_1 \cap S_2 \cap S_3$, where

$S_1 = \{z \in C : |z| < 4\}$,

$S_2 = \left\{ z \in C : lm\left[\dfrac{z-1+\sqrt{3}i}{1-\sqrt{3}i} \right] > 0 \right\}$ and

$S_3 = \{z \in C : Rez > 0\}$.

81. Area of $S =$ **[2013, Advanced]**

(a) $\dfrac{10\pi}{3}$ (b) $\dfrac{20\pi}{3}$

(c) $\dfrac{16\pi}{3}$ (d) $\dfrac{32\pi}{3}$

82. $\min\limits_{z \in S} |1-3i-z| =$ **[2013, Advanced]**

(a) $\dfrac{2-\sqrt{3}}{2}$ (b) $\dfrac{2+\sqrt{3}}{2}$

(c) $\dfrac{3-\sqrt{3}}{2}$ (d) $\dfrac{3+\sqrt{3}}{2}$

83. Let z be a complex number such that the imaginary part of z is nonzero and $a = z^2 + z + 1$ is real. Then a cannot take the value :   **[2012, Advanced]**

(a) -1 (b) $\dfrac{1}{3}$

(c) $\dfrac{1}{2}$ (d) $\dfrac{3}{4}$

84. Let $\alpha(a)$ and $\beta(a)$ be the roots of the equation

$$\left(\sqrt[3]{1+a}-1\right)x^2 + \left(\sqrt{1+a}-1\right)x + \left(\sqrt[6]{1+a}-1\right) = 0$$

where $a > -1$.

Then $\lim\limits_{a \to 0^+} \alpha(a)$ and $\lim\limits_{a \to 0^+} \beta(a)$ are :

[2012, Advanced]

(a) $-\dfrac{5}{2}$ and 1   (b) $-\dfrac{1}{2}$ and -1

(c) $-\dfrac{7}{2}$ and 2   (d) $-\dfrac{9}{2}$ and 3

85. Let (x_0, y_0) be the solution of the following equations   **[2011, Advanced]**

$$(2x)^{\ln 2} = 3(y)^{\ln 3}$$
$$3^{\ln x} = 2^{\ln y}.$$

Then x_0 is :

(a) $\dfrac{1}{6}$ (b) $\dfrac{1}{3}$

(c) $\dfrac{1}{2}$ (d) 6

86. Let α and β be the roots of $x^2 - 6x - 2 = 0$, with $\alpha > \beta$. If $a_n = \alpha^n - \beta^n$ for $n \geq 1$, then the value of $\dfrac{a_{10} - 2a_8}{2a_9}$ is   **[2011, Advanced]**

(a) 1   (b) 2

(c) 3   (d) 4

87. Let ω be a solution of $x^3 - 1 = 0$ with $Im(\omega) > 0$. If $a = 2$ with b and c satisfying (E), then the value of   **[2011, Advanced]**

$$\dfrac{3}{\omega^c} + \dfrac{1}{\omega^b} + \dfrac{3}{\omega^c}$$

is equal to :

(a) -2 (b) 2

(c) 3   (d) -3

88. Let $b = 6$, with a and c satisfying (E). If α and β are the roots of the quadratic equation $ax^2 + bx + c = 0$, then $\sum\limits_{n=0}^{\infty} \left(\dfrac{1}{\alpha} + \dfrac{1}{\beta} \right)^n$ is :   **[2011, Advanced]**

(a) 6   (b) 7

(c) $\dfrac{6}{7}$ (d) ∞

89. If z is any complex number satisfying $|z - 3 - 2i| \leq 2$, then the minimum value of $|2z - 6 + 5i|$ is   **[2011, Advanced]**

90. A value of b for which the equations

$$x^2 + bx - 1 = 0$$
$$x^2 + x + b = 0,$$

have one root in common is :   **[2011, Advanced]**

(a) $-\sqrt{2}$ (b) $-i\sqrt{3}$

(c) $i\sqrt{5}$ (d) $\sqrt{2}$

91. Let $\omega = e^{i\pi/3}$, and a, b, c, x, y, z be non-zero complex numbers such that

$$a + b + c = x$$
$$a + b\omega + c\omega^2 = y$$
$$a + b\omega^2 + c\omega = z.$$

Then the value of $\dfrac{|x|^2 + |y|^2 + |z|^2}{|a|^2 + |b|^2 + |c|^2}$ is........

[2011, Advanced]

92. Match the statements given in Column I with the intervals/union of intervals given in Column II

Column I	Column II
(A) The set $\left\{\text{Re}\left(\dfrac{2iz}{1-z^2}\right):z\text{ is a complex }\right.$ $\left. \text{number}, |z|=1, z \neq \pm 1\right\}$ is	**(p)** $(-\infty, -1) \cup (1, \infty)$
	(q) $(-\infty, 0) \cup (0, \infty)$
(B) The domain of the function $f(x) = \sin^{-1}\left(\dfrac{8(3)^{x-2}}{1-3^{2(x-1)}}\right)$ is	**(r)** $[2, \infty)$
(C) If $f(\theta) = \begin{vmatrix} 1 & \tan\theta & 1 \\ -\tan\theta & 1 & \tan\theta \\ -1 & -\tan\theta & 1 \end{vmatrix}$, then the set $\left\{f(\theta): 0 \le \theta < \dfrac{\pi}{2}\right\}$ is	**(s)** $(-\infty, -1] \cup [1, \infty)$
(D) If $f(x) = x^{3/2}\,(3x-10)$, $x \ge 0$, then $f(x)$ is increasing in	**(t)** $(-\infty, 0] \cup [2, \infty)$

Paragraph for (Q 93 – Q 95)

Let A, B, C, be three sels of complex numbers as defined below :

A = {z : Im$z \ge$, 1}

B = {z : /z - 2 - i/ = 3}

C = {z : Re (1- i) z) = $\sqrt{2}$ }

93. The number of elements in the set A ∩ B ∩ C is : **[2008, Advanced]**

(a) 0   (b) 1

(c) 2   (d) ∞

94. Let z be any point in $A \cap B \cap C$. Then, $|z+1-i|^2 + |z-5-i|^2$ lies between **[2008, Advanced]**

(a) 25 and 29   (b) 30 and 34

(c) 35 and 39   (d) 40 and 44

95. Let z be any point in $A \cap B \cap C$ and let w be any point satisfying $|w - 2 - i| < 3$ Then, $|z| - |w| + 3$ lies between **[2008, Advanced]**

(a) –6 and 3   (b) –3 and 6

(c) –6 and 6   (d) –3 and 9

96. Let α, β be the roots of the equation $x^2 - px + r = 0$ and $\dfrac{\alpha}{2}$, 2β be the roots of the equation $x^2 - qx + r = 0$. Then the value of r is **[2007, Advanced]**

(a) $\dfrac{2}{9}(p-q)\,(2q-p)$ (b) $\dfrac{2}{9}(q-p)\,(2p-q)$

(c) $\dfrac{2}{9}(q-2p)\,(2q-p)$ (d) $\dfrac{2}{9}(2p-q)\,(2q-p)$

97. A man walks a distance of 3 units from the origin towards the north-east ($N\,45°$ E) direction. From there, he walks a distance of 4 units towards the north-west ($N\,45°$ W) direction to reach a point P. Then the position of P in the Argand plane is : **[2007, Advanced]**

(a) $3e^{i\pi/4} + 4i$ (b) $(3 - 4i)e^{i\pi/4}$

(c) $(4 + 3i)e^{i\pi/4}$ (d) $(3 + 4i)e^{i\pi/4}$

98. If $|z| = 1$ and $z \neq \pm 1$, then all the value of $\dfrac{z}{1-z^2}$ lie on : **[2007, Advanced]**

(a) a line not passing through the origin

(b) $|z| = \sqrt{2}$

(c) the X-axis

(d) the Y-axis

Paragraph for Question No. 99 to 101

If a continuous function f defined on the real line R, assumes positive and negative values in R then the equation $f(x) = 0$ has a root in R. For example, if it is known that a continous function f on R is positive at some point and its minimum value is negative then the equation $f(x) = 0$ has a root in R.

Consider $f(x) = ke^x - x$ for all real x where k is a real constant.

99. The positive value of k for which $ke^x - x = 0$ has only one root is **[2007, Advanced]**

(a) $\dfrac{1}{e}$ (b) 1

(c) e (d) $\log_e 2$

100. $k > 0$, the set of all value of k for which $ke^x - x - 0$ has two distinct roots is : **[2007, Advanced]**

(a) $\left(0, \dfrac{1}{e}\right)$ (b) $\left(\dfrac{1}{e}, 1\right)$

(c) $\left(\dfrac{1}{e}, \infty\right)$ (d) $(0, 1)$

101. If $w = \alpha + i\beta$, where $b \neq 0$ and $z \neq 1$, satisfies the condition that $\left(\dfrac{w - \overline{w}z}{1-z}\right)$ is purely real, then the set of values of z is : **[2006, Main]**

(a) $\{z : |z| = 1\}$ (b) $\{z : z = \overline{z}\}$

(c) $\}z : z \neq 1\}$ (d) $\{z : |z| = 1, z \neq 1\}$

102. Let a, b, c be the sides of a triangle. No two of them are equal and $\lambda \in$ R. If the roots of the equation $x^2 + 2(a+b+c)x + 3\lambda\,(ab+bc+ca) = 0$ are real, then: **[2006, Main]**

(a) $\lambda < \dfrac{4}{3}$ (b) $\lambda > \dfrac{5}{3}$

(c) $\lambda \in \left(\dfrac{1}{3}, \dfrac{5}{3}\right)$ (d) $\lambda \in \left(\dfrac{4}{3}, \dfrac{5}{3}\right)$

103. If P is a point on C_1 and Q in another point on C_2– then $\dfrac{PA^2 + PB^2 + PC^2 + PD^2}{QA^2 + QB^2 + QC^2 + QD^2}$ is equal to :

[2006, Main]

(a) 0.75   (b) 1.25

(c) 1   (d) 0.5

104. If roots of the equation $x^2 - 10cx - 11d = 0$ are a, b and those of $x^2 - 10ax - 11b = 0$ are c, d, then the value of $a + b + c + d$ is : (a, b, c and d are distinct numbers). **[2006, Main]**

105. Prove that there exists no complex number z such that $|z| < \dfrac{1}{3}$ and $\displaystyle\sum_{r=1}^{n} a_r z^r = 1$ where $|a_r| < 2$.

[2006, Main]

106. The locus of z which lies in shaded region is best represented by : **[2005, Main]**

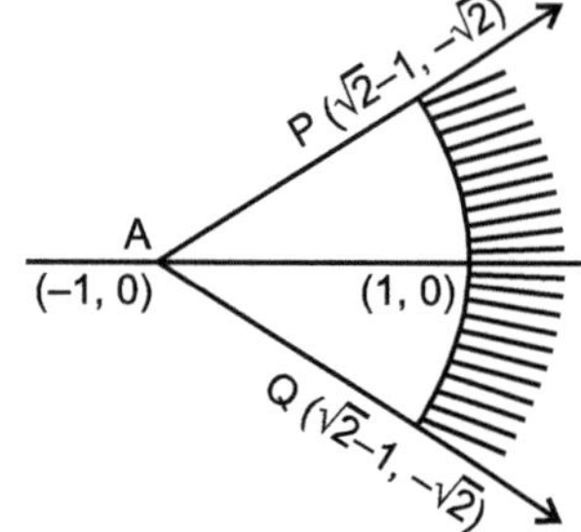

(a) $z : |z + 1| > 2$, $|\arg (z + 1)| < \pi/4$

(b) $z : |z - 1| > 2$, $|\arg (z - 1)| < \pi/4$

(c) $z : |z + 1| < 2$, $|\arg (z + 1)| < \pi/2$

(d) $z : |z - 1| < 2$, $|\arg (z - 1)| < \pi/2$

107. If a, b, c are integers not all equal and ω is a cube root of unity ($\omega \neq 1$), then the minimum value of $|a + b\omega + c\omega^2|$ is : **[2005, Main]**

(a) 0   (b) 1

(c) $\dfrac{\sqrt{3}}{2}$ (d) $\dfrac{1}{2}$

108. Find the range of values of t for which $2 \sin t = \dfrac{1 - 2x + 5x^2}{3x^2 - 2x - 1}$, $t \in \left[-\dfrac{\pi}{2}, \dfrac{\pi}{2} \right]$. **[2005, Main]**

109. $\cos (\alpha - \beta) = 1$ and $\cos (\alpha + \beta) = 1/e$, where α, $\beta \in [-\pi, \pi]$. Pairs of α, β which satisfy both the equations is/are **[2005, Main]**

(a) 0   (b) 1

(c) 2   (d) 4

110. If one root is square of the other root of the equation $x^2 + px + q = 0$, then the relation between p and q is : **[2005, Main]**

(a) $p^3 - q(3p - 1) + q^2 = 0$ (b) $p^3 - q(3p + 1) + q^2 = 0$

(c) $p^3 + q (3p - 1) + q^2 = 0$ (d) $p^3 + q(3p + 1) + q^2 = 0$

111. For all complex numbers z_1, z_2 satisfying $|z_1| = 12$ and $|z_2 - 3 - 4i| = 5$, the minimum value of $|z_1 - z_2|$ is : **[2005, Main]**

(a) 0   (b) 2

(c) 7   (d) 17

112. The number of integral values of k for which the equation $7 \cos x + 5 \sin x = 2k + 1$ has a solution is : **[2005, Main]**

(a) 4   (b) 8

(c) 10   (d) 12.

113. If ω ($\neq 1$) be a cube root of unity and $(1 + \omega^2)^n = (1 + \omega^4)^n$, then the least positive value of n is : **[2004, Main]**

(a) 2   (b) 3

(c) 5   (d) 6

114. For all 'x', $x^2 + 2ax + 10 - 3a > 0$, then the interval in which 'a' lies is : **[2004, Main]**

(a) $a < -5$ (b) $-5 < a < 2$

(c) $a > 5$ (d) $2 < a < 5$

115. If $|z| = 1$ and $\omega = z - 1/z + 1$ (where $z \neq 1$), then Re (ω) is : **[2003, Main]**

(a) 0   (b) $\dfrac{1}{|z + 1|^2}$

(c) $\left| \dfrac{z}{z + 1} \right| \cdot \dfrac{1}{|z + 1|^2}$ (d) $\dfrac{\sqrt{2}}{|z + 1|^2}$

116. If z_1 and z_2 are two complex numbers such that $|z_1| < 1 < |z_2|$ then prove that $\left| \dfrac{1 - z_1 \bar{z_2}}{z_1 - z_2} \right| < 1$.

[2003, Main]

117. Let $f(x) = \displaystyle\int_{1}^{x} \sqrt{2 - t^2}\, dt$ Then the real roots of the equation $x^2 - f'(x) = $ are **[2002, Main]**

(a) ± 1 (b) $\pm 1/\sqrt{2}$

(c) $\pm 1/2$ (d) 0 and 1

118. If one of the vertices of the square circumscribing the circle $|z - 1| = \sqrt{2}$ is $2 + \sqrt{3}\, i$. Find the other vertices of square.

ANSWER KEY

1. (b)	**2.** (d)	**3.** (c)	**4.** (c)	**5.** (d)	**6.** (4)	**7.** (c)	**8.** (b)	**9.** (8)	**10.** ( )
11. (d)	**12.** (b)	**13.** (b)	**14.** (c)	**15.** (c)	**16.** (d)	**17.** (a)	**18.** (c)	**19.** (d)	**20.** (b)
21. (d)	**22.** (b)	**23.** (8)	**24.** (a)	**25.** (d)	**26.** (d)	**27.** (c)	**28.** (c)	**29.** (c)	**30.** (d)
31. (c)	**32.** (d)	**33.** (d)	**34.** (c)	**35.** (b)	**36.** (b)	**37.** (a)	**38.** (a)	**39.** (a,b,c)	**40.** (3)
41. (b)	**42.** (b)	**43.** (c)	**44.** (b)	**45.** (b)	**46.** (c)	**47.** (c)	**48.** (c)	**49.** (c)	**50.** (c)
51. (a)	**52.** (d)	**53.** (a,b)	**54.** (a)	**55.** (d)	**56.** (b)	**57.** (d)	**58.** (d)	**59.** (c)	**60.** (c)
61. (a)	**62.** (c)	**63.** (c)	**64.** (4)	**65.** (b)	**66.** (a,d)	**67.** (c)	**68.** (c)	**69.** (b)	**70.** (b)
71. (a)	**72.** (a)	**73.** (b)	**74.** (c)	**75.** (d)	**76.** (b)	**77.** (a)	**78.** (c,d)	**79.** (c)	
80. (b,c,d)	**81.** (b)	**82.** (c)	**83.** (d)	**84.** (b)	**85.** (c)	**86.** (c)	**87.** (a)	**88.** (b)	**89.** (5)
90. (b)	**91.** (*)	**92.** (A)-(s), (B)-(t), (C)-(r), (D)-(r)		**93.** (b)	**94.** (c)	**95.** (b,c,d)	**96.** (d)	**97.** (d)	
98. (d)	**99.** (a)	**100.** (a)	**101.** (d)	**102.** (a)	**103.** (a)	**104.** (1210)	**105.** (*)	**106.** (a)	**107.** (b)

108. $\left[-\dfrac{\pi}{2}, -\dfrac{\pi}{10} \right] \cup \left[\dfrac{3\pi}{10}, \dfrac{\pi}{2} \right]$ **109.** (d)   **110.** (a)   **111.** (b)   **112.** (b)   **113.** (b)   **114.** (a)   **115.** (a)

116. (*)   **117.** (a)   **118.** (*)

ANSWERS WITH EXPLANATIONS

1. Correct Response : (b)

Let
$$z = x + iy$$
$$\overline{z} = x - iy$$
Length of side = 4
$$AB = 4$$
$$|z - \overline{z}| = 4$$
$$|x + iy - x + iy| = 4$$
$$|2y| = 4; \ |y| = 2 \qquad [\overline{z} - 2\operatorname{Re}(\overline{z})]$$
$$BC = 4$$
$$|\overline{z} - (\overline{z} - 2\operatorname{Re}(\overline{z}))| = 4$$
$$|(x - iy) - (x - iy - 2x)| = 4$$
$$|x - iy + iy + x| = 4$$
$$|2x| = 4; \ |x| = 2$$
$$|z| = \sqrt{x^2 + y^2} = \sqrt{4 + 4} = 2\sqrt{2}$$

2. Correct Response : (d)
$$z = x + iy$$
$$|z| = \operatorname{Re}(z) \le 1$$
$$\Rightarrow \quad \sqrt{x^2 + y^2} - x \le 1$$
$$\Rightarrow \quad \sqrt{x^2 + y^2} \le 1 + x$$
$$\Rightarrow \quad x^2 + y^2 \le 1 + 2x + x^2$$
$$\Rightarrow \quad y^2 \le 2x + 1$$
$$\Rightarrow \quad y^2 \le 2\left(x + \dfrac{1}{2} \right)$$

3. Correct Response : (d)
$$z = x + iy$$
$$z^2 = i|z|^2$$

$$(x + iy)^2 = i(x^2 + y^2)$$
$$(x^2 - y^2) - i(x^2 + y^2 - 2xy) = 0$$
$$(x - y)(x + y) - i(x - y)^2 = 0$$
$$(x - y)[(x + y) - i(x - y)] = 0$$
$$\Rightarrow \qquad x = y$$
z lies on $y = x$.

4. Correct Response : (c)
$$u = \frac{2z + i}{z - ki}$$
$$u = \frac{(2x + iy) + i}{(x + iy) - ki} = \frac{2x + (2y + 1)i}{x + (y - k)i} \times \frac{x - (y - k)i}{x - (y - k)i}$$
$$= \frac{2x^2 + (2y + 1)(y - k)}{x^2 + (y - k)^2} + i\frac{[x(2y + 1) - 2x(y - k)]}{x^2 + (y - k)^2}$$

Since $\operatorname{Re}(u) + \operatorname{Im}(u) = 1$
$$\Rightarrow 2x^2 + (2y + 1)(y - k) + x(2y + 1) - 2x(y - k)$$
$$= x^2 + (y - k)^2$$
$$\left. \begin{array}{l} P(0, y_1) \\ Q(0, y_2) \end{array} \right\} \Rightarrow y^2 + y - k - k^2 = 0 \left\{ \begin{array}{l} y_1 + y_2 = -1 \\ y_1 y_2 = -k - k^2 \end{array} \right.$$
$$\because \qquad PQ = 5$$
$$\Rightarrow \qquad |y_1 - y_2| = 5$$
$$|y_1 - y_2|^2 = (y_1 + y_2)^2$$
$$(5)^2 = 1 + 4k + 4k^2$$
$$4k^2 + 4k - 24 = 0$$
$$k^2 + k - 6 = 0$$
$$\Rightarrow \qquad k = -3, 2$$
So, $\qquad k = 2 \ (k > 0).$

5. Correct Response : (d)

$$(2 + \alpha)^4 = a + b\alpha$$
$$(4 + \alpha^2 + 4\alpha)^2 = a + b\alpha$$
$$\because \quad 1 + \alpha + \alpha^2 = 0$$
$$1 + \alpha = -\alpha^2$$
$$[4(1 + \alpha) + \alpha^2]^2 = a + b\alpha$$
$$9\alpha^4 = a + b\alpha$$
$$9\alpha = a + b\alpha$$
$$a = 0$$
$$b = 9$$
$$a + b = 0 + 9 = 9.$$

6. Correct Response : (4)

$$\left(\frac{1+i}{1-i}\right)^{m/2} = \left(\frac{1+i}{i-1}\right)^{n/3} = 1$$

$$\Rightarrow \left(\frac{1+i}{1-i} \times \frac{1+i}{1+i}\right)^{m/2} = \left(\frac{1+i}{i-1} \times \frac{i+1}{i-1}\right)^{n/3} = 1$$

$$\Rightarrow \left(\frac{(1+i)^2}{2}\right)^{m/2} = \left(\frac{(1+i)^2}{-2}\right)^{n/3} = 1$$

$$\Rightarrow (i)^{m/2} = (-i)^{n/3} = 1$$

$$\Rightarrow \frac{m}{2} = 4k_1 \text{ and } \frac{n}{3} = 4k_2$$

$$\Rightarrow m = 8k_1 \text{ and } n = 12k_2$$

Least value of $m = 8$ and $n = 12$

$$\therefore \quad \text{GCD} = 4.$$

7. Correct Response : (c)

$$\left(\frac{-1+i\sqrt{3}}{1-i}\right)^{30} = \left(\frac{2\omega}{1-i}\right)^{30}$$

$$\because \quad \omega = \frac{-1+i\sqrt{3}}{2}$$

$$= \frac{2^{30}.\omega^{30}}{[(1-i)^2]^{15}}$$

$$= \frac{2^{30}.1}{(1+i^2-2i)^{15}}$$

$$= \frac{2^{30}}{-2^{15}.i^{15}}$$

$$= -2^{15}i$$

8. Correct Response : (b)

$$|z^2 + z + 1| = 1$$

$$\Rightarrow \left|\left(z+\frac{1}{2}\right)^2 + \frac{3}{4}\right| = 1$$

$$\Rightarrow \left|\left(z+\frac{1}{2}\right)^2 + \frac{3}{4}\right| \leq \left|z+\frac{1}{2}\right|^2 + \frac{3}{4}$$

$$\Rightarrow 1 \leq \left|z+\frac{1}{2}\right|^2 + \frac{3}{4}$$

$$\Rightarrow \left|\left(z+\frac{1}{2}\right)\right|^2 \geq \frac{1}{4}$$

$$\Rightarrow \left|z+\frac{1}{2}\right| \geq \frac{1}{2}$$

also $|(z^2 + z) + 1| = 1 \geq ||z^2 + z| - 1|$

$$\Rightarrow |z^2 + z| - 1 \leq 1$$
$$\Rightarrow |z^2 + z| \leq 2$$
$$\Rightarrow ||z^2| - |z|| \leq |z^2 + z| \leq 2$$
$$\Rightarrow |r^2 - r| \leq 2$$
$$\Rightarrow r = |z| \leq 2; \forall z \in S$$

Also we can always find root of the equation

$$z^2 + z + 1 = e^{i\theta}; \forall \theta \in R$$

Hence set 'S' is infinite.

9. Correct Response : (8)

Let $z = x + iy$

$$z^4 - |z|^4 = 4iz^2$$

$$\Rightarrow z^4 - (z\bar{z})^2 = 4iz^2$$

$$\Rightarrow z = 0 \text{ or } z^2 - (\bar{z})^2 = 4i$$

$$\Rightarrow 4ixy = 4i$$

$$\Rightarrow xy = 1$$

(1, 1)

(−1, −1)

for z_1 & $z_2 \Rightarrow x_1y_1 = 1$ & $x_2y_2 = 1$

x_1 & x_2 are the opposite sign

y_1 & y_2 are also of opposite sign

$$x_1 > 0, x_2 < 0, y_1 > 0, y_2 < 0$$

$$|z_1 - z_2|^2 = (x_1 - x_2)^2 + (y_1 - y_2)^2$$
$$= x_1^2 + x_2^2 + y_1^2 + y_2^2 - 2x_1x_2 - 2y_1y_2$$
$$= x_1^2 + x_2^2 + y_1^2 + y_2^2 + 2x_1(-x_2)$$
$$+ 2y_1(-y_2)$$
$$\geq 8(x_1^2x_2^2y_1^2y_2^2.2x_1(-x_2).2y_1(-y_2)^{1/8}$$
$$\geq 8[(x_1y_1)^3.(x_2y)^3]^{1/8}$$
$$\geq 8$$

$|z_1 - z_2|^2_{\min} = 8.$

10. Correct Response : (a)

$$(3 + 2\sqrt{-54}) = 3 + 2 \times 3 \times \sqrt{6}\, i$$

$$= (3 + \sqrt{6}\, i)^2$$

$$(3 - 2\sqrt{54}) = (3 - \sqrt{6}\, i)^2$$

$$(3+2\sqrt{-54})^{1/2}-(3-2\sqrt{-54})^{1/2}$$
$$= \pm(3+\sqrt{6}\,i)\pm(3-\sqrt{6}\,i)$$
$$= 6,-6,2\sqrt{6}i,-2\sqrt{6}i,$$

11. Correct Response : (d)

Let
$$z_1 = x_1 + iy_1$$
$$z_2 = x_2 + iy_2$$
$$|z_1 - 1| = \mathrm{Re}(z_1)$$
$$(x_1-1)^2 + y_1^2 = x_1^2$$
$$y_1^2 - 2x_1 + 1 = 0 \qquad \qquad \text{...(1)}$$
$$|z_2 - 1| = \mathrm{Re}(z_2)$$
$$(x_2-1)^2 + y_2^2 = x_2^2$$
$$y_2^2 - 2x_2 + 1 = 0 \qquad \qquad \text{...(2)}$$
$$y_1^2 - y_2^2 - 2(x_1 - x_2) = 0$$
$$(y_1 - y_2)(y_1 + y_2) = 2(x_1 - x_2)$$
$$y_1 + y_2 = \frac{2(x_1 - x_2)}{(y_1 - y_2)} \qquad \text{...(3)}$$
$$\arg(z_1 - z_2) = \frac{\pi}{6}$$
$$\arg[(x_1 - x_2) + i(y_1 - y_2)] = \frac{\pi}{6}$$
$$\tan^{-1}\left(\frac{y_1 - y_2}{x_1 - x_2}\right) = \frac{\pi}{6}$$
$$\frac{y_1 - y_2}{x_1 - x_2} = \frac{1}{\sqrt{3}} \qquad \text{...(4)}$$

Put value of (4) in equation (3)
$$y_1 + y_2 = 2\sqrt{3}$$
$$\boxed{\mathrm{Im}(z_1 + z_2) = 2\sqrt{3}}$$

12. Correct Response : (b)

The value of $\left(\dfrac{1+\sin 2\pi/9+i\cos 2\pi/9}{1+\sin\dfrac{2\pi}{9}-i\cos\dfrac{2\pi}{9}}\right)$ is :

$$= \left(\frac{1+\sin\left(\dfrac{\pi}{2}-\dfrac{5\pi}{18}\right)+i\cos\left(\dfrac{\pi}{2}-\dfrac{5\pi}{18}\right)}{1+\sin\left(\dfrac{\pi}{2}-\dfrac{5\pi}{18}\right)-i\cos\left(\dfrac{\pi}{2}-\dfrac{5\pi}{18}\right)}\right)^3$$

$$= \left(\frac{1+\cos\dfrac{5\pi}{18}+i\sin\dfrac{5\pi}{18}}{1+\cos\dfrac{5\pi}{18}-i\sin\dfrac{5\pi}{18}}\right)^3$$

$$= \left(\frac{2\cos^2\dfrac{5\pi}{36}+2i\sin\dfrac{5\pi}{36}\cos\dfrac{5\pi}{36}}{2\cos^2\dfrac{5\pi}{36}-2i\sin\dfrac{5\pi}{36}.\cos\dfrac{5\pi}{36}}\right)^3$$

$$= \left(\frac{\cos\dfrac{5\pi}{36}+i\sin\dfrac{5\pi}{36}}{\cos\dfrac{5\pi}{36}-i\sin\dfrac{5\pi}{36}}\right)^3$$

$$= \left(\frac{e^{i5\pi/36}}{e^{-i5\pi/36}}\right)^3 = \left(e^{i5\pi/18}\right)^3$$

$$= \cos\frac{5\pi}{6}+i\sin 5\pi/6$$

$$= -\frac{\sqrt{3}}{2}+i/2$$

13. Correct Response : (b)

Explanation :

$$\mathrm{Re}\left(\frac{z-1}{2z+i}\right) = 1$$

Put $z = x + iy$

$$\mathrm{Re}\left(\frac{(x+iy)-1}{2(x+iy)+i}\right) = 1$$

$$\mathrm{Re}\left(\left(\frac{(x-1)+iy}{2x+i(2y+1)}\right)\left(\frac{2x-i(2y+1)}{2x-i(2y+1)}\right)\right) = 1$$

$$\Rightarrow \qquad 2x^2 + 2y^2 + 2x + 3y + 1 = 0$$
$$x^2 + y^2 + x + \frac{3}{2}y + \frac{1}{2} = 0$$

$\Rightarrow$ locus is a circle whose centre is $\left(-\dfrac{1}{2}, -\dfrac{3}{4}\right)$

and radius $\dfrac{\sqrt{5}}{4}$.

$\Rightarrow$ diameter $= \dfrac{\sqrt{5}}{2}$

14. Correct Response : (c)

Explanation :

$$\alpha + \beta = 1, \ \alpha\beta = -1$$
$$p_k = \alpha^k + \beta^k$$
$$\alpha^2 - \alpha - 1 = 0$$
$$\Rightarrow \alpha^k - \alpha^{k-1} - \alpha^{k-2} = 0$$
$$\text{and } \beta^k - \beta^{k-1} - \beta^{k-2} = 0$$
$$\Rightarrow \qquad p_k = p_{k-1} + p_{k-2}$$
$$p_1 = \alpha + \beta = 1$$
$$p_2 = (\alpha + \beta)^2 - 2\alpha\beta = 1 + 2 = 3$$
$$p_3 = 4$$
$$p_4 = 7$$
$$p_5 = 11$$

15. Correct Response : (c)

Explanation :

$$\Rightarrow \frac{3+i\sin\theta}{4-i\cos\theta} \text{ is a real number}$$

$\Rightarrow \quad 3\cos\theta + 4\sin\theta = 0$

$\Rightarrow \qquad \tan\theta = \dfrac{-3}{4}$

argument of $\sin\theta + i\cos\theta = \pi - \tan^{-1}\dfrac{4}{3}$

16. Correct Response : (d)

Explanation :

Assuming z is a root of the given equation.

$$z = \frac{-b \pm i\sqrt{180 - b^2}}{2}$$

so, $\left(1 - \dfrac{b}{2}\right)^2 + \dfrac{180 - b^2}{4} = 40$

$\Rightarrow \qquad -4b + 184 = 160 \Rightarrow b = 6$

17. Correct Response : (a)

Explanation :

$$\alpha = \omega$$
$$a = (1+\omega)(1 + \omega^2 + \omega^4 + \ldots + \omega^{200})$$
$$a = (1+\omega)\frac{(1 - (\omega^2)^{101})}{1 - \omega^2} = 1$$
$$b = 1 + \omega^3 + \omega^6 + \ldots + \omega^{300} = 101$$
$$x^2 - 102x + 101 = 0$$

18. Correct Response : (c)

Explanation :

$$\left|\frac{z-i}{z+2i}\right| = 1$$

$\Rightarrow \qquad |z - i| = |z + 2i|$

$\Rightarrow z$ lies on perpendicular bisector of $(0, 1)$ and $(0, -2)$.

$\Rightarrow \qquad Imz = -\dfrac{1}{2}$

Let $z = x - \dfrac{i}{2}$

$\because \qquad |z| = \dfrac{5}{2} \Rightarrow x^2 = 6$

$\because \qquad |z + 3i| = \left|x + \dfrac{5i}{2}\right| = \sqrt{x^2 + \dfrac{25}{4}}$

$$= \sqrt{6 + \frac{25}{4}} = \frac{7}{2}$$

19. Correct Response : (d)

Explanation :

$e^{4x} + e^{3x} - 4e^{2x} + e^x + 1 = 0$

Divide by e^{2x}

$\Rightarrow \qquad e^{2x} + e^x - 4 + \dfrac{1}{e^x} + \dfrac{1}{e^{2x}} = 0$

$\Rightarrow \qquad \left(e^{2x} + \dfrac{1}{e^{2x}}\right) + \left(e^x + \dfrac{1}{e^x}\right) - 4 = 0$

$\Rightarrow \left(e^x + \dfrac{1}{e^x}\right)^2 - 2 + \left(e^x + \dfrac{1}{e^x}\right) - 4 = 0$

Let $e^x + \dfrac{1}{e^x} = t \Rightarrow (e^x - 1)^2 = 0 \Rightarrow x = 0.$

$\therefore$ Number of real roots $= 1$

20. Correct Response : (b)

Explanation :

$$ax^2 - 2bx + 5 = 0 {<}^{\alpha}_{\alpha}$$

$\Rightarrow \alpha = \dfrac{b}{a}; \ \alpha^2 = \dfrac{5}{a} \ \Rightarrow b^2 = 5a$

$$x^2 - 2bx - 10 = 0 {<}^{\alpha}_{\beta}$$

$\Rightarrow \quad \alpha^2 - 2b\alpha - 10 = 0$

$\Rightarrow a = \dfrac{1}{4} \Rightarrow \alpha^2 = 20; \ \alpha\beta = -10 \Rightarrow \beta^2 = 5$

$\Rightarrow \qquad \alpha^2 + \beta^2 = 25$

21. Correct Response : (d)

Explanation :

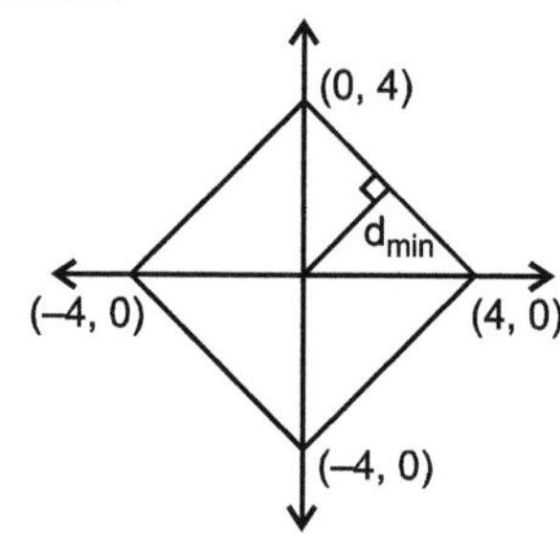

$$z = x + iy$$
$$|x| + |y| = 4$$
$$|z| = \sqrt{x^2 + y^2}$$

$\Rightarrow \qquad |z|_{min} = \sqrt{8} \ \text{and} \ |z|_{max} = 4 = \sqrt{16}$

So $|z|$ cannot be $\sqrt{7}$.

22. Correct Response : (b)

Explanation :

$$\tan\alpha + \tan\beta = \frac{\lambda\sqrt{2}}{k+1}$$

$$\tan\alpha \cdot \tan\beta = \frac{k-1}{k+1}$$

$$\tan(\alpha+\beta) = \frac{\dfrac{\lambda\sqrt{2}}{k+1}}{1 - \dfrac{k-1}{k+1}} = \frac{\lambda\sqrt{2}}{2} = \frac{\lambda}{\sqrt{2}}$$

$\Rightarrow \qquad \dfrac{\lambda^2}{2} = 50 \Rightarrow \lambda = 10 \ \text{and} -10$

23. Correct Response : (8.00)

Explanation :

$$D \geq 0$$

$$\Rightarrow (a-10)^2 - 4 \times 2 \times \left(\frac{33}{2} - 2a\right) \geq 0$$

$$\Rightarrow \quad a^2 - 4a - 32 \geq 0$$

$$\Rightarrow \quad a \in (-\infty, 4] \cup [8, \infty)$$

24. Correct Response : (a)

Explanation :

$$|z| = \frac{\sqrt{2}^2}{\sqrt{a^2 + 1}}$$

$$= \sqrt{\frac{2}{5}}$$

$$\Rightarrow \quad a^2 + 1 = 10$$

$$\Rightarrow \quad a = 3$$

Thus,

$$z = \frac{(1+i)^2}{3-i}$$

$$\bar{z} = \frac{(1-i)^2}{3+i}$$

$$= \frac{-2i(3-i)}{10}$$

$$= \frac{-1-3i}{5}$$

25. Correct Response : (d)

Explanation :

$x^2 + x \sin\theta - 2\sin\theta = 0$ has two roots α and β.

$$\frac{\alpha^{12} + \beta^{12}}{(\alpha^{-12} + \beta^{-12})(\alpha - \beta)^{24}} = \frac{\alpha^{12}\beta^{12}}{(\alpha - \beta)^{24}}$$

$$= \frac{(\alpha\beta)^{12}}{(\alpha - \beta)^{24}}$$

$$= \frac{(-2\sin\theta)^{12}}{\left(\sqrt{\sin^2\theta + 8\sin\theta}\right)^{24}}$$

$$= \frac{2^{12}}{(8 + \sin\theta)^{12}}$$

26. Correct Response : (d)

Explanation :

Given equation implies $5 + |2^x - 1| = 2^{2x} - 2 \cdot 2^x$.

Case (1) : $x \geq 0$

$$\Rightarrow \quad 5 + 2^x - 1 = 2^{2x} - 2 \cdot 2^x$$

$$\Rightarrow \quad 0 = (2x - 4)(2x + 1)$$

$$\Rightarrow \quad x = 2$$

Case (2) : $x < 0$

$$\Rightarrow \quad 5 - 2x + 1 = 2^{2x} - 2 \cdot 2^x$$

$$\Rightarrow \quad 5 + 1 = 2^{2x} - 2^x$$

LHS is positive and RHS is negative. (Not possible)

Therefore, no solution exists in this case.

Thus, number of solution is 1.

27. Correct Response : (c)

Explanation :

Let $|z| = r \Rightarrow z = re^{i\theta}$ and $|w| = \frac{1}{r} \Rightarrow w = \frac{1}{r}e^{i\phi}$.

Given that $\arg z - \arg w = \frac{\pi}{2}$

$$\Rightarrow \quad \theta - \phi = \frac{\pi}{2}$$

$$\Rightarrow \quad \theta = \frac{\pi}{2} + \phi$$

Then,

$$\bar{z}\,w = re^{-i\theta} \cdot \frac{1}{r}e^{i\phi}$$

$$= e^{-i\left(\frac{\pi}{2} + \phi\right) + i\phi}$$

$$= e^{-i\frac{\pi}{2}}$$

$$= -i$$

28. Correct Response : (c)

Explanation :

$$(m^2 + 1) - 3x + (m^2 + 1)^2 = 0$$

$$\alpha + \beta = \frac{3}{m^2 + 1}$$

$$\alpha\beta = \frac{(m^2 + 1)^2}{m^2 + 1}$$

$$= m^2 + 1$$

Here, α and β are the roots of given equation.

Since, $\alpha + \beta$ is maximum. Therefore, $m^2 + 1$, minimum.

$\Rightarrow m = 0$.

So, $\alpha + \beta = 3$, $\alpha\beta = 1$.

This gives

$$|\alpha^3 - \beta^3| = |(\alpha - \beta)(\alpha^2 + \beta^2 + \alpha\beta)|$$

$$= \left|\sqrt{(\alpha + \beta)^2 - 4\alpha\beta}\right|\left|(\alpha + \beta)^2 - \alpha\beta\right|$$

$$= 8\sqrt{5}$$

29. Correct Response : (c)

Explanation :

$$w = \frac{5 + 3z}{5 - 5z}$$

$$\Rightarrow \quad 5w - 5wz = 5 + 3z$$

$$\Rightarrow \quad (5w + 3)z = 5w - 5$$

$$\Rightarrow \quad z = \frac{5w - 5}{5w + 3}$$

As $|z| < 1$ therefore,

$$\left|\frac{5w - 5}{5w + 3}\right| < 1$$

$$\Rightarrow \quad |5w - 5| = |5w + 3|$$

$$\Rightarrow \quad |w-1| < \left|w+\frac{3}{5}\right|$$

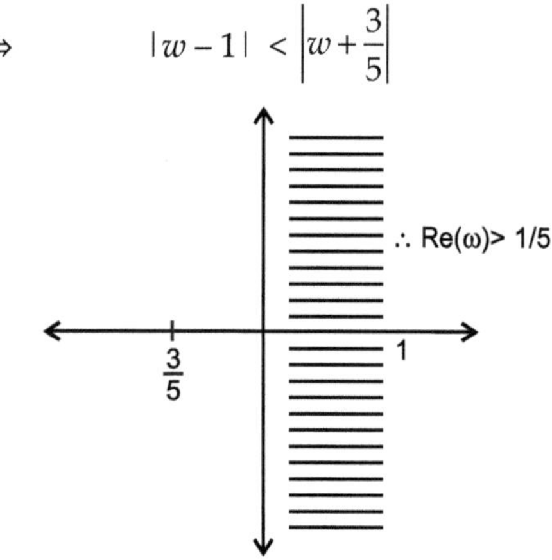

30. Correct Response : (d)

Explanation :

Since, $p, q \in Q$ therefore, the other root is $2+\sqrt{3}$.

Hence, $p = 4$ and $q = 1$.

Hence, $p^2 - 4q - 12 = 0$.

31. Correct Response : (c)

Explanation :

$$x^2 - 2x + 2 = 0$$
$$(x-1)^2 = -1$$
$$= i^2$$
$$\Rightarrow x = 1+i,\ 1-i$$

Let $\alpha = 1+i,\ \beta = 1-i$

$$\left(\frac{\alpha}{\beta}\right)^n = 1$$

$$\Rightarrow \quad \left(\frac{1+i}{1-i}\right)^n = 1$$

$$\Rightarrow \quad \left(\frac{1+i}{1-i}\times\frac{1+i}{1+i}\right)^n = 1$$

$$\Rightarrow \quad \left(\frac{1-1+2i}{2}\right)^n = 1$$

$$\Rightarrow \quad i^n = 1$$
$$\Rightarrow \quad n = 4$$

32. Correct Response : (d)

Explanation :

$$|\sqrt{x}-2|+(\sqrt{x})^2-4\sqrt{x}+4 = 2$$

$$|\sqrt{x}-2|^2 +|\sqrt{x}-2|-2 = 0$$

Put $\quad |\sqrt{x}-2| = t$

$$\Rightarrow \quad t^2+t-2 = 0$$
$$\Rightarrow \quad (t+1)(t+2) = 0$$
$$\Rightarrow |\sqrt{x}-2| = 1 \text{ or } |\sqrt{x}-2|=-2 \text{ (Rejected)}$$
$$\Rightarrow \quad \sqrt{x}-2 = \pm 1$$
$$\Rightarrow \quad \sqrt{x} = 2+1,\ 2-1$$
$$\Rightarrow \quad \sqrt{x} = 3,\ 1$$
$$\Rightarrow \quad x = 9,\ 1$$
$$\therefore \quad \text{sum} = 9+1 = 10$$

33. Correct Response : (d)

Explanation :

$$\left(1+e^{i\frac{\pi}{2}}e^{i\frac{\pi}{6}}+e^{i\frac{5\pi}{6}}+e^{i\frac{8\pi}{6}}e^{i\frac{\pi}{2}}\right)^9$$

$$= \left(1+e^{i\frac{2\pi}{3}}+e^{i\frac{5\pi}{6}}+e^{i\frac{11\pi}{6}}\right)^9$$

$$= \left(1-\frac{1}{2}+\frac{\sqrt{3}}{2}i-\frac{\sqrt{3}}{2}+\frac{i}{2}+\frac{\sqrt{3}}{2}-\frac{i}{2}\right)^9$$

$$= \left(\frac{1}{2}+i\frac{\sqrt{3}}{2}\right)^9$$

$$= \left(e^{i\frac{\pi}{3}}\right)^9$$

$$= e^{i3\pi}$$

$$= -1$$

34. Correct Response : (c)

Explanation :

$$D = 4(1+3m)^2-(1+m^2)(1+8m)$$
$$= 4(1+9m^2+6m-(1+8m+m^2+8m^3))$$
$$= 4(8m^2-2m-8m^3)$$
$$= -8m(4m^2-4m^3+1)$$
$$= -8m(2m-1)^2$$
$$< 0$$

Hence, infinitely many values.

35. Correct Response : (b)

Explanation :

The given equation is,
$$1+\sin^4 x = \cos^2 3x$$

To hold the equality, the value of $\sin^4 x$ should be zero and value of $\cos^2 3x$ should be 1.

In the given range, the value of $\sin x$ is zero at $-2\pi,\ -\pi,\ 0,\ \pi,\ 2\pi$. All the values satisfy the condition, $\cos^2 x = 1$ also.

Therefore, there are five solutions to the above equations.

36. Correct Response : (b)

Explanation :

Let
$$z = x+iy$$

The given expression is,
$$|z-i| = |z-1|$$
$$|x+iy-i| = |x+iy-1|$$
$$(x-1)^2+y^2 = x^2+(y-1)^2$$
$$x = y$$

The above equation represents the line passing through origin with slope 1.

37. Correct Response : (a)

Explanation :

Let,
$$z = x+10i$$

The given expression is,

$$\frac{2z-n}{2z+n} = 2i-1$$

$$\frac{2(x+10i)-n}{2(x+10i)+n} = 2i-1$$

$$2x+20i-n = -(2x+n)-40-20i-2ni$$

Compare imaginary parts of the above equation.

$$20 = -20+2n$$

$$n = 20$$

Compare the real parts.

$$2x-n = -2x-n-40$$

$$x = -10$$

38. Correct Response : (a)

Explanation :

The required diagram is given below :

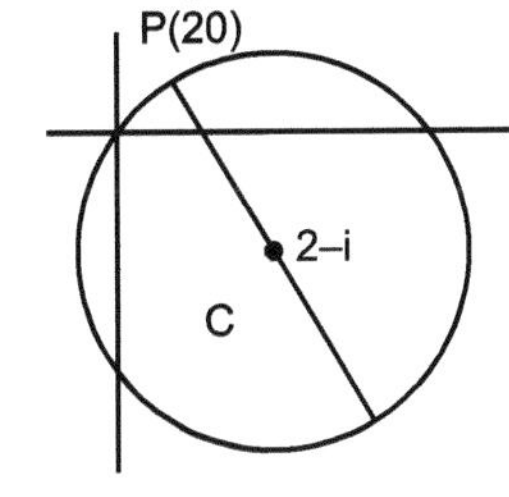

$$|z-(2-i)| \geq \sqrt{5}$$

For $|z_0-1|$ to be minimum, $z_0+x_0 = iy_0$ is at point P as shown in the figure.

$$\arg\left(\frac{4-(z_0+\overline{z_0})}{z_0-\overline{z_0}+2i}\right) = \arg\left(\frac{4-2x}{2iy+2i}\right)$$

$$= \arg\left(\frac{-i(2-x)}{y+1}\right)$$

$$= \arg(-i\lambda)$$

$$= -\frac{\pi}{2} \qquad \text{(since, } \lambda > 0.)$$

39. Correct Response : (a, b, c)

Explanation :

Consider option (a).

$$a_1+a_2+\dots a_n = \sum a_i$$

$$= \frac{\sum \alpha^i - \sum \beta^i}{\alpha-\beta}$$

$$= \frac{\dfrac{\alpha(1-\alpha^n)}{1-\alpha} - \dfrac{\beta(1-\beta^n)}{1-\beta}}{\alpha-\beta}$$

$$= \frac{(\alpha+1)(1-\alpha^n)-(\beta+1)(1-\beta^n)}{(1-\alpha)(1-\beta)(\alpha-\beta)}$$

$$= \frac{\alpha^2-\alpha^{n+2}-\beta^2+\beta^{n+2}}{(1-\alpha)(1-\beta)(\alpha-\beta)}$$

$$= \frac{\sqrt{5}+\beta^{n+2}-\alpha^{n+2}}{\beta-\alpha}$$

$$= -1+a_{n+2}$$

Consider option (b)

$$\sum_{n=1}^{\infty}\frac{a_n}{10^n} = \sum \frac{\alpha^n-\beta^n}{(\alpha-\beta)10^n}$$

$$= \frac{1}{\alpha-\beta}\left(\frac{\dfrac{\alpha}{10}}{1-\dfrac{\alpha}{10}} - \frac{\dfrac{\beta}{10}}{1-\dfrac{\beta}{10}}\right)$$

$$\frac{1}{\alpha-\beta}\left(\frac{\alpha}{10-\alpha} - \frac{\beta}{10-\beta}\right)$$

$$= \frac{1}{\alpha-\beta}\left(\frac{10(\alpha-\beta)-\alpha\beta+\alpha\beta}{100-10(\alpha+\beta)+\alpha\beta}\right)$$

$$= \frac{10}{89}$$

Consider option (c).

$$b_n = a_{n+1}+a_{n-1} - \frac{\alpha^{n-1}-\beta^{n-1}}{\alpha-\beta}$$

$$= \frac{\alpha^{n-1}(\alpha+2)+\beta^{n-1}(\beta+2)}{\alpha-\beta}$$

$$= \frac{\alpha^{n-1}\left(\dfrac{5+\sqrt{5}}{2}\right)-(\beta^{n-1}\left(\dfrac{5+\sqrt{5}}{2}\right)}{\alpha-\beta}$$

$$= \frac{\sqrt{5}(\alpha^n+\beta^n)}{\alpha-\beta}$$

$$= \alpha^n+\beta^n$$

Consider option (d).

$$\sum_{n=1}^{\infty}\frac{b_n}{10^n} = \sum\left(\frac{\alpha}{10}\right)^n + \sum\left(\frac{\beta}{10}\right)^n +$$

$$= \frac{\dfrac{\alpha}{10}}{1-\dfrac{\alpha}{10}} + \frac{\dfrac{\beta}{10}}{1-\dfrac{\beta}{10}}$$

$$= \frac{\alpha}{10-\alpha} + \frac{\beta}{10-\beta}$$

$$= \frac{10(\alpha+\beta)-2\alpha\beta}{100-10(\alpha+\beta)+\alpha\beta}$$

$$= \frac{10+2}{89}$$

$$= \frac{12}{89}$$

40. Correct Response : 3.00

Explanation :

$$|a + bw + cw^2|^2 = a^2 + b^2 + c^2 - ab - bc - ca$$

$$= \frac{1}{2} \left[(a-b)^2 + (b-c)^2 + (c-a)^2 \right]$$

It will be minimum when a, b and c are consecutive integers.

Hence, the minimum value is 3.

41. Correct Response : (b)

Explanation :

The given equation is,

$$x^2 + (2 - \lambda)x + (10 - \lambda) = 0$$

Let, the roots of the equation are x_1 and x_2.

Sum of the roots are,

$$x_1 + x_2 = -(2 - \lambda)$$

$$= (\lambda - 2)$$

The product of the roots,

$$x_1 x_2 = (10 - \lambda)$$

The sum of the cubes of the roots of the equation is,

$$x_1^3 + x_2^3 = (x_1 + x_2)^3 - 3x_1 x_2 (x_1 + x_2)$$

$$= (\lambda - 2)^3 - 3 (10 - \lambda)(\lambda - 2)$$

$$= \lambda^3 - 3\lambda^2 - 24\lambda + 52$$

Let, $\qquad y = \lambda^3 - 3\lambda^2 - 24\lambda + 52$

The sum of the cubes of the roots of the equation is minimum.

$$\frac{dy}{d\lambda} = 0$$

$$\frac{d}{d\lambda}\left(\lambda^3 - 3\lambda^2 - 24\lambda + 52\right) = 0$$

$$3\lambda^2 - 6\lambda - 24 = 0$$

$$\lambda^2 - 2\lambda - 8 = 0$$

Simplify the above equation.

$$\lambda^2 - 2\lambda - 8 = 0$$

$$(\lambda + 2)(\lambda - 4) = 0$$

$$\lambda = -2, 4$$

Differentiate again with respect to λ.

$$\frac{d^2 y}{d\lambda^2} = \frac{d}{d\lambda}\left(3\lambda^2 - 6\lambda - 24\right)$$

$$= 6\lambda - 6$$

The value of $\dfrac{d^2 y}{d\lambda^2}$ at for $(\lambda = -2)$ is,

$$\left.\frac{d^2 y}{d\lambda^2}\right|_{\lambda = -2} = 6(-2) - 6$$

$$= -18 < 0$$

Thus, the sum of the roots is maximum for $(\lambda = -2)$.

The value of $\dfrac{d^2 y}{d\lambda^2}$ at for $(\lambda = 4)$ is,

$$\left.\frac{d^2 y}{d\lambda^2}\right|_{\lambda = 4} = 6(4) - 6$$

$$= 18 > 0$$

Thus, the sum of the roots is minimum for $(\lambda = 4)$.

The equation is,

$$x^2 + (2 - 4)x + (10 - 4) = 0$$

$$x^2 - 2x + 6 = 0$$

$$\left\{x - \left(1 + \sqrt{5}i\right)\right\}\left\{x + \left(1 - \sqrt{5}i\right)\right\} = 0$$

$$x = \left(1 + \sqrt{5}i\right), \left(1 - \sqrt{5}i\right)$$

The magnitude of the difference of the roots,

$$|x_1 - x_2| = \left\|\left(1 + \sqrt{5}i\right) - \left(1 - \sqrt{5}i\right)\right\|$$

$$= 2\sqrt{5}$$

Therefore, magnitude of the difference of the roots is $2\sqrt{5}$.

42. Correct Response : (b)

Explanation :

The given value of ω is,

$$\omega = \frac{1 + (1 - 8\alpha)\, z}{1 - z}$$

If ω is purely imaginary, its real part is equal to zero.

$$\mathrm{Re}(z) = 0$$

$$\frac{1 + (1 - 8\alpha)z}{1 - z} + \frac{1 + (1 - 8\alpha)\bar{z}}{1 - \bar{z}} = 0$$

$$(1 - \bar{z}) + (1 - 8\alpha)z - (1 - 8\alpha)z\bar{z} + (1 - z) + (1 - 8\alpha)\bar{z} -$$

$$(1 - 8\alpha)\bar{z}z = 0$$

$$2 - (\bar{z} + z) + (1 - 8\alpha)(z + \bar{z}) + (z + \bar{z}) - 2(1 - 8\alpha) = 0$$

Simplify the above equation.

$$2 - (\bar{z} + z) + (1 - 8\alpha)(z + \bar{z}) + (z + \bar{z}) - 2(1 - 8\alpha) = 0$$

$$8\alpha(z + \bar{z}) - 16\alpha = 0$$

$$\alpha(z + \bar{z} - 2) = 0$$

The above equation gives,

$$z + \bar{z} - 2 = 0$$

$$\alpha = 0$$

Therefore, for all $z \in C$, the α is equal to {0}.

43. Correct Response : (c)

Explanation :

The given equation is,

$$3x^2 - 10x - 25 = 0$$

Let, tan A and tan B are the roots of this equation, then sum of the roots is,

$$\tan A + \tan B = -\frac{(-10)}{(3)}$$

$$= \frac{10}{3}$$

Product of the roots is,

$$\tan A \cdot \tan B = \frac{(-25)}{3}$$

The value of tan (A + B) is,

$$\tan (A + B) = \frac{\tan A + \tan A}{1 - \tan A \cdot \tan A}$$

$$= \frac{\left(\dfrac{10}{3}\right)}{1 - \left(\dfrac{-25}{3}\right)}$$

$$= \frac{10}{28} = \frac{5}{14}$$

The value of sin (A + B) is,

$$\sin (A + B) = \frac{5}{\sqrt{5^2 + 14^2}}$$

$$= \frac{5}{\sqrt{221}}$$

The value of cos (A + B) is,

$$\cos (A + B) = \frac{14}{\sqrt{5^2 + 14^2}}$$

$$= \frac{14}{\sqrt{221}}$$

The value of the term is,

$$\begin{bmatrix} 3\sin^2 (A+B) \\ -10\sin(A+B)\cdot \cos(A+B) \\ -25\cos^2 (A+B) \end{bmatrix}$$

$$= \begin{bmatrix} 3\left(\dfrac{5}{\sqrt{221}}\right)^2 - 10\left(\dfrac{5}{\sqrt{221}}\right)\left(\dfrac{14}{\sqrt{221}}\right) \\ -25\left(\dfrac{14}{\sqrt{221}}\right)^2 \end{bmatrix}$$

$$= 3\left(\frac{25}{221}\right) - 10\left(\frac{5\times 14}{221}\right) - 25\left(\frac{196}{221}\right)$$

$$= \frac{25}{221}(3 - 28 - 196)$$

$$= -25$$

44. Correct Response : (b)

Explanation :

Written in quadratic form,

$$\frac{1}{x+p} + \frac{1}{x+q} = \frac{1}{r}$$

$$\frac{(x+q)+(x+p)}{(x+q)(x+p)} = \frac{1}{r}$$

$$(2x + p + q)r = (x + q)(x + p)$$

$$x^2 + (p + q - 2r) x + pq - pr - qr = 0$$

By properties of roots of the quadratic equation the value of the product of the roots and sum of the roots define as,

Here being roots are equal in magnitude and opposite in sign,

Sum of roots,

$$\alpha + \beta = 0$$

$$p + q - 2r = 0$$

$$r = \frac{(p+q)}{2} \qquad \qquad ...(1)$$

So product of roots,

$$\alpha\beta = pq - r(q + p)$$

Substituting for r from the equation (1),

Product of roots,

$$pq - r(q + p) = pq - \frac{1}{2}(p+q)^2$$

$$= \left(-\frac{1}{2}\right)\left\{(p+q)^2 - 2pq\right\}$$

$$= \left(-\frac{1}{2}\right)(p^2 + q^2)$$

Square of roots,

$$\alpha^2 + \beta^2 = (\alpha + \beta)^2 - 2\alpha\beta$$

$$= 0 - 2(pq - r(q + p))$$

$$= -2\left(-\frac{1}{2}\right)(p^2 + q^2)$$

$$= (p^2 + q^2)$$

45. Correct Response : (b)

Explanation :

After simplify and apply the Sridharacharya formula,

$$z = \frac{-1 \pm i\sqrt{3}}{2}, z = 1$$

$$z = 1, \frac{-1 + i\sqrt{3}}{2} \text{ and } \frac{-1 - i\sqrt{3}}{2}$$

Here,

$$\frac{-(1 + i\sqrt{3})}{2} = \omega^2$$

$$(1 + i\sqrt{3}) = -2\omega^2 \qquad \qquad ...(1)$$

And,

$$\frac{1 - i\sqrt{3}}{-2} = \omega$$

$$1 - i\sqrt{3} = -2\omega \qquad \qquad ...(2)$$

Substitue the value from equation (1) and (2) in given relation.

$$\left(\frac{1+i\sqrt{3}}{1-i\sqrt{3}}\right)^n = 1$$

$$\left(\frac{-2\omega^2}{-2\omega}\right)^n = 1$$

$$\omega^n = 1$$

Thus, least positive integer value of n is 3.

46. Correct Response : (c)

Explanation :

The given set is,

$$2\left|\sqrt{x}-3\right|+\sqrt{x}\left(\sqrt{x}-6\right)+6 = 0$$

Simplify the above equation.

$$2\left|\sqrt{x}-3\right|+\left(\sqrt{x}-3+3\right)\left(\sqrt{x}-3-3\right)+6 = 0$$

$$2\left|\sqrt{x}-3\right|+\left(\sqrt{x}-3\right)^2 - 3 = 0$$

$$\left(\sqrt{x}-3\right)^2 +2\left|\sqrt{x}-3\right|-3 = 0$$

Further solve the above equation,

$$\left(\left|\sqrt{x}-3\right|+3\right)\left(\left|\sqrt{x}-3\right|-1\right) = 0$$

$$\left|\sqrt{x}-3\right| = 1 \text{ and } \left|\sqrt{x}-3\right|+3 \neq 0$$

$$\sqrt{x}-3 = \pm 1$$

$$\sqrt{x} = 2, 4$$

$$x = 4, 16$$

47. Correct Response : (c)

Explanation :

The given equation is,

$$x^2 - x + 1 = 0$$

$$x = \frac{1 \pm \sqrt{1-4}}{2}$$

$$x = \frac{1 \pm i\sqrt{3}}{2}$$

Roots of the equation is $-\omega^2, -\omega$.

Let $\alpha = -\omega^2$ and $\beta = -\omega$.

The value of equation is,

$$\alpha^{101} + \beta^{107} = (-\omega^2)^{101} + (-\omega)^{107}$$

$$= (-\omega)^{202} + (-\omega)^{107}$$

$$= -(\omega + \omega^2)$$

$$= -(-1)$$

$$= 1$$

48. Correct Response : (c)

Explanation :

The given equation is,

$$2^{(x-1)(x^2+5x-50)} = 1$$

Take logarithm of both LHS and RHS.

$$\log 2^{(x-1)(x^2+5x-50)} = \log 1$$

$$= 0$$

$$(x-1)(x^2+5x-50) \times \log 2 = 0$$

$$(x-1)(x^2+5x-50) = 0$$

Solve the above equation for the values of x.

$$x = 1, 5, -10$$

Sum of all real values of x is,

$$5 + 1 - 10 = -4$$

49. Correct Response : (c)

Explanation :

The given equation is,

$$\text{Im}\left(\frac{iz-2}{z-i}\right)+1 = 0$$

Substitute $z = x + iy$.

$$\text{Im}\left(\frac{i(x+iy)-2}{(x+iy)-i}\right)+1 = 0$$

$$\text{Im}\left(\frac{-(y+2)+ix}{x+i(y-1)}\right)+1 = 0$$

$$\text{Im}\left(\frac{-(y+2)+ix}{x+i(y-1)} \times \frac{x-i(y-1)}{x-i(y-1)}\right)+1 = 0$$

The above imaginary equations converts to real equation.

$$\frac{(y-1)(y+2)+x^2}{x^2+(y-1)^2}+1 = 0$$

$$x^2 + y^2 - \frac{y}{2} - \frac{1}{2} = 0$$

$$x^2 + \left(y-\frac{1}{4}\right)^2 = \frac{9}{16}$$

Compare with the general equation of circle.

$$\text{Radius} = \sqrt{\frac{9}{16}}$$

$$= \frac{3}{4}$$

50. Correct Response : (c)

Explanation :

Let the quadratic polynomial be,

$$p(x) = ax^2 + bx + c \qquad \text{...(1)}$$

Given $p(0) = 1$ then the value of $c = 1$.

Also,

$$p(x) = (x-1)r + 4 \qquad \text{...(2)}$$

$$p(x) = (x+1)s + 6 \qquad \text{...(3)}$$

Where s is a constant.

Substitute $x = 1$ in equation (2) and compare with equation (1).

$$p(1) = 4 = a + b + 1 \qquad \text{...(4)}$$

Put $x = -1$ in equation (3)
$$p(-1) = 6 = a - b + 1 \qquad \ldots(5)$$

On solving equation (4) and (5) we get $a = 4$ and $b = 1$

Then, $p(x) = 4x^2 - x + 1$

By hit and trial method put $x = -2$ from the option.
$$p(-2) = 4(-2)^2 - (-2) + 1$$
$$p(-2) = 19$$

51. Correct Response : (a)

Explanation :

Consider the complex equation :
$$z = x + iy$$

Then,
$$2\,|x + (y+3)i| - |x + (y-1)i| = 0$$
$$2\,|x + (y+3)i| = |x + (y-1)i|$$
$$2\sqrt{x^2 + (y+3)^2} = \sqrt{x^2 + (y-1)^2}$$

On squaring both the sides,
$$4(x^2 + (y+3)^2) = (x^2 + (y-1)^2)$$

Rearrange the above equation :
$$x^2 + y^2 + \frac{16}{3}y + \frac{35}{3} = 0$$

Simplifying the above equation :
$$x^2 + \left(y^2 + \frac{8}{3}\right)^2 = \left(\frac{8}{3}\right)^2$$

Hence, the equation represent circle with radius $= \dfrac{8}{3}$.

52. Correct Response : (d)

Explanation :

The solution of the provided complex equation is,
$$2\omega + 1 = z$$
$$2\omega + 1 = \sqrt{3}i$$
$$\omega = \frac{-1 + \sqrt{3}i}{2}$$

Solve the determinant by gauss elimination.
$$\begin{vmatrix} 1 & 1 & 1 \\ 1 & -1 - \omega^2 & \omega^2 \\ 1 & \omega^2 & \omega^7 \end{vmatrix} \to (C_1 \to C_1 + C_2 + C_3)$$

$$\begin{vmatrix} 3 & 1 & 1 \\ 0 & \omega & \omega^2 \\ 0 & \omega^2 & \omega \end{vmatrix}$$

Solve the obtained determinant.
$$3\,(\omega^2 - \omega^4) = 3k$$

$$3\left(\left(\frac{-1 - \sqrt{3}i}{2}\right) - \left(\frac{-1 + \sqrt{3}i}{2}\right)\right) = 3k$$

$$-3z = 3k$$
$$k = -z$$

53. Correct Response : (a, b)

Explanation :

The given relation is :
$$Im\left(\frac{az + b}{z + 1}\right) = y$$

$$Im\left(\frac{a(x + iy) + b}{x + iy + 1}\right) = y$$

$$Im\left(\frac{ax + b + iay}{x + 1 + iy}(x + 1 - iy)\right) = y$$

$$Im\left(\frac{ax + b + iay}{(x+1)^2 + y^2}(x + 1 - iy)\right) = y$$

Simplify the above equation.
$$\frac{ay(x+1) - (ax + b)y}{(x+1)^2 + y^2} = y$$

$$\frac{a - b}{(x+1)^2 + y^2} = 1$$

$$(x + 1)^2 + y^2 = 1$$

$$x = -1 \pm \sqrt{1 - y^2}$$

54. Correct Response : (a)

Explanation :

The given equation is,
$$\sqrt{2x + 1} - \sqrt{2x - 1} = 1$$

Simplify the above equation and square both sides.

$$\sqrt{2x + 1} = 1 + \sqrt{2x - 1}$$

$$\left(\sqrt{2x + 1}\right)^2 = \left(1 + \sqrt{2x - 1}\right)^2$$

$$2x + 1 = 1 + 2x - 1 + 2\sqrt{2x - 1}$$

$$x = \frac{5}{8}$$

The value of expression $\sqrt{4x^2 - 1}$ at $x = \dfrac{5}{8}$ is,

$$\sqrt{4x^2 - 1} = \sqrt{4\left(\frac{5}{8}\right)^2 - 1}$$

$$= \frac{3}{4}$$

55. Correct Response : (d)

Explanation :

The value of z^3 is,

$$z^3 = (1 + ai)^3$$
$$= 1 - 3a^2 + (3a - a^3)i$$

The variable z^3 is a real number (given). So the imaginary part of z^3 will be zero.

$$3a - a^3 = 0$$
$$a(3 - a^2) = 0$$
$$a = \sqrt{3} \qquad (\because a > 0)$$

The complex number is written as,

$$z = 1 + ai$$
$$= 1 + \sqrt{3}i$$
$$= 2\left(\cos\frac{\pi}{3} + i\sin\frac{\pi}{3}\right)$$

The sum of given geometric series is,

$$\left[\begin{array}{c} (\text{For odd no.}) \\ \because S_{GP} = \dfrac{a\left(1 - r^{n+1}\right)}{1 - r} \end{array}\right]$$

$$1 + z + z^2 + \dots + z^{11} = \frac{1\left(1 - z^{11+1}\right)}{1 - z}$$

$$= \frac{1 - 2^{12}\left(\cos\dfrac{\pi}{3} + i\sin\dfrac{\pi}{3}\right)^{12}}{1 - \left(1 + i\sqrt{3}\right)}$$

Further, substitute the above expression,

$$[\because (\cos\theta + i\sin\theta)^n = (\cos n\theta + i\sin n\theta)]$$

$$= \frac{1 - 2^{12}\left(\cos\dfrac{12\pi}{3} + i\sin\dfrac{12\pi}{3}\right)}{1 - \left(1 + i\sqrt{3}\right)}$$

$$= \frac{1 - 2^{12}\left(\cos 4\pi + i\sin 4\pi\right)}{1 - \left(1 + i\sqrt{3}\right)}$$

$$= \frac{1 - 2^{12}}{-i\sqrt{3}}$$

$$= (-4095) \times \frac{\left(-i\sqrt{3}\right)}{3}$$

Hence, the required value is,

$$S_{GP} = -1365\sqrt{3}i$$

56. Correct Response : (b)

Explanation :

Let $P(2 + i)$

It is given that, the point $(2 + i)$ is moved 1 unit eastward. It means x coordinate will become 3.

It again moves 2 unit northward, it means y coordinate will become $3i$. Hence, new location would be $3 + 3i$. The required diagram is,

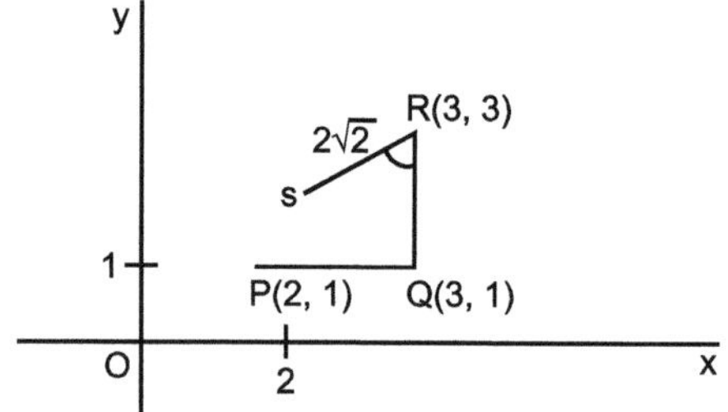

By using rotation theorem,

$$\frac{z - (3 + 3i)}{3 + i - (3 + 3i)} = \frac{2\sqrt{2}}{2} e^{-\pi i/4}$$

$$\frac{z - 3 - 3i}{-2i} = 1 - i$$

$$z - 3 - 3i = -2i - 2$$

$$z = 1 + i$$

57. Correct Response : (d)

Explanation :

Given equation :

$$x^2 + bx - 1 = 0$$
$$x^2 + x + b = 0$$

These equations have a common root. Hence, α will satisfy the given equation as,

$$\alpha^2 + b\alpha - 1 = 0$$
$$\alpha^2 + \alpha + b = 0$$

Hence, for the roots :

$$\frac{\alpha^2}{b^2 + 1} = \frac{\alpha}{-(b+1)} = \frac{1}{(1 - b)}$$

$$(b + 1)^2 = (b^2 + 1)(1 - b)$$
$$b^2 + 2b + 1 = b^2 - b^3 + 1 - b$$
$$b^3 + 3b = 0$$

Further solve the above equation to calculate the value of b.

$$b^3 + 3b = 0$$
$$b = 0 \text{ or } b^2 = -3$$

When $b = 0$, then common root is (-1). Hence, $b = 0$ does not satisfy the condition.

Hence,

$$b^2 = -3$$
$$b = \pm\sqrt{3}i$$
$$|b| = \sqrt{3}$$

58. Correct Response : (d)

Explanation :

Consider the given purely imaginary function is,

$$(a + ib) = \frac{2 + 3i\sin\theta}{1 - 2i\sin\theta}$$

Here, give the real value $a = 0$.

Simplify the above function,

$$a + ib = \frac{2 + 3i\sin\theta}{(1 - 2i\sin\theta)(1 + 2i\sin\theta)} \times (1 + 2i\sin\theta)$$

$$= \frac{2 - 6\sin^2\theta + 7i\sin\theta}{1 + 4\sin^2\theta}$$

$$= \left(\frac{2 - 6\sin^2\theta}{1 + 4\sin^2\theta}\right) + i\left(\frac{7\sin\theta}{1 + 4\sin^2\theta}\right)$$

Compare left hand side and right hand side with real and imaginary part,

$$a = 0$$

$$\frac{2 - 6\sin^2\theta}{1 + 4\sin^2\theta} = 0$$

$$6\sin^2\theta = 2$$

$$\theta = \sin^{-1}\left(\frac{1}{\sqrt{3}}\right)$$

59. Correct Response : (c)

Explanation :

The first equation is given as,

$$x^2 - 2x\sec\theta + 1 = 0$$

Here, the roots of the given equation are α_1 and β_1.

Apply formula to calculate the roots of the equation,

$$x = \frac{2\sec\theta \pm \sqrt{4\sec^2\theta - 4}}{2}$$

$$[\because \sec^2\theta - 1 = \tan^2\theta]$$

$$= \sec\theta \pm \tan\theta$$

Therefore, roots are,

$$\alpha_1 = \sec\theta - \tan\theta \quad \begin{bmatrix} \text{For, } -\dfrac{\pi}{6} < \theta < -\dfrac{\pi}{12} \\ \sec\theta > 0 \\ \tan\theta < 0 \\ \therefore \alpha_1 > \beta_1 \end{bmatrix}$$

And, $\quad \beta_1 = \sec\theta + \tan\theta$

The second equation is,

$$x^2 - 2x\sec\theta + 1 = 0$$

Here, the roots of the given equations are α_2 and β_2.

Apply formula to calculate the roots of the equation,

$$x = \frac{-2\sec\theta \pm \sqrt{4\sec^2\theta + 4}}{2}$$

$$[\because \sec^2\theta = 1 + \tan^2\theta]$$

$$= -\sec\theta \pm \tan\theta$$

Therefore, roots are,

$$\alpha_2 = \tan\theta - \sec\theta \quad \begin{bmatrix} \text{For, } -\dfrac{\pi}{6} < \theta < -\dfrac{\pi}{12} \\ \sec\theta > 0 \\ \tan\theta < 0 \\ \therefore \alpha_2 > \beta_2 \end{bmatrix}$$

And, $\quad \beta_2 = -\tan\theta - \sec\theta$

Hence, the required value is,

$$\alpha_1 + \beta_2 = (\sec\theta - \tan\theta) + (-\tan\theta - \sec\theta)$$

$$= -2\tan\theta$$

60. Correct Response : (c)

Explanation :

The given expression is,

$$4\alpha x^2 + \frac{1}{x} \geq 1 \quad [\forall\, x > 0]$$

Simplify the expression,

$$4\alpha x^2 + \frac{1}{x} \geq 0 \quad [x > 0]$$

$$4\alpha x^3 + 1 \geq x \quad [x > 0]$$

$$4\alpha x^3 - x + 1 \geq 0 \quad [x > 0] \qquad ....(1)$$

Differentiate with respect to x,

$$12\alpha x^2 - 1 = 0$$

$$x = \frac{1}{\sqrt{12\alpha}}$$

Substitute the value of x in the equation (1),

$$4\alpha\left(\frac{1}{12\alpha}\right)^{3/2} - \left(\frac{1}{12\alpha}\right)^{1/2} + 1 \geq 0$$

$$\frac{(4\alpha)}{(12)^{3/2} \times (\alpha)^{3/2}} - \frac{1}{(12)^{1/2}(\alpha)^{1/2}} + 1 \geq 0$$

$$\alpha^{1/2} \geq \frac{8}{12^{3/2}}$$

$$\alpha \geq \frac{1}{27}$$

61. Correct Response : (a)

Explanation :

The given equation is,

$$(x^2 - 5x + 5)^{(x^2 + 4x - 60)} = 1$$

The left hand side of the equation is equal to one if,

Either, $\quad x^2 - 5x + 5 = 1$

or, $\quad x^2 + 4x - 60 = 0$

Thus, solve the above two equation, the roots of the equations is,

$$x = 1, 4$$

or, $\qquad\qquad x = -10, 6$

Also, the given equation is equal to one if,

$$x^2 - 5x + 5 = -1$$

And, $x^2 + 4x - 60 \in$ even number

Therefore the roots of the equation is,

$$x = 2, 3$$

Check the even number for the above roots :

For $x = 2$:

$$x^2 + 4x - 60 = (2)^2 + 4(2) - 60$$
$$= -48 \text{ (Even)}$$

So, $x = 2$ is valid.

For $x = 3$:

$$x^2 + 4x - 60 = (3)^2 + 4(3) - 60$$
$$= -39 \text{ (Odd)}$$

So, $x = 3$ is invalid.

Hence, the total numbers of solution are $x = 1$, $4, -10, 6, 2$

The sum of all real values of x satisfying the equation is,

$$1 + 4 - 10 + 6 + 2 = 3$$

62. Correct Response : (c)

Explanation :

Simplify the given equation :

$$\left| \frac{z_1 - 2z_2}{2 - z_1\bar{z}_2} \right| = 1$$

$$\mid z_1 - 2z_2 \mid^2 = \left| 2 - z_1\bar{z}_2 \right|^2$$

$$\left(z_1 - 2z_2 \right)\left(\bar{z}_1 - 2\bar{z}_2 \right) = \left(2 - z_1\bar{z}_2 \right)\left(2 - \bar{z}_1 z_2 \right)$$

$$\left| z_1 \right|^2 + 4\left| z_2 \right|^2 - 2\bar{z}_1 z_2 - 2z_1\bar{z}_2$$

$$= 4 + \left| z_1 \right|^2 \left| z_2 \right|^2 - 2\bar{z}_1 z_2 - 2z_1\bar{z}_2$$

Simplify further,

$$(\mid z_2 \mid^2 - 1)(\mid z_1 \mid^2 - 4) = 0$$

Since z_2 is not unimodular so it means that $\mid z_2 \mid \neq 1$ $\mid z_1 \mid = 2$.

Hence, the point z_1 lies on a circle of radius 2.

63. Corrrect Response : (c)

Explanation :

The given equation is,

$$x^2 - 6x - 2 = 0$$

$$x^{10} - 6x^9 - 2x^8 = 0 \qquad \text{...(1)}$$

Since the roots of the equation are α and β then,

$$\alpha^{10} - 6\alpha^9 - 2\alpha^8 = 0 \qquad \text{...(2)}$$
$$\beta^{10} - 6\beta^9 - 2\beta^8 = 0 \qquad \text{...(3)}$$

Subtract equation (2) and (3).

$$(\alpha^{10} - \beta^{10}) - (6\alpha^9 - 6\beta^9) - 2\,(\alpha^8 - \beta^8) = 0$$

$$a_{10} - 6a_9 - 2a_8 = 0$$

$$a_{10} - 2a_8 = 6a_9$$

$$\frac{a_{10} - 2a_8}{2a_9} = 3$$

64. Correct Response : (4)

Explanation :

The given considered value of a_k is,

$$a_k = \cos\left(\frac{k\pi}{7} \right) + i \sin\left(\frac{k\pi}{7} \right)$$

$$= e^{i\frac{k\pi}{7}}$$

Simplify the given expression,

$$\frac{\displaystyle\sum_{k=1}^{12} |\alpha_{k+1} - \alpha_k|}{\displaystyle\sum_{k=1}^{3} |\alpha_{4k-1} - \alpha_{4k-2}|} = \frac{\displaystyle\sum_{k=1}^{12} \left| e^{\frac{i(k+1)\pi}{7}} - e^{i\frac{k\pi}{7}} \right|}{\displaystyle\sum_{k=1}^{3} \left| e^{\frac{i(4k-1)\pi}{7}} - e^{i\frac{(4k-2)\pi}{7}} \right|}$$

$$\left[a_k = e^{i\frac{k\pi}{7}} \right]$$

$$= \frac{\displaystyle\sum_{k=1}^{12} \left| e^{\frac{ik\pi}{7}} \right| \cdot \left| e^{i\frac{\pi}{7}} - 1 \right|}{\displaystyle\sum_{k=1}^{3} \left| e^{\frac{i(4k-2)\pi}{7}} \right| \cdot \left| e^{i\frac{\pi}{7}} - 1 \right|}$$

$$= \frac{\displaystyle\sum_{k=1}^{12} \left| e^{i\frac{\pi}{7}} - 1 \right|}{\displaystyle\sum_{k=1}^{3} \left| e^{i\frac{\pi}{7}} - 1 \right|}$$

Further, simplify the above expression,

$$= \frac{12 \left| e^{i\frac{\pi}{7}} - 1 \right|}{3 \left| e^{i\frac{\pi}{7}} - 1 \right|}$$

$$= 4$$

65. Correct Response : (b)

Explanation :

Given that the number of diagonals of the regular polynomial is 54.

Now, the formula for the number of sides of the polynomial is,

$$\frac{n(n-3)}{2} = 54$$

Here, n is number of sides of the polynomial.

Simplify the above formula,

$$n^2 - 3n - 108 = 0$$

$$(n + 9)\,(n - 12) = 0$$

$$n = 12$$

66. Correct Response : (a, d)

Explanation :

The relation for the real roots is,

$$D > 0$$
$$b^2 - 4ac > 0$$
$$1 - 4\alpha^2 > 0$$
$$-\frac{1}{2} < \alpha < \frac{1}{2} \qquad \ldots(1)$$

The given quadratic equation is,

$$\alpha x^2 - x + \alpha = 0$$

Therefore, the sum of the given roots x_1 and x_2 is,

$$x_1 + x_2 = \frac{1}{\alpha}$$

The product of the given roots x_1 and x_2 is,

$$x_1 x_2 = 1$$

Given relation $|x_1 - x_2| < 1$,

So,

$$\sqrt{(x_1 + x_2)^2 - 4x_1 x_2} < 1$$

$$\sqrt{\frac{1}{\alpha^2} - 4} < 1$$

$$\frac{1}{\alpha^2} - 4 < 1$$

$$\frac{1}{\alpha^2} - 5 < 0$$

Futher simplify the above expression,

$$(5\alpha^2 - 1) > 0$$

$$\left(\sqrt{5}\alpha - 1\right)\left(\sqrt{5}\alpha + 1\right) > 0$$

$$\alpha < \frac{-1}{\sqrt{5}} \text{ or } \alpha > \frac{1}{\sqrt{5}} \qquad \ldots(2)$$

From (1) and (2),

$$\alpha \in \left(\frac{-1}{2}, \frac{-1}{\sqrt{5}}\right) \cup \left(\frac{1}{\sqrt{5}}, \frac{1}{2}\right)$$

67. Correct Response : (c)

Explanation :

Let $\qquad z = x + iy$

The expression is $z + \dfrac{1}{z} = x + iy + \dfrac{1}{x + iy}$

$$= x + iy + \frac{1 \times (x - iy)}{x + iy(x - iy)}$$

$$= x + iy + \frac{(x - iy)}{x^2 + y^2}$$

This term cannot be purely imaginary.

Hence, $z + \dfrac{1}{z}$ is any non zero real number.

68. Correct Response : (c)

Explanation :

The equation when $x \geq \dfrac{3}{2}$ is,

$$x^2 + |2x - 3| - 4 = 0$$
$$x^2 + 2x - 7 = 0$$

The equation when $x < \dfrac{3}{2}$ is,

$$x^2 + |2x - 3| - 4 = 0$$
$$x^2 - 2x + 3 - 4 = 0$$
$$x^2 - 2x - 1 = 0$$

The roots of the quadratic equations when $x \geq \dfrac{3}{2}$ are,

$$x_1 = \frac{-b \pm \sqrt{b^2 - 4ac}}{2a}$$

$$= \frac{-2 \pm \sqrt{(2)^2 - 4 \times 1 \times (-7)}}{2 \times 1}$$

$$= \frac{-2 \pm \sqrt{32}}{2}$$

$$= -1 + 2\sqrt{2}$$

The roots of the quadratic equations when $x < \dfrac{3}{2}$ are,

$$x_2 = \frac{-b \pm \sqrt{b^2 - 4ac}}{2a}$$

$$= \frac{-(-2) \pm \sqrt{(2)^2 - 4 \times 1 \times (-1)}}{2 \times 1}$$

$$= \frac{2 \pm \sqrt{8}}{2}$$

$$= 1 - \sqrt{2}$$

The sum of the roots is,

$$x_1 + x_2 = -1 + 2\sqrt{2} + 1 - \sqrt{2}$$

$$= \sqrt{2}$$

69. Correct Response : (b)

Explanation :

The given equation is,

$$(1 + i\alpha)^2 = x + iy$$

Simplify the above equation.

$$1 - \alpha^2 + 2i\alpha = x + iy$$

On comparing imaginary parts

$$y = 2\alpha$$

$$\alpha = \frac{y}{2}$$

And,
$$x = 1 - \alpha^2$$

Substitute the value of α in the above equation.
$$x = 1 - \left(\frac{y}{2}\right)^2$$
$$y^2 + 4x - 4 = 0$$

70. Correct Response : (b)

Explanation :

The given equation is,
$$px^2 + qx + r = 0$$

The sum and product of the roots are,
$$\alpha + \beta = \frac{-q}{p}$$

And,
$$\alpha.\beta = \frac{r}{p}$$

Given that p, q and r are in A.P.,
$$2q = p + r \qquad \qquad ...(1)$$

From the given value,
$$\frac{1}{\alpha} + \frac{1}{\beta} = 4$$
$$\frac{\alpha + \beta}{\alpha\beta} = 4$$
$$\frac{-\dfrac{q}{p}}{\dfrac{r}{p}} = 4$$
$$q = -4r$$

Substitute the value of q in the equation (1),
$$-8r = p + r$$
$$p = -9r$$
$$q = -4r$$

For the value of $|\alpha - \beta|$,
$$|\alpha - \beta| = \sqrt{(\alpha + \beta)^2 - 4\alpha\beta}$$
$$= \sqrt{\left(\frac{-q}{p}\right)^2 - \frac{4r}{p}}$$
$$= \frac{\sqrt{q^2 - 4pr}}{|p|}$$

Substitute the value in the above expression,
$$|\alpha - \beta| = \frac{\sqrt{16r^2 + 36r^2}}{|-9r|}$$
$$= \frac{2\sqrt{13}}{9}$$

71. Correct Response : (a)

Explanation :

The given expression of the function is,
$$f(x) = \alpha \log |x| + \beta x^2 + x$$

Differentiate the given function,
$$f'(x) = \frac{\alpha}{x} + 2\beta x + 1$$
$$0 = \frac{\alpha}{x} + 2\beta x + 1$$

At
$$x = -1, 2,$$
$$\alpha + 2\beta = 1$$
$$\alpha + 8\beta = -2$$

Solve the equations,
$$\beta = -\frac{1}{2}$$
$$\alpha = 2$$

72. Correct Response : (a)

Explanation :

The pairs of the complex conjugate numbers,
$$z_2 = \bar{z}_1,$$
$$z_4 = \bar{z}_3$$

The value of the complex function,
$$\arg\left(\frac{z_1}{z_4}\right) + \arg\left(\frac{z_2}{z_3}\right) = \arg z_1 - \arg z_2 + \arg z_3 - \arg z_4$$
$$= \arg z_1 - \arg \bar{z}_3 + \arg \bar{z}_1 - \arg z_3$$
$$= \arg z_1 + \arg z_3 - \arg z_1 - \arg z_3$$
$$= 0$$

73. Correct Response : (b)

Explanation :

The roots of the given quadratic equation,
$$x^2 - 4\sqrt{2}kx + 2e^{4\ln k} - 1 = 0$$
$$x^2 - 4\sqrt{2}kx + 2k^4 - 1 = 0$$

The roots sum of the quadratic equation,
$$\alpha + \beta = 4\sqrt{2}k$$

Multiplication of roots is,
$$\alpha\beta = 2k^4 - 1$$

The relation between roots,
$$\alpha^2 + \beta^2 = 66$$

The value of k from the roots of the equation,
$$(\alpha + \beta)^2 - 2\alpha\beta = 66$$
$$32k^2 - 2(2k^4 - 1) = 66$$
$$4(k^2 - 4)^2 = 0$$
$$k = 2$$

The value of $\alpha^3 + \beta^3$,
$$\alpha^3 + \beta^3 = (\alpha + \beta)(\alpha^2 - \alpha\beta + \beta^2)$$
$$= \left(8\sqrt{2}\right)(66 - 31)$$
$$= 280\sqrt{2}$$

74. Correct Response : (c)

Explanation :

(P) : Consider the relation,
$$z_k z_j = 1$$
$$z_j = z_{10-k}$$
Hence for each $k \in (1, 2, 3,..., 9\}$ there exists z_j such that $z_k z_j = 1$ is true.

(Q) : consider the relation,
$$z_1 z = z_k$$
$$z = z_{k-1}$$
Hence, for each $k \in \{2. 3,...., 9\}$, there exists z_j such that $z = 1$ for $k = 1$ is false.

(R) : $z_1, z_2, ..., z_9$ are the roots of equation $z^{10} - 1$ other than unity, hence,
$$\frac{z^{10}-1}{z-1} = 1 + z + ... + z^9$$
$$= (z - z_1)(z - z_2)...(z - z_9)$$

Substitute 1 for z in the above expression,
$$\frac{(1-z_1)(1-z_2)...(1-z_9)}{10} = \frac{10}{10} = 1$$

(S) : The value of given function :
$$1 - \sum_{K=1}^{9} \cos\left(\frac{2k\pi}{10}\right)$$
$$= 1 - \{\text{sum of real roots of } z^{10} = 1 \text{ except } 1\}$$
$$= 1 - (-1) = 2$$

75. Correct Response : (d)

Explanation :

The quadratic equation $p(x)$ with real coefficient has the purely imaginary roots.

The form of quadratic equation $p(x)$ is $ax^2 + c$. The quadratic equation $p(x)$ is zero at the imaginary values while $ax^2 + c$ takes real value only at the real x, no roots of the quadratic equation is real.
$$p\big(p(x)\big) = 0$$

The quadratic equation $p(x)$ is purely imaginary.

$ax^2 + c$ = purely imaginary

From the above expression, x can't be purely imaginary since x^2 will be negative in that case and $ax^2 + c$ will be real.

Thus, the option (d) is correct.

76. Correct Response : (b)

Explanation :

The given equations are,
$$ax^2 + bx + c = 0 \qquad (a, b, c, \in R, a \neq 0)$$
And, $\quad 2x^2 + 3x + 4 = 0$,

The equation $2x^2 + 3x + 4 = 0$ holds,
$$D \leq 0$$

Therefore,

Both roots are imaginary and common,

Hence, $\qquad \dfrac{a}{2} = \dfrac{b}{3} = \dfrac{c}{4}$

77. Correct Response : (a)

Explanation :

The given equation is,
$$ax^2 + bx + 1 = 0 \qquad (a, b, \in R, a \neq 0)$$
The product of the roots is,
$$\frac{1}{\sqrt{\alpha\beta}} = \frac{1}{a}$$

And,

The sum of the roots is,
$$\frac{1}{\sqrt{\alpha}} + \frac{1}{\sqrt{\beta}} = -\frac{b}{a}$$
$$\frac{\sqrt{\beta}+\sqrt{\alpha}}{\sqrt{\alpha\beta}} = -\frac{b}{a}$$
$$\sqrt{\alpha} + \sqrt{\beta} = -b$$

Now,

Substitute the value in the equation,
$$x(x + b^3) + a^3 - 3abx = x^2 + (b^3 - 3ab)\,x + a^3$$
$$= x^2 + b\,(b^2 - 3a)\,x + a^3$$

Further, simplify the above equation,
$$= x^2 - \left(\sqrt{\alpha}+\sqrt{\beta}\right)\left\{\sqrt{\alpha}+\sqrt{\beta}+2\sqrt{\alpha}\sqrt{\beta}-3\sqrt{\alpha}\sqrt{\beta}\right\}x$$
$$+\alpha\beta\sqrt{\alpha}\sqrt{\beta}$$
$$= x^2 - \left(\alpha\sqrt{\alpha}+\beta\sqrt{\beta}\right)x+\alpha\beta\sqrt{\alpha\beta}$$

Hence, the roots of the above equation is $\alpha^{\frac{3}{2}}$ and $\beta^{\frac{3}{2}}$.

78. Correct Response : (c, d)

Explanation :

Let, α_i are possible value of z_1 and β_i are possible values of z_2 such that $i = 1, 2, 3$.

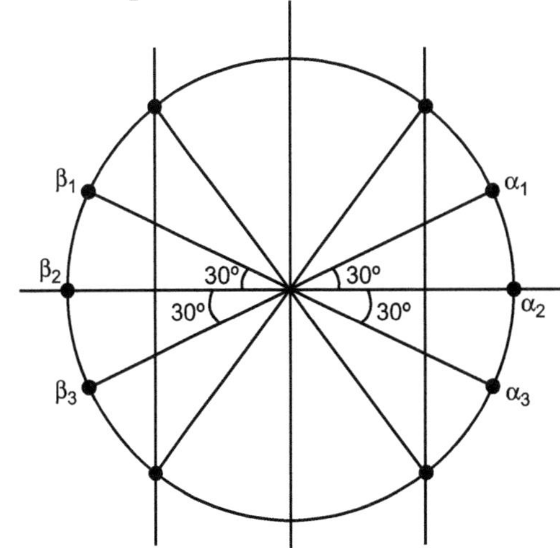

It is given that,

$$\omega = \frac{\sqrt{3}+i}{2}$$

$$= \frac{\sqrt{3}}{2}+\frac{i}{2}$$

$$= e^{\frac{i\pi}{6}}$$

Now,

$$\omega^2 = e^{i\frac{\pi}{3}}$$

$$\omega^3 = e^{i\frac{\pi}{2}}$$

$$\omega^4 = e^{i\frac{2\pi}{3}}$$

$$\omega^5 = e^{i\frac{5\pi}{6}}$$

Therefore, the value of angle $\angle z_1 o z_2$ is,

$$\angle z_1 o z_2 = \frac{2\pi}{3},\frac{5\pi}{6}$$

79.   Correct Response : (c)

Explanation :

The complex number α lies on the circle.

$$(x-x_0)^2+(y-y_0)^2 = r^2 \qquad ...(1)$$

The complex number $\dfrac{1}{\alpha} = \dfrac{\alpha}{|\alpha|^2}$ lies on the circle.

$$(x-x_0)^2+(y-y_0)^2 = 4r^2 \qquad ...(2)$$

Let, α be $\alpha_1 + i\beta_1$ lies on circle from equation (1).

$$(x^2+y^2)+(x_0+y_0)^2-2(xx_0+yy_0) = r^2$$

$$|\alpha|^2+|z_0|^2-2(\alpha_1 x_0+\beta_1 y_0) = r^2 \qquad ....(3)$$

Let, $\dfrac{1}{|\alpha|}$ be $\alpha_1 + i\beta_1$ lies on circle from equation (2).

$$\frac{1}{|\alpha|^2}+|z_0|^2-2\frac{(\alpha_1 x_0+\beta_1 y_0)}{|\alpha|^2} = 4r^2$$

$$1+|\alpha|^2|z_0|^2-2(\alpha_1 x_0+\beta_1 y_0) = 4r^2|\alpha|^2 \ ...(4)$$

Subtract equation (4) from (3),

$$|\alpha|^2-1+|z_0|^2(1-|\alpha|^2) = r^2(1-4|\alpha|^2)$$

$$(|\alpha|^2-1)(1-|z_0|^2) = r^2(1-4|\alpha|^2) \qquad ...(5)$$

Now, from given equation $2|z_0|^2 = r^2+2$.

$$2|z_0|^2 = r^2+2$$

$$r^2 = 2(|z_0|^2-1)$$

$$r^2 = -2(1-|z_0|^2)$$

Substitute the value of r^2 in equation (5).

$$(|\alpha|^2-1)(1-|z_0|^2) = -2(1-|z_0|^2)(1-4|\alpha|^2)$$

$$|\alpha|^2-1 = -2(1-4|\alpha|^2)$$

$$|\alpha|^2-1 = -2+8|\alpha|^2$$

$$1 = 7|\alpha|^2$$

Simplify above equation.

$$|\alpha|^2 = \frac{1}{7}$$

$$|\alpha| = \frac{1}{\sqrt{7}}$$

80.   Correct Response : (b, c, d)

Explanation :

Let, ω be a complex cube root of unity and P be a $n \times n$ matrix with $P_{ij} = \omega^{i+j}$.

$$P = \begin{bmatrix} \omega^2 & 1 & \omega & \omega^2 & ... \\ 1 & \omega & \omega^2 & 1 & ... \\ \omega & \omega^2 & 1 & \omega & ... \\ ... & ... & ... & ... & ... \end{bmatrix}_{n\times n}$$

$$P^2 = \begin{bmatrix} \omega^2 & 1 & \omega & \omega^2 & ... \\ 1 & \omega & \omega^2 & 1 & ... \\ \omega & \omega^2 & 1 & \omega & ... \\ ... & ... & ... & ... & ... \end{bmatrix}\begin{bmatrix} \omega^2 & 1 & \omega & \omega^2 & ... \\ 1 & \omega & \omega^2 & 1 & ... \\ \omega & \omega^2 & 1 & \omega & ... \\ ... & ... & ... & ... & ... \end{bmatrix}$$

$$(\omega^4+1+\omega^2)+(\omega^4+1+\omega^2)+... = 0$$

It is possible if n is a multiple of 3, but it is given that $P^2 \neq 0$.

Therefore, possible values of n can be 55, 58, 56.

81. Correct Response : (b)

Explantion :

Let, S_1 represents the circle with radius 4 and centre $(0, 0)$. $S_1 : |z| < 4$

$$x^2+y^2 < 16$$

It is given that,

$$S_2 : \text{Im}\left[\frac{z-1+\sqrt{3}i}{1-\sqrt{3}i}\right] > 0$$

$$\text{Im}\left(\frac{[(x-1)+(y+\sqrt{3}i)][1+\sqrt{3}i]}{2}\right) > 0$$

So, $\quad S_2 : y + \sqrt{3}x > 0$.

It is also given that,
$$S_3 : \text{Re}(z) > 0$$
$$x > 0$$

Area of shaded region can be calculated as,

$$\text{Area of } (OAB + OBC) = \frac{\pi(4)^2}{4} + \frac{60}{360}\pi(4)^2$$

$$= 4\pi + \frac{16\pi}{6}$$

$$= 4\pi + \frac{8\pi}{3}$$

$$= \frac{20\pi}{3}$$

82. Correct Response : (c)

Explanation :

The minimum distance of point $(1, -3)$ from $y + \sqrt{3}x = 0$ is,

$$\min_{z \in S} |1 - 3i - z| = \left| \frac{-3 + \sqrt{3}}{2} \right|$$

$$= \frac{3 - \sqrt{3}}{2}$$

83. Correct Response (d)

Explantion :

The given equation is,
$$a = z^2 + z + 1$$
$$z^2 + z + (1 - a) = 0$$

Apply the quadratic formula,

$$z = \frac{-(1) \pm \sqrt{(1)^2 - 4(1)(1-a)}}{2(1)}$$

$$= \frac{-1 \pm \sqrt{1 - 4 + 4a}}{2}$$

$$= \frac{-1 \pm \sqrt{4a - 3}}{2}$$

Here, the value of a must not be equal to $\frac{3}{4}$ otherwise z will become purely real.

84. Correct Response : (b)

Explanation :

The given equation is,
$$\left(\sqrt[3]{1+a} - 1\right)x^2 + \left(\sqrt{1+a} - 1\right)x + \left(\sqrt[6]{1+a} - 1\right) = 0 \quad ...(1)$$

Let, $\quad 1 + a = u^6$

The equation is,
$$(u^2 - 1)x^2 + (u^3 - 1)x + (u - 1) = 0$$
$$(u - 1)\{(u + 1)x^2 + (u^2 + u + 1)x + 1\} = 0$$

As the value of $a \to 0$, the value of $u \to 1$.

So, the equation reduces to,
$$(1 + 1)x^2 + (1^2 + 1 + 1)x + 1 = 0$$
$$2x^2 + 3x + 1 = 0$$
$$x = -\frac{1}{2}, -1$$

85. Correct Response : (c)

Explanation :

The given equation is,
$$(2x)^{\ln 2} = (3y)^{\ln 3}$$
$$\ln 2 \cdot \ln(2x) = \ln 3 \cdot \ln(3y) \quad ...(1)$$

The given equation is,
$$3^{\ln x} = 2^{\ln y}$$
$$\ln x \cdot \ln(3) = \ln y \cdot \ln(2)$$
$$\ln y = \frac{\ln x \cdot \ln(3)}{\ln 2} \quad ...(2)$$

Substitute value from equation (2) into equation (1),

$$\ln 2 \cdot \ln(2x) = \ln 3 \cdot (\ln 3 + \ln y)$$

$$\ln 2 \cdot \ln(2x) = \ln 3 \cdot \left(\ln 3 + \frac{\ln x \cdot \ln(3)}{\ln 2}\right)$$

$$(\ln 2)^2 \cdot \ln(2x) = \ln 3(\ln 3 \cdot \ln 2 + \ln x \cdot \ln 3)$$
$$(\ln 2)^2 \cdot \ln(2x) = (\ln 3)^2 \cdot \ln 2 + \ln x \cdot (\ln 3)^2$$

Further solve above equation.
$$(\ln 2)^2 \cdot \ln(2) + (\ln 2)^2 \cdot \ln(x) = (\ln 3)^2 \cdot \ln 2 + \ln x \cdot (\ln 3)^2$$

$$\ln x \left[(\ln 2)^2 - (\ln 3)^2\right] = \ln 2 \left[(\ln 3)^2 - (\ln 2)^2\right]$$

$$\ln x = -\ln 2$$
$$\ln x = \ln(2)^{-1}$$

Solve further,

$$\ln x = \ln \frac{1}{2}$$

$$x = \frac{1}{2}$$

86. Correct Response : (c)

Explanation :

The sum of roots of given equation $x^2 - 6x - 2 = 0$ is,
$$\alpha + \beta = 6$$

The product of roots of given equation $x^2 - 6x - 2 = 0$ is,
$$\alpha\beta = -2$$

The value of given expression is,

$$\frac{a_{10} - 2a_8}{2a_9} = \frac{\left(\alpha^{10} - \beta^{10}\right) - 2\left(\alpha^8 - \beta^8\right)}{2\left(\alpha^9 - \beta^9\right)}$$

$$= \frac{\left(\alpha^{10} - \beta^{10}\right) + \alpha\beta\left(\alpha^8 - \beta^8\right)}{2\left(\alpha^9 - \beta^9\right)}$$

$$= \frac{\left(\alpha^{10}+\alpha^9\beta\right)-\left(\beta^{10}+\alpha\beta^9\right)}{2\left(\alpha^9-\beta^9\right)}$$

$$= \frac{\alpha^9\left(\alpha+\beta\right)-\beta^9\left(\beta+\alpha\right)}{2\left(\alpha^9-\beta^9\right)}$$

Further, simplify above expression.

$$\frac{a_{10}-2a_8}{2a_9} = \frac{\left(\alpha+\beta\right)\left(\alpha^9-\beta^9\right)}{2\left(\alpha^9-\beta^9\right)}$$

$$= \frac{\left(\alpha+\beta\right)}{2}$$

$$= \frac{6}{2}$$

$$= 3$$

87. Correct Response : (a)

Explanation :

The equation from the given matrix is,

$$a + 8b + 7c = 0 \qquad \text{...(1)}$$

The equation from the given matrix is,

$$9a + 2b + 3c = 0 \qquad \text{...(2)}$$

The equation from the given matrix is,

$$7a + 7b + 7c = 0 \qquad \text{...(3)}$$

The above system of equations has no solution. So,

$$\frac{a}{1} = \frac{b}{6} = \frac{c}{-7} = k$$

$a = k,\ b = 6k,\ c = -7k$

It is given that the value of $a = 2$.

So, $b = 12,\ c = -14$

The value of given expression is,

$$\frac{3}{\omega^a}+\frac{1}{\omega^b}+\frac{3}{\omega^c} = \frac{3}{\omega^2}+\frac{1}{\omega^{12}}+\frac{3}{\omega^{-14}}$$

$$= 3\omega + 1 + 3\omega^2$$

$$= 3(-1) + 1$$

$$= -2$$

88. Correct Response : (b)

Explanation :

The equation from the given matrix is,

$$a + 8b + 7c = 0 \qquad \text{...(1)}$$

The equation from the given matrix is,

$$9a + 2b + 3c = 0 \qquad \text{...(2)}$$

The equation from the given matrix is,

$$7a + 7b + 7c = 0 \qquad \text{...(3)}$$

The above system of equations has no solution. So,

$$\frac{a}{1} = \frac{b}{6} = \frac{c}{-7} = k$$

$$a = k,\ b = 6k,\ c = -7k$$

It is given that the value of $b = 6$, So,

$$a = 1,\ c = -7$$

The equation is, $1x^2 + 6x - 7 = 0$

The sum of roots and product of roots for equation above is,

$\alpha + \beta = -6$ and $\alpha\beta = -7$

The value of given expression is,

$$\sum_{n=0}^{\infty}\left(\frac{\alpha+\beta}{\alpha\beta}\right)^n = \sum_{n=0}^{\infty}\left(\frac{6}{7}\right)^n$$

$$= \left(\frac{6}{7}\right)^0 + \left(\frac{6}{7}\right)^1 + \cdots$$

$$= \frac{1}{1-\frac{6}{7}}$$

$$= 7$$

89. Correct Response : 5

It is given that $|z - 3 - 2i| \leq 2$. So, the minimum

Explanation : value of $|2z - 6 + 5i|$ is,

$$|2z - 6 + 5i| = 2\left|z - 3 + \frac{5}{2}i\right|$$

$$= 2\left|z - 3 - 2i + 2i + \frac{5}{2}i\right|$$

$$\geq 2\left|z - 3 - 2i\right| - \left|\frac{9i}{2}\right|$$

Further simplify.

$$|\ 2x - 6 + 5i\ | \geq \left|2 - \frac{9}{2}\right|$$

$$\geq 5$$

90. Correct Response : (b)

Explanation :

Consider the given equation,

$$x^2 + bx - 1 = 0 \qquad \text{...(1)}$$

Consider other equation,

$$x^2 + x + b = 0 \qquad \text{...(2)}$$

Subtract equation (1) from equation (2).

$$bx - x - 1 - b = 0$$

$$x(b - 1) = b + 1$$

$$x = \frac{b+1}{b-1}$$

Substitute value of x in equation (1).

$$\left(\frac{b+1}{b-1}\right)^2 + b\left(\frac{b+1}{b-1}\right) - 1 = 0$$

$$b^3 + 3b = 0$$

$$b(b^2 + 3) = 0$$

$$b = \pm i\sqrt{3}$$

91. Correct Response : (*)

Explanation :

It is given that $\omega = e^{i\pi/3}$. Let, $a = b = c = 1$.

The value of x is,
$$x = 1 + 1 + 1 = 3$$
The value of given expression is,
$$\frac{\left|x^2\right| + \left|y^2\right| + \left|z^2\right|}{\left|a^2\right| + \left|b^2\right| + \left|c^2\right|} = \frac{3^2 + \left|1 + \sqrt{3}i\right|^2 + \left|1 + \sqrt{3}i\right|^2}{\left|1^2\right| + \left|1^2\right| + \left|1^2\right|}$$
$$= \frac{9 + 4 + 4}{3}$$
$$= \frac{17}{3} \notin z$$

For $a = b = c = 1$, the solution is non-integral.

The value of given expression depends on the value taken by a, b and c. Therefore, no integral solution is possible for given problem.

92. **Correct Response :** (A)-(s), (B)-(t), (C)-(r), (D)-(r)

Explanation :

(A)

Let, complex number is $z = \cos\theta + i\sin\theta$. So,
$$\frac{2iz}{1 - z^2} = \frac{2i(\cos\theta + i\sin\theta)}{1 - \cos 2\theta - i\sin 2\theta}$$
$$= \frac{2i(\cos\theta + i\sin\theta)}{2\sin^2\theta - i2\sin\theta\cos\theta}$$
$$= -\frac{1}{\sin\theta}$$
$$= -\operatorname{cosec}\theta$$

The real part is,
$$\operatorname{Re}\left(\frac{2iz}{1 - z^2}\right) = -\operatorname{cosec}\theta$$

The domain for real part is $(-\infty, -1] \cup [1, \infty)$.

(B)

Simplify the given function,
$$f(x) = \sin^{-1}\left(\frac{8(3)^{x-2}}{1 - 3^{2(x-1)}}\right)$$
$$= \sin^{-1}\left(\frac{8(3)^{x}}{9 - 3^{2x}}\right)$$

Put $3^x = t$.
$$f(x) = \sin^{-1}\left(\frac{8t}{9 - t^2}\right)$$

Now, $\qquad -1 \le \left(\dfrac{8t}{9 - t^2}\right) \le 1$

Case 1 :
$$\left(\frac{8t}{9 - t^2}\right) \le 1$$
$$\left(\frac{8t}{9 - t^2}\right) - 1 \le 0$$
$$\frac{t^2 + 8t - 9}{t^2 - 9} \ge 0$$

Further simplify.
$$\frac{(t + 9)(t - 1)}{(t - 3)(t + 3)} \ge 0$$
$$\frac{(t - 1)}{(t - 3)} \ge 0$$

The domain is,
$$t \in (-\infty, 1] \cup (3, \infty)$$
$$\Rightarrow \qquad 3^x \in (0, 1] \cup (3, \infty)$$
$$\Rightarrow \qquad x \in (-\infty, 0] \cup (1, \infty)$$

Case 2 : $\qquad -1 \le \left(\dfrac{8t}{9 - t^2}\right)$
$$\left(\frac{8t}{9 - t^2}\right) + 1 \ge 0$$
$$\left(\frac{t^2 - 8t - 9}{t^2 - 9}\right) \ge 0$$

Further simplify :
$$\frac{(t - 9)(t + 1)}{(t + 3)(t + 3)} \ge 0$$
$$\frac{t - 9}{t + 3} \ge 0$$

The domain is,
$$t \in (-\infty, 3) \cup [9, \infty)$$
$$\Rightarrow \qquad 3^x \in (0, 3) \cup [9, \infty)$$
$$\Rightarrow \qquad x \in (-\infty, 1] \cup [2, \infty)$$

Intersection of $x \in (-\infty, 1] \cup (1, \infty)$ and $x \in (-\infty, 0] \cup [2, \infty)$ is,
$$x \in (-\infty, 0] \cup [2, \infty)$$

(C)

The value of given determinant is calculated as,
$$f(\theta) = \begin{vmatrix} 1 & \tan\theta & 1 \\ -\tan\theta & 1 & \tan\theta \\ -1 & -\tan\theta & 1 \end{vmatrix}$$
$$= \sec^2\theta + \sec^2\theta$$
$$= 2\sec^2\theta$$

Therefore, $f(\theta) \in [2, \infty)$.

(D)

The given function is,
$$f(x) = x^{\frac{3}{2}}(3x - 10)$$

Differentiate given function with respect to x.
$$f'(x) = \frac{3}{2}x^{\frac{1}{2}}(3x - 10) + x^{\frac{3}{2}}(3)$$
$$= \frac{3\sqrt{x}}{2}[3x - 10 + 2x]$$
$$= \frac{3\sqrt{x}}{2}[5x - 10]$$

Function $f(x)$ is increasing for $f'(x) \geq 0$. Therefore, $x \in [2, \infty)$.

93. Correct Response : (b)

Explanation :

A represents the set of points above the line $y = 1$.

B represents the set of the points on the circle $(x - 2)^2 + (y - 1)^2 = 3^2$.

C represents $\mathrm{Re}((1-i)z) = \sqrt{2}$

$$\mathrm{Re}((1-i)(x+iy)) = \sqrt{2}$$

$$x + y = \sqrt{2}$$

Thus, $(A \cap B \cap C)$ has only one point of intesection.

94. Correct Response : (c)

Explanation :

The extreme points of diameter of given circle are $(-1, 1)$ and $(5, 1)$. So,

$$|z+1-i|^2 + |z-5-i|^2 = 6^2$$

$$= 36$$

Therefore, $|z+1-i|^2 + |z-5-i|^2$ lies between 35 and 39.

95. Correct Response : (b, c, d)

Explanation :

Let, z be fixed and $|z - \omega|$ is distance between z and w.

$$\Big||z|-|\omega|\Big| < |z - \omega|$$

The distance between z and w be maximum for opposite points.

$$|z - \omega| < 6$$

$$-6 < |z|-|\omega| < 6$$

$$-3 < |z|-|\omega|+3 < 9$$

Therefore, $|z|-|\omega|+3$ lies between -3 and 9.

96. Correct Response : (d)

Explanation :

If α, β are roots of equation $x^2 - px + r = 0$, then sum and product of roots is,

$\alpha\beta = r$ and $\alpha + \beta = p$

If $\dfrac{\alpha}{2}$, 2β are roots of equation $x^2 - qx + r = 0$, then

sum and product of roots is,

$$\alpha\beta = r \text{ and } \frac{\alpha}{2} + 2\beta = q$$

On solving the value of roots is,

$$\alpha = \frac{2q-p}{3} \text{ and } \beta = \frac{2(2p-q)}{3}$$

Now, the value of r is calculated as,

$$r = \alpha\beta$$

$$= \frac{2q-p}{3} \cdot \frac{2(2p-q)}{3}$$

$$= \frac{2}{9}(2q-p)(2p-q)$$

97. Correct Response : (d)

Explanation :

The given figure according to the information is,

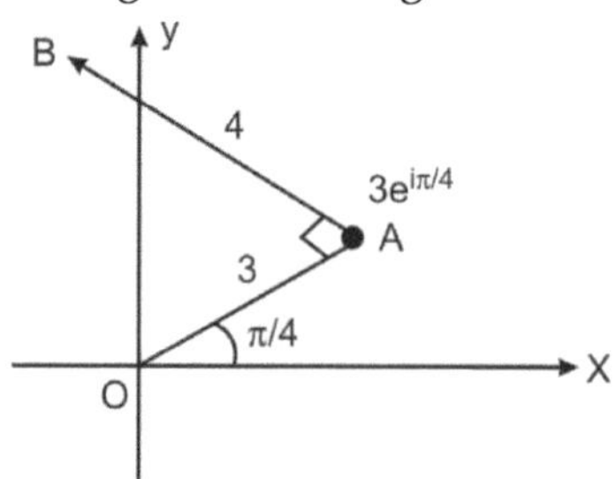

Let, the lenght of OA is 3 and complex number associated with A be $3e^{\frac{i\pi}{4}}$.

The complex number associated with B is z, then

$$\frac{z - 3e^{\frac{i\pi}{4}}}{0 - 3e^{\frac{i\pi}{4}}} = \frac{4}{3}e^{-\frac{i\pi}{2}}$$

$$\frac{z - 3e^{\frac{i\pi}{4}}}{0 - 3e^{\frac{i\pi}{4}}} = -\frac{4i}{3}$$

$$3z - 9e^{\frac{i\pi}{4}} = 12ie^{\frac{i\pi}{4}}$$

$$z = (3+4i)e^{\frac{i\pi}{4}}$$

98. Correct Response : (d)

Explanation :

Let, $z = \cos\theta + i\sin\theta$. So,

$$\frac{z}{1-z^2} = \frac{\cos\theta + i\sin\theta}{1-(\cos\theta + i\sin\theta)^2}$$

$$= \frac{\cos\theta + i\sin\theta}{1-(\cos 2\theta + i\sin 2\theta)}$$

$$= \frac{\cos\theta + i\sin\theta}{2\sin^2\theta - 2i\sin\theta\cos\theta}$$

$$= \frac{\cos\theta + i\sin\theta}{-2i\sin\theta\,(\cos\theta + i\sin\theta)}$$

Further simplify,

$$\frac{z}{1-z^2} = \frac{i}{2\sin\theta}$$

The value of $\dfrac{z}{1-z^2}$ is imaginary. So, it lies on Y-axis.

99. Correct Response : (a)

Explanation :

Let, the function is $f(x) = ke^x - x$.

Differentiate the given function with respect to x.

$$f'(x) = ke^x - 1$$
$$0 = ke^x - 1$$
$$ke^x = 1$$
$$e^x = \frac{1}{k}$$

Take log on both sides,

$$x = ln\,1 - ln\,k$$
$$x = -ln\,k$$

Again, differentiate the function with respect to x.

$$f''(x) = ke^x$$

Now, the function is,

$$f(-ln\,k) = ke^{-1nk} - (-ln\,k)$$
$$= ke^{ln\frac{1}{k}} + ln\,k$$
$$= 1 + ln\,k$$

Solve the quadratic equation.

$$1 + ln\,k = 0$$
$$ln\,k = -1$$
$$k = \frac{1}{e}$$

100. Correct Response : (a)

Explanation :

For two distinct roots of equation,

$$1 + ln\,k < 0$$
$$ln\,k < -1$$
$$k < \frac{1}{e}$$

Therefore, the possible set is $k \in \left(0, \frac{1}{e}\right)$.

101. Correct Response : (d)

Explanation :

It is given that $\left(\dfrac{w - \overline{w}z}{1 - z}\right)$ is purely real. So,

$$\left(\frac{w - \overline{w}z}{1 - z}\right) = \frac{\overline{w} - w\overline{z}}{1 - \overline{z}}$$
$$(z\overline{z} - 1)(\overline{w} - w) = 0$$
$$z\overline{z} = 1$$
$$|z| = 1$$

Therefore, the set of values is

$$\{z : |z| = 1, z \neq 1\}$$

102. Correct Response : (a)

Explanation :

The roots of given equation is real. So,

$$b^2 - 4ac \geq 0$$
$$4(a + b + c)^2 - 12\lambda\,(ab + bc + ca) \geq 0$$
$$\lambda \leq \frac{a^2 + b^2 + c^2}{3(ab + bc + ca)} + \frac{2}{3}$$

For $|a - b| < c$,

$$a^2 + b^2 - 2ab < c^2 \qquad ....(1)$$

For $|b - c| < a$,

$$b^2 + c^2 - 2bc < a^2 \qquad ...(2)$$

For $|c - a| < b$,

$$c^2 + a^2 - 2ac < b^2 \qquad ...(3)$$

Solve equations (1), (2) and (3).

$$\frac{a^2 + b^2 + c^2}{ab + bc + ca} < 2$$

$\therefore$
$$\lambda < \frac{2}{3} + \frac{2}{3}$$
$$\lambda < \frac{4}{3}$$

103. Correct Response : (a)

Explanation :

If P is point on C_1 and Q is point on C_2.

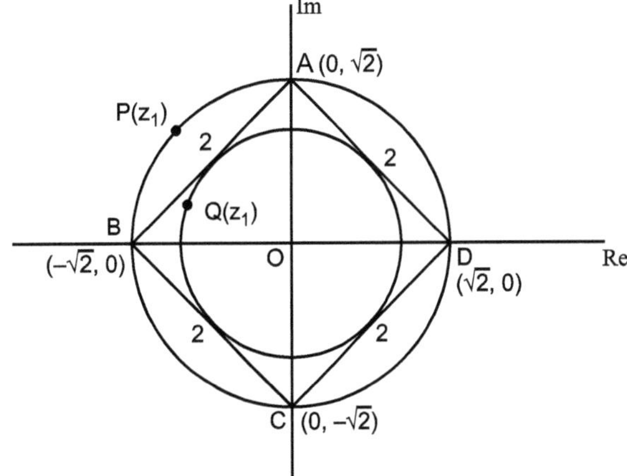

Let, the complex number $\sqrt{2}, -\sqrt{2}, \sqrt{2}i$ and $-\sqrt{2}i$ be A, B, C and D respectively.

$$\frac{PA^2 + PB^2 + PC^2 + PD^2}{QA^2 + QB^2 + QC^2 + QD^2}$$

$$= \frac{\left|z_1 - \sqrt{2}\right|^2 + \left|z_1 + \sqrt{2}\right|^2 + \left|z_1 + \sqrt{2}i\right|^2 + \left|z_1 - \sqrt{2}i\right|^2}{\left|z_2 + \sqrt{2}\right|^2 + \left|z_2 - \sqrt{2}\right|^2 + \left|z_2 - \sqrt{2}i\right|^2 + \left|z_2 + \sqrt{2}i\right|^2}$$

$$= \frac{\left|z_1\right|^2 + 2}{\left|z_2\right|^2 + 2}$$

$$= \frac{3}{4}$$

104. Correct Answer : 1210

Explanation :

If a, b are roots of equation $x^2 - 10cx - 11d = 0$, then
$$a + b = 10c \text{ and } ab = -11d$$

If c, d are roots of equation $x^2 - 10ax - 11b = 0$, then
$$c + d = 10a \text{ and } cd = -11b$$

Solve $ab = -11d$ and $cd = -11b$.
$$ac = 121$$

Add $a + b = 10c$ and $c + d = 10a$.
$$a + b + c + d = 10c + 10a$$
$$b + d = 9(a + c)$$

Root of equation $x^2 - 10cx - 11d = 0$ is a. So,
$$a^2 - 10ca - 11d = 0 \qquad \qquad ...(1)$$

Root of equation $x^2 - 10ax - 11b = 0$ is c. So,
$$c^2 - 10ac - 11b = 0$$

Add equation (1) and (2).
$$a^2 + c^2 - 20ac - 11 (b + d) = 0$$
$$(a + c)^2 - 20(121) - 11 (9) (a + c) = 0$$
$$(a + c) = 121 \text{ or } -22$$

Now,
$$b + d = 9 (121)$$
$$= 1089$$

The required value is,
$$a + b + c + d = 1089 + 121$$
$$= 1210.$$

105. Correct Response : (*)

Explanation :

Solve.
$$a_1 z + a_2 z^2 + ... + a_n z^n = 1$$
$$|a_1 z + a_2 z^2 + ... a_n z^n| = 1$$
$$|a_1 z| + |a_2 z^2| + ... + |a_n z^n| \geq 1$$
$$2 [|z| + |z|^2 + ... + |z|^n] > 1$$

Further solve.
$$\frac{2|z|\left(1 - |z|^n\right)}{(1 - |z|)} > 1$$

As $|z| < \dfrac{1}{3}$,
$$|z| > \frac{1}{3} + \frac{2}{3} |z|^{n+1}$$
$$|z| > \frac{1}{3}$$

There exists a contradiction.
Hence, there exists no complex number as given condition.

106. Correct Response : (a)

Explanation :

The points $\left(\sqrt{2} - 1, \sqrt{2}\right)$, $(1, 0)$ and $\left(\sqrt{2} - 1, -\sqrt{2}\right)$ are at equal distance form point $(-1, 0)$.

The shaded area is the region outside the sector of circle $|z + 1| = 2$. The shaded region lies between

$$\arg (z + 1) = \frac{\pi}{4} \text{ and } \arg (z + 1) = -\frac{\pi}{4}.$$

The locus of z that lies in shaded region is,

$$z : |z + 1| > 2, \left|\arg (z + 1)\right| < \frac{\pi}{4}$$

107. Correct Response : (b)

Explanation :

Let, z be complex number.
$$z = a + b\omega + c\omega^2$$
$$= a + b\omega - c - c\omega$$
$$= (a - c) + (b - c)\left(-\frac{1}{2} + \frac{\sqrt{3}}{2} i\right)$$
$$= a - c - \frac{b}{2} + \frac{c}{2} + (b - c)\frac{\sqrt{3}}{2} i$$

Now, $|z| = \sqrt{\left(a - \dfrac{b}{2} - \dfrac{c}{2}\right)^2 + \dfrac{3}{4}(b - c)^2}$

$$= \sqrt{\frac{1}{2}\left((a - b)^2 + (b - c)^2 + (c - a)^2\right)}$$

The value of $\left|a + b\omega + c\omega^2\right|$ is minimum if $a = b$ and $(b - c)^2 + (c - a)^2 = 1$.

Therefore, minimum value of $\left|a + b\omega + c\omega^2\right|$ is 1.

108. Correct Response : $\left[-\dfrac{\pi}{2}, -\dfrac{\pi}{10}\right] \cup \left[\dfrac{3\pi}{10}, \dfrac{\pi}{2}\right]$

Explanation :

Let, $\sin t = y$. So,
$$\frac{1 - 2x - 5x^2}{3x^2 - 2x - 1} = y$$
$$(3x^2 - 2x - 1) y - (1 - 2x - 5x^2) = 0$$
$$(3y - 5)x^2 - 2x (y - 1) - (y + 1) = 0$$

Since, $x \in R - \left\{1, -\dfrac{1}{3}\right\}$ so $D \geq 0$. Now,

$$y^2 - y - 1 \geq 0$$
$$y \geq \frac{1 + \sqrt{5}}{2} \quad \text{or} \quad y \leq \frac{1 - \sqrt{5}}{2}$$
$$\sin t \geq \frac{1 + \sqrt{5}}{2} \quad \text{or} \quad \sin t \leq \frac{1 - \sqrt{5}}{2}$$
$$\sin t \geq \sin \frac{3\pi}{10} \quad \text{or} \quad \sin t \leq \sin \left(-\frac{\pi}{10}\right)$$

So, $\dfrac{\pi}{2} \geq t \geq \dfrac{3\pi}{10}$ or $-\dfrac{\pi}{2} \leq t \leq -\dfrac{\pi}{10}$.

Therefore, required range of t is
$$\left[-\frac{\pi}{2}, -\frac{\pi}{10}\right] \cup \left[\frac{3\pi}{10}, \frac{\pi}{2}\right].$$

109. Correct Response : (d)

Explanation :

For $(\cos \alpha - \beta) = 1.$

$$(\alpha - \beta) = \cos^{-1} 1$$
$$\alpha - \beta = 0$$
$$\alpha = \beta$$

For $\cos (\alpha + \beta) = \dfrac{1}{e}.$

$$(\alpha + \beta) = \pm \cos^{-1} \dfrac{1}{e}$$

$$2\alpha = \pm \cos^{-1} \dfrac{1}{e}$$

$$2\alpha \in [-2\pi, 2\pi]$$

Therefore, 4 pairs of α and β satisfies both the equations.

110. Correct Response : (a)

Explanation :

Let, a, a^2 be the roots and equation $x^2 + px + q = 0.$

$a + a^2 = -p$ and $a^3 = q$

Solve further.

$$a(a + 1) = -p$$
$$a^3(a^3 + 1 + 3(a^2 + a)) = -p^3$$
$$q(q + 1 - 3p) = -p^3$$
$$p^3 - q(3p - 1) + q^2 = 0$$

Therefore, relation between p and q is

$$p^3 - q(3p - 1) + q^2 = 0.$$

111. Correct Response : (b)

Explanation :

Solve the given complex number.

$$|z_2 - 3 - 4i| = 5$$

$$\left| |z_2| - 5 \right| \leq 5$$

$$|z_2| \leq 10$$

The minimum value of $|z_1 - z_2|$ is,

$$|z_1 - z_2| \geq \left| |z_1| - |z_2| \right|$$

$$\geq 12 - 10$$

$$\geq 2$$

112. Correct Response : (b)

Explanation :

The given equation is,

$$7 \cos x + 5 \sin x = 2k + 1$$

It is known that $-\sqrt{a^2 + b^2} \leq a \sin x + b \cos x \leq \sqrt{a^2 + b^2}$. So,

$$-\sqrt{74} \leq 2k + 1 \leq \sqrt{74}$$

If k is an integer, then

$$-8 \leq 2k + 1 \leq 8$$
$$-9 \leq 2k \leq 7$$

$$-4 \leq k \leq 3$$

Therefore, number of integrals of k is 8.

113. Correct Response : (b)

Explanation :

Solve given equation.

$$(1 + \omega^2)^n = (1 + \omega^4)^n$$
$$(-\omega)^n = (-\omega^2)^n$$
$$\omega^n = 1$$
$$n = 3$$

114. Correct Response : (a)

Explanation :

If $x^2 + 2ax + 10 - 3a > 0$, then

$$D < 0$$
$$4a^2 - 4(10 - 3a) < 0$$
$$4a^2 - 40 + 12a < 0$$
$$(a + 5)(a - 2) = 0$$

Therefore, $-5 < a < 2.$

115. Correct Response : (a)

Explanation :

Solve the given complex number.

$$\omega = \dfrac{z - 1}{z + 1}$$

$$= \dfrac{(x + iy) - 1}{(x + iy) + 1}$$

$$= \dfrac{(x + iy) - 1}{(x + iy) + 1} \cdot \dfrac{(x + iy) - 1}{(x + iy) - 1}$$

$$= 0 + i\left(\dfrac{-1 + x^2 + y^2 + 2y}{(x + 1)^2 + y^2} \right)$$

Therefore, $\text{Re}(\omega)$ is 0.

116. Explanation :

To prove that $\left| \dfrac{1 - z_1 \overline{z_2}}{z_1 - z_2} \right| < 1.$

$$\Leftrightarrow \quad |1 - z_1 \overline{z_2}| < |z_1 - z_2|$$

$$\Leftrightarrow (1 - z_1 \overline{z_2})(1 - \overline{z_1 z_2}) < (z_1 - z_2)(\overline{z_1} - \overline{z_2})$$

$$\Leftrightarrow 1 + |z_1|^2 |z_2|^2 - |z_1|^2 - |z_2|^2 < 0$$

$$\Leftrightarrow (1 + |z_1|^2) + |z_2|^2 (|z_1|^2 - 1) < 0$$

Solve further.

$$\Leftrightarrow (1 - |z_1|^2) + |(1 - |z_2|^2) < 0$$

The above condition is possible as $|z_1| < 1 < |z_2|.$

117. Correct Response : (a)

Explanation :

Let, the given function is $f(x) = \displaystyle\int_1^x \sqrt{2 - t^2} \, dt \cdot$

Differentiate it with respect to x.

$$f'(x) = \sqrt{2 - x^2}$$

Substitute value in given equation.

$$x^2 - \sqrt{2 - x^2} = 0$$

$$x^2 = \sqrt{2 - x^2}$$

$$x^4 = 2 - x^2$$

$$x^2 = 1$$

Therefore, roots of equation are $1, -1$.

118. Explanation :

The centre of circle and midpoint of diagonals of square is $(1, 0)$.

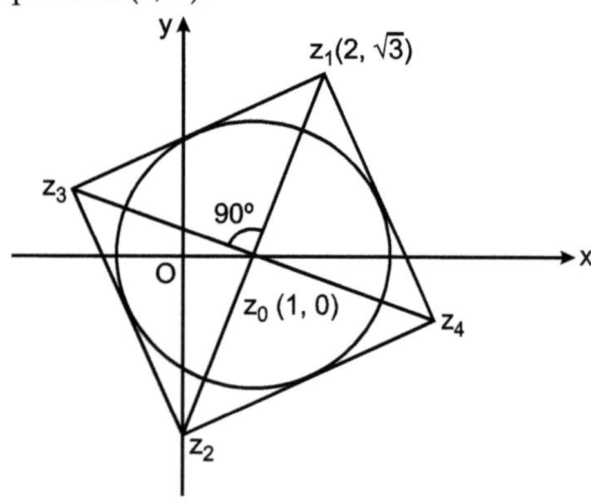

The midpoint of z_1 and z_2 is z_0. So,

$$z_3 - z_0 = (z_1 - z_0)e^{i\pi/2}$$

$$z_3 - z_0 = (2 + \sqrt{3}i - 1)i$$

$$z_3 = i - \sqrt{3} + 1$$

$$= 1 - \sqrt{3} + i$$

Also, z_0 is midpoint of z_1 and z_2 as well as z_3 and z_4.

$$z_4 = (1 + \sqrt{3}) - i$$

$$z_2 = -\sqrt{3}i$$

Therefore, other vertices of square are

$$(0 - \sqrt{3}), (1 - \sqrt{3}, 1) \text{ and } (1 + \sqrt{3}, 1).$$

QUESTIONS

1. Let $\lambda \in R$. The system of linear equations
$$2x_1 - 4x_2 + \lambda x_3 = 1$$
$$x_1 - 6x_2 + x_3 = 2$$
$$\lambda x_1 - 10x_2 + 4x_3 = 3$$
is inconsistent for : **[2020, Main]**
(a) exactly one negative value of λ
(b) exactly one positive value of λ
(c) every value of λ
(d) exactly two values of λ

2. The value of λ and μ for which the system of linear equations
$$x + y + z = 2$$
$$x + 2y + 3z = 4$$
$$x + 3y + \lambda z = \mu$$
has infinitely many solutions are, respectively : **[2020, Main]**
(a) 5 and 7
(b) 6 and 8
(c) 4 and 9
(d) 5 and 8

3. Let m and M be respectively the minimum and maximum values of
$$\begin{vmatrix} \cos^2 x & 1+\sin^2 x & \sin 2x \\ 1+\cos^2 x & \sin^2 x & \sin 2x \\ \cos^2 x & \sin^2 x & 1+\sin 2x \end{vmatrix}.$$ Then the
ordered pair (m, M) is equal to : **[2020, Main]**
(a) $(-3, -1)$
(b) $(-4, -1)$
(c) $(1, 3)$
(d) $(-3, 3)$

4. Let $\theta = \dfrac{\pi}{5}$ and $A = \begin{bmatrix} \cos \theta & \sin \theta \\ -\sin \theta & \cos \theta \end{bmatrix}$. If $B = A +$
A^4, then det (B) : **[2020, Main]**
(a) is one
(b) lies in $(1, 2)$
(c) is zero
(d) lies in $(2, 3)$

5. The sum of distinct values of λ for which the system of equations
$$(\lambda - 1)x + (3\lambda + 1)y + 2\lambda z = 0$$
$$(\lambda - 1)x + (4\lambda - 2)y + (\lambda + 3)z = 0$$
$$2x + (3\lambda + 1)y + 3(\lambda - 1)z = 0,$$
has non-zero solutions, is ....
[2020, Main]

6. If $A = \begin{bmatrix} \cos \theta & i \sin \theta \\ i \sin \theta & \cos \theta \end{bmatrix}, \left(\theta = \dfrac{\pi}{24} \right)$ and $A^5 = $
$\begin{bmatrix} a & b \\ c & d \end{bmatrix}$, where $i = \sqrt{-1}$, then which one of
the following is not true ? **[2020, Main]**
(a) $0 \le a^2 + b^2 \le 1$
(b) $a^2 - d^2 = 0$
(c) $a^2 - b^2 = \dfrac{1}{2}$
(d) $a^2 - c^2 = 1$

7. If the system of equations
$$x - 2y + 3z = 9$$
$$2x + y + z = b$$
$$x - 7y + az = 24,$$
has infinitely many solutions, then $a - b$ is equal
to .... **[2020, Main]**

8. If the system of equations
$$x + y + z = 2$$
$$2x + 4y - z = 6$$
$$3x + 2y + \lambda z = \mu$$
has infinitely many solutions, then : **[2020, Main]**
(a) $\lambda - 2\mu = -5$
(b) $2\lambda - \mu = 5$
(c) $2\lambda + \mu = 14$
(d) $\lambda + 2\mu = 14$

9. Suppose the vectors x_1, x_2 and x_3 are the solutions of the system of linear equations, $Ax = b$ when the vector b on the right side is equal to b_1, b_2 and b_3, respectively. If
$$x_1 = \begin{bmatrix} 1 \\ 1 \\ 1 \end{bmatrix}, x_2 = \begin{bmatrix} 0 \\ 2 \\ 1 \end{bmatrix}, x_3 = \begin{bmatrix} 0 \\ 0 \\ 1 \end{bmatrix}, b_1 = \begin{bmatrix} 1 \\ 0 \\ 0 \end{bmatrix}$$
$$b_2 = \begin{bmatrix} 0 \\ 2 \\ 0 \end{bmatrix} \text{ and } b_3 = \begin{bmatrix} 0 \\ 0 \\ 2 \end{bmatrix},$$
then the determinant of A is equal to : **[2020, Main]**
(a) $\dfrac{1}{2}$
(b) 4
(c) $\dfrac{3}{2}$
(d) 2

10. If $\Delta = \begin{vmatrix} x-2 & 2x-3 & 3x-4 \\ 2x-3 & 3x-4 & 4x-5 \\ 3x-5 & 5x-8 & 10x-17 \end{vmatrix}$

$= Ax^3 + Bx^2 + Cx + D$, then $B + C$ is equal to :

[2020, Main]

(a) -1　　　　　　(b) 1

(c) -3　　　　　　(d) 9

11. Let $A = \begin{bmatrix} x & 1 \\ 1 & 0 \end{bmatrix}$, $x \in R$ and $A^4 = [a_{ij}]$. If $a_{11} = 109$, then a_{22} is equal to .... **[2020, Main]**

12. If the system of linear equations

$$x + y + 3z = 0$$
$$x + 3y + k^2z = 0$$
$$3x + y + 3z = 0$$

has a non-zero solution (x, y, z) for some $k \in R$,

then $x + \left(\dfrac{y}{z}\right)$ is equal to : **[2020, Main]**

(a) 9　　　　　　(b) -3

(c) -9　　　　　　(d) 3

13. If $a + x = b + y = c + z + 1$, where a, b, c, x, y, z are non-zero distinct real numbers, then

$$\begin{vmatrix} x & a+y & x+a \\ y & b+y & y+b \\ z & c+y & z+c \end{vmatrix}$$ is equal to : **[2020, Main]**

(a) 0　　　　　　(b) $y(a-b)$

(c) $y(b-a)$　　　　　　(d) $y(a-b)$

14. The trace of a square matrix is defined to be the sum of its diagonal entries. If A is a 2×2 matrix such that the trace of A is 3 and the trace of A^3 is -18, then the value of the determinant of A is .... **[2020, Advanced]**

15. Let $a, b, c \in R$ be all non-zero and satisfy $a^3 + b^3 + c^3 = 2$. If the matrix $A = \begin{pmatrix} a & b & c \\ b & c & a \\ c & a & b \end{pmatrix}$

satisfies $A^TA = I$, then a value of abc can be :

[2020, Main]

(a) $\dfrac{2}{3}$　　　　　　(b) $-\dfrac{1}{3}$

(c) 3　　　　　　(d) $\dfrac{1}{3}$

16. Let $A = \{X = (x, y, z)^T : PX = 0 \text{ and } x^2 + y^2 + z^2 = 1\}$ where $P = \begin{bmatrix} 1 & 2 & 1 \\ -2 & 3 & -4 \\ 1 & 9 & -1 \end{bmatrix}$, then the set A :

[2020, Main]

(a) is a singleton

(b) contains exactly two elements

(c) contains more then two elements

(d) is an empty set

17. Let A be a 3×3 matrix such that

adj $A = \begin{bmatrix} 2 & -1 & 1 \\ -1 & 0 & 2 \\ 1 & -2 & -1 \end{bmatrix}$ and

$B = $ adj (adj A).

If $|A| = \lambda$ and $|(B^{-1})^T| = \mu$, then the ordered pair, $(|\lambda|, \mu)$ is equal to : **[2020, Main]**

(a) $\left(9, \dfrac{1}{9}\right)$　　　　　　(b) $\left(9, \dfrac{1}{81}\right)$

(c) $\left(3, \dfrac{1}{81}\right)$　　　　　　(d) $(3, 81)$

18. Let S be the set of all integer solutions, (x, y, z), of the system of equations

$$x - 2y + 5z = 0$$
$$-2x + 4y + z = 0$$
$$-7x + 14y + 9z = 0$$

such that $15 \le x^2 + y^2 + z^2 \le 150$. Then, the number of elements in the set S is equal to ....

[2020, Main]

19. Let S be the set of all $\lambda \in R$ for which the system of linear equations

$$2x - y + 2z = 2$$
$$x - 2y + \lambda z = -4$$
$$x + \lambda y + z = 4$$

has no solution. Then the set S **[2020, Main]**

(a) contains more than two elements.

(b) is a singleton.

(c) contains exactly two elements.

(d) is an empty set.

20. Let A be a 2×2 real matrix with entries from $\{0, 1\}$ and $|A| \ne 0$. Consider the following two statements : **[2020, Main]**

(P) If $A \ne I_2$, then $|A| = -1$

(Q) If $|A| = 1$, then $tr(A) = 2$,

where I_2 denotes 2×2 indentity matrix and $tr(A)$ denotes the sum of the diagonal entries of A. Then :

(a) (P) is true and (Q) is false

(b) Both (P) and (Q) are false

(c) Both (P) and (Q) are true

(d) (P) is false and (Q) is true

21. The sum of distinct values of λ for which the system of equations

$$(\lambda - 1)x + (3\lambda + 1)y + 2\lambda z = 0$$

$$(\lambda - 1)x + (4\lambda - 2)y + (\lambda + 3)z = 0$$
$$2x + (3\lambda + 1)y + 3(\lambda - 1)z = 0,$$

has non-zero solutions, is ....

[2020, Main]

22. Let M be a 3×3 invertible matrix with real entries and let I denote the 3×3 identity matrix. If $M^{-1} = \text{adj (adj M)}$, then which of the following statement is/are ALWAYS TRUE ?

[2020, Advanced]

(a) $M = I$ **(b)** det $M = 1$

(c) $M^2 = I$ **(d)** $(\text{adj } M)^2 = I$

23. Let $A = [a_{ij}]$ and $B = [b_{ij}]$ be two 3×3 real matrices such that $b_{ij} = 3^{(i+j-2)}a_{ji}$, where $i, j = 1, 2, 3$. If the determinant of B is 81, then the determinant of A is : **[2020, Main]**

(a) 3   **(b)** 1/3

(c) 1/81   **(d)** 1/9

24. If the system of linear equations,
$$x + y + z = 6$$
$$x + 2y + 3z = 10$$
$$3x + 2y + \lambda z = \mu$$

has more two solutions, then $\mu - \lambda^2$ is equal to .... **[2020, Main]**

25. The system of linear equations
$$\lambda x + 2y + 2z = 5$$
$$2\lambda x + 3y + 5z = 8$$
$$4x + \lambda y + 6z = 10 \text{ has}$$ **[2020, Main]**

(a) infinitely many solutions when $\lambda = 2$.

(b) a unique solution when $\lambda = -8$.

(c) no solution when $\lambda = 8$.

(d) no solution when $\lambda = 2$.

26. If $A = \begin{pmatrix} 2 & 2 \\ 9 & 4 \end{pmatrix}$ and $I = \begin{pmatrix} 1 & 0 \\ 0 & 1 \end{pmatrix}$, then $10A^{-1}$ is equal to : **[2020, Main]**

(a) $4I - A$ **(b)** $A - 6I$

(c) $6I - A$ **(d)** $A - 4I$

27. If the matrices $A = \begin{bmatrix} 1 & 1 & 2 \\ 1 & 3 & 4 \\ 1 & -1 & 3 \end{bmatrix}$, B = adj A and

$C = 3A$, then $\dfrac{|\text{adj B}|}{|C|}$ is equal to : **[2020, Main]**

(a) 72   **(b)** 2

(c) 8   **(d)** 16

28. The following system of linear equations
$$7x + 6y - 2z = 0$$
$$3x + 4y + 2z = 0$$
$$x - 2y - 6z = 0, \text{ has}$$ **[2020, Main]**

(a) infinitely many solutions, (x, y, z) satisfying $x = 2z$.

(b) no solution.

(c) only the trivial solution.

(d) infinitely many solutions, (x, y, z) satisfying $y = 2z$.

29. Let $a - 2b + c = 1$.

If $f(x) = \begin{vmatrix} x+a & x+3 & x+1 \\ x+b & x+3 & x+2 \\ x+c & x+4 & x+3 \end{vmatrix}$, then :

[2020, Main]

(a) $f(-50) = 501$ **(b)** $f(-50) = -1$

(c) $f(50) = 1$ **(d)** $f(50) = -501$

30. Let α be a root of the equation $x^2 + x + 1 = 0$ and the matrix $A = \dfrac{1}{\sqrt{3}}\begin{bmatrix} 1 & 1 & 1 \\ 1 & \alpha & \alpha^2 \\ 1 & \alpha^2 & \alpha^4 \end{bmatrix}$, then the matrix

A^{31} is equal to : **[2020, Main]**

(a) A^3 **(b)** A

(c) A^2 **(d)** I_3

31. If the system of linear equations
$$2x + 2ay + az = 0$$
$$2x + 3by + bz = 0$$
$$2x + 4cy + cz = 0$$

where $a, b, c \in R$ are non-zero and distinct; has a non-zero solution, then : **[2020, Main]**

(a) a, b, c are in A.P.

(b) $a + b + c = 0$

(c) a, b, c are in G.P.

(d) $\dfrac{1}{a}, \dfrac{1}{b}, \dfrac{1}{c}$ are in A.P.

32. For which of the following ordered pairs (μ, δ), the system of linear equations
$$x + 2y + 3z = \lambda$$
$$3x + 4y + 5z = \mu$$
$$4x + 4y + 4z = \delta$$

is inconsistent ? **[2020, Main]**

(a) $(1, 0)$ **(b)** $(4, 6)$

(c) $(3, 4)$ **(d)** $(4, 3)$

33. The number of all 3×3 matrices A, with enteries from the set $\{-1, 0, 1\}$ such that the sum of the diagonal elements of AA^T is 3, is .... **[2020, Main]**

34. If for some a and b in R, the intersection, of the following three places
$$x + 4y - 2z = 1$$
$$x + 7y - 5z = b$$
$$x + 5y + az = 5$$

is a line in R^3, the $a + b$ is equal to : **[2020, Main]**

(a) 10 **(b)** – 10

(c) 2 **(d)** 0

35. If $\Delta_1 = \begin{vmatrix} x & \sin\theta & \cos\theta \\ -\sin\theta & -x & 1 \\ \cos\theta & 1 & x \end{vmatrix}$ and

$\Delta_2 = \begin{vmatrix} x & \sin 2\theta & \cos 2\theta \\ -\sin 2\theta & -x & 1 \\ \cos 2\theta & 1 & x \end{vmatrix}$, $x \ne 0$; then for

all $\theta \in \left(0, \dfrac{\pi}{2}\right)$: **[2019, Main]**

(a) $\Delta_1 - \Delta_2 = -2x^3$

(b) $\Delta_1 - \Delta_2 = x(\cos 2\theta - \cos 4\theta)$

(c) $\Delta_1 + \Delta_2 = -2(x^3 + x - 1)$

(d) $\Delta_1 + \Delta_2 = -2x^3$

36. If the system of linear equations

$x + y + z = 5$

$x + 2y + 2z = 6$

$x + 3y + \lambda z = \mu$, $(\lambda, \mu \in R)$, has infinitely many

solutions, then the value of $\lambda + \mu$ is :

[2019, Main]

(a) 12 **(b)** 9

(c) 7 **(d)** 10

37. Let λ be a real number for which the system of

linear equations **[2019, Main]**

$x + y + z = 6$

$4x + \lambda y - \lambda z = \lambda - 2$

$3x + 2y - 4z = -5$

has infinitely many solution. Then λ is a root of

the quadratic equation :

(a) $\lambda^2 + 3\lambda - 4 = 0$ **(b)** $\lambda^2 - 3\lambda - 4 = 0$

(c) $\lambda^2 + \lambda - 6 = 0$ **(d)** $\lambda^2 - \lambda - 6 = 0$

38. The sum of the real roots of the equation

$\begin{vmatrix} x & -6 & -1 \\ 2 & -3x & x-3 \\ -3 & 2x & x+2 \end{vmatrix} = 0$, is equal to : **[2019, Main]**

(a) 6 **(b)** 0

(c) 1 **(d)** – 4

39. The total number of matrices $A = \begin{bmatrix} 0 & 2y & 1 \\ 2x & y & -1 \\ 2x & -y & 1 \end{bmatrix}$,

$(x, y \in R, x \ne y)$ for which $A^T A = 3I_3$ is :

[2019, Main]

(a) 2 **(b)** 3

(c) 6 **(d)** 4

40. If the system of equations $2x + 3y - z = 0$, $x + ky - 2z = 0$ and $2x - y + z = 0$ has a non-trivial solution

(x, y, z), then $\dfrac{x}{y} + \dfrac{y}{z} + \dfrac{z}{x} + k$ is equal to :

[2019, Main]

(a) $\dfrac{3}{4}$ **(b)** $\dfrac{1}{2}$

(c) $-\dfrac{1}{4}$ **(d)** – 4

41. If $\begin{bmatrix} 1 & 1 \\ 0 & 1 \end{bmatrix}\begin{bmatrix} 1 & 2 \\ 0 & 1 \end{bmatrix}\begin{bmatrix} 1 & 3 \\ 0 & 1 \end{bmatrix} \cdots\cdots \begin{bmatrix} 1 & n-1 \\ 0 & 1 \end{bmatrix}$

$= \begin{bmatrix} 1 & 78 \\ 0 & 1 \end{bmatrix}$, then the inverse of $\begin{bmatrix} 1 & n \\ 0 & 1 \end{bmatrix}$ is :

[2019, Main]

(a) $\begin{bmatrix} 1 & 0 \\ 12 & 1 \end{bmatrix}$ **(b)** $\begin{bmatrix} 1 & -13 \\ 0 & 1 \end{bmatrix}$

(c) $\begin{bmatrix} 1 & -12 \\ 0 & 1 \end{bmatrix}$ **(d)** $\begin{bmatrix} 1 & 0 \\ 13 & 1 \end{bmatrix}$

42. The greatest value of $c \in R$ for which the system

of linear equations **[2019, Main]**

$x - cy - cz = 0$

$cx - y + cz = 0$

$cx + cy - z = 0$

has a non-trivial solution, is :

(a) – 1 **(b)** $\dfrac{1}{2}$

(c) 2 **(d)** 0

43. Let $A = \begin{pmatrix} \cos\alpha & -\sin\alpha \\ \sin\alpha & \cos\alpha \end{pmatrix}$, $(\alpha \in R)$ such that

$A^{32} = \begin{pmatrix} 0 & -1 \\ 1 & 0 \end{pmatrix}$. Then the value of α is :

[2019, Main]

(a) $\dfrac{\pi}{32}$ **(b)** 0

(c) $\dfrac{\pi}{64}$ **(d)** $\dfrac{\pi}{16}$

44. Let the numbers 2, b, c be in an A.P. and

$A = \begin{bmatrix} 1 & 1 & 1 \\ 2 & b & c \\ 4 & b^2 & c^2 \end{bmatrix}$. If $\det(A) \in [2, 16]$, then c lies

in the interval : **[2019, Main]**

(a) $[2, 3)$ **(b)** $(2 + 2^{3/4}, 4)$

(c) $[4, 6]$ **(d)** $[3, 2 + 2^{3/4}]$

45. If the system of linear equations

$$x - 2y + kz = 1$$
$$2x + y + z = 2$$
$$3x - y - kz = 3$$

has a solution (x, y, z), $z \ne 0$, then (x, y) lies on the

straight line whose equations is : **[2019, Main]**

(a) $3x - 4y - 1 = 0$ **(b)** $4x - 3y - 4 = 0$

(c) $4x - 3y - 1 = 0$ **(d)** $3x - 4y - 4 = 0$

46. If A is a symmetric matrix and B is a skew-symmetric matrix such that

$$A + B = \begin{bmatrix} 2 & 3 \\ 5 & -1 \end{bmatrix},$$ then AB is equal to :

[2019, Main]

(a) $\begin{bmatrix} -4 & -2 \\ -1 & 4 \end{bmatrix}$
(b) $\begin{bmatrix} 4 & -2 \\ -1 & -4 \end{bmatrix}$

(c) $\begin{bmatrix} 4 & -2 \\ 1 & -4 \end{bmatrix}$
(d) $\begin{bmatrix} -4 & 2 \\ 1 & 4 \end{bmatrix}$

47. If $B = \begin{bmatrix} 5 & 2\alpha & 1 \\ 0 & 2 & 1 \\ \alpha & 3 & -1 \end{bmatrix}$ is the inverse of a 3×3 matrix A, then the sum of all values of α for which $\det | A | + 1 = 0$, is :

(a) 0
(b) – 1
(c) 1
(d) 2

48. A value of $\theta \in \left(0, \dfrac{\pi}{3}\right)$, for which

$$\begin{bmatrix} 1 + \cos^2\theta & \sin^2\theta & 4\cos\theta \\ \cos^2\theta & 1 + \sin^2\theta & 4\cos 6\theta \\ \cos^2\theta & \sin^2\theta & 1 + 4\cos 6\theta \end{bmatrix}$$ is :

[2019, Main]

(a) $\dfrac{\pi}{9}$
(b) $\dfrac{\pi}{18}$

(c) $\dfrac{7\pi}{24}$
(d) $\dfrac{7\pi}{36}$

49. Let $M = \begin{bmatrix} \sin^4\theta & -1 - \sin^2\theta \\ 1 + \cos^2\theta & \cos^4\theta \end{bmatrix} = \alpha I + \beta M^{-1}$,

where $\alpha = \alpha(\theta)$ and $\beta = \beta(\theta)$ are real numbers, and I is the 2×2 identity matrix. If α' is the minimum of the set $\{\alpha(\theta): \theta \in [0, 2\pi)\}$ and β' is the minimum of the set $\{\beta(\theta) : \theta \in [0, 2\pi)\}$, then the value of $\alpha' + \beta'$ is **[2019, Advanced]**

(a) $-\dfrac{37}{16}$
(b) $-\dfrac{31}{16}$

(c) $-\dfrac{29}{16}$
(d) $-\dfrac{17}{16}$

50. Let $M = \begin{bmatrix} 0 & 1 & a \\ 1 & 2 & 3 \\ 3 & b & 1 \end{bmatrix}$ and adj $M = \begin{bmatrix} -1 & 1 & -1 \\ 8 & -6 & 2 \\ -5 & 3 & -1 \end{bmatrix}$

where a and b are real numbers, Which of the following option is/ are correct? **[2019, Advanced]**

(a) $a + b = 3$
(b) $(\text{adj } M)^{-1} + \text{adj } M^{-1} = -M$

(c) det (adj M^2) = 81

(d) If $M \begin{bmatrix} \alpha \\ \beta \\ \gamma \end{bmatrix} = \begin{bmatrix} 1 \\ 2 \\ 3 \end{bmatrix}$, then $\alpha - \beta + \gamma = 3$

51. Let $P_1 = \begin{bmatrix} 1 & 0 & 0 \\ 0 & 1 & 0 \\ 0 & 0 & 1 \end{bmatrix}$, $P_2 = \begin{bmatrix} 1 & 0 & 0 \\ 0 & 0 & 1 \\ 0 & 1 & 0 \end{bmatrix}$,

$P_3 = \begin{bmatrix} 0 & 1 & 0 \\ 0 & 0 & 1 \\ 1 & 0 & 0 \end{bmatrix}$, $P_4 = \begin{bmatrix} 0 & 1 & 0 \\ 0 & 0 & 1 \\ 1 & 0 & 0 \end{bmatrix}$,

$P_5 = \begin{bmatrix} 0 & 0 & 1 \\ 1 & 0 & 0 \\ 0 & 1 & 0 \end{bmatrix}$,

$P_6 = \begin{bmatrix} 0 & 0 & 1 \\ 0 & 1 & 0 \\ 1 & 0 & 0 \end{bmatrix}$ and $X = \sum_{k=1}^{6} P_k \begin{bmatrix} 2 & 1 & 3 \\ 1 & 0 & 2 \\ 3 & 2 & 1 \end{bmatrix} P_k^T$

where P_k^T denotes the transpose of the matrix P_k. Then which of the following option is/are correct? **[2019, Advanced]**

(a) If $X \begin{bmatrix} 1 \\ 1 \\ 1 \end{bmatrix} = \alpha \begin{bmatrix} 1 \\ 1 \\ 1 \end{bmatrix}$, then $\alpha = 30$

(b) X is a symmetric matrix

(c) The sum of diagonal entries of X is 18

(d) $X - 30I$ is an invertible matrix

52. Let $x \in R$ and let

$P = \begin{bmatrix} 1 & 1 & 1 \\ 0 & 2 & 2 \\ 0 & 0 & 3 \end{bmatrix}$, $Q = \begin{bmatrix} 2 & x & x \\ 0 & 4 & 0 \\ x & x & 6 \end{bmatrix}$ and $R = PQP^{-1}$.

The which of the following options is/are correct? **[2019 Advanced]**

(a) There exists a real number x such that PQ = QP

(b) det $R = \det \begin{bmatrix} 2 & x & x \\ 0 & 4 & 0 \\ x & x & 5 \end{bmatrix} + 8$, for all $x \in \mathbf{R}$

(c) For $x = 0$, if $R \begin{bmatrix} 1 \\ a \\ b \end{bmatrix} = 6 \begin{bmatrix} 1 \\ a \\ b \end{bmatrix}$, then $a + b = 5$

(d) For $x = 1$, there exists a unit vector $\alpha \hat{i} + \beta \hat{j} + \gamma \hat{k}$

for which $R \begin{bmatrix} \alpha \\ \beta \\ \gamma \end{bmatrix} = \begin{bmatrix} 0 \\ 0 \\ 0 \end{bmatrix}$

53. Suppose

$$\det\begin{bmatrix} \sum\limits_{k=0}^{n} k & \sum\limits_{k=0}^{n} {}^{n}C_{k}k^{2} \\ \sum\limits_{k=0}^{n} {}^{n}C_{k}k & \sum\limits_{k=0}^{n} {}^{n}C_{k}3^{k} \end{bmatrix} = 0$$

holds for some positive integer n. Then $\sum\limits_{k=0}^{n} \dfrac{{}^{n}C_{k}}{k+1}$

equals : **[2019 Advanced]**

54. Let S be the set of all column matrices $\begin{bmatrix} b_1 \\ b_2 \\ b_3 \end{bmatrix}$ such

that b_1, b_2, $b_3 \in$ R and the system of equations
(in real variables) **[2018, Advanced]**

$$-x + 2y + 5z = b_1$$
$$2x - 4y + 3z = b_2$$
$$x - 2y + 2z = b_3$$

has at least one solution. Then, which of the following system(s) (in real variables) has (have)

at least one solution for each $\begin{bmatrix} b_1 \\ b_2 \\ b_3 \end{bmatrix} \in$ S?

(a) $x + 2y + 3z = b_1$, $4y + 5z = b_2$ and $x + 2y + 6z = b_3$

(b) $x + y + 3z = b_1$, $5x + 2y + 6z = b_2$ and $-2x - y - 3z = b_3$

(c) $-x + 2y - 5z = b_1$, $2x - 4y + 10z = b_2$ and $x - 2y + 5z = b_3$

(d) $x + 2y + 5z = b_1$, $2x + 3z = b_2$ and $x + 4y - 5z = b_3$

55. Let A be a matrix such that $A \cdot \begin{bmatrix} 1 & 2 \\ 0 & 3 \end{bmatrix}$ is a scalar

matrix and $|3A| = 108$. Then A^2 equals :

[2018, Advanced]

(a) $\begin{bmatrix} 4 & -32 \\ 0 & 36 \end{bmatrix}$ **(b)** $\begin{bmatrix} 36 & 0 \\ -32 & 4 \end{bmatrix}$

(c) $\begin{bmatrix} 4 & 0 \\ -32 & 36 \end{bmatrix}$ **(d)** $\begin{bmatrix} 36 & -32 \\ 0 & 4 \end{bmatrix}$

56. Let S be the set of all real values of k for which the system of linear equations **[2018, Main]**

$$x + y + z = 2$$
$$2x + y - z = 3$$
$$3x + 2y + kz = 4$$

has a unique solution. Then S is :

(a) an empty set   **(b)** equal to $\{0\}$

(c) equal to R   **(d)** equal to $R - \{0\}$

57. Let $A = \begin{bmatrix} 1 & 0 & 0 \\ 1 & 1 & 0 \\ 1 & 1 & 1 \end{bmatrix}$ and $B = A^{20}$. Then the sum of

the elements of the first column of B is :

[2018, Main]

(a) 210   **(b)** 211

(c) 231   **(d)** 251

58. The number of values of k for which the system of linear equations, **[2018, Main]**

$$(k + 2)x + 10y = k$$
$$kx + (k + 3)y = k - 1$$

has no solution, is :

(a) 1   **(b)** 2

(c) 3   **(d)** infinitely many

59. If the system of linear equations

$$x + ky + 3z = 0$$
$$3x + ky - 2z = 0$$
$$2x + 4y - 3z = 0$$

has a non-zero solution (x, y, z), then $\dfrac{xz}{y^2}$ is equal

to : **[2018, Main]**

(a) -10 **(b)** 10

(c) -30 **(d)** 30

60. For two 3×3 matrices A and B, let $A + B = 2B'$ and $3A + 2B = I_3$, where B' is the transpose of B and I_3 is 3×3 identity matrix. Then : **[2017, Main]**

(a) $5A + 10B = 2I_3$ **(b)** $10A + 5B = 3I_3$

(c) $B + 2A = I_3$ **(d)** $3A + 6B = 2I_3$

61. If $x = a$, $y = b$, $z = c$ is a solution of the system of linear equations

$$x + 8y + 7z = 0$$
$$9x + 2y + 3z = 0$$
$$x + y + z = 0$$

such that the point (a, b, c) lies on the plane $x + 2y + z = 6$, then $2a + b + c$ equals : **[2017, Main]**

(a) -1 **(b)** 0

(c) 1   **(d)** 2

62. Let A be a 3×3 matrix such that $A^2 - 5A + 7I = O$.

Statement - I : $A^{-1} = \dfrac{1}{7}(5I - A)$

Statement - II : The polynomial $A^3 - 2A^2 - 3A + I$ can be reduced to $5(A - 4I)$.

Then : **[2016, Main]**

(a) Statement-I is true, but Statement-II is false.

(b) Statement-I is false, but Statement-II is true.

(c) Both the statements are true.

(d) Both the statements are false.

63. If $A = \begin{bmatrix} -4 & -1 \\ 3 & 1 \end{bmatrix}$, then the determinant of the matrix $(A^{2016} - 2A^{2015} - A^{2014})$ is : **[2016, Main]**

(a) 2014

(b) -175

(c) 2016

(d) -25

64. The number of real values of λ for which the system of linear equations

$$2x + 4y - \lambda z = 0$$
$$4x + \lambda y + 2z = 0$$
$$\lambda x + 2y + 2z = 0$$

has infinitely many solutions, is : **[2017, Main]**

(a) 0

(b) 1

(c) 2

(d) 3

65. Let A be any 3×3 invertible matrix. Then which one of the following is not always true?

[2017, Main]

(a) adj $(A) = |A| \cdot A^{-1}$

(b) adj $(\text{adj}(A)) = |A| \cdot A$

(c) adj $(\text{adj}(A)) = |A|^2 \cdot (\text{adj}(A))^{-1}$

(d) adj $(\text{adj}(A)) = |A| \cdot (\text{adj}(A))^{-1}$

66. If $A = \begin{bmatrix} 2 & -3 \\ -4 & 1 \end{bmatrix}$, then adj $(3A^2 + 12A)$ is equal to : **[2017, Main]**

(a) $\begin{bmatrix} 51 & 63 \\ 84 & 72 \end{bmatrix}$

(b) $\begin{bmatrix} 51 & 84 \\ 63 & 72 \end{bmatrix}$

(c) $\begin{bmatrix} 72 & -63 \\ -84 & 51 \end{bmatrix}$

(d) $\begin{bmatrix} 72 & -84 \\ -63 & 51 \end{bmatrix}$

67. If S is the set of distinct values of 'b' for which the following system of linear equations

$$x + y + z = 1$$
$$x + ay + z = 1$$
$$ax + by + z = 0$$

has no solution, then S is : **[2017, Main]**

(a) an infinite set

(b) a finite set containing two or more elements

(c) a singleton set

(d) an empty set

68. Which of the following is (are) NOT the square of a 3×3 matrix with real entries? **[2017, Main]**

(a) $\begin{bmatrix} 1 & 0 & 0 \\ 0 & 1 & 0 \\ 0 & 0 & 1 \end{bmatrix}$

(b) $\begin{bmatrix} 1 & 0 & 0 \\ 0 & 1 & 0 \\ 0 & 0 & -1 \end{bmatrix}$

(c) $\begin{bmatrix} 1 & 0 & 0 \\ 0 & -1 & 0 \\ 0 & 0 & -1 \end{bmatrix}$

(d) $\begin{bmatrix} -1 & 0 & 0 \\ 0 & -1 & 0 \\ 0 & 0 & -1 \end{bmatrix}$

69. For a real number α, if the system

$$\begin{bmatrix} 1 & \alpha & \alpha^2 \\ \alpha & 1 & \alpha \\ \alpha^2 & \alpha & 1 \end{bmatrix}\begin{bmatrix} x \\ y \\ z \end{bmatrix} = \begin{bmatrix} 1 \\ -1 \\ 1 \end{bmatrix}$$

of linear equations, has infinitely many solutions, then $1 + \alpha + \alpha^2 = $ **[2017, Advanced]**

70. The number of distinct real roots of the equation,

$$\begin{vmatrix} \cos x & \sin x & \sin x \\ \sin x & \cos x & \sin x \\ \sin x & \sin x & \cos x \end{vmatrix} = 0 \text{ in the interval } \left[-\frac{\pi}{4}, \frac{\pi}{4} \right]$$

is : **[2016, Main]**

(a) 4

(b) 3

(c) 2

(d) 1

71. The total number of distinct $x \in R$ for which

$$\begin{vmatrix} x & x^2 & 1+x^3 \\ 2x & 4x^2 & 1+8x^3 \\ 3x & 9x^2 & 1+27x^3 \end{vmatrix} = 10 \text{ is :}$$ **[2016, Advanced]**

72. Let $P = \begin{bmatrix} 3 & -1 & -2 \\ 2 & 0 & \alpha \\ 3 & -5 & 0 \end{bmatrix}$, where $\alpha \in R$. Suppose $Q = [q_{ij}]$ is a matrix such that $PQ = kI$, where $k \in R$, $k \neq 0$ and I is the identity matrix of order 3. If $q_{23} = -\dfrac{k}{8}$ and $\det(Q) = \dfrac{k^2}{2}$, then

[2016, Advanced]

(a) $\alpha = 0$, $k = -8$

(b) $4\alpha - k + 8 = 0$

(c) det $(P \text{ adj}(Q)) = 2^9$

(d) det $(Q \text{ adj}(P)) = 2^{13}$

73. If $P = \begin{bmatrix} \dfrac{\sqrt{3}}{2} & \dfrac{1}{2} \\ -\dfrac{1}{2} & \dfrac{\sqrt{3}}{2} \end{bmatrix}$, $A = \begin{bmatrix} 1 & 1 \\ 0 & 1 \end{bmatrix}$ and $Q = PAP^T$, then $P^T Q^{2015} P$ is : **[2016, Main]**

(a) $\begin{bmatrix} 0 & 2015 \\ 0 & 0 \end{bmatrix}$

(b) $\begin{bmatrix} 2015 & 1 \\ 0 & 2015 \end{bmatrix}$

(c) $\begin{bmatrix} 2015 & 0 \\ 1 & 2015 \end{bmatrix}$

(d) $\begin{bmatrix} 1 & 2015 \\ 0 & 1 \end{bmatrix}$

74. If $A = \begin{bmatrix} 1 & 2 & 2 \\ 2 & 1 & -2 \\ a & 2 & b \end{bmatrix}$ is a matrix satisfying the equation $AA^T = 9I$, where I is 3×3 identity matrix, then the ordered pair (a, b) is equal to : **[2015, Main]**

(a) $(2, -1)$

(b) $(-2, 1)$

(c) $(2, 1)$

(d) $(-2, -1)$

75. The set of all values of λ for which the system of linear equations :

$$2x_1 - 2x_2 + x_3 = \lambda x_1$$
$$2x_1 - 3x_2 + 2x_3 = \lambda x_2$$
$$- x_1 + 2x_2 = \lambda x_3$$

has a non-trivial solution, **[2015, Main]**

(a) is an empty set.

(b) is a singleton.

(c) contains two elements

(d) contains more than two elements

76. If A is a 3×3 matrix such that $|5. \text{adj } A| = 5$, then $|A|$ is equal to : **[2015, Main]**

(a) $\pm \dfrac{1}{5}$ **(b)** ± 5

(c) ± 1 **(d)** $\pm \dfrac{1}{25}$

77. If $\begin{vmatrix} x^2 + x & x+1 & x-2 \\ 2x^2 + 3x - 1 & 3x & 3x-3 \\ x^2 + 2x + 3 & 2x-1 & 2x-1 \end{vmatrix} = ax - 12$ then 'a'

is equal to : **[2015, Main]**

(a) 12   **(b)** 24

(c) -12 **(d)** -24

78. If $\alpha, \beta \neq 0$, and $f(n) = \alpha^n + \beta^n$ and

$$\begin{vmatrix} 3 & 1+f(1) & 1+f(2) \\ 1+f(1) & 1+f(2) & 1+f(3) \\ 1+f(2) & 1+f(3) & 1+f(4) \end{vmatrix}$$

$= K(1-\alpha)^2 (1-\beta)^2 (\alpha-\beta)^2$, then K is equal to :

[2014, Main]

(a) 1   **(b)** -1

(c) $\alpha\beta$ **(d)** $\dfrac{1}{\alpha\beta}$

79. If A is a 3×3 non-singular matrix such that $AA' = A'A$ and $B = A^{-1} A'$, then BB' equals :

[2014, Main]

(a) B^{-1} **(b)** $(B^{-1})^{-}$

(c) $I + B$ **(d)** I

80. Let M and N be two 3×3 matrices such that $MN = NM$. Further, if $M \neq N^2$ and $M^2 = N^4$, then :

[2014, Advanced]

(a) determinant of $(M^2 + MN^2)$ is 0

(b) there is a 3×3 non-zero matrix U such that $(M^2 + MN^2)$ U is the zero matrix

(c) determinant of $(M^2 + MN^2) \geq 1$

(d) for a 3×3 matrix U, if $(M^2 + MN^2)$U equals the zero matrix then U is the zero matrix.

81. Let M be a 2×2 symmetric matrix with integer entries. Then M is invertible if : **[2014, Advanced]**

(a) the first column of M is the transpose of the second row of M

(b) the second row of M is the transpose of the first column of M

(c) M is a diagonal matrix with non-zero entries in the main diagonal

(d) the product of entries in the main diagonal of M is not the square of an integer.

82. If $\begin{vmatrix} a^2 & b^2 & c^2 \\ (a+\lambda)^2 & (b+\lambda)^2 & (c+\lambda)^2 \\ (a-\lambda)^2 & (b-\lambda)^2 & (c-\lambda)^2 \end{vmatrix} = K\lambda \begin{bmatrix} a^2 & b^2 & c^2 \\ a & b & c \\ 1 & 1 & 1 \end{bmatrix}$

$\lambda \neq 0$, then K is equal to : **[2014, Main]**

(a) 4λ abc   **(b)** -4λ abc

(c) $4\lambda^2$ **(d)** $-4\lambda^2$

83. If $A = \begin{bmatrix} 1 & 2 & x \\ 3 & -1 & 2 \end{bmatrix}$ and $B = \begin{bmatrix} y \\ x \\ l \end{bmatrix}$ that $AB = \begin{bmatrix} 6 \\ 8 \end{bmatrix}$ then:

[2014, Main]

(a) $y = 2x$ **(b)** $y = -2x$

(c) $y = x$ **(d)** $y = -x$

84. If a, b, c are non - zero real numbers and if the system of equations

$(a-1)x = y + z,$ $(b-1)y = z + x,$

$(c-1)z = x + y,$

has a non-trivial solution, then $ab + bc + ca$ equals:

[2014, Main]

(a) $a + b + c$ **(b)** abc

(c) 1   **(d)** -1

85. If B is a 3×3 matrix such that $B^2 = 0$, then det. $[(C1 + B)^{50} - 50B]$ is equal to : **[2014, Main]**

(a) 1   **(b)** 2

(c) 3   **(d)** 50

86. Let A and B be any two 3×3 matrices. If A is symmetric and B is skew symmetric, then the matrix $AB - BA$ is : **[2014, Main]**

(a) skew symmetric

(b) symmetric

(c) neither symmetric nor skew symmetric

(d) I or $- I$, where I is an identity matrix.

87. Let $\begin{vmatrix} r & 2r-1 & 3r-2 \\ \dfrac{n}{2} & n-1 & a \\ \dfrac{1}{2}(n-1) & (n-1)^2 & \dfrac{1}{2}(3n+4)(n-1) \end{vmatrix}$ then the

value of $\sum\limits_{r=1}^{n-1} \Delta r$: **[2014, Main]**

(a) depends only on a

(b) depends only on n

(c) depends both on a and n

(d) is independent of both a and n.

88. Let A be a 3×3 matrix such that

$$A \begin{bmatrix} 1 & 2 & 3 \\ 0 & 2 & 3 \\ 0 & 1 & 1 \end{bmatrix} = \begin{bmatrix} 0 & 0 & 1 \\ 1 & 0 & 0 \\ 0 & 1 & 0 \end{bmatrix}. \text{ Then } A^{-1} \text{ is :}$$

[2014, Main]

(a) $\begin{bmatrix} 3 & 1 & 2 \\ 3 & 0 & 2 \\ 1 & 0 & 1 \end{bmatrix}$ **(b)** $\begin{bmatrix} 3 & 2 & 1 \\ 3 & 2 & 0 \\ 1 & 1 & 0 \end{bmatrix}$

(c) $\begin{bmatrix} 0 & 1 & 3 \\ 0 & 2 & 3 \\ 1 & 1 & 1 \end{bmatrix}$ **(d)** $\begin{bmatrix} 1 & 2 & 3 \\ 0 & 1 & 1 \\ 0 & 2 & 3 \end{bmatrix}$

89. Let for $i = 1, 2, 3$, $p_i(x)$ be a polynomial of degree 2 in x, $p_i'(x)$ and $p_i''(x)$ be the first and second order derivatives of $p_i(x)$ respectively. Let.

$$A(x) = \begin{bmatrix} p_1(x) & p_1'(x) & p_1''(x) \\ p_2(x) & p_2'(x) & p_2''(x) \\ p_3(x) & p_3'(x) & p_3''(x) \end{bmatrix} \text{ and } B(x) = [A(xT$$

$A(x)$. Then determinant of $B(x)$:   **[2014, Main]**

(a) is a polynomial of degree 6 in x

(b) is a polynomial of degree 3 in x

(c) is a polynomial of degree 2 in x

(d) does not depend on x.

90. For 3×3 matrices M and N, which of the following statement (s) is (are) NOT correct ?

[2014, Advanced]

(a) $N^T M N$ is symmetric or skew symmetric, accordingly as M is symmetric or skew symmetric

(b) $MN - NM$ is skew symmetric for all symmetric matrices M and N

(c) $M N$ is symmetric for all symmetric matrices M and N

(d) $(adj\ M)\ (adj\ N) = adj\ (M\ N)$ for all invertible matrices M and N.

91. Let k be a positive real number and let

$$A = \begin{bmatrix} 2k-1 & 2\sqrt{k} & 2\sqrt{k} \\ 2\sqrt{k} & 1 & -2k \\ -2\sqrt{k} & 2k & -1 \end{bmatrix} \text{ and}$$

$$B = \begin{bmatrix} 0 & 2k-1 & \sqrt{k} \\ 1-2k & 0 & 2\sqrt{k} \\ -\sqrt{k} & -2\sqrt{k} & 0 \end{bmatrix}.$$

If $\det (adj\ A) + \det (adj\ B) = 10^6$, then $[k]$ is equal to

[2010, Advanced]

92. Match the Statements/Expressions in Column I with the Statements/Expressions in Column II and indicate your answer by darkening the appropriate bubbles in the 4×4 matrix given in the ORS.   **[2008, Advanced]**

Column I   **Column II**

(a) The minimum value of $\dfrac{x^2 + 2x + 4}{x+2}$ is   **(p)** 0

(b) The A and B be 3×3 matrices of real numbers where A is symmetric, B is skew-symmetric, and $(A + B)(A - B) = (A - B)(A + B)$. If $(AB)^t = (-I)^k AB$, where $_{(AB)}t$ is the transpose of the matrix AB, then the possible value of k are   **(q)** 1

(c) Let $a = \log_2 \log_2 2$. An integer k satisfying $1 < 2^{(-k + 3^{-\alpha} \log_2 3)} < 2$, must be less than   **(r)** 2

(d) If $\sin \theta = \cos \phi$, then the possible value of $\dfrac{1}{\pi}(\theta \pm \phi - \dfrac{\pi}{2})$ are   **(s)** 3

93. Consider the system of equations

$$x - 2y + 3z = -1$$
$$-x + y - 2z = k$$
$$x - 3y + 4z = 1.$$

STATEMENT-1 : The system of equations has no solution for $k \neq 3$.

and

STATEMENT-2 : The determinant

$$\begin{vmatrix} 1 & 3 & -1 \\ -1 & -2 & k \\ 1 & 4 & 1 \end{vmatrix} \neq 0, \text{ for } k \neq 3.$$

[2018, Advanced]

(a) STATEMENT-1 is True, STATEMENT-2 is True; STATEMENT-2 is a correct explanation for STATEMENT-1

(b) STATEMENT-1 is True, STATEMENT-2 is True, STATEMENT-2 is **NOT** a correct explanation for STATEMENT-1

(c) STATEMENT-1 is True, STATEMENT-2 is FALSE

(d) STATEMENT-1 is False, STATEMENT-2 is True

Read, the situation and answer the question from (94 – 96)

$$A \begin{bmatrix} 1 & 0 & 0 \\ 2 & 1 & 0 \\ 3 & 2 & 1 \end{bmatrix}, \text{ if } U_1, U_2, U_3 \text{ are columns matrices}$$

satisfying

$$AU_1 = \begin{bmatrix} 1 \\ 0 \\ 0 \end{bmatrix}, \ AU_2 = \begin{bmatrix} 2 \\ 3 \\ 0 \end{bmatrix}, \ AU_3 = \begin{bmatrix} 2 \\ 3 \\ 1 \end{bmatrix}$$

and U is a 3×3 matrix whose columns are U_1, U_2, U_3 then answer the following questions :

94. The value of $|U|$ is :

(a) 3   (b) -3

(c) 3/2   (d) 2

95. The sum of the elements of U^{-1} is :

(a) -1 (b) 0

(c) 1   (d) 3

96. The value of $[3 \quad 2 \quad 0] U \begin{bmatrix} 3 \\ 2 \\ 0 \end{bmatrix}$ is :

(a) 5   (d) 5/2

(c) 4   (d) 3/2

97. $A = \begin{bmatrix} 1 & 0 & 0 \\ 0 & 1 & 1 \\ 0 & -2 & 4 \end{bmatrix}$, $I = \begin{bmatrix} 1 & 0 & 0 \\ 0 & 1 & 0 \\ 0 & 0 & 1 \end{bmatrix}$ and $A^{-1} =$

$\left[\dfrac{1}{6}(A^2 + cA + dI) \right]$, then the value of c and d are

[2005 Main]

(a) $-6, -11$ (d) 6, 11

(c) $-6, 11$ (d) 6, -11

98. Given $2x - y - 2z = 2$, $x - 2y + z = -4$, $x + y + \lambda z = 4$ then the value of λ such that the given system of equation has NO solution, is :   **[2004, Main]**

(a) 3   (b) 1

(c) 0   (d) -3

99. If $A = \begin{bmatrix} \alpha & 2 \\ 2 & \alpha \end{bmatrix}$ and $|A^3| = 125$ then the value of α is :   **[2004, Main]**

(a) ± 1 (b) ± 2

(c) ± 3 (d) ± 5

100. If M is a 3×3 matrix, where $M^TM = I$ and $\det(M) = 1$, then prove that $\det(M - I) = 0$. **[2004, Main]**

101. $A = \begin{bmatrix} a & 0 & 1 \\ 1 & c & b \\ 1 & d & b \end{bmatrix}$, $B = \begin{bmatrix} a & 1 & 1 \\ 0 & d & c \\ f & g & h \end{bmatrix}$, $U = \begin{bmatrix} f \\ g \\ h \end{bmatrix}$,

[2004, Main]

$V = \begin{bmatrix} a^2 \\ 0 \\ 0 \end{bmatrix}$. If there is vector matrix X, such that

$AX = U$ has infinitely many solutions, then prove that $BX = V$ has no solution.

102. If $A = \begin{bmatrix} \alpha & 0 \\ 1 & 1 \end{bmatrix}$ and $B = \begin{bmatrix} 1 & 0 \\ 5 & 1 \end{bmatrix}$, then value of α for which $A^2 = B$, is   **[2003, Main]**

(a) 1   (b) -1

(c) 4   (d) no real values

103. If the system of equations $x + ay = 0$, $az + y = 0$ and $ax + z = 0$ has infinite solutions, then the value of a is   **[2003, Main]**

(a) -1 (b) 1

(c) 0   (d) no real values

104. If matrix $A = \begin{bmatrix} a & b & c \\ b & c & a \\ c & a & b \end{bmatrix}$ where a, b, c are real positive numbers, $abc = 1$ and $A^TA = I$, then find the value of $a^3 + b^3 + c^3$.   **[2003, Advanced]**

105. Let $\omega = -\dfrac{1}{2} + i\dfrac{\sqrt{3}}{2}$

Then the value of the determinant

$\begin{vmatrix} 1 & 1 & 1 \\ 1 & -1-\omega^2 & \omega^2 \\ 1 & \omega^2 & \omega^4 \end{vmatrix}$ is

(a) 3ω (b) $3\omega\,(\omega - 1)$

(c) $3\omega^2$ (d) $3\omega\,(1 - \omega)$

[2003, Screening]

ANSWER KEY

1. (a)	**2.** (d)	**3.** (a)	**4.** (b)	**5.** (3)	**6.** (c)	**7.** (5)	**8.** (c)	**9.** (d)	**10.** (c)
11. (10)	**12.** (b)	**13.** (b)	**14.** (5)	**15.** (d)	**16.** (d)	**17.** (c)	**18.** (8)	**19.** (c)	**20.** (d)
21. (3)	**22.** (d)	**23.** (d)	**24.** (13.00)	**25.** (d)	**26.** (b)	**27.** (c)	**28.** (a)	**29.** (c)	**30.** (a)
31. (d)	**32.** (b)	**33.** (672.00)	**34.** (a)	**35.** (d)	**36.** (d)	**37.** (d)	**38.** (b)	**39.** (d)	**40.** (b)
41. (b)	**42.** (a)	**43.** (c)	**44.** (c)	**45.** (b)	**46.** (b)	**47.** (c)	**48.** (a)	**49.** (c)	
50. (a,c,d)	**51.** (a,b,c)	**52.** (b,c)	**53.** (*)	**54.** (a,d)	**55.** (d)	**56.** (d)	**57.** (c)	**58.** (a)	**59.** (b)
60. (b)	**61.** (c)	**62.** (c)	**63.** (d)	**64.** (b)	**65.** (d)	**66.** (a)	**67.** (c)	**68.** (a,b)	**69.** (1)
70. (c)	**71.** (*)	**72.** (b,c)	**73.** (d)	**74.** (d)	**75.** (c)	**76.** (a)	**77.** (b)	**78.** (a)	**79.** (d)
80. (a,b)	**81.** (c,d)	**82.** (c)	**83.** (a)	**84.** (b)	**85.** (a)	**86.** (b)	**87.** (d)	**88.** (a)	**89.** (d)
90. (c,d)	**91.** (4)	**92.** (a)-(r), (b)-(q), (s), (c)-(r), (s), (d)-(p), (r)				**93.** (a)	**94.** (a)	**95.** (b)	**96.** (a)
97. (c)	**98.** (d)	**99.** (c)	**100.** (*)	**101.** (*)	**102.** (d)	**103.** (a)	**104.** (4 or 2)	**105.** (b)	

ANSWERS WITH EXPLANATIONS

1. Correct Response : (a)

$$D = \begin{vmatrix} 2 & -4 & \lambda \\ 1 & -6 & 1 \\ \lambda & -10 & 4 \end{vmatrix}$$

$$= 2(3\lambda + 2)\,(\lambda - 3)$$
$$D_1 = -2(\lambda - 3)$$
$$D_2 = -2(\lambda + 1)\,(\lambda - 3)$$
$$D_3 = -2(\lambda - 3)$$

When $\lambda = 3$, then

$$D = D_1 = D_1 = D_3 = 0$$

$\Rightarrow$ Infinity many solutions

when $\lambda = -\dfrac{2}{3}$ then D_1, D_2, D_3 none of them is

zero so equations are inconsistent.

$$\therefore \qquad \boxed{\lambda = -\dfrac{2}{3}}$$

2. Correct Response : (d)

For infinite many solutions

$$D = D_1 = D_2 = D_3 = 0$$

Now, $\qquad D = \begin{vmatrix} 1 & 1 & 1 \\ 1 & 2 & 3 \\ 1 & 3 & \lambda \end{vmatrix} = 0$

$$1.(2\lambda - 9) - 1.(\lambda - 3) + 1.(3 - 2) = 0$$
$$\therefore \qquad \lambda = 5$$

Now $\qquad D_1 = \begin{vmatrix} 2 & 1 & 1 \\ 5 & 2 & 3 \\ \mu & 3 & 5 \end{vmatrix} = 0$

$$2(10 - 9) - 1(25 - 3\mu) + 1(15 - 2\mu) = 0$$
$$\mu = 8$$

3. Correct Response : (a)

$$\begin{vmatrix} \cos^2 x & 1+\sin^2 x & \sin 2x \\ 1+\cos^2 x & \sin^2 x & \sin 2x \\ \cos^2 x & \sin^2 x & 1+\sin 2x \end{vmatrix}$$

$$R_1 \to R_1 - R_2,\ R_2 \to R_2 - R_3$$

$$\begin{vmatrix} -1 & 1 & 0 \\ 1 & 0 & -1 \\ \cos^2 x & \sin^2 x & 1+\sin 2x \end{vmatrix}$$

$$= -1(\sin^2 x) - 1(1 + \sin 2x + \cos^2 x)$$
$$= -\sin^2 x - 1 - \sin 2x - \cos^2 x$$
$$= -1 - \sin 2x - (\cos^2 x + \sin^2 x)$$
$$= -1 - \sin 2x - 1$$
$$= -\sin 2x - 2$$
$$m = -3,\ M = -1.$$

4. Correct Response : (b)

$$A = \begin{bmatrix} \cos\theta & \sin\theta \\ -\sin\theta & \cos\theta \end{bmatrix}$$

$$A^2 = \begin{bmatrix} \cos\theta & \sin\theta \\ -\sin\theta & \cos\theta \end{bmatrix}\begin{bmatrix} \cos\theta & \sin\theta \\ -\sin\theta & \cos\theta \end{bmatrix}$$

$$A^2 = \begin{bmatrix} \cos 2\theta & \sin 2\theta \\ -\sin 2\theta & \cos 2\theta \end{bmatrix}$$

$$B = A + A^4$$

$$= \begin{bmatrix} \cos\theta & \sin\theta \\ -\sin\theta & \cos\theta \end{bmatrix} + \begin{bmatrix} \cos 4\theta & \sin 4\theta \\ -\sin 4\theta & \cos 4\theta \end{bmatrix}$$

$$B = \begin{bmatrix} (\cos\theta + \cos 4\theta) & (\sin\theta + \sin 4\theta) \\ -(\sin\theta + \sin 4\theta) & (\cos\theta + \cos 4\theta) \end{bmatrix}$$

$$|B| = (\cos\theta + \cos 4\theta)^2 + (\sin\theta + \sin 4\theta)^2$$
$$|B| = \cos^2\theta + \cos^2 4\theta + 2\cos\theta.\cos 4\theta + \sin^2\theta$$
$$\qquad\qquad + \sin^2 4\theta + 2\sin\theta\sin 4\theta$$
$$|B| = (\cos^2\theta + \sin^2\theta) + (\cos^2 4\theta + \sin^2 4\theta)$$
$$\qquad\qquad + 2(\cos\theta.\cos 4\theta + \sin\theta\sin 4\theta)$$
$$|B| = 1 + 1 + 2\cos 3\theta$$
$$|B| = 2 + 2\cos 3\theta$$
$$|B| = 2 + 2\cos 3\theta,$$

when $\qquad \theta = \dfrac{\pi}{5}$

$$|B| = 2 + 2\cos\dfrac{3\pi}{5} = 2(1 - \sin 18)$$

$$|B| = 2\left(1 - \dfrac{\sqrt{5}-1}{4}\right) = 2\left(\dfrac{5-\sqrt{5}}{4}\right) = \dfrac{5-\sqrt{5}}{2}$$

5. Correct Response : (3)

$$(\lambda - 1)x + (3\lambda + 1)y + 2\lambda z = 0$$
$$(\lambda - 1)x + (4\lambda - 2)y + (\lambda + 3)z = 0$$
$$2x + (3\lambda + 1)y + (3\lambda - 3)z = 0$$

$$\begin{vmatrix} \lambda - 1 & 3\lambda + 1 & 2\lambda \\ \lambda - 1 & 4\lambda - 2 & \lambda + 3 \\ 2 & 3\lambda + 1 & 3\lambda - 3 \end{vmatrix} = 0$$

$$R_1 \to R_1 - R_2 \ \&\ R_2 \to R_2 - R_3$$

$$\begin{vmatrix} 0 & 3 - \lambda & \lambda - 3 \\ \lambda - 3 & \lambda - 3 & -2(\lambda - 3) \\ 2 & 3\lambda + 1 & 3\lambda - 3 \end{vmatrix} = 0$$

$$(\lambda - 3)^2 \begin{vmatrix} 0 & -1 & 1 \\ 1 & 1 & -2 \\ 2 & 3\lambda + 1 & 3\lambda - 3 \end{vmatrix} = 0$$

$$(\lambda - 3)^2\,[1(3\lambda - 3) + 4] + [1(3\lambda + 1) - 2]$$
$$(\lambda - 3)^2\,[(3\lambda + 1) + (3\lambda - 1)]$$

$$(\lambda - 3)^2 \left[(3\lambda + 1) + (3\lambda - 1)\right] = 0$$
$$6\lambda(\lambda - 3)^2 = 0 \Rightarrow \lambda = 0, 3$$
$$\text{Sum} = 3$$

6. Correct Response : (c)

$$A^2 = \begin{bmatrix} \cos\theta & i\sin\theta \\ i\sin\theta & \cos\theta \end{bmatrix} \begin{bmatrix} \cos\theta & i\sin\theta \\ i\sin\theta & \cos\theta \end{bmatrix}$$

$$= \begin{bmatrix} \cos^2\theta - \sin^2\theta & 2i\sin\theta\cos\theta \\ 2i\sin\theta\cos\theta & \cos^2\theta - \sin^2\theta \end{bmatrix}$$

$$A^2 = \begin{pmatrix} \cos 2\theta & i\sin 2\theta \\ i\sin 2\theta & \cos 2\theta \end{pmatrix}$$

Similarly, $\quad A^5 = \begin{pmatrix} \cos 5\theta & i\sin 5\theta \\ i\sin 5\theta & \cos 5\theta \end{pmatrix} = \begin{pmatrix} a & b \\ c & d \end{pmatrix}$

(1) $a^2 + b^2 = \cos^2 5\theta - \sin^2 5\theta = \cos 10\theta = \cos 75°$

(2) $a^2 - d^2 = \cos^2 5\theta - \cos^2 5\theta = 0$

(3) $a^2 - b^2 = \cos^2 5\theta + \sin^2 5\theta = 1$

(4) $a^2 - c^2 = \cos^2 5\theta + \sin^2 5\theta = 1$

7. Correct Response : (5)

For infinitely solutions

$$D = D_1 = D_2 = D_3 = 0$$

$$D = \begin{vmatrix} 1 & -2 & 3 \\ 2 & 1 & 1 \\ 1 & -7 & a \end{vmatrix} = 0 \Rightarrow a = 8$$

also, $\quad D_1 = \begin{vmatrix} 9 & -2 & 3 \\ b & 1 & 1 \\ 24 & -7 & 8 \end{vmatrix} = 0 \Rightarrow b = 3$

hence, $\quad a - b = 8 - 3 = 5.$

8. Correct Response : (c)

For infinite solutions

$$\Delta = \Delta_x = \Delta_y = \Delta_z = 0$$

Now $\quad \Delta = 0 \Rightarrow \begin{vmatrix} 1 & 1 & 1 \\ 2 & 4 & -1 \\ 3 & 2 & \lambda \end{vmatrix} = 0$

$$\Rightarrow \qquad \lambda = \frac{9}{2}$$

$$\Delta x = 0 \Rightarrow \begin{vmatrix} 2 & 1 & 1 \\ 6 & 4 & -1 \\ \mu & 2 & -\dfrac{9}{2} \end{vmatrix} = 0$$

$$\Rightarrow \qquad \mu = 5$$

For $\lambda = \dfrac{9}{2}$ & $\mu = 5$, $\Delta_y = \Delta_z = 0$

Now check option $2\lambda + \mu = 14.$

9. Correct Response : (d)

$$Ax_1 = b_1$$
$$Ax_2 = b_2$$

$$Ax_3 = b_3$$
$$|\,AX\,| = |\,b\,|$$
$$|\,A\,|\,|\,X\,| = |\,b\,|$$

$$\Rightarrow \qquad |\,A\,| = \begin{vmatrix} 1 & 0 & 0 \\ 1 & 2 & 0 \\ 1 & 1 & 1 \end{vmatrix} = \begin{vmatrix} 1 & 0 & 0 \\ 0 & 2 & 0 \\ 0 & 0 & 2 \end{vmatrix}$$

$$\Rightarrow \qquad |\,A\,| = \frac{4}{2} = 2$$

10. Correct Response : (c)

$$\Delta = \begin{vmatrix} x-2 & 2x-3 & 3x-4 \\ 2x-3 & 3x-4 & 4x-5 \\ 3x-5 & 5x-8 & 10x-17 \end{vmatrix}$$

$$= Ax^3 + Bx^2 + Cx + D$$

$$R_2 \rightarrow R_2 - R_1 \quad R_3 \rightarrow R_3 - R_2$$

$$\Delta = \begin{vmatrix} x-2 & 2x-3 & 3x-4 \\ x-1 & x-1 & x-1 \\ x-2 & 2(x-2) & 6(x-2) \end{vmatrix}$$

$$= (x-1)\,(x-2) \begin{vmatrix} x-2 & 2x-3 & 3x-4 \\ 1 & 1 & 1 \\ 1 & 2 & 6 \end{vmatrix}$$

$$= -3(x-1)^2\,(x-2)$$
$$= -3x^3 + 12x^2 - 15x + 6$$

$$\therefore \qquad B + C = 12 - 15 = -3.$$

11. Correct Response : (10)

$$A = \begin{bmatrix} x & 1 \\ 1 & 0 \end{bmatrix}$$

$$A^2 = \begin{bmatrix} x & 1 \\ 1 & 0 \end{bmatrix} \begin{bmatrix} x & 1 \\ 1 & 0 \end{bmatrix} = \begin{bmatrix} x^2+1 & x \\ x & 1 \end{bmatrix}$$

$$A^4 = \begin{bmatrix} x^2+1 & x \\ x & 1 \end{bmatrix} \begin{bmatrix} x^2+1 & x \\ x & 1 \end{bmatrix}$$

$$= \begin{bmatrix} (x^2+1)^2 + x^2 & x(x^2+1) + x \\ x(x^2+1) + x & x^2+1 \end{bmatrix}$$

$$a_{11} = (x^2+1)^2 + x^2 = 109$$
$$\Rightarrow \qquad x = \pm 3$$
$$a_{22} = x^2 + 1 = 10.$$

12. Correct Response : (b)

$$x + y + 3z = 0 \qquad\qquad \text{...(i)}$$
$$x + 3y + k^2z = 0 \qquad\qquad \text{...(ii)}$$
$$3x + y + 3z = 0 \qquad\qquad \text{...(iii)}$$

$$\begin{vmatrix} 1 & 1 & 3 \\ 1 & 3 & k^2 \\ 3 & 1 & 3 \end{vmatrix} = 0$$

$$\Rightarrow 9 + 3 + 3k^2 - 27 - k^2 - 3 = 0$$
$$\Rightarrow \qquad k^2 = 9$$

(i) − (iii)

$$\Rightarrow \qquad -2x = 0 \Rightarrow x = 0$$

Now from (i)

$\Rightarrow \qquad y + 3z = 0$

$\Rightarrow \qquad \dfrac{y}{z} = -3$

$\qquad x + \dfrac{y}{z} = -3$

13. Correct Response : (b)

$a + x = b + y = c + z + 1$

$= \begin{vmatrix} x & a+y & x+a \\ y & b+y & y+b \\ z & c+y & z+c \end{vmatrix} \qquad C_3 \to C_3 - C_1$

$= \begin{vmatrix} x & a+y & a \\ y & b+y & b \\ z & c+y & c \end{vmatrix} \qquad C_2 \to C_2 - C_3$

$= \begin{vmatrix} x & y & a \\ y & y & b \\ z & y & c \end{vmatrix}$

$\qquad\qquad R_3 \to R_3 - R_1,\ R_2 \to R_2 - R_1$

$= \begin{vmatrix} x & y & a \\ y-x & 0 & b-a \\ z-x & 0 & c-a \end{vmatrix}$

$= (-y)\,[(y-x)\,(c-a) - (b-a)\,(z-x)]$

$\qquad a + x = b + y \quad a + x = c + z + 1$

$\qquad (a - b) = (y - x) \quad a - c - 1 = (z - x)$

$= (-y)\,[(a-b)\,(c-a) + (a-b)\,(a-c-1)]$

$= (-y)\,[(a-b)\,(c-a) + (a-b)\,(a-c) + b - a]$

$= -y(b-a) = y(a-b).$

14. Correct Response : (5)

M–I

Let $\qquad A = \begin{bmatrix} a & b \\ c & d \end{bmatrix}$

$A^2 = \begin{bmatrix} a^2 + bc & ab + bd \\ ac + dc & bc + d^2 \end{bmatrix}$

$A^3 = \begin{bmatrix} a^3 + 2abc + bdc & a^2b + abd + b^2c + bd^2 \\ a^2c + adc + bc^2 + d^2c & abc + 2bcd + d^3 \end{bmatrix}$

Given $\quad$ trace $(A) = a + d = 3$

and $\quad$ trace $(A^3) = a^3 + d^3 + 3abc + 3bcd = -18$

$\Rightarrow \quad a^3 + d^3 + 3bc(a+d) = -18$

$\Rightarrow \quad a^3 + d^3 + 9bc = -18$

$\Rightarrow (a+d)\,[(a+d)^2 - 3ad] + 9bc = -18$

$\Rightarrow \quad 3(9 - 3ad) + 9bc = -18$

$\Rightarrow \quad ad - bc = 5 = $ determinant of A

M–II

$A = \begin{bmatrix} a & b \\ c & d \end{bmatrix};$

$\Delta = ad - bc$

$|\,A - \lambda\,| = (a - \lambda)\,(d - \lambda) - bc$

$\qquad = \lambda^2 - (a + d)\lambda + ad - bc$

$\qquad = \lambda^2 - 3\lambda + \Delta$

$\Rightarrow \qquad O = A^2 - 3A + \Delta I$

$\Rightarrow \qquad A^2 = 3A - \Delta I$

$\Rightarrow \qquad A^3 = 3A^2 - \Delta A$

$\qquad = 3(3A - \Delta I) - \Delta A$

$\qquad = (9 - \Delta)A - 3\Delta I$

$\qquad = (9 - \Delta)\begin{bmatrix} a & b \\ c & d \end{bmatrix} - 3\Delta \begin{bmatrix} 1 & 0 \\ 0 & 1 \end{bmatrix}$

$\therefore \qquad$ trace $A^3 = (9 - \Delta)\,(a + d) - 6\Delta$

$\Rightarrow \qquad -18 = (9 - \Delta)\,(3) - 6\Delta$

$\qquad = 27 - 9\Delta$

$\Rightarrow \qquad 9\Delta = 45$

$\Rightarrow \qquad \Delta = 5.$

15. Correct Response : (d)

$A^T A = I$

$A^T A = \begin{bmatrix} a & b & c \\ b & c & a \\ c & a & b \end{bmatrix}\begin{bmatrix} a & b & c \\ b & c & a \\ c & a & b \end{bmatrix}$

$= \begin{bmatrix} a^2 + b^2 + c^2 & ab + bc + ac & ab + bc + ac \\ ab + bc + ca & a^2 + b^2 + c^2 & ab + bc + ac \\ ab + bc + ac & ab + bc + ac & a^2 + b^2 + c^2 \end{bmatrix} = I$

$\Rightarrow \qquad a^2 + b^2 + c^2 = 1$

and $\qquad ab + bc + ca = 0$

Now, $\qquad (a + b + c)^2 = 1$

$\Rightarrow \qquad a + b + c = \pm 1$

So, $a^3 + b^3 + c^3 - 3abc$

$= (a + b + c)(a^2 + b^2 + c^2 - ab - bc - ca)$

$= \qquad \pm 1\,(1 - 0) = \pm 1$

$\Rightarrow \qquad 3\,abc = 2 \pm 1 = 3,\ 1$

$\Rightarrow \qquad abc = 1,\ \dfrac{1}{3}$

16. Correct Response : (d)

Given $P = \begin{bmatrix} 1 & 2 & 1 \\ -2 & 3 & -4 \\ 1 & 9 & -1 \end{bmatrix}$, Here $|P| = 0$ & also

given $PX = 0$

$\Rightarrow \begin{bmatrix} 1 & 2 & 1 \\ -2 & 3 & -4 \\ 1 & 9 & -1 \end{bmatrix}\begin{bmatrix} x \\ y \\ z \end{bmatrix} = 0$

$\Rightarrow \left.\begin{array}{l} x + 2y + z = 0 \\ -2x + 3y - 4z = 0 \\ x + 9y - z = 0 \end{array}\right\} \quad$ D = 0, so system have

infinite many solutions,

Let $y = \lambda \in R$

By solving these equation we get $x = \dfrac{-11\lambda}{2}$; $y = \lambda$; $z = \dfrac{7\lambda}{2}$

Also given, $x^2 + y^2 + z^2 = 1$

$$\Rightarrow \left(\dfrac{-11\lambda}{2}\right)^2 + (\lambda)^2 + \left(\dfrac{7\lambda}{2}\right)^2 = 1$$

$$\Rightarrow \qquad \lambda = \pm\dfrac{1}{\sqrt{\dfrac{121}{4} + 1 + \dfrac{49}{4}}}$$

so, there are 2 values of λ.

$\therefore$ so, there are 2 solution sets of (x, y, z).

17. Correct Response : (c)

Explanation :

$$C = \text{adj } A = \begin{vmatrix} +2 & -1 & 1 \\ -1 & 0 & 2 \\ 1 & -2 & -1 \end{vmatrix}$$

$$|C| = |\text{adj } A| = +2(0+4) + 1.(1-2) + 1.(2,4)$$
$$= +8 - 1 + 2$$
$$|\text{adj } A| = |A|^2 = 9 = 9$$
$$\lambda = |A| = \pm 3$$
$$|\lambda| = 3$$
$$B = \text{adj } C$$
$$|B| = |\text{adj } C| = |C|^2 = 81$$
$$|(B^{-1})^T| = |B|^{-1} = \dfrac{1}{81}$$
$$(|\lambda|, \mu) = \left(3, \dfrac{1}{81}\right)$$

18. Correct Response : (8)

$$x - 2y + 5z = 0 \qquad\qquad ...(1)$$
$$-2x + 4y + z = 0 \qquad\qquad ...(2)$$
$$-7x + 14y + 9z = 0 \qquad\qquad ...(3)$$

$2 \times (1) + (2)$

$$z = 0$$

Put $z = 0$ in equation (1)

$$x = 2y$$
$$15 \le x^2 + y^2 + z^2 \le 150$$
$$15 \le 4y^2 + y^2 \le 150$$
$$15 \le 5y^2 \le 150$$
$$3 \le y^2 \le 30$$
$$y = \pm 2, \pm 3, \pm 4, \pm 5$$

19. Correct Response : (c)

$$2x - y + 2z = 2$$
$$x - 2y + \lambda z = -4$$
$$x + \lambda y + z = 4$$

For no solution :

$$D = \begin{vmatrix} 2 & -1 & 2 \\ 1 & -2 & \lambda \\ 1 & \lambda & 1 \end{vmatrix} = 0$$

$$\Rightarrow 2(-2 - \lambda^2) + 1(1 - \lambda) + 2(\lambda + 2) = 0$$
$$\Rightarrow \qquad -2\lambda^2 + \lambda + 1 = 0$$
$$\qquad\qquad \lambda = 1, -\dfrac{1}{2}$$
$$\Rightarrow$$

$$D_x = \begin{vmatrix} 2 & -1 & 2 \\ -4 & 2 & \lambda \\ 4 & \lambda & 1 \end{vmatrix} = 2\begin{vmatrix} 1 & -1 & 2 \\ -2 & -2 & \lambda \\ \lambda & \lambda & 1 \end{vmatrix}$$

$$= 2(1 + \lambda)$$

which not equal to zero for

$$\lambda = 1, -\dfrac{1}{2}$$

20. Correct Response : (d)

$$|A| \ne 0$$

For (P) : $A \ne I_2$

So, $A = \begin{bmatrix} 0 & 1 \\ 1 & 0 \end{bmatrix}$ or $\begin{bmatrix} 1 & 1 \\ 1 & 0 \end{bmatrix}$ or $\begin{bmatrix} 0 & 1 \\ 1 & 1 \end{bmatrix}$ or $\begin{bmatrix} 1 & 1 \\ 0 & 1 \end{bmatrix}$ or $\begin{bmatrix} 1 & 0 \\ 1 & 1 \end{bmatrix}$

$|A|$ can be -1 or 1

So (P) is false.

For (Q) ; $\qquad |A| = 1$

$$A = \begin{bmatrix} 1 & 0 \\ 0 & 1 \end{bmatrix} \text{ or } \begin{bmatrix} 1 & 1 \\ 0 & 1 \end{bmatrix} \text{ or } \begin{bmatrix} 1 & 0 \\ 1 & 1 \end{bmatrix}$$

$$\Rightarrow \qquad\qquad tr(A) = 2$$

$\Rightarrow$ Q is true.

21. Correct Response : (3)

$$(\lambda - 1)x + (3\lambda + 1)y + 2\lambda z = 0$$
$$(\lambda - 1)x + (4\lambda - 2)y + (\lambda + 3)z = 0$$
$$2x + (3\lambda + 1)y + (3\lambda - 3)z = 0$$

$$\begin{vmatrix} \lambda - 1 & 3\lambda + 1 & 2\lambda \\ \lambda - 1 & 4\lambda - 2 & \lambda + 3 \\ 2 & 3\lambda + 1 & 3\lambda - 3 \end{vmatrix} = 0$$

$R_1 \to R_1 - R_2 \ \& \ R_2 \to R_2 - R_3$

$$\begin{vmatrix} 0 & 3 - \lambda & \lambda - 3 \\ \lambda - 3 & \lambda - 3 & -2(\lambda - 3) \\ 2 & 3\lambda + 1 & 3\lambda - 3 \end{vmatrix} = 0$$

$$(\lambda - 3)^2 \begin{vmatrix} 0 & -1 & 1 \\ 1 & 1 & -2 \\ 2 & 3\lambda + 1 & 3\lambda - 3 \end{vmatrix} = 0$$

$$(\lambda - 3)^2 \, [1(3\lambda - 3) + 4] + [(3\lambda + 1) - 2]$$
$$(\lambda - 3)^2 \, [(3\lambda + 1) + (3\lambda - 1)]$$

$$(\lambda - 3)^2 \, [(3\lambda + 1) + (3\lambda - 1)] = 0$$
$$6\lambda(\lambda - 3)^2 = 0 \Rightarrow \lambda = 0, 3$$
$$\text{Sum} = 3$$

22. Correct Response : (d)

$$M^{-1} = \text{adj (adj } M)$$
$$\text{Adj } M.M^{-1} = \text{adj } M.\text{adj (adj } M)$$
$$\text{Adj } M M^{-1} = |\text{Adj } M| \, I$$
$$\text{Adj } M = |M|^2 \, M \qquad \qquad \ldots(1)$$
$$|\text{Adj } M| = ||M|^2 M|$$
$$= |M|^6 \, |M| = |M|^6 \qquad \ldots(2)$$
$$\therefore \ |M| = 1$$
$$\text{Adj } M = M \qquad \text{from equation (1)}$$
$$M.\text{Adj } M = M^2$$
$$M^2 = 1$$
$$\text{Adj } M = M$$
$$(\text{Adj } M)^2 = |M|^2 = 1.$$

23. Correct Response : (d)

Explanation :

$$b_{ij} = (3)^{(i+j-2)} a_{ij}$$

$$B = \begin{bmatrix} a_{11} & 3a_{12} & 3^2 a_{13} \\ 3a_{21} & 3a_{22} & 3a_{23} \\ 3^2 a_{31} & 3^2 a_{32} & 3^2 a_{33} \end{bmatrix}$$

$$\Rightarrow \quad |B| = 3 \times 3^2 \begin{vmatrix} a_{11} & a_{12} & a_{13} \\ 3a_{21} & 3a_{22} & 3a_{23} \\ 3^2 a_{31} & 3^2 a_{32} & 3^2 a_{33} \end{vmatrix}$$

$$= 3^6 |A|$$

$$\Rightarrow \quad |A| = \frac{81}{27 \times 27} = \frac{1}{9}$$

24. Correct Response : (13.00)

Explanation :

System has infinitely many solution

$$\Rightarrow \quad \begin{vmatrix} 1 & 1 & 1 \\ 1 & 2 & 3 \\ 3 & 2 & \lambda \end{vmatrix} = 0$$

$$\Rightarrow \quad \lambda = 1$$

$$D_1 = \begin{vmatrix} 6 & 1 & 1 \\ 10 & 2 & 3 \\ \mu & 2 & 1 \end{vmatrix} = 0$$

$$\mu = 14$$
$$\mu - \lambda^2 = 13$$

25. Correct Response : (d)

Explanation :

$$D = \begin{vmatrix} \lambda & 3 & 2 \\ 2\lambda & 3 & 5 \\ 4 & \lambda & 6 \end{vmatrix} = (\lambda + 8)(2 - \lambda)$$

for $\lambda = 2 : D_1 = 0$

Hence, no solution for $\lambda = 2$

26. Correct Response : (b)

Explanation :

$$A = \begin{pmatrix} 2 & 2 \\ 9 & 4 \end{pmatrix} ; \ |A| = 8 - 18 = -10$$

$$A^{-1} = \frac{\text{adj } A}{|A|} = \frac{\begin{pmatrix} 4 & -2 \\ -9 & 2 \end{pmatrix}}{-10}$$

$$10A^{-1} = \begin{pmatrix} -4 & +2 \\ +9 & -2 \end{pmatrix} = A - 6I$$

27. Correct Response : (c)

Explanation :

$$A = \begin{bmatrix} 1 & 1 & 2 \\ 1 & 3 & 4 \\ 1 & -1 & 3 \end{bmatrix}$$

$$\Rightarrow \quad |A| = 6$$

$$\frac{|\text{adj } B|}{|C|} = \frac{|\text{adj (adj } A)|}{|9A|} = \frac{|A|^4}{3^3 |A|} = \frac{|A|^3}{3^3}$$

$$= \frac{(6)^3}{(3)^3} = 8$$

28. Correct Response : (a)

Explanation :

$$7x + 6y - 2z = 0 \qquad \ldots(1)$$
$$3x + 4y + 2z = 0 \qquad \ldots(2)$$
$$x - 2y - 6z = 0 \qquad \ldots(3)$$

$$\Delta = \begin{vmatrix} 7 & 6 & -2 \\ 3 & 4 & 2 \\ 1 & -2 & -6 \end{vmatrix} = 0 \Rightarrow \text{infinite solutions}$$

Now $(1) + (2) \Rightarrow y = -x$ put in (1), (2) and (3) all will lead to $x = 2z$.

29. Correct Response : (c)

Explanation :

$$R_1 \to R_1 + R_3 - 2R_2$$

$$f(x) = \begin{vmatrix} a+c-2b & 0 & 0 \\ x+b & x+3 & x+2 \\ x+c & x+4 & x+3 \end{vmatrix}$$

$$= (a + c - 2b) \, ((x + 3)^2 - (x + 2)(x + 4))$$
$$= x^2 + 6x + 9 - x^2 - 6x - 8 = 1$$
$$\Rightarrow \quad f(x) = 1 \Rightarrow f(50) = 1$$

30. Correct Response : (a)

Explanation :

$$x^2 + x + 1 = 0$$
$$\alpha = \omega$$
$$\alpha^2 = \omega^2$$

$$A = \frac{1}{\sqrt{3}} \begin{bmatrix} 1 & 1 & 1 \\ 1 & \omega & \omega^2 \\ 1 & \omega^2 & \omega \end{bmatrix}$$

$$A^2 = \begin{bmatrix} 1 & 0 & 0 \\ 0 & 0 & 1 \\ 0 & 1 & 0 \end{bmatrix}$$

$$\Rightarrow \quad A^4 = A^2 . A^2 = I_3$$
$$A^{31} = A^{28} . A^3 = A^3$$

31. Correct Response : (d)

Explanation :

For non-zero solution

$$\begin{vmatrix} 2 & 2a & a \\ 2 & 3b & b \\ 2 & 4c & c \end{vmatrix} = 0, \Rightarrow \begin{vmatrix} 1 & 2a & a \\ 0 & 3b-2a & b-a \\ 0 & 4c-2a & c-a \end{vmatrix} = 0$$

$$\Rightarrow (3b - 2a)(c - a) - (b - a)(4c - 2a) = 0$$
$$\Rightarrow \qquad\qquad 2ac = bc + ab$$
$$\Rightarrow \qquad\qquad \frac{2}{b} = \frac{1}{a} + \frac{1}{c}$$

Hence $\dfrac{1}{a}, \dfrac{1}{b}, \dfrac{1}{c}$ are in A.P.

32. Correct Response : (b)

Explanation :

Apply $2 \times$ (ii) $- 2 \times$ (i) $-$ (iii) : -
$$0 = 2\mu - 2 - \delta$$
$$\Rightarrow \qquad \delta = 2(\mu - 1)$$

33. Correct Response : (672.00)

Explanation :

$$\text{trace } (AA^T) = \sum a_{ij}^2 = 3$$

Hence, number of such matrices
$$= {}^9C_3 \times 2^3 = 672.00$$

34. Correct Response : (a)

Explanation :

For planes to intersect on a line
* there should be infinite solution of the given
system of equations of infinite solutions

$$\Delta = \begin{vmatrix} 1 & 4 & -2 \\ 1 & 7 & -5 \\ 1 & 5 & \alpha \end{vmatrix}$$

$$\Rightarrow \qquad 3a + 9 = 0 \Rightarrow \alpha = -3$$

$$\Delta_z = \begin{vmatrix} 1 & 4 & 1 \\ 1 & 7 & \beta \\ 1 & 5 & 5 \end{vmatrix} = 0$$

$$\Rightarrow \qquad 13 - \beta = 0 \Rightarrow \beta = 13$$
Also for $\alpha = -3$ and $\beta = 13$ $\Delta_x = \Delta_y = 0$
$$\therefore \qquad \alpha + \beta = -3 + 13 = 10$$

35. Correct Response : (d)

Explanation :
$$\Delta_1 = x(-x^2 - 1) - \sin\theta\,(-x\sin\theta - \cos\theta)$$
$$+ \cos\theta\,(-\sin\theta + x\cos\theta)$$

$$= -x^3 - x + x\sin^2\theta + \sin\theta\cos\theta - \sin\theta\cos\theta$$
$$+ x\cos^2\theta$$
$$= -x^3$$

Similarly,
$$\Delta_2 = -x_3$$
$$\Rightarrow \qquad \Delta_1 + \Delta_2 = -2x_3$$

36. Correct Response : (d)

Explanation :

$$D = \begin{vmatrix} 1 & 1 & 1 \\ 1 & 2 & 2 \\ 1 & 3 & \lambda \end{vmatrix}$$

$$= \begin{vmatrix} 1 & 1 & 1 \\ -1 & 0 & 0 \\ 1 & 3 & \lambda \end{vmatrix}$$

$$= 1\,(\lambda - 3)$$

$$D_1 = \begin{vmatrix} 5 & 1 & 1 \\ 6 & 2 & 2 \\ \mu & 3 & \lambda \end{vmatrix}$$

$$= \begin{vmatrix} 5 & 1 & 1 \\ -4 & 0 & 0 \\ \mu & 3 & \lambda \end{vmatrix}$$

$$= 4\,(\lambda - 3)$$

$$D_2 = \begin{vmatrix} 1 & 5 & 1 \\ 1 & 6 & 2 \\ 1 & \mu & \lambda \end{vmatrix}$$

$$= \begin{vmatrix} 1 & 5 & 1 \\ 0 & 1 & 1 \\ 0 & \mu-6 & \lambda-2 \end{vmatrix}$$

$$= \lambda - 2 - \mu + 6$$
$$= \lambda - \mu + 4$$

$$D_3 = \begin{vmatrix} 1 & 1 & 5 \\ 1 & 2 & 6 \\ 1 & 3 & \mu \end{vmatrix}$$

$$= \begin{vmatrix} 1 & 1 & 5 \\ 0 & 1 & 1 \\ 0 & 1 & \mu-6 \end{vmatrix}$$

$$= \mu - 6 - 1$$
$$= \mu - 7$$

For infinitely many solutions
$D = 0, D_1 = 0, D_2 = 0, D_3 = 0$
So,
$\lambda = 3, \lambda = 3, \lambda - \mu = -4, \mu = 7$
This gives $\lambda = 3, \mu = 7$.
$$x + y + z = 5 \qquad\qquad ...(1)$$
$$x + 2y + 2z = 6 \qquad\qquad ...(2)$$
$$x + 3y + 3z = 7 \qquad\qquad ...(3)$$

From equations (1) and (2)

$y + z = 1 \Rightarrow x = 4$ which satisfies equation (3), Thus there are infinitely many solutions for $\lambda + \mu = 10$.

37. Correct Response : (d)

Explanation :

For infinitely many solutions, $\Delta = 0$.

$$\Rightarrow \quad \begin{vmatrix} 1 & 1 & 1 \\ 4 & \lambda & -\lambda \\ 3 & 2 & -4 \end{vmatrix} = 0$$

$$\Rightarrow \quad \lambda = 3$$

which satisfies the equation $\lambda^2 - \lambda - 6 = 0$.

38. Correct Response : (b)

Explanation :

Solve the determinant

$x\,(-3x^2 - 6x - 2x^2 + 6x)$

$\qquad + 6(2x + 4 + 3x - 9) - 1\,(4x - 9x) = 0$

$$\Rightarrow \quad -5x^3 + 35x - 30 = 0$$

$$\Rightarrow \quad x^3 - 7x + 6 = 0$$

$$\Rightarrow \quad (x - 1)\,(x + 3)\,(x - 2) = 0$$

$$\Rightarrow \quad x = 1, 2, -3.$$

Sum of the roots is $1 + 2 - 3 = 0$.

39. Correct Response : (d)

Explanation :

If $A^T A = 3I$ then $AA^T = 3I$

$$AA^T = \begin{bmatrix} 0 & 2y & 1 \\ 2x & y & -1 \\ 2x & -y & 1 \end{bmatrix} \begin{bmatrix} 0 & 2x & 2x \\ 2y & y & -y \\ 1 & -1 & 1 \end{bmatrix}$$

$$= \begin{bmatrix} 4y^2 + 1 & 2y^2 - 1 & -2y^2 + 1 \\ 2y^2 - 1 & 4x^2 + y^2 + 1 & 4x^2 - y^2 - 1 \\ -2y^2 + 1 & 4x^2 - y^2 - 1 & 4x^2 + y^2 + 1 \end{bmatrix}$$

but $AA^T = \begin{bmatrix} 3 & 0 & 0 \\ 0 & 3 & 0 \\ 0 & 0 & 3 \end{bmatrix}$

Therefore, $\qquad 4y^2 + 1 = 3$

$$\Rightarrow \quad y^2 = \frac{1}{2}$$

$$4x^2 + y^2 + 1 = 3$$

$$\Rightarrow \quad 4x^2 + \frac{1}{2} + 1 = 3$$

$$\Rightarrow \quad 4x^2 = 3 - \frac{3}{2}$$

$$\Rightarrow \quad 4x^2 = \frac{3}{2}$$

$$\Rightarrow \quad x^2 = \frac{3}{8}$$

$$(x, y) = \left(\pm\sqrt{\frac{3}{8}}, \pm\frac{1}{\sqrt{2}} \right)$$

So, four such matrices are possible.

40. Correct Response : (b)

Explanation :

$$\begin{vmatrix} 2 & 3 & -1 \\ 1 & k & -2 \\ 2 & -1 & 1 \end{vmatrix} = 0$$

$R_1 \to R_1 - R_3,\ R_3 \to R_3 - 2R_2$

$$\begin{vmatrix} 0 & 4 & -2 \\ 1 & k & -2 \\ 0 & -1 - 2k & 5 \end{vmatrix} = 0$$

$$\Rightarrow \quad k = \frac{9}{2}$$

The given equation $2x + 3y - z = 0$ implies

$$2\frac{x}{y} + 3 - \frac{z}{y} = 0 \qquad \ldots(1)$$

The given equation $2x - y + z = 0$ implies

$$2\frac{x}{y} - 1 + \frac{z}{y} = 0 \qquad \ldots(2)$$

Add equations (1) and (2)

$$\Rightarrow \quad 4\frac{x}{y} + 2 = 0$$

$$\Rightarrow \quad \frac{x}{y} = -\frac{1}{2} \qquad \ldots(3)$$

Substitute this value in equation (1) then

$$\frac{z}{y} = 2 \qquad \ldots(4)$$

Divide equation (3) by equation (4), then

$$\Rightarrow \quad \frac{x}{z} = -\frac{1}{4}$$

Therefore,

$$\frac{x}{y} + \frac{y}{z} + \frac{z}{x} + k = -\frac{1}{2} + \frac{1}{2} - 4 + \frac{9}{2}$$

$$= \frac{1}{2}$$

41. Correct Response : (b)

Explanation :

$$\begin{bmatrix} 1 & 1 \\ 0 & 1 \end{bmatrix}\begin{bmatrix} 1 & 2 \\ 0 & 1 \end{bmatrix}\begin{bmatrix} 1 & 3 \\ 0 & 1 \end{bmatrix} \cdots\cdots \begin{bmatrix} 1 & n-1 \\ 0 & 1 \end{bmatrix} = \begin{bmatrix} 1 & 78 \\ 0 & 1 \end{bmatrix}$$

$$\Rightarrow \quad \frac{n\,(n-1)}{2} = 78$$

$$\Rightarrow \quad n = 13$$

$$A = \begin{bmatrix} 1 & 13 \\ 0 & 1 \end{bmatrix} \Rightarrow A^{-1} = \begin{bmatrix} 1 & -13 \\ 0 & 1 \end{bmatrix}$$

42. Correct Response : (a)

Explanation :

$$\begin{vmatrix} 1 & -c & -c \\ c & -1 & c \\ c & c & -1 \end{vmatrix} = 0$$

$$\Rightarrow \qquad (c+1)^2 (1-2c) = 0$$

$$\Rightarrow \qquad c = \frac{1}{2}, -1$$

but $c \neq \dfrac{1}{2}$ otherwise $x = 0$, $y = 0$, $z = 0$.

43. Correct Response : (c)

Explanation :

$$A^2 = \begin{bmatrix} \cos\alpha & -\sin\alpha \\ \sin\alpha & \cos\alpha \end{bmatrix}\begin{bmatrix} \cos\alpha & -\sin\alpha \\ \sin\alpha & \cos\alpha \end{bmatrix}$$

$$= \begin{bmatrix} \cos 2\alpha & -\sin 2\alpha \\ \sin 2\alpha & \cos 2\alpha \end{bmatrix}$$

Similarly, we observe that

$$A^n = \begin{bmatrix} \cos n\alpha & -\sin n\alpha \\ \sin n\alpha & \cos n\alpha \end{bmatrix}$$

Hence, $\cos 32\alpha = 0$ and $\sin 32\alpha = 1$

$$32\alpha = 2n\pi + \frac{\pi}{2}$$

$$\alpha = \frac{n\pi}{16} + \frac{\pi}{64}, \, n \in i$$

44. Correct Response : (c)

Explanation :

$$A = \begin{vmatrix} 1 & 1 & 1 \\ 2 & b & c \\ 4 & b^2 & c^2 \end{vmatrix} = \begin{vmatrix} 1 & 0 & 0 \\ 2 & (b-2) & (c-2) \\ 4 & (b^2-4) & (c^2-4) \end{vmatrix}$$

$$= \begin{vmatrix} (b-2) & (c-2) \\ (b^2-4) & (c^2-4) \end{vmatrix}$$

$$= (b-2)(c-2)\begin{vmatrix} 1 & 1 \\ (b+2) & (c+2) \end{vmatrix}$$

$$|A| = (b-2)(c-2)(c-b)$$

sin a 2, b, c are in AP.

Therefore, write these as $2, 2+d, 2+2d$

$|A| = d(2d)d = 2d^3 \in [2, 16]$

$\Rightarrow d^3 \in [1, 8] \Rightarrow d \in [1, 2] \Rightarrow 2d \in [2, 4]$

$\Rightarrow 2 + 2d \in [4, 6]$.

45. Correct Response : (b)

Explanation :

For infinite solutions

$$D = 0 \Rightarrow \begin{vmatrix} 1 & -2 & k \\ 2 & 1 & 1 \\ 3 & -1 & -k \end{vmatrix} \Rightarrow k = -\frac{1}{2}$$

For $k = -\dfrac{1}{2}$, $D_1 = D_2 = D_3 = 0$

So, first two equations are

$$2x - 4y - z = 2$$
$$2x + y + z = 2$$

Add these two equations

$$4x - 3y - 4 = 0$$

46. Correct Response : (b)

Explanation :

The matrices are,

$$A = A'$$
$$B = -B'$$

$$A + B = \begin{bmatrix} 2 & 3 \\ 5 & -1 \end{bmatrix} \qquad \text{...(1)}$$

$$A' + B' = \begin{bmatrix} 2 & 5 \\ 3 & -1 \end{bmatrix}$$

$$A - B = \begin{bmatrix} 2 & 5 \\ 3 & -1 \end{bmatrix} \qquad \text{...(2)}$$

Add equation (1) and (2),

$$A = \begin{bmatrix} 2 & 4 \\ 4 & -1 \end{bmatrix}$$

$$B = \begin{bmatrix} 0 & -1 \\ 1 & 0 \end{bmatrix}$$

$$AB = \begin{bmatrix} 4 & -2 \\ -1 & -4 \end{bmatrix}$$

47. Correct Response : (c)

Explanation :

The expression for determinant of the given matrix is given by,

$$|B| = 5(-5) - 2\alpha(-\alpha) - 2\alpha$$
$$= 2\alpha^2 - 2\alpha - 25$$

Given that : det $|A| + 1 = 0$

Substitute the value in the above equation.

$$\Rightarrow \qquad \frac{1}{2\alpha^2 - 2\alpha - 25} + 1 = 0$$

$$\Rightarrow \qquad \frac{2\alpha^2 - 2\alpha - 24}{2\alpha^2 - 2\alpha - 25} = 0$$

$$\Rightarrow \qquad \alpha^2 - \alpha - 12 = 0$$

$$\Rightarrow \qquad \alpha - 4, -3 \Rightarrow \text{sum of values} = 1$$

The sum of the values of α is 1.

48. Correct Response : (a)

Explanation :

The given determinant is,

$$\begin{vmatrix} 1+\cos^2\theta & \sin^2\theta & 4\cos 6\theta \\ \cos^2\theta & 1+\sin^2\theta & 4\cos 6\theta \\ \cos^2\theta & \sin^2\theta & 1+4\cos 6\theta \end{vmatrix} = 0$$

$$R_1 \to R_1 - R_2$$
$$R_2 \to R_2 - R_3$$

$$\begin{vmatrix} 1 & -1 & 0 \\ 0 & 1 & -1 \\ \cos^2\theta & \sin^2\theta & 1+4\cos 6\theta \end{vmatrix} = 0$$

$$C_2 \to C_2 + C_1$$

$$\begin{vmatrix} 1 & 0 & 0 \\ 0 & 1 & -1 \\ \cos^2\theta & 1 & 1+4\cos 6\theta \end{vmatrix} = 0$$

On expanding the determinant,

$$1 + 4\cos 6\theta + 1 = 0$$

$$\cos 6\theta = -\frac{1}{2}$$

$$\cos 6\theta = \cos \frac{2\pi}{3}$$

$$6\theta = 2n\pi \pm \frac{2\pi}{3}$$

or

$$\theta = \frac{n\pi}{3} \pm \frac{\pi}{9}$$

$$= \frac{\pi}{9}, \frac{2\pi}{9}, \frac{4\pi}{9}$$

49. Correct Response : (c)

Explanation :

The given expression is,

$$M = \begin{bmatrix} \sin^4\theta & -1-\sin^2\theta \\ 1+\cos^2\theta & \cos^4\theta \end{bmatrix}$$

The determinant of M is,

$$|M| = \begin{vmatrix} \sin^4\theta & -1-\sin^2\theta \\ 1+\cos^2\theta & \cos^4\theta \end{vmatrix}$$

$$= ((\sin^4\theta)(\cos^4\theta))$$
$$\qquad\qquad - (-1-\sin^2\theta)(1+\cos^2\theta)$$
$$= (\sin^4\theta \cos^4\theta) + (1+\sin^2\theta)(1+\cos^2\theta)$$
$$= \sin^4\theta \cos^4\theta + 1 + (\cos^2\theta + \sin^2\theta)$$
$$\qquad\qquad\qquad\qquad + \sin^2\theta \cos^2\theta$$
$$= \sin^4\theta \cos^4\theta + 1 + 1 + \sin^2\theta \cos^2\theta$$
$$= 2 + \sin^4\theta \cos^4\theta + \sin^2\theta \cos^2\theta$$

The M^{-1} matrix can be written as,

$$M^{-1} = \frac{1}{|M|} \begin{bmatrix} \cos^4\theta & -(-1-\sin^2\theta) \\ -(1+\cos^2\theta) & \sin^4\theta \end{bmatrix}$$

$$= \frac{1}{2 + \sin^4\theta \cos^4\theta + \sin^2\theta \cos^2\theta}$$

$$\begin{bmatrix} \cos^4\theta & 1+\sin^2\theta \\ -1-\cos^2\theta & \sin^4\theta \end{bmatrix}$$

Now $M = \alpha\, I + B\, 14^{-1}$

$$\begin{bmatrix} \sin^4\theta & -1-\sin^2\theta \\ 1+\cos^2\theta & \cos^4\theta \end{bmatrix} = \alpha \begin{bmatrix} 1 & 0 \\ 0 & 1 \end{bmatrix}$$

$$+ \beta \begin{bmatrix} \dfrac{\cos^4\theta}{2+\sin^4\theta\cos^4\theta+\sin^2\theta\cos^2\theta} & \dfrac{1+\sin^2\theta}{2+\sin^4\theta\cos^4\theta+\sin^2\theta\cos^2\theta} \\[3ex] \dfrac{-1-\cos^2\theta}{2+\sin^4\theta\cos^4\theta+\sin^2\theta\cos^2\theta} & \dfrac{\sin^4\theta}{2+\sin^2\theta\cos^4\theta+\sin^2\theta\cos^2\theta} \end{bmatrix}$$

From the above equation,

$$\sin^4\theta = (\alpha+\beta)\left(\frac{\cos^4\theta}{2+\sin^4\theta\cos^4\theta+\sin^2\theta\cos^2\theta}\right)$$

and

$$-1-\sin^2\theta = \beta\left(\frac{1+\sin^2\theta}{2+\sin^4\theta\cos^4\theta+\sin^2\theta\cos^2\theta}\right)$$

$$-(1+\sin^2\theta) = \beta\left(\frac{1+\sin^2\theta}{2+\sin^4\theta\cos^4\theta+\sin^2\theta\cos^2\theta}\right)$$

$$\beta = -(2-\sin^4\theta\cos^4\theta-\sin^2\theta\cos^2\theta)$$

$$= -[t^2 + t + 2]$$

$$\beta = -2 - \frac{1}{4}\sin^2 2\theta - \frac{1}{16}(\sin 2\theta)^4$$

$$\beta = -2 - \frac{1}{16}\{(\sin 2\theta)^4 + 4(\sin^2 2\theta) + 4\} + \frac{1}{4}$$

$$\beta = -\frac{7}{4} - \frac{1}{16}\{\sin^2 2\theta + 2\}^2$$

$$\beta = -\frac{7}{14} - \frac{1}{16} - (9) = - -\frac{37}{16}$$

Therefore, $\qquad \beta_{min} = -\dfrac{37}{16}$.

$$\alpha = \sin^4\theta + \cos^4\theta$$
$$= 1 - 2\sin^2\theta \cos^2\theta$$
$$= 1 - \frac{1}{2}\sin^2 2\theta$$

Therefore, $\qquad \alpha_{min} = \dfrac{1}{2}$.

Hence,

$$\alpha^* + \beta^* = -\frac{37}{16} + \frac{1}{2}$$

$$= -\frac{29}{16}$$

50. Correct Response : (a, c, d)

Explanation :

The given matrix is,

$$M = \begin{bmatrix} 0 & 1 & a \\ 1 & 2 & 3 \\ 3 & b & 1 \end{bmatrix}$$

$$\text{adj } M = \begin{bmatrix} -1 & 1 & -1 \\ 8 & -6 & 2 \\ -5 & 3 & -1 \end{bmatrix}$$

Consider option (a),

The value of unknown variables.

$$(\text{adj } M)_{11} = 2 - 3b$$
$$(\text{adj } M)_{22} = -3a$$

Compare the above equations with the adj$M$ matrix.

$$2 - 3b = -1$$
$$3b = 3$$
$$b = 1$$

and
$$-3a = -6$$
$$a = 2$$

Therefore,

$$a + b = 2 + 1$$
$$= 3$$

Consider option (c),

$$M^{-1} = \begin{vmatrix} 0 & 1 & 2 \\ 1 & 2 & 3 \\ 3 & 1 & 1 \end{vmatrix}$$

$$|M| = -2$$

Now $|\text{adj. }(M^2)| = |M^2|^2$
$$= |M|^4$$
$$= 16 \neq 81$$

Consider option (d),

$$\begin{bmatrix} 0 & 1 & 2 \\ 1 & 2 & 3 \\ 3 & 1 & 1 \end{bmatrix} \begin{bmatrix} \alpha \\ \beta \\ \gamma \end{bmatrix} = \begin{bmatrix} 1 \\ 2 \\ 3 \end{bmatrix}$$

The equations for the above equation are,

$$\beta + 2\gamma = 1$$
$$\alpha + 2\beta + 3\gamma = 2$$
$$3\alpha + \beta + \gamma = 3$$

Solve the above equations,

$$\alpha = 1$$
$$\beta = -1$$
$$\gamma = 1$$

Therefore,

$$\alpha - \beta + \gamma = 1 - (-1) + 1$$
$$= 1 + 1 + 1$$
$$= 3$$

51. Correct Response : (*a, b, c*)

Explanation :

Given that,

$$P_1 = P_1^{T}$$
$$= P_1^{-1}$$
$$P_2 = P_2^{T}$$
$$= P_2^{-1}$$
$$P_6 = P_6^{T}$$
$$= P_6^{-1}$$

and

$$A^T = A,$$

where,
$$A = \begin{bmatrix} 2 & 1 & 3 \\ 1 & 0 & 2 \\ 3 & 2 & 1 \end{bmatrix}$$

Use the formula $(A + B)^T = A^T + B^T$.

$$X^T = (P_1AP_1^T + ... + P_6AP_6^T)^T$$
$$= P_1AP_1^T + ... + P_6AP_6^T$$
$$= X$$

Therefore, X is symmetric.

Consider $B = \begin{bmatrix} 1 \\ 1 \\ 1 \end{bmatrix}$

Therefore,

$$XB = (P_1 + P_2 + ... + P_6) \begin{bmatrix} 6 \\ 3 \\ 6 \end{bmatrix}$$

$$= \begin{bmatrix} 6 \times 2 + 3 \times 2 + 6 \times 2 \\ 6 \times 2 + 3 \times 2 + 6 \times 2 \\ 6 \times 2 + 3 \times 2 + 6 \times 2 \end{bmatrix} - \begin{bmatrix} 30 \\ 30 \\ 30 \end{bmatrix} + 30B$$

$$X \begin{bmatrix} 1 \\ 1 \\ 1 \end{bmatrix} = 30 \begin{bmatrix} 1 \\ 1 \\ 1 \end{bmatrix}$$

$$(X - 30I)B = 0$$

Therefore, $(X - 30I)B = 0$ has a non trivial solution.

Hence, $\qquad (X - 30I) = 0$

Then, X can be written as,

$$X = P_1AP_1^T + ... + P_6AP_6^T$$
$$\text{trace } (X) = t_r P_1AP_1^T + ... + t_r P_6AP_6^T$$
$$= (2 + 0 + 1) + ... + (2 + 0 + 1)$$
$$= 3 \times 6$$
$$= 18$$

52. Correct Response : (*b, c*)

Explanation :

Given, $P = \begin{bmatrix} 1 & 1 & 1 \\ 0 & 2 & 2 \\ 0 & 0 & 3 \end{bmatrix}$ and $Q = \begin{bmatrix} 2 & x & x \\ 0 & 4 & 0 \\ x & x & 6 \end{bmatrix}$.

Consider option (b) and option (d).

The determinant of R matrix can be written as,

$$|R| = |P| \times |Q| \times |P^{-1}|$$
$$|R| = |Q|$$
$$= 4\,(12 - x^2)$$
$$= 48 - 4x^2$$

Solve further as,

$$\begin{bmatrix} 2 & x & x \\ 0 & 4 & 0 \\ x & x & 6 \end{bmatrix} = 48 - 4x^2$$

$$|R| = \begin{bmatrix} 2 & x & x \\ 0 & 4 & 0 \\ x & x & 6 \end{bmatrix} + 8 \, \forall \, x \in R$$

At $x = 1$,

$$|Q| = 48 - 4$$
$$= 44 = |R|$$

$|R|$

Since, $|R| \neq 0$ so,

$$R \begin{bmatrix} \alpha \\ \beta \\ \gamma \end{bmatrix} = \begin{bmatrix} 0 \\ 0 \\ 0 \end{bmatrix}$$

The above equation implies that $\alpha = 0$, $\beta = 0$ and $\gamma = 0$.

Therefore, $\alpha\,\hat{i} + \beta\,\hat{j} + \gamma\,\hat{k}$ is not a unit vector.

The matrix P and Q is,

$$P = \begin{vmatrix} 1 & 1 & 1 \\ 0 & 2 & 2 \\ 0 & 0 & 3 \end{vmatrix},\ Q(x = 0) = \begin{bmatrix} 2 & 0 & 0 \\ 0 & 4 & 0 \\ 0 & 0 & 6 \end{bmatrix}$$

The determinant of P martix is,

$$P = \begin{vmatrix} 1 & 1 & 1 \\ 0 & 2 & 2 \\ 0 & 0 & 3 \end{vmatrix}$$

$$= ((2)\,(3) - (2)\,(0)) + ((0)\,(3) - (0)$$
$$(2)) + ((0)\,(0) - (0)\,(2))$$
$$= 6$$

The matrix P^{-1} is,

$$P^{-1} = \frac{1}{6} \begin{bmatrix} 6 & -3 & 0 \\ 0 & 3 & -2 \\ 0 & 0 & 2 \end{bmatrix}$$

From the standard equation,

$$R = PQP^{-1}$$

$$= \begin{bmatrix} 1 & 1 & 1 \\ 0 & 2 & 2 \\ 0 & 0 & 3 \end{bmatrix} \begin{bmatrix} 2 & 0 & 0 \\ 0 & 4 & 0 \\ 0 & 0 & 6 \end{bmatrix} \frac{1}{6} \begin{bmatrix} 6 & -3 & 0 \\ 0 & 3 & -2 \\ 0 & 0 & 2 \end{bmatrix}$$

$$= \begin{bmatrix} 2 & 4 & 6 \\ 0 & 8 & 12 \\ 0 & 0 & 18 \end{bmatrix} \frac{1}{6} \begin{bmatrix} 6 & -3 & 0 \\ 0 & 3 & -2 \\ 0 & 0 & 2 \end{bmatrix}$$

$$= \frac{1}{6} \begin{bmatrix} 12 & 6 & 4 \\ 0 & 24 & 8 \\ 0 & 0 & 36 \end{bmatrix}$$

$$= \begin{bmatrix} 2 & 1 & \dfrac{2}{3} \\ 0 & 4 & \dfrac{4}{3} \\ 0 & 0 & 6 \end{bmatrix}$$

Consider option (c).

$$(R - 6I)\begin{bmatrix} 1 \\ a \\ b \end{bmatrix} = \begin{bmatrix} -4 & 1 & \dfrac{2}{3} \\ 0 & -2 & \dfrac{4}{3} \\ 0 & 0 & 0 \end{bmatrix}\begin{bmatrix} 1 \\ a \\ b \end{bmatrix}$$

After solving the above matrix equation,

$$-4 + a + \frac{2b}{3} = 0 \qquad\qquad \text{...(1)}$$

$$-2a + \frac{4b}{3} = 0 \qquad\qquad \text{...(2)}$$

Solve equation (1) and equation (2)

$$a = 2 \text{ and } b = 3$$

Consider equation (a)

$$PQ = QP$$
$$x + 4 + x = 2 + 2x + 0$$
$$x \in \phi$$

Which implies no value exist.

53. Explanation :

Given, $$P = \begin{vmatrix} \displaystyle\sum_{k=0}^{n} k & \displaystyle\sum_{k=0}^{n} {}^{n}C_k k^2 \\ \displaystyle\sum_{k=0}^{n} {}^{n}C_k k & \displaystyle\sum_{k=0}^{n} {}^{n}C_k 3^k \end{vmatrix} = 0$$

$$\Rightarrow \begin{vmatrix} \dfrac{n(n+1)}{2} & n2^{n-1} + n(n-1)2^{n-2} \\ n.2^{n-1} & 4^n \end{vmatrix} = 0.$$

$$\Rightarrow \frac{n(n+1)}{2} - \frac{n^2}{4} - \frac{n^2(n+1)}{8} = 0$$

on solving further,

$$n = 0 \text{ or } 4(n + 1) - 2n - n(n - 1) = 0$$
$$\therefore \ 4n + 4 - 2n - n^2 + n = 0$$
$$3n - n^2 + 4 = 0$$
$$(n - 4)\,(n + 1) = 0$$
$$n = 4$$

$$\sum_{r=0}^{4} \frac{{}^{4}C^{r}}{r+1} = \sum_{r=0}^{4} \frac{{}^{5}C_{r+1}}{5}$$

$$= \frac{2^{5}-1}{5}$$

$$= \frac{31}{5}$$

$$= 6.20$$

54. Correct Response : (a, d)

Explanation :

The condition for at least one solution is as follows,

$$\Delta = 0$$
$$\Delta_1 = \Delta_2 = \Delta_3 = 0$$
$$b_1 + 7b_2 = 13b_3 \qquad \qquad ...(1)$$

(a) The determinant of the equation is as follows.

$$\Delta \neq 0$$

Thus, the equations have an unique solution.

Hence, option (a) is correct.

(b) The determinant of the equation is as follows.

$$\Delta = \begin{vmatrix} 1 & 1 & 1 \\ 5 & 2 & 2 \\ 2 & 1 & 1 \end{vmatrix}$$

$$= 0$$

The value of Δ_1 is also zero.

The condition for infinite solution is Δ_2 and Δ_3 must be zero.

$$\begin{vmatrix} 1 & b_1 & 1 \\ 5 & b_2 & 2 \\ 2 & b_3 & 1 \end{vmatrix} = 0$$

$$-b_1 - b_2 + 3b_3 = 0$$

It is clear from the above equation, that the values will not satisfy the equation (i).

Hence, option (b) is wrong.

(c) The determinant of the equation as follows.

$$\Delta = 0$$

Thus, the equations of the plane represents the planes are parallel to each other.

The relationship between b_1, b_2 and b_3 as follows.

$$-b_1 = \frac{b_2}{2} = b_3$$

It is clear from the above relationship, that the values will not satisfy the equation (i).

Hence, option (c) is wrong.

(d) The determinant of the equation is as follows.

$$\Delta \neq 0$$

Thus, the equations have a unique solution.

Hence, option (d) is correct.

Hence, option (a) and option (d) are correct.

55. Correct Response : (d)

Explanation :

Let, the matrix A be,

$$A = \begin{bmatrix} a & b \\ c & d \end{bmatrix}$$

The value of $A \cdot \begin{bmatrix} 1 & 2 \\ 0 & 3 \end{bmatrix}$ is,

$$A \cdot \begin{bmatrix} 1 & 2 \\ 0 & 3 \end{bmatrix} = \begin{bmatrix} a & b \\ c & d \end{bmatrix}\begin{bmatrix} 1 & 2 \\ 0 & 3 \end{bmatrix}$$

$$= \begin{bmatrix} a & 2a+3b \\ c & 2c+3d \end{bmatrix}$$

If this is a scalar matrix then all of the elements in principal diagonal are equal and the other elements are equal to zero.

$$c = 0$$
$$2a + 3b = 0$$

And, $\qquad a = 2c + 3d$
$$= 2(0) + 3d$$
$$= 3d$$

The determinant of matrix A is,

$$|A| = ad - bc$$

The given equation is,

$$|3A| = 108$$
$$|A| = 12$$
$$(3d)\,d - b(0) = 12$$
$$d^2 = 4$$

The value of a^2 is,

$$a^2 = (3d)^2$$
$$= 9 \times 4$$
$$= 36$$

The value of A^2 is

$$A^2 = \begin{bmatrix} a & b \\ 0 & d \end{bmatrix}\begin{bmatrix} a & b \\ 0 & d \end{bmatrix}$$

$$= \begin{bmatrix} a^2 & ab+bd \\ 0 & d^2 \end{bmatrix}$$

$$= \begin{bmatrix} 36 & (6)(-4)+(-4)(2) \\ 0 & 4 \end{bmatrix}$$

$$= \begin{bmatrix} 36 & -32 \\ 0 & 4 \end{bmatrix}$$

Therefore, the value of A^2 is $\begin{bmatrix} 36 & -32 \\ 0 & 4 \end{bmatrix}$.

56. Correct Response : (d)

Explanation :

The determinant of the system of linear equations is,

$$\Delta = \begin{vmatrix} 1 & 1 & 1 \\ 2 & 1 & -1 \\ 3 & 2 & k \end{vmatrix}$$

The condition for the system to have a unique solution, its determinant must be non-zero.

i.e $\qquad \Delta \neq 0$

$$\begin{vmatrix} 1 & 1 & 1 \\ 2 & 1 & -1 \\ 3 & 2 & k \end{vmatrix} \neq 0$$

Solve the determinant.

$$1(k+2) - 1\{2k - (-3)\} + 1(4-3) = 0$$
$$k + 2 - 2k - 3 + 1 = 0$$
$$k = 0$$

S is the set of all real values of k except $\{0\}$.

57. Correct Response : (c)

Explanation :

The given matrix is,

$$A = \begin{bmatrix} 1 & 0 & 0 \\ 1 & 1 & 0 \\ 1 & 1 & 1 \end{bmatrix}$$

$$\therefore \qquad A^2 = \begin{bmatrix} 1 & 0 & 0 \\ 2 & 1 & 0 \\ 3 & 2 & 1 \end{bmatrix}$$

and $\qquad A^3 = \begin{bmatrix} 1 & 0 & 0 \\ 3 & 1 & 0 \\ 6 & 3 & 1 \end{bmatrix}$

$$A^4 = \begin{bmatrix} 1 & 0 & 0 \\ 4 & 1 & 0 \\ 10 & 4 & 1 \end{bmatrix}$$

$$B = A^{20}\begin{bmatrix} 1 & 0 & 0 \\ 20 & 1 & 0 \\ 210 & 20 & 1 \end{bmatrix}$$

Sum of the elements of first column is 231.

58. Correct Response : (a)

Explanation :

The system is,

$$a_1 x + b_1 y + c_1 = 0$$
$$a_2 x + b_2 y + c_2 = 0$$

The system will have no solution if

$$\frac{a_1}{a_2} = \frac{b_1}{b_2} \neq \frac{c_1}{c_2}$$

$$\underset{\text{(I)}}{\left(\frac{k+2}{k}\right)} = \underset{\text{(II)}}{\frac{10}{k+3}} \neq \underset{\text{(III)}}{\frac{k}{k-1}}$$

Consider (I) and (II).

$$(k+2)(k+3) = 10k$$
$$k^2 - 5k + 6 = 0$$
$$k = 2, 3$$

Consider (I) and (III),

$$(k+2)(k-1) \neq k^2$$
$$k \neq 2$$

The value of $k \neq 2$ and $k = 2$ both together consideration is not possible so $k = 3$ is only possible.

So, the number of values of k is 1.

59. Correct Response : (b)

Explanation :

Since, system of linear equations has non-zero solution. Therefore, determinant will be zero.

$$\begin{vmatrix} 1 & k & 3 \\ 3 & k & -2 \\ 2 & 4 & -3 \end{vmatrix} = 0$$

$$1(-3k+8) - k(-9+4) + 3(12 - 2k) = 0$$
$$-4k + 44 = 0$$
$$k = 11$$

Let $x = \alpha$, then,

$$\alpha + 11y + 3z = 0$$
$$3\alpha + 11y - 2z = 0$$
$$\alpha + 3z = 3\alpha - 2z$$

Simplify the above equation.

$$z = \frac{2}{5}\alpha$$

$$y = -\frac{\alpha}{5}$$

The value of $\dfrac{xz}{y^2}$ is calculated as,

$$\frac{xz}{y^2} = \frac{\alpha \times \dfrac{2}{5}\alpha}{\left(-\dfrac{\alpha}{5}\right)^2}$$

$$= 10$$

60. Correct Response : (b)

Explanation :

Consider the equation :

$$A + B = 2B' \qquad \qquad ...(i)$$

Use property of transpose,

$$A' + B' = 2B$$

$$B = \frac{A' + B'}{2} \qquad \qquad ...(ii)$$

Hence, the equation (1) is,

$$A + \frac{A' + B'}{2} = 2B'$$

$$2A + A' = 3B' \qquad ....(iii)$$

or

$$A = \frac{3B' - A'}{2}$$

The given equation is,

$$3A + 2B = I_3 \qquad ...(iv)$$

From equation (ii) and equation (iii),

$$3\left(\frac{3B' - A'}{2}\right) + 2\left(\frac{A'+B'}{2}\right) = I_3 \qquad ...(v)$$

$$11B' - A' = 2I_3$$

Add equation (iv) and (v),

$$35B = 7I_3$$

$$B = \frac{I_3}{5}$$

Calculate the value of A :

$$3A + 2B = I_3$$

$$3A + 2\left(\frac{I_3}{5}\right) = I_3$$

The value of A is $A = \dfrac{I_3}{5}$.

In the given options, only option (b) satisfies the values of A and B, such as,

$$10A + 5B = 3I_3$$

$$10 \times \frac{I_3}{5} + 5 \times \frac{I_3}{5} = 3I_3$$

$$3I_3 = 3I_3$$

61. Correct Response : (c)

Explanation :

Given equations are,

$$x + 8y + 7z = 0 \qquad ...(1)$$
$$9x + 2y + 3z = 0 \qquad ...(2)$$
$$x + y + z = 0 \qquad ...(3)$$

Subtract 2 times equation 3 from equation 2.

$$7x + z = 0$$
$$z = -7x$$

Subtract equation 3 from equation 1.

$$7y + 6z = 0$$
$$y = \frac{-6z}{7}$$

Substitute the value of z in the above equation.

$$y = -\frac{6\,(-7x)}{7}$$

$$= 6x$$

The given equation of plane is.

$$x + 2y + z = 6$$

Since, $x = a$, $y = b$, $z = c$. Assume $a = p$, then $b = 6p$ and $c = -7p$.

Solution of linear equation lies on the given plane. Hence

$$p + 2(6p) + (-7p) = 6$$

$$6p = 6$$
$$p = 1$$

Hence, $\quad 2a + b + c = 2 + 6 - 7$

$$= 1$$

62. Correct Response : (c)

Explanation :

The given function is,

$$A^2 - 5A + 7I = O$$

Solve the given equation,

$$A^2 - 5A + 7I = O$$

$$A\,(A - 5I) = -7I$$

$$A - 5I = -7A^{-1}$$

$$A^{-1} = \frac{1}{7}(5I - A)$$

Thus, the statement-I is true.

Now, solve the equation in statement-II,

$$A^3 - 2A^2 - 3A + I = A\,(A)^2 - 2A^2 - 3A + I$$
$$= A(5A - 7I) - 2A^2 - 3A + I$$
$$= 3A^2 - 10A + I$$
$$= 3(5A - 7I) - 10A + I$$

Further, solve the above equation.

$$A^3 - 2A^2 - 3A + I = 3\,(5A - 7I) - 10A + I$$
$$= 5\,(A - 4I)$$

The statement-II is also true.

63. Correct Response : (d)

Explanation :

The given matrix is,

$$A = \begin{bmatrix} -4 & -1 \\ 3 & 1 \end{bmatrix}$$

The determinant of given expression is written as,

$$|A^{2016} - 2A^{2015} - A^{2014}| = |A|^{2014}|A^2 - 2A - I| \qquad ...(1)$$

The square of matrix A is,

$$A^2 = \begin{bmatrix} -4 & -1 \\ 3 & 1 \end{bmatrix}\begin{bmatrix} -4 & -1 \\ 3 & 1 \end{bmatrix}$$

$$= \begin{bmatrix} 13 & 3 \\ -9 & -2 \end{bmatrix}$$

Substitute $\begin{bmatrix} 13 & 3 \\ -9 & -2 \end{bmatrix}$ for A^2 and $\begin{bmatrix} -4 & -1 \\ 3 & 1 \end{bmatrix}$ for A

in equation (1),

$$|A^{2016} - 2A^{2015} - A^{2014}|$$

$$= \begin{vmatrix} -4 & -1 \\ 3 & 1 \end{vmatrix}^{2014} \left|\begin{bmatrix} 13 & 3 \\ -9 & -2 \end{bmatrix} - 2\begin{bmatrix} -4 & -1 \\ 3 & 1 \end{bmatrix} - \begin{bmatrix} 1 & 0 \\ 0 & 1 \end{bmatrix}\right|$$

$$= (-4 - (-3))^{2014}\begin{vmatrix} 20 & 5 \\ -15 & -5 \end{vmatrix}$$

$$= 1\,(-100 + 75) = -25$$

64. Correct Response : (b)

Explanation :

Consider the linear equation :

$$AX = B$$

For $B = 0$ and determinant of $A = 0$, infinitely many solution exist.

$$\begin{vmatrix} 2 & 4 & -\lambda \\ 4 & \lambda & 2 \\ \lambda & 2 & 2 \end{vmatrix} = 0$$

$$2(2\lambda - 4) - 4(8 - 2\lambda) - \lambda(8 - \lambda^2) = 0$$
$$\lambda^3 + 4\lambda - 40 = 0$$

Here the roots of the above equation are

$$\lambda = 3, -1.5 \pm i3.3$$

And, the above equation is $f(\lambda)$,

$$f(\lambda) = \lambda^3 + 4\lambda - 40$$

Differentiating the above equation with respect to λ,

$$f'(\lambda) = 3\lambda^2 + 4$$
$$f'(\lambda) > 0$$

Hence, it has only one real value of λ.

65. Correct Response : (d)

Explanation :

Consider the properties of matrices,

$$A^{-1} = \frac{1}{|A|} \cdot \text{adj}(A)$$

$$\text{adj}(A) = |A|\, A^{-1} \qquad \qquad \text{...(1)}$$

Also, $\quad |\text{adj}(A)| = |A|^{n-1} = |A|^2 \qquad \text{...(2)}$

From equation (1) and (2) we get,

$$\text{adj}(\text{adj}(A)) = |A|^2\, (\text{adj}(A))^{-1}$$

So, (a), (b) and (c) are correct option and option (d) occurs only when $|A| = 1$.

Hence, the question is asking for the relation which is not always true, so option (d) is correct.

66. Correct Response : (a)

Explanation :

The characteristic matrix is,

$$|A - \lambda I| = \begin{vmatrix} 2 - \lambda & -3 \\ -4 & 1 - \lambda \end{vmatrix}$$

$$= (2 - 2\lambda - \lambda + \lambda^2) - 12$$
$$= \lambda^2 - 3\lambda - 10$$

The matrix A satisfies the characteristic equation.

$$A^2 - 3A - 10I = 0$$
$$A^2 - 3A = 10I$$
$$3A^2 - 9A = 30I$$
$$3A^2 + 12A = 30I + 21A$$

Substitute the value of matrix.

$$3A^2 + 12A = \begin{bmatrix} 30 & 0 \\ 0 & 30 \end{bmatrix} + \begin{bmatrix} 42 & -63 \\ -84 & 21 \end{bmatrix}$$

$$= \begin{bmatrix} 72 & -63 \\ -84 & 51 \end{bmatrix}$$

$$\text{adj}(3A^2 + 12A) = \begin{bmatrix} 51 & 63 \\ 84 & 72 \end{bmatrix}$$

67. Correct Response : (c)

Explanation :

The solution of the linear equations for no solution condition is,

$$\begin{vmatrix} 1 & 1 & 1 \\ 1 & a & 1 \\ a & b & 1 \end{vmatrix} = 0$$

$$-(1 - a)^2 = 0$$
$$a = 1$$

To have no solution, the equations $x + y + z = 1$ and $ax + by + z = 0$ should be parallel.

Hence,

$$\frac{1}{a} = \frac{1}{b}$$

$$b = 1$$

$\therefore$ It is a singleton solution with coordinates $(1, 1)$.

68. Correct Response : (a, b)

Explanation :

The square of a matrix cannot be negative. Let A be the square matrix then $A = B^2 = $ positive

$$B = \begin{vmatrix} 1 & 0 & 0 \\ 0 & 1 & 0 \\ 0 & 0 & -1 \end{vmatrix}$$

$$= 1\,((-1) \times (-1))$$
$$= -1$$

69. Correct Response : (1)

Explanation :

For infinitely many solutions :

$$D = 0$$

$$\begin{vmatrix} 1 & \alpha & \alpha^2 \\ \alpha & 1 & \alpha \\ \alpha^2 & \alpha & 1 \end{vmatrix} = 0$$

$$1(1 - \alpha^2) - \alpha(\alpha - \alpha^3) + \alpha^2(\alpha^2 - \alpha^2) = 0$$
$$1(1 - \alpha^2) - \alpha^2(1 - \alpha^2) = 0$$
$$\alpha = \pm 1$$

For $\alpha = 1$,

$$x + y + z = 1$$
$$x + y + z = -1$$
$$x + y + z = 1$$

Two planes are same and one plane is parallel. Therefore, there is no solution.

For $\alpha = -1$, there are infinitely many solutions.

$$x - y + z = 1$$
$$-x + y - z = -1$$
$$x - y + z = 1$$

Therefore, the value is calculated as :

$$1 + \alpha + \alpha^2 = 1 - 1 + (-1)^2$$
$$= 1$$

70. Correct Response : (c)

Explanation :

Given that the condition for the distinct real roots is,

$$\begin{vmatrix} \cos x & \sin x & \sin x \\ \sin x & \cos x & \sin x \\ \sin x & \sin x & \cos x \end{vmatrix} = 0$$

Simplify the matrix by row column method,
Apply $R_1 \to R_1 + R_2 + R_3$

$$\begin{vmatrix} \cos x + 2\sin x & \cos x + 2\sin x & \cos x + 2\sin x \\ \sin x & \cos x & \sin x \\ \sin x & \sin x & \cos x \end{vmatrix} = 0$$

Take out $(\cos x + 2 \sin x)$ common from the first row (R_1).

$$(\cos x + 2\sin x)\begin{vmatrix} 1 & 1 & 1 \\ \sin x & \cos x & \sin x \\ \sin x & \sin x & \cos x \end{vmatrix} = 0$$

Apply $C_1 \to C_1 - C_3$ to make two zeros in the first column and then expand,

$$(\cos x + 2\sin x)\begin{vmatrix} 0 & 1 & 1 \\ 0 & \cos x & \sin x \\ \sin x - \cos x & \sin x & \cos x \end{vmatrix} = 0$$

$$(\cos x + 2\sin x)\big((\sin x - \cos x)(\sin x - \cos x)\big)$$
$$= 0$$

$(\cos x + 2 \sin x)(\sin x - \cos x)^2 = 0$

Further, simplify the above equation :

For $(\cos x + 2 \sin x) = 0$,

$$(\cos x + 2 \sin x) = 0$$
$$\cos x = -2 \sin x$$
$$\tan x = \frac{-1}{2}$$

$$x = \tan^{-1}\left(\frac{-1}{2}\right)$$

And,

For $(\sin x - \cos x)^2 = 0$,

$$\sin x = \cos x$$
$$\tan x = 1$$
$$x = \frac{\pi}{4}$$

Hence, it has two solutions.

71. Correct Response : (*)

Explanation :

Simplify the given equation is,

$$\begin{vmatrix} x & x^2 & 1+x^3 \\ 2x & 4x^2 & 1+8x^3 \\ 3x & 9x^2 & 1+27x^3 \end{vmatrix} = 10$$

$$\begin{vmatrix} x & x^2 & 1 \\ 2x & 4x^2 & 1 \\ 3x & 9x^2 & 1 \end{vmatrix} + \begin{vmatrix} x & x^2 & x^3 \\ 2x & 4x^2 & 8x^3 \\ 3x & 9x^2 & 27x^3 \end{vmatrix} = 10$$

$$\left(x \times x^2\right)\begin{vmatrix} 1 & 1 & 1 \\ 2 & 4 & 1 \\ 3 & 9 & 1 \end{vmatrix} + \left(x \times x^2 \times x^3\right)\begin{vmatrix} 1 & 1 & 1 \\ 2 & 4 & 8 \\ 3 & 9 & 27 \end{vmatrix} = 10$$

$$x^3\begin{vmatrix} 1 & 1 & 1 \\ 2 & 4 & 1 \\ 3 & 9 & 1 \end{vmatrix} + \left(2 \times 3 \times x^6\right)\begin{vmatrix} 1 & 1 & 1 \\ 1 & 2 & 4 \\ 1 & 3 & 9 \end{vmatrix} = 10$$

Further, simplify the given expression,
Apply the row column substitution,

$$C_2 \to C_2 - C_1, \; C_3 \to C_3 - C_1$$

$$x^3\begin{vmatrix} 1 & 0 & 0 \\ 2 & 2 & -1 \\ 3 & 6 & -2 \end{vmatrix} + \left(6x^6\right)\begin{vmatrix} 1 & 0 & 0 \\ 1 & 1 & 3 \\ 1 & 2 & 8 \end{vmatrix} = 10$$

$$2x^3 + 12x^6 = 10$$
$$6x^6 + x^3 = 5$$

Consider, $\qquad x^3 = t$

Then, $\quad 6t^2 + t - 5 = 0$

$$t = -1, \, t = \frac{5}{6}$$

Hence, the value of x is,

$$x = -1, \, x = \left(\frac{5}{6}\right)^{\frac{1}{3}}$$

72. Correct Response : (b, c)

Explanation :

From the given expression,

$$PQ = kI$$
$$Q = kP^{-1}$$

The value of the inverse of P is,

$$P^{-1} = \frac{\text{adj}(P)}{\det(P)}$$

$$= \frac{\begin{bmatrix} 5\alpha & 10 & -\alpha \\ 3\alpha & 6 & -(3\alpha+4) \\ -10 & 12 & 2 \end{bmatrix}}{\begin{vmatrix} 5\alpha & 10 & -\alpha \\ 3\alpha & 6 & -(3\alpha+4) \\ -10 & 12 & 2 \end{vmatrix}}$$

$$= \begin{bmatrix} 5\alpha & 10 & -\alpha \\ 3\alpha & 6 & -(3\alpha+4) \\ -10 & 12 & 2 \end{bmatrix}$$
$$\overline{\qquad 20+12\alpha \qquad}$$

From the given relation,

$$q_{23} = \frac{-k}{8}$$

$$\frac{k(-3\alpha-4)}{20+12\alpha} = \frac{-k}{8}$$

$$\alpha = -1$$

Now find the value of the determinant of the P,

$$|P| = \begin{vmatrix} 5\alpha & 10 & -\alpha \\ 3\alpha & 6 & -(3\alpha+4) \\ -10 & 12 & 2 \end{vmatrix}$$

$$= 20 + 12\alpha \qquad [\because \alpha = -1]$$
$$= 20 - 12$$
$$= 8$$

And the given relation of the determinant of Q is,

$$|Q| = \frac{k^2}{2}$$

$$|kP^{-1}| = \frac{k^2}{2}$$

$$\frac{k^3}{|P|} = \frac{k^2}{2}$$

$$k = 4$$

(b) The required value is,
$$4\alpha - k + 8 = 4(-1) - 4 + 8$$
$$= 0$$

Hence, option (b) is correct.

(c) The required value is,
$$\det(P\,adj(Q)) = |P||Q|^2$$
$$= 8 \times (8)^2$$
$$= 2^3 \times 2^6$$
$$= 2^9$$

Hence, option (c) is correct.

73. Correct Response : (d)

Explanation :

The given matrix is,

$$P = \begin{bmatrix} \dfrac{\sqrt{3}}{2} & \dfrac{1}{2} \\ \dfrac{-1}{2} & \dfrac{\sqrt{3}}{2} \end{bmatrix}$$

According to the property of matrices :
$$PP^T = P^TP$$

The matrix PP^T is,

$$PP^T = \begin{bmatrix} \dfrac{\sqrt{3}}{2} & \dfrac{1}{2} \\ \dfrac{-1}{2} & \dfrac{\sqrt{3}}{2} \end{bmatrix}\begin{bmatrix} \dfrac{\sqrt{3}}{2} & \dfrac{-1}{2} \\ \dfrac{1}{2} & \dfrac{\sqrt{3}}{2} \end{bmatrix}$$

$$= \begin{bmatrix} 1 & 0 \\ 0 & 1 \end{bmatrix}$$

$$= P^TP = \begin{bmatrix} 1 & 0 \\ 0 & 1 \end{bmatrix}$$

Now,
$$P^TQ^{2015}P = P^TPAP^TPAP^T \ldots\ldots PAP^T \ldots\ldots$$
$$2015 \text{ times} = A^{2015} \qquad (\because Q = PAP^T)$$

Then,
$$A^2 - 2A + 1 = 0$$
$$A^n = nA - (n-1)I$$
$$A^{2015} = 2015\begin{bmatrix} 1 & 1 \\ 0 & 1 \end{bmatrix} - 2014\begin{bmatrix} 1 & 0 \\ 0 & 1 \end{bmatrix}$$

$$= \begin{bmatrix} 1 & 2015 \\ 0 & 1 \end{bmatrix}$$

74. Correct Response : (d)

Explanation :

Simplify the given condition,
$$AA^T = 9I$$

$$\begin{bmatrix} 1 & 2 & 2 \\ 2 & 1 & -2 \\ a & 2 & b \end{bmatrix}\begin{bmatrix} 1 & 2 & a \\ 2 & 1 & 2 \\ 2 & -2 & b \end{bmatrix} = \begin{bmatrix} 9 & 0 & 0 \\ 0 & 9 & 0 \\ 0 & 0 & 9 \end{bmatrix}$$

$$\begin{bmatrix} 9 & 0 & a+4+2b \\ 0 & 9 & 2a+2-2b \\ a+4+2b & 2a+2-2b & a^2+4+b^2 \end{bmatrix} = \begin{bmatrix} 9 & 0 & 0 \\ 0 & 9 & 0 \\ 0 & 0 & 9 \end{bmatrix}$$

From above matrix equation,
$$a+4+2b = 0$$
$$a = -4 - 2b$$

And,
$$2a + 2 - 2b = 0$$
$$2(-4-2b) + 2 - 2b = 0$$
$$b = -1$$

The value of a is,
$$a = -4 - 2(-1)$$
$$= -2$$

75. Correct Response : (c)

Explanation :

The given linear equations are,
$$(2-\lambda)x_1 - 2x_2 + x_3 = 0$$
$$2x_1 - (3+\lambda)x_2 + 2x_3 = 0$$
$$-x_1 + 2x_2 - \lambda x_3 = 0$$

The condition for the non trivial solution is,
$$\Delta = 0$$

$$\begin{vmatrix} 2-\lambda & -2 & 1 \\ 2 & -3-\lambda & 2 \\ -1 & 2 & -\lambda \end{vmatrix} = 0$$

$(2-\lambda)\{3\lambda + \lambda^2 - 4\} + 2\{-2\lambda + 2\} + 1\{4 - 3 - \lambda\} = 0$

$(6\lambda + 2\lambda^2 - 8 - 3\lambda^2 - \lambda^3 + 4\lambda - 4\lambda + 4 + 1 - \lambda) = 0$

Simplify the above equation.
$$\lambda^3 + \lambda^2 - 5\lambda + 3 = 0$$
$$(\lambda - 1)(\lambda + 3)(\lambda - 1) = 0$$

The values of l are,
$$\lambda = 1, -3$$

76. Correct Response : (a)

Explanation :

Simplify the given expression.
$$|5 \cdot \mathrm{adj} A| = 5$$

$$\left[\begin{array}{l} \because |k\,\mathrm{adj}A| = k^n |A|^{n-1} \\ \text{here } n \text{ is order of the matrix} \end{array} \right]$$

$$(5)^3 |A|^2 = 5$$

$$|A| = \pm \frac{1}{5}$$

77. Correct Response : (b)

Explanation :

The given expression is,

$$\begin{vmatrix} x^2 + x & x+1 & x-2 \\ 2x^2 + 3x - 1 & 3x & 3x-3 \\ x^2 + 2x + 3 & 2x-1 & 2x-1 \end{vmatrix} = ax - 12$$

Substitute $x = -1$ in the above expression.

$$\begin{vmatrix} 0 & 0 & -3 \\ -2 & -3 & -6 \\ 2 & -3 & -3 \end{vmatrix} = -a - 12$$

$$-36 = -a - 12$$
$$a = 24$$

78. Correct Response : (a)

Explanation :

The given expression is,

$$\begin{vmatrix} 3 & 1+f(1) & 1+f(2) \\ 1+f(1) & 1+f(2) & 1+f(3) \\ 1+f(2) & 1+f(3) & 1+f(4) \end{vmatrix}$$
$$= K(1-\alpha)^2 (1-\beta)^2 (\alpha-\beta)^2$$

Simplify the given expression,

$$\begin{vmatrix} 3 & 1+f(1) & 1+f(2) \\ 1+f(1) & 1+f(2) & 1+f(3) \\ 1+f(2) & 1+f(3) & 1+f(4) \end{vmatrix}$$
$$= K(1-\alpha)^2 (1-\beta)^2 (\alpha-\beta)^2$$

$$\begin{vmatrix} 1+1+1 & 1+\alpha+\beta & 1+\alpha^2+\beta^2 \\ 1+\alpha+\beta & 1+\alpha^2+\beta^2 & 1+\alpha^3+\beta^3 \\ 1+\alpha^2+\beta^2 & 1+\alpha^3+\beta^3 & 1+\alpha^4+\beta^4 \end{vmatrix}$$
$$= K(1-\alpha)^2 (1-\beta)^2 (\alpha-\beta)^2$$

$$\begin{vmatrix} 1 & 1 & 1 \\ \alpha & \beta & 1 \\ \alpha^2 & \beta^2 & 1 \end{vmatrix} \begin{vmatrix} 1 & \alpha & \alpha^2 \\ 1 & \beta & \beta^2 \\ 1 & 1 & 1 \end{vmatrix}$$
$$= K(1-\alpha)^2 (1-\beta)^2 (\alpha-\beta)^2$$

Further, simplify the above expression,

$$\left\{ \begin{array}{l} 1(\beta - \beta^2) - 1(\alpha - \alpha^2) \\ + 1(\alpha\beta^2 - \beta\alpha^2) \end{array} \right\} \left\{ \begin{array}{l} 1(\beta - \beta^2) - \alpha(1 - \beta^2) \\ + \alpha^2(1-\beta) \end{array} \right\}$$

$$= K \left\{ \begin{array}{l} (1-\alpha)^2 \\ (1-\beta)^2 (\alpha-\beta)^2 \end{array} \right\}$$

$$1 \left\{ \begin{array}{l} (1-\alpha)^2 \\ (1-\beta)^2 (\alpha-\beta)^2 \end{array} \right\} = K \left\{ \begin{array}{l} (1-\alpha)^2 \\ (1-\beta)^2 (\alpha-\beta)^2 \end{array} \right\}$$

$$K = 1$$

79. Correct Response : (d)

Explanation :

Calculate the required value,

$$BB' = (A^{-1} \cdot A')(A^{-1} \cdot A')'$$
$$= A^{-1} \cdot A'A (A^{-1})'$$
$$= (A^{-1} \cdot A) \cdot A' \cdot (A^{-1})'$$
$$= I(A^{-1} A)'$$

Further, simplify the above value,

$$BB' = I.I$$
$$= I$$

80. Correct Response : (a, b)

Explanation :

(a)

The given relation between the matrix is,

$$M^2 = N^4$$
$$(M + N^2)(M - N^2) = 0 \qquad \qquad ...(1)$$

Case (1) : If $\quad |M + N^2| = 0$

Multiply M on both side of the above expression,

$$|M^2 + MN^2| = 0$$

Case (2) if $\quad |M + N^2| \neq 0$

The determinants of $M + N^2$ is invertible from equation (1),

$$(M - N^2)(M + N^2)(M + N^2)^{-1} = 0$$

From the above relation,

$$M - N^2 = 0 \qquad [\because M \neq N^2]$$

The above relation is wrong.

(b) Multiply on M both side of the equation (1),

$$M(M + N^2)(M - N^2) = 0$$
$$(M^2 + MN^2)(M - N^2) = 0$$

Substitute U for $(M - N^2)$ in the abvqe expression.

$$U(M^2 + MN^2) = 0$$

The non-zero value of U such that $U(M^2 + MN^2)$ is zero matrix.

81. Correct Response : (c, d)

Explanation :

Consider the matrix M,

$$M = \begin{bmatrix} a & b \\ b & c \end{bmatrix}$$

Consider the option (a),

$$\begin{bmatrix} a \\ b \end{bmatrix} = \begin{bmatrix} b \\ c \end{bmatrix}$$

From relation of above matrix,

$$a = b$$
$$b = c$$

Let, $\qquad c = \alpha$

Substitute the value in the matrix M,

$$M = \begin{bmatrix} \alpha & \alpha \\ \alpha & \alpha \end{bmatrix}$$

The determinants of the martix M,

$$|M| = 0$$

Hence, the martix is non invertible.

Consider the option (b),

$$[b \quad c] = [a \quad b]$$

From relation of above matrix,

$$a = b$$
$$b = c$$

Let $\qquad c = \alpha$

The determinants of the matrix M,

$$|M| = 0$$

Hence, the martix is non invertible.

Consider the option (c),

$$M = \begin{bmatrix} a & 0 \\ 0 & c \end{bmatrix}$$

The determinants of the above matrix is,

$$|M| = ac \qquad [\because ac \neq 0]$$

Hence, the martix M is invertible.

Consider the option (d),

$$M = \begin{bmatrix} a & b \\ b & c \end{bmatrix}$$

The determinants of the above matrix is,

$$|M| = ac - b^2 \qquad [\because ac - b^2 \neq 0]$$

Hence, the matrix M is invertible.

82. Correct Response : (c)

Explanation :

Apply the first row transformation by gauss elimination $R_2 \rightarrow R_2 - R_3$ and $R_1 \rightarrow R_1 - R_3$.

$$\begin{vmatrix} \lambda(2a-\lambda) & \lambda(2b-\lambda) & \lambda(2c-\lambda) \\ 4a\lambda & 4b\lambda & 4c\lambda \\ (a-\lambda)^2 & (b-\lambda)^2 & (c-\lambda)^2 \end{vmatrix}$$

$$= k\lambda \begin{vmatrix} a^2 & b^2 & c^2 \\ a & b & c \\ 1 & 1 & 1 \end{vmatrix}$$

Apply the second row tansformation by gauss elimination $R_3 \rightarrow R_3 + R_1$ and $R_1 \rightarrow R_1 - \dfrac{1}{2} R_2$.

$$\begin{vmatrix} -\lambda^2 & -\lambda^2 & -\lambda^2 \\ 4a\lambda & 4b\lambda & 4c\lambda \\ a^2 & b^2 & c^2 \end{vmatrix} = k\lambda \begin{vmatrix} a^2 & b^2 & c^2 \\ a & b & c \\ 1 & 1 & 1 \end{vmatrix}$$

$$-4\lambda^3 \begin{vmatrix} 1 & 1 & 1 \\ a & b & c \\ a^2 & b^2 & c^2 \end{vmatrix} = k\lambda \begin{vmatrix} a^2 & b^2 & c^2 \\ a & b & c \\ 1 & 1 & 1 \end{vmatrix}$$

$$4\lambda^3 \begin{vmatrix} a^2 & b^2 & c^2 \\ a & b & c \\ 1 & 1 & 1 \end{vmatrix} = k\lambda \begin{vmatrix} a^2 & b^2 & c^2 \\ a & b & c \\ 1 & 1 & 1 \end{vmatrix}$$

$$k = 4\lambda^2$$

83. Correct Response : (a)

Explanation :

The multiplication of AB is,

$$AB = \begin{bmatrix} 6 \\ 8 \end{bmatrix}$$

$$\begin{bmatrix} 1 & 2 & x \\ 3 & -1 & 2 \end{bmatrix} \begin{bmatrix} y \\ x \\ 1 \end{bmatrix} = \begin{bmatrix} 6 \\ 8 \end{bmatrix}$$

$$\begin{bmatrix} y + 2x + x \\ 3y - x + 2 \end{bmatrix} = \begin{bmatrix} 6 \\ 8 \end{bmatrix}$$

Solve the above matrix for first equation.

$$y + 2x + x = 6$$
$$3x + y = 6 \qquad \qquad ...(1)$$

Solve the above matrix for second equation.

$$3y - x + 2 = 8$$
$$3y - x = 6 \qquad \qquad ...(2)$$

Solve the above two equations.

$$3x + y = 3y - x$$
$$4x = 2y$$
$$y = 2x$$

84. Correct Response : (b)

Explanation :

The condition for the non-trivial solution is,

$$\Delta = 0$$

Substitute the value from the given equations,

$$\begin{vmatrix} 1-a & 1 & 1 \\ 1 & 1-b & 1 \\ 1 & 1 & 1-c \end{vmatrix} = 0$$

$$R_1 \to R_1 - R_3$$

$$\begin{vmatrix} -a & 0 & c \\ 1 & 1-b & 1 \\ 1 & 1 & 1-c \end{vmatrix} = 0$$

$$\Rightarrow -a\{(1-b)(1-c)-1\} + c\{1-(1-b)\} = 0$$

Further, simplify the above expression,

$$ab + ac + bc = abc$$

85. Correct Response : (a)

Explanation :

Simplify the given expression,

$$\det[(1+B)^{50} - 50B]$$

$$= \det\left[1 + 50B + \frac{50 \times 49}{2!}B^2 + \dots - 50B\right]$$

$$= \det\left[1 + B^2\left\{\frac{50 \times 49}{2!} + \frac{50 \times 49 \times 48}{3!}B + \dots\right\}\right]$$

Since, $B^2 = 0$

$$= \det\left[1 + 0\left\{\frac{50 \times 49}{2!} + \frac{50 \times 49 \times 48}{3!}B + \dots\right\}\right]$$

$$= 1$$

86. Correct Response : (b)

Explanation :

Since, A is symmetric and B is skew symmetric matrices.

Hence, $\qquad A = A^T$

and, $\qquad B = -B^T$

Let $P = AB - BA$. Then,

$$P^T = (AB - BA)^T$$

$$= (AB)^T - (BA)^T$$

$$= B^T A^T - A^T B^T$$

$$= -BA + AB$$

Simplify the above eqution.

$$P^T = AB - BA$$

$$= P$$

So $AB - BA$ is symmetric.

87. Correct Response : (d)

Explanation :

The given matrix is,

$$\Delta_r = \begin{vmatrix} r & 2r-1 & 3r-2 \\ \dfrac{n}{2} & n-1 & a \\ \dfrac{1}{2}n(n-1) & (n-1)^2 & \dfrac{1}{2}(3n+4)(n-1) \end{vmatrix}$$

Simplify the above equation for the value of $\sum\limits_{r=1}^{n-1} \Delta_r$.

$$\sum_{r=1}^{n-1} \Delta_r = \begin{vmatrix} \sum\limits_{r=1}^{n-1} r & \sum\limits_{r=1}^{n-1} 2r-1 & \sum\limits_{r=1}^{n-1} 3r-2 \\ \dfrac{n}{2} & n-1 & a \\ \dfrac{1}{2}n(n-1) & (n-1)^2 & \dfrac{1}{2}(3n+4)(n-1) \end{vmatrix}$$

$$\sum_{r=1}^{n-1} \Delta_r =$$

$$\begin{vmatrix} (1+2+\dots+(n-1)) & (n-1)^2 & (1+4+\dots+(3n-5)) \\ \dfrac{n}{2} & n-1 & a \\ \dfrac{1}{2}n(n-1) & (n-1)^2 & \dfrac{1}{2}(3n+4)(n-1) \end{vmatrix}$$

$$\sum_{r=1}^{n-1} \Delta_r = \begin{vmatrix} \dfrac{1}{2}n(n-1) & (n-1)^2 & \dfrac{1}{2}(3n+4)(n-1) \\ \dfrac{n}{2} & n-1 & a \\ \dfrac{1}{2}n(n-1) & (n-1)^2 & \dfrac{1}{2}(3n+4)(n-1) \end{vmatrix}$$

Since, R_1 and R_3 are identical.

Hence, $\sum\limits_{r=1}^{n-1} \Delta_r = 0$ is independent of both a and n.

88. Correct Response : (a)

Explanation :

The properties of the matrix,

$$AA^{-1} = I \qquad\qquad \dots(1)$$

The given relation of the matrix is as shown below,

$$A\begin{bmatrix} 1 & 2 & 3 \\ 0 & 2 & 3 \\ 0 & 1 & 1 \end{bmatrix} = \begin{bmatrix} 0 & 0 & 1 \\ 1 & 0 & 0 \\ 0 & 1 & 0 \end{bmatrix}$$

Applying column transformation and try to make RHS as identity matrix.

$$A\begin{bmatrix} 3 & 2 & 1 \\ 3 & 2 & 0 \\ 1 & 1 & 0 \end{bmatrix} = \begin{bmatrix} 1 & 0 & 0 \\ 0 & 0 & 1 \\ 0 & 1 & 0 \end{bmatrix} \qquad [\because C_1 \leftrightarrow C_3]$$

$$A\begin{bmatrix} 3 & 1 & 2 \\ 3 & 0 & 2 \\ 1 & 0 & 1 \end{bmatrix} = \begin{bmatrix} 1 & 0 & 0 \\ 0 & 1 & 0 \\ 0 & 0 & 1 \end{bmatrix} \qquad [\because C_2 \leftrightarrow C_3]...(2)$$

Compare equation (1) and (2) for A^{-1}.

$$A^{-1} = \begin{bmatrix} 3 & 1 & 2 \\ 3 & 0 & 2 \\ 1 & 0 & 1 \end{bmatrix}$$

89. Correct Response : (d)

Explanation :

Consider the polynomial $P_i^{(x)}$ of degree 2,

$$p_i = a_i x^2 + b_i x + c_i \qquad [\because a_i \neq 0, b_i, c_i \in R]$$

The matrix of the polynomial is given as,

$$A(x) = \begin{bmatrix} a_1 x^2 + b_1 x + c_1 & 2a_1 x + b_1 & 2a_1 \\ a_2 x^2 + b_2 x + c_2 & 2a_2 x + b_2 & 2a_2 \\ a_3 x^2 + b_3 x + c_3 & 2a_3 x + b_3 & 2a_3 \end{bmatrix}$$

Applying the column transformation,

$$C_2 \to C_2 - xC_3$$

Applying column transformation,

$$C_1 \to C_1 - xC_2 + \frac{x^2}{2} C_3$$

The matrix after applying the column transformation,

$$A(x) = \begin{bmatrix} c_1 & b_1 & 2a_1 \\ c_2 & b_2 & 2a_2 \\ c_3 & b_3 & 2a_3 \end{bmatrix}$$

From the above matrix, it is clear that the determinant of the matrix is constant.

$$|B| = |A^T||A|$$
$$= |A|^2$$

Hence, the matrix $|B|$ is independent from n.

90. Correct Response : (c, d)

Explanation :

[a]

It is given that M is symmetric matrix then,

$$(N^T M N)^T = N^T M^T (N^T)^T$$
$$= N^T M^T N$$
$$= N^T M N$$

If M is skew symmetric matrix then,

$$(N^T M N)^T = N^T M^T (N^T)^T$$
$$= N^T M^T N$$
$$= - N^T M N$$

Thus, $N^T MN$ is symmetric or non-symmetric as M is sysmmetric or skew-symmetric

[b]

It is given that M and N are symmetric matrices, then

$$(MN - NM)^T = N^T M^T - M^T N^T$$
$$= NM - MN$$
$$= - (MN - NM)$$

It can be seen that $(MN - NM)$ is skew symmetric.

[c]

It is given that M and N are symmetric matrices, then

$$(MN)^T = N^T M^T$$
$$= NM \neq MN$$

Thus, MN is not symmetric.

[d]

For invertible matrices M and N is,

$$(adj\ M)\ (adj\ N) = adj\ (NM) \neq adj\ (MN)$$

91. Correct Respsonse : (4)

Explanation :

The determinant A of given matrix A is,

$$|A| = (2k-1)\left(-1+4k^2\right) - 2\sqrt{k}\left(-2\sqrt{k} - 4k\sqrt{k}\right)$$
$$+ 2\sqrt{k}\left(4k\sqrt{k} + 2\sqrt{k}\right)$$

$$= (2k+1)^3$$

The determinant of given matrix B is,

$$|B| = 0$$

The given equation is,

$$\det(adjA) + \det(adjB) = 10^6$$
$$|A|^{n-1} + |B|^{n-1} = 10^6$$

$$\begin{bmatrix} \because |adj\ A| = |A|^{n-1} \\ n \text{ is order of the matrix} \end{bmatrix}$$

$$\left|(2k+1)^3\right|^{3-1} + 0 = 10^6$$

$$(2k+1)^6 = 10^6$$

Further, simplify the above expression,

$$(2k+1) = 10$$

$$k = \frac{9}{2}$$

$$k = 4.5$$

$$[k] = 4$$

92. Correct Response : (a)-(r), (b)-(q), (s), (c)-(r), (s), (d)-(p), (r)

Explanation :

(a)

Consider the given function,

$$y = \frac{x^2 + 2x + 4}{x + 2}$$

Differentiate given function with respect to x.

$$\frac{dy}{dx} = \frac{(x + 2)(2x + 2) - (x^2 + 2x + 4)}{(x + 2)^2}$$

The minimum value is 2 at $x = 0$.

(b)

Let, A and B be 3×3 matrices and given,

$$(A + B)(A - B) = (A - B)(A + B)$$
$$A^2 + BA - AB - B^2 = A^2 - BA + AB - B^2$$
$$AB = BA$$

It is also given that,

$$(AB)^t = (-1)^k AB$$
$$B^t A^t = (-1)^k AB$$
$$- BA = (-1)^k BA$$

The possible values of k are 1 and 3.

(c)

Solve for given value of a.

$$a = \log_3 \log_2 2$$
$$3^{-a} = \log_2 3$$

Now,

$$1 < 2^{-k + \log_2 3} < 2$$
$$1 < 3 \cdot 2^{-k} < 2$$
$$\frac{1}{3} < 2^{-k} < \frac{2}{3}$$
$$\frac{3}{2} < 2^k < 3$$

Thus, value of k is 1 which is less than 2 and 3.

(d)

Solve given equation,

$$\sin \theta = \cos \phi$$
$$\cos\left(\frac{\pi}{2} - \theta\right) = \cos \phi$$
$$\frac{\pi}{2} - \theta = 2n\pi \pm \phi$$
$$\theta \pm \varphi - \frac{\pi}{2} = - 2n\phi$$

on further simplifying

$$\frac{1}{\pi}\left(\theta \pm \phi - \frac{\pi}{2}\right) = - 2n$$

Thus, possible values are 0 and 2.

93. Correct Response : (a)

Explanation :

The determinant for given system of equations is,

$$\Delta = \begin{vmatrix} 1 & -2 & 3 \\ -1 & 1 & -2 \\ 1 & -3 & 4 \end{vmatrix}$$
$$= 0$$

The number of solutions of system of equations depends on Δx, Δy, Δz.

The value of Δx for $k = 3$.

$$\Delta x = \begin{vmatrix} -1 & -2 & 3 \\ k & 1 & -2 \\ 1 & -3 & 4 \end{vmatrix}$$
$$\Delta x = 0$$

The value of Δy for $k = 3$.

$$\Delta y = \begin{vmatrix} 1 & -1 & 3 \\ -1 & k & -2 \\ 1 & 1 & 4 \end{vmatrix}$$
$$\Delta y = 0$$

The value of Δz for $k = 3$.

$$\Delta z = \begin{vmatrix} 1 & -2 & -1 \\ -1 & 1 & k \\ 1 & -3 & 1 \end{vmatrix}$$
$$\Delta z = 0$$

Thus, given system of equations has no solution for $k \neq 3$. Both statements are true and statement-2 is correct explanation for statement-1.

94. Correct Response : (a)

Explanation :

Let, matrix U_1 be $\begin{bmatrix} x_1 \\ y_1 \\ z_1 \end{bmatrix}$.

$$\begin{bmatrix} 1 & 0 & 0 \\ 2 & 1 & 0 \\ 3 & 2 & 1 \end{bmatrix}\begin{bmatrix} x_1 \\ y_1 \\ z_1 \end{bmatrix} = \begin{bmatrix} 1 \\ 0 \\ 0 \end{bmatrix}$$

$$\begin{bmatrix} x_1 \\ y_1 \\ z_1 \end{bmatrix} = \begin{bmatrix} 1 \\ -2 \\ 1 \end{bmatrix}$$

Similarly, the values of $U_2 = \begin{bmatrix} 2 \\ -1 \\ -4 \end{bmatrix}$ and $U_3 = \begin{bmatrix} 2 \\ -1 \\ -3 \end{bmatrix}$.

So,

$$U = \begin{bmatrix} 1 & 2 & 2 \\ -2 & -1 & -1 \\ 1 & -4 & -3 \end{bmatrix}$$

Now, determinant of matrix U is,

$$|U| = \begin{vmatrix} 1 & 2 & 2 \\ -2 & -1 & -1 \\ 1 & -4 & -3 \end{vmatrix}$$

$$= 1\,(3-4) - 2(6+1) + 2\,(8+1)$$

$$= 3$$

Therfore, $|U| = 3$.

95. Correct Response : (b)

Explanation :

The matrix U is,

$$U = \begin{bmatrix} 1 & 2 & 2 \\ -2 & -1 & -1 \\ 1 & -4 & -3 \end{bmatrix}$$

The adjoint of matrix is,

$$\text{adj}\,U = \begin{bmatrix} -1 & -2 & 0 \\ -7 & -5 & -3 \\ 9 & 6 & 3 \end{bmatrix}$$

The inverse of matrix U is,

$$U^{-1} = \frac{\text{adj}\,U}{|U|}$$

$$= \frac{1}{3} \begin{bmatrix} -1 & -2 & 0 \\ -7 & -5 & -3 \\ 9 & 6 & 3 \end{bmatrix}$$

Sum of elements of inverse matrix is,

$$\text{Sum} = -\frac{1}{3} - \frac{2}{3} - \frac{7}{3} - \frac{5}{3} - 1 + 3 + 2 + 1$$

$$= 0$$

96. Correct Response : (a)

Explanation :

The required value is calculated as,

$$\begin{bmatrix} 3 & 2 & 0 \end{bmatrix} U \begin{bmatrix} 3 \\ 2 \\ 0 \end{bmatrix} = \begin{bmatrix} 3 & 2 & 0 \end{bmatrix} \begin{bmatrix} 1 & 0 & 0 \\ 0 & -11 & 19 \\ 0 & -38 & 46 \end{bmatrix} \begin{bmatrix} 3 \\ 2 \\ 0 \end{bmatrix}$$

$$= \begin{bmatrix} -1 & 4 & 4 \end{bmatrix} \begin{bmatrix} 3 \\ 2 \\ 0 \end{bmatrix}$$

$$= -3 + 8$$

$$= 5$$

97. Correct Response : (c)

Explanation :

The given equation is,

$$A^{-1} = \frac{1}{6}\left(A^2 + cA + dI\right)$$

$$AA^{-1} = \frac{1}{6}\left(A^3 + cA^2 + dA\right)$$

$$6I = A^3 + cA^2 + dA \qquad \text{...(1)}$$

The value of A^2 is,

$$A^2 = \begin{bmatrix} 1 & 0 & 0 \\ 0 & 1 & 1 \\ 0 & -2 & 4 \end{bmatrix}\begin{bmatrix} 1 & 0 & 0 \\ 0 & 1 & 1 \\ 0 & -2 & 4 \end{bmatrix}$$

$$= \begin{bmatrix} 1 & 0 & 0 \\ 0 & -1 & 5 \\ 0 & -10 & 14 \end{bmatrix}$$

The value of A^3 is,

$$A^3 = A^2 A$$

$$= \begin{bmatrix} 1 & 0 & 0 \\ 0 & -1 & 5 \\ 0 & -10 & 14 \end{bmatrix}\begin{bmatrix} 1 & 0 & 0 \\ 0 & 1 & 1 \\ 0 & -2 & 4 \end{bmatrix}$$

$$= \begin{bmatrix} 1 & 0 & 0 \\ 0 & -11 & 19 \\ 0 & -38 & 46 \end{bmatrix}$$

Substitute the values in equation (1).

$$\begin{bmatrix} 6 & 0 & 0 \\ 0 & 6 & 0 \\ 0 & 0 & 6 \end{bmatrix}$$

$$= \begin{bmatrix} 1+c+d & 0 & 0 \\ 0 & -11-c+d & 19+5c+d \\ 0 & -38-10c-2d & 46+14c+4d \end{bmatrix}$$

Compare elements on both sides and solve.

$$1 + c + d = 6$$

$$d = 5 - c$$

Substitute value in $-11 - c + d = 6.$

$$-11 - c + 5 - c = 6$$

$$-2c = 6 + 6$$

$$c = -6$$

Therefore, $c = -6$ and $d = 11$.

98. Correct Response : (d)

Explanation :

The given system of equations has no solution.
So,

$$\Delta = 0$$

$$\begin{vmatrix} 2 & -1 & -2 \\ 1 & -2 & 1 \\ 1 & 1 & \lambda \end{vmatrix} = 0$$

$$2(-2\lambda - 1) + 1(\lambda - 1) - 2(3) = 0$$

$$\lambda = -3$$

99. Correct Response : (c)

Explanation :

It is given that $|A^3| = 125$.

So, $\qquad |A|^3 = 125$

$$A = 5$$

Solve given matrix.

$$\begin{vmatrix} \alpha & 2 \\ 2 & \alpha \end{vmatrix} = 5$$

$$\alpha^2 - 4 = 5$$

$$\alpha^2 = 9$$

$$\alpha = \pm 3.$$

100. Explanation :

Solve the left hand side.

$$\det(M - I) = \det(M - I)\det(M^T)$$
$$\det(M - I) = \det(MM^T - M^T)$$
$$\det(M - I) = \det(I - M^T)$$
$$\det(M - I) = -\det(M - I)^T$$

Solve on further.

$$\det(M - I) = -\det(M - I)$$
$$2\det(M - I) = 0$$
$$\det(M - I) = 0$$

Hence, it is proved that $\det(M - I) = 0$.

101. Explanation :

Given that $AX = U$ has infinitely many solutions.

$$|A| = 0$$

$$\begin{vmatrix} a & 0 & 1 \\ 1 & c & b \\ 1 & d & b \end{vmatrix} = 0$$

$$ab = 1 \text{ or } c = d$$

Solve $|A_1| = 0$.

$$\begin{vmatrix} a & 0 & f \\ 1 & c & g \\ 1 & d & h \end{vmatrix} = 0$$

$$g = h$$

Solve $|A_2| = 0$.

$$\begin{vmatrix} a & f & 1 \\ 1 & g & b \\ 1 & h & b \end{vmatrix} = 0$$

$$g = h$$

Solve $|A_3| = 0$.

$$\begin{vmatrix} f & 0 & 1 \\ g & c & b \\ h & d & b \end{vmatrix} = 0$$

$$c = d, g = h$$

Now, $|B|$ is,

$$|B| = \begin{vmatrix} a & 1 & 1 \\ 0 & d & c \\ f & g & h \end{vmatrix}$$

$$= 0 \qquad (\text{as } c = d, g = h)$$

The value of $|B_1|$ is,

$$|B_1| = \begin{vmatrix} a^2 & 1 & 1 \\ 0 & d & c \\ 0 & g & h \end{vmatrix}$$

$$= 0$$

The value of $|B_2|$ is,

$$|B_2| = \begin{vmatrix} a^2 & a^2 & 1 \\ 0 & 0 & c \\ f & 0 & h \end{vmatrix}$$

$$= a^2 cf$$
$$= a^2 df$$

The value of $|B_3|$ is,

$$|B_3| = \begin{vmatrix} a & 1 & a^2 \\ 0 & d & 0 \\ f & g & 0 \end{vmatrix}$$

$$= -a^2 df$$

Since, $adf \neq 0$ then $|B_2| = |B_3| \neq 0$. Thus, no solution exists.

102. Correct Response : (d)

Explanation :

Solve for value of α.

$$\begin{bmatrix} \alpha & 0 \\ 1 & 1 \end{bmatrix}\begin{bmatrix} \alpha & 0 \\ 1 & 1 \end{bmatrix} = \begin{bmatrix} 1 & 0 \\ 5 & 1 \end{bmatrix}$$

$$\begin{bmatrix} \alpha^2 & 0 \\ \alpha + 1 & 1 \end{bmatrix} = \begin{bmatrix} 1 & 0 \\ 5 & 1 \end{bmatrix}$$

Compare elements on both sides,

$$\alpha^2 = 1, \ \alpha + 1 = 5$$

Therefore, α have no real values.

103. Correct Response : (a)

Explanation :

If the given system of equations have infinite solutions, then

$$\begin{vmatrix} 1 & a & 0 \\ 0 & 1 & a \\ a & 0 & 1 \end{vmatrix} = 0$$

$$1 + a\,(a^2) = 0$$
$$a^3 = -1$$
$$\therefore \qquad a = -1$$

104. Correct Response : (4 or 2)

Explanation :

Solve $A^T A = I$.

$$(\det A)\,(\det A^T) = 1$$
$$(\det A)^2 = 1$$
$$(\det A) = \pm 1$$

Now, determinant of A is,

$$\det A = \begin{vmatrix} a & b & c \\ b & c & a \\ c & a & b \end{vmatrix}$$

$$= -(a^3 + b^3 + c^3 - 3abc)$$
$$= -(a^3 + b^3 + c^3) + 3 \ [\because abc = 1]$$

Substitute value of det A and solve.

$$-(a^3 + b^3 + c^3) + 3 = \pm 1$$
$$a^3 + b^3 + c^3 = 4 \text{ or } 2$$

105. Correct Response : (b)

Explanation :

Solve the given determinant.

$$\Delta = \begin{vmatrix} 1 & 1 & 1 \\ 1 & -1-\omega^2 & \omega^2 \\ 1 & \omega^2 & \omega^4 \end{vmatrix}$$

It is known that $1 + \omega + \omega^2 = 0$. So, $C_1 \rightarrow C_1 + C_2 + C_3$

$$\Delta = \begin{vmatrix} 3 & 0 & 0 \\ 1 & \omega & \omega^2 \\ 1 & \omega^2 & \omega \end{vmatrix}$$

$$= 3\,(\omega^2 - \omega^4)$$
$$= 3\,(\omega^2 - \omega)$$
$$= 3\omega\,(\omega - 1)$$

●●

Permutations and Combinations

QUESTIONS

1. The number of words, with or without meaning, that can be formed by taking 4 letters at a time from the letters of the word 'SYLLABUS' such that two letters are distinct and two letters are alike, is .... **[2020, Main]**

2. Two families with three members each and one family with four members are to be seated in a row. In how many ways can they be seated so that the same family members are not separated ? **[2020, Main]**
   - (a) $2!3!4!$
   - (b) $(3!)^3.(4!)$
   - (c) $(3!)^2.(4!)$
   - (d) $3!.(4!)^3$

3. The number of words (with or without meaning) that can be formed from all the letters of the word "LETTER" in which vowels never come together is .... **[2020, Main]**

4. The value of $\displaystyle\sum_{r=0}^{20} {}^{50-r}C_6$ is equal to :

   [2020, Main]
   - (a) ${}^{51}C_7 + {}^{30}C_7$
   - (b) ${}^{51}C_7 - {}^{30}C_7$
   - (c) ${}^{50}C_7 - {}^{30}C_7$
   - (d) ${}^{50}C_6 - {}^{30}C_6$

5. A test consists of 6 multiple choice questions, each having 4 alternative answers of which only one is correct. The number of ways, in which a candidate answers all six questions such that exactly four of the answers are correct, is .... **[2020, Main]**

6. The value of $(2.{}^1P_0 - 3.{}^2P_1 + 4.{}^3P_2 - ...$ upto 51th term$) + (1! - 2! + 3! - ...$ upto to 51th term$)$ is equal to : **[2020, Main]**
   - (a) $1 + (51)!$
   - (b) $1 - 51(51)!$
   - (c) $1 + (52)!$
   - (d) 1

7. There are 3 sections in a question paper and each section contains 5 questions. A candidate has to answer a total of 5 questions, choosing at least one question from each section. Then the number of ways, in which the candidate can choose the questions, is : **[2020, Main]**
   - (a) 1500
   - (b) 2255
   - (c) 3000
   - (d) 2250

8. For non-negative integers s and r, let

$$\binom{s}{r} = \begin{cases} \dfrac{s!}{r!(s-r)!} & \text{if } r \leq s, \\ 0 & \text{if } r > s \end{cases}$$

For positive integers m and n, let

$$(m, n)\sum_{p=0}^{m+n} \frac{f(m, n, p)}{\dbinom{n+p}{p}}$$

where for any non-negative integer p,

$$f(m, n, p) = \sum_{i=0}^{p} \binom{m}{i}\binom{n+i}{p}\binom{p+n}{p-i}$$

Then which of the following statements is/are TRUE ? **[2020, Advanced]**
   - (a) $(m, n) = g(n, m)$ for all positive integers m, n
   - (b) $(m, n + 1) = g(m + 1, n)$ for all positive integers m, n
   - (c) $(2m, 2n) = 2g(m, n)$ for all positive integers m, n
   - (d) $(2m, 2n) = [g(m, n)]^2$ for all positive integers m, n

9. An engineer is required to visit a factory for exactly four days during the first 15 days for every month and it is mandatory that no two visits take place on consecutive days. Then the number of all possible ways in which such visists to the factory can be made by the engineer during 1 – 15 June 2021 is ....

   [2020, Advanced]

10. In a hotel, four rooms are available. Six persons are to be accomodated in these four rooms in such a way that each of these rooms contains at least one person and at most two persons. Then the number of all possible ways in which this can be done is .... **[2020, Advanced]**

11. The total number of 3-digit numbes, whose sum of digits is 10, is .... **[2020, Main]**

12. If the letters of the word 'MOTHER' be permuted and all the words so formed (with or without meaning) be listed as in a dictionary, then the position of the word 'MOTHER' is ....

    [2020, Main]

13. Let $n > 2$ be an integer. Suppose that there are n Metro stations in a city located along a circular path. Each pair only. Further, each pair of nearest stations is connected by blue line, whereas all remaining pairs of stations are connected by red line. If the number of red lines is 99 times the number of blue lines, then the value of n is : **[2020, Main]**

(a) 199 (b) 101
(c) 201 (d) 200

14. If a, b and c are the greatest value of $^{19}C_p$, $^{20}C_p$ and $^{21}C_r$ respectively, then **[2020, Main]**

(a) $\dfrac{a}{11} = \dfrac{b}{22} = \dfrac{c}{21}$ (b) $\dfrac{a}{10} = \dfrac{b}{11} = \dfrac{c}{21}$

(c) $\dfrac{a}{10} = \dfrac{b}{11} = \dfrac{c}{42}$ (d) $\dfrac{a}{11} = \dfrac{b}{22} = \dfrac{c}{42}$

15. Total number of 6 digits numbers in which only and all the five digits 1, 3, 5, 7 and 9 appear is : **[2020, Main]**

(a) $\dfrac{5}{2}(6!)$ (b) 5^6

(c) $\dfrac{1}{2}(6!)$ (d) $6!$

16. The number of ordered pairs (r, k) for which $6.^{35}C_r = (k^2 - 3).^{36}C_{r+1}$, when k is an integar, is : **[2020, Main]**

(a) 3 (b) 2
(c) 4 (d) 6

17. An urn contains 5 red marbles, 4 black marbles and 3 white marbles. Then the number of ways in which 4 marbles can be drawn so that at the most three of them are red is .... **[2020, Main]**

18. The number of 4 letter words (with or without meaning) that can be formed from the eleven letters of the word 'EXAMINATION' is .... **[2020, Main]**

19. If 10 different balls are to be placed in 4 distinct boxes at random, then the probability that two of these boxes contain exactly 2 and 3 balls is : **[2020, Main]**

(a) $\dfrac{945}{2^{11}}$ (b) $\dfrac{965}{2^{11}}$

(c) $\dfrac{945}{2^{10}}$ (d) $\dfrac{965}{2^{10}}$

20. If $C_r \equiv {}^{25}C_r$ and
$$C_0 + 5.C_1 + 9.C_2 + ... + (101).C_{25} = 225.k,$$
then k is equal to .... **[2020, Main]**

21. If the number of five digit numbers with distinct digits and 2 at the 10th place is $336\,k$, then k is equal to : **[2020, Main]**

(a) 8 (b) 6
(c) 7 (d) 7

22. The number of 6 digit numbers that can be formed using the digits 0, 1, 2, 5, 7 and 9 which are divisible by 11 and no digit is repeated, is : **[2019, Main]**

(a) 72 (b) 60
(c) 48 (d) 36

23. Suppose that 20 pillars of the same height have been erected along the boundary of a circular stadium. If the top of each pillar has been connected by beams with the top of all its non-adjacent pillars, then the total number of beams is : **[2019, Main]**

(a) 170 (b) 180
(c) 210 (d) 190

24. A committee of 11 members is to be formed from 8 males and 5 females. If m is the number of ways the committee is formed with at least 6 males and n is the number of ways the committee is formed with at least 3 females, then : **[2019, Main]**

(a) $m + n = 68$ (b) $m = n = 78$
(c) $n = m - 8$ (d) $m = n = 68$

25. All possible numbers are formed using the digits 1, 1, 2, 2, 2, 2, 3, 4, 4 taken all at a time. The number of such numbers in which the odd digits occupy even places is : **[2019, Main]**

(a) 180 (b) 175
(c) 160 (d) 162

26. The number of four-digit numbers strictly greater than 4321 that can be formed using the digits 0, 1, 2, 3, 4, 5 (repetition of digits is allowed) is : **[2019, Main]**

(a) 288 (b) 360
(c) 306 (d) 310

27. The numbers of ways of choosing 10 objects out of 31 objects of which 10 are identical and the remaining 21 are distinct, is : **[2019, Main]**

(a) $2^{20} - 1$ (b) 2^{21}
(c) 2^{20} (d) $2^{20} + 1$

28. If $^{20}C_1 + (2^2)\,^{20}C_2 + (3^2)\,^{20}C_3 + ... + (20^2)\,^{20}C_{20} = A(2^{\beta})$, then the ordered pair (A, β) is equal to : **[2019, Main]**

(a) $(420, 19)$ (b) $(420, 18)$
(c) $(380, 18)$ (d) $(380, 9)$

29. A group of students comprises of 5 boys and n girls. If the number of ways, in which a team of 3 students can randomly selected from this group, such that there is at least one boy and at least one girl in each team, is 1750, then n is equal to : **[2019, Main]**

(a) 28 (b) 27
(c) 25 (d) 24

30. n-digit numbers are formed using only three digits 2, 5 and 7. The smallest value of n for which 900 such distinct numbers can be formed, is : **[2018, Main]**
    (a) 6
    (b) 7
    (c) 8
    (d) 9

31. The number of numbers between 2,000 and 5,000 that can be formed with the digits 0, 1, 2, 3, 4 (repetition of digits is not allowed) and are multiple of 3 is : **[2018, Main]**
    (a) 24
    (b) 30
    (c) 36
    (d) 48

32. The number of 5 digit numbers which are divisible by 4, with digits from the set $\{1, 2, 3, 4, 5\}$ and the repetition of digits is allowed, is : **[2018, Advanced]**

33. A debate club consists of 6 girls and 4 boys. A team of 4 members is to be selected from this club including the selection of a captain (from among these 4 members) for the team. If the team has to include at most one day, then the number of ways of selecting the team is : **[2018, Advanced]**
    (a) 380
    (b) 320
    (c) 260
    (d) 95

34. From 6 different novels and 3 different dictionaries, novels and 1 dictionary are to be selected and arranged in a row on a shelf so that the dictionary is always in the middle. The number of such arrangements is : **[2018, Main]**
    (a) at least 1000
    (b) less than 500
    (c) at least 500 but less than 750
    (d) at least 750 but less than 1000

35. If all the words, with or without meaning, are written using the letters of the word QUEEN and are arranged as in English dictionary, then the position of the word QUEEN is : **[2017, Main]**
    (a) 44th
    (b) 45th
    (c) 46th
    (d) 47th

36. A man X has 7 friends, 4 of them are ladies and 3 are men. His wife Y also has 7 friends, 3 of them are ladies and 4 are men. Assume X and Y have no common friends. Then the total number of ways in which X and Y together can throw a party inviting 3 ladies and 3 men, so that 3 friends of each of X and Y are in this party, is : **[2017, Main]**
    (a) 468
    (b) 469
    (c) 484
    (d) 485

37. The value of
$$(^{21}C_1 - {}^{10}C_1) + {}^{21}C_2 - {}^{10}C_2) + ({}^{21}C_3 - {}^{10}C_3)$$
$$+ ({}^{21}C_4 - {}^{10}C_4) + ... + ({}^{21}C_{10} - {}^{10}C_{10}) \text{ is :}$$
[2017, Main]

(a) $2^{21} - 2^{10}$
(b) $2^{20} - 2^9$
(c) $2^{20} - 2^{10}$
(d) $2^{21} - 2^{11}$

38. The number of ways in which 5 boys and 3 girls can be seated on a round table if a particular boy B_1 and a particular girl G_1 never sit adjacent to each other, is : **[2017, Main]**
    (a) $5 \times 6!$
    (b) $6 \times 6!$
    (c) $7!$
    (d) $5 \times 7!$

39. If $\dfrac{^{n+2}C_6}{^{n-2}P_2} = 11$, then n satisfies the equation : **[2016, Main]**

(a) $n^2 + 3n - 108 = 0$
(b) $n^2 + 5n - 84 = 0$
(c) $n^2 + 2n - 80 = 0$
(d) $n^2 + n - 110 = 0$

40. If the four letter words (need not be meaningful) are to be formed using the letters from the word "MEDITERRANEAN" such that the first letter is R and the fourth letter is E, then the total number of all such words is : **[2016, Main]**

(a) $\dfrac{11!}{(2!)^3}$
(b) 110
(c) 56
(d) 59

41. The value of $\displaystyle\sum_{r=1}^{15} r^2 \left(\dfrac{^{15}C_r}{^{15}C_{r-1}} \right)$ is equal to : **[2016, Main]**

(a) 560
(b) 680
(c) 1240
(d) 1085

42. If the number of terms in the expansion of $\left(1 - \dfrac{2}{x} + \dfrac{4}{x^2}\right)^n$, $x \neq 0$, is 28, then the sum of the coefficients of all the terms in this expansion, is : **[2016, Main]**

(a) 64
(b) 2187
(c) 243
(d) 729

43. If all the words (with or without meaning) having five letters, formed using the letters of the word SMALL and arranged as in a dictionary; then the position of the word SMALL is : **[2016, Advanced]**

(a) 46th
(b) 59th
(c) 52nd
(d) 58th

44. let A and B be two sets containing four and two elements respectively. Then the number of subsets of the set A × B, each having at least three elements is : **[2015, Main]**
    (a) 219
    (b) 256
    (c) 275
    (d) 510

45. Let A = $\{x_1, x_2, ..., x_7\}$ and B = $\{y_1, y_2, y_3\}$ be two sets containing seven and three distinct elements

respectively. Then the total number of functions $f : A \rightarrow B$ that are onto, if there exist exactly three elements x in A such that $f(x) = y_2$, is equal to :

[2015, Main]

(a) $14.\,^7C_2$ (b) $16.\,^7C_3$
(c) $12.\,^7C_2$ (d) $14.\,^7C_3$

46. The number of integers greater than 6,000 then can be formed, using the digits 3, 5, 6, 7 and 8, without repetition, is : **[2015, Main]**

(a) 216 (b) 192
(c) 120 (d) 72

47. Let n be the number of ways in which 5 boys and 5 girls can stand in a queue in such a way that all the girls stand consecutively in the queue. Let m be the number of ways in which 5 boys and 5 girls can stand in a queue in such a way that exactly four girls stand consecutively in the queue. Then the value of $\dfrac{m}{n}$ is : **[2015, Advanced]**

48. Two women and some men participated in a chess tournament in which every participant played two games with each of the other participants. If the number of games that the men played bgetween themselves exceeds the number of games that the men played with the women by 66, then the number of men who participated in the tournament lies in the interval :

[2014, Main]

(a) [8, 9] (b) [10, 12]
(c) [11, 13] (d) [14, 17]

49. An eight digit number divisible by 9 is to be formed using digits form 0 to 9 without repeating the digits. The number of ways in which this can be done is : **[2014, Main]**

(a) 72 (7 !) (b) 18 (7 !)
(c) 40 (7 !) (d) 36 (7 !)

50. Six cards and six envelopes are numbered 1, 2, 3, 4, 5, 6 and cards are to be placed in envelopes so that each envelope contains exactly one card and no card is placed in the envelope bearing the same number and moreover the card numbered 1 is always placed in envelope numbered 2. Then the number of ways it can be done is :

[2014, Advanced]

(a) 264 (b) 265
(c) 53 (d) 67

51. 8-digit numbers are formed using the digits 1, 1, 2, 2, 2, 2, 3, 4, 4. The number of such numbers in which the odd digits do not occupy odd places, is : **[2014, Main]**

(a) 160 (b) 120
(c) 60 (d) 48

52. If $\left(2+\dfrac{x}{3}\right)^{55}$ is expanded in the ascending powers of x and the coefficients of powers of x in two consecutive terms of the expansion are equal, then these terms are : **[2014, Main]**

(a) 7th and 8th (b) 8th and 9th
(c) 28th and 29th (d) 27th and 28th

53. The sum of the digits in the unit's place of all the 4-digit numbers formed by using the numbers 3, 4, 5 and 6, without repetition, is :

[2014, Main]

(a) 432 (b) 108
(c) 36 (d) 18

54. Let $n_1 < n_2 < n_3 < n_4 < n_5$ be positive integers such that $n_1 + n_2 + n_3 + n_4 + n_5 = 20$. Then the number or such distinct arrangements $(n_1, n_2, n_3, n_4, n_5)$ is : **[2014, Advanced]**

55. A pack contains n cards numbered from 1 to n. Two consecutive numbered cards are removed from the pack and the sum of the numbers on the remaining cards is 1224. If the smaller of the numbers on the removed cards is k, then $k - 20 =$ **[2013, Advanced]**

56. Consider the set of eight vectors

$$V = \{a\,\hat{i} + b\,\hat{j} + c\,\hat{k} : a, b, c \in \{-1, 1\}\}$$

Three non-coplanar vectors can be chosen from V in $2p$ ways. Then p is : **[2013, Advanced]**

57. Let a_n denote the number of all n-digit positives integers formed by the digits 0, 1 are both such that no conscutive digits in them are 0. Let b_n = the number of such n-digit intergers ending with digit 1 and C_n = the number of such n-digit integers ending with digit 0. **[2012, Advanced]**

(a) 7 (b) 8
(c) 9 (d) 11

58. A rectangle with sides 2m − 1 and 2n − 1 is divided into squares of unit length by drawing parallel lines are shown in the digram, then the number of rectangles possible with odd side lengths is :

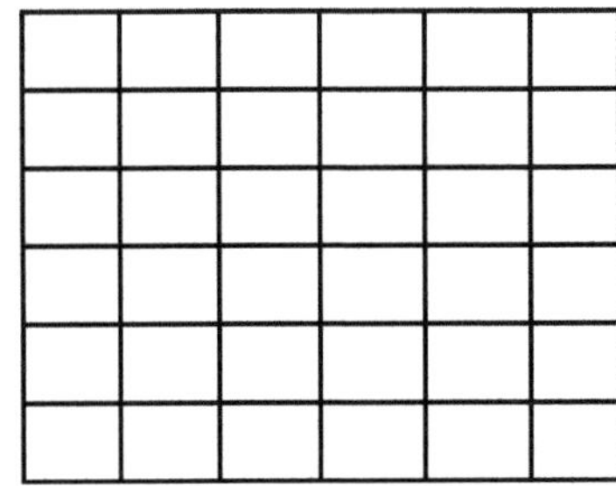

(a) $(m + n + 1)^2$ (b) $_4m + n + 1$
(c) $m^2 n^2$ (d) $mn(m + 1)(n + 1)$

59. Consider all possible permutations of the letters of the word ENDEANOEL.

Match the Statements/Expressions in Column I with the Statements/Expressions in Column II and indicate your answer by darkening the appropriate bubbles in the 4 × 4 matrix given in the ORS. **[2008, Advanced]**

Column I	Column II
(a) The number of permutations containing the word ENDEA is	**(p)** 5!
(b) The number of permutations in which the latter E occurs in the first and the last positions is	**(q)** 2 × 5!
(c) The number of permutations in which none of the letters D, L, N occurs in the last five positions is	**(r)** 7 × 5!
(d) The number of permutations in which the letters A, E, O occur only in odd positions is	**(s)** 21 × 5!

60. The letters of the word COCHIN are permuted and all the permutations are arranged in an alphabetical order as in an English dictionary. The number of words that appear before the word COCHIN is : **[2007, Advanced]**

(a) 360 **(b)** 192

(c) 96 **(d)** 48

61. If total number of runs scored in n matches is $\left(\dfrac{n+1}{4}\right)(2^{n+1} - n - 2)$ where $n > 1$, and the runs scored in the kth match are given by k. 2n+1 –k, where $1 \le k \le n$. Find n. **[2006, Main]**

62. If $^{n-1}C_r = (k^2 - 3)\,^nC_{r+1}$, then $k \in$ **[2005, Main]**

(a) $(-\infty, -2]$ **(b)** $[2, \infty)$

(c) $[-\sqrt{3}, \sqrt{3}]$ **(d)** $(-\sqrt{3}, 2]$

63. Using permutation or otherwise prove that $\dfrac{n^2!}{(n!)^n}$ is an integer, where n is a positive integer. **[2005, Main]**

64. The number of arrangements of the letters of the word BANANA in which the two N's do not appear adjacently is : **[2002, Main]**

(a) 40 **(b)** 60

(c) 80 **(d)** 100

65. The sum $\displaystyle\sum_{i=0}^{m}\binom{10}{i}\binom{20}{m-i}$ (where $\binom{p}{q} = 0.$ If $(p < q)$ is maximum when m is : **[2002, Main]**

(a) 5 **(b)** 10

(c) 15 **(d)** 20

ANSWER KEY

1. (240)	**2.** (c)	**3.** (120)	**4.** (c)	**5.** (135)	**6.** (a)	**7.** (d)	**8.** (a,b,d)	**9.** (495)
10. (1080)	**11.** (54)	**12.** (309)	**13.** (c)	**14.** (d)	**15.** (a)	**16.** (c)	**17.** (490.00)	**18.** (2454.00)
19. (c)	**20.** (51)	**21.** (a)	**22.** (b)	**23.** (a)	**24.** (b)	**25.** (a)	**26.** (d)	**27.** (c)	**28.** (b)
29. (c)	**30.** (b)	**31.** (b)	**32.** (625)	**33.** (a)	**34.** (a)	**35.** (c)	**36.** (d)	**37.** (c)	**38.** (a)
39. (a)	**40.** (a)	**41.** (b)	**42.** (d)	**43.** (d)	**44.** (a)	**45.** (d)	**46.** (b)	**47.** (5)	**48.** (b)
49. (d)	**50.** (c)	**51.** (b)	**52.** (b)	**53.** (b)	**54.** (7)	**55.** (5)	**56.** (5)	**57.** (b)	**58.** (c)
59. [(a)-(p), (b)-(s), (c)-(q), (d)-(g)]			**60.** (c)	**61.** (7)	**62.** (d)	**63.** (*)	**64.** (a)	**65.** (c)

ANSWERS WITH EXPLANATIONS

1. Correct Response : (240)

S^2YL^2ABU

ABCC type words

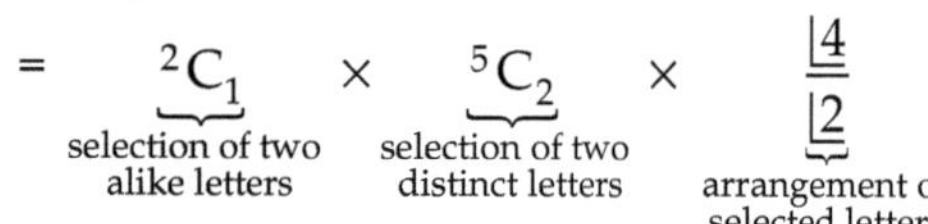

$$= \underbrace{^2C_1}_{\substack{\text{selection of two}\\\text{alike letters}}} \times \underbrace{^5C_2}_{\substack{\text{selection of two}\\\text{distinct letters}}} \times \underbrace{\dfrac{\lfloor 4}{\lfloor 2}}_{\substack{\text{arrangement of}\\\text{selected letters}}}$$

= 240.

2. Correct Response : (c)

Total numbers in three families = 3 + 3 + 4 = 10

so total arrangement = 10 !

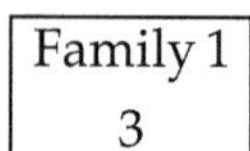

Family 1	Family 2	Family 3
3	3	4

Favourable cases

$$= \underbrace{3!}_{\text{Arrangement of 3 Families}}$$

$$\underbrace{3! \times 3! \times 4!}_{\text{Interval Arrangement of family members}}$$

Number of ways of same family members are together

$$= 3! \times 3! \times 3! \times 4!$$
$$= (3!)^3 \times 4!$$

3. **Correct Response :** (120)

LETTER

vowels = EE, consonant = LTTR

$$\_ L \_ T \_ T \_ R \_$$

$$\frac{4!}{2!} \times {}^5C_2 \times \frac{2!}{2!} = 12 \times 10 = 120.$$

4. **Correct Response :** (c)

$$\sum_{r=0}^{20} {}^{50-r}C_6 = {}^{50}C_6 + {}^{49}C_6 + {}^{48}C_6 + \ldots + {}^{30}C_6$$

$$= {}^{50}C_6 + {}^{49}C_6 + \ldots + {}^{31}C_6$$
$$\qquad + ({}^{30}C_6 + {}^{30}C_7) - {}^{30}C_7$$
$$= {}^{50}C_6 + {}^{49}C_6 + \ldots$$
$$\qquad + ({}^{31}C_6 + {}^{31}C_7) - {}^{30}C_7$$
$$= {}^{50}C_6 + {}^{50}C_7 - {}^{30}C_7$$
$$= {}^{51}C_7 - {}^{30}C_7$$

$${}^nC_r + {}^nC_{r-1} = {}^{n+1}C_r$$

5. **Correct Response :** (135)

$$\text{Ways} = {}^6C_4 \cdot 1^4 \cdot 3^2$$
$$= 15 \times 9$$
$$= 135.$$

6. **Correct Response :** (a)

$$S = (2 \cdot {}^1p_0 - 3 \cdot {}^2p_1 + 4 \cdot {}^3p_2 \ldots \text{upto 51 terms})$$
$$+ (1! + 2! + 3! \ldots \text{upto 51 terms})$$
$$[\because {}^np_{n-1} = n!]$$

$$\therefore \quad S = (2 \times 1! - 3 \times 2! + 4 \times 3! \ldots + 52.51!)$$
$$+ (1! - 2! + 3! \ldots (51)!)$$
$$= (2! - 3! + 4! \ldots + 52!)$$
$$+ (1! - 2! + 3! - 4! + \ldots + (51)!)$$
$$= 1! + 51!.$$

7. **Correct Response :** (d)

A	B	C
5	5	5
1	2	2
2	1	2
2	2	1
1	1	3
1	3	1
3	1	1

Total number of selection

$$= ({}^5C_1 \, {}^5C_2 \, {}^5C_2) \cdot 3 + ({}^5C_1 \, {}^5C_1 \, {}^5C_3) \cdot 3$$
$$= 5 \cdot 10 \cdot 10 \cdot 3 + 5 \cdot 5 \cdot 10 \cdot 3$$
$$= 2250.$$

8. **Correct Response :** (a,b,d)

Solving

$$f(m, n, p) = \sum_{i=0}^{p} {}^mC_i \, {}^{n+i}C_p \cdot {}^{p+n}C_{p-i}$$

$$= {}^mC_i \cdot {}^{n+i}C_p \cdot {}^{p+n}C_{p-i}$$

$$= {}^mC_i \cdot \frac{(n+i)!}{p!(n-p+i)!} \times \frac{(n+p)!}{(p-i)!(n+i)!}$$

$$= {}^mC_i \times \frac{(n+p)!}{p!} \times \frac{1}{(n-p+i)!(p-i)!}$$

$$= {}^mC_i \times \frac{(n+p)!}{p! \, n!} \times \frac{n!}{(n-p+i)!(p-i)!}$$

$$= {}^mC_i \cdot {}^{n+p}C_p \cdot {}^nC_{p-1}$$
$$\{{}^mC_i \cdot {}^nC_{p-i} = {}^{m+n}C_p\}$$

$$f(m, n, p) = {}^{n+p}C_p \cdot {}^{m+n}C_p$$

$$\frac{f(m,n,p)}{{}^{n+p}C_p} = {}^{m+n}C_p$$

Now $\quad g(m, n) = \displaystyle\sum_{p=0}^{m+n} \frac{f(m,n,p)}{{}^{n+p}C_p}$

$$g(m, n) = \sum_{p=0}^{m+n} {}^{m+n}C_p$$

$$g(m, n) = 2^{m+n}$$

(A) $\quad g(m, n) = q(n, m)$

(B) $\quad g(m, n+1) = 2^{m+n+1}$

$$g(m+n, n) = 2^{m+1+n}$$

(D) $\quad g(2m, 2n) = 2^{2m+2n}$
$$= (2^{m+n})^2$$
$$= [g(m, n)]^2.$$

9. **Correct Response :** (495)

Selection of 4 days out of 15 days such that no two of them are consecutive

$$= {}^{15-4+1}C_4 = {}^{12}C_4$$
$$= \frac{12 \times 11 \times 10 \times 9}{4 \times 3 \times 2}$$
$$= 11 \times 5 \times 9 = 495.$$

10. **Correct Response :** (1080)

$$\text{Required ways} = \frac{6!}{2!2!1!2!2!} \times 4! = 1080.$$

11. **Correct Response :** (54)

Let three digit number is xyz

$x + y + z = 10$; $x \geq 1, y \geq 0, z \geq 0$ ....(1)

Let $T = x - 1 \Rightarrow x = T + 1$ where $T \geq 0$

Put in (1)

$T + y + z = 9$; $0 \leq T \leq 8, 0 \leq y, z \leq 9$

No. of non-negative integral solution

$$= {}^{9+3-1}C_{3-1} - 1 \text{ (when } T = 9)$$
$$= 55 - 1 = 54$$

12. **Correct Response :** (309)

MOTHER

(1) $\rightarrow$ E		**(2)** $\rightarrow$ H
(3) $\rightarrow$ M		**(4)** $\rightarrow$ O
(5) $\rightarrow$ R		**(6)** $\rightarrow$ T

So position of word MOTHER in dictionary

$2 \times 5! + 2 \times 4! + 3 \times 3! + 2! + 1$

$= 240 + 48 + 18 + 2 + 1$

$= 309$

13. Correct Response : (c)

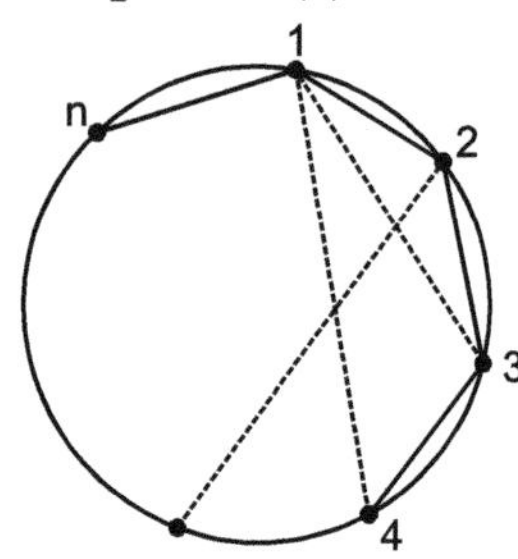

Number of blue lines = Number of sides = n

Number of red lines = Number of diagonals

$$= {}^nC_2 - n$$

$${}^nC_2 - n = 99\,n \Rightarrow \frac{n(n-1)}{2} - n = 99n$$

$$\frac{n-1}{2} - 1 = 99 \Rightarrow n = 201$$

14. Correct Response : (d)

Explanation :

$$a = {}^{19}C_{10},\ b = {}^{20}C_{10}\ \text{and}\ c = {}^{21}C_{10}$$

$$\Rightarrow \quad a = {}^{19}C_9,\ b = 2({}^{19}C_9)\ \text{and}\ c = \frac{21}{11}({}^{20}C_{10})$$

$$\Rightarrow \quad b = 2a\ \text{and}\ c = \frac{21}{11}b = \frac{42a}{11}$$

$$\Rightarrow a : b : c = a : 2a : \frac{42a}{11} = 11 : 22 : 42$$

15. Correct Response : (a)

Explanation :

Total number of 6 digit numbers in which only and all the five digits 1, 3, 5, 7 and 9 is ${}^5C_1 \times \dfrac{6!}{2!}$.

16. Correct Response : (c)

Explanation :

$$6 \times {}^{35}C_r = (k^2 - 3)\, {}^{36}C_{r+1}$$

$$k^2 - 3 > 0 \Rightarrow k^2 > 3$$

$$k^2 - 3 = \frac{6 \times {}^{35}C_r}{{}^{36}C_{r+1}} = \frac{r+1}{6}$$

Possible value of r for integral values of k are

$$r = 5,\ 35$$

Number of ordered pairs are 4, (5, 2), (5, – 2), (35, 3), (35 – 3).

17. Correct Response : (490.00)

Explanation :

The question does not mention that whether same coloured marbles are distinct or identical. So, assuming they are distinct our required answer $= {}^{12}C_4 - {}^5C_4 = 490$

And, if same coloured marbles are identical then required answer $= (2 + 3 + 4 + 4) = 13$

18. Correct Response : (2454.00)

Explanation :

$$N \to 2,\ A \to 2,\ I \to 2,\ E, X, M, T, O \to 1$$

Category	Selection	Arrangement
2 a like of one kind	${}^3C_2 = 3$	$3 \times \dfrac{4!}{2!\,2!} = 18$

and 2 a like of other kind

2 alike and 2 different	${}^3C_1 \times {}^7C_2$	${}^3C_1 \times {}^7C_2 \times \dfrac{4!}{2!} = 756$
All 4 different	${}^8C_4$	${}^8C_4 \times 4! = 1680$
Total		
Ans.		2454

19. Correct Response : (c)

Explanation :

10 different balls in 4 different boxes.

$$\frac{1}{4^{10}}\left(4! \times \frac{10!}{2! \times 3! \times 0! \times 5!} + 4! \times \frac{10!}{2! \times 3! \times 1! \times 4!} \right.$$

$$\left. + 4! \times \frac{10!}{(2!)^2 \times 2! \times (3!)^2 \times 2!} \right)$$

$$= \frac{17 \times 945}{2^{15}}$$

20. Correct Response : (51)

Explanation :

$$S = 1.{}^{25}C_0 + 5.{}^{25}C_1 + 9.{}^{25}C_2 + \dots + (101){}^{25}C_{25}$$

$$S = 101\,{}^{25}C_{25} + 97\,{}^{25}C_1 + \dots + 1\,{}^{25}C_{25}$$

$$2S = (10^2)\,(2^25)$$

$$S = 51\,(2^{25})$$

21. Correct Response : (a)

Explanation :

No. of five digits numbers

$$= \text{No of ways of filling remaning 4 places}$$

$$= 8 \times 8 \times 7 \times 6$$

$$\therefore \quad k = \frac{8 \times 8 \times 7 \times 6}{336} = 8$$

22. Correct Response : (b)

Explanation :

Let the number be $abcdef$.

Sum of given digits is $9 + 7 + 5 + 2 + 1 + 0 = 24$.

Since the number is divisible by 11 therefore,

$$|(a + c + e) - (b + d + f)| = 0$$

The possible ways to write $(a + c + e) - (b + d + f)$ where $(a + c + e) \geq (b + d + f)$ are as follows

$$21 - 3 = 18$$

$$20 - 4 = 16$$

$$19 - 5 = 14$$

$$18 - 6 = 12$$
$$17 - 7 = 10$$
$$16 - 8 = 8$$
$$15 - 9 = 6$$
$$14 - 10 = 4$$
$$13 - 11 = 2$$
$$12 - 12 = 0$$

$a + c + e = 12$ and $b + d + f = 12$

Hence the only possible way is

$\{a, c, e\}$ and $\{b, d, f\} = \{7, 5, 0\}$

Or

$\{a, c, e\}$ and $\{b, d, f\} = \{9, 2, 1\}$

Possible number of ways is

$$2 \times 3! \times 3! - 2! \times 3! = 72 - 12$$
$$= 60$$

23. Correct Response : (a)

Explanation :

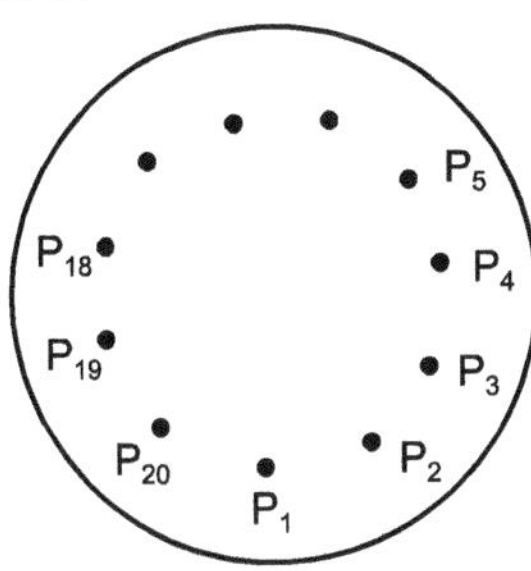

Any two non-adjacent pillars are joined by beams. So, number of beams is equal to number of diagonals which is equal to $^{20}C_2 - 20 = 170$.

24. Correct Response : (b)

Explanation :

At least six males,

M	W
6	5
7	4
8	3

$$m = {}^8C_6 \cdot {}^5C_5 + {}^8C_7 \cdot {}^5C_4 + {}^8C_8 \cdot {}^5C_3$$
$$= 28 + 40 + 10$$
$$= 78$$

At least three females,

M	W
8	3
7	4
6	5

$$m = {}^5C_3 \cdot {}^8C_8 + {}^5C_4 \cdot {}^8C_7 + {}^5C_5 \cdot {}^8C_6$$
$$= 10 + 40 + 28$$
$$= 78$$

$\therefore \qquad m = n = 78$

25. Correct Response : (a)

Explanation :

$$1, 1, 2, 2, 2, 2, 3, 4, 4,$$

Odd numbers occur at even places

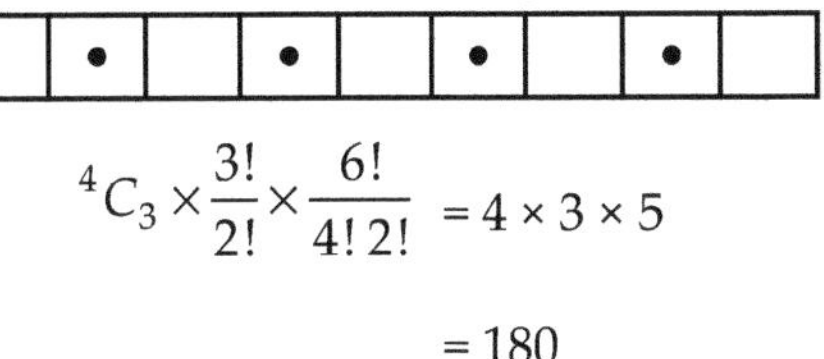

$${}^4C_3 \times \frac{3!}{2!} \times \frac{6!}{4! \, 2!} = 4 \times 3 \times 5$$
$$= 180$$

26. Correct Response : (d)

Explanation :

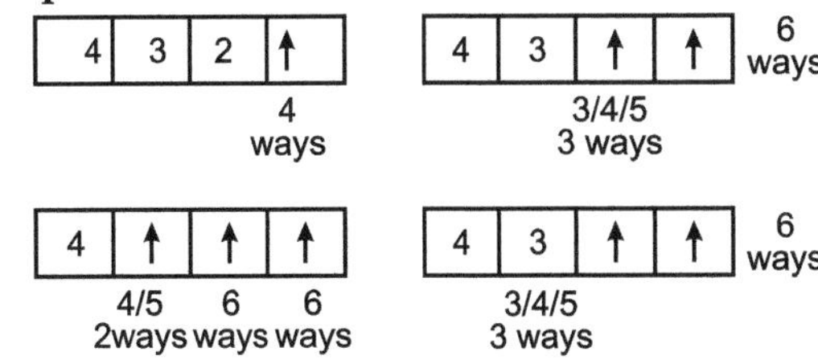

Total ways $= 4 + 18 + 72 + 216 = 94 + 216$
$$= 310$$

27. Correct Response : (c)

Explanation :

The number of ways of choosing are,

$$N = {}^{20}C_0 + {}^{21}C_1 + {}^{21}C_2 + \ldots\ldots\ldots\ldots + {}^{21}C_{10}$$
$$= \frac{2^{21}}{2}$$
$$= 2^{20}$$

28. Correct Response : (b)

Explanation :

The given sequence is represented as,

$$S = \sum_{r=1}^{20} r^2 \, {}^{20}C_{r-1}$$
$$= \sum_{r=1}^{20} r^2 \, {}^{20}C_{r-1}$$
$$= 20 \sum_{r=1}^{20} r \, {}^{19}C_{r-1}$$
$$= 20 \sum_{r=1}^{20} (r-1) \, {}^{19}C_{r-1}$$

Solve further,

$$S = 20 \sum_{r=1}^{20} (r-1) \, {}^{19}C_{r-1} + 20 \sum_{r=1}^{20} {}^{19}C_{r-1}$$
$$= 20 \left(\sum_{r=1}^{20} {}^{18}C_{r-1} \right) + 20(2^{19})$$
$$= (20)(19)(2^{18}) + 20(2^{19})$$
$$= 420(2^{18})$$

29. Correct Response : (c)

Explanation :

For the given condition, there are two ways. First way is to make a team with one boy and two girls and second way is to make a team with two boys and one girl.

The number of ways are,

$$n = (^5C_1)\,(^nC_2) + (^5C_2)\,(^nC_1)$$

$$1750 = (5)\left(\frac{n(n-1)}{2}\right) + 10n$$

$$n^2 + 3n - 700 = 0$$

$$n = 25, -28$$

The number of girls cannot be negative. Therefore, the number of girls are 25.

30. Correct Response : (b)

Explanation :

There are n-digit numbers formed with the help of only three numbers 2, 5 and 7.

To obtain n-digit numbers, the repetition is 3^n.

For value of ($n = 5$).

$$3^n = 3^5 = 243 < 900$$

For value of ($n = 6$).

$$3^n = 3^6 = 729 < 900$$

For value of ($n = 7$),

$$3^n = 3^7 = 2187 > 900$$

It means the smallest value of n for which 900 distinct numbers can be formed is 7.

31. Correct Response : (b)

Explanation :

Number between 2000 and 5000 that can be formed with (0, 1, 2, 3).

The first digit can be only 2 or 3. The remaining 3 digits can be arranged in $3! = 6$ ways, so that makes a total of $6 \times 2 = 12$ numbers with this set.

Number between 2000 and 5000 that can be formed with (0, 2, 3, 4).

The same logic applies : the first digit can only be 2, 3, 4 and there are 6 numbers that can be formed from each of these. That makes of $6 \times 3 = 18$ numbers with this set.

Number of 4 digits number is,

$$2 \times 3! + 3 \times 3! = 30$$

32. Correct Response : 625

Explanation :

In order to obtain a 5 digit number which are divisible by 4, with the digits from the set, the options for the last two digit of the numbers are as (12), (24), (32), (44) and (52).

The total number of five digit number that can be formed is,

$$n = 5 \times 5 \times 5 \times 5$$

$$= 625$$

33. Correct Response : (a)

Explanation :

A debate club consists of 6 girls and 4 boys.

A team of four members is to be selected from the debate club including selection of a captain. If may be a boy or girl.

Case I :

If selecting a team of four members is girls :

The ways of the selection of four girls from the six girls is,

$$^6C_4 = \frac{6\,!}{4\,! \times (6-4)!}$$

$$= 15$$

The ways of the selection of captain from the four girls is,

$$^4C_1 = \frac{4\,!}{1\,! \times (4-1)!}$$

$$= 4$$

The total ways of selecting the team in case I is,

$$15 \times 4 = 60$$

Case II

If selecting a team of three girls and one boy :

The ways of the selection of three girls from the six girls is,

$$^6C_3 = \frac{6\,!}{3\,! \times (6-3)!}$$

$$= 20$$

The ways of the selection of one boy from the four boys is,

$$^4C_1 = 4$$

The ways of the selection of captain from three girls and one boy,

$$^4C_1 = \frac{4\,!}{1\,! \times (4-1)!}$$

$$= 4$$

The total ways of selecting the team in case II is,

$$20 \times 4 \times 4 = 320$$

Hence, the total number of the ways is,

$$60 + 320 = 380$$

34. Correct Response : (a)

Explanation :

Number of ways of selecting 1 dictionary from total 3 dictionaries is $^3C_1$.

Number of ways of selecting 4 novels form total 6 novels is $^6C_4$.

The position of dictionary is fixed. Hence total number of arrangements is,

$$\text{Total arrangements} = {}^6C_4 \times 4! \times {}^3C_1$$
$$= \frac{6!}{(4!)\cdot 2!} \times 4 \times 3 \times 2 \times 3$$
$$= 1080$$

35. Correct Response : (c)

Explanation :

According to dictionary, the word QUEEN is formed by the letters E, E, N, Q, and U.

Consider the sequence of words in dictionary starting with,

For the given words, letter E will come first in dictionary.

$$\text{E}............... = 4!$$
$$= 24$$

Next letter N will come

$$\text{N}............... = \frac{4!}{2!}$$
$$= 12$$

Next letter will be QE

$$\text{QE}............... = 3!$$
$$= 6$$

Next letter will QN

$$\text{QN}............... = \frac{3!}{2!}$$
$$= 3$$

Finally the word QUEEN will come.

$$\text{QUEEN} = 1$$

Total is,

$$24 + 12 + 6 + 3 + 1 = 46^{th}$$

Hence, the position for the word QUEEN will be 46th.

36. Correct Response : (d)

Explanation :

The possible number of ways is,

$$N = C_{mm} + C_{ml} + C_{lm} + C_{ll}$$
$$= ({}^4C_3 \cdot {}^4C_3) + ({}^4C_2 \cdot {}^3C_1)^2 + ({}^4C_1 \cdot {}^3C_2)^2 + ({}^3C_3)^2$$
$$= 16 + 324 + 144 + 1$$
$$= 485$$

37. Correct Response : (c)

Explanation :

The sum of the total positive values is,

$${}^{21}C_1 + {}^{21}C_2 + ... + {}^{21}C_{10}$$

$$= \frac{1}{2}\left\{ {}^{21}C_0 + {}^{21}C_1 + {}^{21}C_2 + ... + {}^{21}C_{21} \right\} - 1$$
$$= 2^{20} - 1$$

The sum of the total negative values is,

$${}^{21}C_1 + {}^{21}C_2 + ... + {}^{21}C_4 = 2^{10} - 1$$

The required sum of the equation is,

$$R = (2^{20} - 1) - (2^{10} - 1)$$
$$= 2^{20} - 2^{10}$$

38. Correct Response : (a)

Explanation :

Four boys and six girls are in a circle. Hence,

$$(6 - 1)! \times \left(\frac{6!}{4! \times 2!}\right) \times 2! = 5! \times \left(\frac{6!}{4!}\right)$$
$$= 5 \times 6!$$

39. Correct Response : (a)

Explanation :

The given expression is,

$$\frac{{}^{n+2}C_6}{{}^{n-2}P_2} = 11$$

Solve the given expression.

$$\frac{{}^{n+2}C_6}{{}^{n-2}P_2} = 11$$

$${}^{n+2}C_6 = 11 \, {}^{n-2}P_2$$

$$\frac{(n+2)!}{6!(n+2-6)!} = 11\left(\frac{(n-2)!}{(n-4)!}\right)$$

$$(n+2)(n+1)n(n-1) = 11(6!)$$

Further solve the above equation.

$$(n+2)(n+1)n(n-1) = 11 \cdot 10 \cdot 9 \cdot 8$$
$$n + 2 = 11$$
$$n = 9$$

From the options, n satisfies the equation $n^2 + 3n - 108 = 0$.

40. Correct Response : (a)

Explanation :

The given word 'MEDITERRANEAN' consists of 13 letters.

The number of the letter is,

$$\text{M} = 1$$
$$\text{E} = 3$$
$$\text{D} = 1$$
$$\text{I} = 1$$
$$\text{and} \qquad \text{T} = 1$$
$$\text{R} = 2$$
$$\text{A} = 2$$
$$\text{N} = 2$$

Here, the number of different letter is 8.

Given, that the position of E and R is fixed.

Therefore, rest of the 11 letters can be arranged in,

$$\frac{11!}{(2!)\times(2!)\times(2!)} = \frac{11!}{(2!)^3}$$

41. Correct Response : (b)

Explanation :

Simplify the given equation :

$$\sum_{r=1}^{15} r^2 \left(\frac{^{15}C_r}{^{15}C_{r-1}}\right) = \sum_{r=1}^{15} r^2 \left(\frac{15-r+1}{r}\right)$$

$$= \sum_{r=1}^{15} r(16-r)$$

$$= 16\left(\frac{15\times16}{2}\right) - \frac{16\times15\times31}{6}$$

$$= \frac{15\times16}{6}(17)$$

$$= 680$$

42. Correct Response : (d)

Explanation :

The total number of non-clubbed terms in the expansion of $(1-a+b)^n$ is given by $^{2n+1}C_0$.

So,

$$^{2n+1}C_0 = 28$$

Simplify the above expression,

$$\frac{(2n+1)!}{(0)!(2n+1+0-1)!} = 28$$

$$\frac{(2n+1)\times(2n)!}{(2n)!} = 28$$

$$2n + 1 = 28$$

$$n = 13.5$$

The value of n is 13.5 which is not possible.

Possible change in the question,

The total number of non-clubbed terms in the expansion of $(1+a+b)^n$ is given by $^{n+2}C_2$.

So,

$$^{n+2}C_2 = 28$$

Simplify the above expression,

$$(n+2)(n+1) = 56$$

$$n = 6$$

So, sum of all the coefficients in the expression of

$\left(1+\dfrac{2}{x}+\dfrac{4}{x^2}\right)^6$ is given by,

$$(1-2+4)^6 = 3^6$$

$$= 729$$

43. Correct Response : (d)

Explanation :

The probability of the words starting with A, L, M is,

$$\frac{4!}{2!}+4!+\frac{4!}{2!} = 48$$

The probability of the words starting with SA, SL is,

$$\frac{3!}{2!}+3! = 9$$

Total words are,

$$48 + 9 = 57$$

Hence, the rank of the word SMALL is 58th.

44. Correct Response : (a)

Explanation :

The number of elements in set A is,

$$n(A) = 4$$

The number of elements in set B is,

$$n(A) = 2$$

The number of elements in set (A × B) is,

$$n(A \times B) = 4 \times 2$$

$$= 8$$

The total number of subsets of (A × B) is,

$$n = 2^8$$

$$= 256$$

The total number of subsets having 0 elements is,

$$^8C_0 = 1$$

The total number of subsets having 1 elements is,

$$^8C_1 = 8$$

The total number of subsets having 2 elements is,

$$^8C_2 = 28$$

Hence, the number of subsets having at least 3 elements,

$$(256 - 1 - 8 - 28) = 219$$

45. Correct Response : (d)

Explanation :

The given two sets of the distinct elements is,

$$A = \{x_1, x_2, ..., x_7\}$$

and

$$B = \{y_1, y_2, y_3\}$$

Selection of three elements in A such that $f(x)$ is,

$$f(x) = y_2$$

$$= {}^7C_3$$

$$= \frac{7!}{3! \times (7-3)!}$$

$$= 35$$

Now, for remaining 4 elements in A we have 2 elements in B.

Hence, the total number of onto function is,

$$^7C_3 \times (2^4 - {}^2C_1 (2-1)^4) = 14 \cdot {}^7C_3$$

46. Correct Response : (b)

Explanation :

Number of integer greater than 6000 may be 4 digit or 5 digit.

Case (I) : When number is of 4 digits,

Number formed by using the given digits which are greater then 6000.

$$C_1 = 3 \times 4 \times 3 \times 2$$
$$= 72$$

Case (II) : When number is of 5 digits,

Number formed by using the given digits which are greater than 6000.

$$C_2 = 5!$$
$$= 120$$

Hence, the total number of ways is

$$n = C_1 + C_2$$
$$= 120 + 72$$
$$= 192$$

47. Correct Response : 5

Explanation :

The number of ways when 5 girls stand together along with 5 boys is,

$$n = 6! \times 5!$$
$$= 720 \times 120$$
$$= 86400$$

and calculate the value of m,

$$m = {}^5C_4 \,(7! - 2 \times 6!) \times 4!$$
$$= 5 \times 3600 \times 24$$
$$= 432000$$

Hence, the required value ratio is,

$$\frac{m}{n} = \frac{432000}{86400}$$
$$= 5$$

48. Correct Response : (b)

Explanation :

Let number of men participated are n and the women are two.

Since each men play with each other the combination will be,

$$^nC_2 = \frac{n!}{2!(n-2)!}$$
$$= \frac{n(n-1)}{2}$$

But there are two games for each them,

$$2 \times {}^nC_2 = 2 \times \frac{n(n-1)}{2}$$
$$= n(n-1)$$

Each man plays with the two women, number of ways would be $2n$.

Given that,

$$2\,({}^nC_2 - 2n) = 66$$
$$n(n-1) - 4n = 66$$

$$n^2 - 5n - 66 = 0$$
$$n = 11, -6$$

Hence, the number of men lies between [10, 12).

49. Correct Response : (d)

Explanation :

Eight digit number divisible by 9, which means the sum of digit is divisible by 9.

Total number formed by 1, 2, 3, 4, 5, 6, 7, 8, is 8 !.

Total number formed by 0, 2, 3, 4, 5, 6, 7, 9, is $7 \times 7!$.

Total number formed by 1, 0, 3, 4, 5, 6, 9, 8 is $7 \times 7!$.

Total number formed by 1, 2, 0, 4, 5, 9, 7, 8 is $7 \times 7!$.

Total number formed by 1, 2, 3, 0, 5, 6, 7, 8 is $7 \times 7!$.

The total number of ways is,

$$8! + 28 \times 7! = 36 \times 7!$$

50. Correct Response : (c)

Explanation :

The arrangement of the cards and the envelopes is given as,

Cards	Envelopes
1	1
2	2
3	3
4	4
5	5
6	6

From the table, if the envelope 2 goes in 1 then the de-arrangement of the four things which can be done by,

$$\text{Number of ways} = 4!\left(\frac{1}{2!} - \frac{1}{3!} + \frac{1}{4!}\right)$$
$$= 9$$

If the envelope 2 does not goes in 1 then the de-arrangement of the five things which can be done by 44 ways.

The total number of the arrangements is given by,

Total number of ways $= 9 + 44$
$$= 53$$

51. Correct Response : (b)

Explanation :

The ways to select 3 odd places out of 4 odd places.

$$n = {}^4C_3 \times \frac{3!}{2!} \times \frac{5!}{3!2!}$$
$$= \frac{4!}{3!(4-3)!} \times \frac{3 \times 2!}{2!} \times \frac{5 \times 4 \times 3!}{3!2!}$$
$$= 4 \times 3 \times \frac{5 \times 4}{2}$$
$$= 120$$

52. Correct Response : (b)

Explanation :

The general term from Binomial theorem is,

$$P(r) = {}^nC_r \cdot p^r \cdot q^{n-r}$$

$$\left(2 + \frac{x}{3}\right)^{55} = {}^{55}C_r \cdot \left(\frac{x}{3}\right)^r \cdot 2^{55-r}$$

Let the coefficients of $T_{r+1} = T_{r+2}$.

$$ {}^{55}C_r \cdot \left(\frac{1}{3}\right)^r \cdot 2^{55-r} = {}^{55}C_{r+1} \cdot \left(\frac{1}{3}\right)^{r+1} \cdot 2^{55-r-1}$$

$$ {}^{55}C_r \cdot \left(\frac{1}{3}\right)^r \cdot 2^{55-r} = {}^{55}C_{r+1} \cdot \left(\frac{1}{3}\right)^{r+1} \cdot 2^{54-r}$$

$$\frac{55!}{(55-r)!\,r!} \cdot 2 = \frac{55!}{(55-(r+1))!\,(r+1)!} \cdot \left(\frac{1}{3}\right)$$

$$r = 7$$

So, the first term is,

$$(r+1)^{th} = (7+1)^{th}$$
$$= 8^{th}$$

and the second term is,

$$(r+2)^{th} = (7+2)^{th}$$
$$= 9^{th}$$

53. Correct Response : (b)

Explanation :

If the unit place is 3 then remaining three palaces can be filled in 3! ways.

Thus 3 appears in unit place in 3! times.

Similarly, each digit appear in unit place 3! times.

Hence, the sum of the digits in units place is,

$$(6+5+4+3)\,(4-1)! = 18 \times 3!$$
$$= 18 \times 6$$
$$= 108$$

54. Correct Response : (7)

Explanation :

Consider the relation between the positive integers as,

$$n_1 \geq 1,\ n_2 \geq 2,\ n_3 \geq 3,\ n_4 \geq 4,\ n_5 \geq 5$$

Consider the relation for the positive integer as,

$$n_1 - 1 = x_1 \geq 0$$
$$n_2 - 2 = x_2 \geq 0$$
$$n_3 - 3 = x_3 \geq 0$$
$$n_4 - 4 = x_4 \geq 0$$
$$n_5 - 5 = x_5 \geq 0$$

The given relation of positive integers,

$$n_1 + n_2 + n_3 + n_4 + n_5 = 20$$
$$x_1 + 1 + x_2 + 2 + x_3 + 3 + x_4 + 4 + x_5 + 5 = 20$$
$$x_1 + x_2 + x_3 + x_4 + x_5 = 5$$

From the above relation of the positive integers,

x_1	x_2	x_3	x_4	x_5
0	0	0	0	5
0	0	0	1	4
0	0	0	2	3
0	0	1	1	3
0	0	1	2	2
0	1	1	1	2
1	1	1	1	1

From the above table, the number of the distinct arrangement is 7.

55. Correct Response : (5)

Explanation :

It is given that a pack contains n cards. Two consecutive numbered cards removed and the sum of numbers on the remaining cards is 1224. So,

$$1 + 2 + 3 + \ldots + n - 2 \leq 1224 \leq 3 + 4 + \ldots + n$$

$$\frac{(n-2)(n-1)}{2} \leq 1224 \leq \frac{(n-2)}{2}(3+n)$$

$$n^2 - 3n - 2446 \leq 0 \text{ and } n^2 + n - 2454 \geq 0$$

$$49 < n < 51$$

So, the value of n is 50.

Now,

$$\frac{n(n+1)}{2} - (2k+1) = 1224$$

$$2k + 1 = 1275 - 1224$$

$$k = 25$$

Therefore, the required value is,

$$k - 20 = 25 - 20$$
$$= 5$$

56. Correct Response : (5)

Explanation :

Let, $(1, 1, 1)$, $(-1, 1, 1)$, $(1, -1, 1)$, $(-1, -1, 1)$ be vectors $\vec{a}$, $\vec{b}$, and $\vec{c}$. The rest vectors are $-\vec{a}$, $-\vec{b}$ and $-\vec{c}$.

The number of ways of selecting anti parallel pair is 4 and number of ways of selecting third vector is 6. Total number of ways is 24.

Number of non co-planar selections is,

$${}^8C_3 - 24 = 56 - 24$$
$$= 32$$
$$= 2^5$$

Therefore, the value of p is 5.

57. Correct Response : (b)

Explanation :

Let a_n be the n digit positive integer which formed by the digits 0, 1 or both in such a way that no consecutive digits are 0, b_n is the n digit integers end with 1 and c_n is the n digit integers end with 0.

The value of b_6 which ends with one is,

1...........1

Total no. of ways exactly two consecutive two is = 5 ways

Total no. of ways exactly three consecutive two is = 2 ways

Total no. of ways exactly four consecutive two is = 1 ways

So, $\qquad b_6 = 5 + 2 + 1$

$\qquad\qquad = 8$

Further solve the above expression,

$\qquad b_6 = 8$

58. Correct Response : (c)

Explanation :

The number of vertical lines is $2m$ and horizontal lines is $2n$.

Select one even numbered line and one odd numbered horizontal line to form a rectangle. Also, select one even numbered line and one odd numbered vertical line to form a rectangle.

The number of rectangles formed is,

$$^mC_1 \cdot {}^mC_1 \cdot {}^nC_1 \cdot {}^nC_1 = m^2 n^2$$

59. Correct Response : (A)-(p), (B)-(s), (C)-(q), (D)-(q)

Explanation :

The given word is ENDEANOEL.

(A) The word containing ENDEA is formed as ENDEA, N, O, E, L. It contains five different letters. So, the required number of permutations is 5!.

(B) The required number of permutation with E at first and last position is,

$$\frac{7!}{2!} = \frac{7 \times 6}{2} \cdot 5! $$

$$= 21 \, (5!)$$

(C) The required number of permutation such that letters D, L, N does not occurs at last five positions,

$$\frac{4!}{2!} \times \frac{5!}{3!} = 2 \, (5!)$$

(D) The required number of permutation such that letters A, E, O occurs only at odd positions,

$$\frac{5!}{3!} \times \frac{4!}{2!} = 2 \, (5!)$$

60. Correct Response : (c)

Explanation :

The given word is COCHIN.

The number of ways to fill the second place is $^4C_1$ and the ways to arrange remaining four alphabets be 4!.

$$^4C_1 \times 4! = \frac{4!}{3!1!} \times 4!$$

$$= 4 \times 24$$

$$= 96$$

Thus, 96 words appear before COCHIN.

61. Correct Answer : 7

Explanation :

Let, total runs scored by player in n matches be S_n.

$$S_n = \sum_{k=1}^{n} k \cdot 2^{n+1-k}$$

$$= 2^{n+1} \sum_{k=1}^{n} k \cdot 2^{-k}$$

$$= 2^{n+1} \left[\frac{\frac{1}{2}\left(1 - \frac{1}{2^n}\right)}{1 - \frac{1}{2}} - \frac{n}{2^{n+1}} \right] \frac{1}{1 - \frac{1}{2}}$$

$$= 2^{n+2} \left[1 - \frac{1}{2^n} - \frac{n}{2^{n+1}} \right]$$

Solve further.

$$S_n = 2^{n+2} - 2n - 4$$

$$\left(\frac{n+1}{4}\right)(2^{n+1} - 2 - n) = 2\,(2^{n+1} - 2 - n)$$

Compare both side,

$$\frac{n+1}{4} = 2$$

$$n = 8 - 1$$

$$n = 7$$

Therefore, value of n is 7.

Therefore, minimum natural number $n_0 = 6$.

62. Correct Response : (d)

Explanation :

Solve the given equation,

$$^{n-1}C_r = (k^2 - 3)\,{}^nC_{r+1}$$

$$\Rightarrow \qquad ^{n-1}C_r = (k^2 - 3)\frac{n}{r+1}\,{}^{n-1}C_r$$

$$\Rightarrow \qquad k^2 - 3 = \frac{r+1}{n}$$

Now, $\qquad 0 < k^2 - 3 \le 1$

$$3 < k^2 \le 4$$

Therefore, $k \in \left(\sqrt{3}, 2\right]$.

63. Explanation :

Let, n^2 objects are distributed in n groups. The number of arrangements of these objects is $\dfrac{n^2!}{(n!)^n}$

and it has to be an integer.

Hence, $\dfrac{n^2!}{(n!)^n}$ is an integer.

64. Correct Response : (a)

Explanation :

The number of words in which two N's appear together is,

$$\frac{5!}{3!} = 5 \times 4 = 20$$

The total number of ways to arrange letter of word BANANA is,

$$\frac{6!}{2!\,3!} = \frac{6 \times 5 \times 4}{2} = 60$$

The number of arrangements in which two N's do not appear together is,

$$60 - 20 = 40$$

65. Correct Response : (c)

Explanation :

Solve the given summation notation.

$$\sum_{i=0}^{m} \binom{10}{i}\binom{20}{m-i} = \sum_{i=0}^{m} {}^{10}C_i \, {}^{20}C_{m-i}$$

$$= {}^{10+20}C_{m-i+i}$$

$$= {}^{30}C_m$$

Therefore, sum is maximum for $m = 15$.

●●

Mathematical Induction

QUESTIONS

1. Suppose four distinct positive numbers a_1, a_2, a_3, a_4 are in G.P. Let $b_1 = a_1$, $b_2 = b_1 + a_2$, $b_3 = b_2 + a_3$ and $b_4 = b_3 + a_4$.

   Statement-1 : The numbers b_1, b_2, b_3, b_4 are neither in A.P. nor in G.P.

   Statement-2 : The numbers b_1, b_2, b_3, b_4 are in H.P.

   [2008, Advanced]

   (a) Statement-1 is True, Statement-2 is True, Statement-2 is a correct explanation for Statement-1

   (b) Statement-1 is True, Statement-2 is True; Statement-2 is **NOT** a correct explanation for Statement-1

   (c) Statement-1 is True, Statement-2 is False

   (d) Statement-1 is False, Statement-2 is True

2. Consider

   $$L_1 : 2x + 3y + p - 3 = 0$$
   $$L_2 : 2x + 3y + p + 3 = 0,$$

   where p is a real number, and $C : x^2 + y^2 + 6x - 10y + 30 = 0$.

   Statement-1 : If line L_1 is a chord of circle C, then line L_2 is not always a diameter of circle C.

   Statement-2 : If line L_1 is a diameter of circle C, then line L_2 is not a chord of circle C.

   [2008, Advanced]

   (a) Statement-1 is True, Statement-2 is True; Statement-2 is a correct explanation for Statement-1

   (b) Statement-1 is True, Statement-2 is True; Statement-2 is **Not** a correct explanation for Statement-1

   (c) Statement-1 is True, Statement-2 is False

   (d) Statement-1 is False, Statement-2 is True

3. Let a, b, c, p, q be real numbers. Suppose α, β are the roots of the equation $x^2 + 2px + q = 0$ and $\alpha, \dfrac{1}{\beta}$ are the roots of the equation $ax^2 + 2bx + c = 0$, where $\beta^2 \notin \{-1, 0, 1\}$.

   Statement-1 : $(p^2 - q)(b^2 - ac) \le 0$

   and

   Statement-2 : $b \ne pa$ or $c \ne qa$ **[2008, Main]**

   (a) Statement-1 is True, Statement-2 is True, Statement-2 is a correct explanation for Statement-1

   (b) Statement-1 is True, Statement-2 is True; Statement-2 is **NOT** a correct explanation for Statement-1

   (c) Statement-1 is True, Statement-2 is False

   (d) Statement-1 is False, Statement-2 is True

4. Consider the planes $3x - 6y - 2z = 15$ and $2x + y - 2z = 5$.

   Statement-1 : The parametric equations of the line of intersection of the given planes are $x = 3 + 14t$, $y = 1 + 2t$, $z = 15t$.

   because

   Statement-2 : The vector $14\hat{i} + 2\hat{j} + 15\hat{k}$ is parallel to the line of intersection of given planes.

   (a) Statement-1 is True, Statement-2 is True; Statement-2 is a correct explanation for Statement-1

   (b) Statement-1 is True, Statement-2 is True; Statement-2 is **NOT** a correct explanation for Statement-1

   (c) Statement-1 is True, Statement-2 is False

   (d) Statement-1 is False, Statement-2 is True

5. Statement-1 : The curve $y = \dfrac{-x^2}{2} + x + 1$ is symmetric with respect to the line $x = 1$.

   because

   Statement-2 : A parabola is symmetric about its axis.   **[2007, Advanced]**

   (a) Statement-1 is True, Statement-2 is True; Statement-2 is a correct explanation for Statement-1

   (b) Statement-1 is True, Statement-2 is True; Statement-2 is **Not** a correct explanation for Statement-1

   (c) Statement-1 is True, Statement-2 is False

   (d) Statement-1 is False, Statement-2 is True

6. Lines $L_1 : y - x = 0$ and $L_2 : 2x + y = 0$ intersect the line $L_3 : y + 2 = 0$ at P and Q, respectively. The bisector of the acute between L_1 and L_2 intersects L_3 at R.

Statement-1 : The ratio $PR : RQ$ equals $2\sqrt{2} : \sqrt{5}$.

because

Statement-2 : In any triangle, bisector of an angle divides the triangle into to similar triangles.

[2007, Advanced]

(a) Statement-1 is True, Statement-2 is True; Statement-2 is a correct explanation for Statement-1

(b) Statement-1 is True, Statement-2 is True; Statement-2 is Not a correct explanation for Statement-1

(c) Statement-1 is True, Statement-2 is False

(d) Statement-1 is False, Statement-2 is True

7. Let $F(x)$ be an indefinite integral of $\sin^2 x$.

STATEMENT-1 : The function $F(x)$ satisfies $F(x + \pi) = F(x)$ for all real x.

because **[2007, Advanced]**

STATEMENT-2 : $\sin^2 (x + \pi) = \sin^2 x$ for all real x.

(a) STATEMENT-1 is True, STATEMENT-2 is True; STATEMENT-2 is a correct.

(b) STATEMENT-1 is True, STATEMENT-2 is True; STATEMENT-2 is NOT a correct explanation for STATEMENT-1

(c) STATEMENT-1 is True, STATEMENT-2 is False

(d) STATEMENT-1 is False, STATEMENT-2 is True

8. Two planes P_1 and P_2 passes through origin. Two lines L_1 and L_2 also passing through origin are such that L_1 lies on P_1 but not on P_2, L_2 lies on P_2 but not on P_1. A, B, C are three points other than origin, then prove that the permutation [A', B', C'] of [A, B, C] exists such that

(i) A lies on L_1, B lies on P_1 not on L_1, C does not lie on P_1.

(ii) A' lies on L_2, B' lies on P_2 not on L_2, C' does not lie on P_2. **[2004, Mains]**

ANSWER KEY

1. (c) 2. (c) 3. (b) 4. (d) 5. (a) 6. (c) 7. (d) 8. (*)

ANSWERS WITH EXPLANATIONS

1. Correct Response : (c)

Explanation :

Let, $a_2 = a_1 \cdot r$, $a_3 = a_1 \cdot r^2$ and $a_4 = a_1 \cdot r^3$.

It is given that $b_1 = a_1$. Also,

$$b_2 = b_1 + a_2$$
$$= a_1 + a_1 \cdot r$$
$$= a_1 (1 + r)$$

Similarly, $b_3 = a_1(1 + r + r^2)$ and $b_4 = a_1(1 + r + r^2 + r^3)$.

Now, $\dfrac{b_1 - b_2}{b_2 - b_3} = \dfrac{a_1 (1 - 1 - r)}{a_1(1 + r - 1 - r - r^2)}$

$$= \dfrac{-r}{-r^2}$$

$$= \dfrac{1}{r}$$

Therefore, it can be noticed that b_1, b_2 and b_3 do not form an A.P., G.P. and H.P.

Thus, Statement 1 is true and Statement 2 is false.

2. Correct Response : (c)

Explanation :

Convert the given equation of circle into general form.

$$x^2 + y^2 + 6x - 10y + 30 = 0$$
$$(x + 3)^2 + (y - 5)^2 = 4$$

The radius of circle is 2.

Distance between given lines L_1 and L_2 is,

$$D = \dfrac{6}{\sqrt{13}} < \text{radius}$$

Therefore, Statement-1 is true and Statement-2 is false.

3. Correct Response : (b)

Explanation :

If the nature of roots is imaginary then $\beta = \overline{\alpha}$ and $\beta = \dfrac{1}{\alpha}$. But, condition $\beta = \dfrac{1}{\beta}$ is not possible.

If the nature of roots is real then,

$$\Delta_1 \cdot \Delta_2 \geq 0$$
$$4 (p^2 - q) \cdot 4 (b^2 - ac) \geq 0$$
$$(p^2 - q) (b^2 - ac) \geq 0$$

Thus, statement-1 is correct.

For equation $ax^2 + 2bx + c = 0$ the sum and product of roots is,

$$\alpha + \dfrac{1}{\beta} = -\dfrac{2b}{a} \quad \text{and} \quad \dfrac{\alpha}{\beta} = \dfrac{c}{a}$$

For equation $x^2 + 2px + q = 0$ the sum and product of roots is,

$$\alpha + \beta = -2p \quad \text{and} \quad \alpha\beta = q$$

If $\beta = 1$, then $\alpha = q$. Also, $c = qa$ and it is not possible.

If $\beta = 1$, then

$$\alpha + 1 = \frac{-2b}{a}$$

$$-2p = \frac{-2b}{a}$$

Therefore, $b = ap$ and it is not possible.

Statement-1 is correct but Statement-2 is not correct explanation for Statement-1.

4. **Correct Response :** (d)

   Explanation :

   The equation of planes are $3x - 6y - 2z = 15$ and $2x + y - 2z = 5$.

   For $z = 0$, equation are $3x - 6y = 15$ and $2x + y = 5$. On solving two equations $x = 3$ and $y = -1$.

   The direction vectors of plane are $\langle 3, -6, -2 \rangle$ and $\langle 2, 1, -2 \rangle$. The direction ratios of line of intersection of planes is $\langle 14, 2, 15 \rangle$.

   $$\frac{x-3}{14} = \frac{y+1}{2} = \frac{z-0}{15} = t$$

   The parametric equation for x is,

   $$x = 3 + 14t$$

   The parametric equation for y is,

   $$y = 2t - 1$$

   The parametric equation for z is ,

   $$z = 15t$$

   Thus, Statement-1 is false but Statement-2 is true.

5. **Correct Response :** (a)

   Explanation :

   The given equation of parabola is,

   $$y = -\frac{x^2}{2} + x + 1$$

   $$y - \frac{3}{2} = -\frac{1}{2}(x-1)^2$$

   The axis of symmetry is $x = 1$. So, parabola is symmetric about X-axis.

   Thus, both statements are true and statement-2 is a correct explanation for statement-1.

6. **Correct Response :** (c)

Explanation :

According to the given information the figure is shown below.

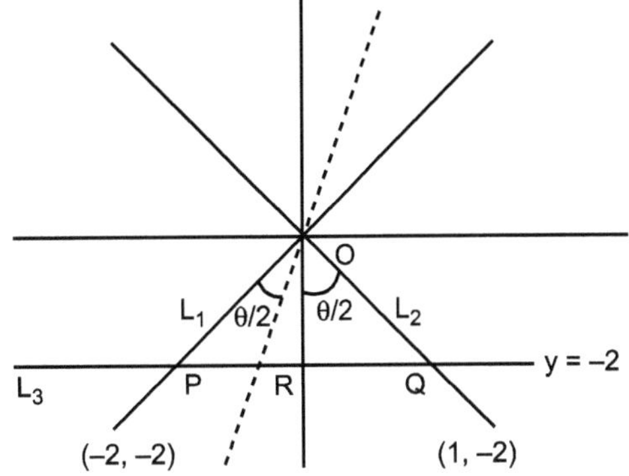

In triangle OPQ,

$$\frac{PR}{RQ} = \frac{OP}{OQ}$$

$$= \frac{2\sqrt{2}}{\sqrt{5}}$$

Therefore, only Statement-1 is correct.

7. **Correct Response :** (d)

   Explanation :

   The indefinite integral of given function is,

   $$F(x) = \int \sin^2 x \, dx$$

   $$= \int \frac{1 - \cos 2x}{2} dx$$

   $$= \frac{1}{4}(2x - \sin 2x) + C$$

   It can be noticed that $F(x + \pi) \neq F(x)$. Statement-1 is false.

   The function $\sin^2 x$ is periodic with period π. Thus, statement-2 is true.

8. **Explanation :**

   Point A corresponds to one A′, B′, C′, point B corresponds to second of A′, B′, C′ and point C corresponds to third of A′, B′, C′. So, six permutations are possible.

   According to given conditions, A lies on L_1, B lies on the intersection of P_1 and P_2 and C lies on the line L_2 on plane P_2.

   Now, A′ lies on L_2, B′ lies on the intersection line of P_1 and P_2 and C′ lie on the plane P_1.

   Therefore, there exist a particular set [A′, B′, C′] and it is permutation of [A, B, C] such that conditions (i) and (ii) are satisfied.

●●

Binomial Theorem and its Simple Applications

⟨?⟩ QUESTIONS

1. The natural number m, for which the coefficient of x in the binomial expansion of $\left(x^m + \dfrac{1}{x^2}\right)^{22}$ is 1540, is .... **[2020, Main]**

2. If p denotes the fractional part of the number p, then $\left\{\dfrac{3^{200}}{8}\right\}$, is equal to :

   (a) $\dfrac{1}{8}$ (b) $\dfrac{5}{8}$

   (c) $\dfrac{3}{8}$ (d) $\dfrac{7}{8}$

3. If the constant term in the binomial expansion of $\left(\sqrt{x} - \dfrac{k}{x^2}\right)^{10}$ is 405, then $|k|$ equals :

   [2020, Main]

   (a) 2   (b) 1

   (c) 3   (d) 9

4. If for some positive integer n, the coeficients of three consecutive terms in the binomial expansion of $(1 + x)^{n+5}$ are in the ratio $5 : 10 : 14$, then the largest coefficient in this expansion is :

   [2020, Main]

   (a) 792   (b) 252

   (c) 462   (d) 330

5. If the number of integral terms in the expansion of $(3^{1/2} + 5^{1/8})$ is exactly 33, then the least value of n is : **[2020, Main]**

   (a) 264   (b) 256

   (c) 128   (d) 248

6. The coefficient of x^4 in the expansion of $(1 + x + x^2 + x^3)^6$ in powers of x, is ....

   [2020, Main]

7. If the term independent of x in the expansion of $\left(\dfrac{3}{2}x^2 - \dfrac{1}{3x}\right)^9$ is k, then $18\,k$ is equal to :

   [2020, Main]

   (a) 9   (b) 11

   (c) 5   (d) 7

8. Let $\alpha > 0$, $\beta > 0$ be such that $\alpha^3 + \beta^2 = 4$, If the maximum value of the term independent of x in the binomial expansion of $\left(\alpha x^{\frac{1}{9}} + \beta x^{-\frac{1}{6}}\right)^{10}$ is $10k$, then k is equal to : **[2020, Main]**

   (a) 176   (b) 336

   (c) 352   (d) 84

9. For a positive integer n, is expanded in increasing powers of x. If three consecutive coefficients in this expansion are in the ratio, $2 : 5 : 12$, then n is equal to ....

   [2020, Main]

10. The coefficient of x^7 in the expression $(1 + x)^{10} + x(1 + x)^9 + x^2(1 + x)^8 + \dots + x^{10}$ is :

    [2020, Main]

    (a) 120   (b) 330

    (c) 210   (d) 420

11. If α and β be the coefficients of x^4 and x^2 respectively in the expansion of $(x + \sqrt{x^2 - 1})^6 + (x - \sqrt{x^2 - 1})^6$, then **[2020, Main]**

    (a) $\alpha + \beta = 60$ (b) $\alpha + \beta = -30$

    (c) $\alpha - \beta = -132$ (d) $\alpha - \beta = 60$

12. The coefficient of x^4 is the expansion of $(1 + x + x^2)^{10}$ is .... **[2020, Main]**

13. In the expansion $\left(\dfrac{x}{\cos\theta} + \dfrac{1}{x\sin\theta}\right)^{16}$, if θ_1 is the least value of the term independent of x when $\dfrac{\pi}{8} \le \theta \le \dfrac{\pi}{4}$ and θ_2 is the least value of the term independent of x when $\dfrac{\pi}{16} \le \theta \le \dfrac{\pi}{8}$, then the ratio $\theta_2 : \theta_1$ is equal to : **[2020, Main]**

    (a) $1 : 8$ (b) $1 : 16$

    (c) $8 : 1$ (d) $16 : 1$

14. If the sum of the coefficients of all even powers of x in the product $(1 + x + x^2 + \dots + x^{2n})\,(1 - x + x^2 - x^3 + \dots + x^{2n})$ is 61, then n is equal to .... **[2020, Main]**

15. If the coefficients of x^2 and x^3 are both zero, in the expansion of the expression $(1 + ax + bx^2)$ $(1 - 3x)^{15}$ in powers of x, then the ordered pair (a, b) is equal to ; **[2019, Main]**

(a) $(28, 861)$ (b) $(-54, 315)$

(c) $(28, 315)$ (d) $(-21, 714)$

16. The smallest natural number n, such that the coefficient of x in the expansion of $\left(x^2 + \dfrac{1}{x^3}\right)^n$ is $^nC_{23}$, is : **[2019, Main]**

(a) 38   (b) 58

(c) 23   (d) 35

17. If some three consecutive coefficients in the binomial expansion of $(x + 1)^n$ in powers of x are in the ratio $2 : 15 : 70$, then the average of these three coefficients is : **[2019, Main]**

(a) 964   (b) 232

(c) 227   (d) 625

18. If the forth term in the Binomial expansion of $\left(\dfrac{2}{x} + x \log_{8x}\right)(x > 0)$ is 20×8^7, then a value of x is: **[2019, Main]**

(a) 8^3 (b) 8^2

(c) 8 (d) 8^{-2}

19. The sum of the co-efficients of all even degree terms in x in the expansion of $(x + \sqrt{x^3 - 1})^6 + (x + \sqrt{x^3 - 1})^6$, $(x > 1)$ is equal to : **[2019, Main]**

(a) 29   (b) 32

(c) 26   (d) 24

20. If the fourth term in the binomial expansion of $\left(\sqrt{\dfrac{1}{x^{1+\log_{10} x}}} + x^{\frac{1}{12}}\right)^6$ is equal to 200, and $x > 1$, then the value of x is : **[2019, Main]**

(a) 100   (b) 10

(c) 10^3 (d) 10^4

21. The coefficient of x^{18} in the product $(1 + x)(1 - x)^{10}$ $(1 + x + x^2)^9$ is : **[2019, Main]**

(a) 84   (b) -126

(c) -84 (d) 126

22. The term independent of x in the expansion of $\left(\dfrac{1}{60} - \dfrac{x^8}{81}\right) \cdot \left(2x^2 - \dfrac{3}{x^2}\right)^6$ is equal to : **[2019, Main]**

(a) -72 (b) 36

(c) -36 (d) -108

23. If n is the degree of the polynomial,
$$\left[\dfrac{2}{\sqrt{5x^3 + 1} - \sqrt{5x^3 - 1}}\right]^8 + \left[\dfrac{2}{\sqrt{5x^3 + 1} + \sqrt{5x^3 - 1}}\right]^8$$
and m is the coefficient of x^n in it, then the ordered pair (n, m) is equal to : **[2018, Main]**

(a) $[24, (10)^8]$ (b) $[8, 5(10)^4]$

(c) $[12, (20)^4]$ (d) $[12, 8(10)^4]$

24. The coefficient of x^2 in the expansion of the product
$$(2 - x)^2 \cdot [(1 + 2x + 3x^2)^6 + (1 - 4x^2)^6] \text{ is :}$$
[2018, Main]

(a) 107   (b) 106

(c) 108   (d) 155

25. The sum of the co-efficients of all odd degree terms in the expansion of **[2018, Main]**
$$(x + \sqrt{x^3 - 1})^5 + (x - \sqrt{x^3 - 1})^5, (x > 1)$$
is :

(a) -1 (b) 0

(c) 1   (d) 2

26. If $(27)^{999}$ is divided by 7, then the remainder is : **[2017, Main]**

(a) 1   (b) 2

(c) 3   (d) 6

27. The coefficient of x^{-5} in the binomial expansion of $\left(\dfrac{x+1}{x^{\frac{2}{3}} - x^{\frac{1}{3}} + 1} - \dfrac{x-1}{x - x^{\frac{1}{2}}}\right)^{10}$, where $x \neq 0, 1$, is : **[2017, Main]**

(a) 1   (b) 4

(c) -4 (d) -1

28. Let $S = \{1, 2, 3, ..., 9\}$, for $k = 1, 2, ..., 5$, let N_k be the number of subsets of S, each containing five elements out of which exactly k are odd. Then
$$N_1 + N_2 + N_3 + N_4 + N_5 = \text{ } \textbf{[2017, Advanced]}$$
(a) 210   (b) 252

(c) 125   (d) 126

29. If the coefficients of x^{-2} and x^{-4} in the expansion of $\left(x^{\frac{1}{3}} + \dfrac{1}{2x^{\frac{1}{3}}}\right)^{18}$, $(x > 0)$, are m and n respectively, then $\dfrac{m}{n}$ is equal to : **[2016, Main]**

(a) 182   (b) $\dfrac{4}{5}$

(c) $\dfrac{5}{4}$ (d) 27

30. For $x \in R$, $x \neq -1$, if

$$(1 + x)^{2016} + x(1 + x)^{2015} + x^2 (1 + x)^{2014} + ... + x^{2016}$$

$$= \sum_{i=0}^{2016} a_i \, x^i, \text{ then } a_{17} \text{ is equal to :} \quad \textbf{[2016, Main]}$$

(a) $\dfrac{2017!}{17! \; 2000!}$

(b) $\dfrac{2016!}{17! \; 1999!}$

(c) $\dfrac{2017!}{2000!}$

(d) $\dfrac{2016!}{16!}$

31. The term independent of x in the binomial expansion of **[2015, Main]**

$$\left(1 - \frac{1}{x} + 3x^5\right)\left(2x^2 - \frac{1}{x}\right)^8 \text{ is :}$$

(a) 400

(b) 496

(c) -400

(d) -496

32. The sum of coefficients of integral powers of x in the binomial expansion of $(1 - 2\sqrt{x})^{50}$ is :

[2015, Main]

(a) $\dfrac{1}{2}(3^{50} + 1)$

(b) $\dfrac{1}{2}(3^{50})$

(c) $\dfrac{1}{2}(3^{50} - 1)$

(d) $\dfrac{1}{2}(2^{50} + 1)$

33. The coefficient of x^{1012} in the expansion of $(1 + x^n + x^{253})^{10}$, (where $n \leq 22$ is any positivite integer), is : **[2014, Main]**

(a) 1

(b) $^{10}C_4$

(c) $4n$

(d) $^{253}C_4$

34. If $1 + x^4 + x^5 = \sum\limits_{i=0}^{5} a_i(1+x)^i$, for all x in B, then a_2

is : **[2014, Main]**

(a) -4

(b) 6

(c) -8

(d) 10

35. The coefficient of x^{50} in the binomial expansion of $(1 + x)^{1000} + x(1 + x)^{999} + x^2(1 + x)^{998} + ... + x^{1000}$

is : **[2014, Main]**

(a) $\dfrac{(1000)!}{(50)!\,(950)!}$

(b) $\dfrac{(1000)!}{(49)!\,(951)!}$

(c) $\dfrac{(1001)!}{(51)!\,(950)!}$

(d) $\dfrac{(1001)!}{(50)!\,(951)!}$

36. For $r = 0, 1, ..., 10$, let A_r, B_r and C_r denote, respectively, the coefficient of x_r in the expansions of $(1 + x)^{10}$, $(1 + x)^{20}$ and $(1 + x)^{30}$, then

$$\sum_{r=1}^{10} A_r \, (B_{10}B_r = C_{10}A_r)$$

is equal to

(a) $B_{10} - C_{10}$

(b) $A_{10} (B^2_{10} - C_{10} A_{10})$

(c) 0

(d) $C_{10} - B_{10}$

[2010, Advanced]

37. Prove that

$$2^k \binom{n}{0}\binom{n}{k} - 2^{k-1}\binom{n}{1}\binom{n-1}{k-1}$$

$$+ 2^{2-k}\binom{n}{2}\binom{n-2}{k-2}$$

$$- ...(-1)^k \binom{n}{k}\binom{n-k}{0} = \binom{n}{k}. \quad \textbf{[2006, Main]}$$

38. The value of

$$\binom{30}{0}\binom{30}{10} - \binom{30}{1}\binom{30}{11} + \binom{30}{2}\binom{30}{12} + ... + \binom{30}{20}\binom{30}{30}$$

is, where, $\binom{n}{r} = {}^nC_r$ **[2005, Main]**

(a) $\binom{30}{10}$

(b) $\binom{30}{15}$

(c) $\binom{60}{30}$

(d) $\binom{31}{10}$

39. Coefficient of t^{24} in $(1 + t^2)^{12} (1 + t^{12}) (1 + t^{24})$ is :

[2003, Main]

(a) $^{12}C_6 + 3$

(b) $^{12}C_6 + 1$

(c) $^{12}C_6$

(d) $^{12}C_6 + 2$

ANSWER KEY

1. (13)	**2.** (a)	**3.** (c)	**4.** (c)	**5.** (b)	**6.** (120)	**7.** (d)	**8.** (b)	**9.** (118)	**10.** (b)
11. (c)	**12.** (615.00)	**13.** (d)	**14.** (30)	**15.** (c)	**16.** (a)	**17.** (b)	**18.** (b)	**19.** (d)	**20.** (b)
21. (a)	**22.** (c)	**23.** (c)	**24.** (b)	**25.** (d)	**26.** (d)	**27.** (a)	**28.** (d)	**29.** (a)	**30.** (a)
31. (b)	**32.** (a)	**33.** (b)	**34.** (a)	**35.** (d)	**36.** (d)	**37.** $\left(\dfrac{n}{k}\right)$	**38.** (a)	**39.** (d)	

ANSWERS WITH EXPLANATIONS

1. **Correct Response :** (13)

Explanation :

$$T_{r+1} = {}^{22}C_r \, (x^m)^{22-r} \left(\frac{1}{x^2}\right)^r$$

$$= {}^{22}C_r \, x^{22m - mr - 2r}$$

$$= {}^{22}C_r \, x$$

$\because \qquad {}^{22}C_3 = {}^{22}C_{19} = 1540$

$\therefore \qquad\qquad r = 3 \text{ or } 19$

$$22m - mr - 2r = 1$$

$$m = \frac{2r+1}{22-5}$$

$r = 3,\qquad m = \dfrac{7}{19} \notin N$

$r = 19,\qquad m = \dfrac{38+1}{22-19} = \dfrac{39}{3} = 13$

$$m = 13.$$

2. **Correct Response :** (a)

   Explanation :

   $$\left\{\frac{3^{200}}{8}\right\} = \left\{\frac{(3^2)^{100}}{8}\right\}$$

   $$= \left\{\frac{(1+8)^{100}}{8}\right\}$$

   $$= \left\{\frac{1 + {}^{100}C_1.8 + {}^{100}C_2.8^2 + \ldots + {}^{100}C_{100}\,8^{100}}{8}\right\}$$

   $$= \left\{\frac{1+8m}{8}\right\}$$

   $$= \frac{1}{8}.$$

3. **Correct Response :** (c)

   Explanation :

   $$\left(\sqrt{x} - \frac{k}{x^2}\right)^{10}$$

   $$T_{r+1} = {}^{10}C_r\,(\sqrt{x})^{10-r}\left(\frac{-k}{x^2}\right)^r$$

   $$T_{r+1} = {}^{10}C_r.x^{\frac{10-r}{2}}.(-k)^r.x^{-2r}$$

   $$T_{r+1} = {}^{10}C_r\,x^{\frac{10-5r}{2}}(-k)^r$$

   Constant term : $\dfrac{10-5r}{2} = 0 \Rightarrow r = 2$

   $$T_3 = {}^{10}C_2.(-k)^2 = 405$$

   $$k^2 = \frac{405}{45} = 9$$

   $$k = \pm 3 \Rightarrow |k| = 3.$$

4. **Correct Response :** (c)

   Explanation :

   Let $\qquad\qquad n + 5 = N$

   $${}^{N}C_{r-1} : {}^{N}C_r : {}^{N}C_{r+1} = 5 : 10 : 14$$

   $\Rightarrow\qquad \dfrac{{}^{N}C_r}{{}^{N}C_{r-1}} = \dfrac{N+1-r}{r} = 2$

   $$N - 3r + 1 = 0$$

$$\frac{{}^{N}C_{r+1}}{{}^{N}C_r} = \frac{N-r}{r+1} = \frac{7}{5}$$

$$5N - 12r - 7 = 0 \qquad\qquad \ldots(2)$$

$\Rightarrow\qquad r = 4,\ N = 11$

   [by solving equation (1) & (2)]

$\Rightarrow (1+x)^{11}$

   Largest coefficient $= {}^{11}C_6 = 462.$

5. **Correct Response :** (b)

   Explanation :

   $$T_{r+1} = {}^{n}C_r\,(3)^{\frac{n-r}{2}}\,(5)^{\frac{r}{8}} \qquad (n \geq r)$$

   Clearly r should be a multiple of 8.

   $\because$ There are exactly 33 integral terms possible values of r can be

   $$0, 8, 16, \ldots, 32 \times 8$$

   $\therefore$ least value of $n = 256.$

6. **Correct Response :** (120)

   Explanation :

   $$(1 + x + x^2 + x^3)^6 = [(1 + x)(1 + x^2)]^6$$

   $$= (1+x)^6\,(1+x^2)^6$$

   $$= \sum_{r=0}^{6} {}^6C_r\, x^r \sum_{r=0}^{6} {}^6C_t\, x^{2t}$$

   $$= \sum_{r=0}^{6}\sum_{t=0}^{6} {}^6C_r\,{}^6C_t\, x^{r+2t}$$

   For coefficient of $x^4 \Rightarrow r + 2t = 4$

r	t
0	2
2	1
4	0

   Coefficient of x^4

   $$= {}^6C_0\,{}^6C_2 + {}^6C_2\,{}^6C_1 + {}^6C_4\,{}^6C_0$$

   $$= 120.$$

7. **Correct Response :** (d)

   Explanation :

   $$T_{r+1} = {}^9C_r\left(\frac{3}{2}x^2\right)^{9-r}\left(-\frac{1}{3x}\right)^r$$

   $$T_{r+1} = {}^9C_r\left(\frac{3}{2}\right)^{9-r}\left(-\frac{1}{3}\right)^r x^{18-3r}$$

   For independent of x

   $18 - 3r = 0,\ r = 6$

   $\therefore\qquad T_r = {}^9C_6\left(\frac{3}{2}\right)^3\left(-\frac{1}{3}\right)^6 = \dfrac{21}{54} = k$

   $\therefore\qquad 18k = \dfrac{21}{54}\times 18 = 7$

8. Correct Response : (b)

Explanation :

Let t_{r+1} denotes

$$r = 1^{\text{th}} \text{ term of } \left(\alpha x^{\frac{1}{9}} + \beta x^{-\frac{1}{6}} \right)^{10}$$

$$t_{r+1} = {}^{10}C_r\, \alpha^{10-r}\, (x)^{\frac{10-r}{9}} \cdot \beta^r\, x^{-\frac{r}{6}}$$

$$= {}^{10}C_r\, \alpha^{10-r}\, \beta^r\, (x)^{\frac{10-r}{9} - \frac{r}{6}}$$

If t_{r+1} is independent of x

$$\frac{10-r}{9} - \frac{r}{6} = 0 \Rightarrow r = 4$$

maximum value of t_5 is 10K (given)

$\Rightarrow {}^{10}C_4\, \alpha^6\, \beta^4$ is maximum

Let α^3, β^2 are 2 Numbers

$$\text{AM} \geq \text{GM}$$

$$\frac{\alpha^3 + \beta^2}{2} \geq (\alpha^3\, \beta^2)^{\frac{1}{2}}$$

$$\frac{4}{2} \geq (\alpha^3\, \beta^2)^{\frac{1}{2}}$$

$$\alpha^6\, \beta^4 \leq 16$$

$$\frac{t_5}{{}^{10}C_4} \leq 16$$

$$t_5 \leq 16 \cdot {}^{10}C_4$$

$$t_5 = 16 \times {}^{10}C_4 = 10\,k$$

$$k = 336$$

9. Correct Response : (118)

Explanation :

$${}^{n}C_{r-1} : {}^{n}C_{r+1} = 2:5:12$$

Now $\quad \dfrac{{}^{n}C_{r-1}}{{}^{n}C_r} = \dfrac{2}{5}$

$$\frac{r}{n-r+1} = \frac{2}{5}$$

$$\Rightarrow \qquad 7r = 2n + 2 \qquad \text{...(1)}$$

$$\frac{{}^{n}C_r}{{}^{n}C_{r+1}} = \frac{5}{12}$$

$$\frac{r+1}{n-r} = \frac{5}{12}$$

$$\Rightarrow \qquad 17r = 5n - 12 \qquad \text{...(2)}$$

On solving (1) & (2)

$$\Rightarrow \qquad n = 118$$

10. Correct Response : (b)

Explanation :

Coefficient of x^7 is

$${}^{10}C_7 + {}^{9}C_6 + {}^{5}C_5 + ... + {}^{4}C_1 + {}^{3}C_0$$

$$\underbrace{{}^{4}C_0 + {}^{4}C_1}_{{}^{5}C_1} + {}^{5}C_2 + ... + {}^{10}C_7 = {}^{11}C_1 = 330$$

11. Correct Response : (c)

Explanation :

$$2[{}^{6}C_0 x^6 + {}^{6}C_2 x^4 (x^2 - 1) + {}^{6}C_4 x^2 (x^2 - 1)^2 + {}^{6}C_6 (x^2 - 1)^3]$$

$\alpha = -96$ and $\beta = 36$

$\therefore\ \alpha - \beta = -132$

12. Correct Response : (615.00)

Explanation :

$(1 + x + x^2)^{10} = {}^{10}C_0 + {}^{10}C_1 x(1 + x) + {}^{10}C_2 x^2 (1 + x)^2$
$\qquad + {}^{10}C_3 x^3 (1 + x)^3 + {}^{10}C_4 x^4 (1 + x^4) + ...$

Coeff. of $x^4 = {}^{10}C_2 + {}^{10}C_2 \times {}^{3}C_1 + {}^{10}C_4 = 615$.

13. Correct Response : (d)

14. Correct Response : (30.00)

Explanation :

Let $(1 + x + x^2 + ... + x^{2n})\,(1 - x + x^2 - x^3 + ... + x^{2n})$

$$= a_0 + a_1 x + a_2 x^2 + a_3 x^3 + a_4 x^4 + ... + a_{4n} x^{4n}$$

So,

$$a_0 + a_1 + a_2 + ... + a_{4n} = 2n + 1 \qquad \text{...(1)}$$
$$a_0 - a_1 + a_2 - a_3 ... + a_{4n} = 2n + 1 \qquad \text{...(2)}$$
$$\Rightarrow \quad a_0 + a_2 + a_4 + ... + a_{4n} = 2n + 1$$
$$\Rightarrow \qquad 2n + 1 = 61 \Rightarrow n = 30$$

15. Correct Response : (c)

Explanation :

Coefficient of x^2 in the binomial expression of $(1 + ax + bx^2)\,(1 - 3x)^{15}$ is zero. That is,

$${}^{15}C_2\,(-3)^2 + a\,{}^{15}C_1\,(-3) + b\,{}^{15}C_0 = 0$$

$$\Rightarrow \qquad \frac{15 \times 14}{2} \times 9 - 3a \times 15 + b = 0$$

$$\Rightarrow \qquad 15 \times 63 - 45a + b = 0 \qquad \text{...(i)}$$

Coefficient of x^3 in the binomial expression of $(1 + ax + bx^2)\,(1 - 3x)^{15}$ is zero. That is,

$${}^{15}C_3\,(-3)^3 + a\,{}^{15}C_2(-3)^2 + b\,{}^{15}C_1\,(-3) = 0$$

$$\Rightarrow \qquad 7 \times 13 \times 3 - 21a + b = 0 \quad \text{...(ii)}$$

Subtract equation (ii) from (i)

$$\Rightarrow \qquad 672 - 24a = 0$$

$$\Rightarrow \qquad a = 28$$

Thus, $\qquad b = 315$.

16. Correct Response : (a)

Explanation :

$$\left(x^2 + \frac{1}{x^3} \right)^n$$

$$T_{r+1} = {}^{n}C_r\, (x^2)^{n-r} \left(\frac{1}{x^3} \right)^r$$

$$= {}^{n}C_r \cdot x^{2n - 2r - 3r}$$

$$= {}^{n}C_r \cdot x^{2n - 5r}$$

For coefficient of $2n - 5r = 1$, put $r = \dfrac{2n-1}{5}$

Then coefficient of x is

$${}^{n}C_{\frac{2n-1}{5}} \text{ or } {}^{n}C_{n - \frac{2n-1}{5}} \Rightarrow {}^{n}C_{\frac{3n+1}{5}}$$

So, put

$$\frac{2n-1}{5} = 23$$

$$\Rightarrow \quad 2n = 116$$
$$\Rightarrow \quad n = 58$$

Now, put

$$\frac{3n+1}{5} = 23$$

$$\Rightarrow \quad 3n + 1 = 115$$
$$\Rightarrow \quad n = 38$$

So, the minimum number is 38.

17. Correct Response : (b)

Explanation :

$$^nC_r : {}^nC_{r+1} : {}^nC_{r+2} = 2 : 15 : 70$$

$$\frac{^nC_r}{^nC_{r+1}} = \frac{2}{15}, \quad \frac{^nC_{r+1}}{^nC_{r+2}} = \frac{15}{70}, \quad \frac{^nC_r}{^nC_{r+2}} = \frac{2}{70}$$

$$\frac{r+1}{n-r} = \frac{2}{15}$$

$$\Rightarrow \quad 15r + 15 = 2n - 2r$$
$$\Rightarrow \quad 17r = 2n - 15 \qquad \text{...(i)}$$

And, $\quad \dfrac{r+2}{n-r-1} = \dfrac{3}{14}$

$$\Rightarrow \quad 14r + 28 = 3n - 3r - 3$$
$$\Rightarrow \quad 17r = 3n - 31 \qquad \text{...(ii)}$$

Solve equations (i) and (ii)

$n = 16, r = 1.$

Average is

$$\frac{^nC_r + {}^nC_{r+1} + {}^nC_{r+2}}{3} = \frac{^{16}C_1 + {}^{16}C_2 + {}^{16}C_3}{3}$$

$$= \frac{16 + 120 + 560}{3}$$

$$= 232.$$

18. Correct Response : (b)

Explanation :

Fourth term in the binomial expansion of

$$\left(\frac{2}{x} + x^{\log_8 x}\right)^6 \text{ is}$$

$$^6C_3 \left(\frac{2}{x}\right)^3 (x^{\log_8 x})^3 = 20 \times 8^7$$

$$\Rightarrow \quad \frac{2}{x}(x^{\log_8 x}) = 2^7$$

This gives,

$$\frac{x^{\log_8 x}}{x} = 2^6$$

$$= 8^2$$

Taking logarithms both sides to the base 8,

$$(\log_8 x)^2 = 2 + (\log_8 x)$$

$$\Rightarrow \quad \log_8 x = 2 \text{ or } -1$$

$$\Rightarrow \quad x = 8^2 \text{ or } \frac{1}{8}$$

19. Correct Response : (d)

Explanation :

$$(x + \sqrt{x^3 - 1})^6 + (x - \sqrt{x^3 - 1})^6$$

$$= 2({}^6C_0 \cdot x^6 + {}^6C_2 \cdot x^4 (x^3 - 1) + {}^6C_4 \cdot x^2 (x^3 - 1)^2$$
$$+ {}^6C_6 (x^3 - 1)^3)$$

Terms of even powers of

$$x = 2({}^6C_0 \cdot x^6 - {}^6C_2 \cdot x^4 + {}^6C_4 \cdot x^2 + {}^6C_4 \cdot x^8$$
$$+ {}^6C_6 (-1 - 3x^6))$$

Sum of coefficients of all even degree terms is,

$$= 2 \, ({}^6C_0 - {}^6C_2 + {}^6C_4 + {}^6C_4 - {}^6C_6 - 3 \cdot {}^6C_6)$$
$$= 2 \, (15 - 3)$$
$$= 24$$

20. Correct Response : (b)

Explanation :

Since fourth term is equal to 200

$$T_4 = {}^6C_3 \left(\sqrt{x^{\left(\frac{1}{1+\log 10x}\right)}}\right)^3 \left(x^{\frac{1}{2}}\right)^3 = 200$$

$$\Rightarrow 20 = \frac{3}{x^{\frac{3}{2(1+\log_{10} x)}}} \frac{1}{x^{\frac{1}{4}}} = 200$$

$$\Rightarrow \quad x^{\frac{1}{4} + \frac{3}{2(1+\log_{10} x)}} = 10$$

Taking $\log_{10}$ can both sides and putting $\log_{10} x = t$

$$\left(\frac{1}{4} + \frac{3}{2(1+t)}\right) t = 1 \Rightarrow t^2 + 3t - 4 = 0$$

$$\Rightarrow t^2 + 4t - t - 4 = 0 \Rightarrow t = 1, -4$$

$\therefore \log_{10} x = 1 \Rightarrow x = 10$

or $\log_{10} x = -4 \Rightarrow x = 10^{-4}$

According to question $x > 1$. $\therefore x = 10$

21. Correct Response : (a)

Explanation :

The term $(1 + x)(1 + x)^{10}(1 + x^2)^9$ can be simplified as,

$$(1 + x)(1 + x)^{10}(1 + x + x^2)^9$$

$$= (1 - x^2)\{(1 - x)(1 + x + x^2)\}^9$$
$$= (1 - x^2)(1 - x^3)^9$$

The coefficient of x^{18} in $(1 - x^2)(1 - x^3)^9$ is,

$$C = {}^9C_6 - 0$$
$$= 84$$

22. Correct Response : (c)

Explanation :

The term independent of x is,

$$T = \frac{1}{60}(2)^3(-3)^6({}^6C_3) + \left(-\frac{1}{81}\right)(2)(-3)^5({}^6C_1)$$

$$= -72 + 36$$

$$= -36$$

23. Correct Response : (c)

Explanation :

Let the polynomial be $P(x)$.

$$P(x) = \left[\frac{2}{\sqrt{5x^3+1}-\sqrt{5x^3-1}}\right]^8 + \left[\frac{2}{\sqrt{5x^3+1}+\sqrt{5x^3-1}}\right]^8$$

$$= \left[\frac{2(\sqrt{5x^3+1}+\sqrt{5x^3-1})}{(\sqrt{5x^3+1}-\sqrt{5x^3-1})(\sqrt{5x^3+1}+\sqrt{5x^3-1})}\right]^8 + \left[\frac{2(\sqrt{5x^3+1}-\sqrt{5x^3-1})}{(\sqrt{5x^3+1}+\sqrt{5x^3-1})(\sqrt{5x^3+1}-\sqrt{5x^3-1})}\right]^8$$

$$= \left[\frac{2(\sqrt{5x^3+1}+\sqrt{5x^3-1})}{(\sqrt{5x^3+1})^2-(\sqrt{5x^3-1})^2}\right]^8 + \left[\frac{2\left(\sqrt{5x^3+1}-\sqrt{5x^3-1}\right)}{\left(\sqrt{5x^3+1}\right)^2-\left(\sqrt{5x^3-1}\right)^2}\right]^8$$

$$= \left[\frac{2(\sqrt{5x^3+1}+\sqrt{5x^3-1})}{2}\right]^8 + \left[\frac{2(\sqrt{5x^3+1}-\sqrt{5x^3-1})}{2}\right]^8$$

Expand the polynomial by binomial expansion.

$$P(x) = (\sqrt{5x^3+1}+\sqrt{5x^3-1})^8 + (\sqrt{5x^3+1}-\sqrt{5x^3-1})^8$$

$$= \left[\begin{array}{l} {}^8C_0(\sqrt{5x^3+1})^8 + {}^8C_1(\sqrt{5x^3+1})^7(\sqrt{5x^3-1}) \\ + {}^8C_2(\sqrt{5x^3+1})^6(\sqrt{5x^3-1})^2 + {}^8C_3(\sqrt{5x^3+1})^5(\sqrt{5x^3-1})^3 \\ + {}^8C_4(\sqrt{5x^3+1})^4(\sqrt{5x^3-1})^4 + {}^8C_5(\sqrt{5x^3+1})^3(\sqrt{5x^3-1})^5 \\ + {}^8C_6(\sqrt{5x^3+1})^2(\sqrt{5x^3-1})^6 + {}^8C_7(\sqrt{5x^3+1})(\sqrt{5x^3-1})^7 \\ \qquad\qquad + {}^8C_8(\sqrt{5x^3-1})^8 \end{array}\right]$$

$$+ \left[\begin{array}{l} {}^8C_0(\sqrt{5x^3+1})^8 - {}^8C_1(\sqrt{5x^3+1})^7(\sqrt{5x^3-1}) \\ + {}^8C_2(\sqrt{5x^3+1})^6(\sqrt{5x^3-1})^2 - {}^8C_3(\sqrt{5x^3+1})^5(\sqrt{5x^3-1})^3 \\ + {}^8C_4(\sqrt{5x^3+1})^4(\sqrt{5x^3-1})^4 - {}^8C_5(\sqrt{5x^3+1})^3(\sqrt{5x^3-1})^5 \\ + {}^8C_6(\sqrt{5x^3+1})^2(\sqrt{5x^3-1})^6 - {}^8C_7(\sqrt{5x^3+1})(\sqrt{5x^3-1})^7 \\ \qquad\qquad + {}^8C_8(\sqrt{5x^3-1})^8 \end{array}\right]$$

$$= 2\left[\begin{array}{l} {}^8C_0(\sqrt{5x^3+1})^8 + {}^8C_2(\sqrt{5x^3+1})^6(\sqrt{5x^3-1})^2 \\ + {}^8C_4(\sqrt{5x^3+1})^4(\sqrt{5x^3-1})^4 + {}^8C_6(\sqrt{5x^3+1})^2(\sqrt{5x^3-1})^6 \\ \qquad\qquad + {}^8C_8(\sqrt{5x^3-1})^8 \end{array}\right]$$

$$= 2\left[\begin{array}{l} {}^8C_0(\sqrt{5x^3+1})^8 + {}^8C_2(\sqrt{5x^3+1})^6(5x^3-1) \\ + {}^8C_4(\sqrt{5x^3+1})^4(5x^3-1)^2 + {}^8C_6(\sqrt{5x^3+1})^2(5x^3-1)^3 \\ \qquad\qquad + {}^8C_8(5x^3-1)^4 \end{array}\right]$$

Further solve the above polynomial.

$P(x)^2 = [(5x^3-1)^4 + 28(5x^3+1)^3(5x^3-1) + 70(5x^3+1)^2(5x^3-1)^2 + 28(5x^3+1)(5x^3-1)^3 + (5x^3-1)^4]$

The above equation gives the degree of the polynomial.

$$(x^3)^4 = x^{12}$$

The value of n is,

$$n = 12$$

The value of m is,

$$m = 2\,(5^4 + 140.5^3 + 70.5^4 + 140.5^3 + 5^4)$$
$$= 160000$$
$$= 20^4$$

Therefore, the ordered pair (n, m) is equal to $[12, (20)^4]$.

24. Correct Response : (b)

Explanation :

The coefficient of $x^2 = 2$ coefficient of x^2 in $[(1 + 2x + 3x^2)^6 + (1 - 4x^2)^6]-$ constant term,

$$(1 + 2x + 3x^2)^6 = \sum_{r=0}^{6} {}^6C_r\,(2x + 3x^2)^r$$

$$= {}^6C_0 + {}^6C_1\,(2x + 3x^2) + {}^6C_2\,(2x + 3x^2) + \dots$$

Coefficient of x^2

$$= 2\,(18 + 60 - 24) - 2$$
$$= 108 - 2$$
$$= 106$$

25. Correct Response : (d)

Explanation :

The given equation is

$$(x + \sqrt{x^3 - 1})^5 + (x - \sqrt{x^3 - 1})^5$$

Expanding the given equation by binomial expansion,

$$(x + \sqrt{x^3 - 1})^5 + (x - \sqrt{x^3 - 1})^5$$

$$= 2[{}^5C_0\,x^5 + {}^5C_2\,x^3\,(x^3 - 1) + {}^5C_4\,x(x^3 - 1)^2]$$
$$= 2[x^5 + 10(x^6 - x^3) + 5x\,(x^6 - 2x^3 + 1)]$$
$$= 2[x^5 + 10x^6 - 10x^3 + 5x^7 - 10x^4 + 5x]$$
$$= 2\,[5x^7 + 10x^6 + x^5 - 10x^4 - 10x^3 + 5x]$$

Sum of the co-efficient of all odd degree terms is,

$$S = 2\,(5 + 1 - 10 + 5)$$
$$= 2$$

26. Correct Response : (d)

Explanation :

The expression of the Binomial Theorem :

$$(1 + x)^n = {}^nC_0 x^n\,(1)^0 + {}^nC_1 x^{n-1}\,(1)^1 + \dots + {}^nC_n x^0\,(1)^n$$
$$(1 + x) = 1 + {}^nC_1 x^{n-1} + \dots + {}^nC_n$$

Where n is considered for positive integer.

From the given value,

$$(27)^{999} = \frac{(28 - 1)^{999}}{7}$$
$$= \frac{28k - 1}{7}$$
$$= \frac{28k - 7 + 7 - 1}{7}$$

$$= \frac{7(4k - 1) + 6}{7}$$

Hence, the remainder is 6.

27. Correct Response : (a)

Explanation :

The given equation is,

$$\left(\frac{x + 1}{x^{\frac{2}{3}} - x^{\frac{1}{3}} + 1} - \frac{x - 1}{x - x^{\frac{1}{2}}} \right)^{10}$$

Simplify the above equation,

$$\left(\frac{\left(x^{\frac{1}{3}} + 1\right)\left(x^{\frac{2}{3}} - x^{\frac{1}{3}} + 1\right)}{\left(x^{\frac{2}{3}} - x^{\frac{1}{3}} + 1\right)} - \frac{\left(\sqrt{x} - 1\right)\left(\sqrt{x} + 1\right)}{\left(\sqrt{x} - 1\right)\sqrt{x}} \right)^{10}$$

$$= \left(x^{\frac{1}{3}} + 1 - 1 - \frac{1}{x^{\frac{1}{2}}} \right)^{10}$$

$$= \left(x^{\frac{1}{3}} - \frac{1}{x^{\frac{1}{2}}} \right)^{10}$$

Solve the above equation.

$$a = \frac{1}{3},\ b = -\frac{1}{2}$$

Coefficient of x^{-5} is,

$${}^{10}C_{10} \left(x^{\frac{1}{3}}\right)^0 \left(2' - 1/2\right)^{10}$$

$$= \frac{10!}{10![(10-10)!]}(x^0)(x)^{\frac{-10}{2}}$$

$$= 1 \times x^{-5}$$

Hence, the coefficient of x^{-5} is 1

28. Correct Response : (d)

Explanation :

The value is given by coefficient of x^5 in $(1 + x)^5$ $(1 + x)^4$ which is ${}^9C_5$.

The value is calculated as :

$$N_1 + N_2 + N_3 + N_4 + N_5 = {}^9C_5$$
$$= 126$$

29. Correct Response : (a)

Explanation :

The expansion of $\left(x^{\frac{1}{3}} + \frac{1}{2x^{\frac{1}{3}}} \right)^{18}$ is written as,

$$T_{r+1} = {}^{18}C_r \left(x^{\frac{1}{3}}\right)^{18-r} \left(\frac{1}{2x^{\frac{1}{3}}}\right)^r$$

$$= {}^{18}C_r \left(\frac{1}{2}\right)^r \left(x^{\frac{18-2r}{3}}\right)$$

For the coefficient of x^{-2}, the value of r is,

$$x^{\frac{18-2r}{3}} = x^{-2}$$

$$\frac{18-2r}{3} = -2$$

$$r = 12$$

For the coefficient of x^{-4}, the value of r is,

$$x^{\frac{18-2r}{3}} = x^{-4}$$

$$\frac{18-2r}{3} = -4$$

$$r = 15$$

The coefficient of x^{-2} and x^{-4} are m and n respectively. So, the ratio is,

$$\frac{m}{n} = \frac{{}^{18}C_{12}\left(\frac{1}{2}\right)^{12}}{{}^{18}C_{15}\left(\frac{1}{2}\right)^{15}}$$

$$= \frac{18!}{12!(18-12)!} \times \frac{15!(18-15)!}{18!} (2^3)$$

$$= 14 \times 13$$

$$= 182$$

30. Correct Response : (a)

Explanation :

Simplify the given equation,

$$\sum_{i=0}^{2016} C_i x^i = (1+x)^{2016} + x(1+x)^{2015}$$

$$+ x^2(1+x)^{2014} + \dots + x^{2016}$$

$$= \frac{(1+x)^{2016}\left[1-\left(\frac{x}{1+x}\right)^{2017}\right]}{1-\frac{x}{1+x}}$$

$$= \frac{\dfrac{(1+x)^{2016}}{1} - \dfrac{x^{2017}}{(1+x)}}{\dfrac{x+1-x}{1+x}}$$

$$= \frac{(1+x)^{2017} - x^{2017}}{1}$$

further simplify the above equation :

$$a_{17} = {}^{2017}C_{17} \qquad \left[\because {}^nC_r = \frac{n!}{r!\times(n-r)!}\right]$$

$$= \frac{2017!}{17!(2017-17)!}$$

$$= \frac{2017!}{17!\,2000!}$$

31. Correct Response : (c)

Explanation :

The given binomial expression is,

$$\left(1-\frac{1}{x}+3x^5\right)\left(2x^2-\frac{1}{x}\right)^8$$

Simplify the given expression,

$$\left(1-\frac{1}{x}+3x^5\right)\cdot {}^8C_r\left(2x^2\right)^{8-r}\left(-\frac{1}{x}\right)^r$$

$$= {}^8C_r\left(2x^2\right)^{8-r}\left(-\frac{1}{x}\right)^r - \frac{1}{x}\,{}^8C_r\left(2x^2\right)^{8-r}\left(-\frac{1}{x}\right)^r$$

$$+ 3x^5\,{}^8C_r\left(2x^2\right)^{8-r}\left(-\frac{1}{x}\right)^r$$

$$= {}^8C_r\,2^{8-r}\,(-1)^r\,x^{16-3r} - {}^8C_r\,2^{8-r}\,(-1)^r\,x^{15-3r}$$

$$+ 3\,{}^8C_r\,2^{8-r}\,(-1)^r\,x^{21-3r}$$

For the term independent of x,

$$16-3r = 0$$

$$15-3r = 0$$

and

$$21-3r = 0$$

Only two possibilities

$$r = 5$$

$$r = 7$$

So,

$$-\left({}^8C_5 2^3\,(-1) - 3\,{}^8C_7 \cdot 2\right) = -(448 - 6\times8)$$

$$= -(448-48)$$

$$= -400$$

32. Correct Response : (a)

Explanation :

The binomial expansion of the given function is,

$$(1-2\sqrt{x})^{50} = {}^{50}C_0 - {}^{50}C_1(2\sqrt{x}) + {}^{50}C_2(2\sqrt{x})^2$$

$$- {}^{50}C_3(2\sqrt{x})^3 + {}^{50}C_4(2\sqrt{x})^4 - \dots$$

Similarly,

$$(1+2\sqrt{x})^{50} = {}^{50}C_0 + {}^{50}C_1(2\sqrt{x}) + {}^{50}C_2(2\sqrt{x})^2$$

$$+ {}^{50}C_3(2\sqrt{x})^3 + {}^{50}C_4(2\sqrt{x})^4 + \dots$$

Put $x=1$ in both the above equation and add them,

$$\frac{1+3^{50}}{2} = {}^{50}C_0 + {}^{50}C_2 \cdot 2^2 + {}^{50}C_4 \cdot 2^4 + \dots$$

33. Correct Response : (b)

Explanation :

The given explanation is $(1+x^n+x^{253})^{10}$.

Let $\qquad x^{1012} = (1)^a\,(x^n)^b\,(x^{253})^c$.

Here, a, b, c, n are all integers and $a \le 10$, $b \le 10$, $c \le 4$, $n \le 22$.

$$a + b + c = 10$$
$$b_n + 253c = 1012$$
$$b_n = 253\,(4 - c)$$

For $c < 4$, $n \le 22$; $b > 10$, which is not possible.

Hence,

$$c = 4$$
$$b = 0$$
$$a = 6$$
$$x^{1012} = (1)^6\,(x^n)^0\,(x^{253})^4$$

Hence, the coefficient of x^{1012} is,

$$x^{1012} = \frac{10!}{6!\,0!\,4!}$$
$$= {}^{10}C_4$$

34. Correct Response : (a)

Explanation :

The given equation is,

$$1 + x^4 + x^5 = \sum_{i=0}^{5} a_i\,(1+x)^i$$

$$= a_0 + a_1(1 + x) + a_2(1 + x)^2 + a_3(1 + x)^3$$
$$+ a_4(1 + x)^4 + a_5(1 + x)^5$$
$$= [a_0 + a_1\,(1 + x) + a_2\,(1 + x^2 + 2x)$$
$$+ a_3\,(1 + 3x + 3x^2 + x^3) +$$
$$a_4\,(1 + 4\,x + 6x^2 + 4x^3 + x^4)$$
$$+ a_5\,(1 + 5x + 10x^2 + 10x^3 + 5x^4 + x^5)]$$

Equate the coefficient of x^5,

$$a_5 = 1$$

Equate the coefficient of x^4,

$$a_4 + 5a_5 = 1$$
$$a_4 + 5 = 1$$
$$a_4 = -4$$

Equate the coefficient of x^3,

$$a_3 + 4a_4 + 10a_5 = 0$$
$$a_3 - 16 + 10 = 0$$
$$a_3 = 6$$

Equate the coefficients of x^2,

$$a_2 + 3a_3 + 6a_4 + 10a_5 = 0$$
$$a_2 + 18 - 24 + 10 = 0$$
$$a_2 = -4$$

35. Correct Response : (d)

Explanation :

The coefficient of x^{50} in the binomial expression,

$$\text{Coefficient of } x^{50} = (1 + x)^{1000} \left[\frac{1 - \left(\dfrac{x}{1+x} \right)^{1000}}{1 - \dfrac{x}{1+x}} \right]$$

$$= (1 + x)^{1001} - x^{10001}$$

The coefficient of x^{50},

$$\text{Coefficient of } x^{50} = {}^{1001}C_{50}$$
$$= \frac{(1001)!}{(50)!(951)!}$$

36. Correct Response : (d)

Explanation :

The given expression is,

$$\sum_{r=1}^{10} A_r\,(B_{10}B_r - C_{10}A_r)$$

$$= \sum_{r=1}^{10} A_r B_{10} B_r - \sum_{r=1}^{10} A_r C_{10} A_r \qquad \ldots(1)$$

According to given condition, A_r is the coefficient of x^r in the expansion of $(1 + x)^{10}$. That means A_r is equal to $10C_r$. B_r is the coefficient of x^r in the expansion of $(1 + x)^{20}$. That means B_r is equal to ${}^{20}C_r$.

Similarly, C_r is equal to ${}^{30}C_r$.

Substitute ${}^{30}C_r$ for C_r, ${}^{20}C_r$ for B_r and ${}^{10}C_r$ for A_r in equation (1).

$$\sum_{r=1}^{10} A_r\,B_{10}\,B_r - \sum_{r=1}^{10} A_r C_{10} A_r$$

$$= \sum_{r=1}^{10} {}^{10}C_r\,{}^{20}C_r\,{}^{20}C_r - \sum_{r=1}^{10} {}^{10}C_r\,{}^{30}C_{10}\,{}^{10}C_r$$

$$= {}^{20}C_{10} \sum_{r=1}^{10} {}^{10}C_{10-r}\,{}^{20}C_r - {}^{30}C_{10} \sum_{r=1}^{10} {}^{10}C_{10-r}\,{}^{10}C_r$$

$$= {}^{20}C_{10}\,({}^{30}C_{20} - {}^{10}C_0\,{}^{20}C_{20})$$
$$- {}^{30}C_{10}\,({}^{20}C_{10} - ({}^{10}C_0)^2)$$

Further solve the above expression,

$$\sum_{r=1}^{10} A_r\,B_{10}\,B_r - \sum_{r=1}^{10} A_r C_{10} A_r$$

$$= {}^{20}C_{10}\,{}^{30}C_{20} - {}^{20}C_{10} - {}^{30}C_{10}\,{}^{20}C_{10} + {}^{30}C_{10}$$
$$= {}^{30}C_{10} - {}^{20}C_{10}$$
$$= C_{10} - B_{10}$$

37. Correct Response : $\left(\dfrac{n}{k} \right)$

Explanation :

Sovle the left hand side.

$$\sum_{r=0}^{k} (-1)^r\,2^{k-r}\,{}^nC_r\,{}^{n-r}C_{k-r}$$

$$= \sum_{r=0}^{k} (-1)^r\,2^{k-r}\,\frac{n!}{(n-r)!\,r!}\,\frac{(n-r)!}{(n-k)!\,(k-r)!}$$

$$= \sum_{r=0}^{k} (-1)^r\,2^{k-r}\,\frac{n!}{(n-k)!\,k!}\,\frac{k!}{r!\,(k-r)!}$$

$$= {}^nC_k 2^k \sum_{r=0}^{k} \left(-\frac{1}{2}\right)^r {}^kC_r$$

$$= {}^nC_k 2^k \left(1-\frac{1}{2}\right)^k$$

Solve further.

$$\sum_{r=0}^{k} (-1)^r 2^{k-r} \, {}^nC_r \, {}^{n-r}C_{k-r} = {}^nC_k$$

$$= \binom{n}{k}$$

Hence, left hand side is equal to right hand side.

38. Correct Response : (a)

Explanation :

Simplify the given expression.

$$\binom{30}{0}\binom{30}{10} - \binom{30}{1}\binom{30}{11} + \binom{30}{2}\binom{30}{12} + \dots + \binom{30}{20}$$

$$\binom{30}{30}$$

$$= {}^{30}C_0 \cdot {}^{30}C_{10} - {}^{30}C_1 \cdot {}^{30}C_{11} + {}^{30}C_2 \cdot {}^{30}C_{12} + \dots$$
$$+ {}^{30}C_{20} \cdot {}^{30}C_{30}$$

$$= {}^{30}C_0 \cdot {}^{30}C_{20} - {}^{30}C_1 \cdot {}^{30}C_{19} + {}^{30}C_2 \cdot {}^{30}C_{18} + \dots$$
$$+ {}^{30}C_{20} \cdot {}^{30}C_{30}$$

The coefficient of x^{20} in $(1+x)^{30}(1-x)^{30} = (1-x^2)^{30}$ is the value of above expression.

Therefore, value of given expression is

$$^{30}C_{10} = \binom{30}{20}.$$

39. Correct Response : (d)

Explanation :

Solve the given expression.

$$(1+t^2)^{12}(1+t^{12})(1+t^{24})$$

$$= (1+t^2)^{12}(1+t^{12}+t^{24}+t^{36})$$

Coefficient of t^{24} is,

$$^{12}C_{12} + {}^{12}C_6 + 1 = {}^{12}C_6 + 2$$

●●

☯ QUESTIONS

1. If $3^{2\sin 2\alpha - 1}$, 14 and $3^{4 - 2\sin 2\alpha}$ are the first three terms of an A.P. for some α, then the sixth term of this A.P. is : **[2020, Main]**

(a) 66 (b) 65

(c) 81 (d) 78

2. If $2^{10} + 2^9.3^1 + 2^8.3^2 + \ldots + 2.3^9 + 3^{10} = S - 2^{11}$, then S is equal to : **[2020, Main]**

(a) $\dfrac{3^{11}}{2} + 2^{10}$ (b) $3^{11} - 2^{12}$

(c) 3^{11} (d) 2.3^{11}

3. If $f(x + y) = f(x)\,f(y)$ and $\displaystyle\sum_{x=1}^{\infty} f(x) = 2$, $x, y \in N$, where N is the set of all natural numbers, then the value of $\dfrac{f(4)}{f(2)}$ is : **[2020, Main]**

(a) $\dfrac{1}{9}$ (b) $\dfrac{4}{9}$

(c) $\dfrac{1}{3}$ (d) $\dfrac{2}{3}$

4. Let a, b, c, d and p be any non-zero distinct real numbers such that $(a^2 + b^2 + c^2)p^2 - 2(ab + bc + cd)\,p + (b^2 + c^2 + d^2) = 0$. Then : **[2020, Main]**

(a) a, c, p are in G.P. (b) a, c, p are in A.P.

(c) a, b, c, d are in G.P. (d) a, b, c, d are in A.P.

5. The common difference of the A.P. $b_1, b_2, \ldots, b_m$ is 2 more than the common difference of A.P. $a_1, a_2, \ldots, a_n$. If $a_{40} = -159$, $a_{100} = -399$ and $b_{100} = a_{70}$, then b_1 is equal to : **[2020, Main]**

(a) -127 (b) -81

(c) 81 (d) 127

6. Suppose that a function $f : R \to R$ satisfies $f(x + y) = f(x)\,f(y)$ for all $x, y \in R$ and $f(1) = 3$. If $\displaystyle\sum_{i=1}^{n} f(i) = 363$, then n is equal to .... **[2020, Main]**

7. Let α and β be the roots of $x^2 - 3x + p = 0$ and γ and δ be the roots of $x^2 - 6x + q = 0$. If $\alpha, \beta, \gamma, \delta$ form a geometric progression. Then ratio $(2q + p) : (2q - p)$ is : **[2020, Main]**

(a) $3 : 1$ (b) $33 : 31$

(c) $9 : 7$ (d) $5 : 3$

8. If $1 + (1 - 2^2.1) + (1 - 4^2.3) + (1 - 6^2.5) + \ldots + (1 - 20^2.19) = \alpha - 220\beta$, then an ordered pair (α, β) is equal to : **[2020, Main]**

(a) $(10, 97)$ (b) $(11, 103)$

(c) $(10, 103)$ (d) $(11, 97)$

9. Let $(2x^2 + 3x + 4)^{10} = \displaystyle\sum_{r=0}^{20} a_r x^r$. Then $\dfrac{a_7}{a_{13}}$ is equal to .... **[2020, Main]**

10. Let $a_1, a_2, \ldots, a_n$ be a given A.P. whose common difference is an integer and $S_n = a_1 + a_2 + \ldots + a_n$. If $a_1 = 1$, $a_n = 300$ and $15 \le n \le 50$, then the ordered pair (S_{n-4}, a_{n-4}) is equal to : **[2020, Main]**

(a) $(2480, 249)$ (b) $(2490, 249)$

(c) $(2490, 248)$ (d) $(2480, 248)$

11. The minimum value of $2^{\sin x} + 2^{\cos x}$ is : **[2020, Main]**

(a) $2^{1 - \frac{1}{\sqrt{2}}}$ (b) $2^{-1 + \sqrt{2}}$

(c) $2^{1 - \sqrt{2}}$ (d) $2^{-1 + \frac{1}{\sqrt{2}}}$

12. If the first term of an A.P. is 3 and the sum of its first 25 terms is equal to the sum of its next 15 terms, then the common difference of this A.P. is : **[2020, Main]**

(a) $\dfrac{1}{4}$ (b) $\dfrac{1}{5}$

(c) $\dfrac{1}{7}$ (d) $\dfrac{1}{6}$

13. The value of $(0.16)^{\log_{2.5}\left(\frac{1}{3} + \frac{1}{3^2} + \frac{1}{3^3} + \ldots \text{ to } \infty\right)}$ is equal to .... **[2020, Main]**

14. If the sum of first 11 terms of an A.P., $a_1, a_2, a_3, \ldots$ is 0 $(a_1 \ne 0)$, then the sum of the A.P., $a_1, a_3, a_5, \ldots, a_{23}$ is ka_1, where k is equal to : **[2020, Main]**

(a) $\dfrac{121}{10}$ (b) $-\dfrac{72}{5}$

(c) $\dfrac{72}{5}$ (d) $-\dfrac{121}{10}$

15. Let S be then sum of the first 9 terms of the series : $\{x + ka\} + \{x^2 + (k + 2)a\} + \{x^3 + (k + 4)a\} + \{x^4 + (k + 6)a\} + ...$ where $a \neq 0$ and $x \neq 1$. If $S = \dfrac{x^{10} - x + 45a(x-1)}{x-1}$, then k is equal to :

[2020, Main]

(a) -5 (b) 1

(c) -3 (d) 3

16. If the variance of the terms in an increasing A.P., $b_1, b_2, b_3,....b_{11}$ is 90, then the common difference of this A.P. is .... **[2020, Main]**

17. If $|x| < 1$, $|y| < 1$ and $x \neq y$, then the sum to infinity of the following series

$$(x + y) + (x^2 + xy + y^2) + (x^3 + x^2y + xy^2 + y^3) + ...$$

[2020, Main]

(a) $\dfrac{x+y-xy}{(1-x)(1-y)}$ (b) $\dfrac{x+y-xy}{(1+x)(1+y)}$

(c) $\dfrac{x+y+xy}{(1+x)(1+y)}$ (d) $\dfrac{x+y+xy}{(1-x)(1-y)}$

18. The sum of the first three terms of a G.P. is S and their product is 27. Then all such S lie in :

[2020, Main]

(a) $[-3, \infty)$

(b) $(-\infty, 9]$

(c) $(-\infty, -9] \cup [3, \infty)$

(d) $(-\infty, -3] \cup [9, \infty)$

19. If the sum of the series

$$20 + 19\dfrac{3}{5} + 19\dfrac{1}{5} + 18\dfrac{4}{5} + ... \text{ upto } n^{\text{th}} \text{ term is } 488$$

and the nth term is negative, then : **[2020, Main]**

(a) n^{th} term is $-4\dfrac{2}{5}$ (b) $n = 41$

(c) n^{th} term is -4 (d) $n = 60$

20. If m arithmetic means (A.Ms) and three geometric means (G.Ms) are inserted between 3 and 243 such that 4th A.M. is equal to 2nd G.M., then m is equal to .... **[2020, Main]**

21. If the first term of an A.P. is 3 and the sum of its first 25 terms is equal to the sum of its next 15 terms, then the common difference of this A.P. is : **[2020, Main]**

(a) $\dfrac{1}{4}$ (b) $\dfrac{1}{5}$

(c) $\dfrac{1}{7}$ (d) $\dfrac{1}{6}$

22. The value of $(0.16)^{\log_{2.5}\left(\frac{1}{3} + \frac{1}{3^2} + \frac{1}{3^3} + ... \text{ to } \infty\right)}$ is equal to .... **[2020, Main]**

23. If the sum of the first 20 terms of the series $\log (71^{1/2}) x + \log (71^{1/3}) x + \log (71^{1/4}) x + ... $ is 460, then x is equal to : **[2020, Main]**

(a) $7^{46/21}$ (b) $7^{1/2}$

(c) e^2 (d) 7^2

24. If the sum of the second, third and fourth terms of a positive term G.P. is 3 and the sum of its sixth, seventh and eighth terms is 243, then the sum of the first 50 terms of this G.P. is : **[2020, Main]**

(a) $\dfrac{2}{13}(3^{50} - 1)$ (b) $\dfrac{1}{26}(3^{50} - 1)$

(c) $\dfrac{1}{13}(3^{50} - 1)$ (d) $\dfrac{1}{26}(3^{49} - 1)$

25. Let $a_1, a_2, a_3, \ldots$ be a sequence of positive integers in arithmetic progression with common difference 2. Also, let $b_1, b_2, b_3, \ldots$ be a sequence of positive integers in geometric progression with common ratio 2. If $a_1 = b_1 = c$, then the number of all possible values of c, for which the equality

$$2(a_1 + a_2 + \ldots + a_n) = b_1 + b_2 + \ldots + b_n$$

holds for some positive integer n, is ....

[2020, Advanced]

26. Five numbers are in A.P., whose sum is 25 and product is 2520. If one of these five numbers is $-\dfrac{1}{2}$, then the greatest number amongst them is :

[2020, Main]

(a) $\dfrac{21}{2}$ (b) 27

(c) 16 (d) 7

27. The greatest positive integer k, for which $49^k + 1$ is a factor of the sum $49^{125} + 49^{124} + ... 49^2 + 49 + 1$, is : **[2020, Main]**

(a) 32 (b) 60

(c) 63 (d) 65

28. If the sum of the first 40 terms of the series, $3 + 4 + 8 + 9 + 13 + 14 + 18 + 19 + ...$ is $(102) m$, then m is equal to : **[2020, Main]**

(a) 20 (b) 5

(c) 10 (d) 25

29. Let $a_1, a_2, a_3, \ldots$ be a G.P. such that $a_1 < 0, a_1 + a_2 = 4$ and $a_3 + a_4 = 16$. If $\displaystyle\sum_{i=1}^{9} a_i = 4\lambda$, then λ is equal to :

[2020, Main]

(a) -171 (b) 171

(c) $\dfrac{511}{3}$ (d) -513

30. Let $f : R \to R$ be such that for all $x \in R$ $(2^{1+x} + 2^{1-x})$, $f(x)$ and $(3^x + 3^{-x})$ are in A.P., then the minimum value of $f(x)$ is **[2020, Main]**

(a) 0   (b) 3

(c) 2   (d) 4

31. The sum $\displaystyle\sum_{k=1}^{20} (1 + 2 + 3 + ... + k)$ is ...

32. If the 10th term of an A.P. is $\dfrac{1}{20}$ and its 20th term is $\dfrac{1}{10}$ then the sum of its first 200 terms is

[2020, Main]

(a) $50\dfrac{1}{4}$ (b) $100\dfrac{1}{2}$

(c) 50   (d) 100

33. The sum $\displaystyle\sum_{n=1}^{7} \dfrac{n(n+1)(2n+1)}{4}$ is equal to _______.

[2020, Main]

34. The product $2^{\frac{1}{4}}.4^{\frac{1}{16}}.8^{\frac{1}{48}}.16^{\frac{1}{128}}. ....$ to ∞ is equal

[2020, Main]

(a) $2^{\frac{1}{2}}$ (b) $2^{\frac{1}{4}}$

(c) 2   (d) 1

35. If $x - \displaystyle\sum_{n=0}^{\infty} (-1)^n \tan^{2n} \theta$ and $y = \displaystyle\sum_{n=0}^{\infty} \cos^{2n} \theta$, for $0 < \theta < \dfrac{\pi}{4}$, then : **[2020, Main]**

(a) $y(1 + x) = 1$ (b) $x(1 + y) = 1$

(c) $y(1 - x) = 1$ (d) $x(1 - y) = 1$

36. Let a_n be the nth term of a G.P. of positive terms. If $\displaystyle\sum_{n=1}^{100} a_{n+1} = 200$ and $\displaystyle\sum_{n=1}^{100} a_{2n} = 100$, then $\displaystyle\sum_{n=1}^{200} a_n$ is equal to : **[2020, Main]**

(a) 225   (b) 175

(c) 300   (d) 150

37. The number of terms common to the two A.P.'s 3, 7, 11, ..., 407 and 2, 9, 16, ..., 709 is .... **[2020, Main]**

38. If $a_1, a_2, a_3, ... a_n$ are in A.P. and $a_1 + a_4 + a_7 + ... + a_{16} = 114$, then $a_1 + a_6 + a_{11} + a_{16}$ is equal to : **[2019, Main]**

(a) 98   (b) 76

(c) 38   (d) 64

39. The sum $\dfrac{3 \times 1^3}{1^2} + \dfrac{5 \times (1^3 + 2^3)}{1^2 + 2^2} + \dfrac{7 \times (1^3 + 2^3 + 3^3)}{1^2 + 2^2 + 3^2} + ...$ upto 10th term, is : **[2019, Main]**

(a) 680   (b) 600

(c) 660   (d) 620

40. The sum $1 + \dfrac{1^3 + 2^3}{1+2} + \dfrac{1^3 + 2^3 + 3^3}{1+2+3} + ...$

$+ \dfrac{1^3 + 2^3 + 3^3 + ... + 15^3}{1+2+3+...+15} - \dfrac{1}{2}(1+2+3+...+15)$ is equal to : **[2019, Main]**

(a) 620   (b) 1240

(c) 1860   (d) 660

41. Let a, b and c be in G.P. with common ratio r, where $a \neq 0$ and $0 < r \leq \dfrac{1}{2}$. If $3a$, $7b$ and $15c$ are the first three terms of an A.P., then the 4th term of this A.P. is : **[2019, Main]**

(a) $\dfrac{2}{3}a$ (b) $5a$

(c) $\dfrac{7}{3}a$ (d) a

42. Let $a_1, a_2, a_3, ...$ be an A.P. with $a_6 = 2$. Then the common difference of this A.P., which maximises the product a_1, a_4, a_5, is : **[2019, Main]**

(a) $\dfrac{3}{2}$ (b) $\dfrac{8}{5}$

(c) $\dfrac{6}{5}$ (d) $\dfrac{2}{3}$

43. Some identical balls are arranged in rows to form an equilateral triangle. The first row consists of one ball, the second row consists of two balls and so on. If 99 more identical balls are added to the total number of balls used in forming the equilateral triangle, then all these balls can be arranged in a square whose each side contains exactly 2 balls less than the number of balls each side of the triangle contains. Then the number of balls used to form the equilateral triangle is : **[2019, Main]**

(a) 157   (b) 262

(c) 225   (d) 190

44. If the sum and product of the first three terms in an A.P. are 33 and 1155, respectively, then the value of its 11th term is : **[2019, Main]**

(a) -35 (b) 25

(c) -36 (d) -25

45. The sum of the series $1 + 2 \times 3 + 3 \times 5 + 4 \times 7 + ...$ upto 11th term is : **[2019, Main]**

(a) 915   (b) 946

(c) 945   (d) 916

46. Let the sum of the first n term of a non-constant A.P., $a_1, a_2, a_3, \ldots\ldots$ be $50n + \dfrac{n(n-7)}{2}A$, where A is a constant. If d is the common difference of this A.P., then the ordered pair (d, a_{50}) is equal to :

[2019, Main]

(a) $(50, 50 + 46A)$

(b) $(50, 50 + 45A)$

(c) $(A, 50 + 45A)$

(d) $(A, 50 + 46A)$

47. The sum of the series $2 \cdot {}^{20}C_0 + 5 \cdot {}^{20}C_1 + 8 \cdot {}^{20}C_2 + 11 \cdot {}^{20}C_3 + \ldots + 62 \cdot {}^{20}C_{20}$ is equal to : **[2019, Main]**

(a) 2^{26}

(b) 2^{25}

(c) 2^{23}

(d) 2^{24}

48. The sum of all natural numbers 'n' such that $100 < n < 200$ and H.C.F. $(91, n) > 1$ is : **[2019, Main]**

(a) 3203

(b) 3303

(c) 3221

(d) 3121

49. If three distinct numbers a, b, c are in G.P. and the equations $ax^2 + 2bx + c = 0$ and $dx^2 + 2ex + f = 0$ have a common root, then which one of the following statements is correct ? **[2019, Main]**

(a) $\dfrac{d}{a}, \dfrac{e}{b}, \dfrac{f}{c}$ are in A.P.

(b) d, e, f are in A.P.

(c) d, e, f are in G.P.

(d) $\dfrac{d}{a}, \dfrac{e}{b}, \dfrac{f}{c}$ are in G.P.

50. The sum $\displaystyle\sum_{k=1}^{20} k\dfrac{1}{2^k}$ is equal to : **[2019, Main]**

(a) $2 - \dfrac{3}{2^{17}}$

(b) $1 - \dfrac{11}{2^{20}}$

(c) $2 - \dfrac{11}{2^{19}}$

(d) $2 - \dfrac{21}{2^{20}}$

51. For $x \in \mathbf{R}$, let $[x]$ denote the greatest integer $\le x$, then the sum of the series $\left[-\dfrac{1}{3}\right] + \left[-\dfrac{1}{3} - \dfrac{1}{100}\right] + \left[-\dfrac{1}{3} - \dfrac{2}{100}\right] + \ldots\ldots + \left[-\dfrac{1}{3} - \dfrac{99}{100}\right]$ is :

[2019, Main]

(a) -153

(b) -133

(c) -131

(d) -135

52. Let S_n denote the sum of the first n terms of an A.P. If $S_4 = 16$ and $S_6 = -48$, then S_{10} is equal to : **[2019, Main]**

(a) -260

(b) -410

(c) -320

(d) -380

53. If $a_1, a_2, a_3, \ldots\ldots$ are in A.P. such that $a_1 + a_7 + a_{16} = 40$, then the sum of the first 15 terms of this A.P. is : **[2019, Main]**

(a) 200

(b) 280

(c) 120

(d) 150

54. If α, β and γ are three consecutive terms of a non-constant G.P. such that the equations $\alpha x^2 + 2\beta x + \gamma = 0$ and $x^2 + x - 1 = 0$ have a common root, then $\alpha(\beta + \gamma)$ is equal to : **[2019, Main]**

(a) 0

(b) $\alpha\beta$

(c) $\alpha\gamma$

(d) $\beta\gamma$

55. Let AP $(a; d)$ denote the set of all the terms of an infinite arithmetic progression with first term a and common difference $d > 0$. If AP$(1; 3) \cap$ AP$(2; 5) \cap$ AP$(3; 7) = $ AP$(a; d)$, then a + d equals$\ldots\ldots\ldots$

[2019, Main]

56. Let $\dfrac{1}{x_1}, \dfrac{1}{x_2}, \ldots\ldots, \dfrac{1}{x_n}$ $(x_i \neq 0$ for $i = 1, 2, \ldots., n)$ be in A.P. such that $x_1 = 4$ and $x_{21} = 20$. If n is the least positive integer for which $x_n > 50$, then $\displaystyle\sum_{i=1}^{n}\left(\dfrac{1}{x_i}\right)$ is equal to : **[2018, Main]**

(a) $\dfrac{1}{8}$

(b) 3

(c) $\dfrac{13}{8}$

(d) $\dfrac{13}{4}$

57. The sum of the first 20 terms of the series :

[2018, Main]

$$1 + \dfrac{3}{2} + \dfrac{7}{4} + \dfrac{15}{8} + \dfrac{31}{16} + \ldots\ldots, \text{ is :}$$

(a) $38 + \dfrac{1}{2^{19}}$

(b) $38 + \dfrac{1}{2^{20}}$

(c) $39 + \dfrac{1}{2^{20}}$

(d) $39 + \dfrac{1}{2^{19}}$

58. Let $a_1, a_2, a_3, \ldots, a_{49}$ be in A.P. such that $\displaystyle\sum_{k=0}^{12} a_{4k+1} = 416$ and $a_9 + a_{43} = 66$. If $a_1^2 + a_2^2 + \ldots + a_{17}^2 = 140$ m, then m is equal to : **[2018, Main]**

(a) 66

(b) 68

(c) 34

(d) 33

59. Let A be the sum of the first 20 terms and B be the sum of the first 40 terms of the series $1^2 + 2 \cdot 2^2 + 3^2 + 2 \cdot 4^2 + 5^2 + 2 \cdot 6^2 + \ldots\ldots$

If $B - 2A = 100\lambda$, then λ is equal to : **[2018, Main]**

(a) 232

(b) 248

(c) 464

(d) 496

60. If $x_1, x_2, ..., x_n$ and $\dfrac{1}{h_1}, \dfrac{1}{h_2}, ..., \dfrac{1}{h_n}$ are two A.P.s such that $x_3 = h_2 = 8$ and $x_8 = h_7 = 20$, then $x_5 \cdot h_{10}$ equals : **[2018, Main]**

(a) 2560   (b) 2650

(c) 3200   (d) 1600

61. If b is the first term of an infinite G.P. whose sum is five, then b lies in the interval : **[2018, Main]**

(a) $(-\infty, -10]$ (b) $(-10, 0)$

(c) $(0, 10)$ (d) $[10, \infty)$

62. If the arithmetic mean of two numbers a and b, $a > b > 0$, is five times their geometric mean, then $\dfrac{a+b}{a-b}$ is equal to : **[2017, Main]**

(a) $\dfrac{\sqrt{6}}{2}$ (b) $\dfrac{3\sqrt{2}}{4}$

(c) $\dfrac{7\sqrt{3}}{12}$ (d) $\dfrac{5\sqrt{6}}{12}$

63. If the sum of the first n terms of the series $\sqrt{3} + \sqrt{75} + \sqrt{243} + \sqrt{507} + ...$ is $435\sqrt{3}$, then n is equal to : **[2017, Main]**

(a) 18   (b) 15

(c) 13   (d) 29

64. If three positive number a, b and c are in A.P. such that $abc = 8$, then the minimum possible value of b is : **[2017, Main]**

(a) 2   (b) $4^{\frac{1}{3}}$

(c) $4^{\frac{2}{3}}$ (d) 4

65. Let $S_n = \dfrac{1}{1^3} + \dfrac{1+2}{1^3+2^3} + \dfrac{1+2+3}{1^3+2^3+3^3} + ... + \dfrac{1+2+........+n}{1^3+2^3+......+n^3}$.

If $100\,S_n = n$, then n is equal to : **[2017, Main]**

(a) 199   (b) 99

(c) 200   (d) 19

66. For any three positive real numbers a, b and c,

$9(25a^2 + b^2) + 25(c^2 - 3ac) = 15b(3a + c)$.

Then : **[2017, Main]**

(a) b, c and a are in A.P.

(b) a, b and c are in A.P.

(c) a, b and c are in G.P.

(d) b, c and a are in G.P.

67. Let a, b, $c \in$ R. If $f(x) = ax^2 + bx + c$ is such that $a + b + c = 3$ and

$$f(x + y) = f(x) + f(y) + xy, \ \forall \ x, y \in R,$$

then $\displaystyle\sum_{n=1}^{10} f(n)$ is equal to : **[2017, Main]**

(a) 165   (b) 190

(c) 255   (d) 330

68. Let $a_1, a_2, a_3, ..., a_n, ...$ be in A.P. If $a_3 + a_7 + a_{11} + a_{15} = 72$, then the sum of its first 17 terms is equal to : **[2016, Main]**

(a) 306   (b) 153

(c) 612   (d) 204

69. If the 2nd, 5th and 9th terms of a non-constant A.P. are in G.P., then the common ratio of this G.P. is: **[2016, Main]**

(a) $\dfrac{8}{5}$ (b) $\dfrac{4}{3}$

(c) 1   (d) $\dfrac{7}{4}$

70. If the sum of the first ten terms of the series

$$\left(1\dfrac{3}{5}\right)^2 + \left(2\dfrac{2}{5}\right)^2 + \left(3\dfrac{1}{5}\right)^2 + 4^2 + \left(4\dfrac{4}{5}\right)^2 + ...,$$

is $\dfrac{16}{5}\,m$, then m is equal to : **[2016, Main]**

(a) 102   (b) 101

(c) 100   (d) 99

71. Let x, y, z be positive real numbers such that $x + y + z = 12$ and $x^3y^4z^5 = (0.1)(600)^3$. Then $x^3 + y^3 + z^3$ is equal to : **[2016, Main]**

(a) 270   (b) 258

(c) 342   (d) 216

72. If the mean deviation of the numbers 1, $1 + d$, ... $1 + 100d$ from their mean is 255, then the value of d is : **[2016, Main]**

(a) 10.1   (b) 20.2

(c) 10   (d) 5.05

73. The sum $\displaystyle\sum_{r=1}^{10} (r^2 + 1) \times (r!)$ is equal to : **[2016, Main]**

(a) $(11)!$ (b) $10 \times (11)!$

(c) $101 \times (10!)$ (d) $11 \times (11!)$

74. The sum of the 3rd and the 4th terms of a G.P. is 60 and the product of its first three terms is 1000. If the first term of this G.P. is positive, then its 7th term is : **[2015, Main]**

(a) 7290   (b) 320

(c) 640   (d) 2430

75. If m is the A.M. of two distinct real numbers l and n (l, $n > 1$) and G_1, G_2 and G_3 are three geometric mean between l and n, then $G_1^4 + 2G_2^4 + G_3^4$ equals: **[2015, Main]**

(a) $4\,l^2mn$

(b) $4lm^2n$

(c) $4\,lmn^2$

(d) $4\,l^2m^2n^2$

76. The sum of first 9 terms of the seires

$$\frac{1^3}{1} + \frac{1^3 + 2^3}{1+3} + \frac{1^3 + 2^3 + 3^3}{1+3+5} + \dots \text{ is :}$$

[2015, Main]

(a) 71

(b) 96

(c) 142

(d) 192

77. If $\displaystyle\sum_{n=1}^{5} \frac{1}{n(n+1)\,(n+2)(n+3)} = \frac{k}{3}$, then k is equal to : **[2015, Main]**

(a) $\dfrac{55}{336}$

(b) $\dfrac{17}{105}$

(c) $\dfrac{1}{6}$

(d) $\dfrac{19}{112}$

78. If $\cos \alpha + \cos \beta = \dfrac{3}{2}$ and $\sin \alpha + \sin \beta = \dfrac{1}{2}$ and θ is the arithmetic mean of α and β, then $\sin 2\theta + \cos 2\theta$ is equal to : **[2015, Main]**

(a) $\dfrac{3}{5}$

(b) $\dfrac{4}{5}$

(c) $\dfrac{7}{5}$

(d) $\dfrac{8}{5}$

79. Let 10 vertical poles standing at equal distances on a straight line, subtend the same angle of elevation α at a point O on this line and all the poles are on the same side of O. If the height of the longest pole is 'h' and the distance of the foot of the smallest pole from O is 'a'; then the distance between two consecutive poles, is : **[2015, Main]**

(a) $\dfrac{h \sin \alpha + a\cos \alpha}{9 \sin \alpha}$

(b) $\dfrac{h \cos \alpha - a\sin \alpha}{9 \cos \alpha}$

(c) $\dfrac{h \cos \alpha - a\sin \alpha}{9 \sin \alpha}$

(d) $\dfrac{h \sin \alpha + a\sin \alpha}{9 \cos \alpha}$

80. Three positive numbers form an increasing G.P. If the middle term in this G.P. is doubled, the new numbers are in A.P. Then the common ratio of the G.P. is : **[2014, Main]**

(a) $2 - \sqrt{3}$

(b) $2 + \sqrt{3}$

(c) $\sqrt{2} + \sqrt{3}$

(d) $3 + \sqrt{2}$

81. Let G be the geometric mean of two positive numbers a and b, and M be the arithmetic mean of $\dfrac{1}{a}$ and $\dfrac{1}{b}$. If $\dfrac{1}{M} : G$ is $4 : 5$, then $a : b$ can be : **[2014, Main]**

(a) $1 : 4$

(b) $1 : 2$

(c) $2 : 3$

(d) $3 : 4$

82. The number of terms in an A.P. is even; the sum of the odd terms in it is 24 and that the even terms is 30. If the last term exceeds the first term by $10\dfrac{1}{2}$, then the number of terms in the A.P. is : **[2014, Main]**

(a) 4

(b) 8

(c) 12

(d) 16

83. Let $f(n) = \left[\dfrac{1}{3} + \dfrac{3n}{100}\right]n$, where $[n]$ denotes the greatest integer less than or equal to n. Then $\displaystyle\sum_{n=1}^{56} f(n)$ is equal to : **[2014, Main]**

(a) 56

(b) 689

(c) 1287

(d) 1399

84. In a geometric progression, if the ratio of the sum of first 5 terms to the sum of their reciprocals is 49, and the sum of the first and the third term is 35. Then the first term of this geometric progression is : **[2014, Main]**

(a) 7

(b) 21

(c) 28

(d) 42

85. The sum of the first 20 terms common between the series $3 + 7 + 11 + 15 + \dots$ and $1 + 6 + 11 + 16 \dots$, is : **[2014, Main]**

(a) 4000

(b) 4020

(c) 4200

(d) 4220

86. If the sum of first n terms of an A.P. is cn^2, then the sum of the squares of these n terms is : **[2014, Advanced)]**

(a) $\dfrac{n\,(4n^2-1)c^2}{6}$

(b) $\dfrac{n\,(4n^2+1)c^2}{3}$

(c) $\dfrac{n\,(4n^2-1)c^2}{3}$

(d) $\dfrac{n\,(4n^2+1)c^2}{6}$

87. Given an A.P. whose terms are all positive integers. The sum of its first nine terms is greater than 200 and less than 220. If the second term in it is 12, then its 4th term is : **[2014, Main]**

(a) 8

(b) 16

(c) 20

(d) 24

88. If the sum

$$\frac{3}{1^2} + \frac{5}{1^2 + 2^2} + \frac{7}{1^2 + 2^2 + 3^2} + ... + \text{upto } 20 \text{ terms is}$$

equal to , then k is equal to : **[2014, Main]**

(a) 120   **(b)** 180

(c) 240   **(d)** 60

89. The least positive integer n such that

$$1 - \frac{2}{3} - \frac{2}{3^2} - ...... - \frac{2}{3^{n-1}} < \frac{1}{100} \text{ , is :} \quad \textbf{[2014, Main]}$$

(a) 4   **(b)** 5

(c) 6   **(d)** 7

90. Let $a_1, a_2, a_3, ..., a_{11}$ be real numbers satisfying $a_1 = 15$, $27 - 2a_2 > 0$ and $a_k = 2a_{k-1} - a_{k-2}$ for $k = 3$, $4, ... 11$.

If $\dfrac{a_1^2 + a_2^2 + ... + a_{11}^2}{11} = 90$, then the value of

$\dfrac{a_1 + a_2 + ... + a_{11}}{11}$ is equal to ....

[2010, Advanced]

91. A straight line through the vertex P of a triangle PQR intersects the side QR at the point S and the circumcircle of the triangle PQR at the point T. If S is not the centre of the circumcircle, then

[2008, Advanced]

(a) $\dfrac{1}{PS} + \dfrac{1}{ST} < \dfrac{2}{\sqrt{QS \times SR}}$

(b) $\dfrac{1}{PS} + \dfrac{1}{ST} > \dfrac{2}{\sqrt{QS \times SR}}$

(c) $\dfrac{1}{PS} + \dfrac{1}{ST} < \dfrac{4}{QR}$

(d) $\dfrac{1}{PS} + \dfrac{1}{ST} > \dfrac{4}{QR}$

92. Which one of the following statements is correct?

[2007, Advanced]

(a) $G_1 > G_2 > G_3 > ....$

(b) $G_1 < G_2 < G_3 < ...$

(c) $G_1 = G_2 = G_3 = ...$

(d) $G_1 < G_3 < G_5 < ...$ and $G_2 > G_4 > G_6 > ....$

93. Which one of the following statements is correct?

[2007, Advanced]

(a) $A_1 > A_2 > A_3 > ....$

(b) $A_1 < A_2 < A_3 < ...$

(c) $A_1 > A_3 > A_5 > ....$ and $A_2 < A_4 < A_6 < ....$

(d) $A_1 < A_3 < A_5 < ...$ and $A_2 > A_4 > A_6 > ......$

94. Which one of the following statements is correct?

[2007, Advanced]

(a) $H_1 > H_2 > H_3 > ....$

(b) $H_1 < H_2 < H_3 < ...$

(c) $H_1 > H_3 > H_5 > ....$ and $H_2 < H_4 < H_6 < ....$

(d) $H_1 < H_3 < H_5 < ...$ and $H_2 > H_4 > H_6 > ......$

95. If $a_n = \dfrac{3}{4} - \left(\dfrac{3}{4}\right)^2 + \left(\dfrac{3}{4}\right)^3 + ...(-1)^{n-1}\left(\dfrac{3}{4}\right)^n$ and $b_n = 1 - a_n$, then find the minimum natural number n_0 such that $b_n > a_n \; \forall \; n > n_0$. **[2006, Main]**

96. In the quadratic equation $ax^2 + bx + c = 0$, if $\Delta = b^2 - 4ac$ and $\alpha + \beta^2$, $\alpha^2 + \beta^2$, $\alpha^3 + \beta^3$ are in G.P., where α, β are the roots of $ax^2 + bx + c = 0$, then:

[2005, Main]

(a) $\Delta \neq 0$ **(b)** $b\Delta = 0$

(c) $c\Delta = 0$ **(d)** $\Delta = 0$

97. Let V_r denote the sum of the first r terms of an arithmetic progression (A.P) whose first term is r and common difference is $(2r - 1)$. Let $T_r = V_{r+1} - V_r - 2$ and $Q_r = T_{n} - T_r$ for $r = 1, 2.......$ Then T_r is always **[2005, Main]**

(a) an odd no   **(b)** an even no

(c) a prime no   **(d)** a composite no.

98. If a, b, c are positive real numbers, then prove that $[(1 + a)(1 + b)(1 + c)]^7 > 7^7 \, a^4 b^4 c^4$. **[2004, Main]**

99. If $\alpha \in \left(0, \dfrac{\pi}{2}\right)$ then $\sqrt{x^2 + x} + \dfrac{\tan^2 \alpha}{\sqrt{x^2 + x}}$ is always greater than or equal to : **[2003, Main]**

(a) $2 \tan \alpha$ **(b)** 1

(c) 2   **(d)** $\sec^2 \alpha$

100. If $a_1, a_2, ... a_n$ are positive real numbers whose product is a fixed number c, then the minimum value of $a_1 + a_2 + ... + a_{n-1} + 2a_n$ is : **[2003, Main]**

(a) $n(2c)^{1/n}$ **(b)** $(n + 1)c^{1/n}$

(c) $2nc^{1/n}$ **(d)** $(n + 1)(2c)^{1/n}$

101. Suppose a, b, c are in A.P. and a^2, b^2, c^2 are in G.P. If $a < b < c$ and $a + b + c = 3/2$, then the value of a is : **(2002, Main)**

(a) $\dfrac{1}{2\sqrt{2}}$ **(b)** $\dfrac{1}{2\sqrt{3}}$

(c) $\dfrac{1}{2} - \dfrac{1}{\sqrt{3}}$ **(d)** $\dfrac{1}{2} - \dfrac{1}{\sqrt{2}}$

ANSWER KEY

1. (a)	**2.** (c)	**3.** (b)	**4.** (c)	**5.** (b)	**6.** (5)	**7.** (c)	**8.** (b)	**9.** (8)	**10.** (c)
11. (a)	**12.** (d)	**13.** (4)	**14.** (b)	**15.** (c)	**16.** (3)	**17.** (a)	**18.** (d)	**19.** (c)	**20.** (39)
21. (d)	**22.** (4)	**23.** (d)	**24.** (b)	**25.** (1)	**26.** (c)	**27.** (c)	**28.** (a)	**29.** (a)	**30.** (b)
31. (1540)	**32.** (b)	**33.** (504)	**34.** (a)	**35.** (c)	**36.** (d)	**37.** (14)	**38.** (b)	**39.** (c)	**40.** (a)
41. (d)	**42.** (b)	**43.** (d)	**44.** (d)	**45.** (b)	**46.** (d)	**47.** (b)	**48.** (d)	**49.** (a)	**50.** (c)
51. (b)	**52.** (c)	**53.** (a)	**54.** (d)	**55.** (157)	**56.** (d)	**57.** (a)	**58.** (c)	**59.** (b)	**60.** (a)
61. (c)	**62.** (d)	**63.** (b)	**64.** (a)	**65.** (a)	**66.** (a)	**67.** (d)	**68.** (a)	**69.** (b)	**70.** (b)
71. (d)	**72.** (a)	**73.** (b)	**74.** (b)	**75.** (b)	**76.** (b)	**77.** (a)	**78.** (c)	**79.** (c)	**80.** (b)
81. (a)	**82.** (b)	**83.** (d)	**84.** (c)	**85.** (b)	**86.** (a)	**87.** (c)	**88.** (a)	**89.** (c)	**90.** (0)
91. (b,d)	**92.** (c)	**93.** (a)	**94.** (b)	**95.** (6)	**96.** (c)	**97.** (d)	**98.** (*)	**99.** (a)	**100.** (a)
101. (d)									

ANSWERS WITH EXPLANATIONS

1. Correct Response : (a)

Explanation :

Given that a, b, c are in A.P. then

$$a + c = 2b$$

$$3^{2\sin 2\alpha - 1} + 3^{4 - 2\sin 2\alpha} = 28$$

Let $\quad 3^{2\sin 2\alpha} = t$

$$\frac{81}{t} + \frac{t}{3} = 28$$

$$t = 81, 3$$

$$3^{2\sin 2\alpha} = 3^1, 3^4$$

$$2\sin 2\alpha = 1, 4$$

$$\sin 2\alpha = \frac{1}{2}, 2 \text{ (rejected)}$$

First term $a = 3^{2\sin 2\alpha - 1}$

$$a = 1$$

Second term $= 14$

$\therefore$ Common difference $d = 13$

$$T_6 = a + 5d$$
$$T_6 = 1 + 5 \times 13$$
$$T_6 = 66.$$

2. Correct Response : (c)

Explanation :

$$a = 2^{10}; r = \frac{3}{2}; n = 11 \text{ (G.P.)}$$

$$S' = (2^{10})\frac{\left(\left(\frac{3}{2}\right)^{11} - 1\right)}{\frac{3}{2} - 1} = 2^{11}\left(\frac{3^{11}}{2^{11}} - 1\right)$$

$$S' = 3^{11} - 2^{11} = S - 2^{11} \text{ (Given)}$$

$$\therefore \quad S = 3^{11}.$$

3. Correct Response : (b)

Explanation :

$$f(x + y) = f(x).f(y)$$

$$\sum_{x=1}^{\infty} f(x) = 2 \text{ where } x, y \in N$$

$$f(1) + f(2) + f(3) + \ldots \infty = 2 \qquad \ldots (1) \text{ (Given)}$$

Now for $f(2)$ put $x = y = 1$

$$f(2) = f(1 + 1) = f(1).f(1) = (f(1))^2$$
$$f(3) = f(2 + 1) = f(2).f(1) = (f(1))^3$$

Now put these values in equation (1)

$$f(1) + f(1)^2 + f(1)^3 + \ldots \infty = 2$$

$$\frac{f(1)}{1 - f(1)} = 2$$

$$\Rightarrow \qquad f(1) = \frac{2}{3}$$

Now $\qquad f(2) = \left(\frac{2}{3}\right)^2$

$$f(4) = \left(\frac{2}{3}\right)^4$$

then the value of $\dfrac{f(4)}{f(2)} = \dfrac{\left(\frac{2}{3}\right)^4}{\left(\frac{2}{3}\right)^2} = \dfrac{4}{9}.$

4. Correct Response : (c)

Explanation :

$$(a^2 + b^2 + c^2)p^2 - 2(ab + bc + cd)p + (b^2 + c^2 + d^2) = 0$$
$$(a^2p^2 - 2abp + b^2) + (b^2p^2 - 2bcp + c^2)$$
$$+ (c^2p^2 - 2cdp + d^2) = 0$$
$$(ap - b)^2 + (bp - c)^2 + (cp - d)^2 = 0$$

This is possible only when
$$ap - b = 0, \; bp - c = 0, \; cp - d = 0$$
$$p = \frac{b}{a} = \frac{c}{b} = \frac{d}{c}$$

a, b, c, d are in G.P.

5. Correct Response : (b)

Explanation :

$a_1, a_2, \ldots, a_n \; (\text{CD} = d)$

$b_1, b_2, \ldots, b_m \; (\text{CD} = d + 2)$

$$a_{40} = a + 39d = -159 \qquad \ldots(1)$$
$$a_{100} = a + 99d = -399 \qquad \ldots(2)$$

Subtract : $\quad 60d = -240 \Rightarrow d = -4$

using equation (1)

$$a + 39(-4) = -159$$
$$a = 156 - 159 = -3$$
$$a_{70} = a + 69d = -3 + 69(-4)$$
$$= -279 = b_{100}$$
$$b_{100} = -279$$
$$b_1 + 99(d + 2) = -279$$
$$b_1 - 198 = -279 \Rightarrow b_1 = -81.$$

6. Correct Response : (5)

Explanation :

$$f(x + y) = f(x)\, f(y)$$

put $x = y = 1$

$$f(2) = [f(1)]^2 = 3^2$$

put $x = 2, y = 1$

$$f(3) = [f(1)]^3 = 3^3$$

Similarly $\quad f(x) = 3^x$

$$\sum_{i=1}^{n} f(i) = 363 \Rightarrow \sum_{i=1}^{n} 3^i = 363$$

$$(3 + 3^2 + \ldots + 3^n) = 363$$
$$\frac{3(3^n - 1)}{2} = 363$$
$$3^n - 1 = 242 \Rightarrow 3^n = 243$$
$$\Rightarrow \qquad n = 5.$$

7. Correct Response : (c)

Explanation :

$$x^2 - 3x + p = 0 \Big\langle \begin{matrix} \alpha \\ \beta \end{matrix}$$

$\alpha, \beta, \gamma, \delta$ in G.P.

$$\alpha + \alpha r = 3 \qquad \ldots(1)$$

$$x^2 - 6x + q = 0 \Big\langle \begin{matrix} \gamma \\ \delta \end{matrix}$$

$$\alpha r^2 + \alpha r^3 = 6 \qquad \ldots(2)$$

$(2) \div (1)$

$$\frac{\alpha r^2(1 + r)}{\alpha(1 + r)} = \frac{6}{3}$$
$$r^2 = 2$$

So, $\quad \dfrac{2q + p}{2q - p} = \dfrac{2r^5 + r}{2r^5 - r} = \dfrac{2r^4 + 1}{2r^4 - 1} = \dfrac{9}{7}$

8. Correct Response : (b)

Explanation :

$$1 + (1 - 2^2.1) + (1 - 4^2.3) + \ldots + (1 - 20^2.19)$$
$$= \alpha - 220\beta$$
$$= 11 - (2^2.1 + 4^2.3 + \ldots + 20^2.19)$$
$$= 11 - 2^2.\sum_{r=1}^{10} r^2(2r - 1) = 11 - 4\left(\frac{110^2}{2} - 35 \times 11\right)$$
$$= 11 - 220(103)$$
$$\Rightarrow \qquad \alpha = 11, \; \alpha = 103.$$

9. Correct Response : (8)

Explanation :

Given $(2x^2 + 3x + 4)^{10} = \displaystyle\sum_{r=0}^{20} a_r x^r \qquad \ldots(1)$

replace x by $\dfrac{2}{x}$ in above identity :

$$\left(2 \times \frac{4}{x^2} + 3 \times \frac{2}{x} + 4\right)^{10} = \sum_{r=0}^{20} a_n \left(\frac{2}{x}\right)^r$$

$$2^{10}\left(\frac{4 + 3x + 2x^2}{x^2}\right)^{10} = \sum_{r=0}^{20} \frac{a_r 2^r}{x^r}$$

$$\frac{2^{10}(2x^2 + 3x + 4)^{10}}{x^{20}} = \sum_{r=0}^{20} \frac{a_r 2^r}{x^r}$$

$$\Rightarrow \quad 2^{10} \sum_{r=0}^{20} a_r x^r = \sum_{r=0}^{20} a_r 2^r x^{(20-r)}$$

[from (i)]

now, comparing coefficient of x^7 from both sides (take $r = 7$ in L.H.S. & $r = 13$ in R.H.S.)

$$2^{10} a_7 = a_{13}\, 2^{13} \Rightarrow \frac{a_7}{a_{13}} = 2^3 = 8$$

10. Correct Response : (c)

Explanation :

$$a_n = a_1 + (n - 1)d$$
$$\Rightarrow \qquad 300 = 1 + (n - 1)d$$
$$\Rightarrow \quad (n - 1)d = 299 = 13 \times 23$$

since, $\quad n \in [15, 50]$

$\therefore \qquad n = 24$ and $d = 13$

$$a_{n-4} = a_{20} = 1 + 19 \times 13 = 248$$
$$\Rightarrow \qquad a_{n-4} = 248$$
$$S_{n-4} = \frac{20}{2}\{1 + 248\} = 2490.$$

11. Correct Response : (a)

Explanation :

Using $\quad\quad AM \geq GM$

$$\Rightarrow \quad \frac{2^{\sin x} + 2^{\cos x}}{2} \geq \sqrt{2^{\sin x} \cdot 2^{\cos x}}$$

$$\Rightarrow \quad 2^{\sin x} + 2^{\cos x} \geq 2^{1 + \left(\frac{\sin x + \cos x}{2}\right)}$$

$$-\sqrt{2} \leq \sin x + \cos x \leq \sqrt{2}$$

So $\quad\quad \dfrac{-1}{\sqrt{2}} \leq \dfrac{\sin x + \cos x}{2} \leq \dfrac{1}{\sqrt{2}}$

Minimum value of

$$2^{\frac{\sin x + \cos x}{2}} = 2^{-\frac{1}{\sqrt{2}}}$$

$$\Rightarrow \min(2^{\sin x} + 2^{\cos x}) = 2 - \frac{1}{\sqrt{2}}$$

12. Correct Response : (d)

Explanation :

Sum of 1st 25 terms = sum of its next 15 terms

$$\Rightarrow \quad (T_1 + \dots + T_{25}) = (T_{26} + \dots + T_{40})$$

$$\Rightarrow \quad (T_1 + \dots + T_{40}) = 2(T_1 + \dots + T_{25})$$

$$\Rightarrow \quad \frac{40}{2}[2 \times 3 + (39d)] = 2 \times \frac{25}{2}[2 \times 3 + 24d]$$

$$\Rightarrow \quad d = \frac{1}{6}.$$

13. Correct Response : (4)

Explanation :

$$(0.16)^{\log_{2.5}\left(\frac{1}{3} + \frac{1}{3^2} + \frac{1}{3^3} + \dots \text{ to } \infty\right)}$$

$$= \frac{4}{25} \log_{\left(\frac{5}{2}\right)} \left[\frac{\frac{1}{3}}{1 - \frac{1}{3}}\right]$$

$$= \left(\frac{4}{25}\right)^{\log_{\left(\frac{5}{2}\right)}\left(\frac{1}{2}\right)}$$

$$= \left(\frac{1}{2}\right)^{\log_{\left(\frac{5}{2}\right)}\left(\frac{4}{25}\right)}$$

$$= \left(\frac{1}{2}\right)^{\log_{\left(\frac{5}{2}\right)}\left(\frac{5}{2}\right)^{-2}}$$

$$= \left(\frac{1}{2}\right)^{-2} = 4.$$

14. Correct Response : (b)

Explanation :

$$a_1 + a_2 + a_3 + \dots + a_{11} = 0$$

$$\Rightarrow \quad (a_1 + a_{11}) \times \frac{11}{2} = 0$$

$$\Rightarrow \quad a_1 + a_{11} = 0$$

$$\Rightarrow \quad a_1 + a_1 + 10d = 0$$

where d is common difference

$$\Rightarrow \quad a_1 = -5d$$

$$a_1 + a_3 + a_5 + \dots + a_{23}$$

$$= (a_1 + a_{23}) \times \frac{12}{2}$$

$$= (a_1 + a_1 + 22d) \times 6$$

$$= \left(2a_1 + 22\left(\frac{-a_1}{5}\right)\right) \times 6$$

$$= -\frac{72}{5}a_1 \Rightarrow K = \frac{-72}{5}$$

15. Correct Response : (c)

Explanation :

$$S = [x + ka + 0] + [x^2 + ka + 2a]$$
$$+ [x^3 + ka + 4a] + [x^4 + ka + 6a] + \dots 9 \text{ terms}$$

$$\Rightarrow S = (x + x^2 + x^3 + x^4 + \dots 9 \text{ terms})$$
$$+ (ka + ka + ka + ka + \dots 9 \text{ terms})$$
$$+ (0 + 2a + 4a + 6a + \dots 9 \text{ terms})$$

$$\Rightarrow \quad S = x\left[\frac{x^9 - 1}{x - 1}\right] + 9ka + 72a$$

$$\Rightarrow \quad S = \frac{(x^{10} - x) + (9k + 72)a(x - 1)}{(x - 1)}$$

Compare with given sum , then we get,

$$(9k + 72) = 45$$

$$\Rightarrow \quad k = -3$$

16. Correct Response : (3)

Explanation :

Given $b_1, b_2, b_3, \dots b_{11}$ are in A.P.

$\therefore$ Variance of $(b_1, b_2, \dots b_{11})$ = Variance of $(o, d, 2d, \dots 10d) = 90$

$$\Rightarrow \quad \frac{\sum_{i=1}^{11} b_i^2}{11} - \left(\frac{\sum_{i=1}^{11} b_i}{11}\right)^2 = 90$$

$$\Rightarrow \quad \frac{(0 + d^2 + 4d^2 + \dots + 100d^2)}{11}$$

$$- \left(\frac{0 + d + 2d + 3d + \dots 10d}{11}\right)^2 = 90$$

$$\Rightarrow \quad \frac{d^2}{11} \times \frac{10 \times 11 \times 21}{6} - \frac{d^2 \times 55 \times 55}{11 \times 11} = 90$$

$$35d^2 - 25d^2 = 90$$
$$10d^2 = 90$$
$$d^2 = 9$$
$$d = \pm 3 \Rightarrow d = 3$$

17. Correct Response : (a)

Explanation :

$|x| < 1,\ |y| < 1,\ x \neq y$

$(x + y) + (x^2 + xy + y^2) + (x^3 + x^2y + xy^2 + y^3) + \ldots$

By multiplying and dividing $x - y$:

$$\frac{(x^2 - y^2) + (x^3 - y^3) + (x^4 - y^4) + \ldots}{x - y}$$

$$= \frac{(x^2 + x^3 + x^4 + \ldots) - (y^2 + y^3 + y^4 + \ldots)}{x - y}$$

$$= \frac{\dfrac{x^2}{1-x} - \dfrac{y^2}{1-y}}{x - y}$$

$$= \frac{(x^2 - y^2) - xy(x - y)}{(1-x)(1-y)(x-y)}$$

$$= \frac{x + y - xy}{(1-x)(1-y)}$$

18. Correct Response : (d)

Explanation :

Let three terms of G.P. are $\dfrac{a}{r},\ a,\ ar$

Product = 27

$$\Rightarrow \qquad a^3 = 27 \Rightarrow a = 3$$

$$S = \frac{3}{r} + 3r + 3$$

For $r > 0$

$$\frac{\dfrac{3}{r} + 3r}{2} \geq \sqrt{3^2} \qquad (\text{By AM} \geq \text{GM})$$

$$\Rightarrow \qquad \frac{3}{r} + 3r \geq 6 \qquad \ldots(1)$$

For $r < 0\ \dfrac{3}{r} + 3r \leq -6 \ldots(2)$

From (1) & (2)

$S \in (-\infty - 3] \cup [9, \infty]$

19. Correct Response : (c)

Explanation :

$$S = \frac{100}{5} + \frac{98}{5} + \frac{96}{5} + \frac{94}{5} + \ldots n$$

$$a = \frac{100}{5},\ d = -\frac{2}{5}$$

$$S_n = \frac{n}{2}[2a + (n-1)d]$$

$$S_n = \frac{n}{2}\left(2 \times \frac{100}{5} + (n-1)\left(-\frac{2}{5}\right)\right) = 188$$

$$n(100 - n + 1) = 488 \times 5$$

$$n^2 - 101n + 488 \times 5 = 0$$

$$n = 61, 40$$

$$T_n = a + (n-1)d = \frac{100}{5} - \frac{2}{5} \times 60$$

$$= 20 - 24 = -4$$

$$T_n = a + (n-1)d$$

at $n = 40$

$$T_{40} = \frac{100}{5} - \frac{2}{5} \times 39$$

$$= \frac{22}{5} > 0$$

20. Correct Response : (39)

Explanation :

$3, A_1, A_2 \ldots\ldots A_m, 243$

$$d = \frac{243 - 3}{m+1} = \frac{240}{m+1}$$

Now $3, G_1, G_2, G_3, 243$

$$r = \left(\frac{243}{3}\right)^{\frac{1}{3+1}} = 3$$

$$\therefore \qquad A_4 = G_2$$

$$\Rightarrow \qquad a + 4d = ar^2$$

$$3 + 4\left(\frac{240}{m+1}\right) = 3(3)^2$$

$$m = 39$$

21. Correct Response : (d)

Explanation :

Sum of 1st 25 terms = sum of its next 15 terms

$$\Rightarrow \qquad (T_1 + \ldots + T_{25}) = (T_{26} + \ldots + T_{40})$$

$$\Rightarrow \qquad (T_1 + \ldots + T_{40}) = 2(T_1 + \ldots + T_{25})$$

$$\Rightarrow \qquad \frac{40}{2}[2 \times 3 + (39d)] = 2 \times \frac{25}{2}[2 \times 3 + 24d]$$

$$\Rightarrow \qquad d = \frac{1}{6}.$$

22. Correct Response : (4)

Explanation :

$$(0.16)^{\log_{2.5}\left(\frac{1}{3} + \frac{1}{3^2} + \frac{1}{3^3} + \ldots \text{ to } \infty\right)}$$

$$= \frac{4}{25} \log_{\left(\frac{5}{2}\right)}\left[\frac{\dfrac{1}{3}}{1 - \dfrac{1}{3}}\right]$$

$$= \left(\frac{4}{25}\right)^{\log_{\left(\frac{5}{2}\right)}\left(\frac{1}{2}\right)}$$

$$= \left(\frac{1}{2}\right)^{\log_{\left(\frac{5}{2}\right)}\left(\frac{4}{25}\right)}$$

$$= \left(\frac{1}{2}\right)^{\log_{\left(\frac{5}{2}\right)}\left(\frac{5}{2}\right)^{-2}}$$

$$= \left(\frac{1}{2}\right)^{-2} = 4.$$

23. Correct Response : (d)

Explanation :

$$460 = \log_7 x \cdot (2 + 3 + 4 + \dots + 20 + 21)$$

$$\Rightarrow \quad 460 = \log_7 x \cdot \left(\frac{21 \times 22}{2} - 1\right)$$

$$\Rightarrow \quad 460 = 230 \cdot \log_7 x$$
$$\Rightarrow \quad \log_7 x = 2$$
$$\Rightarrow \quad x = 49$$

24. Correct Response : (b)

Explanation :

Let first term $= a > 0$

Common ratio $= r > 0$

$$ar + ar^2 + ar^3 = 3 \qquad \dots(i)$$
$$ar^5 + ar^6 + ar^7 = 243 \qquad \dots(ii)$$
$$r^4(ar + ar^2 + ar^3) = 243$$
$$r^4(3) = 243$$
$$\Rightarrow \quad r = 3 \text{ as } r > 0$$

from (1)

$$3a + 9a + 27a = 3$$
$$a = \frac{1}{13}$$
$$S_{50} = \frac{a(r^{50} - 1)}{(r - 1)} = \frac{1}{26}(3^{50} - 1)$$

25. Correct Response : (1)

Explanation :

Given

$$2(a_1 + a_2 + \dots + a_n) = b_1 + b_2 + \dots + b_n$$
$$(\because a_1 = b_1 = c)$$
$$\Rightarrow \quad 2 \times \frac{n}{2}[2c + (n-2)x_2] = c\left(\frac{2^n - 1}{2 - 1}\right)$$
$$\Rightarrow \quad 2n^2 - 2n = c(2^n - 1 - 2n)$$
$$\Rightarrow \quad c = \frac{2n^2 - 2n}{2^n - 1 - 2n} \in \mathbb{N}$$

So, $\quad 2n^2 - 2n \geq 2^n - 1 - 2n$

$$\Rightarrow \quad 2n^2 + 1 \geq 2^n \Rightarrow n < 7$$

$\Rightarrow n$ can be 1, 2, 3, …

Checking c against these values of n we get

$$c = 12 \text{ (when } n = 3)$$

Hence number of such $c = 1$.

26. Correct Response : (c)

Explanation :

Let the A.P. is $a - 2d,\ a - d,\ a,\ a + d,\ a + 2d$

$$\therefore \qquad \text{sum} = 25$$
$$\Rightarrow \qquad a = 5$$

Product $= 2520$

$$(25 - 4d^2)(25 - d^2) = 504$$
$$4d^4 - 125 - d^2 + 121 = 0$$
$$\Rightarrow \qquad d^2 = 1,\ \frac{121}{4}$$
$$\Rightarrow \qquad d = \pm 1,\ \pm\frac{11}{2}$$

$d = \pm 1$ is rejected because none of the term can be $\frac{-1}{2}$.

$$\Rightarrow \qquad d = \pm\frac{11}{2}$$

$\Rightarrow$ AP will be $-6,\ -\dfrac{1}{2},\ 5,\ \dfrac{21}{2},\ 16$

Largest term is 16.

27. Correct Response : (c)

Explanation :

$$1 + 49 + 49^2 + \dots + 49^{125}$$
$$= (49)^{126} - 1$$
$$= (49^{63} + 1)\frac{(49^{63} - 1)}{(48)}$$

So greatest value of $k = 63$

28. Correct Response : (a)

Explanation :

Sum of the 40 terms of

$$3 + 4 + 8 + 9 + 13 + 14 + 18 + 19 \dots$$
$$= (3 + 8 + 13 + \dots \text{ upto } 20 \text{ term}) + [4 + 9 + 15 + \dots \text{ upto } 20 \text{ terms}]$$
$$= 10[\{6 + 19 \times 5\} + \{8 + 19 \times 5\}]$$
$$= 10 \times 204 = 20 \times 102$$

29. Correct Response : (a)

Explanation :

$$a_1 + a_2 = 4$$
$$r^2 a_1 + r^2 a_2 = 16$$
$$\Rightarrow \qquad r^2 = 4 \Rightarrow r = -2 \text{ as } a_1 < 0$$

and $\qquad a_1 + a_2 = 4$

$$a_1 + a_1(-2) = 4 \Rightarrow a_1 = -4$$
$$\Rightarrow \quad 4\lambda = (-4)\left(\frac{(-2)^9 - 1}{-2 - 1}\right) = (-4) \times \frac{513}{3}$$
$$\Rightarrow \qquad \lambda = -171$$

30. Correct Response : (b)

Explanation :

$$f(x) = \frac{2(2^x + 2^{-x}) + (3^x + 3^{-x})}{2} \geq 3$$

(A.M. $\geq$ G.M.)

31. Correct Response : (1540.00)

Explanation :

$$\sum_{k=1}^{20} \frac{k(k+1)}{2} = \frac{1}{2} \sum_{k=1}^{20} \frac{k(k+1)(k+2)(k-1)(k+1)}{3}$$

$$= \frac{1}{6} \times 20 \times 21 \times 22 = 1540.00$$

32. Correct Response : (b)

Explanation :

$$T_{10} = \frac{1}{20} = a + 9d \qquad \text{...(i)}$$

$$T_{20} = \frac{1}{10} = a + 19d \qquad \text{...(ii)}$$

$$a = \frac{1}{200} = d$$

Hence, $\quad S_{200} = \dfrac{200}{2}\left[\dfrac{2}{200} + \dfrac{199}{200}\right] = \dfrac{201}{2}$

33. Correct Response : (504)

Explanation :

$$\frac{1}{4}\left(\sum_{n=1}^{7} 2n^3 + \sum_{n=1}^{7} 3n^2 + \sum_{n=1}^{7} n\right)$$

$$= \frac{1}{4}\left(2\left(\frac{7\times 8}{2}\right)^2 + 3\left(\frac{7\times 8\times 15}{6}\right) + \frac{7\times 8}{2}\right)$$

$$= 504$$

34. Correct Response : (a)

Explanation :

$$2^{\frac{1}{4}}.4^{\frac{1}{16}}.8^{\frac{1}{48}}.16^{\frac{1}{128}}. \,....\, \infty$$

$$= 2^{\frac{1}{4}}.2^{\frac{2}{16}}.2^{\frac{3}{48}}.2^{\frac{4}{128}}. \,....\, \infty$$

$$= 2^{\frac{1}{4}}.2^{\frac{1}{8}}.2^{\frac{1}{16}}.2^{\frac{1}{32}}. \,....\, \infty$$

$$= 2^{\frac{1}{4}+\frac{1}{8}+\frac{1}{16}+\frac{1}{32}+....\infty}$$

$$= (2)^{\left(\frac{1/4}{1-1/2}\right)} = 2^{1/2}$$

35. Correct Response : (c)

Explanation :

$$x = \sum_{n-0}^{\infty} (-1)^n \tan^{2n}\theta$$

$$= 1 - \tan^2\theta + \tan^4\theta + ...$$

$$\Rightarrow \quad x = \cos^2\theta$$

$$y = \sum_{n-0}^{\infty} \cos^{2n}\theta$$

$$\Rightarrow \quad y = 1 + \cos^2\theta + \cos^4\theta + ...$$

$$\Rightarrow \quad y = \frac{1}{\sin^2\theta}$$

$$\Rightarrow \quad y = \frac{1}{1-x}$$

$$\Rightarrow \quad y(1-x) = 1$$

36. Correct Response : (d)

Explanation :

$$\sum_{n=1}^{100} a_{2n+1} = 200$$

$$\Rightarrow a_3 + a_5 + a_7 + ..., + a_{201} = 200$$

$$\Rightarrow \quad ar^2 \frac{(r^{200}-1)}{(r^2-1)} = 200$$

$$\sum_{n=1}^{100} a_{2n} = 100$$

$$\Rightarrow a_2 + a_4 + a_6 + ... + a_{200} = 100$$

$$\Rightarrow \quad ar^2 \frac{(r^{200}-1)}{(r^2-1)} = 200$$

On dividing $r = 2$

on adding $a_2 + a_3 + a_4 + a_5 + ... + a_{200} + a_{201} = 300$

$$\Rightarrow r(a_1 + a_2 + a_3 + ... + a_{200}) = 300$$

$$\Rightarrow \quad \sum_{n=1}^{200} a_n = 150$$

37. Correct Response : (14)

Explanation :

Common term are : 23, 51, 79, ... Tn

$$T_n \le 407 \Rightarrow 23 + (n-1)\,28 \le 407$$

$$\Rightarrow \quad n \le 14.71$$

$$n = 14$$

38. Correct Response : (b)

Explanation :

$$a_1, a_2, ..., a_n \text{ are in A.P.}$$

$$a_1 + a_4 + a_7 + a_{10} + a_{13} + a_{16} = 114$$

$$a_1 + a_{16} = a_4 + a_{13}$$

$$= a_7 + a_{10}$$

$$= a_5 + a_{12}$$

$$= a_6 + a_{11}$$

$$\Rightarrow \quad 3(a_6 + a_{11}) = 114$$

$$\Rightarrow \quad a_6 + a_{11} = 38$$

$$(a_1 + a_6 + a_{11} + a_{16}) = 2\,(a_6 + a_{11})$$

$$= 2 \times 38$$

$$= 76$$

39. Correct Response : (c)

Explanation :

General term is

$$a_n = \frac{(2n+1)(1^3 + 2^3 + 3^3 + ... + n^3)}{(1^2 + 2^2 + 3^2 + ... + n^2)}$$

$$= \frac{(2n+1)\left(\frac{n(n+1)}{2}\right)^2}{\frac{n(n+1)(2n+1)}{6}}$$

$$= \frac{3}{2} n (n+1)$$

$$= \frac{3}{2} (n^2 + n)$$

Sum of the series is,

$$\sum_{n=1}^{10} a_n = \frac{3}{2} \left(\frac{10 \times 11 \times 21}{6} + \frac{10 \times 11}{2} \right)$$

$$= \frac{3}{2} \times 440$$

$$= 660$$

40. Correct Response : (a)

Explanation :

The special series

$$S_n = 1 + 2 + 3 + ... + n$$

$$= \frac{n(n+1)}{2}$$

and $\quad Sn^3 = 1^3 + 2^3 + 3^3 + ... + n^3$

$$= \left(\frac{n(n+1)}{2} \right)^2$$

Use above two formulae to evaluate given series as

$$\sum_{r=1}^{15} \frac{\left(\frac{n(n+1)}{2} \right)^2}{\left(\frac{n(n+1)}{2} \right)} - \frac{1}{2} \left(\frac{15 \times 16}{2} \right) = \sum_{r=1}^{15} \left(\frac{n^2}{2} + \frac{n}{2} \right) - 60$$

$$= 620 + 60 - 60$$

$$= 620$$

41. Correct Response : (d)

Explanation :

Let $b = ar$, $c = ar^2$.

Hence, $3a + 15ar^2 = 14ar$

$$15r^2 - 14r + 3 = 0$$

$$15r^2 - 9r - 5r + 3 = 0$$

$$(3r - 1)(5r - 3) = 0$$

$$r = \frac{1}{3}, \frac{3}{5}$$

$$\therefore \qquad\qquad r = \frac{1}{3}$$

A.P. is $3a, \frac{7}{3}a, \frac{5}{3}a, a, ...$

So the fourth term is a.

42. Correct Response : (b)

Explanation :

It is given that $a_1, a_2, a_3, ..., a_{50}$ are in A.P. and $a_6 = 2$. So $a_1 + 5d = 2$.

$$A = a_1 a_4 a_5 = a_1 (a_1 + 3d)(a_1 + 4d)$$

$$= a_1 (2 - 2d)(2 - d)$$

$$= -2 (5d - 2)(d - 1)(d - 2))$$

$$= -2(5d^3 - 17d^2 + 16d - 4)$$

$$\frac{dA}{d(d)} = -2(15d^2 - 34d + 16)$$

$$= -2(5d - 8)(3d - 2)$$

Thus, maximum occurs at $d = \frac{8}{5}$

43. Correct Response : (d)

Explanation :

$$\frac{n(n+1)}{2} + 99 = (n-2)^2$$

$$\Rightarrow \qquad n^2 - 9n - 190 = 0$$

$$\Rightarrow \qquad\qquad n = 19$$

So, the number of balls is $\dfrac{19 \times 20}{2} = 190$.

44. Correct Response : (d)

Explanation :

Let the three terms be $a - d, a, a + d$

$$\text{Sum is } 3a = 33$$

$$\Rightarrow \qquad\qquad a = 11$$

So the three terms are $11 - d$, 11, $11 + d$.

$$\text{Product is } 11(121 - d^2) = 1155$$

$$\Rightarrow \qquad 121 - d^2 = 105$$

$$\Rightarrow \qquad\qquad d^2 = 16$$

$$\Rightarrow \qquad\qquad d = \pm 4$$

So, the terms are 7, 11, 15 or 15, 11, 7.

$$t_{11} = 7 + 10(4)$$

$$= 47$$

or $\qquad 15 + (10 \times (-4)) = -25$

45. Correct Response : (b)

Explanation :

Write the given series as

$$\sum_{r=1}^{11} r(2r - 1) = 2\sum_{r=1}^{11} r^2 - \sum_{r=1}^{11} r$$

$$= \frac{2 \times 11 \times 12 \times 23}{6} - \frac{11 \times 12}{2}$$

$$= 44 \times 23 - 11 \times 6$$

$$= 946$$

46. Correct Response : (d)

Explanation :

$$S_n = 50n + n(n-7)\frac{A}{2}$$

$$a_n = S_n - S_{n-1}$$

$$= (n-4)A + 50$$
$$\Rightarrow \qquad d = A$$
$$a_{50} = 46A + 50$$

47. Correct Response : (b)

Explanation :

$$2.\ ^{20}C_0 + 5 \cdot\ ^{20}C_1 + 8 \cdot\ ^{20}C_2 + ... + 62 \cdot\ ^{20}C$$

$$= \sum_{r=0}^{20} (3r+2) \cdot\ ^{20}C_r$$

$$= 3\sum_{r=0}^{20} r \cdot\ ^{20}C_r + 2\sum_{r=0}^{20}\ ^{20}C_r$$

$$= 3\times 20 \sum_{r=1}^{20}\ ^{19}C_{r-1} + 2(2^{20})$$

$$= 60\,(2^{19}) + 2\,(2^{20})$$
$$= 16\,(2^{21})$$
$$= 2^{25}$$

48. Correct Response : (d)

Explanation :

Natural numbers between 100 and 200.

101, 102, ..., 199

Either divide by 7 or divide by 13.

(sum of numbers divide by 7) + (sum of numbers divide by 13) − (sum of numbers divide by 91)

$$\sum_{r=1}^{14} (98+7r) + \sum_{r=1}^{8} (91+13r) - 182$$

$$= \left(98\times 14 + 7 \cdot \frac{14\times 15}{2}\right) + \left(91\times 8 + 13 \cdot \frac{8\times 9}{2}\right) - 182$$

$$= 1372 + 735 + 728 + 468 - 182$$
$$= 3121$$

49. Correct Response : (a)

Explanation :

$$b^2 = ac$$

Root of $ax^2 + 2bx + c = 0$ and $dx^2 + 2a + f = 0$ are equal; that is, $-\dfrac{b}{a}$

$$d\left(-\frac{b}{a}\right)^2 + 2e\left(-\frac{b}{a}\right) + f = 0$$

$$db^2 - 2bea + fa^2 = 0$$
$$dc - 2eb + fa = 0$$

Divide by ac

$$\frac{dc}{ac} - \frac{2eb}{b^2} + \frac{fa}{ac} = 0$$

$$\frac{d}{a} - \frac{2e}{b} + \frac{f}{c} = 0$$

$$\Rightarrow$$

$$\frac{d}{a}, \frac{e}{b}, \frac{f}{c} \text{ are in A.P.}$$

50. Correct Response : (c)

Explanation :

$$S = \sum_{k=1}^{20} k\,\frac{1}{2^k}$$

$$S = \frac{1}{2} + \frac{2}{2^2} + \frac{3}{2^3} + ... + \frac{20}{2^{20}}$$

$$\frac{S}{2} = \frac{1}{2} + \frac{2}{2^2} + \frac{3}{2^3} + ... + \frac{1}{2^{20}} - \frac{20}{2^{21}}$$

$$= \frac{\frac{1}{2}\left(1 - \frac{1}{2^{20}}\right)}{\left(\frac{1}{2}\right)} - \frac{20}{2^{21}}$$

$$S = 2\left(1 - \frac{1}{2^{20}}\right) - \frac{20}{2^{20}}$$

$$= 2 - \frac{20}{2^{20}}$$

$$= 2 - \frac{11}{2^{19}}$$

51. Correct Response : (b)

Explanation :

The given sequence is,

$$S = \left[\frac{-1}{3}\right] + \left[\frac{-1}{3} - \frac{1}{100}\right] + \left[\frac{-1}{3} - \frac{2}{100}\right]$$

$$+ ...... + \left[\frac{-1}{3} - \frac{99}{100}\right]$$

$$= (-1 - 1 - 1 - ....\ 67\ \text{times})$$
$$+ (-2 - 2 - 2 - 2 - ....\ 33\ \text{times})$$

$$= -133$$

52. Correct Response : (c)

Explanation :

Given that,

$$S_4 = 16$$
$$\frac{4}{2}(2a+3d) = 16$$
$$2a + 3d = 8$$

Also,

$$S_6 = -48$$
$$\frac{6}{2}(2a+5d) = -48$$
$$2a + 5d = -16$$

Therefore,

$$d = -12$$
$$a = 22$$

The sum of first ten terms is,

$$S_{10} = \frac{10}{2}(44 - 108)$$

$$= -320$$

53. Correct Response : (a)

Explanation :

Given that,

$$a_1 + a_7 + a_{16} = 40$$

$$a_1 + a_1 + 6d + a_1 + 15d = 40$$

$$3a_1 + 21d = 40$$

$$a_1 + 7d = \frac{40}{3}$$

The sum of first 15 terms of A.P. is,

$$S_{15} = \frac{15}{2}[2a_1 + 14d]$$

$$= S_{15}$$

$$= 15\,(a_1 + 7d)$$

$$= 15\left(\frac{40}{3}\right)$$

Solve further,

$$S = 200$$

54. Correct Response : (d)

Explanation :

Let r be the common ratio of G.P. $\alpha x^2 + 2\beta x + y = 0$ is modified The given equation as,

$$\alpha x^2 + 2\alpha r x + \alpha r^2 = 0$$

$$x^2 + 2rx + r^2 = 0 \qquad \text{...(i)}$$

Given that,

$$x^2 + x - 1 = 0 \qquad \text{...(ii)}$$

Subtract equation (i) and equation (ii).

$$(2r^2 - 1)x + (r^2 + 1) = 0$$

$$x = \frac{-(r^2 + 1)}{2r - 1} \qquad \text{...(iii)}$$

Substitute equation (iii) in equation (ii).

$$(r^2 + 1)^2 - (r^2 + 1)\,(2r - 1) - (2r - 1)^2 = 0$$

$$r^4 - 2r^3 - r^2 + 2r + 1 = 0$$

$$r^2 - 2r - 1 + \frac{2}{r} + \frac{1}{r^2} = 0$$

$$\left(r - \frac{1}{r}\right)^2 - 2\left(r - \frac{1}{r}\right) + 1 = 0$$

Solve further,

$$\left(r - \frac{1}{r} - 1\right)^2 = 0$$

$$\frac{r^2 - 1}{r} = 1$$

$$r^2 = 1 + r$$

Therefore, the required term is,

$$\alpha(\beta + \gamma) = \alpha(\alpha r + \alpha r^2)$$

$$= \alpha^2 r\,(1 + r)$$

$$= \alpha^2 r r^2$$

$$= (\alpha r)\,(\alpha r^2)$$

Solve further,

$$\alpha(\beta + \gamma) = \beta\gamma$$

55. Correct Response : (c) 157·0

Explanation :

First series is {1, 4, 7, 10, 13, ...}.

Second series is {2, 7, 12, 17, ... }.

Third series is {3, 10, 17, 24, ... }.

The least number in the third series which leaves remainder 1 on dividing by 3 and leaves remainder 2 on dividing by 5 is 52.

Now $A = 52$.

$$D \text{ is L.C.M. of } (3, 5, 7) = 105$$

$$A + D = 52 + 105$$

$$= 157.$$

56. Correct Response : (d)

Explanation :

By Arithmetic sequence,

$$a_{21} = a_1 + (21 - 1)(d)$$

$$\frac{1}{20} = \frac{1}{4} + (20)d$$

$$d = -\frac{1}{100}$$

$$\frac{1}{x_n} < \frac{1}{50}$$

And Arithmetic sequence for the less than $\dfrac{1}{50}$ terms

$$a_1 + (n - 1)d < \frac{1}{50}$$

Here, $a_1 = \dfrac{1}{4}, \ d = -\dfrac{1}{100}$

Substitute the value in above equation,

$$\frac{1}{4} - \frac{(n - 1)}{100} < \frac{1}{50}$$

$$n > 24$$

$$n = 25$$

$$S = \frac{n}{2}\,(2a_1 + (n - 1)d)$$

Simplify,

$$\sum_{i=1}^{25}\left(\frac{1}{x_i}\right) = \frac{25}{2}\left(2 \times \frac{1}{4} - (25 - 1)\frac{1}{100}\right)$$

$$= \frac{13}{4}$$

Thus the value of the $\displaystyle\sum_{i=1}^{25}\left(\frac{1}{x_i}\right)$ is $\dfrac{13}{4}$.

57. Correct Response : (a)

Explanation :

The sum of first 20 terms is,

$$1 + \frac{3}{2} + \frac{7}{4} + \frac{15}{8} + \frac{31}{16} + \ldots\ldots$$

Arrange the above series as

$$(2-1) + \left(2 - \frac{1}{2}\right) + \left(2 - \frac{1}{4}\right) + \left(2 - \frac{1}{8}\right) + \left(2 - \frac{1}{16}\right)$$

$$+ \ldots\ldots \text{ upto 20 terms}$$

$$= 40 - \left(1 + \frac{1}{2} + \frac{1}{4} + \frac{1}{8} + \ldots\ldots\text{upto 20 terms}\right)$$

$$= 40 - \left(\frac{1 - r^{20}}{1 - r}\right)$$

$$= 40 - \left(\frac{1 - \left(\frac{1}{2}\right)^{20}}{1 - \left(\frac{1}{2}\right)}\right)$$

$$= 40 - 2 + \frac{1}{2^{19}}$$

$$= 38 + \frac{1}{2^{19}}$$

58. Correct Response : (c)

Explanation :

Let the common difference for the arithmetic progression is d.

Given that,

$$a_1 + a_2 + a_3 + \ldots + a_{49} = 416$$
$$a_1 + 24d = 32 \qquad\qquad \ldots(1)$$

And, $\qquad\qquad a_9 + a_{43} = 66$
$$a_1 + 8d + a_1 + 42d = 66$$
$$a_1 + 25d = 33 \qquad\qquad \ldots(2)$$

Solving equation (1) and (2),

$d = 1$ and $a_1 = 8$

The value of m from the given equation,

$$a_1{}^2 + a_2{}^2 + a_3{}^2 + \ldots + a_{17}{}^2 = 140m$$

$$8^2 + 9^2 + 10^2 + \ldots + 24^2 = 140m$$

$$(1^2 + 2^2 + 3^2 + \ldots + 24^2)$$
$$- (1^2 + 2^2 + 3^2 + \ldots + 7^2) = 140m$$

$$\frac{49 \times 24 \times 25}{6} - \frac{15 \times 7 \times 8}{6} = 140m$$

$$m = 34$$

59. Correct Response : (b)

Explanation :

The value of the A from the given series,

$$A = 1^2 + 2.2^2 + 3^2 + \ldots + 2.20^2$$
$$= (1^2 + 2^2 + 3^2 + \ldots + 20^2) + (2^2 + 4^2 + \ldots + 20^2)$$
$$= (1^2 + 2^2 + 3^2 + \ldots + 20^2)$$
$$+ 4(1^2 + 2^2 + \ldots + 10^2)$$

$$= \frac{20 \times 21 \times 41}{6} + \frac{4 \times 10 \times 11 \times 21}{6}$$

$$= 2870 + 1540$$
$$= 4410$$

The value of the B from the given series,

$$B = 1^2 + 2.2^2 + 3^2 + \ldots + 2.40^2$$
$$= (1^2 + 2^2 + 3^2 + \ldots + 40^2)$$
$$+ (2^2 + 4^2 + \ldots + 40^2)$$
$$= (1^2 + 2^2 + 3^2 + \ldots + 40^2)$$
$$+ 4(1^2 + 2^2 + \ldots + 20^2)$$

$$= \frac{40 \times 41 \times 81}{6} + \frac{4 \times 20 \times 21 \times 41}{6}$$

$$= 22140 + 11480$$
$$= 33620$$

The value of the λ is,

$$B - 2A = 100\lambda$$
$$33620 - 8820 = 100\lambda$$
$$\lambda = 248$$

60. Correct Response : (a)

Explanation :

The nth term of an A.P. is,

$$T_n = a + (n - 1)d$$

The value of x_3,

$$x_3 = 8$$
$$a + (3 - 1)d = 8$$
$$a = 8 - 2d$$

The value of x_8,

$$x_8 = 20$$
$$a + (8 - 1)d = 20$$
$$(8 - 2d) + 7d = 20$$
$$d = \frac{12}{5}$$

The first term of the A.P. is,

$$a = 8 - 2\left(\frac{12}{5}\right)$$

$$= \frac{16}{5}$$

The fifth term of the A.P. is,

$$x_5 = \frac{16}{5} + (5 - 1)\left(\frac{12}{5}\right)$$

$$= \frac{64}{5}$$

The tenth term of the second A.P. is,

$$h_{10} = 200$$

The value of the term x_5 is,

$$x_5 \cdot h_{10} = \left(\frac{64}{5}\right)(200)$$

$$= 2560$$

Therefore, the value of $x_5 \cdot h_{10}$ is 2560.

61. Correct Response : (c)

Explanation :

Let b is the first term and r is the common ratio of the G.P. then the sum is five.

$$5 = \frac{b}{1-r}$$

$$r = \frac{5-b}{5}$$

The value of r lies in between -1 to 1.

$$-1 < r < 1$$

$$-1 < \frac{5-b}{5} < 1$$

$$-(-5-5) < b < -(5-5)$$

$$10 < b < 0$$

Therefore, the value of b lies in the interval $(0, 10)$.

62. Correct Response : (d)

Explanation :

Given,

$$\frac{a+b}{2} = 5\sqrt{ab}$$

On squaring both the sides.

$$(a+b)^2 = 100ab \qquad ...(1)$$
$$a^2 + b^2 + 2ab = 100ab$$

Adding $-4ab$ to both sides.

$$a^2 + b^2 - 2ab = 96ab$$
$$(a-b)^2 = 96ab \qquad ...(2)$$

Divide equation (1) by (2).

$$\frac{(a+b)^2}{(a-b)^2} = \frac{100\ ab}{96\ ab}$$

$$\frac{(a+b)^2}{(a-b)^2} = \frac{25}{24}$$

$$\frac{(a+b)}{(a-b)} = \sqrt{\frac{25}{24}}$$

$$\frac{(a+b)}{(a-b)} = \frac{5\sqrt{6}}{12}$$

63. Correct Response : (b)

Explanation :

The summation of n term of series is,

$$S = \sqrt{3} + \sqrt{75} + \sqrt{243} + \sqrt{507} + ... \ n \text{ terms}$$

$$= \sqrt{3} + \sqrt{3 \times 25} + \sqrt{3 \times 81} + \sqrt{3 \times 169} + ... n \text{ terms}$$

$$= \sqrt{3} \ (1 + 5 + 9 + 13 + ... \ n \text{ terms})$$

Terms given in the bracket is A.P. with first term $a = 1$ and the common difference $d = 4$.

The sum of n terms in A.P. is given by :

$$S = \sqrt{3} \times \frac{n}{2} \ (2 + 4(n-1)) = 435\sqrt{3}$$

$$2n^2 - n - 435 = 0$$

$$n = \frac{1 \pm 59}{4}$$

$$= 15 \text{ or } -\frac{58}{4}$$

The valid value is only $n = 15$.

64. Correct Response : (a)

Explanation :

The given relation in a, b and c is,

$$abc = 8$$

The terms are in A.P. hence,

$$b = \left(\frac{a+c}{2}\right)$$

$$ac\left(\frac{a+c}{2}\right) = 8$$

For minimum value of b, take a, c equal to b.

$$b^2\left(\frac{2b}{2}\right) = 8$$

$$b^3 = 8$$

$$b = 2$$

65. Correct Response : (a)

Explanation :

The formula to calculate n^{th} term for the question is,

$$T_n = \frac{\dfrac{n(n+1)}{2}}{\left(\dfrac{n(n+1)}{2}\right)^2}$$

$$= \frac{2}{n\ (n+1)}$$

$$= 2\left(\frac{1}{n} - \frac{1}{n+1}\right)$$

Sum of T_n is calculated as,

$$S_n = 2\sum_{n=1}^{n}\left(\frac{1}{n} - \frac{1}{n+1}\right)$$

$$= 2\left[\left(1 - \frac{1}{2}\right) + \left(\frac{1}{2} - \frac{1}{3}\right) + \left(\frac{1}{3} - \frac{1}{4}\right) + ... \left(\frac{1}{n} - \frac{1}{(n+1)}\right)\right]$$

$$= 2\left(1 - \frac{1}{n+1}\right)$$

$$= \frac{2n}{n+1}$$

$$\because \qquad 100Sn = n$$

$$100 \times \frac{2x}{n\pi} = n$$

$$n = 199$$

66. Correct Response : (a)

Explanation :

The provided equation is

$9(25a^2 + b^2) + 25(c^2 - 3ac) = 15b\,(3a + c)$

Simplify the above equation.

$(15a)^2 + (3b)^2 + (5c)^2 - 45ab - 15bc - 75ac = 0$

$(15a - 3b)^2 + (3b - 5c)^2 + (15a - 5c)^2 = 0$

The possible conditions are,

$15a - 3b = 0,\ 3b - 5c = 0,\ 15a - 5c = 0$

$$\frac{a}{1} = \frac{b}{5} = \frac{c}{3}$$

Hence, b, c, a are in A.P.

67. Correct Response : (d)

Explanation :

The given equation is input with $x = 1$ and $y = 1$.

$$f(2) = 2f(1) + 1$$
$$= 7$$

The given equation is input with $x = 1$ and $y = 2$.

$$f(3) = f(1) + f(2) + 2$$
$$= 12$$

The sum of the series for $n = 1$ to $n = 10$.

$$\sum_{n=1}^{10} f(n) = f(1) + f(2) + f(3) + \dots + f(10)$$

$$= 3 + 7 + 12 + 18$$

$$= \frac{1}{2}(n^2 + 5n)$$

The sum of the series is,

$$S_n = \sum_{n=1}^{10} f(n)$$

$$= \sum_{n=1}^{10} \frac{1}{2}(n^2 + 5n)$$

$$= \frac{n(n+1)(n+8)}{6}$$

$$S_{10} = \frac{10 \times 11 \times 18}{6}$$

$$= 330$$

68. Correct Response : (a)

Explanation :

The given series is

$a_3 + a_7 + a_{11} + a_{15} = 72$

The numbers $a_1, a_2, a_3 \dots, a_n, \dots$ are in A.P. Then,

$$a_3 + a_{15} = a_7 + a_{11}$$
$$= a_1 + a_{17}$$
$$= 36$$

The sum of first 17 terms of A.P. series is,

$$\text{Sum} = \frac{17}{2}(a_1 + a_{17})$$

$$= \frac{17}{2} \times 36$$

$$= 306$$

69. Correct Response : (b)

Explanation :

Consider the A.P. is,

$$A,\ A + d,\ A + 2d,\ \dots$$

It is given that 2nd, 5th and 9th terms $A + d$, $A + 4d$, $A + 8d$ are in G.P.

Let the G.P. be a, ar, ar^2.

Therefore,

$$a = A + d$$
$$ar = A + 4d$$
$$ar^2 = A + 8d$$

Now,

$$\frac{ar^2 - ar}{ar - a} = \frac{(A + 8d) - (A + 4d)}{(A + 4d) - (A + d)}$$

$$\frac{ar(r-1)}{a(r-1)} = \frac{4d}{3d}$$

$$r = \frac{4}{3}$$

Hence, the common ratio of G.P. is $\dfrac{4}{3}$.

70. Correct Response : (b)

Explanation :

Consider the sum of the first ten terms of the given series is equal to S.

$$S = \left(1\frac{3}{5}\right)^2 + \left(2\frac{2}{5}\right)^2 + \left(3\frac{1}{5}\right)^2 + 4^2 + \left(4\frac{4}{5}\right)^2 + \dots\ 10$$

terms Simplify the above series,

$$= \left(\frac{8}{5}\right)^2 + \left(\frac{12}{5}\right)^2 + \left(\frac{16}{5}\right)^2 + \left(\frac{20}{5}\right)^2 + \dots + \left(\frac{44}{5}\right)^2$$

$$= \frac{16}{25}(2^2 + 3^2 + 4^2 + 5^2 + \dots + 11^2)$$

$$= \frac{16}{25}(1^2 + 2^2 + \dots + 11^2 - 1)$$

$$= \frac{16}{5} \times 101$$

Hence, the value of the m is

$$\frac{16}{5} \times m = \frac{16}{5} \times 101$$

$$m = 101$$

71. Correct Response : (d)

Explanation :

Given :

$$x + y + z = 12$$

And,

$$x^3 y^4 z^5 = (0.1)(600)^3$$

The relation between AM, GM, and HM of two positive numbers is,

$$AM \geq GM \geq HM$$

Therefore,

$$AM \geq GM$$

Substitute the value,

$$\frac{3\left(\frac{x}{3}\right) + 4\left(\frac{y}{4}\right) + 5\left(\frac{z}{5}\right)}{12} \geq \left(\left(\frac{x}{3}\right)^3 \left(\frac{y}{4}\right)^3 \left(\frac{z}{5}\right)^3\right)^{1/12}$$

$$\frac{12}{12} \geq \frac{x^3 y^4 z^5}{(60)^3 (4 \times 25)}$$

$$(0.1)(600)^3 \geq x^3 y^4 z^5$$

$$x^3 y^4 z^5 \leq (0.1)(600)^3$$

But given that,

$$x^3 y^4 z^5 = (0.1)(600)^3$$

Therefore, it is clear that,

$$AM = GM$$

Hence,

$$\frac{x}{3} = \frac{y}{4} = \frac{z}{5}$$

$$x = 3, y = 4, z = 5$$

Thus the required value is,

$$x^3 + y^3 + z^3 = 27 + 64 + 125$$

$$= 216$$

72. Correct Response : (a)

Explanation :

The formula of the mean of the series is,

$$\overline{x} = \sum_{i=1}^{n}\left(\frac{x_i}{n}\right)$$

The given series in A.P. is,

$$1, 1 + d, 1 + 2d, ..., 1 + 100d$$

Apply the formula of A.P. to calculate the number of terms in this series is,

$$1 + 100d = 1 + (n - 1)d$$

Compare both sides

$$n - 1 = 100$$

$$n = 101$$

The sum of the 101 terms is,

$$x_i = \frac{101}{2}(2 + (101 - 1)d)$$

$$= 101(50d + 1)$$

Therefore, mean is given as,

$$\overline{x} = \frac{101(50d + 1)}{101}$$

$$= 1 + 50d$$

Sum of deviation about mean is given as :

$$50d + 49d + ... + d + 0 + d + ... + 50d = 50 \times 51d$$

Hence, the mean deviation from mean is

$$\sigma = \frac{50 \times 51d}{101}$$

$$255 = \frac{50 \times 51d}{101}$$

$$d = 10.1$$

Further, simplifying,

$$d = \frac{255 \times 101}{2550}$$

$$= 10.1$$

73. Correct Response : (b)

Explanation :

The sum of expression is,

$$\sum_{r=1}^{10}\left(r^2 + 1\right) \times (r!)$$

$$= \sum_{r=1}^{10}[(r+1)^2 - 2r] \times (r!)$$

$$= \sum_{r=1}^{10}(r+1)(r+1)(r!) - 2\sum_{r=1}^{10} r(r!)$$

$$= \sum_{r=1}^{10}(r+1)(r+1)! - 2\sum_{r=1}^{10} r(r!)$$

$$= \sum_{r=1}^{10}\{(r+1)(r+1)! - r(r!)\} - \sum_{r=1}^{10} r(r!)$$

Further solve the above equation,

$$\sum_{r=1}^{10}\left(r^2 + 1\right) \times (r!) = (11 \times 11! - 1) - \sum_{r=1}^{10}[(r+1)! - r!]$$

$$= (11 \cdot 11! - 1 - 11! + 1!)$$

$$= (11 - 1) \times 11! - 1 + 1$$

$$= 10 \times (11)!$$

74. Correct Response : (b)

Explanation :

Consider the three terms a, ar and ar^2 are in G.P.

The given relation,

$$a(ar)(ar^2) = 1000$$

$$ar = 10$$

And,

$$ar^2 + ar^3 = 60$$

$$10r + 10r^2 = 60$$

$$r^2 + r - 6 = 0$$
$$r = 2, -3$$

Hence,

$$a = 5, -\frac{10}{3} \left(\text{But } a \neq -\frac{10}{3} \right)$$

Hence, the value of the 7th term is,

$$T_7 = ar^6$$
$$= 5\,(2)^6$$
$$= 320$$

75. Correct Response : (b)

Explanation :

The Arithmetic mean of two distinct number is,

$$m = \frac{l+n}{2}$$

$$l + n = 2m$$

Since l, G_1, G_2, G_3, n are in geometric progression.

$$r = \left(\frac{n}{l} \right)^{\frac{1}{4}}$$

So the value of G_1 is,

$$G_1 = ar$$

$$= l \left(\frac{n}{l} \right)^{\frac{1}{4}}$$

So the value of G_2 is,

$$G_2 = ar^2$$

$$= l \left(\frac{n}{l} \right)^{\frac{1}{2}}$$

So the value of G_3 is,

$$G_3 = ar^3$$

$$= l \left(\frac{n}{l} \right)^{\frac{3}{4}}$$

The value of the given term is,

$$G_1^4 + 2G_2^4 + G_3^4 = l^4 \left(\frac{n}{l} \right) + 2l^4 \left(\frac{n}{l} \right)^2 + l^4 \left(\frac{n}{l} \right)^3$$

$$= l^3 n + 2l^2 n^2 + ln^3$$
$$= nl(l + n)^2$$
$$= 4m^2 nl$$

76. Correct Response : (b)

Explanation :

The nth term of the given series is,

$$T_n = \frac{1^3 + 2^3 + \ldots + n^3}{1 + 3 + 5 + \ldots + (2n-1)}$$

$$= \frac{\left\{ \frac{n(n+1)}{2} \right\}^2}{\frac{n}{2}[1 + (2n-1)]}$$

$$= \frac{(n+1)^2}{4}$$

The sum of first nine terms is,

$$\sum_{n=1}^{9} T_n = \frac{1}{4} \sum_{n=1}^{9} (n+1)^2$$

$$= \frac{1}{4} [2^2 + 3^2 + \ldots 10^2]$$

$$= \frac{1}{4} \left[\frac{1}{6}(10)(10+1)(2\times 10+1) - 1^2 \right]$$

$$= 96$$

77. Correct Response : (a)

Explanation :

The given expression is,

$$\sum_{n=1}^{5} \frac{1}{3} \left[\frac{1}{n(n+1)(n+2)} - \frac{1}{(n+1)(n+2)(n+3)} \right] = \frac{k}{3}$$

Simplify the given expression,

$$T_r = \frac{1}{3} \left[\frac{1}{n(n+1)(n+2)} - \frac{1}{(n+1)(n+2)(n+3)} \right]$$

Written in the form of summation,

$$\sum_{r=1}^{5} T_r$$

$$= \sum_{r=1}^{5} \frac{1}{3} \left[\frac{1}{n(n+1)(n+2)} - \frac{1}{(n+1)(n+2)(n+3)} \right]$$

$$\frac{k}{3} = \frac{1}{3} \left[\frac{1}{6} - \frac{1}{6 \times 7 \times 8} \right]$$

$$k = \frac{55}{336}$$

78. Correct Response : (c)

Explanation :

The given expression is,

$$\cos \alpha + \cos \beta = \frac{3}{2}$$

$$2 \cos \left(\frac{\alpha + \beta}{2} \right) \cos \left(\frac{\alpha - \beta}{2} \right) = \frac{3}{2}$$

And,

$$\sin \alpha + \sin \beta = \frac{1}{2}$$

$$2 \sin \left(\frac{\alpha + \beta}{2} \right) \cos \left(\frac{\alpha - \beta}{2} \right) = \frac{1}{2}$$

Divide both equations,

$$\tan \left(\frac{\alpha + \beta}{2} \right) = \frac{1}{3}$$

$$\tan \theta = \frac{1}{3}$$

Hence, the required value is,

$$\sin 2\theta + \cos 2\theta = \frac{2\tan\theta}{1+\tan^2\theta} + \frac{1-\tan^2\theta}{1+\tan^2\theta}$$

$$= \frac{2\tan\theta + 1 - \tan^2\theta}{1+\tan^2\theta}$$

$$= \frac{2\left(\dfrac{1}{3}\right)+1-\left(\dfrac{1}{9}\right)}{1+\left(\dfrac{1}{9}\right)}$$

$$= \frac{7}{5}$$

79. Correct Response : (c)

Explanation :

The figure is shown as,

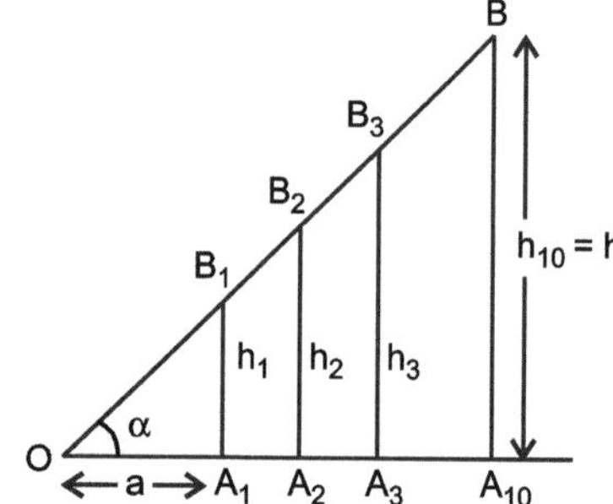

From the triangle formula,

$$\frac{h_1}{a_1} = \frac{h_2}{a_2} = \frac{h_3}{a_3} = \cdots = \frac{h_{10}}{a_{10}} = \tan\alpha$$

So,

$$h = h_{10} = a_{10}\tan\alpha \qquad \ldots(1)$$

And,

$$h_1 = a_1\tan\alpha \qquad \ldots(2)$$

Hence, apply the Arithmetic progression for the given ten poles,

$$h = (a+9d)\tan\alpha$$

$$d = \frac{h - a\tan\alpha}{9\tan\alpha}$$

$$= \frac{h - a\tan\alpha}{9\tan\alpha}$$

$$= \frac{h\cos\alpha - a\sin\alpha}{9\sin\alpha}$$

80. Correct Response : (b)

Explanation :

Consider, the numbers in G.P. are a, ar, ar^2.

And, the numbers in A.P. are a, $2ar$, ar^2.

From the given relation,

$$2\times 2ar = a + ar^2$$

$$4r = 1 + r^2$$

$$r^2 - 4r + 1 = 0$$

Further, simplify the above expression,

$$r = \frac{4 \pm \sqrt{16-4}}{2}$$

$$= 2 \pm \sqrt{3}$$

$$r \neq 2 - \sqrt{3},\ (r>1)\ \text{G.P. is increasing}$$

$$r = 2 + \sqrt{3}$$

81. Correct Response : (a)

Explanation :

The geometric mean of numbers a and b is,

$$G = \sqrt[2]{ab}$$

The value of b is ar.

So, the expression becomes,

$$G = \sqrt[2]{a\cdot ar}$$

$$= a\sqrt{r}$$

The arithmetic mean of numbers $\dfrac{1}{a}$ and $\dfrac{1}{b}$ is,

$$M = \frac{\dfrac{1}{a}+\dfrac{1}{b}}{2}$$

$$= \frac{\dfrac{1}{a}+\dfrac{1}{b}}{2}$$

$$= \frac{b+a}{2ab}$$

$$\frac{1}{M} = \frac{2ab}{b+a}$$

The ratio of $\dfrac{1}{M} : G$ is,

$$\frac{1}{M} : G = \frac{\dfrac{2ab}{b+a}}{\sqrt{ab}}$$

$$\frac{\dfrac{2a\cdot ar}{ar+a}}{a\sqrt{r}} = \frac{4}{5}$$

$$\frac{a^2 r}{a\sqrt{r}\cdot a(r+1)} = \frac{2}{5}$$

$$\frac{\sqrt{r}}{(r+1)} = \frac{2}{5}$$

The solution of the above equation is,

$$5\sqrt{r} = 2(r+1)$$

$$25r = 4(r^2 + 1 + 2r)$$

$$4r^2 + 4 + 8r = 25r$$

$$4r^2 - 17r + 4 = 0$$

The roots of the above equation are,

$$4r(r-4) - 1\,(r-4) = 0$$
$$(4r-1)\,(r-4) = 0$$
$$r = \frac{1}{4} \text{ and } 4$$

So, the value of $a : b$ is,

$$a = br$$
$$\frac{a}{b} = r$$
$$= \frac{1}{4}$$

82. Correct Response : (b)

Explanation :

Let the number of terms are $2n$ which are,

$$a, (a+d), (a+2d), \ldots, \{a+(2n-1)d\}$$

Apply the formula for the sum of even terms for the A.P. series, is,

$$\frac{n}{2}\,[2(a+d) + (n-1)2d] = 30 \qquad \ldots(1)$$

Sum of odd terms is,

$$\frac{n}{2}\,[2a + (n-1)2d] = 24 \qquad \ldots(2)$$

Given that the last term exceed the first term by $\dfrac{21}{2}$,

$$a + (2n-1)d - a = \frac{21}{2}$$
$$(2n-1)d = \frac{21}{2} \qquad \ldots(3)$$

From the equation (1) and (2),

$$\frac{n}{2} \times 2d = 6$$
$$nd = 6 \qquad \ldots(4)$$

And,

$$(2n-1)d = \frac{21}{2}$$
$$\frac{n}{2n-1} = \frac{4}{7}$$
$$8n - 4 = 7n$$
$$n = 4$$

So, number of terms is 8.

83. Correct Response : (d)

Explanation :

Given function is,

$$f(n) = \left[\frac{1}{3} + \frac{3n}{100}\right]n$$

The given expression is,

$$\sum_{n=1}^{56} f(n) = \left[\frac{1}{3} + \frac{3\times1}{100}\right]\times1 + \ldots + \left[\frac{1}{3} + \frac{3\times22}{100}\right]\times22$$
$$+ \left[\frac{1}{3} + \frac{3\times23}{100}\right]\times23 \ldots + \ldots \left[\frac{1}{3} + \frac{3\times55}{100}\right]\times55$$
$$+ \left[\frac{1}{3} + \frac{3\times56}{100}\right]\times56$$

$$= 0 + \ldots + 0 + 23 + 24 + \ldots + 55 + 2 \times 56$$
$$= \frac{55(56)}{2} - \frac{22(23)}{2} + 112$$
$$= 11\,(5 \times 28 - 23) + 112$$

Simplify the above equation.

$$\sum_{n=1}^{56} f(n) = 11 \times 117 + 112$$
$$= 1399$$

84. Correct Response : (c)

Explanation :

Consider the first term of the geometrical progression is a and common ratio is r,

The given condition of the question,

$$\frac{\left(a + ar + ar^2 + ar^3 + ar^4\right)}{\left(\dfrac{1}{a} + \dfrac{1}{ar} + \dfrac{1}{ar^2} + \dfrac{1}{ar^3} + \dfrac{1}{ar^4}\right)} = 49$$
$$a^2 r^4 = 49$$
$$ar^2 = \pm 7$$

The given condition of the question,

$$a + ar^2 = 35 \qquad \ldots(1)$$

Substitute 7 for ar^2 in the above equation,

$$a + 7 = 35$$
$$a = 28$$

Substitute -7 for ar^2 in the equation (1),

$$a - 7 = 35$$
$$a = 42$$

Check the value of common ratio for this value.

$$(42)r^2 = -7$$
$$r^2 = -\frac{7}{42} \quad [\because r^2 < 0]$$

From the above expression, it is clear that the value of first term of the geometric progression is 28.

85. Correct Response : (b)

Explanation :

The common difference of the arithmetic progression $3 + 7 + 11 + 15 + \ldots$,

$$d_1 = 4$$

The common difference of the arithmetic progression $1 + 6 + 11 + 16 + \ldots$,

$$d_2 = 5$$

First common terms of given progression is 11. The common difference of the common progression,

$$d = \text{LCM}(d_1, d_2)$$
$$= 20$$

The sum of first 20 terms of the common arithmetic progression,

$$S = \frac{20}{2} \left[(2 \times 11) + \{(20-1) \times 20\} \right]$$
$$= 10 \times (22 + 380)$$
$$= 10 \times 402$$
$$= 4020$$

86. Correct Response : (a)

Explanation :

The sum of the first n terms is cn^2.

The general formula to calculate the sum of n terms is,

$$\frac{n}{2}(2a + (n-1)d) = ((2an - nd) + n^2 d)\frac{1}{2}$$

Here, a is first term and d is the common difference. Compare the above equation with cn^2.

$$2an - nd = 0,\ a = d$$
$$\frac{c}{2} = d$$
$$a = \frac{c}{2}$$

The formula to calculate the sum of square of n terms is,

$$S_n = \sum_{r=1}^{n} \left(a + (n-1)d \right)^2$$

Here, S_n is sum of square of n terms. Substitute the values in the above equation.

$$S_n = \sum_{r=1}^{n} \left(a + (n-1)d \right)^2$$
$$= \sum_{r=1}^{n} c^2 \left(n^2 - n + \frac{1}{4} \right)$$
$$= \frac{c^2}{4} \left(4\sum_{r=1}^{n} n^2 - 4\sum_{r=1}^{n} n + \sum_{r=1}^{n} 1 \right)$$
$$= \frac{c^2}{4} \left(\frac{4n(n+1)(2n+1)}{6} - \frac{4n(n+1)}{2} + n \right)$$

Simplify the above equation.

$$S_n = \frac{c^2}{4} \left(\frac{4n(n+1)(2n+1)}{6} - \frac{4n(n+1)}{2} + n \right)$$
$$= \frac{n(4n^2 - 1)c^2}{6}$$

87. Correct Response : (c)

Explanation :

Apply A.P. for the second term,

$$a + (2-1)d = 12$$
$$a + d = 12$$

The given condition for its first 9th terms,

$$200 < \frac{9}{2}(2a + 8d) < 220$$
$$\frac{92}{27} < d < \frac{112}{27}$$

But d has to be a integer. Therefore,

$$d = 4$$

Now,

$$a + 4 = 12$$
$$a = 8$$

Hence, its 4th term is,

$$a + 3d = 8 + (3 \times 4)$$
$$= 20$$

88. Correct Response : (a)

Explanation :

The n terms of the given series is,

$$t_n = \frac{2n+1}{\dfrac{n(n+1)(2n+1)}{6}}$$
$$= \frac{6}{n(n+1)}$$
$$= 6\left(\frac{1}{n} - \frac{1}{n+1} \right)$$

Now, substitute the value of $n = 1, 2, 3, .., 20$ in the above expressions,

$$S_n = 6\left\{ \frac{1}{1} - \frac{1}{2} + \frac{1}{2} - \frac{1}{3} + \frac{1}{3} + \ldots - \frac{1}{21} \right\}$$
$$= 6\left\{ \frac{1}{1} - \frac{1}{21} \right\}$$
$$= \frac{120}{21}$$

Hence, $k = 120$

89. Correct Response : (c)

Explanation :

The general expression is,

$$1 - \frac{2}{3} - \frac{2}{3^2} - \ldots - \frac{2}{3^{n-1}} < \frac{1}{100}$$
$$1 - 2\left(\frac{1}{3} + \frac{1}{3^2} + \ldots + \frac{1}{3^{n-1}} \right) < \frac{1}{100}$$

Solve the above binomial expression.

$$1 - 2\left(\frac{1}{3}\right)\frac{\left[1 - \dfrac{1}{3^{n-1}}\right]}{1 - \dfrac{1}{3}} < \frac{1}{100}$$

$$1 - 2\left(\frac{1}{3}\right)\frac{\left[1 - \dfrac{1}{3^{n-1}}\right]}{\dfrac{2}{3}} < \frac{1}{100}$$

$$1 - 1 + \frac{1}{3^{n-1}} < \frac{1}{100}$$

$$3^{n-1} > 100$$

Further solve the above expression,

$$3^{n-1} > 100$$

$$\frac{3^n}{3} > 100$$

$$n - 1 = 5$$

$$n = 6$$

90. Correct Response : (0)

Explanation :

The given expression $a_k = 2a_{k-1} - a_{k-2}$ implies that $a_1, a_2, \ldots\ldots, a_{11}$ are in arithmetic progression.

Now, the given expression can be written as,

$$\frac{a_1^2 + a_2^2 + \ldots + a_{11}^2}{11} = 90$$

$$\frac{11 \times 15^2 + 35 \times 11d^2 + 11 \times 10ad}{11} = 90$$

$$225 + 35d^2 + 150d = 90$$

$$d = -3, \ -\frac{9}{7}$$

The given condition is, $27 - 2a_2 > 0$ or $a_2 < \dfrac{27}{2}$

so the value of d does not equal to $-\dfrac{9}{7}$.

Thus, the sum of expression is,

$$\frac{a_1 + a_2 + \ldots + a_{11}}{11} = \frac{11}{2}\Big[2 \times 15 - (11 - 1)3\Big]$$

$$= 0$$

91. Correct Response : (b, d)

Explanation :

The vertex P of a triangle PQR intersects the side QR at point S.

$$PS \times ST = QS \times SR$$

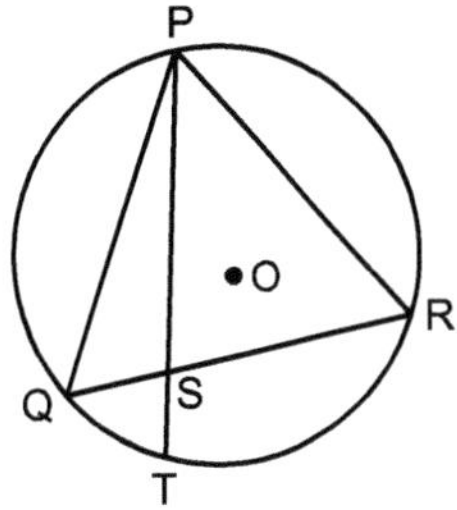

From the property of geometric mean and harmonic mean.

$$\frac{\dfrac{1}{PS} + \dfrac{1}{ST}}{2} > \sqrt{\frac{1}{PS} \times \frac{1}{ST}}$$

$$\frac{1}{PS} + \frac{1}{ST} > \frac{2}{\sqrt{QS \times SR}}$$

$$\frac{QS + SR}{2} > \sqrt{QS \times SR}$$

$$\frac{QR}{2} > \sqrt{QS \times SR}$$

Further simplify.

$$\frac{1}{\sqrt{QS \times SR}} > \frac{2}{QR}$$

$$\frac{1}{PS} + \frac{1}{ST} > \frac{4}{QR}$$

92. Correct Response : (c)

Explanation :

The arithmetic mean of A_{n-1} and H_{n-1} is,

$$A_n = \frac{A_{n-1} + H_{n-1}}{2}$$

The geometric mean of A_{n-1} and H_{n-1} is,

$$G_n = \sqrt{A_{n-1} H_{n-1}}$$

The harmonic mean of A_{n-1} and H_{n-1} is,

$$H_n = \frac{2 A_{n-1} H_{n-1}}{A_{n-1} + H_{n-1}}$$

$$G_n^2 = H_{n-1} A_{n-1}$$
$$G_n^2 = A_n H_n$$
$$G_n^2 = ab$$

Now, $\qquad G_n = \sqrt{ab}$

Therefore, $G_1 = G_2 = G_3 = \ldots$.

93. Correct Response : (a)

Explanation :

The arithmetic mean of A_1 and H_1 is A_2.

$$A_1 > H_1$$
$$A_1 > A_2 > H_1$$

The arithmetic mean of A_2 and H_2 is A_3.

$$A_2 > H_2$$
$$A_2 > A_3 > H_2$$

Therefore, $A_1 > A_2 > A_3 > \ldots$.

94. Correct Response : (b)

Explanation :

The harmonic mean of A_1 and H_1 is H_2.

$$A_1 > H_1$$
$$A_1 > H_2 > H_1$$

The arithmetic mean of A_2 and H_2 is H_3.

$$A_2 > H_2$$
$$A_2 > H_3 > H_2$$

Therefore, $H_1 < H_2 < H_3 < \dots$.

95. Correct Answer : 6

Explanation :

Solve the given value of a_n.

$$a_n = \frac{3}{4} - \left(\frac{3}{4}\right)^2 + \left(\frac{3}{4}\right)^3 + \dots + (-1)^{n-1}\left(\frac{3}{4}\right)^n$$

$$= \frac{\frac{3}{4}\left(1-\left(-\frac{3}{4}\right)^n\right)}{1+\frac{3}{4}}$$

$$= \frac{3}{7}\left(1-\left(-\frac{3}{4}\right)^n\right)$$

It is given that $b_n > a_n$.

$$2a_n < 1$$

$$\frac{6}{7}\left(1-\left(-\frac{3}{4}\right)^n\right) < 1$$

$$1-\left(-\frac{3}{4}\right)^n < \frac{7}{6}$$

$$-\frac{1}{6} < \left(-\frac{3}{4}\right)^n$$

Therefore, minimum natural number is 6.

96. Correct Response : (c)

Explanation :

It is given that $(\alpha + \beta)$, $(\alpha^2 + \beta^2)$ and $(\alpha^3 + \beta^3)$ are in G.P. So,

$$(\alpha^2 + \beta^2)^2 = (\alpha + \beta)(\alpha^3 + \beta^3)$$
$$[(\alpha+\beta)^2 - 2(\alpha\beta)]^2 = (\alpha+\beta)[(\alpha+\beta)^3$$
$$- 3\alpha\beta\,(\alpha+\beta)]$$

$$\left[\frac{b^2}{a^2} - \frac{2c}{a}\right]^2 = \left(-\frac{b}{a}\right)\left[-\frac{b^3}{a^3} - 3\frac{c}{a}\left(-\frac{b}{a}\right)\right]$$

$$\left[\frac{b^2 - 2ac}{a^2}\right]^2 = -\frac{b}{a}\left[\frac{-b^3 + 3abc}{a^3}\right]$$

Solve further.

$$\left[\frac{b^2 - 2ac}{a^2}\right]^2 = \frac{b^2}{a^4}[b^2 - 3ac]$$

$$\frac{(b^2 - 2ac)^2}{a^4} = \frac{b^2}{a^4}[b^2 - 3ac]$$

$$4a^2c^2 - b^2ac = 0$$
$$ac(b^2 - 4ac) = 0$$

As, $a \neq 0$. So,

$$ac \cdot \Delta = 0$$
$$c\,\Delta = 0$$

97. Correct Response : (d)

Explanation :

It is given that $\quad T_r = V_{r+1} - V_r - 2$.

Now,

$$V_{r+1} - V_r = (r+1)^3 - r^3 - \frac{1}{2}\left[(r+1)^2 - r^2\right] + \frac{1}{2}(1)$$

$$= 3r^2 + 2r + 1$$

The value of T_r is,

$$T_r = 3r^2 + 2r + 1 - 2$$
$$= 3r^2 + 2r - 1$$
$$= (3r - 1)(r + 1)$$

Therefore, T_r is always a composite number.

98. Explanation :

Solve.

$$(1 + a)(1 + b)(1 + c) - 1 = 1 + ab + a + b + c + abc$$
$$+ ac + bc$$
$$(1 + a)(1 + b)(1 + c) = ab + a + b + c + abc + ac + bc$$

It is known that AM $\geq$ GM.

$$\frac{(1+a)(1+b)(1+c)-1}{7} > (ab \cdot a \cdot b \cdot c \cdot abc \cdot ac \cdot bc)^{1/7}$$

$$(1 + a)(1 + b)(1 + c) - 1 > 7\,(a^4 \cdot b^4 \cdot c^4)^{1/7}$$
$$(1 + a)(1 + b)(1 + c) > 7\,(a^4 \cdot b^4 \cdot c^4)^{1/7}$$
$$(1 + a)^7(1 + b)^7(1 + c)^7 > 7\,(a^4 \cdot b^4 \cdot c^4)$$

99. Correct Response : (a)

Explanation :

Use the relation between arithmetic mean and geometric mean.

$$\text{A.M.} \geq \text{G.M.}$$

$$\frac{1}{2}\left(\sqrt{x^2 + x} + \frac{\tan^2\alpha}{\sqrt{x^2 + x}}\right) \geq \sqrt{\sqrt{x^2 + x} \cdot \frac{\tan^2\alpha}{\sqrt{x^2 + x}}}$$

$$\sqrt{x^2 + x} + \frac{\tan^2\alpha}{\sqrt{x^2 + x}} \geq 2\tan\alpha$$

100. Correct Response : (a)

Explanation :

Relation between arithmetic mean and geometric mean is,

$$\text{A.M.} \geq \text{G.M.}$$

$$\frac{a_1 + a_2 + \dots + a_{n-1} + 2a_n}{n} \geq (a_1 \cdot a_2 \cdot a_3 \dots a_{n-1} \cdot 2a_n)^{1/n}$$

$$a_1 + a_2 + \ldots + a_{n-1} + 2a_n \geq n(a_1 \cdot a_2 \cdot a_3 \ldots a_{n-1} \cdot 2a_n)^{1/n}$$

It is given that product of positive real numbers is c. So,

$$a_1 + a_2 + \ldots + a_{n-1} + 2a_n \geq n(2c)^{1/n}$$

101. Correct Response : (d)

Explanation :

If a, b and c are in A.P. So,

$$a + c = 2b$$

If a^2, b^2 and c^2 are in G.P. So,

$$(b^2)^2 = a^2 c^2$$
$$b^2 = \pm ac$$

It is given that $a + b + c = \dfrac{3}{2}$. So, $a + c = 1$ and

$$ac = \pm \dfrac{1}{4}.$$

So, a and c are roots of equations $x^2 - x \pm \dfrac{1}{4} = 0$.

$$a = \dfrac{1}{2} - \dfrac{1}{\sqrt{2}}$$

●●

Chapter 8 | Limit, Continuity and Differentiability

⟨?⟩ QUESTIONS

1. For all twice differentiable functions $f : R \to R$, with $f(0) = f(1) = f'(0) = 0$: **[2020, Main]**
   (a) $f''(x) = 0$, for some $x \in (0, 1)$
   (b) $f''(0) = 0$
   (c) $f''(x) \ne 0$ at every point $x \in (0, 1)$
   (d) $f''(x) = 0$ at every point $x \in (0, 1)$

2. Let $f : R \to R$ be a function defined by $f(x) = \max \{x, x^2\}$. Let S denote the set of all points in R, where f is not differentiable. Then : **[2020, Main]**
   (a) $\{0, 1\}$
   (b) $\{0\}$
   (c) ϕ (an empty set)
   (d) $\{1\}$

3. Suppose a differentiable function $f(x)$ satisfies the identity $f(x + y) = f(x) + f(y) + xy^2 + x^2y$, for all real x and y. If $\lim\limits_{x \to 0} \dfrac{f(x)}{x} = 1$, then $f'(3)$ is equal to .... **[2020, Main]**

4. The function $f(x) = \begin{cases} \dfrac{\pi}{4} + \tan^{-1} x, |x| \le 1 \\ \dfrac{1}{2}(|x| - 1), |x| > 1 \end{cases}$ is : **[2020, Main]**
   (a) continuous on $R - \{1\}$ and differentiable on $R - \{-1, 1\}$
   (b) both continuous and differentiable on $R - \{-1\}$
   (c) continuous on $R - \{-1\}$ and differentiable on $R - \{-1, 1\}$
   (d) both continuous and differentiable on $R - \{1\}$

5. Let $f : (0, \infty) (0, \infty)$ be a differentiable function such that $f(1) = e$ and $\lim\limits_{t \to x} \dfrac{t^2 f^2(x) - x^2 f^2(t)}{t - x} = 0$. If $f(x) = 1$, then x is equal to : **[2020, Main]**
   (a) $2e$
   (b) $\dfrac{1}{2e}$
   (c) e
   (d) $\dfrac{1}{e}$

6. Contrapositive of the statement :
   'If a function f is differentiable at a, then it is also continuous at a', is : **[2020, Main]**
   (a) If a function f is continuous at a, then it is not differentiable at a
   (b) If a function f is not continuous at a, then it is differentiable at a
   (c) If a function f is not continuous at a, then it is not differentiable at a
   (d) If a function f is continuous at a, then it is differentiable at a

7. Let $[t]$ denote the greatest integer $\le t$. If for some $\lambda \in R - \{0, 1\}$, $\lim\limits_{x \to 0} \left| \dfrac{1 - x + |x|}{\lambda - x + [x]} \right| = L$ then L is equal to : **[2020, Main]**
   (a) 1
   (b) 2
   (c) $\dfrac{1}{2}$
   (d) 0

8. If $\lim\limits_{x \to 0} \left\{ \dfrac{1}{x^8} \left(1 - \cos \dfrac{x^2}{2} - \cos \dfrac{x^2}{4} + \cos \dfrac{x^2}{2} \cos \dfrac{x^2}{4} \right) \right\} = 2^{-k}$, then the value of k is .... **[2020, Main]**

9. $\lim\limits_{x \to 0} \dfrac{(e^{(\sqrt{1 + x^2 + x^4} - 1)/x} - 1)}{\sqrt{1 + x^2 + x^4} - 1}$ **[2020, Main]**
   (a) does not exist
   (b) is equal to $\sqrt{e}$
   (c) is equal to 0
   (d) is equal to 1

10. Let the function $f : R \to R$ be defined by $f(x) = x^3 - x^2 + (x - 1) \sin x$ and let $g : R \to R$ be an arbitrary function. Let $fg : R \to R$ be the product function defined by $(fg)(x) = f(x) g(x)$. Then which of the following statements is/are TRUE ? **[2020, Advanced]**
   (a) If g is continous at $x = 1$, then fg is differentiable at $x = 1$
   (b) If fg is differentiable at $x = 1$, then g is continuous at $x = 1$
   (c) If g is differentiable at $x = 1$, then fg is differentiable at $x = 1$
   (d) If fg is differentiable at $x = 1$, then g is differentiable at $x = 1$

11. Let e denotes the base of the natural logarithm. The value of the real number a for which the right hand limit

$$\lim_{x \to 0^+} \frac{(1-x)^{\frac{1}{x}} - e^{-1}}{x^a}$$

is equal to a non-zero real number, is ....

[2020, Main]

12. The value of the limit

$$\lim_{x \to \frac{\pi}{2}} \frac{4\sqrt{2}\,(\sin 3x + \sin x)}{\left(2\sin 2x \sin \dfrac{3x}{2} + \cos \dfrac{5x}{2}\right) - \left(\sqrt{2} + \sqrt{2}\cos 2x + \cos \dfrac{3x}{2}\right)}$$

is .... **[2020, Advanced]**

13. $\displaystyle\lim_{x \to a} \frac{(a+2x)^{1/3} - (3x)^{1/3}}{(3a+x)^{1/3} - (4x)^{1/3}}$ $(a \neq 0)$ is equal to

[2020, Main]

(a) $\left(\dfrac{2}{3}\right)\left(\dfrac{2}{9}\right)^{1/3}$
(b) $\left(\dfrac{2}{3}\right)^{4/3}$

(c) $\left(\dfrac{2}{9}\right)^{4/3}$
(d) $\left(\dfrac{2}{9}\right)\left(\dfrac{2}{3}\right)^{1/3}$

14. If $p(x)$ be a polynomial of degree three that has a local maximum value 8 at $x = 1$ and a local minimum value 4 at $x = 2$; then $p(0)$ is equal to :

[2020, Main]

(a) 12
(b) – 24

(c) 6
(d) – 12

15. If $\displaystyle\lim_{x \to 1} \frac{x + x^2 + x^3 + ... + x^n - n}{x - 1} = 820, (n \in N)$ then

the value of n is equal to .... **[2020, Main]**

16. $\displaystyle\lim_{x \to 0} \left(\tan\left(\dfrac{\pi}{4} + x\right)\right)^{1/x}$ is equal to :

[2020, Main]

(a) 2
(b) e

(c) 1
(d) e^2

17. If the tangent to the curve, $y = f(x) = x \log_e x$, $(x > 0)$ at a point $(c, f(c))$ is parallel to the line segment joining the points $(1, 0)$ and (e, e) c is equal to : **[2020, Main]**

(a) $\dfrac{1}{e-1}$
(b) $e^{\left(\frac{1}{1-e}\right)}$

(c) $e^{\left(\frac{1}{e-1}\right)}$
(d) $\dfrac{e-1}{e}$

18. If $(a + \sqrt{2}\,b\cos x)(a - \sqrt{2}\cos y) = a^2 - b^2$, where

$a > b > 0$, then $\dfrac{dx}{dy}$ at $\left(\dfrac{\pi}{4}, \dfrac{\pi}{4}\right)$ is : **[2020, Main]**

(a) $\dfrac{a-b}{a+b}$
(b) $\dfrac{a+b}{a-b}$

(c) $\dfrac{2a+b}{2a-b}$
(d) $\dfrac{a-2b}{a+2b}$

19. If $y^2 + \log_e (\cos^2 x) = y$, $x \in \left(-\dfrac{\pi}{2}, \dfrac{\pi}{2}\right)$, then :

[2020, Main]

(a) $|\, y''(0)\, | = 2$
(b) $|\, y'(0)\, | + |\, y''(0)| = 3$
(c) $|\, y'(0)\, | + |\, y''(0)\, | = 1$
(d) $y''(0) = 0$

20. The derivative of $\tan^{-1}\left(\dfrac{\sqrt{1+x^2}-1}{x}\right)$ with

respect to $\tan^{-1}\left(\dfrac{2x\sqrt{1-x^2}}{1-2x^2}\right)$ at $x = \dfrac{1}{2}$ is :

[2020, Main]

(a) $\dfrac{\sqrt{3}}{12}$
(b) $\dfrac{\sqrt{3}}{10}$

(c) $\dfrac{2\sqrt{3}}{5}$
(d) $\dfrac{2\sqrt{3}}{3}$

21. If $x = 1$ is a critical point of the function $f(x) = (3x^2 + ax - 2 - a)e^x$, then : **[2020, Main]**

(a) $x = 1$ is a local minima and $x = -\dfrac{2}{3}$ is a local maxima of f

(b) $x = 1$ is a local maxima and $x = -\dfrac{2}{3}$ is a local minima of f

(c) $x = 1$ and $x = -\dfrac{2}{3}$ are local minima of f

(d) $x = 1$ and $x = -\dfrac{2}{3}$ are local maxima of f

22. For a polynomial $g(x)$ with real coefficient, let m_g denote the number of distinct real roots of $g(x)$. Suppose S is the set of polynomials with real coefficient defined by

$$S = \{(x^2 - 1)^2\,(a_0 + a_1 x + a_2 x^2 + a_3 x^3) : a_0,\, a_1,\, a_2,\, a_3 \in R\}$$

For a polynomial f, let f' and f'' denote its first and second order derivatives, respectively. Then the minimum possible value of $(m_{f'} + m_{f''})$, where $f \in S$, is ....

$<_1$. Then the value of $\lambda_1 + ... + \lambda_r$

[2020, Advanced]

23. Let $f : R \to R$ and $g : R \to R$ be functions satisfying $f(x + y) = f(x) + f(y) + f(x)\,f(y)$ and $f(x) = xg(x)$ for all $x, y \in$ R. If $\lim\limits_{x \to 0} g(x) = 1$, then which of the following statements is/are TRUE ?

[2020, Advanced]

(a) f is differentiable at every $x \in$ R

(b) If $g(0) = 1$, then g is differentiable at every $x \in$ R

(c) The derivative $f'(1)$ is equal to

(d) The derivative $f'(0)$ is equal to 1

24. Let the function : $(0, \pi) \to$ R be defined by

$$(\theta) = (\sin \theta + \cos \theta)^2 + (\sin \theta - \cos \theta)^4$$

Suppose the function f has a local minimum at θ precisely when $\theta \in \{\lambda_1 \pi, \ldots, \lambda_r \pi\}$, where $0 < \lambda_1 < \ldots < \lambda_r <_1$. Then the value of $\lambda_1 + \ldots + \lambda_r + \ldots + \lambda_r$ is ....   **[2020, Advanced]**

25. If the function f defined on $\left(\dfrac{-1}{3}, \dfrac{1}{3}\right)$ by

$$f(x) = \begin{cases} \dfrac{1}{x}\log_e\left(\dfrac{1+3x}{1-2x}\right), & \text{when } x \neq 0 \\ k, & \text{when } x = 0 \end{cases}$$

is continuous, then k is equal to ....

[2020, Main]

26. If $f(x) = \begin{cases} \dfrac{\sin(a+2)x + \sin x}{x} & ; \quad x < 0 \\ b & ; \quad x = 0 \\ \dfrac{(x+3x^2)^{\frac{1}{3}} - x^{-\frac{1}{3}}}{x^{\frac{4}{3}}} & ; \quad x > 0 \end{cases}$

is continuous at $x = 0$, then $a + 2b$ is equal to :

[2020, Main]

(a) -1

(b) 1

(c) -2

(d) 0

27. Let $[t]$ denote the greatest integer $\leq t$ and $\lim\limits_{x \to 0}\left[\dfrac{4}{x}\right] = A$. Then the function, $f(x) = [x^2]\sin(\pi x)$ is discontinuous, when x is equal to :

[2020, Main]

(a) $\sqrt{A+5}$

(b) $\sqrt{A+1}$

(c) $\sqrt{A}$

(d) $\sqrt{A+21}$

28. let f and g be differentiable function on R such that $f o g$ is the identify function. If for some $a, b \in$ R, $g'(a) = 5$ and $g(a) = b$, then $f'(b)$ is equal to :

[2020, Main]

(a) $\dfrac{2}{5}$

(b) 1

(c) $\dfrac{1}{5}$

(d) 5

29. Let the function, $f : [-7, 0] \to$ R be continuous on $[-7, 0]$ and differentiable on $(-7, 0)$. If $f(-7) = -3$ and $f'(x) \leq 2$, for all $x \in (-7, 0)$, then for all such function f, $f(-1) + f(0)$ lies in the interval :

[2020, Main]

(a) $[-6, 20]$

(b) $(-\infty, 20)$

(c) $(-\infty, 1)$

(d) $[-3, 11]$

30. Let S be the set of points where the function $f(x) = |2 - |x - 3||$, $x \in$ R, is not differentiable. Then $\sum\limits_{x \in S} f(f(x))$ is equal to ....

[2020, Main]

31. $\lim\limits_{x \to 0}\left(\dfrac{3x^2 + 2}{7x^2 + 2}\right)^{\frac{1}{x^2}}$ is equal to :   **[2020, Main]**

(a) $\dfrac{1}{e}$

(b) e^2

(c) e

(d) $\dfrac{1}{e^2}$

32. $\lim\limits_{x \to 2} \dfrac{3^x + 3^{3-x} - 12}{3^{-x/2} - 3^{1-x}}$ is equal to ....

[2020, Main]

33. Let $f(x)$ be a polynomial of degree 5 such that $x = \pm 1$ are its critical points. If $\lim\limits_{x \to 0}\left(2 + \dfrac{f(x)}{x^2}\right) = 4$, then which one of the following is not true?

[2020, Main]

(a) f is an odd function

(b) $x = 1$ is a point of minima and $x = -1$ is a point of maxima of f.

(c) $x = 1$ is a point of maxima and $x = -1$ is a point of minimum of f.

(d) $f(1) - 4f(-1) = 4$

34. A spherical iron ball of 10 cm radius is coated with a layer of ice of uniform thickness that melts at a rate of 50 cm^3/min. When the thickness of ice is 5 cm, then the rate (in cm/min.) at which of the thickness of ice decreases, is :

[2020, Main]

(a) $\dfrac{1}{36\pi}$

(b) $\dfrac{5}{6\pi}$

(c) $\dfrac{1}{18\pi}$

(d) $\dfrac{1}{54\pi}$

35. Let a function $f : [0, 5] \to$ R be continuous, $f(1) = 3$ and F be defined as :

$$F(x) = \int_1^x t^2 g(t)\, dt \,, \text{ where } g(t) = \int_1^x f(u)\, du$$

Then for the function F, the point $x = 1$ is :

[2020, Main]

(a) a point of local minima.
(b) not a critical point.
(c) a point of inflection.
(d) a point of local maxima.

36. Let f be any function continuous on $[a, b]$ and twice differentiable on (a, b). If for all $x \in (a, b)$ $f'(x) > 0$ and $f''(x) < 0$, then for any $c \in (a, b)$, $\dfrac{f(c) - f(a)}{f(b) - f(c)}$ is greater than : **[2020, Main]**

(a) $\dfrac{b+a}{b-a}$
(b) $\dfrac{b-c}{c-a}$

(c) $\dfrac{c-a}{b-c}$
(d) 1

37. If $y(\alpha) = \sqrt{2\left(\dfrac{\tan\alpha + \cot\alpha}{1+\tan^2\alpha}\right) + \dfrac{1}{\sin^2\alpha}}$,

$\alpha \in \left(\dfrac{3\pi}{4}, \pi\right)$, then $\dfrac{dy}{d\alpha}$ at $\alpha = \dfrac{5\pi}{6}$ is :

[2020, Main]

(a) 4
(b) $-1/4$

(c) $\dfrac{4}{3}$
(d) -4

38. Let $x^k + y^k = a^k$, $(a, k > 0)$ and $\dfrac{dy}{dx} + \left(\dfrac{y}{x}\right)^{\frac{1}{3}} = 0$, then k is **[2020, Main]**

(a) $\dfrac{3}{2}$
(b) $\dfrac{1}{3}$

(c) $\dfrac{2}{3}$
(d) $\dfrac{4}{3}$

39. The value of c in the Lagrange's mean value theorem for the function $f(x) = x^3 - 4x^2 + 8x + 11$. When $x \in [0, 1]$ is : **[2020, Main]**

(a) $\dfrac{2}{3}$
(b) $\dfrac{\sqrt{7} - 2}{3}$

(c) $\dfrac{4 - \sqrt{5}}{3}$
(d) $\dfrac{4 - \sqrt{7}}{3}$

40. Let $f(x)$ be a polynomial of degree 5 such that $x = \pm 1$ are its critical points. If $\lim\limits_{x \to 0}\left(2 + \dfrac{f(x)}{x^5}\right) = 4$, then which one of the following is not true ? **[2020, Main]**

(a) f is an odd function.
(b) $x = 1$ is a point of minima and $x = -1$ is a point of minima of f.
(c) $x = 1$ is a point of maxima and $x = -1$ is a point of minimum of f.
(d) $f(1) - 4f(-1) = 4$

41. If c is a point at which Rolle's theorem holds for the function $f(x) = \log_e\left(\dfrac{x^2 + \alpha}{7x}\right)$ in the interval $[3, 4]$, where $\alpha \in R$, then $f''(c)$ is equal to **[2020, Main]**

(a) $\dfrac{\sqrt{3}}{7}$
(b) $\dfrac{1}{12}$

(c) $-\dfrac{1}{24}$
(d) $-\dfrac{1}{12}$

42. Let $f(x) = x \cos^{-1}(-\sin|x|)$, $x \in \left[-\dfrac{\pi}{2}, \dfrac{\pi}{2}\right]$, then which of the following is true? **[2020, Main]**

(a) f' is decreasing in $\left(-\dfrac{\pi}{2}, 0\right)$ and increasing in $\left(0, \dfrac{\pi}{2}\right)$.

(b) f is not differentiable at $x = 0$.

(c) $f'(0) = \dfrac{\pi}{2}$.

(d) f' is increasing in $\left(-\dfrac{\pi}{2}, 0\right)$ and decreasing $\left(0, \dfrac{\pi}{2}\right)$.

43. Let $f(x)$ be a polynomial of degree 3 such that $f(-1) = 10$, $f(1) = -6$, $f(x)$ has a critical point at $x = -1$ and $f'(x)$ has a critical point at $x = 1$. Then $f(x)$ has a local minima at $x = $ .... **[2020, Main]**

44. Let f be any function continuous on $[a, b]$ and twice differentiable on (a, b), then for any $x \in (a, b)$, $f'(x) > 0$ and $f''(x) < 0$, then for any $c \in (a, b)$, $\dfrac{f(c) - f(a)}{f(b) - f(c)}$ is greater than : **[2020, Main]**

(a) $\dfrac{b+a}{b-a}$
(b) $\dfrac{b-c}{c-a}$

(c) $\dfrac{c-a}{b-c}$
(d) 1

45. If $x = 2\sin\theta - \sin 2\theta$ and $y = 2\cos\theta - \cos 2\theta$, $0 \in [0, 2\pi]$, then $\dfrac{d^2y}{dx^2}$ at $\theta = \pi$ is : **[2020, Main]**

(a) $\dfrac{3}{2}$
(b) $-\dfrac{3}{4}$

(c) $\dfrac{3}{4}$
(d) $-\dfrac{3}{8}$

46. Let a function $f : [0, 5] \to \mathbf{R}$ be continuous, $f(1) = 3$ and F be defined as :

$$F(x) = \int_1^x t^2 g(t)\, dt \text{ , where } g(t) = \int_1^t f(u)\, du .$$

Then for the function F, the point $x = 1$ is : **[2020, Main]**

(a) a point of local minima.

(b) not a critical point.

(c) a point of inflection.

(d) a point of local maxima.

47. Let the normal at a point P on the curve $y^2 - 3x^2 + y + 10 = 0$ intersect the y-axis at $\left(0, \dfrac{3}{2}\right)$.

If n is the slope of the tangent at P to the curve then $|n|$ is equal to .... **[2020, Main]**

48. Let $y = y(x)$ be a function of x satisfying $y\sqrt{1-x^2} = k - x\sqrt{1-y^2}$ where k is a constant and $y\left(\dfrac{1}{2}\right) = -\dfrac{1}{4}$. Then $\dfrac{dy}{dx}$ at $x = \dfrac{1}{2}$, is equal to :

[2020, Main]

(a) $\dfrac{\sqrt{5}}{2}$

(b) $-\dfrac{\sqrt{5}}{2}$

(c) $-\dfrac{\sqrt{5}}{4}$

(d) $-\dfrac{\sqrt{5}}{4}$

49. Let $y = y(x)$ be a solution of the differential equation,
$$\sqrt{1-x^2}\,\dfrac{dy}{dx} + \sqrt{1-y^2} = 0, \ |x| < 1.$$

If $y\left(\dfrac{1}{2}\right) = \dfrac{\sqrt{3}}{2}$, then $y\left(\dfrac{-1}{\sqrt{2}}\right)$ is equal to

[2020, Main]

(a) $-\dfrac{\sqrt{3}}{2}$

(b) $\dfrac{1}{\sqrt{2}}$

(c) $\dfrac{\sqrt{3}}{2}$

(d) $-\dfrac{1}{\sqrt{2}}$

50. Let $f(x) = (\sin(\tan^{-1} x) + \sin(\cot^{-1} x))^2 - 1, \ |x| > 1$

If $\dfrac{dy}{dx} = \dfrac{1}{2}\dfrac{d}{dx}(\sin^{-1}(f(x)))$ and $y(\sqrt{3}) = \dfrac{x}{6}$, then $y(-\sqrt{3})$ is equal to

[2020, Main]

(a) $\dfrac{5\pi}{6}$

(b) $-\dfrac{\pi}{6}$

(c) $\dfrac{\pi}{3}$

(d) $\dfrac{2\pi}{3}$

51. Let $f : \text{R} \to \text{R}$ be differentiable at $c \in \text{R}$ and $f(c) = 0$. If $g(x) = |f(x)|$, then at $x = c$, g is : **[2019, Main]**

(a) not differentiable if $f'(c) = 0$

(b) differentiable if $f'(c) \neq 0$

(c) differentiable if $f'(c) = 0$

(d) not differentiable

52. If $\lim\limits_{x \to 1} \dfrac{x^4 - 1}{x - 1} = \lim\limits_{x \to k} \dfrac{x^3 - k^3}{x^2 - k^2}$, then k is :

[2019, Main]

(a) $\dfrac{8}{3}$

(b) $\dfrac{3}{8}$

(c) $\dfrac{3}{2}$

(d) $\dfrac{4}{3}$

53. Let $f(x) = e^x - x$ and $g(x) = x^2 - x, \ \forall \ x \in \text{R}$. Then the set of all $x \in \text{R}$, where the function $h(x) = (fog)\,(x)$ is increasing, in : **[2019, Main]**

(a) $\left[-1, \dfrac{-1}{2}\right] \cup \left[\dfrac{1}{2}, \infty\right)$

(b) $\left[0, \dfrac{1}{2}\right] \cup [1, \infty)$

(c) $[0, \infty)$

(d) $\left[\dfrac{-1}{2}, 0\right] \cup [1, \infty)$

54. If $f(x) = \begin{cases} \dfrac{\sin(p+1)x + \sin x}{x} & , \ x < 0 \\ q & , \ x = 0 \\ \dfrac{\sqrt{x+x^2} - \sqrt{x}}{x^{3/2}} & , \ x > 0 \end{cases}$

is continuous at $x = 0$, then the ordered pair (p, q) is equal to : **[2019, Main]**

(a) $\left(-\dfrac{3}{2}, -\dfrac{1}{2}\right)$

(b) $\left(-\dfrac{1}{2}, \dfrac{3}{2}\right)$

(c) $\left(-\dfrac{3}{2}, \dfrac{1}{2}\right)$

(d) $\left(\dfrac{5}{2}, \dfrac{1}{2}\right)$

55. If the tangent to the curve $y = \dfrac{x}{x^2 - 3}, \ x \in \text{R}, \ (x \neq \sqrt{3})$, at a point $(\alpha, \beta) \neq (0, 0)$ on it is parallel to the line $2x + 6y - 11 = 0$, then : **[2019, Main]**

(a) $|6\alpha + 2\beta| = 19$

(b) $|6\alpha + 2\beta| = 9$

(c) $|2\alpha + 6\beta| = 19$

(d) $|2\alpha + 6\beta| = 11$

56. A spherical iron ball of radius 10 cm is coated with a layer of ice of uniform thickness that melts at a rate of 50 cm^3/min. When the thickness of the ice is 5 cm, then the rate at which the thickness (in cm/min) of the ice decreases, is : **[2019, Main]**

(a) $\dfrac{1}{18\pi}$

(b) $\dfrac{1}{36\pi}$

(c) $\dfrac{5}{6\pi}$

(d) $\dfrac{1}{9\pi}$

57. If $\lim\limits_{x \to 1} \dfrac{x^2 - ax + b}{x - 1} = 5$, then $a + b$ is equal to :

[2019, Main]

(a) -4

(b) 5

(c) -7

(d) 1

58. If $f(x) = [x] - \left[\dfrac{x}{4}\right], \ x \in \text{R}$, where $[x]$ denoted the greatest integer function, then : **[2019, Main]**

(a) f is continuous at $x = 4$.

(b) $\lim\limits_{x \to 4+} f(x)$ exists but $\lim\limits_{x \to 4-} f(x)$ does not exist.

(c) Both $\lim\limits_{x \to 4-} f(x)$ and $\lim\limits_{x \to 4+} f(x)$ exist but are not equal.

(d) $\lim\limits_{x \to 4-} f(x)$ exists but $\lim\limits_{x \to 4+} f(x)$ does not exist.

59. If the function $f(x) = \begin{cases} a\,|\,\pi - x\,| + 1, & x \le 5 \\ b\,|\,x - \pi\,| + 3, & x > 5 \end{cases}$ is continuous at $x = 5$, then the value of $a - b$ is :

[2019, Main]

(a) $\dfrac{2}{\pi + 5}$ **(b)** $\dfrac{-2}{\pi + 5}$

(c) $\dfrac{2}{\pi - 5}$ **(d)** $\dfrac{2}{5 - \pi}$

60. A water tank has the shape of an inverted right circular cone, whose semi-vertical angles is $\tan^{-1}\left(\dfrac{1}{2}\right)$. Water is poured into it at a constant rate of 5 cubic meter per minute. Then the rate (in m/min.), at which the level of water is rising at the instant when the depth of water in the tank is 10 m; is : **[2019, Main]**

(a) $\dfrac{1}{15\pi}$ **(b)** $\dfrac{1}{10\pi}$

(c) $\dfrac{2}{\pi}$ **(d)** $\dfrac{1}{5\pi}$

61. If $f : R \to R$ is a differentiable function and $f(2) = 6$, then $\lim\limits_{x \to 2} \displaystyle\int_{6}^{f(x)} \dfrac{2t\,dt}{(x - 2)}$ is : **[2019, Main]**

(a) $24\,f'(2)$ **(b)** $2\,f'(2)$

(c) 0 **(d)** $12\,f'(2)$

62. If $f(x)$ is non-zero polynomial of degree four, having local extreme points at $x = -1, 0, 1$; then the set **[2019, Main]**

$$S = \{x \in R : f(x) = f(0)\}$$

contains exactly :

(a) four irrational numbers.

(b) four rational numbers.

(c) two irrational and two rational numbers.

(d) two irrational and one rational number.

63. If the tangent to the curve, $y = x^3 + ax - b$ at the point $(1, -5)$ is perpendicular to the line, $-x + y + 4 = 0$, then which one of the following points lies the curve ? **[2019, Main]**

(a) $(-2, 1)$ **(b)** $(-2, 2)$

(c) $(2, -1)$ **(d)** $(2, -2)$

64. If the function f defined on $\left(\dfrac{\pi}{6}, \dfrac{\pi}{3}\right)$ by

$$f(x) = \begin{cases} \dfrac{\sqrt{2}\cos x - 1}{\cot x - 1}, & x \ne \dfrac{\pi}{4} \\ k, & x = \dfrac{\pi}{4} \end{cases}$$

is continuous, then k is equal to : **[2019, Main]**

(a) 2 **(b)** $\dfrac{1}{2}$

(c) 1 **(d)** $\dfrac{1}{\sqrt{2}}$

65. Let $f(x) = 15 - |x - 10|$, $x \in R$. Then the set of all values of x, at which the function, $g(x) = f(f(x))$ is not differentiable, is : **[2019, Main]**

(a) {5, 10, 15}   **(b)** {10, 15}

(c) {5, 10, 15, 20}   **(d)** {10}

66. Let S be the set of all values of x for which the tangent to the curve $y = f(x) = x^3 - x^2 - 2x$ at (x, y) is parallel to the line segment joining the points $(1, f(1))$ and $(-1, f(-1))$, then S is equal to : **[2019, Main]**

(a) $\left\{\dfrac{1}{3}, 1\right\}$ **(b)** $\left\{-\dfrac{1}{3}, -1\right\}$

(c) $\left\{\dfrac{1}{3}, -1\right\}$ **(d)** $\left\{-\dfrac{1}{3}, 1\right\}$

67. $\lim\limits_{x \to 0} \dfrac{\sin^2 x}{\sqrt{2} - \sqrt{1 + \cos x}}$ equals : **[2019, Main]**

(a) $4\sqrt{2}$ **(b)** $\sqrt{2}$

(c) $2\sqrt{2}$ **(d)** 4

68. If S_1 and S_2 are respectively the sets of local minimum and local maximum points of the function, $f(x) = 9x^4 + 12x^3 - 36x^2 + 25$, $x \in R$, then : **[2019, Main]**

(a) $S_1 = \{-2\}; S_2 = \{0, 1\}$ **(b)** $S_1 = \{-2, 0\}; S_2 = \{1\}$

(c) $S_1 = \{-2, 1\}; S_2 = \{0\}$ **(d)** $S_1 = \{-1\}; S_2 = \{0, 2\}$

69. Let $f : [0, 2] \to R$ be a twice differentiable function such that $f''(x) > 0$, for all $x \in (0, 2)$. If $\phi(x)\,f''(x) + f(2 - x)$, then ϕ is :

(a) increasing on $(0, 1)$ and decreasing on $(1, 2)$.

(b) decreasing on $(0, 2)$

(c) decreasing on $(0, 1)$ and increasing on $(1, 2)$.

(d) increasing on $(0, 2)$

70. Let $f : [-1, 3] \to R$ be defined as **[2019, Main]**

$$f(x) = \begin{cases} |x| + [x], & -1 \le x < 1 \\ x + |x|, & 1 \le x < 2 \\ x + [x], & 2 \le x \le 3, \end{cases}$$

where $[t]$ denotes the greatest integer less than or equal to t. Then, f is discountinuous at :

(a) only one point **(b)** only two points

(c) only three points **(d)** four more points

71. The height of a right circular cylinder of maximum volume inscribed in a sphere of radius 3 is :

(a) $\sqrt{6}$ **(b)** $\dfrac{2}{3}\sqrt{3}$

(c) $2\sqrt{3}$ **(d)** $\sqrt{3}$ **[2019, Main]**

72. Let $f : \mathrm{R} \to \mathrm{R}$ be a differentiable function satisfying $f'(3) + f'(2) = 0$. Then $\displaystyle\lim_{x\to\infty}\left(\dfrac{1 + f(3+x) - f(3)}{1 + f(2-x)f(2)}\right)^{\frac{1}{x}}$ is equal to : **[2019, Main]**

(a) 1 **(b)** e^{-1}

(c) e **(d)** e^2

73. Let $f : \mathrm{R} \to \mathrm{R}$ be a continuously differentiable function such that $f(2) = 6$ and $f'(2) = \dfrac{1}{48}$. If $\displaystyle\int_{6}^{f(x)} 4t^3 \, dt = (x-2)\, g(x)$, then $\displaystyle\lim_{x\to\infty} g(x)$ is equal to :

[2019, Main]

(a) 18 **(b)** 24

(c) 12 **(d)** 36

74. If α and β are the roots of the equation $375\, x^2 - 25x - 2 = 0$, then $\displaystyle\lim_{x\to\infty}\sum_{r=1}^{n}\alpha^r + \sum_{r=1}^{n}\beta^r$ is equal to :

[2019, Main]

(a) $\dfrac{21}{346}$ **(b)** $\dfrac{29}{348}$

(c) $\dfrac{1}{12}$ **(d)** $\dfrac{7}{116}$

75. If m is the minimum value of k for which the function $f(x) = x\sqrt{kx - x^2}$ is increasing in the interval $[0, 3]$ and M is the maximum value of f in $[0, 3]$ when $k = m$, then the ordered pair (m, M) is equal to : **[2019, Main]**

(a) $(4, 3\sqrt{2})$ **(b)** $(4, 3\sqrt{3})$

(c) $(3, 3\sqrt{3})$ **(d)** $(5, 3\sqrt{6})$

76. The derivative of $\tan^{-1}\left(\dfrac{\sin x - \cos x}{\sin x + \cos x}\right)$, with respect to $\dfrac{x}{2}$, where $\left(x \in \left(0, \dfrac{\pi}{2}\right)\right)$ is :

[2019, Main]

(a) 1 **(b)** $\dfrac{2}{3}$

(c) $\dfrac{1}{2}$ **(d)** 2

77. $\displaystyle\lim_{x\to 0}\dfrac{x + 2\sin x}{\sqrt{x^2 + 2\sin x + 1} - \sqrt{\sin^2 x - x + 1}}$

[2019, Main]

(a) 6 **(b)** 2

(c) 3 **(d)** 1

78. Let $f(x) = 5 - |x - 2|$ and $g(x) = |x + 1|$, $x \in \mathrm{R}$, If $f(x)$ attains maximum value at α and $g(x)$ attains minimum value at β, then $\displaystyle\lim_{x\to\alpha\beta}\dfrac{(x-1)(x^2 - 5x + 6)}{x^2 - 6x + 8}$ equal to : **[2019, Main]**

(a) $\dfrac{1}{2}$ **(b)** $-\dfrac{3}{2}$

(c) $-\dfrac{1}{2}$ **(d)** $\dfrac{3}{2}$

79. A 2 m ladder leans against a vertical wall. If the top of the ladder begins to slide down the wall at the rate 25 cm/sec., then the rate (in cm/sec.) at which the bottom of the ladder slides away from the wall on the horizontal ground when the top of the ladder 1 m above the ground is :

[2019, Main]

(a) $25\sqrt{3}$ **(b)** $\dfrac{25}{\sqrt{3}}$

(c) $\dfrac{25}{3}$ **(d)** 25

80. Let $f : \mathrm{R} \to \mathrm{R}$ be given by

$$f(x) = \begin{cases} x^5 + 5x^4 + 10x^3 + 10x^2 + 3x + 1, & x < 0; \\ x^2 - x + 1, & 0 \le x < 1; \\ \dfrac{2}{3}x^3 - 4x^2 + 7x - \dfrac{8}{3}, & 1 \le x < 3; \\ (x - z)\log_e(x - 2) - x + \dfrac{10}{3}, & x \ge 3. \end{cases}$$

Then which of the following options is/are correct ?

(a) f is increasing on $(-\infty, 0)$

(b) f' has a local maximum at $x = 1$

(c) f is onto

(d) f' is NOT differentiable at $x = 1$

81. For non-negative integers n, let

$$f(n) = \dfrac{\displaystyle\sum_{k=0}^{n}\sin\left(\dfrac{k+1}{n+2}\pi\right)\sin\left(\dfrac{k+2}{n+2}\pi\right)}{\displaystyle\sum_{k=0}^{n}\sin^2\left(\dfrac{k+1}{n+2}\pi\right)}$$

Assuming $\cos^{-1} x$ takes values in $[0, \pi]$, which of the following options is/are correct ?

[2019, Advanced]

(a) $f(4) = \dfrac{\sqrt{3}}{2}$

(b) $\lim\limits_{n \to \infty} f(n) = \dfrac{1}{2}$

(c) If $\alpha = \tan(\cos^{-1} f(6))$, then $\alpha^2 + 2\alpha - 1 = 0$

(d) $\sin(7 \cos^{-1} f(5)) = 0$

82. Let $f : R \to R$ be a function. We say that f has

PROPERTY 1 : If $\lim\limits_{h \to 0} \dfrac{f(h) - f(0)}{\sqrt{|h|}}$ exists and is finite, and

PROPERTY 2 : If $\lim\limits_{h \to 0} \dfrac{f(h) - f(0)}{h^2}$ exists and is finite. **[2019, Advanced]**

The which of the following options is/are correct?

(a) $f(x) = |x|$ has PROPERTY 1

(b) $f(x) = x^{2/3}$ has PROPERTY 1

(c) $f(x) = x\,|x|$ has PROPERTY 2

(d) $f(x) = \sin x$ has PROPERTY 2

83. Let $f(x) = \dfrac{\sin \pi x}{x^2}, \quad x > 0.$

Let $x_1 < x_2 < x_3 < \dots < x_n < \dots$ be all the points of local maximum of f and $y_1 < y_2 < y_3 \dots < y_n < \dots$ be all the points of focal minimum of f.

Then which of the following options is/are correct ? **[2019, Advanced]**

(a) $x_1 < y_1$

(b) $x_{n+1} - x_n > 2$ for every n

(c) $x_n \in \left(2n, 2n + \dfrac{1}{2}\right)$ for every n

(d) $|x_n - y_n| > 1$ for every n

84. Let $f : R \to R$ be given by $f(x) = (x-1)(x-2)(x-5)$. Define

$$F(x) = \int_0^x f(t)\,dt, \quad x > 0.$$

Then which of the following options is/are correct ? **[2019, Advanced]**

(a) F has a local minimum at $x = 1$

(b) F has a local maximum at $x = 2$

(c) F has two local maxima and one local minimum in $(0, \infty)$

(d) $F(x) \neq 0$ for all $x \in (0, 5)$

85. Let Γ denote a curve $y = y(x)$ which is in the first quadrant and let the point $(1, 0)$ lie on it. Let the tangent to Γ at a point P intersect the y-axis at Y_P. If PY_P has length 1 for each point P on Γ, then which of the following options is/are correct ?

[2019, Advanced]

(a) $y = \log_e\left(\dfrac{1 + \sqrt{1 - x^2}}{x}\right) - \sqrt{1 - x^2}$

(b) $xy' + \sqrt{1 - x^2} = 0$

(c) $y = -\log_e\left(\dfrac{1 + \sqrt{1 - x^2}}{x}\right) + \sqrt{1 - x^2}$

(d) $xy' - \sqrt{1 - x^2} = 0$

86. For any positive integer n, define $f_n : (0, \infty) \to R$ as

$$f_n(x) = \Sigma_{j=1}^n \tan^{-1}\left(\dfrac{1}{1 + (x+j)(x+j-1)}\right) \text{ for all}$$

$x \in (0, \infty)$.

$\Big($Here, the inverse trigonometric function $\tan^{-1} x$

assumes values in $\left(-\dfrac{\pi}{2}, \dfrac{\pi}{2}\right).\Big)$

Then, which of the following statement(s) is (are) TRUE ? **[2018, Advanced]**

(a) $\sum\limits_{j=1}^5 \tan^2(f_j(0)) = 55$

(b) $\sum\limits_{j=1}^{10} (1 + f_j(0)) \sec^2(f_j(0)) = 10$

(c) For any fixed positive integer n,

$$\lim\limits_{x \to \infty} \tan(f_n(x)) = \dfrac{1}{n}$$

(d) For any fixed positive integer n,

$$\lim\limits_{x \to \infty} \sec^2(f_n(x)) = 1$$

87. Let $f : (0, \pi) \to R$ be a twice differentiable function such that

$$\lim\limits_{t \to x} \dfrac{f(x)\sin t - f(t)\sin x}{t - x} = \sin^2 x \text{ for all } x \in (0, \pi).$$

If $f\left(\dfrac{\pi}{6}\right) = -\dfrac{\pi}{12}$, then which of the following statement(s) is (are) TRUE? **[2018, Advanced]**

(a) $f\left(\dfrac{\pi}{4}\right) = \dfrac{\pi}{4\sqrt{2}}$

(b) $f(x) < \dfrac{x^4}{6} - x^2$ for all $x \in (0, \pi)$

(c) There exists $\alpha \in (0, \pi)$ such that $f'(\alpha) = 0$

(d) $f''\left(\dfrac{\pi}{2}\right) + f\left(\dfrac{\pi}{2}\right) = 0$

88. Let $f : R \to R$ be a differentiable function with $f(0) = 0$. If $y = f(x)$ satisfies the differential equation

$$\frac{dy}{dx} = (2 + 5y)(5y - 2)$$

then the value of $\lim\limits_{x \to -\infty} f(x)$ is ....

[2018, Advanced]

89. $\lim\limits_{x \to 0} \dfrac{(27 + x)^{\frac{1}{3}} - 3}{9 - (27 + x)^{\frac{2}{3}}}$ equals :

(a) $\dfrac{1}{3}$

(b) $-\dfrac{1}{3}$

(c) $-\dfrac{1}{6}$

(d) $\dfrac{1}{6}$

90. If the function f defined as

$$f(x) = \frac{1}{x} - \frac{k-1}{e^{2x} - 1}, \, x \neq 0, \text{ is continuous at } x = 0, \text{ then}$$

the ordered pair $(k, f(0))$ is equal to :

[2018, Main]

(a) $(3, 2)$

(b) $(3, 1)$

(c) $(2, 1)$

(d) $\left(\dfrac{1}{3}, 2\right)$

91. If $x = \sqrt{2^{\operatorname{cosec}^{-1} t}}$ and $y = \sqrt{2^{\sec^{-1} t}}$ $(|t| \geq 1)$, then

$\dfrac{dy}{dx}$ is equal to : **[2018, Main]**

(a) $\dfrac{y}{x}$

(b) $\dfrac{x}{y}$

(c) $-\dfrac{y}{x}$

(d) $-\dfrac{x}{y}$

92. Let M and m be respectively the absolute maximum and the absolute minimum values of the function, $f(x) = 2x^3 - 9x^2 + 12x + 5$ in the interval $[0, 3]$. Then $M - m$ is equal to : **[2018, Main]**

(a) 5

(b) 9

(c) 4

(d) 1

93. For every twice differentiable function $f : R \to [-2, 2]$ with $(f(0))^2 + (f'(0))^2 = 85$, which of the following statement(s) is (are) TRUE?

[2018, Advanced]

(a) There exist $r, s \in R$, where $r < s$, such that f is one-one on the open interval (r, s)

(b) There exists $x_0 \in (-4, 0)$ such that $|f'(x_0)| \leq 1$

(c) $\lim\limits_{x \to \infty} f(x) = 1$

(d) There exists $\alpha \in (-4, 4)$ such that $f(\alpha) + f''(\alpha) = 0$ and $f'(\alpha) \neq 0$

94. Let $f : R \to R$ and $g : R \to R$ be two non-constant differentiable functions. If

$$f'(x) = \left(e^{(f(x) - g(x))}\right) g'(x) \text{ for all } x \in R,$$

[2018, Advanced]

(a) $f(2) < 1 - \log_e 2$

(b) $f(2) > 1 - \log_e 2$

(c) $g(1) > 1 - \log_e 2$

(d) $g(1) < 1 - \log_e 2$

95. The number of real solutions of the equation

$$\sin^{-1}\left(\sum_{i=1}^{\infty} x^{i+1} - x \sum_{i=1}^{\infty}\left(\frac{x}{2}\right)^i\right) = \frac{\pi}{2} - \cos^{-1}\left(\sum_{i=1}^{\infty}\left(-\frac{x}{2}\right)^i - \sum_{i=1}^{\infty}(-x)^i\right)$$

lying in the interval $\left(-\dfrac{1}{2}, \dfrac{1}{2}\right)$ is ....

(Here, the inverse trigonometric functions $\sin^{-1} x$ and $\cos^{-1} x$ assume values in $\left[-\dfrac{\pi}{2}, \dfrac{\pi}{2}\right]$ and $[0, \pi]$, respectively.) **[2018, Advanced]**

96. Let $f : R \to (0, 1)$ be a continuous function. Then, which of the following function(s) has(have) the value zero at some point in the interval $(0, 1)$?

(a) $x^9 - f(x)$

(b) $x - \displaystyle\int_0^{\frac{\pi}{2} - x} f(t) \cos t \, dt$

(c) $e^x - \displaystyle\int_0^x f(t) \sin t \, dt$

(d) $f(x) + \displaystyle\int_0^{\frac{\pi}{2}} f(t) \sin t \, dt$

Paragraph for Q. No. 97 to 100

Let $f(x) = x + \log_e x - x \log_e x$, $x \, (0, \infty)$.

- Column 1 contains information about zeros of $f(x)$, $f'(x)$ and $f''(x)$.
- Column 2 contains information about the limiting behavior of $f(x)$, $f'(x)$ and $f''(x)$ at infinity.
- Column 3 contains information about increasing/decreasing nature of $f(x)$ and $f''(x)$.

Column 1	Column 3	Column 3
(I) $f(x) = 0$ for some $x \in (1, e^2)$	(i) $\lim\limits_{x \to \infty} f(x) = 0$	(P) f is increasing in $(0, 1)$
(II) $f'(x) = 0$ for some $x \in (1, e)$	(ii) $\lim\limits_{x \to \infty} f(x) = -\infty$	(Q) f is increasing in (e, e^2)
(III) $f'(x) = 0$ for some $x \in (0, 1)$	(iii) $\lim\limits_{x \to \infty} f'(x) = -\infty$	(R) f' is increasing in $(0, 1)$
(IV) $f''(x) = 0$ for some $x \in (1, e)$	(iv) $\lim\limits_{x \to \infty} f''(x) = 0$	(S) f' is increasing in (e, e^2)

97. Let $f : R \to R$ be a differentiable function such that $f(0) = 0$, $f\left(\dfrac{\pi}{2}\right) = 3$ and $f'(0) = 1$. If

$$g(x) = \int_{x}^{\frac{\pi}{2}} [f'(t)\, \text{cosec}\, t - \cot t\, \text{cosec}\, t\, f(t)]\, dt$$

for $x \in \left(0, \dfrac{\pi}{2}\right]$, then $\displaystyle\lim_{x \to \infty} f(x) =$

[2017, Advanced]

98. Which of the following options is the only CORRECT combination? **[2017, Advanced]**

(a) (I) (i) (P)   **(b)** (II) (ii) (Q)

(c) (III) (iii) (R)   **(d)** (IV) (iv) (S)

99. Which of the following options is the only CORRECT combination? **[2017, Advanced]**

(a) (I) (ii) (R)   **(b)** (II) (iii) (S)

(c) (III) (iv) (P)   **(d)** (IV) (i) (S)

100. Which of the following options is the only INCORRECT combination? **[2017, Advanced]**

(a) (I) (iii) (P)   **(b)** (II) (iv) (Q)

(c) (III) (i) (R)   **(d)** (II) (iii) (P)

101. If $f : R \to R$ is a twice differentiable function such that $f''(x) > 0$ for all $x \in R$, and $f\left(\dfrac{1}{2}\right) = \dfrac{1}{2}$, $f(1) = 1$, then

(a) $f'(1) \le 0$ **(b)** $0 < f'(1) \le \dfrac{1}{2}$

(c) $\dfrac{1}{2} < f'(1) \le 1$ **(d)** $f'(1) > 1$

102. If $f : R \to R$ is a differentiable function such that $f'(x) > 2f(x)$ for all $x \in R$, and $f(0) = 1$, then

[2017, Advanced]

(a) $f(x)$ is increasing in $(0, \infty)$

(b) $f(x)$ is decreasing in $(0, \infty)$

(c) $f(x) > e^{2x}$ in $(0, \infty)$

(d) $f'(x) < e^{2x}$ in $(0, \infty)$

103. Let $f(x) = \dfrac{1 - x\,(1+|1-x|)}{|1-x|}\, \cos\left(\dfrac{1}{1-x}\right)$ for $x \ne 1$.

Then, **[2017, Advanced]**

(a) $\displaystyle\lim_{x \to 1^{-}} f(x) = 0$

(b) $\displaystyle\lim_{x \to 1^{-}} f(x)$ does not exist

(c) $\displaystyle\lim_{x \to 1^{+}} f(x) = 0$

(d) $\displaystyle\lim_{x \to 1^{+}} f(x)$ does not exist

104. If $f(x) = \begin{vmatrix} \cos(2x) & \cos(2x) & \sin(2x) \\ -\cos x & \cos x & -\sin x \\ \sin x & \sin x & \cos x \end{vmatrix}$, then

[2017, Advanced]

(a) $f'(x) = 0$ at exactly three points in $(-\pi, \pi)$

(b) $f'(x) = 0$ at more than three points in $(-\pi, \pi)$

(c) $f(x)$ attains its maximum at $x = 0$

(d) $f(x)$ attains its minimum at $x = 0$

105. If the tangent at a point P, with parameter t, on the curve $x = 4t^2 + 3$, $y = 8t^3 - 1$, $t \in R$, meets the curve again at a point Q, then the coordinates of Q are : **[2016, Main]**

(a) $(t^2 + 3, -t^3 - 1)$ **(b)** $(4t^2 + 3, -8t^3 - 1)$

(c) $(t^2 + 3, t^3 - 1)$ **(d)** $(16t^2 + 3, -64t^3 - 1)$

106. Let $f : (0, \infty) \to R$ be a differentiable function such that $f'(x) = 2 - \dfrac{f(x)}{x}$ for all $x \in (0, \infty)$ and $f(1) \ne 1$.

Then **[2016, Advanced]**

(a) $\displaystyle\lim_{x \to 0^{+}} f'\left(\dfrac{1}{x}\right) = 1$

(b) $\displaystyle\lim_{x \to 0^{+}} x\, f\left(\dfrac{1}{x}\right) = 2$

(c) $\displaystyle\lim_{x \to 0^{+}} x^2 f'(x) = 0$

(d) $|f(x)| \le 2$ for all $x \in (0, 2)$

107. Let $\alpha, \beta \in R$ be such that $\displaystyle\lim_{x \to 0} \dfrac{x^2 \sin(\beta x)}{\alpha x - \sin x} = 1$. Then $6(\alpha + \beta)$ equals **[2016, Advanced]**

108. The normal to the curves, $x^2 + 2xy - 3y^2 = 0$, at $(1, 1)$: **[2015, Main]**

(a) does not meet the curve again.

(b) meets the curve again in the second quadrant.

(c) meets the curve again in the third quadrant.

(d) meets the curve again in the fourth quadrant.

109. Let m and n be two positive integers greater than 1. If

$$\lim_{a \to 0}\left(\dfrac{e^{\cos(\alpha^n)} - e}{\alpha^m}\right) = -\left(\dfrac{e}{2}\right)$$

then the value of $\dfrac{m}{n}$ is **[2015, Advanced]**

110. Let $f, g : [-1, 2] \to R$ be continuous functions which are twice differentiable on the interval $(-1, 2)$. Let the values of f and g at the points $-1, 0$ and 2 be as given in the following table :

	$x = -1$	$x = 0$	$x = 2$
$f(x)$	3	6	0
$g(x)$	0	1	-1

In each of the intervals $(-1, 0)$ and $(0, 2)$ the function $(f - 3g)''$ never vanishes. Then the correct statement(s) is (are) **[2015, Advanced]**

(a) $f'(x) - 3g'(x) = 0$ has exactly three solutions in $(-1, 0) \cup (0, 2)$

(b) $f'(x) - 3g'(x) = 0$ has exactly one solution in $(-1, 0)$

(c) $f'(x) - 3g'(x) = 0$ has exactly one solution in $(0, 2)$

(d) $f'(x) - 3g'(x) = 0$ has exactly two solutions is $(-1, 0)$ and exactly two solutions in $(0, 2)$

111. Let $f'(x) = \dfrac{192x^3}{2 + \sin^4 \pi x}$ for all $x \in$ R with $f\left(\dfrac{1}{2}\right) = 0$. If $m \le \displaystyle\int_{1/2}^{1} f(x)\,dx \le$ M, then the possible values of m and M are **[2015, Advanced]**

(a) $m = 13$, M = 24

(b) $m = \dfrac{1}{4}$, M = $\dfrac{1}{2}$

(c) $m = -11$, M = 0

(d) $m = 1$, M = 12

112. Let F : R $\to$ R be a thrice differentiable function. Suppose that F(1) = 0, F(3) = -4 and F(x) < 0 for all $x\ \{\dfrac{1}{2}, 3)$. Let $f(x) = x$F(x) for all $x \in$ R.

The correct statement(s) is (are)

[2015, Advanced]

(a) $f'(1) < 0$

(b) $f(2) < 0$

(c) $f'(x) \ne 0$ for any $x \in (1, 3)$

(d) $f'(x) = 0$ for some $x \in (1, 3)$

113. Let $y(x)$ be the solution of the differential equation $(x \log x)\dfrac{dy}{dx} + y = 2x \log x$, $(x \ge 1)$. **[2015, Main]**

(a) e

(b) 0

(c) 2

(d) $2e$

114. A cylindrical container is to be made from certain solid material with the following constraints : It has a fixed inner volume of V mm³, has a 2 mm thick solid wall and is open at the top. The bottom of the container is a solid circular disc of thickness 2 mm and is of radius equal to the outer radius of the container.

If the volume of the material used to make the container is minimum when the inner radius of the container is 10 mm, then the value of $\dfrac{V}{250\,\pi}$ is **[2015, Advanced]**

115. Let $g : $R $\to$ R be a differentiable function with $g(0) = 0$, $g'(0) = 0$ and $g'(1) \ne 0$. Let

$$f(x) = \begin{cases} \dfrac{x}{|x|}g(x), & x \ne 0 \\ 0, & x = 0 \end{cases}$$

and $h(x) = e^{|x|}$ for all $x \in$ R. Let $(foh)(x)$ denote $f(h(x))$ and $(hof)(x)$ denote $h(f(x))$. Then which of the following is (are) true? **[2015, Advanced]**

(a) f is differentiable at $x = 0$

(b) h is differentiable at $x = 0$

(c) foh is differentiable at $x = 0$

(d) hof is differentiable at $x = 0$

116.

Column I	Column II
(a) In R², if the magnitude of the projection vector of the vector $\alpha \hat{i} + \beta \hat{j}$ on $\sqrt{3}\hat{i} + \hat{j}$ is $\sqrt{3}$ and if $\alpha = 2 + \sqrt{3}\beta$, then possible value(s) of $|\alpha|$ is (are)	(P) 1
(b) Let a and b be real numbers such that the function $f(x) = \begin{cases} -3ax^2 - 2, & x < 1 \\ bx + a^2, & x \ge 1 \end{cases}$ is differentiable for all $x \in$ R. Then possible value(s) of a is (are)	(Q) 2
(c) Let $w \ne 1$ be a complex cube root of unity. If $(3 - 3w + 2w^2)^{4n+3} + (2 + 3w - 3w^2)^{4n+3} + (-3 + 2w + 3w^2)^{4n+3} = 0$, then possible value(s) of n is (are)	(R) 3
(d) Let the harmonic mean of two positive real numbers a and b be 4. If q is a positive real numbers such that $a, 5, q, b$ is an arithmetic progression, then the value(s) of $|q - a|$ is (are)	(S) 4
	(T) 5

[2015, Advanced]

117. Let the population of rabbits surviving at a time t be governed by the differential equation $\dfrac{dp(t)}{dt} = \dfrac{1}{2}p(t) - 200.$ **[2014, Main]**

If $p(0) = 100$, then $p(t)$ equals :

(a) $600 - 500e^{t/2}$

(b) $400 - 300e^{-t/2}$

(c) $400 - 300e^{t/2}$

(d) $300 - 200e^{-t/2}$

118. The slope of the line touching both the parabolas $y^2 = 4x$ and $x^2 = -32y$ is : **[2014, Main]**

(a) $\dfrac{1}{8}$

(b) $\dfrac{\pi}{2}$

(c) $\dfrac{1}{2}$

(d) $\dfrac{3}{2}$

119. The function

$$f(x) = 2|x| + |x + 2| - ||x + 2| - 2|x||$$

has a local minimum or a local maximum at $x =$ **[2013, Advanced]**

(a) -2

(b) $\dfrac{-2}{3}$

(c) 2

(d) $\dfrac{2}{3}$

120. For $a \in$ R (the set of all real numbers), $a \neq -1$,

$$\lim_{n \to \infty} \frac{(1^a + 2^a + \ldots + n^a)}{(n+1)^{a-1}[(na+1) + (na+2) + \ldots + (na+n)]}$$

$$= \frac{1}{60}$$

Then $a =$ **[2013, Advanced]**

(a) 5   (b) 7

(c) $\dfrac{-15}{2}$ (d) $\dfrac{-17}{2}$

121. Let $f : \left[\dfrac{1}{2}, 1\right] \to$ R (the set of all real numbers) be a positive, non-constant and differentiable function such that $f'(x) < 2 f(x)$ and $f\left(\dfrac{1}{2}\right) = 1$.

Then the value of $\displaystyle\int_{1/2}^{1} f(x)\,dx$ lies in the interval

[2013, Advanced]

(a) $(2e - 1, 2e)$ (b) $(e - 1, 2e - 1)$

(c) $\left(\dfrac{e-1}{2}, e-1\right)$ (d) $\left(0, \dfrac{e-1}{2}\right)$

122. The number of points in $(-\infty, \infty)$, for which $x^2 - x \sin x - \cos x = 0$ is **[2013, Advanced]**

(a) 6   (b) 4

(c) 2   (d) 0

123. A curve passes through the point $\left(1, \dfrac{\pi}{6}\right)$. Let the slope of the curve at each point (x, y) be $\dfrac{y}{x} + \sec\left(\dfrac{y}{x}\right)$, $x > 0$. Then the equation of the curve is : **[2013, Advanced]**

(a) $\sin\left(\dfrac{y}{x}\right) = \log x + \dfrac{1}{2}$

(b) $\csc\left(\dfrac{y}{x}\right) = \log x + 2$

(c) $\sec\left(\dfrac{2y}{x}\right) = \log x + 2$

(d) $\cos\left(\dfrac{2y}{x}\right) = \log x + \dfrac{1}{2}$

124. A rectangular sheet of fixed perimeter with sides having their lengths in the ratio 8 : 15 is converted into an open rectangular box by folding after removing squares of equal area from all four corners. If the total area of removed squares is 100, the resulting box has maximum volume. Then the lengths of the sides of the rectangular sheet are : **[2013, Advanced]**

(a) 24   (b) 32

(c) 45   (d) 60

125. Which of the following is true for $0 < x < 1$?

[2013, Advanced]

(a) $0 < f(x) < \infty$ (b) $-\dfrac{1}{2} < f(x) < \dfrac{1}{2}$

(c) $-\dfrac{1}{4} < f(x) < 1$ (d) $-\infty < f(x) < 0$

126. If the function $e{-}xf(x)$ assumes its minimum in the interval $[0, 1]$ at $x = \dfrac{1}{4}$, which of the following is true? **[2013, Advanced]**

(a) $f'(x) < f(x), \quad \dfrac{1}{4} < x < \dfrac{3}{4}$

(b) $f'(x) > f(x), \quad 0 < x < \dfrac{1}{4}$

(c) $f'(x) < f(x), \quad 0 < x < \dfrac{1}{4}$

(d) $f'(x) < f(x), \quad \dfrac{3}{4} < x < 1$

127. A line $L : y = mx + 3$ meets y-axis at $E(0, 3)$ and the arc of the parabola $y^2 = 16x$, $0 \le y \le 6$ at the point $F(x_0, y_0)$. The tangent to the parabola at $F(x_0, y_0)$ intersects the y-axis at $G(0, y_1)$. The slope m of the line L is chosen such that the area of the triangle EFG has a local maximum.

Match List I with List II and select the correct answer using the code given below the lists :

List I	List II
P. $m =$	1. $\dfrac{1}{2}$
Q. Maximum area of ΔEFG is	2. 4
R. $y_0 =$	3. 2
S. $y_1 =$	4. 1

[2013, Advanced]

Codes :

	P	Q	R	S
(a)	4	1	2	3
(b)	3	4	1	2
(c)	1	3	2	4
(d)	1	3	4	2

128. For every integer n, let a_n and b_n be real numbers. Let function $f : R \to R$ be given by

$$f(x) = \begin{cases} a_n + \sin \pi x, & \text{for } x \in [2n, 2n+1] \\ a_n + \cos \pi x, & \text{for } x \in (2n-1, 2n) \end{cases}$$

for all integars n.

If f is continuous, then which of the following hold(s) for all n? **[2012, Advanced]**

(a) $a_{n-1} - b_{n-1} = 0$

(b) $a_n - b_n = 1$

(c) $a_n - b_{n+1} = 1$

(d) $a_{n-1} - b_n = -1$

129. If $f(x) = \int_0^x e^{t^2}(t-2)(t-3)\,dt$ for all $x \in (0, \infty)$, then

[2012, Advanced]

(a) f has a local maximum at $x = 2$

(b) f is decreasing on $(2, 3)$

(c) there exists some $c \in (0, \infty)$ such that $f''(c) = 0$

(d) f has a local minimum at $x = 3$

130. Let $f(x) = \begin{cases} x^2 \left| \cos \dfrac{\pi}{x} \right|, & x \neq 0 \\ 0, & x = 0 \end{cases}$, $x \in R$

then f is **[2012, Advanced]**

(a) differentiable both at $x = 0$ and at $x = 2$

(b) differentiable at $x = 0$ but not differentiable at $x = 2$

(c) not differentiable at $x = 0$ but differentiable at $x = 2$

(d) differentiable neither at $x = 0$ nor at $x = 2$

131. If $\lim\limits_{x \to \infty} \left(\dfrac{x^2 + x + 1}{x + 1} - ax - b \right) = 4$, then

[2012, Advanced]

(a) $a = 1, b = 4$

(b) $a = 1, b = -4$

(c) $a = 2, b = -3$

(d) $a = 2, b = 3$

132. Let $f : IR \to IR$ be defined as $f(x) = |x| + |x^2 - 1|$. The total number of points at which f attains either a local maximum or a local minimum is

[2012, Advanced]

133. Which of the following is true?

(a) g is increasing on $(1, \infty)$

(b) g is decreasing on $(1, \infty)$

(c) g is increasing on $(1, 2)$ and decreasing on $(2, \infty)$

(d) g is decreasing on $(1, 2)$ and increasing on $(2, \infty)$

134. If $\lim\limits_{x \to 0} \left[1 + x \ln (1 + b^2) \right]^{\frac{1}{x}} = 2b \sin^2 \theta$, $b > 0$ and $\theta \in (-\pi, \pi]$ **[2011, Advanced]**

then the value of θ is

(a) $\pm \dfrac{\pi}{4}$

(b) $\pm \dfrac{\pi}{3}$

(c) $\pm \dfrac{\pi}{6}$

(d) $\pm \dfrac{\pi}{2}$

135. If

$$f(x) = \begin{cases} -x - \dfrac{\pi}{2}, & x \le -\dfrac{\pi}{2} \\ -\cos x, & -\dfrac{\pi}{2} < x \le 0 \\ x - 1, & 0 < x \le 1 \\ \ln x & x > 1 \end{cases}$$

then **[2011, Advanced]**

(a) $f(x)$ is continuous at $x = \dfrac{\pi}{2}$

(b) $f(x)$ is not differentiable at $x = 0$

(c) $f(x)$ is differentiable at $x = 1$

(d) $f(x)$ is differentiable at $x = -\dfrac{3}{2}$

136. Let $f : R \to R$ be a function such that
$$f(x + y) = f(x) + f(y), \ \forall \ x, y \in R$$
If $f(x)$ is differentiable at $x = 0$ then

[2011, Advanced]

(a) If $f(x)$ is differentiable only in a finite interval containing zero

(b) $f(x)$ is continuous $\forall \ x \in R$

(c) $f'(x)$ is constant $\forall \ x \in R$

(d) $f(x)$ is differentiable except at finitely many points

137. The number of distinct real roots of $x^4 - 4x^3 + 12x^2 + x - 1 = 0$ is **[2011, Advanced]**

Paragraph for Q. 138 and 139

Consider the polynomial
$$f(x) = 1 + 2x + 3x^2 + 4x^3$$
Let S be the sum of all distinct real roots of $f(x)$ and let $t = | s |$.

138. The real number s lies in the interval

[2010, Advanced]

(a) $\left(-\dfrac{1}{4}, 0 \right)$

(b) $\left(-11, -\dfrac{3}{4} \right)$

(c) $\left(-\dfrac{3}{4}, -\dfrac{1}{2} \right)$

(d) $\left(0, \dfrac{1}{4} \right)$

139. The function $f'(x)$ is **[2010, Advanced]**

(a) increasing in $\left(-t, -\dfrac{1}{4} \right)$ and decreasing in $\left(-\dfrac{1}{4}, t \right)$

(b) decreasing in $\left(-t, -\dfrac{1}{4} \right)$ and increasing in $\left(-\dfrac{1}{4}, t \right)$

(c) increasing in $(-t, t)$

(d) decreasing in $(-t, t)$

140. Let $f : R \to R$ be a continuous function which satisfies

$$f(x) = \int_0^x f(t)\,dt \; .$$

Then the value of $f(\ln 5)$ is   **[2009, Advanced]**

141. For the function

$$f(x) = x \cos \frac{1}{x}, \; x \geq 1 \quad \textbf{[2009, Advanced]}$$

(a) for at least one x in the interval $[1, \infty)$, $f(x + 2) - f(x) < 2$

(b) $\lim_{x \to \infty} f'(x) = 1$

(c) for all x in the interval $[1, \infty)$, $f(x + 2) - f(x) < 2$

(d) $f'(x)$ is strictly decreasing in the interval $[1, \infty)$

142. Match the statements/expressions given in **Column I** with the values given in **Column II**.

[2009, Advanced]

Column I	**Column II**
(a) Root(s) of the equation $2 \sin^2 \theta + \sin^2 2\theta = 2$	(p) $\dfrac{\pi}{6}$ (q) $\dfrac{\pi}{4}$
(b) Points of discontinuity of the function $f(x) = \left[\dfrac{6x}{\pi}\right] \cos \left[\dfrac{3x}{\pi}\right]$, where $[y]$ denotes the largest integer less then or equal to y	(r) $\dfrac{\pi}{3}$
(c) Volume of the parallelopiped with its edges represented by the vectors $\hat{i} + \hat{j}, \hat{i} + 2\hat{j}$ and $\hat{i} + \hat{j} + \pi \hat{k}$	(s) $\dfrac{\pi}{2}$
(d) Angle between vectors $\vec{a}$ and $\vec{b}$ where $\vec{a}, \vec{b}$ and $\vec{c}$ are unit vectors satisfying $\vec{a} + \vec{b} + \sqrt{3}\,\vec{c} = \vec{0}$	(t) π

143. The maximum value of the function $f(x) = 2x^3 - 15x^2 + 36x - 48$ on the set $A = \{x \,|\, x^2 + 20 \leq 9x\}$ is

[2009, Advanced]

144. Let $p(x)$ be a polynomial of degree 4 having extremum at $x = 1, 2$ and

$$\lim_{x \to 0} \left(\frac{1 + p(x)}{x^2}\right) = 2.$$

Then the value of $p(2)$ is   **[2009, Advanced]**

145. If the function $f(x) = x^3 + e^{\frac{x}{2}}$ and $g(x) = f^{-1}(x)$, then the value of $g'(1)$ is   **[2009, Advanced]**

146. Let $g(x) = \dfrac{(x-1)^n}{\log \cos^m (x-1)} \; ; 0 < x < 2$, m and n are integers, $m \neq 0$, $n > 0$ and let p be the left hand derivative of $|x - 1|$ at $x = 1$.

If $\lim_{x \to 1^+} g(x) = p$, then   **[2009, Advanced]**

(a) $n = 1, m = 1$ (b) $n = 1, m = -1$

(c) $n = 2, m = 2$ (d) $n > 2, m = n$

147. The total number of local maxima and local minima of the function

$$f(x) = \begin{cases} (2+x)^3, & -3 < x \leq -1 \\ x^{2/3} & -1 < x < 2 \end{cases}$$

is   **[2009, Advanced]**

(a) 0   (b) 1

(c) 2   (d) 3

148. Let

$$S_n = \sum_{k=1}^{n} \frac{n}{n^2 + kn + k^2} \text{ and } T_n = \sum_{k=0}^{n-1} \frac{n}{n^2 + kn + k^2},$$

for $n = 1, 2, 3, \ldots$ Then,   **[2009, Advanced]**

(a) $S_n < \dfrac{\pi}{3\sqrt{3}}$ (b) $S_n > \dfrac{\pi}{3\sqrt{3}}$

(c) $T_n < \dfrac{\pi}{3\sqrt{3}}$ (d) $T_n > \dfrac{\pi}{3\sqrt{3}}$

149. Let f and g be real valued functions defined on interval $(-1, 1)$ such that $g''(x)$ is continuous, $g(0) \neq 0$, $g'(0) = 0$, $g''(0) \neq 0$, and $f(x)\,g(x) \sin x$.

STATEMENT-1 :

$$\lim_{x \to 0} [g(x) \cot x - g(0) \operatorname{cosec} x] = f''(0)$$

and

STATEMENT-2 : $f'(0) = g(0)$ **[2008, Advanced]**

(a) STATEMENT-1 is True, STATEMENT-2 is True; STATEMENT-2 is a correct explanation for STATEMENT-1

(b) STATEMENT-1 is True, STATEMENT-2 is True; STATEMENT-2 is **NOT** a correct explanation for STATEMENT-1

(c) STATEMENT-1 is True, STATEMENT-2 is False

(d) STATEMENT-1 is False, STATEMENT-2 is True.

150. If $f(-10\sqrt{2}) = 2\sqrt{2}$, then $f''(-10\sqrt{2}) =$

[2008, Advanced]

(a) $\dfrac{4\sqrt{2}}{7^3 3^2}$

(b) $-\dfrac{4\sqrt{2}}{7^3 3^2}$

(c) $\dfrac{4\sqrt{2}}{7^3 3}$

(d) $-\dfrac{4\sqrt{2}}{7^3 3}$

151. Let the function $g : (-\infty, \infty) \to \left(-\dfrac{\pi}{2}, \dfrac{\pi}{2}\right)$ be given

$g(u) = 2\tan^{-1}(e^u) - \dfrac{\pi}{2}$. Then, g is

[2008, Advanced]

(a) even and is strictly increasing in $(0, \infty)$
(b) odd and is strictly decreasing in $(-\infty, \infty)$
(c) odd and is strictly increasing in $(-\infty, \infty)$
(d) neither even or odd, but is strictly increasing in $(-\infty, \infty)$

152. Let $g(x) = \log f(x)$ where $f(x)$ is a twice differentiable positive function on $(0, \infty)$ such that $f(x + 1) = x$ $f(x)$. Then, for $N = 1, 2\ 3, \dots$, **[2008, Advanced]**

(a) $-4\left\{1 + \dfrac{1}{9} + \dfrac{1}{25} + \dots + \dfrac{1}{(2N-1)^2}\right\}$

(b) $4\left\{1 + \dfrac{1}{9} + \dfrac{1}{25} + \dots + \dfrac{1}{(2N-1)^2}\right\}$

(c) $-4\left\{1 + \dfrac{1}{9} + \dfrac{1}{25} + \dots + \dfrac{1}{(2N+1)^2}\right\}$

(d) $4\left\{1 + \dfrac{1}{9} + \dfrac{1}{25} + \dots + \dfrac{1}{(2N+1)^2}\right\}$

Paragraph for Q. 153 & Q. 154

Consider the function $f : (-\infty, \infty) \to (-\infty, \infty)$

defined by $f(x) = \dfrac{x^2 - ax + 1}{x^2 + ax + 1}$, $0 < a < 2$.

153. Which of the following is true?

[2008, Advanced]

(a) $(2 + a)^2 f''(1) + (2 - a)^2 f''(-1) = 0$
(b) $(2 - a)^2 f''(1) - (2 + a)^2 f''(-1) = 0$
(c) $f'(1) f'(-1) = (2 - a)^2$
(d) $f'(1) f'(-1) = -(2 + a)^2$

154. Which of the following is true?

[2008, Advanced]

(a) $f(x)$ is decreasing on $(-1, 0)$ and has a local minimum at $x = 1$
(b) $f(x)$ is increasing on $(-1, 1)$ has a local maximum at $x = 1$
(c) $f(x)$ is increasing on $(-1, 1)$ but has neither a local maximum nor a local minimum at $x = 1$

(d) $f(x)$ is decreasing on $(-1, 1)$ but has neither a local maximum nor a local minimum at $x = 1$

155. Let $g(x) = \displaystyle\int_0^{e^x} \dfrac{f'(t)}{1 + t^2}\, dt$

Which of the following is true?

[2008, Advanced]

(a) $g'(x)$ is positive on $(-\infty, 0)$ and negative on $(0, \infty)$
(b) $g'(x)$ is negative on $(-\infty, 0)$ and positive on $(0, \infty)$
(c) $g'(x)$ changes sign on both $(-\infty, 0)$ and $(0, \infty)$
(d) $g'(x)$ does not change sign on $(-\infty, \infty)$

156. Let $f(x) = \dfrac{x^2 - 6x + 5}{x^2 - 5x + 6}$.

Match the expressions/statements in **Column I** with expressions/statements in **Column II** and indicate your answer by darkening the appropriate bubbles in the 4×4 matrix given in the ORS. **(2007, Advanced)**

Column I	Column II
(a) If $-1 < x < 1$, then $f(x)$ satisfies	(p) $0 < f(x) < 1$
(b) If $1 < x < 2$, then $f(x)$ satisfies	(q) $f(x) < 0$
(c) If $3 < x < 5$, then $f(x)$ satisfies	(r) $f(x) > 0$
(d) If $x > 5$, then $f(x)$ satisfies	(s) $f(x) < 1$

157. $\displaystyle\lim_{x \to \frac{\pi}{4}} \dfrac{\displaystyle\int_2^{\sec^2 x} f(t)\, dt}{x^2 - \dfrac{\pi^2}{16}}$ equals **[2007, Advanced]**

(a) $\dfrac{8}{\pi} f(2)$

(b) $\dfrac{2}{\pi} f(2)$

(c) $\dfrac{2}{\pi} f\left(\dfrac{1}{2}\right)$

(d) $4 f(2)$

158. In the following $[x]$ denotes the greatest integer less than or equal to x.

Match the functions in **Column I** with the properties in **Column II** and indicate your answer by darkening the appropriate bubbles in 4×4 matrix given in the ORS.

[2007, Advanced]

Column I	Column II
(a) $x\lvert x \rvert$	(p) continuous in $(-1, 1)$
(b) $\sqrt{\lvert x \rvert}$	(q) differentiable in $(-1, 1)$
(c) $x + [x]$	(r) strictly increasing in $(-1, 1)$
(d) $\lvert x - 1 \rvert + \lvert x + 1 \rvert$	(s) not differentiable at least at one point in $(-1, 1)$

159. $\dfrac{d^2x}{dy^2}$ equals **[2007, Advanced]**

(a) $\left(\dfrac{d^2y}{dx^2}\right)^{-1}$

(b) $-\left(\dfrac{d^2y}{dx^2}\right)^{-1}\left(\dfrac{dy}{dx}\right)^{-3}$

(c) $\left(\dfrac{d^2y}{dx^2}\right)\left(\dfrac{dy}{dx}\right)^{-2}$

(d) $-\left(\dfrac{d^2y}{dx^2}\right)\left(\dfrac{dy}{dx}\right)^{-3}$

160. Let $f(x) = 2 + \cos x$ for all real x.

STATEMENT-1 : For each real t, there exists a point c in $[t, t + \pi]$ such that $f''(c) = 0$

because **[2007, Advanced]**

STATEMENT-2 : $f(t) = f(t + 2\pi)$ for each real t.

(a) Statement-1 is True, Statement-2 is True; Statement-2 is a correct explanation for Statement-1

(b) Statement-1 is True, Statement-2 is True; Statement-2 is **NOT** a correct explanation for Statement-1

(c) Statement-1 is True, Statement-2 is False

(d) Statement-1 is False, Statement-2 is True.

161. For $x > 0$, $\lim\limits_{x \to 0} \left((\sin x)^{1/x} + (1/x)^{\sin x}\right)$ is **[2006]**

(a) 0

(b) -1

(c) 1

(d) 2

162. If $f''(x) = -f(x)$ and $g(x) = f'(x)$ and $F(x) = \left(f\left(\dfrac{x}{2}\right)\right)^2 + \left(g\left(\dfrac{x}{2}\right)\right)^2$ and given that $F(5) = 5$, then $F(10)$ is equal to **[2006]**

(a) 5

(b) 10

(c) 0

(d) 15

163. If $f(x) = \min \{1, x^2, x^3\}$, then **[2006]**

(a) $f(x)$ is continuous $\forall\, x \in R$

(b) $f'(x) > 0$, $\forall\, x > 1$

(c) $f(x)$ is not differentiable but continuous $\forall\, x \in R$

(d) $f(x)$ is not differentiable for two values of x

164. $f(x)$ is cubic polynomial which has local maximum at $x = -1$. If $f(2) = 18$, $f(1) = -1$ and $f'(x)$ has local minima at $x = 0$, then **[2006]**

(a) the distance between $(-1, 2)$ and $(a, f(a))$, where $x = a$ is the point of local minima is $2\sqrt{5}$

(b) $f(x)$ has local minima at $x = 1$

(c) $f(x)$ is increasing for $x \in [1, 2\sqrt{5}]$

(d) the value of $f(0) = 5$

165. $f(x) = \begin{cases} e^x, & 0 \le x \le 1 \\ 2 - e^{x-1} & 1 < x \le 2 \\ x - e, & 2 < x \le 3 \end{cases}$ and $g(x) = \int\limits_0^x f(t)\,dt$,

$x \in [1, 3]$ then $g(x)$ has **[2006]**

(a) local maxima at $x = 1 + ln\,2$ and local minima at $x = e$

(b) local maxima at $x = 1$ and local minima at $x = 2$

(c) no local maxima

(d) no local minima

166. If $f''(x) < 0\ \forall\, x \in (a, b)$ and c is a point such that $a < c < b$ and $(c, f(c))$ is the point lying on the curve for which $F(c)$ is maximum, then $f'(c)$ is equal to **[2006]**

(a) $\dfrac{f(b) - f(a)}{b - a}$

(b) $\dfrac{2(f(b) - f(a))}{b - a}$

(c) $\dfrac{2f(b) - f(a)}{2b - a}$

(d) 0

167. If $f(x)$ is a twice differentiable function such that $f(a) = 0$, $f(b) = 2$, $f(c) = -1$, $f(d) = 2$, $f(e) = 0$, where $a < b < c < d < e$, then the minimum number of zeroes of $g(x) = (f'(x))^2 + f''(x)f(x)$ in the interval $[a, e]$ is **[2006]**

168. The function given by $y = ||x| - 1|$ is differentiable for all real numbers except the points : **[2005, Main]**

(a) $\{0, 1, -1\}$

(b) ± 1

(c) 1

(d) -1

169. If $y = y(x)$ and it follows the relation $x \cos y + y \cos x = \pi$, then $y''(0)$: **[2005, Main]**

(a) 1

(b) -1

(c) π

(d) $-\pi$

170. If $f(x)$ is a continuous and differentiable function and $f\left(\dfrac{1}{n}\right) = 0 \ \forall\, n \ge 1$ and $n \in I$, then : **[2005, Main]**

(a) $f(x) = 0$, $x \in (0, 1]$

(b) $f(0) = 0$, $f'(0) = 0$

(c) $f'(0) = 0 = f''(0)$, $x \in (0, 1]$

(d) $f(0) = 0$ and $f'(0)$ need not to be zero

171. If $|f(x_1) - f(x_2)| < (x_1 - x_2)^2$, for all $x_1, x_2 \in R$. Find the equation of tangent to the curve $y = f(x)$ at the point $(1, 2)$. **(2005, Main)**

172. If length of tangent at any point on the curve $y = f(x)$ intercepted between the point and the X-axis is of length 1. Find the equation of the curve. **(2005, Main)**

173. If $f(x - y) = f(x) \cdot g(y) - f(y) \cdot g(x)$ and $g(x - y) = g(x) \cdot g(y) + f(x) \cdot f(y)$ for all $x, y \in R$. If right hand derivative at $x = 0$ exists of $f(x)$. Find derivative of $g(x)$ at $x = 0$. **[2005, Main]**

174. If $P(x)$ be a polynomial of degree 3 satisfying $p(-1) = 10$, $p(1) = -6$ and $p(x)$ has maximum at $x = -1$ and $p'(x)$ has minima at $x = 1$. Find the distance between the local maximum and local minimum of the curve. **[2005, Main]**

175. $f(x)$ is a differentiable function and $g(x)$ is a double differentiable function such that $|f(x)| \leq 1$ and $f'(x) = g(x)$. If $f^2(0) + g^2(0) = 9$. Prove that there exists some $c \in (-3, 3)$ such that $g(c) \cdot g''(c) < 0$.

[2005, Main]

176. If $f(x)$ is differentiable and $\int_0^{t^2} x f(x)\,dx = \frac{2}{5}t^5$, then

$f\left(\dfrac{4}{25}\right)$ equals : **[2004, Main]**

(a) 2/5   (b) $-5/2$

(c) 1   (d) 5/2

177. If $f(x) = x^3 + bx^2 + cx + d$ and $0 < b^2 < c$, then in $(-\infty, \infty)$: **[2004, Main]**

(a) $f(x)$ is a strictly increasing function

(b) $f(x)$ has a local maxima

(c) $f(x)$ is a strictly decreasing function

(d) $f(x)$ is bounded

178. If $f(x) = x^\alpha \log x$ and $f(0) = 0$, then the value of α for which Rolle's theorem can be applied in $[0, 1]$ is : **[2004, Main]**

(a) -2 (b) -1

(c) 0   (d) 1/2

179. If $f(x)$ is differentiable and strictly increasing function, then the value of $\lim\limits_{x \to 0} \dfrac{f(x)^2 - f(x)}{f(x) - f(0)}$ is :

[2004, Main]

(a) 1   (b) 0

(c) -1 (d) 2

180. In $[0, 1]$ Lagranges mean value theorem is NOT applicable to : **[2004, Main]**

(a) $f(x) = \begin{cases} \dfrac{1}{2} - x, & x < \dfrac{1}{2} \\ \left(\dfrac{1}{2} - x\right)^2, & x \geq \dfrac{1}{2} \end{cases}$

(b) $f(x) = \begin{cases} \dfrac{\sin x}{x}, & x \neq 0 \\ 1, & x = 0 \end{cases}$

(c) $f(x) = x|x|$

(d) $f(x) = |x|$

181. If $p(x) = 51x^{101} - 2323x^{100} - 45x + 1035$, using Rolle's Theorem, prove that atleast one root lies between $(45^{1/100}, 46)$. **[2004, Main]**

182. $\lim\limits_{h \to 0} \dfrac{f(2h + 2 + h^2) - f(2)}{f(h - h^2 + 1) - f(1)}$, given that $f'(2) = 6$ and

$f'(1) = 4$: **[2004, Main]**

(a) does not exist   (b) is equal to $-3/2$

(c) is equal to 3/2   (d) is equal to 3

183. If $f : [-1, 1] \to R$ and $f'(0) = \lim\limits_{n \to \infty} nf\left(\dfrac{1}{n}\right)$ and $f(0) = 0$.

Find the value of $\lim\limits_{n \to \infty} \dfrac{2}{\pi}(n + 1)\cos^{-1}\left(\dfrac{1}{n}\right) - n$.

Given that $0 < \left| \lim\limits_{n \to \infty} \cos^{-1}\left(\dfrac{1}{n}\right) \right| < \dfrac{\pi}{2}$.

[2004, Main]

184. $f(x) = \begin{cases} b\sin^{-1}\left(\dfrac{x+c}{2}\right), & -\dfrac{1}{2} < x < 0 \\ \dfrac{1}{2}, & x = 0 \\ \dfrac{e^{\frac{a}{2}x} - 1}{x}, & 0 < x < \dfrac{1}{2} \end{cases}$

If $f(x)$ is differentiable at $x = 0$ and $|c| < \dfrac{1}{2}$ then find the value of 'a' and prove that $64b^2 = (4 - c^2)$. **[2004, Main]**

185. If $\lim\limits_{x \to 0} \dfrac{[(a - n)nx - \tan x]\sin nx}{x^2} = 0$, where n is non-zero real number, then a is equal to : **[2003, Main]**

(a) 0   (b) $\dfrac{n+1}{n}$

(c) n (d) $n + \dfrac{1}{n}$

186. If $f(x) = x^2 + 2bx + 2c^2$ and $g(x) = -x^2 - 2cx + b^2$ such that $\min f(x) > \max g(x)$, then the relation between b and c, is : **[2003, Main]**

(a) no real number of b and c

(b) $0 < c < b\sqrt{2}$

(c) $|c| < |b|\sqrt{2}$

(d) $|c| > |b|\sqrt{2}$

187. The value of 'a' so that the volume of parallelopiped formed by $\hat{i} + a\hat{j} + \hat{k}$, $\hat{j} + a\hat{k}$ and $a\hat{i} + \hat{k}$ becomes minimum is : **[2003, Main]**

(a) -3 (b) 3

(c) $1/\sqrt{3}$ (d) $\sqrt{3}$

188. Find a point on the curve $x^2 + 2y^2 = 6$ whose distance from the line $x + y = 7$ is minimum.

[2003, Main]

189. For the circle $x^2 + y^2 = r^2$, find the value of r for which the area enclosed by the tangents drawn from the point P(6, 8) to the circle and the chord of contact is maximum. **[2003, Main]**

190. Prove that $\sin x + 2x \geq \dfrac{3x \cdot (x+1)}{\pi} \ \forall\, x \in \left[0, \dfrac{\pi}{2}\right]$.

(Justify the inequality, if any used).

[2003, Main]

191. If a function $f : [-2a, 2a] \to$ R is an odd function such that $f(x) = f(2a - x)$ for $x\,\epsilon[a, 2a]$ and the left hand derivative at $x = a$ is 0. Then find the left hand derivative at $x = -a$. **[2003, Main]**

192. Using the relation $2(1 - \cos x) < x^2$, $x \neq 0$ or otherwise, prove that $\sin(\tan x) \geq x,\ \forall\, x \in \left[0, \dfrac{\pi}{4}\right]$.

[2003, Main]

193. The domain of the derivative of the function

$$f(x) = \begin{cases} \tan^{-1} x, & \text{if } |x| \leq 1 \\ \dfrac{1}{2}(|x|-1), & \text{if } |x| > 1 \end{cases}$$ is : **[2002, Main]**

(a) R – {0}　　**(b)** R – {1}
(c) R – {– 1}　　**(d)** R – {– 1, 1}

194. The integer n for which $\displaystyle\lim_{x\to 0}\dfrac{(\cos x - 1)(\cos x - e^x)}{x^n}$ is a finite non zero number is : **[2002, Main]**

(a) 1　　**(b)** 2
(c) 3　　**(d)** 4

195. Let $f :$ R $\to$ R be such that $f(1) = 3$ and $f'(1) = 6$.

[2002, Main]

Then $\displaystyle\lim_{x\to 0}\left(\dfrac{f(1+x)}{f(1)}\right)^{1/x}$ equals :

(a) 1　　**(b)** $e^{1/2}$
(c) e^2　　**(d)** e^3

196. The points(s) on the curve $y^3 + 3x^2 = 12y$ where the tangent is vertical, is (are) : **[2002, Main]**

(a) $\left(\pm\dfrac{4}{\sqrt{3}}, -2\right)$　　**(b)** $\left(\pm\sqrt{\dfrac{11}{3}}, 1\right)$

(c) (0, 0)　　**(d)** $\left(\pm\dfrac{4}{\sqrt{3}}, 2\right)$

197. The length of a longest interval in which the function $3\sin x - 4\sin^3 x$ is increasing, is : **[2002, Main]**

(a) $\pi/3$　　**(b)** $\pi/2$
(c) $3\pi/2$　　**(d)** π

ANSWER KEY

1. (a)	**2.** (a)	**3.** (10)	**4.** (a)	**5.** (d)	**6.** (d)	**7.** (b)	**8.** (8)	**9.** (d)	**10.** (a,c)
11. (1)	**12.** (8)	**13.** (a)	**14.** (d)	**15.** (40)	**16.** (d)	**17.** (c)	**18.** (b)	**19.** (a)	**20.** (b)
21. (a)	**22.** (5)	**23.** (a,b,d)	**24.** (½)	**25.** (5.00)	**26.** (d)	**27.** (b)	**28.** (c)	**29.** (b)	**30.** (3)
31. (d)	**32.** (36)	**33.** (b)	**34.** (c)	**35.** (a)	**36.** (c)	**37.** (a)	**38.** (c)	**39.** (d)	**40.** (c)
41. (b)	**42.** (a)	**43.** (3.00)	**44.** (c)	**45.** (*)	**46.** (a)	**47.** (4)	**48.** (b)	**49.** (b)	**50.** (*)
51. (c)	**52.** (a)	**53.** (b)	**54.** (c)	**55.** (a)	**56.** (a)	**57.** (c)	**58.** (a)	**59.** (d)	**60.** (d)
61. (d)	**62.** (d)	**63.** (d)	**64.** (b)	**65.** (a)	**66.** (d)	**67.** (a)	**68.** (c)	**69.** (c)	**70.** (b)
71. (c)	**72.** (a)	**73.** (a)	**74.** (b)	**75.** (a)	**76.** (d)	**77.** (b)	**78.** (a)	**79.** (b)	
80. (b,c,d)	**81.** (a,c,d)	**82.** (a,b)	**83.** (b,c,d)	**84.** (a,c,d)	**85.** (a,b)	**86.** (d)	**87.** (b,c,d)	**88.** (0.4)	**89.** (c)
90. (2)	**91.** (c)	**92.** (b)	**93.** (a,b,d)	**94.** (b,c)	**95.** (2)	**96.** (a,c,d)	**97.** (2)	**98.** (b)	**99.** (b)
100. (c)	**101.** (d)	**102.** (a,c)	**103.** (a,d)	**104.** (b,c)	**105.** (a)	**106.** (a)	**107.** (7)	**108.** (d)	**109.** (2)
110. (b,c)	**111.** (d)	**112.** (a,b,c)	**113.** (c)	**114.** (4)	**115.** (a,d)				

116. (a) – (P, Q), (b) – (P, Q), (c) – (P, Q, S, T), (d) – (Q, T)　**117.** (c)　**118.** (c)　**119.** (a,b)　**120.** (b,d)　**121.** (d)

122. (c)　**123.** (a)　**124.** (a,c)　**125.** (d)　**126.** (c)　**127.** (a)　**128.** (b,d)　**129.** (a,b,c,d)　**130.** (b)　**131.** (b)

132. (5)　**133.** (b)　**134.** (d)　**135.** (a,b,c,d)　**136.** (b,c)　**137.** (2)　**138.** (c)　**139.** (b)　**140.** (0)

141. (b,c,d)　**142.** (a) – (q, s), (b) – (p, q, s, t), (c) – (t), (d) – (r)　**143.** (7)　**144.** (0)　**145.** (2)

146. (c)　**147.** (c)　**148.** (a,d)　**149.** (a)　**150.** (b)　**151.** (c)　**152.** (a)　**153.** (a)　**154.** (a)　**155.** (b)

156. (a)-(p), (r), (s), (b)-(q), (s), (c)-(q), (s) (d)-(p), (r), (s)　**157.** (a)

158. (A)-(p), (q), (r), (B)-(p), (s), (C)-(r), (s), (D)-(p), (q)   **159.** (d)   **160.** (b)   **161.** (c)   **162.** (a)

163. (a,c)   **164.** (b,c)   **165.** (a,b)   **166.** (a)   **167.** (6)   **168.** (a)   **169.** (c)   **170.** (b)   **171.** $(y-2=0)$

172. (*)   **173.** (*)   **174.** (*)   **175.** (*)   **176.** (a)   **177.** (a)   **178.** (d)   **179.** (c)   **180.** (a)   **181.** (*)

182. (d)   **183.** (*)   **184.** (*)   **185.** (d)   **186.** (d)   **187.** (c)   **188.** (2, 1)   **189.** (*)   **190.** (*)   **191.** (*)

192. (*)   **193.** (d)   **194.** (c)   **195.** (c)   **196.** (d)   **197.** (a)

ANSWERS WITH EXPLANATIONS

1. Correct Response : (a)

Explanation :

$$f(0) = f(1) = f'(0) = 0$$

Apply Rolles theorem on $y = f(x)$ in $x \in [0, 1]$

$$f(0) = f(1) = 0$$

$\Rightarrow \qquad f'(\alpha) = 0$ where $\alpha \in (0, 1)$

Now apply Rolles theorem on $y = f'(x)$ in $x \in [0, \alpha]$

$f'(0) = f'(\alpha) = 0$ and $f'(x)$ is continuous and differentiable.

$\Rightarrow f''(\beta) = 0$ for some, $\beta \in (0, \alpha) \in (0, 1)$

$\Rightarrow f''(x) = 0$ for some $x \in (0, 1)$.

2. Correct Response : (a)

Explanation :

$$f(x) = \max (x, x^2)$$

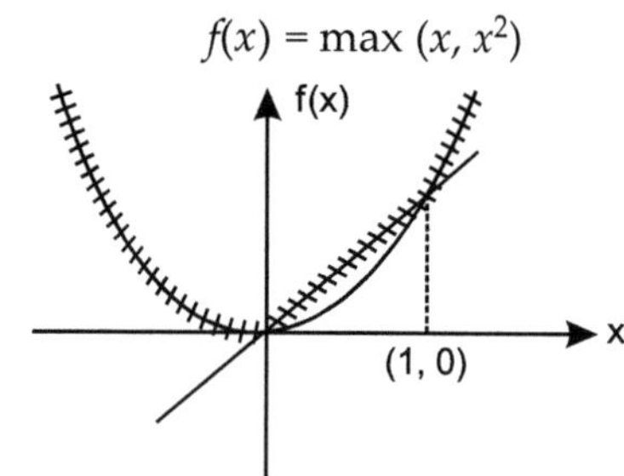

Non-differentiable at $x = 0, 1$

$$S = \{0, 1\}.$$

3. Correct Response : (10)

Explanation :

Since, $\lim\limits_{x \to 0} \dfrac{f(x)}{x}$ exist $\Rightarrow f(0) = 0$

Now, $\quad f'(x) = \lim\limits_{h \to 0} \dfrac{f(x+h) - f(x)}{h}$

$\qquad = \lim\limits_{h \to 0} \dfrac{f(h) + xh^2 + x^2 h}{h}$ (take $y = h$)

$\qquad = \lim\limits_{h \to 0} \dfrac{f(h)}{h} + \lim\limits_{h \to 0} (xh) + x^2$

$\Rightarrow \qquad f'(x) = 1 + 0 + x^2$

$\Rightarrow \qquad f'(3) = 10.$

4. Correct Response : (a)

Explanation :

Graph of $f(x)$:

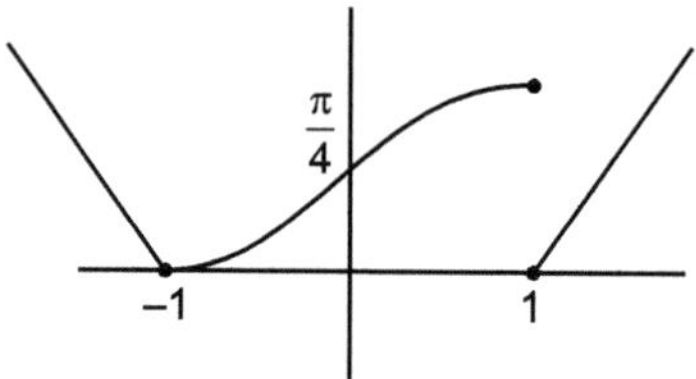

From the graph :

$f(x)$ is continous on $R - \{1\}$

$f(x)$ is differentiable on $R - \{-1, 1\}$.

5. Correct Response : (d)

Explanation :

$$L = \lim_{t \to x} \frac{t^2 f^2(x) - x^2 f^2(t)}{t - x}$$

using L.H. rule

$$L = \lim_{t \to x} \frac{2t f^2(x) - x^2 . 2 f'(t) . f(t)}{1}$$

$\Rightarrow \qquad L = 2xf(x) [f(x)] - xf'(x)) = 0$ (given)

$\Rightarrow \qquad f(x) = xf'(x) \Rightarrow \int \dfrac{f'(x)\, dx}{f(x)} = \int \dfrac{dx}{x}$

$\Rightarrow \quad ln \mid f(x) \mid = ln \mid x \mid + C$

$\because \qquad f(1) = e, x > 0, f(x) > 0$

$\Rightarrow \qquad f(x) = ex$, if $f(x) = 1 \Rightarrow x = \dfrac{1}{e}$

6. Correct Response : (d)

Explanation :

p = function is differentiable at a

q = function is continuous at a

contrapositive of statement $p \to q$ is $\sim q \to \sim p$.

7. Correct Response : (b)

Explanation :

LHL : $\quad \lim\limits_{x \to 0^-} \left| \dfrac{1 - x - x}{\lambda - x - 1} \right| = \left| \dfrac{1}{\lambda - 1} \right|$

RHL : $\quad \lim\limits_{x \to 0^+} \left| \dfrac{1 - x + x}{\lambda - x + 1} \right| = \left| \dfrac{1}{\lambda} \right|$

For existence of limit

$$LHL = RHL$$

$\Rightarrow \qquad \dfrac{1}{|\lambda - 1|} = \dfrac{1}{|\lambda|} \Rightarrow \lambda = \dfrac{1}{2}$

$\therefore \qquad L = \dfrac{1}{|\lambda|} = 2$

8. Correct Response : (8)

Explanation :

$$\lim_{x \to 0}\left\{\frac{1}{x^8}\left(1-\cos\frac{x^2}{2}-\cos\frac{x^2}{4}+\cos\frac{x^2}{2}\cos\frac{x^2}{4}\right)\right\}$$

$$= 2^{-k}$$

$$\Rightarrow \lim_{x \to 0}\frac{\left(1-\cos\frac{x^2}{2}\right)\left(1-\cos\frac{x^2}{4}\right)}{4\left(\frac{x^2}{2}\right)^2\ 16\left(\frac{x^2}{4}\right)^2}=\frac{1}{8}\times\frac{1}{32}=2^{-k}$$

$$\Rightarrow \qquad 2^{-8}=2^{-k}\Rightarrow k=8.$$

9. Correct Response : (d)

Explanation :

$$\lim_{x \to 0}\frac{(e^{(\sqrt{1+x^2+x^4}-1)/x}-1)}{\sqrt{1+x^2+x^4}-1}$$

$$= \lim_{x \to 0}\frac{(e^{(\sqrt{1+x^2+x^4}-1)/x}-1)}{\dfrac{\sqrt{1+x^2+x^4}-1}{x}}$$

Let $\ \dfrac{\sqrt{1+x^2+x^4}-1}{x}=t$

Clearly $x \to 0 \Rightarrow t \to 0$

$$= \mathop{Lt}_{t \to 0}\frac{e^t-1}{t}\qquad \left(\frac{0}{0}\text{ form}\right)$$

L' Hospital Law

$$\mathop{Lt}_{x \to 0} e^t = 1.$$

10. Correct Response : (a, c)

Explanation :

$$f : R \to R$$
$$f(x) = (x^2 + \sin x)\ (x-1)$$
$$f(1^+) = f(1^-) = f(1) = 0$$
$$fg(x) : f(x).g(x)\ fg : R \to R$$

let $\qquad fg(x) = h(x) = f(x).g(x)$
$$h : R \to R$$

option (c) $\quad h'(x) = f'(x)\ g(x) + f(x)\ g'(x)$
$$h'(1) = f'(1)\ g(1) + 0,$$

{as $f(1) = 0$, $g'(x)$ exists}

$\Rightarrow$ if $g(x)$ is differentiable then $h(x)$ is also differentiable (true).

option (a) If $g(x)$ is continuous at $x = 1$ then
$$g(1^+) = g(1^-) = g(1)$$
$$h'(1^+) = \lim_{h \to 0^+}\frac{h(1+h)-h(1)}{h}$$
$$h'(1^+) = \lim_{h \to 0^+}\frac{f(1+h)\ g(1+h)-0}{h}$$
$$= f'(1)\ g(1)$$

$$h'(1^-) = \lim_{h \to 0^+}\frac{f(1-h)\ g(1-h)-0}{-h}$$
$$= f'(1)\cdot g(1)$$

So $\qquad h(x) = f(x).g(x)$ is differentiable

at $x = 1$ (True)

option (b) (d)

$$h'(1^+) = \lim_{h \to 0^+}\frac{h(1+h)-h(1)}{-h}$$

$$h'(1^+) = \lim_{h \to 0^+}\frac{f(1+h)\ g(1+h)}{h}$$
$$= f'(1)\ g(1^+)$$

$$h'(1^-) = \lim_{h \to 0^+}\frac{f(1-h)\ g(1-h)}{-h}$$
$$= f'(1).g(1^-)$$

$\Rightarrow \qquad g(1^+) = g(1^-)$

So we cannot comment on the continuity and differentiability of the function.

11. Correct Response : (1)

Explanation :

$$\lim_{x \to 0^+}\frac{e^{\left(\frac{\ln(1-x)}{x}\right)}-\dfrac{1}{e}}{x^a}$$

$$= \lim_{x \to 0^+}\frac{1}{e}\frac{e^{\left(1+\frac{\ln(1-x)}{x}\right)}-1}{x^a}$$

$$\left(\because e^x = 1+\frac{x}{1!}+\frac{x^2}{2!}+\dots\right)$$

$$= \frac{1}{e}\lim_{x \to 0^+}\frac{1+\dfrac{\ln(1-x)}{x}}{x^a}$$

$$= \frac{1}{e}\lim_{x \to 0^+}\frac{\ln(1-x)+x}{x^{(a+1)}}$$

$$= \frac{1}{e}\lim_{x \to 0^+}\frac{\left(-x-\dfrac{x^2}{2}-\dfrac{x^3}{3}-\dots\right)+x}{x^{a+1}}$$

Thus, $\quad a = 1.$

12. Correct Response : (8)

Explanation :

$$\lim_{x \to \frac{\pi}{2}}\frac{4\sqrt{2}\cdot 2\sin 2x\cos x}{2\sin 2x\sin\dfrac{3x}{2}}$$

$$+\left(\cos\frac{5x}{2}-\cos\frac{3x}{2}\right)-\sqrt{2}(1+\cos 2x)$$

$$= \lim_{x \to \frac{\pi}{2}} \frac{8\sqrt{2}\,\sin 2x\,\cos x}{2\sin 2x \cdot \sin \frac{3x}{2} + 2\sin 2x\left(-\sin \frac{x}{2}\right) - 2\sqrt{2}\cos^2 x}$$

$$= \lim_{x \to \frac{\pi}{2}} \frac{16\sqrt{2}\,\sin x\,\cos^2 x}{2\sin 2x\left(\sin \frac{3x}{2} - \sin \frac{x}{2}\right) - 2\sqrt{2}\cos^2 x}$$

$$= \lim_{x \to \frac{\pi}{2}} \frac{16\sqrt{2}\,\sin x\,\cos^2 x}{4\sin x \cos x\left(2\cos x \cdot \sin \frac{x}{2}\right) - 2\sqrt{2}\cos^2 x}$$

$$= \lim_{x \to \frac{\pi}{2}} \frac{16\sqrt{2}\,\sin x}{8\sin x \cdot \sin \frac{x}{2} - 2\sqrt{2}} = \frac{16\sqrt{2}}{4\sqrt{2} - 2\sqrt{2}} = 8.$$

13. Correct Response : (a)

Explanation :

$$\lim_{x \to a} \frac{\frac{1}{3}(a+2x)^{-2/3} \cdot 2 - \frac{1}{3}\times(3x)^{-2/3}\cdot 3}{\frac{1}{3}(3a+x)^{-2/3} - \frac{1}{3}\times(4x)^{-2/3}\cdot 4}$$

$$= \frac{\frac{1}{3}(3a)^{-2/3}\cdot 2 - \frac{1}{3}\times(3a)^{-2/3}\cdot 3}{\frac{1}{3}(4a)^{-2/3} - \frac{1}{3}\times(4a)^{-2/3}\cdot 4}$$

$$= \frac{\frac{1}{3}(3a)^{-2/3}(-1)}{\frac{1}{3}(4a)^{-2/3}(-3)} = \left(\frac{3}{4}\right)^{-2/3}\cdot\frac{1}{3}$$

$$= \frac{2}{3}\cdot\left(\frac{2}{9}\right)^{1/3}$$

14. Correct Response : (d)

Explanation :

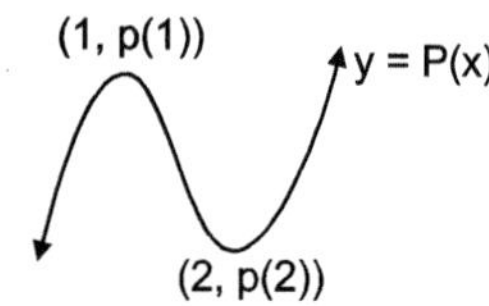

Since $p(x)$ has relative extreme at

$x = 1$ & 2

so $p'(x) = 0$ at $x = 1$ & 2

$\Rightarrow \qquad p'(x) = A(x-1)(x-2)$

$\Rightarrow \qquad p(x) = \int A(x^2 - 3x + 2)dx$

$$p(x) = A\left(\frac{x^3}{3} - \frac{3x^2}{2} + 2x\right) + C$$

$$...(1)$$

$P(1) = 8$

From (1)

$$8 = A\left(\frac{1}{3} - \frac{3}{2} + 2\right) + C$$

$$\Rightarrow \qquad 8 = \frac{5A}{6} + C \Rightarrow 48 = 5A + 6C$$

$$...(3)$$

$$P(2) = 4$$

$$\Rightarrow \qquad 4 = A\left(\frac{8}{3} - 6 + 4\right) + C$$

$$\Rightarrow \qquad 4 = \frac{2A}{3} + C \Rightarrow 12 = 2A + 3C$$

$$...(4)$$

From 3 & 4, $C = -12$

So $P(0) = C = -12$

15. Correct Response : (40)

Explanation :

$$\lim_{x \to 1} \frac{x + x^2 + x^3 + ... + x^n - n}{x - 1} = 820$$

$$\Rightarrow \lim_{x \to 1}\left(\frac{x-1}{x-1} + \frac{x^2-1}{x-1} + ... + \frac{x^n-1}{x-1}\right) = 820$$

$\Rightarrow \qquad 1 + 2 + ... + n = 820$

$\Rightarrow \qquad n(n+1) = 2 \times 820$

$\Rightarrow \qquad n(n+1) = 40 \times 41$

Since $n \in N$, so $n = 40$

16. Correct Response : (d)

Explanation :

$$\lim_{x \to 0}\left\{\tan\left(\frac{\pi}{4} + x\right)\right\}^{1/x}$$

Let $\qquad y = \lim_{x \to 0}\left(\tan\left(\frac{\pi}{4} + x\right)\right)^{1/x}$

Take log on both side

$$y = \lim_{x \to 0}\left[\frac{1}{x}\tan\left(\frac{\pi}{4} + x\right)\right]$$

$$= e^{\lim_{x \to 0}\frac{1}{x}\left\{\tan\left(\frac{\pi}{4} + x\right) - 1\right\}}$$

$$= e^{\lim_{x \to 0}\left(\frac{1 + \tan x - 1 + \tan x}{x(1 - \tan x)}\right)}$$

$$= e^{\lim_{x \to 0}\frac{2\tan x}{x(1 - \tan x)}}$$

$$= e^2$$

17. Correct Response : (c)

Explanation :

$$f(x) = x\log_e x$$

$$f'(x)\big|_{(c, f(c))} = \frac{e - 0}{e - 1}$$

$$f'(x) = 1 + \log_e x$$

$$f'(x)\big|_{(c, f(c))} = 1 + \log_e c = \frac{e}{e-1}$$

$$\log_e c = \frac{e - (e-1)}{e-1} = \frac{1}{e-1}$$

$$\Rightarrow \qquad c = e^{\frac{1}{e-1}}$$

18. Correct Response : (b)

Explanation :

$$(a + \sqrt{2}\, b \cos x)(2 - \sqrt{2}\, b \cos y) = a^2 - b^2$$

$$\Rightarrow a^2 - \sqrt{2}ab \cos y + \sqrt{2}ab \cos x$$

$$- 2b^2 \cos x \cos y = a^2 - b^2$$

Differentiating both sides,

$$0 - \sqrt{2}ab\left(- \sin y \frac{dy}{dx}\right) + \sqrt{2}ab\,(- \sin x)$$

$$- 2b^2\left[\cos x\left(- \sin y \frac{dy}{dx}\right) + \cos y(- \sin x)\right] = 0$$

At $\left(\dfrac{\pi}{4}, \dfrac{\pi}{4}\right)$:

$$ab \frac{dy}{dx} - ab - 2b^2\left(- \frac{1}{2}\frac{dy}{dx} - \frac{1}{2}\right) = 0$$

$$\Rightarrow \qquad \frac{dx}{dy} = \frac{ab + b^2}{ab - b^2} = \frac{a+b}{a-b}\,; a, b > 0$$

19. Correct Response : (a)

Explanation :

$$y^2 + ln\,(\cos^2 x) = y, x \in \left(-\frac{\pi}{2}, \frac{\pi}{2}\right)$$

for $x = 0, y^2 - y = 0 \Rightarrow y = 0$ or 1

Differentiating w.r.t. x

$$\Rightarrow \qquad 2yy' - 2\tan x = y'$$

At $(0, 0)$ $\qquad\qquad y' = 0$

At $(0, 1)$ $\qquad\qquad y' = 0$

Differentiating w.r.t. x

$$2yy'' + 2(y')^2 - 2\sec^2 x = y''$$

At $(0, 0)$ $\qquad\qquad y'' = -2$

At $(0, 1)$ $\qquad\qquad y'' = 2$

$\therefore \qquad\qquad |\,y''(0)\,| = 2.$

20. Correct Response : (b)

Explanation :

Let $\qquad f = \tan^{-1}\left(\dfrac{\sqrt{1+x^2} - 1}{x}\right)$

Put $\qquad x = \tan \theta \Rightarrow \theta = \tan^{-1} x$

$$f = \tan^{-1}\left(\frac{\sec \theta - 1}{\tan \theta}\right)$$

$$f = \tan^{-1}\left(\frac{1 - \cos \theta}{\sin \theta}\right)$$

$$= \tan^{-1}\left(\frac{1 - 1 + 2\sin^2 \frac{\theta}{2}}{2\sin \frac{\theta}{2}\cdot \cos \frac{\theta}{2}}\right)$$

$$f = \tan^{-1}\left(\tan \frac{\theta}{2}\right) = \frac{\theta}{2}$$

$$f = \frac{\tan^{-1} x}{2}$$

$$\Rightarrow \qquad \frac{df}{dx} = \frac{1}{2(1+x^2)} \qquad\qquad \ldots\text{(i)}$$

Let $\qquad g = \tan^{-1}\left(\dfrac{2x\sqrt{1-x^2}}{1-2x^2}\right)$

Put $\qquad x = \sin \theta$

$\Rightarrow \qquad \theta = \sin^{-1} x$

$$g = \tan^{-1}\left(\frac{2\sin \theta \cos \theta}{1 - 2\sin^2 \theta}\right)$$

$$= \tan^{-1}\left(\frac{\sin 2\theta}{\cos 2\theta}\right)$$

$$g = \tan^{-1}(\tan 2\theta) = 2\theta$$

$$g = 2\sin^{-1} x$$

$$\frac{dg}{dx} = \frac{2}{\sqrt{1-x^2}} \qquad\qquad \ldots\text{(ii)}$$

$$\frac{df}{dg} = \frac{1}{2(1+x^2)}\frac{\sqrt{1-x^2}}{2}$$

at $\qquad x = \dfrac{1}{2}\left(\dfrac{df}{dg}\right)_{x=\frac{1}{2}} = \dfrac{\sqrt{3}}{10}$

21. Correct Response : (a)

Explanation :

$$f(x) = (3x^2 + ax - 2 - a)e^x$$

$$f'(x) = (3x^2 + ax - 2 - a)e^x + e^x\,(6x + a)$$

$$= e^x\,[3x^2 + x(6 + a) - 2)]$$

$$f'(x) = 0 \text{ at } x = 1$$

$$\Rightarrow \quad 3 + (6 + a) - 2 = 0$$

$$a = -7$$

$$f'(x) = e^x\,(3x^2 - x - 2)$$

$$= e^x\,(x - 1)\,(3x + 2)$$

$$\begin{array}{ccc} + & - & + \\ \hline & & 1 \\ -2 & & \\ \hline 3 & & \end{array}$$

$x = 1$ is point of local minima

$x = \dfrac{-2}{3}$ is a point of local maxima.

22. Correct Response : (5)

Explanation :

$$f(x) = (x^2 - 1)^2 \, h(x);$$
$$h(x) = a_0 + a_1 x + a_2 x^2 + a_3 x^3$$

Now, $\quad f(1) = f(-1) = 0$

$\Rightarrow \quad f'(\alpha) = 0, \; \alpha \in (-1, 1)$

[Rolle's Theorem]

Also, $\quad f'(1) = f'(-1) = 0$

$\Rightarrow f'(x) = 0$ has atleast 3 roots, $-1, \alpha, 1$ with $-1 < \alpha < 1 \Rightarrow$ minimum $mf' = 3$

$\Rightarrow f''(x) = 0$ will have at least 2 roots, say β, γ such that

$$-1 < \beta < \alpha < \gamma < 1$$

[Rolle's Theorem]

So, $\quad$ min $(m_{f''}) = 2$

and we find $(m_{f'} + m_{f''}) = 5$ for $f(x) = (x^2 - 1)^2$.

23. Correct Response : (a, b, d)

Explanation :

Since, $\quad f(x) = xg(x)$

$$\lim_{x \to 0} f(x) = \lim_{x \to 0} xg(x)$$

$$\lim_{x \to 0} f(x) = \left(\lim_{x \to 0} x \right) \cdot \left(\lim_{x \to 0} g(x) \right)$$

$$\lim_{x \to 0} f(x) = 0 \times 1 = 0 \qquad \text{...(1)}$$

$$f(x + y) = f(x) + f(x) + f(x)\,f(y)$$

Now we check continuity of $f(x)$ at $x = a$

$$\lim_{h \to 0} f(a + h) = f(a) + f(b) + f(a) + f(h)$$

$$\lim_{x \to 0} [f(a) + f(h)(1 + f(1))]$$

$$\lim_{h \to 0} f(a + h) = f(a)$$

$\therefore f(x)$ is continuous $\forall \, x \in R$

$$\lim_{x \to 0} f(x) = f(0) = 0 \qquad \left(\lim_{x \to 0} f(x) = 0 \right)$$

$\therefore \qquad f(0) = 0$

and $\quad \displaystyle\lim_{x \to 0} \frac{f'(x)}{1} = 1$

$\therefore \qquad f'(0) = 1$

Now $\quad f(x + y) = f(x) + f(y) + f(x)\,f(y)$

using partial derivative (w.r.t. y)

$$f'(x + y) + f'(y) + f(x) + f'(y)$$

put $\qquad y = 0$

$$f'(x) = f'(0) + f(x)\,f'(0)$$
$$f'(x) = 1 + f(x)$$

$$\int \frac{f'(x)}{1 + f(x)} \, dx = \int 1 \, dx$$

$$\ln |(1 + f(x))| = x + C$$
$$f(0) = 0; \; c = 0$$

$\therefore \qquad |1 + f(x)| = e^x$
$$1 + f(x) = \pm e^x$$

or $\qquad f(x) = \pm e^x - 1$

Now $\qquad f(0) = 0$

$\therefore \qquad f(x) = e^x - 1$

$\therefore \qquad f(x) = e^x - 1$

option (a) is correct

and $\qquad f'(x) = e^x$

$f'(0) = 1$ option (d) is correct

$$g(x) = \frac{f(x)}{x} = \left\{ \begin{array}{l} \dfrac{e^x - 1}{x} \; ; x \neq 0 \\[2mm] 1 \quad ; x = 0 \end{array} \right\}$$

$$g'(0 + h) = \lim_{h \to 0} \frac{g(0 + h) - g(0)}{h}$$

$$= \lim_{h \to 0} \frac{\dfrac{e^h - 1}{h} - 1}{h} = \frac{1}{2}$$

option (b) is correct.

24. Correct Response : (½)

Explanation :

$$f(\theta) = (\sin \theta + \cos \theta)^2 + (\sin \theta - \cos \theta)^4$$

$$f(\theta) = (1 + \sin 2\theta) + (1 - \sin 2\theta)^2$$

$$= 1 + \sin 2\theta + 1^2 + \sin^2 2\theta - 2 \sin 2\theta$$

$$f(\theta) = \sin^2 2\theta - \sin 2\theta + 2$$

$$f'(\theta) = 2(\sin 2\theta).(2 \cos 2\theta) - 2 \cos 2\theta$$

$$= 2 \cos 2\theta \, (2 \sin 2\theta - 1)$$

Critical points

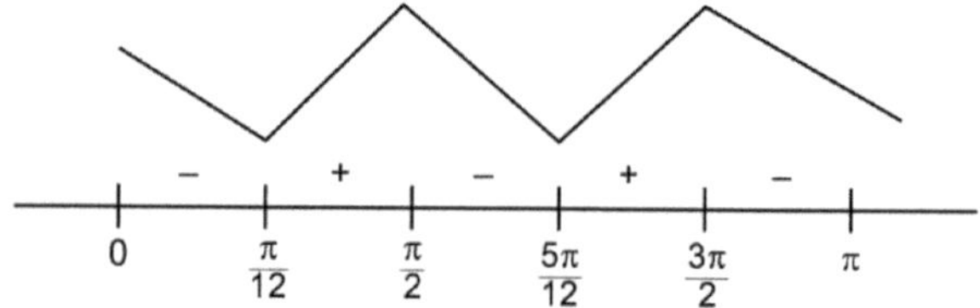

so, minimum at $\theta = \dfrac{\pi}{12}, \dfrac{5\pi}{12}$

$$\lambda_1 + \lambda_2 = \frac{1}{12} + \frac{5}{12} = \frac{6}{12} = \frac{1}{2}$$

25. Correct Response : (5.00)

Explanation :

$$k = \lim_{x \to 0} \left(\frac{\ell n(1 + 3x)}{x} - \frac{\ell n(1 + 2x)}{x} \right)$$

$$k = 3 + 2 = 5$$

26. Correct Response : (d)

Explanation :

$$\lim_{x\to 0^-} f(x) = \lim_{x\to 0}\left(\frac{\sin(a+2)x}{x} + \frac{\sin x}{x}\right)$$

$$= a + 3$$

$$\lim_{x\to 0^-} f(x) = \lim_{x\to 0}\frac{(x+3x^2)^{1/3} - x^{1/3}}{x^{4/3}}$$

$$= \lim_{x\to 0}\frac{(x+3x^2)^{1/3} - 1}{x}$$

$$= 1$$

$$f(0) = b$$

for continuity at $x = 0$

$$\lim_{x\to 0^-} f(x) = f(0) = \lim_{x\to 0^-} f(x)$$

$\Rightarrow \qquad a + 3 = b = 1$

$\therefore \qquad a = -2, b = 1$

$\therefore \qquad a + 2b = 0$

27. Correct Response : (b)

Explanation :

$$A = \lim_{x\to 0} x\left[\frac{4}{x}\right]$$

$$= \lim_{x\to 0} x\left[\frac{4}{x}\right] - x\left\{\frac{4}{x}\right\} = 4$$

$$f(x) = [x^2]\sin(\pi x)$$

will be discontinuous at non integers

$\therefore \qquad x = \sqrt{A+1} \ i.e., \ \sqrt{5}$

28. Correct Response : (c)

Explanation :

$$f(g(x)) = x$$

$$f'(g(x))\, g'(x) = 1$$

put $x = a$

$\Rightarrow \qquad f'(b)g'(a) = 1$

$$f'(b) = \frac{1}{5}$$

29. Correct Response : (b)

Explanation :

Using LMVT in $[-7, -1]$

$$\frac{f(-1) - f(-7)}{-1 - (-7)} \le 2$$

$$f(-1) - f(-7) \le 12$$

$\Rightarrow \qquad f(-1) \le 9 \qquad \qquad \dots(i)$

Using LMVT in $[-7, 0]$

$$\frac{f(0) - f(-7)}{0 - (-7)} \le 2$$

$$f(0) - f(-7) \le 14$$

$$f(0) \le 11 \qquad \qquad \dots(ii)$$

from (i) and (ii)

$$f(0) + f(-1) \le 20$$

30. Correct Response : (3)

Explanation :

$f(x) = |2 - |x - 3||$

f is not differentiable at

$$x = 1, 3, 5$$

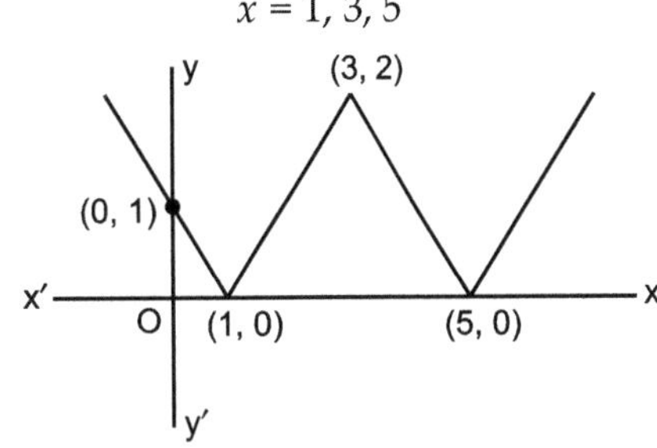

$\Rightarrow \quad \displaystyle\sum_{x\to es} f(f(x)) = f(f(1)) + f(f(3)) + f(f(5))$

$$= f(0) + f(2) + f(0)$$

$$= 1 + 1 + 1 = 3$$

31. Correct Response : (d)

Explanation :

$$\text{Required limit} = e^{\lim\limits_{x\to\infty}\left(\frac{3x^2+2}{7x^2+2}-1\right)\frac{1}{x^2}}$$

$$= e^{\lim\limits_{x\to\infty}\left(\frac{-4}{7x^2+2}\right)} = \frac{1}{e^2}$$

32. Correct Response : (36.00)

Explanation :

$$\lim_{x\to 2}\frac{3^x + 3^{3-x} - 12}{3^{-x/2} - 3^{1-x}} \Rightarrow \lim_{x\to 2}\frac{3^{2x} - 12.3^x + 27}{3^{x/2} - 3}$$

$$= \lim_{x\to 2}\frac{(3^x - 9)(3^x - 3)}{(3^{x/2} - 3)}$$

$$= \lim_{x\to 2}\frac{(3^{x/2} + 3)(3^{x/2} - 3)(3^x - 3)}{(3^{x/2} - 3)}$$

$$= 36$$

33. Correct Response : (b)

Explanation :

$$\lim_{x\to 0}\left(2 + \frac{f(x)}{x^3}\right) = 5$$

$\Rightarrow \qquad f(x) = 2x^3 + ax^4 + bx^5$

$$f'(x) = 6x^2 + 4ax^3 + 5bx^4$$

$$f'(1) = 0, f'(-1) = 0$$

$$a = 0, b = \frac{-6}{5} \Rightarrow f(x) = 2x^3 - \frac{6}{5}x^5$$

$$f'(x) = 6x^2 - 6x^4$$

$$= 6x^2(1 - x)(1 + x)$$

Sign scheme for $f'(x)$

$$\xleftarrow{\qquad\underset{-1}{\overset{-ve}{\quad}}\quad\underset{0}{\overset{+ve}{\quad}}\quad\underset{1}{\overset{+ve}{\quad}}\quad\overset{-ve}{\quad}\qquad}$$

Minima at $x = -1$

Maxima at $x = 1$

34. Correct Response : (c)

Explanation :

Let thickness of ice be 'h'.

$$\text{Vol. of ice} = v = \frac{4\pi}{3}\left((10+h)^3 - 10^3\right)$$

$$\frac{dv}{dt} = \frac{4\pi}{3}(3(10+h)^2)\cdot\frac{dh}{dt}$$

Given $\frac{dv}{dt} = 50$ cm^3/min and $h = 5$ cm

$$\Rightarrow \quad 50 = \frac{4\pi}{3}(3(10+5)^2)\frac{dh}{dt}$$

$$\Rightarrow \quad \frac{dh}{dt} = \frac{50}{4\pi\times15^2} = \frac{1}{18\pi} \text{ cm}/\text{min}$$

35. Correct Response : (a)

Explanation :

$$F'(x) = x^2 g(x) = x^2 \int_1^x f(u)\,du \Rightarrow (1) = 0$$

$$F''(x) = x^2 f(x) - 2x \int_1^x f(u)\,du$$

$$F''(1) = 1.f(1) - 2\times 0$$

$$F''(1) = 3$$

$$F(1) = 0 \text{ and } F''(1) = 3 > 0 \text{ So, Minima}$$

36. Correct Response : (c)

Explanation :

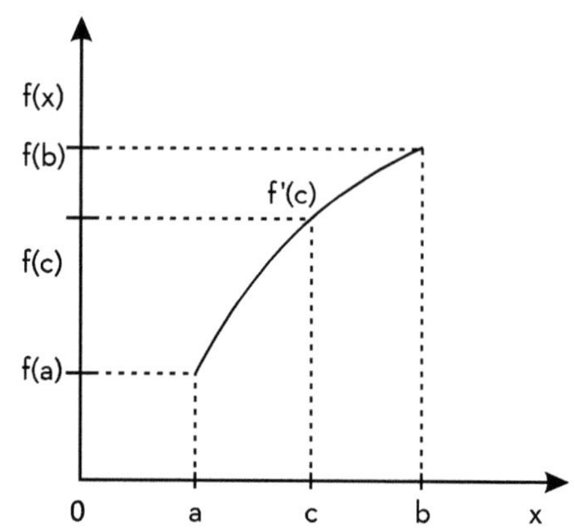

it is clear from graph that $m_1 > m_2$

$$\Rightarrow \quad \frac{f(c)-f(a)}{c-a} > \frac{f(b)-f(c)}{b-c}$$

$$\Rightarrow \quad \frac{f(c)-f(a)}{f(b)-f(c)} > \frac{c-a}{b-c}$$

37. Correct Response : (a)

Explanation :

$$y(\alpha) = \sqrt{2\frac{(\tan\alpha+\cot\alpha)}{1+\tan^2\alpha} + \frac{1}{\sin^2\alpha}}, \quad \alpha \in \left(\frac{3\pi}{4}, \pi\right)$$

$$= \frac{|\sin\alpha+\cos\alpha|}{|\sin\alpha|} = \frac{-(\sin\alpha+\cos\alpha)}{\sin\alpha}$$

$$= -1 - \cot\alpha$$

$$y'(\alpha) = \operatorname{cosec}^2\alpha$$

$$y'\left(\frac{5\pi}{6}\right) = 4$$

38. Correct Response : (c)

Explanation :

$$x^k + y^k = a^k (a, k > 0)$$

$$kx^{k-1} + ky^{k-1}\frac{dy}{dx} = 0$$

$$\frac{dy}{dx} + \left(\frac{x}{y}\right)^{1-k} = 0$$

$$\Rightarrow \quad k - 1 = -\frac{1}{3}$$

$$\Rightarrow \quad k = 2/3$$

39. Correct Response : (d)

Explanation :

$$f(0) = 11$$

$$f(1) = 16$$

$$\frac{f(1)-f(0)}{1-0} = 3c^2 - 8c + 8$$

$$\Rightarrow \quad 3c^2 - 8c + 8 = 5$$

$$\Rightarrow \quad 3c^2 - 8c + 3 = 0$$

$$c \in [0, 1] \Rightarrow c = \frac{4-\sqrt{7}}{3}$$

40. Correct Response : (c)

Explanation :

$$\lim_{\pi\to 0}\left(2+\frac{f(x)}{x^3}\right) = 4$$

$$\Rightarrow \quad f(x) = 2x^3 + ax^4 + bx^5$$

$$f'(x) = 6x^2 + 4ax^3 + 5bx^4$$

$$f'(1) = 0, f'(-1) = 0$$

$$a = 0, b = \frac{-6}{5}$$

$$\Rightarrow \quad f(x) = 2x^3 - \frac{6}{5}x^5$$

$$f'(x) = 6x^2 - 6x^4$$

$$= 6x^2(1 - x)(1 + x)$$

Sign scheme for $f'(x)$

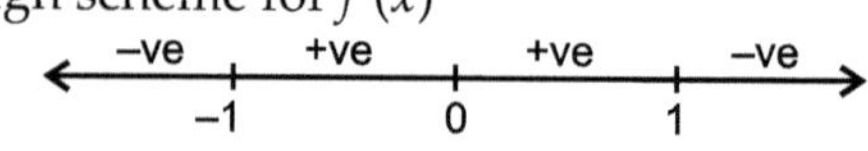

Minima at $x = -1$

Maxima at $x = 1$

41. Correct Response : (b)

Explanation :

$$\frac{9+\alpha}{21} = \frac{16+\alpha}{28} \Rightarrow \alpha = 12$$

Also, $\quad f'(x) = \dfrac{7x}{x^2+12} \times \dfrac{x^2-12}{7x^2} = \dfrac{x^2-12}{x(x^2+12)}$

Hence, $\qquad c = 2\sqrt{3}$

Now, $\qquad f''(c) = \dfrac{1}{12}$

42. Correct Response : (a)

Explanation :

$f(x)$ is an odd function.

Now, if $x \geq 0$, then $f(x) = x \cos^{-1}(-\sin x)$

$$= x\left(\dfrac{\pi}{2} - \sin^{-1}(-\sin x)\right) = x\left(\dfrac{\pi}{2} + x\right)$$

Hence, $\qquad f(x) = \begin{cases} x\left(\dfrac{\pi}{2} + x\right) & ; \quad x \in \left[0, \dfrac{\pi}{2}\right] \\ x\left(\dfrac{\pi}{2} + x\right) & ; \quad x \in \left[\dfrac{\pi}{2}, 0\right] \end{cases}$

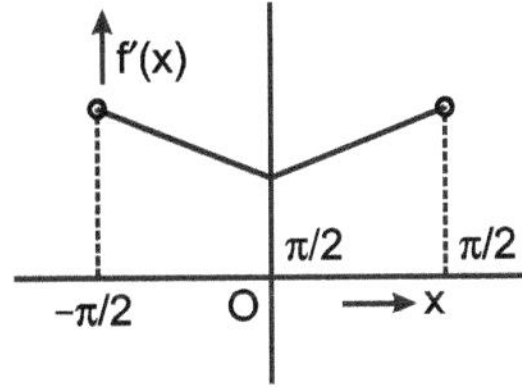

So, $\qquad f'(x) = \begin{cases} \dfrac{\pi}{2} + 2x & ; \quad x \in \left[0, \dfrac{\pi}{2}\right] \\ \dfrac{\pi}{2} - x & ; \quad x \in \left[-\dfrac{\pi}{2}, 0\right) \end{cases}$

43. Correct Response : (3.00)

Explanation :

$$f''(x) = \lambda(x - 1)$$

$$f'(x) = \dfrac{\lambda x^2}{2} - \lambda x + c \Rightarrow f'(-1) = 0 \Rightarrow c = \dfrac{-3\lambda}{2}$$

$$f(x) - \dfrac{\lambda x^3}{6} - \dfrac{\lambda x^2}{2} - \dfrac{3\lambda}{2}x + d$$

$$f(1) = -6 \quad \Rightarrow \quad -11\lambda + 6d = -36 \qquad \text{...(i)}$$

$$f(-1) = 10 \quad \Rightarrow \quad 5\lambda + 6d = 60 \qquad \text{...(ii)}$$

from (i) and (ii) $\lambda = 6$ and $d = 5$

$$f(x) = x^3 - 3x^2 - 9x + 5$$

Which has minima at $x = 3$

44. Correct Response : (c)

Explanation :

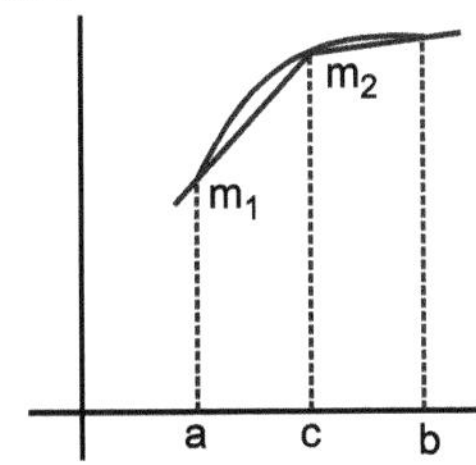

It is clear from graph that $m_1 > m_2$

$$\Rightarrow \qquad \dfrac{f(c) - f(a)}{c - a} > \dfrac{f(b) - f(c)}{b - c}$$

$$\Rightarrow \qquad \dfrac{f(c) - f(a)}{f(b) - f(c)} > \dfrac{c - a}{b - c}$$

45. Correct Response : (*)

Explanation :

$$x = 2\sin\theta - \sin 2\theta$$

$$\Rightarrow \quad \dfrac{dx}{d\theta} = 2\cos\theta - 2\cos 2\theta = 4\sin\left(\dfrac{\theta}{2}\right)\sin\left(\dfrac{3\theta}{2}\right)$$

$$y = 2\cos\theta - \cos 2\theta$$

$$\Rightarrow \quad \dfrac{dy}{d\theta} = -2\sin\theta + 2\sin 2\theta = 4\sin\dfrac{\theta}{2}\cos\dfrac{3\theta}{2}$$

$$\Rightarrow \quad \dfrac{dy}{dx} = \cot\left(\dfrac{3\theta}{2}\right) \Rightarrow \dfrac{d^2y}{dx^2} = \dfrac{-\dfrac{3}{2}\operatorname{cosec}^3\left(\dfrac{3\theta}{2}\right)}{4\sin\left(\dfrac{\theta}{2}\right)\sin\dfrac{3\theta}{2}}$$

$$\Rightarrow \quad \left(\dfrac{d^2y}{dx^2}\right)_{\theta = \pi} = \dfrac{3}{8}$$

Alternate :

$$\dfrac{\dfrac{dy}{d\theta}}{\dfrac{dx}{d\theta}} = \dfrac{-2\sin\theta + 2\sin 2\theta}{2\cos\theta - 2\cos 2\theta} = \dfrac{\sin\theta - \sin 2\theta}{-\cos\theta + \cos 2\theta}$$

$$\dfrac{d^2y}{dx^2} \cdot \dfrac{dy}{d\theta} =$$

$$\dfrac{(-\cos\theta + \cos 2\theta)(\cos\theta - 2\cos 2\theta) - (\sin\theta - \sin 2\theta)(\sin\theta - 2\sin 2\theta)}{(-\cos\theta + \cos 2\theta)^2}$$

$$\dfrac{d^2y}{dx^2} \cdot (-2 - 2) = \dfrac{(+1+1)(-1-2) - (0)}{(1+1)^2}$$

$$\dfrac{d^2y}{dx^2}(-4) = \dfrac{2 \times -3}{4} = -\dfrac{3}{2}$$

$$\dfrac{d^2y}{dx^2} = \dfrac{3}{8}$$

Answer should be $\dfrac{3}{8}$. No options is correct.

46. Correct Response : (a)

Explanation :

$$F'(x) = x^2\, g(x) = x^2 \int_1^x f(u)\, du \Rightarrow F'(1) = 0$$

$$F''(x) = x^2 f(x) - 2x \int_1^x f(u)\, du$$

$$F''(1) = 1.f(1) - 2 \times 0$$

$$F''(1) = 3$$

$\qquad F'(1) = 0$ and $F''(1) = 3 > 0$ So, $x = 1$ is a point of local minima

47. Correct Response : (4.00)

Explanation :

Let $P(\alpha, \beta)$

so, $\qquad \beta^2 - 3\alpha^2 + \beta + 10 = 0 \qquad \ldots(i)$

Now, $\qquad 2yy' - 6x + y' = 0$

$\Rightarrow \qquad m = \dfrac{6\alpha}{2\beta + 1} \qquad \ldots(ii)$

Also, $\qquad \dfrac{\beta - \dfrac{3}{2}}{\alpha} = -\dfrac{1}{m}$

$\Rightarrow \qquad \dfrac{2\beta - 3}{2\alpha} = -\dfrac{(2\beta + 1)}{6\alpha}$ (from (ii))

$\Rightarrow \beta = 1 \Rightarrow \alpha^2 = 4$ (from (i))

Hence, $\qquad |m| = \dfrac{12}{3} = 4.00$

48. Correct Response : (b)

Explanation :

Put $x = \sin\theta$, $y = \sin\alpha$

$$y\sqrt{1 - x^2} = k - x\sqrt{1 - y^2}$$

$\Rightarrow \sin\alpha \cdot \cos\theta + \cos\alpha \cdot \sin\theta = k$

$\Rightarrow \qquad \sin(\alpha + \theta) = k$

$\Rightarrow \qquad \alpha + \theta = \sin^{-1}k$

$\Rightarrow \qquad \sin^{-1}x + \sin^{-1}y = \sin^{-1}k$

$\Rightarrow \qquad \dfrac{1}{\sqrt{1 - x^2}} + \dfrac{1}{\sqrt{1 - y^2}} \times \dfrac{dy}{dx} = 0$

at $x = \dfrac{1}{2}$, $y = \dfrac{-1}{4}$

$$\dfrac{dy}{dx} = \dfrac{-\sqrt{5}}{2}$$

49. Correct Response : (b)

Explanation :

$\dfrac{dy}{dx} = -\dfrac{\sqrt{1 - y^2}}{\sqrt{1 - x^2}}$ so, $\dfrac{dy}{\sqrt{1 - y^2}} + \dfrac{dx}{\sqrt{1 - x^2}} = 0$

Integrating, $\sin^{-1}x + \sin^{-1}y = c$

So, $\dfrac{\pi}{6} + \dfrac{\pi}{3} = c$

Hence, $\sin^{-1}x + \sin^{-1}y = \dfrac{\pi}{2}$

Put $x = -\dfrac{1}{\sqrt{2}}$, $\sin^{-1}y = \dfrac{3\pi}{4}$ (Not possible, bonus)

50. Correct Response : (*)

Explanation :

Let $\tan^{-1}x = \theta$, $\theta \in \left(-\dfrac{\pi}{2}, -\dfrac{\pi}{4}\right] \cup \left(\dfrac{\pi}{4}, \dfrac{\pi}{2}\right)$

$$f(x) = (\sin\theta + \cos\theta)^2 - 1$$

$$= \sin 2\theta = \dfrac{2x}{1 + x^2}$$

Now, $\qquad \dfrac{dy}{dx} = \dfrac{1}{2}\dfrac{d}{dx}\sin^{-1}\left(\dfrac{2x}{1 + x^2}\right)$

$$= -\dfrac{1}{1 + x^2}, |x| > 1$$

Since, we can integrate only in the continuous interval. So, we have to take integral in two cases separately namely for $x < -1$ and for $x > 1$.

$\Rightarrow \qquad y = \begin{cases} -\tan^{-1}x + c_1 & ; \quad x > 1 \\ -\tan^{-1}x + c_2 & ; \quad x < -1 \end{cases}$

so, $\qquad c_1 = \dfrac{\pi}{2}$ as $y(\sqrt{3}) = \dfrac{\pi}{6}$

But we cannot find c_2 as we do not have any other additional information for $x < -1$ So. all of the given options may be correct as c_2 is unknown so, it should be bonus.

51. Correct Response : (c)

Explanation :

$$g(x) = |f(x)|$$

$$g'(c^+) = \lim_{x \to c^+} \dfrac{|f(x)| - f(c)}{x - c}$$

$$= \lim_{x \to c^+} \dfrac{\pm f(x)}{x - c}$$

$$= \pm f'(c)$$

$$g'(c^-) = \lim_{x \to c^-} \dfrac{|f(x)| - f(c)}{x - c}$$

$$= \lim_{x \to c^-} \dfrac{\pm f(x)}{x - c}$$

$$= \pm f'(c)$$

For $g(x)$ to be differentiable at $x = c$, $f'(c)$ must be zero.

52. Correct Response : (a)

Explanation :

By L. Hopital's rule,

$$\lim_{x \to 1} \dfrac{4x^3}{1} = \lim_{x \to 1} \dfrac{3x^3}{2x}$$

$\Rightarrow \qquad 4 = \dfrac{3k^2}{2k}$

$\Rightarrow \qquad k = \dfrac{8}{3}$

53. Correct Response : (b)

Explanation :

$$h(x) = fog(x)$$

$$= f(g(x))$$

$$= e^{x^2 - x} - x^2 + x$$

$$h'(x) = e^{x^2 - x}(2x - 1) - 2x + 1$$

$$\geq 0$$

$\Rightarrow \quad (2x - 1)(e^{x^2 - x} - 1) \geq 0$

Case 1 :
$$x \geq \frac{1}{2} \text{ and } x^2 - x \geq 0$$
$$\Rightarrow \qquad x \geq 1$$
Or
Case 2 :
$$x \leq \frac{1}{2} \text{ and } x^2 - x \leq 0$$
$$\Rightarrow \qquad 0 \leq x \leq \frac{1}{2}$$
So,
$$x \in \left[0, \frac{1}{2}\right] \cup [1, \infty)$$

54. Correct Response : (c)
Explanation :
$$f(0) = q$$
$$f(0^-) = \lim_{h \to 0} \frac{\sin(p+1)(-h) - \sin h}{-h}$$
$$= \lim_{h \to 0} \frac{(p+1)\sin(p+1)h}{(p+1)h} + \frac{\sin h}{h}$$
$$= p + 1 + 1$$
$$= p + 2$$
$$f(0^+) = \lim_{h \to 0} \frac{\sqrt{h^2 + h} - h}{h\sqrt{h}}$$
$$= \lim_{h \to 0} \frac{\sqrt{h+1} - 1}{h}$$
$$= \lim_{h \to 0} \frac{h + 1 - 1}{h\left(\sqrt{h+1} + 1\right)}$$
$$= \frac{1}{2}$$

For $f(x)$ to be continuous at $x = 0$, $f(0^-) = f(0) = f(0^+)$. This implies
$$p + 2 = q = \frac{1}{2}$$
$$\Rightarrow \qquad p = -\frac{3}{2}, \ q = \frac{1}{2}.$$

55. Correct Response : (a)
Explanation :
Rewrite the equation of given line as $y = -\dfrac{1}{3}x + \dfrac{11}{6}$.

Then the slope of the line is $-\dfrac{1}{3}$.

As tangent is parallel to this line therefore,
$$\frac{dy}{dx} = \frac{x^2 - 3 - x(2x)}{(x^2 - 3)^2}$$
$$= -\frac{(x^2 + 3)}{(x^2 - 3)^2}$$

$$= -\frac{1}{3}$$
$$\Rightarrow \qquad 3x^2 + 9 = x^4 + 9 - 6x^2$$
$$\Rightarrow \qquad x^4 - 9x^2 = 0$$
$$\Rightarrow \qquad x^2(x^2 - 9) = 0$$
$$\Rightarrow \qquad x = 0, 3, -3.$$
Substitute these values in the given equation of tangent. Then, $y = 0, \dfrac{1}{2}, -\dfrac{1}{2}$.

Points $\left(3, \dfrac{1}{2}\right)$ and $\left(-3, -\dfrac{1}{2}\right)$ satisfy option (a)

Point $(0, 0)$ doesn't satisfy any of the above options.

56. Correct Response : (a)
Explanation :

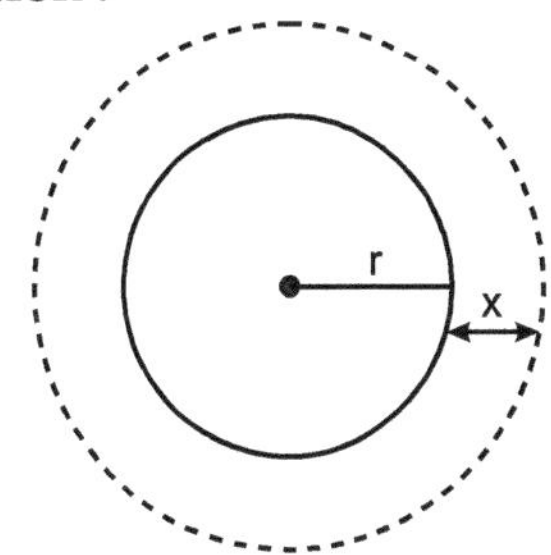

Volume of ice is $\dfrac{4}{3}\pi(r + x)^3 - \dfrac{4}{3}\pi r^3$

Rate of change of volume is
$$\frac{dV}{dt} = 50 \text{ cm}^3/\text{min}$$
$$\Rightarrow \qquad 4\pi(r+x)^2 \frac{dx}{dt} = 50$$
At $r = 10$ and $x = 5$,
$$\Rightarrow \qquad 4\pi(15)^2 \frac{dx}{dt} = 50$$
$$\Rightarrow \qquad \frac{dx}{dt} = \frac{50}{4\pi(225)}$$
$$= \frac{1}{18\pi} \text{ cm/min}$$

57. Correct Response : (c)
Explanation :
Given that
$$\lim_{x \to 1} \frac{x^2 - ax + b}{x - 1} = 5$$
For existence of limit
$$1 - a + b = 0$$
$$\Rightarrow \qquad a - b = 1 \qquad \qquad \text{...(i)}$$
Equation (i) implies
$$\lim_{x \to 1} \frac{x^2 - ax + a - 1}{x - 1} = 5$$
$$\Rightarrow \qquad \lim_{x \to 1} \frac{(x^2 - 1) - a(x - 1)}{x - 1} = 5$$

$$\Rightarrow \quad \lim_{x\to 1}(x+1-a) = 5$$

$$\Rightarrow \quad 2-a = 5$$

$$\Rightarrow a = -3, b = -4, a+b = -7.$$

58. Correct Response : (a)

Explanation :

$$f(x) = [x]-\left[\frac{x}{4}\right]$$

$$\lim_{h\to 0^+}[4+h]-\left[\frac{4+h}{4}\right] = 4-1$$

$$= 3$$

$$\lim_{h\to 0^+}[4-h]-\left[\frac{4-h}{4}\right] = 3-0$$

$$= 3$$

$$f(4) = [4]-[1]$$

$$= 3$$

$f(x)$ is continuous at $x = 4$.

59. Correct Response : (d)

Explanation :

$$f(5) = a|\pi-5|+1$$

$$\lim_{x\to 5^-}f(x) = a|\pi-5|+1$$

$$= a(5-\pi)+1$$

$$\lim_{x\to 5^+}f(x) = b|5-\pi|+3$$

$$= b(5-\pi)+3$$

$f(x)$ is continuous at $x = 5$ implies

$$f(5) = \lim_{x\to 5^-}f(x)$$

$$= \lim_{x\to 5^+}f(x)$$

$$\Rightarrow \quad a(5-\pi)+1 = b(5-\pi)+3$$

$$\Rightarrow \quad (a-b)(5-\pi) = 2$$

$$\Rightarrow \quad a-b = \frac{2}{5-\pi}$$

60. Correct Response : (d)

Explanation :

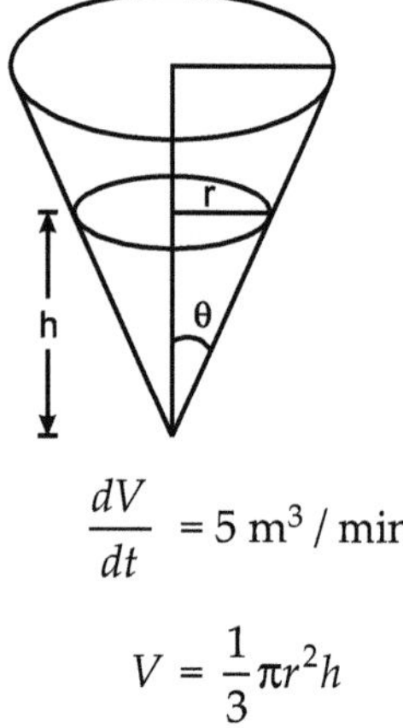

$$\frac{dV}{dt} = 5 \text{ m}^3/\text{min}$$

$$V = \frac{1}{3}\pi r^2 h$$

$$\tan\theta = \frac{r}{h}$$

$$= \frac{1}{2}$$

$$\Rightarrow \quad 2r = h$$

$$V = \frac{1}{3}\pi\frac{h^3}{4}$$

$$= \frac{\pi h^3}{12}$$

$$\Rightarrow \quad \frac{dV}{dt} = \frac{\pi}{4}h^2\frac{dh}{dt}$$

$$\Rightarrow \quad 5 = \frac{\pi}{4}10^2\frac{dh}{dt}$$

So,

$$\frac{dh}{dt} = \frac{20}{100\pi}$$

$$= \frac{1}{5\pi} \text{ m/min.}$$

61. Correct Response : (d)

Explanation :

$$f(2) = 6$$

Use L. Hospital's rule

$$\lim_{x\to 2}\int_6^{f(x)}\frac{2t\,dt}{x-2} = \lim_{x\to 2}\frac{\int_6^{f(x)}2t\,dt}{x-2}$$

$$= \lim_{x\to 2}\frac{2f(x)f'(x)}{1}$$

$$= 12\,f'(2)$$

62. Correct Response : (d)

Explanation :

Let $f'(x) = \lambda x(x^2-1) \Rightarrow f(x) = \lambda\left(\frac{x^4}{4}-\frac{x^2}{2}\right)+C$

Now $f(0) = f(x)$ implies $\frac{x^4}{4}-\frac{x^2}{2} = 0$

$$\Rightarrow x = 0 \text{ or } \pm\sqrt{2}$$

$\therefore$ Option (d) is correct.

63. Correct Response : (d)

Explanation :

$$f(x) = x^3+ax-b$$

It passes through $(1,-5)$ and $f'(1) = 1$

Hence, $-5 = 1+a-b \qquad \Rightarrow a-b = 6$

$$f'(x) = 3x^2+a \qquad \Rightarrow -1 = 3+a$$

$$\Rightarrow a = -4 \text{ hence, } b = 2.$$

$$f(x) = x^3-4x-2 \quad \Rightarrow (2,-2) \text{ lies on it.}$$

64. Correct Response : (b)

Explanation :

Since $f(x)$ is continuous at $x = \dfrac{\pi}{4}$.

$$\lim_{x \to \frac{\pi}{4}} f(x) = f\left(\dfrac{\pi}{4}\right)$$

$\Rightarrow \qquad k = \lim_{x \to \frac{\pi}{4}} \dfrac{\sqrt{2}\cos x - 1}{\cot x - 1}$

This implies,

$$k = \lim_{x \to \frac{\pi}{4}} \dfrac{-\sqrt{2}\sin x}{-\operatorname{cosec}^2 x}$$

$$= \dfrac{1}{2}$$

65. Correct Response : (a)

Explanation :

$$\begin{aligned}
g(x) &= f(15 - |x - 10|) \\
&= 15 - |15 - |x - 10| - 10| \\
&= 15 - |5 - |x - 10||
\end{aligned}$$

$$= \begin{cases} 15 - |x - 5| & x < 10 \\ 15 - |15 - x| & x > 10 \end{cases}$$

$$= \begin{cases} 10 + x & x < 5 \\ 20 - x & 5 < x < 10 \\ x & 10 < x < 5 \\ 30 - x & 15 < x \end{cases}$$

It is not differentiable at 5, 10, 15.

66. Correct Response : (d)

Explanation :

$$\begin{aligned}
f(1) &= 1 - 1 - 2 \\
&= -2 \\
f(-1) &= -1 - 1 + 2 \\
&= 0
\end{aligned}$$

Hence, points are $(1, -2)$ and $(-1, 0)$

Slope is $\dfrac{2}{-2} = -1$.

So,

$$\begin{aligned}
f'(x) &= 3x^2 - 2x - 2 \\
&= -1
\end{aligned}$$

$\Rightarrow \qquad 3x^2 - 2x - 1 = 0$

$\Rightarrow \qquad (3x + 1)(x - 1) = 0$

$\Rightarrow \qquad x = -\dfrac{1}{3},\ x = 1$

67. Correct Response : (a)

Explanation :

$$\lim_{x \to 0} \dfrac{\sin^2 x}{\sqrt{2} - \sqrt{1 + \cos x}}$$

$$= \lim_{x \to 0} \dfrac{\sin^2 x\,(\sqrt{2} + \sqrt{1 + \cos x})}{1 - \cos x}$$

$$= \lim_{x \to 0} \dfrac{\sin^2 x}{x^2}\left(\dfrac{1}{\dfrac{1 - \cos x}{x^2}}\right)(\sqrt{2} + \sqrt{1 + \cos x})$$

$$= \dfrac{2\sqrt{2}}{1/2}$$

$$= 4\sqrt{2}$$

68. Correct Response : (c)

Explanation :

$$y = 9x^4 + 12x^3 - 36x^2 + 25$$

$$\dfrac{dy}{dx} = 36x^3 + 36x^2 - 72x$$

$$= 36x\,(x^2 + x - 2)$$

$$= 36x\,(x + 2)\,(x - 1)$$

$$\begin{array}{ccccccc} - & & + & & - & & + \\ \hline & -2 & & 0 & & 1 & \end{array}$$

$\{-2, 1\}$ are points of minima

$\{0\}$ is the point of maxima

69. Correct Response : (c)

Explanation :

$f''(x) > 0,\ y = f(x);\ x \in (0, 2)$

$$\phi(x) = f(x) + f(2 - x)$$

$$\phi'(x) = f'(x) - f'(2 - x)$$

For $\phi(x)$ to be increasing

$$\phi'(x) > 0 \Rightarrow f'(2) > f'(2 - x)$$

$\Rightarrow \qquad x > 2 - x$

$\qquad\qquad (f'(x)$ is increasing in $(0, 2))$

$\Rightarrow \qquad x > 1$

$\Rightarrow \qquad x \in (1, 2)$

For $\phi(x)$ to be decreasing

$$\phi'(x) < 0 \Rightarrow f'(x) < f'(2 - x)$$

Therefore, $x \in (0, 1)$

70. Correct Response : (b)

Explanation :

$$\text{Interval } f(x) = \begin{cases} x \in [-1, 0) & \Rightarrow (-x - 1) \\ x \in [0, 1) & \Rightarrow x \\ x \in [1, 2) & \Rightarrow 2x \\ x \in [2, 3) & \Rightarrow x + 2 \end{cases}$$

At $x = 0, 1$

$f(x)$ is discontinuous at two points.

71. Correct Response : (c)

Explanation :

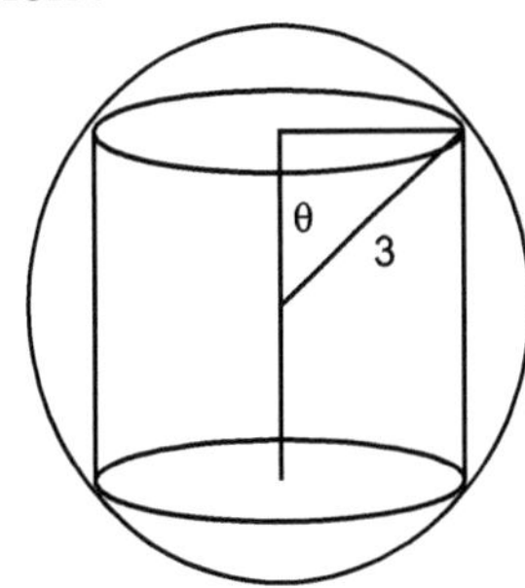

$$h = 2\,(3\cos\theta)$$
$$r = 3\sin\theta$$
$$V = \pi r^2 h$$
$$= \pi(9\sin^2\theta).6\cos\theta$$
$$= 54\pi\sin^2\theta\cos\theta$$

Put $\dfrac{dV}{d\theta} = 0$

$$\Rightarrow \quad 2\sin\theta\cos^2\theta - \sin^3\theta = 0$$

Put $\sin\theta = s$

$$\Rightarrow \quad 2s\,(1 - s^2) - s^3 = 0$$
$$\Rightarrow \quad 2s - 2s^3 - s^3 = 0$$
$$\Rightarrow \quad 2s - 3s^3 = 0$$

$$\Rightarrow s = 0 \text{ or } 2 - 3s^2 = 0 \Rightarrow s = \pm\sqrt{\dfrac{2}{3}}$$

This gives,

$$\cos\theta = \sqrt{1 - \dfrac{2}{3}}$$
$$= \dfrac{1}{\sqrt{3}}$$

$$\Rightarrow \qquad h = 6\left(\dfrac{1}{\sqrt{3}}\right) = 2\sqrt{3}$$

72. Correct Response : (a)

Explanation :

$$\lim_{x\to 0}\left(\dfrac{1 + f(3 + x) - f(3)}{1 + f(2 - x) - f(2)}\right)^{\frac{1}{x}}$$

$$= e^{\displaystyle\lim_{x\to 0}\left(\frac{1}{x}\left[\frac{1 + f(3+x) - f(3)}{1 + f(2-x) - f(2)}\right]\right)}$$

$$= e^{\displaystyle\lim_{x\to 0}\left(\frac{f(3+x) - f(2-x) - (f(3) - f(2))}{x(1 + f(2-x) - f(2)}\right)}$$

$$= e^{\displaystyle\lim_{x\to 0}\left(\frac{f'(3+x) + f'(2-x)}{1}\right)}$$

$$= e^{f'(3) + f'(2)}$$
$$= e^0$$
$$= 1$$

Which lies in (3, 4).

73. Correct Response : (a)

Explanation :

Given, the value of,

$$\int_{6}^{f(x)} 4x^3\,dx = g(x)\,(x - 2)$$

$$g(x) = \dfrac{(f(x))^4 - (6)^4}{x - 2}$$

The value of $\displaystyle\lim_{x\to 2} g(x)$ is,

$$\lim_{x\to 2} g(x) = \dfrac{(f(x))^4 - (6)^4}{x - 2}$$

$$= \lim_{x\to 2}\dfrac{4f^3(x)f'(x)}{x - 1}$$

$$= (4)\,(6)^3\left(\dfrac{1}{48}\right)$$

$$= 18$$

74. Correct Response : (b)

Explanation :

The roots of the equation $375x^2 - 25x - 2$ are in the range of $(-1, 1)$.

The sequence formed by these roots gives a finite sum.

Therefore,

$$\lim_{n\to\infty}\sum_{r=1}^{n}\alpha^r + \lim_{n\to\infty}\sum_{r=1}^{n}\beta^r = \lim_{n\to\infty}\left(\dfrac{\alpha}{1 - \alpha} + \dfrac{\beta}{1 - \beta}\right)$$

$$= \dfrac{\alpha\,(1 - \beta) + \beta(1 - \alpha)}{(1 - \alpha)\,(1 - \beta)}$$

$$= \dfrac{\alpha + \beta - 2\alpha\beta}{1 - (\alpha + \beta) + \alpha\beta}$$

From the property of roots of quadratic equation,

$$\alpha + \beta = 25/375$$
$$\alpha\beta = -\,2/375$$

Therefore,

$$\lim_{n\to\infty}\sum_{r=1}^{n}\alpha^r + \lim_{n\to\infty}\sum_{r=1}^{n}\beta^r = \dfrac{\dfrac{25}{375} - \dfrac{2\times(-2)}{375}}{1 - \dfrac{25}{375} - \dfrac{2}{375}}$$

$$= \dfrac{25 - 2(-2)}{375 - 25 - 2}$$

$$= \dfrac{29}{348}$$

75. Correct Response : (a)

Explanation :

Given that,

$$f(x) = x\sqrt{kx - x^2}$$

Differentiate with respect to x.

$$f'(x) = \sqrt{kx - x^2} + \dfrac{(k - 2x)\,x}{2\sqrt{kx - x^2}}$$

$$= \dfrac{2\,(kx - x^2) + kx - 2x^2}{2\sqrt{kx - x^2}}$$

$$= \dfrac{3kx - 4x^2}{2\sqrt{kx - x^2}}$$

$$= \dfrac{x\,(3k - 4x)}{2\sqrt{kx - x^2}}$$

For increasing function, the value of $f'(x) \geq 0$, $\forall\, x \in [0, 3]$.

Therefore, taking the denominator part,

$$kx - x^2 \geq 0 \qquad \forall\, x \in [0, 3]$$
$$x(x - k) \leq 0 \qquad \forall\, x \in [0, 3]$$
$$k \geq 3$$

Now, take the numerator part,

$$3k - 4x \geq 0 \qquad \forall\, x \in [0, 3]$$
$$4x - 3k \leq 0 \qquad \forall\, x \in [0, 3]$$
$$k \geq 4$$

Taking the minimum and common value of k, $m = 4$.

The maximum value of $f(x)$ when $k = 4$ is,

$$M = 3\left(\sqrt{(4)(3) - (3)^2}\right)$$
$$= 3\sqrt{3}$$

76. Correct Response : (d)

Explanation :

The given function is,

$$y = \tan^{-1}\left(\frac{\sin x - \cos x}{\sin x + \cos x}\right)$$
$$= \tan^{-1}\left(\frac{\tan x - 1}{\tan x + 1}\right)$$
$$= \tan^{-1}\left(\frac{\tan x - 1}{\tan x + 1}\right)$$
$$= -\frac{\pi}{4} + x$$

Differentiate the above equation with respect to x.

$$\frac{dy}{dx} = -1$$

The differentiation of $\dfrac{x}{2}$ with respect to x is $\dfrac{1}{2}$.

Therefore, the differentiation of y with respect to $\dfrac{x}{2}$ is,

$$\frac{dy}{d(x/2)} = \frac{1}{\dfrac{1}{2}}$$
$$= 2$$

77. Correct Response : (b)

Explanation :

The limit is computed as,

$$\lim_{x \to 0} \frac{(x + 2\sin x)\left(\sqrt{x^2 + 2\sin x + 1} + \sqrt{\sin^2 x - x + 1}\right)}{x^2 + 2\sin x + 1 - \sin^2 x + x - 1}$$

$$= \lim_{x \to 0} \frac{\left(1 + \dfrac{2\sin x}{x}\right)\left(\sqrt{x^2 + 2\sin x + 1} + \sqrt{\sin^2 x - x + 1}\right)}{x + 2\dfrac{\sin x}{x} + \dfrac{1}{x} - \dfrac{\sin^2 x}{x} + 1 - \dfrac{1}{x}}$$

$$= \frac{(1 + 2)(1 + 1)}{3}$$

$$= 2$$

78. Correct Response : (a)

Explanation :

The function $f(x)$ attains its maximum value at $x = 2$.

The function $g(x)$ attains its minimum value at $x = -1$.

So, the value of $-\alpha\beta$ is -2.

Therefore, the value of required limit is,

$$\lim_{x \to -\alpha\beta} \frac{(x - 1)(x^2 - 5x + 6)}{x^2 - 6x + 8}$$

$$= \lim_{x \to 2} \frac{(x - 1)(x - 2)(x - 3)}{(x - 2)(x - 4)}$$

$$= \lim_{x \to 2} \frac{(x - 1)(x - 3)}{(x - 4)}$$

$$= \frac{(1)(-1)}{(-2)}$$

$$= \frac{1}{2}$$

79. Correct Response : (b)

Explanation :

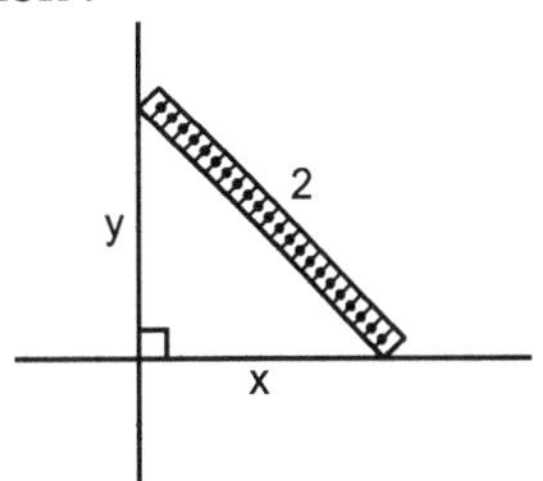

From the figure,

$$x^2 + y^2 = 4$$
$$2x\frac{dx}{dt} + 2y\frac{dy}{dt} = 0$$
$$\frac{dx}{dt} = -\frac{y}{x}\left(\frac{dy}{dt}\right)$$

When the upper ends is 1 m above the ground, the rate of sliding is,

$$\frac{dx}{dt} = \left(-\frac{1}{\sqrt{3}}\right)(25)$$
$$= -\frac{25}{\sqrt{3}}$$

80. Correct Response : (b, c, d)

Explanation :

The given function is,

$$f(x) = \begin{cases} x^5 + 5x^4 + 10x^2 + 3x + 1 & x < 0 \\ x^2 - x + 1 & 0 \leq x < 1 \\ \dfrac{2}{3}x^3 - 4x^2 + 7x - \dfrac{8}{3} & 1 \leq x < 3 \\ (x - 2)\ln(x - 2) - x + \dfrac{10}{3} & x \geq 3 \end{cases}$$

The differential value of the above function is,

$$f'(x) = \begin{cases} 5(x+1)^4 - 2 & x < 0 \\ 2x - 1 & 0 \le x < 1 \\ 2x^2 - 8x + 7 & 1 \le x < 3 \\ \ln(x-2) - x + \dfrac{10}{3} & x \ge 3 \end{cases}$$

$x^5 + 5x^4 + 10x^3 + 10x^2 + 3x + 1$ takes value between

$-\infty$ to 1 and $(x-2)\ln(x-2) - x + \dfrac{10}{3}$ also takes

values between $\dfrac{1}{3}$ to ∞.

So, the range of $f(x)$ is R.

$f''(1-) = 2$ and $f''(1+) = -4$.

Hence, $f'(x)$ is non-differentiable at $x = 1$.

$f'(x)$ has local maxima at $x = 1$.

81. Correct Response : (a, c, d)

Explanation :

The given function is,

$$f(n) = \frac{\displaystyle\sum_{k=0}^{n} \sin\left(\frac{k+1}{n+2}\pi\right) \sin\left(\frac{k+2}{n+1}\pi\right)}{\displaystyle\sum_{k=0}^{n} \sin^2\left(\frac{k+1}{n+2}\pi\right)}$$

Solve the above function.

$$f(n) = \frac{\displaystyle\sum_{k=0}^{n}\left(\cos\frac{\pi}{n+2} - \cos\left(\frac{2k+3}{n+2}\pi\right)\right)}{\displaystyle\sum_{k=0}^{n} 2\sin^2\left(\frac{k+1}{n+2}\pi\right)}$$

$$= \frac{(n+1)\cos\dfrac{\pi}{n+2} - \dfrac{\cos\left(\frac{n+3}{n+2}\right)\pi \sin\left(\frac{n+1}{n+1}\right)\pi}{\sin\dfrac{\pi}{n+1}}}{(n+1) - \dfrac{\cos\pi \sin\left(\frac{n+1}{n+2}\right)\pi}{\sin\dfrac{\pi}{n+2}}}$$

$$= \frac{(n+1)\cos\dfrac{\pi}{n+2} + \cos\left(\frac{n+3}{n+2}\right)\pi}{(n+1)+1}$$

$$= \frac{(n+1)\cos\dfrac{\pi}{n+2} + \cos\dfrac{\pi}{n+2}}{n+2}$$

$$= \cos\frac{\pi}{n+2}$$

Consider option (a)

$$f(4) = \cos\frac{\pi}{6}$$

$$= \frac{\sqrt{3}}{2}$$

Consider option (b).

$$\lim_{n \to \infty} f(n) = \cos\left(\frac{\pi}{n+2}\right)$$

$$= 1$$

Consider option (c).

$$\alpha = \tan(\cos^{-1} f(6))$$

$$= \tan\left(\cos^{-1}\left(\cos\frac{\pi}{8}\right)\right)$$

$$= \tan\frac{\pi}{8}$$

Consider option (d).

$$\sin(7\cos^{-1} f(5)) = \sin\left(7\cos^{-1}\left(\cos\frac{\pi}{7}\right)\right)$$

$$= \sin\pi$$

$$= 0$$

82. Correct Response : (a, b)

Explanation :

Consider option (a)

$$f(x) = \lim_{h \to 0} \frac{h-0}{\sqrt{|h|}}$$

$$= 0$$

Consider option (b).

$$f(x) = \lim_{h \to 0} \frac{h^{\frac{2}{3}} - 0}{\sqrt{|h|}}$$

$$= 0$$

Consider option (c).

$$f(x) = \lim_{h \to 0} \frac{f(h) - f(0)}{h^2}$$

$$= \lim_{h \to 0} \frac{h|h| - 0}{h^2}$$

does not exist.

Consider option (d).

$$f(x) = \lim_{h \to 0} \frac{\sin h - 0}{h^2}$$

does not exist.

83. Correct Response : (b, c, d)

Explanation :

The given function is,

$$f(x) = \frac{\sin \pi x}{x^2}$$

The derivative of the above function is,

$$f'(x) = \frac{2x \cos \pi x \left(\dfrac{\pi x}{2} - \tan \pi x\right)}{x^4}$$

The required diagram is shown in figure below.

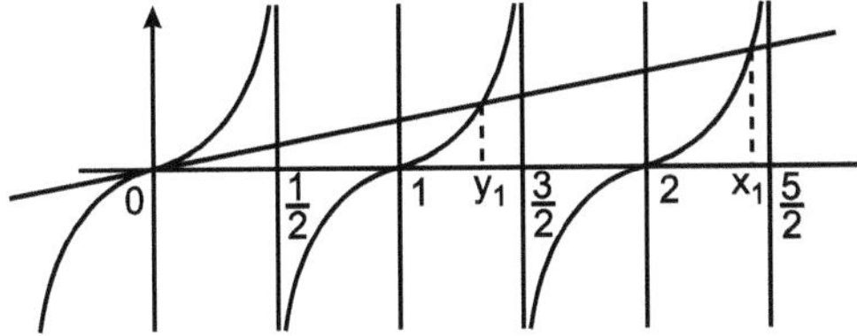

For $f'(x)$

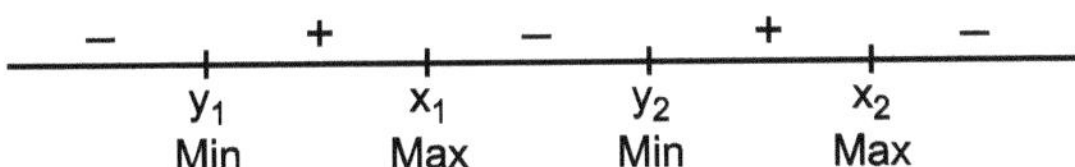

$$\begin{array}{cccc} - & + & - & + & - \\ y_1 & x_1 & y_2 & x_2 \\ \text{Min} & \text{Max} & \text{Min} & \text{Max} \end{array}$$

84. Correct Response : (a, b, d)

Explanation :

Then given function is,

$$f(x) = (x - 1)(x - 2)(x - 5)$$

The function to define is,

$$F(x) = \int_0^x f(t)\,dt$$

As $F(1)$ is negative and $F(2)$ is also negative. Hence, $F(x)$ cannot be zero for $x \in (0, 5)$.

Therefore,

$$F'(x) = f(x)$$
$$= (x - 1)(x - 2)(x - 5)$$

The required diagram is shown in the figure below.

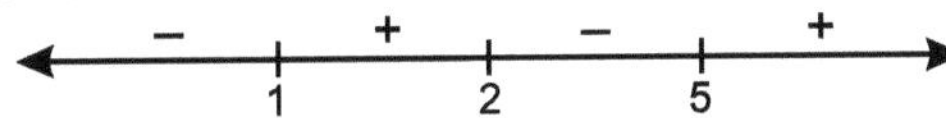

From the above figure.

$F(x)$ has two local minima points at $x = 1$ and $x = 5$ and

$F(x)$ has one local maxima point at $x = 2$.

85. Correct Response : (a, b)

Explanation :

Let $(a, f(a)) = r$.

Consider $f'(x)$ be differentiation of $f(x)$.

The equation of tangent is,

$$(y - f(a)) = f'(a)(x - a).$$

If $x = 0$, the above equation will be,

$$y - f(a) = -af'(a)$$
$$y = f(a) - af'(a)$$
$$y_p = (0, f(a) - af'(a))$$

Now,

$$\frac{py_p = 1}{\sqrt{a^2 + (af'(a))^2}} = 1$$

$$a^2 + (af'(a))^2 = 1$$

$$f'(a)^2 = \frac{1 - a^2}{a^2}$$

Put $a = x$ and integrate both sides of the above equation.

$$\int (f'(x)) = \pm \int \sqrt{\frac{1 - x^2}{x^2}}$$

Substitute $\sqrt{1 - x^2} = t$ in the above equation.

$$y = \pm \int \frac{-t^2}{1 - t^2}\,dt$$

$$= \pm \left(t - \frac{1}{2} \ln \left| \frac{1 + t}{1 - t} \right| \right) + c$$

$$= \pm \left(t - \frac{1}{2} \ln \frac{(1 + t)^2}{1 - t^2} \right) + c$$

$$= \pm \left(\sqrt{1 - x^2} - \ln \frac{1 + \sqrt{1 - x^2}}{x} \right) + c$$

Substitute $x = 1$ and $y = 0$.

Therefore, $c = 0$. Option a and b are correct.

86. Correct Response : (d)

Explanation :

The first order derivative of the function is as follows.

$$f_n'(x) = \frac{1}{1 + (x + n)^2} - \frac{1}{1 + x^2}$$

The value of the function is calculated as follows,

$$\sum_{j=1}^5 \tan^2(f_j(0)) = \sum_{j=1}^5 j^2$$

$$= 55$$

It is clear from the above expression that 0 is not in the domain of the function.

Hence, option (a) and (b) are false.

The definition of function is as follows,

$$f_n(x) = \sum_{j=1}^n \tan^{-1} \left(\frac{(x + j) - (x + j - 1)}{1 + (x + j)(x + j - 1)} \right)$$

$$= \sum_{j=1}^n \tan^{-1}(x + j) - \tan^{-1}(x + j - 1)$$

$$= \tan^{-1}(x + n) - \tan^{-1} x$$

On further simplifying the function,

$$\tan(f_n(x)) = \tan(\tan^{-1}(x + n) - \tan^{-1} x)$$

$$\tan(f_n(x)) = \frac{(x + n) - x}{1 + x(x + n)}$$

$$\tan(f_n(x)) = \frac{n}{1 + x^2 + nx}$$

Apply the limits in the above expression.

$$\lim_{x \to \infty} \tan(f_n(x)) = \lim_{x \to \infty} \frac{n}{1 + x^2 + nx}$$

$$= 0$$

Hence, option (c) is false.

The trigonometric identity in terms of secant and tangent of an angle is as follows.

$$\sec^2(f_n(x)) = 1 + \tan^2(f_n(x))$$

Substitute the values.

$$\sec^2(f_n(x)) = 1 + \left(\frac{n}{1+x^2+nx}\right)^2$$

$$\lim_{x\to\infty}\sec^2(f_n(x)) = \lim_{x\to\infty}\left(1+\left(\frac{n}{1+x^2+nx}\right)^2\right)$$

$$= 1$$

Hence, option (d) is true.

87. **Correct Response :** (b, c, d)

Explanation :

The definition of the function is,

$$\lim_{t\to x}\frac{f(x)\sin t - f(t)\sin x}{t-x} = \sin^2 x$$

$$\frac{f(x)\cos x - f'(x)\sin x}{\sin^2 x} = 1$$

$$-d\left(\frac{f(x)}{\sin x}\right) = 1$$

Integrate the equation,

$$\frac{f(x)}{\sin x} = -x + c$$

At $$x = \frac{\pi}{6}$$

$$f(x) = -\frac{\pi}{12}$$

$$\Rightarrow \qquad c = 0$$

The function becomes,

$$f(x) = -x\sin x$$

(a) The value of the function at $x = \dfrac{\pi}{4}$ is,

$$f\left(\frac{\pi}{4}\right) = -\frac{\pi}{4}\sin\left(\frac{\pi}{4}\right)$$

$$= -\frac{\pi}{4\sqrt{2}}$$

Hence, option (a) is not correct.

(b) The definition of the function is,

$$f(x) = -x\sin x$$

We know that,

$$\sin x > x - \frac{x^3}{6}$$

$$-x\sin x < -x^2 + \frac{x^4}{6}$$

$$f(x) < -x^2 + \frac{x^4}{6}\ \forall x \in (0,\pi)$$

Hence, option (b) is correct.

(c) The function is,

$$f'(x) = -\sin x - x\cos x$$

$$f'(x) = 0$$

$$\tan x = -x$$

For $\tan x = -x$, there exist $\alpha \in (0,\pi)$ for which $f'(\alpha) = 0$.

Hence, option (c) is correct.

(d) The first order derivative of the function is as follows.

$$f''(x) = -2\cos x + x\sin x$$

At $$x = \frac{\pi}{2},$$

$$f''\left(\frac{\pi}{2}\right) = \frac{\pi}{2}$$

$$f\left(\frac{\pi}{2}\right) = -\frac{\pi}{2}$$

Add the values,

$$f''\left(\frac{\pi}{2}\right) + f\left(\frac{\pi}{2}\right) = 0$$

Hence, option (d) is correct.

88. **Correct Response :** 0.4

Explanation :

The function is as follows,

$$\frac{dy}{dx} = (5y+2)(5y-2)$$

$$\frac{1}{25}\int\frac{dy}{\left(y+\frac{2}{5}\right)\left(y-\frac{2}{5}\right)} = \int dx$$

$$\frac{1}{20}\ln\left(\frac{5y-2}{5y+2}\right) = x + c$$

$$x = 0$$

At $$y = 0$$

Substitute the value in the function.

$$c = 0$$

Substitute the values.

$$\frac{2-5y}{2+5y} = e^{20x}$$

$$\lim_{x\to\infty}e^{20x} = 0$$

$$\lim_{x\to\infty}y = \frac{2}{5}$$

$$= 0.4$$

89. **Correct Response :** (c)

Explanation :

The given expression is,

$$\lim_{x\to 0}\frac{\left((27+x)^{\frac{1}{3}}-3\right)}{9-(27+x)^{\frac{2}{3}}}$$

Simplify the above expression.

$$\lim_{x \to 0} \frac{3\left(\left(1+\dfrac{x}{27}\right)^{\frac{1}{3}} - 1\right)}{9\left(1 - \left(1+\dfrac{x}{27}\right)^{\frac{2}{3}}\right)} \qquad \left(\because \dfrac{1}{x} \to \infty\right)$$

$$\lim_{x \to 0} \frac{1}{3}\left(\frac{\dfrac{x}{81}}{-\dfrac{2}{3}\cdot\dfrac{x}{27}}\right) = \frac{-1}{6}$$

90. **Correct Response :** (2)
Explanation :
The given expression is,

$$f(x) = \frac{1}{x} - \frac{k-1}{e^{2x}-1}; x \neq 0$$

The function $f(x)$ is continuous at $x = 0$.
Substitute $f(0)$ in the above equation.

$$f(0) = \lim_{x \to 0} \frac{1}{x} - \frac{k-1}{e^{2x}-1}$$

$$f(0) = \lim_{x \to 0} \frac{(e^{2x}-1)-(k-1)}{x(e^{2x}-1)}$$

$$= \lim_{x \to 0} \frac{\left(1+(2x)+\dfrac{1}{x!}(2x)^2+\ldots\ldots\ldots(-1-x(k-1))\right)}{2x^2\left(\dfrac{e^{2x}-1}{2x}\right)}$$

$$= \frac{\lim_{x \to 0}\left((2x)+\dfrac{1}{x!}(2x)^2+\ldots\ldots\ldots(-x(k-1))\right)}{\lim_{x \to 0} 2x^2\left(\dfrac{e^{2x}-1}{2x}\right)}$$

From the continuity equation,

$$f(0) = \lim_{x \to 0^+} f(x) = \lim_{x \to 0^-} f(x)$$

Clearly, $k = 3$ and $f(0) = 1$

91. **Correct Response :** (c)
Explanation :
The given equation is,

$$x = \sqrt{2^{\operatorname{cosec}^{-1}t}}$$

$$y = \sqrt{2^{\sec^{-1}t}}$$

Differentiate the above equation.

$$\frac{dy}{dx} = \frac{\left(\dfrac{dy}{dt}\right)}{\left(\dfrac{dx}{dt}\right)}$$

$$= \frac{\dfrac{1}{2\sqrt{2^{\sec^{-1}t}}} 2^{\sec^{-1}t} ln2\left(\dfrac{1}{t\sqrt{t^2-1}}\right)}{\dfrac{1}{2\sqrt{2^{\operatorname{cosec}^{-1}t}}} 2^{\operatorname{cosec}^{-1}t} ln2\left(\dfrac{1}{t\sqrt{t^2-1}}\right)}$$

$$= \frac{2^{\sec^{-1}t}}{2^{\operatorname{cosec}^{-1}t}}$$

$$= -\frac{y}{x}$$

92. **Correct Response :** (b)
Explanation :
For the given function $f(x)$

$$f(x) = 2x^3 - 9x^2 + 12x + 5, x \in [0, 3]$$

Differentiate the above function,

$$f'(x) = 6x^2 - 18x + 12$$

$$f'(x) = 6(x-1)(x-2)$$

Substitute the value in the function ($f'(x) = 0$, $x = 1, 2$)

$$f(1) = 2(1)^3 - 9(1)^2 + 12(1) + 5$$

$$= 10$$

$$f(2) = 9$$

For $x = 0$

$$f(0) = 5$$

For $x = 3$

$$f(3) = 14$$

Therefore, the maximum and minimum value is M = 14. So $m = 5$

Thus, the value of (M − m) is 9.

93. **Correct Response :** (a, b, d)
Explanation :
(a) It is clear from the definiton of the function $f(x)$ that the function is a continuous function. For every continuous function, there exists an open interval (r, s) where, $(r < s)$ such that function f is a one-one function on the open interval.
Hence, option (a) is true.
(b) The first order derivative of function is,

$$|f'(c)| = \left|\frac{f(-4)-f(0)}{-4-0}\right|$$

The limits of the function are as follows,

$$-2 \leq f(-4) \leq 2$$

$$-2 \leq f(0) \leq 2$$

Combine the above limits of the function,

$$-4 \leq f(-4) - f(0) \leq 4$$

Hence, $\qquad |f'(c)| \leq 1$

Hence, option (b) is true.
(c) The limit of the function $f(x)$ such that $x \to \infty$ is,

$$f(x) = 2\sin\left(\frac{\sqrt{85}x}{2}\right)$$

$$f'(x) = \sqrt{85}\cos\left(\frac{\sqrt{85}x}{2}\right)$$

$$f^2(0) + (f'(0)^2 = 85 \qquad \ldots(1)$$

It is clear from equation (1) that $\lim\limits_{x\to\infty} f(x)$ does not exist.

Hence, option (c) is false.

(d) Consider the function,

$$h(x) = f^2(x) + f'(x)^2$$
$$h(0) = 85$$

From option (b), there exist some real number such that $(f'(x))^2 \le 1$ for some x in the range $(-4, 0)$.

$$h(x_0) = f^2(x_0) + (f'(x_0)^2) \le 4 + 1$$
$$h(x_0) \le 5$$

Assume an element p such that $p \in (-4, 0)$ for which $h(p) = 5$.

Assume a small element q such that $q \in (0, 4)$ for which $h(q) = 5$.

Hence, by Rolle's theorem is (p, q).

$$h'(c) = 0$$
$$c \in (-4, 4)$$

Hence, $h(x) > 5$ as we move from $x = p$ to $x = q$ and $f^2(x) \le 4$,

$$\Rightarrow (f'(x))^2 \ge 1 \text{ in } (p, q)$$

Thus,

$$h'(c) = 0$$

This mean,

$$f'f + f'f'' = 0$$
$$f + f'' = 0 \text{ and } f' \ne 0$$

Hence, option (d) is true.

94. Correct Response : (b, c)

Explanation :

The first order derivative of the function is,

$$f'(x) = 0$$
$$e^{-f(x)} f'(x) - e^{g(x)} g'(x) = 0$$
$$\int \left(e^{-f(x)} f'(x) - e^{g(x)} g'(x) \right) dx = C$$
$$-e^{-f(x)} + e^{-g(x)} = C$$

On further expansion of the expression,

$$-e^{f(1)} + e^{-g(1)} = -e^{-f(2)} + e^{-g(2)}$$
$$-\frac{1}{e} + e^{-g(1)} = -e^{-f(2)} + \frac{1}{e}$$
$$e^{-f(2)} + e^{-g(1)} = \frac{2}{e}$$

The conclusion from the above expression is,

$$\therefore e^{-f(2)} < \frac{2}{e} \text{ and } e^{-g(1)} < \frac{2}{e}$$

$$\Rightarrow -f(2) < \log_e 2 - 1 \text{ and } -g(1) < \log_e 2 - 1$$
$$\Rightarrow f(2) < 1 - \log_e 2 \text{ and } g(1) < 1 - \log_e 2$$

95. Correct Response : 2

Explanation :

The number of real solution of the equation is,

$$\sin^{-1}\left(\sum_{i=1}^{\infty} x^{i+1} - x \sum_{i=1}^{\infty} \left(\frac{x}{2}\right)^i \right)$$
$$= \frac{\pi}{2} - \cos^{-1}\left(\sum_{i=1}^{\infty} \left(\frac{-x}{2}\right)^i - \sum_{i=1}^{\infty} (x)^i \right)$$
$$\frac{x^2}{1-x} - x\frac{\frac{x}{2}}{\left(1-\frac{x}{2}\right)} = \frac{x}{1+x} + \frac{\left(-\frac{x}{2}\right)}{1+\frac{x}{2}}$$
$$\frac{x^2}{1-x} - \frac{x}{1+x} = \frac{x^2}{2-x} - \frac{x}{2+x}$$
$$x^3 + 2x^2 + 5x - 2 = 0 \text{ or } x = 0$$

The root of the equation is,

$$f(x) = x^3 + 2x^2 + 5x - 2$$
$$f'(x) > 0$$
$$f(0) = -2$$
$$f\left(\frac{1}{2}\right) = \frac{9}{8}$$

It is clear from the above calculation that one root lies between 0 and $\dfrac{1}{2}$.

So, the equation has 2 roots.

96. Correct Response : (a, c, d)

Explanation :

Check the discontinuity at $x = m$.

$$f(m) = m \cos 2m\pi = m$$
$$f(m^+) = m \cos 2m\pi = m$$
$$f(m^-) = m \cos (2m-1)\pi = -m$$

It can be seen that the above function is discontinuous for every given integer except 0.

97. Correct Response : 2

Explanation :

The given function is :

$$g(x) = \int_{x}^{\frac{\pi}{2}} \left[f'(t) \operatorname{cosec} t - \cot t \operatorname{cosec} t \, f(t) \right] dt$$
$$= \left| f(t) \operatorname{cosec}(t) \right|_{x}^{\pi/2}$$
$$= \left(3 - \frac{f(x)}{\sin x} \right)$$

The limit is calculated as :

$$\lim_{x\to 0} g(x) = \lim_{x\to 0}\left(3 - \frac{f(x)}{\sin x} \right)$$

$$= 3 - \lim_{x \to 0} \frac{f'(x)}{\cos x}$$

$$= 3 - 1$$

$$= 2$$

98. Correct Response : (b)

Explanation :

For column 1 :

$$f(x) = x + ln\ x - x\ ln,\ x,\ x \in (0, \infty)$$

(I)

$$f(1) = 1 + ln\ 1 - (1)\ ln\ 1$$
$$= 1 > 0$$
$$f(e^2) = e^2 + ln\ e^2 - e^2\ ln\ e^2$$
$$= e^2 + 2 - 2e^2$$
$$= 2 - e^2$$
$$= -5.38 < 1$$

Therefore, $f(x) = 0$ for some $x \in (1, e^2)$

I is correct.

(II)

$$f(x) = x + ln\ x - x\ ln\ x,\ x \in (0, \infty)$$

$$f'(x) = 1 + \frac{1}{x} - ln\ x - 1 = \frac{1}{x} - ln\ x$$

$$f'(1) = \frac{1}{1} - ln\ 1 = 1$$

$$f'(e) = \frac{1}{e} - ln\ e = \frac{1}{e} - 1 < 0$$

Therefore, $f'(x) = 0$ for some $x \in (1, e)$.

II is correct.

(III)

$$f''(x) = -\frac{1}{x^2} - \frac{1}{x}$$

$$= -\frac{(1+x)}{x^2} < 0\ \text{for}\ x \in (0, \infty)$$

As the double derivative is negative and doesn't change sign $f'(x)$ is strictly decreasing in the interval $x \in (0, \infty)$.

Therefore, III is wrong.

(IV)

$$f''(x) = -\frac{1}{x^2} - \frac{1}{x}$$

$$f''(1) = -\frac{1}{1^2} - \frac{1}{1}$$

$$= -2$$

$$f''(e) = -\frac{1}{e^2} - \frac{1}{e}$$

$$= -0.5$$

Since, $f''(x)$ is always negative in the interval $x \in (1, e)$. It cannot be zero for $x \in (1, e)$.

Therefore, (IV) is wrong.

For Column 2 :

$$\lim_{x \to \infty} f(x) = \lim_{x \to \infty} \left(x + ln\ x - x ln\ x\right)$$

$$= \lim_{x \to \infty} x - (x - 1)\left(ln\ x - 1\right)$$

$$= -\infty$$

(i) is not correct.

(ii) is correct.

(iii)

$$\lim_{x \to \infty} f'(x) = \lim_{x \to \infty} \left(\frac{1}{x} - ln\ x\right)$$

$$= -\infty$$

Therefore, (iii) is correct.

(iv)

$$\lim_{x \to \infty} f''(x) = \lim_{x \to \infty} \left(-\frac{1}{x^2} - \frac{1}{x}\right)$$

$$= 0$$

Therefore, (iv) is correct.

For Column 3 :

(P)

$$f'(x) = 1 + \frac{1}{x} - ln\ x - 1$$

$$= \frac{1}{x} - 1 < 0$$

$$f'(0) = \infty > 0$$

$$f'(1) = \frac{1}{1} - 2\ ln\ e$$

$$= 1 > 0$$

Therefore, $f(x)$ is increasing in the interval $(0, 1)$. P is correct.

(Q)

$$f'(x) = \frac{1}{x} - ln\ x$$

$$f'(e) = \frac{1}{e} - ln\ e$$

$$= \frac{1}{e} - ln\ e$$

$$f'(e^2) = \frac{1}{e^2} - ln\ e^2$$

$$= \frac{1}{e^2} - ln\ e^2$$

$$= \frac{1}{e^2} - 2 < 0$$

Therefore, $f(x)$ is decreasing in the interval (e, e^2). Q is correct.

(R)

$$f''(x) = -\frac{1}{x^2} - \frac{1}{x}$$

$$f''(0) = -\infty < 0$$

$$f''(1) = -\frac{1}{1^2} - \frac{1}{1}$$

$$= -2 < 0$$

Therefore, $f'(x)$ is decreasing in the interval $(0, 1)$. R is correct.

(S)

$$f''(x) = -\frac{1}{x^2} - \frac{1}{x}$$

$$= -\left(\frac{1}{x^2} + \frac{1}{x}\right) < 0 \text{ for } x \in (e, e^2)$$

Therefore, $f'(x)$ is decreasing in the interval (e, e^2). S is correct.

99. Correct Response : (b)

Explanation :

(II)

$$f(x) = x + \ln x - x \ln x, x \in (0, \infty)$$

$$f'(x) = 1 + \frac{1}{x} - \ln x - 1 = \frac{1}{x} - \ln x$$

$$f'(1) = \frac{1}{1} - \ln 1 = 1$$

$$f'(e) = \frac{1}{e} - \ln e = \frac{1}{e} - 1 < 0$$

Therefore, $f'(x) = 0$ for some $x \in (1, e)$. II is correct.

(iii)

$$\lim_{x \to \infty} f'(x) = \lim_{x \to \infty}\left(\frac{1}{x} - \ln x\right)$$

$$= -\infty$$

Therefore, (iii) is correct.

(S)

$$f''(x) = -\frac{1}{x^2} - \frac{1}{x}$$

$$= -\left(\frac{1}{x^2} + \frac{1}{x}\right) < 0 \text{ for } x \in (e, e^2)$$

Therefore, $f'(x)$ is decreasing in the interval (e, e^2). S is correct.

II, (iii) and S are correct.

100. Correct Response : (c)

Explanation :

(III)

$$f''(x) = -\frac{1}{x^2} - \frac{1}{x}$$

$$= -\frac{(1+x)}{x^2} < 0 \text{ for } x \in (0, \infty)$$

As the double derivative is negative and doesn't change sign $f'(x)$ is strictly decreasing in the interval $x \in (0, \infty)$.

Therefore, III is wrong.

(i)

$$\lim_{x \to \infty} f(x) = \lim_{x \to \infty}(x + \ln x - x\ln x)$$

$$= \lim_{x \to \infty} x - (x-1)(\ln x - 1)$$

$$= -\infty$$

(i) is not correct.

(R)

$$f''(x) = -\frac{1}{x^2} - \frac{1}{x}$$

$$f''(0) = -\infty < 0$$

$$f''(1) = -\frac{1}{1^2} - \frac{1}{1}$$

$$= -2 < 0$$

Therefore, $f'(x)$ is decreasing in the interval $(0, 1)$. R is correct.

III, i, R is incorrect.

101. Correct Response : (d)

Explanation :

It is given that $f''(x) > 0$ which implies that $f'(x)$ is an increasing function. By Lagrange's mean value theorem in the interval $\left[\frac{1}{2}, 1\right]$.

$$f'(x) = \frac{f(1) - f\left(\frac{1}{2}\right)}{1 - \frac{1}{2}}$$

$$= \frac{1 - \frac{1}{2}}{1 - \frac{1}{2}}$$

$$= 1$$

As $f'(x)$ is increasing function, the slope at end point is greater than average slope of the graph.

$$f'(1) > 1$$

102. Correct Response : (a, c)

Explanation :

The given condition is :

$$f'(x) > 2f(x)$$

$$e^{-2x} f'(x) > e^{-2x} 2f(x)$$

$$e^{-2x} f'(x) - e^{-2x} 2f(x) > 0$$

$$\frac{d}{dx}\left(e^{-2x} f(x)\right) > 0$$

This implies that $e^{-2x} f(x)$ is strictly increasing function.

$$e^{-2x} f(x) > e^{-2(0)} f(0) \ \vee \ x \in (0, \infty)$$
$$e^{-2x} f(x) > f(0)$$
$$f(x) > e^{2x}$$

Therefore, the value is calculated as :

$$f'(x) > 2f(x)$$
$$> 2e^{2x}$$
$$> 0$$

This shows that $f(x)$ is increasing function in the interval $x \in (0, \infty)$.

103. Correct Response : (a, d)

Explanation :

The given function is :

$$f(x) = \frac{1 - x(1 + |1 - x|)}{|1 - x|} \cos\left(\frac{1}{1 - x}\right)$$

The left hand limit is given by :

$$\lim_{x \to 1^-} f(x) = \lim_{x \to 1^-} \frac{1 - x(1 + (1 - x))}{1 - x} \cos\left(\frac{1}{1 - x}\right)$$
$$= \lim_{x \to 1^-} \frac{1 - x - x + x^2}{1 - x} \cos\left(\frac{1}{1 - x}\right)$$
$$= \lim_{x \to 1^-} \frac{(1 - x)^2}{1 - x} \cos\left(\frac{1}{1 - x}\right)$$
$$= \lim_{x \to 1^-} (1 - x) \cos\left(\frac{1}{1 - x}\right)$$
$$= 0$$

The right hand limit is given by :

$$\lim_{x \to 1^+} f(x) = \lim_{x \to 1^+} \frac{1 - x(1 - (1 - x))}{x - 1} \cos\left(\frac{1}{1 - x}\right)$$
$$= \lim_{x \to 1^-} \frac{1 - x + x - x^2}{x - 1} \cos\left(\frac{1}{1 - x}\right)$$
$$= \lim_{x \to 1^-} \frac{1 - x^2}{1 - x} \cos\left(\frac{1}{1 - x}\right)$$
$$= \lim_{x \to 1^-} (1 + x) \cos\left(\frac{1}{1 - x}\right)$$

The right hand limit doesn't exist.

104. Correct Response : (b, c)

Explanation :

The given function is :

$$f(x) = \begin{vmatrix} \cos(2x) & \cos(2x) & \sin(2x) \\ -\cos x & \cos x & -\sin x \\ \sin x & \sin x & \cos x \end{vmatrix}$$

$$= \begin{vmatrix} 0 & \cos(2x) & \sin(2x) \\ -2\cos x & \cos x & -\sin x \\ 0 & \sin x & \cos x \end{vmatrix}$$

$$= 2 \cos x \, (\cos (2x) \cos x - \sin (2x) \sin x)$$
$$= 2 \cos x \cos (3x)$$
$$= \cos 4x + \cos (2x)$$

Differentiate the given function with respect to x on both sides.

$$f'(x) = -4 \sin (4x) - 2 \sin (2x)$$
$$0 = -2 \sin (2x) (4 \cos (2x) + 1)$$

Solve the above equation for x.

$$\sin (2x) = 0$$

$$x = 0, \frac{\pi}{2}, -\frac{\pi}{2}$$

Or

$$\cos (2x) = -\frac{1}{4}$$

$$1 - 2 \sin^2 (x) = -\frac{1}{4}$$

$$2 \sin^2 (x) = \frac{5}{4}$$

$$x = \pm\sin^{-1}\sqrt{\frac{5}{8}}, \pi - \sin^{-1}\sqrt{\frac{5}{8}}, -\pi + \sin^{-1}\sqrt{\frac{5}{8}}$$

The function $f'(x)$ has more than 3 solution in the interval $(-\pi, \pi)$.

Obtain the double derivative of the function $f(x)$ as :

$$f''(x) = -16 \cos (4x) - 4 \cos (2x)$$
$$f'' (0) = -20$$

Therefore, $f(x)$ has maxima at $x = 0$.

105. Correct Response : (a)

Explanation :

Given curves are,

$$x = 4t^2 + 3$$

And,

$$y = 8t^3 - 1$$

Differentiate the curves with respect to t,

$$\frac{dx}{dt} = 8t + 0$$
$$= 8t$$

And,

$$\frac{dy}{dt} = 24t^2 - 0$$
$$= 24t^2$$

Now the value of $\frac{dy}{dx}$ is,

$$\frac{dy}{dx} = \frac{dy/dt}{dx/dt}$$

$$= \frac{24t^2}{8t}$$

$$= 3t$$

The equation of the tangent at point $P(x_1, y_1)$ is,

$$y - y_1 = \frac{dy}{dx}(x - x_1)$$

Here, $(x_1, y_1) \equiv (4t^2 + 3, 8t^3 - 1)$.

Substitute the value in the above equation of the tangent

$$y - 8t^3 + 1 = 3t(x - 4t^2 - 3)$$

Consider the point $Q\left(4t_1^2 + 3, 8t_1^3 - 1\right)$ will satisfy

The above equation of the tangent at point P.

Therefore,

$$8t_1^3 - 1 - 8t^3 + 1 = 3t\left(4t_1^2 + 3 - 4t^2 - 3\right)$$

$$8\left(t_1 - t\right)\left(t_1^2 + t_1 t + t^2\right) = 3t \cdot 4\left(t_1 - t\right)\left(t_1 + t\right)$$

$$2t_1^2 + 2t_1 t - t^2 = 0$$

$$\left(t_1 - t\right)\left(2t_1 + t\right) = 0$$

Simplify the above equation to find the value of t

$$t_1 = -\frac{t}{2}$$

Hence, the point Q is $(t^2 + 3, -t^3 - 1)$.

106. Correct Response : (a)

Explanation :

Given, the differential equation is,

$$f'(x) = 2 - \frac{f(x)}{x}$$

$$\frac{dy}{dx} + \frac{1}{x}y = 2 \begin{bmatrix} \text{replace } f(x) \to y \\ \text{and } f'(x) \to \dfrac{dy}{dx} \end{bmatrix}$$

The integral function of the equation is,

$$IF = e^{\int \frac{1}{x}dx}$$

$$= e^{\ln x}$$

$$= x$$

The solution of the differential equation is,

$$y(IF) = \int 2(IF)dx$$

$$yx = 2\frac{x^2}{2} + c$$

$$y = x + \frac{c}{x}$$

For the value of $x = 1$ and $y \neq 1$,

$$1 \neq 1 + \frac{c}{1}$$

$$c \neq 0$$

(a)

From the given differential equation,

$$f'(x) = 1 - \frac{c}{x^2}$$

$$f'\left(\frac{1}{x}\right) = 1 - cx^2 \quad \left[x \to \frac{1}{x}\right]$$

Hence, the value of the limit,

$$\lim_{x \to 0^+} f'\left(\frac{1}{x}\right) = 1 - 0$$

$$= 1$$

(b)

From the solution of the differential equation,

$$xf\left(\frac{1}{x}\right) = x\left(\frac{1}{x} + cx\right)$$

$$= 1 + cx^2$$

Hence, the value of the limit,

$$\lim_{x \to 0^+} xf\left(\frac{1}{x}\right) = 1 + 0$$

$$= 1$$

(c)

From the given differential equation,

$$x^2 f'(x) = x^2\left(1 - \frac{c}{x^2}\right)$$

$$= x^2 - c$$

Hence, the value of the limit,

$$\lim_{x \to 0^+} x^2 f'(x) = -c$$

$$\neq 0$$

(d)

From the solution of the differential equation,

$$|f(x)| = \left|x + \frac{c}{x}\right|, x > 0$$

$$= x + \frac{c}{x}$$

Let, $c = 2$

Hence, $|f(x)| = x + \frac{2}{x}$

Let, $x = 1$

Hence, $|f(x)| = 1 + \frac{2}{1}$

$$= 3$$

Therefore, the above value contradicts

$$|f(x)| \leq 2.$$

107. **Correct Response :** 7

Explanation :

The given expression is,

$$\lim_{x\to 0}\frac{x^2\sin(\beta x)}{\alpha x-\sin x}=1$$

Simplify the given expression,

$$\lim_{x\to 0}\frac{x^2\left[\beta x-\dfrac{(\beta x)^3}{3!}+...\right]}{\alpha x-\left(x-\dfrac{x^3}{3!}+...\right)}=1$$

$$\lim_{x\to 0}\frac{\left[\beta x^3-\dfrac{\left(\beta^3 x^5\right)}{6}+...\right]}{\left((\alpha-1)x-\dfrac{x^3}{6}+...\right)}=1$$

Hence, the given expression is satisfy the relation,

$$\alpha-1=0$$
$$\alpha=1$$

And, $$6\beta=1$$

$$\beta=\frac{1}{6}$$

Hence, the required value is,

$$6(\alpha+\beta)=6\left(1+\frac{1}{6}\right)$$

$$=7$$

108. **Correct Response :** (d)

Explanation :

The equation of the curve is,

$$x^2+2xy-3y^2=0 \qquad ...(1)$$

Differentiate the above expression with respect to x.

$$2x+2\left(x\frac{dy}{dx}+y\right)-6y\frac{dy}{dx}=0$$

$$\frac{dy}{dx}=\frac{-(x+y)}{(x-3y)}$$

At point (1, 1)

$$\frac{dy}{dx}=\frac{-(1+1)}{(1-3\times 1)}$$

$$m=1$$

The slope of the normal is,

$$m_1=-\frac{1}{m}$$

$$=-1$$

The equation of the normal passing through the point (1, 1) is,

$$y-1=-1(x-1)$$
$$x+y=2$$
$$y=2-x$$

From equation (1),

$$x^2+2x(2-x)-3(2-x)^2=0$$
$$x^2+4x-2x^2-3(4+x^2-4x)=0$$
$$x^2-4x+3=0$$
$$(x-1)(x-3)=0$$

The values of x obtained are,

$$x=1 \text{ and } 3,$$

For $x=1$,

$$y=2-1$$
$$=1$$

For $x=3$,

$$y=2-3$$
$$=-1$$

The intersecting points are (1, 1) and (3, − 1). Hence, it is the curve again in the fourth quadrant.

109. **Correct Response :** 2

Explanation :

The given expression is,

$$\underbrace{\lim_{\alpha\to 0}\left(\frac{e^{\cos(\alpha^n)}-e}{\alpha^m}\right)}_{\text{L.H.S.}}=\underbrace{-\left(\frac{e}{2}\right)}_{\text{R.H.S.}}$$

Simplify the LHS of the given expression,

$$\lim_{\alpha\to 0}\left(\frac{e^{\cos(\alpha^n)}-e}{\alpha^m}\right)=\lim_{\alpha\to 0}\left(\frac{e\left\{e^{\cos(\alpha^n)-1}-1\right\}}{\alpha^m}\right)$$

$$=\lim_{\alpha\to 0}\left(\frac{e\left\{e^{\cos(\alpha^n)-1}-1\right\}}{\left\{\cos(\alpha^n)-1\right\}}\cdot\frac{\left\{\cos(\alpha^n)-1\right\}(\alpha^n)^2}{(\alpha^n)^2}\frac{(\alpha^n)^2}{\alpha^m}\right)$$

$$=e(\ln e)\left(\frac{-1}{2}\right)\alpha^{2n-m}$$

Now, replace the L.H.S. with the simplified value in the given expression is,

$$e(\ln e)\left(\frac{-1}{2}\right)\alpha^{2n-m}=-\frac{e}{2}$$

$$\left(-\frac{e}{2}\right)\alpha^{2n-m}=-\frac{e}{2}$$

$$\alpha^{2n-m}=1$$

$$2n-m=0$$

Further, simplify the above expression,

$$\frac{m}{n} = 2$$

110. Correct Response : (b, c)

Explanation :

The given values of the function is,

$$f(-1) = 3$$
$$f(0) = 6$$
$$f(2) = 0$$
$$g(-1) = 0$$

And,
$$g(0) = 1$$
$$g(2) = -1$$

Consider a function $h(x)$,

$$h(x) = f(x) - 3g(x) \qquad ....(1)$$

Substitute $x = -1$ in the above equation,

$$h(-1) = f(-1) - 3g(-1)$$
$$= 3 - 3\,(0)$$
$$= 3$$

Substitute $x = 0$ in equation (1).

$$h(0) = f(0) - 3g(0)$$
$$= 6 - 3\,(1)$$
$$= 3$$

Substitute $x = 2$ in equation (1).

$$h(2) = f(2) - 3g(2)$$
$$= 0 - 3\,(-1)$$
$$= 3$$

By Rolles theorem, we get at least one solution for $h'(x) = 0$ in $(-1, 0)$ and at least one solution for $h'(x) = 0$ in $(0, 2)$.

Differentiate equation (1) with respect to x,

$$h'(x) = f'(x) - 3g'(x)$$

The solution for the $h'(x) = 0$ is,

$$h'(x) = 0$$
$$f'(x) - 3g'(x) = 0$$
$$f'(x) = 3\,g'(x)$$

Again differentiate the above equation,

$$h''(x) = f''(x) - 3g''(x)$$

Now the function at $(-1, 0)$ and $(0, 2)$ is,

$$(f - 3g)'' = h''(x)$$
$$\neq 0$$

Hence, $h'(x)$ is monotonic. so, the function has exactly one solution in $(-1, 0)$ and exactly one solution at $(0, 2)$.

111. Correct Response : (d)

Explanation :

The given derivative of the function is,

$$f'(x) = \frac{192x^3}{2 + \sin^4(\pi x)} > 0$$

The limit x increases from $\dfrac{1}{2}$ to 1.

Substitute $x = \dfrac{1}{2}$ and $x = 1$ in the above derivative function,

$$f'\!\left(\frac{1}{2}\right) = \frac{192\left(\frac{1}{2}\right)^3}{2 + \sin^4\left(\pi\left(\frac{1}{2}\right)\right)}$$

$$= 8$$

$$f'(1) = \frac{192\,(1)^3}{2 + \sin^4(\pi(l))}$$

$$= 96$$

Therefore, $f'(x)$ increases 8 to 96

$$8 < \frac{f(1) - f\left(\frac{1}{2}\right)}{1 - \frac{1}{2}} < 96$$

$$4 < f(1) < 48$$

$$\frac{1}{2} \times \frac{1}{2} \times 4 \le \int_{\frac{1}{2}}^{1} f(x)\,dx \le \frac{1}{2} \times \frac{1}{2} \times 48$$

$$1 \le \int_{\frac{1}{2}}^{1} f(x)\,dx \le 12$$

112. Correct Response : (a, b, c)

Explanation :

The given value of the function is,

$$F(1) = 0$$
$$F(3) = -4$$
$$F'(x) < 0,\ x \in \left(\frac{1}{2}, 3\right)$$

Given that $f(x)$ is design in $\left(\dfrac{1}{2}, 3\right)$.

$$f(x) = xF(x)$$
$$f'(x) = F(x) + xF'(x),\ x \in (1, 3) \qquad ...(1)$$

So, $f(x)$ is decreasing.

(a)
$$f'(1) = F(1) + (1)\,F'(1)$$
$$< 0$$

So, option (a) is correct

(b)
$$F(1) = 1F(1)$$
$$= 0$$
$$F(3) = 3F(3)$$
$$= -12$$

Therefore,
$$f(2) < 0$$
So, option (b) is also correct.

(c)
$$f'(x) < 0$$
So,
$$f'(x) \neq 0 \text{ and } x \in (1, 3)$$
So, option (c) is correct.

Hence, (d) is incorrect.

113. Correct Response : (c)

Explanation :

The given differential equation is,
$$\left(x \log x\right)\frac{dy}{dx} + y = 2x \log x$$

$$\frac{dy}{dx} + \frac{y}{x \log x} = 2$$

The integrating factor (I.F.) is,
$$I.F. = e^{\int \frac{1}{x \log x} dx}$$
$$= e^{\log (\log x)}$$
$$= \log x$$

Solution of the differential equation is,
$$y \cdot (I.F.) = \int Q \cdot (I.F.) dx + c$$

$$y \log x = \int 2 \log x \, dx + c$$

$$y \log x = 2x \left[\log x - 1\right] + c$$

At $x = 1$, $y = 0$, the above equation becomes,
$$0 = -2 + c$$
$$c = 2$$

Hence, the solution of the differential equation is,
$$y \log x = 2x \left[\log x - 1\right] + 2$$

Put $x = e$,
$$y \log e = 2e \left[\log e - 1\right] + 2$$
$$y = 2$$

114. Correct Response : 4

Explanation :

The figure of the cylindrical container is,

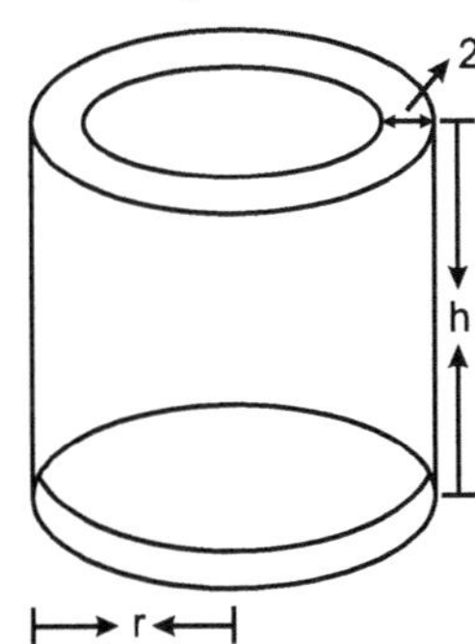

The expression for the inner volume V is,
$$V = \pi(r - 2)^2 h$$

Volume of the material used,
$$V_m = 4h\left(\frac{r + r - 2}{2}\right)\pi + 2\pi r^2$$

$$V_m = 4h(r - 1)\pi + 2\pi r^2$$

$$V_m = \frac{4(r - 1)V}{(r - 2)^2} + 2\pi r^2$$

Here,
$$\frac{dV_m}{dr} = 0$$

$$4V\left(\frac{(r - 2)^2 - (r - 1)2(r - 2)}{(r - 2)^4}\right) + 4\pi r = 0$$

Substitute $r = 12$ as inner radius is 10.
$$4V\left(\frac{100 - 220}{10000}\right) + 48\pi = 0$$

$$\frac{48V}{1000} - 48\pi = 0$$

$$\frac{V}{250\pi} = 4$$

115. Correct Response : (a, d)

Explanation :

The given values is,
$$g(0) = 0$$
$$g'(0) = 0$$
$$g'(1) \neq 0$$

And the function is,
$$f(x) = \begin{cases} g(x) & x > 0 \\ 0 & x = 0 \\ -g(x) & x < 0 \end{cases}$$

Differentiate the above function with respect to x,
$$f'(x) = \begin{cases} g'(x) & x > 0 \\ 0 & x = 0 \\ -g'(x) & x < 0 \end{cases}$$

Hence, it is clear that the function $f(x)$ is differentiable at $x = 0$, as $g'(0) = 0$.

Hence, option (a) is true.

The given function is,
$$h(x) = e^{|x|}$$

The graph of the given function $h(x) = e^{|x|}$ is,

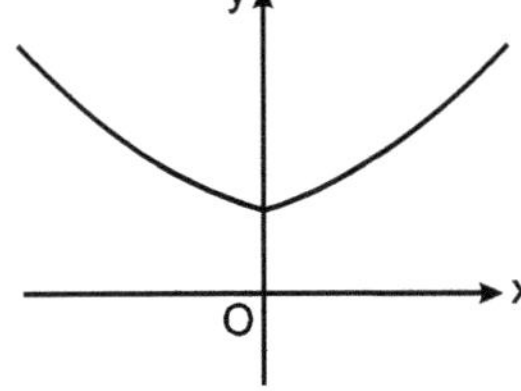

Hence, it is clear that it is not differentiable at $x = 0$.

Hence, option (b) is not true.

The given function is,

$$foh(x) = f(h\,(x)) \qquad [\text{as } h(x) > 0]$$

So, $\qquad f(h\,(x)) = g(h(x))$

Differentiate both sides with respect to x,

$$\frac{df\big(h(x)\big)}{dx} = g'(h(x))\,h'(x)$$

Since, $\qquad g'\,(1) \neq 0$

Hence, at $x = 0$, $f(h(x))$ is not differentiable.

Hence, option (c) is not true.

For the given function,

$$hof(x) = h\,(f\,(x))$$
$$= e^{|f(x)|}$$

It is differentiable at $x = 0$

Hence, option (d) is true.

116. **Correct Response :** (a) – (P, Q), (b) – (P, Q), (c) – (P, Q, S, T), (d) – (Q, T)

Explanation :

(a) – (P, Q)

Calculate the value of $|\alpha|$ by the given relation,

$$\frac{\big(\alpha\,\hat{i}+\beta\,\hat{j}\big).\big(\sqrt{3}\,\hat{i}+\hat{j}\big)}{\sqrt{\big(\sqrt{3}\big)^2+1}} = \sqrt{3}$$

Given,

$$\alpha = 2 + \sqrt{3}\beta \qquad ...(1)$$

Then,

$$\sqrt{3}\alpha + \beta = \pm 2\sqrt{3} \qquad ....(2)$$

Solving the equation (1) and (2).

$$\alpha = 2 \text{ or } -1$$
$$|\alpha| = 2 \text{ or } 1$$

(b) – (P, Q)

The given function is,

$$f(x) = \begin{cases} -3ax^2 - 2, & x < 1 \\ bx + a^2, & x \geq 1 \end{cases}$$

Differentiate with respect to x,

$$f'(x) = \begin{cases} -6ax, & x < 1 \\ b, & x \geq 1 \end{cases}$$

Differentiate with respect to x,

$$f'(x) = \begin{cases} -6ax, & x < 1 \\ b, & x \geq 1 \end{cases}$$

Solve the right hand limit,

$$f'(1^-) = \frac{f(1+h) - f(1)}{h}$$

$$= b \qquad ...(1)$$

Also solve the left hand limit,

$$f'(1^-) = \lim_{h \to 0} \frac{-3a(1-h)^2 - 2 - \big(b+a^2\big)}{-h}$$

$$= \lim_{h \to 0} \frac{-3a\big(1 - 2h + h^2\big) - 2 - \big(b + a^2\big)}{-h}$$

$$= -6a \qquad ...(2)$$

The condition for the differentiable function,

$$f'(1^+) = f'(1^-)$$
$$b = -6a \qquad ...(3)$$

The given value is differentiable at $x = 1$ if,

$$f(1^-) = f(1^+)$$
$$-3a - 2 = b + a^2$$
$$-3a - 2 - b - a^2 = 0$$
$$a^2 + 3a + 2 + b = 0 \qquad ...(4)$$

From (3) and (4)

$$a^2 + 3a + 2 - 6a = 0$$
$$a^2 - 3a + 2 = 0$$
$$a = 1, 2$$

(c) – (P, Q, S and T)

Simplify the given expression,

$$\big(3 - 3\omega + 2\omega^2\big)^{4n+3} + \left(\frac{3 - 3\omega + 2\omega^2}{\omega^2}\right)^{4n+3}$$

$$+ \left(\frac{3 - 3\omega + 2\omega^2}{\omega^2}\right)^{4n+3} = 0$$

$$\big(3 - 3\omega + 2\omega^2\big)^{4n+3} + \left\{1 + \left(\frac{1}{\omega^2}\right)^{4n+3} + \left(\frac{1}{\omega}\right)^{4n+3}\right\} = 0$$

$$1 + (\omega)^{4n+3} + \big(\omega^2\big)^{4n+3} = 0$$

Hence, the value $4n + 3$ is not multiple of 3 and the possible values of the n are 1, 2, 4 and 5 but not for $n = 3$.

(d) – (Q, T)

Given that the harmonic value of the real number is,

$$\frac{2ab}{a+b} = 4$$

$$\frac{ab}{a+b} = 2$$

$$\frac{a(15 - 2a)}{a + 15 - 2a} = 2$$

$$a = \frac{5}{2}, 6 \qquad ...(1)$$

Given, that the values a, 5, q, b in arithmetic progression,

$$2q = 5 + b$$

And, $\qquad 10 = a + q$

Then, $\qquad a + b + q + 5 = 10 + 2q$

$$b - 5 = q - a \qquad \qquad ...(2)$$

From (1) and (2)

$$q - a = 5 \text{ or } -2$$

117. Correct Response : (c)

Explanation :

The given differential equation is,

$$\frac{dp(t)}{dt} = \frac{1}{2}p(t) - 200$$

By integrating the given equation,

$$\frac{dp(t)}{\left(\frac{1}{2}p(t) - 200\right)} = dt$$

$$\int \frac{dp(t)}{\frac{1}{2}p(t) - 200} = \int dt$$

$$2\log\left(\frac{p(t)}{2} - 200\right) = t + c$$

$$\frac{p(t)}{2} - 200 = e^{\frac{t}{2}}k \qquad \qquad ...(1)$$

Substitute the given value $p(0) = 100$,

$$\frac{100}{2} - 200 = e^{\frac{0}{2}}k$$

$$-150 = k$$

Substitute the value of the k in the equation (1),

$$p(t) = 400 - 300e^{\frac{t}{2}}$$

118. Correct Response : (c)

Explanation :

Let tangent to $y^2 = 4x$ be,

$$y = mx + \frac{1}{m}$$

This is also tangent to $x^2 = -32y$,

$$x^2 + 32mx + \frac{32}{m} = 0$$

Since roots are equal,

So,

$$D = 0$$

$$b^2 - 4ac = 0$$

$$(32m)^2 - 4 \times \frac{32}{m} = 0$$

Hence, the value of m is,

$$m^3 = \frac{4}{32}$$

$$m = \frac{1}{2}$$

119. Correct Response : (a, b)

Explanation :

The given function is,

$$f(x) = 2|x| + |x + 2| - |x + 2| - 2|x|$$

The interval for given function is,

$$f(x) = -2x - 4, \qquad x < -2$$

$$f(x) = 2x + 4, \qquad -2 \le x < -\frac{2}{3}$$

$$f(x) = -4x, \qquad -\frac{2}{3} \le x \le 0$$

$$f(x) = 4x, \qquad 0 \le x < 2$$

For $f(x) = 2x + 4, \quad x \ge 2.$

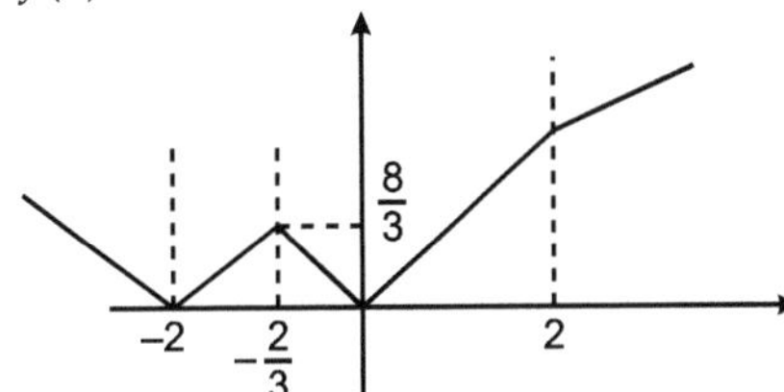

From the above graph it can be noticed that point of minima are $x = -2$ and $x = 0$.

The point of maxima is $x = -\dfrac{2}{3}$.

120. Correct Response : (b, d)

Explanation :

Solve the given limit.

$$\lim_{n \to \infty} \frac{\left(1^a + 2^a + ... + n^a\right)}{(n+1)^{a-1}\left[(na+1) + (na+2) + ... + (na+n)\right]}$$

$$= \frac{1}{60}$$

$$\lim_{n \to \infty} \frac{\sum\limits_{n=1}^{n}(r)^a}{(n+1)^{a-1}\left[\sum\limits_{n=1}^{n}(na+r)\right]} = \frac{1}{60}$$

$$\lim_{n \to \infty} \frac{n^a \sum\limits_{n=1}^{n}\left(\frac{r}{n}\right)^a}{n(n+1)^{a-1}\left[\sum\limits_{n=1}^{n}\left(a+\frac{r}{n}\right)\right]} = \frac{1}{60}$$

$$\lim_{n \to \infty} \frac{1}{\left(1+\frac{1}{n}\right)^{a-1}} \frac{1}{n} \frac{\sum\limits_{n=1}^{n}\left(\frac{r}{n}\right)^a}{\left[\sum\limits_{n=1}^{n}\left(a+\frac{r}{n}\right)\right]} = \frac{1}{60}$$

Futher simplify above limit.

$$\frac{\int\limits_{0}^{1}x^a dx}{\int\limits_{0}^{1}(a+x)dx} = \frac{1}{60}$$

$$\frac{\left[x^{a+1}\right]_0^1}{(a+1)\left[\left(ax+\dfrac{x^2}{2}\right)_0^1\right]} = \frac{1}{60}$$

$$\frac{1}{a+1}\left[\frac{1-0}{a+\dfrac{1}{2}}\right] = \frac{1}{60}$$

$$\frac{2}{(2a+1)(a+1)} = \frac{1}{60}$$

Simplify for the value of x.

$$2a^2 + 3a - 119 = 0$$

$$a = \frac{-3 \pm \sqrt{9 + 8(119)}}{4}$$

$$= \frac{-3 \pm \sqrt{961}}{4}$$

$$= 7, -\frac{17}{2}$$

121. Correct Response : (d)

Explanation :

It is given that $f'(x) < 2f(x)$.

$$f'(x) - 2f(x) < 0$$

$$f(x) < ce^{2x}$$

Substitute $x = \dfrac{1}{2}$ in above function.

$$1 < ce^{2\left(\frac{1}{2}\right)}$$

$$1 < ce$$

$$\frac{1}{e} < c$$

Now, the function is,

$$f(x) < \frac{1}{e}e^{2x}$$

$$f(x) < e^{2x-1}$$

$$0 < \int_{1/2}^{1} f(x)dx < \int_{1/2}^{1} e^{2x-1}dx$$

$$0 < \int_{1/2}^{1} f(x)dx < \frac{e-1}{2}$$

the

It can be seen that the value of integral lies in interval $\left(0, \dfrac{e-1}{2}\right)$.

122. Correct Response : (c)

Explanation :

Let, the function is,

$$f(x) = x^2 - x \sin x - \cos x$$

Differentiate above function.

$$f'(x) = 2x - x \cos x - \sin x + \sin x$$

$$= 2x - x \cos x$$

Substitute 0 for x in given function,

$$f(0) = (0)^2 - (0) \sin (0) - \cos (0)$$

$$= -1$$

(0, 1)

For $x > 0$, $f(x)$ is increasing.

For $x < 0$, $f(x)$ is decreasing.

So, $f(\infty) = \infty$ and $f(-\infty) = \infty$.

The number of points in $(-\infty, \infty)$ is 2.

123. Correct Response : (a)

Explanation :

The given slope of curve is,

$$\frac{dy}{dx} = \frac{y}{x} + \sec \frac{y}{x}$$

Put $y = vx$.

$$\frac{d(vx)}{dx} = v + \sec v$$

$$v + x\frac{dv}{dx} = v + \sec v$$

$$x\frac{dv}{dx} = \sec v$$

$$\cos v\, dv = \frac{dx}{x}$$

Integrate above function.

$$\sin v = 1 \log x + c$$

The curve passes through the point $\left(1, \dfrac{\pi}{6}\right)$. So,

$$\frac{1}{2} = c$$

Substitute value of c and v.

$$\sin \frac{y}{x} = \log x + \frac{1}{2}$$

124. Correct Response : (a, c)

Explanation :

Let, the sides of rectangle be $15k$ and $8k$. The side of square be x.

The volume of box is,

$$V = (15k - 2x)(8k - 2x)$$

$$V = (4x^3 - 46kx^2 + 120k^2x)$$

Differentiate above function with respect to x.

$$\frac{dV}{dx} = 12x^3 - 92kx + 120k^2$$

$$12x^3 - 92kx + 120k^2 = 0$$

The value of derivative at $x = 5$ is,

$$60k^2 - 230k + 150 = 0$$
$$6k^2 - 23k + 15 = 0$$
$$(6k - 5)(k - 3) = 0$$
$$k = 3, \frac{5}{6}$$

For $k = 3$, sides of rectangle are 45 and 24.

125. Correct Response : (d)

Explanation :

The given inequality is,

$$f''(x) - 2f'(x) + f(x) \geq e^x$$
$$\frac{d^2y}{dx^2} - 2\frac{dy}{dx} + y \geq e^x$$
$$e^{-x}\frac{d^2y}{dx^2} - 2e^{-x}\frac{dy}{dx} + e^{-x}y \geq 1$$
$$\frac{d^2}{dx^2}\left(ye^{-x}\right) \geq 1$$

So, ye^{-x} concave upward.

For, $0 < x < 1$. So, $-\infty < f(x) < 0$.

126. Correct Response : (c)

Explanation :

The increasing function is $\dfrac{d}{dx}\left(ye^{-x}\right)$. For

$0 < x < \dfrac{1}{4}$,

$$\frac{d}{dx}\left(ye^{-x}\right) < 0$$
$$e^{-x}\frac{dy}{dx} - e^{-x}y < 0$$
$$\frac{dy}{dx} < y$$
$$f'(x) < f(x)$$

127. Correct Response : (a)

Explanation :

The given parabola is $y^2 = 16x$ and equation of line is $y = mx + 3$.

Substitute value of y in equation of parabola.

$$(mx + 3)^2 = 16x$$
$$m^2x^2 + (6m - 16)x + 9 = 0$$

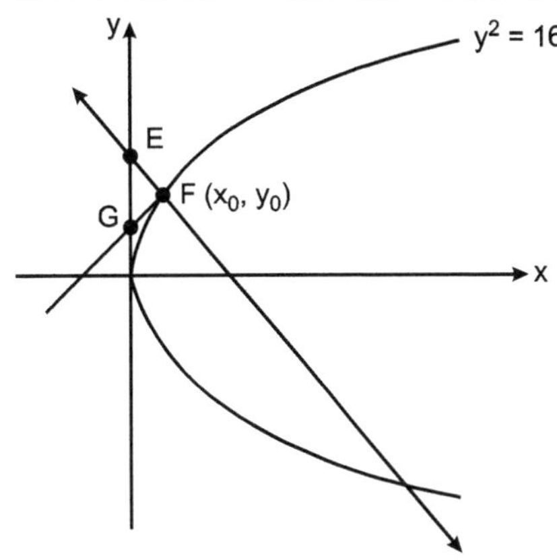

The tangent at point of parabola is,

$$yy_0 = 8(x + x_0)$$
$$y_1 = \frac{8x_0}{y_0}$$

The area of triangle EFG is calculated as,

$$\Delta = \frac{1}{2}(3 - y_1) \cdot x_0$$
$$= \frac{1}{2}\left(3 - \frac{8x_0}{y_0}\right)x_0$$
$$= \frac{1}{2}\left(3x_0 - \frac{8x_0^2}{y_0}\right)$$
$$= \frac{1}{2}\left(3x_0 - \frac{8x_0^2}{4\sqrt{x_0}}\right)$$

For the maximum value of Δ,

$$\frac{d\Delta}{dx_0} = 0$$
$$3 - 2\left(\frac{3}{2}\sqrt{x_0}\right) = 0$$
$$3 = 3\sqrt{x_0}$$
$$x_0 = 1$$

So, the value of $y_0 = 4$.

Substitute value of x_0 and y_0.

$$y_1 = \frac{8 \cdot 1}{4}$$
$$= 2$$

The slope of line is,

$$y_0 = mx_0 + 3$$
$$4 = m(1) + 3$$
$$m = 1$$

128. Correct Response : (b, d)

Explanation :

The given function is,

$$f(x) = \begin{cases} a_n + \sin \pi x, & x \in [2n, 2n+1] \\ b_n + \cos \pi x, & x \in (2n-1, 2n) \end{cases}$$

When the function f is continuous then,

The value of the function at $x = 2n$ is,

$$f(2n) = a_n + \sin \pi (2n)$$
$$= a_n + 0$$
$$= a_n$$

At $x = 2n^+$,

$$f(2n^+) = a_n + \sin \pi (2n^+)$$
$$= a_n + 0$$
$$= a_n$$

At $x = 2n^-$,

$$f(2n^-) = b_n + \cos \pi (2n^-)$$
$$= b^n + 1$$

Above three values must be equal.

$$a_n = b_n + 1$$
$$a_n - b_n = 1$$

Option (b) is correct.

The value of the function at $x = 2n + 1$ is,

$$f(2n + 1) = a_n + \sin \pi (2n + 1)$$
$$= a_n + \sin \pi$$
$$= a_n + 0$$
$$= a_n$$

At $x = (2n + 1)^+$,

$$f\{(2n+1)^+\} = b_{n+1} + \cos \pi (2n + 1)^+$$
$$= b_{n+1} - 1$$

At $x = (2n + 1)^-$,

$$f\{(2n + 1)^-\} = a_n + \sin \theta (2n + 1)^-$$
$$= a_n + 0$$
$$= a_n$$

Above three values must be equal.

$$a_n = b_{n+1} - 1$$
$$a_n - b_{n+1} = -1$$
$$a_{n-1} - b_n = -1$$

Option (d) is correct.

129. Correct Response : (a, b, c, d)

Explanation :

The given function is,

$$f(x) = \int_0^x e^{t^2} (t - 2)(t - 3) dt$$

$$f'(x) = 1 \cdot e^{x^2} \cdot (x - 2)(x - 3) \qquad ....(1)$$

For maxima and minima,

$$f'(x) = 0$$
$$e^{x^2} (x - 2)(x - 3) = 0$$
$$x = 2, 3$$

The figure shows the values maxima and minima at the line.

The function $f(x)$ has a local maximum at $x = 2$.

Option (a) is correct.

The function $f(x)$ has a local minimum at $x = 3$.

Option (d) is correct.

The function $f(x)$ is decreasing in the interval (2, 3).

Option (b) is correct.

Differentiate equation (1) with respect to x.

$$f''(x) = \frac{d}{dx}\left\{ e^{x^2} (x - 2)(x - 3) \right\}$$

$$= e^{x^2} (x - 2) + e^{x^2} (x - 3) + 2xe^{x^2} (x - 2)(x - 3)$$

$$= e^{x^2} [x - 2 + x - 3 + 2x(x - 2)(x - 3)]$$

$$= e^{x^2} (2x^3 - 10x^2 + 14x - 5)$$

At $x = 0$,

$$f''(0) = e^0 (2(0)^3 - 10(0)^2 + 14(0) - 5)$$
$$= -5 < 0$$

At $x = 1$,

$$f''(1) = e^1 (2(1)^3 - 10(1)^2 + 14(1) - 5)$$
$$= e > 0$$

Also, when $c \in (0, 1)$

$$f''(c) = 0$$

Option (c) is correct.

130. Correct Response : (b)

Explanation :

The given function is,

$$f(x) = \begin{cases} x^2 \left| \cos \dfrac{\pi}{x} \right|, & x \neq 0 \\ 0, & x = 0 \end{cases}, \ x \in \mathbb{R}$$

Check differentiability at $x = 0$.

The left hand derivative at $x = 0$ is,

$$\text{L.H.D.} = f'(0^-)$$

$$= \lim_{h \to 0} \frac{f(0 - h) - f(0)}{-h}$$

$$= \lim_{h \to 0} \frac{(-h)^2 \left| \cos\left(-\dfrac{\pi}{h} \right) \right| - 0}{-h}$$

$$= 0$$

The right hand derivative at $x = 0$ is,

$$\text{R.H.D.} = f'(0^+)$$

$$= \lim_{h \to 0} \frac{f(0 + h) - f(0)}{h}$$

$$= \lim_{h \to 0} \frac{h^2 \left| \cos\left(\dfrac{\pi}{h} \right) \right| - 0}{h}$$

$$= 0$$

Both L.H.D. and R.H.D. are equal. Thus, function $f(x)$ is differentiable at $x = 2$.

Check differentiability at $x = 2$.

The left hand derivative at $x = 2$ is,

$$\text{L.H.D.} = f'(2^-)$$

$$= \lim_{h \to 0} \frac{f(2-h) - f(2)}{-h}$$

$$= \lim_{h \to 0} \frac{(2-h)^2 \left|\cos\left(\dfrac{\pi}{2-h}\right)\right| - 2^2 \left|\cos\left(\dfrac{\pi}{2}\right)\right|}{-h}$$

$$= \lim_{h \to 0} \frac{(2-h)^2 \left\{-\cos\left(\dfrac{\pi}{2-h}\right)\right\} - 0}{-h}$$

Further solve the above expression.

$$\text{L.H.D.} = f'(2^+)$$

$$= \lim_{h \to 0} \frac{(2-h)^2 \sin\left(\dfrac{\pi}{2} - \dfrac{\pi}{2-h}\right)}{h}$$

$$= \lim_{h \to 0} \frac{(2-h)^2 \sin\left(-\dfrac{\pi h}{2(2-h)}\right)}{\left(-\dfrac{\pi h}{2(2-h)}\right)} \left(\dfrac{-\pi}{2(2-h)}\right)$$

$$= -\pi$$

The right hand derivative at $x = 2$ is,

$$\text{R.H.D.} = f'(2^+)$$

$$= \lim_{h \to 0} \frac{f(2+h) - f(2)}{h}$$

$$= \lim_{h \to 0} \frac{(2+h)^2 \left|\cos\left(\dfrac{\pi}{2+h}\right)\right| - 2^2 \left|\cos\left(\dfrac{\pi}{2}\right)\right|}{-h}$$

$$= \lim_{h \to 0} \frac{(2+h)^2 \cos\left(\dfrac{\pi}{2+h}\right) - 0}{h}$$

Further solve the above expression.

$$\text{R.H.D.} = \lim_{h \to 0} \frac{(2+h)^2 \sin\left(\dfrac{\pi}{2} - \dfrac{\pi}{2+h}\right)}{h}$$

$$= \lim_{h \to 0} \frac{(2+h)^2 \sin\left(\dfrac{\pi h}{2(2+h)}\right)}{\left(\dfrac{\pi h}{2(2+h)}\right)} \left(\dfrac{\pi}{2(2+h)}\right)$$

$$= 2^2 \frac{\pi}{2(2)}$$

$$= \pi$$

Both L.H.D. and R.H.D. are not equal. Thus, function $f(x)$ is not differentiable at $x = 2$.

Therefore, the function $f(x)$ is differentiable at $x = 0$ but not differentiable at $x = 2$.

131. Correct Response : (b)

Explantion :

The given equation is,

$$\lim_{x \to \infty} \left(\frac{x^2 + x + 1}{x + 1} - ax - b\right) = 4$$

$$\lim_{x \to \infty} \left(\frac{x^2 + x + 1 - ax^2 - bx - ax - b}{x + 1}\right) = 4$$

$$\lim_{x \to \infty} \left(\frac{x^2 + (1-a) + x(1-a-b) + (1-b)}{(x+1)}\right) = 4$$

The applied limit has finite value and it exist when the term,

$$(1 - a) = 0$$

$$a = 1$$

The equation is,

$$\lim_{x \to \infty} \left(\frac{0 + (1-a-b) + \left(\dfrac{1-b}{x}\right)}{1 + \dfrac{1}{x}}\right) = 4$$

$$1 - a - b = 4$$

$$1 - (1) - b = 4$$

$$b = -4$$

Hence, the values are $a = 1$, $b = -4$.

132. Correct Response : (5)

Explantion :

The given function is,

$$f(x) = |x + x^2 - 1|$$

$$= \begin{cases} -x + (x^2 - 1), & x < -1 \\ -x - (x^2 - 1), & -1 \le x \le 0 \\ x - (x^2 - 1), & 0 < x < 1 \\ x + (x^2 - 1), & x \ge 1 \end{cases}$$

$$= \begin{cases} x^2 - x - 1, & x < -1 \\ -x^2 - x + 1, & -1 \le x \le 0 \\ -x^2 + x + 1, & 0 < x < 1 \\ x^2 + x - 1, & x \ge 1 \end{cases}$$

The figure shows the positions where the function attains either local maximum or a local minimum.

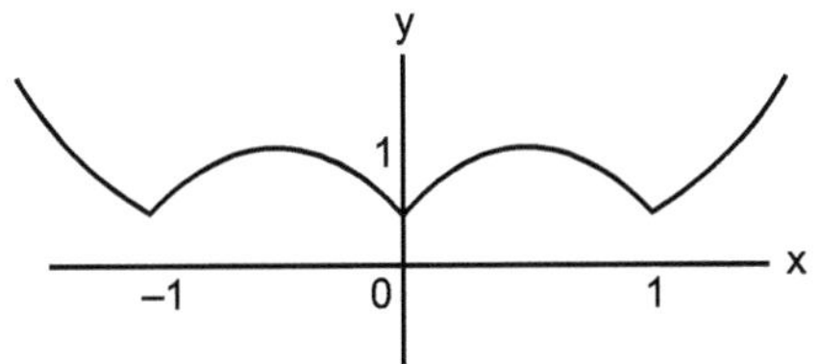

It shows two local maximum and three local minimum between $[-1, 1]$.

Therefore, the total number of points when the function attains local maximum and local minimun is 5.

133. Correct Response : (b)

Explanation :

The function $f(x)$ is,

$$f(x) = (1-x)^2 \sin^2 x + x^2$$

The function $g(x)$ is,

$$g(x) = \int_1^x \left(\frac{2(t-1)}{t+1} - lnt \right) f(t)\, dt$$

$$g'(x) = \left(\frac{2(x-1)}{x+1} - lnx \right) f(x) \cdot 1$$

Let,

$$h(x) = \frac{2(x-1)}{x+1} - lnx$$

Differentiate with respect to x.

$$h'(x) = \frac{d}{dx} \left\{ \frac{2(x-1)}{x+1} - lnx \right\}$$

$$= \frac{(x+1)(2) - (x-1)(1)}{(x+1)^2} - \frac{1}{x}$$

$$= \frac{-x^2 + 2x - 1}{x(x+1)^2}$$

$$= -\frac{(x-1)^2}{x(x+1)^2}$$

The value of $h'(x)$ is,

$$h'(x) \leq 0$$

Since, $h'(x)$ is decreasing in when $x \in (1, \infty)$ then, The function g is,

$$g'(x) < 0$$

Therefore, the function g is decreasing on interval $(1, \infty)$.

134. Correct Response : (d)

Explanation :

Solve the given equation.

$$\lim_{x \to \infty} \left[1 + x\, ln\left(1 + b^2\right) \right]^{1/x} = 2b \sin^2 \theta$$

$$\lim_{x \to \infty} \left[1 + x\, ln\left(1 + b^2\right)^{\frac{1}{x\, ln\left(1+b^2\right)}} \right]^{ln\left(1+b^2\right)} = 2b \sin^2 \theta$$

$$e^{ln(1 + b^2)} = 2b \sin^2 \theta$$

$$\left(1 + b^2\right) = 2b \sin^2 \theta$$

Further solve above equation.

$$\sin^2 \theta = \frac{1 + b^2}{2b} \qquad \qquad ...(1)$$

Consider right hand side of above equation.

$$\frac{1 + b^2}{2b} \geq 1$$

Therefore, left hand side is,

$$\sin^2 \theta = 1$$

$$\theta = \pm \frac{\pi}{2}$$

135. Correct Response : (a, b, c, d)

Explanation :

(a)

At $x = -\dfrac{\pi}{2}$

The left hand limit is 0 and right hand limit is 0. Also,

$$f\left(-\frac{\pi}{2} \right) = 0$$

Therefore, function $f(x)$ is continuous at $x = -\dfrac{\pi}{2}$.

(b)

At $x = 0$, the left hand derivative is 0 and right hand derivative is 1.

Therefore, $f(x)$ is not differentiable at $x = 0$.

(c)

At $x = 1$, the left hand derivative is 1 and right hand derivative is 1.

Therefore, $f(x)$ is differentiable at $x = 1$.

(d)

In the interval $\left(-\dfrac{\pi}{2}, 0 \right]$, the function is $f(x)$

$$= -\cos x.$$

So, function $f(x)$ is differentiable at $x = -\dfrac{3}{2}$.

136. Correct Response : (b, c)

Explanation :

The given condition is,

$$f(x + h) = f(x) + f(h)$$

Now,

$$f'(x) = \lim_{h \to 0} \frac{f(x+h) - f(x)}{h}$$

$$= \lim_{h \to 0} \frac{f(h)}{h}$$

$$= f'(0)$$

So, $f'(x)$ exists for all $x \in R$. So, $f'(0)$ exists.

For all $x \in R, f(x)$ is continuous and $f'(x)$ is constant.

137. Correct Response : (2)

Explanation :

The given function is,

$$f(x) = x^4 - 4x^3 + 12x^2 + x - 1$$

Differentiate above function with respect to x.

$$f'(x) = 4x^3 - 12x^2 + 24x + 1$$

Again differentiate above function with respect to x.

$$f''(x) = 12x^2 - 24x + 24$$
$$= 12(x^2 - 2x + 2) > 0$$

Since, $f'(x)$ is always increasing and $f(x) = 0$ have one root only. If $f'(x) = 0$ has one real root then $f(x)$ has positive and negative values.

Therefore, $f(x) = 0$ has exactly two real roots.

138. Correct Response : (c)

Explanation :

The given polynomial is,

$$f(x) = 4x^3 + 3x^2 + 2x + 1$$

The differentiation of given polynomial with respect to x is,

$$f'(x) = 2(6x^2 + 3x + 1)$$

So, the function $f(x) = 0$ has only one real root.

The value of function $f(x)$ at $x = -\dfrac{1}{2}$ is,

$$f\left(-\frac{1}{2}\right) = 4\left(-\frac{1}{2}\right)^3 + 3\left(-\frac{1}{2}\right)^2 + 2\left(-\frac{1}{2}\right) + 1$$

$$= -\frac{4}{8} + \frac{3}{4} - 1 + 1$$

$$= \frac{1}{4}$$

$$f\left(-\frac{1}{2}\right) > 0$$

The value of function $f(x)$ at $x = -\dfrac{3}{4}$ is,

$$f\left(-\frac{3}{4}\right) = 1 - \frac{6}{4} + \frac{27}{16} - \frac{108}{64}$$

$$= -\frac{1}{2}$$

$$f\left(-\frac{3}{4}\right) < 0$$

The function changes it sign in the interval $\left(-\dfrac{3}{4}, -\dfrac{1}{2}\right)$. So, $f(x) = 0$ has a root in this interval.

139. Correct Response : (b)

Explanation :

The differentiation of given polynomial with respect to x is,

$$f'(x) = 2(6x^2 + 3x + 1)$$

Again differentiate above function with respect to x,

$$f''(x) = 2(12x + 3)$$

The maximum value of the function is,

$$f''(x) = 0$$
$$2(12x + 3) = 0$$
$$x = -\frac{1}{4}$$

Thus, the function is decreasing in $\left(-t, \dfrac{-1}{4}\right)$ and increasing in interval $\left(\dfrac{-1}{4}, t\right)$.

140. Correct Answer : (0)

Explanation :

The given continuous function is,

$$f(x) = \int_0^x f(t)\, dt$$

It is a continuous function as $f : R \to R$. The value of $f(0) = 0$.

Also, according to Newton-Leibnitz theorem,

$$f'(x) = f(x)$$
$$\frac{f'(x)}{f(x)} = 1$$
$$\Rightarrow \qquad f(x) = ke^x$$

If $f(0) = 0$, then $e^x = 0$.

But this is a contradiction. Hence,

$$f(x) = 0 \ \forall \ x \in R$$

Hence, the value of $f(\ln 5)$ is,

$$f(\ln 5) = 0$$

Hence, the correct answer is 0.

141. Correct Response : (b, c, d)

Explanation :

The given function is,

$$f(x) = x \cos \frac{1}{x}$$

at $x \geq 1$.

Differentiate the above equation.

$$f'(x) = \cos\left(\frac{1}{x}\right) + \frac{1}{x}\sin\left(\frac{1}{x}\right)$$

(1)

The value of $f'(x) \to 1$ if $x \to \infty$.

Differentiate equation (1).

$$f''(x) = \frac{1}{x^2}\sin\left(\frac{1}{x}\right) - \frac{1}{x^2}\sin\left(\frac{1}{x}\right) - \frac{1}{x^3}\cos\left(\frac{1}{x}\right)$$

The value of $f''(x)$ will be $-\dfrac{1}{x^3}\cos\left(\dfrac{1}{x}\right)$ at $f''(x)$

< 0 for $x \geq 1$.

This implies that the function $f(x)$ is decreasing at $[1, \infty)$.

The value of $\lim\limits_{x \to \infty} f(x+2) - f(x)$ is calculated as,

$$\lim\limits_{x \to \infty} f(x+2) - f(x)$$

$$= \lim\limits_{x \to \infty}\left[(x+2)\cos\frac{1}{x+2} - x\cos\frac{1}{x}\right]$$

$$= 2$$

Hence,

$$f(x+2) - f(x) > 2 \;\forall\; x \geq 1$$

Hence, option (b, c, d) is correct.

142. **Correct Response :**

(a) - (q, s)

(b) - (p, r, s, t)

(c) - (t)

(d) - (r)

Explanation :

(a) The given expression is,

$$2\sin^2\theta + \sin^2 2\theta = 2$$

Simplify the above equation.

$$2\sin^2\theta + 4\sin^2\theta\cos^2\theta = 2$$

$$(\because \sin^2 2\theta = 4\sin^2\theta\cos^2\theta)$$

$$\sin^2\theta + 2\sin^2\theta(1-\sin^2\theta) = 1$$

$$3\sin^2\theta - 2\sin^4\theta - 1 = 0$$

Simplify the above expression.

$$3\sin^2\theta - 2\sin^4\theta - 1 = 0$$

$$\sin\theta = \pm\frac{1}{\sqrt{2}}, \pm 1$$

The value of θ is ,

$$\theta = \frac{\pi}{4}, \frac{\pi}{2}$$

(b) The given function is,

$$f(x) = \left[\frac{6x}{\pi}\right]\cos\left[\frac{3x}{\pi}\right]$$

Assume $n \in I$. The above value becomes,

$$f(x) = \left[\frac{6x}{\pi}\right]\cos\left[\frac{3x}{\pi}\right]$$

$$= n$$

$$x = \frac{n\pi}{6}$$

Here, x is $\dfrac{\pi}{6}, \dfrac{\pi}{3}, \dfrac{\pi}{2}, \pi$.

Take limits on both sides,

$$\lim\limits_{x \to \frac{\pi^-}{6}} f(x) = 0 \cdot \cos 0$$

$$= 0$$

$$\lim\limits_{x \to \frac{\pi^+}{6}} f(x) = 1 \cdot \cos 0$$

$$= 1$$

Hence, the function is discontinuous at $x = \dfrac{\pi}{6}$.

Similarly, the function is discontinuous is $\dfrac{\pi}{3}, \dfrac{\pi}{2}, \pi$.

(c) The edges of parallelopiped is represented by equation,

$$\hat{i} + \hat{j}$$

$$\hat{i} + 2\hat{j}$$

$$\hat{i} + \hat{j} + \pi\hat{k}$$

The volume of parallelopiped is calculated as,

$$\begin{vmatrix} 1 & 1 & 0 \\ 1 & 2 & 0 \\ 1 & 1 & \pi \end{vmatrix} = 1\,(2\pi - 0) - 1\,(\pi - 0) + 0$$

$$= \pi$$

(d) The given unit vectors $\vec{a}, \vec{b}, \vec{c}$ satisfies the equation,

$$\vec{a} + \vec{b} + \sqrt{3}\,\vec{c} = 0$$

Simplify the above equation.

$$\vec{a} + \vec{b} = -\sqrt{3}\,\vec{c}$$

$$|\vec{a} + \vec{b}|^2 = |\sqrt{3}\,\vec{c}|^2$$

$$a^2 + b^2 - 2ab = 3c^2$$

The dot product of the above equation is,

$$a^2 + b^2 - 2ab = 3c^2$$

$$2 + 2\cos\theta = 3$$

$$\cos\theta = \frac{1}{2}$$

$$\theta = \frac{\pi}{3}$$

Hence,

(A) - (q, s)

(B) - (p, r, s, t)

(C)-(t)

(D)- (r)

The given equation of planes is,

$$kx + 4y + z = 0$$
$$4x + ky + 2z = 0$$
$$2x + 2y + z = 0$$

These planes intersect a straight line if the determinant of these equations is zero.

Hence,

$$\begin{vmatrix} k & 4 & 1 \\ 4 & k & 2 \\ 2 & 2 & 1 \end{vmatrix} = 0$$

$$k(k - 4) - 4 (4 - 2) + 1 (8 - 2k)$$
$$k^2 - 6k + 8 = 0$$
$$k = 2, 4$$

(c) The required graph of the equation $|x - 1| + |x - 2| + |x + 1| + |x + 1| = 4k$ is,

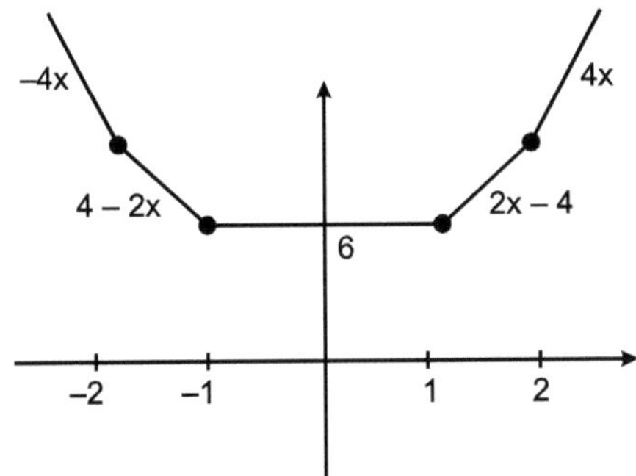

The value of k for which the equation $|x - 1| + |x - 2| + |x + 1| + |x + 1| = 4k$ has integral answer is,

$$k = 2, 3, 4, 5$$

(d) The given equation is,

$$y' = y + 1$$

Simplify the above equation.

$$\frac{dy}{y + 1} = dx$$

$$ln\,|y + 1| = x + c$$

(1) Substitute $y(0) = 1$ in the above equation.

$$ln\,|y + 1| = x + c$$
$$ln\,2 = c$$

Substitute the value of c in equation (1).

$$ln\,|y + 1| = x + c$$
$$ln\,|y + 1| = x + ln\,2$$

Substitute $x = ln\,2$ in the above equation.

$$ln\,|y + 1| = ln\,2 + ln\,2$$
$$y + 1 = 4$$
$$y = 3$$

Hence,

(A)-(p)

(B)-(q, s)

(C)-(q, r, s, t)

(D)- (r)

143. Correct Response : (7)

Explanation :

The given function is,

$$f(x) = 2x^3 - 15x^2 + 36x - 48$$

(1) The equation of given set is,

$$A = \{x \mid x^2 + 20 \le 9x\}$$

Simplify the equation $x^2 + 20 \le 9x$ to get the roots of x.

$$x^2 + 20 \le 9x$$
$$x^2 - 9x + 20 \le 0$$
$$x^2 - 4x - 5x + 20 \le 0$$
$$(x - 4) (x - 5) \le 0$$

Hence, the range of x is $4 \le x \le 5$.

Differentiate the function given in equation (1).

$$f'(x) = 6x^2 - 30x + 36$$
$$= 6 (x^2 - 5x + 6)$$

Solve the above quadratic equation.

$$f'(x) = 6(x^2 - 5x + 6)$$
$$= 6 (x - 2) (x - 3)$$

Since, the function is increasing at $4 \le x \le 5$. Hence, the maximum value of the function lies at $x = 5$.

The value of $f(5)$ is calculated from the equation (1).

$$f(5) = 2(5)^3 - 15(5)^2 + 36(5) - 48$$
$$= 250 - 375 + 180 - 48$$
$$= 430 - 423$$
$$= 7$$

Hence, the correct answer is 7.

144. Correct Answer : (0)

Explanation :

The given polynomial function is,

$$\lim_{x \to 0}\left(1 + \frac{p(x)}{x^2}\right) = 2$$

(1) Assume the general polynomial of four degree,

$$p(x) = ax^4 + bx^3 + cx^2 + dx + e$$

(2) The value of $p'(1) = p'(2) = 0$ because the polynomial $p(x)$ has extremum at $x = 1, 2$.

Solve the polynomial in equation (1).

$$\lim_{x \to 0}\left(1 + \frac{p(x)}{x^2}\right) = 2$$

$$\lim_{x \to 0}\left(\frac{x^2 + p(x)}{x^2}\right) = 2$$

(3) Since, the value of $p(0) = 0$. Hence, the value $e = 0$.

Take the differential of polynomial function in equation (3).

$$\lim_{x \to 0} \left(\frac{2x + p'(x)}{2x} \right) = 2 \qquad \ldots(4)$$

Since, the value of $p'(0) = 0$. Hence, the value $d = 0$.

Take the differential of polynomial function in equation (4).

$$\lim_{x \to 0} \left(\frac{2 + p''(x)}{2} \right) = 2$$

The value of c is 1.

Solve the above equation to get the values of a, b. That is,

$$a = \frac{1}{4}$$

$$b = -1$$

Substitute the values of a, b, c, d, e in equation (2).

$$p(x) = ax^4 + bx^3 + cx^2 + dx + e$$

$$= \frac{x^4}{4} - x^3 + x^2$$

The value of $P(2)$ is calculated as,

$$p(2) = \frac{x^4}{4} - x^3 + x^2$$

$$= \frac{2^4}{4} - 2^3 + 2^2$$

Hence, the correct answer is 0.

145. Correct Answer : (2)

Explanation :

The given function is,

$$f(x) = x^3 + e^{\frac{x}{2}}$$

$$g(x) = f^{-1}(x)$$

Differentiate $f(x)$

$$f'(x) = 3x^2 + \frac{1}{2}e^{\frac{x}{2}}$$

$$f'(g(x)) \, g'(x) = 1$$

Substitute $x = 0$ in the above equation.

$$g'(1) = \frac{1}{f'(0)} \qquad (f(0) = 1)$$

$$= 2$$

Hence, the correct answer is 2.

146. Correct Response : (c)

Explanation :

It is given that left hand limit of $|x - 1|$ at $x = 1$ is -1.

$$\lim_{x \to 1^+} \frac{(x-1)^n}{\log\left(\cos^m(x-1)\right)} = -1$$

Apply L' Hospital rule,

$$\lim_{x \to 1^+} \frac{n(x-1)^{n-1}}{-\dfrac{m \cos^{m-1}(x-1)\sin(x-1)}{\cos^m(x-1)}} = -1$$

$$\lim_{x \to 1^+} -\frac{n(x-1)^{n-1}}{m \tan(x-1)} = -1$$

The value of n for which limit tends to -1 is 2.

$$\lim_{x \to 1^+} -\frac{2}{m} = -1$$

$$m = 2$$

147. Correct Response : (c)

Explanation :

The graph of given function

$$f(x) = \begin{cases} (2+x)^3 & ,-3 < x \le -1 \\ x^{2/3} & ,-1 < x < 2 \end{cases}$$

is shown below.

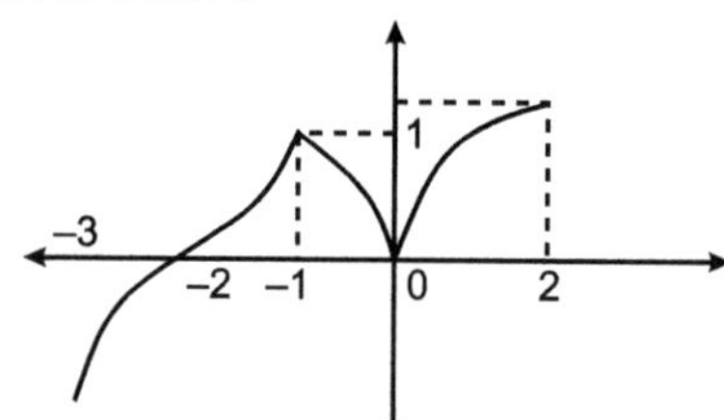

From the graph it can be observed that local maxima at $x = -1$ and local minima at $x = 0$. Thus, total number of local maxima and minima is 2.

148. Correct Response : (a, d)

Explanation :

Let, $\quad S_n < \lim_{n \to \infty} S_n$ then,

$$S_n < \lim_{n \to \infty} \sum_{k=1}^{n} \frac{n}{n^2 + kn + k^2}$$

$$< \lim_{n \to \infty} \sum_{k=1}^{n} \frac{1}{n}\left(\frac{1}{1 + k/n + (k/n)^2} \right)$$

$$= \int_0^1 \frac{dx}{1 + x + x^2}$$

$$= \frac{\pi}{3\sqrt{3}}$$

As $h\sum\limits_{k=0}^{n-1} f(kh) > \int\limits_0^1 f(x)dx > h\sum\limits_{k=1}^{n} f(kh)$.

So, $T_n = \dfrac{\pi}{3\sqrt{3}}$.

149. Correct Response : (a)

Explanation :

The given function is,

$$f(x) = g(x)\sin x$$

Differentiate above function with respect to x.

$$f'(x) = g'(x)\sin x + g(x)\cos x$$

For $x = 0$,

$$f'(0) = g'(0)(0) + g(0)\cos(0)$$
$$= g(0)$$

So, statement-2 is correct.

Now, simplify given limit.

$$\lim_{x\to 0}\Big[g(x)\cot x - g(0)\operatorname{cosec}x\Big]$$

$$= \lim_{x\to 0}\frac{g(x)\cos x - g(0)}{\sin x}$$

$$= \lim_{x\to 0}\frac{g(x)\cos x + g'(x)\sin x - g'(x)\sin x - g(0)}{\sin x}$$

$$= \lim_{x\to 0}\frac{f'(x) - g'(x)\sin x - f'(0)}{\sin x}$$

$$= \lim_{x\to 0}\left[\frac{\dfrac{f'(x) - f'(0)}{x}}{\dfrac{\sin x}{x}} - g'(x)\right]$$

Further simplify

$$\lim_{x\to 0}\Big[g(x)\cot x - g(0)\operatorname{cosec}x\Big] = f''(0) - g'(0)$$

$$= f''(0)$$

Thus, statement-2 is correct and statement-2 is correct explanation of statement-1.

150. Correct Response : (b)

Explanation :

The given equation is,

$$y^3 - 3y + x = 0$$

Differentiate above equation.

$$3y^2 y' - 3y'^2 + 1 = 0$$

$$y' = \frac{1}{3\left(1 - y^2\right)}$$

Again differentiate above equation.

$$y'' = \frac{2y}{9\left(1 - y^2\right)^3}$$

Substitute values of x and y,

$$f''\left(-10\sqrt{2}\right) = \frac{2\left(2\sqrt{2}\right)}{9\left(1 - \left(2\sqrt{2}\right)^2\right)^3}$$

$$= -\frac{4\sqrt{2}}{9\times 7^3}$$

$$= -\frac{4\sqrt{2}}{3^2 \times 7^3}$$

151. Correct Response : (c)

Explanation :

The given function is,

$$g(u) = 2\tan^{-1}\left(e^u\right) - \frac{\pi}{2}$$

Differentiate the given function.

$$g'(u) = \frac{2e^u}{1 + 2e^u} > 0$$

So, $g(u)$ is strictly increasing function.

Substitute $-u$ for u in given function.

$$g(-u) = 2\tan^{-1}\left(e^{-u}\right) - \frac{\pi}{2}$$

$$= 2\cot^{-1}\left(e^u\right) - \frac{\pi}{2}$$

$$= 2\left(\frac{\pi}{2} - \tan^{-1}\left(e^u\right)\right) - \frac{\pi}{2}$$

$$= \frac{\pi}{2} - 2\tan^{-1} e^u$$

Therefore, $g(-u) = -g(u)$ is an odd function.

152. Correct Response : (a)

Explanation :

Let, $\qquad g(x) = \log(f(x))$

So, $\qquad g(x + 1) = \log(f(x + 1))$

$$= \log(xf(x))$$

$$= \log x + \log(f(x))$$

$$= \log x + g(x)$$

Further simplify,

$$g(x + 1) = \log x + g(x)$$

$$g(x + 1) - g(x) = \log x$$

Double differentiate above equation with respect to x.

$$g''(x + 1) - g''(x) = -\frac{1}{x^2}$$

Solve further,

$$g''\left(1+\frac{1}{2}\right)-g''\left(\frac{1}{2}\right)=-4$$

$$g''\left(2+\frac{1}{2}\right)-g''\left(1+\frac{1}{2}\right)=-\frac{4}{9}$$

....

$$\because \ g''\left(N+\frac{1}{2}\right)-g''\left(N-\frac{1}{2}\right)=-\frac{4}{(2N-1)^2}$$

Add all the terms

$$g''\left(N+\frac{1}{2}\right)-g''\left(\frac{1}{2}\right)$$

$$=-4\left(1+\frac{1}{9}+....+\frac{1}{(2N-1)^2}\right)$$

153. Correct Response : (a)

Explanation :

Consider the given function,

$$f(x)=\frac{x^2-ax+1}{x^2+ax+1}$$

Differentiate the given function with respect to x.

$$f'(x)=\frac{2a(x^2-1)}{(x^2+ax+1)^2}$$

$$(x^2+ax+1)^2 f(x)=2a(x^2-1)$$

Again differentiate the above equation with respect to x.

$$(x^2+ax+1)2\,f''(x)$$

$$+\,2(x^2+ax+1).(2x+a).f'(x)=4ax \ \ ...(1)$$

Substitute -1 for x in equation (1)

$$(2-a)^2 f''(-1)+0=-4a \qquad ...(2)$$

Substitute 1 for x in equation (2)

$$(2+a)^2 f''(1)+0=4a \qquad ...(3)$$

Add equation (2) and (3).

$$(2+a)2\,f''(1)+(2-a)^2 f''(-1)=0$$

154. Correct Response : (a)

Explanation :

Consider the given function.

$$f(x)=\frac{x^2-ax+1}{x^2+ax+1}$$

Differentiate the given function with respect to x.

$$f'(x)=\frac{2a\left(x^2-1\right)}{\left(x^2+ax+1\right)^2}>0$$

$$(x^2-1)>0$$

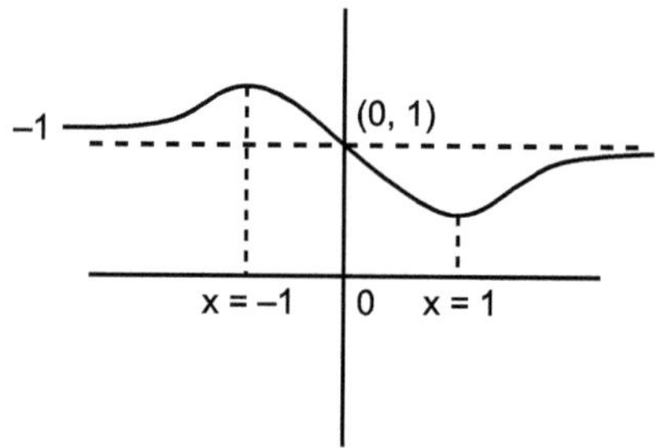

Therefore, function is decreasing on $(-1, 1)$ and local minima at $x=1$.

155. Correct Response : (b)

Explanation :

The given function is,

$$g(x)=\int_{0}^{e^x}\frac{f'(t)\,dt}{1+t^2}$$

Differentiate the given function.

$$g'(x)=\frac{f'\left(e^x\right)\cdot e^x}{1+\left(e^x\right)^2}$$

$$=\frac{2a\left(e^{2x}-1\right)e^x}{\left(e^{2x}+ae^x+1\right)^2\left(1+e^{2x}\right)}$$

$$=\frac{2ae^x}{1+e^{2x}}\cdot\frac{e^{2x}-1}{\left(e^{2x}+ae^x+1\right)^2}$$

Now, for $x>0$,

$$e^{2x}-1>0$$
$$g'(x)>0$$

For $x<0$,

$$e^{2x}-1<0$$
$$g'(x)<0$$

Therefore, $g'(x)$ is negative on $(-\infty, 0)$ and positive on $(0, \infty)$.

156. Correct Response : (a)-(p), (r), (s), (b)-(q), (s), (c)-(q), (s) (d)-(p), (r), (s)

Explanation :

Simplify the given function :

$$f(x)=\frac{x^2-6x+5}{x^2-5x+6}$$

$$f(x)=\frac{(x-1)(x-5)}{(x-2)(x-3)}$$

Draw the graph of given function.

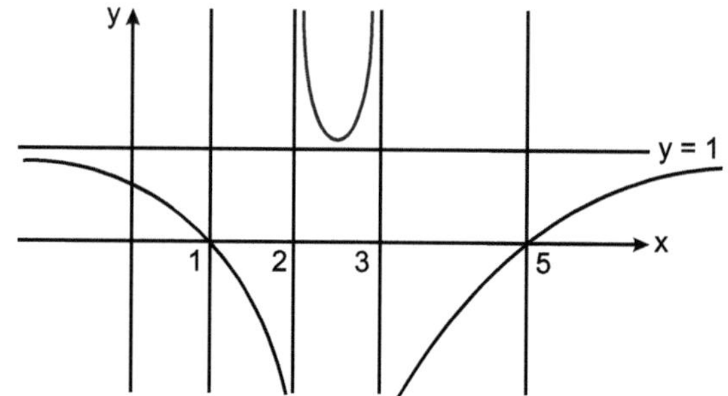

(a) If $-1 < x < 1$, then $0 < f(x) < 1$.
(b) If $1 < x < 2$, then $f(x) < 0$.
(c) If $3 < x < 5$, then $f(x) < 0$.
(d) If $x > 5$, then $f(x) < 1$.

157. Correct Response : (a)

Explanation :

The value of given limit is calculated as,

$$\lim_{x \to \frac{\pi}{4}} \frac{\displaystyle\int_{2}^{\sec^2 x} f(t)\,dt}{x^2 - \dfrac{\pi^2}{16}} = \lim_{x \to \frac{\pi}{4}} \frac{f\left(\sec^2 x\right) \cdot 2\sec^2 x \tan x}{2x}$$

$$= \frac{f(2) \times 2}{\pi/4}$$

$$= \frac{8}{\pi} f(2)$$

158. Correct Response : (A)-(p), (q), (r), (B)-(p), (s), (C)-(r), (s), (D)-(p), (q)

Explanation :

(a) The given function is,

$$f(x) = x|x|$$

$$= \begin{cases} -x^2, & x < 0 \\ x^2, & x > 0 \end{cases}$$

This function is continuous and differentiable everywhere. It is also increasing.

(b)

The given function is,

$$f(x) = \sqrt{|x|}$$

$$= \begin{cases} \sqrt{-x}, & x < 0 \\ \sqrt{x}, & x > 0 \end{cases}$$

Differentiate above function with respect to x.

$$f'(x) = \begin{cases} -\dfrac{1}{2\sqrt{-x}}, & x < 0 \\ \dfrac{1}{2\sqrt{x}}, & x > 0 \end{cases}$$

It is continues everywhere and differentiable everywhere except at $x = 0$.

(c)

The given function is,

$$f(x) = x + [x]$$

It is strictly increasing in $(-1, 1)$. The function is not continues and differentiable at $x = 0$.

(d)

The given function is,

$$f(x) = |x-1| + |x+1|$$

$$= \begin{cases} -2x, & x < -1 \\ 2, & -1 \le x < 1 \\ 2x, & 1 \le x \end{cases}$$

The function is continues and differentiable at $(-1, 1)$.

159. Correct Response : (d)

Explanation :

It is known that differential is,

$$\frac{dx}{dy} = \frac{1}{\dfrac{dy}{dx}}$$

$$= \left(\frac{dy}{dx}\right)^{-1}$$

Now,

$$\frac{d}{dy}\left(\frac{dx}{dy}\right) = \frac{d}{dx}\left(\frac{dy}{dx}\right)^{-1} \frac{dx}{dy}$$

$$\frac{d^2 x}{dy^2} = -\left(\frac{d^2 y}{dx^2}\right)\left(\frac{dy}{dx}\right)^{-2}\left(\frac{dy}{dx}\right)$$

$$= -\left(\frac{d^2 y}{dx^2}\right)\left(\frac{dy}{dx}\right)^{-3}$$

160. Correct Response : (b)

Explanation :

Consider the given function.

$$f(x) = 2 + \cos x$$

Differentiate the function with respect to x.

$$f'(x) = -\sin x$$

Thus, there exists a point c such that $c \in [t, t+\pi]$, where $f'(c) = 0$

As $f(x)$ is periodic function with period 2π. So, $f(t) = f(t + 2\pi)$.

Therefore, both statements are true, but statement-2 is not correct explanation of statement-1.

161. Correct Response : (c)

Explanation :

Use L' Hospital rule to solve given limit.

$$\lim_{x \to 0}\left((\sin x)^{\frac{1}{x}} + \left(\frac{1}{x}\right)^{\sin x}\right) = 0 + e^{\lim_{x \to 0} \sin x \ln\left(\frac{1}{x}\right)}$$

$$= 1$$

162. Correct Response : (a)

Explanation :

It is given that $f''(x) = -f(x)$ and $g(x) = f'(x)$.

$$f''(x) \cdot f'(x) + f(x) \cdot f'(x) = 0$$

$$[f(x)]^2 + [f'(x)]^2 = c$$

$$f(x)^2 + g(x)^2 = c$$

$$F(x) = c$$

Also it is given that $F(5) = 5$.

Thus, $F(10) = 5$.

163. Correct Response : (a, c)

Explanation :

The given function is,

$$f(x) = \min \{1, x^2, x^3\}$$

$$= \begin{cases} x^3, x \le 1 \\ 1, x > 1 \end{cases}$$

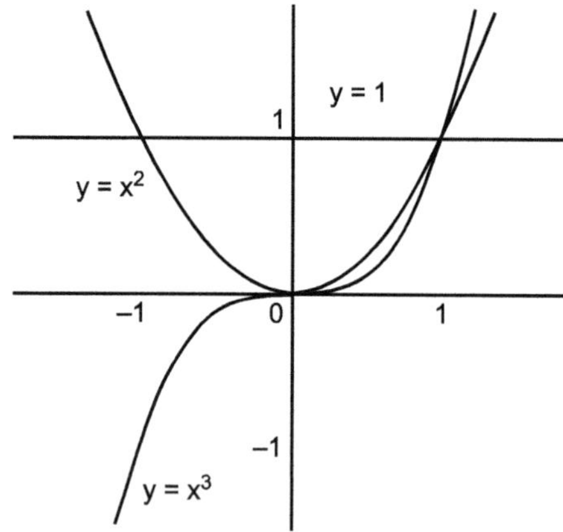

Therefore, $f(x)$ is continuous for all $x \in R$ and function is not differentiable at $x = 1$.

164. Correct Response : (b, c)

Explanation :

The cubic polynomial that satisfies the given conditions is,

$$f(x) = \frac{1}{4}(19x^3 - 57x + 34)$$

The graph of polynomial is,

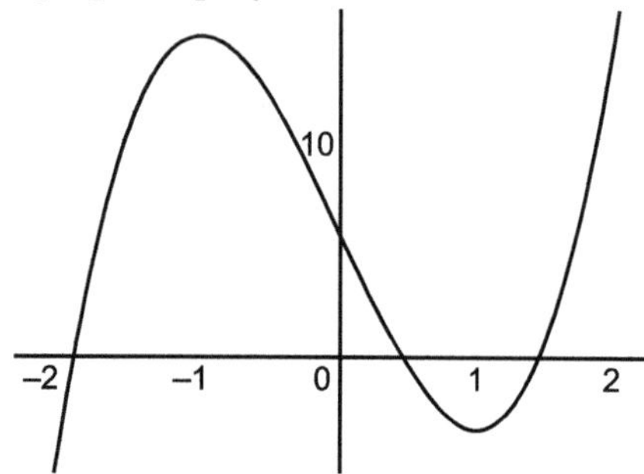

So, the polynomial has local maxima at $x = -1$ and local minima at $x = 1$.

Therefore, function $f(x)$ is increasing for $x \in \left[1, 2\sqrt{5}\right]$.

165. Correct Response : (a, b)

Explanation :

Differentiate given function $g(x)$.

$$g'(x) = f(x)$$

$$= \begin{cases} e^x, & 0 \le x \le 1 \\ 2 - e^{x-1}, & 1 < x \le 2 \\ x - e, & 2 < x \le 3 \end{cases}$$

If $x = 1 + \ln 2$ and $x = e$, then $g'(x) = 0$.

Again differentiate function $g'(x)$.

$$g''(x) = \begin{cases} -e^{x-1}, & 1 < x \le 2 \\ 1, & 2 < x \le 3 \end{cases}$$

The value of function of $x = 1 + \ln 2$ is,

$$g''(x) = -e^{\ln 2} < 0$$

So, $g(x)$ has a local maxima at $x = 1 + \ln 2$.

The value of function at $x = e$ is,

$$g''(e) = 1 > 0$$

So, $g(x)$ has a local minima at $x = e$.

If $f(x)$ is discontinuous at $x = 1$, then function has local maxima at $x = 1$ and local minima at $x = 2$.

166. Correct Response : (a)

Explanation :

According to the given information,

$$F'(c) = (b - a) f'(c) + f(a) - f(b) \qquad ...(1)$$

Differentiate above equation

$$F''(c) = f''(c)(b - a) < 0$$

So, $\quad F'(c) = 0$

Substitute the value of $F'(c)$ in equation (1).

$$(b - a) f'(c) + f(a) - f(b) = 0$$

$$(b - a) f'(c) = f(b) - f(a)$$

$$f'(c) = \frac{f(b) - f(a)}{b - a}$$

167. Correct Answer : 6

Explanation :

The given function is,

$$g(x) = (f'(x))^2 + f''(x) f(x)$$

$$= \frac{d}{dx}\left(f(x) \cdot f'(x)\right)$$

Now, for the zeros of $g(x)$ consider a function,

$$h(x) = f(x) \cdot f'(x)$$

There exist at least one root of $h'(x)$ between two roots of function $h(x)$.

$$h(x) = 0$$

$$f(x) = 0 \text{ or } f'(x) = 0$$

Function $f(x) = 0$ has minimum 4 solutions and $f'(x) = 0$ has minimum 3 solutions.

Function $h(x) = 0$ has minimum 7 solutions. Therefore, $h'(x) = g(x) = 0$ has minimum 6 solutions.

168. Correct Response : (a)

Explanation :

The graph of function $y = |\,|x| - 1\,|$ is shown below.

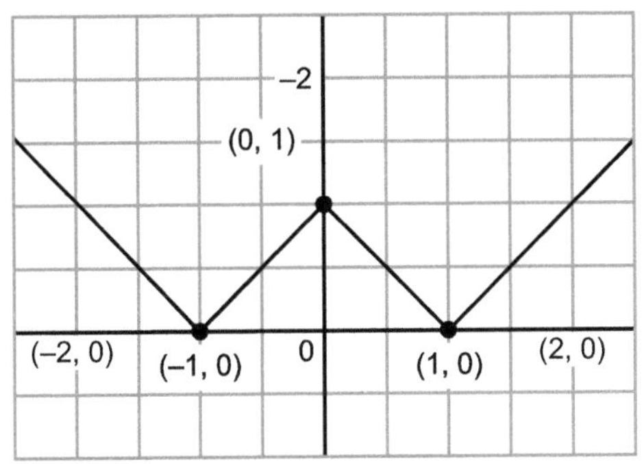

From the graph it can be observed that function is not differentiable at $x = -1, 0, 1$.

Therefore, given function is differentiable for all real numbers except $\{-1, 0, 1\}$.

169. Correct Response : (c)

Explanation :

The value of given function at $x = 0$ is,

$$y(0) = \pi$$

Differentiate given equation with respect to x,

$$-x \sin y \frac{dy}{dx} + \cos y - y \sin x + \cos x \frac{dy}{dx} = 0$$

Substitute $y(0) = \pi$ in above equation.

$$y'(0) = 1$$

Again, differentiate above equation with respect to x.

$$2 \sin y (y') - x \cos y \, (y')^2 - x \sin y \, (y'') + y'' \cos x - y'$$
$$\sin x - y' \sin x - y \cos x = 0$$

Substitute $y(0) = \pi$ and $y'(0) = 1$ in above equation.

$$y''(0) = \pi$$

170. Correct Response : (b)

Explanation :

It is given that $f(x)$ is continuous and differentiable function. Also, $f\left(\dfrac{1}{x}\right) = 0$ for $x = n$ and $n \in \mathrm{I}$.

$$f(0^+) = f\left(\frac{1}{\infty}\right)$$

$$= 0$$

Function $f(x)$ is continuous, so $f(0) = 0$. Also,

$$f'(0) = \lim_{h \to 0} \frac{f(h) - f(0)}{h - 0}$$

$$\lim_{h \to 0} \frac{f(h)}{h} = 0$$

Therefore, $f'(0) = 0$ and $f(0) = 0$.

171. Correct Response : $y - 2 = 0$

Explanation :

It is given that $|f(x_1) - f(x_2)| < (x_1 - x_2)^2$.

$$\lim_{x_1 \to x_2} \left| \frac{f(x_1) - f(x_2)}{x_1 - x_2} \right| < \lim_{x_1 \to x_2} |x_1 - x_2|$$

$$f'|(x)| < \delta$$
$$f'(x) = 0$$

So, function $f(x)$ is constant and point $(1, 2)$ lies on the curve.

$$f(x) = 2$$

Therefore, equation of tangent to the curve is $y - 2 = 0$.

172. Correct Answer : (*)

Explanation :

The length of tangent at any point on the curve $y = f(x)$ between the point and X-axis is 1. So,

$$\text{Length of tangent} = \left| y \sqrt{1 + \left(\frac{dx}{dy}\right)^2} \right|$$

$$1 = y^2 \left[1 + \left(\frac{dx}{dy}\right)^2 \right]$$

$$\frac{dy}{dx} = \pm \frac{y}{\sqrt{1 - y^2}}$$

Integrate both sides of above equation.

$$\int \frac{\sqrt{1 - y^2}}{y} \, dy = \pm x + c$$

Put $\qquad y = \sin\theta.$

$$dy = \cos\theta \, d\theta$$

Solve the integral.

$$\sqrt{1 - y^2} + \ln \left| \frac{1 - \sqrt{1 - y^2}}{y} \right| = \pm x + c$$

Therefore, above equation is the required equation of curve.

173. Correct Answer : (*)

Explantion :

The given equation is,

$$f(x - y) = f(x)\, g(y) - f(y)\, g(x) \qquad \ldots(1)$$

Substitute $y = x$ in equation (1)

$$f(0) = f(y)\, g(y) - f(y)\, g(y)$$
$$f(0) = 0$$

Substitute $y = 0$ in equation (1)

$$g(0) = 1$$

Now, the right hand derivative at $x = 0$ is,

$$f'(0^+) = \lim_{h \to 0^+} \frac{f(0 + h) - f(0)}{h}$$

$$= \lim_{h \to 0^+} \frac{f(0)g(-h) - g(0)f(-h) - f(0)}{h}$$

$$= \lim_{h \to 0^+} \frac{f(0-h) - f(0)}{-h}$$

$$= f'(0^-)$$

So, function is differentiable at $x = 0$.

Substitute $y = x$ in $g(x - y) = g(x) g(y) + f(x) f(y)$.

$$g(0) = g(x) g(x) + f(x) f(x)$$
$$1 = g^2(x) + f^2(x)$$
$$g^2(x) = 1 - f^2(x)$$

Differentiate above equation.

$$2g'(x) g(x) = -2f(x) f'(x)$$
$$2g'(0) g(0) = -2$$
$$g'(0) = 0$$

Therefore, the derivative of $g(x)$ at $x = 0$ is 0.

174. Correct Answer : (*)

Explanation :

Let, the cubic polynomial be $p(x) = ax^3 + bx^2 + cx + d$.

Substitute -1 for x in polynomial.

$$p(-1) = -a + b - c + d$$
$$10 = -a + b - c + d$$

Substitute 1 for x in polynomial.

$$p(1) = a + b + c + d$$
$$-6 = a + b + c + d$$

Differentiate the polynomial,

$$p'(x) = 3ax^2 + 2bx + c$$

Polynomial has maxima at $x = -1$.

$$p'(-1) = 0$$
$$3a - 2b + c = 0$$

And $p'(x)$ has minima at $x = 1$.

$$p''(1) = 0$$
$$6a + 2b = 0$$
$$3a + b = 0$$

On solving the equations $a = 1$, $b = -3$, $c = -9$ and $d = 5$.

The polynomial is $p(x) = x^3 - 3x^2 - 9x + 5$. Differentiate the polynomial.

$$p'(x) = 3x^2 - 6x - 9$$
$$= 3(x + 1)(x - 3)$$

The point of local maximum is $(-1, 10)$ and point of local minimum is $(3, -22)$. The distance between local maximum and minimum is,

$$\sqrt{(3+1)^2 + (-22-10)^2} = \sqrt{16 + 1024}$$
$$= \sqrt{1040}$$
$$= 4\sqrt{65}$$

Therefore, required distance is $4\sqrt{65}$ units.

175. Correct Answer : (*)

Explanation :

Assume that $g(x)$ and $g''(x)$ are positive for all $x \in (-3, 3)$.

The integral in the interval $[0, 3]$ is,

$$\int_0^3 g(x)\,dx = \int_0^3 f'(x)\,dx$$

$$\int_0^3 g(x)\,dx = f(3) - f(0)$$

$$\left| \int_0^3 g(x)\,dx \right| < 2 \qquad \text{....(1)}$$

Similarly,

$$\left| \int_{-3}^0 g(x)\,dx \right| < 2 \qquad \text{...(2)}$$

Add equations (1) and (2),

$$\left| \int_0^3 g(x)\,dx \right| + \left| \int_{-3}^0 g(x)\,dx \right| < 4 \qquad \text{...(3)}$$

It is given that $(f(0))^2 + (g(0))^2 = 9$.

So, $2\sqrt{2} < g(0) < 3$ or $-3 < g(0) < -2\sqrt{2}$

Case 1 : $2\sqrt{2} < g(0) < 3$

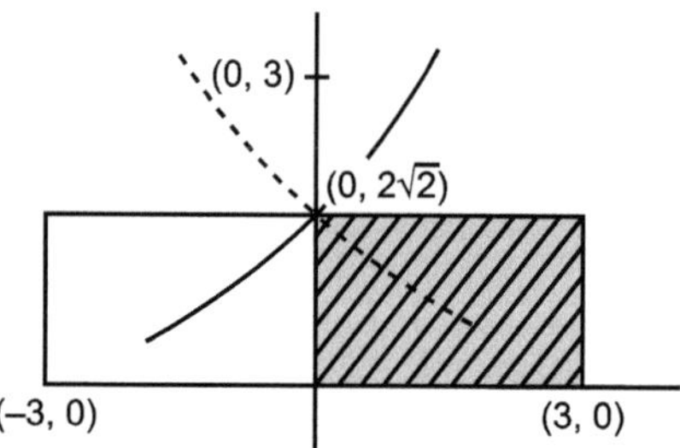

Let, $g(x)$ concave upward in the interval $(-3, 3)$. The area is,

$$\left| \int_{-3}^0 g(x)\,dx \right| + \left| \int_0^3 g(x)\,dx \right| > 6\sqrt{2}$$

The above condition contradicts equation (3). So, $g(x)$ will concave downward for some $c \in (-3, 3)$.

$$g''(c) < 0 \qquad \text{...(4)}$$

At point c the value of $g(c)$ is greater than $2\sqrt{2}$.

$$g(c) < 0 \qquad \text{...(5)}$$

From equation (4) and (5) it can be considered that $g(c) g''(c) < 0$ for $c \in (-3, 3)$.

Case 2 : $-3 < g(0) < -2\sqrt{2}$

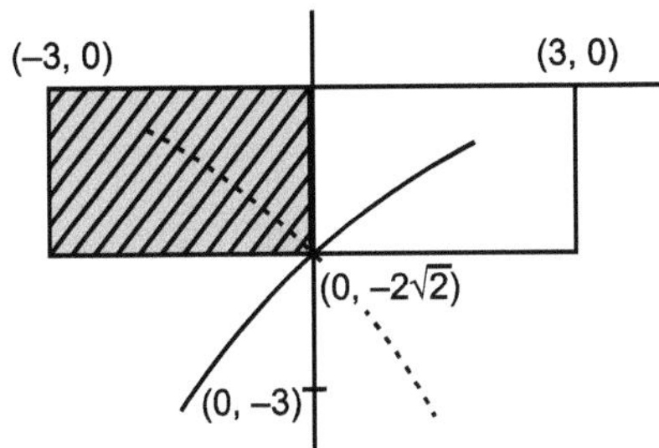

Let, $g(x)$ concave downward in the interval $(-3, 3)$. The area is,

$$\left| \int_{-3}^{0} g(x)dx \right| + \left| \int_{0}^{3} g(x)dx \right| < 6\sqrt{2}$$

The above condition contradicts equation (3). So, $g(x)$ will concave upward for some $c \in (-3, 3)$.

$$g''(c) > 0 \qquad \qquad ...(6)$$

At point c the value of $g(c)$ is less than $-2\sqrt{2}$

$$g(c) > 0 \qquad \qquad ...(7)$$

From equation (6) and (7) it can be considered that $g(c)\, g''(c) < 0$ for $c \in (-3, 3)$.

176. Correct Response : (a)

Explanation :

Differentiate both sides of given equation,

$$t^2 f(t^2) \cdot \frac{d}{dt} t^2 - 0 f(0) \frac{d}{dt}(0) = 2t^4$$

$$t^2 f(t^2) \cdot 2t = 2t^4$$

$$f(t^2) = t$$

Substitute $t^2 = \dfrac{4}{25}$.

$$f\left(\frac{4}{25}\right) = \pm \frac{2}{5}$$

177. Correct Response : (a)

Explanation :

The given function is,

$$f(x) = x^3 + bx^2 + cx + d$$

Differentiate above function.

$$f'(x) = 3x^2 + 2bx + c$$

Now,
$$D = 4b^2 - 12c$$
$$D = 4(b^2 - c) - 8c$$
$$D < 0$$

If $D < 0$, then $f'(x) > 0$ for all $x \in (-\infty, \infty)$.

Therefore, $f(x)$ is an increasing function.

178. Correct Response : (d)

Explanation :

It the given function is continuous in $[0, 1]$ then it satisfy Rolle's theorem.

The right hand limit is,

$$\lim_{x \to 0^+} f(x) = f(0)$$

$$\lim_{x \to 0^+} \frac{\log x}{x^{-\alpha}} = 0$$

Use L' Hospital rule to solve above limit.

$$\lim_{x \to 0^+} \frac{1/x}{-\alpha x^{-\alpha-1}} = 0$$

$$\lim_{x \to 0^+} -\frac{1}{\alpha x^{-\alpha}} = 0$$

$$\lim_{x \to 0^+} -\frac{1}{\alpha} x^{\alpha} = 0$$

$$\alpha > 0$$

So, $f(x)$ is differentiable in $(0, 1)$ for all $\alpha > 0$ and $f(1) = 0 = f(0)$.

Therefore, value of $\alpha = \dfrac{1}{2}$.

179. Correct Response : (c)

Explanation :

Use L' Hospital rule to solve given expression.

$$\lim_{x \to 0} \frac{f(x^2) - f(x)}{f(x) - f(0)} = \lim_{x \to 0} \frac{2xf'(x^2) - f'(x)}{f'(x)}$$

$$= -1$$

180. Correct Response : (a)

Explanation :

According to Lagrange's mean value theorem, let $f : [a, b] \to R$ be a continuous function on $[a, b]$ and differentiable on (a, b) then there exist a point c such that,

$$f'(c) = \frac{f(b) - f(a)}{b - a}$$

In option (a) function is not differentiable at $x = \dfrac{1}{2}$. So, it does not satisfy Lagrange mean value theorem.

181. Correct Response : (*)

Explanation :

Let, a function be $g(x)$.

$$g(x) = \int p(x)\,dx$$

$$= \int \left[51x^{101} - 2323x^{100} - 45x + 1035 \right] dx$$

$$= \frac{51x^{102}}{102} - \frac{2323x^{101}}{101} - \frac{45x^2}{2} + 1035x + c$$

$$= \frac{1}{2}x^{102} - 23x^{101} - \frac{45}{2}x^2 + 1035x + c$$

Now, the value of function at $x = 45^{1/100}$.

$$g\,(45^{1/100}) = \frac{1}{2}\,(45)^{\frac{102}{100}} - 23\,(45)^{\frac{101}{100}} - \frac{45}{2}(45)^{\frac{2}{100}}$$

$$+ 1035(45)^{\frac{1}{100}} + c$$

$$= c$$

The value of function at $x = 46$.

$$g(x) = \frac{1}{2}\,(46)^{102} - 23(46)^{101} - \frac{45}{2}\,(46)^2$$

$$+ 1035\,(46) + c$$

$$= c$$

Therefore, $g'\,(x) = p(x)$ has at least one root in the interval.

182. Correct Response : (d)

Explanation :

Use L' Hospital rule to solve given limit.

$$\lim_{h \to 0} \frac{f\left(2h + 2 + h^2\right) - f\left(2\right)}{f\left(h - h^2 + 1\right) - f\left(1\right)}$$

$$= \lim_{h \to 0} \frac{f'\left(2h + 2 + h^2\right)(2 + 2h)}{f'\left(h - h^2 + 1\right)(1 - 2h)}$$

$$= \frac{f'(2)(2)}{f'(1)(1)}$$

$$= \frac{6 \times 2}{4 \times 1} = \frac{12}{4}$$

$$= 3$$

183. Correct Response : (*)

Explanation :

Solve the given limit.

$$\lim_{n \to \infty} \frac{2}{\pi}(n + 1)\cos^{-1}\left(\frac{1}{n}\right) - n$$

$$= \lim_{n \to \infty} n\left[\frac{2}{\pi}\left(n + \frac{1}{n}\right)\cos^{-1}\left(\frac{1}{n}\right) - 1\right]$$

$$= \lim_{n \to \infty} n f\left(\frac{1}{n}\right)$$

$$= f'(0)$$

Here, $f(x) = \frac{2}{\pi}(1 + x)\cos^{-1} x - 1$ and $f(0) = 0$.

Now, differentiate $f(x)$.

$$f'(x) = \frac{2}{\pi}\left[(1 + x)\frac{-1}{\sqrt{1 - x^2}} + \cos^{-1} x\right]$$

The value of function at $x = 0$ is,

$$f'(0) = \frac{2}{\pi}\left[-1 + \frac{\pi}{2}\right]$$

$$= \frac{2}{\pi}\left[\frac{\pi - 2}{2}\right]$$

$$= 1 - \frac{2}{\pi}$$

Therefore, the value of

$$\lim_{n \to \infty} \frac{2}{\pi}(n + 1)\cos^{-1}\left(\frac{1}{n}\right) - n \text{ is } 1 - \frac{2}{\pi}.$$

184. Correct Response : (*)

Explanation :

It is given that $f(x)$ is differentiable at $x = 0$. So,

$f(0^+) = f(0^{-1}) = f(0)$

The value of $f(0^+)$ is,

$$f(0^+) = \lim_{x \to \infty} \frac{e^{\frac{ax}{2}} - 1}{x}$$

$$= \lim_{x \to \infty} \frac{e^{\frac{ax}{2}} - 1}{\frac{ax}{2}} \cdot \frac{a}{2}$$

$$= \frac{a}{2}$$

Now, $\dfrac{a}{2} = \dfrac{1}{2}$

$$a = 1$$

The left hand limit is,

$$f'(0^-) = \lim_{h \to 0^-} \frac{b\sin^{-1}\dfrac{h + c}{2} - \dfrac{1}{2}}{h}$$

$$= \frac{b/2}{\sqrt{1 - \dfrac{c^2}{4}}}$$

The right hand limit is,

$$f'(0^+) = \lim_{h \to 0^+} \frac{\dfrac{e^{h/2} - 1}{h} - \dfrac{1}{2}}{h}$$

$$= \frac{1}{8}$$

Given that left hand limit is equal to right hand limit.

$$\frac{b/2}{\sqrt{1 - \dfrac{c^2}{4}}} = \frac{1}{8}$$

$$4b = \sqrt{1 - \frac{c^2}{4}}$$

$$16b^2 = \frac{4 - c^2}{4}$$

$$64b^2 = 4 - c^2$$

185. Correct Response : (d)

Explanation :

Solve given limit.

$$\lim_{x \to 0} \frac{[(a-n)nx - \tan x]\sin nx}{x^2} = 0$$

$$\lim_{x \to 0} \frac{\sin(nx)}{nx} \times n\left[n(a-n) - \frac{\tan x}{x}\right] = 0$$

$$n^2(a-n) - n = 0$$

$$a = n + \frac{1}{n}$$

Therefore, the value of a is $n + \dfrac{1}{n}$.

186. Correct Response : (d)

Explanation :

The minimum value of $f(x)$ is,

$$f(x) = (x+b)^2 + 2c^2 - b^2$$

$$f(x)_{\min} = 2c^2 - b^2$$

The maximum value of $g(x)$ is,

$$g(x) = -(x+c)^2 + b^2 + c^2$$

$$g(x)_{\max} = b^2 + c^2$$

According to given condition.

$$2c^2 - b^2 > b^2 + c^2$$

$$c^2 > 2b^2$$

$$|c| > \sqrt{2}\,|b|$$

187. Correct Response : (c)

Explanation :

Volume of parallelopiped by given vectors is,

$$V = \begin{vmatrix} 1 & a & 1 \\ 0 & 1 & a \\ a & 0 & 1 \end{vmatrix}$$

$$= 1 + a^3 - a$$

Differentiate with respect to a.

$$\frac{dV}{da} = 3a^2 - 1$$

$$= 3\left(a + \frac{1}{\sqrt{3}}\right)\left(a - \frac{1}{\sqrt{3}}\right)$$

Therefore, volume is minimum at $a = \dfrac{1}{\sqrt{3}}$.

188. Correct Response : (2, 1)

Explanation :

Let, the required point be $P = (\sqrt{6}\cos\theta + \sqrt{3}\sin\theta)$.

The slope of tangent at point P is -1.

Differentiate given equation of curve $x^2 + 2y^2 = 6$.

$$2x + 4y\frac{dy}{dx} = 0$$

$$\frac{dy}{dx} = -\frac{x}{2y}$$

$$\left[\frac{dy}{dx}\right]_P = -\frac{\sqrt{6}\cos\theta}{2\sqrt{3}\sin\theta}$$

$$-1 = -\frac{1}{\sqrt{2}}\cot\theta$$

Solve further.

$$\cot\theta = \sqrt{2}$$

$$\sin\theta = \frac{1}{\sqrt{3}},\ \cos\theta = \sqrt{\frac{2}{3}}$$

$$P = \left(\sqrt{6}\cdot\sqrt{\frac{2}{3}},\ \sqrt{3}\cdot\frac{1}{\sqrt{3}}\right)$$

Therefore, point P on the curve is (2, 1).

189. Correct Response : (*)

Explanation :

The length of OP is 10 and $\sin\theta = \dfrac{r}{10}$

where $\theta \in \left(0, \dfrac{\pi}{2}\right)$.

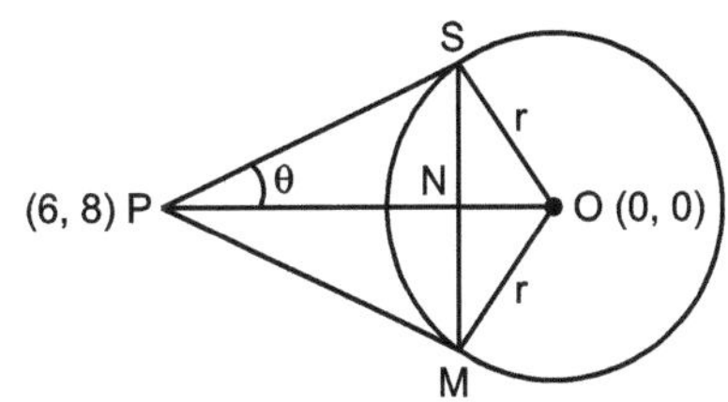

In $\triangle$PSO,

$$\tan\theta = \frac{r}{PS}$$

$$= \frac{r}{\sqrt{100 - r^2}}$$

$$\sin\theta = \frac{r}{10}$$

$$\cos\theta = \frac{\sqrt{100 - r^2}}{10}$$

The required area of $\triangle$PSM is,

$$\Delta = \frac{1}{2} \times SM \times PN$$

$$= \frac{1}{2} \times 2 \times SN \times PN$$

$$= SN \times PN$$

$$= SP\sin\theta \times SP\cos\theta$$

Substitute the values.

$$\Delta = (\sqrt{100 - r^2})^2\ \sin\theta\cos\theta$$

$$= (100 - r^2) \frac{r}{10} \cdot \frac{\sqrt{100 - r^2}}{10}$$

$$= \frac{r(100 - r^2)^{3/2}}{100}$$

Differentiate with respect to r.

$$\frac{d\Delta}{dr} = \frac{1}{100} \cdot \frac{3}{2}(100 - r^2)^{1/2}(-2r)r$$

$$+ \frac{(100 - r^2)^{3/2}}{100}$$

$$0 = (100 - r^2)^{1/2}(-3r^2 + 100 - r^2)$$

The value of r cannot be 10 as P is outside the circle. So,

$$4r^2 = 100$$
$$r^2 = 25$$
$$r = 5$$

Therefore, the area would be maximum for $r = 5$.

190. Correct Response : (*)

Explanation :

Let, the function be $f(x) = 3x^2 + (3 - 2\pi)x - \pi \sin x$.

$$f(0) = 0, \ f\left(\frac{\pi}{2}\right) = - \text{ve}$$

Differentiate the function.

$$f'(x) = 6x + 3 - 2\pi - \pi \cos x$$

Again, differentiate the function.

$$f''(x) = 6 + \pi \sin x > 0$$

So, $f'(x)$ is increasing function in $\left[0, \dfrac{\pi}{2}\right]$ and no

local maxima of $f(x)$ in interval $\left[0, \dfrac{\pi}{2}\right]$. The graph

of $f(x)$ lies in the interval $\left[0, \dfrac{\pi}{2}\right]$, below the x-axis.

$$f(x) \le 0$$
$$3x^2 + 3x \le 2\pi x + \pi \sin x$$
$$\sin x + 2x \ge \frac{3x(x+1)}{\pi}$$

191. Correct Response : (*)

Explanation :

The left hand derivative at $x = a$ is,

$$f'(a) = \lim_{h \to 0^-} \frac{f(a+h) - f(a)}{h}$$

$$= 0$$

The left hand derivative at $x = -a$ is,

$$f'(-a) = \lim_{h \to 0^-} \frac{f(-a+h) - f(-a)}{h}$$

$$= \lim_{h \to 0^-} \frac{-f(-h+a) + f(a)}{h}$$

Also, f is an odd function. So, left hand derivative is,

$$f'(-a) = \lim_{h \to 0^-} \frac{-f(2a + h - a) + f(a)}{h}$$

$$= -\lim_{h \to 0^-} \frac{f(a+h) - f(a)}{h}$$

$$= -f'(a)$$

$$= 0$$

192. Correct Response : (*)

Explanation :

Let, function be $f(x) = \sin(\tan x) - x$.

Differentiate the function with respect to x.

$$f'(x) = \cos(\tan x)\sec^2 x - 1$$
$$f'(x) = \tan^2 x \cos(\tan x) + \cos(\tan x) - 1$$
$$f'(x) > \tan^2 x \cos(\tan x) - \frac{\tan^2 x}{2}$$

Solve further.

$$f'(x) > \tan^2 x \left(\cos(\tan x) - \cos\frac{\pi}{3}\right) > 0$$

So, $f(x)$ is an increasing function for all $x \in \left[0, \dfrac{\pi}{4}\right]$.

As
$$f(0) = 0,$$
$$f(x) \ge 0$$
$$\sin(\tan x) - x \ge 0$$
$$\sin(\tan x) \ge x$$

193. Correct Response : (d)

Explanation :

The given function is,

$$f(x) = \begin{cases} \tan^{-1} x, & \text{if } |x| \le 1 \\ \dfrac{1}{2}(|x| - 1), & \text{if } |x| > 1 \end{cases}$$

At $x = 1, -1$, function is discontinuous and non-differentiable.

Therefore, the domain of derivative of function is $R - \{-1, 1\}$.

194. Correct Response : (c)

Explanation :

Solve the given limit.

$$\lim_{x \to 0} \frac{(\cos x - 1)(\cos x - e^x)}{x^n}$$

$$= \lim_{x \to 0} \frac{2\sin^2\frac{x}{2}\left(e^x - 1 + 1 - \cos x\right)}{x^n}$$

$$= \lim_{x \to 0} \frac{2\sin^2\frac{x}{2}\left(e^x - 1 + 2\sin^2\frac{x}{2}\right)}{x^n}$$

$$= \lim_{x \to 0} \frac{1}{2} \left(\frac{\sin \frac{x}{2}}{\frac{x}{2}} \right)^2 \frac{\left(e^x - 1 + 2\sin^2 \frac{x}{2} \right)}{x^{n-2}}$$

The value of above expression is non-zero if,

$$n - 2 = 1$$
$$n = 3$$

195. Correct Response : (c)

Explanation :

Solve the given limit.

$$\lim_{x \to 0} \left(\frac{f(1+x)}{f(1)} \right)^{1/x} = e^{\lim_{x \to 0} \frac{1}{x} \left(\frac{f(1+x) - f(1)}{f(1)} \right)}$$

$$= e^{\frac{f'(1)}{f(1)}}$$

$$= e^{\frac{6}{3}}$$

$$= e^2$$

196. Correct Response : (d)

Explanation :

The given equation is,

$$y^3 + 3x^2 = 12y \qquad \ldots(1)$$

Differentiate above equation.

$$3y^2 \frac{dy}{dx} + 6x = 12 \frac{dy}{dx}$$

$$\frac{dy}{dx} = \frac{6x}{3(4 - y^2)}$$

It is given that the tangent at a point is vertical. So, the slope of tangent is infinity at this point.

$$3y^2 - 12 = 0$$
$$y = \pm 2$$

Substitute 2 for y in equation (1),

$$(2)^3 + 3x^2 = 12(2)$$
$$3x^2 = 24 - 8$$
$$x^2 = \frac{16}{3}$$
$$x = \pm \frac{4}{\sqrt{3}}$$

For $y = -2$, value will be imaginary.

Therefore, the point on the curve is $\left(\pm \frac{4}{\sqrt{3}}, 2 \right)$.

197. Correct Response : (a)

Explanation :

The given function is,

$$f(x) = 3\sin x - 4\sin^3 x = \sin 3x$$

Differentiate above function.

$$f'(x) = 3\cos 3x > 0$$

Now,

$$-\frac{\pi}{2} > 3x > \frac{\pi}{2}$$

$$-\frac{\pi}{6} > x > \frac{\pi}{6}$$

Therefore, length of longest interval is $\frac{\pi}{3}$.

●●

Integral Calculus

QUESTIONS

1. If $\int (e^{2x} + 2e^x - e^{-x} - 1)e^{(e^x + e^{-x})}\, dx$

$= g(x)e^{(e^x + e^{-x})} + c$, where c is a constant of integration, then $g(0)$ is equal to : **[2020, Main]**

(a) 2   (b) e^2

(c) e (d) 1

2. The value of $\displaystyle\int_{-\pi/2}^{\pi/2} \frac{1}{1 + e^{\sin x}}\, dx$ is : **[2020, Main]**

(a) π (b) $\dfrac{3\pi}{2}$

(c) $\dfrac{\pi}{4}$ (d) $\dfrac{\pi}{2}$

3. $\displaystyle\lim_{x \to 1}\left(\frac{\displaystyle\int_0^{(x-1)^2} t\cos(t^2)\, dt}{(x-1)\sin(x-1)}\right)$ **[2020, Main]**

(a) does not exist   (b) is equal to $\dfrac{1}{2}$

(c) is equal to 1   (d) is equal to $-\dfrac{1}{2}$

4. If $I_1 = \displaystyle\int_0^1 (1 - x^{50})^{100}\, dx$ and $I_2 = \displaystyle\int_0^1 (1 - x^{50})^{101}\, dx$

such that $I_2 = \alpha I_1$ then α equals to : **[2020, Main]**

(a) $\dfrac{5050}{5051}$ (b) $\dfrac{5050}{5049}$

(c) $\dfrac{5049}{5050}$ (d) $\dfrac{5051}{5050}$

5. The integral $\displaystyle\int_1^2 e^x \cdot x^x (2 + \log_e x)$ equal :

[2020, Main]

(a) $e(4e + 1)$ (b) $e(2e - 1)$

(c) $4e^2 - 1$ (d) $e(4e - 1)$

6. Let $f(x) = |\,x - 2\,|$ and $g(x) = f[f(x)]$, $x \in [0, 4]$.

Then $\displaystyle\int_0^3 [g(x) - f(x)]\, dx$ is equal to : **[2020, Main]**

(a) $\dfrac{3}{2}$ (b) 0

(c) $\dfrac{1}{2}$ (d) 1

7. Let $f(x) = \displaystyle\int \frac{\sqrt{x}}{(1 + x)^2}\, dx\ (x \geq 0)$. Then $f(3) - f(1)$ is equal to : **[2020, Main]**

(a) $-\dfrac{\pi}{6} + \dfrac{1}{2} + \dfrac{\sqrt{3}}{4}$ (b) $\dfrac{\pi}{6} + \dfrac{1}{2} - \dfrac{\sqrt{3}}{4}$

(c) $-\dfrac{\pi}{12} + \dfrac{1}{2} + \dfrac{\sqrt{3}}{4}$ (d) $\dfrac{\pi}{12} + \dfrac{1}{2} - \dfrac{\sqrt{3}}{4}$

8. The integral $\displaystyle\int\left(\frac{x}{x\sin x + \cos x}\right)^2 dx$ is equal to :

(where C is a constant of integration)

[2020, Main]

(a) $\sec x + \dfrac{x\tan x}{x\sin x + \cos x} + C$

(b) $\sec x - \dfrac{x\tan x}{x\sin x + \cos x} + C$

(c) $\tan x + \dfrac{x\sec x}{x\sin x + \cos x} + C$

(d) $\tan x - \dfrac{x\sec x}{x\sin x + \cos x} + C$

9. $\displaystyle\int_{\pi/6}^{\pi/3} \tan^3 x \cdot \sin^2 3x (2\sec^2 x \cdot \sin^2 3x$

$+ 3\tan x \cdot \sin 6x)\, dx$ is equal to :

[2020, Main]

(a) $\dfrac{9}{2}$ (b) $-\dfrac{1}{9}$

(c) $-\dfrac{1}{18}$ (d) $\dfrac{7}{18}$

10. Let $\{x\}$ and $[x]$ denote the fractional part of x and the greatest integer $\leq x$ respectiely of a real number x. If $\displaystyle\int_0^n \{x\}\, dx$, $\displaystyle\int_0^n [x]\, dx$ and $10(n^2 - n)$, $(n \in N,\ n > 1)$ are three consecutive terms of a G.P., then n is equal to ....

[2020, Main]

11. $\displaystyle\int_{-\pi}^{\pi} |\pi - |x|\,|\,dx$ is equal to : **[2020, Main]**

(a) π^2 (b) $2\pi^2$

(c) $\sqrt{2}\pi^2$ (d) $\dfrac{\pi^2}{2}$

12. If $\displaystyle\int \dfrac{\cos\theta}{5 + 7\sin\theta - 2\cos^2\theta}\,d\theta = A\log_e |\,B(\theta)\,| + C,$ where C is a constant of integration, then $\dfrac{B(\theta)}{A}$ can be : **[2020, Main]**

(a) $\dfrac{2\sin\theta + 1}{5(\sin\theta + 3)}$ (b) $\dfrac{2\sin\theta + 1}{\sin\theta + 3}$

(c) $\dfrac{5(\sin\theta + 3)}{2\sin\theta + 1}$ (d) $\dfrac{5(2\sin\theta + 1)}{\sin\theta + 3}$

13. Which of the following inequalities is/are TRUE ? **[2020, Main]**

(a) $\displaystyle\int_0^1 x\cos x\,dx \ge \dfrac{3}{8}$ (b) $\displaystyle\int_0^1 x\sin x\,dx \ge \dfrac{3}{10}$

(c) $\displaystyle\int_0^1 x^2\cos x\,dx \ge \dfrac{1}{2}$ (d) $\displaystyle\int_0^1 x^2\sin x\,dx \ge \dfrac{2}{9}$

14. Let m be the minimum possible value of $\log_3 (3^{y_1} + 3^{y_2} + 3^{y_3})$ where y_1, y_2, y_3 are real numbers for which $y_1 + y_2 + y_3 = 9$. Let M be the maximum possible value of $(\log_3 x_1 + \log_3 x_2 + \log_3 x_3)$, where x_1, x_2, x_3 are positive real numbers for which $x_1 + x_2 + x_3 = 9$. Then the value of $\log_2 (m^3) + \log_3 (M^2)$ is .... **[2020, Advanced]**

15. Let $f : R \to R$ be a differentiable function such that its derivative f' is continuous and $f(\pi) = -6$. If $F : [0, \pi] \to R$ is defined by $F(x) = \int_0^x f(t)\,dt$ and if
$$\int_0^\pi [f'(x) + F(x)]\cos x\,dx = 2,$$
then the value of $f(0)$ is .... **[2020, Advanced]**

16. Let $[t]$ denotes the greatest integer less than or equal to t. Then the value of $\displaystyle\int_1^2 |\,2x - [3x]\,|\,dx$ is .... **[2020, Main]**

17. If the value of the integral $\displaystyle\int_9^{1/2} \dfrac{x^2}{(1-x^2)^{3/2}}\,dx$ is $\dfrac{k}{6}$, then k is equal to : **[2020, Main]**

(a) $2\sqrt{3} - \pi$ (b) $3\sqrt{2} + \pi$

(c) $3\sqrt{2} - \pi$ (d) $2\sqrt{3} + \pi$

18. If $\displaystyle\int \sin^{-1}\left(\sqrt{\dfrac{x}{1+x}}\right)dx = A(x)\tan^{-1}(\sqrt{x}) + B(x) +$ C, where C is a constant of integration, then the ordered pair $(A(x), B(x))$ can be : **[2020, Main]**

(a) $(x - 1, \sqrt{x})$ (b) $(x + 1, \sqrt{x})$

(c) $(x + 1, -\sqrt{x})$ (d) $(x - 1, -\sqrt{x})$

19. If $x^3\,dy + xy\,dx = x^2\,dy + 2y\,dx;\ y(2) = e$ and $x > 1$, then $y(4)$ is equal to : **[2020, Main]**

(a) $\dfrac{3}{2} + \sqrt{e}$ (b) $\dfrac{3}{2} - \sqrt{e}$

(c) $\dfrac{1}{2} + \sqrt{e}$ (d) $\dfrac{\sqrt{e}}{2}$

20. The integral $\displaystyle\int_0^2 |\,|x-1| - x\,|\,dx$ is equal to .... **[2020, Main]**

21. The area (in sq. units) of the region $\{(x, y) \le R^2\,|\,4x^2 \le y \le 8x + 12\}$ is : **[2020, Main]**

(a) $\dfrac{127}{3}$ (b) $\dfrac{125}{3}$

(c) $\dfrac{124}{3}$ (d) $\dfrac{128}{3}$

22. If θ_1 and θ_2 be respectively the smallest and the largest values of θ in $(0, 2\pi) = \{\pi\}$ which satisfy the equation, $2\cot^2\theta - \dfrac{5}{\sin\theta} + 4 = 0,$ then $\displaystyle\int_{\theta_2}^{\theta_1} \cos^2 3\theta\,d\theta$ is equal to : **[2020, Main]**

(a) $\dfrac{2\pi}{3}$ (b) $\dfrac{\pi}{3} + \dfrac{1}{6}$

(c) $\dfrac{\pi}{9}$ (d) $\dfrac{\pi}{3}$

23. The value of α for which $4\alpha \displaystyle\int_{-1}^2 e^{-\alpha|x|}\,dx = 5$, is : **[2020, Main]**

(a) $\log_e\left(\dfrac{3}{2}\right)$ (b) $\log_e\left(\dfrac{4}{2}\right)$

(c) $\log_e 2$ (d) $\log_e \sqrt{2}$

24. The area (in sq. units) of the region $\{(x, y) \in R^2 : x^2 \le y \le 3 - 2x\}$. is **[2020, Main]**

(a) $\dfrac{29}{3}$ (b) $\dfrac{31}{3}$

(c) $\dfrac{34}{3}$ (d) $\dfrac{32}{3}$

25. If $I = \int\limits_{1}^{2} \dfrac{dx}{\sqrt{2x^3 - 9x^2 + 12x + 4}}$. then : **[2020, Main]**

(a) $\dfrac{1}{9} < I^2 < \dfrac{1}{8}$ (b) $\dfrac{1}{16} < I^2 < \dfrac{1}{9}$

(c) $\dfrac{1}{6} < I^2 < \dfrac{1}{2}$ (d) $\dfrac{1}{8} < I^2 < \dfrac{1}{4}$

26. $\lim\limits_{x \to 0} \dfrac{\int\limits_{0}^{x} t \sin(10t)\,dt}{x}$ is equal to : **[2020, Main]**

(a) 0 (b) $-\dfrac{1}{5}$

(c) $-\dfrac{1}{10}$ (d) $\dfrac{1}{10}$

27. The value of $\int\limits_{0}^{2x} \dfrac{x \sin^8 x}{\sin^8 x + \cos^8 x}\,dx$ is equal to :

[2020, Main]

(a) 2π (b) 4π

(c) $2\pi^2$ (d) π^2

28. The integral $\int \dfrac{dx}{(x+4)^{\frac{8}{7}} (x-3)^{\frac{6}{7}}}$ is equal to :

(where C is a constant of integration)

[2020, Main]

(a) $\left(\dfrac{x-3}{x+4}\right)^{\frac{1}{7}} + C$ (b) $-\left(\dfrac{x-3}{x+4}\right)^{\frac{-1}{7}} + C$

(c) $\dfrac{1}{2}\left(\dfrac{x-3}{x+4}\right)^{\frac{3}{7}} + C$ (d) $-\dfrac{1}{13}\left(\dfrac{x-3}{x+4}\right)^{-\frac{13}{7}} + C$

[2020, Main]

29. If for all real triplets (a, b, c), $f(x) = a + bx + cx^2$, then $\int\limits_{0}^{1} f(x)\,dx$ is equal to : **[2020, Main]**

(a) $\dfrac{1}{2}\left\{f(1) + 3f\left(\dfrac{1}{2}\right)\right\}$ (b) $2\left\{3f(1) + 2f\left(\dfrac{1}{2}\right)\right\}$

(c) $\dfrac{1}{6}\left\{f(0) + f(1) + 4f\left(\dfrac{1}{2}\right)\right\}$ (d) $\dfrac{1}{3}\left\{f(0) + f\left(\dfrac{1}{2}\right)\right\}$

30. Given : $f(x) = \begin{cases} x, & 0 \le x \le \dfrac{1}{2} \\ \dfrac{1}{2}, & x = \dfrac{1}{2} \\ 1-x, & \dfrac{1}{2} < x \le 1 \end{cases}$

and $g(x) = \left(x - \dfrac{1}{2}\right)^2$, $x \in$ R. Then the area (in sq.

units) of the region bounded by the curves, $y = f(x)$ and $y = g(x)$ between the line $2x = 1$ and $2x = \sqrt{3}$, is : **[2020, Main]**

(a) $\dfrac{1}{3} + \dfrac{\sqrt{3}}{4}$ (b) $\dfrac{\sqrt{3}}{4} - \dfrac{1}{3}$

(c) $\dfrac{1}{2} + \dfrac{\sqrt{3}}{4}$ (d) $\dfrac{1}{2} - \dfrac{\sqrt{3}}{4}$

31. If $\int \dfrac{d\theta}{\cos^2 \theta (\tan 2\theta + \sec 2\theta)} = \lambda \tan \theta + 2 \log_e |f(\theta)|$

+ C. where, C is a constant of integration, then the ordered pair $(\lambda, f(0))$ is equal to :

[2020, Main]

(a) $(-1, 1 + \tan \theta)$ (b) $(-1, 1 - \tan \theta)$
(c) $(1, 1 - \tan \theta)$ (d) $(1, 1 + \tan \theta)$

32. The area of the region, enclosed by the circle $x^2 + y^2 = 2$ which is not common to the region bounded by the parabola $y^2 = x$ and the straight line $y = x$, is : **[2020, Main]**

(a) $\dfrac{1}{3}(12\pi - 1)$ (b) $\dfrac{1}{6}(12\pi - 1)$

(c) $\dfrac{1}{6}(24\pi - 1)$ (d) $\dfrac{1}{3}(6\pi - 1)$

33. If $f(a + b + 1 - x) = f(x)$, for all x, where a and b are fixed positive real numbers, then $\dfrac{1}{a+b}\int\limits_{x}^{b}[f(x) + f(x+1)]$ is equal to : **[2020, Main]**

(a) $\int\limits_{a+1}^{b+1} f(x)\,dx$ (b) $\int\limits_{a+1}^{b+1} f(x+1)\,dx$

(c) $\int\limits_{a-1}^{b-1} f(x+1)\,dx$ (d) $\int\limits_{a-1}^{b-1} f(x)\,dx$

34. For $a > 0$. Let the curves $C_1 : y^2 = ax$ and $C_2 : x^2 = ay$ intersect at origin O and a point P. Let the line $x = b (o < b < a)$ intersect the chord OP and x-axis at points Q and R. respectively. If the line $x = b$ bisects the area bounded by the curves, C_1 and C_2, and the area of $\triangle OQR = \dfrac{1}{2}$, then '$a$' satisfies the equation : **[2020, Main]**

(a) $x^6 - 12x^3 + 4 = 0$ (b) $x^6 - 12x^3 - 4 = 0$
(c) $x^6 + 6x^3 - 4 = 0$ (d) $x^6 - 6x^3 + 4 = 0$

35. If $\int \dfrac{\cos x\, dx}{\sin^3 x (1 + \sin x^6)^{2/3}} = f(x)\,(1 + \sin^6 x)^{1/\lambda} + c$

where c is a constant of integration, then $\lambda f\left(\dfrac{\pi}{3}\right)$ is equal to : **[2020, Main]**

(a) -2 (b) $-\dfrac{9}{8}$

(c) 2 (d) $\dfrac{9}{8}$

36. If $f'(x) = \tan^{-1}(\sec x + \tan x)$, $-\dfrac{\pi}{2} < x < \dfrac{\pi}{2}$, and $f(0)$ $= 0$, then $f(1)$ is equal to : **[2020, Main]**

(a) $\dfrac{\pi-1}{4}$

(b) $\dfrac{\pi+2}{4}$

(c) $\dfrac{\pi+1}{4}$

(d) $\dfrac{1}{4}$ [2020, Main]

37. The value of $\displaystyle\int_0^{2\pi} [\sin 2x(1+\cos 3x)]dx,$ where $[t]$ denotes the greatest integer function, is :

[2019, Main]

(a) π

(b) $-\pi$

(c) -2π

(d) 2π

38. If $\displaystyle\int \dfrac{dx}{(x^2-2x+10)^2}$

$= A\left(\tan^{-1}\left(\dfrac{x-1}{3}\right) + \dfrac{f(x)}{x^2-2x+10}\right)+C$

where C is a constant of integration, then :

[2019, Main]

(a) $A = \dfrac{1}{54}$ and $f(x) = 3(x-1)$

(b) $A = \dfrac{1}{81}$ and $f(x) = 3(x-1)$

(c) $A = \dfrac{1}{27}$ and $f(x) = 9(x-1)$

(d) $A = \dfrac{1}{54}$ and $f(x) = 9(x-1)^2$

39. $\displaystyle\lim_{n\to\infty}\left(\dfrac{(n+1)^{1/3}}{n^{4/3}}+\dfrac{(n+2)^{1/3}}{n^{4/3}}+.....+\dfrac{(2n)^{1/3}}{n^{4/3}}\right)$ is equal to :   [2019, Main]

(a) $\dfrac{3}{4}(2)^{4/3}-\dfrac{3}{4}$

(b) $\dfrac{4}{3}(2)^{4/3}$

(c) $\dfrac{3}{4}(2)^{4/3}-\dfrac{4}{3}$

(d) $\dfrac{4}{3}(2)^{3/4}$

40. The area (in sq. units) of the region bounded by the curves $y = 2^x$ and $y = |x+1|$, in the first quadrant is :   [2019, Main]

(a) $\log_e 2+\dfrac{3}{2}$

(b) $\dfrac{3}{2}$

(c) $\dfrac{1}{2}$

(d) $\dfrac{3}{2}-\dfrac{1}{\log_e 2}$

41. The integral $\displaystyle\int_{\pi/6}^{\pi/3} \sec^{2/3}x\ \mathrm{cosec}^{4/3}x\,dx$ is equal to :

[2019, Main]

(a) $3^{5/6}-3^{2/3}$

(b) $3^{4/3}-3^{1/3}$

(c) $3^{7/6}-3^{5/6}$

(d) $3^{5/3}-3^{1/3}$

42. If $\displaystyle\int x^5 e^{-x^2}\,dx = g(x)e^{-x^2}+c$, where c is a constant of interation, then g(–1) is equal to :

[2019, Main]

(a) -1

(b) 1

(c) $-\dfrac{5}{2}$

(d) $-\dfrac{1}{2}$

43. The value of the integral $\displaystyle\int_0^1 x\cot^{-1}(1-x^2+x^4)\,dx$ is :   [2019, Main]

(a) $\dfrac{\pi}{2}-\dfrac{1}{2}\log_e 2$

(b) $\dfrac{\pi}{4}-\log_e 2$

(c) $\dfrac{\pi}{2}-\log_e 2$

(d) $\dfrac{\pi}{4}-\dfrac{1}{2}\log_e 2$

44. If $\displaystyle\int e^{\sec x}\,(\sec x \tan x\, f(x) + (\sec x \tan x + \sec^2 x))\,dx = e^{\sec x} f(x)+C$, then a possible choice of $f(x)$ is :

[2019, Main]

(a) $\sec x + \tan x + \dfrac{1}{2}$

(b) $\sec x - \tan x - \dfrac{1}{2}$

(c) $\sec x + x \tan x - \dfrac{1}{2}$

(d) $x \sec x + \tan x + \dfrac{1}{2}$

45. The area (in sq. units) of the region $A=\{(x,y);\ \dfrac{y^2}{2}\le x \le y+4\}$ is :   [2019, Main]

(a) $\dfrac{53}{3}$

(b) 30

(c) 16

(d) 18

46. The integral $\displaystyle\int \sec^{2/3}x\ \mathrm{cosec}^{4/3}x\,dx$ is equal to : (Here, C is a constant of integration) [2019, Main]

(a) $-3\tan^{-1/3}x + C$

(b) $-\dfrac{3}{4}\tan^{-4/3}x + C$

(c) $-3\cot^{-1/3}x + C$

(d) $3\tan^{-1/3}x + C$

47. The value of $\displaystyle\int_0^{\pi/2} \dfrac{\sin^3 x}{\sin x+\cos x}\,dx$ is : [2019, Main]

(a) $\dfrac{\pi-2}{8}$

(b) $\dfrac{\pi-1}{4}$

(c) $\dfrac{\pi-2}{4}$

(d) $\dfrac{\pi-1}{2}$

48. The area (in sq. units) of the region $A=\{(x,y): x^2\le y\le x+2\}$ is :   [2019, Main]

(a) $\dfrac{10}{3}$

(b) $\dfrac{9}{2}$

(c) $\dfrac{31}{6}$

(d) $\dfrac{13}{6}$

49. $\displaystyle\int \frac{\sin\frac{5x}{2}}{\sin\frac{x}{2}}\,dx$ is equal to : **[2019, Main]**

(where c is a constant of integration.)

(a) $2x + \sin x + 2\sin 2x + c$

(b) $x + 2\sin x + 2\sin 2x + c$

(c) $x + 2\sin x + \sin 2x + c$

(d) $2x + \sin x + \sin 2x + c$

50. The area (in sq. units) of the region $A = \{(x, y) \in \mathbf{R} \times \mathbf{R} \mid 0 \le x \le 3, 0 \le y \le 4, y \le x^2 + 3x\}$ is :

[2019, Main]

(a) $\dfrac{53}{6}$

(b) 8

(c) $\dfrac{59}{6}$

(d) $\dfrac{26}{3}$

51. If $f(x) = \dfrac{2 - x\cos x}{2 + x\cos x}$ and $g(x) = \log_e x$, $(x > 0)$ then the value of the integral $\displaystyle\int_{-\pi/4}^{\pi/4} g(f(x))\,dx$ is :

[2019, Main]

(a) $\log_e 3$

(b) $\log_e e$

(c) $\log_e 2$

(d) $\log_e 1$

52. If $\displaystyle\int \frac{dx}{x^3(1 + x^6)^{2/3}} = xf(x)(1 + x^6)^{\frac{1}{3}} + C$ where C is a constant of integration, then the function $f(x)$ is equal to : **[2019, Main]**

(a) $\dfrac{3}{x^2}$

(b) $-\dfrac{1}{6x^3}$

(c) $-\dfrac{1}{2x^2}$

(d) $-\dfrac{1}{2x^3}$

53. Let $f(x) = \displaystyle\int_0^x g(t)\,dt$, where g is a non-zero even function. If $f(x + 5) = g(x)$, then $\displaystyle\int_0^x f(t)\,dt$ equals :

[2019, Main]

(a) $\displaystyle\int_{x+5}^{5} g(t)\,dt$

(b) $\displaystyle\int_{5}^{x+5} g(t)\,dt$

(c) $2\displaystyle\int_{5}^{x+5} g(t)\,dt$

(d) $5\displaystyle\int_{x+5}^{5} g(t)\,dt$

54. Let $S(\alpha) = \{(x, y) : y^2 \le x, 0 \le x \le \alpha\}$ and $A(\alpha)$ is area of the region $S(\alpha)$. If for a λ, $0 < \lambda < 4$, $A(\lambda) : A(4) = 2 : 5$, then λ equals : **[2019, Main]**

(a) $2\left(\dfrac{4}{25}\right)^{\frac{1}{3}}$

(b) $2\left(\dfrac{2}{5}\right)^{\frac{1}{3}}$

(c) $4\left(\dfrac{2}{5}\right)^{\frac{1}{3}}$

(d) $4\left(\dfrac{4}{25}\right)^{\frac{1}{3}}$

55. The integral $\displaystyle\int \frac{2x^3 - 1}{x^4 + x}\,dx$ is equal to :

(Here C is a constant of integration) **[2019, Main]**

(a) $\dfrac{1}{2}\log_e \dfrac{|x^3 + 1|}{x^2} + C$

(b) $\dfrac{1}{2}\log_e \dfrac{(x^3 + 1)^2}{|x^3|} + C$

(c) $\log_e \left|\dfrac{x^3 + 1}{x}\right| + C$

(d) $\log_e \dfrac{|x^3 + 1|}{x^2} + C$

56. If $\displaystyle\int_0^{\frac{\pi}{2}} \frac{\cot x}{\cot x + \cosec x}\,dx = m(\pi + n)$, then $m \cdot n$ is equal to : **[2019, Main]**

(a) $-\dfrac{1}{2}$

(b) 1

(c) $\dfrac{1}{2}$

(d) -1

57. A value of α such that $\displaystyle\int_{\alpha}^{\alpha+1} \frac{dx}{(x + \alpha)(x + \alpha + 1)} = \log_e\left(\dfrac{9}{8}\right)$ is : **[2019, Main]**

(a) -2

(b) $1/2$

(c) $-1/2$

(d) 2

58. let $\alpha \in (0, \pi/2)$ be fixed. If the integral $\displaystyle\int \frac{\tan x + \tan\alpha}{\tan x - \tan\alpha}\,dx = A(x)\cos 2\alpha + B(x)\sin 2\alpha + C$, where C is a constant of integration, then the functions $A(x)$ and $B(x)$ are respectively : **[2019, Main]**

(a) $x + \alpha$ and $\log_e |\sin(x + \alpha)|$

(b) $x - \alpha$ and $\log_e |\sin(x - \alpha)|$

(c) $x - \alpha$ and $\log_e |\cos(x - \alpha)|$

(d) $x + \alpha$ and $\log_e |\sin(x - \alpha)|$

59. If the area (in sq. units) of the region $\{(x, y) : y^2 \le 4x, x + y \le 1, x \ge 0, y \ge 0\}$ is $a\sqrt{2} + b$, then $a - b$ is equal to : **[2019, Main]**

(a) $\dfrac{10}{3}$

(b) 6

(c) $\dfrac{8}{3}$

(d) $-\dfrac{2}{3}$

60. If the area (in sq. units) bounded by the parabola $y^2 = 4\lambda x$ and the line $y = \lambda x$, $\lambda > 0$, is $\dfrac{1}{9}$, then λ is equal to : **[2019, Main]**

(a) $2\sqrt{6}$　　　　　　(b) 48

(c) 24　　　　　　(d) $4\sqrt{3}$

61. The area of the region $\{(x, y) : xy \le 8,\ 1 \le y \le x^2\}$ is **[2019, Advanced]**

(a) $16 \log_e 2 - \dfrac{14}{3}$　　　(b) $8 \log_e 2 - \dfrac{14}{3}$

(c) $16 \log_e 2 - 6$　　　(d) $8 \log_e 2 - \dfrac{7}{3}$

62. If $I = \dfrac{2}{\pi} \displaystyle\int_{-\pi/4}^{\pi/4} \dfrac{dx}{(1 + e^{\sin x})(2 - \cos 2x)}$ then $27\,I^2$ equals.

[2019, Advanced]

63. For $a \in \mathbf{R}$, $|a| > 1$, let

$$\lim_{n \to \infty}\left(\dfrac{1 + \sqrt[3]{2} + \ldots + \sqrt[3]{n}}{n^{7/3}\left(\dfrac{1}{(an+1)^2} + \dfrac{1}{(an+2)^2} + \ldots + \dfrac{1}{(an+n)^2} \right)} \right) = 54$$

Then the possible value (s) of a is/are

[2019, Advanced]

(a) -9　　　　　　(b) -6

(c) 7　　　　　　(d) 8

64. The value of the integral $\displaystyle\int_0^{\pi/2} \dfrac{3\sqrt{\cos\theta}}{(\sqrt{\cos\theta} + \sqrt{\sin\theta})^5}\, d\theta$

equals **[2019, Advanced]**

65. If $f\left(\dfrac{x-4}{x+2}\right) = 2x + 1$, $(x \in R - \{1, -2\})$, then $\displaystyle\int f(x)\,dx$ is equal to : **[2018, Main]**

(where C is a constant of integration)

(a) $12 \log_e |1 - x| + 3x + C$

(b) $-12 \log_e |1 - x| - 3x + C$

(c) $12 \log_e |1 - x| - 3x + C$

(d) $-12 \log_e |1 - x| + 3x + C$

66. The area (in sq. units) of the region $\{x \in R : x \ge 0,\ y \ge 0,\ y \ge x - 2 \text{ and } y \le \sqrt{x}\ \}$, is : **[2018, Main]**

(a) $\dfrac{13}{3}$　　　　　　(b) $\dfrac{8}{3}$

(c) $\dfrac{10}{3}$　　　　　　(d) $\dfrac{5}{3}$

67. The value of the integral

$$\int_{-\frac{\pi}{2}}^{\frac{\pi}{2}} \sin^4 x\left(1 + \log\left(\dfrac{2 + \sin x}{2 - \sin x}\right)\right) dx \text{ is :}$$

[2018, Main]

(a) 0　　　　　　(b) $\dfrac{3}{4}$

(c) $\dfrac{3}{8}\pi$　　　　　　(d) $\dfrac{3}{16}\pi$

68. If $\displaystyle\int \dfrac{\tan x}{1 + \tan x + \tan^2 x}\, dx = x - \dfrac{K}{\sqrt{A}} \tan^{-1}\left(\dfrac{K \tan x + 1}{\sqrt{A}}\right) + C$, (C is a constant of integration),

then the ordered pair (K, A) is equal to : **[2018, Main]**

(a) $(2, 1)$　　　　　　(b) $(-2, 3)$

(c) $(2, 3)$　　　　　　(d) $(-2, 1)$

69. If $f(x) = \displaystyle\int_0^x t(\sin x - \sin t)\,dt$ then :

[2018, Main]

(a) $f'''(x) + f''(x) = \sin x$

(b) $f'''(x) + f''(x) = \cos x$

(c) $f'''(x) + f'(x) = \cos x - 2x \sin x$

(d) $f'''(x) - f''(x) = \cos x - 2x \sin x$

70. If the area of the region bounded by the curves, $y = x^2$, $y = \dfrac{1}{x}$ and the lines $y = 0$ and $x = t(t > 1)$ is 1 sq. unit, then t is equal to : **[2018, Main]**

(a) $e^{\frac{3}{2}}$　　　　　　(b) $\dfrac{4}{3}$

(c) $\dfrac{3}{2}$　　　　　　(d) $e^{\frac{2}{3}}$

71. The integral

$$\int \dfrac{\sin^2 x \cos^2 x}{(\sin^5 x + \cos^3 x \sin^2 x + \sin^3 x \cos^2 x + \cos^5 x)^2}\, dx$$

is equal to : **[2018, Main]**

(a) $\dfrac{1}{3(1 + \tan^3 x)} + C$　　　(b) $\dfrac{-1}{3(1 + \tan^3 x)} + C$

(c) $\dfrac{1}{1 + \cot^3 x} + C$　　　(d) $\dfrac{-1}{1 + \cot^3 x} + C$

(where C is a constant of integration)

72. The value of $\displaystyle\int_{-\frac{\pi}{2}}^{\frac{\pi}{2}} \frac{\sin^2 x}{1+2^x}\,dx$ is : **[2018, Main]**

(a) $\dfrac{\pi}{8}$

(b) $\dfrac{\pi}{2}$

(c) 4π

(d) $\dfrac{\pi}{4}$

73. Let $g(x) = \cos x^2$, $f(x) = \sqrt{x}$, and α, β ($\alpha < \beta$) be the roots of the quadratic equation $18x^2 - 9\pi x + \pi^2 = 0$. Then the area (in sq. units) bounded by the curve $y = (gof)(x)$ and the lines $x = \alpha$, $x = \beta$ and $y = 0$ is : **[2018, Main]**

(a) $\dfrac{1}{2}\left(\sqrt{3}-1\right)$

(b) $\dfrac{1}{2}\left(\sqrt{3}+1\right)$

(c) $\dfrac{1}{2}\left(\sqrt{3}-\sqrt{2}\right)$

(d) $\dfrac{1}{2}\left(\sqrt{2}-1\right)$

74. Let $f : [0, \infty) \to R$ be a continuous function such that

$$f(x) = 1 - 2x + \int_0^x e^{x-t} f(t)\,dt$$

for all $x \in [0, \infty)$. Then, which of the following statement(s) is (are) TRUE ? **[2018, Advanced]**

(a) The curve $y = f(x)$ passes through the point $(1, 2)$

(b) The curve $y = f(x)$ passes through the point $(2, -1)$

(c) The area of the region

$$\{(x, y) \in [0, 1] \times R : f(x) \le y \le \sqrt{1-x^2}\}\text{ is}$$

$$\dfrac{\pi-2}{4}$$

(d) The area of the region

$$\{(x, y \in [0, 1] \times R : f(x) \le y \le \sqrt{1-x^2}\}\text{ is}$$

$$\dfrac{\pi-1}{4}$$

75. For each positive integer n, let

$$y_n = \frac{1}{n}\left((n+1)(n+2)...(n+n)\right)^{\frac{1}{n}}.$$

For $x \in R$, let $[x]$ be the greatest integer less than or equal to x. If $\displaystyle\lim_{n\to\infty} y_n = L$, then the value of $[L]$

is .... **[2018, Advanced]**

76. The value of the integral

$$\int_0^{\frac{1}{2}} \frac{1+\sqrt{3}}{((x+1)^2(1-x)^6)^{\frac{1}{4}}}\,dx$$

is .... **[2018, Advanced]**

77. Let $\text{In} = \int \tan^n x\,dx$, $(n > 1)$. If $I_4 + I_6 = a\tan^5 x + bx^5$ $+\ C$, where C is a constant of integration, then the ordered pair (a, b) is equal to : **[2017, Main]**

(a) $\left(\dfrac{1}{5}, 0\right)$

(b) $\left(\dfrac{1}{5}, -1\right)$

(c) $\left(-\dfrac{1}{5}, 0\right)$

(d) $\left(-\dfrac{1}{5}, 1\right)$

78. The integral $\displaystyle\int_{\frac{\pi}{4}}^{\frac{3\pi}{4}} \frac{dx}{1+\cos x}$ is equal to : **[2017, Main]**

(a) 2

(b) 4

(c) – 1

(d) – 2

79. The area (in sq. units) of the region $\{(x, y) : x \ge 0,$ $x + y \le 3$, $x^2 \le 4y$ and $y \le 1 + \sqrt{x}\ \}$ is :

(a) $\dfrac{3}{2}$

(b) $\dfrac{7}{3}$

(c) $\dfrac{5}{2}$

(d) $\dfrac{59}{12}$

80. If $f\left(\dfrac{3x-4}{3x+4}\right) = x + 2$, $x \pi - \dfrac{4}{3}$, and $\int f(x)\,dx = A$ $\log |1 - x| + Bx + C$, then the ordered pair (A, B) is equal to :

(where C is a constant of integration) **[2017, Main]**

(a) $\left(\dfrac{8}{3}, \dfrac{2}{3}\right)$

(b) $\left(-\dfrac{8}{3}, \dfrac{2}{3}\right)$

(c) $\left(-\dfrac{8}{3}, -\dfrac{2}{3}\right)$

(d) $\left(\dfrac{8}{3}, -\dfrac{2}{3}\right)$

81. If $\displaystyle\int_1^2 \frac{dx}{(x^2-2x+4)^{\frac{3}{2}}} = \frac{k}{k+5}$, then k is equal to : **[2017, Main]**

(a) 1

(b) 2

(c) 3

(d) 4

82. If the line $x = \alpha$ divides the area of region $R = \{(x, y) \in R^2 : x^3 \le y \le x, 0 \le x \le 1\}$ into two equal parts, then : **[2017, Advanced]**

(a) $0 < \alpha \le \dfrac{1}{2}$

(b) $\dfrac{1}{2} < \alpha < 1$

(c) $2\alpha^4 - 4\alpha^2 + 1 = 0$

(d) $\alpha^4 + 4\alpha^2 - 1 = 0$

83. The integral

$$\int \sqrt{1+2\cot x\,(\csc x+\cot x)}\,dx$$

$$\left(0<x<\frac{\pi}{2}\right)\text{ is equal to :}$$

(where C is a constant of integration)

[2017, Main]

(a) $4\log\left(\sin\dfrac{x}{2}\right)+C$

(b) $2\log\left(\sin\dfrac{x}{2}\right)+C$

(c) $2\log\left(\cos\dfrac{x}{2}\right)+C$

(d) $4\log\left(\cos\dfrac{x}{2}\right)+C$

84. The integral $\displaystyle\int_{\frac{\pi}{12}}^{\frac{\pi}{4}}\frac{8\cos 2x}{(\tan x+\cot x)^3}\,dx$ equals :

[2017, Main]

(a) $\dfrac{15}{128}$

(b) $\dfrac{15}{64}$

(c) $\dfrac{13}{32}$

(d) $\dfrac{13}{256}$

85. The area (in sq. units) of the smaller portion enclosed between the curves, $x^2 + y^2 = 4$ and $y^2 = 3x$ is : **[2017, Main]**

(a) $\dfrac{1}{2\sqrt{3}}+\dfrac{\pi}{3}$

(b) $\dfrac{1}{\sqrt{3}}+\dfrac{2\pi}{3}$

(c) $\dfrac{1}{2\sqrt{3}}+\dfrac{2\pi}{3}$

(d) $\dfrac{1}{\sqrt{3}}+\dfrac{4\pi}{3}$

86. If $I=\displaystyle\sum_{k=1}^{98}\int_{k}^{k+1}\frac{k+1}{x(x+1)}\,dx$, then :

[2017, Advanced]

(a) $I>\log_e 99$

(b) $I<\log_e 99$

(c) $I<\dfrac{49}{50}$

(d) $I>\dfrac{49}{50}$

87. The integral $\displaystyle\int\frac{dx}{(1+\sqrt{x})\,\sqrt{x-x^2}}$ is equal to :

(where C is a constant of integration)

[2016, Main]

(a) $-2\sqrt{\dfrac{1+\sqrt{x}}{1-\sqrt{x}}}+C$

(b) $-2\sqrt{\dfrac{1-\sqrt{x}}{1+\sqrt{x}}}+C$

(c) $-\sqrt{\dfrac{1-\sqrt{x}}{1+\sqrt{x}}}+C$

(d) $2\sqrt{\dfrac{1+\sqrt{x}}{1-\sqrt{x}}}+C$

88. The value of the integral

$$\int_{4}^{10}\frac{[x^2]\,dx}{[x^2-28x+196]+[x^2]},\text{ where }[x]\text{ denotes the}$$

greatest integer less than or equal to x, is :

[2016, Main]

(a) 6

(b) 3

(c) 7

(d) $\dfrac{1}{3}$

89. The integral $\displaystyle\int\frac{2x^{12}+5x^9}{(x^5+x^3+1)^3}\,dx$ is equal to :

[2016, Main]

(a) $\dfrac{x^5}{(x^5+x^3+1)^2}+C$

(b) $\dfrac{x^{10}}{2(x^5+x^3+1)^2}+C$

(c) $\dfrac{x^5}{2(x^5+x^3+1)^2}+C$

(d) $\dfrac{-x^{10}}{2(x^5+x^3+1)^2}+C$

90. The area (in sq. units) of the region

$$\{(x,y):y^2\geq 2x\text{ and }x^2+y^2\leq 4x,\,x\geq 0,\,y\geq 0\}$$

is : **[2016, Main]**

(a) $\pi-\dfrac{4}{3}$

(b) $\pi-\dfrac{8}{3}$

(c) $\pi-\dfrac{4\sqrt{2}}{3}$

(d) $\dfrac{\pi}{2}-\dfrac{2\sqrt{2}}{3}$

91. If $\displaystyle\int\frac{dx}{\cos^3 x\sqrt{2\sin 2x}}=(\tan x)^A+C(\tan x)^B+k$,

where k is a constant of integration, then A + B + C equals : **[2016, Main]**

(a) $\dfrac{21}{5}$

(b) $\dfrac{16}{5}$

(c) $\dfrac{7}{10}$

(d) $\dfrac{27}{10}$

92. If $2\displaystyle\int_0^1\tan^{-1}x\,dx=\int_0^1\cot^{-1}(1-x+x^2)\,dx$, then $\displaystyle\int_0^1\tan^{-1}(1-x+x^2)\,dx$ is equal to :

[2016, Main]

(a) $\log 4$

(b) $\dfrac{\pi}{2}+\log 2$

(c) $\log 2$

(d) $\dfrac{\pi}{2}-\log 4$

93. The area (in sq. units) of the region described by $A=\{(x,y)\mid y\geq x^2-5x+4,\,x+y\geq 1,\,y\leq 0\}$ is : **[2016, Main]**

(a) $\dfrac{7}{2}$

(b) $\dfrac{19}{6}$

(c) $\dfrac{13}{6}$

(d) $\dfrac{17}{6}$

94. The total number of distinct $x \in [0, 1]$ for which

$$\int_0^x \frac{t^2}{1+t^4}\,dt = 2x - 1 \text{ is :}$$ **[2016, Advanced]**

95. The integral $\displaystyle\int \frac{dx}{x^2(x^4+1)^{3/4}}$ equals :

[2015, Main]

(a) $\left(\dfrac{x^4+1}{x^4}\right)^{\frac{1}{4}} + c$
(b) $(x^4+1)^{\frac{1}{4}} + c$

(c) $-(x^4+1)^{\frac{1}{4}} + c$
(d) $-\left(\dfrac{x^4+1}{x^4}\right)^{\frac{1}{4}} + c$

96. The integral

$$\int_2^4 \frac{\log x^2}{\log x^2 + \log(36 - 12x + x^2)}\,dx \text{ is equal to :}$$

[2015, Main]

(a) 2
(b) 4

(c) 1
(d) 6

97. The area (in sq. units) of the region described by $\{(x, y) : y^2 \le 2x \text{ and } y \ge 4x - 1\}$ is :

[2015, Main]

(a) $\dfrac{7}{32}$
(b) $\dfrac{5}{64}$

(c) $\dfrac{15}{64}$
(d) $\dfrac{9}{32}$

98. If $\alpha = \displaystyle\int_0^1 \left(e^{9x+3\tan^{-1}x}\right)\left(\frac{12+9x^2}{1+x^2}\right)dx$

where, $\tan^{-1}x$ takes only principal values, then the value of $\left(\log_e |1+\alpha| - \dfrac{3\pi}{4}\right)$ is : **[2015, Advanced]**

99. Let $f : \mathbb{R} \to \mathbb{R}$ be a continuous odd function, which vanishes exactly at one point and $f(1) = \dfrac{1}{2}$. Suppose

that $F(x) = \displaystyle\int_{-1}^x f(t)\,dt$ for all $x \in [-1, 2]$ and $G(x)$

$= \displaystyle\int_{-1}^x t|f(f(t))|\,dt$ for all $x \in [-1, 2]$. If $\displaystyle\lim_{x \to 1}\frac{F(x)}{G(x)} =$

$\dfrac{1}{14}$, then the value of $f\left(\dfrac{1}{2}\right)$ is :

[2015, Advanced]

100. The option(s) with the values of a and L that satisfy the following equation is (are)

$$\frac{\displaystyle\int_0^{4\pi} e^t(\sin^6 at + \cos^4 at)\,dt}{\displaystyle\int_0^{\pi} e^t(\sin^6 at + \cos^4 at)\,dt} = L?$$

[2015, Advanced]

(a) $a = 2,\ L = \dfrac{e^{4\pi}-1}{e^{\pi}-1}$
(b) $a = 2,\ L = \dfrac{e^{4\pi}+1}{e^{\pi}+1}$

(c) $a = 4,\ L = \dfrac{e^{4\pi}-1}{e^{\pi}-1}$
(d) $a = 4,\ L = \dfrac{e^{4\pi}+1}{e^{\pi}+1}$

101. Let $f(x) = 7\tan^8 x + 7\tan^6 x - 3\tan^4 x - 3\tan^2 x$ for

all $x \in \left(-\dfrac{\pi}{2}, \dfrac{\pi}{2}\right)$. Then the correct expression(s)

is (are) **[2015, Advanced]**

(a) $\displaystyle\int_0^{\pi/4} x f(x)\,dx = \dfrac{1}{12}$
(b) $\displaystyle\int_0^{\pi/4} f(x)\,dx = 0$

(c) $\displaystyle\int_0^{\pi/4} x f(x)\,dx = \dfrac{1}{6}$
(d) $\displaystyle\int_0^{\pi/4} f(x)\,dx = 1$

102. If $\displaystyle\int_1^3 x^2 F'(x)\,dx = -12$ and $\displaystyle\int_1^3 x^3 F''(x)\,dx = 40$, then

the correct expression(s) is (are)

[2015, Advanced]

(a) $9f'(3) + f'(1) - 32 = 0$
(b) $\displaystyle\int_1^3 f(x)\,dx = 12$

(c) $9f'(3) - f'(1) + 32 = 0$
(d) $\displaystyle\int_1^3 f(x)\,dx = -12$

103. Let $f : \mathbb{R} \to \mathbb{R}$ be a function defined by

$$f(x) = \begin{cases} [x], & x \le 2 \\ 0, & x > 2 \end{cases}$$

where $[x]$ is the greatest integer less than or

equal to x. If $I = \displaystyle\int_{-1}^2 \frac{x f(x^2)}{2 + f(x+1)}\,dx$, then the value

of $(4I - 1)$ is **[2015, Advanced]**

104. Let $F(x) = \displaystyle\int_x^{x^2+\frac{\pi}{6}} 2\cos^2 t\,dt$ for all $x \in \mathbb{R}$ and

$f : \left[0, \dfrac{1}{2}\right] \to [0, \infty)$ be a continuous function. For

$a \in \left[0, \dfrac{1}{2}\right]$, if $F'(a) + 2$ is the area of the region

bounded by $x = 0$, $y = 0$, $y = f(x)$ and $x = a$, then $f(0)$ is **[2015, Advanced]**

105. If $\int \dfrac{\log(t+\sqrt{1+t^2})}{\sqrt{1+t^2}}\,dt = \dfrac{1}{2}\,(g(t))^2 + C$, where C is

a constant, then $g(2)$ is equal to : **[2015, Main]**

(a) $2\log(2+\sqrt{5})$ (b) $\log(2+\sqrt{5})$

(c) $\dfrac{1}{\sqrt{5}}\log(2+\sqrt{5})$ (d) $\dfrac{1}{2}\log(2+\sqrt{5})$

106. If $f : R \to R$ be a function suchthat $f(2-x) = f(2+x)$

and $f(4-x) = f(4+x)$, for all $x \in R$ and $\displaystyle\int_0^2 f(x)\,dx =$

5. Then the value of $\displaystyle\int_{10}^{50} f(x)\,dx$ is : **[2015, Main]**

(a) 80   (b) 100

(c) 125   (d) 200

107. Let $f : (-1, 1) \to R$ be a continuous funciton. If

$\displaystyle\int_0^{\sin x} f(t)\,dt = \dfrac{\sqrt{3}}{2}x$, then $f\left(\dfrac{\sqrt{3}}{2}\right)$ is equal to :

[2015, Main]

(a) $\dfrac{\sqrt{3}}{2}$ (b) $\sqrt{3}$

(c) $\sqrt{\dfrac{3}{2}}$ (d) $\dfrac{1}{2}$

108. If m is a non-zero number and $\displaystyle\int \dfrac{x^{5m-1}+2x^{4m-1}}{(x^{2m}+x^m+1)^3}\,dx$

$= f(x) + e$ then $f(x)$ is : **[2014, Main]**

(a) $\dfrac{x^{5m}}{2m(x^{2m}+x^m+1)^2}$ (b) $\dfrac{x^{4m}}{2m(x^{2m}+x^m+1)^2}$

(c) $\dfrac{2m(x^{5m}+x^{4m})}{(x^{2m}+x^m+1)^2}$ (d) $\dfrac{(x^{5m}-x^{4m})}{2m(x^{2m}+x^m+1)^2}$

109. The integral $\displaystyle\int\left(1+x-\dfrac{1}{x}\right)e^{x+\frac{1}{x}}\,dx$ is equal to :

[2014, Main]

(a) $(x+1)e^{x+\frac{1}{x}}+C$ (b) $-xe^{x+\frac{1}{x}}+C$

(c) $(x-1)e^{x+\frac{1}{x}}+C$ (d) $xe^{x+\frac{1}{x}}+C$

110. The integral

$\displaystyle\int_0^\pi \sqrt{1+4\sin^2\dfrac{x}{2}-4\sin\dfrac{x}{2}}\,dx$ equals :

[2014, Main]

(a) $4\sqrt{3}-4$ (b) $4\sqrt{3}-4-\dfrac{\pi}{3}$

(c) $\pi-4$ (d) $\dfrac{2\pi}{3}-4-4\sqrt{3}$

111. The area of the region descirbed by $A = \{(x, y) : x^2 + y^2 \le 1$ and $y^2 \le 1-x\}$ is : **[2014, Main]**

(a) $\dfrac{\pi}{2}-\dfrac{2}{3}$ (b) $\dfrac{\pi}{2}+\dfrac{2}{3}$

(c) $\dfrac{\pi}{2}+\dfrac{4}{3}$ (d) $\dfrac{\pi}{2}-\dfrac{4}{3}$

112. The are region above the x-axis and bounded by the curve $y = \tan x$, $0 \le x \le \pi/<$ and the tangent to the curve at $x = \pi/4$ is : **[2014, Main]**

(a) $\dfrac{1}{2}(\log 2-1)$ (b) $\dfrac{1}{2}\left(\log 2+\dfrac{1}{2}\right)$

(c) $\dfrac{1}{2}(1-\log 2)$ (d) $\dfrac{1}{2}(1+\log 2)$

113. Let function F be defined as $F(x) = \displaystyle\int_1^x \dfrac{e^t}{t}\,dt, x > 0$

then the value of the integral $\displaystyle\int_1^x \dfrac{e^t}{t+a}\,dt$, where $a > 0$, is : **[2014, Main]**

(a) $e^a\,[F(x) - F(1 + a)]$
(b) $e^{-a}[F(x + a) - F(a)]$
(c) $e^a\,[F(x + a) - F(1 + a)]$
(d) $e^{-a}\,[F(x + a) - F(1 + a)]$

114. The area enclosed by the curves $y = \sin x + \cos x$ and $y = |\cos x - \sin x|$ over the interval $\left[0, \dfrac{\pi}{2}\right]$ is

: **[2014, Advanced]**

(a) $4(\sqrt{2}-1)$ (b) $2\sqrt{2}\,(\sqrt{2}-1)$

(c) $2(\sqrt{2}+1)$ (d) $2\sqrt{2}\,(\sqrt{2}+1)$

115. The integral $\displaystyle\int \dfrac{\sec^2 x}{(\sec x+\tan x)^{9/2}}\,dx$ equals (for

some arbitrary constant K) **[2012, Advanced]**

(a) $-\dfrac{1}{(\sec x+\tan x)^{11/2}}\left\{\dfrac{11}{7}-\dfrac{1}{7}(\sec x+\tan x)^2\right\}+K$

(b) $\dfrac{1}{(\sec x+\tan x)^{11/2}}\left\{\dfrac{11}{7}-\dfrac{1}{7}(\sec x+\tan x)^2\right\}+K$

(c) $-\dfrac{1}{(\sec x+\tan x)^{11/2}}\left\{\dfrac{11}{7}+\dfrac{1}{7}(\sec x+\tan x)^2\right\}+K$

(d) $\dfrac{1}{(\sec x+\tan x)^{11/2}}\left\{\dfrac{11}{7}+\dfrac{1}{7}(\sec x+\tan x)^2\right\}+K$

116. Let S be the area of the region enclosed by $y = e^{-x^2}$, $y = 0$, $x = 0$, and $x = 1$. Then

[2012, Advanced]

(a) $S \geq \dfrac{1}{e}$

(b) $S \geq 1 - \dfrac{1}{e}$

(c) $S \leq \dfrac{1}{4}\left(1 + \dfrac{1}{\sqrt{e}}\right)$

(d) $S \leq \dfrac{1}{\sqrt{2}} + \dfrac{1}{\sqrt{e}}\left(1 - \dfrac{1}{\sqrt{2}}\right)$

117. The value of the integral

$$\int_{-\pi/2}^{\pi/2}\left(x^2 + \ln\frac{\pi+x}{\pi-x}\right)\cos x\, dx \text{ is}$$

[2012, Advanced]

(a) 0

(b) $\dfrac{\pi^2}{2} - 4$

(c) $\dfrac{\pi^2}{2} + 4$

(d) $\dfrac{\pi^2}{2}$

118. Let $f : [-1, 2] \to [0, \infty)$ be a continuous function such that $f(x) = f(1 - x)$ for all $x \in [-1, 2]$.

Let $R_1 = \displaystyle\int_{-1}^{2} x f(x)\, dx$, and R_2 be the area of the region bounded by $y = f(x)$, $x = -1$, $x = 2$, and the x-axis. Then :   **[2011, Advanced]**

(a) $R_1 = 2R_2$

(b) $R_1 = 3R_2$

(c) $2R_1 = R_2$

(d) $3R_1 = R_2$

119. The value of $\displaystyle\int_{\sqrt{\ln 2}}^{\sqrt{\ln 3}} \frac{x \sin x^2}{\sin x^2 + \sin(\ln 6 - x^2)}\, dx$ is

[2011, Advanced]

(a) $\dfrac{1}{4}\ln\dfrac{3}{2}$

(b) $\dfrac{1}{2}\ln\dfrac{3}{2}$

(c) $\ln\dfrac{3}{2}$

(d) $\dfrac{1}{6}\ln\dfrac{3}{2}$

120. Let the straight line $x = b$ divide the area enclosed by $y = (1 - x)^2$, $y = 0$ and $x = 0$ into two parts R_1 $(0 \leq x \leq b)$ and R_2 $(b \leq x \leq 1)$ such that $R_1 - R_2 = \dfrac{1}{4}$. Then b equals   **[2011, Advanced]**

(a) $\dfrac{3}{4}$

(b) $\dfrac{1}{2}$

(c) $\dfrac{1}{3}$

(d) $\dfrac{1}{4}$

121. If $I_n = \displaystyle\int_{-\pi}^{\pi} \frac{\sin nx}{(1 + \pi^x)\sin x}\, dx$, $n = 0, 1, 2, \ldots,$

[2009, Advanced]

(a) $I_n = I_{n+2}$

(b) $\displaystyle\sum_{m=1}^{10} I_{2m+1} = 10\pi$

(c) $\displaystyle\sum_{m=1}^{10} I_{2m} = 0$

(d) $I_n + I_{n+1}$

122. Let

$$I = \int \frac{e^x}{e^{4x} + e^{2x} + 1}\, dx, \quad J = \int \frac{e^{-x}}{e^{-4x} + e^{-2x} + 1}\, dx.$$

Then, for an arbitrary constant C, the value of $J - I$ equals   **[2008, Advanced]**

(a) $\dfrac{1}{2}\log\left(\dfrac{e^{4x} - e^{2x} - 1}{e^{4x} + e^{2x} + 1}\right) + C$

(b) $\dfrac{1}{2}\log\left(\dfrac{e^{2x} + e^{x} + 1}{e^{2x} - e^{x} + 1}\right) + C$

(c) $\dfrac{1}{2}\log\left(\dfrac{e^{2x} - e^{x} + 1}{e^{2x} + e^{x} + 1}\right) + C$

(d) $\dfrac{1}{2}\log\left(\dfrac{e^{4x} + e^{2x} + 1}{e^{2x} - e^{2x} + 1}\right) + C$

123. The area of the region bounded by the curve $y = f(x)$, the x-axis, and the lines $x = a$ and $x = b$, where $-\infty < a < b < -2$, is   **[2008, Advanced]**

(a) $\displaystyle\int_{a}^{b} \frac{x}{3\left((f(x))^2 - 1\right)}\, dx + b\, f(b) - a\, f(a)$

(b) $-\displaystyle\int_{a}^{b} \frac{x}{3\left((f(x))^2 - 1\right)}\, dx + b\, f(b) - a\, f(a)$

(c) $\displaystyle\int_{a}^{b} \frac{x}{3\left((f(x))^2 - 1\right)}\, dx - b\, f(b) + a\, f(a)$

(d) $-\displaystyle\int_{a}^{b} \frac{x}{3\left((f(x))^2 - 1\right)}\, dx - b\, f(b) + a\, f(a)$

124. $\displaystyle\int_{-1}^{1} g'(x)\, dx =$ **[2008, Advanced]**

(a) $2g(-1)$

(b) 0

(c) $-2g(1)$

(d) $2g(1)$

125. Let $f(x)$ be differentiable on the interval $(0, \infty)$ such that $f(1) = 1$, and

$$\lim_{t \to x} \frac{t^2 f(x) - x^2 f(t)}{t - x} = 1$$

for each $x > 0$. Then $f(x)$ is   **[2008, Advanced]**

(a) $\dfrac{1}{3x}+\dfrac{2x^3}{3}$ (b) $\dfrac{-1}{3x}+\dfrac{4x^2}{3}$

(c) $\dfrac{-1}{x}+\dfrac{2}{x^2}$ (d) $\dfrac{1}{x}$

126. Match the integrals in **Column I** with the values in **Column II** and indicate your answer by darkening the appropriate bubbles in the 4 × 4 matrix given in the ORS. **[2008, Advanced]**

Column I	Column II
(a) $\displaystyle\int_{-1}^{1}\dfrac{dx}{1+x^2}$	(p) $\dfrac{1}{2}\log\left(\dfrac{2}{3}\right)$
(b) $\displaystyle\int_{0}^{1}\dfrac{dx}{\sqrt{1-x^2}}$	(q) $2\log\left(\dfrac{2}{3}\right)$
(c) $\displaystyle\int_{20}^{3}\dfrac{dx}{1-x^2}$	(r) $\dfrac{\pi}{3}$
(d) $\displaystyle\int_{1}^{2}\dfrac{dx}{x\sqrt{x^2-1}}$	(s) $\dfrac{\pi}{2}$

127. $\displaystyle\int\dfrac{x^2-1}{x^3\sqrt{2x^4-2x^2+1}}\,dx$ is equal to

[2007, Advanced]

(a) $\dfrac{\sqrt{2x^4-2x^2+1}}{x^2}+c$

(b) $\dfrac{\sqrt{2x^4-2x^2+1}}{x^3}+c$

(c) $\dfrac{\sqrt{2x^4-2x^2+1}}{x}+c$

(d) $\dfrac{\sqrt{2x^4-2x^2+1}}{2x^2}+c$

128. The value of $5050\,\dfrac{\displaystyle\int_{0}^{1}(1-x^{50})^{100}\,dx}{\displaystyle\int_{0}^{1}(1-x^{50})^{101}\,dx}$ is

[2006, Advanced]

129. Match the following

(i) $\displaystyle\int_{0}^{\pi/2}(\sin x)^{\cos x}(\cos x\cot x-\log(\sin x)^{\sin x})\,dx$ (A) 1

(ii) Area bounded by $-4y^2=x$ and $x-1=-5y^2$ (B) 0

(iii) Cosine of the angle of intersection of curves $y=3^{x-1}\log x$ and $y=x^x-1$ is   (C) 6 In 2

(iv) Data could not be retrieved.   (D) 4/3

130. Match the following   **[2006, Advanced]**

(i) Two rays in the first quadrant $x+y=1$ intersects each other in the interval $a\in(a_0,\infty)$, the value of a_0 is   (A) 2

(ii) Point (α,β,γ) lies on the plane $x+y+z=2$. Let $\vec{a}=\alpha\hat{i}+\beta\hat{j}+\gamma\hat{k}$, $\hat{k}\times(\hat{k}\times\vec{a})$, then $\gamma=$.   (B) 4/3

(iii) $\left|\displaystyle\int_{0}^{1}(1-y)^2\,dy\right|+\left|\displaystyle\int_{-1}^{0}(y^2-1)\,dy\right|$ (C) $\left|\displaystyle\int_{0}^{1}\sqrt{1-x}\,dx\right|+\left|\displaystyle\int_{-1}^{0}\sqrt{1-x}\,dx\right|$

(iv) If $\sin A\sin B\sin C+\cos A\cos B=1$, then the value of $\sin C=$ (D) 1

131. $\displaystyle\int_{-2}^{0}\left(x^3+3x^2+3x+3+(x+1)\cos(x+1)\right)dx$ is equal to   **[2005, Advanced]**

(a) – 4   (b) 0

(c) 4   (d) 6

132. The area bounded by the parabola $y=(x+1)^2$ an=d $y=(x-1)^2$ and the line $y=14$ is

[2005, Advanced]

(a) 4 sq. units   (b) 1/6 sq. units

(c) 4/3 sq. units   (d) 1/3 sq. units

133. Evaluate

$$\int_{0}^{\pi}e^{|\cos x|}\left(2\sin\left(\dfrac{1}{2}\cos x\right)+3\cos\left(\dfrac{1}{2}\cos x\right)\right)\sin x\,dx.$$

[2005, Main]

134. If $\begin{bmatrix}4a^2 & 4a & 1\\4b^2 & 4b & 1\\4c^2 & 4c & 1\end{bmatrix}\begin{bmatrix}f(-1)\\f(1)\\f(2)\end{bmatrix}=\begin{bmatrix}3a^2+3a\\3b^2+3b\\3c^2+3c\end{bmatrix}$, $f(x)$ is a quadratic function and its maximum value occurs at a point V. A is a point of intersection of $y=f(x)$ with x-axis and point B is such that chord AB subtends a right angle at V. Find the area enclosed by $f(x)$ and chord AB.

[2005, Main]

135. The area enclosed between the curves $y=ax^2$ and $x=ay^2$ $(a>0)$ is 1 sq. unit, then the value of a is

[2005, Main]

(a) $1/\sqrt{3}$ (b) 1/2

(c) 1   (d) 1/3

136. The value of the integral $\int\limits_{0}^{1}\sqrt{\dfrac{1-x}{1+x}}\,dx$ is

[2004, Main]

(a) $\dfrac{\pi}{2}+1$ (b) $\dfrac{\pi}{2}-1$

(c) -1 (d) 1

137. If $y(x) = \int\limits_{\pi^2/16}^{x^2}\dfrac{\cos x.\cos\sqrt{\theta}}{1+\sin^2\sqrt{\theta}}\,d\theta$ then find $\dfrac{dy}{dx}$ at

$x = \pi.$ **[2004, Main]**

138. A curve passes through (2, 0) and the slope of

tangent at point P (x, y) equals $\dfrac{(x+1)^2 + y - 3}{(x+1)}$

. Find the equation of the curve and area enclosed by the curve and the x-axis is the fourth quadrant.   **[2004, Main]**

139. Evaluate $\int\limits_{-\pi/3}^{\pi/3}\dfrac{(\pi+4x^3)\,dx}{2-\cos\left(|x|+\dfrac{\pi}{3}\right)}\,dx.$ **[2004, Main]**

140. If $f(m, n) = \int\limits_{0}^{1}t^m(1+t)^n\,dt$, then the expression for

$l(m, n)$ in terms of $l(m + 1, n – 1)$ is **[2003, Main]**

(a) $\dfrac{2^n}{m+1}-\dfrac{n}{m+1}l\,(m+1,n-1)$

(b) $\dfrac{n}{m+1}\,l\,(m+1,n-1)$

(c) $\dfrac{2^n}{m+1}+\dfrac{n}{m+1}\,l\,(m+1,n-1)$

(d) $\dfrac{m}{n+1}\,l\,(m+1,n-1)$

141. The area bounded by the curves $y = \sqrt{x}$, $2y + 3 = x$ and x-axis is the 1st quadrant is

(a) 9   (b) 27/4

(c) 36   (d) 18

142. If f is an even function then prove that

$$\int\limits_{0}^{\pi/2}f(\cos 2x)\cos x\,dx - \sqrt{2}\int\limits_{0}^{\pi/4}f(\sin 2x)\cos x\,dx$$

.

[2003, Main]

143. The area bounded by the curves $y = |x| – 1$ and $y = -|x| + 1$ is   **[2002, Main]**

(a) 1   (b) 2

(c) $2\sqrt{2}$ (d) 4

144. Let T > 0 be a fixed real number. Suppose f is a continuous function such that for all $x \in$ R,

$f(x + T) = f(x)$. If $I = \int\limits_{0}^{T}f(x)dx$ then the value of

$\int\limits_{0}^{3+3T}f(2x)dx$ is   **[2002, Main]**

(a) $(3/2)\,1$ (b) $2I$

(c) $3I$ (d) $6I$

145. The integral $\int\limits_{-1/2}^{1/2}\left([x]+\text{In}\left(\dfrac{1+x}{1-x}\right)\right)dx$ equals to

[2002, Main]

(a) $-1/2$ (b) 0

(c) 1   (d) 2 In (1/2)

ANSWER KEY

1. (a)	2. (d)	3. (a)	4. (a)	5. (d)	6. (d)	7. (d)	8. (c)	9. (c)	10. (21)
11. (a)	12. (d)	13. (a)	14. (8)	15. (4)	16. (1)	17. (a)	18. (c)	19. (a)	20. (3/2)
21. (d)	22. (d)	23. (c)	24. (d)	25. (a)	26. (a)	27. (d)	28. (a)	29. (c)	30. (b)
31. (a)	32. (b)	33. (c)	34. (a)	35. (a)	36. (c)	37. (b)	38. (a)	39. (a)	40. (d)
41. (c)	42. (c)	43. (b)	44. (a)	45. (d)	46. (a)	47. (b)	48. (b)	49. (c)	50. (c)
51. (d)	52. (d)	53. (a)	54. (d)	55. (c)	56. (d)	57. (a)	58. (a)	59. (b)	60. (c)
61. (a)	62. (4)	63. (a,d)	64. (0.5)	65. (b)	66. (c)	67. (c)	68. (c)	69. (c)	70. (a)
71. (b)	72. (d)	73. (a)	74. (b,c)	75. (4)	76. (2)	77. (a)	78. (a)	79. (c)	80. (b)
81. (a)	82. (b,c)	83. (b)	84. (a)	85. (d)	86. (b,d)	87. (b)	88. (b)	89. (b)	90. (b)
91. (b)	92. (c)	93. (b)	94. (1)	95. (d)	96. (c)	97. (d)	98. (9)	99. (7)	100. (a,c)
101. (a,b)	102. (c,d)	103. (0)	104. (3)	105. (b)	106. (b)	107. (b)	108. (b)	109. (d)	110. (b)
111. (c)	112. (a)	113. (d)	114. (b)	115. (c)	116. (a,b,d)	117. (b)	118. (c)	119. (a)	120. (b)
121. (a,b,c)	122. (c)	123. (a)	124. (d)	125. (a)	126. (a) – (s), (b) – (s), (c) – (p), (d) – (r)				

127. (d)   **128.** (5051) **129.** (i)-(A), (ii)-(D), (iii)-(A)   **130.** (i)-(D), (ii)-(A), (iii)-(B),(C), (iv)-(D)   **131.** (c)

132. (d)   **133.** $\dfrac{24}{5}\left(e\cos\left(\dfrac{1}{2}\right)+\dfrac{e}{2}\sin\left(\dfrac{1}{2}\right)-1\right)$ **134.** $\dfrac{125}{3}$ **135.** (a)   **136.** (b)   **137.** (2π) **138.** $\dfrac{4}{3}$

139. $\dfrac{4\pi}{\sqrt{3}}\tan^{-1}\left(\dfrac{1}{2}\right)$ **140.** (a)   **141.** (a)   **142.** (*)   **143.** (b)   **144.** (c)   **145.** (a)

ANSWERS WITH EXPLANATIONS

1. Correct Response : (a)

Explanation :

$e^{2x}+2e^{x}-e^{-x}-1$

$$= e^{2x}+e^{x}+e^{x}-e^{-x}-1$$
$$= e^{x}(e^{x}+1)-e^{-x}(e^{x}+1)+e^{x}$$
$$= [(e^{x}+1)(e^{x}-e^{-x})+e^{x}]$$

so $\quad I = \int(e^{x}+1)(e^{x}-e^{-x})e^{e^{x}+e^{-x}}\,dx$

$$+\int e^{x}.e^{e^{x}+e^{-x}}\,dx$$

$$= (e^{x}+1)e^{e^{x}+e^{-x}}-\int e^{x}.e^{e^{x}+e^{-x}}\,dx$$

$$+\int e^{x}.e^{e^{x}+e^{-x}}\,dx$$

$$\Rightarrow (e^{x}+1)e^{e^{x}+e^{-x}}+C = g(x)e^{e^{x}+e^{-x}}+C$$

$\therefore \qquad g(x) = e^{x}+1 \Rightarrow g(0) = 2.$

2. Correct Response : (d)

Explanation :

$$I = \int_{-\pi/2}^{\pi/2}\frac{1}{1+e^{\sin x}}\,dx \qquad \qquad \ldots(1)$$

Apply King property

$$I = \int_{-\pi/2}^{\pi/2}\frac{1}{1+e^{-\sin x}}\,dx = \int_{-\pi/2}^{\pi/2}\frac{e^{\sin x}}{1+e^{\sin x}}\,dx$$

$$\ldots(2)$$

Add (1) & (2)

$$2I = \int_{-\pi/2}^{\pi/2}dx = \pi$$

$$I = \frac{\pi}{2}.$$

3. Correct Response : (a)

Explanation :

$$\lim_{x\to 1}\frac{\displaystyle\int_{0}^{(x-1)^2} t\cos(t^2)\,dt}{(x-1)\sin(x-1)}\left(\frac{0}{0}\right)$$

Apply L Hospital Rule

$$= \lim_{x\to 1}\frac{2(x-1).(x-1)^2\cos(x-1)^4-0}{(x-1).\cos(x-1)+\sin(x-1)}\left(\frac{0}{0}\right)$$

$$= \lim_{x\to 1}\frac{2(x-1)^3.\cos(x-1)^4}{(x-1)\left[\cos(x-1)+\dfrac{\sin(x-1)}{(x-1)}\right]}$$

$$= \lim_{x\to 1}\frac{2(x-1)^2\cos(x-1)^4}{(x-1)\left[\cos(x-1)+\dfrac{\sin(x-1)}{(x-1)}\right]}$$

$$= \lim_{x\to 1}\frac{2(x-1)^2\cos(x-1)^4}{\cos(x-1)+\dfrac{\sin(x-1)}{(x-1)}}$$

On taking limit

$$= \frac{0}{1+1} = 0.$$

4. Correct Response : (a)

Explanation :

$$I_1 = \int_{0}^{1}(1-x^{50})^{100}\,dx$$

and $\quad I_2 = \int_{0}^{1}(1-x^{50})^{101}\,dx$

and $\quad I_1 = \alpha I_2$

$$I_2 = \int_{0}^{1}(1-x^{50})^{101}\,dx$$

$$I_2 = \int_{0}^{1}(1-x^{50})(1-x^{50})^{100}\,dx$$

$$I_2 = \int_{0}^{1}(1-x^{50})^{100}\,dx-\int_{0}^{1}x^{50}(1-x^{50})^{100}\,dx$$

$$I_2 = I_1-\int_{0}^{1}\underset{I}{x}.\underset{II}{\underbrace{x^{49}.(1-x^{50})^{100}}}\,dx$$

Now apply IBP

$$I_2 = I_1-\left[x\int x^{49}(1-x^{50})^{100}\,dx\right.$$

$$\left.-\int\left[\int\frac{d(x)}{dx}.\int x^{49}(1-x^{50})^{100}\,dx\right]dx\right]$$

Let $\quad (1-x^{50}) = t$

$$-50x^{49}\,dx = dt$$

$$I_2 = I_1 - \left[x \cdot \left(-\frac{1}{50} \right) \frac{(1-x^{50})^{101}}{101} \Big|_{x=0}^{x=1} \right.$$

$$\left. -\int_0^1 \left(-\frac{1}{50} \right) \frac{(1-x^{50})^{101}}{101} \, dx \right]$$

$$I_2 = I_1 - 0 - \frac{1}{50} \cdot \frac{1}{101} . I_2 = I_1 - \frac{1}{5050} I_2$$

$$I_2 + \frac{1}{5050} I_2 = I_1$$

$$\Rightarrow \quad \frac{5051}{5050} I_2 = I_1$$

$$\therefore \quad \alpha = \frac{5050}{5051}$$

$$I_2 = \frac{5050}{5051} I_1$$

$$\because \quad I_2 = \alpha . I_1$$

5. Correct Response : (d)

Explanation :

Let $\qquad y = (ex)^x$

Take log on both sides

$$\ln y = x \ln ex$$
$$\ln y = x(1 + \ln x)$$
$$\frac{1}{y} \frac{dy}{dx} = x \times \frac{1}{x} + (1 + \ln x).1$$
$$\frac{1}{y} \frac{dy}{dx} = 2 + \ln x$$
$$dy = (ex)^x (2 + \ln x) \, dx$$
$$dy = e^x x^x (2 + \ln x) \, dx$$

$$\int_1^2 d(ex)^x$$

$$[(ex)^x]_1^2 = (2e)^2 - (e)^1$$
$$= 4e^2 - e.$$

6. Correct Response : (d)

Explanation :

$$g(x) = f[f(x)]$$
$$g(x) = f[|x-2|]$$
$$g(x) = |(x-2) - 2|$$

$$\int_0^3 g(x) - f(x) = \int_0^3 ||x-2| - 2| \, dx - \int_0^3 |x-2| \, dx$$

$$= \int_0^2 x \, dx + \int_2^3 (4-x) \, dx + \int_0^2 (x-2) \, dx - \int_2^3 (x-2) \, dx$$

$$= \left[\frac{x^2}{2} \right]_0^2 + \left[4x - \frac{x^2}{2} \right]_2^3 + \left[\frac{x^2}{2} - 2x \right]_0^2 - \left[\frac{x^2}{2} - 2x \right]_2^3$$

$$= 2 + 12 - \frac{9}{2} - 8 + 2 + 2 - 4 - \frac{9}{2} + 6 + 2 - 4$$

$$= 1.$$

7. Correct Response : (d)

Explanation :

$$f(x) = \int \frac{\sqrt{x}}{(1+x)^2} \, dx$$

Let $\qquad x = \tan^2 \theta$

$$dx = 2 \tan \theta \sec^2 \theta \, d\theta$$

$$f(x) = \int \frac{\tan \theta}{(1 + \tan^2 \theta)^2} 2 \tan \theta \sec^2 \theta \, d\theta$$

$$f(x) = \int \frac{\tan \theta}{\sec^4 \theta} \times 2 \tan \theta \sec^2 \theta \, d\theta$$

$$f(x) = \int 2 \tan^2 \theta \cos^2 \theta \, d\theta$$
$$f(x) = \int 2 \sin^2 \theta \, d\theta$$
$$f(x) = \int (1 - \cos 2\theta) \, d\theta$$
$$f(x) = \theta - \frac{\sin 2\theta}{2} + c$$

$$= \theta - \frac{\tan \theta}{1 + \tan^2 \theta} + c$$

$$f(x) = \tan^{-1} x - \frac{\sqrt{x}}{1+x} + c$$

$$f(3) - f(1) = \tan^{-1} \sqrt{3} - \frac{\sqrt{3}}{1+3} - \tan^{-1} 1 + \frac{1}{1+1}$$

$$= \frac{\pi}{3} - \frac{\pi}{4} + \frac{1}{2} - \frac{\sqrt{3}}{4} = \frac{\pi}{12} + \frac{1}{2} - \frac{\sqrt{3}}{4}$$

8. Correct Response : (c)

Explanation :

$$\int \left(\frac{x}{x \sin x + \cos x} \right)^2 dx$$

$$= \int \left(\frac{x}{\cos x} \right) \cdot \frac{x \cos x \, dx}{(x \sin x + \cos x)^2}$$

$$= \frac{x}{\cos x} \int \left(\frac{x \cos x}{x \sin x + \cos x} \right) dx$$

$$- \int \left[\frac{d}{dx} x \sec x \int \frac{x \cos x}{(x \sin x + \cos x)^2} \, dx \right] dx$$

$$\frac{d}{dx} (x \sec x) = \sec x + x \sec x \tan x$$

$$= \sec x \left(1 + \frac{x \sin x}{\cos x}\right)$$

$$= \sec^2 x (\cos x + \sin x)$$

$$= \frac{\cos x + \sin x}{\cos^2 x}$$

$$= \frac{x}{\cos x}\left(-\frac{1}{x \sin x + \cos x}\right)$$

$$+ \int \left(\frac{\cos x + x \sin x}{\cos^2 x}\right)\left(\frac{1}{x \sin x + \cos x}\right) dx$$

$$= -\frac{x \sec x}{x \sin x + \cos x} + \int \sec^2 x \, dx$$

$$= -\frac{x \sec x}{x \sin x + \cos x} + \tan x + C.$$

9. Correct Response : (c)

Explanation :

$$I = \int_{\pi/6}^{\pi/3} [(2 \tan^3 x \cdot \sec^2 x \cdot \sin^4 3x)$$

$$+ (3 \tan^4 x \cdot \sin^3 3x \cdot \cos 3x)] \, dx$$

$$= \int_{\pi/6}^{\pi/3} \left[\frac{\frac{d}{dx}(\tan^4 x)}{2} \cdot \sin^4 3x + \tan^4 x \cdot \frac{\frac{d}{dx}(\sin^4 3x)}{2} \right]$$

$$\Rightarrow \qquad I = \frac{1}{2} \int_{\pi/6}^{\pi/3} d[(\sin 3x)^4 (\tan x)^4]$$

$$\Rightarrow \qquad I = [(\sin 3x)^4 (\tan x)^4]_{\pi/6}^{\pi/3}$$

$$\Rightarrow \qquad I = -\frac{1}{18}$$

10. Correct Response : (21)

Explanation :

$$\int_0^n \{x\} \, dx = n \int_0^1 \{x\} \, dx = n \int_0^1 x \, dx = \frac{n}{2}$$

$$\int_0^n \{x\} \, dx = \int_0^n [x - \{x\}] \, dx = \frac{n^2}{2} - \frac{n}{2}$$

$$\Rightarrow \left(\frac{n^2 - n}{2}\right)^2 = \frac{n}{2} \cdot 10 \cdot n(n-1) \qquad \text{(where } n > 1\text{)}$$

$$\Rightarrow \frac{n-1}{4} = 5 \Rightarrow n = 21.$$

11. Correct Response : (a)

Explanation :

$$\int_{-\pi}^{\pi} |\pi - |x|| \, dx = 2 \int_0^{\pi} |\pi - x| \, dx$$

$$\therefore \qquad f(-x) = f(x)$$

$$\int_{-a}^{a} f(x) \, dx = 2 \int_0^{a} f(x) \, dx$$

$$= 2 \int_0^{\pi} (\pi - x) \, dx$$

$$= 2 \left[\pi x - \frac{x^2}{2} \right]_0^{\pi} = \pi^2.$$

12. Correct Response : (d)

Explanation :

$$\int \frac{\cos \theta \, d\theta}{5 + 7 \sin \theta - 2 \cos^2 \theta}$$

$$= \int \frac{\cos \theta \, d\theta}{5 + 7 \sin \theta - 2(1 - \sin^2 \theta)}$$

$$= \int \frac{\cos \theta \, d\theta}{3 + 7 \sin \theta + 2 \sin^2 \theta}$$

$$\boxed{\begin{aligned} \sin \theta &= t \\ \cos \theta \, d\theta &= dt \end{aligned}}$$

$$\int \frac{dt}{2t^2 + 7t + 3} = \int \frac{dt}{(2t+1)(t+3)}$$

$$= \frac{1}{5} \int \left(\frac{2}{2t+1} - \frac{1}{t+3}\right) dt$$

$$= \frac{1}{5} \ln \left|\frac{2t+1}{t+3}\right| + C$$

$$= \frac{1}{5} \ln \left|\frac{2 \sin \theta + 1}{\sin \theta + 3}\right| + C$$

$$A = \frac{1}{5} \text{ and } B(\theta) = \frac{2 \sin \theta + 1}{\sin \theta + 3}$$

$$\frac{B(\theta)}{A} = \frac{5(2 \sin \theta + 1)}{\sin \theta + 3}.$$

13. Correct Response : (a)

Explanation :

$$\cos x = 1 - \frac{x^2}{2!} + \frac{x^4}{4!} - \cdots$$

$$\sin x = x - \frac{x^3}{3!} + \frac{x^5}{5!} - \cdots$$

$$\cos x \geq 1 - \frac{x^2}{2}$$

$$\int_0^1 x \cos x \, dx \geq \int_0^1 x \left(1 - \frac{x^2}{2}\right) = \frac{1}{2} - \frac{1}{8}$$

$$\int_0^1 x \cos x \, dx \geq \frac{3}{8} \qquad \text{(True)}$$

(b)
$$\sin x \geq x - \frac{x^3}{6}$$

$$\int_0^1 x \sin x \geq \int_0^1 x\left(x - \frac{x^3}{6}\right)dx$$

$$\int_0^1 x \sin x \geq \frac{1}{3} - \frac{1}{30}$$

$$\Rightarrow \quad \int_0^1 x \sin x \, dx \geq \frac{3}{8}$$ (True)

(d)
$$\int_0^1 x^2 \sin x \, dx \geq \int_0^1 x^2\left(x - \frac{x^3}{6}\right)dx$$

$$\int_0^1 x^2 \sin x \, dx \geq \frac{1}{4} - \frac{1}{36}$$

$$\int_0^1 x^2 \sin x \, dx \geq \frac{2}{9}$$ (True)

(c)
$$\cos x < 1$$
$$x^2 \cos x < x^2$$

$$\int_0^1 x^2 \cos x \, dx < \int_0^1 x^2 \, dx$$

$$\int_0^1 x^2 \cos x \, dx < \frac{1}{3}$$ (True)

So option (c) is incorrect.

14. Correct Response : ( )

Explanation :

$$\frac{3^{y_1} + 3^{y_2} + 3^{y_3}}{3} \geq [3^{(y_1 + y_2 + y_3)}]^{\frac{1}{3}}$$

$$(\because y_1 + y_2 + y_3 = 9)$$

$$\Rightarrow \quad 3^{y_1} + 3^{y_2} + 3^{y_3} \geq 3^4$$

$$\Rightarrow \log_3 (3^{y_1} + 3^{y_2} + 3^{y_3}) \geq 4$$

$$\Rightarrow \quad m = 4$$

Also, $\quad \dfrac{x_1 + x_2 + x_3}{3} \geq \sqrt[3]{x_1 x_2 x_3}$

$$(\because x_1 + x_2 + x_3 = 9)$$

$$\Rightarrow \quad x_1 x_2 x_3 \leq 27$$

$$\Rightarrow \log_3 x_1 + \log_3 x_2 + \log_3 x_3 \leq 3$$

$$\Rightarrow \quad M = 3$$

Thus, $\log_2 (m^3) + \log_3 (M^2)$
$$= 6 + 2$$
$$= 8.$$

15. Correct Response : (4)

Explanation :

$$F(x) = \int_0^x f(t).dt$$

$$\Rightarrow \quad F'(x) = f(x)$$

$$I = \int_0^\pi f'(x).\cos x \, dx$$

$$+ \int_0^\pi F(x).\cos x \, dx = 2 \ ...(1)$$

$$I_1 = \int_0^\pi f^1(x).\cos x \, dx \qquad \text{(Let)}$$

Using by parts

$$I_1 = [\cos x.f(x)]_0^\pi + \int_0^\pi \sin x.f(x)\, dx$$

$$I_1 = 6 - f(0) + \int_0^\pi \sin x.F'(x)\, dx$$

$$I_1 = 6 - f(0) + I_2 \qquad ...(2)$$

$$I_2 = \int_0^\pi \sin x.F'(x)\, dx$$

Using by part we get

$$I_2 = [\sin x.F(x)]_0^\pi - \int_0^\pi \cos x.F(x)\, dx$$

$$I_2 = -\int_0^\pi \cos x.F(x)\, dx$$

$$(2) \Rightarrow \quad I_1 = 6 - f(0) - \int_0^\pi \cos x.F(x)\, dx$$

$$(1) \Rightarrow \quad I = 6 - f(0) = 2$$

$$\Rightarrow \quad f(0) = 4.$$

16. Correct Response : (1)

Explanation :

$$3 < 3x < 6$$

Take cases when $3 < 3x < 4$, $4 < 3x < 5$, $5 < 3x < 6$;

Now $\int_1^2 |2x - [3x]|\, dx$

$$= \int_1^{4/3} (3 - 2x)dx + \int_{4/3}^{5/3} (4 - 2x)dx + \int_{5/3}^2 (5 - 2x)dx$$

$$= \left(3x - \frac{2x^2}{2}\right)\Big|_1^{\frac{4}{3}} + \left(4x - \frac{2x^2}{2}\right)\Big|_{\frac{4}{3}}^{\frac{5}{3}} + \left(5x - \frac{2x^2}{2}\right)\Big|_{\frac{5}{3}}^2$$

$$= \left(3x - x^2\right)\Big|_1^{\frac{4}{3}} + \left(4x - x^2\right)\Big|_{\frac{4}{3}}^{\frac{5}{3}} + \left(5x - x^2\right)\Big|_{\frac{5}{3}}^2$$

$$= \frac{2}{9} + \frac{3}{9} + \frac{4}{9} = 1$$

17. Correct Response : (a)

Explanation :

$$\Rightarrow \int_0^{1/2} \frac{x^2}{(1-x^2)^{3/2}}\, dx$$

$$x = \sin \theta$$
$$dx = \cos \theta \, d\theta$$

$$\Rightarrow \int_0^{\pi/6} \frac{\sin^2\theta}{(1-\sin^2\theta)^{3/2}} \cdot \cos\theta \, d\theta$$

$$\Rightarrow \int_0^{\pi/6} \frac{\sin^2\theta}{\cos^3\theta} \cos\theta \, d\theta$$

$$\Rightarrow \int_0^{\pi/6} \tan^2\theta \, d\theta$$

$$\Rightarrow \int_0^{\pi/6} (\sec^2\theta - 1) \, d\theta$$

$$\Rightarrow (\tan\theta - \theta)_0^{\pi/6}$$

$$\Rightarrow \left(\frac{1}{\sqrt{3}} - \frac{\pi}{6}\right) = \frac{k}{6}$$

$$k = 2\sqrt{3} - \pi$$

18. Correct Response : (c)

Explanation :

Put $x = \tan^2\theta \Rightarrow dx = 2\tan\theta\sec^2\theta \, d\theta$

$\int \theta.(2\tan\theta.\sec^2\theta)d\theta$

$$\downarrow \quad \downarrow$$
$$|\quad ||\qquad \text{(By parts)}$$

$= \theta.\tan^2\theta - \int \tan^2\theta \, d\theta$

$= \theta \int 2\tan\theta.\sec^2\theta \, d\theta - \int \left[\frac{d}{d\theta}(\theta)\int 2\tan\theta\sec^2\theta \, d\theta\right] d\theta$

$= \theta \tan^2\theta - \int \tan^2\theta \, d\theta$

$= \theta \tan^2\theta - \int (\sec^2\theta - 1) \, d\theta$

$= \theta.\tan^2\theta - \tan\theta + \theta + c$

$= \theta(1 + \tan^2\theta) - \tan\theta + c$

$= \tan^{-1}(\sqrt{x})(1+x) - \sqrt{x} + c$

Compare $\tan^{-1}(\sqrt{x})\,A(x) + B(x) + c$

$A(x) = (1 + x)\ B(x) = -\sqrt{x}$

19. Correct Response : (a)

Explanation :

$$x^3 \, dy + xy \, dx = x^2 \, dy + 2y \, dx$$

$$\Rightarrow \quad dy(x^3 - x^2) = dx(2y - xy)$$

$$\Rightarrow \quad -\int \frac{1}{y} dy = \int \frac{x-2}{x^2(x-1)} dx$$

$$\Rightarrow \quad -\ln y = \int \left(\frac{A}{x} + \frac{B}{x^2} + \frac{C}{(x-1)}\right)$$

Where A = 1, B = + 2, C = − 1

$$-\ln y = \int \left(\frac{1}{x} + \frac{2}{x^2} - \frac{1}{(x-1)}\right) dx$$

$$\Rightarrow \quad -\ln y = \ln x - \frac{2}{x} - \ln(x-1) + \lambda$$

$$\Rightarrow \quad y(2) = e \Rightarrow -1 = -\ln 2 - 1 - 0 + \lambda$$

$$\therefore \quad \lambda = -\ln 2$$

$$\Rightarrow \quad -\ln y = -\ln x + \frac{2}{x} + \ln(x-1) + \ln 2$$

Now put $x = 4$ in Solution

$$\Rightarrow \quad \ln y = -\ln 4 + \frac{1}{2} + \ln 3 + \ln 2$$

$$\Rightarrow \quad \ln y = \ln 2^2 + \frac{1}{2} + \ln 3 + \ln 2$$

$$\ln y = -2\ln 2 + \frac{1}{2} + \ln 3 + \ln 2$$

$$\ln y = \ln 3 - \ln 2 + \frac{1}{2}$$

$$\ln y = \ln\left(\frac{3}{2}\right) + \frac{1}{2}\ln e \qquad (\because \ln e = 1)$$

$$\Rightarrow \quad y = \frac{3}{2} + \sqrt{e}$$

20. Correct Response : (3/2)

Explanation :

$$\int_0^2 |\,x-1\,|-x\,|\, dx$$

Let $f(x) = |\,|x-1| - x\,|$

$$= \begin{cases} 1, & x \geq 1 \\ |1-2x|, & x \leq 1 \end{cases}$$

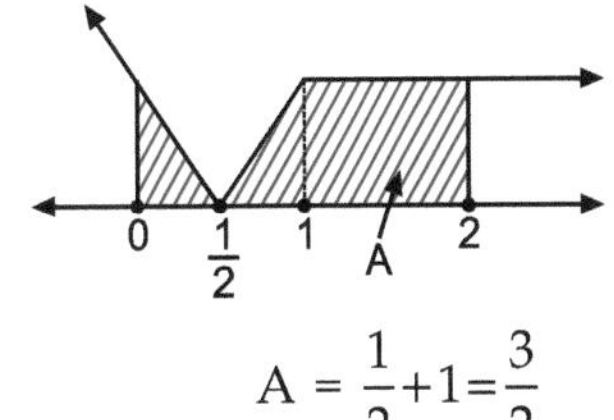

$$A = \frac{1}{2} + 1 = \frac{3}{2}$$

or

$$\int_0^2 |\,x-1\,|-x\,|\, dx = \int_0^1 |1-x-x|dx + \int_1^2 |x-1-x|dx$$

$$= \int_0^{\frac{1}{2}}(1-2x)dx + \int_{\frac{1}{2}}^1(2x-1) + \int_1^2 dx$$

$$= \left(x - x^2\right)_0^{\frac{1}{2}} + \left(x^2 - x\right)_{\frac{1}{2}}^1 + (x)_1^2$$

$$= \frac{1}{2} - \frac{1}{4} + (1-1) - \left(\frac{1}{4} - \frac{1}{2}\right) + 2 - 1$$

$$= \frac{1}{4} + \frac{1}{4} + 1 = \frac{3}{2}$$

21. Correct Response : (d)

Explanation :

$4x^2 - y \le 0$ and $8x - y + 12 \ge 0$

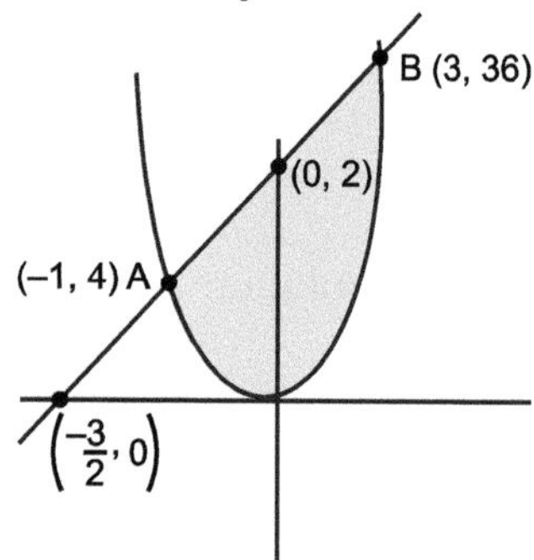

On Solving $\quad y = 4x^2$

and $\qquad y = 8x + 12$

We get A(–1, 4) and B(3, 36)

Required area = Area of the shaded region

$$= \int_{-1}^{3} (8x + 12 - 4x^2)dx = \frac{128}{3}$$

22. Correct Response : (d)

Explanation :

$$2\cos^2\theta - 5\sin\theta + 4\sin^2\theta = 0$$

$$3\sin^2\theta - 5\sin\theta + 2 = 0$$

$$\sin\theta = \frac{1}{2},\ 2(\text{Rejected})$$

$$\int_{\theta_1}^{\theta_2} \cos^2 3\theta\, d\theta = \int_{\pi/6}^{5\pi/6} \frac{1 + \cos 6\theta}{2}\, d\theta$$

$$= \frac{1}{2}\left(\frac{5\pi}{6} - \frac{\pi}{6}\right) = \frac{2\pi}{6} = \frac{\pi}{3}$$

23. Correct Response : (c)

Explanation :

$$4\alpha\left[\int_{-1}^{0} e^{\alpha x}dx + \int_{0}^{2} e^{-\alpha x}dx\right] = 5$$

$$\Rightarrow \quad 4\alpha\left(\left[\frac{e^{\alpha x}}{\alpha}\right]_{-1}^{0} + \left[\frac{e^{-\alpha x}}{-\alpha}\right]_{0}^{2}\right) = 5$$

$$\Rightarrow \quad 4e^{-2\alpha} + 4e^{-\alpha} - 3 = 0$$

Let $e^{-\alpha} = t$, $4t^2 + 4t - 3 = 0$, $t = \dfrac{1}{2}, \dfrac{-3}{2}$ (Rejected)

$$e^{-\alpha} = \frac{1}{2};\ \alpha = \ell n 2$$

24. Correct Response : (d)

Explanation :

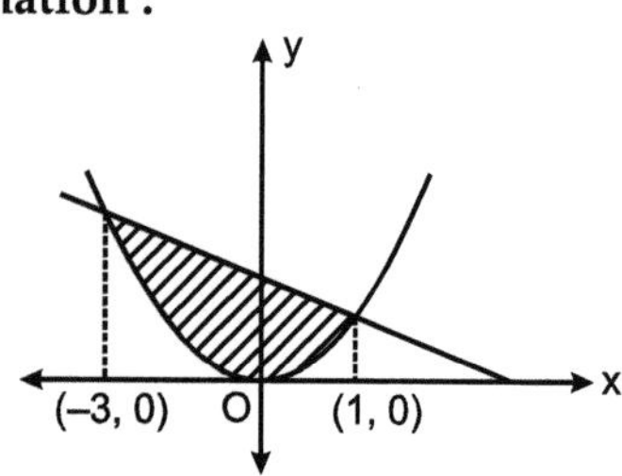

$$\text{Area} = \int_{-3}^{1} (3 - 2x - x^2)dx = \frac{32}{3}$$

25. Correct Response : (a)

Explanation :

$$f(x) = \frac{1}{\sqrt{2x^3 - 9x^2 + 12x + 4}}$$

$$f'(x) = \frac{-6(x-1)(x-2)}{2(2x^3 - 9x^2 + 12x + 4)^{3/2}}$$

$\therefore f(x)$ is decreasing in (1, 2)

$$f(1) = \frac{1}{3};\ f(2) = \frac{1}{\sqrt{8}}$$

$$\frac{1}{3} < I < \frac{1}{\sqrt{8}} \Rightarrow I^2 \in \left(\frac{1}{9}, \frac{1}{8}\right)$$

26. Correct Response : (a)

Explanation :

Using L.H. Rule

$$\lim_{x \to 0} \frac{x\sin(10x)}{1} = 0$$

27. Correct Response : (d)

Explanation :

$$I = \int_{0}^{2\pi} \frac{x\sin^8 x}{\sin^8 x + \cos^6 x}dx \qquad\qquad \dots(1)$$

$$= \left[\int_{0}^{\pi} \frac{x\sin^8 x}{\sin^8 x \cos^8 x}dx + \int_{0}^{\pi} \frac{(2\pi - x)\sin^8 x}{\sin^8 x + \cos^8 x}dx\right]$$

$$= 2\pi \int_{0}^{\pi} \frac{\sin^8 x}{\sin^8 x + \cos^8 x}dx$$

$$I = 2\pi\left[\int_{0}^{\pi/2} \frac{\sin^8 x}{\sin^8 x + \cos^8 x}dx + \int_{0}^{\pi/2} \frac{\cos^8 x\, dx}{\sin^8 x + \cos^8 x}dx\right]$$

$$= 2\pi \int_{0}^{\pi/2} 1\, dx = 2\pi \cdot \frac{\pi}{2} = \pi^2$$

28. Correct Response : (a)

Explanation :

$$I = \int \frac{dx}{(x+4)^{\frac{8}{7}}(x-3)^{\frac{6}{7}}}$$

$$= \int \frac{dx}{\left(\dfrac{x+4}{x-3}\right)^{\frac{8}{7}}(x-3)^2}$$

Let $\dfrac{x+4}{x-3} = t \Rightarrow \dfrac{dx}{(x-3)^2} = -\dfrac{1}{7}dt$

$$\Rightarrow \qquad = -\frac{1}{7}\int \frac{dt}{t^{8/7}} = \frac{-1}{7}\int t^{-8/7}dt$$

$$= t^{-1/7}C = \left(\frac{x+4}{x-3}\right)^{-1/7} + C = \left(\frac{x-3}{x+4}\right)^{1/7} + C$$

29. Correct Response : (c)

Explanation :

$$f(x) = a + bx + cx^2$$

$$\int_0^1 f(x)dx = \left[ax + \frac{bx^2}{2} + \frac{cx^3}{3}\right]_0^1$$

$$= a + \frac{b}{2} + \frac{c}{3} = \frac{1}{6}[6a + 3b + c]$$

$$= \frac{1}{6}\left[f(0) + f(1) + 4f\left(\frac{1}{2}\right)\right]$$

30. Correct Response : (b)

Explanation :

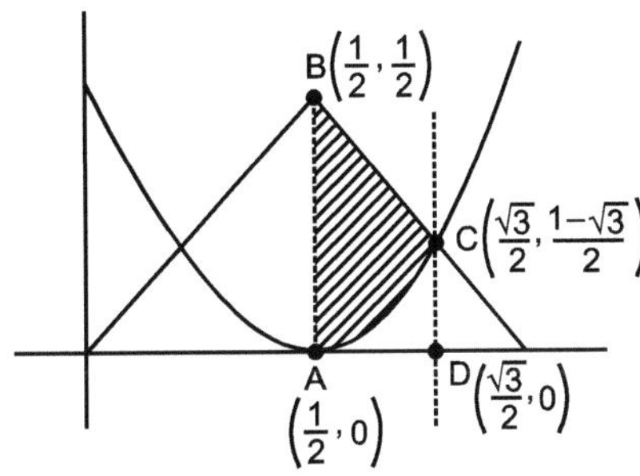

Required area = Area of trepezium ABCD –

Area of parabola between $x = \dfrac{1}{2}$ and $x = \dfrac{\sqrt{3}}{2}$

$$A = \frac{1}{2}\left(\frac{\sqrt{3}}{2} - \frac{1}{2}\right)\left(\frac{1}{2} + 1 - \frac{\sqrt{3}}{2}\right) - \int_{1/2}^{\sqrt{3}/2}\left(x + \frac{1}{2}\right)^2 dx$$

$$= \frac{\sqrt{3}}{4} - \frac{1}{3}$$

31. Correct Response : (a)

Explanation :

$$I = \int \frac{d\theta}{\cos^2\theta(\tan 2\theta + \sec 2\theta)}$$

$$= \int \frac{\sec^2\theta \, d\theta}{\dfrac{2\tan\theta}{1 - \tan^2 0} + \dfrac{1 + \tan^2\theta}{1 - \tan^2 0}}$$

$$= \int \frac{(1 - \tan^2\theta)\sec^2\theta \, d\theta}{(1 - \tan\theta)^2}$$

$$\tan\theta = t \Rightarrow \sec^2\theta \, d\theta = dt$$

$$I = \int \frac{1 - t^2}{(1 + t)^2}dt = \int \frac{(1 - t)(1 + t)}{(i + t)^2}dt = \int \frac{1}{1 + t} - (1 + t)$$

$$= \ln|1 + t| - \int\left(\frac{1 + t}{1 + t} - \frac{1}{1 - t}\right)dt$$

$$= \ell n|1 + t| - t + \ell n|1 + t|$$

$$= 2\ell n|1 + t| - t + C$$

$$= 2\ell n|1 + \tan\theta| - \tan\theta + C$$

$$\lambda = -1, f(\theta) = 1 + \tan\theta$$

32. Correct Response : (b)

Explanation :

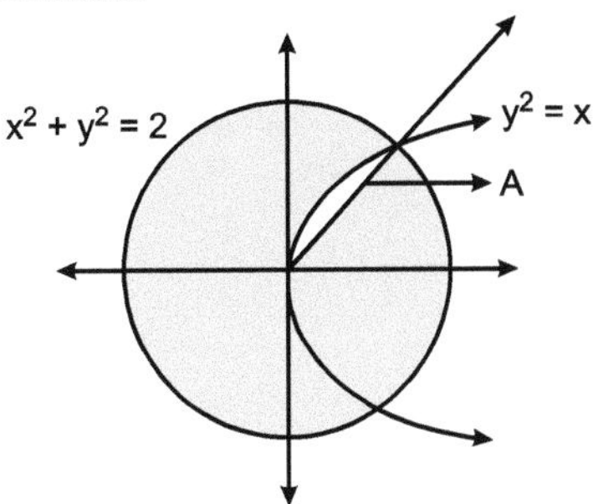

$$A = \int_0^1 (\sqrt{x} - x)dx$$

$$= \left[\frac{2}{3}x^{3/2} - \frac{x^2}{2}\right]_0^1 = \frac{1}{6}$$

Required Area : $\pi r^2 - \dfrac{1}{6} = \dfrac{1}{6}(12\pi - 1)$

33. Correct Response : (a)

Explanation :

$$f(x + 1) = f(a + b - x)$$

$$I = \frac{1}{(a+b)}\int_a^b x(f(x) + f(x+1)dx) \qquad \dots(i)$$

$$I = \frac{1}{(a+b)}\int_a^b (a + b - x)(f(x+1) + f(x)dx \dots(ii)$$

from (i) and (ii)

$$2I = \int_a^b (f(x) + f(x+1)dx$$

$$2I = \int_a^b f(a + b - x)dx + \int_a^b f(x+1)dx$$

$$2I = 2\int_a^b f(x+1)dx$$

$$\Rightarrow \quad I = \int_a^b f(x+1)dx$$

$$= \int_{a+1}^{b+1} f(x)dx$$

34. Correct Response : (a)

Explanation :

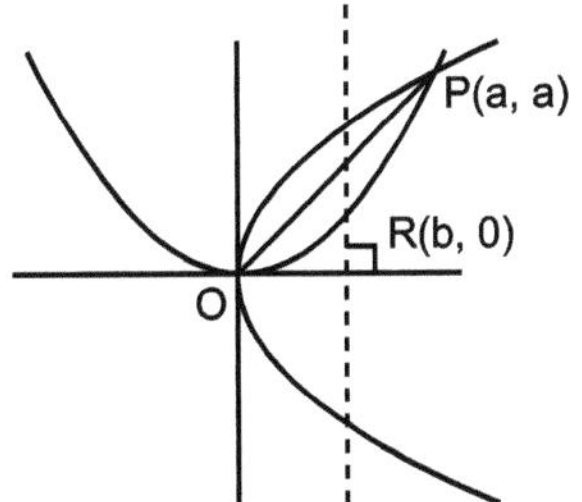

$$\int_a^b\left(\sqrt{ax} - \frac{x^2}{a}\right)dx = \frac{1}{2} \times \frac{16\left(\dfrac{a}{4}\right)\left(\dfrac{a}{4}\right)}{3}$$

$$\Rightarrow \quad \left[\frac{2\sqrt{a}}{3}x^{3/2} - \frac{x^3}{3a}\right]_0^b = \frac{a^2}{6} \qquad \text{...(i)}$$

$$\frac{2\sqrt{a}}{3}b^{3/2} - \frac{b^3}{3a} = \frac{a^2}{6}$$

Also, $\qquad \dfrac{1}{2}\times b^2 = \dfrac{1}{2}$

$$\Rightarrow \qquad\qquad b = 1$$

So, $\dfrac{2\sqrt{a}}{3}b^{3/2} - \dfrac{1}{3a} = \dfrac{a^2}{6} \Rightarrow a^3 - 4a^{3/2} + 2 = 0$

$$\Rightarrow \qquad a^6 + 4a^3 + 4 = 16a^3$$

$$\Rightarrow \qquad a^6 - 12a^3 + 4 = 0$$

35. Correct Response : (a)

Explanation :

If $\displaystyle \int \frac{\cos x\, dx}{\sin^3 x(1+\sin^6 x)^{2/3}}$

$$= -\frac{6}{6}\int \frac{\cos x\, dx}{\sin^7 x\left(\dfrac{1}{\sin^6 x}+1\right)^{2/3}}$$

$$= -\frac{1}{6}\times 3\left(\frac{1}{\sin^6 x}+1\right)^{\frac{1}{3}}+c$$

$$= -\frac{1}{2}\frac{(1+\sin^6 x)^{\frac{1}{3}}}{\sin^2 x}+c$$

Hence, $\lambda = 3$ and $f(x) = -\dfrac{1}{2\sin^2 x}$

so, $\qquad \lambda f\left(\dfrac{\pi}{3}\right) = -2$

Remark : Technically, this questions should be marked as bonus. Because $f(x)$ and λ cannot be found uniquely.

For example, another such $f(x)$ and λ can be

$\dfrac{(1+\sin^6 x)^{\frac{1}{6}}}{2\sin^2 x}$ and 6 respectively.

36. Correct Response : (c)

Explanation :

$$f'(x) = \tan^{-1}(\sec x + \tan x)$$

$$f'(x) = \tan^{-1}\left(\frac{1+\sin x}{\cos x}\right) = \tan^{-1}\left(\frac{1+\tan\dfrac{x}{2}}{1-\tan\dfrac{x}{2}}\right)$$

$$= \tan^{-1}\left(\tan\left(\frac{\pi}{4}+\frac{\pi}{2}\right)\right)$$

$\therefore \qquad -\dfrac{\pi}{2}<x<\dfrac{\pi}{2} \Rightarrow 0<\dfrac{\pi}{4}+\dfrac{x}{2}<\dfrac{\pi}{2}$

$$\Rightarrow \quad f'(x) = \frac{\pi}{4}+\frac{x}{2}$$

$$\therefore \quad f(x) = \frac{\pi}{4}x+\frac{x^2}{4}+c$$

$$\therefore \quad f(0) = 0 \Rightarrow c = 0$$

$$\Rightarrow \quad f(1) = \frac{\pi}{4}x+\frac{x^2}{4}$$

$$\therefore \quad f(1) = \frac{\pi+1}{4}$$

37. Correct Response : (b)

Explanation :

$$I = \int_0^{2\pi} (\sin 2x(1+\cos 3x))\, dx$$

Apply $a+b-x$

$$I = \int_0^{2\pi} (-\sin 2x(1+\cos 3x))\, dx$$

$$2I = \int_0^{2\pi} (\sin 2x(1+\cos 3x))$$

$$+ (-\sin 2x\,(1+\cos 3x))dx$$

$$2I = -2\pi$$

$$I = -\pi$$

38. Correct Response : (a)

Explanation :

$$\int \frac{dy}{(x^2-2x+10)^2} = \int \frac{dx}{((x^2-1)^2+9)^2}$$

Put $x-1 = 3\tan\theta$

$$\Rightarrow \qquad dx = 3\sec^2\theta\, d\theta$$

$$\int \frac{3\sec^2\theta\, d\theta}{(9\sec^2\theta)^2} = \frac{1}{27}\int \frac{d\theta}{\sec^2\theta}$$

$$= \frac{1}{27}\int \cos^2\theta\, d\theta$$

$$= \frac{1}{27}\int\left(\frac{1+\cos 2\theta}{2}\right)d\theta$$

$$= \frac{1}{54}\left[\theta+\frac{1}{2}\sin\theta\right]+C$$

$$= \frac{1}{54}\left[\tan^{-1}\left(\frac{x-1}{3}\right)+\frac{3(x-1)}{x^2-2x+10}\right]+C$$

39. Correct Response : (a)

Explanation :

$$\lim_{n\to\infty}\left\{\left(1+\frac{1}{n}\right)^{1/3}+\left(1+\frac{2}{n}\right)^{1/3}+....+\left(1+\frac{n}{n}\right)^{1/3}\right\}\frac{1}{n}$$

$$= \lim_{n\to\infty}\sum_{r=1}^{n}\left(1+\frac{r}{n}\right)^{1/3}\frac{1}{n}$$

$$= \int_0^1 (1+x)^{1/3}\, dx$$

$$= \frac{1}{4/3}(1+x)^{4/3}\Big|_0^1$$

$$= \frac{3}{4}(2^{4/3}-1)$$

40. Correct Response : (d)

Explanation :

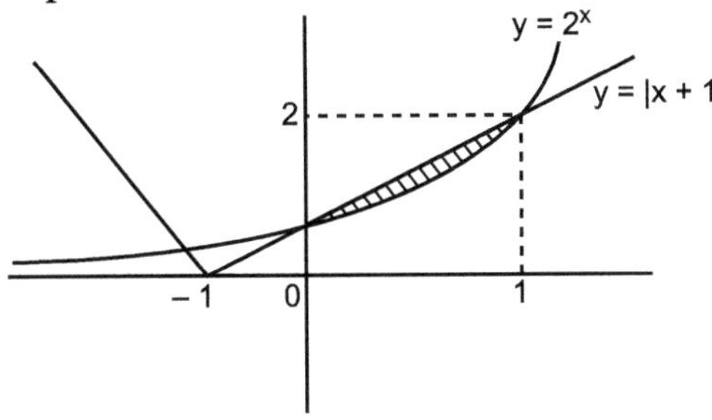

Area of the required region is

$$\int_0^1 (|x+1| - 2^x)\, dx = \int_0^1 (x+1-2^x)\, dx$$

$$= \left(\frac{x^2}{2} + x - \frac{2^x}{ln\,2}\right)_0^1$$

$$= \left(\frac{1}{2} + 1 - \frac{2}{ln\,2}\right) - \left(-\frac{1}{ln\,2}\right)$$

$$= \frac{3}{2} - \frac{1}{ln\,2}$$

41. Correct Response : (c)

Explanation :

$$\int_{\frac{\pi}{6}}^{\frac{\pi}{3}} \sec^{2/3} x\,\operatorname{cosec}^{4/3} x\, dx$$

$$= \int_{\frac{\pi}{6}}^{\frac{\pi}{3}} \frac{1}{\dfrac{\sin^{4/3} x}{\cos^{4/3} x}\cos^{2/3} x \cos^{4/3} x}\, dx$$

$$= \int_{\frac{\pi}{6}}^{\frac{\pi}{3}} \frac{\sec^2 x}{\tan^{4/3} x}\, dx$$

Put $\tan x = t \Rightarrow \sec^2 x\, dx = dt$

$$\int_{1/\sqrt{3}}^{\sqrt{3}} \frac{dt}{t^{4/3}} = -3\left(\frac{1}{t^{1/3}}\right)_{1/\sqrt{3}}^{\sqrt{3}}$$

$$= -3\left(\frac{1}{(\sqrt{3})^{1/3}} - \sqrt{3}^{1/3}\right)$$

$$= -3\left(\frac{1-3^{1/3}}{\sqrt{3}^{1/3}}\right)$$

$$= 3^{\frac{4}{3}-\frac{1}{6}} - 3^{1-\frac{1}{6}}$$

$$= 3^{\frac{7}{6}} - 3^{\frac{5}{6}}$$

42. Correct Response : (c)

Explanation :

Consider $\displaystyle\int x^5 e^{-x^2}\, dx$

Put $x^2 = t \Rightarrow 2x\,dx = dt$

Then the integral becomes

$$\frac{1}{2}\int t^2 e^{-t}\, dt = \frac{1}{2}\left(-t^2 e^{-t} + \int 2t e^{-t}\, dt\right) + C$$

$$= \frac{1}{2}\left(-t^2 e^{-t} + 2(-te^{-t} + \int e^{-t}\, dt)\right) + C$$

$$= \frac{-t^2 e^{-t}}{2} - te^{-t} - e^{-t} + C$$

By given information,

$$\frac{-t^2 e^{-t}}{2} - te^{-t} - e^{-t} = g(x)e^{-x^2}$$

$$\Rightarrow \frac{-x^4 e^{-x^2}}{2} - x^2 e^{-x^2} - e^{-x^2} = g(x)e^{-x^2}$$

$$\Rightarrow \frac{-x^4}{2} - x^2 - 1 = g(x)$$

$$g(-1) = -\frac{1}{2} - 1 - 1$$

$$= -\frac{5}{2}$$

43. Correct Response : (b)

Explanation :

$$\int_0^1 x\tan^{-1}\left(\frac{1}{1-x^2+x^4}\right) dx$$

Put $x^2 = t$

$$\frac{1}{2}\int_0^1 \tan^{-1}\left(\frac{1}{1-t+t^2}\right) dt = \frac{1}{2}\int_0^1 \tan^{-1}\left(\frac{t+(1+t)}{1-t(1-t)}\right) dt$$

$$= \frac{1}{2}\int_0^1 (\tan^{-1} t + \tan^{-1}(1-t))\, dt$$

$$= \frac{1}{2}\int_0^1 (\tan^{-1}(1-t))\, dt +$$

$$= \frac{1}{2}\int_0^1 (\tan^{-1}(1-t))\, dt$$

$$= \int_0^1 (\tan^{-1}(1-t))\, dt$$

$$= \int_0^1 (\tan^{-1} t)\, dt$$

Put $\tan^{-1} t = k$

Then, using integration by parts

$$\int_0^{\frac{\pi}{4}} k \sec^2 k\, dk = \frac{\pi}{4} - \frac{1}{2} \ln 2$$

44. Correct Response : (a)

Explanation :

$$\int e^{\sec x}(\sec x \tan x\, f(x) + \sec x \tan x + \sec^2 x)\, dx$$

$$= e^{\sec x} f(x)$$

Differentiate both sides with respect to x

$e^{\sec x}(\sec x \tan x\, f(x) + \sec x \tan x + \sec^2 x)$

$$= e^{\sec x} f'(x) + e^{\sec x} \sec x \tan x\, f(x)$$

Compare both sides

$$\sec x \tan x + \sec^2 x = f'(x)$$

Integrate both sides

$$f(x) = \sec x + \tan x + C.$$

45. Correct Response : (d)

Explanation :

$$\frac{y^2}{2} \le x \le y + 4$$

$$y^2 \le 2x$$

$$x - y - 4 \le 0$$

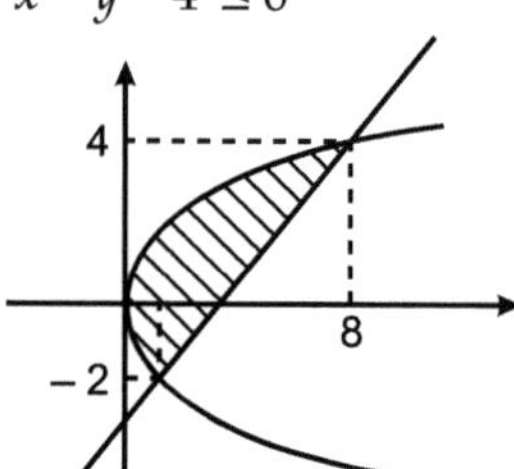

Required area is

$$\int_{-2}^{4} (x_{\text{right}} - y_{\text{left}})\, dy = \int_{-2}^{4}\left((y+4) - \frac{y^2}{2}\right) dy$$

$$= \frac{y^2}{2} + 4y - \frac{y^3}{6}\Big|_{-2}^{4}$$

$$= 18$$

46. Correct Response : (a)

Explanation :

$$I = \int (\sec x)^{2/3} \cdot (\csc x)^{4/3}\, dx$$

$$= \int \frac{1}{(\sin x)^{4/3} \cdot (\cos x)^{2/3}}\, dx$$

Multiplying numerator and denominator by $\csc^2 x$, we get

$$I = \int \frac{\csc^2 x}{(\cot x)^{2/3}}\, dx$$

Let $\cot x = t^3 \Rightarrow \csc^2 x\, dx = -3t^2\, dt$

Thus,

$$I = -3\int \frac{t^2 dt}{t^2}$$

$$= -3t + C$$
$$= -3\,(\cot x)^{1/3} + C$$
$$= -3\,(\tan x)^{-1/3} + C$$

47. Correct Response : (b)

Explanation :

$$I = \int_0^{\frac{\pi}{2}} \frac{\sin^3 x}{\sin x + \cos x}\, dx$$

$$= \int_0^{\frac{\pi}{4}} \frac{\sin^3 x + \cos^3 x}{\sin x + \cos x}\, dx$$

$$= \int_0^{\frac{\pi}{4}} (1 - \sin x \cos x)\, dx$$

$$= \frac{\pi}{4} + \frac{1}{4}(\cos 2x)_0^{\pi/4}$$

$$= \frac{\pi}{4} - \frac{1}{4}$$

48. Correct Response : (b)

Explanation :

$$x^2 = x + 2$$

$$\Rightarrow \qquad x = -1 \text{ or } 2.$$

Required area is,

$$\int_{-1}^{2} (x + 2 - x^2)\, dx = \frac{x^2}{2} + 2x - \frac{x^3}{3}\Big|_{-1}^{2}$$

$$= \left(2 + 4 - \frac{8}{3}\right) - \left(\frac{1}{2} - 2 + \frac{1}{3}\right)$$

$$= \frac{10}{3} + \frac{7}{6}$$

$$= \frac{27}{6}$$

$$= \frac{9}{2}$$

49. Correct Response : (c)

Explanation :

$$\int \frac{\sin \dfrac{5x}{2}}{\sin \dfrac{x}{2}}\, dx \;=\; \int \frac{2\sin \dfrac{5x}{2}\cos \dfrac{x}{2}}{2\sin \dfrac{x}{2}\cos \dfrac{x}{2}}\, dx$$

$$= \int \left(\frac{\sin 3x + \sin 2x}{\sin x} \right) dx$$

$$= \int 2\cos x\, dx + \int (3 - 4\sin^2 x)\, dx$$

$$= 2\int \cos x\, dx + \int dx + 2\int \cos 2x\, dx$$

$$= 2\sin x + x + \sin 2x + C$$

50. Correct Response : (c)

Explanation :

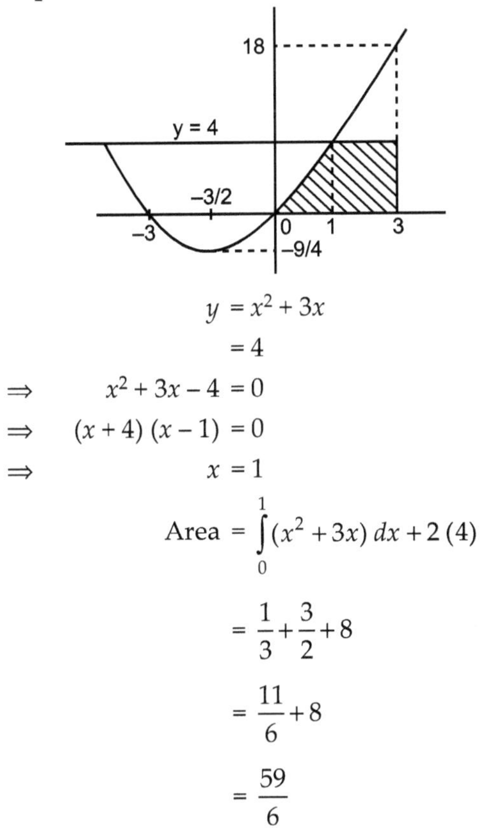

$$y = x^2 + 3x$$
$$= 4$$
$$\Rightarrow \quad x^2 + 3x - 4 = 0$$
$$\Rightarrow \quad (x + 4)(x - 1) = 0$$
$$\Rightarrow \quad x = 1$$

$$\text{Area} = \int_0^1 (x^2 + 3x)\, dx + 2(4)$$

$$= \frac{1}{3} + \frac{3}{2} + 8$$

$$= \frac{11}{6} + 8$$

$$= \frac{59}{6}$$

51. Correct Response : (d)

Explanation :

$$g(x) = \ln(x),\; f(x) = \frac{2 - x\cos x}{2 + x\cos x}\;\frac{2 - x\cos x}{2 + x\cos x}$$

$$\text{and} \qquad g(f(x)) = \ln\left(\frac{2 - x\cos x}{2 + x\cos x} \right)$$

$$I = \int_{-\frac{\pi}{4}}^{\frac{\pi}{4}} \ln\left(\frac{2 - x\cos x}{2 + x\cos x} \right) dx$$

$$x \to a + b - x$$
$$x \to -x$$

$$I = \int_{-\frac{\pi}{4}}^{\frac{\pi}{4}} \ln\left(\frac{2 + x\cos x}{2 - x\cos x} \right) dx$$

Adding,

$$2I = \int_{-\frac{\pi}{4}}^{\frac{\pi}{4}} \ln(1)\, dx$$

$$= 0$$
$$\Rightarrow \qquad I = 0$$

52. Correct Response : (d)

Explanation :

$$\int \frac{dx}{x^3(1 + x^6)^{2/3}} \;=\; \int \frac{dx}{x^7\left(1 + \dfrac{1}{x^6}\right)^{2/3}}$$

Substitute $\left(1 - \dfrac{1}{x^6}\right)^{1/3} = t$

$$-\frac{d}{x^7}\, dx = dt \Rightarrow -\frac{1}{6}\int \frac{dt}{t^{2/3}}$$

$$-\frac{1}{6}\left(\frac{t^{1/3}}{\dfrac{1}{3}} \right) = \frac{1}{2}\left[\left(1 + \frac{1}{x^6}\right)^{1/5} \right] + C$$

$$= -\frac{1}{2}\left[\left(\frac{1 + x^6}{x^2} \right)^{1/3} \right] + C$$

$$= x \cdot f(x)\,(1 + x^6)^{1/3}$$

$$\Rightarrow \qquad f(x) = -\frac{1}{2x^3}$$

53. Correct Response : (a)

Explanation :

$f(0) = 0$ and $g(x)$ is even, so $f(x)$ is odd function.

$$g(x) = f(x + 5)$$

Replacing x by $-x$

$$g(-x) = f(-x + 5)$$
$$g(x) = -f(x - 5)$$

Replacing x by $x + 5$

$$f(x) = -g(x + 5)$$

$$I = \int_0^x f(t)\, dt$$

$$= -\int_0^x g(t + 5)\, dt$$

Put $t + 5 = k$

$$I = -\int_5^{x+5} g(k)\, dk$$

$$= -\int_{x+5}^5 g(t)\, dt$$

54. Correct Response : (d)

Explanation :

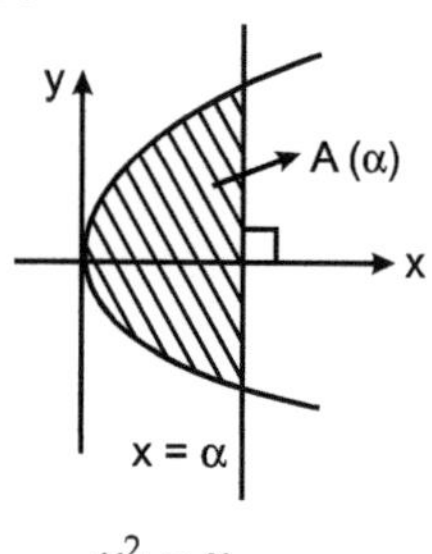

$$y^2 = x$$

$$S(\lambda) = 2\int_0^\lambda \sqrt{x}\,dx$$

$$= \frac{2x^{3/2}}{\frac{3}{2}}\Big|_0^\lambda$$

$$= \frac{4}{3}\lambda^{3/2}$$

$$\frac{S(\lambda)}{S(4)} = \frac{2}{5}$$

$$\Rightarrow \qquad \frac{\lambda^{3/2}}{4^{3/2}} = \frac{2}{5}$$

Therefore,

$$\lambda = 4\left(\frac{2}{5}\right)^{2/3}$$

$$= 4\left(\frac{4}{25}\right)^{1/3}$$

55. Correct Response : (c)

Explanation :

The given integral is,

$$I = \int \frac{2x^3 - 1}{x^4 + x}\,dx$$

$$= \int \frac{2x - x^2}{x^2 + x^{-1}}\,dx$$

Substitute $z = x^2 + x^{-1}$

$dz = 2x - x^2$.

Therefore,

$$I = \int \frac{dz}{z}$$

$$= In\, z + c$$

$$= In\,(x^2 + x^{-1}) + c$$

$$= In\left(\frac{x^3 + 1}{x}\right) + c$$

56. Correct Response : (d)

Explanation :

The given integral is,

$$I = \int_0^{\frac{\pi}{2}} \frac{\cot x}{\cot x + \operatorname{cosec} x}\,dx$$

$$= \int_0^{\frac{\pi}{2}} \frac{\cos x}{\cos x + 1}\,dx$$

$$= \int_0^{\frac{\pi}{2}} \frac{2\cos^2 \frac{x}{2} - 1}{2\cos^2 \frac{x}{2}}\,dx$$

$$= \int_0^{\frac{\pi}{2}} \left(1 - \frac{1}{2}\sec^2 \frac{x}{2}\right)dx$$

$$= \left(x - \tan^2 \frac{x}{2}\right)\Big|_0^{\frac{\pi}{2}}$$

Solve further,

$$I = \frac{\pi}{2} - 1$$

$$= \frac{1}{2}(\pi - 2)$$

Given that,

$$I = m\,(p + n)$$

Therefore,

$$mn = \left(\frac{1}{2}\right)(-1)$$

$$= -1$$

57. Correct Response : (a)

Explanation :

The given integral is,

$$I = \int_\alpha^{\alpha+1} \frac{dx}{(x + \alpha)(x + \alpha + 1)}$$

Let $x + \alpha = t$, $dx = dt$.

The integral changes to,

$$I = \int_{2\alpha}^{2\alpha+1} \frac{dt}{t\,(t + 1)}\,dt$$

$$= \int_{2\alpha}^{2\alpha+1} \left(\frac{1}{t} - \frac{1}{t + 1}\right)dt$$

$$= In\,t - In\,(t + 1)\Big|_{2\alpha}^{2\alpha+1}$$

$$= In\left(\frac{t}{t + 1}\right)\Big|_{2\alpha}^{2\alpha+1}$$

Solve further,

$$I = In\left(\frac{2\alpha + 1}{2\alpha - 2}\right) - In\left(\frac{2\alpha}{2\alpha + 1}\right)$$

$$= In\left(\frac{(2\alpha+1)^1}{2\alpha-2}\right)$$

Given that,

$$I = In\left(\frac{9}{8}\right)$$

Therefore,

$$\frac{(2\alpha+1)^2}{2\alpha+2} = \frac{9\alpha}{4}$$

$$4\,(4\alpha^2+1+4\alpha) = 18\alpha^2+18\alpha$$

$$\alpha^2+\alpha-2 = 0$$

$$\alpha = -2,\,1$$

58. Correct Response : (a)

Explanation :

The given integral is,

$$I = \int \frac{\tan x + \tan\alpha}{\tan x - \tan\alpha}\,dx$$

$$= \int \frac{\dfrac{\sin x}{\cos x}+\dfrac{\sin\alpha}{\cos\alpha}}{\dfrac{\sin x}{\cos x}-\dfrac{\sin\alpha}{\cos\alpha}}\,dx$$

$$= \int \frac{\sin(x+\alpha)}{\sin(x-\alpha)}\,dx$$

$$= \int \frac{\sin(x-\alpha+2\alpha)}{\sin(x-\alpha)}\,dx$$

Solve further,

$$I = \int \frac{\sin(x-\alpha)\cos 2\alpha + \cos(x-\alpha)\sin 2\alpha}{\sin(x-\alpha)}\,dx$$

$$= \cos 2\alpha \int dx + \sin 2\alpha \int \cot(x-\alpha)\,dx$$

$$= x\cos 2\alpha + \sin 2\alpha\, In\,|\sin(x-\alpha)| + c$$

59. Correct Response : (b)

Explanation :

The required diagram is shown in the figure.

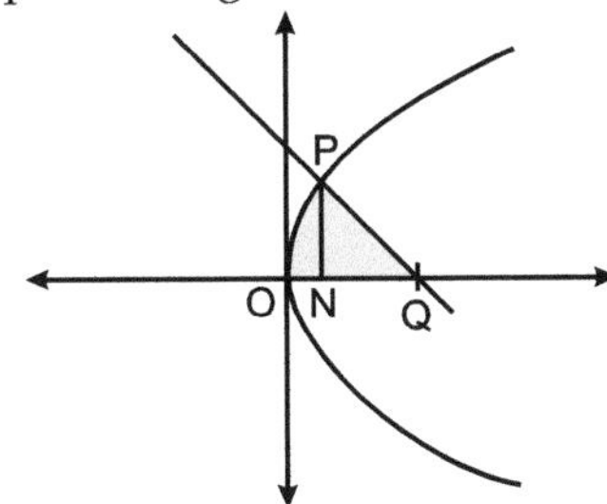

For point P,

$$y^2 = 4\,(1-y)$$

$$y^2+4y-4 = 0$$

$$y = -2\pm 2\sqrt{2}$$

The coordinates of P are $(3-2\sqrt{2},\,-2+2\sqrt{2})$

The area of the shaded region is,

$$A = \int_0^{3-2\sqrt{2}} 2\sqrt{x}\,dx + \frac{1}{2}[1-(3-2\sqrt{2})]^2$$

$$= \frac{2}{3}(2)\,(\sqrt{2}-1)\,(3-2\sqrt{2}) + \frac{1}{2}[2\,(\sqrt{2}-1)]^2$$

$$= \frac{4}{3}(-7+5\sqrt{2}) + 2\,(3-2\sqrt{2})$$

$$= \frac{8}{3}\sqrt{2} - \frac{10}{3}$$

Therefore,

$$a = \frac{8}{3}$$

$$b = -\frac{10}{3}$$

Hence, the required value is,

$$a-b = \frac{18}{3}$$

$$= 6$$

60. Correct Response : (c)

Explanation :

The required diagram is shown in the figure.

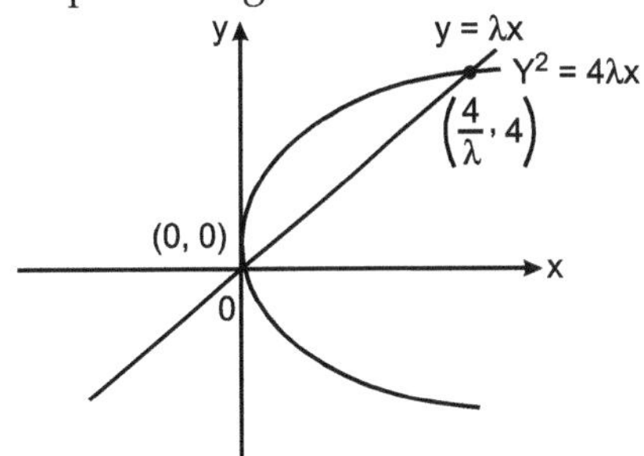

The expression for area is,

$$\frac{1}{9} = \int_0^{\frac{4}{\pi}} (2\sqrt{\lambda}\sqrt{x} - \lambda x)\,dx$$

$$\frac{1}{9} = \left(\frac{2\sqrt{\lambda}x^{\frac{3}{2}}}{\frac{3}{2}} - \frac{\lambda x^2}{2}\right)\Bigg|_0^{\frac{4}{\lambda}}$$

$$\frac{1}{9} = \left(\frac{4}{3}\right)\sqrt{\lambda}\left(\frac{8}{\lambda^{\frac{3}{2}}}\right) - \lambda\left(\frac{8}{\lambda^2}\right)$$

$$\frac{1}{9} = \frac{32}{3\lambda} - \frac{8}{\lambda}$$

Solve further,

$$\frac{8}{3\lambda} = \frac{1}{9}$$

$$\lambda = 24.$$

61. Correct Response : (a)

Explanation :

The given equations are,

$$xy \leq 8 \text{ and } 1 \leq y \leq x^2.$$

Therefore,

$$x^2 \cdot x = 8$$
$$x^3 = 8$$
$$x = 2$$

The required diagram is shown in figure below.

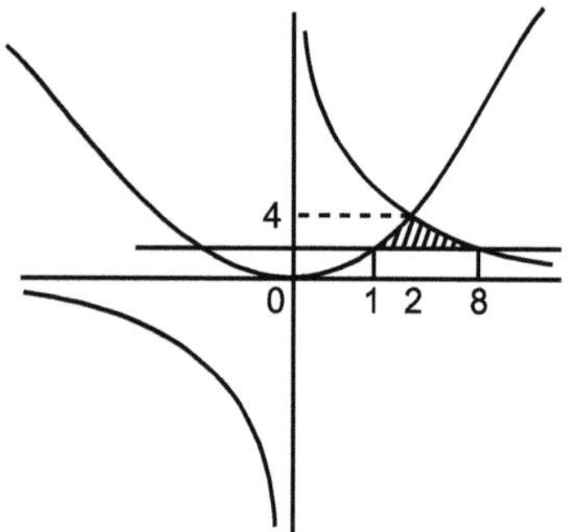

The required area is,

$$A = \int_1^4 \left(\frac{8}{y} - \sqrt{y} \right)$$

$$= \left[8\ln y - \frac{y^{\frac{3}{2}}}{\frac{3}{2}} \right]_1^4$$

$$= 8\ln 4 - \frac{2}{3}(8) - 0 + \frac{2}{3}$$

$$= 16\ln 2 - \frac{14}{3}$$

62. Correct Response : (4.00)

Explanation :

The given expression is,

$$I = \frac{2}{\pi} \int_{-\frac{\pi}{4}}^{\frac{\pi}{4}} \frac{dx}{(1 + e^{\sin x})(2 - \cos 2x)} \qquad ...(i)$$

By $a + b - x$ property,

$$I = \frac{2}{\pi} \int_{-\frac{\pi}{4}}^{\frac{\pi}{4}} \frac{dx}{(1 + e^{-\sin x})(2 - \cos 2x)}$$

$$= \frac{2}{\pi} \int_{-\frac{\pi}{4}}^{\frac{\pi}{4}} \frac{e^{\sin x}}{(1 + e^{\sin x})(2 - \cos 2x)} dx \qquad ...(ii)$$

Add equation (i) and equation (ii).

$$2I = \frac{2}{\pi} \int_{-\frac{\pi}{4}}^{\frac{\pi}{4}} \frac{(1 + e^{\sin x})}{(1 + e^{\sin x})(2 - \cos 2x)} dx$$

$$I = \frac{1}{\pi} \int_{-\frac{\pi}{4}}^{\frac{\pi}{4}} \frac{1}{2 - (\cos^2 x - 1)} dx$$

$$= \frac{1}{\pi} \int_{-\frac{\pi}{4}}^{\frac{\pi}{4}} \frac{\sec^2 x}{3\sec^2 x - 2} dx$$

Substitute $\tan x = t$ and $\sec^2 x\, dx = dt$ in the above equation.

$$I = \frac{1}{\pi} \int_{-\frac{\pi}{4}}^{\frac{\pi}{4}} \frac{dt}{3t^2 + 1}$$

$$= \frac{2}{3\pi} \frac{1}{\frac{1}{\sqrt{3}}} \left(\tan^{-1} \left(\frac{t}{\frac{1}{\sqrt{3}}} \right) \right)_0^1$$

$$= \frac{2}{\sqrt{3}\pi} (\tan^{-1}(\sqrt{3}) - \tan^{-1} 0)$$

$$= \frac{2}{\sqrt{3}\pi} \left(\frac{\pi}{3} \right)$$

$$= \frac{2}{3\sqrt{3}}$$

Therefore,

$$27I^2 = 27 \left(\frac{4}{27} \right)$$

$$= 4$$

63. Correct Response : (a, d)

Explanation :

The given equation is,

$$\lim_{n \to \infty} \left(\frac{1 + \sqrt[3]{2} + ... + \sqrt[3]{n}}{n^{\frac{7}{3}} \left(\frac{1}{(an+1)^2} + \frac{1}{(an+2)^2} + ... + \frac{1}{(an+n)^2} \right)} \right) = 54$$

Solve further as,

$$\lim_{n \to \infty} \left(\frac{\frac{1}{n} \sum_{r=1}^{n} \left(\frac{r}{n} \right)}{\frac{1}{n} \left(\frac{n^2}{(an+1)^2} + \frac{n^2}{(an+2)^2} + ... + \frac{n^2}{(an+n)^2} \right)} \right) = 54$$

$$\frac{\int_0^1 x^{\frac{1}{3}} dx}{\int_0^1 \frac{dx}{(a+x)^2}} = 54$$

$$\frac{\left[\frac{3}{4} x^{\frac{4}{3}} \right]_0^1}{\left[-\frac{1}{a+x} \right]_0^1} = 54$$

$$\frac{\frac{3}{4}}{\frac{1}{a}-\frac{1}{a+1}} = 54$$

$$\frac{1}{a}-\frac{1}{a+1} = \frac{3}{(4)(54)}$$

$$\frac{1}{a(a+1)} = \frac{1}{72}$$

$$a(a+1) = 72$$

Therefore,

$a = 8$ or $a = -9$.

64. Correct Response : (0.50)

Explanation :

The value of the given integral is,

$$I = 3\int_0^{\frac{\pi}{2}} \frac{\sqrt{\cos\theta}}{(\sqrt{\sin\theta}+\sqrt{\cos\theta})^5}\,d\theta$$

$$= 3\int_0^{\frac{\pi}{2}} \frac{3\sqrt{\cos\theta}}{(\sqrt{\sin\theta}+\sqrt{\cos\theta})^5}\,d\theta$$

$$= 3\int_0^{\frac{\pi}{2}} \frac{\sqrt{\sin\theta}}{(\sqrt{\sin\theta}+\sqrt{\cos\theta})^5}\,d\theta$$

Solve further as,

$$2I = 3\int_0^{\frac{\pi}{2}} \frac{1}{(\sqrt{\sin\theta}+\sqrt{\cos\theta})^4}\,d\theta$$

$$\frac{2I}{3} = \int_0^{\frac{\pi}{2}} \frac{\sec^2\theta}{(\sqrt{\tan\theta}+1)^4}\,d\theta$$

Consider, $\tan\theta = t^2$ and $\sec^2\theta\,d\theta = 2t\,dt$.

The above equation will be,

$$\frac{2I}{3} = \int_0^{\infty} \frac{2t\,dt}{(t+1)^4}$$

$$\frac{I}{3} = \int_0^{\infty}\left[\frac{1}{(t+1)^3}-\frac{1}{(t+1)^4}\right]dt$$

$$I = \left|\frac{-3}{2(t+1)^2}-\frac{1}{(t+1)^3}\right|_0^{\infty}$$

$$= \frac{3}{2}-1$$

$$= \frac{1}{2}$$

65. Correct Response : (b)

Explanation :

The given function is,

$$f\left(\frac{x-4}{x+2}\right) = 2x+1$$

The function $f(x)$ is,

$$f(x) = 2\left\{1-3\left(\frac{x+1}{x-1}\right)\right\}+1$$

$$= 2-\frac{6x+6}{x-1}+1$$

$$= \frac{-3x-9}{x-1}$$

$$= \frac{3(x+3)}{(1-x)}$$

Integrate with respect to x.

$$\int f(x)\,dx = \int \frac{3(x+3)}{(1-x)}\,dx$$

$$= 3\left\{\int \frac{4}{(1-x)}\,dx-\int dx\right\}$$

$$= 3\{-4\ln|1-x|-x\}+C$$

$$= -12\ln|1+x|-3x+C$$

Therefore, the term $\int f(x)\,dx$ is

$$-12\ln|1-x|-3x+C.$$

66. Correct Response : (c)

Explanation :

The given region is,

$\{x \in \mathrm{R}, x \geq 0, y \geq 0, y \geq x-2\}$

And,

$$y \leq \sqrt{x}$$

The figure shows the shaded region area which is bounded between the given region.

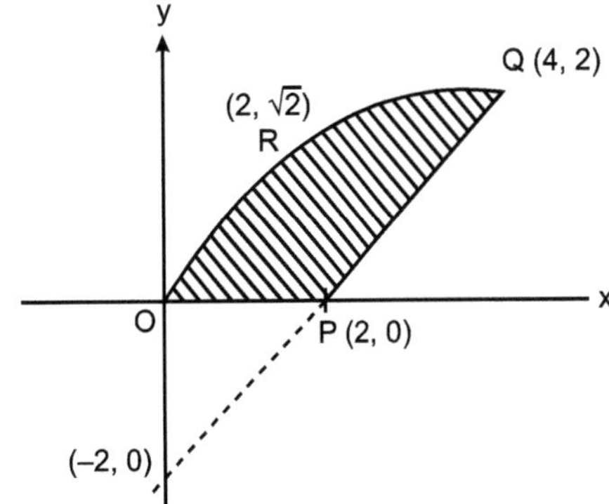

The area bounded by the region is,

$$A = \int_0^2 \sqrt{x}\,dx+\int_2^4 \left(\sqrt{x}\right)dx-\int_2^4 (x-2)\,dx$$

$$= \int_0^4 \sqrt{x}\,dx + \int_2^4 (2-x)\,dx$$

$$= \left[\frac{x^{\left(\frac{3}{2}\right)}}{\left(\frac{3}{2}\right)}\right]_0^4 + \left[2x - \frac{x^2}{2}\right]_2^4$$

$$= \left[\frac{2}{3}\left(4^{\frac{3}{2}} - 0\right)\right] + \left[2(4-2) - \frac{1}{2}(4^2 - 2^2)\right]$$

Simplify the above expression.

$$A = \left[\frac{2}{3}(8)\right] + \left[2(2) - \frac{1}{2}(12)\right]$$

$$= \frac{16-6}{3}$$

$$= \frac{10}{3}$$

Therefore, the area bounded by the region is $\dfrac{10}{3}$.

67. Correct Response : (c)

Explanation :

Let, the value of the integral,

$$\int_{-\frac{\lambda}{2}}^{\frac{\lambda}{2}} \sin^4 x \left(1 + \log\left(\frac{2+\sin x}{2-\sin x}\right)\right) dx = I \quad ...(1)$$

Apply the property of integral,

$$\int_a^b f(x) = \int_a^b f(a+b-x)$$

Then,

$$I = \int_{-\frac{\pi}{2}}^{\frac{\pi}{2}} \sin^4 x \left(1 + \log\left(\frac{2-\sin x}{2+\sin x}\right)\right) dx \quad ...(2)$$

Add equation (1) and (2).

$$2I = \int_{-\frac{\pi}{2}}^{\frac{\pi}{2}} \sin^4 x \left(1 + \log\left(\frac{2+\sin x}{2-\sin x}\right)\right) dx$$

$$+ \int_{-\frac{\pi}{2}}^{\frac{\pi}{2}} \sin^4 x \left(1 + \log\left(\frac{2+\sin x}{2-\sin x}\right)\right) dx$$

$$2I = \int_{-\frac{\pi}{2}}^{\frac{\pi}{2}} \sin^4 x \left(1 - \log\left(\frac{2+\sin x}{2-\sin x}\right)\right) dx$$

$$+ \int_{-\frac{\pi}{2}}^{\frac{\pi}{2}} \sin^4 x \left(1 - \log\left(\frac{2+\sin x}{2-\sin x}\right)\right) dx$$

$$2I = 2\int_0^{\frac{\pi}{2}} 2\sin^4 x\,dx$$

$$\left[\because \int_{-a}^a f(x)\,dx = 2\int_0^a f(x)\,dx\right]$$

$$I = 2\int_0^{\frac{\pi}{2}} \sin^4 x\,dx$$

Further solve the integral.

$$I = 2\left[-\frac{1}{4}\sin^3 x \cdot \cos x + \frac{3}{8}\left(x - \frac{1}{2}\sin 2x\right) + C\right]_0^{\frac{\pi}{2}}$$

$$= 2\left[\left\{-\frac{1}{4}\sin^3\left(\frac{\pi}{2}\right)\cdot\cos\left(\frac{\pi}{2}\right)\right\} \\ \left\{-\frac{1}{4}\sin^3(0)\cdot\cos(0)\right\}\right.$$

$$\left. + \frac{3}{8}\left(\left(\frac{\pi}{2}\right) - \frac{1}{2}\sin 2\left(\frac{\pi}{2}\right)\right) + C\right\}$$

$$\left. \frac{3}{8}\left((0) - \frac{1}{2}\sin 2(0)\right) + C\right\}\right]$$

$$= 2\left[\left\{-\frac{1}{4}(1)(0) + \frac{3}{8}\left(\frac{\pi}{2} - \frac{1}{2}(0)\right)\right\}\right.$$

$$\left. - \left\{\frac{1}{4}(0)(1) + \frac{3}{8}\left(-\frac{1}{2}(0)\right)\right\}\right]$$

$$= \frac{3}{8}\pi$$

Therefore, the value of the integral is $\dfrac{3}{8}\pi$.

68. Correct Response : (c)

Explanation :

Consider the given integral function is equal to I

$$I = \int \frac{\tan x}{1 + \tan x + \tan^2 x}\,dx$$

$$= \int \frac{\left(1 + \tan^2 x + \tan x\right) - \left(1 + \tan^2 x\right)}{1 + \tan x + \tan^2 x}\,dx$$

$$= \int 1 - \frac{\sec^2 x}{1 + \tan x + \tan^2 x}\,dx \quad (\because 1 + \tan^2 x = \sec^2 x)$$

Putting,

$$t = \tan x$$

$$dt = \sec^2 x\,dx$$

$$I = x - \int \frac{dt}{1 + t + t^2}$$

$$= x - \int \frac{dt}{\left(t + \frac{1}{2}\right)^2 + \frac{3}{4}}$$

$$= x - \frac{1}{\frac{\sqrt{3}}{2}}\tan^{-1}\left(\frac{t + \frac{1}{2}}{\frac{\sqrt{3}}{2}}\right) + C$$

$$= x - \frac{2}{\sqrt{3}}\tan^{-1}\left(\frac{2\tan x + 1}{\sqrt{3}}\right) + C$$

Compare the above value with given integral function solution.

Thus, K = 2, A = 3.

69. Correct Response : (c)

Explanation :

The given function is,

$$f(x) = \int_0^x t(\sin x - \sin t)\,dt$$

Simplify the above equation.

$$f(x) = \int_0^x t(\sin x - \sin t)\,dt$$

$$f(x) = (\sin x)x + \cos x \int_0^x t\,dt - x\sin x$$

$$f'(x) = (\cos x)\int_0^x t\,dt$$

Further simplify.

$$f''(x) = (\cos x)x - (\sin x)\int t\,dt$$

$$f'''(x) = x\,(-\sin x) + \cos x - (\sin x)x$$
$$- (\cos x)\int t\,dt$$

$$f'''(x) = \cos x - 2x\sin x - f'(x)$$
$$f'''(x) + f'(x) = \cos x - 2x\sin x$$

70. Correct Response : (a)

Explanation :

The curve form by the given curves and lines is

Curve $y = x^2$ and $y = \dfrac{1}{x}$

And line $y = 0$ and $x = t\ [t > 1]$

The final combine curve is,

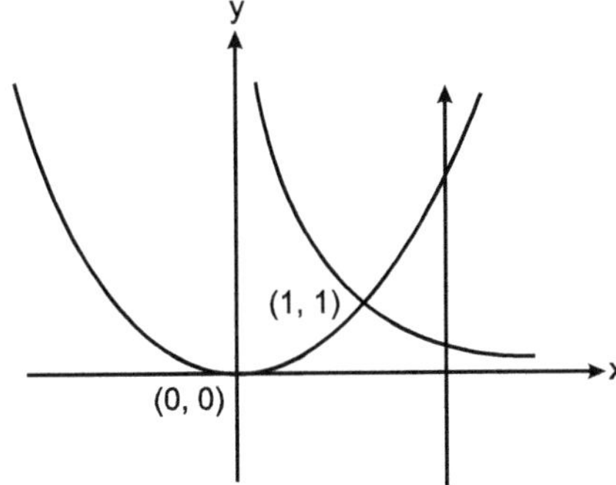

Now, area of the region bounded by the curves is,

$$\int_0^1 x^2\,dx + \int_1^t \frac{1}{x}\,dx = 1$$

$$\frac{1}{3} + \ln t = 1$$

$$t = e^{\left(1 - \frac{1}{3}\right)}$$

$$= e^{\frac{2}{3}}$$

Therefore, the value of the t is $e^{\frac{2}{3}}$.

71. Correct Response : (b)

Explanation :

The given integral is,

$$I = \int \frac{\sin^2 x \cdot \cos^2 x}{\left\{\left(\sin^5 x + \cos^3 x \sin^2 x\right) + \sin^3 x \cos^2 x + \cos^5 x\right\}^2}\,dx$$

Simplify the above equation.

$$I = \int \frac{\sin^2 x \cdot \cos^2 x}{\left\{\left(\sin^2 x + \cos^2 x\right)\left(\sin^3 x + \cos^3 x\right)\right\}^2}$$

Take $\cos^6 x$ as common from numerator and denominator.

$$I = \int \frac{\tan^2 x \sec^2 x\,dx}{\left(1 + \tan^3 x\right)^2}$$

Let, tan3 $x = z$. Then,

$$3\tan^2 x \cdot \sec^2 x\,dx = dz$$

Hence,

$$I = \frac{1}{3}\int \frac{dz}{z^2}$$

$$= \frac{-1}{3z} + C$$

$$= \frac{-1}{3\left(1 + \tan^3 x\right)} + C$$

72. Correct Response : (d)

Explanation :

The given integral is,

$$I = \int_{-\frac{\pi}{2}}^{\frac{\pi}{2}} \frac{\sin^2 x\,dx}{1 + 2^x} \qquad \text{...(1)}$$

By the property,

$$I = \int_{-\frac{\pi}{2}}^{\frac{\pi}{2}} \frac{2^x \sin^2 x\,dx}{1 + 2^x} \qquad \text{..(2)}$$

Add equation (1) and (2),

$$2I = \int_{-\frac{\pi}{2}}^{\frac{\pi}{2}} \frac{2^x \sin^2 x\,dx}{1 + 2^x}$$

$$= 2\int_0^{\frac{\pi}{2}} \sin^2 x\,dx$$

$$I = \int_0^{\frac{\pi}{2}} \sin^2 x \, dx$$

Simplify the above equation.

$$I = \int_0^{\frac{\pi}{2}} \sin^2 x \, dx$$

$$= \frac{1}{2}\int_0^{\frac{\pi}{2}} (1 - \cos 2x)\, dx$$

$$= \frac{\pi}{4}$$

73. Correct Response : (a)

Explanation :

The given quadratic equation is,

$$18x^2 - 9\pi x + \pi^2 = 0$$

Simplify the above equation.

$$(6x - \pi)(3x - \pi) = 0$$

$$x = \frac{\pi}{6}, \frac{\pi}{3}$$

Let $\alpha = \dfrac{\pi}{6}$ and $\beta = \dfrac{\pi}{3}$.

The curve is described by,

$$y = (gof)(x)$$

$$= \cos x$$

Area bounded by the curve,

$$\text{Area} = \int_{\frac{\pi}{6}}^{\frac{\pi}{3}} \cos x \, dx$$

$$= \frac{\sqrt{3}}{2} - \frac{1}{2}$$

$$= \frac{1}{2}\left(\sqrt{3} - 1\right) \text{ sq. units}$$

74. Correct Response : (b, c)

Explanation :

The modified form of the given function is,

$$f(x) = 1 - 2x + \int_0^x e^{x-1} f(t)\, dt$$

$$e^{-x} f(x) = e^{-x}(1 - 2x) + \int_0^x e^{-1} f(t)\, dt$$

Differentiate the above expression with respect to x.

$$-e^{-x} f(x) + e^{-x} f'(x) = -e - x\,(1 - 2x) + e^{-x}(-2) + e^{-x} f(x)$$

$$-f(x) + f'(x) = -(1 - 2x) - 2 + f(x)$$

$$f'(x) - 2f(x) = 2x - 3$$

The integrating factor of the function is e^{-2x}

$$f(x)e^{-2x} = \int e^{-2x}(2x - 3)\, dx$$

$$= (2x - 3)\int e^{-2x} dx - \int\left((2)\int e^{-2x} dx\right)dx$$

$$= \frac{(2x - 3)e^{-2x}}{-2} - \frac{e^{-2x}}{2} + c$$

$$f(x) = \frac{2x - 3}{-2} - \frac{1}{2} + ce^{2x}$$

The function for the area is,

$$f(x) = (1 - x) + ce^{2x} \qquad \text{...(1)}$$

$$x = 0$$

At $\qquad f(x) = 1$

Substitute the values in equation (1).

$$1 = 1 + c$$

$$c = 0$$

The equation of the line is,

$$y = 1 - x$$

The curve passes through the point $(2, -1)$ but does not pass through $(1, 2)$.

The graph shows the function.

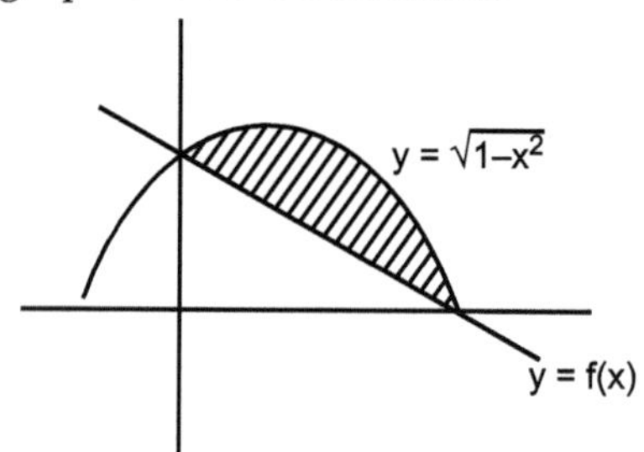

The required area of the curve is,

$$A = \left(\frac{1}{4} \times \pi \times (1)^2\right) - \left(\frac{1}{2} \times 1 \times 1\right)$$

$$= \frac{\pi}{4} - \frac{1}{2}$$

75. Correct Response : (4)

Explanation :

The value of [L] is,

$$y_n = \frac{1}{n}\left((n+1)(n+2)\ldots\ldots(n+n)\right)^{1/n}$$

$$\log L = \lim_{x \to \infty} \frac{1}{n}\sum_{r=1}^{n} \log\left(1 + \frac{r}{n}\right)$$

$$= \int_0^1 \log(1 + x)\, dx$$

$$= \int_1^2 \log(1 + x)\, dx$$

On further expansion,

$$\log L = \left|x \log x - x\right|_1^2$$

$$= \log 4$$

$$[L] = 4$$

76. Correct Response : (2)

Explanation :

The simplified integral is,

$$I = \int_0^{\frac{1}{2}} \frac{\left(1+\sqrt{3}\right)}{\left[(1+x)^2 (1-x)^6\right]^{\frac{1}{4}}} \, dx$$

$$= \int_0^{\frac{1}{2}} \frac{\left(1+\sqrt{3}\right)}{(1+x)^2 \left[\dfrac{(1-x)^6}{(1+x)^6}\right]^{\frac{1}{4}}} \, dx$$

Substitute,

$$\frac{1-x}{1+x} = t$$

$$-\frac{2dx}{\left(1+x^2\right)} = dt$$

Substitute the values in integral,

$$I = \int_1^{\frac{3}{2}} \frac{\left(1+\sqrt{3}\right)}{-2t^{\frac{6}{4}}} \, dt$$

$$= \frac{-\left(1+\sqrt{3}\right)}{2} \times \left|\frac{-2}{\sqrt{t}}\right|_1^{\frac{1}{3}}$$

$$= \left(1+\sqrt{3}\right)\left(\sqrt{3}-1\right)$$

$$= 2$$

77. Correct Response : (a)

Explanation :

The required integration is,

$$I_4 + I_6 = \int \left(\tan^4 x + \tan^6 x\right) dx$$

$$= \int \left(\tan^4 x \left(1+\tan^2 x\right)\right) dx$$

$$= \int \left(\tan^4 x \sec^2 x\right) dx \qquad \ldots(1)$$

Let $\tan x = t,$

$$\tan x = t$$

$$\sec^2 x \, dx = dt$$

Substitute this value in equation (1).

$$I_4 + I_6 = \int t^4 dt$$

$$= \frac{t^5}{5} + C$$

$$= \frac{1}{5} \tan^5 x + C$$

The coefficients according to the above equation

is $a = \dfrac{1}{5}$ and $b = 0$.

78. Correct Response : (a)

Explanation :

The integration of the given equation is,

$$\int_{\frac{\pi}{4}}^{\frac{3\pi}{4}} \frac{dx}{2\cos^2 \dfrac{x}{2}} = \frac{1}{2} \int_{\frac{\pi}{4}}^{\frac{3\pi}{4}} \sec^2 \frac{x}{2} \, dx$$

$$= \frac{1}{2} \left[\frac{\tan \dfrac{x}{2}}{\dfrac{1}{1}}\right]_{\frac{\pi}{4}}^{\frac{3\pi}{4}}$$

$$= \tan \frac{3\pi}{8} - \tan \frac{\pi}{8}$$

Simplif $\tan \dfrac{\pi}{8}$ as,

$$\tan \frac{3\pi}{8} = \sqrt{\frac{1-\cos \dfrac{\pi}{4}}{1+\cos \dfrac{\pi}{4}}}$$

$$= \sqrt{\frac{\sqrt{2}-1}{\sqrt{2}+1}}$$

$$= \sqrt{2}-1$$

Simplify, $\tan \dfrac{3\pi}{8}$ as,

$$\tan \frac{3\pi}{8} = \sqrt{\frac{1-\cos \dfrac{3\pi}{4}}{1+\cos \dfrac{3\pi}{4}}}$$

$$= \sqrt{\frac{\sqrt{2}+1}{\sqrt{2}-1}}$$

$$= \sqrt{2}+1$$

Hence,

$$\tan \frac{3\pi}{8} - \tan \frac{\pi}{8} = \sqrt{2}+1-\left(\sqrt{2}-1\right)$$

$$= 2$$

79. Correct Response : (c)

Explanation :

The diagram according to the equations provided is shown below.

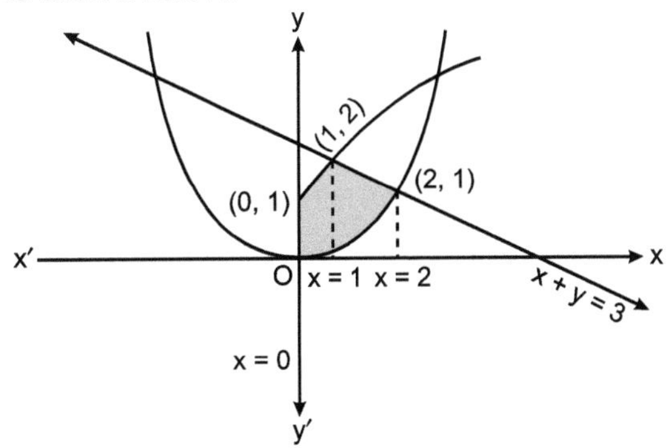

The area of the shaded region is,

$$A = \int \left(\sqrt{x} + 1 - \frac{x^2}{4} \right) dx + \int_1^2 \left((3-x) - \frac{x^2}{4} \right) dx$$

$$= \frac{5}{4} + \frac{5}{4}$$

$$= \frac{5}{2} \text{ sq.unit}$$

80. Correct Response : (b)

Explanation :

The given function is,

$$f\left(\frac{3x-4}{3x+4} \right) = x + 2$$

$$\int f(x)\, dx = A \log |1-x|\, Bx + C \qquad ...(1)$$

Let $\dfrac{3x-4}{3x+4}$ be t, then,

$$\frac{3x-4}{3x+4} = t$$

$$3x - 4 = 3tx + 4t$$

$$x = \frac{4t+4}{3-3t} + 2$$

The function in terms of t is,

$$f(t) = \frac{4t+4}{3-3t} + 2$$

$$= \frac{10 - 2t}{3 - 3t}$$

Replace t with x.

$$f(x) = \frac{2x - 10}{3x - 3}$$

Integrate $f(x)$,

$$\int f(x)\, dx = \int \frac{2x-10}{3x-3}\, dx$$

$$= \int \frac{2x}{3x-3}\, dx - 10 \int \frac{dx}{3x-3}$$

$$= \frac{2}{3} \int \frac{x-1}{x-1}\, dx + \frac{2}{3} \int \frac{dx}{x-1} - \frac{10}{3} \int \frac{dx}{x-1}$$

$$= \frac{2x}{3} - \frac{8}{3} \ln(x-1) + c$$

Compare the above with equation (1).

$$A = \frac{-8}{3},\ B = \frac{2}{3}$$

81. Correct Response : (a)

Explanation :

Simplify the given equation :

$$\int_1^2 \frac{dx}{\left(x^2 - 2x + 4 \right)^{\frac{3}{2}}} = \int_1^2 \frac{dx}{\left((x-1)^2 + 3 \right)^{\frac{3}{2}}}$$

Let $(x - 1) = \sqrt{3} \tan \theta$. Then,

$$x = \sqrt{3} \tan \theta + 1$$

$$dx = \sqrt{3} \sec^2 \theta \cdot d\theta$$

Changing the order of integration :

For $x = 1$,

$$\theta = 0$$

For $x = 2$,

$$\theta = \tan^{-1}\left(\frac{1}{\sqrt{3}} \right)$$

$$= \frac{\pi}{6}$$

Integrate the changed function :

$$\int_1^2 \frac{dx}{\left(x^2 - 2x + 4 \right)^{\frac{3}{2}}} = \int_0^{\frac{\pi}{6}} \frac{\sqrt{3} \sec^2 \theta \cdot d\theta}{3\sqrt{3} \sec^3 \theta}$$

$$= \frac{1}{3} \int_0^{\frac{\pi}{6}} \sec^2 \theta \cdot d\theta$$

$$= \frac{1}{3} \int_0^{\frac{\pi}{6}} \sec^2 \theta \cdot d\theta \, \frac{1}{3} [\tan \theta]_0^{\frac{\pi}{6}}$$

$$= \frac{1}{6}$$

From the given question,

$$\frac{k}{k+5} = \frac{1}{6}$$

$$k = 1$$

82. Correct Response : (b, c)

Explanation :

According to the given condition, the two area are equated as :

$$\int_0^\alpha \left(x - x^3 \right) dx = \frac{1}{2} \int_0^1 \left(x - x^3 \right) dx$$

$$\left| \frac{x^2}{2} - \frac{x^4}{4} \right|_0^\alpha = \left| \frac{x^2}{2} - \frac{x^4}{4} \right|_0^\alpha$$

$$\frac{\alpha^2}{2} - \frac{\alpha^4}{4} = \frac{1}{2}\left(\frac{1}{2} - \frac{1}{4} \right)$$

$$\frac{\alpha^2}{2} - \frac{\alpha^4}{4} = \frac{1}{8}$$

Simplify the above equation,

$$4\alpha^2 - 2\alpha^4 = 1$$

$$2\alpha^4 - 4\alpha^2 + 1 = 0$$

Let the obtained function be as shown below,

$$f(\alpha) = 2\alpha^4 - 4\alpha^2 + 1$$

$$f(0) = 1$$

$$f\left(\frac{1}{2}\right) = 2\left(\frac{1}{2}\right)^4 - 4\left(\frac{1}{2}\right)^2 + 1$$

$$= \frac{1}{8}$$

The value at end point is :

$$f(1) = 2(1)^4 - 4(1)^2 + 1$$
$$= -1$$

Since $f(0)$ and $f\left(\frac{1}{2}\right)$ are positive and $f(1)$ is

negative, $f(\alpha)$ has zero between $\left(\frac{1}{2}, 1\right)$.

83. Correct Response : (b)

Explanation :

Consider the given integral,

$$I = \int \sqrt{1 + 2\cot x\,(\cosec x + \cot x)}\ dx$$

Simplify the above integral.

$$I = \int \sqrt{1 + 2\cot x \cosec x + 2\cot^2 x}\ dx$$

$$= \int \sqrt{1 + 2\frac{\cos x}{\sin^2 x} + 2\frac{\cos^2 x}{\sin^2 x}}\ dx$$

$$= \int \sqrt{\frac{\sin^2 x + 2\cos x + 2\cos^2 x}{\sin^2 x}}\ dx$$

Further simplify the above equation.

$$I = \int \sqrt{\frac{(1 + \cos x)^2}{\sin^2 x}}\ dx$$

Further, solving the above equation.

$$I = \int \frac{1 + \cos x}{\sin x}\ d$$

$$= \int \frac{2\cos^2\left(\dfrac{x}{2}\right)}{2\sin\left(\dfrac{x}{2}\right)\cos\left(\dfrac{x}{2}\right)}\ dx$$

$$= \int \cot\left(\frac{x}{2}\right)$$

Integrate the above equation.

$$I = 2\log\left(\sin\frac{x}{2}\right) + C$$

84. Correct Response : (a)

Explanation :

Consider the given integral,

$$\int_{\frac{\pi}{12}}^{\frac{\pi}{4}} \frac{8\cos 2x}{(\tan x + \cot x)^3}\ dx$$

Simplify the above integral.

$$\int_{\frac{\pi}{12}}^{\frac{\pi}{4}} \frac{8\cos 2x}{(\tan x + \cot x)^3}\ dx = \int_{\frac{\pi}{12}}^{\frac{\pi}{4}} \frac{8\cos 2x}{\left(\dfrac{\sin x}{\cos x} + \dfrac{\cos x}{\sin x}\right)^3}\ dx$$

$$= \int_{\frac{\pi}{12}}^{\frac{\pi}{4}} \frac{8\cos 2x}{\left(\dfrac{\sin^2 x + \cos^2 x}{\sin x \cos x}\right)^3}\ dx$$

$$= \int_{\frac{\pi}{12}}^{\frac{\pi}{4}} \frac{8\cos 2x}{\left(\dfrac{1}{\sin(2x/2)}\right)^3}\ dx$$

$$= \int_{\frac{\pi}{12}}^{\frac{\pi}{4}} \cos 2x \sin 2x \sin^2 2x\ dx$$

Futher, simplify the above equation.

$$\int_{\frac{\pi}{12}}^{\frac{\pi}{4}} \frac{8\cos 2x}{(\tan x + \cot x)^3}\ dx$$

$$= \frac{1}{2}\int_{\frac{\pi}{12}}^{\frac{\pi}{4}} (2\cos 2x \sin 2x)\sin^2 2x\,dx$$

$$= \frac{1}{2}\int_{\frac{\pi}{12}}^{\frac{\pi}{4}} (\sin 4x)\sin^2 2x\,dx$$

$$= \frac{1}{4}\int_{\frac{\pi}{12}}^{\frac{\pi}{4}} (\sin 4x)\left(1 - \cos^2 4x\right)dx$$

Further, simplify the above equation.

$$\int_{\frac{\pi}{12}}^{\frac{\pi}{4}} \frac{8\cos 2x}{(\tan x + \cot x)^3}\ dx$$

$$= \frac{1}{4}\left(\int_{\frac{\pi}{12}}^{\frac{\pi}{4}} \sin 4x\,dx - \int_{\frac{\pi}{12}}^{\frac{\pi}{4}} \sin 8x\,dx\right)$$

$$= \frac{1}{4}\left(-\frac{\cos 4x}{4}\right)_{\frac{\pi}{12}}^{\frac{\pi}{4}} - \left(-\frac{\cos 8x}{8}\right)_{\frac{\pi}{12}}^{\frac{\pi}{4}}$$

$$= \frac{1}{4}\left[-\frac{\cos 4x}{4} + \frac{\cos 8x}{8}\right]_{\frac{\pi}{12}}^{\frac{\pi}{4}}$$

$$= \frac{1}{4}\left[-\frac{\cos\left(4\frac{\pi}{4}\right)}{4} + \frac{\cos\left(8\frac{\pi}{4}\right)}{8} + \frac{\cos\left(4\frac{\pi}{4}\right)}{4} \right]$$

$$-\frac{\cos\left(8\frac{\pi}{4}\right)}{8}$$

Further, simplify the above equation.

$$\int_{\frac{\pi}{12}}^{\frac{\pi}{4}} \frac{8\cos 2x}{(\tan x + \cot x)^3} dx = \frac{15}{128}$$

85. Correct Response : (d)

Explanation :

Consider the diagram :

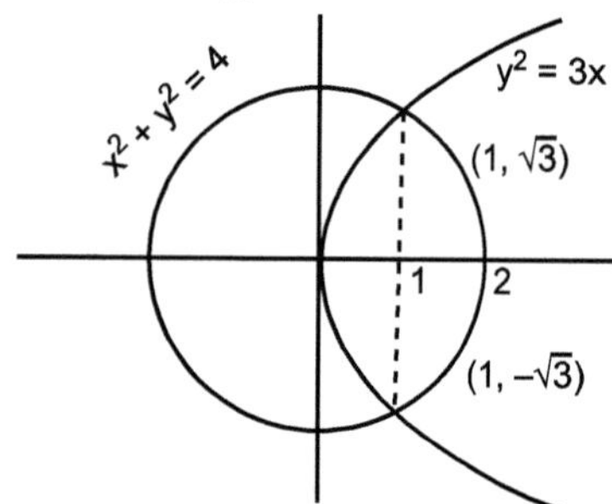

The curve $x^2 + y^2 = 4$ and $y^2 = 3x$ is given below,

$$x^2 + y^2 = 4$$

$$x^2 + 3x - 4 = 0$$

$$x = -4 \text{ or } x = 1$$

For $x = -4$, y^2 is negative. Hence, $x = 1$ is the intersection point of two curves.

Then at $x = 1$, $= \pm\sqrt{3}$, the intersection points are $\left(1, \sqrt{3}\right)$ and $\left(1, -\sqrt{3}\right)$.

Area of the smaller portion is given as :

$$A = \int_0^1 \sqrt{3}\cdot\sqrt{x}\,dx + \left(\int_0^1\int_0^1 \sqrt{3}\cdot\sqrt{x}\,dx + \int_1^2 \sqrt{4-x^2}\,dx\right)\cdot 2$$

$$= 2\times\left(\sqrt{3}\left(\frac{x^{3/2}}{3/2}\right)_0^1 + \left(\frac{x}{2}\sqrt{4-x^2} + 2\sin^{-1}\left(\frac{x}{2}\right)\right)_1^2 \right)$$

$$= 2\times\left(\sqrt{3}\left(\frac{2}{3}\right) + \left(2\times\frac{\pi}{2} - \left(\frac{\sqrt{3}}{2} + \frac{\pi}{3}\right)\right) \right)$$

$$= \frac{1}{\sqrt{3}} + \frac{4\pi}{3}$$

86. Correct Response : (b, d)

Explanation :

It is given that x is between k and $k + 1$.

$$x > k$$

$$x + 1 > k + 1$$

$$\frac{k+1}{x+1} < 1$$

$$\left(\frac{k+1}{x+1}\right)\frac{1}{x} < \left(\frac{k+1}{x+1}\right)\frac{1}{x}$$

And,

$$x < k + 1$$

$$\frac{k+1}{(k+1)(x+1)} < \frac{k+1}{x(x+1)}$$

$$\frac{1}{x+1} < \frac{k+1}{x(x+1)}$$

Thus, the inequality becomes :

$$\frac{1}{x+1} < \frac{k+1}{x(x+1)} < \frac{1}{x}$$

$$\sum_{k=1}^{98}\int_k^{k+1} \frac{1}{(x+1)}dx < \sum_{k=1}^{98}\int_k^{k+1} \frac{k+1}{x(x+1)}dx < \sum_{k=1}^{98}\int_k^{k+1} \frac{1}{x}dx$$

$$\sum_{k=1}^{98}\left|ln\,(x+1)\right|_k^{k+1} < I < \sum_{k=1}^{98}\left|ln\,(x)\right|_k^{k+1}$$

$$\sum_{k=1}^{98}ln\left(\frac{k+2}{k+1}\right) < \sum_{k=1}^{98}ln\left(\frac{k+1}{k}\right)$$
$$I <$$

$$ln\left(\frac{3}{2}\cdot\frac{4}{3}\,.......\,\frac{100}{99}\right) < I < ln\left(\frac{2}{1}\cdot\frac{3}{2}\,.......\,\frac{99}{98}\right)$$

Hence, the result is :

$$ln\left(\frac{100}{2}\right) < I < ln\left(\frac{99}{1}\right)$$

$$ln\,50 < I < ln\,99$$

$$\frac{49}{50} < I < ln\,99$$

87. Correct Response : (b)

Explanation :

The integration of given expression is,

$$I = \int \frac{dx}{\left(1+\sqrt{x}\right)\sqrt{x-x^2}}$$

Take $x = \cos^2\theta$ and the differentiation of this expresion is $dx = -2\cos\theta\sin\theta\,d\theta$.

The integration is,

$$I = \int \frac{-2\cos\theta\sin\theta\,d\theta}{(1+\cos\theta)\sqrt{\cos^2\theta - \left(\cos^2\theta\right)^2}}$$

$$= \int \frac{-2\cos\theta\sin\theta\,d\theta}{(1+\cos\theta)\cos\theta\sin\theta}$$

$$= -2\int \frac{d\theta}{2\cos^2 \theta/2}$$

$$= -\int \sec^2 \theta/2\, d\theta \in$$

Futher solve the above expression,

$$I = -\int \sec^2 \theta/2\, d\theta$$

$$= -2\tan \theta/2 + C \qquad ...(1)$$

The value of cosine in terms of x is,

$$\cos \theta = \sqrt{x}$$

$$\frac{1 - \tan^2 \theta/2}{1 + \tan^2 \theta/2} = \sqrt{x}$$

$$\tan \theta/2 = \sqrt{\frac{1 - \sqrt{x}}{1 + \sqrt{x}}}$$

Substitute this value in equation (1),

$$I = -\int \sec^2 \theta/2\, d\theta$$

$$= -2\sqrt{\frac{1 - \sqrt{x}}{1 + \sqrt{x}}} + C$$

88. Correct Response : (b)

Explanation :

The value of the given integral is,

$$I = \int_{4}^{10} \frac{\left[x^2\right]dx}{\left[x^2 - 28x + 196\right] + \left[x^2\right]} \qquad ...(1)$$

Rewrite the equation (1) by using the property

$$\int_{a}^{b} f(a + b - x)\,dx = \int_{a}^{b} f(x)\,dx$$

$$I = \int_{4}^{10} \frac{\left[x^2 - 28x + 196\right]dx}{\left[x^2\right] + \left[x^2 - 28x + 196\right]} \qquad ...(2)$$

Add equation (1) and equation (2).

$$2I = \int_{4}^{10} dx$$

$$= [x]_{4}^{10}$$

$$= 6$$

$$I = 3$$

89. Correct Response : (b)

Explanation :

Consider the given integral function I :

$$I = \int \frac{2x^{12} + 5x^9}{\left(x^5 + x^3 + 1\right)^3} dx$$

Divide numerator and denominator by x^{15}.

$$\int \frac{\dfrac{2}{x^3} + \dfrac{5}{x^6}}{\left(1 + \dfrac{1}{x^2} + \dfrac{1}{x^5}\right)^3} dx$$

Consider,

$$1 + \frac{1}{x^2} + \frac{1}{x^5} = t$$

$$\frac{dt}{dx} = \frac{-2}{x^3} - \frac{5}{x^6}$$

$$\frac{dt}{\dfrac{-2}{x^3} - \dfrac{5}{x^6}} = dx$$

Substitute the above value in the integral function,

$$I = \int \left(\frac{-1}{t^3}\right) dt$$

$$= \frac{1}{2t^2} + C$$

Hence,

$$I = \frac{1}{2\left(1 + \dfrac{1}{x^2} + \dfrac{1}{x^5}\right)^2} + C$$

$$= \frac{x^{10}}{2\left(x^5 + x^3 + 1\right)^2} + C$$

90. Correct Response : (b)

Explanation :

The diagram for the given region is,

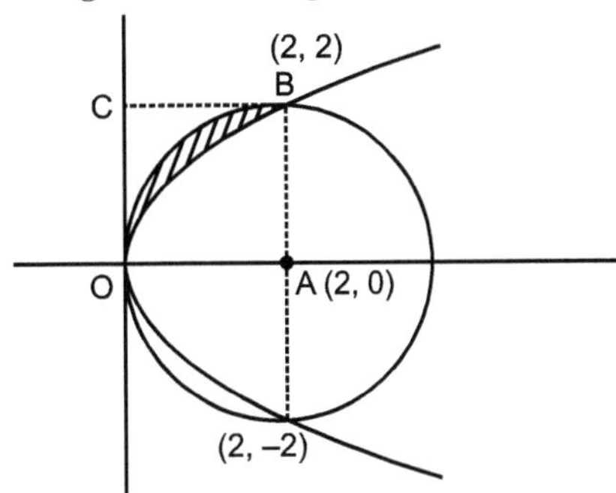

The point of intersection of the curve $x^2 + y^2 = 4x$ and $y^2 = 2$ are (0, 0) and (2, 2) for $x \geq 0$ and $y \geq 0$.

Therefore, required area is,

$$A = \frac{1}{4}\pi \times 4 - \int_{0}^{2} \sqrt{2x}\, dx$$

$$= \pi - \sqrt{2} \times \frac{2}{3} \times \left(x^{\frac{3}{2}}\right)\Bigg|_{0}^{2}$$

$$= \pi - \frac{8}{3}$$

91. Correct Response : (b)

Explanation :

Given

$$\int \frac{dx}{\cos^3 x\sqrt{2\sin 2x}} = (\tan x)^A + C(\tan x)^B + k$$

Substitute $\tan x = t$.

$$I = \frac{1}{2}\int t^{\frac{3}{2}}dt + \frac{1}{2}\int t^{\frac{-1}{2}}dt$$

$$= \frac{t^{\frac{5}{2}}}{5} + t^{\frac{1}{2}} + c$$

$$= \frac{(\tan x)^{\frac{5}{2}}}{5} + (\tan x)^{1/2}$$

Equate the above equation with the given equation :

$$A = \frac{1}{2}$$

$$B = \frac{5}{2}$$

$$C = \frac{1}{5}$$

Then the value of $A + B + C$ is,

$$A + B + C = \frac{1}{2} + \frac{5}{2} + \frac{1}{5}$$

$$= \frac{16}{5}$$

92. Correct Response : (c)

Explanation :

The given equation is,

$$2\int_0^1 \tan^{-1} x\, dx = \int_0^1 \cot^{-1}\left(1 - x + x^2\right)dx$$

Then,

$$2\int_0^1 \tan^{-1}\left(1 - x + x^2\right)dx$$

$$= 2\int_0^1 \left(\frac{\pi}{2} - \cot^{-1}\left(1 - x + x^2\right)dx\right)$$

$$= 2\left(\frac{\pi x}{2}\Big|_0^1\right) - 2\int_0^1 \tan^{-1} x\, dx$$

$$= \pi - 4\int_0^1 \tan^{-1} x\, dx$$

$$= \pi - 4\left(x\tan^{-1} x - \frac{1}{2}\ln\left(1 + x^2\right)\right)\Big|_0^1$$

Futher, simplifying the above equation,

$$2\int_0^1 \tan^{-1}\left(1 - x + x^2\right)dx = \pi - \pi + \ln 2$$

$$= \ln 2$$

93. Correct Response : (b)

Explanation :

Given :

$A = \{(x, y)\mid y \geq x^2 - 5x + 4,\ x + y \geq 1,\ y \leq 0\}$

Here $y \geq x^2 - 5x + 4,\ x + y \geq 1,\ y \leq 0$

Consider the required plot :

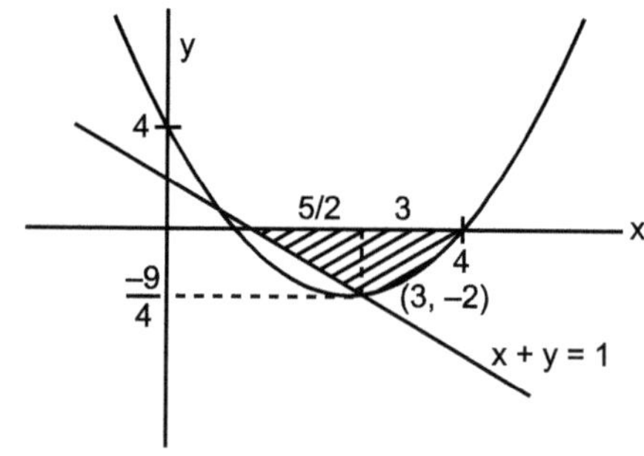

So, the required are is,

$$\text{Area} = \frac{1}{2} \times 2 \times 2 + \int_3^4 \left(5x - x^2 - 4\right)dx$$

$$= 2 + \left(\frac{5x^2}{2} - \frac{x^3}{3} - 4x\right)\Big|_3^4$$

$$= 2 + \frac{5}{2}(16 - 9) - \frac{1}{3}(64 - 27) - 4(4 - 3)$$

$$= \frac{19}{6}$$

94. Correct Response : (1)

Explanation :

Consider the given function as :

$$f(x) = \int_0^x \frac{t^2}{1 + t^4}dt - 2x + 1 \qquad \ldots(1)$$

Differentiate the above function with respect to x,

$$f'(x) = \frac{x^2}{1 + x^4} - 2$$

$$= \frac{1}{\frac{1}{x^2} + x^2} - 2$$

The known relation as,

$$x^2 + \frac{1}{x^2} \geq 2$$

$$\frac{1}{x^2 + \frac{1}{x^2}} \leq \frac{1}{2}$$

Here, $\qquad f'(x) < 0$

Therefore, function $f(x)$ is the decreasing function.

Now,

$$f(0) = 1 \qquad \qquad ...(2)$$

And,

$$f(1) = \int_0^1 \frac{t^2}{1+t^4}\,dt - 1 \qquad ...(3)$$

Now from the above relation,

$$\int_0^1 \frac{t^2}{1+t^4}\,dt \ \le \ \int_0^1 \frac{1}{2}\,dt$$

Or,

$$\int_0^1 \frac{t^2}{1+t^4}\,dt - 1 \ \le \ \int_0^1 \frac{1}{2}\,dt - 1 \qquad ...(4)$$

Therefore,

$$f(1) < 0 \qquad \qquad ...(5)$$

Hence, $f(x)$ will cross X-axis exactly at one point between [0, 1].

95. Correct Response : (d)

Explanation :

The given integral is,

$$I = \int \frac{dx}{x^2\left(x^4+1\right)^{\frac{3}{4}}}$$

$$= \int \frac{dx}{x^2 x^3\left(1+\dfrac{1}{x^4}\right)^{\frac{3}{4}}}$$

Let, $\qquad 1 + \dfrac{1}{x^4} = t$

$$\Rightarrow \qquad -\frac{4}{x^3}\,dx = dt$$

Substitute the values.

$$I = -\frac{1}{4}\int \frac{dt}{t^{\frac{3}{4}}}$$

$$= -\frac{1}{4}\left[\frac{t^{-\frac{3}{4}+1}}{-\frac{3}{4}+1}\right] + c$$

$$= -t^{\frac{1}{4}} + c$$

$$= -\left(1+\frac{1}{x^4}\right)^{\frac{1}{4}} + c$$

Further simplify,

$$I = -\left(\frac{x^4+1}{x^4}\right)^{\frac{1}{4}} + c$$

96. Correct Response : (c)

Explanation :

The given integral is,

$$I = \int_2^4 \frac{\log x^2}{\log x^2 + \log\left(36-12x+x^2\right)}\,dx$$

$$= \int_2^4 \frac{\log x^2}{\log x^2 + \log(6-x)^2}\,dx$$

$$= \int_2^4 \frac{\log x}{\log x + \log(6-x)}\,dx \qquad ...(1)$$

Apply the integral property.

$f(a+b-x) = f(x)$

$$I = \int_2^4 \frac{\log(6-x)}{\log(6-x)+\log x}\,dx \qquad ...(2)$$

Add equation (1) and (2),

$$2I = \int_2^4 \frac{\log x + \log(6-x)}{\log x + \log(6-x)}\,dx$$

$$= [x]_2^4$$

$$I = \frac{2}{2}$$

$$I = 1$$

97. Correct Response : (d)

Explanation :

The equations are considered as follows,

$$y^2 = 2x$$

$$x = \frac{y^2}{2}$$

And, $\qquad y = 4x - 1$

$$y = 2y^2 - 1$$

$$2y^2 - y - 1 = 0$$

$$(2y+1)(y-1) = 0$$

The values of the y-coordinates are,

$$y = \frac{-1}{2} \text{ and } 1$$

Then the values of x-coordinates are,

$$x = \frac{1}{8} \text{ and } \frac{1}{2}$$

The intersecting points are $\left(\dfrac{1}{2}, 1\right)$ and $\left(\dfrac{1}{8}, -\dfrac{1}{2}\right)$

. Consider the diagram :

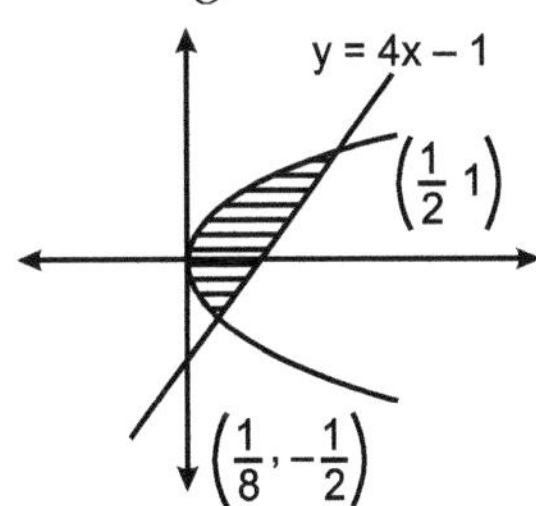

The area is,

$$A = \int_{-\frac{1}{2}}^{1}\left(\frac{y+1}{4}-\frac{y^2}{2}\right)dy$$

$$= \left[\frac{1}{4}\left(\frac{y^2}{2}+y\right)-\frac{1}{6}\left(y^3\right)\right]_{-\frac{1}{2}}^{1}$$

$$= \left[\frac{1}{4}\left(\frac{1}{2}+1\right)-\frac{1}{6}-\frac{1}{4}\left(\frac{1}{8}-\frac{1}{2}\right)-\frac{1}{48}\right]$$

$$= \frac{9}{32}$$

98. Correct Response : (9)

Explanation :

Consider,

$$x = \tan\theta$$

Differentiate the above value with respect to x,

$$dx = \sec^2\theta\, d\theta$$

Now, simplify the given integral function by substituting the above value.

$$\alpha = \int_0^{\frac{\pi}{4}} e^{(3\theta+9\tan\theta)}\cdot\frac{\left(12+9\tan^2\theta\right)}{\left(1+\tan^2\theta\right)}\sec^2\theta\, d\theta$$

$$= \int_0^{\frac{\pi}{4}} e^{(3\theta+9\tan\theta)}\cdot\left(9\left(\sec^2\theta-1\right)+12\right)d\theta$$

$$= \int_0^{\frac{\pi}{4}} e^{(3\theta+9\tan\theta)}\cdot\left(9\sec^2\theta+3\right)d\theta$$

Consider,

$$3\theta + 9\tan\theta = t$$

Differentiate the above value with respect to θ,

$$(3 + 9\sec^2\theta) = d\theta = dt$$

Therefore,

Substitute the above value in the simplified integral function,

$$\alpha = \int_0^{9+\frac{3\pi}{4}} e^t\, dt$$

$$= \left(e^{9+\frac{3\pi}{4}}-1\right)$$

$$\alpha + 1 = e^{9+\frac{3\pi}{4}}$$

Take in both sides,

$$\text{In }|1+\alpha| = 9+\frac{3\pi}{4}$$

$$\ln|1+\alpha|-\frac{3\pi}{4} = 9$$

$$\log_e|1+\alpha|-\frac{3\pi}{4} = 9$$

99. Correct Response : (7)

Explanation :

Given function is,

$$\lim_{x\to 1}\frac{F(x)}{G(x)} = \frac{1}{14}$$

Substitute the given values in the above function,

$$\lim_{x\to 1}\frac{\int_{-1}^{x} f(t)\,dt}{\int_{-1}^{x} t\left|f(f(t))\right|dt} = \frac{1}{14}$$

Apply L' Hospital's

$$\lim_{x\to 1}\frac{\int_{-1}^{x}\frac{d}{dt}\left(f(t)\,dt\right)}{\int_{-1}^{x}\frac{d}{dt}\left(tf(f(t))\right)dt} = \frac{1}{14}$$

$$\lim_{x\to 1}\frac{f(x)}{x\left|f(f(x))\right|} = \frac{1}{14}$$

$$\frac{f(1)}{\left|f(f(1))\right|} = \frac{1}{14}$$

Substitute $f(1) = \dfrac{1}{2}$ in the above function,

$$\frac{\dfrac{1}{2}}{f\left(\dfrac{1}{2}\right)} = \frac{1}{14}$$

$$f\left(\frac{1}{2}\right) = 7$$

100. Correct Response : (a, c)

Explanation :

The given equation is,

$$L = \frac{\int_0^{4\pi} e^t\left(\sin^6 at+\cos^4 at\right)dt}{\int_0^{\pi} e^t\left(\sin^6 at+\cos^4 at\right)dt}$$

Simplify the given equation. Consider numerator first to simplify.

$$\text{Numerator} = \underbrace{\int_0^{\pi} e^t\left(\sin^6 at+\cos^4 at\right)dt}_{I_1}$$

$$+\underbrace{\int_{\pi}^{2\pi} e^t\left(\sin^6 at+\cos^4 at\right)dt}_{I_2}$$

$$+\underbrace{\int_{2\pi}^{3\pi} e^t\left(\sin^6 at+\cos^4 at\right)dt}_{I_3}+\underbrace{\int_{3\pi}^{4\pi} e^t\left(\sin^6 at+\cos^4 at\right)dt}_{I_4}$$

In I_2 substitute $t = \theta + \alpha$

In I_3 substitute $t = 2\theta + \alpha$

And in I_4 substitute $t = 3\theta + \alpha$

Substitute these values in the numerator function,

Numeator

$$= \int_0^\pi e^t \left(\sin^6 at + \cos^4 at \right) dt + e^\pi \int_0^\pi e^t \left(\sin^6 at + \cos^4 at \right) dt$$

$$+ e^{2\pi} \int_0^\pi e^t \left(\sin^6 at + \cos^4 at \right) dt + e^{3\pi} \int_0^\pi e^t \left(\sin^6 at + \cos^4 at \right) dt$$

$$= \left(1 + e^\pi + e^{2\pi} + e^{3\pi} \right) \int_0^\pi e^t \left(\sin^6 at + \cos^4 at \right) dt$$

Therefore, substitute the numerator value in the given relation.

$$L = \frac{\left(1 + e^\pi + e^{2\pi} + e^{3\pi} \right) \int_0^\pi e^t \left(\sin^6 at + \cos^4 at \right) dt}{\int_0^\pi e^t \left(\sin^6 at + \cos^4 at \right) dt}$$

$$L = 1 \cdot \frac{e^{4\pi} - 1}{e^\pi - 1}, \, a = 2, 4$$

101. Correct Response : (a, b)

Explanation :

The given function is,

$f(x) = 7 \tan^8 x + 7 \tan^6 x - 3 \tan^4 x - 3 \tan^2 x$

Simplify the given function,

$f(x) = 7 \tan^6 x \,(1 + \tan^2 x) - 3 \tan^2 (1 + \tan^2 x)$

$= 7 \tan^6 (x) \cdot \sec^2 (x) - 3 \tan^2 (x) \cdot \sec^2 (x)$

As per required value of,

$$\int_0^{\frac{\pi}{4}} f(x)\,dx = \int_0^{\frac{\pi}{4}} 7 \tan^6 (x) . \sec^2 (x)\,dx$$

$$\int_0^{\frac{\pi}{4}} 7 \tan^6 (x) . \sec^2 (x)\,dx$$

$$= \int_0^{\frac{\pi}{4}} \left(7 \tan^6 (x) - 3 \tan^2 (x) \right) \sec^2 (x)\,dx$$

Futher simplify the definite integral function.

$$\int_0^{\frac{\pi}{4}} f(x)\,dx = \left(\tan^7 x - \tan^3 x \right)\Big|_0^{\frac{\pi}{4}}$$

$$= 0$$

And,

$$\int_0^{\frac{\pi}{4}} xf(x)\,dx = \int_0^{\frac{\pi}{4}} x \sec^2 (x) \left(7 \tan^6 (x) - 3 \tan^2 (x) \right) dx$$

$$= \left(x \left(\tan^7 (x) - \tan^3 (x) \right) \right)\Big|_0^{\frac{\pi}{4}}$$

$$- \int_0^{\frac{\pi}{4}} \left(\tan^7 (x) - \tan^3 (x) \right) . 1 dx$$

$$= \int_0^{\frac{\pi}{4}} \tan^3 x \left(1 - \tan^4 \right) dx$$

$$= \int_0^{\frac{\pi}{4}} \tan^3 x \left(1 - \tan^2 x \right) \sec^2 (x)\,dx$$

Further, simplify the definite integral function,

$$\int_0^{\frac{\pi}{4}} xf(x)\,dx = \left(\frac{\tan^4 x}{4} - \frac{\tan^6 x}{6} \right)\Big|_0^{\frac{\pi}{4}}$$

$$= \frac{1}{4} - \frac{1}{6}$$

$$= \frac{1}{12}$$

102. Correct Response : (c, d)

Explanation :

From the given value,

$f'(x) = F(x) + xF'(x),\ x \in (1, 3)$ ...(1)

The given value is,

$$\int_1^3 x^3 F''(x)\,dx = 40$$

Simplify the given definite integral function,

$$\int_1^3 x^3 F''(x)\,dx = 40$$

$$x^3 F'(x)\Big|_1^3 - \int_1^3 3x^2 F'(x)\,dx = 40$$

$$27F'(3) - F'(1) - 3(-12) = 40$$

$$27F'(3) - F'(1) = 4 \qquad ...(2)$$

From the equation (1),

$$f'(x) = F(x) + xF'(x)$$
$$f'(1) = F(1) + F'(1)$$
$$f'(1) = F'(1)$$
$$f'(3) = F(3) + 3F'(3)$$

Further, simplify the above relation,

$$f'(3) = -4 + 3F'(3)$$
$$3F'(3) = f'(3) + 4$$

Substitute the value of $3F'(x)$ equation (2)

$$9(f'(3) + 4) - f'(1) = 4$$
$$9f'(3) - f'(1) + 32 = 0$$

So, option (c) is correct.

$$\int_1^3 f(x)\,dx = \int_1^3 xF(x)\,dx$$

$$= \frac{x^2}{2} F(x)\Big|_1^3 - \int_1^3 \frac{x^2}{2} F'(x)\,dx$$

$$= \frac{9}{2} F(3) - \frac{F(1)}{2} - \frac{1}{2} \int_1^3 x^2 F'(x)\,dx$$

$$= \frac{9}{2}(-4) - 0 - \frac{1}{2}(-12)$$

Futher, substitute the above value.

$$\int_1^3 f(x)\,dx = -12$$

So, option (d) is correct.

103. Correct Response : (0)

Explanation :

The given definite integral function is,

$$I = \int_{-1}^{2} \frac{xf\left(x^2\right)}{2+f(x+1)} dx$$

Simplify the definite integral function,

$$I = \int_{-1}^{2} \frac{xf\left(x^2\right)}{2+f(x+1)} dx$$

$$I = \int_{-1}^{0} \frac{xf\left(x^2\right)}{2+f(x+1)} dx + \int_{0}^{1} \frac{xf\left(x^2\right)}{2+f(x+1)} dx$$

$$+ \int_{1}^{\sqrt{2}} \frac{xf\left(x^2\right)}{2+f(x+1)} dx + \int_{\sqrt{2}}^{2} \frac{xf\left(x^2\right)}{2+f(x+1)} dx$$

$$I = \int_{-1}^{0} \frac{x.0}{2+0} dx + \int_{0}^{1} \frac{x.0}{2+0} dx + \int_{1}^{\sqrt{2}} \frac{x.1}{2+0} dx + \int_{\sqrt{2}}^{2} \frac{x.0}{2+0} dx$$

$$I = \frac{1}{4}\left(x^2\right)_{1}^{\sqrt{2}}$$

Further, simplify the integral function,

$$I = \frac{1}{4}(2-1)$$

$$I = \frac{1}{4}$$

$$4I - 1 = 0$$

104. Correct Response : (3)

Explanation :

Simplify the given integral function is,

$$F(x) = \int_{x}^{x^2+\frac{\pi}{6}} 2\cos^2 t \, dt$$

$$= \int_{x}^{x^2+\frac{\pi}{6}} (1+\cos 2t) dt$$

$$= t\Big|_{x}^{x^2+\frac{\pi}{6}} + \frac{\sin 2t}{2}\Big|_{x}^{x^2+\frac{\pi}{6}}$$

$$= x^2 - x + \frac{\pi}{6} + \frac{1}{2}\left(\sin\left(2x^2+\frac{\pi}{3}\right) - \sin 2x\right)$$

Differentiate the function with respect to x,

$$F'(x) = 2x - 1 + \frac{1}{2}\left(\cos\left(2x^2+\frac{\pi}{3}\right) - 2\cos 2x\right)$$

Given that,

$$\int_{0}^{a} f(x) dx = F'(a) + 2$$

$$= 2a - 1 + \frac{1}{2}\left(\cos\left(2a^2+\frac{\pi}{3}\right)4a - 2\cos 2a + 2\right)$$

Differentiate with respect to a,

$$f(a) = 2 + \frac{1}{2}\left(4\cos\left(2a^2+\frac{\pi}{3}\right) - 4a\sin\left(2a^2+\frac{\pi}{3}\right)4a + 4\sin 2a\right)$$

Substitute $a = 0$,

$$f(0) = 2 + \frac{1}{2}\left(4\times\frac{1}{2} - 0 + 0\right)$$

$$= 3$$

105. Correct Response : (b)

Explanation :

The given function is,

$$\int \frac{\log\left(t+\sqrt{1+t^2}\right)}{\sqrt{1+t^2}} dt = \frac{1}{2}(g(t))^2 + C$$

Consider the integral function is,

$$I = \int \frac{\log\left(t+\sqrt{1+t^2}\right)}{\sqrt{1+t^2}} dt$$

Consider,

$$u = \log(t+\sqrt{1+t^2})$$

Differentiate with respect to t,

$$du = \frac{1}{\sqrt{1+t^2}} dt$$

Substitute the value in the integral function I,

$$I = \int u\,du$$

$$= \frac{u^2}{2} + C$$

$$\frac{1}{2}g^2(t) + C = \frac{\log^2\left(t+\sqrt{1+t^2}\right)}{2} + C$$

$$g(t) = \log\left(t+\sqrt{1+t^2}\right)$$

Hence, the required value is,

$$g(2) = \log\left(2+\sqrt{5}\right)$$

106. Correct Response : (b)

Explanation :

The given function is,

$$f(2-x) = f(2+x) \qquad ...(1)$$

And,

$$f(4-x) = f(4+x) \qquad ...(2)$$

Replace x with $(x + 2)$ in equation 1

$$f(-x) = f(4 + x)$$
$$= f(4 - x)$$

Replace x with $(-x)$

$$f(x) = f(x + 4)$$

Hence, the function $f(x)$ is periodic with period 4.

Then the required value is,

$$\int_{10}^{50} f(x)\,dx = 10\int_{10}^{14} f(x)\,dx\,\hat{i}$$

$$= 10 \times 2\int_{0}^{2} f(x)\,dx$$

$$= 20 \times 5$$

$$= 100$$

107. Correct Response : (b)

Explanation :

The given function is,

$$\int_{0}^{\sin x} f(t)\,dt = \frac{\sqrt{3}}{2}x$$

Differentiate the above function with respect to x,

$$f(\sin x)\cos x = \frac{\sqrt{3}}{2}$$

Hence, for the required value substitute $x = \dfrac{\pi}{3}$,

$$f\left(\sin\frac{\pi}{3}\right)\cos\left(\frac{\pi}{3}\right) = \frac{\sqrt{3}}{2}$$

$$f\left(\frac{\sqrt{3}}{2}\right)\left(\frac{1}{2}\right) = \frac{\sqrt{3}}{2}$$

$$f\left(\frac{\sqrt{3}}{2}\right) = \sqrt{3}$$

108. Correct Response : (b)

Explanation :

$$I = \int \frac{x^{5m-1} + 2x^{4m-1}}{\left(x^{2m} + x^{m} + 1\right)^{5}}\,dx$$

$$= \int \frac{x^{5m-1} + 2x^{4m-1}}{x^{6m}\left(1 + \dfrac{1}{x^{m}} + \dfrac{1}{x^{2m}}\right)^{5}}\,dx$$

$$= \int \frac{x^{-m-1} + 2x^{-2m-1}}{\left(1 + \dfrac{1}{x^{m}} + \dfrac{1}{x^{2m}}\right)^{5}}\,dx$$

Let, $1 + \dfrac{1}{x^{m}} + \dfrac{1}{x^{2m}} = t$. Then,

$$I = -\frac{1}{m}\int \frac{dt}{t^{3}}$$

$$= -\frac{1}{m} \times \frac{t^{-3+1}}{(-3+1)} + c$$

$$= \frac{1}{2m\left(1 + \dfrac{1}{x^{m}} + \dfrac{1}{x^{2m}}\right)^{2}} + c$$

$$= \frac{x^{4m}}{2m\left(x^{2m} + x^{m} + 1\right)^{2}} + c$$

109. Correct Response : (d)

Explanation :

Consider the given integral function,

$$f(x) = \int\left(1 + x - \frac{1}{x}\right)e^{x + \frac{1}{x}}\,dx$$

Simplify the above expression,

$$= \int\left(e^{x + \frac{1}{x}} + x\left(1 - \frac{1}{x^{2}}\right)e^{x + \frac{1}{x}}\right)dx$$

$$= \int\left(xf'(x) + f(x)\right)dx = xf(x) + c$$

$$= x.e^{x + \frac{1}{x}} + c$$

110. Correct Response : (b)

Explanation :

The given integral function is,

$$I = \int_{0}^{\pi} \sqrt{1 + 4\sin^{2}\frac{x}{2} - 4\sin\frac{x}{2}}\;dx$$

$$= \int_{0}^{\pi}\left|2\sin\frac{x}{2} - 1\right|dx$$

Here,

$$\begin{bmatrix} \sin\dfrac{x}{2} = \dfrac{1}{2} \\[2mm] \dfrac{x}{2} = \dfrac{\pi}{6}, \dfrac{x}{2} = \dfrac{5\pi}{6} \\[2mm] x = \dfrac{\pi}{3}, x = \dfrac{5\pi}{3} \end{bmatrix}$$

Now,

$$I = \int_{0}^{\frac{\pi}{3}}\left(1 - 2\sin\frac{x}{2}\right)dx + \int_{\frac{\pi}{3}}^{\pi}\left(2\sin\frac{x}{2} - 1\right)dx$$

$$= \frac{\pi}{3} + 4\frac{\sqrt{3}}{2} - 4 + \left(0 - \pi + \frac{\pi}{3} + 4\frac{\sqrt{3}}{2}\right)$$

$$= 4\sqrt{3} - 4 - \frac{\pi}{3}$$

111. Correct Response : (c)

Explanation :

The figure is draw from the given equations,

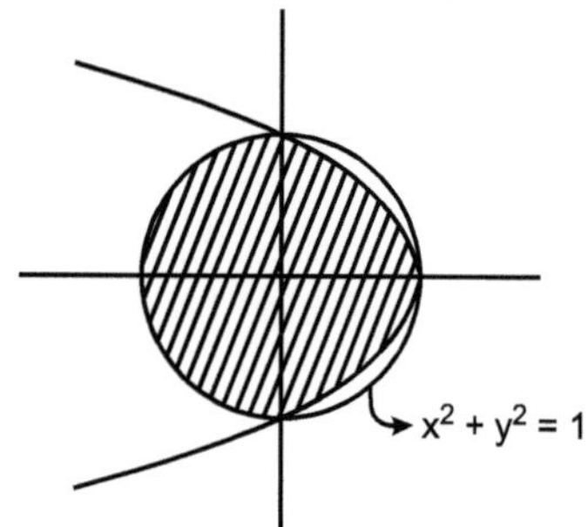

Now, the area of the shaded region is,

$$A = \frac{\pi(1)^2}{2} + 2\int_0^1 \sqrt{(1-x)}\,dx$$

$$= \frac{\pi}{2} + \left. \frac{2(1-x)^{\frac{3}{2}}}{\left(\frac{3}{2}\right)}(-1) \right|_0^1$$

$$= \frac{\pi}{2} + \frac{4}{3}(0-(-1))$$

$$= \frac{\pi}{2} + \frac{4}{3}$$

112. Correct Response : (a)

Explanation :

The required curve is drawn as :

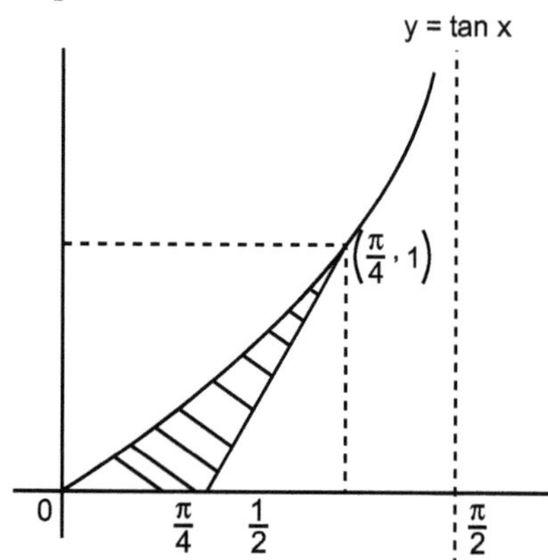

The given function is,

$$y = \tan x$$

$$\frac{dy}{dx} = \sec^2 x$$

$$\left.\frac{dy}{dx}\right|_{x=\frac{\pi}{4}} = 2$$

The equation of the tangent at point $\left(\frac{\pi}{4}, 1\right)$ on

x-axis is,

$$0 - 1 = 2\left(x - \frac{\pi}{4}\right)$$

$$\frac{\pi}{4} - \frac{1}{2} = x$$

Shaded area can be given as,

$$A = \int_0^{\frac{\pi}{4}} \tan x\,dx - \frac{1}{2}\cdot\frac{1}{2}\cdot 1$$

$$= \left(\log \sec x\right)^{\frac{\pi}{4}}_0 - \frac{1}{4}$$

$$= \log \sqrt{2} - \frac{1}{4}$$

$$= \frac{1}{2}\left[\log 2 - \frac{1}{2}\right]$$

113. Correct Response : (d)

Explanation :

The given function is,

$$F(x) = \int_1^x \frac{e^t}{t}\,dt$$

Differentiate the above function,

$$F'(x) = \frac{e^x}{x}\cdot 1 - 0$$

$$= \frac{e^x}{x}$$

The value of the integral is,

$$I = \int_1^x \frac{e^t}{t+a}\,dt$$

Let $t + a = p$. Then,

$$dt = dp$$

Hence, $\qquad I = \int_{1+a}^{x+a} \frac{e^{p-a}}{p}\,dp$

$$= e^{-a}\int_{1+a}^{x+a} \frac{e^p}{p}\,dp$$

$$= e^{-a}\int_{1+a}^{x+a} \frac{e^t}{t}\,dt$$

$$= e^{-a}\int_{1+a}^{x+a} F'(t)\,dt$$

Further simplify the above equation,

$$I = e^{-a}\left[F(x+a) - F(1+a)\right]$$

114. Correct Response : (b)

Explanation :

The given first curve is,

$$y_1 = \sin x + \cos x$$

The given second curve is,

$$y_2 = |\cos x - \sin x|$$

The area enclosed by the curves in the given interval $\left[0, \dfrac{\pi}{2}\right]$ is,

$$\text{Area} = \int_0^{\pi/2} (\sin x + \cos x)\,dx$$

$$-\left[\int_0^{\pi/4} (\cos x - \sin x)\,dx + \int_{\pi/4}^{\pi/2} (\sin x - \cos x)\,dx\right]$$

$$= -|\cos x|_0^{\pi/2} + |\sin x|_0^{\pi/2} - \left[|\sin x|_0^{\pi/4} + |\cos x|_0^{\pi/4}\right.$$

$$\left. -|\cos x|_{\pi/4}^{\pi/2} - |\sin x|_{\pi/4}^{\pi/2}\right]$$

$$= -(0-1) + (1-0)$$

$$\left[\frac{1}{\sqrt{2}} + \frac{1}{\sqrt{2}} - 1 - \left(0 - \frac{1}{\sqrt{2}}\right) - \left(1 - \frac{1}{\sqrt{2}}\right)\right]$$

Further simplify above value.

$$\text{Area} = 2 - \left[\sqrt{2} - 1 + \frac{1}{\sqrt{2}} - 1 + \frac{1}{\sqrt{2}}\right]$$

$$= 2 - \left[2\sqrt{2} - 2\right]$$

$$= 4 - 2\sqrt{2}$$

$$= 2\sqrt{2}\left(\sqrt{2} - 1\right)$$

115. Correct Response : (c)

Explanation :

Let, the given integral is,

$$I = \int \frac{\sec^2 x}{(\sec x + \tan x)^{9/2}}\,dx$$

$$= \int \frac{\sec x}{(\sec x + \tan x)^{9/2}}(\sec x \cdot dx)$$

Let,

$$t = (\sec x + \tan x)$$
$$dt = (\sec x \cdot \tan x + \sec^2 x)\,dx$$
$$dt = \sec x \cdot (t)\,dx$$
$$\sec x \cdot dx = \frac{1}{t}\,dt$$

Also,

$$t = (\sec x + \tan x)$$
$$t = \frac{(\sec^2 x - \tan^2 x)}{(\sec x - \tan x)}$$
$$(\sec x - \tan x) = \frac{1}{t}$$
$$\sec x = \frac{\left(t + \dfrac{1}{t}\right)}{2}$$

The integral is,

$$I = \int \frac{\left(t + \dfrac{1}{t}\right)}{2t^{9/2}} \cdot \frac{1}{t}\,dt$$

$$= \frac{1}{2}\int \left(\frac{1}{t^{9/2}} + \frac{1}{t^{13/2}}\right)dt$$

$$= \frac{1}{2}\left[\frac{2}{7t^{7/2}} + \frac{2}{11t^{11/2}}\right] + K$$

$$= -\frac{1}{t^{11/2}}\left[\frac{1}{11} + \frac{t^2}{7}\right] + K$$

Further solve the above integral.

$$I = -\frac{1}{t^{11/2}}\left[\frac{1}{11} - \frac{t^2}{7}\right] + K$$

$$= -\frac{1}{(\sec x + \tan x)^{11/2}}\left[\frac{1}{11} + \frac{1}{7}(\sec x + \tan x)^2\right] + K$$

116. Correct Response : (a, b, d)

Explanation :

The figure shows the area of the region enclosed by the curve $y = e^{-x^2}$, $y = 0$, $x = 0$ and $x = 1$.

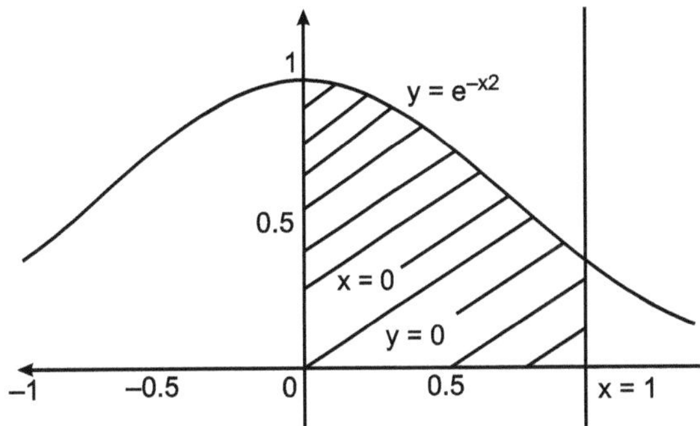

The area of the region is,

$$S = \int_0^1 y\,dx$$

$$= \int_0^1 e^{-x^2}\,dx \qquad \qquad \dots(1)$$

It is true that,

$$-x^2 \le 0$$
$$e^{-x^2} \le 1$$

From equation (1),

$$S \le 1$$

Also,

$$x^2 \le x$$
$$-x^2 \ge -x$$
$$e^{-x^2} \ge e^{-x}$$

So,

$$S \ge \int_0^1 e^{-x}\,dx$$

$$\geq -\left(e^{-x}\right)_0^1$$

$$\geq -\left(e^{-1}-e^0\right)$$

$$S \geq \left(1-\frac{1}{e}\right)$$

Option (b) is correct.

Also,

$$S \geq \left(1-\frac{1}{e}\right)$$

$$S \geq \frac{1}{e}$$

Option (a) is correct.

$$S < \frac{1}{\sqrt{2}}+\frac{1}{\sqrt{e}}\left(1-\frac{1}{\sqrt{2}}\right)$$

Option (d) is correct.

117. Correct Response : (b)

Explanation :

The value of the integral is,

$$\int_{-\pi/2}^{\pi/2}\left(x^2+ln\,\frac{\pi+x}{\pi-x}\right)\cos x \cdot dx$$

$$= \int_{-\pi/2}^{\pi/2}\left(x^2\cos x\right)dx+\int_{-\pi/2}^{\pi/2}\left(ln\,\frac{\pi+x}{\pi-x}\right)\cos x \cdot dx$$

$$= 2\int_{0}^{\pi/2}\left(x^2\cos x\right)dx+0$$

$$= 2\left[\left(x^2\sin x\right)_0^{\pi/2}-\int_{0}^{\pi/2}\left(2x\sin x\right)dx\right]$$

$$= 2\left[\left(\frac{\pi^2}{4}\sin\frac{\pi}{2}-0\right)-2\int_{0}^{\pi/2}\left(x\sin x\right)dx\right]$$

Futher solve the integral.

$$\int_{-\pi/2}^{\pi/2}\left(x^2+ln\frac{\pi+x}{\pi-x}\right)\cos x \cdot dx$$

$$= 2\left[\left(\frac{\pi^2}{4}\sin\frac{\pi}{2}-0\right)-2\int_{0}^{\pi/2}\left(x\sin x\right)dx\right]$$

$$= \frac{\pi^2}{2}-4\left[\left(-x\cos x\right)_0^{\pi/2}+\int_{0}^{\pi/2}\cos x\right]$$

$$= \frac{\pi^2}{4}-4\left[(0)+\sin\frac{\pi}{2}-\sin 0\right]$$

$$= \frac{\pi^2}{4}-4$$

118. Correct Response : (c)

Explanation :

The given function is,

$$f(x)=f(1-x)$$

The area of the first bounded region is,

$$R_1 = \int_{-1}^{2} xf(x)dx \qquad \ldots(1)$$

Use property of definite integral in above equation.

$$R_1 = \int_{-1}^{2}(1-x)\,f(1-x)dx$$

$$R_2 = \int_{-1}^{2}(1-x)\,f(x)dx \qquad \ldots(2)$$

Add equation (1) and (2).

$$2R_1 = \int_{-1}^{2} f(x)dx$$

$$2R_1 = R_2$$

119. Correct Response : (a)

Explanation :

The given integral is,

$$I = \int_{\sqrt{ln2}}^{\sqrt{ln3}}\frac{x\sin x^2}{\sin x^2+\sin\left(ln6-x^2\right)}dx$$

Substitute $x=\sqrt{t}$ in above integral function.

Differentiate above function with respect to x.

$$x^2 = t$$

$$2xdx = dt$$

$$xdx = \frac{1}{2}dt$$

For $x=\sqrt{ln2}$, $t=ln\,2$. For $x=\sqrt{ln3}$, $t=ln\,3$.

Now, the integral can be written as,

$$I = \frac{1}{2}\int_{ln2}^{ln3}\frac{\sin t}{\sin t+\sin\left(ln\,6-t\right)}dt \qquad \ldots(1)$$

Use property of definite integral to solve.

$$I=\frac{1}{2}\int_{ln2}^{ln3}\frac{\sin\left(ln3+ln2-t\right)}{\sin\left(ln3+ln2-t\right)+\sin\left(ln6-\left(ln3+ln2-t\right)\right)}dt$$

$$= \frac{1}{2}\int_{ln2}^{ln3}\frac{\sin\left(ln6-t\right)}{\sin\left(ln6-t\right)+\sin(t)}dt \qquad \ldots(2)$$

Add equatin (1) and (2).

$$2I = \frac{1}{2}\int_{ln2}^{ln3} dt$$

$$2I = \frac{1}{2}\left[ln3-ln2\right]$$

$$I = \frac{1}{4}ln\frac{3}{2}$$

120. **Correct Response :** (b)

Explanation :

The area enclosed by the curve $y = (1 - x^2)$, $y = 0$ and $x = 0$ into two parts is,

$$R_1 - R_2 = \frac{1}{4}$$

$$\int_0^b (1-x)^2\, dx - \int_b^1 (1-x)^2\, dx = \frac{1}{4}$$

$$\int_0^b (1+x^2 - 2x)dx - \int_b^1 (1+x^2 - 2x)dx = \frac{1}{4}$$

$$\left[x - x^2 + \frac{x^3}{3} \right]_0^b - \left[x - x^2 + \frac{x^3}{3} \right]_b^1 = \frac{1}{4}$$

Further simplify,

$$\left[-b + b^2 - \frac{b^3}{3} \right] - \left[\left(b - b^2 + \frac{b^3}{3} \right) - \left(1 - 1 + \frac{1}{3} \right) \right] = \frac{1}{4}$$

$$b - b^2 + \frac{b^3}{3} = \frac{7}{24}$$

$$b = \frac{1}{2}$$

121. **Correct Response :** (a, b, c)

Explanation :

The given expression is,

$$I_n = \int_{-\pi}^{\pi} \frac{\sin nx}{\left(1 + \pi^x\right)\sin x} \qquad \text{...(1)}$$

Change the limit.

$$I_n = \int_0^{\pi} \left[\frac{\sin nx}{\left(1 + \pi^x\right)\sin x} + \frac{\sin(-nx)}{\left(1 + \pi^{-x}\right)\sin(-x)} \right] dx$$

$$= \int_0^{\pi} \left[\frac{\sin nx}{\left(1 + \pi^x\right)\sin x} + \frac{\pi^x \sin(nx)}{\left(1 + \pi^x\right)\sin(x)} \right]$$

$$= \int_0^{\pi} \frac{\sin nx}{\sin x}$$

Simplify $I_{n+2} - I_n$.

$$I_{n+2} - I_n = \int_0^{\pi} \frac{\sin(n+2)x - \sin nx}{\sin x}\, dx$$

$$= \int_0^{\pi} \frac{2\cos(n+1)x \cdot \sin x}{\sin x}\, dx$$

$$= \left[\frac{2\sin(n+1)x}{n+1} \right]_0^{\pi}$$

$$= 0$$

Hence,

$$I_{n+2} = I_n$$

The value of $\sum_{m=1}^{10} I_{2m}$ is calculated as,

Simplify the above equation.

$$10 I_3 = 10 \int_0^{\pi} \frac{\sin 2x}{\sin x}\, dx$$

$$= 20 \int_0^{\pi} \cos x\, dx$$

$$= 20 \times [-\sin]_0^{\pi}$$

$$= 0$$

Now, assume,

$$I_1 = I_3 = I_5$$

The value of $\sum_{m=1}^{10} I_{2m+1}$ is calculated as,

Simplify the above equation.

$$10 I_3 = 10 \int_0^{\pi} \frac{\sin 3x}{\sin x}\, dx$$

$$= 10 \int_0^{\pi} \frac{\sin 3x}{\sin x}\, dx$$

$$= 10 \left[[3 \times -2] \int (1 - \cos 2x)\, dx \right]$$

$$= 10\pi$$

Hence, option (a, b, c) is correct.

122. **Correct Response :** (c)

Explanation :

The value of $J - 1$ is calculated as,

$$J - 1 = \int \frac{e^{3x}}{e^{4x} + e^{2x} + 1}\, dx - \int \frac{e^x}{e^{4x} + e^{2x} + 1}\, dx$$

$$= \int \frac{e^x \left(e^{2x} - 1 \right)}{e^{4x} + e^{2x} + 1}\, dx$$

Put $e^x = t$.

Differentiate above equation.

$$e^x dx = dt$$

Substitute values in above integral.

$$J - 1 = \int \frac{(t^2 - 1)}{t^4 + t^2 + 1}\, dt$$

$$= \int \frac{\left(1 - \dfrac{1}{t^2} \right)}{\left(t + \dfrac{1}{t} \right)^2 - 1}\, dt$$

Let, $t + \dfrac{1}{t} = u$. So, $\left(1 - \dfrac{1}{t^2} \right) dt = du$.

$$J - 1 = \int \frac{du}{u^2 - 1}$$

$$= \frac{1}{2} \ln \left| \frac{u - 1}{u + 1} \right|$$

$$= \frac{1}{2} ln \left| \frac{e^x + \dfrac{1}{e^x} - 1}{e^x + \dfrac{1}{e^x} + 1} \right| + C$$

$$= \frac{1}{2} ln \left(\frac{e^{2x} - e^x + 1}{e^{2x} + e^x + 1} \right)$$

123. Correct Response : (a)

Explanation :

The given equation is,

$$y^3 - 3y + x = 0$$

Differentiate above equation.

$$3y^2 y' - 3y' + 1 = 0$$

$$y' = \frac{1}{3(1 - y^2)}$$

$$f'(x) = \frac{1}{3\left(1 - (f(x))^2\right)}$$

The area of region bounded by the curve is,

$$A = \int_a^b f(x)\,dx$$

$$= \left[xf(x) \right]_a^b - \int_a^b xf'(x)\,dx$$

$$= bf(b) - af(a) + \int_a^b \frac{x}{3\left[(f(x))^2 - 1 \right]}\,dx$$

124. Correct Response : (d)

Explanation :

The given equation is,

$$y^3 - 3y + x = 0$$

Differentiate above equation.

$$3y^2 y' - 3y' + 1 = 0$$

$$y' = \frac{1}{3\left(1 - y^2\right)}$$

$$g'(x) = \frac{1}{3\left(1 - (g(x))^2\right)}$$

It is an even function. So,

$$g(-1) = -g(1)$$

The value of integral is,

$$\int_{-1}^1 g'(x)\,dx = \left[g(x) \right]_{-1}^1$$

$$= g(1) - g(-1)$$

$$= 2g(1)$$

125. Correct Response : (a)

Explanation :

Simplify given limit.

$$\lim_{t \to x} \frac{t^2 f(x) - x^2 f(t)}{t - x} = 1$$

$$x^2 f'(x) - 2x f(x) + 1 = 0$$

$$f'(x) = \frac{2}{x} f(x) - \frac{1}{x^2}$$

Integrate the above function.

$$f(x) = cx^2 + \frac{1}{3x} \qquad \qquad ...(1)$$

Substitute 1 for x in above function.

$$1 = c(1)^2 + \frac{1}{3(1)}$$

$$c = 1 - \frac{1}{3}$$

$$c = \frac{2}{3}$$

Substitute the value of c into equation (1).

$$f(x) = \frac{2}{3} x^2 + \frac{1}{3x}$$

126. Correct Response : (a)-(s), (b)-(s), (c)-(p), (d)-(r)

Explanation :

(a)

Solve the given integral.

$$\int_{-1}^1 \frac{dx}{1 + x^2} = 2 \int_0^1 \frac{dx}{1 + x^2}$$

$$= 2\left[\tan^{-1} x \right]_0^1$$

$$= 2\left(\frac{\pi}{4} - 0 \right)$$

$$= \frac{\pi}{2}$$

(b)

Solve the given integral.

$$\int_0^1 \frac{dx}{\sqrt{1 - x^2}} = \left[\sin^{-1} x \right]_0^1$$

$$= \frac{\pi}{2} - 0$$

$$= \frac{\pi}{2}$$

(c)

Solve the given integral.

$$\int_2^3 \frac{dx}{1 - x^2} = \frac{1}{2}\left[ln \left| \frac{1 + x}{1 - x} \right| \right]_2^3$$

$$= \frac{1}{2} \ln \left(\frac{2}{3} \right)$$

(d)

Solve the given integral.

$$\int_1^2 \frac{dx}{x\sqrt{x^2-1}} = \frac{1}{2} \left[\sec^{-1} x \right]_1^2$$

$$= \frac{\pi}{3} - 0$$

$$= \frac{\pi}{3}$$

127. Correct Response : (d)

Explanation :

Solve the given integral.

$$I = \int \frac{x^2-1}{x^3 \sqrt{2x^4 - 2x^2 + 1}} dx$$

$$= \int \frac{\left(\dfrac{1}{x^3} - \dfrac{1}{x^5} \right)}{\sqrt{2 - \dfrac{2}{x^2} + \dfrac{1}{x^4}}} dx$$

Put $2 - \dfrac{2}{x^2} + \dfrac{1}{x^4} = t$.

$$\left(\frac{4}{x^3} - \frac{4}{x^5} \right) dx = dt$$

$$\left(\frac{1}{x^3} - \frac{1}{x^5} \right) dx = \frac{1}{4} dt$$

Now, substitute values in integral.

$$I = \frac{1}{4} \int \frac{dt}{\sqrt{t}}$$

$$= \frac{1}{2} \sqrt{t} + C$$

$$= \frac{1}{2} \sqrt{2 - \frac{2}{x^2} + \frac{1}{x^4}} + C$$

128. Correct Answer : 5051

Explanation :

The given integral is,

$$5050 \, \frac{\displaystyle\int_0^1 \left(1 - x^{50}\right)^{100} dx}{\displaystyle\int_0^1 \left(1 - x^{50}\right)^{101} dx} = 5050 \, \frac{I_{100}}{I_{101}}$$

Solve for I_{101}.

$$I_{101} = \int_0^1 (1 - x^{50})(1 - x^{50})^{100} dx$$

$$I_{101} = I_{100} - \int_0^1 x \cdot x^{49} (1 - x^{50})^{100} dx$$

$$I_{101} = I_{100} - \left[\frac{-x\left(1 - x^{50}\right)^{101}}{101} \right]_0^1 - \int_0^1 \frac{\left(1 - x^{50}\right)^{101}}{5050} dx$$

$$I_{101} = I_{100} - \frac{I_{101}}{5050}$$

Further simplify,

$$I_{101} + \frac{I_{101}}{5050} = I_{100}$$

$$\frac{5051 \, I_{101}}{5050} = I_{100}$$

$$5050 \, \frac{I_{100}}{I_{101}} = 5051$$

129. Correct Response : (i)-(A), (ii)-(D), (iii)-(A)

Explanation :

(i)

Solve the given integral.

$$I = \int_0^{\pi/2} (\sin x)^{\cos x} (\cos x \cot x - \log (\sin x)^{\sin x}) dx$$

$$= \int_0^{\pi/2} \frac{d}{dx} (\sin x)^{\cos x} dx$$

$$= 1$$

(ii)

The points of intersection of curves $-4y^2 = x$ and $x - 1 = -5y^2$ and $(-4, -1)$ and $(-4, 1)$.

The area bounded by the curves is,

$$\text{Area} = 2 \left| \int_0^1 \left(1 - 5y^2\right) dy - \int_0^1 -4y^2 dy \right|$$

$$= \frac{4}{3}$$

(iii)

The point of intersection of curves $y = 3^{x-1} \log x$ and $y = x^x - 1$ is $(1, 0)$.

Differentiate the equation of curve $y = 3^{x-1} \log x$.

$$\frac{dy}{dx} = \frac{3^{x-1}}{x} + 3^{x-1} \log 3 \cdot \log x$$

$$\left. \frac{dy}{dx} \right|_{(1,0)} = 1$$

Differentiate the equation of curves $y = x^x - 1$.

$$\frac{dy}{dx} = x^x (\ln x + 1)$$

$$\left.\frac{dy}{dx}\right|_{(1,0)} = 1$$

Let, θ be the angle between the curves then,

$$\tan \theta = 0$$

$$\Rightarrow \qquad \cos \theta = 1$$

130. Correct Response : (i)-(D), (ii)-(A), (iii)-(B),(C), (iv)-(D)

Explanation :

(i)

Solve two equations of rays $x + y = |a|$ and $ax - y = 1$.

$$x = \frac{|a|+1}{a+1} > 0 \text{ and } y = \frac{|a|-1}{a+1} > 0$$

If $a + 1 > 0$, then $a > 1$. So,

$$a_0 = 1$$

(ii)

The given vector is $\vec{a} = \alpha\hat{i} + \beta\hat{j} + \gamma\hat{k}$.

$$\vec{a} \cdot \hat{k} = \gamma$$

Now,

$$\hat{k} \times (\hat{k} \times \hat{a}) \ \hat{k} \times (\hat{k} \times \hat{a}) = 0$$

$$(\hat{k} \cdot \vec{a})\hat{k} - (\hat{k} \cdot \hat{k})\vec{a} = 0$$

$$\gamma\hat{k} - (\alpha\hat{i} + \beta\hat{j} + \gamma\hat{k}) = 0$$

$$\alpha\hat{i} + \beta\hat{j} = 0$$

Further simplify.

$$\alpha = \beta = 0$$

The value of γ is,

$$\alpha + \beta + \gamma = 2$$

$$\gamma = 2$$

(iii)

The value of given expression is,

$$\left|\int_0^1 (1-y^2)\,dy\right| + \left|\int_1^0 (y^2-1)\,dy\right| = 2\int_0^1 (1-y^2)\,dy$$

$$= 2\left[y - \frac{y^3}{3}\right]_0^1$$

$$= \frac{4}{3}$$

Now, the value of other integral expression is,

$$\left|\int_0^1 \sqrt{1-x}\,dx\right| + \left|\int_{-1}^0 \sqrt{1+x}\,dx\right| = 2\int_0^1 \sqrt{1-x}\,dx$$

$$= 2\left[-\frac{2}{3}(1-x)^{\frac{3}{2}}\right]_0^1$$

$$= \frac{4}{3}$$

(iv)

Solve.

$$\sin A \sin B \sin C + \cos A \cos B$$
$$\leq \sin A \sin B + \cos A \cos B$$
$$1 \leq \cos (A - B)$$
$$\cos (A - B) = 1$$
$$\sin C = 1$$

131. Correct Response : (c)

Explanation :

The given integral is,

$$I = \int_{-2}^{0} \left(x^3 + 3x^2 + 3x + 3 + (x+1)\cos(x+1)\right)dx$$

Substitute $x + 1 = t$.

$$dx = dt$$

Now, value of integral is,

$$I = \int_{-1}^{1} \left((t-1)^3 + 3(t-1)^2 + 3(t-1) + 3 + t\cos t\right)dt$$

$$= \int_{-1}^{1} \left(t^3 + t\cos t + 2\right)dt$$

$$= \left[\frac{t^4}{4} + t\sin t + \cos t + 2x\right]_{-1}^{1}$$

$$= 4$$

132. Correct Response : (d)

Explanation :

The two parabolas cut each other at $(0, 1)$ and intersect the line $y = \frac{1}{4}$ at $x = -\frac{3}{2}, -\frac{1}{2}, \frac{1}{2}, \frac{3}{2}$.

The required area is,

$$\text{Area} = 2\int_0^{1/2} \left[(x-1)^2 - \frac{1}{4}\right]dx$$

$$= 2\int_0^{1/2} \left[x^2 - 2x + \frac{3}{4}\right]dx$$

$$= 2\left[\frac{x^3}{3} - x^2 + \frac{3}{4}x\right]_0^{1/2}$$

$$= 2\left[\frac{1}{24} - \frac{1}{4} + \frac{3}{8}\right]$$

Solve further,

$$\text{Area} = 2\left(\frac{4}{24}\right)$$

$$= \frac{1}{3}$$

Therefore, area of bounded region is $\dfrac{1}{3}$ sq. units.

133. Explanation :

Solve the given integral.

$$I = \int_0^\pi e^{|\cos x|}\left(2\sin\left(\frac{1}{2}\cos x\right) + 3\cos\left(\frac{1}{2}\cos x\right)\right)\sin x \, dx$$

$$= \int_0^\pi e^{|\cos x|}\left(2\sin\left(\frac{1}{2}\cos x\right)\right)\sin x\, dx$$

$$+ \int_0^\pi e^{|\cos x|}\left(3\cos\left(\frac{1}{2}\cos x\right)\right)\sin x \, dx$$

Use the property $\displaystyle\int_0^{2a} f(x)\,dx = 0$ if $f(2a - x) = -f(x)$

and $\displaystyle\int_0^{2a} f(x)\,dx = 2\int_0^{a} f(x)\,dx$ if $f(2a - x) = f(x)$.

$$I = 6\int_0^{\pi/2} e^{|\cos x|} \sin x \left(\cos\left(\frac{1}{2}\cos x\right)\right) dx$$

Put $\cos x = t$.

$$\sin x\,dx = dt$$

Now, value of integral is,

$$I = 6\int_0^1 e^t \cos\left(\frac{t}{2}\right) dt$$

$$= \frac{24}{5}\left(e\cos\left(\frac{1}{2}\right) + \frac{e}{2}\sin\left(\frac{1}{2}\right) - 1\right)$$

134. Explanation :

The equations form given matrix is,

$$4a^2 f(-1) + 4af(1) + f(2) = 3a^2 + 3a \quad ...(1)$$
$$4b^2 f(-1) + 4bf(1) + f(2) = 3b^2 + 3b \quad ...(2)$$
$$4c^2 f(-1) + 4cf(1) + f(2) = 3c^2 + 3c \quad ...(3)$$

Now, consider a quadratic equation.

$$4x^2 f(-1) + 4x f(1) + f(2) = 3x^2 + 3x$$
$$[4f(-1) - 3]x^2 + [4f(1) - 3]x + f(2) = 0 \quad ...(4)$$

Compare terms of x^2.

$$4f(-1) = 3$$
$$f(-1) = \frac{3}{4}$$

Compare terms of x.

$$4f(1) = 3$$
$$f(1) = \frac{3}{4}$$

Compare constant terms.

$$f(2) = 0$$

So, the function is $f(x) = -\dfrac{x^2}{4} + 1$.

Let, point A be $(-2, 0)$ and point B be $(2t, -t^2 + 1)$.

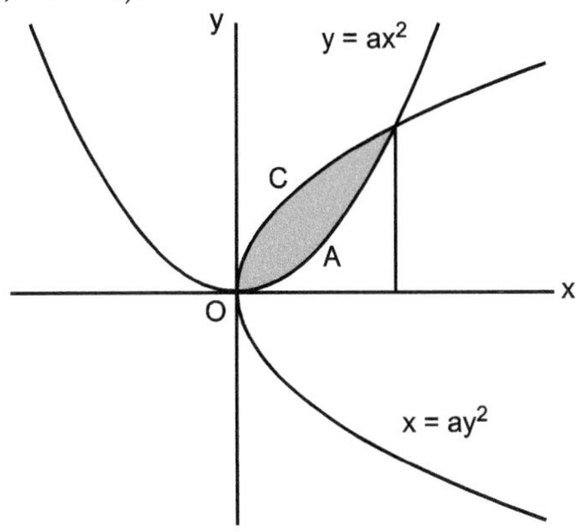

So, AB makes a right angle at vertex V.

$$\frac{1}{2} \times \frac{-t^2}{2t} = -1$$

$$t = 4$$

Coordinates of vertex is $(8, -15)$.

The area bounded by chord AB and $f(x)$ is,

$$\text{Area} = \int_{-2}^{8}\left(\frac{4 - x^2}{4} + \frac{3x + 6}{2}\right) dx$$

$$= \frac{125}{3}$$

Therefore, required area is $\dfrac{125}{3}$ sq. units.

135. Correct Response : (a)

Explanation :

The area enclosed between the curves is BAOCB.

Points of intersection of curves $y = ax^2$ and $x = ay^2$ are $(0, 0)$ and $\left(\dfrac{1}{a}, \dfrac{1}{a}\right)$.

The area enclosed between the curves is,

$$\text{Area} = \int_0^{1/a}\left(\sqrt{\frac{x}{a}} - ax^2\right) dx$$

$$1 = \left(\frac{1}{\sqrt{a}}\frac{x^{3/2}}{3/2} - \frac{ax^3}{3}\right)\Bigg|_0^{1/a}$$

$$1 = \frac{2}{3a^2} - \frac{1}{3a^2}$$

$$a = \frac{1}{\sqrt{3}}$$

136. Correct Response : (b)

Explanation :

Solve the given integral.

$$I = \int_0^1 \sqrt{\frac{1 - x}{1 + x}}\, dx$$

$$= \int_0^1 \frac{1-x}{\sqrt{1-x^2}}\,dx$$

$$= \int_0^1 \frac{1}{\sqrt{1-x^2}}\,dx - \int_0^1 \frac{x}{\sqrt{1-x^2}}\,dx$$

Substitute $t^2 = 1 - x^2$.

$$t\,dt = x\,dx$$

Further solve above integral.

$$I = \left(\sin^{-1} x\right)_0^1 + \int_1^0 \frac{t}{t}\,dt$$

$$= (\sin^{-1} 1 - \sin^{-1} 0) + (t)_1^0$$

$$= \frac{\pi}{2} - 1$$

137. Explanation :

Solve the given integral.

$$y = \int_{\pi^2/16}^{x^2} \frac{\cos x \cdot \cos \sqrt{\theta}}{1 + \sin^2 \sqrt{\theta}}\,d\theta$$

$$y = \cos x \int_{\pi^2/16}^{x^2} \frac{\cos \sqrt{\theta}}{1 + \sin^2 \sqrt{\theta}}\,d\theta$$

Differentiate above equation.

$$\frac{dy}{dx} = -\sin x \int_{\pi^2/16}^{x^2} \frac{\cos \sqrt{\theta}}{1 + \sin^2 \sqrt{\theta}}\,d\theta + \frac{2x \cos x \cdot \cos x}{1 + \sin^2 x}$$

The value of $\dfrac{dy}{dx}$ at $x = \pi$ is,

$$\left(\frac{dy}{dx}\right)_{x=\pi} = 0 + \frac{2\pi(-1)(-1)}{1+0}$$

$$= 2\pi$$

138. Explanation :

The slope of tangent at point P is,

$$\frac{dy}{dx} = \frac{(x+1)^2 + y - 3}{x+1}$$

$$\frac{dy}{dx} = (x+1) + \frac{y-3}{x+1}$$

Put $X = x + 1$ and $Y = y - 3$.

$$\frac{dY}{dX} = X + \frac{Y}{X}$$

$$\frac{dY}{dX} - \frac{Y}{X} = X$$

Integrating factor is,

$$\text{I.F.} = e^{-\int \frac{1}{X}\,dx}$$

$$= e^{-\log X}$$

$$= \frac{1}{X}$$

Now, the equation of curve is,

$$\frac{1}{X} \cdot Y = X + c$$

$$\frac{y-3}{x+1} = (x+1) + c$$

The curve is passing through (0, 2). So,

$$c = -4$$

The equation of curve is,

$$y - 3 = (x+1)^2 - 4(x+1)$$

$$y = x^2 - 2x$$

The area enclosed by the curve and x-axis is,

$$\text{Area} = \left| \int_0^2 \left(x^2 - 2x\right)dx \right|$$

$$= \left| \left[\frac{x^3}{3} - x^2 \right]_0^2 \right|$$

$$= \frac{4}{3}$$

Therefore, the required area is $\dfrac{4}{3}$ sq. units.

139. Explanation :

Solve the given integral.

$$I = \int_{-\pi/3}^{\pi/3} \frac{\left(\pi + 4x^3\right)dx}{2 - \cos\left(|x| + \dfrac{\pi}{3}\right)}$$

$$2I = \int_{-\pi/3}^{\pi/3} \frac{2\pi\,dx}{2 - \cos\left(x + \dfrac{\pi}{3}\right)}$$

Substitute $x + \dfrac{\pi}{3} = t$.

$$I = \int_{\pi/3}^{2\pi/3} \frac{2\pi\,dt}{2 - \cos t}$$

$$= 2\pi \int_{\pi/3}^{2\pi/3} \frac{\sec^2 \dfrac{t}{2}\,dt}{1 + 3\tan^2 \dfrac{t}{2}}$$

$$= 2\pi \int_{1/\sqrt{3}}^{\sqrt{3}} \frac{2\,dt}{1 + 3t^2}$$

$$= \frac{4\pi}{3} \int_{1/\sqrt{3}}^{\sqrt{3}} \frac{dt}{\left(\dfrac{1}{\sqrt{3}}\right)^2 + t^2}$$

Solve further.

$$I = \frac{4\pi}{3}\sqrt{3}\Big[\tan^{-1}\sqrt{3}t\Big]_{1/\sqrt{3}}^{\sqrt{3}}$$

$$= \frac{4\pi}{\sqrt{3}}\Big[\tan^{-1}3 - \frac{\pi}{4}\Big]$$

$$= \frac{4\pi}{\sqrt{3}}\tan^{-1}\Big(\frac{1}{2}\Big)$$

140. Correct Response : (a)

Explanation :

Solve the given integral.

$$I(m, n) = \int_0^1 t^m (1+t)^n \, dt$$

$$= \Big[\frac{t^{m+1}}{(m+1)}(1+t)^n\Big]_0^1 - \int_0^1 \frac{t^{m+1}}{m+1}n(1+t)^{n-1}\, dt$$

$$= \frac{2^n}{m+1} - \frac{n}{m+1}I(m+1, n-1)$$

141. Correct Response : (a)

Explanation :

The intersection points of curve and line is (0, 3) and (9, 3).

The area of region bounded by curve, line and x-axis is,

$$\text{Area} = \int_0^3 \big(2y + 3 - y^2\big)dy$$

$$= \Big[y^2 + 3y - \frac{y^3}{3}\Big]_0^3$$

$$= 9 + 9 - 9$$

$$= 9$$

142. Explanation :

Solve the left hand side.

$$\int_0^{\pi/2} f(\cos 2x)\cos x \, dx$$

$$= \int_0^{\pi/4}\Big[f(\cos 2x)\cos x + f\Big(\cos 2\Big(\frac{\pi}{2}-x\Big)\Big)\cos\Big(\frac{\pi}{2}-x\Big)\Big]dx$$

$$= \int_0^{\pi/4}\big[f(\cos 2x)\cos x + f(-\cos 2x)\sin x\big]dx$$

$$= \int_0^{\pi/4} f(\cos 2x)(\cos x + \sin x)dx$$

$$= \sqrt{2}\int_0^{\pi/4} f(\cos 2x)\cos\Big(\frac{\pi}{4}-x\Big)dx$$

Solve further.

$$\int_0^{\pi/2} f(\cos 2x)\cos x \, dx$$

$$= \sqrt{2}\int_0^{\pi/4} f\Big(\cos 2\Big(\frac{\pi}{4}-x\Big)\Big)\cos\Big(\frac{\pi}{4}-\Big(\frac{\pi}{4}-x\Big)\Big)dx$$

$$= \sqrt{2}\int_0^{\pi/4} f(\sin 2x)\cos x \, dx$$

Hence, left hand side is equal to right hand side.

143. Correct Response : (b)

Explanation :

Draw the graph of equation $y = |x| - 1$ and $y = -|x| + 1$.

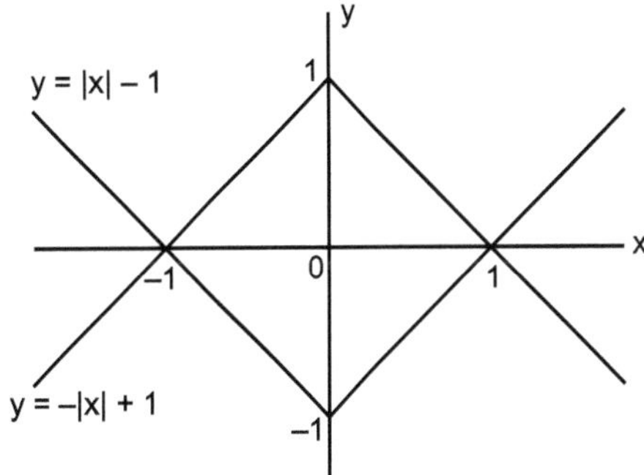

The required area bounded by the curve is,

$$\text{area} = \frac{1}{2}\times 2 \times 2$$

$$= 2 \text{ sq. units.}$$

144. Correct Response : (c)

Explanation :

Solve the given integral.

$$\int_3^{3+3T} f(2x)dx = \int_6^{6+6T} f(t)\frac{dt}{2}$$

$$= \frac{1}{2}\int_0^{6T} f(t)dt$$

$$= 3\int_0^{T} f(t)dt$$

$$= 3I$$

145. Correct Response : (a)

Explanation :

Solve the given integral.

$$\int_{-1/2}^{1/2}\Big([x] + \ln\Big(\frac{1+x}{1-x}\Big)\Big)dx = \int_{-1/2}^{1/2} [x]dx$$

$$= -\frac{1}{2}$$

●●

🔖 QUESTIONS

1. If $y = y(x)$ is the solution of the differential equation $\dfrac{5+e^x}{2+y} \cdot \dfrac{dy}{x} + e^x = 0$ satisfying $y(0) = 1$, then a value of $y(\log_e 13)$ is : **[2020, Main]**

(a) 1
(b) – 1
(c) 2
(d) 0

2. The general solution of the differential equation $\sqrt{1+x^2+y^2+x^2y^2} + xy\dfrac{dy}{dx} = 0$ is : **[2020, Main]**

(where C is a constant of integration)

(a) $\sqrt{1+y^2} + \sqrt{1+x^2} = \dfrac{1}{2}\log_e\left(\dfrac{\sqrt{1+x^2}+1}{\sqrt{1+x^2}-1}\right) + C$

(b) $\sqrt{1+y^2} - \sqrt{1+x^2} = \dfrac{1}{2}\log_e\left(\dfrac{\sqrt{1+x^2}+1}{\sqrt{1+x^2}-1}\right) + C$

(c) $\sqrt{1+y^2} + \sqrt{1+x^2} = \dfrac{1}{2}\log_e\left(\dfrac{\sqrt{1+x^2}-1}{\sqrt{1+x^2}+1}\right) + C$

(d) $\sqrt{1+y^2} - \sqrt{1+x^2} = \dfrac{1}{2}\log_e\left(\dfrac{\sqrt{1+x^2}-1}{\sqrt{1+x^2}+1}\right) + C$

3. If $y = \left(\dfrac{2}{\pi}x - 1\right)\operatorname{cosec} x$ is the solution of the differential equation,

$$\dfrac{dy}{dx} + p(x)y = \dfrac{2}{\pi}\operatorname{cosec} x, 0 < x < \dfrac{\pi}{2},$$

then the function $p(x)$ is equal to : **[2020, Main]**

(a) $\cot x$
(b) $\tan x$
(c) $\operatorname{cosec} x$
(d) $\sec x$

4. Let $y = y(x)$ be the solution of the differential equation, $xy' - y = x^2(x\cos x + \sin x)$, $x > 0$. If $y(\pi) = \pi$, then $y''\left(\dfrac{\pi}{2}\right) + y\left(\dfrac{\pi}{2}\right)$ is equal to : **[2020, Main]**

(a) $2 + \dfrac{\pi}{2}$
(b) $1 + \dfrac{\pi}{2}$
(c) $1 + \dfrac{\pi}{2} + \dfrac{\pi^2}{4}$
(d) $2 + \dfrac{\pi}{2} + \dfrac{\pi^2}{4}$

5. The solution of the differential equation

$$\dfrac{dy}{dx} - \dfrac{y+3x}{\log_e(y+3x)} + 3 = 0 \text{ is :}$$

(where C is a constant of integration.) **[2020, Main]**

(a) $x - 2\log_e(y + 3x) = C$
(b) $x - \log_e(y + 3x) = C$
(c) $x - \dfrac{1}{2}[\log_e(y+3x)]^2 = C$
(d) $y + 3x - \dfrac{1}{2}(\log_e x)^2 = C$

6. Let $y = y(x)$ be the solution of the differential equation $\cos x \dfrac{dy}{dx} + 2y\sin x = \sin 2x$, $x \in \left(0, \dfrac{\pi}{2}\right)$. If $y(\pi/3) = 0$, then $y(\pi/4)$ is equal to : **[2020, Main]**

(a) $\sqrt{2} - 2$
(b) $\dfrac{1}{\sqrt{2}} - 1$
(c) $2 - \sqrt{2}$
(d) $2 + \sqrt{2}$

7. If a curve $y = f(x)$, passing through the point $(1, 2)$, is the solution of the differential equation, $2x^2dy = (2xy + y^2)dx$, then $f\left(\dfrac{1}{2}\right)$ is equal to : **[2020, Main]**

(a) $\dfrac{1}{1-\log_e 2}$
(b) $\dfrac{1}{1+\log_e 2}$
(c) $\dfrac{-1}{1+\log_e 2}$
(d) $1 + \log_e 2$

8. Let $y = y(x)$ be the solution of the differential equation,

$$\dfrac{2+\sin x}{y+1} \cdot \dfrac{dy}{dx} = -\cos x, y > 0, y(0) = 1. \text{ If } y(\pi) = a$$

and $\dfrac{dy}{dx}$ at $x = \pi$ is b, then the ordered pair (a, b) is equal to : **[2020, Main]**

(a) $(2, 1)$ **(b)** $\left(2, \dfrac{3}{2}\right)$

(c) $(1, -1)$ **(d)** $(1, 1)$

9. If $y = \displaystyle\sum_{k=1}^{6} k \cos^{-1}\left\{\dfrac{3}{5}\cos kx - \dfrac{4}{5}\sin kx\right\}$, then $\dfrac{dy}{dx}$ at

$x = 0$ is .... [2020, Main]

10. Let $y = y(x)$ be the solution curve of the differential equation, $(y^2 - x)\dfrac{dy}{dx} = 1$, satisfying

$y(0) = 1$. This curve intersects the x-axis at a point whose abscissa is : [2020, Main]

(a) $2 + e$ **(b)** 2

(c) $2 - e$ **(d)** $-e$

11. The differential equation of the family of curves, $x^2 = 4b(y + b)$, $b \in R$, is : [2020, Main]

(a) $x(y')^2 = x + 2yy'$ **(b)** $x(y')^2 = x - 2yy'$

(c) $xy'' - y'$ **(d)** $x(y')^2 = x - 2yy'$

12. If $f'(x) = \tan^{-1}(\sec x + \tan x)$, $\dfrac{-\pi}{2} < x < \dfrac{x}{2}$ and

$f(0) = 0$, then $f(1)$ is equal to : [2020, Main]

(a) $\dfrac{\pi - 1}{4}$ **(b)** $\dfrac{\pi + 2}{4}$

(c) $\dfrac{\pi + 1}{4}$ **(d)** $\dfrac{1}{4}$

13. If for $x \geq 0$, $y = y(x)$ is the solution of the differential equation

$(x + 1)dy = ((x + 1)^2 + y - 3)\, dx$, $y(2) = 0$.

then $y(3)$ is equal to.................. . [2020, Main]

14. If $\dfrac{dy}{dx} = \dfrac{xy}{x^2 + y^2}$; $y(1) = 1$; then a value of x

satisfying $y(x) = e$ is : [2020, Main]

(a) $\sqrt{2}e$ **(b)** $\dfrac{e}{\sqrt{2}}$

(c) $\dfrac{1}{2}\sqrt{3}e$ **(d)** $\sqrt{3}e$

15. If $y = y(x)$ is the solution of the differential equation $e^y\left(\dfrac{dy}{dx} - 1\right) = e^x$ such that $y(0) = 0$, then

$y(1)$ is equal to : [2020, Main]

(a) $2 + \log_e 2$ **(b)** $2e$

(c) $\log_e 2$ **(d)** $1 + \log_e 2$

16. Let $f(x)$ be a polynomial of degree 3 such that $f(-1) = 10$ m, $f(1) = -6$, $f(x)$ has a critical point at $x = -1$ and $f'(x)$ has a critical point at $x = 1$. Then $f(x)$ has a local minima at $x = $ ....

[2020, Main]

17. If for $x \leq 0$, $y = (x)$ is the solution of the differential equation $(x + 1)dy = ((x + 1))^2 + y - 3)dx$, $y(2) = 0$, then $y(3)$ is equal to ....

[2020, Main]

18. If $y = y(x)$ is the solution of the differential

equation $\dfrac{dy}{dx} = (\tan x - y)\sec^2 x$,

$x \in \left(-\dfrac{\pi}{3}, \dfrac{\pi}{2}\right)$, such that $y(0) = 0$ then

$y\left(-\dfrac{\pi}{4}\right)$ is equal to : [2019, Main]

(a) $e - 2$ **(b)** $\dfrac{1}{2} - e$

(c) $2 + \dfrac{1}{e}$ **(d)** $\dfrac{1}{e} - 2$

19. Let $y = y(x)$ be the solution of the differential

equation, $\dfrac{dy}{dx} + y \tan x = 2x + x^2 \tan x$,

$x \in \left(-\dfrac{\pi}{2}, \dfrac{\pi}{2}\right)$, such that $y(0) = 1$. Then :

[2019, Main]

(a) $y\left(\dfrac{\pi}{4}\right) + y\left(-\dfrac{\pi}{4}\right) = \dfrac{\pi^2}{2} + 2$

(b) $y'\left(\dfrac{\pi}{4}\right) + y'\left(-\dfrac{\pi}{4}\right) = -\sqrt{2}$

(c) $y\left(\dfrac{\pi}{4}\right) - y\left(-\dfrac{\pi}{4}\right) = \sqrt{2}$

(d) $y'\left(\dfrac{\pi}{4}\right) - y'\left(-\dfrac{\pi}{4}\right) = \pi - \sqrt{2}$

20. If $\cos x \dfrac{dy}{dx} - y \sin x = 6x$, $\left(0 < x < \dfrac{\pi}{2}\right)$ and $y\left(\dfrac{\pi}{3}\right)$

$= 0$, then $y\left(\dfrac{\pi}{6}\right)$ is equal to : [2019, Main]

(a) $\dfrac{\pi^2}{2\sqrt{3}}$ **(b)** $-\dfrac{\pi^2}{2}$

(c) $-\dfrac{\pi^2}{2\sqrt{3}}$ **(d)** $-\dfrac{\pi^2}{4\sqrt{3}}$

21. The solution of the differential equation $x\dfrac{dy}{dx} +$

$2y = x^2$ $(x \neq 0)$ with $y(1) = 1$, is : [2019, Main]

(a) $y = \dfrac{4}{5}x^3 + \dfrac{1}{5x^2}$ **(b)** $y = \dfrac{x^3}{5} + \dfrac{1}{5x^2}$

(c) $y = \dfrac{x^2}{4} + \dfrac{3}{4x^2}$ **(d)** $y = \dfrac{3}{4}x^2 + \dfrac{1}{4x^2}$

22. Let $y = y(x)$ be the solution of the differential equation, $(x^2 + 1)^2 \dfrac{dy}{dx} + 2x(x^2 + 1)y = 1$ such that $y(0) = 0$. If $\sqrt{a}\, y(1) = \dfrac{\pi}{32}$, then the value of '$a$' is :

[2019, Main]

(a) $\dfrac{1}{4}$

(b) $\dfrac{1}{2}$

(c) 1

(d) $\dfrac{1}{16}$

23. If $f(1) = 1, f'(1) = 3$, then the derivative of $f(f(f(x))) + (f(x))^2$ at $x = 1$ is : **[2019, Main]**

(a) 33

(b) 12

(c) 15

(d) 9

24. Consider the differential equation, $y^2 dx + \left(x - \dfrac{1}{y}\right) dy = 0$. If value of y is 1 when $x = 1$, then the value of x for which $y = 2$, is : **[2019, Main]**

(a) $\dfrac{5}{2} + \dfrac{1}{\sqrt{e}}$

(b) $\dfrac{3}{2} - \dfrac{1}{\sqrt{e}}$

(c) $\dfrac{1}{2} + \dfrac{1}{\sqrt{e}}$

(d) $\dfrac{3}{2} - \sqrt{e}$

25. If $e^y + xy = e$, the ordered pair $\left(\dfrac{dy}{dx}, \dfrac{d^2y}{dx^2}\right)$ at $x = 0$ is equal to : **[2019, Main]**

(a) $\left(\dfrac{1}{e}, -\dfrac{1}{e^2}\right)$

(b) $\left(-\dfrac{1}{e}, \dfrac{1}{e^2}\right)$

(c) $\left(\dfrac{1}{e}, \dfrac{1}{e^2}\right)$

(d) $\left(-\dfrac{1}{e}, -\dfrac{1}{e^2}\right)$

26. The general solution of the differential equation $(y^2 - x^3)\, dx - xy dx = 0\ (x \neq 0)$ is :
(where c is a constant of integration)
(a) $y^2 - 2x^2 + cx^3 = 0$
(b) $y^2 + 2x^3 + cx^2 = 0$
(c) $y^2 + 2x^2 + cx^3 = 0$
(d) $y^2 - 2x^3 + cx^2 = 0$

27. Let $y = y(x)$ be the solution of the differential equation $\dfrac{dy}{dx} + 2y = f(x)$, where **[2018, Main]**

$$f(x) = \begin{cases} 1, & x \in [0, 1] \\ 0, & \text{otherwise} \end{cases}$$

If $y(0) = 0$, then $y\left(\dfrac{3}{2}\right)$ is :

(a) $\dfrac{e^2 + 1}{2e^4}$

(b) $\dfrac{1}{2e}$

(c) $\dfrac{e^2 - 1}{e^3}$

(d) $\dfrac{e^2 - 1}{2e^3}$

28. Let $y = y(x)$ be the solution of the differential equation

$$\sin x \dfrac{dy}{dx} + y \cos x = 4x, \ x \in (0, \pi). \text{ If } y\left(\dfrac{\pi}{2}\right) = 0, \text{ then}$$

$y\left(\dfrac{\pi}{6}\right)$ is equal to : **[2018, Main]**

(a) $\dfrac{4}{9\sqrt{3}}\pi^2$

(b) $\dfrac{-8}{9\sqrt{3}}\pi^2$

(c) $-\dfrac{8}{9}\pi^2$

(d) $-\dfrac{4}{9}\pi^2$

29. The differential equation representing the family of ellipses having foci either on the x-axis or on the y-axis, centre at the origin and passing through the point $(0, 3)$ is : **[2018, Main]**

(a) $xy\, y'' + x\,(y')^2 - y\, y' = 0$
(b) $x + y\, y'' = 0$
(c) $xy\, y' + y^2 - 9 = 0$
(d) $xy\, y' - y^2 + 9 = 0$

30. If $(2 + \sin x)\dfrac{dy}{dx} + (y + 1)\cos x = 0$ and $y(0) = 1$, then $y\left(\dfrac{\pi}{2}\right)$ is equal to : **[2017, Main]**

(a) $-\dfrac{2}{3}$

(b) $-\dfrac{1}{3}$

(c) $\dfrac{4}{3}$

(d) $\dfrac{1}{3}$

31. If $y = [x + \sqrt{x^2 - 1}]^{15} + [x - \sqrt{x^2 - 1}]^{15}$, then $(x^2 - 1)\dfrac{d^2y}{dx^2} + x\dfrac{dy}{dx}$ is equal to : **[2017, Main]**

(a) $125y$

(b) $224y^2$

(c) $225y^2$

(d) $225y$

32. The curve satisfying the differential equation, $ydx - (x + 3y^2)dy = 0$ and passing through the point $(1, 1)$, also passes through the point : **[2017, Main]**

(a) $\left(\dfrac{1}{4}, -\dfrac{1}{2}\right)$

(b) $\left(-\dfrac{1}{3}, \dfrac{1}{3}\right)$

(c) $\left(\dfrac{1}{3}, -\dfrac{1}{3}\right)$

(d) $\left(\dfrac{1}{4}, \dfrac{1}{2}\right)$

33. If $f(x)$ is a differentiable function in the interval $(0, \infty)$ such that $f(1) = 1$ and $\lim\limits_{t \to x}\dfrac{t^2 f(x) - x^2 f(t)}{t - x} = 1$, for each $x > 0$, then $f\left(\dfrac{3}{2}\right)$ is equal to :

[2016, Main]

(a) $\dfrac{13}{6}$ **(b)** $\dfrac{23}{18}$

(c) $\dfrac{25}{9}$ **(d)** $\dfrac{31}{18}$

34. The solution of the differential equation $\dfrac{dy}{dx} + \dfrac{y}{2}$

$\sec x = \dfrac{\tan x}{2y}$, where $0 \le x < \dfrac{\pi}{2}$, and $y(0) = 1$, is

given by : **[2016, Main]**

(a) $y = 1 - \dfrac{x}{\sec x + \tan x}$

(b) $y^2 = 1 + \dfrac{x}{\sec x + \tan x}$

(c) $y^2 = 1 - \dfrac{x}{\sec x + \tan x}$

(d) $y = 1 + \dfrac{x}{\sec x + \tan x}$

35. The solution of the differential equation $ydx - (x + 2y^2)dy = 0$ is $x = f(y)$.
If $y(-1) = 1$, then $f(1)$ is equal to : **[2015, Main]**
(a) 4 **(b)** 3
(c) 2 **(d)** 1

36. Let $y(x)$ be the solution of the differential equatio
$(x \log x)\dfrac{dy}{dx} + y = 2x \log x,\ (x \ge 1).$ **[2014, Main]**

Then $y(e)$ is equal to :
(a) e **(b)** 0
(c) 2 **(d)** $2e$

37. The general solution of the differential equation,

$\sin 2x\left(\dfrac{dy}{dx} - \sqrt{\tan x}\right) - y = 0$, is : **[2014, Main]**

(a) $y\sqrt{\tan x} = x + c$

(b) $y\sqrt{\cot x} = \tan x + c$

(c) $y\sqrt{\tan x} = \cot x + c$

(d) $y\sqrt{\cot x} = x + c$

38. If the differential equation representing the family of all circles touching x-axis at the origin

is $(x^2 - y^2)\dfrac{dy}{dx} = g(x)\,y$, then $g(x)$ equals :

[2014, Main]

(a) $\dfrac{1}{2}x$ **(b)** $2x^2$

(c) $2x$ **(d)** $\dfrac{1}{2}x^2$

39. $\dfrac{dy}{dx} + y\tan x = \sin 2x$ and $y(0) = 1$, then $y(\pi)$ is

equal to : **[2014, Main]**
(a) 1 **(b)** -1
(c) -5 **(d)** 5

40. If the general solution of the differential equation

$y' = \dfrac{y}{x} + \phi\left(\dfrac{x}{y}\right)$, for some function ϕ, is given by

y In $|cx| = x$, where c is an arbitrary constant,
then ϕ (2) is equal to : **[2014, Main]**

(a) 4 **(b)** $\dfrac{1}{4}$

(c) -4 **(d)** $-\dfrac{1}{4}$

41. Let $f : [1, \infty) \to [2, \infty)$ be a differentiable function such that $f(1) = 2$. If

$$6\int\limits_{1}^{x} f(t)\,dt = 3x\,f(x) - x^3$$

for all $x \ge 1$, then the value of $f(2)$ is :

[2011, Advanced]

42. Let $y'(x) + y(x)g'(x) = g(x)g'(x)$, $y(0) = 0$, $x \in \mathbb{R}$,

where $f'(x)$ denotes $\dfrac{df(x)}{dx}$ and $g(x)$ is a given

non-constant differentiable function on R with $g(0) = g(2) = 0$. Then the value of $y(2)$ is

[2011, Advanced]

43. The differential equation $\dfrac{dy}{dx} = \dfrac{\sqrt{1 - y^2}}{y}$

determines a family of circle with

[2007, Advanced]

(a) variable radii and a fixed centre at $(0, 1)$

(b) variable radii and a fixed centre at $(0, -1)$

(c) fixed radius 1 and variable centres along the x-axis

(d) fixed radius 1 and variable centres along the y-axis.

44. The solution of primitive integral equation $(x^2 + y^2)\,dy = xy\,dx$, is $y = y(x)$. If $y(1) = 1$ and $y(x_0) = e$, then x_0 is : **[2005, Main]**

(a) $\sqrt{2(e^2 - 1)}$ **(b)** $\sqrt{2(e^2 + 1)}$

(c) $\sqrt{3}e$ **(d)** $\sqrt{\dfrac{e^2 + 1}{2}}$

45. For the primitive inetgral equation $ydx + y^2dy = x\,dy$; $x \in R$, $y > 0$, $y = y(x)$, $y(1) = 1$, then $y(-3)$ is : **[2005, Main]**

(a) 3   (b) 2

(c) 1   (d) 5

46. If $y = y(x)$ and $\dfrac{2+\sin x}{y+1}\left(\dfrac{dy}{dx}\right) = -\cos x$, $y(0) = 1$, then $y\left(\dfrac{\pi}{2}\right)$ equals : **[2004, Main]**

(a) 1/3   (b) 2/3

(c) − 1/3   (d) 1

47. If y is a function of x and $\log(x+y) - 2xy = 0$, then the value of $y'(0)$ is equal to : **[2004, Main]**

(a) 1   (b) − 1

(c) 2   (d) − 0

48. If $y(t)$ is a solution of $(1+t)\dfrac{dy}{dt} - ty = 1$ and $y(0) = -1$, then $y(1)$ equal to : **[2003, Main]**

(a) − 1/2   (b) $e + 1/2$

(c) $e - 1/2$ (d) 1/2

49. If $y(x)$ satisfies the differential equation $y' - y\tan x = 2x \sec x$ and $y(0) = 0$, then

(a) $y\left(\dfrac{\pi}{4}\right) = \dfrac{\pi^2}{8\sqrt{2}}$

(b) $y'\left(\dfrac{\pi}{4}\right) = \dfrac{\pi^2}{18}$

(c) $y\left(\dfrac{\pi}{3}\right) = \dfrac{\pi^2}{9}$

(d) $y'\left(\dfrac{\pi}{3}\right) = \dfrac{4\pi}{3} + \dfrac{2\pi^2}{3\sqrt{3}}$

ANSWER KEY

1. (b)	2. (a)	3. (a)	4. (a)	5. (c)	6. (a)	7. (b)	8. (d)	9. (91)	10. (c)
11. (a)	12. (c)	13. (3.00)	14. (d)	15. (d)	16. (3)	17. (3)	18. (a)	19. (d)	20. (c)
21. (c)	22. (d)	23. (a)	24. (b)	25. (b)	26. (b)	27. (d)	28. (c)	29. (d)	30. (d)
31. (d)	32. (b)	33. (d)	34. (c)	35. (b)	36. (c)	37. (d)	38. (c)	39. (c)	40. (d)
41. (6)	42. (9)	43. (c)	44. (c)	45. (a)	46. (a)	47. (a)	48. (a)	49. (a, d)	

ANSWERS WITH EXPLANATIONS

1. Correct Response : (b)

Explanation :

$$\frac{(5+e^x)}{2+y}\frac{dy}{dx} = -e^x$$

$$\int\frac{dy}{2+y} = \int\frac{-e^x}{e^x+5}dx$$

$$\ln(y+2) = -\ln(e^x+5) + \ln C$$

$$(y+2)(e^x+5) = C$$

$$\because \quad y(0) = 1$$

$$\Rightarrow \quad C = 18$$

$$y+2 = \frac{18}{e^x+5}$$

at $x = 13$

$$y+2 = \frac{18}{13+5} = 1$$

$$y = -1.$$

2. Correct Response : (a)

Explanation :

$$\sqrt{1+x^2+y^2+x^2y^2} + xy\frac{dy}{dx} = 0$$

$$\Rightarrow \quad \sqrt{(1+x)^2(1+y^2)} + xy\frac{dy}{dx} = 0$$

$$\Rightarrow \quad \sqrt{1+x^2}\sqrt{1+y^2} = -xy\frac{dy}{dx}$$

$$\Rightarrow \quad \int\frac{y\,dy}{\sqrt{1+y^2}} = -\int\frac{\sqrt{1+x^2}}{x}dx \quad \text{...(1)}$$

Now put $1+x^2 = u^2$ and $1+y^2 = v^2$

$$2x\,dx = 2u\,du \text{ and } 2y\,dy = 2v\,dv$$

$$\Rightarrow \quad x\,dx = u\,du \text{ and } y\,dy = v\,dv$$

Substituting these values in equation (1)

$$\int\frac{v\,dv}{v} = -\int\frac{u\times u\,du}{x^2}$$

$$\int\frac{v\,dv}{v} = -\int\frac{u^2\,du}{u^2-1}$$

$$\int\frac{v\,dv}{v} = -\int\frac{u^2.du}{u^2-1}$$

$$\Rightarrow \quad \int dv = -\int\frac{u^2-1+1}{u^2-1}du$$

$$\Rightarrow \quad v = -\int\left(1+\frac{1}{u^2-1}\right)du$$

$$\Rightarrow \qquad v = -u - \frac{1}{2}\log_e\left|\frac{u-1}{u+1}\right| + c$$

$$\Rightarrow \sqrt{1+y^2} = -\sqrt{1+x^2} + \frac{1}{2}\log_e\left|\frac{\sqrt{1+x^2}+1}{\sqrt{1+x^2}-1}\right| + c$$

$$\Rightarrow \sqrt{1+y^2} + \sqrt{1+x^2} = \frac{1}{2}\log_e\left|\frac{\sqrt{1+x^2}+1}{\sqrt{1+x^2}-1}\right| + c.$$

3. **Correct Response :** (a)

   Explanation :

$$y = \left(\frac{2x}{\pi}-1\right)\cosec x \qquad \ldots(1)$$

$$\frac{dy}{dx} = \frac{2}{\pi}\cosec x - \left(\frac{2x}{\pi}-1\right)\cosec x \cot x$$

$$\frac{dy}{dx} = \frac{2\cosec x}{\pi} - y\cot x$$

using equation (1)

$$\frac{dy}{dx} + y\cot x = \frac{2\cosec x}{\pi}$$

$$\frac{dy}{dx} + p(x).y = \frac{2\cosec x}{\pi}, \ x \in \left(0, \frac{\pi}{2}\right)$$

Compare : $p(x) = \cot x$

4. **Correct Response :** (a)

   Explanation :

$$x\frac{dy}{dx} - y = x^2(x\cos x + \sin x), \ x > 0$$

$$\frac{dy}{dx} - \frac{y}{x} = x(x\cos x + \sin x)$$

$$\Rightarrow \quad \frac{dy}{dx} + Py = Q$$

so, $\quad$ I.F. $= e^{\int -\frac{1}{x}dx} = \frac{1}{|x|} = \frac{1}{x}(x > 0)$

Thus, $\quad \dfrac{y}{x} = \int \dfrac{1}{x}[x(x\cos x + \sin x)]\,dx$

$$\Rightarrow \quad \frac{y}{x} = x\sin x + C$$

$\because \qquad y(\pi) = \pi \Rightarrow C = 1$

so, $\qquad y = x^2\sin x + x$

$$\Rightarrow \quad (y)_{\pi/2} = \frac{\pi^2}{4} + \frac{\pi}{2}$$

Also, $\quad \dfrac{dy}{dx} = x^2\cos x + 2x\sin x + 1$

$$\Rightarrow \quad \frac{d^2y}{dx^2} = -x^2\sin x + 4x\cos x + 2\sin x$$

$$\Rightarrow \quad \frac{d^2y}{dx^2}\bigg|_{\frac{\pi}{2}} = -\frac{\pi^2}{4} + 2$$

Thus, $y_{\left(\frac{\pi}{2}\right)} + \dfrac{d^2y}{dx^2}_{\left(\frac{\pi}{2}\right)} = \dfrac{\pi}{2} + 2$

5. **Correct Response :** (c)

   Explanation :

$$n(y + 3x) = z \qquad \text{(let)}$$

$$\frac{1}{y+3x}\left(\frac{dy}{dx}+3\right) = \frac{dz}{dx} \qquad \ldots(1)$$

$$\frac{dy}{dx} + 3 = \frac{y+3x}{\ln(y+3x)} \qquad \text{(given)}$$

$$\frac{1}{(y+3x)}\frac{(y+3x)}{\ln(y+3x)} = \frac{dz}{dx}$$

$$\frac{dz}{dx} = \frac{1}{z}$$

$$\Rightarrow \quad z\,dz = dx \Rightarrow \frac{z^2}{2} = x + C$$

$$\Rightarrow \quad \frac{1}{2}\ln 2(y+3x) = x + C$$

$$\Rightarrow \quad x - \frac{1}{2}[\ln(y+3x)]^2 = C.$$

6. **Correct Response :** (a)

   Explanation :

$$\cos x\frac{dy}{dx} + 2y\sin x = \sin 2x$$

$$\frac{dy}{dx} + \frac{2\sin x}{\cos x}y = 2\sin x$$

$$\text{I.F.} = e^{\int 2\frac{\sin x}{\cos x}dx} = e^{\int 2\tan x\,dx}$$
$$= e^{2\,ln\,\sec x} = \sec^2 x$$
$$y \cdot \sec^2 x = \int \sin x \cdot \sec^2 x\,dx$$
$$y\sec^2 x = 2\int \tan x\sec x\,dx$$
$$y\sec^2 x = 2\sec x + c$$

At $x = \dfrac{\pi}{3}$, $y = 0$

$$\Rightarrow \quad 0 = 2\sec\frac{\pi}{3} + C \Rightarrow C = -4$$

$$y\sec^2 x = 2\sec x - 4$$

Put $\qquad x = \dfrac{\pi}{4}$

$$y \cdot 2 = 2\sqrt{2} - 4$$
$$y = \sqrt{2} - 2.$$

7. **Correct Response :** (b)

   Explanation :

$$2x^2 dy = (2xy + y^2)\,dx$$

$$\Rightarrow \quad \frac{dy}{dx} = \frac{2xy + y^2}{2x^2}$$

{Homogeneous D.E.}

$$\begin{bmatrix} \text{let } y = xt \\ \Rightarrow \dfrac{dy}{dx} = t + x\dfrac{dt}{dx} \end{bmatrix}$$

$$\Rightarrow \quad t + x\frac{dt}{dx} = \frac{2x^2 t + x^2 t^2}{2x^2}$$

$$\Rightarrow \quad t + x\frac{dt}{dx} = t + \frac{t^2}{2}$$

$$\Rightarrow \quad x\frac{dt}{dx} = \frac{t^2}{2}$$

$$\Rightarrow \quad 2\int \frac{dt}{t^2} = \int \frac{dx}{x}$$

$$\Rightarrow \quad 2\left(-\frac{1}{t}\right) = ln(x) + C \quad \left\{ \text{Put } t = \frac{y}{x}\right\}$$

$$\Rightarrow \quad -\frac{2x}{y} = ln\,x + C$$

$$\begin{bmatrix} \text{Put } x = 1 \,\&\, y = 2 \\ \text{then we get } C = -1 \end{bmatrix}$$

$$\Rightarrow \quad \frac{-2x}{y} = ln(x) - 1$$

$$\Rightarrow \quad y = \frac{2x}{1 - ln\,x}$$

$$\Rightarrow \quad f(x) = \frac{2x}{1 - \log_e x}$$

$$f\left(\frac{1}{2}\right) = \frac{2 \times \dfrac{1}{2}}{1 - \log_e\left(\dfrac{1}{2}\right)}$$

so, $\quad f\left(\dfrac{1}{2}\right) = \dfrac{1}{1 + \log_e 2}$

8. Correct Response : (d)

Explanation :

$$\frac{2 + \sin x}{y + 1}\frac{dy}{dx} = -\cos x, \ y > 0$$

$$\Rightarrow \quad \frac{dy}{y+1} = \frac{-\cos x}{2 + \sin x}dx$$

By integrating both sides :
$$ln|y + 1| = -ln|2 + \sin x| + ln\,K$$

$$\Rightarrow \quad y + 1 = \frac{K}{2 + \sin x} \qquad (y + 1 > 0)$$

$$\Rightarrow \quad y(x) = \frac{K}{2 + \sin x} - 1$$

Given $y(0) = 1 \Rightarrow K = 4$

So, $\quad y(x) = \dfrac{4}{2 + \sin x} - 1$

$$a = y(\pi) = 1$$

$$b = \frac{dy}{dx}\bigg]_{x = \pi}$$

$$= \frac{-\cos x}{2 + \sin x}(y(x) + 1)\bigg]_{x = \pi} = 1$$

So, $(a, b) = (1, 1)$

9. Correct Response : (91)

Explanation :

Put $\cos \alpha = \dfrac{3}{5}$, $\sin \alpha = \dfrac{4}{5}$ $\ 0 < \alpha < \dfrac{\pi}{2}$

Now $\dfrac{3}{5}\cos kx - \dfrac{4}{5}\sin kx$

$$= \cos \alpha . \cos kx - \sin \alpha . \sin kx$$
$$= \cos(\alpha + kx)$$

As we have to find derivate at $x = 0$
We have $\cos^{-1}(\cos(\alpha + kx))$
$$= (\alpha + kx)$$

$$\Rightarrow \quad y = \sum_{k=1}^{6} k(\alpha + kx)$$

$$\Rightarrow \quad \frac{dy}{dx}\bigg|_{at\,x=0} = \sum_{k=x}^{6} k^2 = \frac{6 \times 7 \times 13}{6} = 91$$

10. Correct Response : (c)

Explanation :

$$(y^2 - x)\frac{dy}{dx} = 1$$

$$\Rightarrow \quad \frac{dy}{dx} + x = y^2$$

$$\text{I.F.} = e^{\int dy} = e^y$$

Solution is given by
$$x\,e^y = \int y^2 e^y dx + C$$

$$\Rightarrow \quad xe^y = (y^2 - 2y + 2)\,e^y + C$$
$$\Rightarrow x = 0, y = 1, \text{ gives } C = -e$$
If $y = 0$, then $x = 2 - e$

11. Correct Response : (a)

Explanation :

$$2x = 4by'$$

$$\Rightarrow \quad y' = \frac{2x}{4b}$$

Required D.E. is $x^2 = \dfrac{2x}{y'}y + \left(\dfrac{x}{y'}\right)^2$

$$\Rightarrow \quad x(y')^2 = 2yy' + x$$

12. Correct Response : (c)

Explanation :

$$f'(x) = \tan^{-1}(\sec x + \tan x)$$

$$= \tan^{-1}\left(\frac{1+\sin x}{\cos x}\right)$$

$$= \tan^{-1}\left(\frac{1+\tan\dfrac{x}{2}}{1-\tan\dfrac{x}{2}}\right)$$

$$= \tan^{-1}\left[\tan\left(\frac{\pi}{4}+\frac{x}{2}\right)\right]$$

$$\because \quad \frac{x}{2} < x < \frac{x}{2} \Rightarrow 0 < \frac{\pi}{4}+\frac{x}{2} < \frac{x}{2}$$

$$\Rightarrow \quad f'(x) = \frac{\pi}{4}+\frac{x}{2}$$

$$\therefore \quad f'(x) = \frac{\pi}{4}x+\frac{x^2}{2}+c$$

$$\because \quad f'(0) = 0 \Rightarrow c = 0$$

$$\Rightarrow \quad f'(x) = \frac{\pi}{4}x+\frac{x^2}{4}$$

$$\Rightarrow \quad f'(1) = \left(\frac{\pi+1}{4}\right)$$

13. Correct Response : (3.00)

Explanation :

$$(x+1)dy - ydx = ((x+1)^2 - 3)dx$$

$$\Rightarrow \frac{(x+1)dy - ydx}{(x+1)^2} = \left(1-\frac{3}{(x+1)^2}\right)dx$$

$$\Rightarrow \quad d\left(\frac{y}{(x+1)}\right) = \left(1-\frac{3}{(x+1)^2}\right)dx$$

integrating both sides

$$\frac{y}{x+1} = x+\frac{3}{(x+1)}+C$$

Given $y(2) = 0 \Rightarrow c = -3$

$$\therefore \quad y = (x+1)\left(x+\frac{3}{(x+1)}-3\right)$$

$$\therefore \quad y(3) = 3.00$$

14. Correct Response : (d)

Explanation :

$$\frac{dy}{dx} = \frac{xy}{x^2+y^2}$$

Let $\qquad y = vx$

$$\frac{dy}{dx} = v+x.\frac{dv}{dx}$$

$$v+x\frac{dv}{dx} = \frac{xvx}{x^2+v^2x^2} = \frac{v}{1+v^2}$$

$$x\frac{dv}{dx} = \frac{v}{1+v^2}-v$$

$$= \frac{v-v-v^3}{1+v^2} = \frac{v^3}{1+v^2}$$

$$\int\frac{1+v^2}{v^3}.dv = \int-\frac{dx}{x}$$

$$\Rightarrow \quad \int v^{-3}.dv + \int\frac{1}{v}dv = -\int\frac{dx}{x}$$

$$\Rightarrow \quad \frac{v^{-2}}{-2}+\ell nv = -\ell nx + \lambda$$

$$\Rightarrow \quad \frac{1}{2v^2}+\ell n\left(\frac{y}{x}\right) = -\ell nx + 1$$

$$\Rightarrow \quad -\frac{1}{2}\frac{x^2}{y^2}+\ell ny - \ell nx = -\ell nx + \lambda$$

$$\Rightarrow \quad -\frac{1}{2}+0 = \lambda \Rightarrow \lambda = -\frac{1}{2}$$

$$\Rightarrow \quad -\frac{1}{2}\frac{x^2}{y^2}+\ell ny + \frac{1}{2} = 0 \text{ at } y = e$$

$$\Rightarrow \quad -\frac{1}{2}\frac{x^2}{e^2}+1+\frac{1}{2} = 0$$

$$\Rightarrow \quad \frac{x^2}{2e^2} = \frac{3}{2} \Rightarrow x^2 = 3e^2$$

$$\therefore \quad x = \sqrt{3}e$$

15. Correct Response : (d)

Explanation :

$$e^y\frac{dy}{dx}-e^y = e^x, \text{ Let } e^y = t$$

$$\Rightarrow \quad e^y\frac{dy}{dx} = \frac{dt}{dx}$$

$$\frac{dt}{dx}-t = e^x$$

$$\therefore \quad \text{I.F.} = e^{\int -dx} = e^{-x}$$

$$te^{-x} = x+c$$

$$\Rightarrow \quad e^{y-x} = x+c$$

$$y(0) = 0 \Rightarrow c = 1$$

$$e^{y-x} = x+1 \Rightarrow y(1) = 1+\log_e 2$$

16. Correct Response : (3.00)

Explanation :

$$f''(x) = \lambda(x-1)$$

$$f'(x) = \frac{\lambda x^2}{2}-\lambda x+C \Rightarrow f'(-1) = 0 \Rightarrow c = \frac{-3\lambda}{2}$$

$$f(x) = \frac{\lambda x^3}{6}-\frac{\lambda x^2}{2}-\frac{3\lambda}{2}x+d$$

$$f(1) = -6 \Rightarrow -11\lambda + 6d = -36 \qquad ...(i)$$

$$f(-1) = 10 \Rightarrow 5\lambda + 6d = 60 \qquad ...(ii)$$

From (i) and (ii) $\lambda = 6$ and $d = 5$

$$f(x) = x^3 - 3x^2 - 9x + 5$$

Which has minima at $x = 3$

17. Correct Response : (3.00)

Explanation :

$(x + 1)\,dy - y\,dx = ((x + 1)^2 - 3)dx$

$$\Rightarrow \quad \frac{(x+1)dy - y\,dx}{(x+1)^2} = \left(1 - \frac{3}{(x+1)^2}\right)dx$$

$$\Rightarrow \quad d\left(\frac{y}{(x+1)}\right) = \left(1 - \frac{3}{(x+1)^2}\right)dx$$

integrating both sides

$$\frac{y}{x+1} = x + \frac{3}{(x+1)} + C$$

Given $y(2) = 0 \Rightarrow c = -3$

$$y = (x + 1)\left(x + \frac{3}{(x+1)} - 3\right)$$

$$y(3) = 3.00$$

18. Correct Response : (a)

Explanation :

$$\frac{dy}{dx} + y\sec^2 x = \tan x \sec^2 x$$

I.F. for the above linear differential equation is

$$e^{\int \sec^2 x\, dx} = e^{\tan x}$$

Solution to the given differential equation is

$$y \times \text{I.F.} = \int q(x)\,(\text{I.F.})dx$$

$$\Rightarrow \quad y e^{\tan x} = \int e^{\tan x} \tan x \sec^2 x\, dx$$

Put $\tan x = t$

$$y e^{\tan x} = \int e^t t\, dt$$

$$= t e^t - e^t + C$$

$$= e^t (t - 1) + C$$

$$0 = -1 + C \Rightarrow C = 1$$

Hence, $\quad y\left(-\dfrac{\pi}{4}\right) = -1 - 1 + e = e - 2$

19. Correct Response : (d)

Explanation :

$$\frac{dy}{dx} + y\tan x = +2x + x^2 \tan x$$

I.F. for the above linear differential equation is

$$e^{\int \ln \sec x\, dx} = \sec x$$

Solution to the given differential equation is

$$y \times \text{I.F.} = \int q(x)\,(\text{I.F.})dx$$

$$\Rightarrow \quad y \sec x = \int (2x + x^2 \tan x)\sec x\, dx$$

$$\Rightarrow \quad y \sec x = \int (2x)\sec x\, dx$$

$$+ \int x^2 \sec x \tan x\, dx$$

$$\Rightarrow \quad y \sec x = \int 2x \sec x\, dx + (x^2 \sec x$$

$$- \int 2x \sec x\, dx + C)$$

$$\Rightarrow \quad y \sec x = x^2 \sec x + C$$

$$\Rightarrow \quad y = x^2 + C \cos x$$

Now, $\quad y(0) = 1 \Rightarrow y = x^2 + \cos x$

$$\Rightarrow \quad y\left(\frac{\pi}{4}\right) = \frac{\pi^2}{16} + \frac{1}{\sqrt{2}}$$

$$\Rightarrow \quad y' = 2x - \sin x$$

$$\Rightarrow \quad y'\left(\frac{\pi}{4}\right) = \frac{\pi}{2} - \frac{1}{\sqrt{2}}$$

$$\Rightarrow \quad y'\left(-\frac{\pi}{4}\right) = -\frac{\pi}{2} + \frac{1}{\sqrt{2}}$$

$$\Rightarrow \quad y\left(\frac{\pi}{4}\right) - y'\left(-\frac{\pi}{4}\right) = \pi - \sqrt{2}$$

20. Correct Response : (c)

Explanation :

$$\frac{dy}{dx} + y\tan x = 6x \sec x$$

I.F. for the above linear differential equation is

$$e^{\int \tan x\, dx} = e^{-\ln(\sec x)}$$

$$= \cos x$$

Solution to the given differential equation is

$$y \times \text{I.F.} = \int q(x)\,(\text{I.F.})dx$$

$$\Rightarrow \quad y \cos x = \int 6x\, dx$$

$$\Rightarrow \quad y \cos x = 3x^2 + C$$

As $y\left(\dfrac{\pi}{3}\right) = 0$ therefore,

$$0 = 3\left(\frac{\pi^2}{9}\right) + C$$

$$\Rightarrow \quad C = -\frac{\pi^2}{3}$$

So the solution beomces

$$y \cos x = 3x^2 - \frac{\pi^2}{3}$$

At $x = \dfrac{\pi}{6}$,

$$y \times \frac{\sqrt{3}}{2} = 3 \times \frac{\pi^2}{36} - \frac{\pi^2}{3}$$

$$\Rightarrow \qquad \frac{\sqrt{3}y}{2} = -\frac{\pi^2}{4}$$

$$\Rightarrow \qquad y = -\frac{\pi^2}{2\sqrt{3}}$$

21. Correct Response : (c)

Explanation :

$$\frac{x\,dy}{dx} + 2y = x^2$$

$$\Rightarrow \qquad \frac{dy}{dx} + \frac{2y}{x} = x$$

$$\text{I.F.} = e^{\int \frac{2}{x}dx}$$

$$= x^{2\,\ln n}$$

Solution is

$$yx^2 = \int x^3 dx$$

$$yx^2 = \frac{x^4}{4} + C$$

$$1 = \frac{1}{4} + C \Rightarrow C = \frac{3}{4}$$

$$y = \frac{x^2}{4} + \frac{3}{4x^2}$$

22. Correct Response : (d)

Explanation :

$$(x^2 + 1)\frac{dy}{dx} + 2x(x^2 + 1)y = 1$$

$$\frac{dy}{dx} + \frac{2x}{x^2 + 1}y = \frac{1}{(x^2 + 1)^2}$$

Linear differential equation

$$\text{I.F.} = e^{\int \frac{2x}{x^2+1}dx}$$

$$= e^{\ln(x^2 + 1)}$$

$$= x^2 + 1$$

Therefore, $\qquad y(\text{I.F.}) = \int Q(\text{I.F.})\,dx$

$$y(x^2 + 1) = \int \frac{1}{(x^2 + 1)^2}(x^2 + 1)dx + C$$

$$y(x^2 + 1) = \tan^{-1} x + C$$

$$y(0) = 0$$

$$\Rightarrow \qquad C = 0$$

$$\Rightarrow \qquad y(x^2 + 1) = \tan^{-1} x$$

$$\Rightarrow \qquad y(1) = \frac{\pi}{8}$$

$$\Rightarrow \qquad a = \frac{1}{16}$$

23. Correct Response : (a)

Explanation :

$$y = f(f(f(x))) + (f(x))^2$$

$$\frac{dy}{dx} = f'(f(f(x))) \cdot f'(f(x)) \cdot f'(x) + 2f(x)\,f'(x)$$

Put $x = 1$

$$f'(f(f(1))) \cdot f'(f(1)) \cdot f'(1) + 2f(1)\,f'(1) = 27 + 6$$

$$= 33$$

24. Correct Response : (b)

Explanation :

The given equation is,

$$y^2 dx + \left(x - \frac{1}{y}\right)dy = 0$$

$$\frac{dx}{dy} + \frac{x}{y^2} = \frac{1}{y^3}$$

The integrating factor is,

$$\text{I.F.} = \frac{1}{y^2}$$

The solution is,

$$e^{\frac{1}{y}} = \int \left(e^{-\frac{1}{y}}\right)\left(\frac{1}{y^3}\right)dy$$

Put $\dfrac{-1}{y} = t$.

The integral changes to,

$$xe^t = \int e^t(-t)\,dt$$

$$= -(te^t - e^t) + c$$

$$xe^{-\frac{1}{y}} = e^{-\frac{1}{y}}\left(1 + \frac{1}{y}\right) + c$$

$$x = 1 + \frac{1}{y} + ce^{\frac{1}{y}}$$

The curve passes through point (1, 1). Therefore,

$$c = -\frac{1}{e}$$

Hence, the curve equation is,

$$x = 1 + \frac{1}{y} - e^{\frac{1}{y}-1}$$

The curve passes through $(k, 2)$.

Therefore, the value of k is,

$$k = 1 + \frac{1}{2} - e^{-\frac{1}{2}}$$

$$= \frac{3}{2} - \frac{1}{\sqrt{e}}$$

25. Correct Response : (b)

Explanation :

It is given that

$$e^y + xy = e \qquad ...(i)$$

In the above equation, when $x = 0$,

$$e^y = e$$
$$y = 1$$

Differentiate equation (i) with respect to x.

$$e^y \frac{dy}{dx} + x \frac{dy}{dx} + y = 0 \qquad ...(ii)$$

Put $x = 0$ and $y = 1$ in the above equation.

$$e \frac{dy}{dx} + 1 = 0$$

$$\frac{dy}{dx} = \frac{-1}{e}$$

Differentiate equation (ii) with respect to x,

$$e^y \frac{d^2 y}{d^2 x} + e^y \left(\frac{dy}{dx}\right)^2 + x \frac{d^2 y}{d^2 x} + 2 \frac{dy}{dx} = 0$$

Put $x = 0$ and $y = 1$ in the above equation.

$$e^y \frac{d^2 y}{d^2 x} + e \left(\frac{-1}{e}\right)^2 + (0) \frac{d^2 y}{d^2 x} + 2 \left(\frac{-1}{e}\right) = 0$$

$$\frac{d^2 y}{dx^2} = \frac{1}{e^2}$$

26. Correct Response : (b)

Explanation :

The given equation is,

$$(y^2 - x^3) dx - xy \, dy = 0$$

$$y(y \, dx - x \, dy) = x^3 \, dx$$

$$\frac{y}{x} \left(\frac{y \, dx - x \, dy}{x^2}\right) = dx$$

$$-\left(\frac{y}{x}\right) d\left(\frac{y}{x}\right) = dx$$

Solve further,

$$-\frac{1}{2} \left(\frac{y}{x}\right)^2 = x + k$$

$$-y^2 = 2x^3 + 2x^2 k$$

$$y^2 + 2x^3 + cx^2 = 0$$

27. Correct Response : (d)

Explanation :

The given differential equation is,

$$\frac{dy}{dx} + 2y = f(x)$$

The solution of the above equation is,

$$y = y(x)$$

Let,

$$e^{\int 2 dx} = e^{2x}$$

The solution of the above equations is,

$$y \cdot e^{2x} = \int f(x) \cdot e^{2x} \, dx + C$$

$$y(x) = e^{-2x} \int_0^x f(x) e^{2x} dx + Ce^{-2x} \qquad ...(1)$$

At $x = 0$,

$$y(0) = e^{-2(0)} \int_0^0 f(0) e^{2(0)} dx + Ce^{-2(0)}$$

$$= 0 + C$$

$$= C$$

The given condition is,

$$y(0) = 0$$

$$C = 0$$

From equation (1),

$$y(x) = e^{-2x} \int_0^x f(x) e^{2x} dx + (0) e^{-2x}$$

$$= e^{-2x} \int_0^x f(x) e^{2x} dx$$

At $x = \frac{3}{2}$,

$$y\left(\frac{3}{2}\right) = e^{-2\left(\frac{3}{2}\right)} \int_0^1 e^{2x} dx + \int_1^{3/2} 0 \cdot dx$$

$$= e^{-3} \left(\frac{e^2 - e^0}{2}\right) + 0$$

$$= e^{-3} \left(\frac{e^2 - 1}{2}\right)$$

$$= \frac{e^2 - 1}{2e^3}$$

28. Correct Response : (c)

Explanation :

The given differential equation is,

$$\sin x \frac{dy}{dx} + y \cos x = 4x$$

$$\frac{dy}{dx} + y \cot x = \frac{4}{\sin x}$$

$$\text{I.F.} = e^{\int \cot x \, dx}$$

$$\text{I.F.} = \sin x$$

The solution of the equation is given by,

$$y \sin x = \int \frac{4x}{\sin x} \cdot \sin x \, dx$$

$$y \sin x = 2x^2 + c$$

Apply boundary conditions,

$$y = 0 \text{ at } x = \frac{\pi}{2}$$

$$c = -\frac{\pi^2}{2}$$

The equation is,

$$y \sin x = 2x^2 - \frac{\pi^2}{2}$$

At $x = \frac{\pi}{6}$, the above equation becomes,

$$y \frac{1}{2} = 2 \frac{\pi^2}{36} - \frac{\pi^2}{2}$$

$$y = -\frac{8\pi^2}{9}$$

29. **Correct Response :** (d)

Explanation :

Equation of ellipse,

$$\frac{x^2}{a^2} + \frac{y^2}{b^2} = 1$$

It passes from (0, 3).

$$\frac{x^2}{a^2} + \frac{y^2}{9} = 1 \qquad\qquad ...(1)$$

$$\frac{x}{a^2} dx = \frac{-y}{9} dx$$

$$\frac{1}{a^2} = -\frac{y}{9x} \frac{dy}{dx} \qquad\qquad ...(2)$$

From equation (1) and (2),

$$-\frac{yx}{9} \frac{dy}{dx} + \frac{y^2}{9} = 1$$

$$xyy' - y^2 + 9 = 0$$

30. **Correct Response :** (d)

Explanation :

The provided equation is,

$$(2 + \sin x) \frac{dy}{dx} + (y + 1) \cos x = 0$$

Rearrange,

$$\frac{1}{y+1} dy + \frac{\cos x}{2 + \sin x} dx = 0$$

Integrate the above equation.

$$\ln|y + 1| + \ln|2 + \sin x| = \ln C$$
$$(y + 1)(2 + \sin x) = C$$

Substitute $x = 0$, $y = 1$ in the above equation,

$$(y + 1)(2 + \sin x) = C$$
$$(1 + 1)(2 + \sin 0) = C$$
$$C = 4$$

For $x = \frac{\pi}{2}$,

$$(y + 1)(2 + 1) = 4$$
$$y + 1 = \frac{4}{3}$$
$$y = \frac{1}{3}$$

31. **Correct Response :** (d)

Explanation :

Given equation is,

$$y = [x + \sqrt{x^2 - 1}]^{15} + [x - \sqrt{x^2 - 1}]^{15} \qquad ...(1)$$

Consider $[x + \sqrt{x^2 - 1}]^{15} = t$

Differentiate the above equations with respect to x,

$$\frac{dt}{dx} = 15[x + \sqrt{x^2 - 1}]^{14} \cdot \left[1 + \frac{x}{\sqrt{x^2 - 1}}\right]$$

$$\frac{dt}{dx} = \frac{15}{\sqrt{x^2 - 1}} \cdot [x + \sqrt{x^2 - 1}]^{15}$$

$$\frac{dt}{dx} = \frac{15}{\sqrt{x^2 - 1}} \cdot t$$

Rationalize the term $[x - \sqrt{x^2 - 1}]^{15}$,

$$[x - \sqrt{x^2 - 1}]^{15} = \frac{[x - \sqrt{x^2 - 1}]^{15} \times [x + \sqrt{x^2 - 1}]^{15}}{[x + \sqrt{x^2 - 1}]^{15}}$$

$$= \frac{[x^2 - (x^2 - 1)]^{15}}{[x + \sqrt{x^2 - 1}]^{15}}$$

$$= \frac{1}{[x + \sqrt{x^2 - 1}]^{15}} = \frac{1}{t}$$

The equation becomes :

$$y = \left(t + \frac{1}{t}\right)$$

$$\frac{dy}{dx} = \left(1 - \frac{1}{t^2}\right) \times \frac{dt}{dx}$$

$$= \left(1 - \frac{1}{t^2}\right) \times \frac{15}{\sqrt{x^2 - 1}} \cdot t$$

$$\sqrt{x^2 - 1} \frac{dy}{dx} = 15\left(t + \frac{1}{t}\right)$$

Differentiating the above equation w.r.t. x,

$$\sqrt{x^2 - 1} \frac{d^2y}{dx^2} + \frac{x}{\sqrt{x^2 - 1}} \frac{dy}{dx} = 15\left(1 + \frac{1}{t^2}\right) \times \frac{dt}{dx}$$

$$\frac{(x^2 - 1)\frac{d^2y}{dx^2} + x\frac{dy}{dx}}{\sqrt{x^2 - 1}} = 15\left(1 + \frac{1}{t^2}\right) \times \frac{15}{\sqrt{x^2 - 1}} \cdot t$$

$$(x^2 - 1)\frac{d^2y}{dx^2} + x\frac{dy}{dx} = 225\left(t + \frac{1}{t}\right)$$

Rearrange the above equation.

$$(x^2 - 1)\frac{d^2y}{dx^2} + x\frac{dy}{dx} = 225\, y$$

32. Correct Response : (b)

Explanation :

Simplify the given differential equation.

$$y\,dx - (x + 3y^2)\,dy = 0$$

$$\frac{dx}{dy} = \frac{x}{y} + 3y$$

$$\frac{dx}{dy} - \frac{x}{y} = 3y$$

Integrate the above factor.

$$\text{I.F.} = e^{-\int \frac{1}{y}dy}$$

$$= e^{-\ln y}$$

$$= \frac{1}{y}$$

Hence, the solution is,

$$\frac{x}{y} = \int 3y \cdot \text{IF}\,dy$$

$$= \int 3y \times \frac{1}{y}\,dy$$

$$= 3y + C$$

Satisfying the given point in equation,

$$1 = 3 + C$$

$$C = -2$$

Hence, the solution is,

$$x = 3y^2 - 2y$$

Thus, the option (b) satisfies the solution.

33. Correct Response : (d)

Explanation :

The given function is,

$$\lim_{t \to x} \frac{t^2 \cdot f(x) - x^2 f(t)}{t - x} = 1$$

Apply the L-Hospital's rule in the above equation,

$$\lim_{t \to x} \frac{2t \cdot f(x) - x^2 f'(t)}{1 - x} = 1$$

$$\Rightarrow \quad \frac{2xf(x) - x^2 f'(x)}{1 - 0} = 1$$

$$\Rightarrow \quad -x^2 f'(x) = 1 - 2xf(x)$$

$$\Rightarrow \quad f'(x) = \frac{2xf(x) - 1}{x^2}$$

Replace, $f'(x)$ with $\dfrac{dy}{dx}$,

$$\frac{dy}{dx} = \frac{2xy}{x^2} - \frac{1}{x^2}$$

$$\frac{dy}{dx} - y\left(\frac{2}{x}\right) = -\frac{1}{x^2}$$

Compare the above equation with equation,

$$\frac{dy}{dx} + Px = Q$$

Now, calculate the value of the integrating factor,

$$\text{I.F.} = e^{\int P dx}$$

Substitute the value in the above I.F.,

$$\text{I.F.} = e^{-\int \frac{2}{x}dx}$$

$$= e^{-2\ln x}$$

$$= \frac{1}{3x^3}$$

Now, the solution of the differential equation is,

$$y(P) = \int Q \times (\text{I.F.})\,dx$$

Substitute the value,

$$y\left(\frac{1}{x^2}\right) = \int -\frac{1}{x^4}\,dx$$

$$\frac{y}{x^2} = \frac{1}{3x^3} + c$$

Substitute the value $x = 1$, $y = 1$ in the above equation,

$$\frac{1}{1} = \frac{1}{3} + c$$

$$c = 1 - \frac{1}{3}$$

$$= \frac{2}{3}$$

Substitute the value of c in the equation,

$$\frac{y}{x^2} = \frac{1}{3x^3} + \frac{2}{3}$$

$$f(x) = \frac{1}{3x} + \frac{2x^2}{3}$$

Hence, the value of $f\left(\dfrac{3}{2}\right)$ is,

$$f(x) = \frac{1}{3x} + \frac{2x^2}{3}$$

$$= \frac{1}{3 \times \left(\dfrac{3}{2}\right)} + \frac{2}{3} \times \left(\frac{3}{2}\right)^2$$

$$f\left(\frac{3}{2}\right) = \frac{31}{18}$$

34. Correct Response : (c)

Explanation :

The given differential equation is,

$$\frac{dy}{dx} + \frac{y}{2}\sec x = \frac{\tan x}{2y}$$

$$2y\frac{dy}{dx} + y^2 \sec x = \tan x \qquad \text{...(1)}$$

Put
$$y^2 = t$$

Differentiate the above equation with respect to x,

$$\frac{d}{dx}\left(y^2\right) = \frac{dt}{dx}$$

$$2y\frac{dy}{dx} = \frac{dt}{dx}$$

From equation (1),

$$\frac{dt}{dx} + t \sec x = \tan x \qquad \text{...(2)}$$

The integrated factor of the above equation is,

$$\text{I.F.} = e^{\int \sec x \, dx}$$

$$\left[\because \int \sec x \, dx = \ln|\sec x + \tan x|\right]$$

$$= e^{\ln(\sec x + \tan x)}$$

$$= \sec x + \tan x$$

The solution of differential equation (2) is,

$$t \cdot (\sec x + \tan x) = \int (\sec x + \tan x)\tan x \, dx$$

$$t \cdot (\sec x + \tan x) = \int \sec x \tan x \, dx + \int \tan^2 x \, dx$$

$$y^2 (\sec x + \tan x) = \sec x + \tan x - x + C$$

$$y^2 = 1 - \frac{x}{\sec x + \tan x}$$

$$[\because y(0) = 1 \Rightarrow C = 0]$$

35. Correct Response : (b)

Explanation :

The given differential equation is,
$$y\,dx - (x + 2y^2)\,dy = 0$$

Simplify the given differential equation,
$$\frac{y\,dx - x\,dy}{y^2} = 2\,dy$$

$$d\left(\frac{x}{y}\right) = 2\,dy$$

Integrate both sides,
$$\frac{x}{y} = 2y + c$$

At $(-1, 1)$,
$$-1 = -2 + c$$
$$c = 1$$

The solution of the differential equation is,
$$\frac{x}{y} = 2y + 1$$
$$x = 2y^2 + y$$
$$f(y) = 2y^2 + y$$

Hence, the required value is,
$$f(1) = 2(1)^2 + 1$$
$$= 3$$

36. Correct Response : (c)

Explanation :

The given differential equation is,
$$(x \log x)\frac{dy}{dx} + y = 2x \log x$$

$$\frac{dy}{dx} + \frac{y}{x \log x} = 2$$

The integrating factor (I.F.) is,
$$\text{I.F.} = e^{\int \frac{1}{x \log x}dx}$$
$$= e^{\log(\log x)}$$
$$= \log x$$

Solution of the differential equation is,
$$y \cdot (\text{I.F.}) = \int Q \cdot (\text{I.F.})\,dx + c$$

$$y \log x = \int 2 \log x \, dx + c$$

$$y \log x = 2x\,[\log x - 1] + c$$

At $x = 1$, $y = 0$, the above equation becomes,
$$0 = -2 + c$$
$$c = 2$$

Hence, the solution of the differential equation is,
$$y \log x = 2x\,[\log x - 1] + 2$$

Put $x = e$,
$$y \log e = 2e\,[\log e - 1] + 2$$
$$y = 2$$

37. Correct Response : (d)

Explanation :

The given differential equation is,
$$\sin 2x \left(\frac{dy}{dx} - \sqrt{\tan x}\right) - y = 0$$

$$\frac{dy}{dx} - \frac{y}{\sin 2x} = \sqrt{\tan x}$$

The integration factor of the above equation is,
$$\text{I.F.} = e^{\int P(x)dx}$$

$$= e^{-\int \frac{1}{\sin 2x}dx}$$

$$= e^{-\frac{1}{2}\ln \tan x}$$

$$= \frac{1}{\sqrt{\tan x}}$$

The general solution of the equation is,
$$y \cdot \frac{1}{\sqrt{\tan x}} = \int \sqrt{\tan x} \cdot \frac{1}{\sqrt{\tan x}} + c$$

$$y \sqrt{\cot x} = x + c$$

38. Correct Response : (c)

Explanation :

The figure of the circle of radius is a,

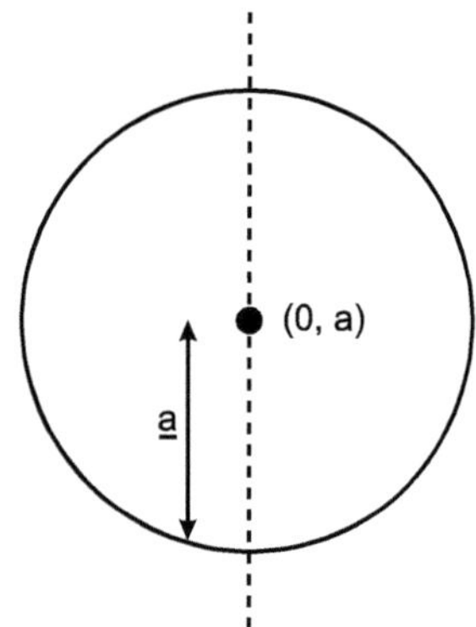

The equation of the circle which centre is $(0, a)$ and radius is a,

$$x^2 + (y - a)^2 = a^2$$
$$x^2 + y^2 - 2ay = 0 \qquad \dots(1)$$

Differentiate equation (1) with respect to x,

$$2x + 2y\frac{dy}{dx} - 2a\frac{dy}{dx} = 0$$

$$a = \frac{x + yy'}{y'} \qquad \dots(2)$$

Put the value of the equation (2) in (1),

$$x^2 + y^2 - 2y\left(\frac{x + yy'}{y'}\right) = 0$$

$$(x^2 + y^2)\, y' = 2xy \qquad \dots(3)$$

Compare (3) with the given equation

$$(x^2 - y^2)\frac{dy}{dx} = g(x)\, y.$$

Hence, the required value is,

$$g(x) = 2x$$

39. Correct Response : (c)

Explanation :

The given derivative equation is,

$$\frac{dy}{dx} + y\tan x = \sin 2x$$

$$\text{I.F.} = e^{\int \tan x\, dx}$$
$$= e^{\log \sec x}$$
$$= \sec x$$

The solution of the equation is,

$$y \sec x = \int \sin 2x \cdot \sec x\, dx + c$$
$$= \int 2 \sin x\, dx + c$$
$$= -2 \cos x + c \qquad \dots(1)$$

Apply boundary condition,

$$y(0) = 1$$
$$1 \cdot 1 = -1 \cdot 2 + c$$
$$c = 3$$

Substitute the value of c in equation (1),

$$y \sec x = -2 \cos x + 3$$
$$y = \frac{-2\cos x + 3}{\sec x}$$

The value of $y(\pi)$ is,

$$y(\pi) = \frac{(-2)\cdot(-1)+3}{(-1)}$$
$$= -5$$

40. Correct Response : (d)

Explanation :

The differential equation is given by,

$$y' = \frac{y}{x} + \phi\frac{x}{y} \qquad \dots(1)$$

The function ϕ is given by,

$$y \ln |cx| = x$$

$$\frac{y}{|cx|} \times \frac{|cx|}{cx} \times c + \ln|cx|y' = 1 \qquad \left[\text{Let, } \ln|cx| = \frac{x}{y}\right]$$

$$y' = \left(1 - \frac{y}{x}\right)\frac{y}{x} \qquad \dots(2)$$

Compare the equations (1) and (2),

$$\left[1 - \left(\frac{y}{x}\right)\right]\left(\frac{y}{x}\right) = \left(\frac{y}{x}\right) + \phi\left(\frac{x}{y}\right)$$

Substitute 2 for $\left(\dfrac{x}{y}\right)$ in the above equation.

$$\left(1 - \frac{1}{2}\right)\left(\frac{1}{2}\right) = \frac{1}{2} + \phi(2)$$

$$\phi(2) = -\frac{1}{4}$$

41. Correct Response : (6)

Explanation :

It is given that,

$$6\int_{1}^{x} f(t)\, dt = 3xf(x) - x^3$$

Differentiate above equation with respect to x.

$$6f(x) = 3xf'(x) + 3f(x) - 3x^2$$
$$f(x) = xf'(x) - x^2$$
$$x\frac{dy}{dx} - y = x^2$$
$$\frac{dy}{dx} - \frac{y}{x} = x$$

The integrating factor for above equation is,

$$\text{.F.} = e^{\int -\frac{1}{x}dx}$$
$$= \frac{1}{x}$$

Now,

$$\frac{1}{x}\cdot y = \int \frac{1}{x}\cdot x\,dx$$

$$\frac{y}{x} = x + c$$

It is given that $y = 2$ for $x = 1$. Substitute these values in above equation.

$$c = 1$$

The value of function at $x = 2$ is,

$$\frac{f(x)}{2} = 2 + 1$$

$$f(x) = 3 \cdot 2$$

$$= 6$$

42. **Correct Response :** (9)

Explanation :

The given equation is,

$$\frac{dy}{dx} + g'(y)\cdot y = g(x)\cdot g'(x)$$

Integrating factor is calculated as,

$$\text{I.F.} = e^{\int g'(x)dx}$$

$$= e^{g(x)}$$

Therefore, the solution is,

$$y\cdot e^{g(x)} = \int e^{g(x)}\cdot g(x)\cdot g'(x)\,dx$$

$$y\cdot e^{g(x)} = e^{g(x)}\,g(x) - e^{g(x)} + C$$

$$y\cdot e^{g(0)} = e^{g(0)}\,g(x) - e^{g(0)} + C$$

$$0 = 0 - e^1 + C$$

Further simplify above equation.

$$C = 1$$

For $x = 2$,

$$y\cdot e^{g(2)} = e^{g(2)}\,g(x) - e^{g(2)} + 1$$

$$y\cdot 1 = 0 - 1 + 1$$

$$y = 0$$

Therefore, the value of $y(2)$ is 0.

For the third given matrix,

$$\begin{bmatrix} a & b & c \\ d & e & f \\ g & h & i \end{bmatrix}\cdot\begin{bmatrix} 1 \\ 1 \\ 1 \end{bmatrix} = \begin{bmatrix} 0 \\ 0 \\ 12 \end{bmatrix}$$

$$\begin{bmatrix} a+b+c \\ b+e+h \\ g+h+i \end{bmatrix} = \begin{bmatrix} 0 \\ 0 \\ 12 \end{bmatrix}$$

So, $c = 1$, $f = -5$ and $i = 7$.

Therefore, the sum of diagonal entries of M is,

$$a + e + i = 0 + 2 + 7$$

$$= 9$$

43. **Correct Response :** (c)

Explanation :

Solve the given differential function,

$$\frac{dy}{dx} = \frac{\sqrt{1-y^2}}{y}$$

$$\frac{y}{\sqrt{1-y^2}}dy = dx$$

Integrate above equation.

$$\int \frac{y}{\sqrt{1-y^2}}dy = \int dx$$

$$-\sqrt{1-y^2} = x + c$$

$$(x + c)^2 = 1 - y^2$$

$$(x + c)^2 + y^2 = 1$$

Radius of circle is,

$$r = \sqrt{c^2 - c^2 + 1}$$

$$= 1$$

Thus, the center of the circle is $(-c, 0)$ and radius is 1.

44. **Correct Response :** (c)

Explanation :

The given differential equation is,

$$(x^2 + y^2)dy = xy\,dx$$

Put $y = vx$.

$$\frac{dy}{dx} = v + x\frac{dv}{dx}$$

$$dy = v\,dx + x\,dv$$

Substitute value in given differential equation.

$$(1 + v^2)\,(v\,dx + x\,dv) = v\,dx$$

$$\frac{dx}{x} = -\frac{1+v^2}{v^3}dv$$

Integrate above equation.

$$\ln x = \frac{1}{2v^2} - \ln v + c$$

$$\ln xv = \frac{1}{2v^2} + c$$

$$\ln y = \frac{x^2}{2y^2} + c \qquad \text{...(1)}$$

Substitute $y(1) = 1$.

$$c = -\frac{1}{2}$$

Substitute value in equation (1),

$$\ln y = \frac{x^2}{2y^2} - \frac{1}{2}$$

$$-\frac{x^2}{2y^2} + \ln y = -\frac{1}{2}$$

It is given that $y(x_0) = e$.

$$-\frac{x_0^2}{2e^2} + \ln e = -\frac{1}{2}$$

$$x_0^2 = 3e^2$$

$$x_0 = \sqrt{3}e$$

45. Correct Response : (a)

Explanation :

Simplify given primitive equation.

$$y\,dx + y^2\,dy = x\,dy$$

$$\frac{dx}{dy} - \frac{x}{y} = -y$$

The integrating factor is calculated as,

$$\text{I.F.} = e^{\int \frac{dy}{y}}$$

$$= e^{-\ln y}$$

$$= \frac{1}{y}$$

Multiply the equation by integrating factor,

$$\frac{1}{y}\left(\frac{dx}{dy}\right) - \frac{x}{y^2} = -1$$

$$\frac{d}{dy}\left(\frac{x}{y}\right) - \frac{x}{y^2} = -1$$

Integrate both sides of above equation.

$$\frac{x}{y} = -y + c$$

Substitute $y(1) = 1$.

$$c = 2$$

Now, the equation becomes,

$$\frac{x}{y} = -y + 2$$

$$y^2 - 2y + x = 0$$

The value of $y(-3)$ is,

$$y^2 - 2y - 3 = 0$$

$$(y - 3)(y + 1) = 0$$

$$y = 3, -1$$

46. Correct Response : (a)

Explanation :

Solve the given differential equation,

$$\frac{dy}{dx} = \frac{-\cos x(y+1)}{2 + \sin x}$$

$$\frac{dy}{y+1} = \frac{-\cos x}{2+\sin x}\,dx$$

Integrate both sides of above equation,

$$\int \frac{dy}{y+1} = -\int \frac{\cos x}{2+\sin x}\,dx$$

$$\log(y+1) = -\log(2 + \sin x) + \log c \quad ...(1)$$

Substitute $x = 0$, $y = 1$.

$$c = 4$$

Substitute 4 for c in equation (1),

$$y + 1 = \frac{4}{2 + \sin x}$$

The required value is,

$$y\left(\frac{\pi}{2}\right) = \frac{4}{3} - 1$$

$$= \frac{1}{3}$$

47. Correct Response : (a)

Explanation :

The value of y at $x = 0$ is,

$$\log(y) = 0$$

$$y = 1$$

Differentiate given equation $\log(x + y) - 2xy = 0$.

$$\log(x + y) = 2xy$$

$$\frac{1}{x+y}\left(1 + \frac{dy}{dx}\right) = 2x\frac{dy}{dx} + 2y$$

$$\frac{dy}{dx} = \frac{2y(x+y) - 1}{1 - 2(x+y)x}$$

$$\left(\frac{dy}{dx}\right)_{(0,1)} = 1$$

Therefore, the value of $y'(0) = 1$.

48. Correct Response : (a)

Explanation :

The given differential equation is,

$$(t+1)\frac{dy}{dt} - ty = 1$$

Multiply both sides by e^{-t} and rearrange the terms.

$$e^{-t}(1+t)dy + y[e^{-t} - (1+t)e^{-t}]dt = e^{-t}\,dt$$

$$d[e^{-t}(1+t)y] = d(-e^{-t})$$

$$ye^{-t}(1+t) = -e^{-t} + c$$

Substitute $y(0) = -1$.

$$c = 0$$

Now, the equation is,

$$ye^{-t}(1+t) = -e^{-t}$$

$$y(1+t) = -1$$

$$y = -\frac{1}{1+t}$$

Therefore, the value of $y(1)$ is $-\frac{1}{2}$.

49. Correct Response : (a, d)

Explanation :

The given equation is,

$$y' - y \tan x = 2x \sec x$$

The integrating factor is,

$$\text{I.F.} = e^{-\int \tan x \cdot dx}$$

$$= e^{-\ln(\sec x)}$$

$$= e^{\ln\left(\frac{1}{\sec x}\right)}$$

$$= \cos x$$

So,

$$\cos x \cdot y = \int \cos x \, (2x \sec x) dx$$

$$\cos x \cdot y = 2\int (x) \, dx$$

$$\cos x \cdot y = 2\left(\frac{x^2}{2}\right) + C$$

$$y = x^2 \sec x + C \sec x$$

The value of y at $x = 0$ is,

$$y(0) = 0$$

$$0 = 0 + C(1)$$

$$C = 0$$

The value of y is,

$$y = x^2 \sec x$$

The value of y at $x = \dfrac{\pi}{4}$ is,

$$y = \left(\frac{\pi}{4}\right)^2 \sec\left(\frac{\pi}{4}\right)$$

$$= \frac{\pi^2}{16}\sqrt{2}$$

$$= \frac{\pi^2}{8\sqrt{2}}$$

The value of y' at $x = \dfrac{\pi}{4}$ is,

$$y' = \left(\left(\frac{\pi}{4}\right)^2 \sec\frac{\pi}{4}\right)\tan\frac{\pi}{4} + 2\left(\frac{\pi}{4}\right)\sec\frac{\pi}{4}$$

$$= \frac{\pi^2}{16}\sqrt{2} + \frac{\pi}{2}\sqrt{2} = \frac{\pi^2}{8\sqrt{2}}$$

The value of y at $x = \dfrac{\pi}{3}$ is,

$$y = \left(\frac{\pi}{3}\right)^2 \sec\left(\frac{\pi}{3}\right)$$

$$= \frac{\pi^2}{9}\cdot 2$$

$$= \frac{2\pi^2}{9}$$

The value of y' at $x = \dfrac{\pi}{3}$ is,

$$y' = \left(\left(\frac{\pi}{3}\right)^2 \sec\frac{\pi}{3}\right)\tan\frac{\pi}{3} + 2\left(\frac{\pi}{3}\right)\sec\frac{\pi}{3}$$

$$= \frac{2\pi^2}{3\sqrt{3}} + \frac{4\pi}{3}$$

●●

Coordinate Geometry

QUESTIONS

1. If the common tangent to the parabolas, $y^2 = 4x$ and $x^2 = 4y$ also touches the circle, $x^2 + y^2 = c^2$, then c is equal to : **[2020, Main]**

   (a) $\dfrac{1}{2}$

   (b) $\dfrac{1}{2\sqrt{2}}$

   (c) $\dfrac{1}{\sqrt{2}}$

   (d) $\dfrac{1}{4}$

2. If the point P on the curve, $4x^2 + 5y^2 = 20$ is farthest from the point $Q(0, -4)$, then PQ^2 is equal to : **[2020, Main]**

   (a) 21

   (b) 36

   (c) 48

   (d) 29

3. If the co-ordinates of two points A and B are $(\sqrt{7}, 0)$ and $(-\sqrt{7}, 0)$ respectively and P is any point on the conic, $9x^2 + 16y^2 = 144$, then PA + PB is equal to : **[2020, Main]**

   (a) 8

   (b) 6

   (c) 16

   (d) 9

4. If the line, $2x - y + 3 = 0$ is at a distance $\dfrac{1}{\sqrt{5}}$ and $\dfrac{2}{\sqrt{5}}$ from the lines $4x - 2y + \alpha = 0$ and $6x - 3y + \beta = 0$, respectively, then the sum of all possible values of α and β is .... **[2020, Main]**

5. Which of the following points lies on the locus of the foot of perpendicular drawn upon any tangent to the ellipse, $\dfrac{x^2}{4} + \dfrac{y^2}{2} = 1$ from any of its foci ? **[2020, Main]**

   (a) $(-1, \sqrt{3})$

   (b) $(-1, \sqrt{2})$

   (c) $(-2, \sqrt{3})$

   (d) $(1, 2)$

6. The area (in sq. units) of the region $A = \{(x, y) : |x| + |y| \le 1, 2y^2 \ge |x|\}$ is : **[2020, Main]**

   (a) $\dfrac{1}{6}$

   (b) $\dfrac{1}{3}$

   (c) $\dfrac{7}{6}$

   (d) $\dfrac{5}{6}$

7. Let L_1 be a tangent to the parabola $y^2 = 4(x + 1)$ and L_2 be a tangent to the parabola $y^2 = 8(x + 2)$ such that L_1 and L_2 intersect at right angles. Then L_1 and L_2 meet on the straight line : **[2020, Main]**

   (a) $x + 3 = 0$

   (b) $x + 2y = 0$

   (c) $2x + 1 = 0$

   (d) $x + 2 = 0$

8. Let AD and BC be two vertical poles at A and B respectively on a horizontal ground. If AD = 8 m, BC = 11 m and AB = 10 m; then the distance (in meters) of a point M on AB from the point A such that $MD^2 + MC^2$ is minimum is .... **[2020, Main]**

9. If the normal at an end of a latus rectum of an ellipse passes through an extremity of the minor axis, then the eccentricity e of the ellipse satisfies : **[2020, Main]**

   (a) $e^2 + 2e - 1 = 0$

   (b) $e^2 + e - 1 = 0$

   (c) $e^4 + 2e^2 - 1 = 0$

   (d) $e^4 + e^2 - 1 = 0$

10. The area (in sq. units) of the region enclosed by the curves $y = x^2 - 1$ and $y = 1 - x^2$ is equal to : **[2020, Main]**

    (a) $\dfrac{4}{3}$

    (b) $\dfrac{8}{3}$

    (c) $\dfrac{16}{3}$

    (d) $\dfrac{7}{2}$

11. Let L denote the line in the xy-plane with x and y intercepts as 3 and 1 respectively. Then the image of the point $(-1, -4)$ in this line is : **[2020, Main]**

    (a) $\left(\dfrac{8}{5}, \dfrac{29}{5}\right)$

    (b) $\left(\dfrac{29}{5}, \dfrac{11}{5}\right)$

    (c) $\left(\dfrac{11}{5}, \dfrac{28}{5}\right)$

    (d) $\left(\dfrac{29}{5}, \dfrac{8}{5}\right)$

12. The centre of the circle passing through the point $(0, 1)$ and touching the parabola $y = x^2$ at the point $(2, 4)$ is : **[2020, Main]**

    (a) $\left(\dfrac{3}{10}, \dfrac{16}{5}\right)$

    (b) $\left(\dfrac{-16}{5}, \dfrac{53}{10}\right)$

    (c) $\left(\dfrac{6}{5}, \dfrac{53}{10}\right)$

    (d) $\left(\dfrac{-53}{10}, \dfrac{16}{5}\right)$

13. Let $\dfrac{x^2}{a^2} + \dfrac{y^2}{b^2} = 1$ $(a > b)$ be a given ellipse, length of whose latus rectum is 10. If its eccentricity is the maximum value of the function, $\phi(t) = \dfrac{5}{12} + t - t^2$, then $a^2 + b^2$ is equal to : **[2020, Main]**

(a) 126

(b) 135

(c) 145

(d) 116

14. A triangle ABC lying in the first quadrant has two vertices as A(1, 2) and B(3, 1). If $\angle BAC = 90°$ and ar $(\Delta ABC) = 5\sqrt{5}$ sq. units, then the abscissa of the vertex C is : **[2020, Main]**

(a) $2 + \sqrt{5}$

(b) $1 + \sqrt{5}$

(c) $1 + 2\sqrt{5}$

(d) $2\sqrt{5} - 1$

15. Let P(3, 3) be a point on the hyperbola, $\dfrac{x^2}{a^2} - \dfrac{y^2}{b^2} = 1$. If the normal to it at P intersects the x-axis at (9, 0) and e is its eccentricity, then the ordered pair (a^2, e^2) is equal to : **[2020, Main]**

(a) $\left(\dfrac{9}{2}, 3\right)$

(b) $\left(\dfrac{9}{2}, 2\right)$

(c) $\left(\dfrac{3}{2}, 2\right)$

(d) $(9, 3)$

16. The circle passing through the intersection of the circles, $x^2 + y^2 - 6x = 0$ and $x^2 + y^2 - 4y = 0$, having its centre on the line, $2x - 3y + 12 = 0$, also passes through the point : **[2020, Main]**

(a) $(1, -3)$

(b) $(-1, 3)$

(c) $(-3, 1)$

(d) $(-3, 6)$

17. Let $x = 4$ be a directrix to an ellipse whose centre is at the origin and its eccentricity is $\dfrac{1}{2}$. If P(1, β), β > 0 is a point on this ellipse, then the equation of the normal to it at P is : **[2020, Main]**

(a) $7x - 4y = 1$

(b) $4x - 2y = 1$

(c) $4x - 3y = 2$

(d) $8x - 2y = 5$

18. The area (in sq. units) of the largest rectangle ABCD whose vertices A and B lie on the x-axis and vertices C and D lie on the parabola, $y = x^2 - 1$ below the x-axis is :

(a) $\dfrac{4}{3\sqrt{3}}$

(b) $\dfrac{1}{3\sqrt{3}}$

(c) $\dfrac{4}{3}$

(d) $\dfrac{2}{3\sqrt{3}}$

19. Let PQ be a diameter of the circle $x^2 + y^2 = 9$. If α and β are the lengths of the perpendicular from P and Q on the straight line, $x + y = 2$ respectively, then the maximum value of $\alpha\beta$ is .... **[2020, Main]**

20. A hyperbola having the transverse axis of length $\sqrt{2}$ has the same foci as that of the ellipse $3x^2 + 4y^2 = 12$, then this hyperbola does not pass through which of the following points ? **[2020, Main]**

(a) $\left(1, -\dfrac{1}{\sqrt{2}}\right)$

(b) $\left(\sqrt{\dfrac{3}{2}}, \dfrac{1}{\sqrt{2}}\right)$

(c) $\left(\dfrac{1}{\sqrt{2}}, 0\right)$

(d) $\left(-\sqrt{\dfrac{3}{2}}, 1\right)$

21. The area (in sq. units) of the region $\{(x, y) : 0 \le y \le x^2 + 1, 0 \le y \le x + 1, \dfrac{1}{2} \le x \le 2\}$ is : **[2020, Main]**

(a) $\dfrac{79}{16}$

(b) $\dfrac{23}{6}$

(c) $\dfrac{79}{24}$

(d) $\dfrac{23}{16}$

22. Let P be a point on the parabola, $y^2 = 12x$ and N be the foot of the perpendicular drawn from P on the axis of the parabola. A line is now drawn through the mid-point M of PN, parallel to its axis which meets the parabola at Q. If the y-intercept of the line NQ is $\dfrac{4}{3}$, then : **[2020, Main]**

(a) $MQ = \dfrac{1}{3}$

(b) $PN = 3$

(c) $MQ = \dfrac{1}{4}$

(d) $PN = 4$

23. The diameter of the circle, whose centre lies on the line $x + y = 2$ in the first quadrant and which touches both the lines $x = 3$ and $y = 2$, is .... **[2020, Main]**

24. The area (in sq. units) of the region A = $\{(x, y) : (x - 1)[x] \le y \le 2\sqrt{x}, 0 \le x \le 2\}$, where $[t]$ denotes the greatest integer function, is : **[2020, Main]**

(a) $\dfrac{8}{3}\sqrt{2} - \dfrac{1}{2}$

(b) $\dfrac{8}{3}\sqrt{2} - 1$

(c) $\dfrac{4}{3}\sqrt{2} - \dfrac{1}{2}$

(d) $\dfrac{4}{3}\sqrt{2} + 1$

25. If the length of the chord of the circle, $x^2 + y^2 = r^2$ $(r > 0)$ along the line, $y - 2x = 3$ is r, then r^2 is equal to : **[2020, Main]**

(a) $\dfrac{9}{5}$

(b) $\dfrac{12}{5}$

(c) 12

(d) $\dfrac{24}{5}$

26. If the line $y = mx + c$ is a common tangent to the hyperbola $\dfrac{x^2}{100} - \dfrac{y^2}{64} = 1$ and the circle $x^2 + y^2 = 36$, then which one of the following is true ?

[2020, Main]

(a) $5m = 4$ (b) $4c^2 = 369$

(c) $c^2 = 369$ (d) $8m + 5 = 0$

27. Which of the following points lies on the tangent to the curve $x^4 e^y + 2\sqrt{y+1} = 3$ at the point $(1, 0)$?

[2020, Main]

(a) $(2, 2)$ (b) $(-2, 6)$

(c) $(-2, 4)$ (d) $(2, 6)$

28. If the lines $x + y = a$ and $x - y = b$ touch the curve $y = x^2 - 3x + 2$ at the points where the curve intersects the x-axis, then $\dfrac{a}{b}$ is equal to

.... **[2020, Main]**

29. Let the functions $f : R \to R$ and $g : R \to R$ be defined by

$$f(x) = e^{x-1} - e^{-|x-1|} \text{ and } g(x) = \dfrac{1}{2}(e^{x-1} + e^{1-x})$$

Then the area of the region in the first quadrant bounded by the curves $y = f(x)$, $y = g(x)$ and $x = 0$ is :

[2020, Advanced]

(a) $(2 - \sqrt{3}) + \dfrac{1}{2}(e - e^{-1})$

(b) $(2 + \sqrt{3}) + \dfrac{1}{2}(e - e^{-1})$

(c) $(2 - \sqrt{3}) + \dfrac{1}{2}(e + e^{-1})$

(d) $(2 + \sqrt{3}) + \dfrac{1}{2}(e + e^{-1})$

30. Let a, b and λ be positive real numbers. Suppose P is an end point of the latus rectum of the parabola $y^2 = 4\lambda x$ and suppose the ellipse $\dfrac{x^2}{a^2} + \dfrac{y^2}{b^2} = 1$ passes through the point P. If the tangents to the parabola and the ellipse at the point P are perpendicular to each other, then the eccentricity of the ellipse is :

[2020, Advanced]

(a) $\dfrac{1}{\sqrt{2}}$ (b) $\dfrac{1}{2}$

(c) $\dfrac{1}{3}$ (d) $\dfrac{2}{5}$

31. Let O be the centre of the circle $x^2 + y^2 = r^2$, where $r > \dfrac{\sqrt{5}}{2}$. Suppose PQ is a chord of this circle and the equation of the line passing through P and

Q is $2x + 4y = 5$. If the centre of the circumcircle of the triangle OPQ lies on the line $x + 2y = 4$, then the value of r is ....

[2020, Advanced]

32. Let a and b be positive real numbers such that $a > 1$ and $b < a$. Let P be a point in the first quadrant that lies on the hyperbola $\dfrac{x^2}{a^2} - \dfrac{y^2}{b^2} = 1$. Suppose the tangent to the hyperbola at P passes through the point $(1, 0)$ and suppose the normal to the hyperbola at P cuts off equal intercepts on the coordinate axes. Let Δ denotes the area of the triangle formed by the tangent at P, the normal at P and the x-axis. If e denotes the eccentricity of the hyperbola, then which of the following statements is/are TRUE ?

[2020, Advanced]

(a) $1 < e < \sqrt{2}$ (b) $\sqrt{2} < e < 2$

(c) $\Delta = a^4$ (d) $\Delta = b^4$

33. The equation of the normal to the curve $y = (1 + x)^{2y} + \cos^2(\sin^{-1} x)$ at $x = 0$ is :

[2020, Main]

(a) $y = 4x + 2$ (b) $x + 4y = 8$

(c) $y + 4x = 2$ (d) $2y + x = 4$

34. For some $\theta \in \left(0, \dfrac{\pi}{2}\right)$, if the eccentricity of the hyperbola, $x^2 - y^2 \sec^2\theta = 10$ is $\sqrt{5}$ times the eccentricity of the ellipse, $x^2\sec^2\theta + y^2 = 5$, then the length of the latus rectum of the ellipse, is :

[2020, Main]

(a) $\sqrt{30}$ (b) $\dfrac{4\sqrt{5}}{3}$

(c) $2\sqrt{6}$ (d) $\dfrac{2\sqrt{5}}{3}$

35. Consider a region $R = \{x, y) \in R^2 : x^2 \le y \le 2x\}$. If a line $y = \alpha$ divides the area of region R into two equal parts, then which of the following is true?

[2020, Main]

(a) $\alpha^3 - 6\alpha^2 + 16 = 0$ (b) $3\alpha^2 - 8\alpha + 8 = 0$

(c) $\alpha^3 - 6\alpha^{3/2} - 16 = 0$ (d) $3\alpha^2 - 8\alpha^{3/2} + 8 = 0$

36. The set of all possible values of θ in the interval $(0, \pi)$ for which the points $(1, 2)$ and $(\sin \theta, \cos \theta)$ lie on the same side of the line $x + y = 1$ is :

[2020, Main]

(a) $\left(0, \dfrac{\pi}{4}\right)$ (b) $\left(0, \dfrac{3\pi}{4}\right)$

(c) $\left(\dfrac{\pi}{4}, \dfrac{3\pi}{4}\right)$ (d) $\left(0, \dfrac{\pi}{2}\right)$

37. If the surface are of a cube is increasing at a rate of 3.6 cm²/sec, retaining its shape; then the rate of change of its volume (in cm^3/sec), when the length of a side of the cube is 10 cm is :

[2020, Main]

(a) 9   (b) 18

(c) 10   (d) 20

38. Let the latus rectum of the parabola $y^2 = 4x$ be the common chord to the circles C_1 and C_2 each of them having radius $2\sqrt{5}$. Then, the distance between the centres of the circles C_1 and C_2 is :

[2020, Main]

(a) 8   (b) $4\sqrt{5}$

(c) 12   (d) $8\sqrt{5}$

39. If a ΔABC has vertices $A(-1, 7)$, $B(-7, 1)$ and $C(5, -5)$, then its orthocentre has coordinates :

[2020, Main]

(a) $(3, -3)$ (b) $\left(-\dfrac{3}{5}, \dfrac{3}{5}\right)$

(c) $(-3, 3)$ (d) $\left(\dfrac{3}{5}, -\dfrac{3}{5}\right)$

40. Let e_1 and e_2 be the eccentricities of the ellipse, $\dfrac{x^2}{25} + \dfrac{y^2}{b^2} = 1 (b < 5)$ and the hyperbola $\dfrac{x^2}{16} - \dfrac{y^2}{b^2} = 1$ respectively satisfying $e_1 e_2 = 1$. If α and β are the distances between the foci of the ellipse and the foci of the hyperbola respectively, then the ordered pair (α, β) is equal to :

[2020, Main]

(a) $(8, 10)$ (b) $(8, 12)$

(c) $\left(\dfrac{20}{3}, 12\right)$ (d) $\left(\dfrac{24}{5}, 10\right)$

41. If the tangent of the curve, $y = e^x$ at a point (c, e^c) and the normal to the parabola, $y^2 = 4x$ at the point $(1, 2)$ intersect at the same point on the x-axis, then the value of c is ....

[2020, Main]

42. If the tangent to the curve $y = x + \sin y$ at a point (a, b) is parallel to the line joining $\left(0, \dfrac{3}{2}\right)$ and $\left(\dfrac{1}{2}, 2\right)$, then :

[2020, Main]

(a) $b = a$ (b) $b = \dfrac{\pi}{2} + a$

(c) $|b - a| = 1$ (d) $|a + b| = 1$

43. Let $P(h, k)$ be a point on the curve $y = x^2 + 7x + 2$, nearest to the line, $y = 3x - 3$. Then the equation of the normal to the curve at P is : **[2020, Main]**

(a) $x + 3y - 62 = 0$ (b) $x - 3y - 11 = 0$

(c) $x - 3y + 22 = 0$ (d) $x + 3y + 26 = 0$

44. A line parallel to the straight line $2x - y = 0$ is tangent to the hyperbola $\dfrac{x^2}{4} - \dfrac{y^2}{2} = 1$ at the point (x_1, y_1). Then $x_1^2 + 5y_1^2$ is equal to :

[2020, Main]

(a) 5   (b) 6

(c) 8   (d) 10

45. The number of integral values of k for which the line, $3x + 4y = k$ intersects the circle, $x^2 + y^2 - 2x - 4y + 4 = 0$ at two distinct points is ....

[2020, Main]

46. If $3x + 4y = 12\sqrt{2}$ is a tangent to the ellipse $\dfrac{x^2}{a^2} + \dfrac{y^2}{9} = 1$ for some $a \in R$, then the distance between the foci of the ellipse is : **[2020, Main]**

(a) 4   (b) $2\sqrt{7}$

(c) $2\sqrt{5}$ (d) $2\sqrt{2}$

47. The locus of the mid-points of the perpendicular drawn from points on the line, $x = 2y$ to the line $x = y$ is : **[2020, Main]**

(a) $2x - 3y = 0$ (b) $7x = 5y = 0$

(c) $5x - 7y = 0$ (d) $3x - 2y = 0$

48. Let the tangents drawn from the origin to the circle, $x^2 + y^2 - 8x - 4y + 16 = 0$ touch it at the points A and B. The $(AB)^2$ is equal to :

[2020, Main]

(a) $\dfrac{52}{5}$ (b) $\dfrac{32}{5}$

(c) $\dfrac{56}{5}$ (d) $\dfrac{64}{5}$

49. The length of the perpendicular from the origin, on the normal to the curve, $x^2 + 2xy - 3y^2 = 0$ at the point $(2, 2)$ is **[2020, Main]**

(a) $4\sqrt{2}$ (b) $2\sqrt{2}$

(c) 2   (d) $\sqrt{2}$

50. If a line, $y = mx + c$ is a tangent to the circle, $(x - 3)^2 + y^2 = 1$ and it perpendicular to a line L_1, where L_1 is the tangent to the circle. $x^2 + y^2 = 1$ at the point $\left(\dfrac{1}{\sqrt{2}}, \dfrac{1}{\sqrt{2}}\right)$, then

[2020, Main]

(a) $c^2 - 6c + 7 = 0$ (b) $c^2 + 6c + 7 = 0$

(c) $c^2 + 7c + 6 = 0$ (d) $c^2 - 7c + 6 = 0$

51. If a hyperbola passes through the point $P(10, 16)$ and it has vertices at $(\pm 6, 0)$, then the equation of the normal to it at P is **[2020, Main]**

(a) $x + 2y = 42$ (b) $3x + 4y = 94$

(c) $2x + 5y = 100$ (d) $x + 3y = 58$

52. Let a line $y = mx$ $(m > 0)$ intersect the parabola, $y^2 = x$ at a point P, other than the origin. Let the tangent to it at P meet the x-axis at the point Q. If area $(\Delta OPQ) = 4$ sq. units, then m is equal to .... **[2020, Main]**

53. A circle touches the y-axis at the point $(0, 4)$ and passes through the point $(2, 0)$. Which of the following lines is not a tangent to this circle ? **[2020, Main]**

(a) $3x - 4y - 24 = 0$ (b) $3x + 4y - 6 = 0$

(c) $4x + 3y - 8 = 0$ (d) $4x - 3y + 17 = 0$

54. If e_1 and e_2 are the eccentricities of the ellipse, $\dfrac{x^2}{18} + \dfrac{y^2}{4} = 1$ and the hyperbola, $\dfrac{x^2}{9} - \dfrac{y^2}{4} = 1$ respectively and (e_1, e_2) is a point on the ellipse, $15x^2 + 3y^2 = k$, then k is equal to : **[2020, Main]**

(a) 15   (b) 14

(c) 17   (d) 16

55. The length of the minor axis (along y-axis) of an ellipse in the standard form is $\dfrac{4}{\sqrt{3}}$. If this ellipse touches the line, $x + 6y = 8$; then its eccentricity is : **[2020, Main]**

(a) $\sqrt{\dfrac{5}{6}}$ (b) $\dfrac{1}{2}\sqrt{\dfrac{11}{3}}$

(c) $\dfrac{1}{3}\sqrt{\dfrac{11}{3}}$ (d) $\dfrac{1}{2}\sqrt{\dfrac{5}{3}}$

[2020, Main]

56. If one end of a focal chord AB of the parabola $y^2 = 8x$ is at $A\left(\dfrac{1}{2}, -2\right)$, then the equation of the tangent to it at B is : **[2020, Main]**

(a) $2x + y - 24 = 0$ (b) $x - 2y + 8 = 0$

(c) $2x - y - 24 = 0$ (d) $x + 2y + 8 = 0$

57. If the curves, $x^2 - 6x + y^2 + 8 = 0$ and $x^2 - 8y + y^2 + 16 - k = 0$, $(k > 0)$ touch each other at a point, then the largest value of k is ....

[2020, Main]

58. If $y = mx + 4$ is a tangent to both the parabolas, $y^2 = 4x$ and $x^2 = 2by$, then b is equal to :

[2020, Main]

(a) 128   (b) $- 64$

(c) $- 128$ (d) $- 32$

59. If the distance between the foci of an ellipse is 6 and the distance between its directrices is 12, then the length of its latus rectum is :

[2020, Main]

(a) $\sqrt{3}$ (b) $2\sqrt{3}$

(c) $3\sqrt{2}$ (d) $\dfrac{3}{\sqrt{2}}$

60. Let $A(1, 0)$, $B(6, 2)$ and $C\left(\dfrac{3}{2}, 6\right)$ be the vertices of a triangle ABC. If P is a point inside the triangle ABC such that the triangles APC, APB and BPC have equal areas, then the length of the line segment PQ, where Q is the point $\left(-\dfrac{7}{6}, -\dfrac{1}{3}\right)$, is .... **[2020, Main]**

61. Let the line $y = mx$ and the ellipse $2x^2 + y^2 = 1$ intersect at a point P in the first quadrant. If the normal to this ellipse at P meets the co-ordinate axes at $\left(-\dfrac{1}{3\sqrt{2}}, 0\right)$ and $(0, \beta)$, then β is equal to **[2020, Main]**

(a) $\dfrac{2}{\sqrt{3}}$ (b) $\dfrac{2\sqrt{2}}{3}$

(c) $\dfrac{2}{3}$ (d) $\dfrac{\sqrt{2}}{3}$

62. Let two points be $A(1, -1)$ and $B(0, 2)$. If a point $P(x', y')$ be such that the area of $\Delta PAB = 5$ sq. units and it lies on the line, $3x + y - 4\lambda = 0$, then a value of λ is **[2020, Main]**

(a) 1   (b) 4

(c) 3   (d) $- 3$

63. The locus of a point which divides the line segment joining the point $(0, -1)$ and a point on the parabola, $x^2 = 4y$, internally in the ratio $1 : 2$, is **[2020, Main]**

(a) $9x^2 - 3y = 2$ (b) $9x^2 - 12y = 8$

(c) $x^2 - 3y = 2$ (d) $4x^2 - 3y = 2$

64. If the circles $x^2 + y^2 + 5Kx + 2y + K = 0$ and $2(x^2 + y^2) + 2Kx + 3y - 1 = 0$, $(K \in R)$, intersect at the points P and Q, then the line $4x + 5y - K = 0$ passes through P and Q, for : **[2019, Main]**

(a) infinitely many values of K

(b) no value of K.

(c) exactly two values of K

(d) exactly one value of K

65. If the line $x - 2y = 12$ is tangent to the ellipse $\dfrac{x^2}{a^2} + \dfrac{y^2}{b^2} = 1$ at the point $\left(3, \dfrac{-9}{2}\right)$, then the length of the latus rectum of the ellipse is : **[2019, Main]**

(a) 9   (b) $12\sqrt{2}$

(c) 5   (d) $8\sqrt{3}$

66. The region represented by $|x - y| \le 2$ and $|x + y| \le 2$ is bounded by a : **[2019, Main]**

(a) square of side length $2\sqrt{2}$ units

(b) rhombus of side length 2 units

(c) square of area 16 sq. units

(d) rhombus of area $8\sqrt{2}$ sq. units

67. The line $x = y$ touches a circle at the point (1, 1). If the circle also passes through the point (1, – 3,) then is radius is : **[2019, Main]**

(a) 3

(b) $2\sqrt{2}$

(c) 2

(d) $3\sqrt{2}$

68. If a the directrix of the hyperbola centred at the origin and passing through the point $(4, -4\sqrt{5})$ is $5x = 4\sqrt{5}$ and its eccentricity is e, then

[2019, Main]

(a) $4e^4 - 24e^2 + 27 = 0$

(b) $4e^4 - 12e^2 - 27 = 0$

(c) $4e^4 - 24e^2 + 35 = 0$

(d) $4e^4 + 8e^2 + 35 = 0$

69. If $5x + 9 = 0$ is the directrix of the hyperbola $16x^2 - 9y^2 = 144$, then its corresponding focus is: **[2019, Main]**

(a) (5, 0)

(b) $\left(-\dfrac{5}{3}, 0\right)$

(c) $\left(\dfrac{5}{3}, 0\right)$

(d) (– 5, 0)

70. The tangent and normal to the ellipse $3x^2 + 5y^2 = 32$ at the point P(2, 2) meet the x-axis at Q and R, respectively, then the area (in sq, units) of the triangle PQR is : **[2019, Main]**

(a) $\dfrac{34}{15}$

(b) $\dfrac{14}{3}$

(c) $\dfrac{16}{3}$

(d) $\dfrac{68}{15}$

71. If the line $ax + y = c$, touches both the curves $x^2 + y^2 = 1$ and $y^2 = 4\sqrt{2}x$, then $|c|$ is equal to : **[2019, Main]**

(a) 2

(b) $\dfrac{1}{\sqrt{2}}$

(c) $\dfrac{1}{2}$

(d) $\sqrt{2}$

72. Lines are drawn parallel to the line $4x - 3y + 2 = 0$, at a distance $\dfrac{3}{5}$ from the origin. Then which one of the following points lies on any of these lines ? **[2019, Main]**

(a) $\left(-\dfrac{1}{4}, \dfrac{2}{3}\right)$

(b) $\left(\dfrac{1}{4}, -\dfrac{1}{3}\right)$

(c) $\left(\dfrac{1}{4}, \dfrac{1}{3}\right)$

(d) $\left(-\dfrac{1}{4}, -\dfrac{2}{3}\right)$

73. The locus of the centres of the circles, which touch the circle, $x^2 + y^2 = 1$ externally, also touch the y-axis and lie in the first quadrant, is : **[2019, Main]**

(a) $x = \sqrt{1+4y}, y \geq 0$

(b) $y = \sqrt{1+2x}, x \geq 0$

(c) $y = \sqrt{1+4x}, x \geq 0$

(d) $x = \sqrt{1+2y}, y \geq 0$

74. The area (is sq. units) of the smaller of the two circles that touch the parabola, $y^2 = 4x$ at the point (1, 2) and the x-axis is : **[2019, Main]**

(a) $8\pi(2 - \sqrt{2})$

(b) $4\pi(2 - \sqrt{2})$

(c) $4\pi(3 + \sqrt{2})$

(d) $8\pi(3 - 2\sqrt{2})$

75. If the two lines $x + (a - 1)\,y = 1$ and $2x + a^2y = 1$ ($a \in R - (0, 1)$) are perpendicular, then the distance of their point of intersection from the origin is : **[2019, Main]**

(a) $\sqrt{\dfrac{2}{5}}$

(b) $\dfrac{2}{5}$

(c) $\dfrac{2}{\sqrt{5}}$

(d) $\dfrac{\sqrt{2}}{5}$

76. The common tangent to the circles $x^2 + y^2 = 4$ and $x^2 + y^2 + 6x + 8y - 24 = 0$ also passes through the point : **[2019, Main]**

(a) (4, – 2)

(b) (– 6, 4)

(c) (6, – 2)

(d) (– 4, 6)

77. If the tangent to the parabola $y^2 = x$ at a point (α, β), $(\beta > 0)$ is also a tangent to the ellipse, $x^2 + 2y^2 = 1$, then α is equal to : **[2019, Main]**

(a) $\sqrt{2} - 1$

(b) $2\sqrt{2} - 1$

(c) $2\sqrt{2} + 1$

(d) $\sqrt{2} + 1$

78. Slope of a line passing through P(2, 3) and intersecting the line , $x + y = 7$ at a distance of 4 units from P, is : **[2019, Main]**

(a) $\dfrac{1 - \sqrt{5}}{1 + \sqrt{5}}$

(b) $\dfrac{1 - \sqrt{7}}{1 + \sqrt{7}}$

(c) $\dfrac{\sqrt{7} - 1}{\sqrt{7} + 1}$

(d) $\dfrac{\sqrt{5} - 1}{\sqrt{5} + 1}$

79. If the line $y = mx + 7\sqrt{3}$ is normal to the hyperbola $\dfrac{x^2}{24} - \dfrac{y^2}{18} = 1$, then a value of m is : **[2019, Main]**

(a) $\dfrac{\sqrt{5}}{2}$

(b) $\dfrac{\sqrt{15}}{2}$

(c) $\dfrac{2}{\sqrt{5}}$

(d) $\dfrac{3}{\sqrt{5}}$

80. All the points in the set $S = \left\{\dfrac{\alpha + i}{\alpha - i} : \alpha \in R\right\}$ $(i = \sqrt{-1})$ lie on a : **[2019, Main]**

(a) straight line whose slope is 1.

(b) circle whose radius is 1.

(c) circle whose radius is $\sqrt{2}$.

(d) straight line whose slope is – 1.

81. If a tangent to the circle $x^2 + y^2 = 1$ intersects the coordinate axes at distinct points P and Q, then the locus of the mid-point of PQ is : **[2019, Main]**

(a) $x^2 + y^2 - 4x^2y^2 = 0$ **(b)** $x^2 + y^2 - 2xy = 0$

(c) $x^2 + y^2 - 16x^2y^2 = 0$ **(d)** $x^2 + y^2 - 2x^2y^2 = 0$

82. The sum of the squares of the lengths of the chords intercepted on the circle, $x^2 + y^2 = 16$, by the lines, $x + y = n$, $n \in N$, where N is the set of all natural numbers, is : **[2019, Main]**

(a) 320 **(b)** 105

(c) 160 **(d)** 210

83. If the tangents on the ellipse $4x^2 + y^2 = 8$ at the points $(1, 2)$ and (a, b) are perpendicular to each other, then a^2 is equal to : **[2019, Main]**

(a) $\dfrac{128}{17}$ **(b)** $\dfrac{64}{17}$

(c) $\dfrac{4}{17}$ **(d)** $\dfrac{2}{17}$

84. A point on the straight line, $3x + 5y = 15$ which is equidistant from the coordinate axes will lies only in : **[2019, Main]**

(a) 4th quadrant

(b) I^{st} quadrant

(c) I^{st} and 2nd quadrants

(d) I^{st}, 2nd and 4th quadrants

85. Let O(0, 0) and A(0, 1) be two fixed points. Then the locus of a point P such that the perimeter of $\triangle AOP$ is 4, is : **[2019, Main]**

(a) $8x^2 - 9y^2 + 9y = 18$ **(b)** $9x^2 + 8y^2 + 8y = 16$

(c) $9x^2 + 8y^2 - 8y = 16$ **(d)** $8x^2 + 9y^2 - 9y = 18$

86. Suppose that the points (h, k), $(1, 2)$ and $(-3, 4)$ lies on the line L_1. If a line L_2 passing through the points (h, k) and $(4, 3)$ is perpendicular to L_1, then $\dfrac{k}{h}$ equals : **[2019, Main]**

(a) $\dfrac{1}{3}$ **(b)** 0

(c) 3 **(d)** $-\dfrac{1}{7}$

87. If the eccentricity of the standard hyperbola passing through the point $(4, 6)$ is 2, then the equation of the tangent to the hyperbola at $(4, 6)$ is : **[2019, Main]**

(a) $x - 2y + 8 = 0$ **(b)** $2x - 3y + 10 = 0$

(c) $2x - y - 2 = 0$ **(d)** $3x - 2y = 0$

88. If a point R(4, y, z) lies on the line segment joining the points P(2, – 3, 4) and Q(8, 0, 10), then the distance of R from the origin is : **[2019, Main]**

(a) $2\sqrt{14}$ **(b)** $2\sqrt{21}$

(c) 6 **(d)** $\sqrt{53}$

89. Given that the slope of the tangent to a curve $y = y(x)$ at any point (x, y) is $\dfrac{2y}{x^2}$. If the curve passes through the centre of the circle $x^2 + y^2 - 2x - 2y = 0$, then its equation is : **[2019, Main]**

(a) $x \log_e |y| = 2(x - 1)$ **(b)** $x \log_e |y| = -2(x - 1)$

(c) $x^2 \log_e |y| = -2(x - 1)$ **(d)** $x \log_e |y| = x - 1$

90. The tangent and the normal lines at the point $(\sqrt{3}, 1)$ to the circle $x^2 + y^2 = 4$ and the x-axis form a triangle. The area of this triangle (in square units) is : **[2019, Main]**

(a) $\dfrac{4}{\sqrt{3}}$ **(b)** $\dfrac{1}{3}$

(c) $\dfrac{2}{\sqrt{3}}$ **(d)** $\dfrac{1}{\sqrt{3}}$

91. In an ellipse, with centre at the origin, if the difference of the lengths of major axis and minor axis is 10 and one of the foci is at $(0, 5\sqrt{3})$, then the length of its latus rectum is : **[2019, Main]**

(a) 10 **(b)** 5

(c) 8 **(d)** 6

92. The tangent to the parabola $y^2 = 4x$ at the point where it intersects the circle $x^2 + y^2 = 5$ in the first quadrant, passes through the point : **[2019, Main]**

(a) $\left(-\dfrac{1}{3}, \dfrac{4}{3}\right)$ **(b)** $\left(\dfrac{1}{4}, \dfrac{3}{4}\right)$

(c) $\left(\dfrac{3}{4}, \dfrac{7}{4}\right)$ **(d)** $\left(-\dfrac{1}{4}, \dfrac{1}{2}\right)$

93. If the angle of intersection at a point where the two circles with radii 5 cm and 12 cm intersect is 90°, then the length (in cm) of their common chord is : **[2019, Main]**

(a) $\dfrac{13}{5}$ **(b)** $\dfrac{120}{13}$

(c) $\dfrac{60}{13}$ **(d)** $\dfrac{13}{2}$

94. The equation $y = \sin x \sin (x + 2) - \sin^2 (x + 1)$ represents a straight line lying in : **[2019, Main]**

(a) second and third quadrants only

(b) first, second and fourth quadrants

(c) first, third and fourth quadrants

(d) third and fourth quadrants only

95. If the normal to the ellipse $3x^2 + 4y^2 = 12$ at a point P on it is parallel to the line, $2x + y = 4$ and the tangent to the ellipse at P passes through Q(4, 4) then PQ is equal to : **[2019, Main]**

(a) $\dfrac{5\sqrt{5}}{2}$

(b) $\dfrac{\sqrt{61}}{2}$

(c) $\dfrac{\sqrt{221}}{2}$

(d) $\dfrac{\sqrt{157}}{2}$

96. Let P be the point of intersection of the common tangents to the parabola $y^2 = 12x$ and the hyperbola $8x^2 - y^2 = 8$. If S and S' denote the foci of the hyperbola where S lies on the positive x-axis then P divides SS' in a ratio : **[2019, Main]**

(a) $13 : 11$

(b) $14 : 13$

(c) $5 : 4$

(d) $2 : 1$

97. An ellipse, with foci at (0, 2) and (0, – 2) and minor axis of length 4, passes through which of the following points ? **[2019, Main]**

(a) $(\sqrt{2}, 2)$

(b) $(2, \sqrt{2})$

(c) $(2, 2\sqrt{2})$

(d) $(1, 2\sqrt{2})$

98. A circle touching the x-axis at (3, 0) and making an intercept of length 8 on the y-axis passes through the point : **[2019, Main]**

(a) $(3, 10)$

(b) $(3, 5)$

(c) $(2, 3)$

(d) $(1, 5)$

99. The equation of common tangent to the curves, $y^2 = 16x$ and $xy = -4$, is : **[2019, Main]**

(a) $x - y + 4 = 0$

(b) $x + y + 4 = 0$

(c) $x - 2y + 16 = 0$

(d) $2x - y + 2 = 0$

100. A triangle has vertex at (1, 2) and the mid points of the two sides through it are (– 1, 1) and (2, 3). Then the centroid of this triangle is : **[2019, Main]**

(a) $\left(1, \dfrac{7}{3}\right)$

(b) $\left(\dfrac{1}{3}, 2\right)$

(c) $\left(\dfrac{1}{3}, 1\right)$

(d) $\left(\dfrac{1}{3}, \dfrac{5}{3}\right)$

101. A straight line L at a distance of 4 units from the origin makes positive intercepts on the coordinate axes and the perpendicular from the origin to the line makes an angle of 60° with the line $x + y = 0$. Then an equation of the line L is : **[2019, Main]**

(a) $x + \sqrt{3}y = 8$

(b) $(\sqrt{3} + 1)x + (\sqrt{3} - 1)y = 8\sqrt{2}$

(c) $\sqrt{3x} + y = 8$

(d) $(\sqrt{3} - 1)x + (\sqrt{3} + 1)y = 8\sqrt{2}$

102. The tangents of the curve $y = (x - 2)^2 - 1$ at its points of intersection with the line $x - y = 3$, intersect at the point : **[2019, Main]**

(a) $\left(\dfrac{5}{2}, 1\right)$

(b) $\left(-\dfrac{5}{2}, -1\right)$

(c) $\left(\dfrac{5}{2}, -1\right)$

(d) $\left(-\dfrac{5}{2}, 1\right)$

103. A rectangle is inscribed in a circle with a diameter lying along the line $3y = x + 7$. If the two adjacent vertices of the rectangle are (– 8, 5) and (6, 5), then the area of the rectangle (in sq. units) is : **[2019, Main]**

(a) 84

(b) 98

(c) 72

(d) 56

104. A line $y = mx + 1$ intersects the circle $(x - 3)^2 + (y + 2)^2 = 25$ at the points P and Q. If the midpoint of the line segment PQ has x-coordinate $-\dfrac{3}{5}$, then which one of the following options is correct ? **[2019, Advanced]**

(a) $-3 \leq m < -1$

(b) $2 \leq m < 4$

(c) $4 \leq m < 6$

(d) $6 \leq m < 8$

105. In a non-right-angled triangle ΔPQR, let p, q, r denote the lengths of the sides opposite to the angles at P, Q, R respectively. The median from R meets the side PQ at S, the perpendicular from P meets the side QR at E, and RS and PE intersect at O. If $p = \sqrt{3}$, $q = 1$, and the radius of the circumcircle of the ΔPQR equals 1, then which of the following options is/are correct ? **[2019, Advanced]**

(a) Length of RS = $\dfrac{\sqrt{7}}{2}$

(b) Area of $\Delta SOE = \dfrac{\sqrt{3}}{12}$

(c) Length of OE = $\dfrac{1}{6}$

(d) Radius of incircle of $\Delta PQR = \dfrac{\sqrt{3}}{2}(2 - \sqrt{3})$

106. Define the collections $\{E_1, E_2, E_3, ...\}$ of ellipses and $\{R_1, R_2, R_3, ...\}$ of rectangles of follows :

$$E_1 : \dfrac{x^2}{9} + \dfrac{y^2}{4} = 1;$$

R_1 : rectangle of largest area, with sides parallel to the axes, inscribed in E_1 ;

E_n : ellipse $\dfrac{x^2}{a_n^2} + \dfrac{y^2}{b_n^2} = 1$ of largest area inscribed in R_{n-1}, $n > 1$;

R_n : rectangle of largest area, with sides parallel to the axes, inscribed in E_n, $n > 1$.

Then which of the following options is/area correct ? **[2019, Advanced]**

(a) The eccentricities of E_{18} and E_{19} are NOT equal

(b) $\sum\limits_{n=1}^{N}$ (area of R_n) < 24, for each positive integer N

(c) Then length of latus rectum of E_9 is $\dfrac{1}{6}$

(d) The distance of a focus from the centre in E_9 is $\dfrac{\sqrt{5}}{32}$

107. Let the point B be the reflection of the point A (2, 3) with respect to the line $8x - 6y - 23 = 0$. Let Γ_A and Γ_B be circles of radii 2 and 1 with centres A and B respectively. Let T be a common tangent to the circles Γ_A and Γ_B such that both the circles are on the same side of Γ. If C is the point of intersection of I and the line passing through A and B, then the length of the line segment AC is :

[2019, Advanced]

Answer Q. 108 and Q. 109 by appropriately matching the lists based on the information given in the paragraph.

Let the circle $C_1 : x^2 + y^2 = 9$ and $C_2 : (x - 3)^2 + (y - 4)^2 = 16$. intersect at the points X and Y. Suppose that another circle $C_3 : (x - h)^2 + (y - k)^2 = r^2$ satisfies the following conditions :

(A) centre of C_3 is collinear with the centres of C_1 and C_2.

(B) C_1 and C_2 both lie inside C_3, and

(C) C_3 touches C_1 at M and C_2 at N.

Let the line through X and Y intersect C_3 at Z and W, and let a common tangent of C_1 and C_3 be a tangent to the parabola $x^2 = 8ay$.

There are some expressions given in the List-I whose values are given in List-II below :

List-I	List-II
(I) $2h + k$	**(P)** 6
(II) $\dfrac{\text{Length of ZW}}{\text{Length of XY}}$	**(Q)** $\sqrt{6}$
(III) $\dfrac{\text{Area of triangle MZN}}{\text{Area of triangle ZMW}}$	**(R)** $\dfrac{5}{4}$
(IV) α	**(S)** $\dfrac{21}{5}$
	(T) $2\sqrt{6}$
	(U) $\dfrac{10}{3}$

108. Which of the following is the only CORRECT combination ? **[2019, Advanced]**

(a) (I), (S)   **(b)** (I), (U)

(c) (II), (Q)   **(d)** (II), (T)

109. Which of the following is the only INCORRECT combination ? **[2019, Advanced]**

(a) (I) (P)   **(b)** (IV) (U)

(c) (IV) (R)   **(d)** (IV) (S)

110. A circle passes through the points (2, 3) and (4, 5). If its centre lies on the line, $y - 4x + 3 = 0$, then its radius is equal to : **[2018, Main]**

(a) 2   **(b)** $\sqrt{5}$

(c) $\sqrt{2}$ **(d)** 1

111. If the tangents drawn to the hyperbola $4y^2 = x^2 + 1$ intersect the co-ordinate axes at the distinct points A and B, then the locus of the mid point of AB is : **[2018, Main]**

(a) $x^2 - 4y^2 + 16x^2y^2 = 0$

(b) $x^2 - 4y^2 - 16x^2y^2 = 0$

(c) $4x^2 - y^2 + 16x^2y^2 = 0$

(d) $4x^2 - y^2 - 16x^2y^2 = 0$

112. If β is one of the angles between the normals to the ellipse, $x^2 + 3y^2 = 9$ at the points $(3\cos\theta, \sqrt{3}\sin\theta)$ and $(-3\sin\theta, \sqrt{3}\cos\theta$ and $0 \in \left(0, \dfrac{\pi}{2}\right)$; then $\dfrac{2\cot\beta}{\sin 2\theta}$ is equal to : **[2018, Main]**

(a) $\dfrac{2}{\sqrt{3}}$ **(b)** $\dfrac{1}{\sqrt{3}}$

(c) $\sqrt{2}$ **(d)** $\dfrac{\sqrt{3}}{4}$

113. The locus of the point of intersection of the lines, $\sqrt{2}x - y + 4\sqrt{2}k = 0$ and $\sqrt{2}kx + ky - 4\sqrt{2} = 0$

(k is any non-zero real parameter), is :

[2018, Main]

(a) an ellipse whose eccentricity is $\dfrac{1}{\sqrt{3}}$.

(b) an ellipse with length of its major axis $8\sqrt{2}$.

(c) a hyperbola whose eccentricity is $\sqrt{3}$.

(d) a hyperbola with length of its transverse axis $8\sqrt{2}$.

114. Let P be a point on the parabola, $x^2 = 4y$. If the distance of P from the centre of the circle, $x^2 + y^2 + 6x + 8 = 0$ is minimum, then the equation of the tangent to the parabola at P, is :

[2018, Main]

(a) $x + 4y - 2 = 0$ **(b)** $x - y + 3 = 0$

(c) $x + y + 1 = 0$ **(d)** $x + 2y = 0$

115. If the length of the latus rectum of an ellipse is 4 units and the distance between a focus and its nearest vertex on the major axis is $\dfrac{3}{2}$ units, then its eccentricity is : **[2018, Main]**

(a) $\dfrac{1}{2}$ **(b)** $\dfrac{1}{3}$

(c) $\dfrac{2}{3}$ **(d)** $\dfrac{1}{9}$

116. Two sets A and B are as under :

$A = \{a, b) \in R \times R : |a - 5| < 1 \text{ and } |b - 5| < 1\};$

$B = \{(a, b) \in R \times R : 4(a - 6)^2 + 9(b - 5)^2 \leq 36\}.]$

Then : **[2018, Main]**

(a) $B \subset A$

(b) $A \subset B$

(c) $A \cap B = \infty$ (an empty set)

(d) neither $A \subset B$ nor $B \subset A$

117. If the curves $y^2 = 6x$, $9x^2 + by^2 = 16$ intersect each other at right angles, then the value of b is :

[2018, Main]

(a) 6   **(b)** $\dfrac{7}{2}$

(c) 4   **(d)** $\dfrac{9}{2}$

118. A straight line through a fixed point (2, 3) intersect the coordinate axes at distinct points P and Q. If O is the origin and the rectangle OPRQ is completed, then the locus of R is :

[2018, Main]

(a) $3x + 2y = 6$ **(b)** $2x + 3y = xy$

(c) $3x + 2y = xy$ **(d)** $3x + 2y = 6xy$

119. Let the orthocentre and centroid of a triangle be A(– 3, 5) and B(3, 3) respectively. If C is the circumcentre of this triangle, then the radius of the circle having line segment AC as diameter, is : **[2018, Main]**

(a) $\sqrt{10}$ **(b)** $2\sqrt{10}$

(c) $3\sqrt{\dfrac{5}{2}}$ **(d)** $\dfrac{3\sqrt{5}}{2}$

120. Tangent and normal are drawn at P(16, 16) on the parabola $y^2 = 16x$, which intersect the axis of the parabola at A and B, respectively. If C is the centre of the circle through the points P, A and B are $\angle CPB = \theta$, then a value of $\tan \theta$ is :

[2018, Main]

(a) $\dfrac{1}{2}$ **(b)** 2

(c) 3   **(d)** $\dfrac{4}{3}$

121. Tangents are drawn to the hyperbola $4x^2 - y^2 = 36$ at the points P and Q. If these tangents intersect at the point T(0, 3) then the area (in sq. units) of ΔPTQ is : **[2018, Main]**

(a) $45\sqrt{5}$ **(b)** $54\sqrt{3}$

(c) $60\sqrt{3}$ **(d)** $36\sqrt{5}$

122. A tangent to the curve, $y = f(x)$ at P (x, y) meets x-axis at A and y-axis at B. If AP : BP = 1 : 3 and $f(1) = 1$, then the curve also passes through the point : **[2017, Main]**

(a) $\left(\dfrac{1}{3}, 24\right)$ **(b)** $\left(\dfrac{1}{2}, 4\right)$

(c) $\left(2, \dfrac{1}{8}\right)$ **(d)** $\left(3, \dfrac{1}{28}\right)$

123. A square, of each side 2, lies above the x-axis and has one vertex at the origin. If one of the side passing through the origin makes an angle 30° with the positive direction of the x-axis, then the sum of the x-coordinates of the vertices of the square is : **[2017, Main]**

(a) $2\sqrt{3} - 1$ **(b)** $2\sqrt{3} - 2$

(c) $\sqrt{3} - 2$ **(d)** $\sqrt{3} - 1$

124. A line drawn through the point P(4, 7) cuts the circle $x^2 + y^2 = 9$ at the points A and B. Then PA·PB is equal to : **[2017, Main]**

(a) 53   **(b)** 56

(c) 74   **(d)** 65

125. The tangent at the point (2, – 2) to the curve, $x^2y^2 - 2x = 4(1 - y)$ does not pass through the point : **[2017, Main]**

(a) $\left(4, \dfrac{1}{3}\right)$ **(b)** (8, 5)

(c) (– 4, – 9)   **(d)** (– 2, – 7)

126. The locus of the point of intersection of the straight lines,

$$tx - 2y - 3t = 0$$

$$x - 2ty + 3 = 0 \ (t \in R), \text{ is :} \quad \textbf{[2017, Main]}$$

(a) an ellipse with eccentricity $\dfrac{2}{\sqrt{5}}$

(b) an ellipse with the length of major axis 6

(c) a hyperbola with eccentricity $\sqrt{5}$

(d) a hyperbola with the length of conjugate axis 3.

127. If two parallel chords of a circle, having diameter 4 units, lie on the opposite sides of the centre and subtend angles $\cos^{-1}\left(\dfrac{1}{7}\right)$ and $\sec^{-1}(7)$ at the centre respectively, then the distance between these chords, is : **[2017, Main]**

(a) $\dfrac{4}{\sqrt{7}}$

(b) $\dfrac{8}{\sqrt{7}}$

(c) $\dfrac{8}{7}$

(d) $\dfrac{16}{7}$

128. If the common tangents to the parabola, $x^2 = 4y$ and the circle, $x^2 + y^2 = 4$ intersect at the point P, then the distance of P from the origin, is :

[2017, Main]

(a) $\sqrt{2} + 1$

(b) $2(3 + 2\sqrt{2})$

(c) $2(\sqrt{2} + 1)$

(d) $3 + 2\sqrt{2}$

129. Consider an ellipse, whose centre is at the origin and its major axis is along the x-axis. If its eccentricity is $\dfrac{3}{5}$ and the distance between its foci is 6, then the area (in sq. units) of the quadrilateral inscribed in the ellipse, with the vertices as the vertices of the ellipse, is :

[2017, Main]

(a) 8

(b) 32

(c) 80

(d) 40

130. The eccentricity of an ellipse having centre at the origin, axes along the co-ordinate axes and passing through the points $(4, -1)$ and $(-2, 2)$ is : **[2017, Main]**

(a) $\dfrac{1}{2}$

(b) $\dfrac{2}{\sqrt{5}}$

(c) $\dfrac{\sqrt{3}}{2}$

(d) $\dfrac{\sqrt{3}}{4}$

131. If $y = mx + c$ is the normal at a point on the parabola $y^2 = 8x$ whose focal distance is 8 units, then $|c|$ is equal to : **[2017, Main]**

(a) $2\sqrt{3}$

(b) $8\sqrt{3}$

(c) $10\sqrt{3}$

(d) $16\sqrt{3}$

132. The two adjacent sides of a cyclic quadrilateral are 2 and 5 and the angle between them is $60°$. If the area of the quadrilateral is $4\sqrt{3}$, then the perimeter of the quadrilateral is : **[2017, Main]**

(a) 12.5

(b) 13.2

(c) 12

(d) 13

133. The minimum distance of a point on the curve $y = x^2 - 4$ from the origin is : **[2016, Main]**

(a) $\dfrac{\sqrt{19}}{2}$

(b) $\sqrt{\dfrac{15}{2}}$

(c) $\dfrac{\sqrt{15}}{2}$

(d) $\sqrt{\dfrac{19}{2}}$

134. If a variable line drawn through the intersection of the line $\dfrac{x}{3} + \dfrac{y}{4} = 1$ and $\dfrac{x}{4} + \dfrac{y}{3} = 1$, meets the coordinate axes at A and B, $(A \neq B)$, then the locus of the midpoint of AB is : **[2016, Main]**

(a) $6xy = 7(x + y)$

(b) $4(x + y)^2 - 28(x + y) + 49 = 0$

(c) $7xy = 6(x + y)$

(d) $14(x + y)^2 - 97(x + y) + 168 = 0$

135. The point $(2, 1)$ is translated parallel to the line L $: x - y = 4$ is $2\sqrt{3}$ units. If the new point Q lies in the third quadrant, then the equation of the line passing through Q and perpendicular to L is : **[2016, Main]**

(a) $x + y = 2 - \sqrt{6}$

(b) $x + y = 3 - 3\sqrt{6}$

(c) $x + y = 3 - 2\sqrt{6}$

(d) $2x + 2y = 1 - \sqrt{6}$

136. A circle passes through $(-2, 4)$ and touches the y-axis at $(0, 2)$. Which one of the following equations can represent a diameter of this circle? **[2016, Main]**

(a) $4x + 5y - 6 = 0$

(b) $2x - 3y + 10 = 0$

(c) $3x + 4y - 3 = 0$

(d) $5x + 2y + 4 = 0$

137. Let a and b respectively be the semi-transverse and semi-conjugate axes of a hyperbola whose eccentricity satisfies the equation $9e^2 - 18e + 5 = 0$. If $S(5, 0)$ is a focus and $5x = 9$ is the corresponding directrix of this hyperbola, then $a^2 - b^2$ is equal to : **[2016, Main]**

(a) 7

(b) -7

(c) 5

(d) -5

138. If the tangent at a point on the ellipse $\dfrac{x^2}{27} + \dfrac{y^2}{3} = 1$ meets the coordinate axes at A and B, and O is the origin, then the minimum area (in sq. units) of the triangle OAB is : **[2016, Main]**

(a) $\dfrac{9}{2}$

(b) $3\sqrt{3}$

(b) $9\sqrt{3}$

(d) 9

139. A ray of light is incident along a line which meets another line, $7x - y + 1 = 0$, at the point $(0, 1)$. The ray is then reflected from this point along the line, $y + 2x = 1$. Then the equation of the line of incidence of the ray of light is : **[2016, Main]**

(a) $41x - 38y + 38 = 0$

(b) $41x + 25y - 25 = 0$

(c) $41x + 38y - 38 = 0$

(d) $41x - 25y + 25 = 0$

140. A straight line through origin O meets the lines $3y = 10 - 4x$ and $8x + 6y + 5 = 0$ at points A and B respectively. Then O divides the segment AB in the ratio : **[2016, Main]**

(a) $2 : 3$

(b) $1 : 2$

(c) $4 : 1$

(d) $3 : 4$

141. Equation of the tangent to the circle, at the point $(1, -1)$, whose centre is the point of intersection of the straight lines $x - y = 1$ and $2x + y = 3$ is :

[2016, Main]

(a) $4x + y - 3 = 0$

(b) $x + 4y + 3 = 0$

(c) $3x - y - 4 = 0$

(d) $x - 3y - 4 = 0$

142. P and Q are two distinct points on the parabola, $y^2 = 4x$, with parameters t and t_1 respectively. If the normal at P passes through Q, then the minimum value of t_1^2 is : **[2016, Main]**

(a) 2

(b) 4

(c) 6

(d) 8

143. A hyperbola whose transverse axis is a long the major axis of the conic, $\left|\dfrac{x^2}{3}\right| + \left|\dfrac{y^2}{4}\right| = 4$ and has vertices at the foci of this conic. If the eccentricity of the hyperbola is $\dfrac{3}{2}$, then which of the following points does **NOT** lie on it? **[2016, Main]**

(a) $(0, 2)$

(b) $\left(\sqrt{5}, 2\sqrt{2}\right)$

(c) $\left(\sqrt{10}, 2\sqrt{3}\right)$

(d) $\left(5, 2\sqrt{3}\right)$

144. Let C be a curve given by $y(x) = 1 + \sqrt{4x - 3}$, $x > \dfrac{3}{4}$. If P is a point on C, such that the tangent at P has slope $\dfrac{2}{3}$, then a point through which the normal at P passes, is : **[2016, Main]**

(a) $(2, 3)$

(b) $(4, -3)$

(c) $(1, 7)$

(d) $(3, -4)$

145. Two sides of a rhombus are along the lines, $x - y + 1 = 0$ and $7x - y - 5 = 0$. If its diagonals intersect at $(-1, -2)$, then which one of the following is a vertex of this rhombus ?

[2016, Main]

(a) $(-3, -9)$

(b) $(-3, -8)$

(c) $\left(\dfrac{1}{3}, -\dfrac{8}{3}\right)$

(d) $\left(-\dfrac{10}{3}, -\dfrac{7}{3}\right)$

146. The centres of those circles which touch the circle, $x^2 + y^2 - 8x - 8y - 4 = 0$, externally and also touch the x-axis, lie on : **[2016, Main]**

(a) a circle.

(b) an ellipse which is not a circle.

(c) a hyperbola.

(d) a parabola.

147. If one of the diameters of the circle, given by the equation, $x^2 + y^2 - 4x + 6y - 12 = 0$, is a chord of a circle S, whose centre is at $(-3, 2)$, then the radius of S are : **[2016, Main]**

(a) $5\sqrt{2}$

(b) $5\sqrt{3}$

(c) 5

(d) 10

148. Let P be the point on the parabola, $y^2 = 8x$ which is at a minimum distance from the centre C of the circle, $x^2 + (y + 6)^2 = 1$. Then the equation of the circle, passing through C and having its centre at P is : **[2016, Main]**

(a) $x^2 + y^2 - 4x + 8y + 12 = 0$

(b) $x^2 + y^2 - x + 4y - 12 = 0$

(c) $x^2 + y^2 - \dfrac{x}{4} + 2y - 24 = 0$

(d) $x^2 + y^2 - 4x + 9y + 18 = 0$

149. The eccentricity of the hyperbola whose length of the latus rectum is equal to 8 and the length of its conjugate axis is equal to half of the distance between its foci, is : **[2016, Main]**

(a) $\dfrac{4}{3}$

(b) $\dfrac{4}{\sqrt{3}}$

(c) $\dfrac{2}{\sqrt{3}}$

(d) $\sqrt{3}$

150. The numbers of points, having both co-ordinates as integers, that lie in the interior of the triangle with vertices $(0, 0)$, $(0, 41)$ and $(41, 0)$, is : **[2015, Main]**

(a) 901

(b) 861

(c) 820

(d) 780

151. Locus of the image of the points $(2, 3)$ in the line $(2x - 3y + 4) + k(x - 2y + 3) = 0, k \in$ R is a : **[2015, Main]**

(a) straight line parallel to x-axis.

(b) straight line parallel to y-axis.

(c) circle of radius $\sqrt{2}$.

(d) circle of radius $\sqrt{3}$.

152. The number of common tangents to the circles $x^2 + y^2 - 4x - 6y - 12 = 0$ and $x^2 + y^2 + 6x + 18y + 26 = 0$ is : **[2015, Main]**

(a) 1

(b) 2

(c) 3

(d) 4

153. The area (in sq. units) of the quadrilateral formed by the tangents at the end point of the latusrectumer to the ellipse $\dfrac{x^2}{9} + \dfrac{y^2}{5} = 1$, is : **[2015, Main]**

(a) $\dfrac{27}{4}$

(b) 18

(c) $\dfrac{27}{2}$

(d) 27

154. Let O be the vertex and Q be any point on the parabola, $x^2 = 8y$. If the point P divides the line segment OQ internally in the ratio 1 : 3, then the locus of P is : **[2015, Main]**

(a) $x^2 = y$

(b) $y^2 = x$

(c) $y^2 = 2x$

(d) $x^2 = 2y$

155. A straight l ine L through the point $(3, -2)$ is inclined at an angle of $60°$ to the line $\sqrt{3}\, x + y = 1$. If L also intersects the x-axis, then the equation of L is : **[2015 Main]**

(a) $y + \sqrt{3}\, x + 2 - 3\sqrt{3}\, x = 0$

(b) $y - \sqrt{3}\, x + 2 + 3\sqrt{3} = 0$

(c) $\sqrt{3}\, y - x + 3 + 2\sqrt{3} = 0$

(d) $\sqrt{3}\, y + x - 3 + 2\sqrt{3} = 0$

156. If the incentre of an equilateral triangle is $(1, 1)$ and the equation of its one side is $3x + 4y + 3 = 0$, then the equation of the circumcircle of this triangle is : **[2015, Main]**

(a) $x^2 + y^2 - 2x - 2y - 2 = 0$

(b) $x^2 + y^2 - 2x - 2y - 14 = 0$

(c) $x^2 + y^2 - 2x - 2y + 2 = 0$

(d) $x^2 + y^2 - 2x - 2y - 7 = 0$

157. If a circle passing though the point $(-1, 0)$ touches y-axis at $(0, 2)$, then the length of the chord of the circle along the x-axis is : **[2015, Main]**

(a) $\dfrac{3}{2}$

(b) $\dfrac{5}{2}$

(c) 3

(d) 5

158. If the distance between the foci of an ellipse is half the length of its latus rectum, then the eccentricity of the ellipse is : **[2015, Main]**

(a) $\dfrac{1}{2}$

(b) $\dfrac{2\sqrt{2} - 1}{2}$

(c) $\sqrt{2} - 1$

(d) $\dfrac{\sqrt{2} - 1}{2}$

159. Let PQ be a double ordinate of the parabola, $y^2 = -4x$, where P lies in the second quadrant. If R divides PQ in the ratio 2 : 1, then the locus of R is : **[2015, Main]**

(a) $9y^2 = 4x$

(b) $9y^2 = -4x$

(c) $3y^2 = 2x$

(d) $3y^2 = -2x$

160. Let PS be the median of the triangle with vertices P(2, 2), Q(6, -1) and R(7, 3). The equation of the line passing through (1, -1) and parallel to PS is : **[2014, Main]**

(a) $4x + 7y + 3 = 0$

(b) $2x - 9y - 11 = 0$

(c) $4x - 7y - 11 = 0$

(d) $2x + 9y + 7 = 0$

161. Let a, b, c and d be non-zero numbers. If the point of intersection of the lines $4ax + 2ay + c = 0$ and $5bx + 2by + d = 0$ lies in the fourth quadrant and is equidistant from the two axes then : **[2014, Main]**

(a) $3bc - 2ad = 0$

(b) $3bc + 2ad = 0$

(c) $2bc - 3ad = 0$

(d) $2bc + 3ad = 0$

162. The locs of the foot of perpendicular drawn from the centre of the ellipse $x^2 + 3y^2 = 6$ on any tangent to it is : **[2014, Main]**

(a) $(x^2 + y^2)^2 = 6x^2 + 2y^2$

(b) $(x^2 + y^2)^2 = 6x^2 - 2y^2$

(c) $(x^2 - y^2)^2 = 6x^2 + 2y^2$

(d) $(x^2 - y^2)^2 = 6x^2 - 2y^2$

163. Let C be the circle with centre at (1, 1) and radius = 1. If T is the circle centred at $(0, y)$, passing through origin and touching the circle C externally, then the radius of T is equal to : **[2014, Main]**

(a) $\dfrac{1}{2}$

(b) $\dfrac{1}{4}$

(c) $\dfrac{\sqrt{3}}{\sqrt{2}}$

(d) $\dfrac{\sqrt{3}}{2}$

164. Two parallel chords of a circle of radius 2 are at a distance $\sqrt{3} + 1$ apart. If the chords subtend at the centre, angles of $\dfrac{\pi}{k}$ and $\dfrac{2\pi}{k}$, where $k > 0$, then the value of $[k]$ is : **[2010, Advanced]**

[Note : $[k]$ denotes the largest integer less than or equal to $k]$

Paragraph for question (165, 166 and 167)

Tangents are drawn from the point P(3, 4) to the ellipse $\dfrac{x^2}{9} + \dfrac{y^2}{4} = 1$ touching the ellipse at point A and B.

165. The coordinates of A and B are :

[2010, Advanced]

(a) $(3, 0)$ and $(0, 2)$

(b) $\left(-\dfrac{8}{5}, \dfrac{2\sqrt{161}}{15}\right)$ and $\left(-\dfrac{9}{5}, \dfrac{8}{5}\right)$

(c) $\left(-\dfrac{8}{5}, \dfrac{2\sqrt{161}}{15}\right)$ and $(0, 2)$

(d) $(3, 0)$ and $\left(-\dfrac{9}{5}, \dfrac{8}{5}\right)$

166. The orthocentre of the triangle PAB is :

[2010, Advanced]

(a) $\left(5, \dfrac{8}{7}\right)$ 　　　 **(b)** $\left(\dfrac{7}{5}, \dfrac{25}{8}\right)$

(c) $\left(\dfrac{11}{5}, \dfrac{8}{5}\right)$ 　　　 **(d)** $\left(\dfrac{8}{25}, \dfrac{7}{5}\right)$

167. The equation of the locus of the point whose distances from the point P and the line AB are equal, is : [2010, Advanced]

(a) $9x^2 + y^2 - 6xy - 54x - 62y + 241 = 0$

(b) $x^2 + 9y^2 + 6xy - 54x + 64y - 241 = 0$

(c) $9x^2 + 9y^2 - 6xy - 54x - 62y - 241 = 0$

(d) $x^2 + y^2 - 2xy + 27x + 31y - 120 = 0$

168. Consider a branch of the hyperbola

$$x^2 - 2y^2 - 2\sqrt{2}x - 4\sqrt{2}\,y - 6 = 0$$

with vertex at the point A. Let B be one of the end points of its lauts rectum. If C is the focus of the hyperbola nearest to the point A, then the area of the triangle ABC is : [2008, Advanced]

(a) $1 - \sqrt{\dfrac{2}{3}}$ 　　　 **(b)** $\sqrt{\dfrac{3}{2}} - 1$

(c) $1 + \sqrt{\dfrac{2}{3}}$ 　　　 **(d)** $\sqrt{\dfrac{3}{2}} + 1$

169. The line $y = x$ meets $y = ke^x$ for $k \le 0$ at

[2007, Advanced]

(a) no point 　　　 **(b)** one point

(c) two points 　　　 **(d)** more than two points

170. Let $O(0, 0)$, $P(3, 4)$, $Q(6, 0)$ be the vertices of the triangle OPQ. The point R inside the triangle OPQ is such that the triangles OPR, PQR, OQR are of equal area. The coordinates of R are :

[2007, Advanced]

(a) $\left(\dfrac{4}{3}, 3\right)$ 　　　 **(b)** $\left(3, \dfrac{2}{3}\right)$

(c) $\left(3, \dfrac{4}{3}\right)$ 　　　 **(d)** $\left(\dfrac{4}{3}, \dfrac{2}{3}\right)$

171. Match the statements in **Column I** with the properties in **Column II** and indicate your answer by darkening the appropriate bubbles in the 4 × 4 matrix given in the ORS.

Column I	Column II
(a) Two intersecting circles	(p) have a common tangent
(b) Two mutually external circles	(q) have a common normal
(c) Two circles, one strictly inside the other	(r) do not have a common tangent
(d) Two branches of a hyperbola	(s) do not have a common normal

172. The axis of a parabola is along the line $y = x$ and the distance of its vertex from origin is $\sqrt{2}$ and that form its focus is $2\sqrt{2}$. If vertex and focus both the lie in the first quadrant, then the equation of the parabola is : [2006, Main]

(a) $(x + y)^2 = (x - y - 2)$ 　 **(b)** $(x - y)^2 = (x + y - 2)$

(c) $(x - y)^2 = 4(x + y - 2)$ 　 **(d)** $(x + y)^2 = 8(x + y - 2)$

173. The equations of the common tangents to the parabola $y = x^2$ and $y = -(x - 2)^2$ is/are :

[2006, Main]

(a) $y = 4(x - 1)$ 　　　 **(b)** $y = 0$

(c) $y = -4(x - 1)$ 　　 **(d)** $y = -30x - 50$

174. A tangent drawn to the curve $y = f(x)$ at $P(x, y)$ cuts the x-axis and Y-axis at A and B respectively such that $BP : AP = 3 : 1$, given that $f(1) = 1$, then:

[2006, Main]

(a) equation of curve is $x\dfrac{dy}{dx} - 3y = 0$

(b) normal at $(1, 1)$ is $x + 3y = 4$

(c) curve passes through $(2, 1/8)$

(d) equation of curve is $x\dfrac{dy}{dx} + 3y = 0$

175. If a hyperbola passes through the focus of the ellipse $\dfrac{x^2}{25} + \dfrac{y^2}{16} = 1$ and its transverse and conjugate axes coincide with the major and minor axes of the ellipse, and the product of eccentricities is 1, then : [2006, Main]

(a) the equation of hyperbola is $\dfrac{x^2}{9} - \dfrac{y^2}{16} = 1$

(b) the equation of hyperbola is $\dfrac{x^2}{9} - \dfrac{y^2}{25} = 1$

(c) focus of hyperbola is $(5, 0)$

(d) focus of hyperbola is $(5\sqrt{3}, 0)$

176. A circle touches the line L and the circle C_1 externally such that both the circles are on the same side of the line, then the locus of centre of the circle is : **[2006, Main]**

(a) ellipse   (b) hyperbola

(c) parabola   (d) parts of straight line

177. A line M through A is drawn parallel to BD. Point S moves such that its distances from the line BD and the vertex A are equal. If locus of S cuts M at T_2 and T_3 and AC at T_1, then area of $\Delta T_1 T_2 T_3$ is: **[2006, Main]**

(a) $\dfrac{1}{2}$ sq. unit   (b) $\dfrac{2}{3}$ sq. unit

(c) 1 sq. unit   (d) 2 sq. unit

178. Match the following :

Normals are drawn at point P, Q and R lying on the parabola $y^2 = 4x$ which intersect at (3, 0). Then **[2006, Main]**

(a) Area of ΔPQR   (i) 2

(b) Radius of circumcircle of ΔPQR   (ii) 5/2

(c) Centroid of ΔPQR   (iii) (5/2, 0)

(d) Circumcentre of ΔPQR   (iv) (2/3, 0)

179. Circles with radii 3, 4 and 5 touch each other externally if P is the point of intersection of tangents to these circles at their points of contact. Find the distance of P from the points of contact. **[2005, Main]**

180. The area of the triangle formed by the intersection of a line parallel to X-axis and passing through P(h, k) with the lines $y = x$ and $x + y = 2$ in $4h^2$. Find the locus of the point P. **[2005, Main]**

181. Tangents are drawn from any point on the hyperbola $\dfrac{x^2}{9} - \dfrac{y^2}{4} = 1$ to the circle $x^2 + y^2 = 9$. Find the locus of mid-point of the chord of contact. **[2005, Main]**

182. Find the equation of the common tangent in 1st quadrant to the circle $x^2 + y^2 = 16$ and the ellipse $\dfrac{x^2}{25} + \dfrac{y^2}{4} = 1$. Also find the length of the intercept of the tangent between the coordinate axes. **(2005, Main)**

183. In an equilateral triangle, 3 coins of radii 1 unit each are kept so that they touch each other and also the sides of the triangle. So the area of equilateral Δ is : **[2005, Screening]**

(a) $4 + 2\sqrt{3}$ (b) $6 + 4\sqrt{3}$

(c) $12 + \dfrac{7\sqrt{3}}{4}$ (d) $3 + \dfrac{7\sqrt{3}}{4}$

184. The minimum area of triangle formed by the tangent to the ellipse $\dfrac{x^2}{a^2} + \dfrac{y^2}{b^2} = 1$ and coordinate axes is : **[2005, Screening]**

(a) ab sq. units   (b) $\dfrac{a^2 + b^2}{2}$ sq. units

(c) $\dfrac{(a+b)^2}{2}$ sq. units   (d) $\dfrac{a^2 + ab + b^2}{3}$ sq. units

185. Tangent to the curve $y = x^2 + 6$ at a point P (1, 7) touches the circle $x^2 + y^2 + 16x + 12y + c = 0$ at a point Q. Then the coordinates of Q are : **[2005, Screening]**

(a) $(-6, -11)$ (b) $(-9, -13)$

(c) $(-10, -15)$ (d) $(-6, -7)$

186. A circle touches the line $2x + 3y + 1 = 0$ at the point $(1, -1)$ and is orthogonal to the circle which has the line segment having end points $(0, -1)$ and $(-2, 3)$ as the diameter. **(2004, Main)**

187. At any point P on the parabola $y^2 - 2y - 4x + 5 = 0$, a tangent is drawn which meets the directrix at Q. Find the locus of point R which divides OP externally in the ratio $\dfrac{1}{2} : 1$ **(2004, Main)**

188. Area of the triangle formed by the line $x + y = 3$ and angle bisectors of the pair of straight lines $x^2 - y^2 + 2y = 1$ is : **[2004, Screening]**

(a) 2 sq. units   (b) 4 sq. units

(c) 6 sq. units   (d) 8 sq. units

189. If tangents are drawn to the ellipse $x^2 + 2y^2 = 2$, then the locus of the mid-poinf of the intercept made by the tangents between the coordinate axes is : **[2004, Screening]**

(a) $\dfrac{1}{2x^2} + \dfrac{1}{4y^2} = 1$ (b) $\dfrac{1}{4x^2} + \dfrac{1}{2y^2} = 1$

(c) $\dfrac{x^2}{2} + \dfrac{y^2}{4} = 1$ (d) $\dfrac{x^2}{4} + \dfrac{y^2}{2} = 1$

190. The angle between the tangents drawn from the point (1, 4) to the parabola $y^2 = 4x$ is : **[2004, Screening]**

(a) $\pi/6$ (b) $\pi/4$

(c) $\pi/3$ (d) $\pi/2$

191. If the line $2x + \sqrt{6}\,y = 2$ touches the hyperbola $x^2 - 2y^2 = 4$, then the point of contact is : **[2004, Screening]**

(a) $(-2, \sqrt{6})$ (b) $(-5, 2\sqrt{6})$

(c) $\left(\dfrac{1}{2}, \dfrac{1}{\sqrt{6}}\right)$ (d) $(4, -\sqrt{6})$

192. If one of the diameter of the circle $x^2+y^2-2x-6y+6=0$ is a chord to the circle with centre $(2, 1)$, then the radius of the circle is :

[**2004, Screening**]

(a) $\sqrt{3}$ (b) $\sqrt{2}$

(c) 3   (d) 2

193. The area of the quadrilateral formed by the tangent at the end points of latus rectm to the ellipse $\dfrac{x^2}{9} + \dfrac{y^2}{5} = 1$, is :   [**2003, Screening**]

(a) 27/4 sq. units   (b) 9 sq. units

(c) 27/2 sq. units   (d) 27 sq. units

194. The number of integral points (integral point means both the coordinates should be integer exactly in the interior of the triangle with vertices $(0, 0)$ and $(0, 21)$ and $(21, 0)$, is : [**2003, Screening**]

(a) 133   (b) 190

(c) 233   (d) 105

195. If the angles of a triangle are in the ratio $4 : 1 : 1$, then the ratio of the longest side of the perimeter is :   [**2003, Screening**]

(a) $\sqrt{3} : (2 + \sqrt{3})$ (b) $1 : 6$

(c) $1 : 2 + \sqrt{3}$ (d) $2 : 3$

196. For hyperbola $\dfrac{x^2}{\cos^2\alpha} - \dfrac{y^2}{\sin^2\alpha} = 1$ which of the following reMain constant with change in 'α'   [**2003, Screcning**]

(a) abscissae of vertices

(b) abscissae of foci

(c) eccentricity

(d) directrix

197. The centre of circle inscribed in square formed by the line $x^2 - 8x + 12 = 0$ and $y^2 - 14y + 45 = 0$, is :   [**2003, Screening**]

(a) $(4, 7)$ (b) $(7, 4)$

(c) $(9, 4)$ (d) $(4, 9)$

198. The focal chord to $y^2 = 16x$ is tangent to $(x - 6)^2 + y^2 = 2$, then the possible values of the slope of this chord, are :   [**2003, Screening**]

(a) $\{-1, 1\}$ (b) $\{-2, 2\}$

(c) $\{-2, 1/2\}$ (d) $\{2, -1/2\}$

199. Tangent is drawn to ellipse $\dfrac{x^2}{27} + y^2 = 1$ at $\left(3\sqrt{3}\cos\theta, \sin\theta\right)$ (where $\theta \in (0, \pi/2)$). Then the value of θ such that sum of intercepts on axes made by this tangent is minimum, is :

[**2003, Screening**]

(a) $\pi/3$ (b) $\pi/6$

(c) $\pi/8$ (d) $\pi/4$

200. Orthocentre of triangle with vertices $(0, 0)$, $(3, 4)$ and $(4, 0)$ is :   [**2003, Screening**]

(a) $\left(3, \dfrac{5}{4}\right)$ (b) $(3, 12)$

(c) $\left(3, \dfrac{3}{4}\right)$ (d) $(3, 9)$

201. Let $0 < \alpha < \pi/2$ be a fixed angle. If $P = (\cos\theta, \sin\theta)$ and $Q = (\cos(\alpha - \theta), \sin(\alpha - \theta))$ then Q is obtained from P by :

(a) clockwise rotation around origin through an angle α

(b) anticlockwise rotation around origin through an angle α

(c) reflection in the line through origin with slope $\tan\alpha$

(d) reflection in the line through origin with slope $\tan(\alpha/2)$.

202. Let $P = (-1, 0)$, $Q = (0, 0)$ and $R = (3, 3\sqrt{3})$ be three points. Then the equation of the bisector of the angle PQR is :   [**2002, Screening**]

(a) $(\sqrt{3}/2)\, x + y = 0$ (b) $x + \sqrt{3}\, y = 0$

(c) $\sqrt{3x} + y = 0$ (d) $x + (\sqrt{3}/2)y = 0$

203. A straight line through the origin O meets the parallel lines $4x + 2y = 9$ and $2x + y + 6 = 0$ at points P and Q respectively. Then the point O divides the segment PQ in the ratio :   [**2002, Screening**]

(a) $1 : 2$ (b) $3 : 4$

(c) $2 : 1$ (d) $4 : 3$

204. If the tangent at the point P on the circle $x^2 + y^2 + 6x + 6y = 2$ meets the straight line $5x - 2y + 6 = 0$ at a point Q on the y-axis, then the length of PQ is :   [**2002, Screening**]

(a) 4   (b) $2\sqrt{5}$

(c) 5   (d) $3\sqrt{5}$

205. If $a > 2b > 0$ then the positive value of m for which $y = mx - b\sqrt{1 + m^2}$ is a common tangent to $x^2 + y^2 = b^2$ and $(x - a)^2 + y^2 = b^2$ is :

[**2002, Screening**]

(a) $\dfrac{2b}{\sqrt{a^2 - 4b^2}}$ (b) $\dfrac{\sqrt{a^2 - 4b^2}}{2b}$

(c) $\dfrac{2b}{a - 2b}$ (d) $\dfrac{b}{a - 2b}$

206. The locus of the mid-point of the line segment joining the focus to a moving point on the parabola $y^2 = 4ax$ is another parabola with directrix : **[2002, Screening]**

(a) $x = -a$ **(b)** $x = -a/2$

(c) $x = 0$ **(d)** $x = a/2$

207. The equation of the common tangent to the curves $y^2 = 8x$ and $xy = -1$ is : **[2002, Screening]**

(a) $3y = 9x + 2$ **(b)** $y = 2x + 1$

(c) $2y = x + 8$ **(d)** $y = x + 2$

ANSWER KEY

1. (c)   2. (b)   3. (a)   4. (30)   5. (a)   6. (d)   7. (a)   8. (5)   9. (d)   10. (b)

11. (c)   12. (b)   13. (a)   14. (c)   15. (a)   16. (d)   17. (b)   18. (a)

19. $\dfrac{5 + 9 \sin 2\theta}{2} \le 7$ 20. (b)   21. (c)   22. (c)   23. (3)   24. (a)   25. (b)   26. (b)   27. (b)

28. (0.50)   29. (a)   30. (a)   31. (2)   32. (a,d)   33. (b)   34. (b)   35. (d)   36. (d)   37. (a)

38. (a)   39. (c)   40. (a)   41. (4)   42. (c)   43. (d)   44. (b)   45. (9)   46. (b)   47. (c)

48. (d)   49. (b)   50. (b)   51. (c)   52. (0.50)   53. (c)   54. (d)   55. (b)   56. (b)   57. (36)

58. (c)   59. (c)   60. (5.00)   61. (d)   62. (c)   63. (b)   64. (b)   65. (a)   66. (a)   67. (b)

68. (c)   69. (d)   70. (d)   71. (d)   72. (a)   73. (b)   74. (d)   75. (a)   76. (c)   77. (d)

78. (c)   79. (c)   80. (b)   81. (a)   82. (d)   83. (d)   84. (c)   85. (c)   86. (a)   87. (c)

88. (a)   89. (a)   90. (c)   91. (b)   92. (c)   93. (b)   94. (d)   95. (a)   96. (c)   97. (a)

98. (a)   99. (a)   100. (b)   101. (d)   102. (c)   103. (a)   104. (b)   105. (a,c,d)   106. (b,c)

107. (10.00)   108. (c)   109. (d)   110. (a)   111. (b)   112. (a)   113. (d)   114. (c)   115. (b)

116. (b)   117. (d)   118. (c)   119. (c)   120. (b)   121. (a)   122. (c)   123. (b)   124. (b)   125. (d)

126. (d)   127. (b)   128. (c)   129. (d)   130. (c)   131. (c)   132. (c)   133. (c)   134. (c)   135. (c)

136. (b)   137. (b)   138. (d)   139. (a)   140. (c)   141. (b)   142. (d)   143. (d)   144. (c)   145. (c)

146. (d)   147. (b)   148. (a)   149. (c)   150. (d)   151. (c)   152. (c)   153. (d)   154. (d)   155. (b)

156. (b)   157. (c)   158. (c)   159. (b)   160. (d)   161. (a)   162. (a)   163. (b)   164. (3)   165. (d)

166. (c)   167. (a)   168. (b)   169. (b)   170. (c)   171. (a) – (p), (q), (b) – (p), (q), (c) – (q), (r), (d) – (q), (r)

172. (d)   173. (a,b)   174. (c,d)   175. (a,c)   176. (c)   177. (c)   178. (a) – (i), (b) – (i), (c) – (iv), (d) – (iii)

179. $(\sqrt{5})$ 180. $(y = -2x + 1)$ 181. $\dfrac{x^2}{9} - \dfrac{y^2}{4} = \left(\dfrac{x^2 + y^2}{q} \right)$ 182. $\left(\dfrac{14}{\sqrt{3}} \right)$ 183. (b)   184. (a)   185. (d)

186. $(2x^2 + 2y^2 - 10x - 5y + 1 = 0)$ 187. $((y - 1)^2 (x + 1) + 4 = 0)$ 188. (a)   189. (a)   190. (c)   191. (d)

192. (c)   193. (d)   194. (b)   195. (a)   196. (b)   197. (a)   198. (a)   199. (b)   200. (c)   201. (d)

202. (c)   203. (b)   204. (c)   205. (a)   206. (c)   207. (d)

ANSWERS WITH EXPLANATIONS

1. **Correct Response :** (c)

Explanation :

$$y = mx + \frac{1}{m} \text{ (tangent at } y^2 = 4x)$$

$$y = mx - m^2 \text{ (tangent at } x^2 = 4y)$$

$$\frac{1}{m} = -m^2 \text{ (for common tangent)}$$

$$m^3 = -1$$

$$m = -1$$

$$y = -x - 1$$

$$x + y + 1 = 0$$

This line touches circle

$\therefore$ apply $p = r$

$$c = \left| \frac{0 + 0 + 1}{\sqrt{2}} \right| = \frac{1}{\sqrt{2}}$$

2. **Correct Response :** (b)

   Explanation :

   Given ellipse is $\dfrac{x^2}{5}+\dfrac{y^2}{4}=1$

   Let point P is $(\sqrt{5}\cos\theta,\ 2\sin\theta)$

   $(PQ)^2 = (\sqrt{5}\cos\theta-0)^2+(2\sin\theta+4)^2$

   $(PQ)^2 = 5\cos^2\theta+4(\sin\theta+2)^2$

   $(PQ)^2 = 5\cos^2\theta+4\sin^2\theta+16+16\sin\theta$

   $\qquad = \cos^2\theta+4(\cos^2\theta+\sin^2\theta)+16+16\sin\theta$

   $\qquad = \cos^2\theta+4+16\sin\theta$

   $(PQ)^2 = \cos^2\theta+16\sin\theta+20$

   $(PQ)^2 = -\sin^2\theta+16\sin\theta+21$

   $\qquad = 85-(\sin\theta-8)^2$

   will be maximum when $\sin\theta = 1$

   $\Rightarrow \qquad (PQ)^2_{max} = 85-49 = 36.$

3. **Correct Response :** (a)

   Explanation :

   $\dfrac{x^2}{16}+\dfrac{y^2}{9}=1$

   $$a = 4;\ b = 3;\ e = \sqrt{\dfrac{16-9}{16}} = \dfrac{\sqrt{7}}{4}$$

   A and B are foci

   $\Rightarrow \qquad PA+PB = 2a = 2\times4 = 8.$

4. **Correct Response :** (30)

   Explanation :

   Apply distance between parallel line formula

   $\qquad 4x-2y+\alpha = 0$

   $\qquad 4x-2y+6 = 0$

   $\qquad \left|\dfrac{\alpha-6}{\sqrt{16+4}}\right| = \dfrac{1}{\sqrt{5}}$

   $\qquad \left|\dfrac{\alpha-6}{2\sqrt{5}}\right| = \dfrac{1}{\sqrt{5}}$

   $\qquad |\alpha-6| = 2 \Rightarrow \alpha = 8, 4$

   $\qquad\qquad \text{sum} = 12$

   again $\qquad 6x-3y+\beta = 0$

   $\qquad 6x-3y+9 = 0$

   $\qquad \left|\dfrac{\beta-9}{3\sqrt{5}}\right| = \dfrac{2}{\sqrt{5}}$

   $\qquad |\beta-9| = 6 \Rightarrow \beta = 15, 3$

   $\qquad\qquad \text{sum} = 18$

   sum of all values of α and β is 30.

5. **Correct Response :** (a)

   Explanation :

   Let foot of perpendicular is (h, k).

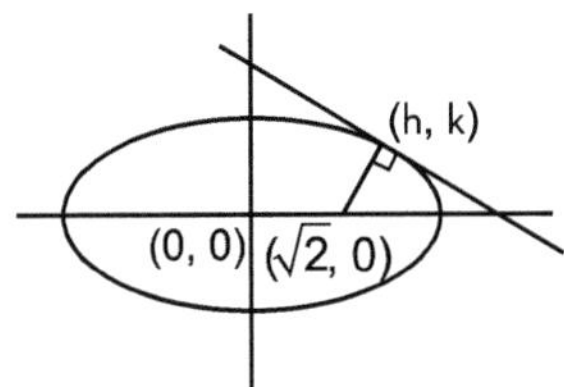

$\dfrac{x^2}{4}+\dfrac{y^2}{2}=1$ (Given)

$$a = 2,\ b = \sqrt{2},\ e = \sqrt{1-\dfrac{2}{4}} = \dfrac{1}{\sqrt{2}}$$

$\therefore\qquad$ Focus $(ae, 0) = (\sqrt{2}, 0)$

Equation of tangent

$$y = mx+\sqrt{a^2m^2+b^2}$$

$$y = mx+\sqrt{4m^2+2}$$

Pass through (h, k)

$\qquad (k-mh)^2 = 4m^2+2 \qquad\qquad …(1)$

Line perpendicular to tangent wil have slope $-\dfrac{1}{m}$

Equation of line passing through $(\sqrt{2}, 0)$

$$y-0 = -\dfrac{1}{m}(x-\sqrt{2})$$

$$my = -x+\sqrt{2}$$

$\qquad (h-mk)^2 = 2 \qquad\qquad …(2)$

Add equation (1) and (2)

$\qquad k^2(1+m^2)+h^2(1+m^2) = 4(1+m^2)$

$\qquad h^2+k^2 = 4$

$\qquad x^2+y^2 = 4$ (Auxilary circle)

$\therefore\ (-1, \sqrt{3})$ lies on the locus.

6. **Correct Response :** (d)

   Explanation :

   $\qquad |x|+|y| \le 1$

   $\qquad 2y^2 \ge |x|$

For point of intersection

$\qquad x+y = 1 \Rightarrow x = 1-y$

$$y^2 = \frac{x}{2} \Rightarrow 2y^2 = x$$

$$2y^2 = 1 - y \Rightarrow 2y^2 + y - 1 = 0$$

$$(2y - 1)(y + 1) = 0$$

$$y = \frac{1}{2} \text{ or} - 1$$

Now Area of $\Delta OAB = \dfrac{1}{2} \times 1 \times 1 = \dfrac{1}{2}$

Area of Region $R_1 = \dfrac{1}{2} \times \dfrac{1}{2} \times \dfrac{1}{2} = \dfrac{1}{8}$

Area of Region $R_2 = \dfrac{1}{\sqrt{2}} \displaystyle\int_0^{\frac{1}{2}} \sqrt{x} \, dx = \dfrac{1}{6}$

Now area of shaded region in first quadrant

= Area of $\Delta OAB - R_1 - R_2$

$$= \frac{1}{2} - \left(\frac{1}{8}\right) - \left(\frac{1}{6}\right) = \frac{5}{24}$$

So required area $= 4\left(\dfrac{5}{24}\right) = \dfrac{5}{6}$

7. Correct Response : (a)

Explanation :

$$y^2 = 4(x + 1)$$

Equation of tangent $y = m(x + 1) + \dfrac{1}{m}$

$$y = mx + m + \frac{1}{m}$$

$$y^2 = 8(x + 2)$$

Equation of tangent $y = m'(x + 2) + \dfrac{2}{m}$,

$$y = m'x + 2\left(m' + \frac{1}{m'}\right)$$

Since lines intersect at right angles.

$$\therefore \qquad mm' = -1$$

Now $\qquad y = mx + m + \dfrac{1}{m} \qquad \qquad …(1)$

$$y = m'x + 2\left(m' + \frac{1}{m'}\right)$$

$$y = -\frac{1}{m}x + 2\left(-\frac{1}{m} - m\right)$$

$$y = -\frac{1}{m}x - 2\left(m + \frac{1}{m}\right) \qquad …(2)$$

From equation (1) and (2)

$$mx + m + \frac{1}{m} = -\frac{1}{m}x - 2\left(m + \frac{1}{m}\right)$$

$$\left(m + \frac{1}{m}\right)x + 3\left(m + \frac{1}{m}\right) = 0$$

$$\therefore \qquad x + 3 = 0.$$

8. Correct Response : (5)

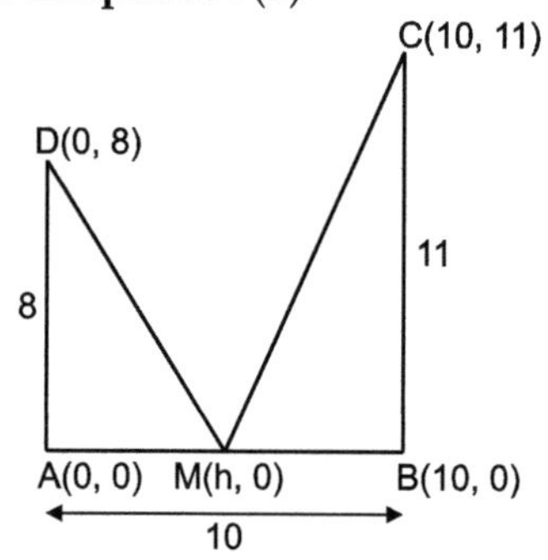

$$(MD)^2 + (MC)^2 = h^2 + 64 + (h - 10)^2 + 121$$

$$= 2h^2 - 20h + 64 + 100 + 121$$

$$= 2(h^2 - 10h) + 285$$

$$= 2(h - 5)^2 + 235$$

It is minimum if $h = 5$.

9. Correct Response : (d)

Explanation :

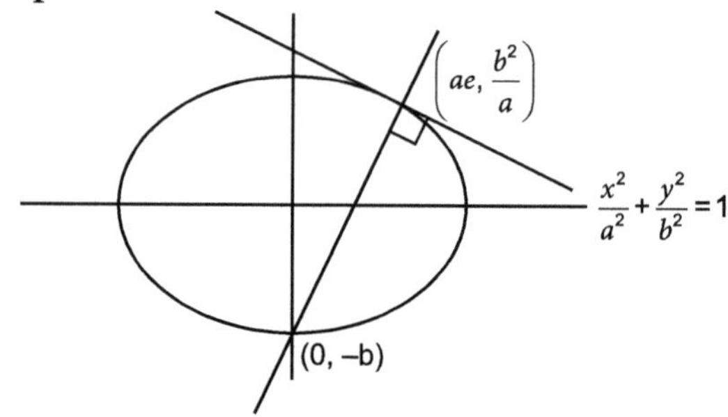

$$\frac{a^2 x}{x_1} - \frac{b^2 y}{y_1} = a^2 e^2$$

$$\frac{a^2 x}{ae} - \frac{b^2 y}{b^2}.a = a^2 e^2$$

$$\frac{ax}{e} - ay = a^2 e^2$$

$$\Rightarrow \qquad \frac{x}{e} - y = ae^2$$

passes through $(0, -b)$

$$+ b = ae^2$$

$$\Rightarrow \qquad b^2 = a^2 e^4 = a^2(1 - e^2)$$

$$a^2(1 - e^2) = a^2 e^4$$

$$\Rightarrow \qquad e^4 + e^2 = 1.$$

10. Correct Response : (b)

Explanation :

$$y = x^2 - 1 \text{ and } y = 1 - x^2$$

$$A = \int_{-1}^{1} [(1 - x^2) - (x^2 - 1)] \, dx$$

$$A = \int_{-1}^{1} (2 - 2x^2)\,dx = 4\int_{0}^{1} (1 - x^2)\,dx$$

$$A = 4\left(x - \frac{x^3}{3} \right)_0^1 = 4\left(\frac{2}{3} \right) = \frac{8}{3} \text{ sq. unit.}$$

11. Correct Response : (c)

Explanation :

$$L : \frac{x}{3} + \frac{y}{1} = 1$$

$$\Rightarrow \qquad x + 3y - 3 = 0$$

Image of point $(-1, -4)$

$$\frac{x+1}{1} = \frac{y+4}{3} = -2\left(\frac{-1 - 12 - 3}{10} \right)$$

$$\frac{x+1}{1} = \frac{y+4}{3} = \frac{16}{5}$$

$$(x, y) \equiv \left(\frac{11}{5}, \frac{28}{5} \right)$$

12. Correct Response : (b)

Explanation :

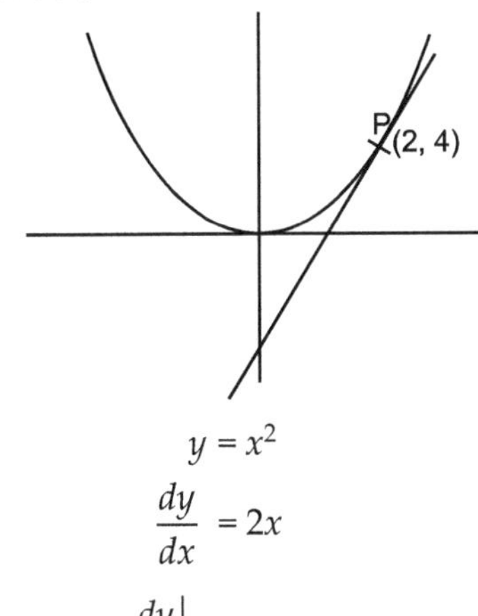

$$y = x^2$$

$$\frac{dy}{dx} = 2x$$

$$\left.\frac{dy}{dx}\right|_p = 4$$

Equation of tangent at P

$$(y - 4) = 4(x - 2)$$

$$4x - y - 4 = 0$$

Circle : $(x - 2)^2 + (y - 4)^2 + \lambda(4x - y - 4) = 0$ passes through $(0, 1)$.

$$4 + 9 + \lambda(-5) = 0 \Rightarrow \lambda = \frac{13}{5}$$

$$x^2 - 4x + 4 + y^2 - 8y + 16 + \lambda(4x - y - 4) = 0$$
$$x^2 + y^2 + x(4\lambda - 4) + y(-\lambda - 8) + (20 - 4\lambda) = 0 \dots(1)$$
$$x^2 + y^2 + 2hx + 2ky + a = 0 \qquad \dots(2)$$
From (1) & (2)

$$2h = 4\lambda - 4, \; 2k = -\lambda - 8$$

$$h = 2\lambda - 2, \; k = \frac{-\lambda - 8}{2}$$

Centre : $(-h, -k)$

$$= \left(2 - 2\lambda, \frac{\lambda + 8}{2} \right)$$

$$= \left(2 - 2 \times \frac{13}{5}, \frac{\frac{13}{5} + 8}{2} \right)$$

$$= \left(\frac{-16}{5}, \frac{53}{10} \right)$$

13. Correct Response : (a)

Explanation :

$$\frac{x^2}{a^2} + \frac{y^2}{b^2} = 1 \;(a > b); \; \frac{2b^2}{a} = 10$$

$$\Rightarrow \qquad b^2 = 5a \qquad\qquad \dots(i)$$

$$\text{Now,} \qquad \phi(t) = \frac{5}{12} + t - t^2 = \frac{8}{12} - \left(t - \frac{1}{2} \right)^2$$

$$\phi(t)_{max} = \frac{8}{12} = \frac{2}{3} = e$$

$$\Rightarrow \qquad e^2 = 1 - \frac{b^2}{a^2} = \frac{4}{9} \qquad \dots(ii)$$

$$\Rightarrow \qquad a^2 = 81 \qquad \text{[from (i) and (ii)]}$$

So, $\quad a^2 + b^2 = 81 + 45 = 126.$

14. Correct Response : (c)

Explanation :

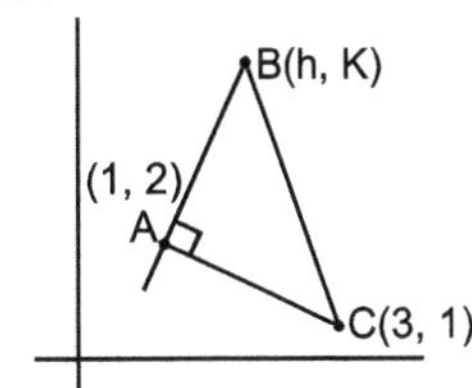

$$m_{AB} m_{AC} = -1$$

$$\left(\frac{k-2}{h-1} \right)\left(\frac{1-2}{3-1} \right) = -1 \Rightarrow K = 2h \qquad \dots(1)$$

$$\because \qquad [\Delta ABC] = 5\sqrt{5}$$

$$\text{Now} \qquad \text{Area of } \Delta ABC = \frac{1}{2} AB.AC$$

$$\Rightarrow \frac{1}{2}\sqrt{(3-1)^2 + (1-2)^2}\;\sqrt{(h-1)^2 + (k-2)^2} = 5\sqrt{5}$$

$$\Rightarrow \frac{1}{2} \times \sqrt{5}\sqrt{(h-1)^2 + (2h-2)^2} = 5\sqrt{5}$$

$$(h - 1) = 2\sqrt{5}$$

$$h = 2\sqrt{5} + 1.$$

15. Correct Response : (a)

Explanation :

Since, $(3, 3)$ lies on $\dfrac{x^2}{a^2} - \dfrac{y^2}{b^2} = 1$

$$\frac{9}{a^2} - \frac{9}{b^2} = 1 \qquad \qquad \text{...(1)}$$

Now, normal at (3, 3) is

$$y - 3 = \frac{a^2}{b^2}(x - 3),$$

which passes through (9, 0)

$$\Rightarrow \qquad b^2 = 2a^2 \qquad \qquad \text{...(2)}$$

So, $\qquad e^2 = 1 + \dfrac{b^2}{a^2} = 3$

Also, $\qquad a^2 = \dfrac{9}{2} \qquad \qquad$ [from (i) & (ii)]

Thus, $\quad (a^2, e^2) = \left(\dfrac{9}{2}, 3\right)$

16. Correct Response : (d)

Explanation :

Let S be the circle passing through point of intersection of S_1 & S_2.

$$\therefore \qquad S = S_1 + \lambda S_2 = 0$$
$$\Rightarrow S : (x^2 + y^2 - 6x) + \lambda(x^2 + y^2 - 4y) = 0$$
$$\Rightarrow S : (\lambda + 1)x^2 + (\lambda + 1)y^2 - 6x - 4\lambda y = 0$$
$$\Rightarrow S : x^2 + y^2 - \left(\frac{6}{1+\lambda}\right)x - \left(\frac{4\lambda}{1+\lambda}\right)y = 0 \quad \text{...(1)}$$

Centre $\left(\dfrac{3}{1+\lambda}, \dfrac{2\lambda}{1+\lambda}\right)$ lies on

$$2x - 3y + 12 = 0$$
$$2\left(\frac{3}{\lambda+1}\right) - 3\left(\frac{2\lambda}{\lambda+1}\right) + 12 = 0$$
$$6 - 6\lambda + 12 = 0$$
$$6\lambda = -18$$
$$\lambda = -3$$

put in (1) $\Rightarrow S : x^2 + y^2 + 3x - 6y = 0$

Option (d) satisfy this equation.

17. Correct Response : (b)

Explanation :

Ellipse : $\quad \dfrac{x^2}{a^2} + \dfrac{y^2}{b^2} = 1$

directrix : $x = \dfrac{a}{e} = 4 \,\& \, e = \dfrac{1}{2}$

$$\Rightarrow \qquad a = 2 \,\& \, b^2 = a^2(1 - e^2) = 3$$

$\Rightarrow$ Ellipse is $\dfrac{x^2}{4} + \dfrac{y^2}{3} = 1$

(1, β) lies on $\dfrac{x^2}{4} + \dfrac{y^2}{3} = 1$

$$\frac{1}{4} + \frac{\beta^2}{3} = 1$$

$$\beta^2 = \frac{9}{4}$$

$$\beta = \frac{3}{2} \qquad \qquad (\because \beta > 0)$$

P is $\left(1, \dfrac{3}{2}\right)$

Normal is : $\dfrac{4x}{1} - \dfrac{3y}{3/2} = 4 - 3$

$$\Rightarrow \qquad 4x - 2y = 1.$$

18. Correct Response : (a)

Explanation :

$$A = \text{area of ABCD}$$
$$\text{Area (A)} = 2t \cdot (1 - t^2) \qquad (0 < t < 1)$$
$$A = 2t - 2t^3$$
$$\frac{dA}{dt} = 2 - 6t^2$$
$$\frac{dA}{dt} = 0$$
$$2 - 6t^2 = 0$$
$$t = \frac{1}{\sqrt{3}}$$

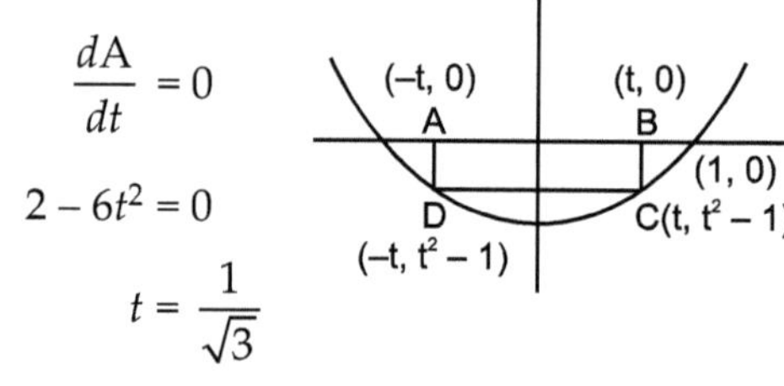

$$\Rightarrow \qquad A_{max} = \frac{2}{\sqrt{3}}\left(1 - \frac{1}{3}\right) = \frac{4}{3\sqrt{3}}.$$

19. Correct Response : $\dfrac{5 + 9\sin 2\theta}{2} \leq 7$

Explanation :

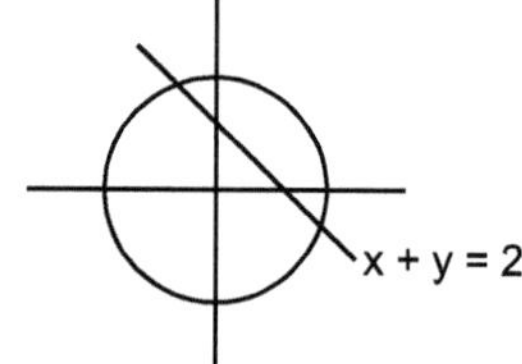

Let $P(3\cos\theta, 3\sin\theta)$

$Q(-3\cos\theta, -3\sin\theta)$

Given line $x + y - 2 = 0$

$$\alpha = \frac{|3\cos\theta + 3\sin\theta - 2|}{\sqrt{2}}$$

$$\beta = \frac{|-3\cos\theta - 3\sin\theta - 2|}{\sqrt{2}}$$

$$\Rightarrow \qquad \alpha\beta = \frac{|(3\cos\theta + 3\sin\theta)^2 - 4|}{2}$$

$$\Rightarrow \qquad \alpha\beta = \frac{5 + 9\sin 2\theta}{2} \leq 7$$

20. Correct Response : (b)

Explanation :

Ellipse : $\dfrac{x^2}{4} + \dfrac{y^2}{3} = 1$

eccentricity $= \sqrt{1 - \dfrac{3}{4}} = \dfrac{1}{2}$

$\therefore$ foci $= (\pm 1, 0)$

for hyperbola given $2a = \sqrt{2}$

$\Rightarrow$ $a = \dfrac{1}{\sqrt{2}}$

$\therefore$ hyperbola will be

$\dfrac{x^2}{1/2} - \dfrac{y^2}{b^2} = 1$

eccentricity $= \sqrt{1 + 2b^2}$

$\therefore$ foci $= \left(\pm \sqrt{\dfrac{1 + 2b^2}{2}}, 0 \right)$

$\because$ Ellipse and hyperbola have same foci.

$\Rightarrow$ $\sqrt{\dfrac{1 + 2b^2}{2}} = 1$

$\Rightarrow$ $b^2 = \dfrac{1}{2}$

$\therefore$ Equation of hyperbola : $\dfrac{x^2}{1/2} - \dfrac{y^2}{1/2} = 1$

$\Rightarrow$ $x^2 - y^2 = \dfrac{1}{2}$

Clearly $\left(\sqrt{\dfrac{3}{2}}, \dfrac{1}{\sqrt{2}} \right)$ does not lie on it.

21. Correct Response : (c)

Explanation :

$0 \le y \le x^2 + 1, \ 0 \le y \le x + 1, \ \dfrac{1}{2} \le x \le 2$

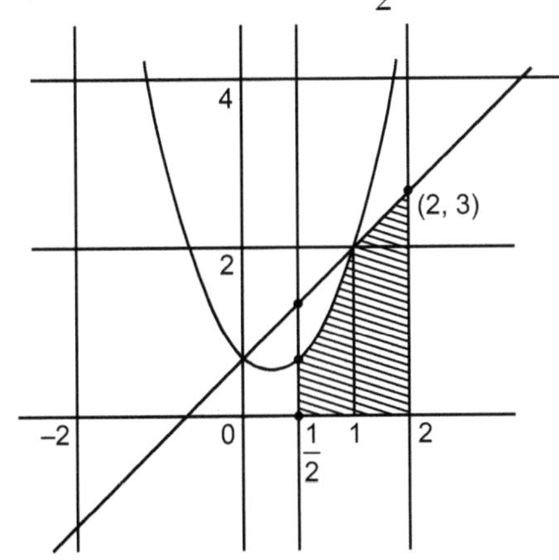

Required area $= \displaystyle\int_{1/2}^{1} (x^2 + 1)\, dx + \dfrac{1}{2}(2 + 3) \times 1$

$= \dfrac{19}{24} + \dfrac{5}{2} = \dfrac{79}{24}.$

22. Correct Response : (c)

Explanation :

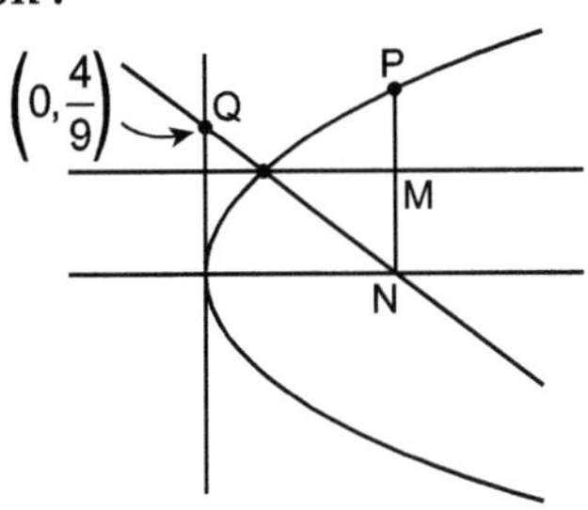

Let $P = (3t^2, 6t); N = (3t^2, 0)$

$M = (3t^2, 3t)$

Equation of MQ : $y = 3t$

$\therefore$ $Q = \left(\dfrac{3}{4} t^2, 3t \right)$

Equation of NQ

$y = \dfrac{3t}{\left(\dfrac{3}{4} t^2 - 3t^2 \right)} (x - 3t^2)$

y-intercept of NQ $= 4t = \dfrac{4}{3} \Rightarrow t = \dfrac{1}{3}$

$\therefore$ $MQ = \dfrac{9}{4} t^2 = \dfrac{1}{4}$

$PM = 6t = 2.$

23. Correct Response : (3)

Explanation :

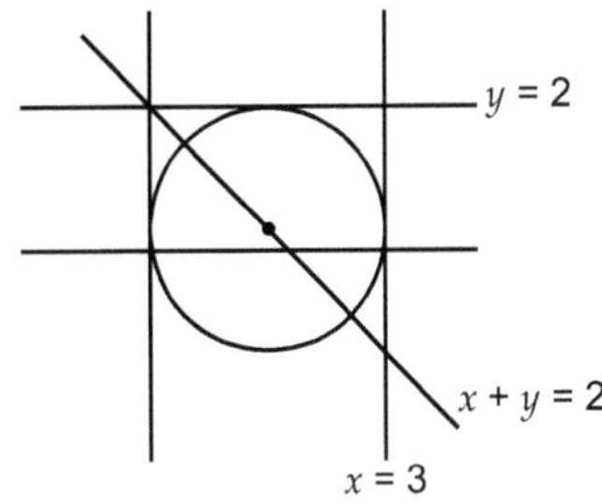

$\because$ centre lies on $x + y = 2$ and in 1st quadrant

centre $= (\alpha, 2 - \alpha)$

where $\alpha > 0$ and $2 - \alpha > 0 \Rightarrow 0 < \alpha < 2$

$\because$ circle touches $x = 3$ and $y = 2$

$\Rightarrow$ $|\, 3 - \alpha \,| = |\, 2 - (2 - \alpha) \,| = $ radius

$\Rightarrow$ $|\, 3 - \alpha \,| = |\, \alpha \,| \Rightarrow \alpha = \dfrac{3}{2}$

$\therefore$ radius $= \alpha$

$\Rightarrow$ Diameter $= 2\alpha = 3.$

24. Correct Response : (a)

Explanation :

$(x - 1)\,[x] \le y \le 2\sqrt{x}, \ 0 \le x \le 2$

Draw $y = 2\sqrt{x}$

$\Rightarrow$ $y^2 = 4x, \ x \ge 0$

$$y = (x-1)\,[x] = \begin{cases} 0 & ,\, 0 \le x < 1 \\ x-1, & 1 \le x < 2 \\ 2, & x = 2 \end{cases}$$

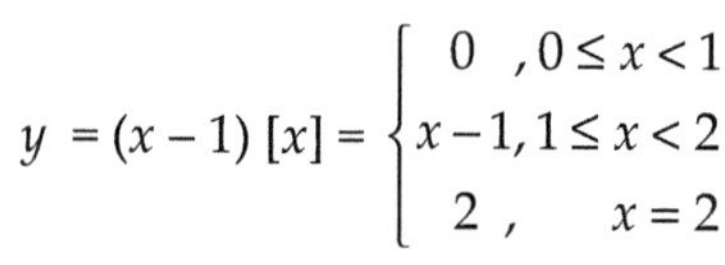

$$A = \int_0^2 2\sqrt{x}\,dx - \frac{1}{2}\cdot 1\cdot 1$$

$$A = 2\cdot\left[\frac{x^{3/2}}{(3/2)}\right]_0^2 - \frac{1}{2} = \frac{8\sqrt{2}}{3} - \frac{1}{2}$$

25. Correct Response : (b)

Explanation :

Let chord

$$AB = r$$

$\because \Delta AOM$ is right angled triangle.

$$OM = \sqrt{r^2 + \left(\frac{r}{2}\right)^2}$$

$$OM = \frac{\sqrt{3}\,r}{2}$$

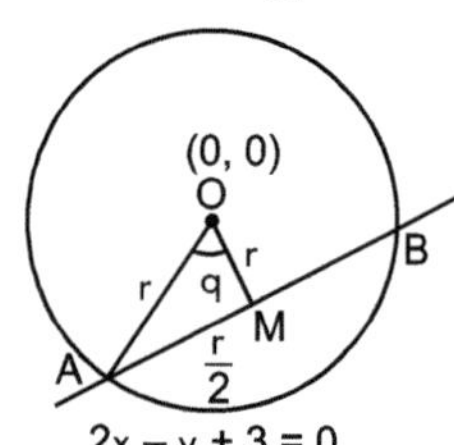

$\therefore \ OM = \dfrac{r\sqrt{3}}{2}$ = perpendicular distance of line

AB from (0, 0).

$$\frac{r\sqrt{3}}{2} = \left|\frac{3}{\sqrt{5}}\right|$$

$$r^2 = \frac{12}{5}.$$

26. Correct Response : (b)

Explanation :

$$y = mx + c \text{ is tangent to}$$

$$\frac{x^2}{100} - \frac{y^2}{64} = 1 \text{ and } x^2 + y^2 = 36$$

$$c^2 = 100m^2 - 64 \mid c^2 = 36(1 + m^2)$$

$$\Rightarrow \quad 100m^2 - 64 = 36 + 36m^2$$

$$m^2 = \frac{100}{64}$$

$$\Rightarrow \qquad m = \pm\frac{10}{8}$$

$$c^2 = 36\left(1 + \frac{100}{64}\right) = \frac{36 \times 164}{64}$$

$$4c^2 = 369.$$

27. Correct Response : (b)

Explanation :

$$x^4 e^y + 2\sqrt{y+1} = 3$$

d.w.r. to x

$$x^4 e^y\, y' + e^y\, 4x^3 + \frac{2y'}{2\sqrt{y+1}} = 0$$

at P(1, 0)

$$y'_p + 4 + y'_p = 0$$

$$\Rightarrow \qquad y'_p = -2$$

Tangent at P(1, 0) is

$$y - 0 = -2(x-1)$$

$$2x + y = 2$$

$(-2, 6)$ lies on it.

28. Correct Response : (0.50)

Explanation :

$$y = x^2 - 3x + 2$$

At x-axis $y = 0 = x^2 - 3x + 2$

$$x = 1, 2$$

$$\frac{dy}{dx} = 2x - 3$$

A(1, 0) B(2, 0)

$$\left(\frac{dy}{dx}\right)_{x=1} = -1 \text{ and } \left(\frac{dy}{dx}\right)_{x=2} = 1$$

$$x + y = a \Rightarrow \frac{dy}{dx} = -1$$

So A(1, 0) lies on it.

$$\Rightarrow \qquad 1 + 0 = a \Rightarrow \boxed{a = 1}$$

$$x - y = b \Rightarrow \frac{dy}{dx} = 1$$

So B(2, 0) lies on it.

$$2 - 0 = b \Rightarrow \boxed{b = 2}$$

$$\frac{a}{b} = 0.50$$

29. Correct Response : (a)

Explanation :

Here $\qquad f(x) = \begin{cases} 0 & ,\, x \le 1 \\ e^{x-1} - e^{1-x}, & x \ge 1 \end{cases}$

&$\qquad g(x) = \dfrac{1}{2}\left(e^{x-1} + e^{1-x}\right)$

Solve $f(x)$ & $g(x) \Rightarrow x = 1 + \ln\sqrt{3}$

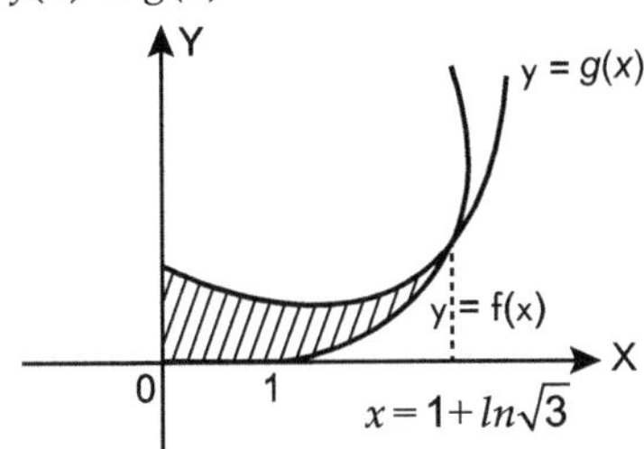

Solve $f(x)$ & $g(x)$

$\Rightarrow \qquad x = 1 + l\,n\sqrt{3}$

So bounded area $= \int_0^1 \frac{1}{2}(e^{x-1} + e^{1-x})\,dx$

$\qquad + \int_1^{1+\ln\sqrt{3}} \frac{1}{2}(e^{x-1} + e^{1-x}) - (e^{x-1} - e^{1-x})\,dx$

$= \int_0^1 \frac{1}{2}(e^{x-1} + e^{1-x})\,dx$

$\qquad + \int_1^{1+\ln\sqrt{3}} \left(-\frac{1}{2}e^{x-1} + \frac{3}{2}e^{x-1}\right)dx$

$= \frac{1}{2}[e^{x-1} - e^{1-x}]_0^1 + \left[-\frac{1}{2}e^{x-1} - \frac{3}{2}e^{1-x}\right]_0^{1+\ln\sqrt{3}}$

$= \frac{1}{2}\left[e - \frac{1}{e}\right] + \left[\left(-\frac{\sqrt{3}}{2} - \frac{\sqrt{3}}{2}\right) + 2\right]$

$= 2 - \sqrt{3} + \frac{1}{2}\left(e - \frac{1}{e}\right).$

30. Correct Response : (a)

Explanation :

$y^2 = 4\lambda x,\ P(\lambda, 2\lambda)$

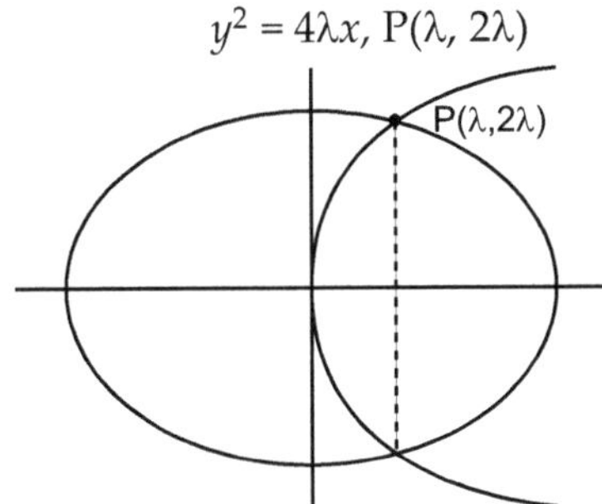

Slope of the tangent to the parabola at point P

$\frac{dy}{dx} = \frac{4\lambda}{2y} = \frac{4\lambda}{2x2\lambda} = 1$

Slope of the tangent to the ellipse at P

$\frac{2x}{a^2} + \frac{2yy'}{b^2} = 0$

As tangents are perpendicular $y' = -1$

$\Rightarrow \qquad \frac{2\lambda}{a^2} - \frac{4\lambda}{b^2} = 0$

$\Rightarrow \qquad \frac{a^2}{b^2} = \frac{1}{2}$

$e = \sqrt{1 - \frac{a^2}{b^2}}$

$\Rightarrow \qquad e = \sqrt{1 - \frac{1}{2}} = \frac{1}{\sqrt{2}}.$

31. Correct Response : (2)

Explanation :

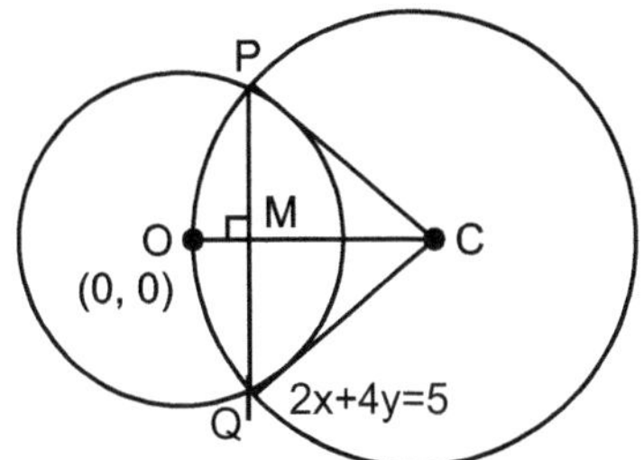

Circumcenter C of $\triangle OPQ$ lies on $x + 2y = 4$

Let $\qquad C = (4 - 2\alpha, \alpha)$

$\because \qquad OC \perp PQ$

$\Rightarrow \qquad M_{OC} \cdot M_{PQ} = -1$

$\Rightarrow \qquad \left(\frac{\alpha}{4 - 2\alpha}\right)\left(-\frac{2}{4}\right) = -1$

$\Rightarrow \qquad \alpha = \frac{8}{5} \Rightarrow C\left(\frac{4}{5}, \frac{8}{5}\right)$

$OM = \frac{|0 + 0 - 5|}{\sqrt{2^2 + 4^2}} = \frac{\sqrt{5}}{2}$

$CM = \frac{\left|2\left(\frac{4}{5}\right) + 4\left(\frac{8}{5}\right) - 5\right|}{\sqrt{2^2 + 4^2}} = \frac{3}{2\sqrt{5}}$

$OC = PC = \sqrt{\left(\frac{4}{5}\right)^2 + \left(\frac{8}{5}\right)^2} = \frac{4}{\sqrt{5}}$

Now $\qquad PM^2 = OP^2 - OM^2$

$\qquad\qquad = PC^2 - CM^2$

$\Rightarrow \qquad r^2 - \frac{5}{4} = \frac{16}{5} - \frac{9}{20}$

$\qquad\qquad r = 2$

32. Correct Response : (a,d)

Explanation :

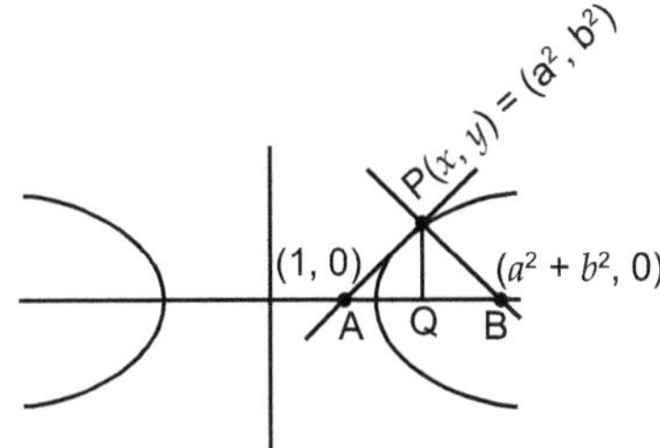

Since Normal at point P makes equal intercept on co-ordinate axes, therefore slope of Normal = 1

Hence slope of tangent = 1

Equation of tangent

$\qquad y - 0 = 1(x - 1)$

$\qquad y = x - 1$

Equation of tangent at (x_1, y_1)

$$\frac{xx_1}{a^2} - \frac{yy_1}{b^2} = 1$$

$$x - y = 1 \qquad \text{(equation of tangent)}$$

on comparing $x_1 = a^2$, $y_1 = b^2$

Also $\qquad a^2 - b^2 = 1 \qquad \qquad ...(1)$

Now equation of normal at

$$(x_1, y_1) = (a^2, b^2)$$
$$y - b^2 = -1(x - a^2)$$
$$x + y = a^2 + b^2 \qquad ...(\text{Normal})$$

Point of intersection with x-axis is $(a^2 + b^2)$

Now $\qquad e = \sqrt{1 + \dfrac{b^2}{a^2}}$

$$e = \sqrt{1 + \frac{b^2}{b^2 + 1}}$$

$$\left[\text{from (1)} \frac{b^2}{b^2 + 1} < 1 \right]$$

$$1 < e < \sqrt{2} \qquad \qquad \text{option (A)}$$

$$\Delta = \frac{1}{2} . AB . PQ$$

and $\qquad \Delta = \dfrac{1}{2}(a^2 + b^2 - 1).b^2$

$$\Delta = \frac{1}{2}(b^2 + 1 + b^2 - 1)b^2$$

$$\qquad \qquad \text{from equation (1)}$$

$$\Delta = \frac{1}{2}(2b^2)b^2$$

$$[\text{from (1)} \ a^2 - 1 = b^2]$$

$$\Delta = b^4$$

33. Correct Response : (b)

Explanation :

Given equation of curve

$y = (1 + x)^{2y} + \cos^2(\sin^{-1} x)$

at $\qquad \qquad x = 0$

$$y = (1 + 0)^{2y} + \cos^2(\sin^{-1} 0)$$
$$y = 1 + 1$$
$$y = 2$$

So we have to find the normal at $(0, 2)$

Now $y = e^{2y \ln(1 + x)} + \cos^2(\cos^{-1}\sqrt{1 - x^2})$

$$y = e^{2y \ln(1 + x)} + (\sqrt{1 - x^2})^2$$

$$y = e^{2y \ln(1 + x)} + (1 - x^2) \qquad ...(1)$$

Now differentiate w.r.t. x

$$y' = e^{2y \ln(1 + x)}\left[2y.\left(\frac{1}{1 + x}\right) + \ln(1 + x).2y' \right] - 2x$$

Put $x = 0$ & $y = 2$

$$y' = e^{2 \times 2/\ln}\left[2 \times 2\left(\frac{1}{1 + 0}\right) + \ln(1 + 0).2y' \right] - 2 \times 0$$

$y' = e^0[4 + 0] - 0$

$y' = 4$ = slope of tangent to the curve

so slope of normal to the curve $= -\dfrac{1}{4} \ \{m_1 m_2 = -1\}$

Hence equation of normal at $(0, 2)$ is

$$y - 2 = \frac{-1}{4}(x - 0)$$

$\Rightarrow \qquad 4y - 8 = -x$

$\Rightarrow \qquad x + 4y = 8$

34. Correct Response : (b)

Explanation :

Given $\theta \in \left(0, \dfrac{\pi}{2}\right)$

equation of hyperbola $\Rightarrow x^2 - y^2 \sec^2\theta = 10$

$\Rightarrow \qquad \dfrac{x^2}{10} - \dfrac{y^2}{10\cos^2\theta} = 1$

Hence eccentricity of hyperbola

$$(e_E) = \sqrt{1 + \frac{10\cos^2\theta}{10}} \qquad ...(1)$$

$$e_E = \sqrt{1 + \cos^2\theta} \qquad \left\{ e = \sqrt{1 + \frac{b^2}{a^2}} \right\}$$

Now equation of ellipse $\Rightarrow x^2 \sec^2\theta + y^2 = 5$

$\Rightarrow \qquad \dfrac{x^2}{5\cos^2\theta} + \dfrac{y^2}{5} = 1 \qquad \left\{ e = \sqrt{1 - \dfrac{a^2}{b^2}} \right\}$

Hence eccenticity of ellipse

$$(e_E) = \sqrt{1 - \frac{5\cos^2\theta}{5}}$$

$$(e_E) = \sqrt{1 - \cos^2\theta}$$

$$= |\sin\theta| = \sin\theta \qquad ...(2)$$

$$\left\{ \because \theta \in \left(0, \frac{\pi}{2}\right) \right\}$$

given $\Rightarrow e_H = \sqrt{5}e_e$

Hence $1 + \cos^2\theta = 5\sin^2\theta$

$$1 + \cos^2\theta = 5(1 - \cos^2\theta)$$
$$1 + \cos^2\theta = 5 - 5\cos^2\theta$$
$$6\cos^2\theta = 4$$

$$\cos^2\theta = \frac{2}{3} \qquad ...(3)$$

Now length of latus rectum of ellipse

$$= \frac{2a^2}{b} = \frac{10\cos^2\theta}{\sqrt{5}} = \frac{20}{3\sqrt{5}} = \frac{4\sqrt{5}}{3}$$

35. Correct Response : (d)

Explanation :

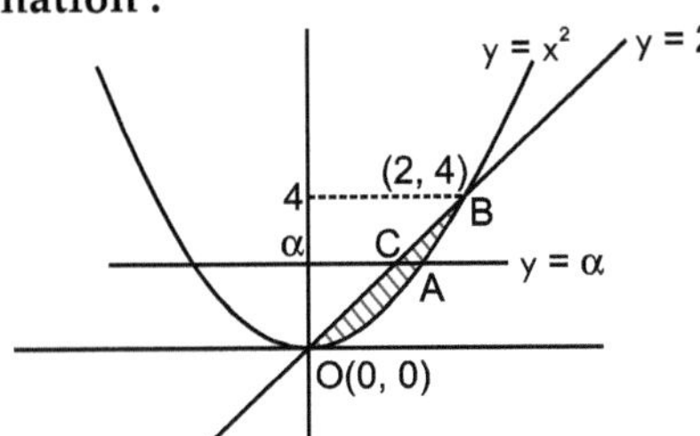

$*\ y \geq x^2 \Rightarrow$ upper region of $y = x^2$

$y \leq 2x \Rightarrow$ lower region of $y = 2x$

According to ques, area of OABC = 2 area of OAC

$$\Rightarrow \int_0^4 \left(\sqrt{y} - \frac{y}{2} \right) dy = 2 \int_0^a \left(\sqrt{y} - \frac{y}{2} \right) dy$$

$$\Rightarrow \left(\frac{2y^{3/2}}{3} - \frac{y^2}{2} \right)\Bigg|_0^4 = 2 \left(\frac{2y^{3/2}}{3} - \frac{y^2}{4} \right)\Bigg|_0^4$$

$$\frac{16}{3} - 4 = 2 \left(\frac{2}{3}\alpha^{\frac{3}{2}} - \frac{\alpha^2}{4} \right)$$

$$\Rightarrow \quad \frac{4}{3} = 2 \left[\frac{2}{3}\alpha^{3/2} - \frac{1}{4}\cdot\alpha^2 \right]$$

$$\Rightarrow \quad 3\alpha^2 - 8\alpha^{3/2} + 8 = 0$$

36. Correct Response : (d)

Explanation :

Given that both points (1, 2) & $(\sin\theta, \cos\theta)$ lie on same side of the line $x + y - 1 = 0$

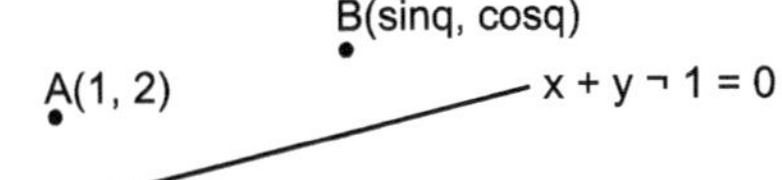

So, $\left(\dfrac{\text{Put}(1,2)\text{ in}}{\text{given line}} \right)\left(\dfrac{\text{Put}(\sin\theta,\cos\theta)\text{ in}}{\text{given line}} \right) > 0$

$\Rightarrow (1 + 2 - 1)(\sin\theta + \cos\theta - 1) > 0$

$\Rightarrow \sin\theta + \cos\theta > 1 \ \{\div \text{ by } \sqrt{2}\}$

$\Rightarrow \dfrac{1}{\sqrt{2}}\sin\theta + \dfrac{1}{\sqrt{2}}\cos\theta > \dfrac{1}{\sqrt{2}}$

$\Rightarrow \cos\dfrac{\pi}{4}\sin\theta + \sin\dfrac{\pi}{4}\cos\theta > \dfrac{1}{\sqrt{2}}$

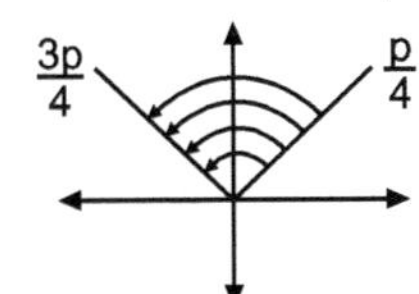

$\Rightarrow \sin\left(\theta + \dfrac{\pi}{4} \right) > \dfrac{1}{\sqrt{2}}$

$\Rightarrow \dfrac{\pi}{4} < \theta + \dfrac{\pi}{4} < \dfrac{3\pi}{4}$

$\Rightarrow 0 < \theta < \dfrac{\pi}{2}$

37. Correct Response : (a)

Explanation :

$$\frac{d}{dt}(6a^2) = 3.6 \Rightarrow 12a\frac{da}{dt} = 3.6$$

$$a\frac{da}{dt} = 0.3$$

$$\frac{dv}{dt} = \frac{d}{dt}(a^3) = 3a\left(a\frac{da}{dt} \right)$$

$$= 3 \times 10 \times 0.3 = 9$$

38. Correct Response : (a)

Explanation :

Length of latus rectum = 4

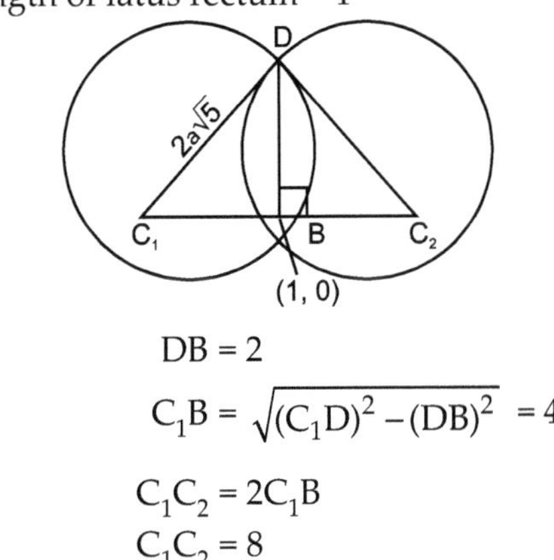

DB = 2

$C_1B = \sqrt{(C_1D)^2 - (DB)^2} = 4$

$C_1C_2 = 2C_1B$

$C_1C_2 = 8$

39. Correct Response : (c)

Explanation :

Let orthocentre is $H(x_0, y_0)$

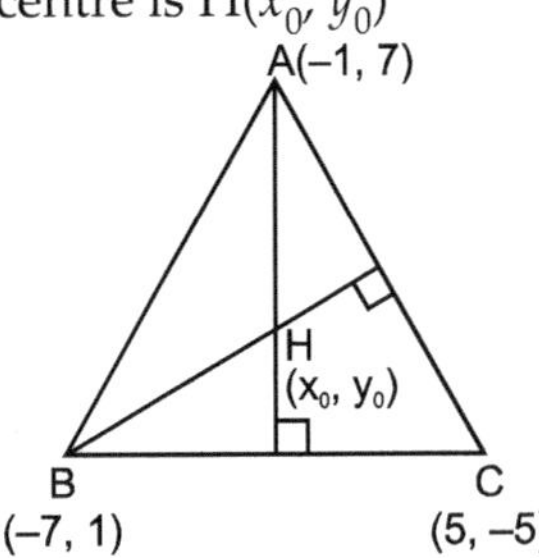

$$m_{A+1} \cdot m_{BC} = -1$$

$$\Rightarrow \left(\frac{y_0 - 7}{x_0 + 1} \right)\left(\frac{1 + 5}{-7 - 5} \right) = -1$$

$$\Rightarrow \quad 2x_0 - y_0 + 9 = 0 \quad\quad ....(1)$$

and $$m_{BH} \cdot m_{AC} = -1$$

$$\Rightarrow \left(\frac{y_0 - 1}{x_0 + 7} \right)\left(\frac{7 - (-5)}{-1 - 5} \right) = -1$$

$$\Rightarrow \quad x_0 - 2y_0 + 9 = 0 \quad\quad ...(2)$$

Solving equation (1) and (2) we get

$$(x_0, y_0) = (-3, 3)$$

40. Correct Response : (a)

Explanation :

For ellipse $\dfrac{x^2}{25} + \dfrac{y^2}{b^2} = 1$ $(b < 5)$

Let e_1 is eccentricity of ellipse

$$\therefore \qquad b^2 = 25(1 - e_1^2) \qquad \dots(1)$$

Again for hyperbola

$$\frac{x^2}{16} - \frac{y^2}{b^2} = 1$$

Let e_2 is eccentricity of hyperbola.

$$\therefore \qquad b^2 = 16(e_2^2 - 1) \qquad \dots(2)$$

by (1) and (2)

$$25(1 - e_1^2) = 16(e_2^2 - 1) \qquad \dots(3)$$

Now, $\qquad e_1 . e_2 = 1 \qquad$ (given)

Put $e_2 = \dfrac{1}{e_1}$, in equation

$$\therefore \qquad 25(1 - e_1^2) = 16\left(\frac{1 - e_1^2}{e_1^2}\right)$$

or $e_1 = \dfrac{4}{5} \quad \therefore e_2 = \dfrac{5}{4}$

Now distance between foci is $2ae$

$$\therefore \qquad \text{distance for ellipse} = 2 \times 5 \times \frac{4}{5} = 8 = \alpha$$

$$\text{distance of hyperbola} = 2 \times 4 \times \frac{5}{4} = 10 = \beta$$

$$\therefore \qquad (\alpha, \beta) \equiv (8, 10)$$

41. Correct Response : (4)

Explanation :

$$y = e^x \Rightarrow \frac{dy}{dx} = e^x$$

$$m = \left(\frac{dy}{dx}\right)_{(c, e^c)} = e^c$$

$\Rightarrow$ Tangent at (c, e^c)

$$y - e^c = e^c(x - c)$$

it intersects x-axis

Put $\qquad y = 0 \Rightarrow x = c - 1 \qquad \dots(1)$

Now $\qquad y^2 = 4x \Rightarrow \dfrac{dy}{dx} = \dfrac{2}{y} \Rightarrow \left(\dfrac{dy}{dx}\right)_{(1,2)} = 1$

$\Rightarrow \qquad$ Slope of normal $= -1$

Equation of normal $y - 2 = -1(x - 1)$

$x + y = 3$ it intersects x-axis

Put $y = 0 \Rightarrow x = 3 \qquad \dots(2)$

Points are same

$\Rightarrow \qquad x = c - 1 = 3$

$\Rightarrow \qquad c = 4$

42. Correct Response : (c)

Explanation :

Slope of tangent to the curve $y = x + \sin y$ at (a, b)

is $\dfrac{2 - \dfrac{3}{2}}{\dfrac{1}{2} - 0} = 1$

$$\Rightarrow \qquad \frac{dy}{dx}\Big]_{x=a} = 1$$

$\dfrac{dy}{dx} = 1 + \cos y . \dfrac{dy}{dx}$ (from equation of curve)

$$\frac{dy}{dx}\Big]_{x=a} = 1 + \cos b . \frac{dy}{dx}\Big]_{x=a}$$

$$\Rightarrow \qquad \cos b = 0 \Rightarrow b = (2n + 1)\frac{\pi}{2}$$

$$\Rightarrow \qquad \sin b = \pm 1$$

Now, from curve $y = x + \sin y$

$$b = a + \sin b$$

$$\Rightarrow \qquad |b - a| = |\sin b| = 1$$

43. Correct Response : (d)

Explanation :

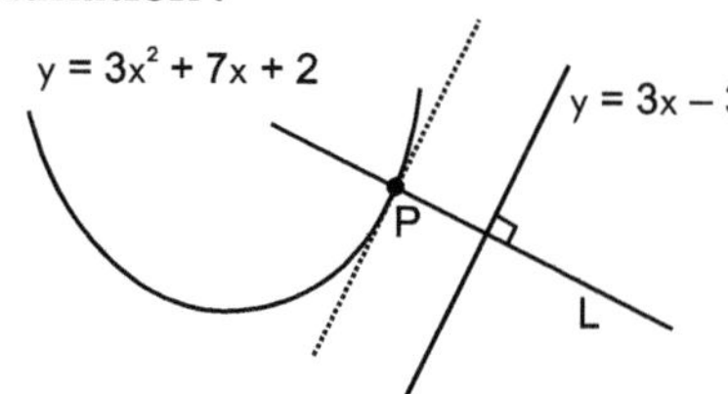

Let L be the common normal to parabola $y = x^2 + 7x + 2$ and line $y = 3x - 3$

$\Rightarrow$ slope of tangent of $y = x^2 + 7x + 2$ at P $= 3$

$$\Rightarrow \qquad \frac{dy}{dx}\Big]_{\text{For P}} = 3$$

$$\Rightarrow \qquad 2x + 7 = 3 \Rightarrow x = -2 \Rightarrow = -8$$

So P$(-2, -8)$

Normal at P : $x + 3y + C = 0$

$\Rightarrow$ C $= 26$ (P satisfies the line)

Normal : $x + 3y + 26 = 0$

44. Correct Response : (b)

Explanation :

Slope of tangent is 2, Tangent of hyperbola

$\dfrac{x^2}{4} - \dfrac{y^2}{2} = 1$ at the point (x_1, y_1) is

$$\frac{xx_1}{4} - \frac{yy_1}{2} = 1 \qquad (T = 0)$$

Slope of hyperbola tangent = Slope of straight line

Slope : $\qquad \dfrac{1}{2}\dfrac{x_1}{y_1} = 2 \Rightarrow x_1 = 4y_1 \qquad \dots(1)$

(x_1, y_1) lies on hyperbola

$$\Rightarrow \qquad \frac{x_1^2}{4} - \frac{y_1^2}{2} = 1 \qquad \qquad \dots(2)$$

From (1) & (2)

$$\frac{(4y_1)^2}{4} - \frac{y_1^2}{2} = 1 \Rightarrow 4y_1^2 - \frac{y_1^2}{2} = 1$$

$$\Rightarrow \qquad 7y_1^2 = 2 \Rightarrow y_1^2 = 2/7$$

Now $x_1{}^2 + 5y_1{}^2 = (4y_1)^2 + 5y_1{}^2$

$$= (21)y_1{}^2 = 21 \times \frac{2}{7} = 6$$

45. Correct Response : (9)

Explanation :

Circle $x^2 + y^2 - 2x - 4y + 4 = 0$

$\Rightarrow (x-1)^2 + (y-2)^2 = 1$

Centre : (1, 2) radius = 1

line $3x + 4y - k = 0$ intersects the circle at two distinct points.

$\Rightarrow$ distance of centre from the line < radius

$$\Rightarrow \left| \frac{3 \times 1 + 4 \times 2 - k}{\sqrt{3^2 + 4^2}} \right| < 1$$

$$\Rightarrow \qquad |11 - k| < 5$$
$$\Rightarrow \qquad 6 < k < 16$$
$$\Rightarrow \qquad k \in \{7, 8, 9, \dots 15\} \text{ since } k \in I$$

Number of K is 9.

46. Correct Response : (b)

Explanation :

$3x + 4y = 12\sqrt{12}$ is tangent to $\dfrac{x^2}{a^2} + \dfrac{y^2}{9} = 1$

$$c^2 = m^2 a^2 + b^2$$
$$\Rightarrow \qquad a^2 = 16$$

$$e = \sqrt{1 - \frac{9}{16}} = \frac{\sqrt{7}}{4}$$

Distance between focii = $2ae = 2\sqrt{7}$

47. Correct Response : (c)

Explanation :

$$\frac{\alpha - \beta}{2\alpha - \beta} = 1$$

$$3\alpha = 2\beta$$

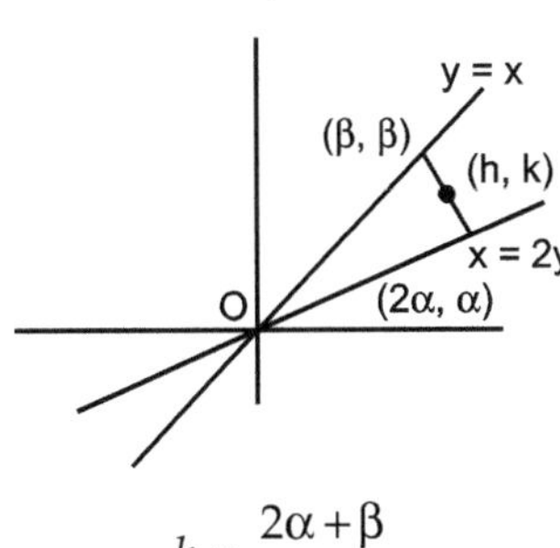

$$h = \frac{2\alpha + \beta}{2}$$

$$2h = \frac{7\alpha}{2}$$

$$k = \frac{\alpha + \beta}{2}$$

$$2k = \frac{5\alpha}{2}$$

$$\frac{h}{k} = \frac{7}{5}$$

$$5x = 7y$$

48. Correct Response : (d)

Explanation :

$$R = \sqrt{16 + 4 - 16} = 2$$

$$L = \sqrt{s_1} = 4$$

$$AB(\text{Chord of contact}) = \frac{2LR}{\sqrt{L^2 + R^2}} = \frac{8}{\sqrt{5}}$$

$$(AB)^2 = \frac{64}{5}$$

49. Correct Response : (b)

Explanation :

$$x^2 + 2xy - 3y^2 = 0$$

m_N = slope of normal drawn to curve at (2, 2) is – 1

$$L : x + y = 4$$

Perpendicular distance of L from (0, 0)

$$= \frac{|0 + 0 - 4|}{\sqrt{2}} = 2\sqrt{2}$$

50. Correct Response : (b)

Explanation :

Slope of tangent to $x^2 + y^2 = 1$ at $P\left(\dfrac{1}{\sqrt{2}}, \dfrac{1}{\sqrt{2}}\right)$

$$2x + 2yy' = 0 \Rightarrow m_{T|p} = -1$$

$y = mx + c$ is tangent to $(x-3)^2 + y^2 = 1$

$y = x + c$ is tangent to $(x-3)^2 + y^2 = 1$

$$\left| \frac{c + 3}{\sqrt{2}} \right| = 1$$

$$\Rightarrow \qquad c^2 + 6c + 7 = 0$$

51. Correct Response : (c)

Explanation :

$$\frac{x^2}{36} - \frac{y^2}{b^2} = 1 \qquad \ldots(i)$$

P(10, 16) lies on (i) get $b^2 = 144$

$$\frac{x^2}{36} - \frac{y^2}{144} = 1$$

Equation of normal is

$$\frac{a^2 x}{x_1} + \frac{b^2 y}{y_1} = a^2 e^2$$

$$2x + 5y = 100$$

52. Correct Response : (0.50)

Explanation :

$$\Delta OPQ = 4$$

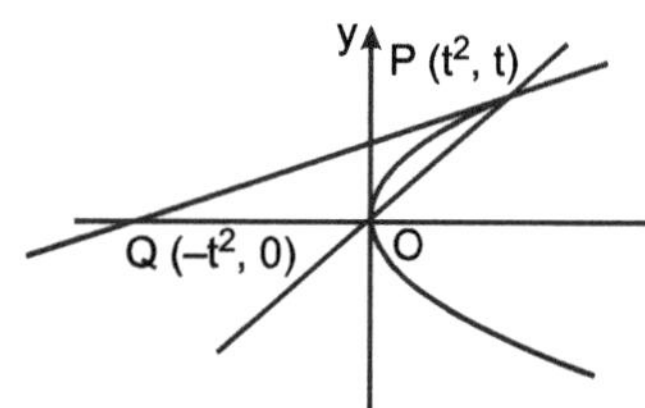

$$\frac{1}{2} \begin{Vmatrix} 0 & 0 & 1 \\ t^2 & t & 1 \\ -t^2 & 0 & 1 \end{Vmatrix} = 4$$

$$t = 2 \qquad (\because t > 0)$$

$$\therefore \qquad m = \frac{1}{2} = 0.50$$

53. Correct Response : (c)

Explanation :

Equation of family of circle touching y-axis at (0, 4) is given by $(x - 0)^2 + (y - 4)^2 + \lambda x = 0$.

$\therefore$ It passes through (2, 0)

$\Rightarrow \qquad \lambda = -10$

$\Rightarrow$ Required circle is $(x - 0)^2 + (y - 4)^2 - 10x = 0$

$\Rightarrow x^2 + y^2 - 10x - 8y + 16 = 0$

center of circle $\equiv$ (5, 4) and radius = 5

distance of $4x + 3y - 8 = 0$ from (5, 4)

$$= \left| \frac{24}{5} \right| \neq \text{radius}$$

54. Correct Response : (d)

Explanation :

$$e_1 = \sqrt{1 - \frac{4}{18}} = \frac{\sqrt{7}}{3}$$

$$e_2 = \sqrt{1 + \frac{4}{9}} = \frac{\sqrt{13}}{3}$$

$\because (e_1, e_2)$ lies on $15x^2 + 3y^2 = k$

$\Rightarrow \qquad 15e_1^2 + 3e_2^3 = k$

$\Rightarrow \qquad k = 16$

55. Correct Response : (b)

Explanation :

Let $\qquad \dfrac{x^2}{a^2} + \dfrac{y^2}{b^2} = 1;\ a > b;$

and $\qquad 2b = \dfrac{4}{\sqrt{3}} \Rightarrow b = \dfrac{2}{\sqrt{3}}$

$\Rightarrow \qquad b^2 = \dfrac{4}{3}$

tangent $y = \dfrac{-x}{6} + \dfrac{4}{3}$ compare with

$$y = mx \pm \sqrt{a^2 m^2 + b^2}$$

$\Rightarrow \qquad m = \dfrac{-1}{6}$

$\Rightarrow \qquad \sqrt{\dfrac{a^2}{36} + \dfrac{4}{3}} = \dfrac{4}{3}$

$\Rightarrow \qquad a = 4$

$$e = \sqrt{1 - \frac{b^2}{a^2}} = \frac{1}{2}\sqrt{\frac{11}{3}}$$

56. Correct Response : (b)

Explanation :

$$y^2 = 8x$$

$$4t^1 = 2 \Rightarrow t_1 = -\frac{1}{2},$$

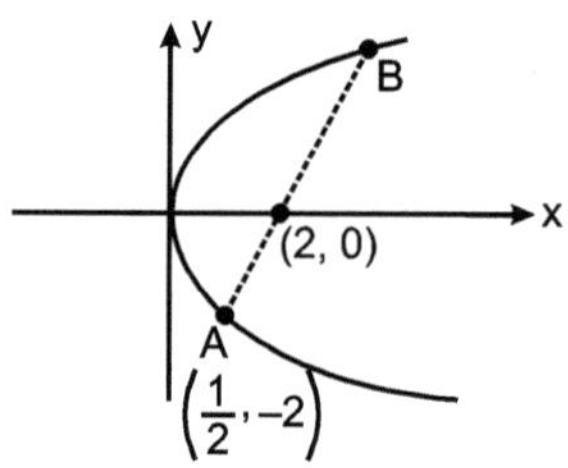

$$t_1 . t_2 = -1$$

$$t_2 = -\frac{1}{t_1}$$

$\Rightarrow \qquad t_2 = 2$

So, the coordinate of B is (8, 8).

$\therefore$ Equation of langent at B is

$$8y = 4 (n + 8) \Rightarrow 2y = x + 8$$

57. Correct Response : (36)

Explanation :

Common tangent is $S_1 - S_2 = 0$

$\Rightarrow \qquad -6x + 8y - 8 + k = 0$

Use $p = r$ for 1st circle

$\Rightarrow \qquad \dfrac{|-18 - 8 + k|}{10} = 1$

$\Rightarrow k = 36$ or $16 \Rightarrow k_{\text{max}} = 36$

58. Correct Response : (c)

Explanation :

$y = mx + 4$ is tangent to $y^2 = 4x$

$$\Rightarrow \qquad m = \frac{1}{4}$$

$$y = \frac{1}{4}x + 4 \text{ is tangent to } x^2 = 2by$$

$$\Rightarrow \quad x^2 - \frac{b}{2}x - 8b = 0$$

$$\Rightarrow \qquad D = 0$$

$$b^2 + 128 = 0$$

$$\Rightarrow \qquad b = -128, 0$$

$$b \neq 0 \Rightarrow b = -128$$

59. Correct Response : (c)

Explanation :

Given, $\qquad 2ae = 6 \Rightarrow ae = 3 \qquad \ldots(i)$

and $\qquad \dfrac{2a}{e} = 12 \Rightarrow a = 6e \qquad \ldots(ii)$

from (i) and (ii)

$$6e^2 = 3 \Rightarrow e = \frac{1}{\sqrt{2}}$$

$$\Rightarrow \qquad a = 3\sqrt{2}$$

Now, $b^2 = a^2(1 - e^2)$

$$\Rightarrow \qquad b^2 = 18\left(1 - \frac{1}{2}\right) = 9$$

Length of L.R $= \dfrac{2(9)}{3\sqrt{3}} = 3\sqrt{2}$

60. Correct Response : (5)

Explanation :

P is centroid of the triangle ABC

$$\Rightarrow \qquad P \equiv \left(\frac{17}{6}, \frac{8}{3}\right)$$

$$\Rightarrow \qquad PQ = 5$$

61. Correct Response : (d)

Explanation :

Any normal to the ellipse is

$$\frac{x\sec\theta}{\sqrt{2}} - y\cosec\,\theta = -\frac{1}{2}$$

$$\Rightarrow \quad \frac{x}{\left(\dfrac{-\cos\theta}{\sqrt{2}}\right)} + \frac{y}{\left(\dfrac{\sin\theta}{2}\right)} = 1$$

$$\Rightarrow \frac{\cos\theta}{\sqrt{2}} = \frac{1}{3\sqrt{2}} \text{ and } \frac{\sin\theta}{2} = \beta$$

$$\Rightarrow \qquad \beta = \frac{\sqrt{2}}{3}$$

62. Correct Response : (c)

Explanation :

$\overline{AB} : 3x + y - 2 = 0$

Also, $\dfrac{1}{2} \times \sqrt{10} \times h = 5$

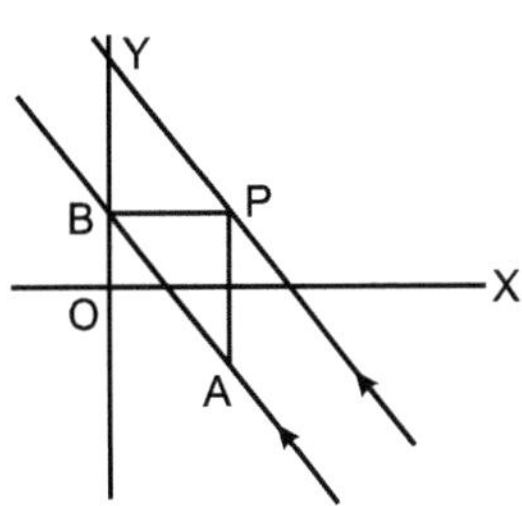

$$\Rightarrow \qquad h = \sqrt{10}$$

$$\Rightarrow \qquad \frac{|4\lambda - 2|}{\sqrt{10}} = \sqrt{10} \Rightarrow \lambda = 3, -2$$

63. Correct Response : (b)

Explanation :

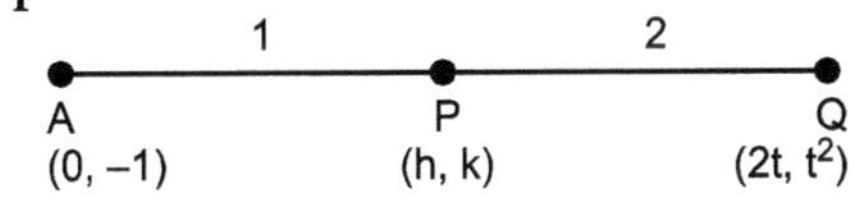

$\Rightarrow 3h = 2t = \text{ and } 3k = t^2 - 2$

$$\Rightarrow \qquad 3y = \left(\frac{3x}{2}\right)^2 - 2$$

$$\Rightarrow \qquad 12y = 9x^2 - 8$$

64. Correct Response : (b)

Explanation :

Equation of the common chord is $S_1 - S_2 = 0$.

$$\Rightarrow \quad 4Kx + \frac{y}{2} + K + \frac{1}{2} = 0$$

which is identical to $4x + 5y - K = 0$.

Thus, $\qquad \dfrac{4K}{4} = \dfrac{1/2}{5} = \dfrac{K + 1/2}{-K}$

Thus, $\qquad K = \dfrac{1}{10} \text{ or } \dfrac{-5}{11}$.

which is a contradiction so, there is no value of k.

65. Correct Response : (a)

Explanation :

$\left(3, -\dfrac{9}{2}\right)$ lies on $\dfrac{x^2}{a^2} + \dfrac{y^2}{b^2} = 1$

$$\Rightarrow \qquad \frac{9}{a^2} + \frac{81}{4b^2} = 1$$

Equation of tangent is $\left(3, -\dfrac{9}{2}\right)$ is

$$\frac{3x}{a^2} + \frac{y\left(-\dfrac{9}{2}\right)}{b^2} = 1$$

Compare it with $\dfrac{x}{12}+\dfrac{y}{-6}=1$

$$\Rightarrow \quad \frac{a^2}{3}=12 \ \text{ and }\ \frac{2b^2}{9}=6$$

$$\Rightarrow \quad a=6 \ \text{ and }\ b=3\sqrt{3}$$

Length of latus rectum is

$$\frac{2b^2}{a}=\frac{2\times 27}{6}$$

$$=9$$

66. Correct Response : (a)

Explanation :

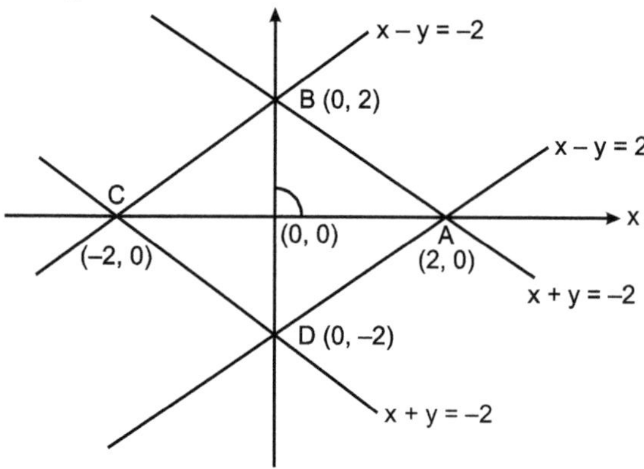

In the figure ABCD is a square whose area is $4\times\dfrac{1}{2}\times 2\times 2=8$ and side is $2\sqrt{2}$.

67. Correct Response : (b)

Explanation :

Family of the circle touching the given line is

$$(x-1)^2+(y-1)^2+\lambda(x-y)=0$$

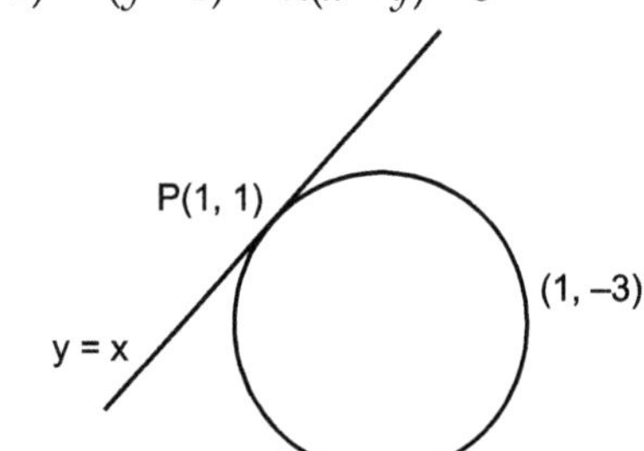

It passes through the point $(1,-3)$

$$\Rightarrow \qquad 0+16+\lambda\,(1+3)=0$$

$$\Rightarrow \qquad \lambda =-4$$

So the equation of the circle is

$$x^2+1-2x+y^2+1-2y-4x+4y=0$$

$$\Rightarrow \qquad x^2+y^2-6x+2y+2=0$$

So the radius is

$$r=\sqrt{9+1-2}$$

$$=2\sqrt{2}$$

68. Correct Response : (c)

Explanation :

Equation of hyperbola is

$$\frac{x^2}{a^2}-\frac{y^2}{b^2}=1 \ \Rightarrow\ \frac{16}{a^2}-\frac{12}{b^2}=1 \qquad \text{...(i)}$$

$$\frac{4}{\sqrt{5}}=\frac{a}{e}\ \Rightarrow\ 16e^2=5a^2 \qquad \text{...(ii)}$$

Equation (i) implies

$$16-12\,\frac{a^2}{b^2}=a^2$$

Substitute the value of a^2 from equation (ii)

$$16-\frac{12}{e^2-1}=\frac{16e^2}{5}$$

$$\Rightarrow \qquad 80\,(e^2-1)-60=16e^2\,(e^2-1)$$

$$\Rightarrow \qquad 16e^4-96e^2+140=0$$

$$\Rightarrow \qquad 4e^4-24e^2+35=0$$

69. Correct Response : (d)

Explanation :

Directrix of hyperbola is $5x+9=0$.

Equation of hyperbola is $16x^2-9y^2=144$. So,

$$\pm\frac{a}{e}=\pm\frac{a^2}{ae}$$

$$=\pm\frac{9}{5}$$

As $ae=5$ therefore, required corresponding focus is $(-ae, 0)=(-5, 0)$.

70. Correct Response : (d)

Explanation :

Equation of the ellipse is

$$3x^2+5y^2=32$$

$$\Rightarrow \qquad 6x+10y\,\frac{dy}{dx}=0$$

$$\Rightarrow \qquad \frac{dy}{dx}=-\frac{6x}{10y}$$

$$\Rightarrow \qquad \frac{dy}{dx}=-\frac{3x}{5y}$$

Slope of tangent at $(2, 2)$ is $-\dfrac{3}{5}$ and that of normal is $\dfrac{5}{3}$.

So, the equation of tangent is

$$y-2=-\frac{3}{5}(x-2)$$

$$\Rightarrow \qquad 3x+5y=16$$

The equation of normal is

$$y - 2 = \frac{5}{3}(x - 2)$$

$$\Rightarrow \quad 5x - 3y = 4$$

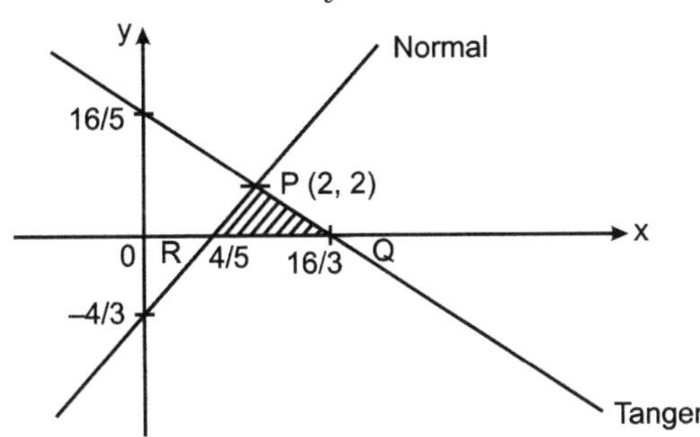

From the figure, the required area of triangle is

$$\frac{1}{2} \times \left(\frac{16}{3} - \frac{4}{5}\right) \times 2 = \frac{68}{15}$$

71. Correct Response : (d)

Explanation :

Tangent to the circle $x^2 + y^2 = 1$ is

$$y = mx \pm \sqrt{1 + m^2}$$

Tangent to the parabola $y^2 = 4\sqrt{2}x$ is

$$y = mx + \frac{\sqrt{2}}{m}$$

$$\Rightarrow \quad 1 + m^2 = \frac{2}{m^2}$$

$$\Rightarrow \quad m^4 + m^2 - 2 = 0$$

$$\Rightarrow \quad m = \pm 1$$

So, the common tangents are $y = x + \sqrt{2}$ or $y = -x - \sqrt{2}$

$$\Rightarrow \quad c = \pm \sqrt{2}$$

$$\Rightarrow \quad |c| = \sqrt{2}$$

72. Correct Response : (a)

Explanation :

Straight line parallel to $4x - 3y + 2 = 0$ is

$4x - 3y + \lambda = 0$ whose distance from $(0, 0)$ is $\frac{3}{5}$.

Therefore, $\left|\frac{\lambda}{5}\right| = \frac{3}{5} \Rightarrow \lambda = \pm 3$.

So, the straight line are

$$4x - 3y + 3 = 0 \text{ or } 4x - 3y - 3 = 0.$$

$\left(-\frac{1}{4}, \frac{2}{3}\right)$ is the point that satisfies these equations.

73. Correct Response : (b)

Explanation :

Let the centre of the circles be (h, k) and radius be h. $(h, k > 0)$

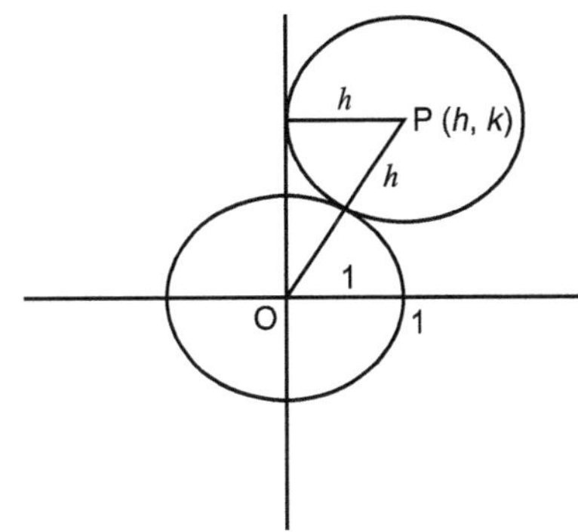

In the figure, $\quad OP = h + 1$

$$\sqrt{h^2 + k^2} = h + 1$$

$$\Rightarrow \quad h^2 + k^2 = h^2 + 2h + 1$$

$$\Rightarrow \quad k^2 = 2h + 1$$

So the locus is $y^2 = 2x + 1$.

$$\Rightarrow \quad y = \sqrt{2x + 1}; x \geq 0$$

74. Correct Response : (d)

Explanation :

Equation of tangent at point $(1, 2)$ is

$$2y = 2(x + 1)$$

$$\Rightarrow \quad y = x + 1$$

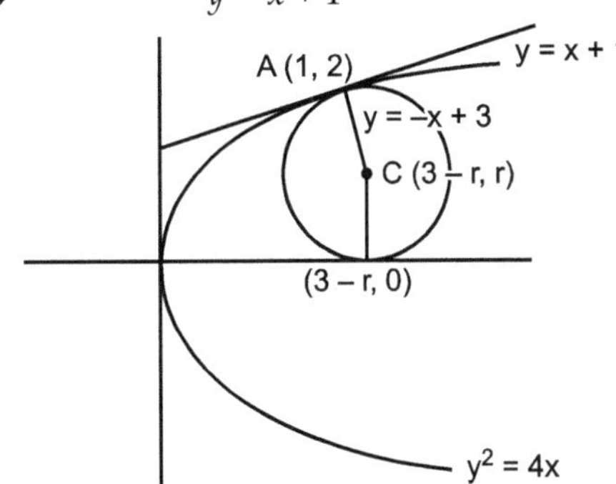

Equation of normal is

$$y = -x + 3$$

Let $C(3 - r, r)$ be centre of the circle then,

$$AC^2 = r^2 \Rightarrow (3 - r - 1)^2 + (r - 2)^2 = r^2$$

$$\Rightarrow \quad 2(2 - r)^2 = r^2$$

$$\Rightarrow \quad r^2 - 8r + 8 = 0$$

$$\Rightarrow \quad r = 4 \pm 2\sqrt{2}$$

For $\quad r = 4 + 2\sqrt{2}, 3 - r < 0$, (Not possible)

$$\therefore \quad r = 4 - 2\sqrt{2}$$

Area is

$$\pi r^2 = 8\pi (3 - 2\sqrt{2})$$

75. Correct Response : (a)

Explanation :

$x + (a - 1)y = 1$ and $2x + a^2 y = 1$ lines are perpendicular.

So,
$$1 \times 2 + a^2(a-1) = 0$$
$$\Rightarrow \quad a^3 + a^2 - 2a^2 - 2a + 2a + 2 = 0$$
$$\Rightarrow \quad a^2(a+1) - 2a(a+1) + 2(a+1) = 0$$
$$\Rightarrow \quad (a+1)(a^2 - 2a + 2) = 0$$
$$\Rightarrow \quad a = -1$$

Therefore, the given lines are $x - 2y = 1$ and $2x + y = 1$
$$\Rightarrow \quad -x - 3y = 0$$
$$\Rightarrow \quad x = -3y$$
So,
$$-5y = 1 \Rightarrow y = -\frac{1}{5}, x = \frac{3}{5}$$

Required distance is
$$\sqrt{\frac{9}{25} + \frac{1}{25}} = \sqrt{\frac{10}{25}}$$
$$= \sqrt{\frac{2}{5}}$$

76. Correct Response : (c)

Explanation :

Both the circles $x^2 + y^2 = 4$ and $x^2 + y^2 + 6x + 8y - 24 = 0$ touch each other internally. So, the common tangent is $S_1 - S_2 = 0$
$$\Rightarrow \quad 6x + 8y = 20$$
$$\Rightarrow \quad 3x + 4y - 10 = 0$$

Hence, the point $(6, -2)$ lies on the tangent.

77. Correct Response : (d)

Explanation :

Let the given point be (β^2, β).

Equation of the tangent on parabola is
$$y\beta = \frac{1}{2}(x + \beta^2)$$
$$y = \frac{x}{2\beta} + \frac{\beta}{2} \quad \left(m = \frac{1}{2\beta}, c = \frac{\beta}{2} \right)$$

Equation of ellipse is $x^2 + \dfrac{y^2}{1/2} = 1$

Condition for tangency is $c^2 = a^2m^2 + b^2$
This implies
$$\frac{\beta^2}{4} = 1\left(\frac{1}{4\beta^2}\right) + \frac{1}{2}$$
$$\Rightarrow \quad \beta^4 = 2\beta^2 + 1$$
$$\Rightarrow \quad (\beta^2 - 1)^2 = 2$$
$$\Rightarrow \quad \beta^2 = \sqrt{2} + 1$$
$$\Rightarrow \quad \alpha = \sqrt{2} + 1$$

78. Correct Response : (c)

Explanation :
$$|\tan\theta| = \frac{1}{\sqrt{7}}$$
$$= \left|\frac{m-1}{m+1}\right|$$

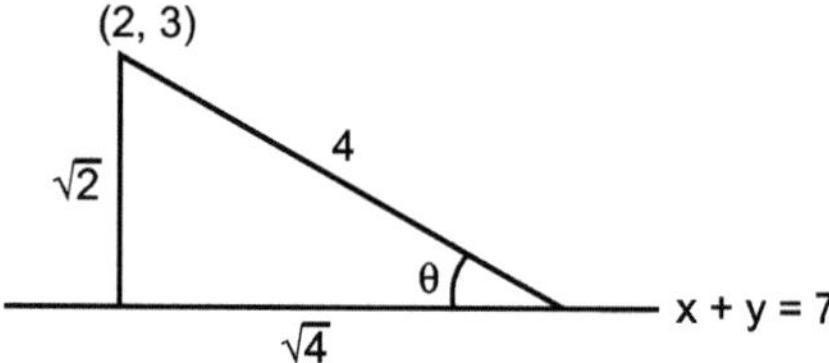

Taking (+) sign $1 + m = m\sqrt{7} - \sqrt{7} \Rightarrow m = \dfrac{\sqrt{7}+1}{\sqrt{7}-1}$

Taking (–) sign $1 + m = \sqrt{7} - \sqrt{7}m \Rightarrow m = \dfrac{\sqrt{7}-1}{\sqrt{7}+1}$

79. Correct Response : (c)

Explanation :
$$7\sqrt{3} = \frac{42m}{\sqrt{24 - 18m^2}} \Rightarrow \sqrt{3} = \frac{\sqrt{6}m}{\sqrt{4 - 3m^2}}$$
$$\Rightarrow 4 - 3m^2 = 2m^2 \qquad \Rightarrow \quad m = \frac{2}{\sqrt{5}}$$

80. Correct Response : (b)

Explanation :
$$x + iy = \frac{(\alpha + i)^2}{\alpha^2 + 1}$$
$$= \frac{\alpha^2 - 1 + 2\alpha i}{\alpha^2 + 1}$$
$$x = \frac{\alpha^2 - 1}{\alpha^2 + 1} \text{ and } y = \frac{2\alpha}{\alpha^2 + 1}$$
$$\Rightarrow \quad x^2 + y^2 = \frac{(\alpha^2 - 1)^2 + 4\alpha^2}{(\alpha^2 + 1)^2}$$
$$\Rightarrow \quad x^2 + y^2 = 1$$

81. Correct Response : (a)

Explanation :

Let equation of the tangent to the given circle be
$x\cos\theta + y\sin\theta = 1$

The line meets x-axis at $(\sec\theta, 0)$ and y-axis at $(0, \csc\theta)$. If $P(h, k)$ is the mid-point of this segment then,

$2h = \sec\theta$ and $2k = \csc\theta$
$$\Rightarrow \quad \frac{1}{x^2} + \frac{1}{y^2} = 4$$
$$\Rightarrow \quad x^2 + y^2 - 4x^2y^2 = 0$$

82. Correct Response : (d)

Explanation :

$$p = \frac{n}{\sqrt{2}}$$

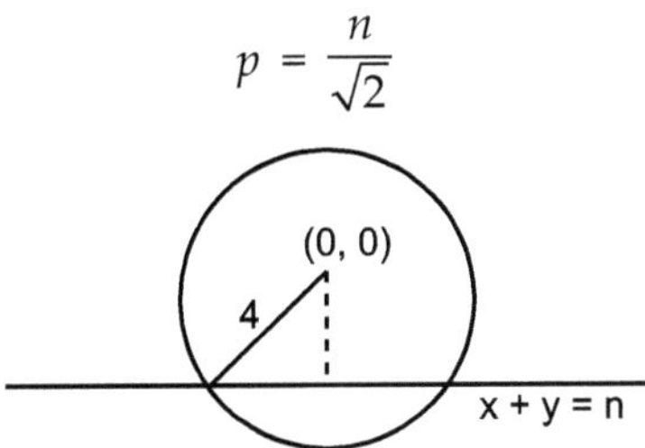

To make the intercept

$$\frac{n}{\sqrt{2}} < 4$$

$$\Rightarrow \qquad n < 4\sqrt{2}$$

Length of intercepts is $2\sqrt{r^2 - p^2} = 2\sqrt{16 - \frac{n^2}{2}}$

Square of intercept is $4 \times \left(16 - \frac{n^2}{2}\right), n \in N$

Sum of squares of intercept

$$= 4 \times \left(\left(16 - \frac{n^2}{2}\right) + \left(16 - \frac{4}{2}\right) + \left(16 - \frac{9}{2}\right)\right.$$

$$\left. + \left(16 - \frac{16}{2}\right) + \left(16 - \frac{25}{2}\right)\right)$$

$$= 4\left(80 - \frac{1}{2} \times 55\right)$$

$$= 210$$

83. Correct Response : (d)

Explanation :

Equation of given ellipse is

$$4x^2 + y^2 = 8$$

$$\Rightarrow \qquad \frac{x^2}{2} + \frac{y^2}{8} = 1 = ?$$

$$\frac{x^2}{(\sqrt{2})^2} + \frac{y^2}{(2\sqrt{2})^2} = 1$$

Now, equation of tangent to the ellipse $\frac{x^2}{a^2} + \frac{y^2}{b^2} = 1$ at (x_1, x_1) is $\frac{xx_1}{a^2} + \frac{yy_1}{b^2} = 1$

and equation of another tangent at point (a, b) is

$$4ax + by = 8$$

Since lines (ii) and (iii) are perpendicular to each other

$$\therefore \qquad \left(-\frac{2}{1}\right) \times \left(-\frac{4a}{b}\right) = -1$$

If lines $a_1x + b_1y + c_1 = 0$ and $a_2x + b_2y + c_2 = 0$

are perpendicular, then $\frac{-a_1}{b_1} - \frac{a_2}{b_2} = -1$

$$b = 8a$$

Also, the point (a, b) lies on the ellipes (i) so,

$$\Rightarrow \qquad 4a^2 + b^2 = 8$$

$$\Rightarrow \qquad 4a^2 + b^2 = 8 \text{ [from equation (iv)]}$$

$$\Rightarrow \qquad 4a^2 + 64a^2 = 8$$

$$\Rightarrow \qquad 687a^2 = 8$$

$$\Rightarrow \qquad a^2 = \frac{8}{68}$$

$$\Rightarrow \qquad a^2 = \frac{2}{17}$$

84. Correct Response : (c)

Explanation :

From the figure

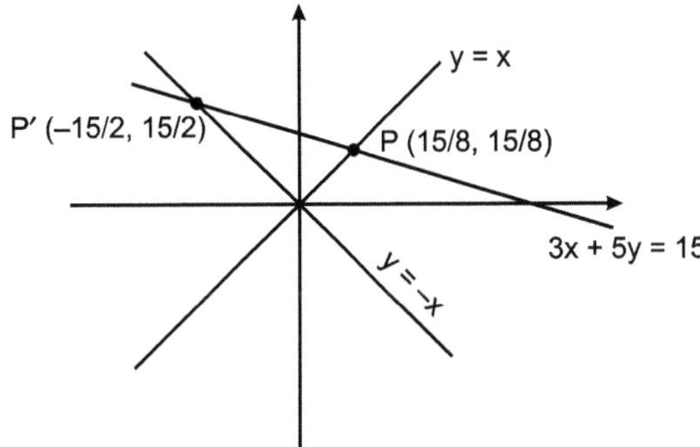

Intersection of the original line with $y = x$ and $y = -x$ will given desired point P and P' in 1st and 2nd quadrant.

85. Correct Response : (c)

Explanation :

$$\sqrt{x^2 + y^2} + \sqrt{x^2 + (y-1)^2} = 3$$

$$\Rightarrow \qquad x^2 + y^2 - 2y + 1 = 9 + x^2 + y^2 - 6\sqrt{x^2 + y^2}$$

$$3\sqrt{x^2 + y^2} = 4 + y$$

$$9x^2 + 9y^2 = 16 + y^2 + 8y$$

$$9x^2 + 8y^2 - 8y = 16$$

86. Correct Response : (a)

Explanation :

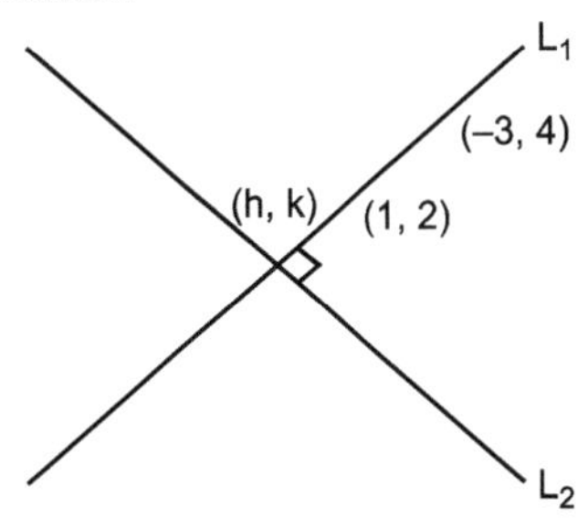

$$L_1 : (y - 2) = -\frac{1}{2}(x - 1) = x + 2y - 5 = 0$$

$$L_2 : (y - 3) = 2(x - 4) = 2x - y - 5 = 0$$

Put h, k in both lines

$$(h, k) = (3, 1) \Rightarrow \frac{k}{h} = \frac{1}{3}$$

87. Correct Response : (c)

Explanation :

Let the equation of hyperbola be $\dfrac{x^2}{a^2} - \dfrac{y^2}{b^2} = 1$

Passes throught $(4, 6) \Rightarrow \dfrac{16}{a^2} - \dfrac{36}{b^2} = 1$ ...(i)

$$e^2 = 1 + \dfrac{b^2}{a^2}$$

$$\Rightarrow \qquad b^2 = 3a^2$$

Put this in equation (i)

$$\dfrac{16}{a^2} - \dfrac{36}{3a^2} = 1$$

$$\Rightarrow \qquad a^2 = 4$$
$$\Rightarrow \qquad b^2 = 12$$

Equation $\quad \dfrac{x^2}{4} - \dfrac{y^2}{12} = 1$

Equation of tangent $T = 0$ at $(4, 6)$ is $2x - y = 2$.

88. Correct Response : (a)

Explanation :

$$PQ : \dfrac{x-2}{6} = \dfrac{y+3}{3} = \dfrac{z-4}{6}$$

R on PQ

$$\dfrac{1}{3} = \dfrac{y+3}{3} = \dfrac{z-4}{6}$$

$R(4, -2, 6)$

$$OR = \sqrt{16+4+36}$$

$$= 2\sqrt{14}$$

89. Correct Response : (a)

Explanation :

$$\dfrac{dy}{dx} = \dfrac{2y}{x^2} \Rightarrow \ln y = -\dfrac{2}{x} + \ln C$$

Passes through $(1, 1)$

$$0 = \dfrac{-2}{1} + \ln C , \ln C = 2$$

$$\ln y = -\dfrac{2}{x} + 2$$

$$x \ln y = 2(x - 1)$$

90. Correct Response : (c)

Explanation :

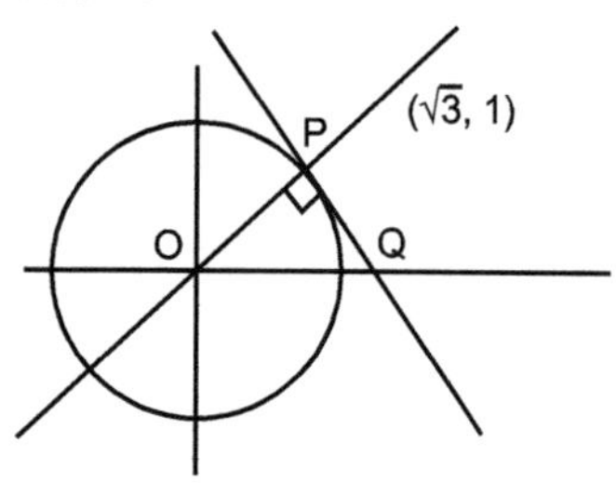

Slope of $OP = \dfrac{1}{\sqrt{3}}$, Slope of $PQ = -\sqrt{3}$

$$y - 1 = -\sqrt{3}(x - \sqrt{3})$$

$$= -\sqrt{3}x + 3$$

$$\Rightarrow \qquad \sqrt{3}x + y = 4 \text{ and } Q\left(\dfrac{4}{\sqrt{3}}, 0\right)$$

$$\Delta OPQ = \dfrac{2}{\sqrt{3}}$$

91. Correct Response : (b)

Explanation :

$$be = 5\sqrt{3}$$

$$\Rightarrow \qquad b^2 e^2 = 75$$
$$\Rightarrow \qquad b^2 - a^2 = 75 \{ \because a^2 = b^2 - b^2 e^2, |b| > |a| \}$$
$$\Rightarrow \quad (b + a)(b - a) = 75$$
$$\Rightarrow \qquad b + a = 15 \qquad [\because 2b - 2a = 10]$$
$$\Rightarrow \qquad b = 10, a = 5$$

$$LR = 2 \times \dfrac{a^2}{b}$$

$$= \dfrac{2 \times 25}{10}$$

$$= 5$$

92. Correct Response : (c)

Explanation :

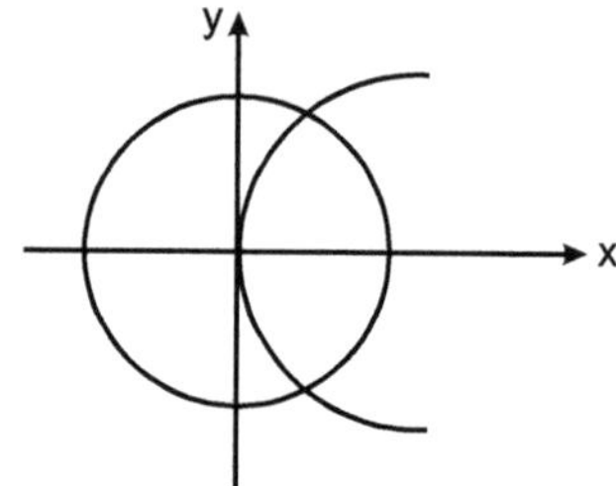

$$x^2 + 4x - 5 = 0$$

$$\Rightarrow \qquad (x + 5)(x - 1) = 0$$
$$\Rightarrow \qquad x = -5 \text{ and } x = 1$$

Required point in first quadrant is $(1, 2)$

Required equation of the tangent is $x - y + 1 = 0$ and the only given point which satisfies this equation is $\left(\dfrac{3}{4}, \dfrac{7}{4}\right)$.

93. Correct Response : (b)

Explanation :

The figure shows the circles with the common chord.

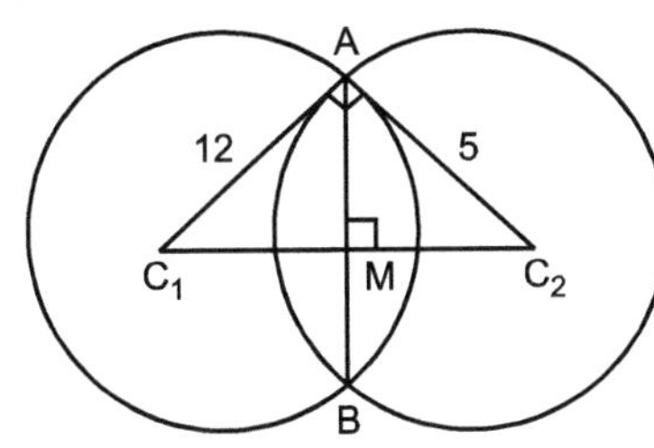

The length C_1C_2 is,

$$l = \sqrt{16 + 4 + 36}$$

$$= 13$$

Area of triangle AC_1C_2 is,

$$\Delta = \left(\frac{1}{2}\right)(12)(5)$$

$$= 30$$

Also,

$$\Delta = \left(\frac{1}{2}\right)(13)\left(\frac{AB}{2}\right)$$

$$30 = \left(\frac{1}{2}\right)(13)\left(\frac{AB}{2}\right)$$

$$AB = \frac{120}{13}$$

94. Correct Response : (d)

Explanation :

The given expression is,

$$y = \sin x \left(\sin (x + 2)\right) - \sin^2 (x + 1)$$

$$= \frac{1}{2} \left[2\sin (x + 2) \sin x - 2 \sin^2 (x + 1)\right]$$

$$= \frac{1}{2} \left[\cos 2 - \cos (2x + 2) + \cos (2x + 2) - 1\right]$$

$$= - \sin^2 (1)$$

The above value is less then zero. Hence, the line passes through third and fourth quadrants only.

95. Correct Response : (a)

Explanation :

The given expression of ellipse is,

$$3x^2 + 4y^2 = 12$$

$$\frac{x^2}{4} + \frac{y^2}{3} = 1$$

The normal at point $P(2\cos\theta, \sqrt{3}\sin\theta)$ is,

$$2x \sin\theta - \sqrt{3}y \cos\theta = \sin\theta \cos\theta$$

Since the normal is parallel to line $2x + y = 4$; therefore,

$$\frac{2}{\sqrt{3}}\tan\theta = -2$$

$$\tan\theta = -\sqrt{3} \qquad \text{...(i)}$$

The tangent at point P is,

$$\sqrt{3}x \cos\theta + 2y \sin\theta = 2\sqrt{3}$$

The tangent passes through point (4, 4).

$$(4\sqrt{3} \cos\theta) + 8 \sin\theta = 2\sqrt{3} \qquad \text{...(ii)}$$

From equation (i) and (ii),

$$\theta = \frac{2\pi}{3}$$

The points of the tangent are $P\left(-1, \frac{3}{2}\right)$ and $Q(4, 4)$.

Therefore, the length for line PQ,

$$PQ = \sqrt{25 + \frac{25}{4}}$$

$$= \frac{5\sqrt{5}}{2}$$

96. Correct Response : (c)

Explanation :

Let the equation of common tangent be,

$$y = mx + \frac{3}{m}$$

$$\left(\frac{3}{m}\right)^2 = m^2 - 8$$

$$m^4 - 8m^2 - 9 = 0$$

$$m^2 = 9$$

The value of slope can be ± 3.

The equations of common tangent are $y = 3x + 1$ and $y = -3x - 1$.

The figure shows the points of tangent,

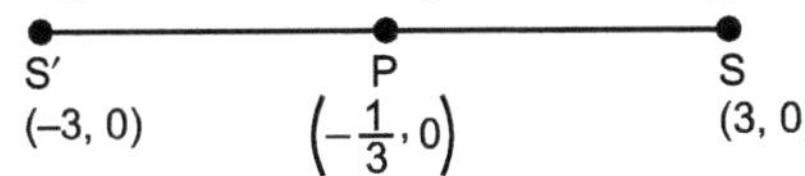

Therefore,

$$\frac{PS}{PS'} = \frac{3 + \frac{1}{3}}{-\frac{1}{3} + 3}$$

$$= \frac{5}{4}$$

97. Correct Response : (a)

Explanation :

Let the equation of ellipse be,

$$\frac{x^2}{a^2} + \frac{y^2}{b^2} = 1 \quad a < b$$

Given that,

$$2a = 4$$

$$a = 2$$

It is given that foci lie at $(0, \pm 2)$. Therefore, $be = 2$

$$e^2 = 1 - \frac{a^2}{b^2}$$

$$b^2e^2 = b^2 - a^2$$

$$4 = b^2 - 4$$

$$b^2 = 8$$

The equation of ellipse is,

$$\frac{x^2}{4} + \frac{y^2}{8} = 1$$

The above ellipse passes through point $(\sqrt{2}, 2)$.

98. Correct Response : (a)

Explanation :

The figure shows the circle and its points.

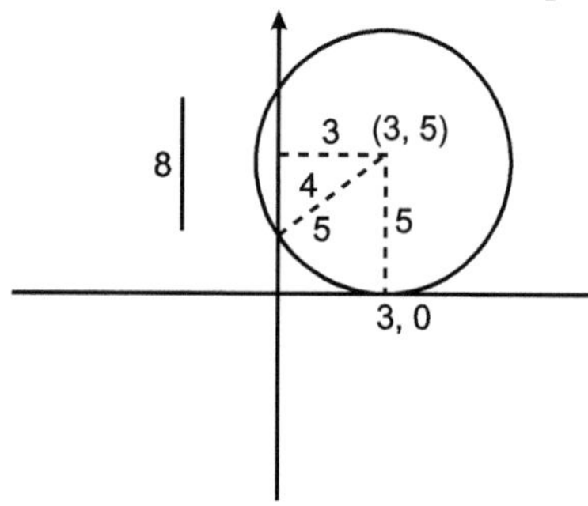

The equation of the circle is,

$$(x - 3)^3 + (y - 5)^2 = (5)^2$$

Hence, (3, 10) will satisfy the above equation.

99. Correct Response : (a)

Explanation :

Let the equation of common tangent be,

$$y = mx + \frac{4}{m} \qquad \text{...(i)}$$

The above line is a tangent to curve $xy = -4$.

$$x\left(mx + \frac{4}{m}\right) + 4 = 0$$

$$mx^2 + \frac{4}{m}(x) + 4 = 0$$

For a tangent

$$D = 0$$

$$\frac{16}{m^2} - 16m = 0$$

$$m^3 = 1$$

$$m = 1$$

Put $m = 1$ in equation (i)

$$y = x + 4$$

100. Correct Response : (b)

Explanation :

The figure shows the points of a triangle.

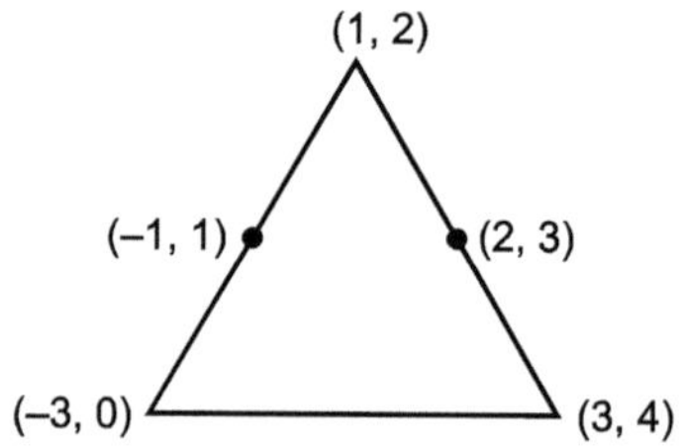

The coordinates of centroid are,

$$C = \left(\frac{1 + 3 - 3}{3}, \frac{2 + 0 + 4}{3}\right)$$

$$= \left(\frac{1}{3}, 2\right)$$

101. Correct Response : (d)

Explanation :

The given figure shows the lines.

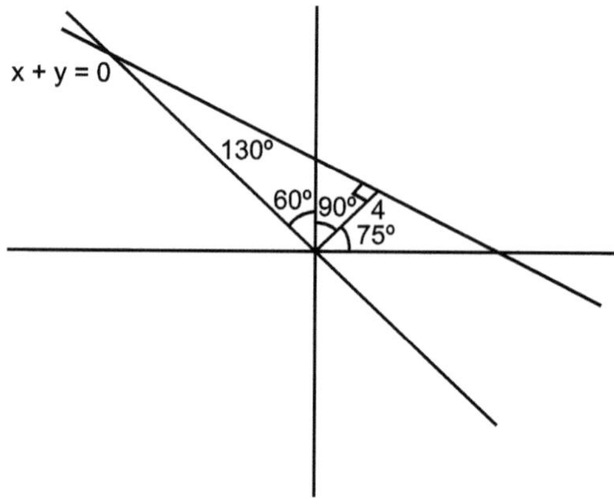

The equation of line is,

$$x \cos \theta + y \sin \theta = p$$

$$x \cos 75° + y \sin 75° = 4$$

$$x\left(\frac{\sqrt{3} - 1}{2\sqrt{2}}\right) + y\left(\frac{\sqrt{3} + 1}{2\sqrt{2}}\right) = 4$$

$$x(\sqrt{3} - 1) + y(\sqrt{3} + 1) = 8\sqrt{2}$$

102. Correct Response : (c)

Explanation :

Let the coordinates of C be (h, k).

The chord of contact of C with respect to the given curve is $T = 0$.

$$\frac{y + k}{2} = xh + 3 - 2(x + h)$$

$$2(h - 2)x - y = -(6 - 4h - k)$$

Compare the above equation with $x - y = 3$.

$$2(h - 2) = 1$$

$$h = \frac{5}{2}$$

Also,

$$6 - 4h - k = -3$$

$$k = -1$$

Therefore, the point of intersection is $\left(\frac{5}{2}, -1\right)$.

103. Correct Response : (a)

Explanation :

Denote the given points by A(– 8, 5) and B(6, 5).

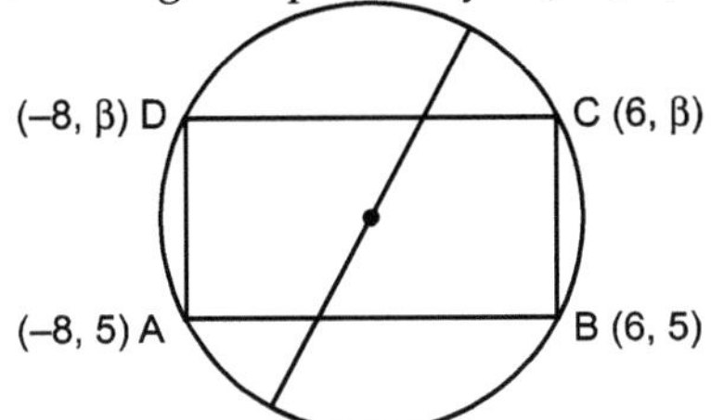

By section formula, the midpoint of AC is $\left(-1, \dfrac{\beta+5}{2}\right)$. It lies on $3y = x + 7$.

$$\Rightarrow \quad \frac{3}{2}(\beta+5) = 6$$

$$\Rightarrow \quad \beta + 5 = 4$$
$$\Rightarrow \quad \beta = -1$$

So, the area of rectangle is $14 \times 6 = 84$.

104. Correct Response : (b)

Explanation :

The required diagram is shown in figure below.

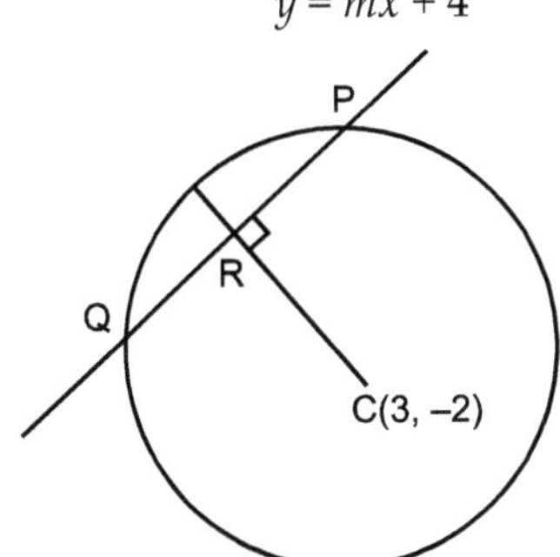

For point R,

$$x = -\frac{3}{5} \text{ and } y = 1 - \frac{3m}{5}$$

Therefore, co-ordinate of point R is,

$$R = \left(-\frac{3}{5}, 1 - \frac{3m}{5}\right)$$

Slope of CR is,

$$\frac{3 - \dfrac{3m}{5}}{-\dfrac{3}{5} - 3} = -\frac{1}{m}$$

$$\frac{15 - 3m}{-3 - 15} = -\frac{1}{m}$$

$$15m - 3m^2 = 18$$

$$m^2 - 5m + 6 = 0$$

The roots of above quadratic equation are, $m = 2$ and 3.

Therefore,

$$2 \le m \le 4.$$

105. Correct Response : (a, c, d)

Explanation :

The required diagram is shown in figure below.

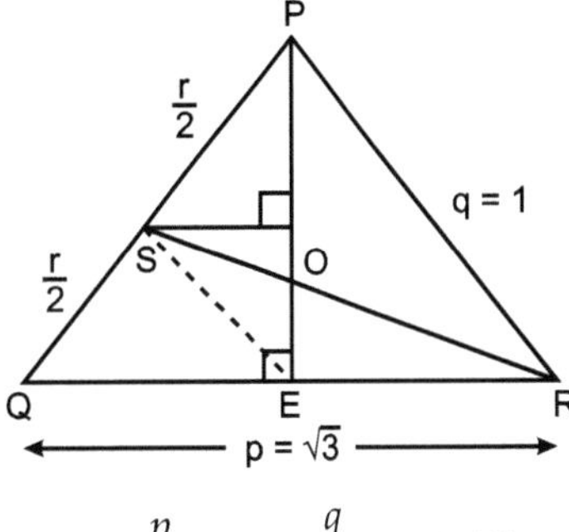

$$\frac{p}{\sin P} = \frac{q}{\sin Q} = 2 \ (1)$$

Solve further as,

$$\frac{\sqrt{3}}{\sin P} = 2$$

$$\sin P = \frac{\sqrt{3}}{2}$$

$$\angle P = \sin^{-1} \frac{\sqrt{3}}{2}$$

$$= 60° \text{ or } 120°$$

Solve further as,

$$\frac{1}{\sin Q} = 2$$

$$\sin Q = \frac{1}{2}$$

$$\angle Q = \sin^{-1} \frac{1}{2}$$

$$= 30° \text{ or } 150°$$

Since, $\angle P + \angle Q$ must be less than 180° but not equal to 90°.

$$\angle P = 120°, \quad \angle Q = 30°$$

and $\qquad \angle R = 30°$

From the figure,

$$\frac{r}{\sin R} = 2$$

$$r = 2 \sin 30°$$

$$= 2\left(\frac{1}{2}\right)$$

$$= 1$$

The length of median RS is,

$$RS = \frac{1}{2}\sqrt{2p^2 + 2q^2 - r^2}$$

$$= \frac{1}{2}\sqrt{6 + 2 - 1}$$

$$= \frac{\sqrt{7}}{2}$$

The radius of incircle ΔPQR is,

$$r_{in} = \frac{2\Delta}{p+q+r}$$

$$= \frac{\dfrac{2\,pqr}{4(1)}}{p+q+r}$$

$$= \frac{1}{2}\left(\frac{(1)\,(1)\,(\sqrt{3})}{(1)\,(1)\,(\sqrt{3})}\right)$$

$$= \frac{\sqrt{3}}{2}\left(\frac{2-\sqrt{3}}{1}\right)$$

The length of the bisector PE by equal area of triangle is,

$$\left(\frac{1}{2}\right)\sqrt{3}\ PE = \frac{pqr}{4\,(1)}$$

$$PE = \frac{(1)\,(1)\,(\sqrt{3})}{4}\frac{2}{\sqrt{3}}$$

$$= \frac{1}{2}$$

The length of OE is,

$$OE = \frac{2\,(\text{area of } \Delta OQR)}{QR}$$

$$= \frac{(2)\left(\dfrac{1}{3}\right)\left(\dfrac{1}{2}\cdot 1\cdot\sqrt{3}\sin 30^\circ\right)}{\sqrt{3}}$$

$$= \frac{1}{6}$$

106. Correct Response : (b, c)

Explanation :

The required diagram is shown in figure below.

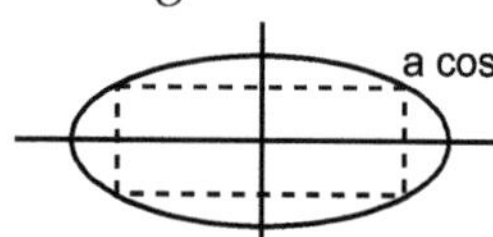

Area will be maximum when $\theta = 45^\circ$.

E_1	3	2
E_2	$\dfrac{3}{\sqrt{2}}$	$\dfrac{2}{\sqrt{2}}$
E_3	$\dfrac{3}{(\sqrt{2})^2}$	$\dfrac{2}{(\sqrt{2})^2}$
$\vdots$	$\vdots$	$\vdots$
E_9	$\dfrac{3}{(\sqrt{2})^8}$	$\dfrac{2}{(\sqrt{2})^8}$

Consider option (A).

$$E_1 + E_2 + \ldots\ldots\ldots + E_m$$

$$e^2 = 1 - \frac{b^2}{a^2}$$

encentricities of all ellipse will be equal

Consider option (b).

When $m \to \infty$

$$\frac{2ab}{1-\dfrac{1}{\sqrt{2}}\dfrac{1}{\sqrt{2}}} = 4ab$$

$$= 4(3)\,(2)$$

$$= 24$$

Consider option (c).

The length of latus rectum is,

$$LR = \frac{2b^2}{a}$$

$$= 2\frac{4\cdot 2^4}{2^8\cdot 3}$$

$$= \frac{1}{6}$$

Consider option (D).

Distance between focus and centre of ellipse is

$$a_9 e_9 = \frac{3}{(\sqrt{2})^8}\left(\frac{\sqrt{5}}{3}\right)$$

$$= \frac{\sqrt{5}}{16}$$

107. Correct Response : 10.00

Explanation :

The required diagram is shown in the figure below.

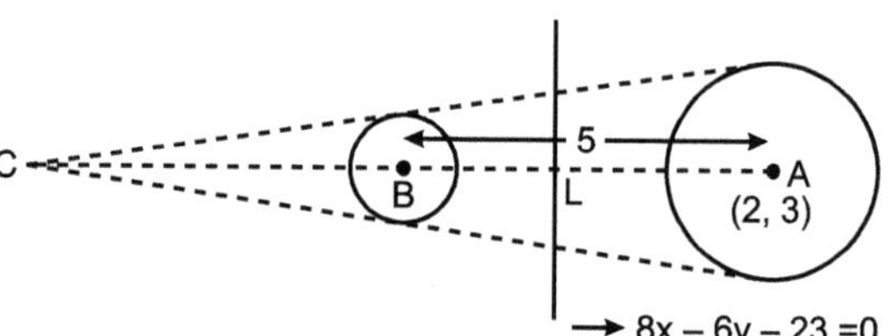

The length AL is,

$$AL = \left|\frac{16-18-23}{10}\right|$$

$$= \frac{5}{2}$$

The length CA is,

$$\frac{CB}{CA} = \frac{1}{2}$$

$$\frac{CA-5}{CA} = \frac{1}{2}$$

$$CA = 10$$

108. Correct Response : (c)

Explanation :

The required diagram is shown in figure below.

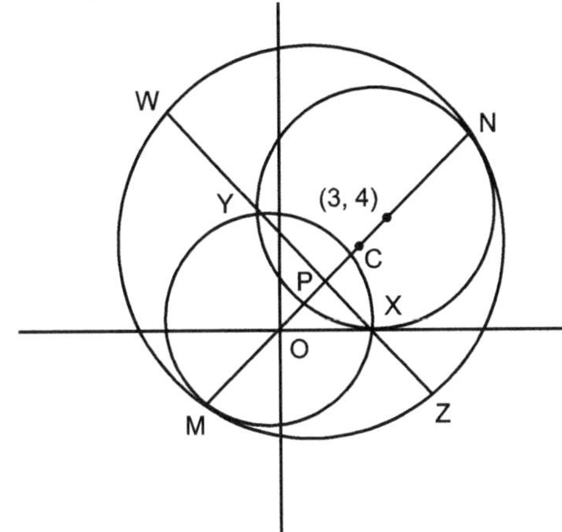

Consider option (I) of list I.

From the above figure.

$$2r = MN$$
$$= 3 + \sqrt{3^2 + 4^2} + 4$$
$$= 12$$
$$r = 6$$

The coordinate of C be $\left(h, \dfrac{4}{3}h \right)$

From the figure,

$$OC = MC - OM$$
$$= \dfrac{12}{2} - 3$$
$$= 3$$

Therefore,

$$\sqrt{h^2 + \dfrac{16}{9}h^2} = 3$$
$$\dfrac{5h}{3} = 3$$
$$h = \dfrac{9}{5}$$
$$k = \dfrac{4}{3}h$$
$$= \dfrac{4}{3}\left(\dfrac{9}{5}\right)$$
$$= \dfrac{12}{5}$$

Therefore,

$$2h + k = \dfrac{18}{5} + \dfrac{12}{5}$$

Consider option (II) of list I.

The equation of line ZW can be written as,

$$C_1 = C_2$$
$$3x + 4y = 9$$

The distance of ZW from (0, 0) is,

$$\dfrac{|-9|}{\sqrt{3^2 + 4^2}} = \dfrac{9}{5}$$

The length of XY is,

$$XY = 2\sqrt{3^2 - \left(\dfrac{9}{5}\right)^2}$$
$$= \dfrac{24}{5}$$

Distance of ZW from C is,

$$\dfrac{\left|\left(\dfrac{(3)(9)}{5} + 4\right)\left(\dfrac{12}{5} - 9\right)\right|}{\sqrt{3^2 + 4^2}} = \dfrac{6}{5}$$

The length of ZW is,

$$ZW = 2\sqrt{6^2 - \dfrac{6^2}{5^2}}$$
$$= \dfrac{24\sqrt{6}}{5}$$

Therefore,

$$\dfrac{\text{length of ZW}}{\text{length of XY}} = \sqrt{6}.$$

Consider option (III) of list I

The area of ΔMZN is,

$$\Delta MZN = \dfrac{1}{2}NM\left(\dfrac{1}{2}ZW\right)$$
$$= \dfrac{72\sqrt{6}}{5}$$

The area of ΔZMW is,

$$\Delta ZMW = \dfrac{1}{2}ZW(OM + OP)$$
$$= \dfrac{1}{2}\left(\dfrac{24\sqrt{6}}{5}\right)\left(3 + \dfrac{9}{5}\right)$$
$$= \dfrac{288\sqrt{6}}{25}$$

Therefore,

$$\dfrac{\text{area of }\Delta MZN}{\text{area of }\Delta ZMW} = \dfrac{5}{4}$$

109. Correct Response : (d)

Explanation :

The required diagram is shown in figure below.

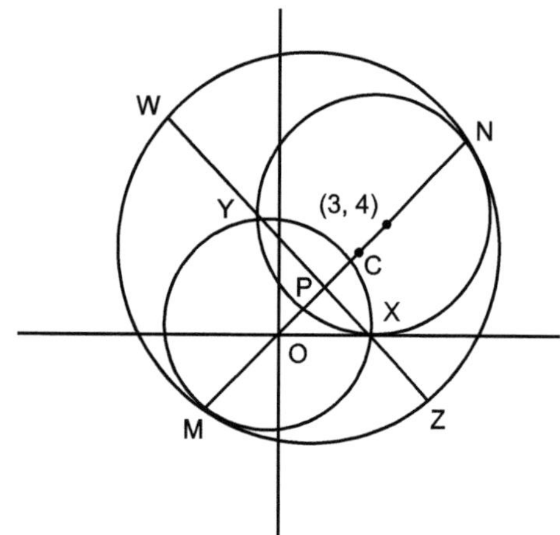

Consider option (IV) of list I

Slope of tangent to C_1 at M is,

$$m = \frac{-1}{\dfrac{4}{3}}$$

$$= -\frac{3}{4}$$

Equation of tangent is,

$$y = mx - 3\sqrt{1+m^2}$$

$$= -\frac{3}{4}x - 3\sqrt{1+\left(-\frac{3}{4}\right)^2}$$

$$= -\frac{3}{4}x - 3\sqrt{1+\frac{9}{16}}$$

$$= -\frac{3x}{4} - \frac{15}{4}$$

Solve further as,

$$x = -\frac{4y}{3} - 5$$

The tangent $x^2 = 4(2\alpha)y$ is,

$$x = m'y + \frac{2\alpha}{m'}$$

Compare the above two equations.

$$m' = -\frac{4}{3}$$

And

$$\frac{2\alpha}{m'} = 5$$

$$\alpha = \frac{10}{3}$$

110. Correct Response : (a)

Explanation :

The circle passes through two points (2, 3) and (4, 5).

The centre of the circle lies on the line,

$$y - 4x + 3 = 0$$

$$y = 4x - 3$$

Let, the x coordinate of the center of the circle is a.

The y coordinate of the circle is,

$$y = 4a - 3$$

The center off the circle is $(a, 4a - 3)$.

The figure shows the circle with the center O.

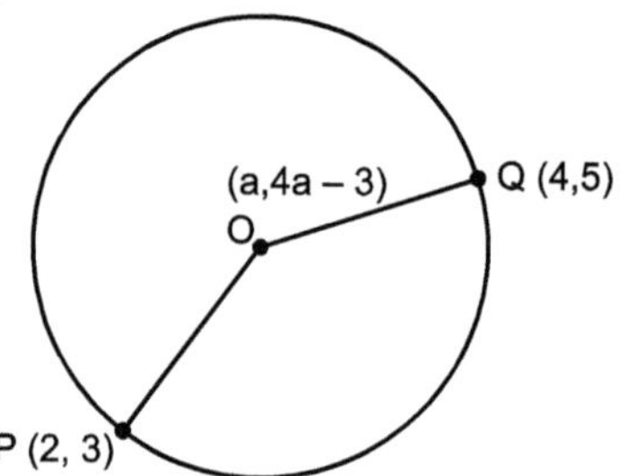

The distance of the center from the points which lies on the circumference is equal.

$$OP = OQ$$

$$= \sqrt{(a-2)^2 + \{(4a-3)-3\}^2}$$

$$= \sqrt{(a-4)^2 + \{(4a-3)-5\}^2}$$

$$(a^2 - 4a + 4) + (16a^2 - 48a + 36)$$
$$= (a^2 - 8a + 16) + (16a^2 - 64a + 64)$$

$$a = 2$$

The coordinate of the center is,

$$(2, 4\,(2) - 3) = (2, 5)$$

The radius of the circle is,

$$r = \sqrt{(0-0)^2 + (5-3)^2}$$

$$= 2$$

Therefore, the radius of the circle is 2.

111. Correct Response : (b)

Explanation :

The equation of the hyperbola is,

$$4y^2 = x^2 + 1$$

Let, the equation of a tangent which passes through point (x_1, y_1) to the hyperbola is,

$$4yy_1 = xx_1 + 1$$

This line intersect the hyperbola at point A and B whose coordinates are $\left(-\dfrac{1}{x_1}, 0\right)$ and $\left(0, \dfrac{1}{4y_1}\right)$.

Let, the coordinates of the mid-point of the line AB is (h, k).

The abscissa h of the mid-point is,

$$h = \frac{\left(-\dfrac{1}{x_1} + 0\right)}{2}$$

$$x_1 = -\frac{1}{2h}$$

The ordinate k of the mid-point is,

$$k = \frac{\left(0 + \dfrac{1}{4y_1}\right)}{2}$$

$$y_1 = \frac{1}{8k}$$

This point lies on the hyperbola due to which the point (x_1, y_1) must satisfy the hyperbola.

$$4\left(\frac{1}{8k}\right)^2 = \left(-\frac{1}{2h}\right)^2 + 1$$

$$\frac{1}{16k^2} = \frac{1}{4h^2} + 1$$

$$h^2 - 4k^2 - 16h^2k^2 = 0$$

$$x^2 - 4y^2 - 16x^2y^2 = 0$$

Therefore, the locus of the mid-point of AB is $x^2 - 4y^2 - 16x^2y^2 = 0$.

112. Correct Response : (a)

Explanation :

The equation of the ellipse is,

$$x^2 + 3y^2 = 9$$

$$\frac{x^2}{(3)^2} + \frac{y^2}{\left(\sqrt{3}\right)^2} = 1$$

Equation of the line normal to the ellipse at point $\left(3\cos\theta, \sqrt{3}\sin\theta\right)$ is,

$$(3\sec\theta)x - \left(\sqrt{3}\csc\theta\right)y = 6$$

The slope of the line is,

$$m_1 = -\frac{a}{b}$$

$$= -\frac{(3\sec\theta)}{-\sqrt{3}\csc\theta}$$

$$= \sqrt{3}\tan\theta$$

Equation of the line normal to the ellipse at point $\left(-3\sin\theta, \sqrt{3}\cos\theta\right)$ is,

$$(-3\csc\theta)x - \left(\sqrt{3}\sec\theta\right) = 6$$

The slope of the line is,

$$m_2 = -\frac{a}{b}$$

$$= -\frac{(-3\csc\theta)}{\left(-\sqrt{3}\sec\theta\right)}$$

$$= -\sqrt{3}\cot\theta$$

If the angle between the lines normal to the ellipse is β then,

$$\tan\beta = \left|\frac{m_1 - m_2}{1 + m_1 m_2}\right|$$

$$= \left|\frac{\left(\sqrt{3}\tan\theta\right) - \left(-\sqrt{3}\cot\theta\right)}{1 + \left(\sqrt{3}\tan\theta\right)\left(-\sqrt{3}\cot\theta\right)}\right|$$

$$= \left|\frac{\sqrt{3}\left(\dfrac{\sin\theta}{\cos\theta} + \dfrac{\cos\theta}{\sin\theta}\right)}{-2}\right|$$

$$= \left|-\frac{\sqrt{3}\left(\sin^2\theta + \cos^2\theta\right)}{2\sin\theta\cos\theta}\right|$$

Further solve the above equation.

$$\tan\beta = \frac{\sqrt{3}(1)}{\sin 2\theta}$$

$$\frac{1}{\cot\beta} = \frac{\sqrt{3}}{\sin 2\theta}$$

$$\frac{\cot\beta}{\sin 2\theta} = \frac{1}{\sqrt{3}}$$

$$\frac{2\cot\beta}{\sin 2\theta} = \frac{2}{\sqrt{3}}$$

113. Correct Response : (d)

Explanation :

The given lines are

$$\sqrt{2}x - y + 4\sqrt{2}k = 0 \qquad \ldots(1)$$

$$\sqrt{2}kx + ky - 4\sqrt{2} = 0 \qquad \ldots(2)$$

Solve the given lines by eliminate k from the equation (1) and (2)

$$k = \frac{\sqrt{2}x - y}{-4\sqrt{2}}$$

$$\left(\sqrt{2}x + y\right)\left(\frac{\sqrt{2}x - y}{-4\sqrt{2}}\right) = 4\sqrt{2}$$

$$2x^2 - y^2 = -32$$

The expression for the hyperbola is,

$$\frac{y^2}{32} - \frac{x^2}{16} = 1$$

Here $a = \sqrt{32} = 4\sqrt{2}$ and $b = 4$

Eccentricity of hyperbola.

$$e = \sqrt{1 + \frac{16}{32}}$$

$$= \sqrt{\frac{3}{2}}$$

And the length of the transverse axis = $2a$

$$2a = 8\sqrt{2}$$

114. Correct Response : (c)

Explanation :

Let P($2t$, t^2) equation normal at P to $x^2 = 4y$ be,

$$y - t^2 = -\frac{1}{t}(x - 2t)$$

It passes through (-3, 0),

$$0 - t^2 = -\frac{1}{t}(-3 - 2t)$$

$$t^3 + 2t + 3 = 0$$
$$(t + 1)(t^2 - t + 3) = 0$$
$$t = -1$$

Point P is (-2, 1) equation of tangent to $x^2 = 4y$ at (-2, 1)

$$x(-2) = 2(y + 1)$$
$$x + y + 1 = 0$$

115. Correct Response : (b)

Explanation :

Equation of the ellipse,

$$\frac{x^2}{a^2} + \frac{y^2}{b^2} = 1$$

$$y^2 = \sqrt{b^2\left(1 - \frac{x^2}{a^2}\right)}$$

Also the coordinate of the focus are (ae, 0) and the equation of the directrix is,

$$x - \frac{a}{e} = 0$$

The distance of point (0, b) from the focus and directrix are $\sqrt{b^2 + a^2 e^2}$ and $\frac{a}{e}$ respectively.

In the conic, the ratio of the distance of any point from the focus to the distance from the directrix is e

$$\frac{\sqrt{b^2 + a^2 e^2}}{\frac{a}{e}} = e$$

$$b^2 = a^2(1 - e^2) \qquad \text{...(1)}$$

Given that the length of the latus rectum of an ellipse = 4

Putting the value of b^2 in the equation (1)

$$2a = a^2(1 - e^2)$$

$$a = \frac{2}{\left(1 - e^2\right)}$$

$$a = \frac{2}{(1 - e)(1 + e)} \qquad \text{...(2)}$$

The vertex nearest the focus is (a, 0)

The distance between the focus and the nearest vertex on major axis is,

$$a - ae = \frac{3}{2}$$

$$a = \frac{3}{2(1 - e)} \qquad \text{...(3)}$$

From the equation (2) and (3)

$$\frac{2}{(1 - e)(1 + e)} = \frac{3}{2(1 - e)}$$

$$\frac{3}{2} = \frac{2}{(1 + e)}$$

$$(1 + e) = \frac{4}{3}$$

$$e = \frac{1}{3}$$

The eccentricity is $\frac{1}{3}$.

116. Correct Response : (b)

Explanation :

For set A,

$$|a - 5| < 1$$

And,

$$|b - 5| < 1,$$

Hence,

$6 > a > 4$ and $4 < b < 6$

From set B,

$$4(a - 6)^2 + 9(b - 5)^2 \le 36$$

$$\frac{(a - 6)^2}{9} + \frac{(b - 5)^2}{4} \le 1$$

Take a and b as axis.

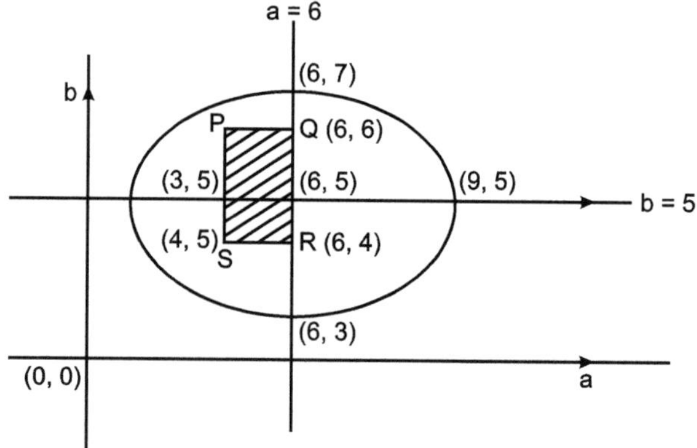

The set A represents square PQRS inside set B which represents an ellipse.

Hence, $A \subset B$.

117. Correct Response : (d)

Explanation :

The slope of the tangent at (x_1, y_1) for the first curve $y^2 = 6x$ is,

$$m_1 = \frac{3}{y_1}$$

The slope of the tangent at (x_1, y_1) for the first curve $9x^2 + by^2 = 16$ is,

$$m_2 = \frac{-9x_1}{by_1}$$

Both the curves intersect each other at right angles. Hence,

$$m_1 \cdot m_2 = -1$$

$$\frac{-27x_1}{b(y_1)^2} = -1$$

$$\frac{-27x_1}{6bx_1} = -1$$

$$b = \frac{9}{2}$$

118. Correct Response : (c)

Explanation :

Let the equation of the line is,

$$\frac{x}{a} + \frac{y}{b} = 1$$

The equation of line when passes through the fixed point (2, 3).

$$\frac{2}{a} + \frac{3}{b} = 1$$

Now coordinates of the point P, O, Q is $P(a, 0)$, $Q(0, b)$, $O(0, 0)$

Let the coordinate of R is $R(h, k)$. The required diagram is,

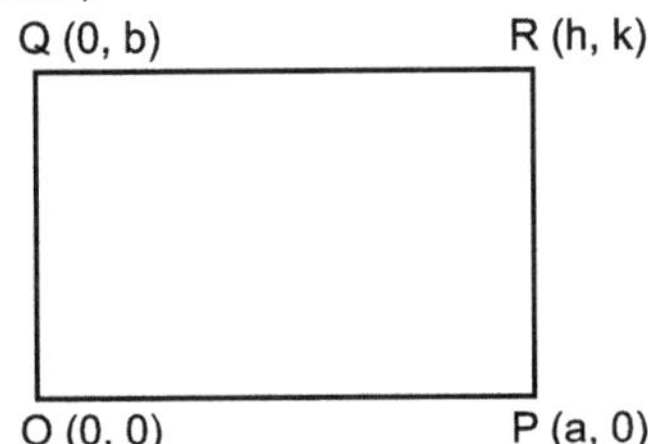

Midpoint of OR is $\left(\dfrac{h}{2}, \dfrac{k}{2}\right)$.

Midpoint of PQ is $\left(\dfrac{a}{2}, \dfrac{b}{2}\right)$. These coordinates gives

$h = a$ and $k = b$.

From the equation of line,

$$\frac{2}{h} + \frac{3}{k} = 1$$

$$\frac{2}{x} + \frac{3}{y} = 1$$

$$3x + 2y = xy$$

119. Correct Response : (c)

Explanation :

Orthocenter of the triangle $A(-3, 5)$ and centroid of the triangle $B(3, 3)$ are shown in the figure.

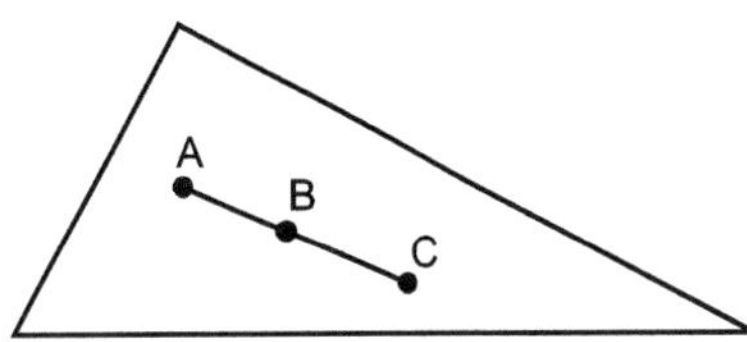

Distance between A and B is,

$$AB = \sqrt{\left(y_2 - y_1\right)^2 + \left(x_2 - x_1\right)^2}$$

$$= 2\sqrt{10}$$

The centroid of the triangle is,

$$AC = \frac{3}{2}AB$$

By taking AC as diameter of circle

$$\text{Radius} = \frac{3}{4}AB$$

$$= \frac{3}{4} \times 2\sqrt{10}$$

$$= 3\sqrt{\frac{5}{2}}$$

120. Correct Response : (b)

Explanation :

The equation of the tangent drawn on parabola at $P : 2y = x + 16$

The equation of the normal drawn on parabola at $P : y = -2x + 16$.

From the above equations, point A is $(-16, 0)$ and B is $(24, 0)$.

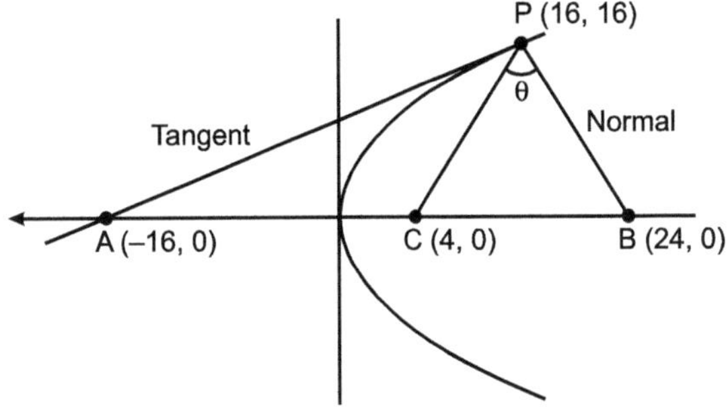

Centre of the circle is (4, 0)

Slope of the line PC is,

$$m_{PC} = \frac{4}{3}$$

Slope of the line PB is,

$$m_{PB} = -2$$

Thus,

$$\tan\theta = \left|\frac{m_{PC} - m_{PB}}{1 + m_{PC}m_{PB}}\right|$$

$$= \left| \dfrac{\dfrac{4}{3}+2}{1-\dfrac{8}{3}} \right|$$

$$= 2$$

121. Correct Response : (a)

Explanation :

With the help of the following diagram,

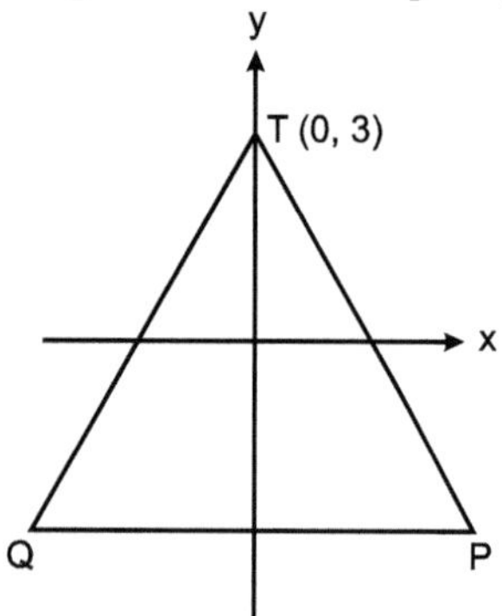

Equation of chord of contact PQ is at $x = 0$.

$$0 - 3y = 36$$
$$y = -12$$

Then the value of x is,

$$4x^2 + 144 = 36$$
$$x = \pm 3\sqrt{5}$$

The coordinates are $P\left(3\sqrt{5}, -12\right)$ $Q\left(-3\sqrt{5}, -12\right)$

and $T(0, 3)$.

Area of the ΔPQT is,

$$\text{Area} = \frac{1}{2} \times 15 \times 6\sqrt{5}$$

$$= 45\sqrt{5}$$

122. Correct Response : (c)

Explanation :

Consider the figure below :

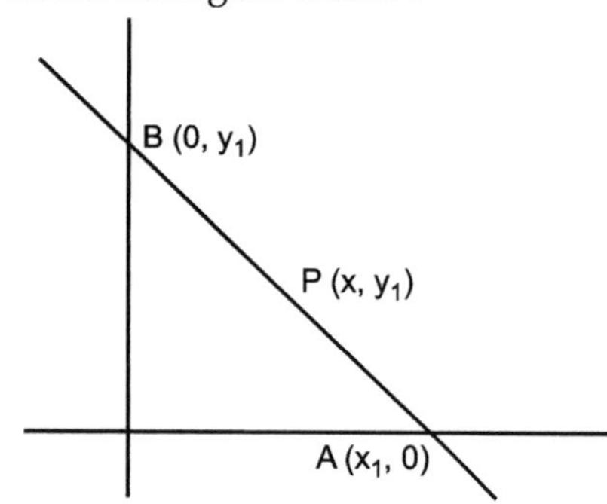

Use section formula for line AB.

$$\frac{AP}{BP} = \frac{1}{3}$$

$$\frac{m}{n} = \frac{1}{3}$$

$$m = 1, n = 3$$

Hence,

$$x = \frac{m \times 0 + n \times x_1}{m+n}$$

$$= \frac{3x_1}{4}$$

$$x_1 = \frac{4x}{3}$$

$$y = \frac{m \times y_1 + n \times 0}{m+n}$$

$$y_1 = 4y$$

Slope of tangent is,

$$\frac{dy}{dx} = \frac{0 - y_1}{x_1 - 0}$$

$$= \frac{-y_1}{x_1}$$

$$= \frac{-4y}{\left(\dfrac{4x}{3}\right)}$$

$$\frac{dy}{y} = \frac{-3dx}{x}$$

Integrate left hand side and right hand side.

$$\ln y = -3 \ln x + c$$
$$yx^3 = c$$
$$f(1) = 1$$
$$c = 1$$

Hence, the equation of curve is,

$$yx^3 = 1$$

From the given options only option (3) satisfies the above equation as,

$$\frac{1}{8} \times 2^3 = 1$$

$$1 = 1$$

The curve passes through the point $\left(2, \dfrac{1}{8}\right)$.

123. Correct Response : (b)

Explanation :

Consider the figure below :

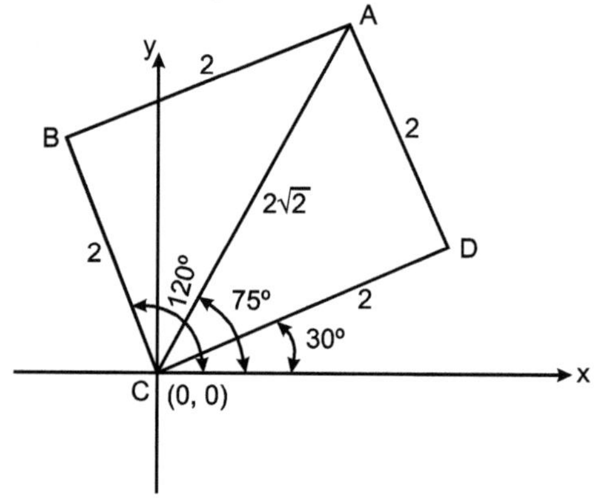

The vertex AD makes $30°$ with x axis. Then,

$$\frac{x}{\cos 30°} = \frac{y}{\sin 30°} = 2$$

$$x = \sqrt{3}$$

$$y = 1$$

The side AB which is passing through the origin will make $120°$ with x axis and its vertex. Then,

$$\frac{x}{\cos 120°} = \frac{y}{\sin 120°} = 2$$

$$x = -1$$

$$y = \sqrt{3}$$

The vertex of the side AC making an angle $75°$ is,

$$\frac{x}{\cos 75°} = \frac{y}{\sin 75°}$$

$$= \sqrt{2^2 + 2^2}$$

$$= 2\sqrt{2}$$

$$x = \sqrt{3} - 1, \ y = \sqrt{3} + 1$$

Sum of the x-coordinates are,

$$0 + \sqrt{3} - 1 + \sqrt{3} - 1 = 2\sqrt{3} - 2$$

124. Correct Response : (b)

Explanation :

Let $\qquad PB \cdot PA = S^2$

Since, $PB \cdot PA$ is on the given line, hence,

$$S^2 = x^2 + y^2 - 9$$

The value of S^2 at $P(4, 7)$ is,

$$S^2 = 4^2 + 7^2 - 9$$

$$= 56$$

Therefore, $PA \cdot PB = 56$.

125. Correct Response : (d)

Explanation :

Given curve equation,

$$x^2 y^2 - 2x = 4\,(1 - y)$$

Partially differentiate the above equation with respect to x.

$$\left(2xy^2 + 2yx^2 \cdot \frac{dy}{dx}\right) - 2(1) = 4(-1)\frac{dy}{dx}$$

$$\frac{dy}{dx}\left(2yx^2 + 4\right) = 2 - 2xy^2$$

$$\frac{dy}{dx} = \frac{2 - 2xy^2}{\left(2yx^2 + 4\right)}$$

The expression for the slope of the tangent is,

$$m = \frac{dy}{dx}$$

$$= \frac{2 - 2xy^2}{\left(2yx^2 + 4\right)}$$

Tangent at point $(2, -2)$ is,

$$\left(\frac{dy}{dt}\right)_{(2,-2)} = \frac{2 - 2(2)(-2)^2}{\left(2(-2)(2)^2 + 4\right)}$$

$$= \frac{14}{12}$$

$$= \frac{7}{6}$$

Hence, the equation of tangent is given as :

$$(y + 2) = m(x - 2)$$

$$(y + 2) = \frac{7}{6}(x - 2)$$

$$7x - 6y = 26$$

Only $(-2, -7)$ does not satisfy the above equation.

126. Correct Response : (d)

Explanation :

The given equation of straight line is,

$$tx - 2y - 3t = 0 \qquad \qquad \dots(1)$$

$$x - 2ty + 3 = 0 \qquad \qquad \dots(2)$$

Multiply equation (1) and (2) with t :

$$t^2 x - 2ty - 3t^2 = 0 \qquad \qquad \dots(3)$$

$$tx - 2t^2 y + 3t = 0 \qquad \qquad \dots(4)$$

Subtract equation (1) with equation (4).

$$y = \frac{3t}{t^2 - 1} \Rightarrow 2y = -3\left(\frac{2t}{1 - t^2}\right) = -3\tan 2A$$

Subtract equation (2) with (4) gives :

$$x = \frac{3t^2 + 1}{t^2 - 1} = -3\sec 2A$$

$$\sec^2(2A) - \tan^2(2A) = 1$$

$$\frac{x^2}{9} - \frac{y^2}{9/4} = 1$$

Simplfiy the above equation :

$$\lambda(T \cdot A) = 2b$$

$$= 2 \times \frac{3}{2}$$

$$= 3$$

The eccentricity is calculated as,

$$e^2 = 1 + \frac{\left(\frac{9}{4}\right)}{9}$$

$$= 1 + \frac{1}{4}$$

$$= \frac{5}{4}$$

$$e = \frac{\sqrt{5}}{2}$$

Also, semi conjugate axis $= \sqrt{\dfrac{9}{4}} = \dfrac{3}{2}$

Therefore the length of conjugate axis is 3.

127. Correct Response : (b)

Explanation :

The diagram is shown below according to question.

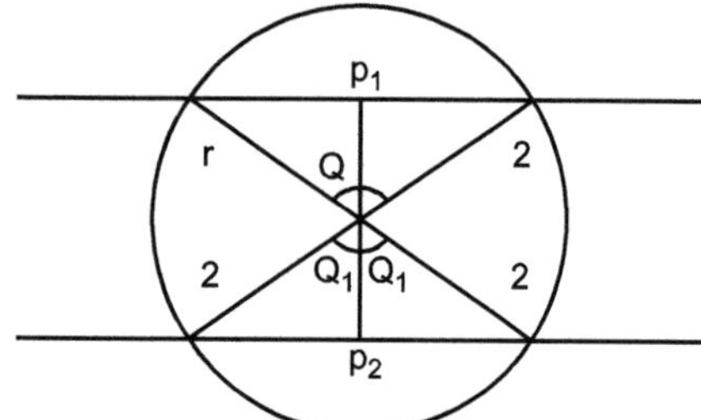

From figure,

$$\cos 2A = \frac{1}{7}$$

$$\cos^2 A - 1 = \frac{1}{7}$$

$$\cos^2 A = \frac{4}{7}$$

Simplfiy the above equation.

$$\frac{d_1^2}{4} = \frac{4}{7}$$

$$d_1 = \frac{4}{\sqrt{7}}$$

For sec 2B,

$$\sec 2B = 7$$

$$\frac{1}{2\cos^2 A - 1} = 7$$

$$2\cos^2 B - 1 = \frac{1}{7}$$

Simplfiy the above equation.

$$\cos^2 B = \frac{4}{7}$$

$$\frac{d_2^2}{4} = \frac{4}{7}$$

$$d_2 = \frac{4}{\sqrt{7}}$$

The total distance between these chords is d. Hence,

$$d = d_1 + d_2$$

$$= \frac{8}{\sqrt{7}}$$

128. Correct Response : (c)

Explanation :

Consider the given figure :

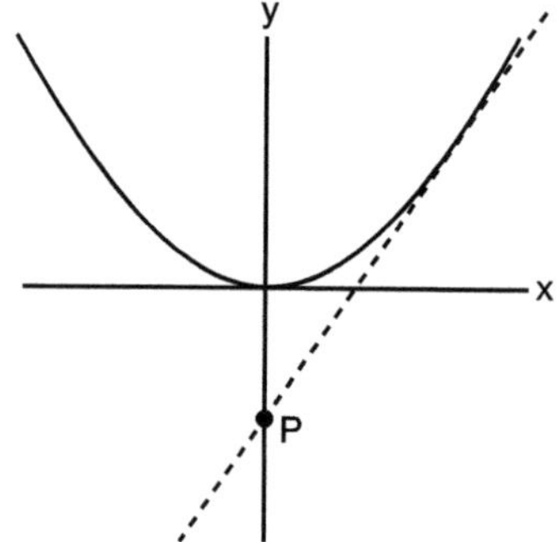

The standard equation of the parabola is,

$$x^2 = 4ay$$

Condition of the tangency is given as :

$$c^2 = a^2 (1 + m^2)$$

If $y = mx + c$ is a tangent to the circle $x^2 + y^2 = a^2$, then tangent to $x^2 + y^2 = 4$ is,

$$y = mx \pm 2\sqrt{1 + m^2}$$

Also,

$$x^2 = 4y$$

$$x^2 = 4mx + 8\sqrt{1 + m^2}$$

$$x^2 - 4mx - 8\sqrt{1 + m^2} = 0$$

For D = 0, the above equation becomes,

$$D = b^2 - 4ac$$

$$= 0$$

Substitute the value of a, b and c in the above expression

$$16m^2 - 4 \times 8\sqrt{1 + m^2} = 0$$

$$m^2 = 2\sqrt{1 + m^2}$$

$$m^4 - 2m^2 - 4 = 0$$

$$(m^2)^2 - 4(m^2) - 4 = 0$$

The root of the above equation is,

$$m^2 = 2 + 2\sqrt{2}$$

$$= 2\left(\sqrt{2} + 1\right)$$

129. Correct Response : (d)

Explanation :

Consider the required diagram :

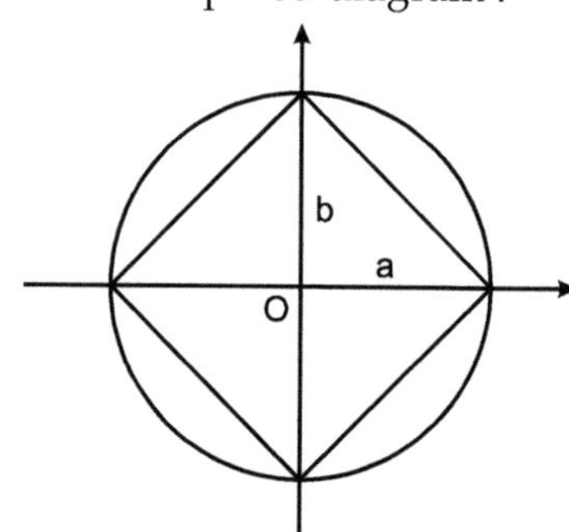

Given ecccentricity of ellipse $\dfrac{3}{5}$

$$e = \frac{3}{5}$$
$$2ae = 6$$
$$a = 5$$

The equation of ellipse is,
$$b^2 = a^2(1 - e^2)$$
$$b^2 = 16$$
$$b = 4$$

Area of an ellipse is given as :
$$A = 4 \times \frac{1}{2}ab$$
$$= 40$$

130. Correct Response : (c)

Explanation :

The equation for an ellipse is
$$\frac{x^2}{a^2} + \frac{y^2}{b^2} = 1$$

The ellipse passes through $(4, -1)$, hence,
$$\frac{16}{a^2} + \frac{1}{b^2} = 1$$
$$16b^2 + a^2 = a^2b^2 \qquad ...(1)$$

The ellipse pass through $(-2, 2)$, hence,
$$\frac{4}{a^2} + \frac{4}{b^2} = 1$$
$$4b^2 + 4a^2 = a^2b^2 \qquad ...(2)$$

From equation (1) and (2).
$$16b^2 + a^2 = 4b^2 + 4a^2$$
$$\frac{b^2}{a^2} = \frac{1}{4}$$

The formula for eccentricity is given as,
$$e = \sqrt{1 - \frac{b^2}{a^2}}$$

Hence,
$$1 - e^2 = \frac{1}{4}$$
$$e = \frac{\sqrt{3}}{2}$$

131. Correct Response : (c)

Explanation :

Write the expression for focal distance.
$$x + a = d$$

Here, d is focal distance.

The equation of parabola is,
$$y^2 = 4ax$$
$$y^2 = 8x$$
$$a = 2$$

Substitute the values.

$$x + 2 = 8$$
$$x = 6$$

Also,
$$y^2 = 8 \times 6$$
$$= 48$$
$$y = \pm 4\sqrt{3}$$

Differentitate equation (1) of parabola with respect to x.

$$2y\frac{dy}{dx} = 8$$
$$\frac{dy}{dx} = \frac{4}{y}$$

Substitute the values.
$$\frac{dy}{dx} = \frac{4}{4\sqrt{3}}$$
$$= \frac{1}{\sqrt{3}}$$

Write the expression for slope of normal.
$$\text{slope of normal} = \frac{-dx}{dy}$$
$$= -\sqrt{3}$$

Write the expression of the normal,.
$$y = mx + c$$

Substitute the values.
$$4\sqrt{3} = -\sqrt{3} \times 6 + c$$
$$c = 10\sqrt{3}$$

132. Correct Response : (c)

Explanation :

Consider the following diagram :

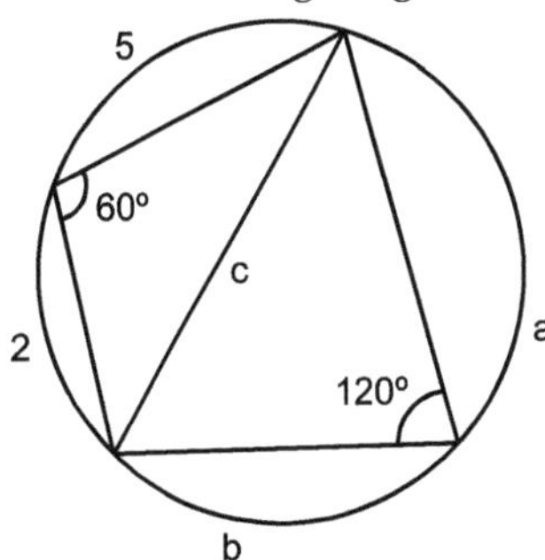

By properties of triangle,
$$2^2 + 5^2 - 2 \times 2 \times 5 \cos 60° = c^2$$

Hence,
$$\cos 60° = \frac{(2^2 + 5^2 - c^2)}{(2 \times (2 \times 5))}$$
$$\frac{1}{2} = \frac{(4 + 25 - c^2)}{(2 \times 10)}$$
$$10 = 29 - c^2$$
$$c = \sqrt{19}$$

Similarly,

$$\cos 120° = \frac{(a^2 + b^2 - 19)}{2ab}$$

$$-\frac{1}{2} = \frac{(a^2 + b^2 - 19)}{2ab}$$

$$a^2 + b^2 + ab = 19$$

Area of the quadrilateral is $4\sqrt{3}$. It is the sum of two triangles. Hence,

$$\frac{1}{2} \times 2 \times 5 \sin 60° + \frac{1}{2} ab \sin 120° = 4\sqrt{3}$$

$$5\frac{\sqrt{3}}{2} + \frac{1}{2} ab \frac{\sqrt{3}}{2} = 4\sqrt{3}$$

$$5 + \frac{ab}{2} = 8$$

$$ab = 6$$

So,

$$a^2 + b^2 + 6 = 19$$
$$a^2 + b^2 = 13$$
$$(a + b)^2 = a^2 + b^2 + 2ab$$
$$= 13 + 2 \times 6$$
$$= 25$$

Hence,

$$a + b = 5$$

The perimeter of the quadrilateral is $(2 + 5 + a + b) = 2 + 5 + 5 = 12$.

133. Correct Response : (c)

Explanation :

Let the point at minimum distance from the origin O to point P be $(h, h^2 - 4)$. Hence,

$$OP^2 = h^2 + (h^2 - 4)^2$$

Differentiate the above equation and put it equal to zero.

$$\frac{d\,(OP)^2}{dh} = 0$$

$$2h + 2(h^2 - 4)\,2h = 0$$

$$h = \pm \sqrt{\frac{7}{2}}, 0$$

Again differentiate the above equation :

$$\left(\frac{d^2\,(OP)^2}{dh^2}\right)_{h=\pm\sqrt{\frac{7}{2}}} > 0$$

Then OP is minimum at $h = \pm\sqrt{\frac{7}{2}}$

So, for the minimum distance,

$$OP_{min} = \sqrt{\frac{7}{2} + \left(\frac{7}{2} - 4\right)^2}$$

$$= \frac{\sqrt{15}}{2}$$

134. Correct Response : (c)

Explanation :

Given :

$$\frac{x}{3} + \frac{y}{4} = 1 \qquad \text{...(1)}$$

$$4x + 3y = 12$$

$$\frac{x}{4} + \frac{y}{3} = 1$$

$$3x + 4y = 12 \qquad \text{...(2)}$$

Equation of line passing through the intersection is given as :

$$4x + 3y - 12 + \lambda(3x + 4y - 12) = 0$$

Let A and B are the intersection point.

$$A = \left(\frac{12\,(1+\lambda)}{4 + 3\lambda}, 0\right)$$

$$B = \left(0, \frac{12\,(1+\lambda)}{3 + 4\lambda}\right)$$

Then, midpoint $P(h, k)$ is given by :

$$h = \frac{6\,(1+\lambda)}{4 + 3\lambda} \qquad \text{...(3)}$$

$$k = \frac{6\,(1+\lambda)}{3 + 4\lambda} \qquad \text{...(4)}$$

From equation (3) and (4),

$$\lambda = \frac{3k - 4h}{3h - 4k}$$

Substitute the value of λ in equation (1).

$$7xy = 6\,(x + y)$$

135. Correct Response : (c)

Explanation :

Given the equation of the line is,

$$x - y = 4$$
$$y = x - 4 \qquad \text{...(1)}$$

Compare the above equation with $y = mx + c$ the value of the slope of the line is,

$$m = 1$$

or,

$$\tan \theta = 1$$

Here θ is the angle between x and line as shown in the figure.

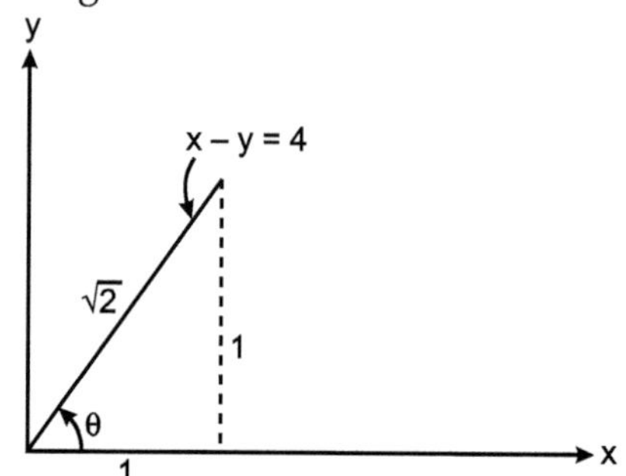

Therefore,

In the first quadrant the value is,

$$\cos\theta = \frac{1}{\sqrt{2}}$$

$$\sin\theta = \frac{1}{\sqrt{2}}$$

In the third quadrant,

$$\cos\theta = -\frac{1}{\sqrt{2}}$$

$$\sin\theta = -\frac{1}{\sqrt{2}}$$

Then the new point Q is,

$$Q \equiv \left(x + 2\sqrt{3}\left(\cos\theta\right)\right), y + 2\sqrt{3}\left(\sin\theta\right)$$

$$\equiv \left(2 + 2\sqrt{3}\left(-\frac{1}{\sqrt{2}}\right), 1 + 2\sqrt{3}\left(-\frac{1}{\sqrt{2}}\right)\right)$$

$$\equiv \left(2 - \sqrt{6}, 1 - \sqrt{6}\right)$$

Hence, the equation of required line is

$$x + y = 3 - 2\sqrt{6}$$

136. Correct Response : (b)

Explanation :

The equation of the circle is,

$$(x - h)^2 + (y - k)^2 = r^2 \qquad ...(1)$$

Here, the centre of the circle is (h, k) and radius is r.

Required circle is given as :

$$x^2 + (y - 2)^2 + \lambda x = 0$$

This passes through $(- 2, 4)$, Hence,

$$4 + 4 - 2\lambda = 0$$

$$\lambda = 4$$

Substitute the value of the λ in the equation of the circle,

$$x^2 + (y - 2)^2 + 4x = 0$$

$$x^2 + y^2 - 4y + 4x + 4 + 4 = 4$$

$$(x^2 + 4x + 4) + (y^2 - 4y + 4) = 4$$

$$(x + 2)^2 + (y - 2)^2 = 2^2$$

Compare this equation with equation (1), therefore,

The centre of the circle is $(- 2, 2)$ and radius is 2.

The centre $(- 2, 2)$ which satisfy the equation.

$$2x - 3y + 10 = 0$$

Thus, the option (b) is correct.

137. Correct Response : (b)

Explanation :

Given equation is,

$$9e^2 - 18e + 5 = 0$$

$$e = \frac{5}{3}$$

Then, eccentricity is,

$$e = \frac{\sqrt{(a^2 + b^2)}}{a}$$

From above formula,

$$1 + \frac{b^2}{a^2} = e^2$$

$$1 + \frac{b^2}{a^2} = \frac{25}{9} \qquad ...(1)$$

The distance between foci and directrix is,

$$\left(ae - \frac{a}{e}\right) = 5 - \frac{9}{5}$$

$$a\left(\frac{5}{3} - \frac{3}{5}\right) = \frac{16}{5}$$

$$a = 3$$

From equation (1),

$$1 + \frac{b^2}{9} = \frac{25}{19}$$

$$b^2 = 16$$

So,

$$a^2 - b^2 = 9 - 16$$

$$= - 7$$

138. Correct Response : (d)

Explanation :

The general equation of the ellipse is,

$$\frac{x^2}{a^2} + \frac{y^2}{b^2} = 1$$

The equation of the ellipse is given as,

$$\frac{x^2}{27} + \frac{y^2}{3} = 1$$

The point P on the ellipse is,

$$P \equiv (a\cos\theta, b\sin\theta)$$

Substitute the value of a and b in the point P,

$$P \equiv \left(3\sqrt{3}\cos\theta, \sqrt{3}\sin\theta\right)$$

At the point $P\left(3\sqrt{3}\cos\theta, \sqrt{3}\sin\theta\right)$

The equation of the tangent is given by,

$$\frac{x\cos\theta}{a} + \frac{y\sin\theta}{b} = 1$$

Substitute the value in the above equation,

$$\frac{x}{3\sqrt{3}}\cos\theta + \frac{y}{\sqrt{3}}\sin\theta = 1$$

Then,

$$a = (3\sqrt{3}\sec\theta, 0)$$

And,

$$b = (0,\ \sqrt{3}\ \text{cosec}\ \theta)$$

Area of triangle is given as :

$$\text{Area}\ (\Delta OAB) = \frac{1}{2} \times OA \times OB$$

$$= \frac{1}{2}\ (3\sqrt{3}\ \sec\theta \cdot \sqrt{3}\ \text{cosec}\ \theta)$$

$$= \frac{9}{2\sin\theta\cos\theta}$$

$$= \frac{9}{\sin 2\theta}$$

Hence, the minimum area of ΔOAB is,

$$\text{Area}_{\text{Min}} = \frac{9}{\sin 2\theta}$$

$$= \frac{9}{1}$$

$$[\because \text{maximum value of } \sin^2\theta \text{ is } 1]$$

$$= 9$$

139. Correct Response : (a)

Explanation :

Let slow of incident ray be m.

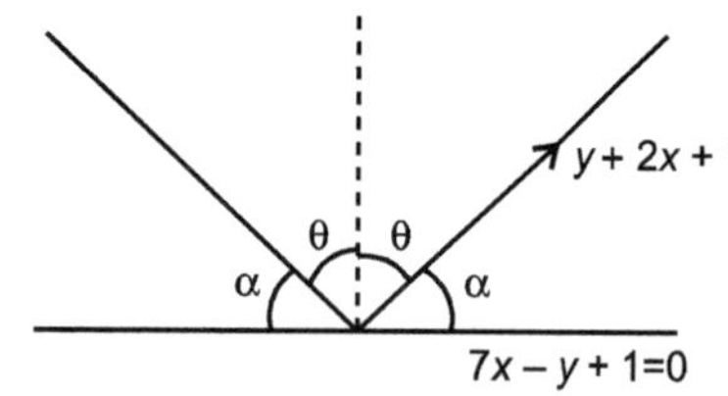

$\therefore$ angle of incidence = angle of reflection

$$\therefore \quad \left|\frac{m-7}{1+7m}\right| = \left|\frac{-2-7}{1+14}\right| = \frac{9}{13}$$

$$\Rightarrow \quad \left|\frac{m-7}{1+7m}\right| = \frac{9}{13}$$

$$\text{or} \quad \left|\frac{m-7}{1+7m}\right| = -\frac{9}{13}$$

$$\Rightarrow \quad 13\,m - 91 = 9 + 63\,m$$

$$\text{or} \quad 13\,m - 91 = -9 - 63\,m$$

$$\Rightarrow \quad 50\,m = -100$$

$$\text{or} \quad 76\,m = 82$$

$$\Rightarrow \quad m = \frac{1}{2}$$

$$\text{or} \quad m = \frac{41}{38}$$

$$\Rightarrow \quad y - 1 = -\frac{1}{2}(x-0)$$

or

$$y - 1 = \frac{41}{38}(x-0)$$

i.e., $\quad x + 2y - 2 = 0$

or $\quad 38y - 38 - 41x = 0$

140. Correct Response : (c)

Explanation :

Let the straight line through origin $(0, 0)$ is,

$$\frac{x}{\cos\theta} = \frac{y}{\sin\theta} = r$$

The above line meets line $3y = 10 - 4x$ at point A then,

$$3r_1 \sin\theta = 10 - 4r_1 \cos\theta$$

$$r_1\,(3\sin\theta + 4\cos\theta) = 10 \qquad \qquad \text{...(1)}$$

Again the line through origin meets line $8x + 6y + 5 = 0$ at point B then,

$$8r_2 \cos\theta + 6r_2 \sin\theta + 5 = 0$$

$$2r_2\,(3\sin\theta + 4\cos\theta) = -5 \qquad \qquad \text{...(2)}$$

Divide equation (1) by equation (2),

$$\frac{r_1\,(3\sin\theta + 4\cos\theta)}{2r_2\,(3\sin\theta + 4\cos\theta)} = \frac{10}{-5}$$

$$\frac{r_1}{r_2} = \frac{4}{1}$$

141. Correct Response : (b)

Explanation :

The given straight line are,

$$x - y = 1 \qquad \qquad \text{...(1)}$$

Second equation of line is,

$$2x + y = 3 \qquad \qquad \text{...(2)}$$

Add equation (1) and equation (2) to get the value of x,

$$3x = 4$$

$$x = \frac{4}{3}$$

Substitute $\dfrac{4}{3}$ for x in equation (1),

$$y = \frac{4}{3} - 1$$

$$= \frac{1}{3}$$

The centre of circle is the point of intersection of straight lines $x - y = 1$ and $2x + y = 3$ so the centre of circle is $\left(\dfrac{4}{3}, \dfrac{1}{3}\right)$.

The equation of the circle is,

$$\left(x - \frac{4}{3}\right)^2 + \left(y - \frac{1}{3}\right)^2 = \left(1 - \frac{4}{3}\right)^2 + \left(-1 - \frac{1}{3}\right)^2$$

$$x^2 + y^2 - \frac{8}{3}x - \frac{2}{3}y = 0$$

$$3x^2 + 3y^2 - 8x - 2y = 0$$

The equation of tangent to the circle at point $(1, -1)$ is,

$$3x(1) + 3y(-1) - \frac{8}{2}(x+1) - \frac{2}{2}(y-1) = 0$$

$$3x - 3y - 4x - 4 - y + 1 = 0$$

$$-x - 4y - 3 = 0$$

$$x + 4y + 3 = 0$$

142. Correct Response : (d)

Explanation :

Let the point P is $(t^2, 2t)$ and the point Q is $\left(t_1^2, 2t_1\right)$ on the parabola $y^2 = 4x$.

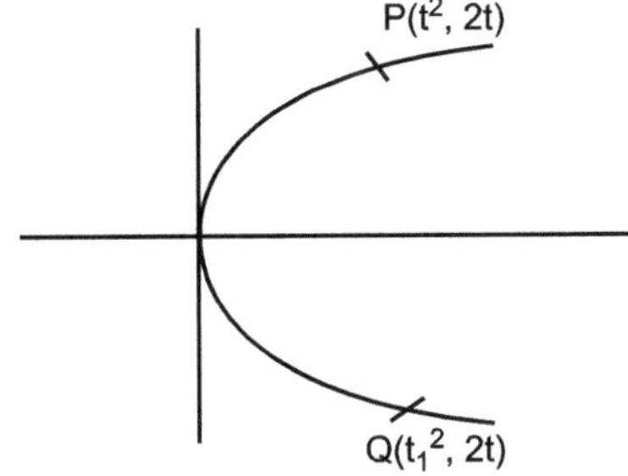

The equation of normal at point P $(t^2, 2t)$ passes through point Q $\left(t_1^2, 2t_1\right)$ is,

$$t_1 = -t - \frac{2}{t} \qquad ...(1)$$

Differentiate the above equation with respect to t,

$$\frac{dt_1}{dt}\bigg|_{max} = -1 + \frac{2}{t^2}$$

$$0 = -1 + \frac{2}{t^2}$$

$$t^2 = 2$$

Square both sides of equation (1),

$$t_1^2 = \left(-t - \frac{2}{t}\right)^2$$

$$= t^2 + \frac{4}{t^2} + 4$$

$$= 2 + \frac{4}{2} + 4$$

$$= 8$$

143. Correct Response : (d)

Explanation :

For hyperbola,

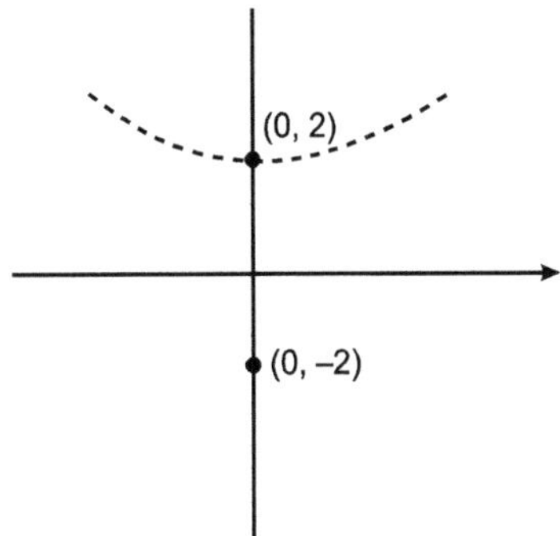

Equation of the hyperbola,

$$\frac{x^2}{a^2} - \frac{y^2}{b^2} = -1$$

The eccentricity of the hyperbola is,

$$\frac{3}{2} = \sqrt{1 + \frac{a^2}{b^2}}$$

$$\frac{9}{4} = 1 + \frac{a^2}{b^2}$$

$$a^2 = \frac{5}{4}b^2$$

Given that $b^2 = 4$,

Therefore,

$$a^2 = 5$$

Hence, the equation of the ellipse is,

$$\frac{x^2}{5} - \frac{y^2}{4} = -1$$

Check options one by one by substitute the given points on the hyperbola,

Check option (d)

For point $\left(5, 2\sqrt{3}\right)$

$$\frac{x^2}{5} - \frac{y^2}{4} = \frac{25}{5} - \frac{12}{4}$$

$$= 5 - 3$$

$$= 2$$

$$\neq -1$$

Hence, option (d) is correct.

144. Correct Response : (c)

Explanation :

Let point $P\left(\alpha, 1 + \sqrt{4\alpha - 3}\right)$ is on the curve C.

Differentiate the given equation with respect to x,

$$\frac{dy}{dx} = \frac{2}{\sqrt{4x - 3}}$$

$$\frac{dy}{dx}\bigg|_{P\left(\alpha, 1+\sqrt{4\alpha-3}\right)} = \frac{2}{\sqrt{4\alpha - 3}}$$

$$\frac{2}{3} = \frac{2}{\sqrt{4\alpha - 3}}$$

$$\alpha = 3$$

The point P is obtained as (3, 4).

The slope of normal at point P (3, 4) is $\frac{-3}{2}$.

The equation of normal is,

$$y - 4 = -\frac{3}{2}(x - 3)$$

$$3x + 2y = 17$$

From the option, it is clear that normal passes through point (1, 7).

145. Correct Response : (c)

Explanation :

Draw a rhombus by the given equations.

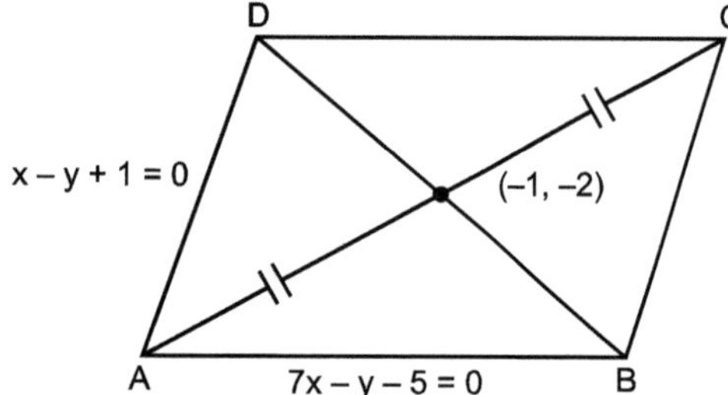

Point of intersection of AD and AB is A. The coordinates of A is (1, 2).

Consider C be $(x_1\ y_1)$.

For the line AC, apply the formula for the center of the line,

$$\frac{x_1 + 1}{2} = -1$$

$$x_1 = -3$$

And,

$$\frac{y_1 + 2}{2} = -2$$

$$y_1 = -6$$

Slope of AC is,

$$\frac{2 + 2}{1 + 1} = 2$$

Now, the equation of the AC is,

$$\frac{y + (-6)}{x + (-3)} = 2$$

$$2x - 6 = y - 6$$

$$2x - y = 0$$

Hence, the slope of BD is $\frac{-1}{2}$

Now the equation of the BD is,

$$\frac{y + 2}{x + 1} = \frac{-1}{2}$$

$$x + 2y + 5 = 0$$

Remaining two sides of rhombus are,

$$x - y - 3 = 0$$

And,

$$7x - y + 15 = 0$$

On solving the equation of lines AD, DC, BC and AB, the vertice are $\left(\frac{1}{3}, -\frac{8}{3}\right)$, (1, 2), $\left(-\frac{7}{3}, -\frac{4}{3}\right)$ and (− 3, − 6).

146. Correct Response : (d)

Explanation :

Consider (h, k) be the centre of the circle which touch x− axis and $x^2 + y^2 - 8x - 8y - 4 = 0$ externally.

Radius of that circle is $|k|$, that is,

$$(h - 4)^2 + (k - 4)^2 = (|k| + 6)^2$$

$$x^2 - 8x - 20y - 4 = 0 \qquad \text{if } y \geq 0$$

And,

$$x^2 - 8x + 4y - 4 = 0 \qquad \text{If } y < 0$$

Therefore, the circle touches each other shown below,

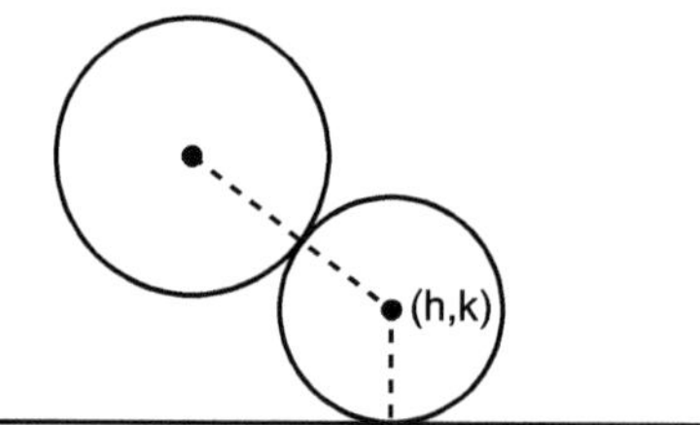

The curve is parabola.

147. Correct Response : (b)

Explanation :

Draw a circle by the given equation of the circle whose centre is at (− 3, 2).

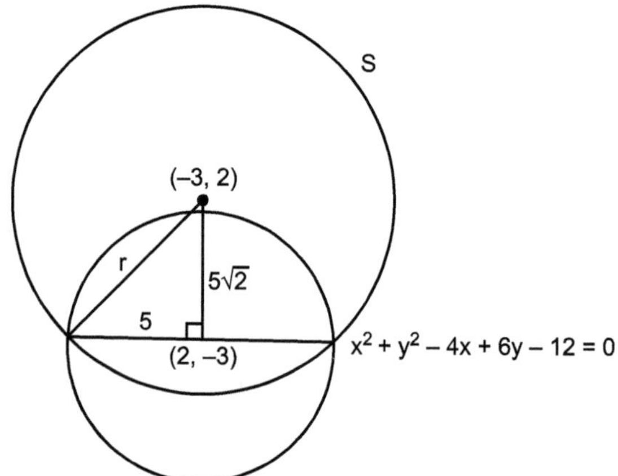

Consider r be the radius of the circle S. Then,

$$r = \sqrt{25 + 50}$$

$$= 5\sqrt{3}$$

148. Correct Response : (a)

Explanation :

Draw the required diagram for the combination of parabola and circle,

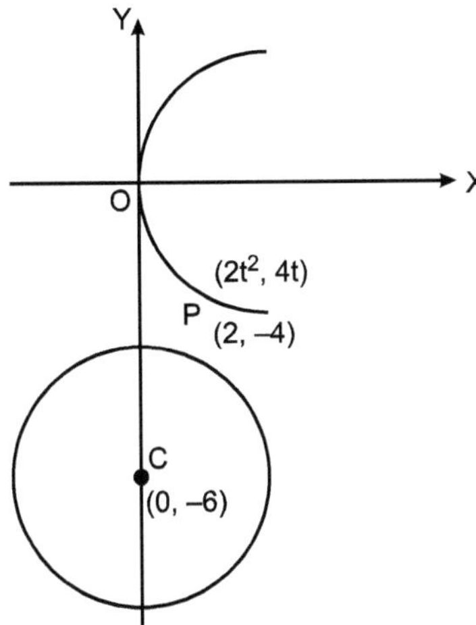

Equation of normal at P($2t^2$, $4t$) is,

$$y + xt = 2at + at^3$$
$$y = -tx + 4t + 2t^3$$

It passes through the point C($0, -6$).

Therefore, it satisfies the equation of the normal,

$$-6 = 4t + 2t^3$$
$$t^3 + 2t + 3 = 0$$
$$t = -1$$

Hence, P is,

$$(2t^2, 4t) = (2, -4)$$

Now the value of the radius of the circle r is,

$$r = \sqrt{2^2 + (-4 + 6)^2}$$
$$= 2\sqrt{2}$$

Equation of required circle is,

$$(x - 2)^2 + (y + 4)^2 = 8$$
$$x^2 + y^2 - 4x + 8y + 12 = 0$$

149. Correct Response : (c)

Explanation :

The given length of the latus rectum is,

$$\frac{2b^2}{a} = 8$$

And, the length of its conjugate axis is,

$$2b = \frac{1}{2}(2ae)$$
$$2b = ae$$
$$4b^2 = a^2e^2$$

The expression of the eccentricity of the hyperbola is,

$$e = \sqrt{1 + \frac{b^2}{a^2}}$$
$$a^2(e^2 - 1) = b^2$$

Substitute the value and simplify,

$$a^2(e^2 - 1) = \frac{a^2 e^2}{4}$$
$$3e^2 = 4$$
$$e = \frac{2}{\sqrt{3}}$$

150. Correct Response : (d)

Explanation :

The equation of the line joining points A and B is,

$$y - 0 = -1(x - 41)$$
$$x + y = 41$$

Consider the diagram :

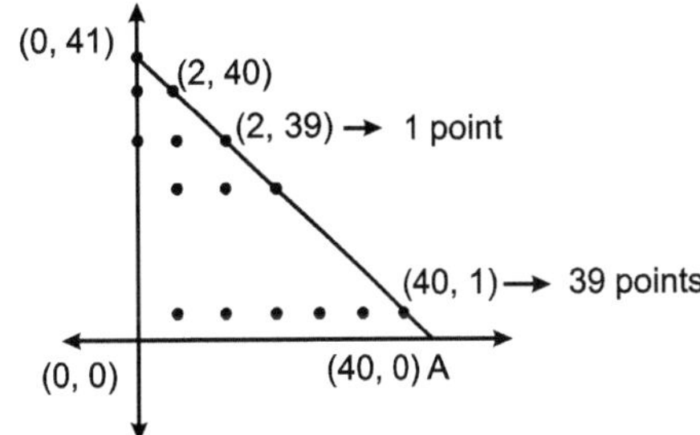

Hence, the number of the integer coordinates within the triangle is,

$$n = 1 + 2 + 3 + ... + 39$$
$$= \frac{39 \times (39 + 1)}{2}$$
$$= 780$$

151. Correct Response : (c)

Explanation :

Consider the following figure.

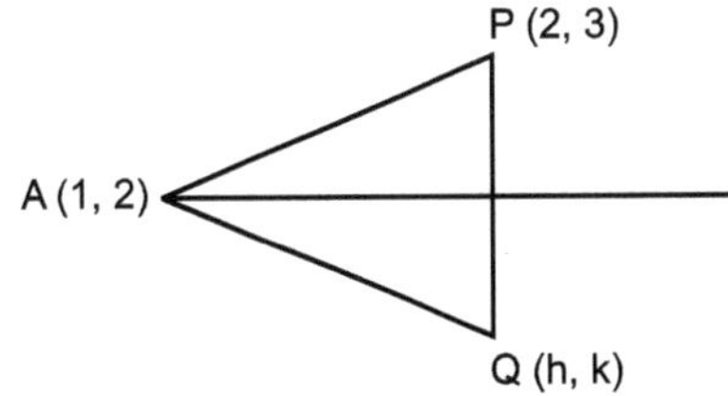

The given equation of line is passing through the (1, 2).

$$AP = AQ$$
$$\sqrt{(h-1)^2 + (k-2)^2} = \sqrt{(2-1)^2 + (3-2)^2}$$
$$(h - 1)^2 + (k - 2)^2 = 2$$

The above equation represents the equation of a circle whose radius is,

$$r = \sqrt{2}$$

152. Correct Response : (c)

Explanation :

The equation of the first circle is,

$$x^2 + y^2 - 4x - 6y - 12 = 0$$

The centre of the first circle is,
$$C_1 = (2, 3)$$
The radius of the first circle is,
$$r_1 = \sqrt{4+9+12}$$
$$= 5$$
The equation of the second circle is,
$$x^2 + y^2 + 6x + 18y + 26 = 0$$
The centre of the second circle is,
$$C_2 = (-3, -9)$$
The radius of the second circle is,
$$r_2 = \sqrt{9+91-26}$$
$$= 8$$
The distance between the centers of the circles is,
$$C_1C_2 = \sqrt{5^2 + 12^2}$$
$$= 13$$
And the sum of the radius is,
$$r_1 + r_2 = 8 + 5$$
$$= 13$$
Hence,
$$r_1 + r_2 = C_1C_2$$
It means that the circles are touching externally due to which only 3 common tangents are possible.

153. Correct Response : (d)

Explanation :

The equation of the ellipse is,
$$\frac{x^2}{9} + \frac{y^2}{5} = 1$$

Compare the above equation with,
$$\frac{x^2}{a^2} + \frac{y^2}{b^2} = 1$$

The values of a and b are,
$$a = 3$$
$$b = \sqrt{5}$$

The eccentricity is,
$$e = \sqrt{1 - \frac{5}{9}}$$
$$= \frac{2}{3}$$

The value of one of the end point of a latusrectum is,
$$A\left(ae, \frac{b^2}{a}\right)$$
$$A\left(2, \frac{5}{3}\right)$$

The equation of the tangent are $A\left(2, \frac{5}{3}\right)$ is,

$$\frac{2x}{9} + \frac{y}{3} \times \frac{5}{5} = 1$$

$$\frac{x}{\frac{9}{2}} + \frac{y}{3} = 1$$

The obtained figure is,

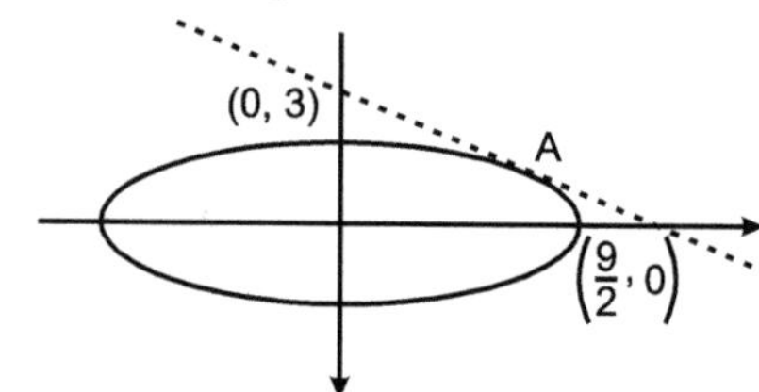

The area of the rhombus formed by tangents is,
$$A = 4\left(\frac{1}{2} \times \frac{9}{2} \times 3\right)$$
$$= 27$$

154. Correct Response : (d)

Explanation :

Any point on the parabola is $(4t, 2t^2)$. Point P divides the line segments joining $O(0, 0)$ and $Q(4t, 2t^2)$ in the ratio $\frac{1}{3}$. The required figure is,

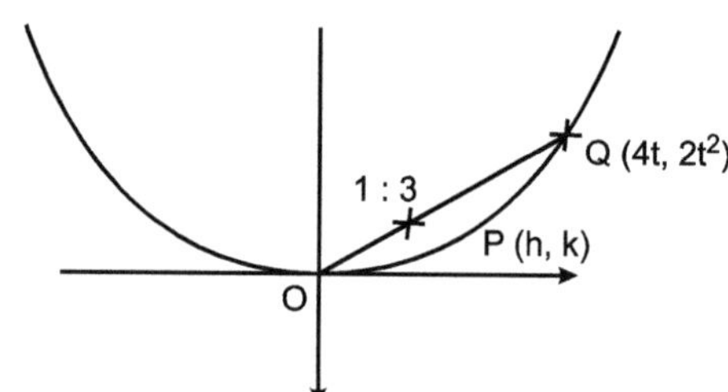

Using the above figure,
$$h = \frac{1 \times 4t + 3 \times 0}{1+3}$$
$$= t$$
$$k = \frac{1 \times 2t^2 + 3 \times 0}{1+3}$$
$$k = \frac{t^2}{2}$$

It means that,
$$k = \frac{1}{2} h^2$$

Replace h by x and k by y.
$$y = \frac{1}{2} x^2$$
$$x^2 = 2y$$

155. Correct Response : (b)

Explanation :

Consider the slope of the line L is m.

The given line L$_1$ is,

$$\sqrt{3}x + y = 1$$

$$y = \left(-\sqrt{3}\right) x + 1$$

Slope of the line L$_1$ is,

$$m_1 = -\sqrt{3}$$

Now, angle between L and L$_1$ is 60°.

$$\tan 60° = \left| \frac{m - (-\sqrt{3})}{1 + (-m\sqrt{3})} \right|$$

$$\sqrt{3} = \left| \frac{m + \sqrt{3}}{1 - m\sqrt{3}} \right|$$

$$\left| \sqrt{3} - 3m \right| = \left| m + \sqrt{3} \right|$$

Then,

$$\sqrt{3} - 3m = -m - \sqrt{3}$$

$$2m = 2\sqrt{3}$$

$$m = \sqrt{3}$$

Or

$$m = 0$$

Hence, the equation of the line L is,

$$y + 2 = \sqrt{3}\ (x - 3)$$

$$y - \sqrt{3}x + 2 + 3\sqrt{3} = 0$$

156. Correct Response : (b)

Explantion :

In an equilateral triangle, incentre and circumcentre are same and,

$$R = 2r$$

The diagram of the equilateral triangle is,

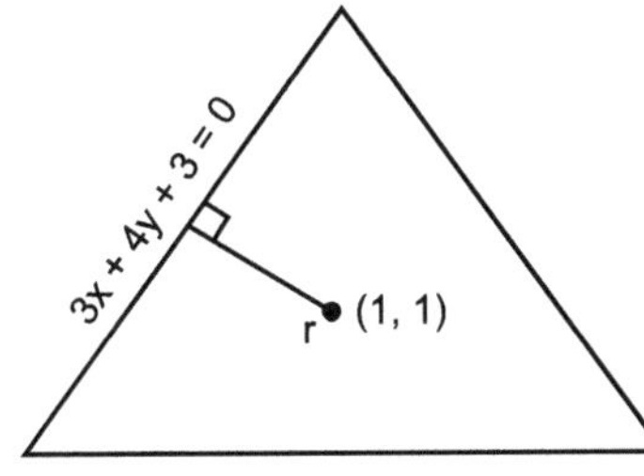

Now,

$$r = \frac{|3 + 4 + 3|}{\sqrt{9 + 16}}$$

$$= 2$$

Therefore,

$$R = 2r$$

$$= 4$$

So, the equation of the circumcentre of this triangle is,

$$(x - 1)^2 + (y - 1)^2 = 4^2$$

$$x^2 + y^2 - 2x - 2y - 14 = 0$$

157. Correct Response : (c)

Explanation :

The figure is shown as,

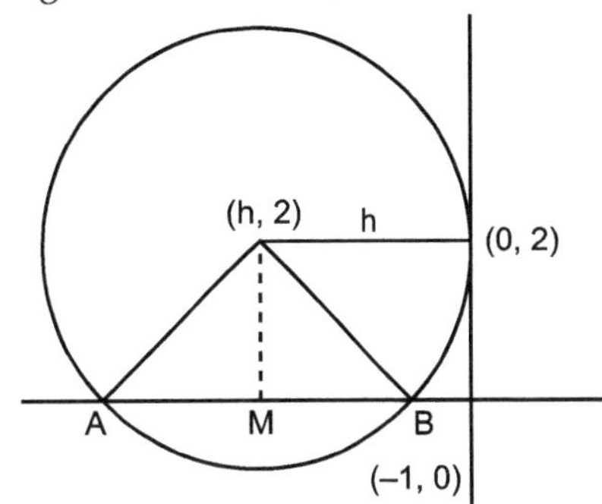

Apply the formula to calculate the value of h,

$$(h + 1)^2 + 2^2 = h^2$$

$$h^2 + 1 + 2h + 4 = h^2$$

$$2h + 5 = 0$$

$$h = \frac{-5}{2}$$

Here,

$$AB = 2\,(AM)$$

$$= 2\,\sqrt{(h^2 - 2^2)}$$

$$= 2 \left(\frac{3}{2} \right)$$

$$= 3$$

158. Correct Response : (c)

Explanation :

The equation of the ellipse,

$$\frac{x^2}{a^2} - \frac{y^2}{b^2} = 1$$

From the given relation,

$$ae = \frac{b^2}{2a}$$

$$e = \frac{b^2}{2a^2}$$

$$= \frac{a^2\,(1 - e^2)}{2a^2}$$

$$e = \frac{1 - e^2}{2}$$

Further, simplify the above expression,

$$2e = 1 - e^2$$

$$e^2 + 2e - 1 = 0$$

$$e = \frac{-2 \pm \sqrt{4 + 4}}{2}$$

$$e = -1 \pm \sqrt{2}$$

Hence the eccentricity of the ellipse is,

$$e > 0, \text{ then } e = \sqrt{2} - 1$$

159. Correct Response : (b)

Explanation :

The given equation of the parabola is,

$$y^2 = -4x$$

Consider the points $P\left(-at_1^2, 2at_1\right)$,

$$Q\left(-at_2^2, 2at_2\right) \text{ and } R\,(h, k).$$

Here,

$$h = -at_1^2$$

And,

$$h = \frac{-2at_1}{3}$$

So,

$$9k^2 = -4h$$

Hence, the locus or R is,

$$9y^2 = -4x$$

160. Correct Response : (d)

The figure of the triangle for the given vertices is,

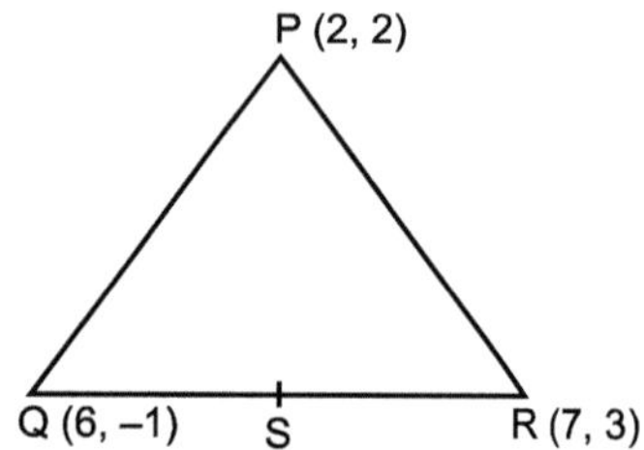

Here, S is the midpoint of QR. So,

$$S = \left(\frac{7+6}{2}, \frac{3-1}{2}\right)$$

$$= \left(\frac{13}{2}, 1\right)$$

Slope of PS is,

$$m = \frac{2-1}{2-\dfrac{13}{2}}$$

Hence, the equation of the line is,

$$y - (-1) = -\frac{2}{9}(x-1)$$

$$2x + 9y + 7 = 0$$

161. Correct Response : (a)

Explanation :

The equation of the lines are given as,

$$4ax + 2ay + c = 0$$

And,

$$5bx + 2by + d = 0$$

Let $(\alpha, -\alpha)$ be the point of intersection of the lines. Therefore it satisfy the equation of the lines,

$$4a\alpha - 2a\alpha + c = 0$$

$$\alpha = -\frac{c}{2a} \qquad \ldots(1)$$

And,

$$5b\alpha - 2b\alpha + d = 0$$

$$\alpha = -\frac{d}{3b} \qquad \ldots(2)$$

From the equation (1) and (2),

$$-\frac{c}{2a} = -\frac{d}{3b}$$

$$3bc - 2ad = 0$$

162. Correct Response : (a)

Explanation :

The given equation is form of an ellipse is,

$$\frac{x^2}{a^2} + \frac{y^2}{b^2} = 1$$

Here, $a^2 = 6$, $b^2 = 2$.

Equation of tangent for any variable is,

$$y = mx \pm \sqrt{a^2m^2 + b^2} \qquad \ldots(1)$$

The equation of perpendicular line drawn from centre of the tangent is,

$$y = \frac{-x}{m}$$

$$m = \frac{-x}{y}$$

Substitute the value of m, a and b in the equation (1),

$$(x^2 + y^2)^2 = a^2x^2 + b^2y^2$$

$$(x^2 + y^2)^2 = 6x^2 + 2y^2$$

163. Correct Response : (b)

Explanation :

The diagram of the circle is,

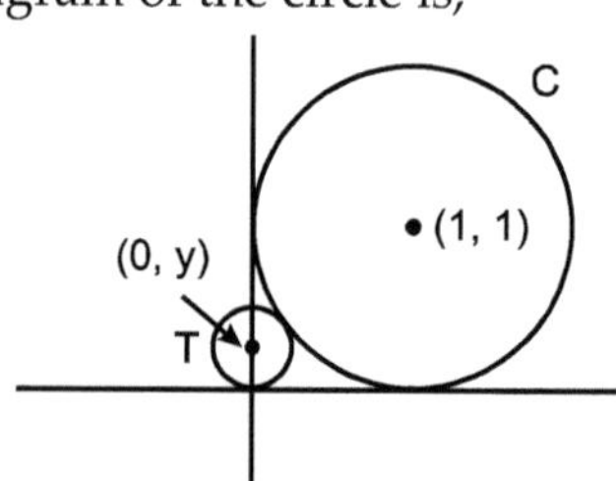

The equation of the circle is,

$$(x-1)^2 + (y-1)^2 = 1$$

Radius of T is $|y|$ and T touches circle C externally. Therefore,

$$(0-1)^2 + (y-1)^2 = \left(1 + |y|\right)^2$$

$$1 + y^2 + 1 - 2y = 1 + y^2 + 2|y|$$

If $y > 0$,

$$y^2 + 2 - 2y = y^2 + 1 + 2y$$

$$4y = 1$$

$$y = \frac{1}{4}$$

If $y < 0$,
$$y^2 + 2 - 2y = y^2 + 1 - 2y$$
$$2 = 1 \quad [\text{does not exist}]$$

Hence, the value of y is $\dfrac{1}{4}$.

164. Correct Response : 3

Explanation :

The diagram of given conditions is shown below,

Let angle θ is equal to $\dfrac{\pi}{2k}$.

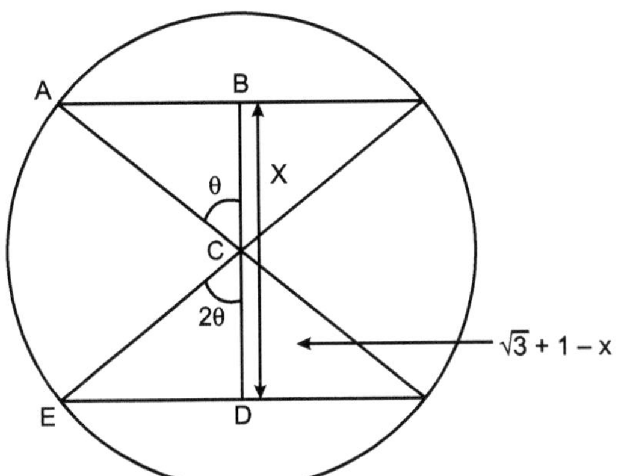

From triangle ABC,
$$\cos \theta = \frac{x}{2} \qquad \qquad ...(1)$$

From triangle EDC,
$$\cos 2\theta = \frac{\sqrt{3}+1-x}{2}$$

$$2\cos^2 \theta - 1 = \frac{\sqrt{3}+1-x}{2}$$

$$2\left(\frac{x^2}{4}\right) - 1 = \frac{\sqrt{3}+1-x}{2}$$

$$x^2 + x - 3 + \sqrt{3} = 0$$

The root of the above equation is,
$$x = \frac{-1 \pm \sqrt{1 + 12 + 4\sqrt{3}}}{2}$$

$$= \frac{-1 + 2\sqrt{3} + 1}{2}$$

$$= \sqrt{3}$$

Put $x = \sqrt{3}$ in equation (1),
$$\cos \theta = \frac{\sqrt{3}}{2}$$

$$\theta = \frac{\pi}{6}$$

$$\frac{\pi}{2k} = \frac{\pi}{6}$$

$$k = 3$$

165. Correct Response : (d)

Explanation :

The tangent of the ellipse from the point P (3, 4) is,

$$y = mx + \sqrt{a^2 m^2 + b^2}$$

$$4 - 3m = \sqrt{9m^2 + 4}$$

$$(4 - 3m)^2 = \left(\sqrt{9m^2 + 4}\right)^2$$

$$m = \frac{12}{24}$$

The equation of line pass through point P (3, 4) is,
$$y - y_1 = m (x - x_1)$$

$$y - 4 = \frac{1}{2} (x - 3)$$

$$x - 2y + 5 = 0 \qquad ...(1)$$

Let the point B is (α, β) so,
$$\frac{x\alpha}{9} + \frac{y\beta}{4} - 1 = 0 \qquad ...(2)$$

From equation (1) and (2),
$$\frac{\alpha/9}{1} = \frac{\beta/4}{-2} = \frac{-1}{5}$$

Thus, the point B is,
$$B \equiv \left(-\frac{9}{5}, \frac{8}{5}\right)$$

It is clear from option that the point A should be (3, 0) because it is drawn from the point P (3, 4).

166. Correct Response : (c)

Explanation :

The figure is shown below,

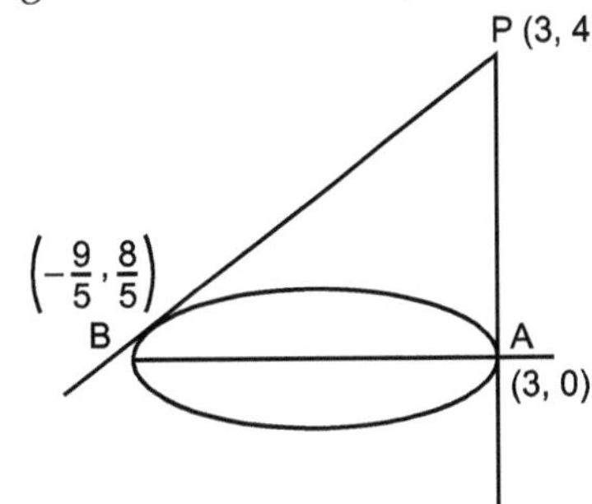

From the figure, the equation of AB is,

$$y - 0 = \frac{\dfrac{8}{5} - 0}{-\dfrac{9}{5} - 3}(x - 3)$$

$$y = -\frac{1}{3}(x - 3)$$

$$x + 3y = 3$$

The equation of the straight line perpendicular to AB through point P is,

$$3x - y = 5$$

The equation of PA is,

$$x - 3 = 0$$

From the figure it is clear that the line perpendicular to PA through point B is,

$$y = \frac{8}{5}$$

Thus, the orthocentre of triangle PAB is $\left(\dfrac{11}{5}, \dfrac{8}{5}\right)$.

167. **Correct Response :** (a)

Explanation :

The equation of AB is,

$$y - 0 = \frac{\dfrac{8}{5} - 0}{-\dfrac{9}{5} - 3}(x - 3)$$

$$y = -\frac{1}{3}(x - 3)$$

$$x + 3y = 3$$

The equation of locus according to given condition is,

$$(x - 3)^2 + (y - 4)^2 = \frac{(x + 3y - 3)^2}{10}$$

$$9x^2 + y^2 - 6xy - 54x - 62y + 241 = 0$$

168. **Correct Response :** (b)

Convert the given equation of hyperbola into standard form.

$$\frac{\left(x - \sqrt{2}\right)^2}{4} - \frac{\left(y + \sqrt{2}\right)^2}{2} = 1$$

The value of a is 2 and b is $\sqrt{2}$. So, eccentricity of hyperbola is,

$$e = \sqrt{\frac{a^2 + b^2}{a^2}}$$

$$= \sqrt{\frac{3}{2}}$$

Now, the area in triangle ABC is,

$$\text{Area} = \frac{1}{2}a(e - 1)\frac{b^2}{a}$$

$$= \sqrt{\frac{3}{2}} - 1$$

169. **Correct Response :** (b)

Explanation :

The graph of equation $y = x$ and curve $y = ke^x$ is,

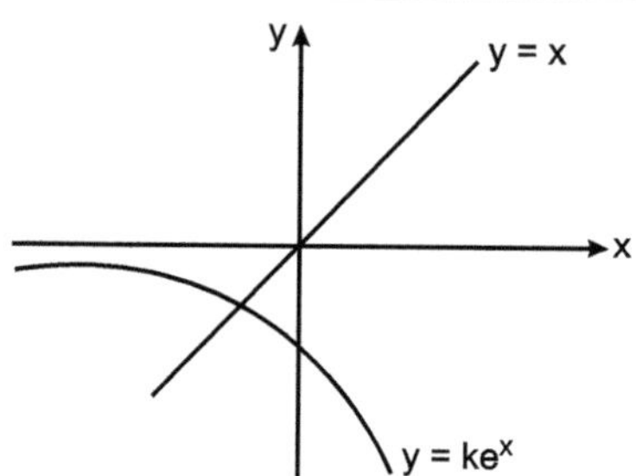

From above figrue line $y = x$ intersect the curve $y = ke^x$ at exactly one point for $k \le 0$.

170. **Correct Response :** (c)

Explanation :

Let, R be the centroid of the triangle OPQ.

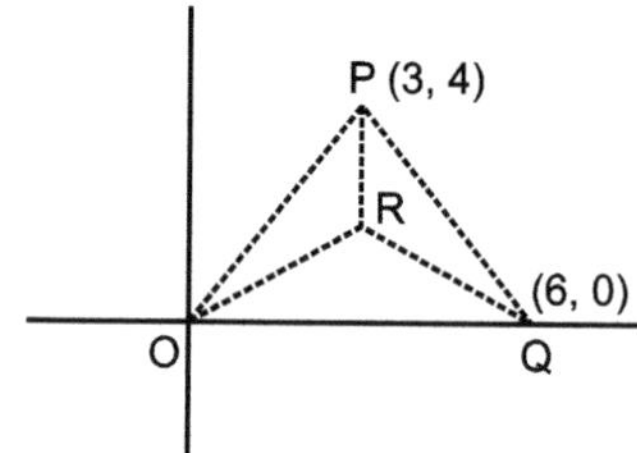

The centroid is calculated as,

$$R = \left(\frac{0 + 3 + 6}{3}, \frac{0 + 4 + 0}{3}\right)$$

$$= \left(\frac{9}{3}, \frac{4}{3}\right)$$

$$= \left(3, \frac{4}{3}\right)$$

171. **Correct Response :** (a)-(p), (q), (b)-(p)-(q), (c)-(q), (r), (d)-(q), (r)

Explanation :

(a) If two circles are intersecting then the circles have common tangent and common normal.

(b) Two mutually external circles can also have a common tangent and common normal.

(c) If one circle lies inside the other circle, then they have a common normal but common tangent is not possible.

(d) The branches of hyperbola have common normal but common tangent is not possible.

172. **Correct Response :** (d)

Explanation :

The directrix equation of parabola is $x + y = 0$.

The equation of parabola is,

$$\frac{x + y}{\sqrt{2}} = \sqrt{(x - 2)^2 + (y - 2)^2}$$

$$(x + y)^2 = 2\left[(x - 2)^2 + (y - 2)^2\right]$$

$$(x + y)^2 = 8(x + y - 2)$$

173. Correct Response : (a, b)

Explanation :

The equation of tangent to parabola $x^2 = y$ is,

$$y = mx - \frac{1}{4}m^2 \qquad ...(1)$$

The equation of tangent to parabola $y = -(x-2)^2$ is,

$$y = m(x-2) + \frac{1}{4}m^2 \qquad ...(2)$$

Equate equations (1) and (2).

$$mx - \frac{1}{4}m^2 = m(x-2) + \frac{1}{4}m^2$$

$$m = 0 \text{ or } 4$$

Therefore, common tangents to both the parabolas are $y = 0$ and $y = 4x - 4$.

174. Correct Response : (c, d)

Explanation :

The equation of tangent of the curve $y = f(x)$ is,

$$Y - y = \frac{dy}{dx}(X - x)$$

It is given that ratio of BP : AP is 3 : 1. So,

$$\frac{dx}{x} = -\frac{dy}{3y}$$

$$x\frac{dy}{dx} + 3y = 0$$

Integrate above equation,

$$\ln x = -\frac{1}{3} \ln y - \ln c$$

$$\ln x^3 = -(\ln cy)$$

$$\frac{1}{x^3} = cy$$

Substitute $f(1) = 1$.

$$c = 1$$

Substitute value of c in above equation.

$$y = \frac{1}{x^3}$$

Therefore, curve is passing through $\left(2, \frac{1}{8}\right)$.

175. Correct Response : (a), (c)

Explanation :

The ecentricity of ellipse is,

$$b^2 = a^2(1 - e^2)$$

$$\frac{16}{25} = 1 - e^2$$

$$e^2 = \frac{9}{25}$$

$$e = \frac{3}{5}$$

It is given that product of eccentricities of hyperbola and parabola is 1. So, eccentricity of hyperbola is $\frac{5}{3}$ and it is passing through (± 3, 0).

$$1 + \frac{b^2}{a^2} = e^2$$

$$1 + \frac{b^2}{9} = \frac{25}{9}$$

$$b^2 = 16$$

Therefore, equation of hyperbola is $\frac{x^2}{9} - \frac{y^2}{16} = 1$ and foci are (± 5, 0).

176. Correct Response : (c)

Explanation :

Let, the centre of circle be C. Draw a parallel line to line L at a distance equal to radius of circle C_1.

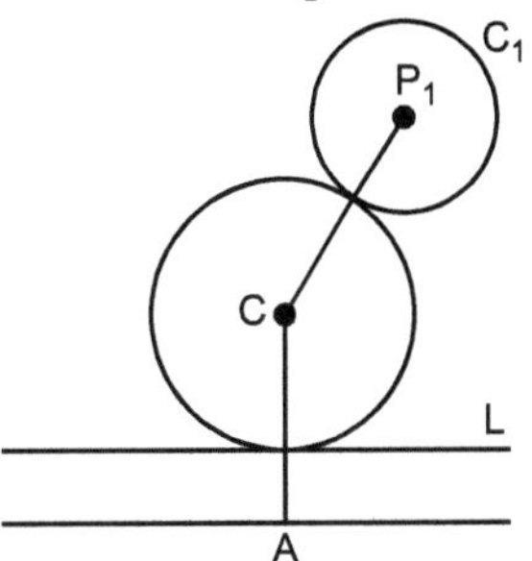

So, $\qquad CP_1 = AC.$

Therefore, the locus of centre of the circle is a parabola.

177. Correct Response : (c)

Explanation :

A line M is drawn through A parallel to BD. The point S move such that its distance from line BD and vertex A are equal.

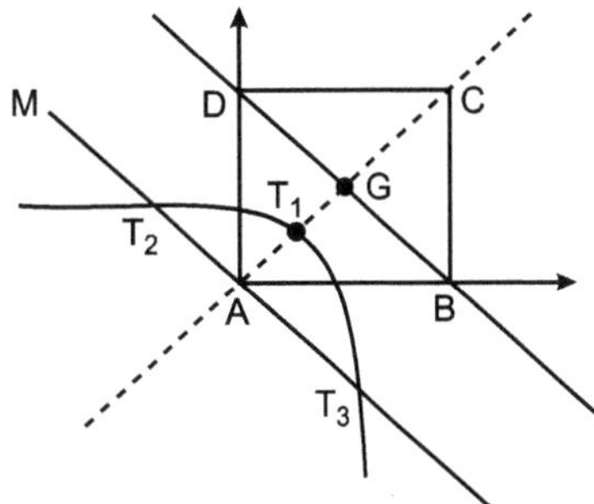

The length of side AD of square is 2. So, $AG = \sqrt{2}$.

$$AT_1 = T_1G = \frac{1}{\sqrt{2}}$$

The focus of parabola is A, vertex is T_1 and BD is directrix. Latus rectum is T_2T_3.

$$T_2 T_3 = 4\left(\frac{1}{\sqrt{2}}\right)$$

$$= 2\sqrt{2}$$

The area of required triangle is,

$$\Delta T_1 T_2 T_3 = \frac{1}{2} \times \frac{1}{\sqrt{2}} \times 2\sqrt{2}$$

$$= 1$$

Therefore, area of triangle is 1 square unit.

178. Correct Response : (a)-(i), (b)-(i), (c)-(iv)(d), (iii)

Explanation :

The equation of normal is,

$$y = mx - 2am - am^3$$

The equation of normal is passing through (3, 0). So,

$$0 = 3m - 2m - m^3$$

$$m^3 = m$$

$$m = 0, \pm 1$$

The centroid of triangle is,

$$\left(\frac{m_1^2 + m_2^2 + m_3^2}{3}, -\frac{2(m_1 + m_2 + m_3)}{3}\right)$$

$$= \left(\frac{0+1+1}{3}, \frac{2(0+1-1)}{3}\right)$$

$$= \left(\frac{2}{3}, 0\right)$$

The circum radius is,

$$\left|\frac{-2m_1 + 2m_2}{2}\right| = 2 \text{ units}$$

Points of contact of normal are,

$$Q = \left(m_2^2, -2m_2\right)$$

$$= (1 - 2)$$

$$R = \left(m_3^2, -2m_3\right)$$

$$= (1, 2)$$

The area of triangle PQR is,

$$\text{Area} = \frac{1}{2} \times 4 \times 1$$

$$= 2 \text{ sq. units}$$

Now,

$$R = \frac{QR}{2\sin \angle QRP}$$

$$= \frac{4}{2\sin\left(2\tan^{-1} 2\right)}$$

$$= \frac{4}{2\sin\left(\tan^{-1}\dfrac{4}{1-4}\right)}$$

$$= \frac{4}{2 \times \dfrac{4}{5}} = \frac{5}{2}$$

Circumcentre of triangle is $\left(\dfrac{5}{2}, 0\right)$.

179. Correct Response : $(\sqrt{5})$

Explanation :

Let, centre of three circles be P, Q, R. Point A is the in-centre of triangle PQR.

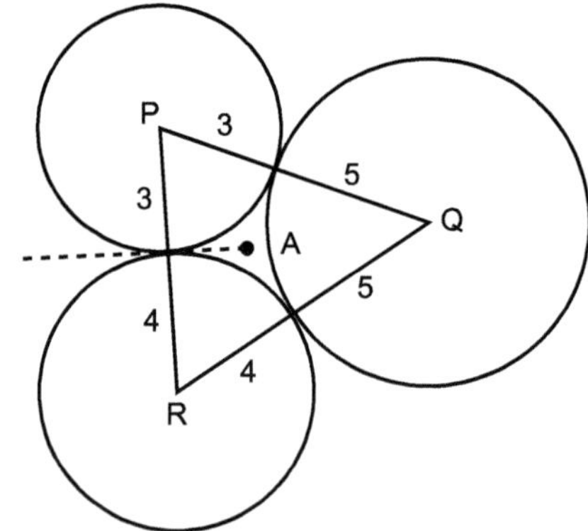

The semi-perimeter of circle is,

$$s = \frac{7+8+9}{2}$$

$$= \frac{24}{2}$$

$$= 12$$

The distance of point P from point of contact is,

$$r = \frac{\Delta}{s}$$

$$= \frac{\sqrt{s(s-a)(s-b)(s-c)}}{s}$$

$$= \frac{\sqrt{12 \times 5 \times 4 \times 3}}{12}$$

$$= \sqrt{5}$$

Therefore, the required distance is $\sqrt{5}$ units.

180. Correct Response : $y = 2,\ x + 1,\ y = -2x + 1$

Explanation :

Let, P be a point parallel to X-axis.

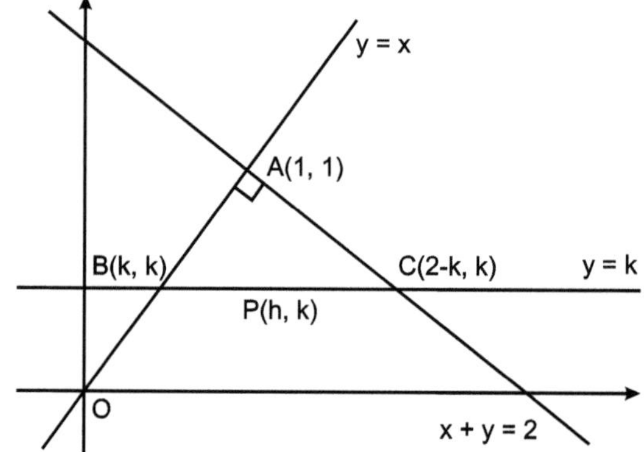

The area of triangle ABC is,

$$\text{Area} = \frac{1}{2} \times AB \times AC$$

$$4h^2 = \frac{1}{2}(k-1)(2-k-k)$$

$$4h^2 = (k-1)^2$$

$$k-1 = \pm 2h$$

Therefore, locus of point P is $y = 2x+1$, $y = -2x+1$.

181. Correct Response : $\dfrac{x^2}{9} - \dfrac{y^2}{4} = \left(\dfrac{x^2+y^2}{q}\right)$

Explanation :

Let, $(3\sec\theta, 2\tan\theta)$ be any point on the hyperbola. The equation of chord of contact of cricle $x^2+y^2=9$ with point on hyperbola is,

$$3\sec\theta \cdot x + 2\tan\theta \cdot y = 9 \qquad \text{...(1)}$$

Let, midpoint of chord of contact be (h, k). The equation of chord mid-point form is,

$$xh + yk = h^2 + k^2 \qquad \text{...(2)}$$

From equations (1) and (2),

$$\frac{3\sec\theta}{h} = \frac{2\tan\theta}{k} = \frac{9}{h^2+k^2}$$

$$\sec\theta = \frac{9h}{3(h^2+k^2)}, \ \tan\theta = \frac{9k}{2(h^2+k^2)}$$

Now, square and subtract both terms.

$$\frac{81h^2}{9(h^2+k^2)^2} - \frac{81k^2}{4(h^2+k^2)^2} = 1$$

$$\frac{h^2}{9} - \frac{k^2}{4} = \left(\frac{h^2+k^2}{9}\right)^2$$

Therefore, required equation of locus is,

$$\frac{x^2}{9} - \frac{y^2}{4} = \left(\frac{x^2+y^2}{9}\right)^2.$$

182. Correct Response : $\dfrac{14}{\sqrt{3}}$

Explanation :

The equation of tangent to given circles is,

$$y = mx + 4\sqrt{1+m^2}$$

The equation of tangent to given ellipse is,

$$y = mx + \sqrt{25m^2+4}$$

It is given that circle and ellipse have common tangent. So,

$$4\sqrt{1+m^2} = \sqrt{25m^2+4}$$

$$16(1+m^2) = 25m^2 + 4$$

$$9m^2 = 12$$

$$m = \pm\frac{2}{\sqrt{3}}$$

The common tangent lies in 1st quadrant. So,

$$m = -\frac{2}{\sqrt{3}}$$

The equation of common tangent is,

$$y = -\frac{2}{\sqrt{3}}x + 4\sqrt{\frac{7}{3}}$$

Tangent cuts the coordinate axis at $(2\sqrt{7},0)$ and $\left(0, 4\sqrt{\frac{7}{3}}\right)$. The required length is,

$$\sqrt{(2\sqrt{7})^2 + \left(4\sqrt{\frac{7}{3}}\right)^2} = \sqrt{28 + \frac{112}{3}}$$

$$= \frac{14}{\sqrt{3}}$$

183. Correct Response : (b)

Let, three coins of radius 1 unit each are kept in triangle ABC.

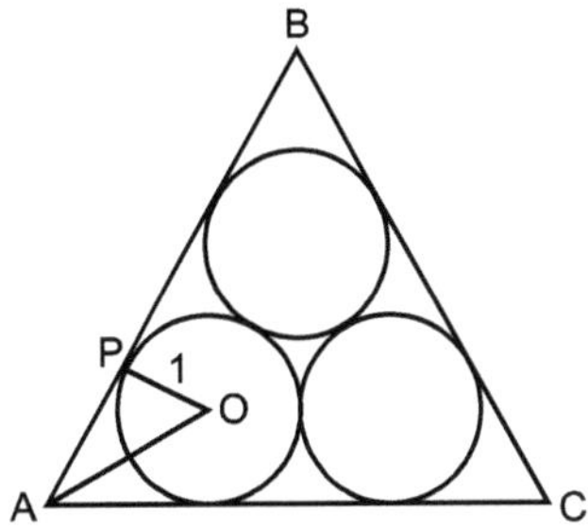

In $\triangle APO$,

$$\tan\frac{\pi}{6} = \frac{OP}{AP}$$

$$\tan\frac{\pi}{6} = \frac{1}{AP}$$

$$AP = \cot\frac{\pi}{6}$$

The length of each side of triangle is,

$$AB = 1 + 1 + \cot\frac{\pi}{6} + \cot\frac{\pi}{6}$$

$$= 2 + 2\cot\frac{\pi}{6}$$

$$= 2(1+\sqrt{3})$$

Now, the area of equilateral triangle is,

$$\text{Area} = \frac{\sqrt{3}}{4} 4(1+\sqrt{3})^2$$

$$= 6 + 4\sqrt{3}$$

184. Correct Response : (a)

Explanation :

Let, point on ellipse be $(a \cos \theta, b \sin \theta)$. The equation of tangent to the ellipse is,

$$\frac{x \cos\theta}{a} + \frac{y \sin\theta}{b} = 1$$

The tangent cuts the coordinate axis at $(0, b \csc \theta)$ and $(a \sec \theta, 0)$.

The minimum area of triangle formed is,

$$\text{Area} = \frac{1}{2} (a \csc \theta)(b \sec \theta)$$

$$= \frac{ab}{2 \sin \theta \cos \theta}$$

$$= \frac{ab}{\sin 2\theta}$$

$$\geq ab$$

Therefore, minimum area of triangle be ab sq. units.

185. Correct Response : (d)

Explanation :

The equation of parabola is,

$$y = x^2 + 6$$

Differentiate above equation.

$$\frac{dy}{dx} = 2x$$

$$\left(\frac{dy}{dx}\right)_{(1,7)} = 2$$

The equation of tangent is,

$$y - 7 = 2(x - 1)$$

$$y = 2x + 5$$

The center of circle is $(-8, -6)$.

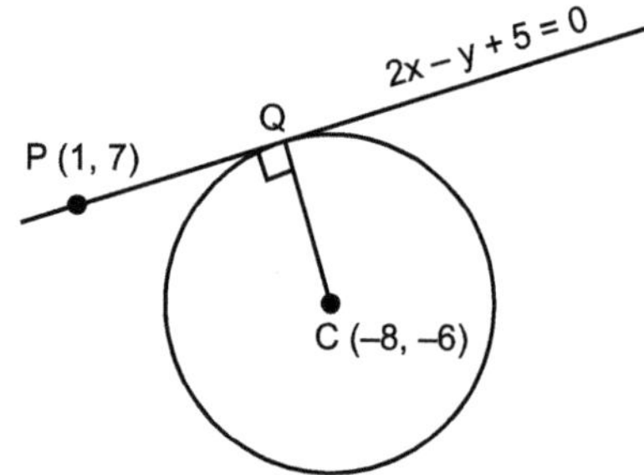

The equation of line CQ is,

$$x + 2y + k = 0$$

$$-8 - 12 + k = 0$$

$$k = 20$$

The equation of line PQ is,

$$4x - 2y + 10 = 0 \qquad \text{...(1)}$$

The equation of line CQ is,

$$x + 2y + 20 = 0 \qquad \text{...(1)}$$

Solve equation (1) and (2).

$x = -6$ and $y = -7$

Hence, point of contact is $(-6, -7)$.

186. Correct Response : $2x^2 + 2y^2 - 10x - 5y + 1 = 0$

Explanation :

The tangent at point $(1, -1)$ of circle is $2x + 3y + 1 = 0$. The equation of circle be,

$$(x - 1)^2 + (y + 1)^2 + \lambda(2x + 3y + 1) = 0$$

$$x^2 + y^2 + x(2\lambda - 2) + y(3\lambda + 2) + 2 + \lambda = 0$$

The above circle is orthogonal to the circle with line segment having end points $(0, -1)$ and $(-2, 3)$.

$$x(x + 2) + (y + 1)(y - 3) = 0$$

$$x^2 + y^2 + 2x - 2y - 3 = 0$$

$$\frac{2(2\lambda - 2)}{2}\left(\frac{2}{2}\right) + \frac{2(3\lambda + 2)}{2}\left(\frac{-2}{2}\right) = 2 + \lambda - 3$$

$$\lambda = \frac{-3}{2}$$

$$\lambda = -\frac{3}{2}$$

The required equation of circle is,

$$x^2 + y^2 + x\left(2\left(-\frac{3}{2}\right) - 2\right) + y\left(3\left(-\frac{3}{2}\right) + 2\right)$$

$$+ 2 + \left(-\frac{3}{2}\right) = 0$$

$$x^2 + y^2 - 5x - \frac{5}{2}y + \frac{1}{2} = 0$$

$$2x^2 + 2y^2 - 10x - 5y + 1 = 0$$

187. Explanation :

Let, any point on the parabola be P $(1 + t^2, 1 + 2t)$. The equation of tangent at point P is,

$$t(y - 1) = x - 1 + t^2$$

The equation of tangent meets the directrix $x = 0$ at point $Q\left(0, 1 + t - \frac{1}{t}\right)$.

Let, point R be (h, k). It divides QP externally in the ratio $\frac{1}{2} : 1$. The midpoint of RP is Q.

$$\frac{h + 1 + t^2}{2} = 0$$

$$t^2 = -(h + 1) \qquad \text{...(1)}$$

And

$$1 + t - \frac{1}{t} = \frac{k + 1 + 2t}{2}$$

$$t = \frac{2}{1 - k}$$

Substitute value of k in equation (1).

$$\frac{4}{(1-k)^2}+(h+1)=0$$

$$(k-1)^2(h+1)+4=0$$

Therefore, locus of point R is $(y-1)^2(x+1)+4=0$.

188. Correct Response : (a)

Explanation :

The equation of pair of striaght lines is,

$$x^2-y^2+2y=1$$
$$x^2-(y^2+2y-1)=0$$
$$x^2=(y-1)^2$$

Equations of lines are $y=x+1$ and $y=-x+1$.

The angle bisectors are $y=1$ and $x=0$.

Now, the area of triangle formed by $x+y=3$, $y=1$ and $x=0$ is,

$$\text{Area}=\frac{1}{2}\times 2\times 2$$

$$=2\text{ sq. units.}$$

189. Correct Response : (a)

Explanation :

The equation of ellipse is,

$$x^2+2y^2=2$$
$$\frac{x^2}{2}+\frac{y^2}{1}=1$$

Let, point be $P\left(\sqrt{2}\cos\theta,\sin\theta\right)$ on the ellipse.

The equation of tangent at any point is,

$$\frac{x\sqrt{2}}{2}\cos\theta+y\sin\theta=1$$

The intercepts on coordinate axis are $\left(\sqrt{2}\sec\theta,0\right)$ and $(0,\text{cosec }\theta)$. So, the midpoint of intercepts between axes is,

$$\left(\frac{\sqrt{2}}{2}\sec\theta,\frac{1}{2}\text{cosec }\theta\right)=(h,k)$$

$$\cos\theta=\frac{1}{\sqrt{2}\,h}\text{ and }\sin\theta=\frac{1}{2k}$$

The locus of midpoint is,

$$\cos^2\theta+\sin^2\theta=\frac{1}{2h^2}+\frac{1}{4k^2}$$

$$\frac{1}{2h^2}+\frac{1}{4k^2}=1$$

$$\frac{1}{2x^2}+\frac{1}{4y^2}=1$$

190. Correct Response : (c)

Explanation :

The equation of tangent to parabola $y^2=4x$ is,

$$y=mx+\frac{1}{m}$$

Tangents is passing through $(1,4)$. So,

$$m^2-4m+1=0$$

Let, m_1 and m_2 are roots of equation.

$$m_1+m_2=4\text{ and }m_1m_2=1$$

Now,

$$|m_1-m_2|=\sqrt{(m_1+m_2)^2-4m_1m_2}$$

$$=\sqrt{16-4}$$

$$=\sqrt{12}$$

$$=2\sqrt{3}$$

The angle formed between tangents is,

$$\tan\theta=\left|\frac{m_2-m_1}{1+m_1m_2}\right|$$

$$\tan\theta=\left|\frac{2\sqrt{3}}{1+1}\right|$$

$$\tan\theta=\sqrt{3}$$

$$\theta=\frac{\pi}{3}$$

191. Correct Response : (d)

Explanation :

The equation of tangent of hyperbola is,

$$xx_1-2yy_1=4$$

Compare the given equation of line $2x+\sqrt{6}y=2$ with above equation.

$$x_1=4\text{ and }y_1=-\sqrt{6}$$

Therefore, point of contact is $\left(4,-\sqrt{6}\right)$.

192. Correct Response : (c)

Explanation :

The given equation of circle is,

$$x^2+y^2-2x-6y+6=0$$
$$(x-1)^2+(y-3)^2=4$$

The radius of circle is 2 and center is $(1,3)$.

Let, r be the radius of second circle.

$$r^2=2^2+(3-1)^2+(2-1)^2$$
$$r^2=9$$
$$r=3$$

193. Correct Response : (d)

Explanation :

The shape of quadrilateral is rhombus. The area of quadrilateral is four times the area of right and triangle formed by tangent and axes in Quadrant 1.

The relation of a, b and e is,

$$ae=\sqrt{a^2-b^2}$$

$$= \sqrt{9-5}$$

$$= 2$$

The equation of tangent in first quadrant at end of latusrectum $\left(2, \dfrac{5}{3}\right)$ is,

$$\frac{2}{9}x + \frac{5}{3} \cdot \frac{y}{5} = 1$$

$$\frac{x}{9/2} + \frac{y}{3} = 1$$

The required area of quadrilateral is,

$$\text{Area} = 4 \times \frac{1}{2} \times \frac{9}{2} \times 3$$

$$= 27 \text{ sq. units.}$$

194. Correct Response : (b)

Explanation :

A triangle formed by (0, 0), (0, 21) and (21, 0) is,

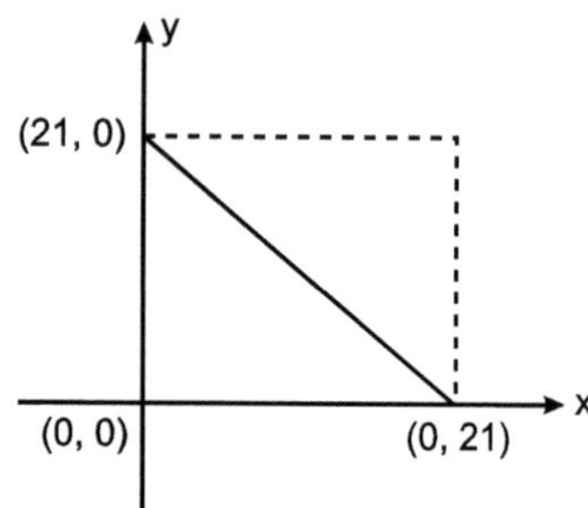

Number of integral points is,

$19 + 18 + 17 + \ldots\ldots + 1 = 190$

195. Correct Response : (a)

Explanation :

Let, $4x$, x and x are angles of a triangle.

$$4x + x + x = 180°$$

$$6x = 180°$$

$$x = 30°$$

So, angle A is 120°, B is 30° and C is 30°.

Ratio of sides of triangle is,

$$a : b : c = \frac{\sqrt{3}}{2} : \frac{1}{2} : \frac{1}{2}$$

$$= \sqrt{3} : 1 : 1$$

The required ratio of longest sides to the perimeter of triangle is,

$$\frac{\sqrt{3}}{\sqrt{3} + 1 + 1} = \left(\sqrt{3} : 2 + \sqrt{3}\right)$$

196. Correct Response : (b)

Explanation :

The eccentricity of hyperbola is,

$$b^2 = a^2 (e^2 - 1)$$

$$\sin^2 \alpha = \cos^2 \alpha \, (e^2 - 1)$$

$$\cos^2 \alpha \cdot e^2 = 1$$

Therefore, abscissa of foci reMain constant.

197. Correct Response : (a)

Explanation :

Solve the given equations.

$$x^2 - 8x + 12 = 0$$

$$(x - 6)(x - 2) = 0$$

$$y^2 - 14y + 45 = 0$$

$$(y - 5)(y - 9) = 0$$

Therefore, the center of circle is (4, 7).

198. Correct Response : (a)

Explanation :

The equation of focal chord is,

$$y = m(x - 4)$$

Now,

$$\frac{\left| 0 - m(6 - 4) \right|}{\sqrt{1 + m^2}} = \sqrt{2}$$

$$|-2m| = \sqrt{2}\,\sqrt{1 + m^2}$$

Square both side of above equation and solve.

$$4m^2 = 2(1 + m^2)$$

$$2m^2 = 2$$

$$m = \pm 1$$

Therefore, the possible values of slope are 1 and -1.

199. Correct Response : (b)

Explanation :

The equation of tangent is,

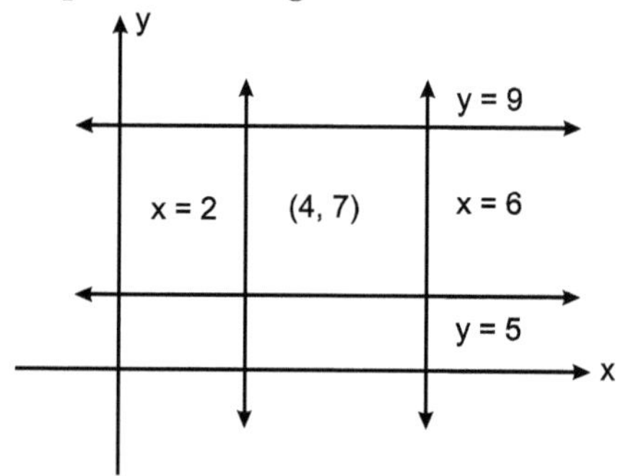

$$\frac{x \cos \theta}{a} + \frac{y \sin \theta}{b} = 1$$

The x intercept is $\dfrac{a}{\cos \theta}$ and y intercept is $\dfrac{b}{\sin \theta}$.

Sum of intercepts is,

$$f(\theta) = \frac{3\sqrt{3}}{\cos \theta} + \frac{1}{\sin \theta}$$

Therefore, $\theta = \dfrac{\pi}{6}$.

200. Correct Response : (a)

Explanation :

The vertices of triangle are (0, 0), (3, 4) and (4, 0).

The value of tan θ from the above figure is,

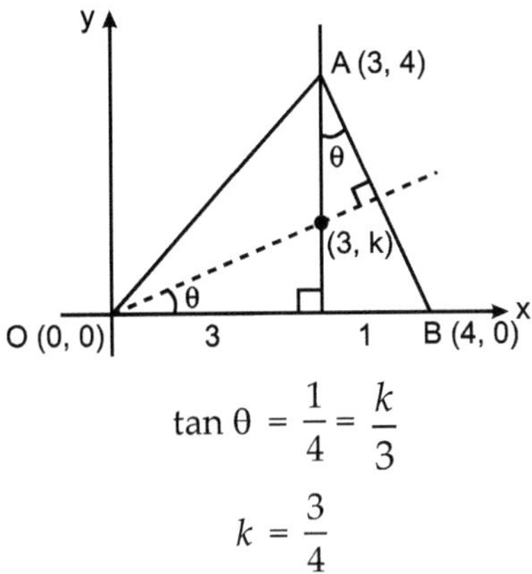

$$\tan \theta = \frac{1}{4} = \frac{k}{3}$$

$$k = \frac{3}{4}$$

Therefore, orthocenter is $\left(3, \frac{3}{4}\right)$.

201. Correct Response : (d)

Explanation :

Point Q is mirror reflection of P = (cos θ, sin θ) to

the line $y = \tan\left(\frac{\alpha}{2}\right) x$.

Therefore, reflection in the line through origin

with slope $\tan\left(\frac{\alpha}{2}\right)$.

202. Correct Response : (c)

Explanation :

Let, P = (− 1, 0), Q = (0, 0) and R = $\left(3, 3\sqrt{3}\right)$.

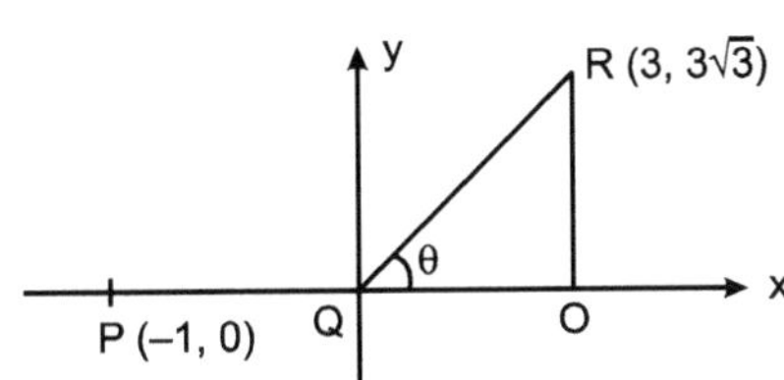

In ΔORQ,

$$\tan \theta = \frac{3\sqrt{3}}{3}$$

$$\tan \theta = \sqrt{3}$$

$$\theta = 60°$$

So, ΔPQR = 120°.

The equation of bisector is,

$$y = \left(-\sqrt{3}\right)x$$

$$\sqrt{3}x + y = 0$$

203. Correct Response : (b)

Explanation :

The line $4x + 2y = 9$ cuts the x-axis at P $\left(\frac{9}{4}, 0\right)$ and

line $2x + y + 6 = 0$ cuts the x-axis at Q (− 3, 0).

The required ratio is,

$$\frac{OP}{OQ} = \frac{9}{4 \cdot 3}$$

$$= \frac{3}{4}$$

204. Correct Response : (c)

Explantion :

The equation of line $5x - 2y + 6 = 0$ cuts the y axis at point Q i.e. (0, 3).

The length of tangent PQ is,

$$d = \sqrt{0 + 3^2 + 0 + 6 \times 3 - 2}$$

$$= \sqrt{25}$$

$$= 5$$

205. Correct Response : (a)

Explanation :

The center of circle $x^2 + y^2 = b^2$ is (0, 0) and $(x - a)^2 + y^2 = b^2$ is (a, 0). Midpoint of centers of

circles is $\left(\frac{a}{2}, 0\right)$.

The line $y = mx - b\sqrt{1+m^2}$ passes through point

$\left(\frac{a}{2}, 0\right)$. So,

$$\frac{m^2 a^2}{4} = b^2(1 + m^2)$$

$$m^2\left(\frac{a^2}{4} - b^2\right) = b^2$$

$$m = \frac{2b}{\sqrt{a^2 - 4b^2}}$$

206. Correct Response : (c)

Explanation :

Let, (h, k) be the mid-point of line joining $(a, 0)$ and $(at^2, 2at)$

$$(h, k) = \left(\frac{at^2 + a}{2}, \frac{2at + 0}{2}\right)$$

Compare value of h.

$$2h = a(t^2 + 1)$$

Compare value of k.

$$2k = 2at$$

The locus of parabola is,

$$y^2 = 2a\left(x - \frac{a}{2}\right)$$

Therefore, equation of directrix is,

$$x - \frac{a}{2} = -\frac{a}{2}$$

$$x = 0$$

207. Correct Response : (d)

Explanation :

The equation of tangent of the curve $y^2 = 8x$ is,

$$y = mx + \frac{2}{m}$$

The above tangent touch $xy = -1$, if it has equal roots.

$$x\left(mx + \frac{2}{m}\right) = -1$$

$$mx^2 + \frac{2}{m}x + 1 = 0$$

The above equation has real roots. So,

$$\frac{4}{m^2} = 4m$$

$$m = 1$$

Therefore, equation of tangent is $y = x + 2$.

●●

❓ QUESTIONS

1. If (a, b, c) is the image of the point $(1, 2, -3)$ in the line, $\dfrac{x+1}{2} = \dfrac{y-3}{-2} = \dfrac{z}{-1}$, then $a + b + c$ is equal to :

[2020, Main]

(a) -1 (b) 2

(c) 3   (d) 1

2. The shortest distance between the lines $\dfrac{x-1}{0} = \dfrac{y+1}{-1} = \dfrac{z}{1}$ and $x + y + z + 1 = 0$, $2x - y + z + 3 = 0$ is : [2020, Main]

(a) $\dfrac{1}{2}$ (b) 1

(c) $\dfrac{1}{\sqrt{2}}$ (d) $\dfrac{1}{\sqrt{3}}$

3. A plane P meets the coordinate axes at A, B and C respectively. The centroid of $\triangle ABC$ is given to be $(1, 1, 2)$. Then the equation of the line through this centroid and perpendicular to the plane P is : [2020, Main]

(a) $\dfrac{x-1}{1} = \dfrac{y-1}{2} = \dfrac{z-2}{2}$

(b) $\dfrac{x-1}{2} = \dfrac{y-1}{2} = \dfrac{z-2}{1}$

(c) $\dfrac{x-1}{2} = \dfrac{y-1}{1} = \dfrac{z-2}{1}$

(d) $\dfrac{x-1}{1} = \dfrac{y-1}{1} = \dfrac{z-2}{2}$

4. If the equation of a plane P, passing through the intersection of the planes, $x + 4y - z + 7 = 0$ and $3x + y + 5z = 8$ is $ax + by + 6z = 15$ for some $a, b \in$ R, then the distance of the point $(3, 2, -1)$ from the plane P is .... [2020, Main]

5. The distance of the point $(1, -2, 3)$ from the plane $x - y + z = 5$ measured parallel to the line $\dfrac{x}{2} = \dfrac{y}{3} = \dfrac{z}{-6}$ is : [2020, Main]

(a) 7   (b) 1

(c) $\dfrac{1}{7}$ (d) $\dfrac{7}{5}$

6. The foot of the perpendicular drawn from the point $(4, 2, 3)$ to the line joining the points $(1, -2, 3)$ and $(1, 1, 0)$ lies on the plane : [2020, Main]

(a) $x + 2y - z = 1$ (b) $x - 2y + z = 1$

(c) $x - y - 2z = 1$ (d) $2x + y - z = 1$

7. If for some $\alpha \in$ R, the lines

$L_1 : \dfrac{x+1}{2} = \dfrac{y-2}{-1} = \dfrac{z-1}{1}$ and

$L_2 : \dfrac{x+2}{\alpha} = \dfrac{y+1}{5-\alpha} = \dfrac{z+1}{1}$ are coplanar, then the line L_2 passes through the point : [2020, Main]

(a) $(-2, 10, 2)$ (b) $(10, 2, 2)$

(c) $(10, -2, 2)$ (d) $(2, -10, -2)$

8. Let L_1 and L_2 be the following straight line.

$L_1 : \dfrac{x-1}{1} = \dfrac{y}{-1} = \dfrac{z-1}{3}$ and $L_2 : \dfrac{x-1}{-3} = \dfrac{y}{-1} = \dfrac{z-1}{1}$

Suppose the straight line

$$L : \dfrac{x-\alpha}{l} = \dfrac{y-1}{m} = \dfrac{z-\gamma}{-2}$$

lies in the plane containing L_1 and L_2 and passes through the point of intersection of L_1 and L_2. If the line L bisects the acute angle between the lines L_1 and L_2, then which of the following statements is/are TRUE ? [2020, Advanced]

(a) $\alpha - \gamma = 3$ (b) $l + m = 2$

(c) $\alpha - \gamma = 1$ (d) $l + m = 0$

9. Let $\alpha, \beta, \gamma, \delta$ be real numbers such that $\alpha^2 + \beta^2 + \gamma^2 \neq 0$ and $\alpha + \gamma = 1$. Suppose the point $(3, 2, -1)$ is the mirror image of the point $(1, 0, -1)$ with respect to the plane $\alpha x + \beta y + \gamma z = \delta$. Then which of the following statements is/are TRUE ?

[2020, Advanced]

(a) $\alpha + \beta = 2$ (b) $\delta - \gamma = 3$

(c) $\delta + \beta = 4$ (d) $\alpha + \beta + \gamma = \delta$

10. A plane passing through the point $(3, 1, 1)$ contains two lines whose direction ratios are 1, $-2, 2$ and $2, 3, -1$ respectively. If this plane also passes through the point $(\alpha, -3, 5)$, then α is equal to : **[2020, Main]**

(a) -10 (b) 5

(c) 10 (d) -5

11. The plane which bisects the line joining the points $(4, -2, 3)$ and $(2, 4, -1)$ at right angles also passes through the point : **[2020, Main]**

(a) $(4, 0, -1)$ (b) $(4, 0, 1)$

(c) $(0, 1, -1)$ (d) $(0, -1, 1)$

12. Let a plane P contain two lines

$$\vec{r} = \hat{i} + \lambda(\hat{i} + \hat{j}),\ \lambda \in R \text{ and}$$

$$\vec{r} = -\hat{j} + \mu(\hat{j} - \hat{k}),\ \mu \in R$$

If $Q(\alpha, \beta, \gamma)$ is the foot of the perpendicular drawn from the point $M(1, 0, 1)$ to P, then $3(\alpha + \beta + \gamma)$ equals .... **[2020, Main]**

13. The plane passing through the points $(1, 2, 1)$, $(2, 1, 2)$ and parallel to the line, $2x = 3y, z = 1$ also passes through the point : **[2020, Main]**

(a) $(0, 6, -2)$ (b) $(-2, 0, 1)$

(c) $(0, -6, 2)$ (d) $(2, 0, -1)$

14. If the foot of the perpendicular drawn from the point $(1, 0, 3)$ on a line passing through $(\alpha, 7, 1)$ is $\left(\dfrac{5}{3}, \dfrac{7}{3}, \dfrac{17}{3}\right)$, then α is equal to ....

[2020, Main]

15. Let the volume of a parallelopiped whose coterminous edges are given by $\vec{u} = \hat{i} + \hat{j} + \lambda\hat{k}$,

$\vec{v} = \hat{i} + \hat{j} + 3\hat{k}$ and $\vec{w} = 2\hat{i} + \hat{j} + \hat{k}$ be 1 cu.

unit. If θ be the angle between the edges $\vec{u}$ and $\vec{w}$, then $\cos \theta$ can be : **[2020, Main]**

(a) $\dfrac{7}{6\sqrt{3}}$ (b) $\dfrac{5}{7}$

(c) $\dfrac{7}{6\sqrt{6}}$ (d) $\dfrac{5}{3\sqrt{3}}$

16. The shortest distance between the lines $\dfrac{x-3}{3} = \dfrac{y-8}{-1} = \dfrac{z-3}{1}$ and $\dfrac{x+3}{-3} = \dfrac{y+7}{2} = \dfrac{z-6}{4}$ is

[2020, Main]

(a) $\dfrac{7}{2}\sqrt{30}$ (b) $3\sqrt{30}$

(c) 3 (d) $2\sqrt{30}$

17. The mirror image of the point $(1, 2, 3)$ in a plane is $\left(-\dfrac{7}{3}, -\dfrac{4}{3}, -\dfrac{1}{3}\right)$. Which of the following points lies on this plane? **[2020, Main]**

(a) $(-1, -1, -1)$ (b) $(-1, -1, 1)$

(c) $(1, 1, 1)$ (d) $(1, -1, 1)$

18. Let C be the centroid of the triangle with vertices $(3, -1)$, $(1, 3)$ and $(2, 4)$. Let P be the point of intersection of the lines $x + 3y - 1 = 0$ and $3x - y + 1 = 0$. Then the line passing through the points C and P also passes through the point : **[2020, Main]**

(a) $(7, 6)$ (b) $(-9, -6)$

(c) $(-9, -7)$ (d) $(9, 7)$

19. If the vectors, $\vec{p} = (a+1)\hat{i} + a\hat{j} + a\hat{k}$,

$\vec{q} = a\hat{i} + (a+1)\hat{j} + a\hat{k}$ and $\vec{r} = a\hat{i} + a\hat{j} + (a+1)\hat{k}$

$(a \in R)$ are coplanar $3(\vec{p}.\vec{q})^2 - \lambda\,|\vec{r} \times \vec{q}|^2 = 0$, then the value of λ is .... **[2020, Main]**

20. If the distance between the plane, $23x - 10y - 2z + 48 = 0$ and the plane containing the lines $\dfrac{x+1}{2} = \dfrac{y-3}{4} = \dfrac{z+1}{3}$ and $\dfrac{x+3}{2} = \dfrac{y+2}{6} = \dfrac{z-1}{\lambda}$

$(\lambda \in R)$ is equal to $\dfrac{k}{\sqrt{633}}$, then k is equal to ....

[2020, Main]

21. Let P be a plane passing through the points $(2, 1, 0)$, $(4, 1, 1)$ and $(5, 0, 1)$ and R be any point $(2, 1, 6)$. Then the image of R in the plane P is : **[2020, Main]**

(a) $(6, 5, -2)$ (b) $(4, 3, 2)$

(c) $(3, 4, -2)$ (d) $(6, 5, 2)$

22. If $Q(0, -1, -3)$ is the image of the point P in the plane $3x - y + 4z = 2$ and R is the point $(3, -1, -2)$, then the area (in sq. units) of $\triangle PQR$ is : **[2019, Main]**

(a) $2\sqrt{13}$ (b) $\dfrac{\sqrt{91}}{4}$

(c) $\dfrac{\sqrt{91}}{2}$ (d) $\dfrac{\sqrt{65}}{2}$

23. The distance of the point having position vector $-\hat{i} + 2\hat{j} + 6\hat{k}$ from the straight line passing through the point $(2, 3, -4)$ and parallel to the vector, $6\hat{i} + 3\hat{j} - 4\hat{k}$ is : **[2019, Main]**

(a) 7 (b) $4\sqrt{3}$

(c) 6 (d) $2\sqrt{13}$

24. A perpendicular is drawn from a point on the line $\dfrac{x-1}{2} = \dfrac{y+1}{-1} = \dfrac{z}{1}$ to the plane $x + y + z = 3$. Such that the foot of the perpendicular also lies

on the plane $x - y + z = 3$. Then the co-ordinates of Q are : **[2019, Main]**

(a) $(1, 0, 2)$ (b) $(2, 0, 1)$

(c) $(-1, 0, 4)$ (d) $(4, 0, -1)$

25. If the plane $2x - y + 2z + 3 = 0$ has the distance $\dfrac{1}{3}$ and $\dfrac{2}{3}$ units from the planes $4x - 2y + 4z + \lambda = 0$ and $2x - y + 2z + \mu = 0$, respectively, then the maximum value of $\lambda + \mu$ is equal to : **[2019, Main]**

(a) 9   (b) 15

(c) 5   (d) 13

26. Let P be the plane, which contains the line of intersection of the planes, $x + y + z - 6 = 0$ and $2x + 3y + z + 5 = 0$ and it is perpendicular to the xy-plane. Then the distance of the point $(0, 0, 256)$ from P is equal to : **[2019, Main]**

(a) $\dfrac{17}{\sqrt{5}}$ (b) $\dfrac{63}{\sqrt{5}}$

(c) $\dfrac{205}{\sqrt{5}}$ (d) $\dfrac{11}{\sqrt{5}}$

27. If the line, $\dfrac{x-1}{2} = \dfrac{y+1}{3} = \dfrac{z-2}{4}$ meets the plane, $x + 2y + 3z = 15$ at a point P, then the distance of P from the origin is : **[2019, Main]**

(a) $\dfrac{\sqrt{5}}{2}$ (b) $2\sqrt{5}$

(c) $\dfrac{9}{2}$ (d) $\dfrac{7}{2}$

28. A plane passing through the points $(0, -1, 0)$ and $(0, 0, 1)$ and making an angle $\dfrac{\pi}{4}$ with the plane $y - z + 5 = 0$, also passes through the point : **[2019, Main]**

(a) $(-\sqrt{2}, 1, -4)$ (b) $(\sqrt{2}, -1, 4)$

(c) $(-\sqrt{2}, -1, -4)$ (d) $(\sqrt{2}, 1, 4)$

29. The shortest distance between the line $y = x$ and the curve $y^2 = x - 2$ is : **[2019, Main]**

(a) 2   (b) $\dfrac{7}{8}$

(c) $\dfrac{7}{4\sqrt{2}}$ (d) $\dfrac{11}{4\sqrt{2}}$

30. The equation of a plane containing the line of intersection of the planes $2x - y - 4 = 0$ and $y + 2z - 4 = 0$ passing through the point $(1, 1, 0)$ is : **[2019, Main]**

(a) $x - 3y - 2z = -2$ (b) $2x - z = 2$

(c) $x - y - z = 0$ (d) $x + 3y + z = 4$

31. If the line $\dfrac{x-2}{3} = \dfrac{y+1}{2} = \dfrac{z-1}{-1}$ intersects the plane $2x + 3y - z + 13 = 0$ at a point P and the plane $3x + y + 4z = 16$ at a point Q, then PQ is equal to : **[2019, Main]**

(a) 14   (b) $\sqrt{14}$

(c) $2\sqrt{7}$ (d) $2\sqrt{14}$

32. A plane which bisects the angle between the two given planes $2x - y + 2z - 4 = 0$ and $x + 2y + 2z - 2 = 0$, passes through the point : **[2019, Main]**

(a) $(1, -4, 1)$ (b) $(1, 4, -1)$

(c) $(2, 4, 1)$ (d) $(2, -4, 1)$

33. The length of the perpendicular drawn from the point $(2, 1, 4)$ to the plane containing the lines $\vec{r} = (\hat{i} + \hat{j}) + \lambda(\hat{i} + 2\hat{j} - \hat{k})$ and $\vec{r} = (\hat{i} + \hat{j}) + \mu(-\hat{i} + \hat{j} - 2\hat{k})$ is : **[2019, Main]**

(a) 3   (b) $\dfrac{1}{3}$

(c) $\sqrt{3}$ (d) $\dfrac{1}{\sqrt{3}}$

34. If the length of the perpendicular from the point $(\beta, 0, \beta)$, $(\beta \neq 0)$ to the line, $\dfrac{x}{1} = \dfrac{y-1}{0} = \dfrac{z+1}{-1}$ is $\sqrt{\dfrac{3}{2}}$, then β is equal to : **[2019, Main]**

(a) 1   (b) 2

(c) -1 (d) -2

35. The length of the perpendicular from point $(2, -1, 4)$ on the straight line, $\dfrac{x+3}{10} = \dfrac{y-2}{-7} = \dfrac{z}{1}$ is : **[2019, Main]**

(a) greater than 3 but less than 4

(b) less than 2

(c) greater than 2 but less than 3

(d) greater than 4

36. Let L_1 and L_2 denote the lines
$\vec{r} = \lambda(-\hat{i} - 2\hat{j} + 2\hat{k})$, $\lambda \in R$ and
$\vec{r} = \lambda(-\hat{i} - 2\hat{j} + 2\hat{k})$, $\mu \in R$
respectively. If L_3 is a line which is perpendicular to both L_1 and L_2 and cuts both of them, then which of the following options describe (s) L_3 ? **[2019, Advanced]**

(a) $\vec{r} = \dfrac{2}{9}(4\hat{i} + \hat{j} + \hat{k}) + t(2\hat{i} + 2\hat{j} - \hat{k})$, $t \in R$

(b) $\vec{r} = \dfrac{2}{9}(2\hat{i} - \hat{j} + 2\hat{k}) + t(2\hat{i} + 2\hat{j} - \hat{k})$, $t \in R$

(c) $\vec{r} = \dfrac{1}{3}(2\hat{i}+\hat{k})+t(2\hat{i}+2\hat{j}-\hat{k}),\, t \in R$

(d) $\vec{r} = t(2\hat{i}+2\hat{j}-\hat{k}),\, t \in R$

37. Three lines are given by

$$\vec{r} = \lambda\hat{i},\, \lambda \in R$$

$$\vec{r} = \mu(\hat{i}+\hat{j}),\, \mu \in R \text{ and}$$

$$\vec{r} = \nu(\hat{i}+\hat{j}+\hat{k}),\, \nu \in R$$

Let the lines cut the plane $x + y + z = 1$ at the points A, B and C respectively. If the area of the triangle ABC is Δ then the value of $(6\Delta)^2$ equals.

[2019, Advanced]

38. Three lines

$$L_1 : \vec{r} = \lambda\hat{i},\, \lambda \in R$$

$$L_2 : \vec{r} = \hat{k}+\mu\hat{j},\, \mu \in R \text{ and}$$

$$L_3 : \vec{r} = \hat{i}+\hat{j}+\nu\hat{k},\, \nu \in R$$

are given. For which points(s) Q on L_2 can we find a point P on L_1 and a point R on L_3 so that P, Q and R are collinear ?   **[2019, Advanced]**

(a) $\hat{k}-\dfrac{1}{2}\hat{j}$

(b) $\hat{k}$

(c) $\hat{k}+\dfrac{1}{2}\hat{j}$

(d) $\hat{k}+\hat{j}$

39. A variable plane passes through a fixed point (3, 2, 1) and meet X, Y and Z axes at A, B and C respecitvely. A plane is drawn parallel to yz-plane through A, a second plane is drawn parallel zx-plane through B and a third plane is drawn parallel to xy-plane through C. Then the locus of the point of intersection of these three planes, is :   **[2018, Main]**

(a) $\dfrac{x}{3}+\dfrac{y}{2}+\dfrac{z}{1} = 1$ **(b)** $x + y + z = 6$

(b) $\dfrac{1}{x}+\dfrac{1}{y}+\dfrac{1}{z} = \dfrac{11}{6}$ **(d)** $\dfrac{3}{x}+\dfrac{2}{y}+\dfrac{1}{z} = 1$

40. An angle between the plane, $x + y + z = 5$ and the line of intersection of the planes, $3x + 4y + z - 1 = 0$ and $5x + 8y + 2z + 14 = 0$, is :   **[2018, Main]**

(a) $\sin^{-1}\left(\sqrt{\dfrac{3}{17}}\right)$ **(b)** $\cos^{-1}\left(\sqrt{\dfrac{3}{17}}\right)$

(c) $\cos^{-1}\left(\dfrac{3}{\sqrt{17}}\right)$ **(d)** $\sin^{-1}\left(\dfrac{3}{\sqrt{17}}\right)$

41. The sum of the intercepts on the coordinate axes of the plane passing through the point $(-2, -2, 2)$ and containing the line joining the points $(1, -1, 2)$ and $(1, 1, 1)$, is :   **[2018, Main]**

(a) 4   **(b)** -4

(c) 8   **(d)** 12

42. If the angle between the lines, $\dfrac{x}{2}=\dfrac{y}{2}=\dfrac{z}{1}$ and $\dfrac{5-x}{-2}=\dfrac{7y-14}{p}=\dfrac{z-3}{4}$ is $\cos^{-1}\left(\dfrac{2}{3}\right)$ then p is equal to :   **[2018, Main]**

(a) $\dfrac{7}{2}$ **(b)** $\dfrac{2}{7}$

(c) $-\dfrac{7}{4}$ **(d)** $-\dfrac{4}{7}$

43. The length of the projection of the line segment joining the points $(5, -1, 4)$ and $(4, -1, 3)$ on the plane, $x + y + z = 7$ is :   **[2018, Main]**

(a) $\dfrac{2}{\sqrt{3}}$ **(b)** $\dfrac{2}{3}$

(c) $\dfrac{1}{3}$ **(d)** $\sqrt{\dfrac{2}{3}}$

44. If L_1 is the line of intersection of the planes $2x - 2y + 3z - 2 = 0$, $x - y + z + 1 = 0$ and L_2 is the line of intersection of the planes $x + 2y - z - 3 = 0$, $3x - y + 2z - 1 = 0$, then the distance of the origin from the plane, containing the lines L_1 and L_2, is :   **[2018, Main]**

(a) $\dfrac{1}{4\sqrt{2}}$ **(b)** $\dfrac{1}{3\sqrt{2}}$

(c) $\dfrac{1}{2\sqrt{2}}$ **(d)** $\dfrac{1}{\sqrt{2}}$

45. If the line, $\dfrac{x-3}{1}=\dfrac{y+2}{-1}=\dfrac{z+\lambda}{-2}$ lies in the plane, $2x - 4y + 3z = 2$, then the shortest distance between this line and the line, $\dfrac{x-1}{12}=\dfrac{y}{9}=\dfrac{z}{4}$ is :   **[2018, Main]**

(a) 2   **(b)** 1

(c) 0   **(d)** 3

46. If a variable plane, at a distance of 3 units from the origin, intersects the coordinate axes at A, B and C, then the locus of the centroid of $\triangle ABC$ is :   **[2017, Main]**

(a) $\dfrac{1}{x^2}+\dfrac{1}{y^2}+\dfrac{1}{z^2} = 1$ **(b)** $\dfrac{1}{x^2}+\dfrac{1}{y^2}+\dfrac{1}{z^2} = 3$

(c) $\dfrac{1}{x^2}+\dfrac{1}{y^2}+\dfrac{1}{z^2} = \dfrac{1}{9}$ **(d)** $\dfrac{1}{x^2}+\dfrac{1}{y^2}+\dfrac{1}{z^2} = 9$

47. The coordinates of the foot of the perpendicular from the point $(1, -2, 1)$ on the plane containing the lines, $\dfrac{x+1}{6} = \dfrac{y-1}{7} = \dfrac{z-3}{8}$ and $\dfrac{x-1}{3} = \dfrac{y-2}{5}$

$= \dfrac{z-3}{7}$, is : **[2017, Main]**

(a) $(2, -4, 2)$
(b) $(-1, 2, -1)$
(c) $(0, 0, 0)$
(d) $(1, 1, 1)$

48. The distance of the points $(1, 3, -7)$ from the plane passing through the point $(1, -1, 1)$ having normal perpendicular to both the lines $\dfrac{x-1}{1} = \dfrac{y+2}{-2} = \dfrac{z-4}{3}$ and $\dfrac{x-2}{2} = \dfrac{y+1}{-1} = \dfrac{z+7}{-1}$, is :

[2017, Main]

(a) $\dfrac{10}{\sqrt{83}}$
(b) $\dfrac{5}{\sqrt{83}}$

(c) $\dfrac{10}{\sqrt{74}}$
(d) $\dfrac{20}{\sqrt{74}}$

49. If the image of the point $P(1, -2, 3)$ in the plane, $2x + 3y - 4z + 22 = 0$ measured parallel to the line, $\dfrac{x}{1} = \dfrac{y}{4} = \dfrac{z}{5}$ is Q, then PQ is equal to :

[2017, Main]

(a) $2\sqrt{42}$
(b) $\sqrt{42}$
(c) $6\sqrt{5}$
(d) $3\sqrt{5}$

50. The line of intersection of the planes

$\vec{r} \cdot (3\hat{i} - \hat{j} + \hat{k}) = 1$ and $\vec{r} \cdot (\hat{i} + 4\hat{j} - 2\hat{k}) = 2$, is :

[2016, Main]

(a) $\dfrac{x - \dfrac{4}{7}}{-2} = \dfrac{y}{7} = \dfrac{z - \dfrac{5}{7}}{13}$

(b) $\dfrac{x - \dfrac{4}{7}}{2} = \dfrac{y}{-7} = \dfrac{z + \dfrac{5}{7}}{13}$

(c) $\dfrac{x - \dfrac{6}{13}}{2} = \dfrac{y - \dfrac{5}{13}}{-7} = \dfrac{z}{-13}$

(d) $\dfrac{x - \dfrac{6}{13}}{2} = \dfrac{y - \dfrac{5}{13}}{7} = \dfrac{z}{-13}$

51. ABC is a triangle in a plane with vertices $A(2, 3, 5)$, $B(-1, 3, 2)$ and $C(\lambda, 5, \mu)$. If the median through A is equally inclined to the coordinate axes, then the value of $(\lambda^3 + \mu^3 + 5)$ is :

[2016, Main]

(a) 1130
(b) 1348
(c) 676
(d) 1077

52. The number of distinct real values of λ for which the lines $\dfrac{x-1}{1} = \dfrac{y-2}{2} = \dfrac{z-3}{\lambda^2}$ and $\dfrac{x-3}{1} = \dfrac{y-2}{\lambda^2}$

$= \dfrac{z-1}{2}$ are coplanar is : **[2016, Main]**

(a) 4
(b) 1
(c) 2
(d) 3

53. The shortest distance between the lines $\dfrac{x}{2} = \dfrac{y}{2} = \dfrac{z}{1}$ and $\dfrac{x+2}{-1} = \dfrac{y-4}{8} = \dfrac{z-5}{4}$ lies in the interval : **[2016, Main]**

(a) $[0, 1)$
(b) $[1, 2)$
(c) $(2, 3]$
(d) $(3, 4]$

54. The distance of the point $(1, -2, 4)$ from the plane passing through the point $(1, 2, 2)$ and perpendicular to the planes $x - y + 2z = 3$ and $2x - 2y + z + 12 = 0$, is : **[2016, Main]**

(a) $2\sqrt{2}$
(b) 2
(c) $\sqrt{2}$
(d) $\dfrac{1}{\sqrt{2}}$

55. If the line, $\dfrac{x-3}{2} = \dfrac{y+2}{-1} = \dfrac{z+4}{3}$ lies in the plane, $lx + my - z = 9$, then $l^2 + m^2$ is equal to :

[2016, Advanced]

(a) 26
(b) 18
(c) 5
(d) 2

56. The shortest distance between the Z-axis and the line $x + y + 2z - 3 = 0 = 2x + 3y + 4z - 4$, is :

[2015, Main]

(a) 1
(b) 2
(c) 3
(d) 4

57. The distance of the point $(1, 0, 2)$ from the point of intersection of the line $\dfrac{x-2}{3} = \dfrac{y+1}{4} = \dfrac{z-2}{12}$ and the plane $x - y + z = 16$, is : **[2015, Main]**

(a) $2\sqrt{14}$
(b) 8
(c) $3\sqrt{21}$
(d) 13

58. The equation of the plane containing the line $2x - 5y + z = 3$; $x + y + 4z = 5$, and parallel to the plane, $x + 3y + 6z = 1$, is : **[2015, Main]**

(a) $2x + 6y + 12z = 13$
(b) $x + 3y + 6z = -7$
(c) $x + 3y + 6z = 7$
(d) $2x + 6y + 12z = -13$

59. A plane containing the point $(3, 2, 0)$ and the line $\dfrac{x-1}{1} = \dfrac{y-2}{5} = \dfrac{z-3}{4}$ also contains the point :

[2015, Main]

(a) $(0, -3, 1)$ (b) $(0, 7, 10)$

(c) $(0, 7, -10)$ (d) $(0, 3, 1)$

60. A symmetrical form of the line of intersection of the planes $x = ay + b$ and $z = cy + d$ is : **[2014, Main]**

(a) $\dfrac{x-b}{a} = \dfrac{y-1}{1} = \dfrac{z-d}{c}$

(b) $\dfrac{x-b-a}{a} = \dfrac{y-1}{1} = \dfrac{z-d-c}{c}$

(c) $\dfrac{x-a}{b} = \dfrac{y-0}{1} = \dfrac{z-c}{d}$

(d) $\dfrac{x-b-a}{b} = \dfrac{y-1}{0} = \dfrac{z-d-c}{d}$

61. The image of the line $\dfrac{x-1}{3} = \dfrac{y-3}{1} = \dfrac{z-4}{-5}$ in the plane $2x - y + z + 3 = 0$ is the line : **[2014, Main]**

(a) $\dfrac{x-3}{3} = \dfrac{y+5}{1} = \dfrac{z-2}{-5}$

(b) $\dfrac{x-3}{-3} = \dfrac{y+5}{-1} = \dfrac{z-2}{5}$

(c) $\dfrac{x+3}{3} = \dfrac{y-5}{1} = \dfrac{z-2}{-5}$

(d) $\dfrac{x+3}{-3} = \dfrac{y-5}{-1} = \dfrac{z+2}{5}$

62. If the distance between planes, $4x - 2y + 4z + 1 = 0$ and $4x - 2y - 4z + d = 0$ is 7, then d is : **[2014, Main]**

(a) 41 or -42 (b) 42 or -43

(c) -41 or 43   (d) -42 or 44

63. Equation of the plane which passes through the point of intersection of lines $\dfrac{x-1}{3} = \dfrac{y-2}{1} = \dfrac{z-3}{2}$ and $\dfrac{x-3}{1} = \dfrac{y-1}{2} = \dfrac{z-2}{3}$ and has the largest distance from the origin is : **[2014, Main]**

(a) $7x + 2y + 4z = 54$ (b) $3x + 4y + 5z = 49$

(c) $4x + 3y + 5z = 50$ (d) $5x + 4y + 3z = 57$

64. A line in the 3-dimensional space makes an angle $\theta \left(0 < \theta \le \dfrac{\pi}{2}\right)$ with both the x and y axes. Then the set of all values of θ is the interval : **[2014, Main]**

(a) $\left(0, \dfrac{\pi}{2}\right]$ (b) $\left[\dfrac{\pi}{6}, \dfrac{\pi}{3}\right]$

(c) $\left[\dfrac{\pi}{4}, \dfrac{\pi}{2}\right]$ (d) $\left(\dfrac{\pi}{3}, \dfrac{\pi}{2}\right)$

65. Equation of the line of shortest distance between the lines $\dfrac{x}{1} = \dfrac{y}{-1} = \dfrac{z}{1}$ and $\dfrac{x-1}{0} = \dfrac{y+1}{-2} = \dfrac{z}{1}$ is : **[2014, Main]**

(a) $\dfrac{x}{1} = \dfrac{y}{-1} = \dfrac{z}{-2}$ (b) $\dfrac{x-1}{1} = \dfrac{y+1}{-1} = \dfrac{z}{-2}$

(c) $\dfrac{x-1}{1} = \dfrac{y+1}{-1} = \dfrac{z}{1}$ (d) $\dfrac{x}{-2} = \dfrac{y}{1} = \dfrac{z}{2}$

66. If the angle between the line $2(x + 1) = y = z + 4$ and the plane $2x - y + \sqrt{\lambda}\, z + 4 = 0$ is $\dfrac{\pi}{6}$, then the value of λ is : **[2014, Main]**

(a) $\dfrac{135}{7}$ (b) $\dfrac{45}{11}$

(c) $\dfrac{45}{7}$ (d) $\dfrac{135}{11}$

67. Let A $(2, 3, 5)$, B $(-1, 3, 2)$ and C $(\lambda, 5, \mu)$ be the vertices of a $\triangle ABC$. If the median through A is equally inclined to the coordinate axes, then : **[2014, Main]**

(a) $5\lambda - 8\mu = 0$ (b) $8\lambda - 5\mu = 0$

(c) $10\lambda - 7\mu = 0$ (d) $7\lambda - 10\mu = 0$

68. The plane containing the line $\dfrac{x-1}{1} = \dfrac{y-2}{2} = \dfrac{z-3}{3}$ and parallel to the line $\dfrac{x}{1} = \dfrac{y}{1} = \dfrac{z}{4}$ passes through the point : **[2014, Main]**

(a) $(1, -2, 5)$ (b) $(1, 0, 5)$

(c) $(0, 3, -5)$ (d) $(-1, -3, 0)$

69. If the distance of the point $P(1, -2, 1)$ from the plane $x + 2y - 2z = \alpha$, where $\alpha > 0$, is 5, then the foot of the perpendicular from P to the plane is: **(2010, Advanced)**

(a) $\left(\dfrac{8}{3}, \dfrac{4}{3}, -\dfrac{7}{3}\right)$ (b) $\left(\dfrac{4}{3}, -\dfrac{4}{3}, \dfrac{1}{3}\right)$

(c) $\left(\dfrac{1}{3}, \dfrac{2}{3}, \dfrac{10}{3}\right)$ (d) $\left(\dfrac{2}{3}, -\dfrac{1}{3}, \dfrac{5}{2}\right)$

70. Match the statements in **Column-I** with the values in **Column-II**. **(2010, Advanced)**

Column I	Column II
(a) A line from the origin meets the lines $\dfrac{x-2}{1} = \dfrac{y-1}{-2} = \dfrac{z+1}{1}$ and $\dfrac{x-\dfrac{8}{3}}{2} = \dfrac{y+3}{-1} = \dfrac{z-1}{1}$ at P and Q respectively. If length PQ = d, then d^2 is	(p) -4

(b) The values of x satisfying
$\tan^{-1}(x+3) - \tan^{-1}(x-3) =$
$\sin^{-1}\left(\dfrac{3}{5}\right)$ are   (q) 0

(c) Non-zero vectors $\vec{a}, \vec{b}$ and $\vec{c}$ (r) 4

satisfy $\vec{a}.\vec{b} = 0$, $(\vec{b}-\vec{a}).(\vec{b}+\vec{c})$

$= 0$ and $2\,|\,\vec{b}+\vec{c}\,| = |\,\vec{b}-\vec{c}\,|$.

If $\vec{a} = \mu\,\vec{b} + 4\,\vec{c}$, then the

possible value of μ are

(d) Let f be the function on $[-\pi, \pi]$
given by $f(0) = 9$ and
$f(x) = \sin\left(\dfrac{9x}{2}\right)\Big/\sin\left(\dfrac{x}{2}\right)$ for $x \neq 0$.   (s) 5

The value of $\dfrac{2}{\pi}\displaystyle\int_{-\pi}^{\pi} f(x)\,dx$ is   (t) 6

71. Consider the lines :
$$4 = \frac{x+1}{3} = \frac{y+2}{1} = \frac{z+1}{2}, \ L_2 = \frac{x-2}{1} = \frac{y+2}{2} = \frac{z-3}{3}$$

The distance of the point $(1, 1, 1)$ from the plane passing through the point $(-1, -2, -1)$ and whose normal is perpendicular to both the line L_1 and L_2 is :   (2008, Advanced)

(a) $\dfrac{2}{\sqrt{75}}$ (b) $\dfrac{7}{\sqrt{75}}$

(c) $\dfrac{13}{\sqrt{75}}$ (d) $\dfrac{23}{\sqrt{75}}$

72. Consider the following linear equations
$$ax + by + cz = 0$$
$$bx + cy + az = 0$$
$$cx + ay + bz = 0$$
Match the conditions/expressions in **Column I** with statements in **Column II** and indicate your answer by darkening the appropriate bubbles in the 4×4 matrix given in the ORS.

                                       [2007, Advanced]

Column I   **Column II**

(a) $a + b + c \neq 0$ and   (p) the equations represent
$\quad a^2 + b^2 + c^2 = ab + bc + ca$ planes meeting only at
                               a single point.

(b) $a + b + c = 0$ and   (q) the equations represent
$\quad a^2 + b^2 + c^2 \neq ab + bc + ca$ the line $x = y = z$.

(c) $a + b + c \neq 0$ and   (r) the equations represent
$\quad a^2 + b^2 + c^2 \neq ab + bc + ca$ identical planes.

(d) $a + b + c = 0$ and   (s) the equations represent
$\quad a^2 + b^2 + c^2 = ab + bc + ca$ the whole of the three
                               dimensional space.

73. Let $ABCD$ be a quadrilateral with area 18, with side AB parallel to the side CD and $AB = 2CD$. Let AD be perpendicular to AB and CD. If a circle is drawn inside the quadrilateral $ABCD$ touching all the sides, then its radius is :   **[2007, Advanced]**

(a) 3   (b) 2

(c) $\dfrac{3}{2}$ (d) 1

74. A plane passes through $(1, -2, 1)$ and is perpendicular to two planes $2x - 2y + z = 0$ and $x - y + 2z = 4$. The distance of the plane from the point $(1, 2, 1)$ is :   **[2006, Main]**

(a) 0   (b) 1

(c) $\sqrt{2}$ (d) $2\sqrt{2}$

75. A variable plane at a distance of 1 unit from the origin cuts the coordinate axes at A, B and C. If the centroid D (x, y, z) of triangle ABC satisfies the relation $\dfrac{1}{x^2} + \dfrac{1}{y^2} + \dfrac{1}{z^2} = k$, then the value of k is :   **[2005, Main]**

(a) 3   (b) 1

(c) 1/3   (d) 9

76. Find the equation of the plane containing the line $2x - y + z - 3 = 0$, $3x + y + z = 5$ and at a distance of $\dfrac{1}{\sqrt{6}}$ from the point $(2, 1, -1)$.   **[2005, Main]**

77. If the lines $\dfrac{x-1}{2} = \dfrac{y+1}{3} = \dfrac{z-1}{4}$

and $\dfrac{x-3}{1} = \dfrac{y-k}{2} = \dfrac{z}{1}$

intersect, then the value of k is :   **[2004, Main]**

(a) 3/2   (b) 9/2

(c) $-2/9$ (d) $-3/2$

78. T is a parallelopiped in which A, B, C and D are vertices of one face. And the face just above it has corresponding vertices A′, B′, C′, D′. T is now compressed to S with face ABCD remaining same and A′, B′, C′, D′ shifted to A″, B″, C″, D″ in S. The volume of parallelopiped S is reduced to 90% of T. Prove that the locus of A″ is a plane.   **[2004, Main]**

79. A plane is parallel to two lines whose direction ratios are $(1, 0 - 1)$ and $(-1, 1, 0)$ and it contains the point $(1, 1, 1)$. If it cuts coordinate axis at A, B, C, then find the volume of the tetrahedron OABC.   **[2004, Main]**

80. The value of k such that $\dfrac{x-4}{1} = \dfrac{y-2}{1} = \dfrac{z-k}{2}$ lies in the plane $2x - 4y + z = 7$, is :   **[2003, Main]**

(a) 7   (b) -7

(c) no real value   (d) 4

ANSWER KEY

1. (b)	**2.** (d)	**3.** (c)	**4.** (*)	**5.** (b)	
6. (d)	**7.** (d)	**8.** (a)	**9.** (a,b,c)	**10.** (b)	
11. (a)	**12.** (*)	**13.** (b)	**14.** (4.00)	**15.** (a)	
16. (b)	**17.** (d)	**18.** (b)	**19.** (1.00)	**20.** (3)	
21. (a)	**22.** (c)	**23.** (a)	**24.** (b)	**25.** (d)	
26. (d)	**27.** (c)	**28.** (d)	**29.** (c)	**30.** (c)	
31. (d)	**32.** (d)	**33.** (c)	**34.** (c)	**35.** (a)	
36. (a,b,c)	**37.** (0.75)	**38.** (a,c)	**39.** (d)	**40.** (a)	
41. (b)	**42.** (a)	**43.** (d)	**44.** (b)	**45.** (c)	
46. (a)	**47.** (c)	**48.** (a)	**49.** (a)	**50.** (c)	
51. (b)	**52.** (d)	**53.** (c)	**54.** (a)	**55.** (d)	
56. (b)	**57.** (d)	**58.** (c)	**59.** (b)	**60.** (b)	
61. (c)	**62.** (c)	**63.** (c)	**64.** (c)	**65.** (b)	
66. (c)	**67.** (c)	**68.** (b)	**69.** (a)		

70. (a) – (t), (b) – (p) (r), (c) – either (q) or (q) (s), (d) – (r)   **71.** (c)

72. (a) – (r), (b) – (q), (c) – (p), (d) – (s)   **73.** (b)   **74.** (d)   **75.** (d)   **76.** $(62x + 29y + 19z - 105 = 0)$

77. (b)   **78.** (*)   **79.** (9/2 cubic units)   **80.** (a)

ANSWERS WITH EXPLANATIONS

1. Correct Response : (b)

Explanation :

P(1, 2, –3)

R

Q (a, b, c) (image point)

Line is $\dfrac{x+1}{2} = \dfrac{y-3}{-2} = \dfrac{z}{-1} = \lambda$: Let point R is

$(2\lambda - 1, -2\lambda + 3, -\lambda)$

Direction ratio of PQ $\equiv (2\lambda - 2, -2\lambda + 1, 3 - \lambda)$

PQ is $\perp$ to line

$\Rightarrow 2(2\lambda - 2) - 2(-2\lambda + 1) - 1(3 - \lambda) = 0$

$4\lambda - 4 + 4\lambda - 2 - 3 + \lambda = 0$

$9\lambda = 9 \Rightarrow \lambda = 1$

$\Rightarrow$ Point R is $(1, 1, -1)$

$\dfrac{a+1}{2} = 1, \dfrac{b+2}{2} = 1, \dfrac{c-3}{2} = -1$

$a = 1, b = 0, c = 1$

$\Rightarrow \quad a + b + c = 2.$

2. Correct Response : (d)

Explanation :

Plane through line of intersection is

$$x + y + z + 1 + \lambda(2x - y + z + 3) = 0$$

$(1 + 2\lambda)x + (1 - \lambda)y + (1 + \lambda)z + (1 + 3\lambda) = 0$

It should be parallel to given line

$$0(1 + 2\lambda) - 1(1 - \lambda) + 1(1 + \lambda) = 0$$

$$\lambda = 0$$

Plane $x + y + z + 1 = 0$

S.D. = Perpendicular distance of

$(1, -1, 0)$ from this plane

$= \dfrac{1 - 1 + 0 + 1}{\sqrt{1^2 + 1^2 + 1^2}} = \dfrac{1}{\sqrt{3}}.$

3. Correct Response : (c)

Explanation :

$$\frac{x}{a} + \frac{y}{b} + \frac{z}{c} = 1$$

$A \equiv (a, 0, 0)$, $B \equiv (0, b, 0)$, $C \equiv (0, 0, c)$

Centroid $\equiv \left(\dfrac{a}{3}, \dfrac{b}{3}, \dfrac{c}{3}\right) = (1, 1, 2)$

$$a = 3, b = 3, c = 6$$

Plane : $\dfrac{x}{3} + \dfrac{y}{3} + \dfrac{z}{6} = 1$

$$2x + 2y + z = 6$$

Line $\perp$ to the plane (DR of line $= 2\,\hat{i} + 2\,\hat{j} + \hat{k}$)

$$\frac{x-1}{2} = \frac{y-1}{2} = \frac{z-2}{1}$$

4. Correct Response : (*)

Explanation :

$$D_1 = \begin{vmatrix} -7 & 4 & -1 \\ 8 & 1 & 5 \\ 15 & b & 6 \end{vmatrix} = 0 \Rightarrow b = -3$$

$$D = \begin{vmatrix} 1 & 4 & -1 \\ 3 & 1 & 5 \\ a & b & 6 \end{vmatrix} = 0$$

$\Rightarrow 21a - 8b - 66 = 0$ ...(1)

$P : 2x - 3y + 6z = 15$

so required distance $= \dfrac{21}{7} = 3$

Equation of plane passing through intersection of planes

$x + 4y - z + 7 = 0$ ...(1)

and $\quad 3x + y + 52 - 8 = 0$ ...(2)

$$p_1 + \lambda p_2 = 0$$

$(x + 4y - z + 7) + \lambda(3x + y + 5y - 8) = 0$

$(3\lambda + 1)x + (\lambda + 4)y + (5\lambda - 1)z + (7 - 8\lambda) = 0$ ...(3)

$$ax + by + 6z - 15 = 0 \qquad \text{...(4)}$$

Comparing (3) & (4)

$$\frac{a}{3\lambda + 1} = \frac{b}{\lambda + 4} + \frac{b}{5\lambda - 1} = \frac{-15}{(7 - 8\lambda)}$$

$$\frac{6}{5\lambda - 1} = \frac{-15}{(7 - 8\lambda)}$$

$$\lambda = -1$$

$$\frac{a}{-2} = \frac{b}{3} = -1$$

$$\Rightarrow \qquad a = 2, b = -3$$

so plane is

$$2x - 3y + 6z - 15 = 0$$

Distance of plane (5) from point $(3, 2, -1)$ is p

$$= \frac{6 - 6 - 6 - 15}{\sqrt{4 + 9 + 36}} = \left| \frac{-21}{7} \right| = 3.$$

5. **Correct Response :** (b)

   Explanation :

   Equation of line parallel to $\dfrac{x}{2} = \dfrac{y}{3} = \dfrac{z}{-6}$ passes

   through $(1, -2, 3)$ is

   $$\frac{x - 1}{2} = \frac{y + 2}{3} = \frac{z - 3}{-6} = r$$

   $$x = 2r + 1$$
   $$y = 3r - 2,$$
   $$z = -6r + 3$$

   So $2r + 1 - 3r + 2 - 6r + 3 = 5$

   $$\Rightarrow \qquad -7r + 1 = 0$$

   $$r = \frac{1}{7}$$

   $$x = \frac{9}{7}, y = \frac{-11}{7}, z = \frac{15}{7}$$

   Distance is

   $$= \sqrt{\left(1 - \frac{9}{7}\right)^2 + \left(-2 + \frac{11}{7}\right)^2 + \left(3 - \frac{15}{7}\right)^2}$$

   $$= \sqrt{\left(\frac{-2}{7}\right)^2 + \left(\frac{-3}{7}\right)^2 + \left(\frac{-6}{7}\right)^2}$$

   $$= \sqrt{\left(\frac{2}{7}\right)^2 + \left(\frac{3}{7}\right)^2 + \left(\frac{6}{7}\right)^2}$$

   $$= \frac{1}{7}\sqrt{4 + 9 + 36}$$

   $$= \frac{1}{7}\sqrt{49} = 1.$$

6. **Correct Response :** (d)

   Explanation :

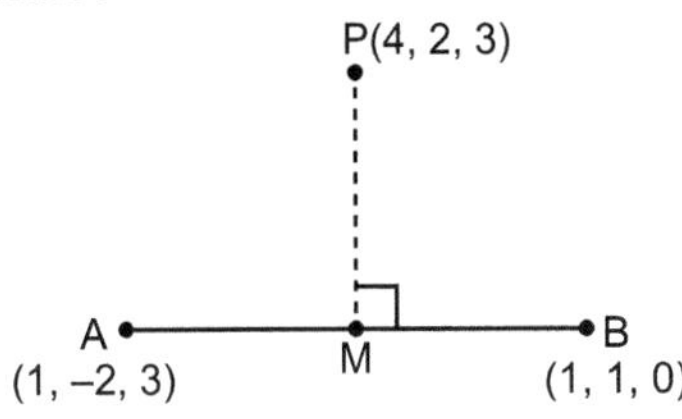

   Equation of AB $= \overrightarrow{r} = (\hat{i} + \hat{j}) + \lambda(3\hat{j} - 3\hat{k})$

   Let coordinates of M $= [1, (1 + 3\lambda), -3\lambda]$

   $$\overrightarrow{PM} = -3\hat{i} + (3\lambda - 1)\hat{j} - 3(\lambda + 1)\hat{k}$$

   $$\overrightarrow{AB} = 3\hat{j} - 3\hat{k}$$

   $\because \quad \overrightarrow{PM} \perp \overrightarrow{AB} \Rightarrow \overrightarrow{PM}.\overrightarrow{AB} = 0$

   $\Rightarrow \qquad 3(3\lambda - 1) + 9(\lambda + 1) = 0$

   $\Rightarrow \qquad \lambda = -\dfrac{1}{3}$

   $\therefore \qquad M = (1, 0, 1)$

   Clearly M lies on $2x + y - z = 1$.

7. **Correct Response :** (d)

   Explanation :

   $$L_1 \equiv \frac{x + 1}{2} = \frac{y - 2}{-1} = \frac{z - 1}{1}$$

   $$L_2 \equiv \frac{x + 2}{\alpha} = \frac{y + 1}{5 - \alpha} = \frac{z + 1}{1}$$

   Point A$(-1, 2, 1)$, B$(-2, -1, -1)$

   $\because$ L$_1$ and L$_2$ are coplanar.

   $$\Rightarrow \quad \begin{vmatrix} 2 & -1 & 1 \\ \alpha & 5 - \alpha & 1 \\ 1 & 3 & 2 \end{vmatrix} = 0$$

   $$\alpha = -4$$

   $$L_2 = \frac{x - 2}{-4} = \frac{y + 1}{9} = \frac{z + 1}{1}$$

   Check options $(2, -10, -2)$ lies on L$_2$.

8. **Correct Response :** (a)

   Explanation :

   $$L_1 : \frac{x - 1}{1} = \frac{y}{-1} \frac{z - 1}{3} = \lambda \Rightarrow (\lambda + 1, -\lambda, 3\lambda + 1)$$

   $$L_2 : \frac{x - 1}{-3} = \frac{y}{-1} = \frac{z - 1}{1} = \mu \Rightarrow (-3\mu + 1, -\mu, \mu + 1)$$

   Both interacts

   $$(\lambda + 1, -\lambda, 3\lambda + 1) = (-3\mu + 1, -\mu, \mu + 1)$$

   $$\lambda + 1 = -3\mu + 1$$

   $$\lambda + 3\mu = 0$$

   $$\lambda = \mu$$

   $\Rightarrow \qquad \lambda = \mu = 0 \ \& \ 3\lambda = \mu$

Both lines pass through (1, 0, 1).

Point of intersection of L_1 & L_2 is (1, 0, 1).

Line L passes through (1, 0, 1).

$$\frac{1-\alpha}{l} = -\frac{1}{m} = \frac{1-\gamma}{-2} \qquad \ldots(1)$$

Acute angle bisector of L_1 & L_2

$$\vec{r} = \hat{i} + \hat{k} + \lambda\left(\frac{\hat{i} - \hat{j} + 3\hat{k} - 3\hat{i} - \hat{j} + \hat{k}}{\sqrt{11}}\right)$$

$$\vec{r} = \hat{i} + \hat{k} + \lambda(\hat{i} + \hat{j} - 2\hat{k})$$

DR's of acute angle bisect or between two lines is $(-1, -1, 2)$.

$$\Rightarrow \qquad \frac{l}{1} = \frac{m}{1} = \frac{-2}{-2}$$

$$l = m = 1$$

$$\Rightarrow \qquad l + m = 2$$

From (1) $\qquad \dfrac{1-\alpha}{1} = -1$

$$\Rightarrow \qquad \alpha = 2$$

and $\qquad \dfrac{1-\gamma}{-2} = -1$

$$\Rightarrow \qquad \gamma = -1$$

$$\alpha - \gamma = 3$$

9. Correct Response : (a,b,c)

Explanation :

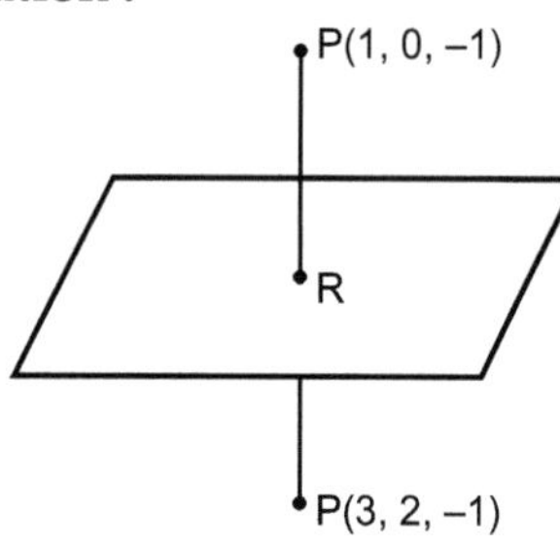

R is mid point of PQ.

$\therefore$ R(2, 1, $-$ 1) and it lies on plane equation of plane is

$$\alpha a + \beta b + \gamma z = \delta$$

$\therefore \qquad 2\alpha + \beta - \gamma = \delta \qquad \ldots(1)$

Normal vector to plane is

$$\vec{n} = 2\hat{i} + 2\hat{j}$$

$$\therefore \qquad \frac{\alpha}{2} = \frac{\beta}{2} = \frac{\gamma}{0} = k$$

$\therefore \qquad \alpha = 2k,\ \beta = 2k,\ \gamma = 0 \qquad \ldots(2)$

and $\qquad \alpha + \gamma = 1$ (given) $\qquad \ldots(3)$

from (2) and (3)

$\therefore \qquad \alpha = 1,\ \beta = 1,\ \gamma = 0$

and from (1)

$$2(1) + 1 - 0 = \delta$$

$$\delta = 3$$

Now $\qquad \alpha + \beta = 2$

$$\delta - \gamma = 3$$

$$\delta + \beta = 4$$

so, a, b, c are correct.

10. Correct Response : (b)

Explanation :

Hence normal is $\perp$ to both the lines so normal vector to the plane is

$$\vec{n} = (\hat{i} - 2\hat{j} + 2\hat{k}) \times (2\hat{i} + 3\hat{j} - \hat{k})$$

$$\vec{n} = \begin{vmatrix} \hat{i} & \hat{j} & \hat{k} \\ 1 & -2 & 2 \\ 2 & 3 & -1 \end{vmatrix}$$

$$= \hat{i}(2-6) - \hat{j}(-1-4) + \hat{k}(3+4)$$

$$\vec{n} = -4\hat{i} + 5\hat{j} + 7\hat{k}$$

Now equation of plane passing through (3, 1, 1) is

$$\Rightarrow -4(x-3) + 5(y-1) + 7(z-1) = 0$$

$$\Rightarrow -4x + 12 + 5y - 5 + 7z - 7 = 0$$

$$\Rightarrow \quad -4x + 5y + 7z = 0 \qquad \ldots(1)$$

Plane is also passing through $(\alpha, -3, 5)$ so this point satisfies the equation of plane so put is equation (1)

$$-4\alpha + 5 \times (-3) + 7 \times (5) = 0$$

$$\Rightarrow \quad -4\alpha - 15 + 35 = 0$$

$$\Rightarrow \qquad \alpha = 5$$

11. Correct Response : (a)

Explanation :

$$PA = PB$$

$$\Rightarrow \qquad PA^2 = PB^2$$

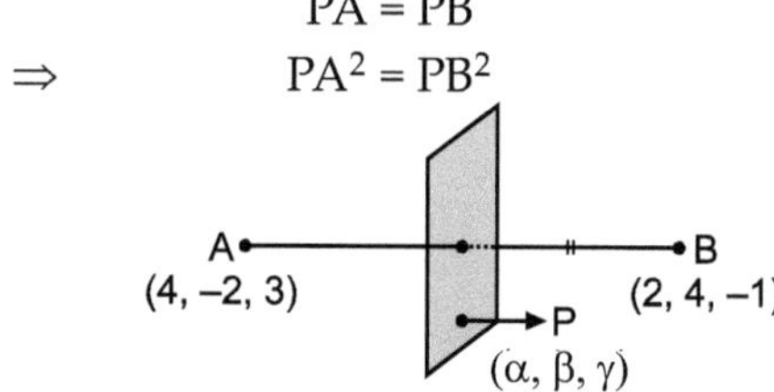

$$\Rightarrow (\alpha - 4)^2 + (\beta + 2)^2 + (\gamma - 3)^2$$

$$= (\alpha - 2)^2 + (\beta - 4)^2 + (\gamma + 1)^2$$

$$\Rightarrow \qquad -4\alpha + 12\beta - 8\gamma = -8$$

$$\Rightarrow \qquad 2x - 6y + 4z = 4$$

$$2x - 6y + 4z - 4 = 0$$

(4, 0, $-$ 1) also passes through the plane

$$2 \times 4 - 6 \times 0 + 4 \times (-1) - 4 = 0$$

12. Correct Response : (*)

Explanation :

Dr's normal to plane

$$\begin{vmatrix} \hat{i} & \hat{j} & \hat{k} \\ 1 & 1 & 0 \\ 0 & 1 & -1 \end{vmatrix} = -\hat{i} + \hat{j} + \hat{k}$$

Equation for plane

$$-1(x-1) + 1(y-0) + 1(z-0) = 0$$
$$x - y - z = 0 \qquad \ldots(1)$$

Now, $\dfrac{\alpha-1}{1} = \dfrac{\beta-0}{-1} = \dfrac{\gamma-1}{-1} = -\dfrac{(1-0-1-1)}{3}$

$$\dfrac{\alpha-1}{1} = \dfrac{\beta}{-1} = \dfrac{\gamma-1}{-1} = \dfrac{1}{3}$$

$$\alpha = \dfrac{4}{3},\ \beta = -\dfrac{1}{3},\ \gamma = \dfrac{2}{3}$$

$$3(\alpha + \beta + \gamma) = 3\left(\dfrac{4}{3} - \dfrac{1}{3} + \dfrac{2}{3}\right) = 5$$

13. Correct Response : (b)

Explanation :

Two points on the line (L say) $\dfrac{x}{3} = \dfrac{y}{2}$, $z = 1$ are

(0, 0, 1) & (3, 2, 1).

So dr's of the line is < 3, 2, 0 >

Line passing through (1, 2, 1), parallel to L and coplanar with given plane is

$$\vec{r} = \hat{i} + 2\hat{j} + \hat{k} + t(3\hat{i} + 2\hat{j}),\ t \in \text{R}\,(-2, 0, 1)\text{ satisfies}$$

the line (for $t = -1$)

$\Rightarrow (-2, 0, 1)$ lies on given plane.

Answer of the question is (b)

We can check other options by finding equation of plane

Equation plane : $\begin{vmatrix} x-1 & y-2 & z-1 \\ 1+2 & 2-0 & 1-1 \\ 2+2 & 1-0 & 2-1 \end{vmatrix} = 0$

$$\Rightarrow 2(x-1) - 3(y-2) - 5(z-1) = 0$$
$$\Rightarrow \quad 2x - 3y - 5z + 9 = 0$$

14. Correct Response : (4.00)

Explanation :

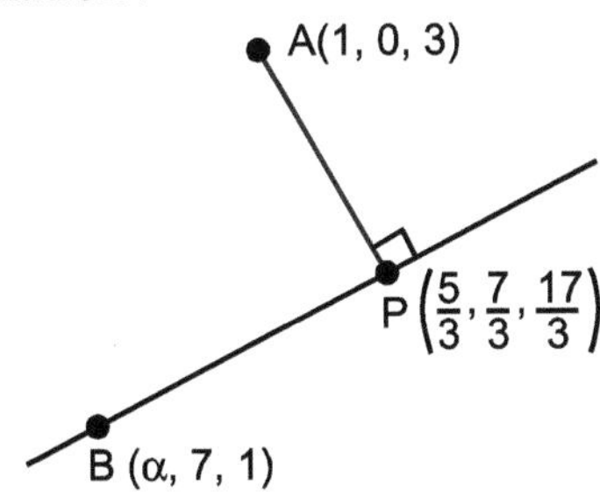

$$\text{D.R. of BP} = <\dfrac{5}{3} - \alpha,\ \dfrac{7}{3} - 7,\ \dfrac{17}{3} - 1 >$$

$$\text{D.R. of AP} = <\dfrac{5}{3} - 1,\ \dfrac{7}{3} - 0,\ \dfrac{17}{3} - 3 >$$

$$\text{BP} \perp \text{AP}$$
$$\Rightarrow \qquad \alpha = 4$$

15. Correct Response : (a)

Explanation :

$$\begin{Vmatrix} 1 & 1 & \lambda \\ 1 & 1 & 3 \\ 2 & 1 & 1 \end{Vmatrix} = 1 \Rightarrow \lambda = 2, 4$$

Now, $\cos\theta = \dfrac{\vec{u}.\vec{w}}{|\vec{u}||\vec{w}|}$

$$= \dfrac{5}{\sqrt{6}\sqrt{6}} \text{ or } \dfrac{7}{\sqrt{6}\sqrt{18}}$$

$$= \dfrac{5}{6} \text{ or } \dfrac{7}{6\sqrt{3}}$$

16. Correct Response : (b)

Explanation :

Shortest distance $= \dfrac{\begin{Vmatrix} 6 & 15 & -3 \\ 3 & -1 & 1 \\ -3 & 2 & 4 \end{Vmatrix}}{\sqrt{11\times29-49}} = \dfrac{270}{\sqrt{270}}$

$$= \sqrt{270} = 3\sqrt{30}$$

17. Correct Response : (d)

Explanation :

Point on plane $\text{R}\left(\dfrac{-2}{3}, \dfrac{1}{3}, \dfrac{4}{3}\right)$ Normal vector of

plane is $\dfrac{10}{3}\hat{i} + \dfrac{10}{3}\hat{j} + \dfrac{10}{3}\hat{k}$. Equation of require

plane is $x + y + z = 1$. Hence $(1, -1, 1)$ lies on plane.

18. Correct Response : (b)

Explanation :

Centroid of $\Delta = (2, 2)$

Line passing through intersection of

$$x + 3y - 1 = 0 \text{ and}$$
$$3x - y + 1 = 0, \text{ be given by}$$
$$(x + 3y - 1) + \lambda(3x - y + 1) = 0$$

$\because$ It passes through (2, 2)

$$\Rightarrow \qquad 7 + 5\lambda = 0 \Rightarrow \lambda = -\dfrac{7}{5}$$

$\therefore$ Required line is $8x - 11y + 6 = 0$

$\because (-9, -6)$ satisfies this equation.

19. Correct Response : (1.00)

Explanation :

$$\vec{p} = (a+1)\hat{i} + a\hat{j} + a\hat{k},$$

$$\vec{q} = a\hat{i} + (a+1)\hat{j} + a\hat{k}$$

and $\qquad \vec{r} = a\hat{i} + a\hat{j}(a+1)\hat{k}.$

$\because \vec{p}, \vec{q}, \vec{r}$ are coplanar.

$$\Rightarrow \quad [\vec{p} \ \vec{q} \ \vec{r}] = 0$$

$$\Rightarrow \quad \begin{vmatrix} a+1 & a & a \\ a & a+1 & a \\ a & a & a+1 \end{vmatrix} = 0$$

$$\Rightarrow \quad 3a + 1 = 0 \Rightarrow a = -\frac{1}{3}$$

$$\vec{p} \cdot \vec{q} = -\frac{1}{3}, \ \vec{r} \cdot \vec{q} = -\frac{1}{3}$$

$$|\vec{r}|^2 = |\vec{q}|^2 = \frac{2}{3}$$

$$\therefore \quad 3(\vec{p} \cdot \vec{q})^2 - \lambda[\vec{r} \times \vec{q}]^2 = 0$$

$$\Rightarrow \quad \lambda = \frac{3(\vec{p} \cdot \vec{q})^2}{|\vec{r} \times \vec{q}|^2} = \frac{3(\vec{p} \cdot \vec{q})^2}{|\vec{r}|^2 |\vec{q}|^2 - (\vec{r} \cdot \vec{q})^2} = 1.00$$

20. Correct Response : (3)

Explanation :

If $\lambda = -7$, then planes will be parallel and distance between them will be $\dfrac{3}{\sqrt{633}} \Rightarrow k = 3$. But if $\lambda \neq -7$, then planes will be intersecting and distance between them will be 0.

21. Correct Response : (a)

Explanation :

Plane passing through : (2, 1, 0), (4, 1, 1) and (5, 0, 1)

$$\begin{vmatrix} x-2 & y-1 & z \\ 2 & 0 & 1 \\ 3 & -1 & 1 \end{vmatrix} = 0$$

$$\Rightarrow \quad x + y - 2z = 3$$

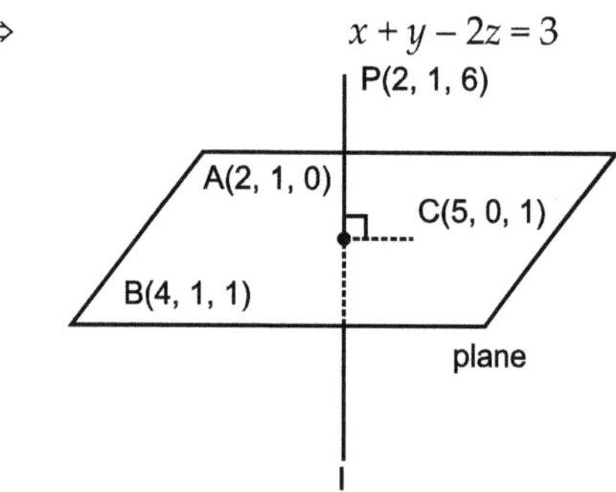

Let I and F are respectively image of foot of perpendicular of point P in the plane.

eq^n of line PI $\dfrac{x-2}{1} = \dfrac{y-1}{1} = \dfrac{z-6}{-2} = \lambda$ (say)

Let I $(\lambda + 2, \lambda + 1, -2\lambda + 6)$

$$\Rightarrow \quad F\left(2 + \frac{\lambda}{2}, 1 + \frac{\lambda}{2}, -\lambda + 6\right)$$

F lies in the plane

$$\Rightarrow 2 + \frac{\lambda}{2} + 1 + \frac{\lambda}{2} + 2l - 12 - 3 = 0$$

$$\Rightarrow \quad \lambda = \lambda$$

$$\Rightarrow \quad = (6, 5, -2)$$

22. Correct response : (c)

Explanation :

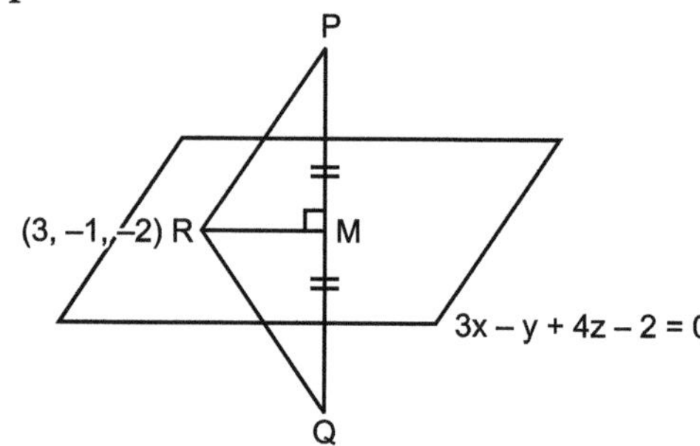

Image of Q(0, − 1, − 3) in plane is

$$\frac{x-0}{3} = \frac{y+1}{-1} = \frac{z+3}{+4} = \frac{-2(1-12)}{(9+1+16)} = 1$$

$$\Rightarrow \quad x = 3, y = -2, z = 1$$

$\Rightarrow$ P(3, − 2, 1), Q(0, − 1, − 3), R(3, − 1, − 2)

$\therefore$ Area of ΔPQR is

$$\frac{1}{2} |\vec{QP} \times \vec{QR}| = \frac{1}{2} \begin{vmatrix} \hat{i} & \hat{j} & \hat{k} \\ 3 & -1 & 4 \\ 3 & 0 & 1 \end{vmatrix}$$

$$= \frac{1}{2} [\hat{i} \, (-1) - \hat{j} \, (3 - 12) + \hat{k} \, (3)]$$

$$= \frac{1}{2} \sqrt{1 + 81 + 9} = \frac{\sqrt{91}}{2}$$

23. Correct Response : (a)

Explanation :

Passing point of the line is (2, 3, − 4) and parallel vector to the line is $6\hat{i} + 3\hat{j} - 4\hat{k}$.

So, the equation of the line is $\dfrac{x-2}{6} = \dfrac{y-3}{3} = \dfrac{z+4}{-4} = \lambda.$

Let the foot of perpendicular from point P(− 1, 2, 6) on the line be Q($6\lambda + 2, 3\lambda + 3, -4\lambda - 4$).

Then, PQ has direction ratios ($6\lambda + 3, 3\lambda + 1, -4\lambda - 10$).

Since PQ is perpendicular to the line therefore,
$6(6\lambda + 3) + 3(3\lambda + 1) - 4(-4\lambda - 10) = 0,$

$\Rightarrow$ Q(− 4, 0, 0)

So, $\quad$ PQ $= \sqrt{9 + 4 + 36}$

$$= 7$$

24. Correct Response: (b)

Explanation:

Equation of the line is

$$\frac{x-1}{2} = \frac{y+1}{-1} = \frac{z}{1} = \lambda.$$

Let the point be Q$(2\lambda + 1, -\lambda - 1, \lambda)$.

Then the foot of the perpendicular is

$$\frac{x - 2(2\lambda+1)}{1} = \frac{y + (\lambda+1)}{1} = \frac{z-\lambda}{1}$$

$$= \frac{-(2\lambda+1-\lambda-1+\lambda-3)}{3}$$

$$\frac{x - 2\lambda - 1}{1} = \frac{y + \lambda + 1}{1}$$

$$= \frac{z-\lambda}{1} = \frac{-(2\lambda-3)}{3}$$

This implies,

$$y = -\lambda - 1 - \frac{(2\lambda-3)}{3}$$

$$= \frac{-3\lambda - 3 - 2\lambda + 3}{3}$$

$$= -\frac{5\lambda}{3}$$

$$z = \lambda - \frac{(2\lambda-3)}{3}$$

$$= \frac{\lambda+3}{3}$$

So, the point P is $\left(\frac{4\lambda+6}{3}, \frac{-5\lambda}{3}, \frac{\lambda+3}{3}\right)$.

It lies on $x - y + z = 3$.

$$\frac{4\lambda+6}{3} - \left(\frac{-5\lambda}{3}\right) + \frac{\lambda+3}{3} = 3$$

$$\Rightarrow \qquad 10\lambda + 9 = 9$$

$$\Rightarrow \qquad \lambda = 0$$

So the point Q is $(2, 0, 1)$.

25. Correct Response : (d)

Explanation :

Denote the planes as

$$P_1 : 2x - y + 2z = -3$$
$$P_2 : 4x - 2y + 4z = -\lambda$$
$$P_3 = 2x - y + 27$$
$$= -\mu$$

Distance between P_1 and P_2 is $\frac{1}{3}$.

$$\Rightarrow \qquad \left|\frac{\frac{\lambda}{2} - 3}{3}\right| = \frac{1}{3}$$

$$\Rightarrow \qquad \frac{\lambda}{2} - 3 = \pm 1$$

$$\Rightarrow \qquad \lambda = 8, 4.$$

Distance between P_1 and P_3 is $\frac{2}{3}$.

$$\Rightarrow \qquad \left|\frac{\mu - 3}{3}\right| = \left|\frac{2}{3}\right|$$

$$\Rightarrow \qquad \mu - 3 = \pm 2$$

$$\Rightarrow \qquad \mu = 5, 1.$$

This gives

$$(\lambda + \mu)_{max} = 8 + 5$$

$$= 13$$

26. Correct Response : (d)

Explanation :

Plane through line of intersection of $x + y + z - 6 = 0$ and $2x + 3y + z + 5 = 0$ is $x + y + z - 6 + \lambda(2x + 3y + z + 5) = 0$

$$\Rightarrow (1 + 2\lambda)x + (1 + 3\lambda)y + (1 + \lambda)z + 5\lambda - 6 = 0$$

Perpendicular to xy plane implies $z = 0$.

So, $1 + \lambda = 0 \Rightarrow \lambda = -1$.

Equation of plane P is $x + 2y + 11 = 0$

Distance of the point $(0, 0, 256)$ from plane is

$$\frac{0+0+11}{\sqrt{1+4}} = \frac{11}{\sqrt{5}}$$

27. Correct Response : (c)

Explanation :

Let $\dfrac{x-1}{2} = \dfrac{y+1}{3} = \dfrac{z-2}{4} = \lambda$

$$\Rightarrow x = 2\lambda + 1, \ y = 3\lambda - 1, \ z = 4\lambda + 2$$

Substitute in $x + 2y + 3z = 15$

$$\Rightarrow 2(\lambda + 1) + 2(3\lambda - 1) + 3(4\lambda + 2) = 15$$

$$\Rightarrow \qquad 2\lambda + 1 + 6\lambda - 2 + 12\lambda + 6 = 15$$

$$\Rightarrow \qquad 20\lambda + 5 = 15$$

$$\Rightarrow \qquad \lambda = \frac{1}{2}$$

Hence, point of intersection is $\left(2, \dfrac{1}{2}, 4\right)$.

Distance from origin is $\sqrt{4 + \dfrac{1}{4} + 16} = \sqrt{\dfrac{81}{4}} = \dfrac{9}{2}$

28. Correct Response : (d)

Explanation :

$ax + by + cz = 1, \ b = -1, \ c = 1$

$$ax - y + z = 1$$

$$\frac{1}{\sqrt{2}} = \cos\frac{\pi}{4}$$

$$= \frac{-1-1}{\sqrt{2}\sqrt{a^2+2}}$$

$$\Rightarrow \qquad a^2 + 2 = 4$$

$$\Rightarrow \qquad a = \sqrt{2}$$

Plane is $-\sqrt{2}x - y + z = 1$

The point $(\sqrt{2}, 1, 4)$ satisfies the plane.

29. Correct Response : (c)

Explanation :

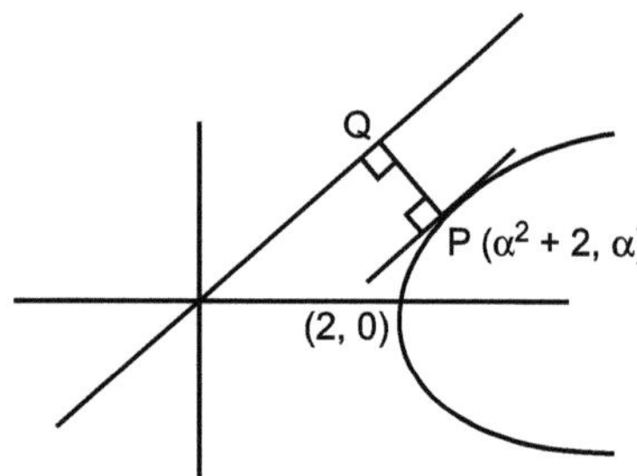

Shortest distance between $y^2 = x - 2$ and $y = x \cdot \dfrac{dy}{dx}$

at point P will be 1.

Differentiating the curve $2yy' = 1$.

This implies

$$y' = \frac{1}{2y}$$

$$= \frac{1}{2\alpha}$$

$$= 1$$

Therefore, $P\left(\dfrac{9}{4}, \dfrac{1}{2}\right)$ and the minimum distance

is

$$PQ = \left| \frac{\begin{vmatrix} \dfrac{9}{4} - \dfrac{1}{2} \end{vmatrix}}{\sqrt{2}} \right|$$

$$= \frac{7}{4\sqrt{2}}$$

30. Correct Response : (c)

Explanation :

$$P_1 + \lambda P_2 = 0$$

$(2x - y - 4) + \lambda(y + 2z - 4) = 0$

It passes through $(1, 1, 0)$

$\Rightarrow \qquad\qquad 1 + \lambda = 0$

$\Rightarrow \qquad\qquad \lambda = -1$

Equation of plane is $x - y - z = 0$.

31. Correct Response : (d)

Explanation :

Let the equation of line be,

$$\frac{x-2}{3} = \frac{y+1}{2} = \frac{z-1}{-1} = \lambda$$

Therefore, the coordinates of point A are $(3\lambda + 2, 2\lambda - 1, -\lambda + 1)$.

Since point A lies on the plane $(2x + 3y - z + 13 = 0)$; therefore,

$2(3\lambda + 2) + 3(2\lambda - 1) - (-\lambda + 1) + 13 = 0$

$$13\lambda + 13 = 0$$

$$\lambda = -1$$

The coordinates of point P are $(-1, -3, 2)$.

The point A also lies on the plane $3x + y + 4z = 16$.

$$3(3\lambda + 2) + (2\lambda - 1) + 4(-\lambda + 1) = 16$$

$$7\lambda = 7$$

$$\lambda = 1$$

The coordinates of point Q are $(5, 1, 0)$.

The value of PQ is,

$$PQ = \sqrt{36 + 16 + 4}$$

$$= \sqrt{56}$$

$$= 2\sqrt{14}$$

32. Correct Response : (d)

Explanation :

The planes bisecting the two given planes are given by,

$$\frac{2x - y + 2z - 4}{3} = \pm \frac{x + 2y + 2z - 2}{3}$$

The lines obtained are $(x - 3y = 2)$ and $3x + y + 4z = 6$.

Among the given points, only the point $(2, -4, 1)$ satisfies the equation $3x + y + 4z = 6$.

33. Correct Response : (c)

Explanation :

The normal vector to the plane is,

$$N = \begin{vmatrix} \hat{i} & \hat{j} & \hat{k} \\ 1 & 2 & -1 \\ -1 & 1 & -2 \end{vmatrix}$$

The equation of the plane is,

$$-3x + 3y + 3z = c$$

The point $(1, 1, 0)$ satisfies the equation of the plane. Therefore,

$$c = 3 + 3 + 0$$

$$= 0$$

The distance of plane $-3x + 3y + 3z = 0$ from point $(2, 1, 4)$ is,

$$D = \left| \frac{-6 + 3 + 12}{\sqrt{27}} \right|$$

$$= \left| \frac{9}{3\sqrt{3}} \right|$$

$$= \sqrt{3} \text{ units}$$

34. Correct Response : (c)

Explanation :

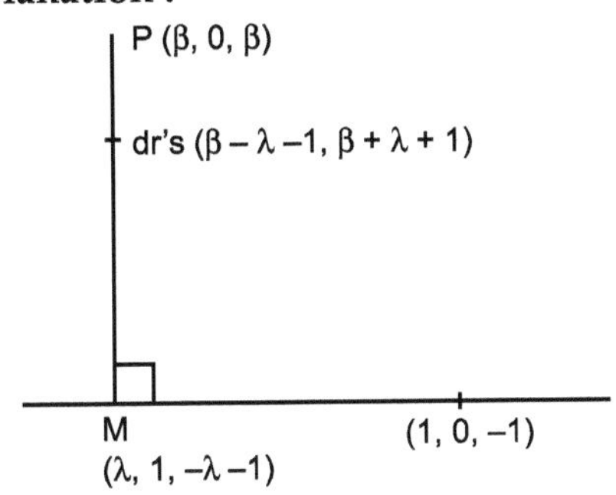

In the figure PM is perpendicular to the line

$$\Rightarrow \quad \beta - \lambda + 0 - \beta - \lambda - 1 = 0$$

$$\Rightarrow \quad \lambda = -\frac{1}{2}$$

So the foot of the perpendicular is M $\left(-\frac{1}{2}, 1, -\frac{3}{2}\right)$.

Given that PM = $\sqrt{\dfrac{3}{2}}$

$$\Rightarrow \quad \left(\beta + \frac{1}{2}\right)^2 + 1 + \left(\beta + \frac{3}{2}\right)^2 = \frac{3}{2}$$

$$\Rightarrow \quad \beta^2 + \beta + \frac{1}{4} + 1 + \beta^2 + 3\beta + \frac{9}{4} = \frac{3}{2}$$

$$\Rightarrow \quad 2\beta^2 + 4\beta + 2 = 0$$

$$\Rightarrow \quad (\beta + 1)^2 = 0$$

$$\Rightarrow \quad \beta = -1$$

35. Correct Response : (a)

Explanation :

Equation of given line is

$$\frac{x+3}{10} = \frac{y-2}{7} = \frac{z}{1} = r \text{ (let)} \qquad ...(i)$$

Coordinates of a point on line (i) is

$$A(10r - 3, -7r + 2, r)$$

Now, let the line joining the points P(2, − 1, 4) and A(10 − r − 3, − 7r + 2, r) is perpendicular to line (i). Then,

$$PA. \ (10\hat{i} - 7\hat{j} + \hat{k}) = 0$$

$$[\because \text{ vector along line (i) is } (10\hat{i} - 7\hat{j} + \hat{k})]$$

$$\Rightarrow [(10r - 5)\hat{i} + (-7r + 3)\hat{j} + (r - 4)\hat{k}] \cdot [10\hat{i} - 7\hat{j} + \hat{k}]$$
$$= 0$$

$$\Rightarrow 10(10r - 5) - 7(3 - 7r) + (r - 4) = 0$$

$$\Rightarrow \quad 100r - 50 - 21 + 49r + r - 4 = 0$$

$$\Rightarrow \quad 150r = 75$$

$$\Rightarrow \quad r = \frac{1}{2}$$

So, the foot of perpendicular is $\left(2, -\frac{3}{2}, \frac{1}{2}\right)$

$$\left[\text{Put } r = \frac{1}{2} \text{ in the coordinates of point A}\right]$$

Now, perpendicular distance of point P(2, − 1, 4) from the line (i) is

$$PA = \sqrt{(2-2)^2 + \left(-\frac{3}{2}+1\right)^2 + \left(\frac{1}{2}-4\right)^2}$$

$$= \sqrt{\frac{1}{4} + \frac{49}{4}}$$

$$= \sqrt{\frac{50}{4}} = \frac{5}{\sqrt{2}}$$

which lies in (3, 4).

36. Correct Response : (a, b, c)

Explanation :

Both the given lines are skew lines.

So the direction ratios of any line perpendicular to these lines are $6\hat{i} + 6\hat{j} - 3\hat{k}$.

The required diagram is shown below.

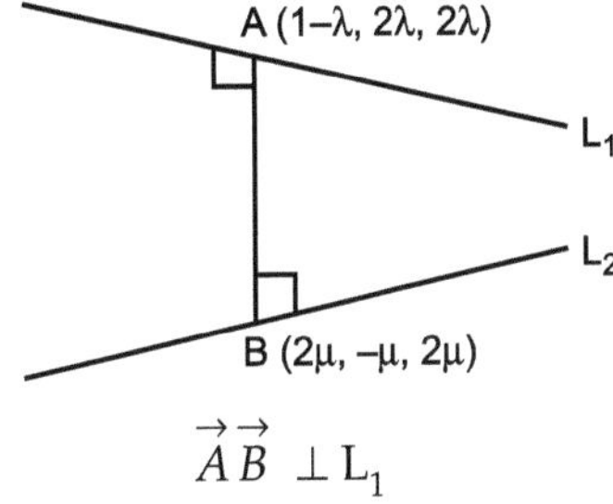

$$\vec{AB} \perp L_1$$

On solving we get

$$\lambda = \frac{1}{9} \text{ and } \mu = \frac{2}{9}$$

So, A$\left(\frac{8}{9}, \frac{2}{9}, \frac{2}{9}\right)$, B$\left(\frac{4}{9}, \frac{-2}{9}, \frac{4}{9}\right)$

The equation of required line is,

$$\vec{r} = \left(\frac{8}{9}\hat{i} + \frac{2}{9}\hat{j} + \frac{2}{9}\hat{k}\right) + \alpha(2\hat{i} + 2\hat{j} + \hat{k}).$$

or $\vec{r} = \dfrac{2}{9}(2\hat{i} - \hat{j} + 2\hat{k}) + t(2\hat{i} + 2\hat{j} - \hat{k})$

37. Correct Response : 0.75

Explanation :

The given equations of the three lines are,

$$\vec{r} = \lambda\hat{i} \qquad \lambda \in R$$

$$\vec{r} = \mu(\hat{i} + \hat{j}) \qquad \mu \in R$$

$$\vec{r} = \nu(\hat{i} + \hat{j} + \hat{k}) \quad \nu \in R$$

Substituting (λ, 0, 0) in $x + y + z = 1$,

$$\lambda + 0 + 0 = 1$$

$$\lambda = 1$$

Therefore, the coordinate of point A of the $\triangle ABC$ is A(1, 0, 0).

Substituting $(\mu, \mu, 0)$ in $x + y + z = 1$,

$$\mu + \mu + 0 = 1$$
$$2\mu = 1$$
$$\mu = \frac{1}{2}$$

Therefore, the coordinate of point B of the $\triangle ABC$ is $B\left(\dfrac{1}{2}, \dfrac{1}{2}, 0\right)$.

Substituting (v, v, v) in $x + y + z = 1$,

$$v + v + v = 1$$
$$3v = 1$$
$$v = \frac{1}{3}$$

Therefore, the coordinate of point C of the $\triangle ABC$ is $C\left(\dfrac{1}{3}, \dfrac{1}{3}, \dfrac{1}{3}\right)$.

Area of the $\triangle ABC$ is $\overrightarrow{AB}$

$$\triangle ABC = \frac{1}{2}\left| \overrightarrow{AC} \times \overrightarrow{AC} \right|$$

$$= \frac{1}{2}\left| \left(\frac{\hat{i} - \hat{j}}{2}\right) \times \left(\frac{2\hat{i} - \hat{j} - \hat{k}}{2}\right) \right|$$

$$= \frac{1}{12}\left| \hat{i} + \hat{j} + \hat{k} \right|$$

$$= \frac{\sqrt{3}}{12}$$

Therefore, $\quad (6\Delta)^2 = 0.75$.

38. Correct Response : (a, c)

Explanation :

The given equations of the three lines are,

$$\overrightarrow{r} = \lambda \hat{i} \qquad \lambda \in R$$

$$\overrightarrow{r} = \hat{k} + \mu \hat{j} \qquad \mu \in R$$

$$\overrightarrow{r} = \hat{i} + \hat{j} + v\hat{k} \qquad v \in R$$

Consider the coordinates as,

$P(\lambda, 0, 0)$, $Q(0, \mu, 1)$ and $R(1, 1, v)$.

Therefore, $\quad \overrightarrow{PQ} = k\overrightarrow{PR}$

$$-\frac{\lambda}{\lambda - 1} = \frac{-\mu}{-1}$$

$$= \frac{-1}{-v}$$

Solve further as,

$$1 + \frac{1}{\lambda - 1} = \mu$$

$$= \frac{1}{v}$$

μ cannot take the value of 1 and 0.

39. Correct Response : (d)

Explanation :

The plane intersect X, Y and Z axes at A, B and C respectively.

The equation of plane parallel to yz-plane is

$$x = a$$

The equation of plane parallel to zx-plane is,

$$y = b$$

The equation of plane parallel to xy-plane is,

$$z = c$$

The coordinates of point A, B and C are $(a, 0, 0)$, $(0, b, 0)$ and $(0, 0, c)$ respectively.

The equation of plane is,

$$\frac{x}{a} + \frac{y}{b} + \frac{z}{c} = 1$$

This plane passes through a fixed point (3, 2, 1). So, this point must satisfy the plane.

$$\frac{3}{a} + \frac{2}{b} + \frac{1}{c} = 1$$

The locus of the point of intersection of three planes is,

$$\frac{3}{x} + \frac{2}{y} + \frac{1}{z} = 1$$

40. Correct Response : (a)

Explanation :

The determinant from the equation of planes $3x + 4y + z - 1 = 0$ and $5x + 8y + 2z + 14 = 0$ is,

$$\begin{vmatrix} \hat{i} & \hat{j} & \hat{k} \\ 3 & 4 & 1 \\ 5 & 8 & 2 \end{vmatrix} = \hat{i}(8 - 8) - \hat{j}(6 - 5) + \hat{k}(24 - 20)$$

$$= (0)\hat{i} + (-1)\hat{j} + (4)\hat{k}$$

The direction of the line by the intersection of two planes is $(0)\hat{i} + (-1)\hat{j} + (4)\hat{k}$.

The angle between the plane $x + y + z = 5$ and the line of intersection of the planes $3x + 4y + z - 1 = 0$ and $5x + 8y + 2z + 14 = 0$ is,

$$\pi = \frac{\pi}{2}$$

$$- \cos^{-1}\left[\frac{(0) + (-1) + (4)}{\sqrt{(1)^2 + (1)^2 + (1)^2}\sqrt{(0)^2 + (-1)^2 + (4)^2}} \right]$$

$$= \frac{\pi}{2} - \cos^{-1}\left(\frac{3}{\sqrt{3}\sqrt{17}}\right)$$

$$= \frac{\pi}{2} - \cos^{-1}\left(\frac{\sqrt{3}}{\sqrt{17}}\right)$$

$$= \sin^{-1}\sqrt{\frac{3}{17}}$$

41. Correct Response : (b)

Explanation :

Equation for the plane,

$$P(x_1, x_2, x_3) = (-2, -2, 2)$$
$$P_1(a_1, a_2, a_3) = (1, -1, 2)$$

and $\qquad P_2(b_1, b_2, b_3) = (1, 1, 1)$

Equation of the plane,

$$\begin{bmatrix} x - x_1 & y - x_2 & z - x_3 \\ x_1 - a_1 & x_2 - a_2 & x_3 - a_3 \\ x_1 - b_1 & x_2 - b_1 & x_3 - b_1 \end{bmatrix} = 0$$

$$\begin{bmatrix} x+2 & y+2 & z-2 \\ -3 & -1 & 0 \\ -3 & -3 & 1 \end{bmatrix} = 0$$

$$-(x+2) + 3(y+2) + 6(z-2) = 0$$
$$x - 3y - 6z + 8 = 0$$

Thus, sum of the intercepts,

$$-\frac{8}{1} + \frac{8}{3} + \frac{8}{6} = -4$$

42. Correct Response : (a)

Explanation :

Consider the given lines as equal to L_1 and L_2 and rearrange.

$$\left. \begin{aligned} L_1 &\equiv \frac{x}{2} = \frac{y}{2} = \frac{z}{1} \\ L_2 &\equiv \frac{x-5}{2} = \frac{y-2}{\left(\frac{p}{7}\right)} = \frac{z-3}{4} \end{aligned} \right\} \quad ...(i)$$

Compare the above expression with the general from of the lines which considered as equal to L_1 and L_2

$$\left. \begin{aligned} L_1 &\equiv \frac{x-x_1}{a_1} = \frac{y-x_2}{b_1} = \frac{z-x_3}{c_1} \\ L_2 &\equiv \frac{x-y_1}{a_2} = \frac{y-y_2}{b_2} = \frac{z-y_3}{c_2} \end{aligned} \right\} \quad ...(2)$$

The formula of angle between both lines L_1 and L_2 is

$$\cos^{-1}\theta = \cos^{-1}\left(\frac{a_1 a_2 + b_1 b_2 + c_1 c_2}{\sqrt{\left(a_1^2 + b_1^2 + c_1^2\right)} \times \sqrt{\left(a_2^2 + b_2^2 + c_2^2\right)}}\right) \quad ...(3)$$

Now, comparing equations (1), (2) and substitute the values in equation (3). Here θ is given $\frac{2}{3}$.

$$\cos^{-1}\left(\frac{2}{3}\right) = \cos^{-1}\left(\frac{4 + \frac{2p}{7} + 4}{\sqrt{(4+4+1)} \times \sqrt{\left(4 + \frac{p}{7} + 16\right)}}\right)$$

$$\frac{2}{3} = \frac{56 + 2p}{3\sqrt{p^2 + 980}}$$

$$\sqrt{p^2 + 980} = p + 28$$

$$p^2 + 980 = p^2 + 56p + 784$$

$$p = \frac{7}{2}$$

43. Correct Response : (d)

Explanation :

The equation of the line normal to the plane $x + y + z = 7$ is $\hat{n} = \hat{i} + \hat{j} + \hat{k}$.

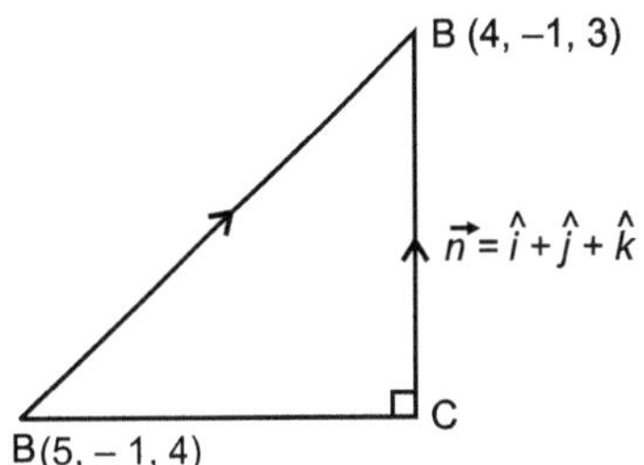

For the line AB,

$$\overrightarrow{AB} = -\hat{i} - \hat{k}$$

$$\left|\overrightarrow{AB}\right| = AB$$

$$= \sqrt{2}$$

For line BC, length of projection of $\overrightarrow{AB}$ is $\vec{n}$ is,

$$|\overrightarrow{AB}.\hat{n}| = \left|(-\hat{i} - \hat{k}) \cdot \frac{(\hat{i} + \hat{j} + \hat{k})}{\sqrt{3}}\right|$$

$$= \frac{2}{\sqrt{3}}$$

Length of projection of the line segment on the plane AC is,

$$AC^2 = AB^2 - BC^2$$

$$= 2 - \frac{4}{3}$$

$$= \frac{2}{3}$$

$$AC = \sqrt{\frac{2}{3}}$$

44. Correct Response : (b)

Explanation :

Let L_1 is parallel to,

$$\begin{vmatrix} \hat{i} & \hat{j} & \hat{k} \\ 2 & -2 & 3 \\ 1 & -1 & 1 \end{vmatrix} = \hat{i}(-2+3) - \hat{j}(2-3) + \hat{k}(-2+2)$$

$$= \hat{i} + \hat{j}$$

Line L_2 is parallel to,

$$\begin{vmatrix} \hat{i} & \hat{j} & \hat{k} \\ 1 & 2 & -1 \\ 3 & -1 & 2 \end{vmatrix} = \hat{i}(4-1) - \hat{j}(2+3) + \hat{k}(-1-6)$$

$$= 3\hat{i} - 5\hat{j} - 7\hat{k}$$

Also, L_2 passes through points $\left(\dfrac{5}{7}, \dfrac{8}{7}, 0\right)$.

Required plane is,

$$\begin{vmatrix} x - \dfrac{5}{7} & y - \dfrac{8}{7} & z \\ 1 & 1 & 0 \\ 3 & -5 & -7 \end{vmatrix} = 0$$

$$7x - 7y + 8z + 3 = 0$$

Distance of the plane from $(0, 0, 0)$ is,

$$D = \left| \frac{3}{\sqrt{7^2 + 7^2 + 8^2}} \right|$$

$$= \frac{1}{3\sqrt{2}}$$

45. Correct Response : (c)

Explanation :

The equation of plane is,

$$2x - 4y + 3z = 2$$

The point $(3, -2, -\lambda)$ is on the plane. Hence,

$$6 + 8 - 3\lambda = 2$$

$$\lambda = 4$$

The equation of line 1 is,

$$\frac{x-3}{1} = \frac{y+2}{-1} = \frac{z+4}{-2} = a$$

Point on this line is,

$$\frac{x-3}{1} = a$$

$$x = a + 3$$

$$\frac{y+2}{-1} = a$$

$$y = -a - 2$$

Similarly, $\dfrac{z+4}{-2} = a$

$$z = -2a - 4$$

The point is $(a+3, -a-2, -2a-4)$.

The equation of line 2 is,

$$\frac{x-1}{12} = \frac{y}{9} = \frac{z}{4} = b$$

Hence, $\dfrac{x-1}{12} = b$

$$x = 12b + 1$$

$$\frac{y}{9} = b$$

$$y = 9b$$

Similarly, $\dfrac{z}{4} = b$

$$z = 4b$$

Point on this line is,

$$(12b + 1, 9b, 4b)$$

Compare points of both lines,

$$a + 3 = 12b + 1$$

$$-a - 2 = 9b$$

$$-2a - 4 = 4b$$

Solve the above equations,

$$a = -2, b = 0$$

Both the lines intersect at point $(12b + 1, 9b, 4b)$,

$$(12 \times 0 + (1), 9\,(0), 4(0)) = (1, 0, 0)$$

Hence, the shortest distance is 0.

46. Correct Response : (a)

Explanation :

Let the plane equation be $ax + by + cz + d = 0$.

The distance of the plane from the origin is 3. Therefore,

$$\frac{d}{\sqrt{a^2 + b^2 + c^2}} = 3$$

That is, $\qquad d^2 = 9(a^2 + b^2 + c^2) \qquad$ ...(1)

Now, the plane intersects x-axis at point $A\left(-\dfrac{d}{a}, 0, 0\right)$; y-axis at point $\left(0, -\dfrac{d}{a}, 0\right)$ and z-axis at point $C\left(0, 0, -\dfrac{d}{c}\right)$.

Let $h = -\dfrac{d}{3a}, \ k = -\dfrac{d}{3b}, \ l = -\dfrac{d}{3c}$

Therefore from Equation (1), we get

$$\frac{1}{9h^2} + \frac{1}{9k^2} + \frac{1}{9l^2} = \frac{1}{9} \Rightarrow \frac{1}{h^2} + \frac{1}{k^2} + \frac{1}{l^2} = 1$$

$$\Rightarrow \frac{1}{x^2} + \frac{1}{y^2} + \frac{1}{z^2} = 1$$

47. Correct Response : (c)

Explanation :

Normal to given lines equation is,

$$n = n_1 \times n_2$$

$$= \begin{vmatrix} \hat{i} & \hat{j} & \hat{k} \\ 6 & 7 & 8 \\ 3 & 5 & 7 \end{vmatrix}$$

$$= 9\hat{i} - 18\hat{j} + 9\hat{k}$$

Simplify the above equation :

$$n = \hat{i} - 2\hat{j} + \hat{k}$$

Plane containing given lines are,

$$1\,(x+1) - 2(y-1) + 1\,(z-3) = 0$$

$$x - 2y + z = 0$$

Normal line from $(1, -2, 1)$,

$$\frac{x_1 - 1}{1/\sqrt{6}} = \frac{y_1 + 2}{-2/\sqrt{6}} = \frac{z_1 - 1}{1/\sqrt{6}} = k \quad ...(1)$$

This point lies on the plane. Substitute (x_1, y_1, z_1) in terms of k in the plane equation.

$$k = -\sqrt{6}$$

Substitute the value of k in equation (1), find the value of x_1, x_2 and x_3.

$$\underbrace{\frac{x_1 - 1}{1/\sqrt{6}}}_{\text{I}} = \underbrace{\frac{y_1 + 2}{-2/\sqrt{6}}}_{\text{II}} = \underbrace{\frac{z_1 - 1}{1/\sqrt{6}}}_{\text{III}} = \underbrace{\frac{-\sqrt{6}}{\text{IV}}}_{}$$

Consider I and IV,

$$x_1 = 0$$

Consider II and IV,

$$y_1 = 0$$

Consider III and IV,

$$z_1 = 0$$

Hence, the coordinates is,

$$(x_1, y_1, z_1) = (0, 0, 0).$$

48. Correct Response : (a)

Explanation :

The plane passing through the point $(1, -1, -1)$ is

$$a(x-1) + b\,(y+1) + c\,(z+1) = 0$$

The plane is perpendicular to the given lines,

$$a - 2b + 3c = 0$$

$$2a - b - c = 0 \qquad [\because\, 'a : b : c = 5 : 7 : 3]$$

The equation of the plane becomes,

$$5(x-1) + 7(y+1) + 3\,(z+1) = 0$$

$$5x + 7y + 3z + 5 = 0$$

The distance of the point $(1, 3, -7)$ from the plane is,

$$D = \frac{5(1) + 7(3) + 3(-7) + 5}{\sqrt{5^2 + 7^2 + 3^2}}$$

$$= \frac{10}{\sqrt{83}}$$

49. Correct Response : (a)

Explanation :

The equation of the line PQ is,

$$\frac{x-1}{1} = \frac{y+2}{4} = \frac{z-3}{5} = \lambda$$

$$x = \lambda + 1$$

$$y = 4\lambda - 2$$

$$z = 5\lambda + 3$$

The line on the plane is shown in the figure below. The point M lies on the line as well on the plane, so the equation is,

$$2x + 3y - 4z + 22 = 0$$

$$2(\lambda + 1) + 3\,(4\lambda - 2) - 4(5\lambda + 3) + 22 = 0$$

$$\lambda = 1$$

For the point Q the value of $\lambda = 2$. The distance of the point P from Q.

$$PQ = 2d$$

$$= 2\sqrt{1^2 + 4^2 + 5^2}$$

$$= 2\sqrt{42}$$

50. Correct Response : (c)

Explanation :

The equation of line of intersection is given by :

$$n = n_1 \times n_2$$

$$= \begin{vmatrix} \hat{i} & \hat{j} & \hat{k} \\ 3 & -1 & 1 \\ 1 & 4 & -2 \end{vmatrix}$$

$$= 2\hat{i} - 7\hat{j} - 13\hat{k}$$

Now, the equation is given as :

$$3x - y + z = 1$$

$$x + 4y - 2z = 2$$

But $z = 0$ hence,

$$x = \frac{6}{13},\, y = \frac{5}{13}$$

Hence, the equation of line is given as :

$$\frac{x - \dfrac{6}{13}}{2} = \frac{y - \dfrac{5}{13}}{-7} = \frac{z}{-13}$$

51. Correct Response : (b)

Explanation :

The triangle ABC with vertices is shown below,

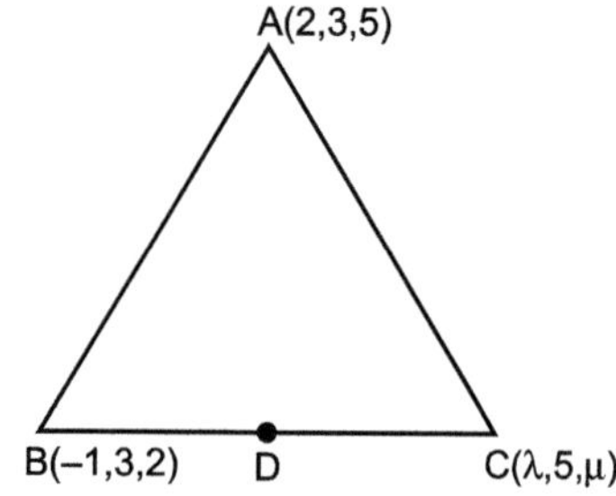

The coordinates of point D is,

$$D \equiv \left(\frac{-1+\lambda}{2}, 4, \frac{2+\mu}{2} \right)$$

The direction cosine of median AD is,

$$AD \equiv \left(\frac{-1+\lambda}{2} - 2, 4 - 3, \frac{2+\mu}{2} - 5 \right)$$

The vector AD is written as,

$$\overrightarrow{AD} = \frac{\lambda-5}{2}\hat{i} + \hat{j} + \frac{\mu-8}{2}\hat{k}$$

From the above expression,

$$\frac{\left(\frac{\lambda-5}{2}\right)}{\sqrt{\left(\frac{\lambda-5}{2}\right)^2 + 1^2 + \left(\frac{\mu-8}{2}\right)^2}}$$

$$= \frac{1}{\sqrt{\left(\frac{\lambda-5}{2}\right)^2 + 1^2 + \left(\frac{\mu-8}{2}\right)^2}} = \frac{\left(\frac{\mu-8}{2}\right)}{\sqrt{\left(\frac{\lambda-5}{2}\right)^2 + 1^2 + \left(\frac{\mu-8}{2}\right)^2}}$$

$$\overrightarrow{AD}\cdot\hat{i} = \overrightarrow{AD}\cdot\hat{j} = \overrightarrow{AD}\cdot\hat{k}$$

From the above expression, the value of λ is 7 and the value of μ is 10.

Thus, the value of given expression is,

$$\lambda^3 + \mu^3 + 5 = 7^3 + 10^3 + 5$$
$$= 1348$$

52. Correct Response : (d)

Explanation :

The given equation of line is,

$$\frac{x-1}{1} = \frac{y-2}{2} = \frac{z-3}{\lambda^2}$$

$$\frac{x-3}{1} = \frac{y-2}{\lambda^2} = \frac{z-1}{2}$$

The given two lines are coplanar. Hence,

$$\begin{vmatrix} 1 & 2 & \lambda^2 \\ 1 & \lambda^2 & 2 \\ 3-1 & 2-2 & 1-(-3) \end{vmatrix} = 0$$

$$4\lambda^2 - 2(0) + \lambda^2(-2\lambda^2) = 0$$

$$2\lambda^2(2-\lambda^2) = 0$$
$$\lambda = 0, \pm\sqrt{2}$$

Thus, there are three values of λ.

53. Correct Response : (c)

Explanation :

Given that the equation of lines are,

$$\frac{x}{2} = \frac{y}{2} = \frac{z}{1}$$

and

$$\frac{x+2}{-1} = \frac{y-4}{8} = \frac{z-5}{4}$$

Shortest distance d between the lines is given by,

$$d = \left| \frac{\begin{vmatrix} x_2-x_1 & y_2-y_1 & z_2-z_1 \\ a_1 & b_1 & c_1 \\ a_2 & b_2 & c_2 \end{vmatrix}}{\sqrt{(a_1b_2-a_2b_1)^2 + (b_1c_2-b_2c_1)^2 + (c_1a_2-c_2a_1)^2}} \right|$$

Substitute the value in the above expression,

$$d = \left| \frac{\begin{vmatrix} -2-0 & 4-0 & 5-0 \\ 2 & 2 & 1 \\ -1 & 8 & 4 \end{vmatrix}}{\sqrt{(16-(-2))^2 + (8-8)^2 + (-1-8)^2}} \right|$$

$$= \left| \frac{-2(8-8) - 4(8+1) + 5(16+2)}{\sqrt{324+81}} \right|$$

$$= 2.7$$

Hence, this value lies in (2, 3].

54. Correct Response : (a)

Explanation :

The given equation of planes are,

$$x - y + 2z = 3$$

and

$$2x - 2y + z + 12 = 0$$

and it passes through (1, 2, 2) is,

$$\begin{vmatrix} x-1 & y-2 & z-2 \\ 1 & -1 & 2 \\ 2 & -2 & 1 \end{vmatrix} = 0$$

Solve the matrices,

$$\Rightarrow (x-1)(-1+4) - (y-2)(1-4) + (z-2)(-2+2) = 0$$

$$\Rightarrow 3(x-1) + 3(y-2) = 0$$

$$x + y = 3 \quad \text{...(1)}$$

Then the distance of plane $x + y - 3 = 0$ from $(1, -2, 4)$ is,

$$d_{(1, -2, 4)} = \left| \frac{x+y-3}{\sqrt{(1)^2 + (1)^2}} \right|$$

$$d_{(1, -2, 4)} = \left| \frac{1-2-3}{\sqrt{(1)^2 + (1)^2}} \right|$$

$$= 2\sqrt{2}$$

55. Correct Response : (d)

Explanation :

The equation of the given line is,
$$\frac{x-3}{2} = \frac{y+2}{-1} = \frac{z+4}{3}$$

The given line lies on plane $lx + my - z = 9$.

So,

For the $x = 2$, $y = -1$ and $z = 3$,
$$2l - m - 3 = 0 \qquad \qquad ...(i)$$

The given line is perpendicular to normal of the plane.

Also point $(3, -2, -4)$ lies in plane.

Therefore,
$$3l - 2m - 5 = 0 \qquad \qquad ...(ii)$$

From equation (i) and (ii),
$$l = 1$$
$$m = -1$$

Hence,
$$l^2 + m^2 = 2$$

56. Correct Response : (b)

Explanation :

The equation of the line is,
$$x + y + 2z - 3 = 0 = 2x + 3y + 4z - 4$$

and the equation of Z-axis is,
$$\frac{x}{0} = \frac{y}{0} = \frac{z}{1}$$

The equation of the given line is,

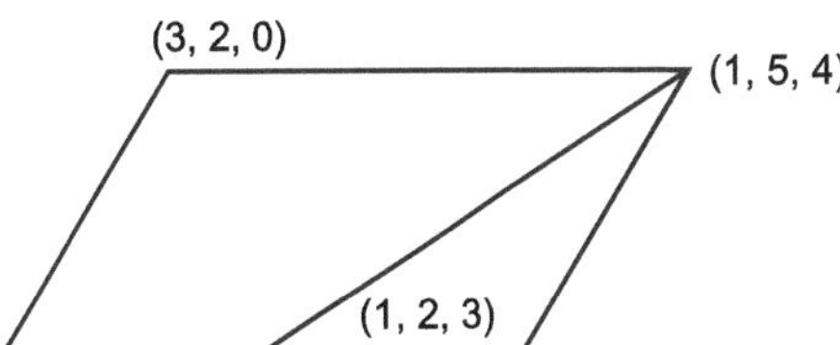

Hence, the shortest distance between the Z-axis and the given line is,
$$\text{Shortest distance} = \left| \frac{(5i - 2i).2j}{2} \right|$$
$$= 2$$

57. Correct Response : (d)

Explanation :

Consider the Cartesian equation :
$$\frac{x-2}{3} = \frac{y+1}{4} = \frac{z-2}{12} = k$$

From above expression, the point of intersection is,
$$P(3k + 2, 4k - 1, 12k + 2)$$

It lies on the given plane
$$3k + 2 - 4k + 1 + 12k + 2 = 16$$
$$11k = 11$$
$$k = 1$$

The points becomes,
$$P(5, 3, 14)$$

Hence, the distance between points is,
$$d = \sqrt{(5-1)^2 + (3-0)^2 + (14-2)^2}$$
$$= \sqrt{4^2 + 3^2 + 12^2}$$
$$= \sqrt{169}$$
$$= 13$$

58. Correct Response : (c)

Explanation :

The equation of the real plane is,
$$2x - 5y + z - 3 + k(x + y + 4z - 5) = 0$$
$$x(2 + k) + y(k - 5) + z(4k + 1) - 3 - 5k = 0$$

The above equation gives the relation,
$$\frac{k+2}{1} = \frac{k-5}{3} = \frac{4k+1}{6} = -3 - 5k$$

Equating first two terms,
$$3k + 6 = k - 5$$
$$k = -\frac{11}{2}$$

The equation of the plane is,
$$-\frac{7}{2}x - \frac{21}{2}y - 21z + \frac{49}{2} = 0$$
$$7x + 21y + 42z - 49 = 0$$
$$x + 3y + 6z = 7$$

59. Correct Response : (b)

Explanation :

The plane which contains given point $(3, 2, 0)$ and line $\dfrac{x-1}{1} = \dfrac{y-2}{5} = \dfrac{z-3}{4}$,

The equation of the plane passing through the three points is,
$$15x - 11y + 10z = 23$$

Hence, the plane contains the point is,
$$P(0, 7, 10)$$

60. Correct Response : (b)

Explanation :

The first equation is,
$$x = ay + b$$
$$y = \frac{x-b}{a}$$

The second equation is,
$$z = cy + d$$
$$y = \frac{z-d}{c}$$

Equate the both equations,

$$\frac{x-b}{a} = y = \frac{z-d}{c}$$

$$\frac{x-b}{a} - 1 = y - 1 = \frac{z-d}{c} - 1$$

$$\frac{x-b-a}{a} = \frac{y-1}{1} = \frac{z-d-c}{c}$$

61. Correct Response : (c)

Explanation :

The image of the line is given as,

$$\frac{x-1}{3} = \frac{y-3}{1} = \frac{z-4}{-5}$$

add equation of the plane is,

$$2x - y + z + 3 = 0$$

The diagram is shown as,

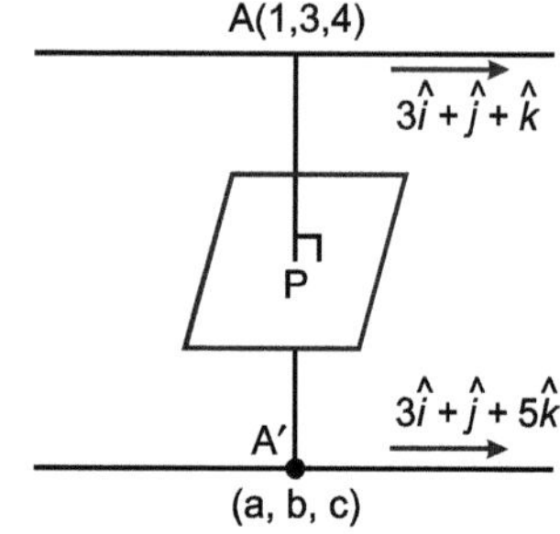

Consider the above figure,

For point A,

$$\frac{a-1}{2} = \frac{b-3}{-1} = \frac{c-4}{1} = \lambda$$

$$a = 2\lambda + 1$$

$$b = 3 - 1$$

$$c = 4 + 1$$

Therefore, point P is,

$$\left(\lambda + 1, 3 - \frac{\lambda}{2}, 4 + \frac{\lambda}{2} \right)$$

For given plane,

$$2(\lambda + 1) - \left(3 - \frac{\lambda}{2} \right) + \left(4 + \frac{\lambda}{2} \right) + 3 = 0$$

$$2\lambda + 2 - 3 + \frac{\lambda}{2} + 4 + \frac{\lambda}{2} + 3 = 0$$

$$3\lambda + 6 = 0$$

$$\lambda = -2$$

Now, value of $a = -3, b = 5, c = 2$

Hence, the equation of the line is,

$$\frac{x+3}{3} = \frac{y-5}{1} = \frac{z-2}{-5}$$

62. Correct Response : (c)

Explanation :

The distance between the two lines is,

$$\left| \frac{d-1}{\sqrt{4^2 + 2^2 + 4^2}} \right| = 7$$

$$\left| \frac{d-1}{6} \right| = 7$$

$$d - 1 = \pm 42$$

$$d = \pm 43 \text{ and } - 41$$

63. Correct Response : (c)

Explanation :

The given equation of the planes is,

$$\frac{x-1}{3} = \frac{y-2}{1} = \frac{z-3}{2} = \alpha$$

$$\frac{x-3}{1} = \frac{y-1}{2} = \frac{z-2}{3} = \beta$$

Solve the above equation to find the point of intersection *i.e.* (4, 3, 5).

Consider a plane with distances l, m, n as distances from the origin d is,

$$lx + my + nz = d$$

Point (4, 3, 5) joining with origin is,

$$\left(\frac{4}{\sqrt{50}}, \frac{3}{\sqrt{50}}, \frac{5}{\sqrt{50}} \right)$$

Hence, the equation of plane is,

$$\frac{4}{\sqrt{50}} x + \frac{3}{\sqrt{50}} y + \frac{5}{\sqrt{50}} z = \sqrt{50}$$

$$4x + 3y + 5z = 50$$

64. Correct Response : (c)

Explanation :

The given angle θ which makes by the plane in the Three-dimensional space is,

$$0 < \theta \le \frac{\pi}{2}$$

The condition for minimum value of angle θ is :

- If the line lies on x, y plane, it makes angle of 45°.

The condition for maximum value of angle θ is :

- If line is at Z - axis, it makes an angle of 90°.

Hence, the required interval is,

$$\frac{\pi}{4} \le \theta \le \frac{\pi}{2}$$

65. Correct Response : (b)

Explanation :

Consider the diagram :

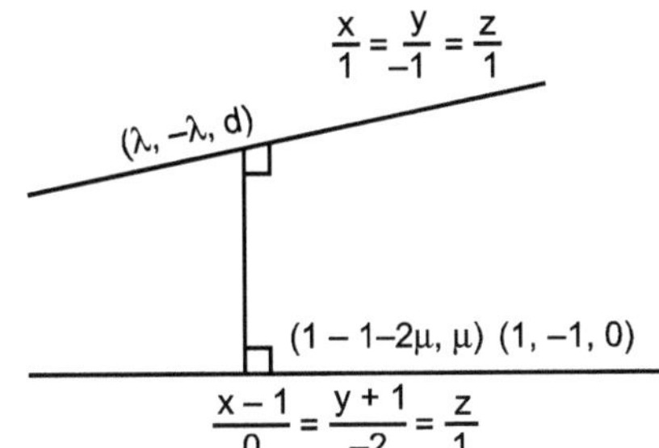

Consider the lines,

$$\frac{x}{1} = \frac{y}{-1} = \frac{z}{1} = \lambda \qquad \text{...(1)}$$

and $$\frac{x-1}{0} = \frac{y+1}{-2} = \frac{z+1}{1} = \mu \qquad \text{...(2)}$$

Here, from the line (1),

$$x = 1$$
$$y = -\lambda$$
$$z = \lambda$$

and, similarly use the equation (2),

$$x = 1$$
$$y = -2\mu - 1$$
$$z = \mu - 1$$

Consider from the above figure,

$$\frac{1-\lambda}{1} = \frac{-1-2\mu+\lambda}{-1} = \frac{\mu-\lambda}{-2}$$

$$-2 = 3\lambda + \mu$$
$$-1 + \lambda = -1 - 2\mu + 1$$

Hence, $$\mu = 0$$

$$\lambda = -\frac{2}{3}$$

Now, the equation will be,

$$\frac{x-1}{1} = \frac{y+1}{-1} = \frac{z}{-2}$$

66. Correct Response : (c)

Explanation :

The expression for the angle between the line and plane is,

$$\sin\theta = \frac{|A.u_1 + B.u_2 + C.u_3|}{\sqrt{A^2 + B^2 + C^2}\sqrt{u_1^2 + u_2^2 + u_3^2}}$$

$$\sin\frac{\pi}{6} = \frac{1-1+\sqrt{\lambda}}{\sqrt{\frac{1}{4}+1+1}\sqrt{4+1+\lambda}}$$

$$\frac{1}{2} = \frac{\sqrt{\lambda}}{\sqrt{\frac{9}{4}}\sqrt{5+\lambda}}$$

$$\lambda = \frac{45}{7}$$

67. Correct Response : (c)

Explanation :

The median of the point B and C is given by,

$$D \equiv \left(\frac{\lambda-1}{2}, 4, \frac{\mu+2}{2}\right)$$

The direction ratio of the point A (2, 3, 5) and point D.

$$AD = \left(\frac{\lambda-5}{2}, 1, \frac{\mu-8}{2}\right)$$

From the result of the above expression,

$$\frac{\lambda-5}{2} = 1$$

$$\lambda = 7$$

$$\frac{\mu-8}{2} = 1$$

$$\mu = 10$$

The relation between the constant λ and μ,

$$\frac{\lambda}{7} = \frac{\mu}{10}$$

$$10\lambda - 7\mu = 0$$

68. Correct Response : (b)

Explanation :

The normal vector passing through the plane and line,

$$\overline{N} = \begin{vmatrix} \hat{i} & \hat{j} & \hat{k} \\ 1 & 2 & 3 \\ 1 & 1 & 4 \end{vmatrix}$$

$$= 5\hat{i} - \hat{j} - \hat{k}$$

The equation of plane at the point (1, 2, 3),

$$5(x-1) - 1(y-2) - 1(z-3) = 0$$
$$5x - y - z = 0$$

Hence, the line passes through the points (1, 0, 5).

69. Correct Response : (a)

Explanation :

The distance of point P from plane $x + 2y - 2z = \alpha$ is,

$$\left|\frac{1-4-2-\alpha}{3}\right| = 5$$

$$\alpha = 10$$

The foot perpendicular $f(x, y, z)$ from the point P to the plane $x + 2y - 2z = \alpha$ is,

$$\frac{x-1}{1} = \frac{y+2}{2} = \frac{z-1}{-2} = \frac{5}{3}$$

Solve the above equation for x, y and z to get the solution as $x = \dfrac{8}{3}$, $y = \dfrac{4}{3}$ and $z = -\dfrac{7}{3}$.

Thus, the foot of the perpendicular is,

$$f(x, y, z) = f\left(\frac{8}{3}, \frac{4}{3}, -\frac{7}{3}\right)$$

70. Correct Response :

(a)- (t)

(b)- (p), (r)

(c)- either (q) or (q), (s)

(d)- (r)

Explanation :

(a) Let the equation of line passing through origin is,

$$\frac{x}{a} = \frac{y}{b} = \frac{z}{c}$$

The equation of plane from line $\dfrac{x-2}{1} = \dfrac{y-1}{-2}$

$$= \frac{z+1}{1} \text{ and } \frac{x}{a} = \frac{y}{b} = \frac{z}{c} \text{ is,}$$

$$\begin{vmatrix} 2 & 1 & -1 \\ 1 & -2 & 1 \\ a & b & c \end{vmatrix} = 0$$

$$a + 3b + 3c = 0 \qquad \text{...(1)}$$

The equation of plane from line

$$\frac{x-\dfrac{8}{3}}{2} = \frac{y+3}{-1} = \frac{z-1}{1} \text{ and } \frac{x}{a} = \frac{y}{b} = \frac{z}{c} \text{ is,}$$

$$\begin{vmatrix} \dfrac{8}{3} & -3 & 1 \\ 2 & -1 & 1 \\ a & b & c \end{vmatrix} = 0$$

$$3a + b - 5c = 0 \qquad \text{...(2)}$$

From equations (1) and (2),

$$\frac{a}{-20} = \frac{b}{20} = \frac{c}{-8}$$

$$\frac{a}{5} = \frac{b}{-5} = \frac{c}{4}$$

The equation of line is,

$$\frac{x}{5} = \frac{y}{-5} = \frac{z}{4} \qquad \text{...(3)}$$

The point on above equation is $(5\lambda, -5\lambda, 4\lambda)$, the point on first given line is $(2+k_1, 1-2k_1, -1+k_1)$ and the point on second given line is $\left(\dfrac{8}{3}+2k_2, -3-k_2, 1+k_2\right)$.

Solve the above points to get the point P as $(5, -5, 2)$ and point Q as $\left(\dfrac{10}{3}, -\dfrac{10}{3}, \dfrac{4}{3}\right)$.

The length of PQ is,

$$PQ = \sqrt{\left(\frac{5}{3}\right)^2 + \left(\frac{5}{3}\right)^2 + \left(\frac{2}{3}\right)^2}$$

$$d = \frac{\sqrt{54}}{3}$$

$$d^2 = \frac{54}{9}$$

$$= 6$$

Thus, the correct option for (a) is (t).

(b) The given expression is,

$$\tan^{-1}(x+3) - \tan^{-1}(x-3) = \sin^{-1}\left(\frac{3}{5}\right)$$

$$\tan^{-1}\frac{(x+3)-(x-3)}{1+(x^2-9)} = \tan^{-1}\left(\frac{3}{4}\right)$$

$$x^2 - 8 = 8$$

$$x = \pm 4$$

Thus, the correct options for (b) are (p) and (r).

(c) The given expression is,

$$\vec{a} = \mu\vec{b} + 4\vec{c}$$

$$\mu(|\vec{b}|) = -4\vec{a}\cdot\vec{c}$$

The solution of expression is,

$$(\vec{b} - \vec{a})\cdot(\vec{b} + \vec{c}) = 0$$

$$|\vec{b}|^2 = 4\vec{a}\cdot\vec{c}$$

Again, solve the given expression as,

$$2|\vec{b} + \vec{c}| = |\vec{b} - \vec{a}|$$

Solve the above expression and eliminate $\vec{b}\cdot\vec{c}$

and $|\vec{a}|^2$ to get the expression as,

$$\left(2\mu^2 - 10\mu\right)|\vec{b}|^2 = 0$$

$$\mu = 0, 5$$

Thus, the correct options for (c) are (*q*) and (*s*).

(d) The value of given expression is,

$$I = \frac{2}{\pi}\int_{-\pi}^{\pi} f(x)\,dx$$

$$= \frac{2}{\pi}\int_{-\pi}^{\pi} \frac{\sin 9(x/2)}{\sin(x/2)}\,dx$$

$$= \frac{2}{\pi} \times 2\int_{0}^{\pi} \frac{\sin 9(x/2)}{\sin(x/2)}\,dx$$

Put $\dfrac{x}{2} = \theta$ in the above expression,

$$I = \frac{8}{\pi}\int_{0}^{\pi/2} \frac{\sin 9\theta}{\sin \theta}\,dx$$

$$= \frac{8}{\pi}$$

$$\int_{0}^{\pi/2} \frac{(\sin 9\theta - \sin 7\theta)}{\sin \theta} + \frac{(\sin 7\theta - \sin 5\theta)}{\sin \theta} + \frac{(\sin 5\theta - \sin 3\theta)}{\sin \theta}$$

$$+ \frac{(\sin 3\theta - \sin \theta)}{\sin \theta} + \frac{\sin \theta}{\sin \theta}\,d\theta$$

$$= \frac{16}{\pi}\int_{0}^{\pi/2} (\cos 8\theta + \cos 6\theta + \cos 4\theta + \cos 2\theta + 1)\,d\theta$$

$$+ \frac{16}{\pi}\int_{0}^{\pi/2} d\theta$$

$$= 4$$

Thus, the correct option for (d) is (*r*).

71. **Correct Response :** (c)

Explanation :

The equation of plane passing through point $(-1, -2, -1)$ is,

$$-1(x+1) - 7(y+2) + 5(z+1) = 0$$
$$-x - 7y + 5z - 10 = 0$$

The distance of point $(1, 1, 1)$ from plane $-x - 7y + 5z - 10 = 0$ is,

$$\left|\frac{-1 - 7 + 5 - 10}{\sqrt{1^2 + 7^2 + 5^2}}\right| = \frac{13}{\sqrt{75}}$$

72. **Correct Response :** (a)-(r), (b)-(q), (c)-(p), (d)-(s)

Explanation :

Δ can be calculated as,

$$\Delta = \begin{vmatrix} a & b & c \\ b & c & a \\ c & a & b \end{vmatrix}$$

$$= -(a^3 + b^3 + c^3 - 3abc)$$
$$= -(a + b + c)(a^2 + b^2 + c^2 - ab - bc - ca)$$
$$= -\frac{1}{2}(a+b+c)\left[(a-b)^2 + (b-c)^2 + (c-a)^2\right]$$

(a)

It is given that

$a + b + c \neq 0$ and $a^2 + b^2 + c^2 = ab + bc + ca$. So,

$$\Delta = 0 \text{ and } a = b = c \neq 0$$

Thus, the given equations represent identical planes.

(b)

It is given that $a + b + c = 0$ and $a^2 + b^2 + c^2 \neq ab + bc + ca$. So,

$$\Delta = 0$$

The given equations have infinitely many solutions. So, $x = y = z$.

(c)

It is given that $a + b + c \neq 0$ and $a^2 + b^2 + c^2 \neq ab + bc + ca$. So,

$$\Delta \neq 0$$

Thus, the given equations represents planes that meet at only one point.

(d)

It is given that $a + b + c = 0$ and $a^2 + b^2 + c^2 = ab + bc + ca$. So,

$$a = b = c = 0$$

Thus, the given equations represent the whole of three dimensional space.

73. **Correct Response :** (b)

Explanation :

Let, a quadrilateral be *ABCD*. The area of quadrilateral is 18.

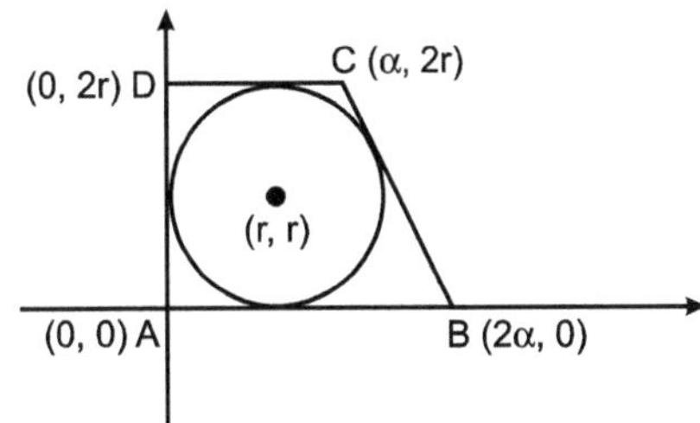

The area of quadrilateral is,

$$18 = \frac{1}{2}(2\alpha + \alpha)(2r)$$

$$18 = (3\alpha)r$$

$$\alpha r = 6$$

The line *BC* is tangent to the circle. The equation of the tangent of the circle $(x - r)^2 + (y - r)^2 = r^2$ is,

$$y = -\frac{2r}{\alpha}(x - 2\alpha)$$

So, $2\alpha = 3r$ and $\alpha r = 6$.

$$\frac{3}{2} r \cdot r = 6$$

$$r^2 = 4$$

$$r = 2$$

Thus, the radius of circle is 2.

74. Correct Response : (d)

Explanation :

The equation of plane passing through $(1, -2, 1)$ is,

$$a(x-1) + b(y+2) + c(z-1) = 0 \qquad ...(1)$$

Above equation of plane is parallel to planes $2a - 2b + c = 0$ and $a - b + 2c = 0$.

So,

$$\frac{a}{1} = \frac{b}{1} = \frac{c}{0}$$

Substitute values in equation (1). The equation of plane is,

$$x + y + 1 = 0$$

So, the distance of plane from the point $(1, 2, 1)$ is,

$$D = \frac{1+2+1}{\sqrt{1^2 + 1^2}}$$

$$= 2\sqrt{2}$$

75. Correct Response : (d)

Explanation :

Let, a plane be $\dfrac{x}{a} + \dfrac{y}{b} + \dfrac{z}{c} = 1$. It is given that perpendicular distance is 1.

$$\frac{1}{a^2} + \frac{1}{b^2} + \frac{1}{c^2} = 1$$

The plane cuts coordinate axis at point $(a, 0, 0)$, $(0, b, 0)$ and $(0, 0, c)$. So, the centroid of triangle is $\left(\dfrac{a}{3}, \dfrac{b}{3}, \dfrac{c}{3}\right)$.

Substitute values of x, y and z in $\dfrac{1}{x^2} + \dfrac{1}{y^2} + \dfrac{1}{z^2} = k$.

$$k = \frac{9}{a^2} + \frac{9}{b^2} + \frac{9}{c^2}$$

$$= 9\left(\frac{1}{a^2} + \frac{1}{b^2} + \frac{1}{c^2}\right)$$

$$= 9$$

Therefore, value of k is 9.

76. Correct Response : $(62x + 29y + 19z - 105 = 0)$

Explanation :

The equation of plane is,

$$(2x - y + z - 3) + \lambda(3x + y + z - 5) = 0$$

$$(3\lambda + 2)x + (\lambda - 1)y + (\lambda + 1)z - 5\lambda - 3 = 0$$

Now, distance of plane from point $(2, 1 - 1)$ is,

$$\left|\frac{6\lambda + 4 + \lambda - 1 - \lambda - 5\lambda - 3}{\sqrt{(3\lambda + 2)^2 + (\lambda - 1)^2 + (\lambda + 1)^2}}\right| = \frac{1}{\sqrt{6}}$$

$$6(\lambda - 1)^2 = 11\lambda^2 + 12\lambda + 6$$

$$\lambda = 0, -\frac{24}{5}$$

The equation of plane for $\lambda = 0$ is,

$$2x - y + z - 3 = 0$$

The equation of plane for $\lambda = -\dfrac{24}{5}$ is,

$$62x + 29y + 19z - 105 = 0$$

77. Correct Response : (b)

Explanation :

Consider equation of first line.

$$\frac{x-1}{2} = \frac{y+1}{3} = \frac{z-1}{4} = \lambda$$

$$x = 2\lambda + 1, \ y = 3\lambda - 1, \ z = 4\lambda + 1$$

Consider equation of second line,

$$\frac{x-3}{1} = \frac{y-k}{2} = \frac{z}{1} = \mu$$

$$x = \mu + 3, \ y = 2\mu + k, \ z = \mu$$

The given lines intersect, so their coordinates are same. Equate the coordinates and solve.

$$\lambda = -\frac{3}{2} \text{ and } \mu = -5$$

The value of k is,

$$k = 3\lambda - 2\mu - 1$$

$$= 3\left(-\frac{3}{2}\right) - 2(-5) - 1$$

$$= \frac{9}{2}$$

78. Explanation :

Let, $ax + by + cz + d = 0$ be the equation of plane, h be the height of parallelopiped and (α, β, γ) be coordinates of point A''.

$$\frac{|a\alpha + b\beta + c\gamma + d|}{\sqrt{a^2 + b^2 + c^2}} = 0.9\,h$$

$$a\alpha + b\beta + c\gamma + d = \pm 0.9h\sqrt{a^2 + b^2 + c^2}$$

Therefore, locus of A'' is plane parallel to ABCD.

79. Correct Response : $\dfrac{9}{2}$ cubic units

Explanation :

Let, direction ratios be (l, m, n).

The equation of line with direction ratios $(1, 0, -1)$ is,

$$1 - n = 0$$

The equation of line with direction ratios $(-1, 1, 0)$ is,

$$-1 + m = 0$$

So, $l = m = n$.

The equation of plane containing point $(1, 1, 1)$ is,

$$\frac{x}{3} + \frac{y}{3} + \frac{z}{3} = 1$$

The coordinates axes are A $(3, 0, 0)$, B $(0, 3, 0)$, and C $(0, 0, 3)$. The volume of tetrahedron OABC is,

$$V = \frac{1}{6} \begin{vmatrix} 3 & 0 & 0 \\ 0 & 3 & 0 \\ 0 & 0 & 3 \end{vmatrix}$$

$$= \frac{27}{6}$$

$$= \frac{9}{2}$$

Therefore, the required area is $\dfrac{9}{2}$ cubic units.

80. Correct Response : (a)

Explanation :

The point $(4, 2, k)$ lies on the plane $2x - 4y + z = 7$. So,

$$2(4) - 4(2) + (k) = 7$$
$$k = 7 / - 8 + 8$$
$$k = 7$$

Vector Algebra

❓ QUESTIONS

1. If the volume of a parallelopiped, whose coterminus edges are given by the vectors

$$\vec{a} = \hat{i} + \hat{j} + n\hat{k}, \ \vec{b} = 2\hat{i} + 4\hat{j} - n\hat{k}$$

and $\vec{c} = \hat{i} + n\hat{j} + 3\hat{k}$

$(n \geq 0)$, is 158 cu, units, then : **[2020, Main]**

(a) $\vec{a} \cdot \vec{c} = 17$ (b) $\vec{b} \cdot \vec{c} = 10$

(c) $n = 7$ (d) $n = 9$

2. If $\vec{a}$ and $\vec{b}$ are unit vectors, then the greatest value of $\sqrt{3}\,|\vec{a} + \vec{b}| + |\vec{a} - \vec{b}|$ is .... **[2020, Main]**

3. If $\vec{x}$ and $\vec{y}$ be two non-zero vectors such that $|\vec{x} + \vec{y}| = |\vec{x}|$ and $2\vec{x} + \lambda\vec{y}$ is perpendicular to $\vec{y}$, then the value of λ is ....

[2020, Main]

4. Let x_0 be the point of local maxima of $f(x) = \vec{a} \cdot (\vec{b} \times \vec{c})$, where $\vec{a} = x\hat{i} - 2\hat{j} + 3\hat{k}$, $\vec{b} = -2\hat{i} + x\hat{j} - \hat{k}$ and $\vec{c} = 7\hat{i} - 2\hat{j} + x\hat{k}$. Then the value of $\vec{a} \cdot \vec{b} + \vec{b} \cdot \vec{c} + \vec{c} \cdot \vec{a}$ at $x = x_0$ is : **[2020, Main]**

(a) -30 (b) 14

(c) -4 (d) -22

5. If $\vec{a} = 2\hat{i} + \hat{j} + 2\hat{k}$, then the value of

$$|\hat{i} \times (\vec{a} \times \hat{i})|^2 + |\hat{j} \times (\vec{a} \times \hat{j})|^2 + |\hat{k} \times (\vec{a} \times \hat{k})|^2$$

is equal to .... **[2020, Main]**

6. The lines $\vec{r} = (\hat{i} - \hat{j}) + l(2\hat{i} + \hat{k})$ and

$$\vec{r} = (2\hat{i} - \hat{j}) + m(\hat{i} + \hat{j} - \hat{k})$$ **[2020, Main]**

(a) Intersect when $l = 1$ and $m = 2$

(b) Intersect when $l = 2$ and $m = \dfrac{1}{2}$

(c) Do not intersect for any values of l and m

(d) Intersect for all values of l and m

7. Let the vectors $\vec{a}, \vec{b}, \vec{c}$ be such that $|\vec{a}| = 2, |\vec{b}| = 4$ and $|\vec{c}| = 4$. If the projection of $\vec{b}$ on $\vec{a}$ is equal to the projection of $\vec{c}$ on $\vec{a}$ and $\vec{b}$ is perpendicular to $\vec{c}$, then the value of $|\vec{a} + \vec{b} - \vec{c}|$ is .... **[2020, Main]**

8. In a triangle PQR, let $\vec{a} = \overrightarrow{QR}, \vec{b} = \overrightarrow{RP}$ and $\vec{c} = \overrightarrow{PQ}$. If $|\vec{a}| = 3, |\vec{b}| = 4$ and

$$\dfrac{\vec{a} \cdot (\vec{c} - \vec{b})}{\vec{c} \cdot (\vec{a} - \vec{b})} = \dfrac{|\vec{a}|}{|\vec{a}| + |\vec{b}|},$$ then the value of $|\vec{a} \times \vec{b}|^2$ is .... **[2020, Advanced]**

9. Let a and b be positive real numbers. Suppose $\overrightarrow{PQ} = a\hat{i} + b\hat{j}$ and $\overrightarrow{PS} = a\hat{i} - b\hat{j}$ are adjacent sides of a parallelogram PQRS. Let $\vec{u}$ and $\vec{v}$ be the projection vectors of $\vec{w} = \hat{i} + \hat{j}$ along $\overrightarrow{PQ}$ and $\overrightarrow{PS}$ respectively. If $|\vec{u}| + |\vec{v}| = |\vec{w}|$ and if the area of the paralellogram PQRS is 8, then which of the following statements is/are TRUE ? **[2020, Advanced]**

(a) $a + b = 4$

(b) $a - b = 2$

(c) The length of the diagonal PR of the parallelogram PQRS is 4

(d) $\vec{w}$ is an angle bisector of the vectors $\overrightarrow{PQ}$ and $\overrightarrow{PS}$

10. The area (in sq. units) of an equilateral triangle inscribed in the parabola $y^2 = 8x$, with one of its vertices on the vertex of this parabola, is :

[2020, Main]

(a) $64\sqrt{3}$ (b) $256\sqrt{3}$

(c) $192\sqrt{3}$ (d) $128\sqrt{3}$

11. Let the position vectors of points 'A' and 'B' be $\hat{i}+\hat{j}+\hat{k}$ and $2\hat{i}+\hat{j}+3\hat{k}$, respectively. A point 'P' divides the line segment AB internally in the ratio $\lambda : 1$ $(\lambda > 0)$. If O is the origin and $\overrightarrow{OB}.\overrightarrow{OP}-3|\overrightarrow{OA}\times\overrightarrow{OP}|^2 = 6$, then λ is equal to ....

[2020, Main]

12. Let $a, b, c \in R$ be such that $a^2 + b^2 + c^2 = 1$. If $a\cos\theta = b\cos\left(\theta+\dfrac{2\pi}{3}\right) = c\cos\left(\theta+\dfrac{4\pi}{3}\right)$, where $\theta = \dfrac{\pi}{9}$, then the angle between the vectors $a\hat{i}+b\hat{j}+c\hat{k}$ and $b\hat{i}+c\hat{j}+a\hat{k}$ is :

[2020, Main]

(a) $\dfrac{\pi}{2}$ (b) 0

(c) $\dfrac{\pi}{9}$ (d) $\dfrac{2\pi}{3}$

13. Area (in sq. units) of the region outside $\dfrac{|x|}{2}+\dfrac{|y|}{3}=1$ and inside the ellipse $\dfrac{x^2}{4}+\dfrac{y^2}{9}=1$ is :

[2020, Main]

(a) $3(4-\pi)$ (b) $6(\pi-2)$

(c) $3(\pi-2)$ (d) $6(4-\pi)$

14. Let $\overrightarrow{a}, \overrightarrow{b}$ and $\overrightarrow{c}$ be three unit vectors such that $|\overrightarrow{a}-\overrightarrow{b}|^2 +|\overrightarrow{a}-\overrightarrow{c}|^2 = 8.$

Then $|\overrightarrow{a}+2\overrightarrow{b}|^2 +|\overrightarrow{a}+2\overrightarrow{c}|^2$ is equal to ....

[2020, Main]

15. Let $\overrightarrow{a}, \overrightarrow{b}$ and $\overrightarrow{c}$ be three units vectors such that $\overrightarrow{a}+\overrightarrow{b}+\overrightarrow{c}=\overrightarrow{0}$. If $\lambda = \overrightarrow{a}.\overrightarrow{b}+\overrightarrow{b}.\overrightarrow{c}+\overrightarrow{c}.\overrightarrow{a}$ and $\overrightarrow{d}=\overrightarrow{a}\times\overrightarrow{b}+\overrightarrow{b}\times\overrightarrow{c}+\overrightarrow{c}\times\overrightarrow{a}$, then the ordered pair, $(\lambda, \overrightarrow{d})$ is equal to :

[2020, Main]

(a) $\left(-\dfrac{3}{2}, 3\overrightarrow{a}\times\overrightarrow{b}\right)$ (b) $\left(-\dfrac{3}{2}, 3\overrightarrow{c}\times\overrightarrow{b}\right)$

(c) $\left(\dfrac{3}{2}, 3\overrightarrow{b}\times\overrightarrow{c}\right)$ (d) $\left(\dfrac{3}{2}, 3\overrightarrow{a}\times\overrightarrow{c}\right)$

16. Let $\overrightarrow{a}, \overrightarrow{b}$ and $\overrightarrow{c}$ be three vectors such that $|\overrightarrow{a}|=\sqrt{3}$, $|\overrightarrow{b}| = 3$, $\overrightarrow{b}.\overrightarrow{c} = 10$ and the angle between $\overrightarrow{b}$ and $\overrightarrow{c}$ is $\dfrac{\pi}{3}$. If $\overrightarrow{a}$ is perpendicular to the vector $\overrightarrow{b}\times\overrightarrow{c}$, then $|\overrightarrow{a}\times(\overrightarrow{b}\times\overrightarrow{c})|$ is equal to ....

[2020, Main]

17. A vector $\overrightarrow{a}=\alpha\hat{i}+2\hat{j}+\beta\hat{k}$ $(\alpha, \beta \in R)$ lies in the plane of the vectors $\overrightarrow{b}=\hat{i}+\hat{j}$ and $\overrightarrow{c}=\hat{i}-\hat{j}+4\hat{k}$. If $\overrightarrow{a}$ bisects the angle between $\overrightarrow{b}$ and $\overrightarrow{c}$, then :

[2020, Main]

(a) $\overrightarrow{a}.\hat{i}+1 = 0$ (b) $\overrightarrow{a}.\hat{i}+3 = 0$

(c) $\overrightarrow{a}.\hat{k}+4 = 0$ (d) $\overrightarrow{a}.\hat{k}+2 = 0$

18. The projection of the line segment joining the points $(1, -1, 3)$ and $(2, -4, 11)$ on the line joining the points $(-1, 2, 3)$ and $(3, -2, 10)$ is ....

[2020, Main]

19. Let $\overrightarrow{a}=\hat{i}-2\hat{j}+\hat{k}$ and $\overrightarrow{b}=\hat{i}-\hat{j}+\hat{k}$ be two vectors $\overrightarrow{c}$ is a vector such that $\overrightarrow{b}\times\overrightarrow{c}=\overrightarrow{b}\times\overrightarrow{a}$ and $\overrightarrow{c}.\overrightarrow{a}=0$, then $\overrightarrow{c}.\overrightarrow{b}$ is equal to

(a) $\dfrac{1}{2}$ (b) -1

(c) $-\dfrac{1}{2}$ (d) $-\dfrac{3}{2}$

[2020, Main]

20. If a unit vector $\overrightarrow{a}$ makes angles $\dfrac{\pi}{3}$ with $\hat{i}$, $\dfrac{\pi}{4}$ with $\hat{j}$ and $\theta \in (0, \pi)$ with $\hat{k}$, then a value of θ is :

[2019 Main]

(a) $\dfrac{5\pi}{6}$ (b) $\dfrac{\pi}{4}$

(c) $\dfrac{5\pi}{12}$ (d) $\dfrac{2\pi}{3}$

21. Let $\overrightarrow{\alpha}=3\hat{i}+\hat{j}$ and $\overrightarrow{\beta}=2\hat{i}-\hat{j}+3\hat{k}$. If $\overrightarrow{\beta}=\overrightarrow{\beta}_1-\overrightarrow{\beta}_2$, where $\overrightarrow{\beta}_1$ is parallel to $\overrightarrow{\alpha}$ and $\overrightarrow{\beta}_2$ is perpendicular to $\overrightarrow{\alpha}$, then $\overrightarrow{\beta}_1\times\overrightarrow{\beta}_2$ is equal to :

[2019, Main]

(a) $-3\hat{i}+9\hat{j}+5\hat{k}$ (b) $3\hat{i}-9\hat{j}-5\hat{k}$

(c) $\dfrac{1}{2}(-3\hat{i}+9\hat{j}+5\hat{k})$ (d) $\dfrac{1}{2}(3\hat{i}-9\hat{j}-5\hat{k})$

22. The magnitude of the projection of the vector $2\hat{i}+3\hat{j}+\hat{k}$ on the vector perpendicular to the plane containing the vectors $\hat{i}+\hat{j}+\hat{k}$ and $\hat{i}+2\hat{j}+3\hat{k}$, is : **[2019 Main]**

(a) $\dfrac{\sqrt{3}}{2}$

(b) $\sqrt{6}$

(c) $3\sqrt{6}$

(d) $\sqrt{\dfrac{3}{2}}$

23. Let $\vec{a}=3\hat{i}+2\hat{j}+x\hat{k}$ and $\vec{b}=\hat{i}-\hat{j}+\hat{k}$, for some real x. Then $|\vec{a}\times\vec{b}|=r$ is possible if :

[2019 Main]

(a) $\sqrt{\dfrac{3}{2}}<r\le 3\sqrt{\dfrac{3}{2}}$

(b) $r\ge 5\sqrt{\dfrac{3}{2}}$

(c) $0<r\le \sqrt{\dfrac{3}{2}}$

(d) $3\sqrt{\dfrac{3}{2}}<r<5\sqrt{\dfrac{3}{2}}$

24. Let $\vec{a}=3\hat{i}+2\hat{j}+2\hat{k}$ and $\vec{b}=\hat{i}+2\hat{j}-2\hat{k}$ be two vectors. If a vector perpendicular to both the vectors $\vec{a}+\vec{b}$ and $\vec{a}-\vec{b}$ has the magnitude 12 then one such vector is : **[2019 Main]**

(a) $4(2\hat{i}+2\hat{j}+\hat{k})$

(b) $4(2\hat{i}-2\hat{j}-\hat{k})$

(c) $4(2\hat{i}+2\hat{j}-\hat{k})$

(d) $4(-2\hat{i}-2\hat{j}+\hat{k})$

25. If the volume of parallelopiped formed by the vectors $\hat{i}+\lambda\hat{j}+\hat{k}$, $\hat{j}+\lambda\hat{k}$ and $\lambda\hat{i}+\hat{k}$ is minimum, then λ is equal to : **[2019 Main]**

(a) $-\dfrac{1}{\sqrt{3}}$

(b) $\dfrac{1}{\sqrt{3}}$

(c) $\sqrt{3}$

(d) $-\sqrt{3}$

26. Let $\alpha\in\mathbf{R}$ and the three vectors $\vec{a}=\alpha\hat{i}+\hat{j}+3\hat{k}$, $\vec{b}=2\hat{i}+\hat{j}-\alpha\hat{k}$ and $\vec{c}=\alpha\hat{i}-2\hat{j}+3\hat{k}$. Then the set $S=\{\alpha:\vec{a},\vec{b}\text{ and }\vec{c}\text{ are coplanar}\}$

[2019 Main]

(a) is singleton

(b) is empty

(c) contains exactly two positive numbers

(d) contains exactly two numbers only one of which is positive

27. Let $\vec{a}=2\hat{i}+\hat{j}-\hat{k}$ and $\vec{b}=\hat{i}+2\hat{j}+\hat{k}$ be two vectors. Consider a vector $\vec{c}=\alpha\vec{a}+\beta\vec{b}$, $\alpha,\beta\in\mathbf{R}$. If the projection of $\vec{c}$ on the vector $(\vec{a}+\vec{b})$ is $3\sqrt{2}$, then the minimum value of $(\vec{c}-(\vec{a}\times\vec{b}))\cdot\vec{c}$ equals .... **[2019 Advanced]**

28. Consider the cube in the first octant with sides OP, OQ and OR of length 1, along the x-axis, y-axis and z-axis, respectively, where $O(0,0,0)$ is the origin. Let $S\left(\dfrac{1}{2},\dfrac{1}{2},\dfrac{1}{2}\right)$ be the centre of the cube and T be the vertex of the cube opposite to the origin O such that S lies on the diagonal OT. If $\vec{p}=\vec{SP}$, $\vec{q}=\vec{SQ}$, $\vec{r}=\vec{SR}$ and $\vec{t}=\vec{ST}$, then the value of $\left|(\vec{p}\times\vec{q})\times(\vec{r}\times\vec{t})\right|$ is ....

[2018, Advanced]

29. If $\vec{a},\vec{b}$ and $\vec{c}$ are unit vectors such that $\vec{a}+2\vec{b}+2\vec{c}=\vec{0}$, then $|\vec{a}\times\vec{c}|$ is equal to :

[2018, Main]

(a) $\dfrac{\sqrt{15}}{4}$

(b) $\dfrac{1}{4}$

(c) $\dfrac{15}{16}$

(d) $\dfrac{\sqrt{15}}{16}$

30. Let $\vec{a}=\hat{i}+\hat{j}+\hat{k}$, $\vec{c}=\hat{j}-\hat{k}$ and a vector $\vec{b}$ be such that $\vec{a}\times\vec{b}=\vec{c}$ and $\vec{a}\cdot\vec{b}=3$. Then $|\vec{b}|$ equals : **[2018, Main]**

(a) $\dfrac{11}{3}$

(b) $\dfrac{11}{\sqrt{3}}$

(c) $\sqrt{\dfrac{11}{3}}$

(d) $\dfrac{\sqrt{11}}{3}$

31. Let $\vec{u}$ be a vector coplanar with the vectors $\vec{a}=2\hat{i}+3\hat{j}-\hat{k}$ and $\vec{b}=\hat{j}+\hat{k}$. If $\vec{u}$ is perpendicular to $\vec{a}$ and $\vec{u}\cdot\vec{b}=24$, then $|\vec{u}|^{2}$ is equal to :

[2018, Main]

(a) 336

(b) 315

(c) 256

(d) 84

32. If the vector $\vec{b} = 3\hat{j} + 4\hat{k}$ is written as the sum of a vector $\vec{b}_1$, parallel to $\vec{a} = \hat{i} + \hat{j}$ and a vector $\vec{b}_2$, perpendicular to $\vec{a}$, then $\vec{b}_1 \times \vec{b}_2$ is equal to :

[2018, Main]

(a) $-3\hat{i} + 3\hat{j} - 9\hat{k}$ (b) $6\hat{i} - 6\hat{j} + \dfrac{9}{2}\hat{k}$

(c) $-6\hat{i} + 6\hat{j} - \dfrac{9}{2}\hat{k}$ (d) $3\hat{i} - 3\hat{j} + 9\hat{k}$

33. Let ABC be a triangle whose circumcentre is at P. If the position vectors of A, B, C and P are $\vec{a}, \vec{b}, \vec{c}$ and $\dfrac{\vec{a} + \vec{b} + \vec{c}}{4}$ respectively, then the position vector of the orthocentre of this triangle, is : **[2018, Main]**

(a) $\vec{a} + \vec{b} + \vec{c}$ (b) $-\left(\dfrac{\vec{a} + \vec{b} + \vec{c}}{2}\right)$

(c) $\vec{0}$ (d) $\left(\dfrac{\vec{a} + \vec{b} + \vec{c}}{2}\right)$

34. The area (in sq. units) of the parallelogram whose diagonals are along the vectors $8\hat{i} - 6\hat{j}$ and $3\hat{i} + 4\hat{j} - 12\hat{k}$, is : **[2017, Main]**

(a) 26   (b) 65

(c) 20   (d) 52

35. Let $\vec{a} = 2\hat{i} + \hat{j} - 2\hat{k}$ and $\vec{b} = \hat{i} + \hat{j}$. Let $\vec{c}$ be a vector such that $|\vec{c} - \vec{a}| = 3$, $\left|(\vec{a} \times \vec{b}) \times \vec{c}\right| = 3$ and the angle between $\vec{c}$ and $\vec{a} \times \vec{b}$ be 30°. Then $\vec{a} \cdot \vec{c}$ is equal to : **[2017, Main]**

(a) 2   (b) 5

(c) $\dfrac{1}{8}$ (d) $\dfrac{25}{8}$

36. In a triangle ABC, right angled at the vertex A, if the position vectors of A, B and C are respectively $3\hat{i} + \hat{j} - \hat{k}$, $-\hat{i} + 3\hat{j} + p\hat{k}$ and $5\hat{i} + q\hat{j} - 4\hat{k}$, then the point (p, q) lies on a line : **[2016, Main]**

(a) parallel to x-axis.

(b) parallel to y-axis.

(c) making an acute angle with the positive direction of x-axis

(d) making an obtuse angle with the positive direction of x-axis.

37. Let $\vec{a}, \vec{b}$ and $\vec{c}$ be three unit vectors such that $\vec{a} \times (\vec{b} \times \vec{c}) = \dfrac{\sqrt{3}}{2}(\vec{b} + \vec{c})$. If $\vec{b}$ is not parallel to $\vec{c}$, then the angle between $\vec{a}$ and $\vec{b}$ is, **[2016, Advanced]**

(a) $\dfrac{3\pi}{4}$ (b) $\dfrac{\pi}{2}$

(c) $\dfrac{2\pi}{3}$ (d) $\dfrac{5\pi}{6}$

38. In a parallelogram ABCD, $\left|\vec{AB}\right| = a$, $\left|\vec{AD}\right| = b$ and $\left|\vec{AC}\right| = c$, then $\vec{DB} \cdot \vec{AB}$ has the value : **[2015, Main]**

(a) $\dfrac{1}{2}(a^2 - b^2 + c^2)$ (b) $\dfrac{1}{4}(a^2 + b^2 - c^2)$

(c) $\dfrac{1}{3}(b^2 + c^2 - a^2)$ (d) $\dfrac{1}{2}(a^2 + b^2 + c^2)$

39. Suppose that $\vec{p}, \vec{q}$ and $\vec{r}$ are three non-coplanar vectors in R³. Let the components of a vector $\vec{s}$ along $\vec{p}, \vec{q}$ and $\vec{r}$ be 4, 3 and 5, respectively. If the components of this vector $\vec{s}$ along $(-\vec{p} + \vec{q} + \vec{r})$, $(\vec{p} - \vec{q} + \vec{r})$ and $(-\vec{p} - \vec{q} + \vec{r})$ are x, y and z, respectively, then the value of $2x + y + z$ is : **[2015, Advanced]**

40. Let ΔPQR be a triangle. Let $\vec{a} = \vec{QR}$, $\vec{b} = \vec{RP}$ and $\vec{c} = \vec{PQ}$. If $|\vec{a}| = 12$, $|\vec{b}| = 4\sqrt{3}$ and $\vec{b} \cdot \vec{c} = 24$, then which of the following is (are) true? **[2015, Advanced]**

(a) $\dfrac{|\vec{c}|^2}{2} - |\vec{a}| = 12$

(b) $\dfrac{|\vec{c}|^2}{2} + |\vec{a}| = 30$

(c) $\left|\vec{a} \times \vec{b} + \vec{c} \times \vec{a}\right| = 48\sqrt{3}$

(d) $\vec{a} \cdot \vec{b} = -72$

41. If $[\vec{a} \times \vec{b} \ \ \vec{b} \times \vec{c} \ \ \vec{c} \times \vec{a}] = \lambda [\vec{a} \ \vec{b} \ \vec{c}]^2$ then λ is equal to : **[2014, Main]**

(a) 0   (b) 1

(c) 2   (d) 3

42. Let $\vec{a}, \vec{b}$ and $\vec{c}$ be three non-coplanar unit vectors such that the angle between every pair of them is $\dfrac{\pi}{3}$. If $\vec{a} \times \vec{b} + \vec{b} \times \vec{c} = p\vec{a} + q\vec{b} + r\vec{c}$, where p, q and r are scalars, then the value of $\dfrac{p^2 + 2q^2 + r^2}{q^2}$ is **[2014, Advanced]**

43. If $\left|\vec{a}\right| = 2, \left|\vec{b}\right| = 3$ and $\left|2\vec{a} - \vec{b}\right| = 5$, then $\left|2\vec{a} + \vec{b}\right|$ equals : **[2014, Main]**

(a) 17   (b) 7

(c) 5   (d) 1

44. If $\hat{x}, \hat{y}$ and $\hat{z}$ are three unit vectors in three-dimensional space, then the minimum value of $\left|\hat{x} + \hat{y}\right|^2 + \left|\hat{y} + \hat{z}\right|^2 + \left|\hat{z} + \hat{x}\right|^2$ is: **[2014, Main]**

(a) $\dfrac{3}{2}$ (b) 3

(c) $3\sqrt{3}$ (d) 6

45. If $\vec{x} = 3\hat{i} - 6\hat{j} - \hat{k}$, $\vec{y} = \hat{i} + 4\hat{j} - 3\hat{k}$ and $\vec{z} = 3\hat{i} - 4\hat{j} - 12\hat{k}$, then the magnitude of the projection of $\vec{x} \times \vec{y}$ on $\vec{z}$ is : **[2014, Main]**

(a) 12   (b) 15

(c) 14   (d) 13

46. If $|\vec{c}|^2 = 60$ and $\vec{c} \times (\hat{i} + 2\hat{j} + 5\hat{k}) = 0$ then a value of $\vec{c} \cdot (-7\hat{i} + 2\hat{j} + 3\hat{k})$ is : **[2014, Main]**

(a) $4\sqrt{2}$ (b) 12

(c) 24   (d) $12\sqrt{2}$

47. Match List—I with List—II and select the correct answer using the code given below the lists : **[2013, Advanced]**

List —I	**List—II**
P. Volume of parallelopiped determined by $\vec{a}, \vec{b}$ and $\vec{c}$ is 2. Then the volume of the parallelopiped determined by vectors $2(\vec{a} \times \vec{b})$, $3(\vec{b} \times \vec{c})$ and $(\vec{c} \times \vec{a})$ is	1.100
Q. Volume of parallelopiped determined by vectors $\vec{a}, \vec{b}$ and $\vec{c}$ is 5. Then the volume of the parallelopiped determined by vectors $3(\vec{a} + \vec{b})$, $(\vec{b} + \vec{c})$ and $2(\vec{c} + \vec{a})$ is	2.30
R. Area of a triangle with adjacent sides determined by vectors $\vec{a}$ and $\vec{b}$ is 20. Then the area of the triangle with adjacent sides determined by vectors $(2\vec{a} + 3\vec{b})$ and $(\vec{a} - \vec{b})$ is	3.24
S. Area of a parallelogram with adjacent sides determined by vectors $\vec{a}$ and $\vec{b}$ is 30. Then the area of the parallelogram with adjacent sides determined by vectors $(\vec{a} + \vec{b})$ and $\vec{a}$ is :	4.60

48. Let $\vec{PR} = 3\hat{i} + \hat{j} - 2\hat{k}$ and $\vec{SQ} = \hat{i} - 3\hat{j} - 4\hat{k}$ determine diagnoals of a parallelogram PQRS and $\vec{PT} = \hat{i} + 2\hat{j} + 3\hat{k}$ be another vector. Then the volume of the parallelopiped determined by the vectors $\vec{PT}, \vec{PQ}$ and $\vec{PS}$ is : **[2012, Advanced]**

(a) 5   (b) 20

(c) 10   (d) 30

49. If $\vec{a}$ and $\vec{b}$ are vectors such that $\left|\vec{a} + \vec{b}\right| = \sqrt{29}$ and $\vec{a} \times (2\hat{i} + 3\hat{j} + 4\hat{k}) = (2\hat{i} + 3\hat{j} + 4\hat{k}) \times \vec{b}$, then a possible value of $(\vec{a} + \vec{b}) \cdot (-7\hat{i} + 2\hat{j} + 3\hat{k})$ is :

[2012, Advanced]

(a) 0   (b) 3

(c) 4   (d) 8

50. If $\vec{a}, \vec{b}$ and $\vec{c}$ are unit vectors satisfying

[2012, Advanced]

$|\vec{a} - \vec{b}|^2 + |\vec{b} - \vec{c}|^2 + |\vec{c} - \vec{a}|^2 = 9$, then $\left|2\vec{a} + 5\vec{b} + 5\vec{c}\right|$ is :

51. Let $\vec{a} = -\hat{i} - \hat{k}$, $\vec{b} = -\hat{i} - \hat{j}$ and $\vec{c} = \hat{i} + 2\hat{j} + 3\hat{k}$ be three given vectors. If $\vec{r}$ is a vector such that $\vec{r} \times \vec{b} = \vec{c} \times \vec{b}$ and $\vec{r} \cdot \vec{a} = 0$, then the value of $\vec{r} \cdot \vec{b}$ is : **[2011, Advanced]**

52. The vector(s) which is/are coplanar with vectors $\hat{i} + \hat{j} + 2\hat{k}$ and $\hat{i} + 2\hat{j} + \hat{k}$, and perpendicular to the vector $\hat{i} + \hat{j} + \hat{k}$ is/are **[2011, Advanced]**

(a) $\hat{j} - \hat{k}$ (b) $-\hat{i} + \hat{j}$

(c) $-\hat{j} + \hat{k}$ (d) $-\hat{j} + \hat{k}$

53. Two adjacent sides of a parallelogram ABCD are given by :

$$\vec{AB} = 2\hat{i} + 10\hat{j} + 11\hat{k} \text{ and } \vec{AD} = -\hat{i} + 2\hat{j} + 2\hat{k}$$

The side AD is rotated, by an acute angle α in the plane of the parallelogram so that AD becomes AD'. If AD' makes a right angle with the side AB, then the cosine of the angle α is given by :

[2010, Advanced]

(a) $\dfrac{8}{9}$

(b) $\dfrac{\sqrt{17}}{9}$

(c) $\dfrac{1}{9}$

(d) $\dfrac{4\sqrt{5}}{9}$

54. Let two non-collinear unit vectors $\hat{a}$ and $\hat{b}$ form an acute angle. A point P moves so that at any time t the position vector $\overline{OP}$ (where O is the origin) is given by $\hat{a}\cos t + \hat{b}\sin t$. When P is farthest from origin O, let M be the length of $\overline{OP}$ and $\hat{u}$ be the unit vector along $\overline{OP}$. Then,

[2008, Advanced]

(a) $\hat{u} = \dfrac{\hat{a} + \hat{b}}{\left|\hat{a} + \hat{b}\right|}$ and $M = (1 + \hat{a}\cdot\hat{b})^{\frac{1}{2}}$

(b) $\hat{u} = \dfrac{\hat{a} - \hat{b}}{\left|\hat{a} - \hat{b}\right|}$ and $M = (1 + \hat{a}\cdot\hat{b})^{\frac{1}{2}}$

(c) $\hat{u} = \dfrac{\hat{a} + \hat{b}}{\left|\hat{a} + \hat{b}\right|}$ and $M = (1 + 2\hat{a}\cdot\hat{b})^{\frac{1}{2}}$

(d) $\hat{u} = \dfrac{\hat{a} - \hat{b}}{\left|\hat{a} - \hat{b}\right|}$ and $M = (1 + 2\hat{a}\cdot\hat{b})^{\frac{1}{2}}$

consider the lines

$$L_1 : \dfrac{x+1}{3} = \dfrac{y+2}{1} = \dfrac{z+1}{2}$$

$$L_2 : \dfrac{x+2}{1} = \dfrac{y+2}{2} = \dfrac{z+3}{3}$$

55. The unit vector perpendicular to both L_1 and L_2 is : **[2008, Advanced]**

(a) $\dfrac{-\hat{i} + 7\hat{j} + 7\hat{k}}{\sqrt{99}}$

(b) $\dfrac{-\hat{i} - 7\hat{j} + 5\hat{k}}{5\sqrt{3}}$

(c) $\dfrac{-\hat{i} - 7\hat{j} + 5\hat{k}}{5\sqrt{3}}$

(d) $\dfrac{7\hat{i} - 7\hat{j} - \hat{k}}{\sqrt{99}}$

56. The shortest distance between L_1 and L_2 is :

[2008, Advanced]

(a) 0

(b) $\dfrac{17}{\sqrt{3}}$

(c) $\dfrac{41}{5\sqrt{3}}$

(d) $\dfrac{17}{5\sqrt{3}}$

57. The edges of a parallelopiped are of unit length and are parallel to non-coplanar unit vectors $\hat{a}, \hat{b}, \hat{c}$ such that

$$\hat{a}\cdot\hat{b} = \hat{b}\cdot\hat{c} = \hat{c}\cdot\hat{a} = \dfrac{1}{2}.$$

Then, the volume of the parallelopiped is :

[2008, Advanced]

(a) $\dfrac{1}{\sqrt{2}}$

(b) $\dfrac{1}{2\sqrt{2}}$

(c) $\dfrac{\sqrt{3}}{2}$

(d) $\dfrac{1}{\sqrt{3}}$

58. A particle P starts from the point $z_0 = 1 + 2i$, where $i = \sqrt{-1}$. It move first horizontally away from origin by 5 units and then vertically away from origin by 3 units to reach a point z_1. From z_1 the particle moves $\sqrt{2}$ units in the direction of the vector $\hat{i} + \hat{j}$ and then it move through an angle $\dfrac{\pi}{2}$ in anticlockwise direction on a circle with centre at origin, to reach a point z_2. The point z_2 is given by :

(2008, Advanced)

(a) $6 + 7i$

(b) $-7 + 6i$

(c) $7 + 6i$

(d) $-6 + 7i$

59. Let the vectors $\vec{PQ}, \vec{QR}, \vec{RS}, \vec{ST}, \vec{TU}$ and $\vec{UP}$ represent the sides of a regular hexagon.

STATEMENT-1 : $\vec{PQ} \times (\vec{RS} + \vec{ST}) \neq \vec{0}$.

because

STATEMENT-2: $\vec{PQ} \times \vec{RS} = \vec{0}$ and $\vec{PQ} \times \vec{ST} \neq \vec{0}$.

[2007, Advanced]

(a) Statement-1 is True, Statement-2 is True; Statement-2 is a correct explanation for Statement-1

(b) Statement-1 is True, Statement-2 is True; Statement-2 is **NOT** a correct explanation for Statement-1

(c) Statement-1 is True, Statement-2 is False

(d) Statement-1 is False, Statement-2 is True.

60. Let $\vec{a}, \vec{b}, \vec{c}$ be unit vectors such that $\vec{a} + \vec{b} + \vec{c} = \vec{0}$. Which one of the following is correct ?

[2007, Advanced]

(a) $\vec{a} \times \vec{b} = \vec{b} \times \vec{c} = \vec{c} \times \vec{a} = \vec{0}$

(b) $\vec{a} \times \vec{b} = \vec{b} \times \vec{c} = \vec{c} \times \vec{a} \neq \vec{0}$

(c) $\vec{a} \times \vec{b} = \vec{b} \times \vec{c} = \vec{a} \times \vec{c} \neq \vec{0}$

(d) $\vec{a} \times \vec{b}, \vec{b} \times \vec{c}, \vec{c} \times \vec{a}$ are mutually perpendicular

61. Let $\vec{A}$ be vector parallel to line of intersection of planes P_1 and P_2 through origin, P_1 is parallel to the vectors $2\hat{j} + 3\hat{k}$ and $4\hat{j} - 3\hat{k}$ and P_2 is parallel to $\hat{j} - \hat{k}$ and $3\hat{i} + 3\hat{j}$, then the angle between vector $\vec{A}$ and $2\hat{i} + \hat{j} - 2\hat{k}$ is :   **[2006, Main]**

(a) $\dfrac{\pi}{2}$

(b) $\dfrac{\pi}{4}$

(c) $\dfrac{\pi}{6}$

(d) $\dfrac{3\pi}{4}$

62. If $\vec{a}, \vec{b}, \vec{c}$ are three non-zero, non-coplanar vectors and

$$\vec{b_1} = \vec{b} - \frac{\vec{b} \cdot \vec{a}}{|\vec{a}|^2}\vec{a} \quad \vec{b_2} = \vec{b} + \frac{\vec{b} \cdot \vec{a}}{|\vec{a}|^2}\vec{a},$$

$$\vec{c_1} = \vec{c} - \frac{\vec{c} \cdot \vec{a}}{|\vec{a}|^2}\vec{a} + \frac{\vec{b} \cdot \vec{c}}{|\vec{c}|^2}\vec{b_1},$$

$$\vec{c_2} = \vec{c} - \frac{\vec{c} \cdot \vec{a}}{|\vec{a}|^2}\vec{a} - \frac{\vec{b_1} \cdot \vec{c}}{|\vec{b_1}|^2}\vec{b_1},$$

$$\vec{c_3} = \vec{c} - \frac{\vec{c} \cdot \vec{a}}{|\vec{c}|^2}\vec{a} + \frac{\vec{b} \cdot \vec{c}}{|\vec{c}|^2}\vec{b_1},$$

$$\vec{c_4} = \vec{c} - \frac{\vec{c} \cdot \vec{a}}{|\vec{c}|^2}\vec{a} - \frac{\vec{b} \cdot \vec{c}}{|\vec{b}|^2}\vec{b_1},$$

(a) $(\vec{a}, \vec{b_1}, \vec{c_3})$

(b) $(\vec{a}, \vec{b_1}, \vec{c_2})$

(c) $(\vec{a}, \vec{b_1}, \vec{c_1})$

(d) $(\vec{a}, \vec{b_2}, \vec{c_2})$

63. Incident ray is along the unit vector $\hat{v}$ and the reflected ray is along the unit vector $\hat{w}$. The normal is along unit vector $\hat{a}$ outwards. Express $\hat{w}$ in terms of $\hat{a}$ and $\hat{v}$.   **[2005, Advanced]**

64. If $\vec{a} = (\hat{i} + \hat{j} + \hat{k})$, $\vec{a} \cdot \vec{b} = 1$ and $\vec{a} \times \vec{b} = \hat{j} - \hat{k}$, then $\vec{b}$ is :   **[2004, Advanced]**

(a) $\hat{i} - \hat{j} + \hat{k}$

(b) $2\hat{j} - \hat{k}$

(c) $\hat{i}$

(d) $2\hat{i}$

65. The unit vector which is orthogonal to the vector $5\hat{i} + 2\hat{j} + 6\hat{k}$ and is coplanar with the vectors $2\hat{i} + \hat{j} + \hat{k}$ and $\hat{i} - \hat{j} + \hat{k}$ is :   **[2004, Main]**

(a) $\dfrac{2\hat{i} - 6\hat{j} + \hat{k}}{\sqrt{41}}$

(b) $\dfrac{2\hat{i} - 5\hat{j}}{\sqrt{29}}$

(c) $\dfrac{3\hat{j} - \hat{k}}{\sqrt{10}}$

(d) $\dfrac{2\hat{i} - 8\hat{j} + \hat{k}}{\sqrt{69}}$

66. $\vec{a}, \vec{b}, \vec{c}, \vec{d}$ are four distinct vectors satisfying the conditions $\vec{a} \times \vec{b} = \vec{c} \times \vec{d}$ and $\vec{a} \times \vec{c} = \vec{d} \times \vec{d}$, then prove that $\vec{a} \cdot \vec{b} + \vec{c} \cdot \vec{d} \neq \vec{a} \cdot \vec{c} + \vec{d} \cdot \vec{d}$.

[2004, Advanced]

67. Let $\vec{a}$ and $\vec{b}$ are two unit vectors such that $\vec{a} + 2\vec{b}$ and $5\vec{a} - 4\vec{b}$ are perpendicular to each other then the angle between $\vec{a}$ and $\vec{b}$ is :

[2002, Advanced]

(a) $45°$

(b) $60°$

(c) $\cos^{-1}(1/3)$

(d) $\cos^{-1}(2/7)$

68. Let $\vec{V} = 2\hat{i} + \hat{j} + \hat{k}$ and $\vec{W} = \hat{i} + 3\hat{k}$. If $\vec{U}$ is a unit vector, then the maximum value of the scalar triple product $[\vec{U}\,\vec{V}\,\vec{W}]$ is :   **[2002, Main]**

(a) -1

(b) $\sqrt{10} + \sqrt{6}$

(c) $\sqrt{59}$

(d) $\sqrt{60}$

ANSWER KEY

1. (b)	**2.** (4)	**3.** (1)	**4.** (d)	**5.** (18)	**6.** (c)	**7.** (6)	**8.** (108)	**9.** (c)	**10.** (c)
11. (0.8)	**12.** (a)	**13.** (b)	**14.** (2)	**15.** (a)	**16.** (30)	**17.** (*)	**18.** (8.00)	**19.** (c)	**20.** (d)
21. (c)	**22.** (d)	**23.** (b)	**24.** (b)	**25.** (b)	**26.** (b)	**27.** (18)	**28.** (0.5)	**29.** (a)	**30.** (c)
31. (a)	**32.** (b)	**33.** (d)	**34.** (b)	**35.** (a)	**36.** (c)	**37.** (d)	**38.** (*)	**39.** (9)	
40. (a,c,d)	**41.** (b)	**42.** (4)	**43.** (c)	**44.** (b)	**45.** (c)	**46.** (d)	**47.** (c)	**48.** (c)	**49.** (c)
50. (3)	**51.** (9)	**52.** (a,d)	**53.** (b)	**54.** (a)	**55.** (b)	**56.** (d)	**57.** (a)	**58.** (d)	**59.** (c)
60. (b)	**61.** (b,d)	**62.** (b)	**63.** $\hat{w} = \hat{v} - 2\left(\hat{n}\cdot\hat{v}\right)\hat{n}$		**64.** (c)	**65.** (c)	**66.** (*)	**67.** (b)	**68.** (c)

ANSWERS WITH EXPLANATIONS

1. Correct Response : (b)

Explanation :

$$v = [\vec{a}\ \vec{b}\ \vec{c}]$$

$$158 = \begin{vmatrix} 1 & 1 & n \\ 2 & 4 & -n \\ 1 & n & 3 \end{vmatrix},\ n \geq 0$$

$$158 = 1(12 + n^2) - (6 + n) + n(2n - 4)$$

$$158 = n^2 + 12 - 6 - n + 2n^2 - 4n$$

$$3n^2 - 5n - 152 = 0$$

$$n = 8, \frac{-38}{6}\ \text{(Rejected)}$$

$$\vec{a}\cdot\vec{c} = 1 + n + 3n = 1 + 4n = 33$$

$$\vec{b}\cdot\vec{c} = 2 + 4n - 3n = 2 + n = 10.$$

2. Correct Response : (4)

Explanation :

$$\sqrt{3}\,|\vec{a} + \vec{b}| + |\vec{a} - \vec{b}|$$

$$= \sqrt{3}(\sqrt{2 + 2\cos\theta}) + \sqrt{2 - 2\cos\theta}$$

$$= \sqrt{6}(\sqrt{1 + \cos\theta}) + \sqrt{2}(\sqrt{1 - \cos\theta})$$

$$= 2\sqrt{3}\left|\cos\frac{\theta}{2}\right| + 2\left|\sin\frac{\theta}{2}\right|$$

$$\leq \sqrt{(2\sqrt{3})^2 + (2)^2} = 4.$$

3. Correct Response : (1)

Explanation :

$$|\vec{x} + \vec{y}| = |\vec{x}|$$

$$\sqrt{|\vec{x}|^2 + |\vec{y}|^2 + 2\,\vec{x}\cdot\vec{y}} = |\vec{x}|$$

$$|\vec{y}|^2 + 2\,\vec{x}\cdot\vec{y} = 0 \qquad\qquad ...(1)$$

Now $\qquad (2\vec{x} + \lambda\vec{y})\cdot\vec{y} = 0$

$$2\,\vec{x}\cdot\vec{y} + \lambda|\vec{y}|^2 = 0$$

From (1)

$$-|\vec{y}|^2 + \lambda|\vec{y}|^2 = 0$$

$$(\lambda - 1)|\vec{y}|^2 = 0$$

Given $\qquad\qquad |\vec{y}| \neq 0$

$$\Rightarrow \qquad\qquad \lambda = 1.$$

4. Correct Response : (d)

Explanation :

$$f(x) = \vec{a}\cdot(\vec{b}\times\vec{c}) = \begin{vmatrix} x & -2 & 3 \\ -2 & x & -1 \\ 7 & -2 & x \end{vmatrix}$$

$$= x^3 - 27x + 26$$

$$f'(x) = 3x^2 - 27 = 0 \Rightarrow x = \pm 3$$

and $\quad f''(-3) < 0$

$\Rightarrow$ local maxima at $x = x_0 = -3$

Thus, $\qquad \vec{a} = -3\hat{i} - 2\hat{j} + 3\hat{k},$

$$\vec{b} = -2\hat{i} - 3\hat{j} - \hat{k},$$

and $\qquad \vec{c} = 7\hat{i} - 2\hat{j} - 3\hat{k}$

$$\Rightarrow \vec{a}\cdot\vec{b} + \vec{b}\cdot\vec{c} + \vec{c}\cdot\vec{a} = 9 - 5 - 26 = -22.$$

5. Correct Response : (18)

Explanation :

Let $\qquad \vec{a} = x\hat{i} + y\hat{j} + z\hat{k}$

$$\hat{i}\times(\vec{a}\times\hat{i}) = (\hat{i}\cdot\hat{i})\vec{a} - (\vec{a}\cdot\hat{i})\hat{i}$$

$$= x\hat{i} + y\hat{j} + z\hat{k} - x\hat{i}$$

$$= y\hat{j} + z\hat{k}$$

Similarly

$$\hat{j}\times(\vec{a}\times\hat{j}) = x\hat{i}+z\hat{k}$$

$$\hat{k}\times(\hat{a}\times\hat{k}) = x\hat{i}+y\hat{j}$$

$$|\hat{i}\times(a\times\hat{i})|^2+|\hat{j}\times(\vec{a}\times\hat{j})|^2+|\hat{k}\times(\vec{a}\times\hat{k})|^2$$

$$=|y\hat{j}+z\hat{k}|^2+|x\hat{i}+z\hat{k}|^2+|x\hat{i}+4\hat{j}|^2$$

$$=2|\vec{a}|^2$$

$$=2\times 9=18.$$

6. Correct Response : (c)

Explanation :

$$\vec{r} = \hat{i}(1+2l)+\hat{j}(-1)+\hat{k}(l)$$

$$\vec{r} = \hat{i}(2+m)+\hat{j}(m-1)+\hat{k}(-m)$$

For intersection

$$1+2l=2+m \quad \ldots(i)$$

$$-1=m-1 \quad \ldots(ii)$$

$$l=-m \quad \ldots(iii)$$

from (ii) $m=0$

from (iii) $l=0$

These values of m and l do not satisfy equation (1).

Hence the two lines do not intersect for any values of l and m.

7. Correct Response : (6)

Explanation :

Projection of $\vec{b}$ on $\vec{a}$ = projection of $\vec{c}$ on $\vec{a}$

$$\Rightarrow \quad \frac{\vec{b}\cdot\vec{a}}{|\vec{a}|} = \frac{\vec{c}\cdot\vec{a}}{|\vec{a}|}$$

$$\Rightarrow \quad \vec{b}\cdot\vec{a} = \vec{c}\cdot\vec{a}$$

$\because$ $\vec{b}$ is perpendicular to $\vec{c} \Rightarrow \vec{b}\cdot\vec{c}=0$

Let $|\vec{a}+\vec{b}-\vec{c}|=k$

Square both sides

$$k^2=|\vec{a}|^2+|\vec{b}|^2+|\vec{c}|^2+2\vec{a}\cdot\vec{b}$$

$$-2\vec{a}\cdot\vec{c}-2\vec{b}\cdot\vec{c}$$

$$=(2)^2+(4)^2+(4)^2+2\vec{a}\cdot\vec{b}-2\vec{a}\cdot\vec{b}$$

$$=4+16+16$$

$$k^2=36$$

$$k=6=|\vec{a}+\vec{b}-\vec{c}|.$$

8. Correct Response : (108)

Explanation :

We have

$$\vec{a}+\vec{b}+\vec{c} = \vec{0}$$

$$\Rightarrow \quad \vec{c}=-\vec{a}-\vec{b}$$

$$\text{Now,} \quad \frac{\vec{a}\cdot(-\vec{a}-2\vec{b})}{(-\vec{a}-\vec{b})\cdot(\vec{a}-\vec{b})} = \frac{3}{7}$$

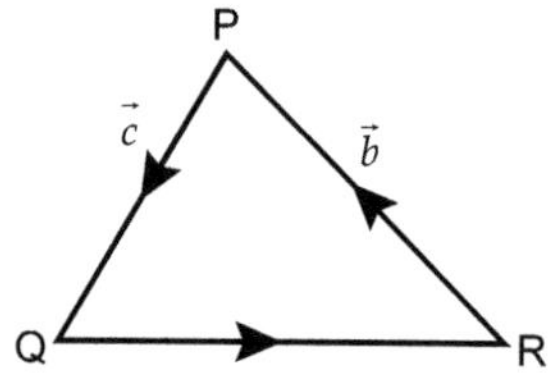

$$\text{Now,} \quad \frac{|\vec{a}|^2+2\vec{a}\cdot\vec{b}}{|\vec{a}|^2-|\vec{b}|^2} = \frac{3}{7}$$

$$\frac{9+2\vec{a}\cdot\vec{b}}{9-16} = \frac{3}{7}$$

$$\Rightarrow \quad \vec{a}\cdot\vec{b}=-6$$

$$\Rightarrow \quad |\vec{a}\times\vec{b}|^2 = a^2b^2-(\vec{a}\,\vec{b})^2$$

$$=9\times16-36=108.$$

9. Correct Response : (c)

Explanation :

$$\vec{u} = [(\hat{i}+\hat{j}).\text{PQ}]\,\text{PQ}$$

$$\vec{u} = |(\hat{i}+\hat{j}).\text{PQ}|$$

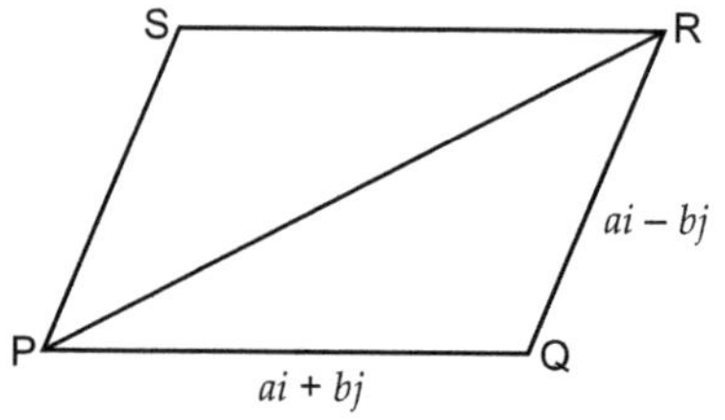

$$|\vec{u}| = \left|(\hat{i}+\hat{j}).\frac{(ai+bj)}{\sqrt{a^2+b^2}}\right| = \frac{a+b}{a^2+b^2}$$

$$\vec{v} = (i+j).\text{PS}$$

$$|\vec{v}| = \left|\frac{(i+j).(ai-bj)}{\sqrt{a^2+b^2}}\right| = \frac{a-b}{\sqrt{a^2+b^2}}$$

$$|\vec{u}|+|\vec{v}| = |\vec{w}| \qquad (\because \vec{w}=\hat{i}+\hat{j})$$

$$|\vec{w}| = \sqrt{2}$$

$$\frac{|(a+b)|+|(a-b)|}{\sqrt{a^2+b^2}} = \sqrt{2}$$

For $\qquad a > b$

$$2a = \sqrt{2}.\sqrt{a^2 + b^2}$$
$$4a^2 = 2a^2 + 2b^2$$
$$a^2 = b^2$$
$\therefore \qquad a = b \qquad \qquad \dots(1)$

$(a > 0, b > 0)$

Similarly for $a > b$ we will get

$$a = b$$

Now area of parallelogram

$$= |(ai + bj) \times (ai - bj)|$$
$$= 2ab$$
$\therefore \qquad 2ab = 8$

$$ab = 4 \qquad \qquad \dots(2)$$

from (1) and (2)

$$a = 2, b = 2$$
$\therefore \qquad a + b = 4 \qquad \qquad$ option (a)

length of diagonal is

$$|2a\,\hat{i}| = |4\,\hat{i}| = 4$$

so option (c).

10. **Correct Response :** (c)

   Explanation :

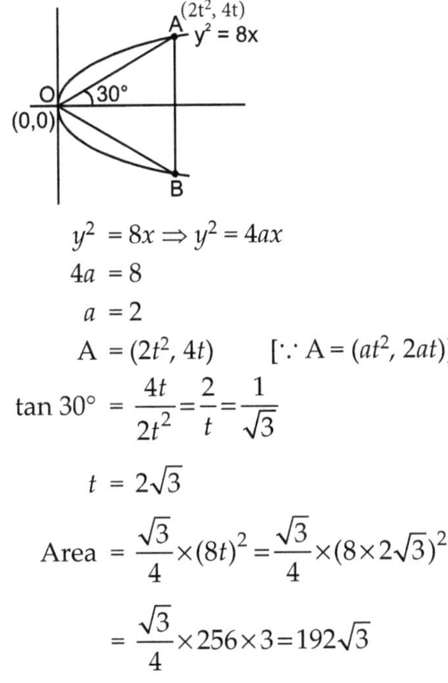

$$y^2 = 8x \Rightarrow y^2 = 4ax$$
$$4a = 8$$
$$a = 2$$
$$A = (2t^2, 4t) \qquad [\because A = (at^2, 2at)]$$
$$\tan 30° = \frac{4t}{2t^2} = \frac{2}{t} = \frac{1}{\sqrt{3}}$$
$$t = 2\sqrt{3}$$
$$\text{Area} = \frac{\sqrt{3}}{4} \times (8t)^2 = \frac{\sqrt{3}}{4} \times (8 \times 2\sqrt{3})^2$$
$$= \frac{\sqrt{3}}{4} \times 256 \times 3 = 192\sqrt{3}$$

11. **Correct Response :** (0.8)

   Explanation :

$$\overset{\lambda \qquad\qquad 1}{\underset{A(\hat{i}+\hat{j}+\hat{k}) \qquad\qquad B(2\hat{i}+\hat{j}+3\hat{k})}{\bullet\!-\!-\!-\!-\!-\!\bullet\!-\!-\!-\!-\!-\!\bullet}}$$

Using section formula we get

$$\overrightarrow{OP} = \frac{2\lambda+1}{\lambda+1}\hat{i} + \frac{\lambda+1}{\lambda+1}\hat{j} + \frac{3\lambda+1}{\lambda+1}\hat{k}$$

$$\overrightarrow{OB} = 2\hat{i} + \hat{j} + 3\hat{k}$$

Now $\qquad \overrightarrow{OB} \cdot \overrightarrow{OP} = \dfrac{4\lambda + 2 + \lambda + 1 + 9\lambda + 3}{\lambda + 1}$

$$= \frac{14\lambda + 6}{\lambda + 1}$$

$$\overrightarrow{OA} \times \overrightarrow{OP} = \begin{vmatrix} \hat{i} & \hat{j} & \hat{k} \\ 1 & 1 & 1 \\ \dfrac{2\lambda+1}{\lambda+1} & 1 & \dfrac{3\lambda+1}{\lambda+1} \end{vmatrix}$$

$$= \frac{2\lambda+1}{\lambda+1}\hat{i} + \frac{-\lambda}{\lambda+1}\hat{j} + \frac{-\lambda}{\lambda+1}\hat{k}$$

$$|\overrightarrow{OA} \times \overrightarrow{OP}|^2 = \frac{(2\lambda+1)^2 + \lambda^2 + \lambda^2}{(\lambda+1)^2}$$

$$= \frac{6\lambda^2 + 1}{(\lambda+1)^2}$$

$$\overrightarrow{OB}.\overrightarrow{OP} - 3\,|\overrightarrow{OA} \times \overrightarrow{OP}|^2 = 6$$

$$\Rightarrow \frac{14\lambda + 6}{\lambda + 1} - 3 \times \frac{(6\lambda^2 + 1)}{(\lambda+1)^2} = 6$$

$$\Rightarrow \qquad 10\lambda^2 - 8\lambda = 0$$
$$\Rightarrow \qquad \lambda = 0. = 0.8$$
$$\Rightarrow \qquad \lambda = 0.8$$

12. **Correct Response :** (a)

   Explanation :

$$\cos\phi = \frac{\overline{p}.\overline{q}}{|\overline{p}||\overline{q}|} = \frac{ab + bc + ca}{a^2 + b^2 + c^2} = \frac{\Sigma ab}{1}$$

$$= abc\left(\frac{1}{a} + \frac{1}{b} + \frac{1}{c}\right)$$

$$a\cos\theta = b\cos\left(\theta + \frac{2\pi}{3}\right) = c\cos\left(\theta + \frac{4\pi}{3}\right) = \lambda$$

$$a = \frac{\lambda}{\cos\theta}, b = \frac{\lambda}{\cos\left(\theta + \dfrac{2\pi}{3}\right)}, c = \frac{\lambda}{\cos\left(\theta + \dfrac{4\pi}{3}\right)}$$

$\because \cos C + \cos D = 2\cos\dfrac{C+D}{2}.\cos\dfrac{C-D}{2}$

$$= \frac{abc}{\lambda}\left(\cos\theta + 2\cos(\theta + \pi).\cos\frac{\pi}{3}\right)$$

$$= \frac{abc}{\lambda}\left(\cos\theta - 2\cos\theta \times \frac{1}{2}\right)$$

$$= \frac{abc}{\lambda}(\cos\theta - \cos\theta)$$

$$= 0$$

$$\cos\phi = 0$$

$$\boxed{\theta = \frac{\pi}{2}}$$

13. Correct Response : (b)

Explanation :

$$\frac{|x|}{2}+\frac{|y|}{3}=1$$

$$\frac{x^2}{4}+\frac{y^2}{9}=1$$

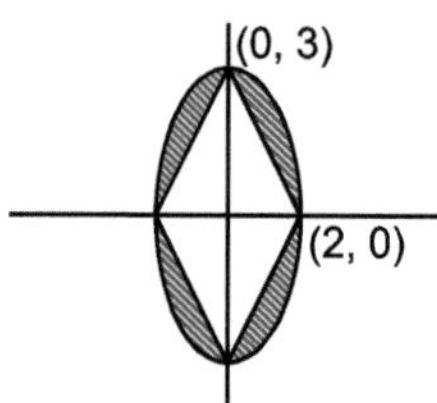

Area of Ellipse $= \pi ab = 6\pi$

Required area

$$= \pi \times 2 \times 3 - (\text{Area of quadrilateral})$$

$$= 6\pi - \frac{1}{2}6\times 4$$

$$= 6\pi - 12$$

$$= 6(\pi - 2)$$

14. Correct Response : (2)

Explanation :

$$|\vec{a}|=|\vec{b}|=|\vec{c}|=1$$

$$|\vec{a}-\vec{b}|^2+|\vec{a}-\vec{b}|^2=8$$

$$\Rightarrow |\vec{a}|^2+|\vec{b}|^2-2\vec{a}.\vec{b}+|\vec{a}|^2+|\vec{c}|^2-2\vec{a}.\vec{c}=8$$

$$\Rightarrow 4-2(\vec{a}.\vec{b}+\vec{a}.\vec{c})=8$$

$$\Rightarrow \vec{a}.\vec{b}+\vec{a}.\vec{c}=-2$$

$$|\vec{a}+2\vec{b}|^2+|\vec{a}+2\vec{c}|^2$$

$$= |\vec{a}|^2+4|\vec{b}|^2+4\vec{a}.\vec{b}+|\vec{a}|^2+4|\vec{c}|^2+4\vec{a}.\vec{c}$$

$$= 10+4(\vec{a}.\vec{b}+\vec{a}.\vec{c})$$

$$= 10-8$$

$$= 2.$$

15. Correct Response : (a)

Explanation :

$$\vec{a}+\vec{b}+\vec{c}=\vec{0}$$

$$\Rightarrow |\vec{a}|^2+|\vec{b}|^2+|\vec{c}|^2+2(\vec{a}.\vec{b})+2(\vec{b}.\vec{c})+2(\vec{c}.\vec{a})$$

$$= 0$$

$$1=\vec{a}.\vec{b}+\vec{b}.\vec{c}+\vec{c}.\vec{a}=\frac{-3}{2}$$

$$\vec{d}=\vec{a}\times\vec{b}+\vec{b}\times\vec{c}+\vec{c}\times\vec{a}$$

$$\vec{a}+\vec{b}+\vec{c}=\vec{0}$$

$$\Rightarrow \vec{a}\times\vec{b}=\vec{b}\times\vec{c}=\vec{c}\times\vec{a}$$

$$\Rightarrow \vec{d}=3(\vec{a}\times\vec{b})$$

16. Correct Response : (30)

Explanation :

$$\vec{b}.\vec{c}=10$$

$$\Rightarrow 5|\vec{c}|\cos\frac{\pi}{3}=10$$

$$\Rightarrow |\vec{c}|=4$$

$$|\vec{a}\times(\vec{b}\times\vec{c})|=|\vec{a}||\vec{b}\times\vec{c}|$$

$$= \sqrt{3}.5.4.\sin\frac{\pi}{3}=30$$

17. Correct Response : (*)

Explanation :

$$\vec{a}=\lambda(\vec{b}+\vec{c})=\lambda\left(\frac{\hat{i}+\hat{j}}{\sqrt{2}}+\frac{\hat{i}-\hat{j}+4\hat{k}}{3\sqrt{2}}\right)$$

$$\vec{a}=\frac{\lambda}{3\sqrt{2}}(4\hat{i}+2\hat{j}+4\hat{k})$$

$$\Rightarrow \frac{\lambda}{3\sqrt{2}}(4\hat{i}+2\hat{j}+4\hat{k})=\alpha\hat{i}+2\hat{j}+\beta\hat{k}$$

$$\Rightarrow \alpha=4 \text{ and } \beta=4$$

So, $$\vec{a}=4\hat{i}+2\hat{j}+4\hat{k}$$

None of the given options is correct.

18. Correct Response : (8.00)

Explanation :

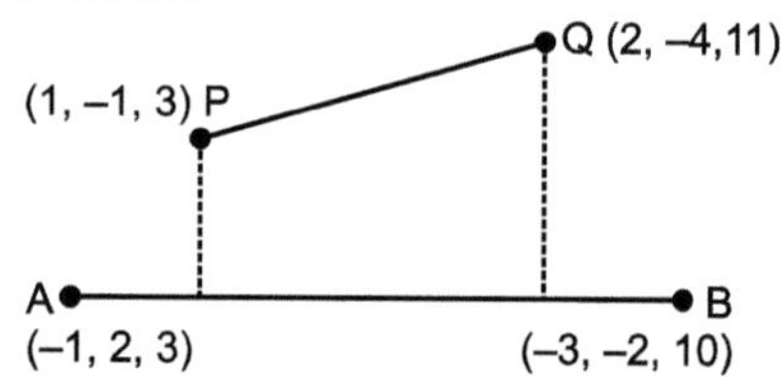

P Projection of $\vec{PQ}$ and $\vec{AB}=\left|\dfrac{\vec{PQ}.\vec{AB}}{|\vec{AB}|}\right|$

$$= \left|\frac{(\hat{i}-3\hat{j}+8\hat{k}).(4\hat{i}-4\hat{j}+7\hat{k})}{9}\right|=8$$

19. Correct Response : (c)

Explanation :

$$\vec{b}\times\vec{c}-\vec{b}\times\vec{a}=\vec{0}$$

$$\vec{b}\times(\vec{c}-\vec{a})=\vec{0}$$

$$\vec{b}=\lambda(\vec{c}-\vec{a})$$

$$\qquad\qquad\qquad\qquad ...(i)$$

$$\vec{a} \cdot \vec{b} = \lambda(\vec{a} \cdot \vec{c} - \vec{a}^2)$$

$$4 = \lambda(0 - 6)$$

$$4 = \lambda(0 - 6) \Rightarrow \lambda = \frac{-4}{6} = \frac{-2}{3}$$

From (i) $$\vec{b} = \frac{-2}{3}(\vec{c} - \vec{a})$$

$$\vec{c} = \frac{-3}{2}\vec{b} + \vec{a} = \frac{-1}{2}(\hat{i} + \hat{j} + \hat{k})$$

$$\vec{b} \cdot \vec{c} = \frac{-1}{2}$$

20. Correct Response : (d)
Explanation :

$$\alpha = \frac{\pi}{3}, \beta = \frac{\pi}{4}$$

Since, $\cos^2 \alpha + \cos^2 \beta + \cos^2 \gamma = 1$
Therefore,

$$\frac{1}{4} + \frac{1}{2} + \cos^2 \gamma = 1$$

$$\Rightarrow \qquad \cos^2 \gamma = \frac{1}{4}$$

$$\Rightarrow \qquad \cos \gamma = \pm\frac{1}{2}$$

$$\Rightarrow \qquad \gamma = \frac{2\pi}{3}$$

21. Correct Response : (c)
Explanation :

$$\vec{\beta_1} = \frac{\vec{\alpha} \cdot \vec{\beta}}{|\vec{\alpha}|^2}\vec{\alpha}$$

$$= \frac{5}{10}\vec{\alpha}$$

$$= \frac{\vec{\alpha}}{2}$$

$$= \frac{3}{2}\hat{i} + \frac{1}{2}\hat{j}$$

$$\vec{\beta_2} = \vec{\beta_1} - \vec{\beta}$$

$$= -\frac{1}{2}\hat{i} + \frac{3}{2}\hat{j} - 3\hat{k}$$

$$\vec{\beta_1} \times \vec{\beta_2} = \frac{1}{2}(-3\hat{i} + 9\hat{j} + 5\hat{k})$$

22. Correct Response : (d)
Explanation :

Normal vector to the plane containing $\hat{i} + \hat{j} + \hat{k}$

and $\hat{i} + 2\hat{j} + 3\hat{k}$ is

$$\vec{n} = (\hat{i} + \hat{j} + \hat{k}) \times (\hat{i} + 2\hat{j} + 3\hat{k})$$

$$\vec{n} = \hat{i} - 2\hat{j} + \hat{k}$$

Projection of $2\hat{i} + 3\hat{j} + \hat{k}$ on $\vec{n}$

$$\left| \frac{(2\hat{i} + 3\hat{j} + \hat{k}) \cdot (\hat{i} - 2\hat{j} + \hat{k})}{\sqrt{1 + 4 + 1}} \right| = \frac{3}{\sqrt{6}}$$

$$= \sqrt{\frac{3}{2}}$$

23. Correct Response : (b)
Explanation :

$$(a \times b) = \begin{vmatrix} i & j & k \\ 3 & 2 & x \\ 1 & -1 & 1 \end{vmatrix}$$

$$= (2 + x)i - (3 - x)j - 5k$$

$$|a \times b| = \sqrt{(2+x)^2 + (3-x)^2 + 25}$$

$$= \sqrt{2}\sqrt{x^2 - x + 19}$$

Minimum value is $\sqrt{2}\sqrt{\dfrac{-D}{4a}} = \dfrac{5\sqrt{3}}{\sqrt{2}}$

So, $$r \geq 5\sqrt{\frac{3}{2}}$$

24. Correct Response : (b)
Explanation :
The required vector is,

$$\vec{r} = \lambda((\vec{a} + \vec{b}) \times (\vec{a} - \vec{b}))$$

$$= \lambda \begin{vmatrix} \hat{i} & \hat{j} & \hat{k} \\ 4 & 4 & 0 \\ 2 & 0 & 4 \end{vmatrix}$$

$$= \lambda(16\hat{i} - 16\hat{j} - 8\hat{k})$$

$$= 8\lambda(2\hat{i} - 2\hat{j} - \hat{k})$$

Solve further as,

$$|\vec{r}| = |8\lambda| \cdot \sqrt{2^2 + 2^2 + 1}$$

$$= |8\lambda| \cdot 3$$

Since, $$|\vec{r}| = 12.$$

Therefore, $$\lambda = \frac{1}{2}$$

Substitute the values,

$$\vec{r} = \pm 4(2\hat{i} - 2\hat{j} - \hat{k}).$$

25. Correct Response : (b)
Explanation :
From the given data,

$$V = [\vec{a}\,\vec{b}\,\vec{c}]$$

$$= \begin{vmatrix} 1 & \lambda & 1 \\ 0 & 1 & \lambda \\ \lambda & 0 & 1 \end{vmatrix}$$

$$= 1 - \lambda(-\lambda^2) + 1(0-\lambda)$$

$$= \lambda^3 - \lambda + 1$$

Minimum value occur at $\lambda = \dfrac{1}{\sqrt{3}}$.

26. Correct Response : (b)

Explanation :

It is given that vectors are coplanar.

Therefore,

$$\begin{vmatrix} \alpha & 1 & 3 \\ 2 & 1 & -\alpha \\ \alpha & -2 & 3 \end{vmatrix} = 0$$

$$\alpha(3 - 2\alpha) - 1(6 + \alpha^2) + 3(-4 - \alpha) = 0$$

$$-3\alpha^2 - 18 = 0$$

$$\alpha^2 = -6$$

Since there is no real value of α, the set S is null.

27. Correct Response : 18.00

Explanation :

The given vectors are,

$$\vec{a} = 2\hat{i} + \hat{j} - \hat{k}$$

And

$$\vec{b} = \hat{i} + 2\hat{j} + \hat{k}$$

The considered vector is,

$$\vec{c} = \alpha\vec{a} + \beta\vec{b}$$

Solve the above equation.

$$\vec{c} = \alpha(2\hat{i} + \hat{j} - \hat{k}) + \beta(\hat{i} + 2\hat{j} + \hat{k})$$

$$= (2\alpha + \beta)\hat{i} + (\alpha + 2\beta)\hat{j} + (\beta - \alpha)\hat{k}$$

Therefore,

$$\frac{\vec{c} \cdot (\vec{a} + \vec{b})}{|\vec{a} + \vec{b}|} = 3\sqrt{2}$$

$$9(\alpha + \beta) = 18$$

$$\alpha + \beta = 2$$

Again,

$$(\vec{c} - \vec{a} \times \vec{b}) \cdot \vec{c} = (\alpha\vec{a} + \beta\vec{b} - \vec{a} \times \vec{b}) \cdot (\alpha\vec{a} + \beta\vec{b})$$

$$= 6\alpha^2 + 6\alpha\beta + 6\beta^2$$

$$= 6(\alpha^2 + \alpha(2 - \alpha) + (2 - \alpha)^2)$$

$$= 6(\alpha^2 - 2\alpha + 4)$$

Solve the rest,

The minimum value is 18 for $\alpha = 1$.

28. Correct Response : 0.5

Explanation :

The figure below shows the cube.

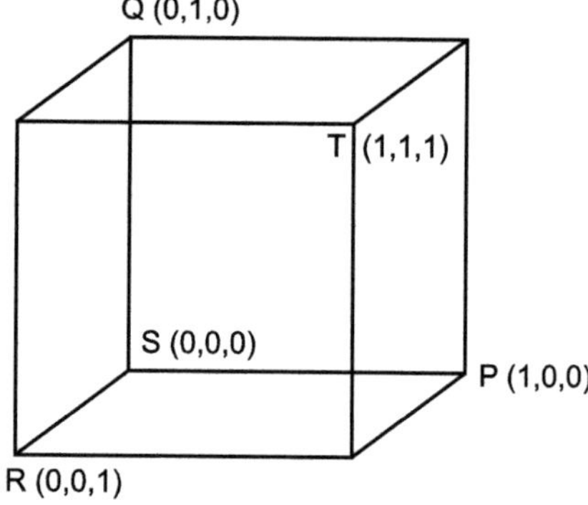

The vectors $\overline{OP}, \overline{OQ}, \overline{OR}$ and $\overline{OT}$ are as follows,

$$\vec{p} = \vec{OP} = \frac{\hat{i} - \hat{j} - \hat{k}}{2}$$

$$\vec{q} = \vec{SQ} = \frac{\hat{i} + \hat{j} + \hat{k}}{2}$$

$$\vec{r} = \vec{OR} = \frac{-\hat{i} - \hat{j} + \hat{k}}{2}$$

$$\vec{t} = \vec{OT} = \frac{\hat{i} + \hat{j} + \hat{k}}{2}$$

The cross product of vector $\vec{p}$ and $\vec{q}$ is,

$$\vec{p} \times \vec{q} = \begin{vmatrix} \hat{i} & \hat{j} & \hat{k} \\ 1 & -1 & -1 \\ -1 & 1 & -1 \end{vmatrix} \times \frac{1}{4}$$

$$= \frac{1}{4}(2\hat{i} + 2\hat{j})$$

$$= \frac{\hat{i} + \hat{j}}{2}$$

The cross product of vector $\vec{r}$ and $\vec{t}$ is,

$$\vec{r} \times \vec{t} = \begin{vmatrix} \hat{i} & \hat{j} & \hat{k} \\ -1 & -1 & 1 \\ 1 & 1 & 1 \end{vmatrix} \times \frac{1}{4}$$

$$= \frac{1}{4}(-2\hat{i} + 2\hat{j})$$

$$= \frac{-\hat{i} + \hat{j}}{2}$$

The cross product of vector $(\vec{r} \times \vec{t})$ and $(\vec{r} \times \vec{t})$ is,

$$(\vec{p} \times \vec{q}) \times (\vec{r} \times \vec{t}) = \begin{vmatrix} \hat{i} & \hat{j} & \hat{k} \\ 1 & 1 & 0 \\ -1 & 1 & 0 \end{vmatrix} \times \frac{1}{4}$$

$$= \frac{\hat{k}}{2}$$

$$|(\vec{p} \times \vec{q}) \times (\vec{r} \times \vec{t})| = \frac{1}{2}$$

$$= 0.5$$

29. Correct Response : (a)

Explanation :

$$\vec{a} + 2\vec{b} + 2\vec{c} = \vec{0}$$

$$(\vec{a} + 2\vec{c})^2 = (-2\vec{b})^2$$

$$\left|\vec{a}\right|^2 + 4\,\vec{a} \cdot \vec{c} + 4\left|\vec{c}\right|^2 = 4\left|\vec{b}\right|^2$$

$$\left|\vec{a}\right|^2 + 4\left|\vec{a}\right|\left|\vec{c}\right|\cos\theta + 4\left|\vec{c}\right|^2 = 4\left|\vec{b}\right|^2$$

If $\vec{a}$, $\vec{b}$ and $\vec{c}$ are unit vectors then, there magnitude will be unity.

$$(1) + 4(1)(1)\cos\theta + 4(1) = 4(1)$$

$$\cos\theta = -\frac{1}{4}$$

The magnitude of $\left|\vec{a} \times \vec{c}\right|$ is,

$$\left|\vec{a} \times \vec{c}\right| = \left|\vec{a}\right| \cdot \left|\vec{c}\right|\sin\theta$$

$$= (1)(1)\sqrt{1 - \cos^2\theta}$$

$$= \sqrt{1 - \left(-\frac{1}{4}\right)^2}$$

$$= \frac{\sqrt{15}}{4}$$

30. Correct Response : (c)

Explanation :

Apply the cross product formula,

$$\vec{a} \times \vec{b} = \vec{c}$$

Multiply both sides with $\vec{a}$

$$\vec{a} \times (\vec{a} \times \vec{b}) = \vec{a} \times \vec{c} \qquad \qquad ...(1)$$

Here,

$$\vec{a} \times \vec{c} = -2\hat{i} + \hat{j} + \hat{k}$$

From equation (1)

$$3\vec{a} - 3\vec{b} = -2\hat{i} + \hat{j} + \hat{k}$$

$$3\hat{i} + 3\hat{j} + 3\hat{k} - 3\vec{b} = -2\hat{i} + \hat{j} + \hat{k}$$

$$\vec{b} = \frac{1}{3}(5\hat{i} + 2\hat{j} + 2\hat{k})$$

$$\left|\vec{b}\right| = \frac{\sqrt{25 + 4 + 4}}{3}$$

$$\left|\vec{b}\right| = \sqrt{\frac{11}{3}}$$

31. Correct Response : (a)

Explanation :

For the vector $\hat{u}$

$$\vec{u} = \beta(\vec{a} \times (\vec{a} \times \vec{b}))$$

$$= \beta((\vec{a} \cdot \vec{b})\,\vec{a} - |\vec{a}|^2\,\vec{b})$$

$$= \beta(2\vec{a} - 14\vec{b})$$

$$= 2\beta\{(2\hat{i} + 3\hat{j} - \hat{k}) - 7(\hat{j} + \hat{k})\}$$

Simplify the above equation.

$$= 2\beta(2\hat{i} - 4\hat{j} - 8\hat{k})$$

Since $\vec{u} \cdot \vec{b} = 24$,

$$2\beta(2\hat{i} - 4\hat{j} - 8\hat{k}) \cdot (\hat{j} + \hat{k}) = 24$$

$$2\beta(-4 - 8) = 24$$

$$\beta = -1$$

The magnitude is,

$$\vec{u} = 4(\hat{i} - 2\hat{j} - 4\hat{k})$$

$$|\vec{u}| = (4)\sqrt{1^2 + (-2)^2 + (-4)^2}$$

$$|\vec{u}|^2 = 16 \times 21$$

$$|\vec{u}|^2 = 336$$

32. Correct Response : (b)

Explanation :

For a vector $\vec{b}$,

$$\vec{b} = \left(\frac{\vec{b} \cdot \vec{a}}{|\vec{a}|}\right)\frac{\vec{a}}{|\vec{a}|}$$

$$= \left(\frac{(3\hat{j} + 4\hat{k}) \cdot (\hat{i} + \hat{j})}{\sqrt{2}}\right)\left(\frac{(\hat{i} + \hat{j})}{\sqrt{2}}\right)$$

$$= \frac{3}{2}(\hat{i} + \hat{j})$$

From the question,

$$\vec{b}_1 + \vec{b}_2 = \vec{b}$$

$$\vec{b}_2 = \vec{b} - \vec{b}_1$$

$$\vec{b}_2 = (3\hat{j} + 4\hat{k}) - \frac{3}{2}(\hat{i} + \hat{j})$$

$$= -\frac{3}{2}\hat{i} + \frac{3}{2}\hat{j} + 4\hat{k}$$

The cross product of $\vec{b}_1$ and $\vec{b}_2$ is,

$$\vec{b}_1 \times \vec{b}_2 = \begin{vmatrix} \hat{i} & \hat{j} & \hat{k} \\ \dfrac{3}{2} & \dfrac{3}{2} & 0 \\ -\dfrac{3}{2} & \dfrac{3}{2} & 4 \end{vmatrix}$$

$$= \hat{i}\left(\frac{12}{2} - 0\right) - \hat{j}(6) + \hat{k}\left(\frac{9}{4} + \frac{9}{4}\right)$$

$$= 6\hat{i} - 6\hat{j} + \frac{9}{2}\hat{k}$$

33. Correct Response : (d)

Explanation :

For the given position vectors $\vec{a}$, $\vec{b}$ and $\vec{c}$ the expression for the centroid of the triangle ABC is,

$$\text{Centroid} \equiv \left(\frac{\vec{a} + \vec{b} + \vec{c}}{3}\right)$$

The relationship between the centroid, circumcenter and orthocenter is shown in the diagram,

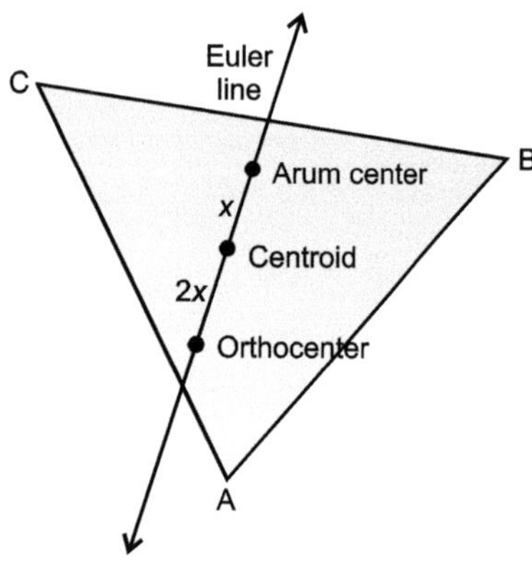

Therefore,

Orthocentre = 3 (centroid) – 2 (circumcenter)

$$\text{Orthocentre} = 3\left(\frac{\vec{a} + \vec{b} + \vec{c}}{3}\right) - 2\left(\frac{\vec{a} + \vec{b} + \vec{c}}{4}\right)$$

$$= \left(\frac{\vec{a} + \vec{b} + \vec{c}}{2}\right)$$

34. Correct Response : (b)

Explanation :

The product of diagonal is given as :

$$d_1 \times d_2 = \begin{vmatrix} i & j & k \\ 8 & -6 & 0 \\ 3 & 4 & -12 \end{vmatrix}$$

$$= 72i + 96j + 50k$$

Area of the parallelogram is given as,

$$A = \frac{1}{2}|d_1 \times d_2|$$

$$= \frac{1}{2}\sqrt{72^2 + 96^2 + 50^2}$$

$$= 65 \text{ sq. units}$$

35. Correct Response : (a)

Explanation :

The cross product of a, b, c is,

$$\left|(\vec{b} \times \vec{b}) \times \vec{c}\right| = 3$$

$$\left|\vec{a} \times \vec{b}\right|\left|\vec{c}\right|\sin 30° = 3$$

$$\left|\vec{c}\right|\left(\frac{1}{2}\right) = \frac{3}{\sqrt{4 + 4 + 1}}$$

$$\left|\vec{c} - \vec{a}\right| = 3$$

The cross product of a, c is,

$$\left|\vec{c} - \vec{a}\right| = 3$$

$$|\vec{c}|^2 + |\vec{c}|^2 - 2\left(\vec{a} \cdot \vec{c}\right) = 9$$

$$\vec{a} \cdot \vec{c} = \frac{9 - 3 - 2}{2}$$

$$= 2$$

36. Correct Response : (c)

Explanation :

The given value of the position vector is,

$$\vec{A} = 3\hat{i} + \hat{j} - \hat{k}$$

$$\vec{B} = -\hat{i} + 3\hat{j} + p\hat{k}$$

and

$$\vec{C} = 5\hat{i} + q\hat{j} - 4\hat{k}$$

Dot product of the position vector of A and B is,

$$\vec{A}.\vec{B} = -4\hat{i} + 2\hat{j} + (p + 1)\hat{k}$$

Dot product of the position vector of A and C is,

$$\vec{A}.\vec{C} = 2\hat{i} + (q - 1)\hat{j} - 3\hat{k}$$

The relation for right angle tirangle is,

$$(\vec{A}.\vec{B}).(\vec{A}.\vec{C}) = 0$$

$$-8 + 2(q-1) - 3(p+1) = 0$$
$$-3p + 2q - 13 = 0$$
$$3p - 2q + 13 = 0$$

Hence, the point (p, q) lies on a line :
$$3x - 2y + 13 = 0$$
$$y = \left(\frac{3}{2}\right)x + \frac{13}{2}$$

Hence, the slope is $= \dfrac{3}{2}$

37. Correct Response : (d)

Explanation :

The given expression of the vector is

$$\vec{a} \times (\vec{b} \times \vec{c}) = \frac{\sqrt{3}}{2}(\vec{b} + \vec{c})$$

$$\left(\vec{a}.\vec{c}\right)\vec{b} - (\vec{a}.\vec{b})\vec{c} = \frac{\sqrt{3}}{2}(\vec{b} + \vec{c})$$

Compare both the sides of the above expression,

$$\vec{a}.\vec{c} = \frac{\sqrt{3}}{2}$$

$$\vec{a}.\vec{c} = -\frac{\sqrt{3}}{2}$$

So, the angle between $\vec{a}$ and $\vec{b}$ is,

$$\cos\theta = -\frac{\sqrt{3}}{2}$$

Here, θ is angle between $\vec{a}$ and $\vec{b}$.

$$\theta = \frac{5\pi}{6}$$

38. Correct Response : (*)

Explanation :

The figure of the parallelogram with the direction of the vector,

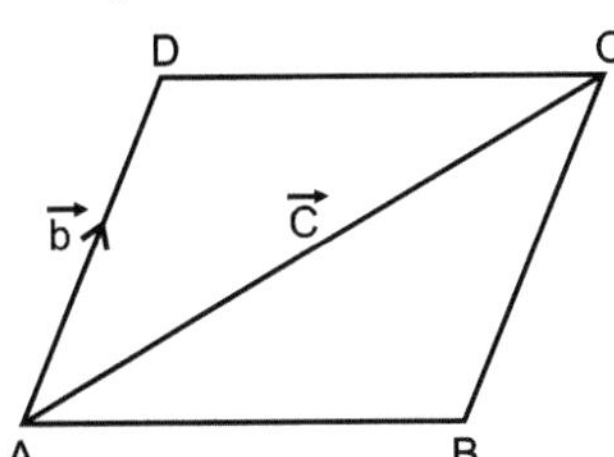

Here,
$$|\overline{AB}| = a$$
$$|\overline{AD}| = b$$

And,
$$|\overline{AC}| = c$$

Since,
$$\overline{AB} + \overline{AD} = \overline{AC}$$
$$|\overline{AB}|^2 + |AD|^2 + 2\overline{AB}.\overline{AD} = |AC|^2$$

$$a^2 + b^2 + 2\overline{AB}.(\overline{AB} + \overline{BD}) = c^2$$
$$a^2 + b^2 + 2a^2 + 2\overline{AB}.\overline{BD} = c^2$$

Further, simplify the above vector expression,
$$2\overline{AB}.\overline{BD} = c^2 - 3a^2 - b^2$$
$$2\overline{AB}.\overline{DB} = 3a^2 + b^2 - c^2$$
$$\overline{AB}.\overline{DB} = \frac{1}{2}(3a^2 + b^2 - c^2)$$
$$\overline{DB}.\overline{AB} = \frac{1}{2}(3a^2 + b^2 - c^2)$$

39. Correct Response : (9)

Explanation :

Given the components of a vector $\vec{s}$ is,

$$\vec{s} = 4\vec{p} + 3\vec{q} + 5\vec{r} \qquad ...(1)$$

And also the value of the vector $\vec{s}$ is,

$$\vec{s} = x(-\vec{p} + \vec{q} + \vec{r}) + y(\vec{p} - \vec{q} + \vec{r}) + z(-\vec{p} - \vec{q} + \vec{r})$$

$$= (-x + y - z)\vec{p} + (x - y - z)\vec{q} + (x + y + z)\vec{r} \;...(2)$$

Compare equation (1) with equation (2),
$$-x + y - z = 4 \qquad ...(3)$$
$$x - y - z = 3 \qquad ...(4)$$
$$x + y + z = 5 \qquad ....(5)$$

Simplify the equation (3), (4) and (5),
$$x = 4$$
$$y = 4.5$$
$$z = -3.5$$

Hence, the required value is,
$$2(4) + 4.5 + (-3.5) = 8 + 1$$
$$= 9$$

40. Correct Response : (a, c, d)

Explanation :

Given,
$$|\vec{a}| = 12$$
$$|\vec{b}| = 4\sqrt{3}$$
$$\vec{b}.\vec{c} = 24$$

Calculate the values,
$$\vec{a} + \vec{b} + \vec{c} = 0$$
$$\vec{b} + \vec{c} = -\vec{a}$$

Square both sides,
$$\left|\vec{b} + \vec{c}\right|^2 = |\vec{a}|^2$$
$$|\vec{c}|^2 = 48$$
$$= 4\sqrt{3}$$

Hence,

From the given value,

$$\vec{b} \cdot \vec{c} = 24$$

$$|\vec{b}| \cdot |\vec{c}| \cos \theta = 24$$

The value of the angle is,

$$\cos \theta = \frac{1}{2}$$

$$\angle QPR = 120°, \angle PQR = \angle QRP = 30°$$

(a)

The required value is,

$$\frac{|\vec{c}|^2}{2} - |\vec{a}| = \frac{48}{2} - 12$$

$$= 12$$

(b)

The required value is,

$$\frac{|\vec{c}|^2}{2} + |\vec{a}| = \frac{48}{2} + 12$$

$$= 36$$

(d)

The given relation for the triangle is,

$$\vec{a} + \vec{b} + \vec{c} = 0$$

Multiply both sides with $\vec{b}$,

$$\vec{a} \cdot \vec{b} + \vec{b} \cdot \vec{b} + \vec{c} \cdot \vec{b} = 0$$

$$\vec{a} \cdot \vec{b} + |\vec{b}|^2 + 24 = 0$$

$$\vec{a} \cdot \vec{b} = -(24 + (4\sqrt{3})^2)$$

$$= -72$$

(c)

Calculate the required value,

$$\left| \vec{a} \times \vec{b} + \vec{a} \times \vec{c} \right| = 2 \left| \vec{a} \times \vec{b} \right|$$

$$= 2\left(\sqrt{144 \times 48 - 72^2}\right)$$

$$= 48\sqrt{3}$$

41. Correct Response : (b)

Explanation :

The given expression is,

$$\lambda[\vec{a} \cdot \vec{b} \cdot \vec{c}]^2 = (\vec{a} \times \vec{b}) \cdot [(\vec{b} \times \vec{c}) \times (\vec{c} \times \vec{a})]$$

Simplify the given expression,

$$\lambda[\vec{a} \ \vec{b} \ \vec{c}]^2 = (\vec{a} \times \vec{b}) \cdot [(\vec{b} \times \vec{c}) \times (\vec{c} \times \vec{a})]$$

$$= (\vec{a} \times \vec{b}) \cdot [(\vec{b} \times \vec{c} \cdot \vec{a})\vec{c} - (\vec{b} \times \vec{c} \cdot \vec{c})\vec{a}]$$

$$= (\vec{a} \times \vec{b}) \cdot \left[[\vec{b} \cdot \vec{c} \cdot \vec{a}]\vec{c}\right]$$

$$= [\vec{a} \ \vec{b} \ \vec{c}] \cdot (\vec{a} \times \vec{b} \cdot \vec{c})$$

Further, simplify the given expression,

$$\lambda[\vec{a} \ \vec{b} \ \vec{c}]^2 = [\vec{a} \cdot \vec{b} \cdot \vec{c}]^2$$

$$\lambda = 1$$

42. Correct Response : (4)

Explanation :

The relation between the three non linear unit vectors is given by,

$$[\vec{a} \ \vec{b} \ \vec{c}]^2 = \begin{vmatrix} \vec{a} \cdot \vec{a} & \vec{a} \cdot \vec{b} & \vec{a} \cdot \vec{c} \\ \vec{b} \cdot \vec{a} & \vec{b} \cdot \vec{b} & \vec{b} \cdot \vec{c} \\ \vec{c} \cdot \vec{a} & \vec{c} \cdot \vec{b} & \vec{c} \cdot \vec{c} \end{vmatrix}$$

$$= \begin{vmatrix} 1 & \frac{1}{2} & \frac{1}{2} \\ \frac{1}{2} & 1 & \frac{1}{2} \\ \frac{1}{2} & \frac{1}{2} & 1 \end{vmatrix}$$

$$[\vec{a} \ \vec{b} \ \vec{c}]^2 = \frac{1}{2}$$

$$[\vec{a} \ \vec{b} \ \vec{c}] = \frac{1}{\sqrt{2}} \qquad ..(1)$$

The relation between the function as,

$$\vec{a} \times \vec{b} + \vec{b} \times \vec{c} = p\vec{a} + q\vec{b} + r\vec{c} \qquad ...(2)$$

Take dot product with $\vec{a}$ in both side of the above expression,

$$\vec{a} \cdot (\vec{a} \times \vec{b}) + \vec{a} \cdot (\vec{b} \times \vec{c}) = p(\vec{a})^2 + \vec{a} \cdot q\vec{b} + \vec{a} \cdot r\vec{c}$$

$$0 + \frac{1}{\sqrt{2}} = p + \frac{q}{2} + \frac{r}{2} \qquad ...(3)$$

Take dot product with $\vec{b}$ in both side of the equation (2),

$$\vec{b} \cdot (\vec{a} \times \vec{b}) + \vec{b} \cdot (\vec{b} \times \vec{c}) = \vec{b} \cdot p(\vec{a}) + q(\vec{b})^2 + \vec{b} \cdot r\vec{c}$$

$$0 = \frac{p}{2} + q + \frac{r}{2} \qquad ...(4)$$

Take dot product with $\vec{c}$ in both side of the equation (2),

$$\vec{c} \cdot (\vec{a} \times \vec{b}) + \vec{c} \cdot (\vec{b} \times \vec{c}) = \vec{c} \cdot p(\vec{a}) + \vec{c} \cdot q(\vec{b}) + r(\vec{c})^2$$

$$0 + \frac{1}{\sqrt{2}} = \frac{p}{2} + \frac{q}{2} + r \qquad ..(5)$$

Subtract equation (4) from the equation (3),

$$\frac{p}{2} - \frac{r}{2} = 0$$

$$p = r$$

Substitute p for r in the equation (4) for the value of relation between p and q,

$$p + q = 0$$

The value of the funciton,

$$\frac{p^2 + 2q^2 + r^2}{q^2} = \frac{p^2 + 2p^2 + p^2}{p^2}$$

$$= 4$$

43. Correct Response : (c)

Explanation :

The given relation is,

$$\left| 2\vec{a} - \vec{b} \right| = 5$$

Simplify the given relation,

$$\left| 2\vec{a} - \vec{b} \right|^2 = 25$$

$$4\,|\vec{a}|^2 + |\vec{b}|^2 - 4\,\vec{a}.\vec{b} = 25$$

$$16 + 9 - 4\,\vec{a}.\vec{b} = 25$$

$$4 \times \vec{a}.\vec{b} = 0$$

Now,

$$|2\vec{a} + \vec{b}| = k$$

$$(2\vec{a} + \vec{b})(2\vec{a} + \vec{b}) = k^2$$

$$4\,|\vec{a}|^2 + |\vec{b}|^2 + 4\,\vec{a}.\vec{b} = k^2$$

$$\sqrt{16 + 9 + 0} = k$$

Hence, the required value is,

$$k = 5.$$

44. Correct Response : (b)

Explanation :

The given equation is,

$$\left|\hat{x} + \hat{y}\right|^2 + \left|\hat{y} + \hat{z}\right|^2 + \left|\hat{z} + \hat{x}\right|^2$$

$$= \hat{x}^2 + \hat{y}^2 + 2\hat{x}\hat{y} + \hat{y}^2 + \hat{x}^2 + 2\hat{y}\hat{z} + \hat{z}^2 + \hat{x}^2 + 2\hat{z}\hat{x}$$

$$= 2\hat{x}^2 + 2\hat{y}^2 + 2\hat{z}^2 + 2\hat{x}.\hat{y} + 2\hat{y}.\hat{z} + 2\hat{z}.\hat{x}$$

$$= 2\cdot1 + 2\cdot1 + 2\cdot1 + 2\,(\cos\theta_1 + \cos\theta_2 + \cos\theta_3)$$

$$= 6 + 2\,(\cos\theta_1 + \cos\theta_2 + \cos\theta_3)$$

The minimum value of given expression lies at

$$\theta_1 = \theta_2 = \theta_3 = \frac{2\pi}{3}.$$

The minimum value of the given expression is,

$$|\hat{x} + \hat{y}|^2 + |\hat{y} + \hat{z}|^2 + |\hat{z} + \hat{x}|^2$$

$$= 6 + 2\left(\cos\frac{2\pi}{3} + \cos\frac{2\pi}{3} + \cos\frac{2\pi}{3}\right)$$

$$= 6 - 3$$

$$= 3$$

45. Correct Response : (c)

Explanation :

The magnitude of the projection of $\vec{x} \times \vec{y}$ on $\vec{z}$ is given by,

$$\left| \frac{(\vec{x} \times \vec{y}) \cdot \vec{z}}{|\vec{z}|} \right| = \frac{1}{\sqrt{9 + 16 + 144}} \begin{vmatrix} 3 & -6 & -1 \\ 1 & 4 & -3 \\ 3 & -4 & -12 \end{vmatrix}$$

$$= 14$$

46. Correct Response : (d)

Explanation :

The given relation of the vector,

$$\vec{c} \times (\hat{i} + 2\hat{j} + 5\hat{k}) = 0$$

$$\vec{c} = \lambda(\hat{i} + 2\hat{j} + 5\hat{k})$$

$$|\vec{c}| = \lambda\sqrt{30}$$

$$(\lambda\sqrt{30})^2 = (|\vec{c}|)^2$$

Further solve the above expression,

$$(\lambda\sqrt{30})^2 = 60$$

$$\lambda = \pm\sqrt{2}$$

The value of $\vec{c}\cdot(-7\hat{i} + 2\hat{j} + 3\hat{k})$,

$$\vec{c}\cdot(-7\hat{i} + 2\hat{j} + 3\hat{k}) = (\lambda(\hat{i} + 2\hat{j} + 5\hat{k}))\cdot(-7\hat{i} + 2\hat{j} + 3\hat{k})$$

$$= \lambda\,(-7 + 4 + 15)$$

$$= \pm\,12\sqrt{2}$$

Hence, the value of $\vec{c}\cdot(-7\hat{i} + 2\hat{j} + 3\hat{k})$ is $12\sqrt{2}$.

47. Correct Response : (c)

Explanation :

P.

It is given that $[\vec{a}\ \ \vec{b}\ \ \vec{c}] = 2$.

The volume of parallelopiped given by vectors is,

$$V = [2(\vec{a} \times \vec{b})\ \ \ 3(\vec{b} \times \vec{c})\ \ \left(\vec{c} \times \vec{a}\right)]$$

$$= 6[\vec{a}\ \ \vec{b}\ \ \vec{c}]^2$$

$$= 6(2)^2$$

$$= 24$$

Q.

It is given that $[\vec{a}\ \ \vec{b}\ \ \vec{c}] = 5$.

The Volume of parallelopiped by given vectors is,

$$V = [3(\vec{a} + \vec{b})\ \ \ (\vec{b} + \vec{c})\ \ \ 2\left(\vec{c} + \vec{a}\right)]$$

$$= 6[\vec{a}+\vec{b} \quad \vec{b}+\vec{c} \quad \vec{c}+\vec{a}]$$

$$= 12[\vec{a} \quad \vec{b} \quad \vec{c}]$$

$$= 60$$

R.

It is given that $|\vec{a}\times\vec{b}| = 40$.

Now, the area of triangles.

$$A = \frac{1}{2}\left|(2\vec{a}+3\vec{b})\times(\vec{a}-\vec{b})\right|$$

$$= \frac{1}{2}\cdot 5\left|\vec{a}+\vec{b}\right|$$

$$= \frac{5}{2}\times 40$$

$$= 100.$$

S.

It is given that $\left|\vec{a}\times\vec{b}\right| = 30$.

Now, the area of parallelogram is,

$$A = \left|(\vec{a}+\vec{b})\times\vec{a}\right|$$

$$= \left|\vec{a}+\vec{b}\right|$$

$$= 30$$

48. Correct Response : (c)

Explanation :

The area of parallelogram is,

Area of base (PQRS) $= \dfrac{1}{2}\left|\overline{PQ}\times\overline{SQ}\right|$

$$= \frac{1}{2}\begin{vmatrix} \hat{i} & \hat{j} & \hat{k} \\ 3 & 1 & -2 \\ 1 & -3 & -4 \end{vmatrix}$$

$$= \frac{1}{2}\left|-10\hat{i}+10\hat{j}-10\hat{k}\right|$$

Further simplify.

Area of base (PQRS) $= \dfrac{1}{2}(10)\left|\hat{i}-\hat{j}+\hat{k}\right|$

$$= 5\left|\hat{i}-\hat{j}+\hat{k}\right|$$

$$= 5\sqrt{1^2+(-1)^2+1^2}$$

$$= 5\sqrt{3}$$

Height is calculated as,

$$\text{Height} = \left|\frac{1-2+3}{\sqrt{3}}\right|$$

$$= \frac{2}{\sqrt{3}}$$

Volume of parallelopiped is,

$$\text{Volume} = (5\sqrt{3})\left(\frac{2}{\sqrt{3}}\right)$$

$$= 10 \text{ cubic units}$$

49. Correct Response : (c)

Explanation :

The magnitude of two vectors is,

$$\left|\vec{a}+\vec{b}\right| = \sqrt{29}$$

Let,

$$2\hat{i}+3\hat{j}+4\hat{k} = \vec{c}$$

The given equation is,

$$\vec{a}\times(2\hat{i}+3\hat{j}+4\hat{k}) = (2\hat{i}+3\hat{j}+4\hat{k})\times\vec{b}$$

$$\vec{a}\times\vec{c} = \vec{c}\times\vec{b}$$

$$(\vec{a}+\vec{b})\times\vec{c} = \vec{0}$$

The cross product is zero, due to which ($\vec{a}+\vec{b}$) and $\vec{c}$ are parallel.

$$\vec{a}+\vec{b} = \lambda\vec{c} \qquad \ldots(1)$$

$$|\vec{a}+\vec{b}| = |\lambda||\vec{c}|$$

$$\sqrt{29} = |\lambda|\sqrt{2^2+3^2+4^2}$$

$$\lambda = \pm 1$$

From equation (1).

$$\vec{a}+\vec{b} = (\pm 1)\vec{c}$$

$$\vec{a}+\vec{b} = \pm(2\hat{i}+3\hat{j}+4\vec{k})$$

The value of term is,

$$(\vec{a}+\vec{b})\cdot(-7\hat{i}+2\hat{j}+3\hat{k}) = \pm(2\hat{i}+3\hat{j}+4\vec{k})$$
$$(-7\hat{i}+2\hat{j}+3\hat{k})$$

$$= \pm(-14+6+12)$$

$$= \pm 4$$

50. Correct Response : (3)

Explanation :

The given equation is,

$$|\vec{a}-\vec{b}|^2+|\vec{b}-\vec{c}|^2+|\vec{c}-\vec{a}|^2 = 9$$

$$|\vec{a}|^2+|\vec{b}|^2-2\vec{a}\cdot\vec{b}+|\vec{b}|^2+|\vec{c}|^2-2\vec{b}\cdot\vec{c}$$

R   Q   T   (α, β, γ)   S   P

$$+ |\vec{c}|^2 + |\vec{a}|^2 - 2\vec{c}\cdot\vec{a} = 9$$

$$1 + 1 - 2\vec{a}\cdot\vec{b} + 1 + 1 - 2\vec{b}\cdot\vec{c} + 1 + 1 - 2\vec{c}\cdot\vec{a} = 9$$

$$\vec{a}\cdot\vec{b} + \vec{b}\cdot\vec{c} + \vec{c}\cdot\vec{a} = -\frac{3}{2}$$

It is true that,

$$|\vec{a} + \vec{b} + \vec{c}|^2 \geq 0$$

$$|\vec{a}|^2 + |\vec{b}|^2 + |\vec{c}|^2 + 2(\vec{a}\cdot\vec{b} + \vec{b}\cdot\vec{c} + \vec{c}\cdot\vec{a}) \geq 0$$

$$1 + 1 + 1 + 2(\vec{a}\cdot\vec{b} + \vec{b}\cdot\vec{c} + \vec{c}\cdot\vec{a}) \geq 0$$

$$(\vec{a}\cdot\vec{b} + \vec{b}\cdot\vec{c} + \vec{c}\cdot\vec{a}) \geq -\frac{3}{2}$$

It means that the magnitude of $(\vec{a} + \vec{b} + \vec{c})$ is,

$$\left|\vec{a} + \vec{b} + \vec{c}\right| = \vec{0}$$

$$\vec{a} + \vec{b} + \vec{c} = 0$$

$$\vec{b} + \vec{c} = -\vec{a}$$

The value of the term,

$$\left|2\vec{a} + 5\vec{b} + 5\vec{c}\right| = \left|2\vec{a} + 5(\vec{b} + \vec{c})\right|$$

$$= \left|2\vec{a} + 5\left(-\vec{a}\right)\right|$$

$$= 3\,(1)$$

$$= 3$$

51. Correct Response : (9)

Explanation :

If $\vec{r}$ is a vector such that,

$$\vec{r}\times\vec{b} = \vec{c}\times\vec{b}$$

$$(\vec{r} - \vec{c})\,\vec{b} = 0$$

$$\vec{r} - \vec{c} = \lambda\vec{b}$$

$$\vec{r} = \vec{c} + \lambda\vec{b}$$

It is given that,

$$\vec{r}\cdot\vec{a} = 0$$

Substitute value of $\vec{r}$.

$$\vec{c}\cdot\vec{a} + \lambda\vec{b}\cdot\vec{a} = 0$$

$$\lambda = -\frac{\vec{c}\cdot\vec{a}}{\vec{b}\cdot\vec{a}}$$

$$\lambda = 4$$

Therefore, the value of $\vec{r}\cdot\vec{b}$ is,

$$\vec{r}\cdot\vec{b} = \vec{c}\cdot\vec{b} + \lambda|\vec{b}|^2$$

$$= 9$$

52. Correct Response : (a, d)

Explanation :

Let, the vector be $\vec{r} = x\hat{i} + y\hat{j} + z\hat{k}$. The vector $\vec{r}$ is coplanar with vectors $\hat{i} + \hat{j} + 2\hat{k}$ and $\hat{i} + 2\hat{j} + \hat{k}$.

$$\begin{vmatrix} x & y & z \\ 1 & 1 & 2 \\ 1 & 2 & 1 \end{vmatrix} = 0$$

$$-3x + y + z = 0 \qquad \text{...(i)}$$

It is also given the vector $\vec{r}$ is perpendicular to $\hat{i} + \hat{j} + \hat{k}$.

$$\vec{r}\cdot(\hat{i} + \hat{j} + \hat{k}) = 0$$

$$x + y + z = 0 \qquad \text{...(ii)}$$

Solve equation (i) and (ii) by cross multiplication.

$$\frac{x}{0} = \frac{y}{4} = \frac{z}{-4}$$

$$\frac{x}{0} = \frac{y}{1} = \frac{z}{-1}$$

Therefore, the vectors be $\vec{r} = \hat{j} - \hat{k}$ or $\vec{r} = -\hat{j} + \hat{k}$.

53. Correct Response : (b)

Explanation :

The parallelogram ABCD is shown below.

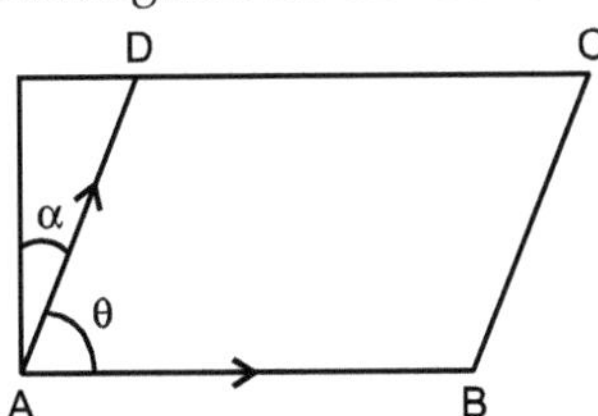

Angle θ between AB and AD is,

$$\cos\theta = \left|\frac{\overrightarrow{AB}\cdot\overrightarrow{AD}}{|\overrightarrow{AB}||\overrightarrow{AD}|}\right|$$

$$= \left|\frac{-2 + 20 + 22}{(15)(3)}\right|$$

$$= \frac{8}{9}$$

Similarly,

$$\sin\theta = \left|\frac{\overrightarrow{AB}\times\overrightarrow{AD}}{|\overrightarrow{AB}||\overrightarrow{AD}|}\right|$$

$$= \frac{\sqrt{17}}{9}$$

From the figure,

$$\alpha + \theta = 90°$$
$$\theta = 90° - \theta$$

Take cosine both sides,

$$\cos \alpha = \cos(90° - \theta)$$
$$= \sin \theta$$
$$= \frac{\sqrt{17}}{9}$$

Thus, the cosine of the angle α is $\dfrac{\sqrt{17}}{9}$.

54. Correct Response : (a)

Explanation :

The length $|\overrightarrow{OP}|$ is calculated as,

$$|\overrightarrow{OP}| = \left| \hat{a} \cos t + \hat{b} \sin t \right|$$

$$= (\cos^2 t + \sin^2 t + 2\cos t \sin t \, \hat{a} \cdot \hat{b})^{1/2}$$

$$= (1 + 2\cos t \sin t \, \hat{a} \cdot \hat{b})^{1/2}$$

$$= (1 + 2\sin 2t \, \hat{a} \cdot \hat{b})^{1/2}$$

The unit vector along $|\overrightarrow{OP}|$ is,

$$\hat{u} = |\overrightarrow{OP}|_{max}$$

$$= (1 + \hat{a} \cdot \hat{b})^{1/2}$$

$$= \frac{\hat{a} + \hat{b}}{\sqrt{2} \dfrac{|\hat{a} + \hat{b}|}{\sqrt{2}}}$$

$$= \frac{\hat{a} + \hat{b}}{|\hat{a} + \hat{b}|}$$

Therefore, length is $M = (1 + \hat{a} \cdot \hat{b})^{1/2}$ and unit

vector is $\hat{u} = \dfrac{\hat{a} + \hat{b}}{|\hat{a} + \hat{b}|}$.

55. Correct Response : (b)

Explanation :

The perpendicular vector for both line L_1 and L_2 is,

$$\begin{vmatrix} i & j & k \\ 3 & 1 & 2 \\ 1 & 2 & 3 \end{vmatrix} = i(3-4) - j(9-2) + k(6-1)$$

$$= -i - 7j + 5k$$

The unit vector perpendicular to L_1 and L_2 is,

$$\frac{-i - 7j + 5k}{\sqrt{1^2 + 7^2 + 5^2}} = \frac{-i - 7j + 5k}{5\sqrt{3}}$$

56. Correct Response : (d)

Explanation :

The shortest distance between the lines L_1 and L_2 is calculated as,

$$\text{S.D.} = \left| \left(\frac{-\hat{i} - 7\hat{j} + 5\hat{k}}{5\sqrt{3}} \right) (-3\hat{i} + 0\hat{j} - 4\hat{k}) \right|$$

$$= \left| \frac{3 - 20}{5\sqrt{3}} \right|$$

$$= \frac{17}{5\sqrt{3}}$$

57. Correct Response : (a)

Explanation :

Given that, edges of parallelopiped are of unit length *i.e.* $\hat{a} \cdot \hat{a} = 1$ and $\hat{a} \cdot \hat{b} = \hat{b} \cdot \hat{c} = \hat{c} \cdot \hat{a} = \dfrac{1}{2}$

Volume of parallelopiped is calculated as,

$$V = \left| \hat{a} \cdot (\hat{b} \times \hat{c}) \right|$$

$$= \sqrt{\begin{vmatrix} \hat{a} \cdot \hat{a} & \hat{a} \cdot \hat{b} & \hat{a} \cdot \hat{c} \\ \hat{b} \cdot \hat{a} & \hat{b} \cdot \hat{b} & \hat{b} \cdot \hat{c} \\ \hat{c} \cdot \hat{a} & \hat{c} \cdot \hat{b} & \hat{c} \cdot \hat{c} \end{vmatrix}}$$

$$= \sqrt{\begin{vmatrix} 1 & 1/2 & 1/2 \\ 1/2 & 1 & 1/2 \\ 1/2 & 1/2 & 1 \end{vmatrix}}$$

$$= \frac{1}{\sqrt{2}}$$

Therefore, volume of parallelopiped is $\dfrac{1}{\sqrt{2}}$.

58. Correct Response : (d)

Explanation :

A particle P starts from point $z_0 = 1 + 2i$. It moves horizontally by 5 units and vertically by 3 units. So,

$$z_1 = 6 + 5i$$

Now, particle moves at an angle of $\dfrac{\pi}{2}$ in anticlockwise direction and $\sqrt{2}$ units in direction of $\hat{i} + \hat{j}$. So,

$$z_2 = -6 + 7i$$

59. Correct Response : (c)

Explanation :

Let, $\overline{PQ}$, $\overline{QR}$, $\overline{RS}$, $\overline{ST}$, $\overline{TU}$ and $\overline{UP}$ represents the sides of regular hexagon.

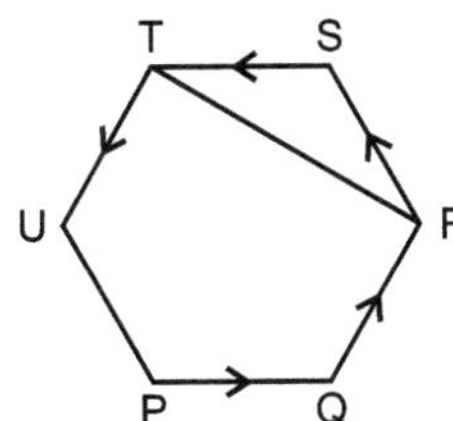

Statement 1 :

It can be noticed that $\overline{TR}$ is resultant vector of $\overline{RS}$ and $\overline{ST}$. So,

$$\overline{PQ} \times (\overline{RS} + \overline{ST}) \neq 0$$

It is true statement,

Statement 2 :

It is given that $\overline{PQ} \times \overline{RS} = 0$. From the figure it can be noticed that $\overline{PQ} \parallel \overline{RS}$ is not possible.

Thus, statement-2 is false.

60. Correct Response : (b)

Explanation :

It is given that $\vec{a}$, $\vec{b}$, $\vec{c}$ be unit vectors and $\vec{a} + \vec{b} + \vec{c} = 0$. So,

$\vec{a}$, $\vec{b}$, $\vec{c}$ are coplanar.

Therefore, $\vec{a} \times \vec{b} = \vec{b} \times \vec{c} = \vec{c} \times \vec{a} \neq 0$.

61. Correct Response : (b), (d)

Explanation :

Vector $\vec{A}$ is parallel to line of intersection of planes P_1 and P_2. So,

$$\left[\left(2\hat{j}+3\hat{k}\right)\times\left(4\hat{j}-3\hat{k}\right)\right]\times\left[\left(\hat{j}-\hat{k}\right)\times\left(3\hat{i}+3\hat{j}\right)\right]$$

$$= 54\hat{j} - 54\hat{k}$$

The angle between vector $\vec{A}$ and $2\hat{i} + \hat{j} - 2\hat{k}$ is,

$$\cos\theta = \pm\left(\frac{54+108}{3.54\sqrt{2}}\right)$$

$$\cos\theta = \pm\frac{1}{\sqrt{2}}$$

$$\theta = \cos^{-1}\left(\pm\frac{1}{\sqrt{2}}\right)$$

Thus, value of θ are $\dfrac{\pi}{4}$ and $\dfrac{3\pi}{4}$.

62. Correct Response : (b)

Explanation :

The dot product of vector $\vec{a} \cdot \vec{b}_1$ is,

$$\vec{a} \cdot \vec{b}_1 = \left(\vec{b} \cdot \vec{a} - \frac{\vec{b} \cdot \vec{a}}{|\vec{a}|^2} \vec{a} \cdot \vec{a}\right)$$

$$= 0$$

The dot product of vector $\vec{a} \cdot \vec{c}_2$ is,

$$\vec{a} \cdot \vec{c}_2 = \left(\vec{c} \cdot \vec{a} - \frac{\vec{c} \cdot \vec{a}}{|\vec{a}|^2} \vec{a} \cdot \vec{a} - \frac{\vec{b}_1 \cdot \vec{c}}{|\vec{b}_1|^2} \vec{a} \cdot \vec{b}_1\right)$$

$$= 0$$

Also, $\vec{b}_1 \cdot \vec{c}_2 = 0$.

Therefore, $(\vec{a}, \vec{b}_1, \vec{c}_2)$ are orthogonal vectors.

63. Correct Response : $\hat{w} = \hat{v} - 2\left(\hat{n} \cdot \hat{v}\right)\hat{n}$

Explanation :

Let, $\hat{n}$ be the unit vector along the external bisector of $\hat{n}$ and $\hat{v}$.

So, normal vector is $\hat{w} - \hat{v} = \lambda\hat{n}$.

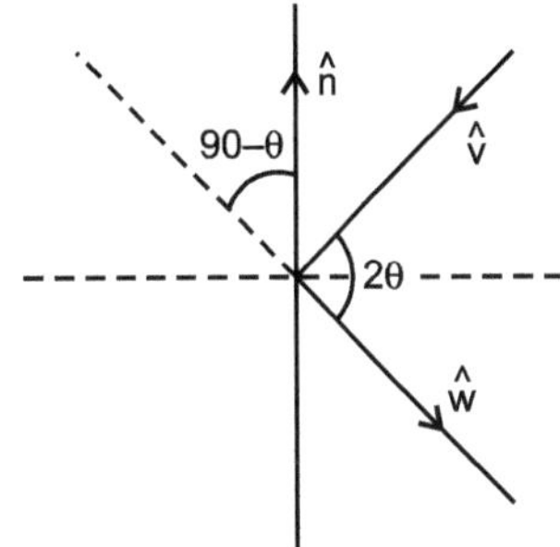

$$1 + 1 - \hat{w} \cdot \hat{v} = \lambda^2$$

$$2 - 2\cos 2\theta = \lambda^2$$

$$2(2\sin^2\theta) = \lambda^2$$

$$\lambda = 2\sin\theta$$

Substitute the value of λ in $\hat{w} - \hat{v} = \lambda\hat{n}$.

$$\hat{w} - \hat{v} = 2\sin\theta\,\hat{n}$$

$$\hat{w} - \hat{v} = 2\cos(90° - \theta)\hat{n}$$

$$\hat{w} - \hat{v} = -2\left(\hat{n} \cdot \hat{v}\right)\hat{n}$$

64. Correct Response : (c)

Explanation :

It is known that,

$$\vec{a} \times (\vec{a} \times \vec{b}) = (\vec{a} \cdot \vec{b})\vec{a} - (\vec{a} \cdot \vec{a})\vec{b}$$

$$(\hat{i}+\hat{j}+\hat{k}) \times (\hat{j}-\hat{k}) = 1(\hat{i}+\hat{j}+\hat{k}) - 3\vec{b}$$

$$-2\hat{i}+\hat{j}+\hat{k} = \hat{i}+\hat{j}+\hat{k}-3\vec{b}$$

$$\vec{b} = i$$

65. Correct Response : (c)

Explantion : $5\hat{i}+2\hat{j}+6\hat{k}$

Let, $\vec{a} = 5\hat{i}+2\hat{j}+6\hat{k}$, $\vec{b} = 2\hat{i}+\hat{j}+\hat{k}$ and $\vec{c} = \hat{i}-\hat{j}+\hat{k}$

$$\vec{a}\times(\vec{b}\times\vec{c}) = (5\hat{i}+2\hat{j}+6\hat{k})\times((2\hat{i}+\hat{j}+\hat{k})\times(\hat{i}-\hat{j}+\hat{k}))$$

$$= 27\hat{j}-9\hat{k}$$

Unit vector is calculated as,

$$\frac{27\hat{j}-9\hat{k}}{\sqrt{27^2+9^2}} = \frac{9(3\hat{j}-\hat{k})}{9\sqrt{10}}$$

$$= \frac{3\hat{j}-\hat{k}}{10}$$

66. Correct Response : (*)

Explanation :

Given that $\vec{a}\times\vec{b} = \vec{c}\times\vec{d}$ and $\vec{a}\times\vec{c} = \vec{b}\times\vec{d}$.

Consider the condition.

$$(\vec{a}-\vec{d})\times(\vec{c}-\vec{b}) = \vec{a}\times\vec{c}-\vec{a}\times\vec{b}-\vec{d}\times\vec{c}+\vec{d}\times\vec{b}$$

$$= \vec{a}\times\vec{c}-\vec{a}\times\vec{b}+\vec{c}\times\vec{d}+\vec{d}\times\vec{b}$$

$$= \vec{a}\times\vec{c}-\vec{a}\times\vec{b}+\vec{a}\times\vec{b}-\vec{a}\times\vec{c}$$

$$= 0$$

So, $(\vec{a}-\vec{d})$ is parallel to $(\vec{c}-\vec{b})$.

$$(\vec{a}-\vec{d})\cdot(\vec{c}-\vec{b}) \neq 0$$

$$\vec{a}\cdot\vec{c}-\vec{a}\cdot\vec{b}-\vec{d}\cdot\vec{c}+\vec{d}\cdot\vec{b} \neq 0$$

$$\vec{a}\cdot\vec{b}+\vec{c}\cdot\vec{d} \neq \vec{a}\cdot\vec{c}+\vec{d}\cdot\vec{b}$$

Hence, it is proved that $\vec{a}\cdot\vec{b}+\vec{c}\cdot\vec{d} \neq \vec{a}\cdot\vec{c}+\vec{d}\cdot\vec{b}$.

67. Correct Response : (b)

Explanation :

It is given that $\vec{a}+2\vec{b}$ and $5\vec{a}-4\vec{b}$ are perpendicular to each other.

$$(\vec{a}+2\vec{b})\cdot(5\vec{a}-4\vec{b}) = 0$$

$$5|\vec{a}|^2 -8|\vec{b}|^2 +6\vec{a}\cdot\vec{b} = 0$$

$$6\vec{a}\cdot\vec{b} = 3$$

$$\vec{a}\cdot\vec{b} = \frac{1}{2}$$

The angle between $\vec{a}$ and $\vec{b}$ is,

$$\cos\theta = \frac{1}{2}$$

$$\cos\theta = \cos 60°$$

$$\theta = 60°$$

68. Correct Response : (c)

Explanation :

The maximum value of scalar triple product is,

$$[\overline{U}\,\overline{V}\,\overline{W}] = \overline{U}\cdot(\overline{V}\times\overline{W})$$

$$\leq |\overline{U}||\overline{V}\times\overline{W}|$$

$$\leq |\overline{V}\times\overline{W}|$$

The cross product of $\overline{V}\times\overline{W}$ is,

$$\overline{V}\times\overline{W} = \begin{vmatrix} \hat{i} & \hat{j} & \hat{k} \\ 2 & 1 & -1 \\ 1 & 0 & 3 \end{vmatrix}$$

$$= 3\hat{i}-7\hat{j}-\hat{k}$$

Now,

$$[\overline{U}\,\overline{V}\,\overline{W}] \leq \sqrt{9+49+1}$$

$$\leq \sqrt{59}.$$

Chapter 14

Statistics and Probability

QUESTIONS

1. The mean and variance of 7 observations are 8 and 6, respectively. If five observations are 2, 4, 10, 12, 14, then the absolute difference of the remaining two observations is : **[2020, Main]**

(a) 2   (b) 4

(c) 3   (d) 1

2. Four pair dice are thrown independently 27 times. Then the expected number of times, at least two dice show up a three or a five, is .... **[2020, Main]**

3. Out of 11 consecutive natural numbers if three numbers are selected at random (without repetition), then the probability that they are in A.P. with positive common difference is : **[2020, Main]**

(a) $\dfrac{15}{101}$ (b) $\dfrac{5}{101}$

(c) $\dfrac{5}{33}$ (d) $\dfrac{10}{99}$

4. If $\displaystyle\sum_{i=1}^{n} (x_i - a) = n$ and $\displaystyle\sum_{i=1}^{n} (x_i - a)^2 = na, \ (n, \ a > 1)$

then the standard deviation of n observations $x_1, x_2, ..., x_n$ is : **[2020, Main]**

(a) $n\sqrt{a-1}$ (b) $\sqrt{a-1}$

(c) $a - 1$ (d) $\sqrt{n(a-1)}$

5. The probabilities of three events A, B and C are given by $P(A) = 0.6$, $P(B) = 0.4$ and $P(C) = 0.5$. If $P(A \cup B) = 0.8$, $P(A \cap C) = 0.3$, $P(A \cap B \cap C) = 0.2$, $P(B \cap C) = \beta$ and $P(A \cup B \cup C) = \alpha$, where $0.85 \leq \alpha \ 0.95$, then β lies in the interval : **[2020, Main]**

(a) [0.36, 0.40]   (b) [0.35, 0.36]

(c) [0.25, 0.35]   (d) [0.20, 0.25]

6. Consider the data on x taking the values 0, 2, 4, 8, ..., 2^n with frequencies $^nC_0, \ ^nC_1, \ ^nC_2, \ ..., \ ^nC_n$ respectively. If the mean of this data is $\dfrac{728}{2^n}$, then n is equal to .... **[2020, Main]**

7. The mean and variance of 8 observations are 10 and 13.5, respectively. If 6 of these observations are 5, 7, 10, 12, 14, 15, then the absolute difference of the remaining two observations is : **[2020, Main]**

(a) 7   (b) 3

(c) 5   (d) 9

8. The probability of a man hitting a target is $\dfrac{1}{10}$. The least number of shots required, so that the probability of his hitting the target at least once is greater than $\dfrac{1}{4}$, is .... **[2020, Main]**

9. In a game two players A and B take turns in throwing a pair of fair dice starting with player A and total of scores on the two dice, in each throw is noted. A wins the game if he throws a total of 6 before B throws a total of 7 and B wins the game if he throws a total of 7 before A throws a total of six. The game stops as soon as either of the players wins. The probability of A winning the game is : **[2020, Main]**

(a) $\dfrac{31}{61}$ (b) $\dfrac{5}{6}$

(c) $\dfrac{5}{31}$ (d) $\dfrac{30}{61}$

10. If the variance of the following frequency distribution

Class :	10 – 20	20 – 30	30 – 40
Frequency :	2	x	2

is 50, then x is equal to .... **[2020, Main]**

11. A die is thrown two times and the sum of the scores appearing on the die is observed to be a multiple of 4. Then the conditional probability that the score 4 has appeared atleast once is : **[2020, Main]**

(a) $\dfrac{1}{8}$ (b) $\dfrac{1}{9}$

(c) $\dfrac{1}{3}$ (d) $\dfrac{1}{4}$

12. For the frequency distribution :

$$\text{Variate } (x) \quad : \quad x_1 \quad x_2 \quad x_3 \ \dots \ x_{15}$$
$$\text{Frequency } (f): \quad f_1 \quad f_2 \quad f_3 \ \dots \ f_{15}$$

where $0 < x_1 < x_2 < x_3 < \dots < x_{15} = 10$ and $\displaystyle\sum_{i=1}^{15} f_i > 0,$

the standard deviation cannot be : **[2020, Main]**

(a) 2   **(b)** 1

(c) 4   **(d)** 6

13. If the mean and the standard deviation of the data 3, 5, 7, a, b are 5 and 2 respectively, then a and b are the roots of the equation :

[2020, Main]

(a) $2x^2 - 20x + 19 = 0$ **(b)** $x^2 - 10x + 19 = 0$

(c) $x^2 - 10x + 18 = 0$ **(d)** $x^2 - 20x + 18 = 0$

14. In a bombing attack, there is 50% chance that a bomb will hit the target. At least two independent hits are required to destroy the target completely. Then the minimum number of bombs, that must be dropped to ensure that there is at least 99% chance of completely destroying the target, is ....

[2020, Main]

15. Let C_1 and C_2 be two biased coins such that the probabilities of getting head in a single toss are $\dfrac{2}{3}$ and $\dfrac{1}{3}$, respectively. Suppose α is the number of heads that appear when C_1 is tossed twice, independently, Then probability that the roots of the quadratic polynomial $x^2 - \alpha x + \beta$ are real and equal to : **[2020, Main]**

(a) $\dfrac{40}{81}$ **(b)** $\dfrac{20}{81}$

(c) $\dfrac{1}{2}$ **(d)** $\dfrac{1}{4}$

16. The probability that a missible hits a target successfully is 0.75. In order to destroy the target completely, at least three successful hits are required. Then the minimum number of missiles that have to be fired so that the probability of completely destroying the target is NOT less than 0.95, is ....

[2020, Advanced]

17. Two fair dice, each with faces numbered 1, 2, 3, 4, 5 and 6, are rolled together and the sum of the numbers on the faces is observed. This process is repeated till the sum is either a prime number or a perfect square. Suppose the sum turns out to be a perfect square before it turns out to be a prime number. If p is the probability that this perfect square is an odd number, then the value of $14p$ is .... **[2020, Main]**

18. Let $n > 2$ be an integer. Suppose that there are n Metro stations in a city located along a circular path. Each pair only. Further, each pair of nearest stations is connected by blue line, whereas all remaining pairs of stations are connected by red line. If the number of red lines is 99 times the number of blue lines, then the value of n is :

[2020, Main]

(a) 199   **(b)** 101

(c) 201   **(d)** 200

19. The probability that a randomly chosen 5-digit number is made from exactly two digits is :

[2020, Main]

(a) $\dfrac{121}{10^4}$ **(b)** $\dfrac{150}{10^4}$

(c) $\dfrac{135}{10^4}$ **(d)** $\dfrac{134}{10^4}$

20. Box I contains 30 cards numbered 1 to 30 and Box II contains 20 cards numbered 31 to 50. A box is selected at random and a card is drawn from it. The number on the card is found to be a non-prime number. The probability that the card was drawn from Box I is : **[2020, Main]**

(a) $\dfrac{8}{17}$ **(b)** $\dfrac{2}{3}$

(c) $\dfrac{4}{17}$ **(d)** $\dfrac{2}{5}$

21. Let $X = \{x \in N : 1 \le x \le 17\}$ and $Y = \{ax + b : x \in X$ and $a, b \in R, a > 0\}$. If mean and variance of elements of Y are 17 and 216 respectively then $a + b$ is equal to : **[2020, Main]**

(a) -7 **(b)** 7

(c) 9   **(d)** -27

22. Let $x_i \ (1 \le i \le 10)$ be ten observations of a random variable X. If $\displaystyle\sum_{i=1}^{10}(x_i - p) = 3$ and $\displaystyle\sum_{i=1}^{10}(x_i - p)^2 = 9$ where $0 \ne p \in R$, then the standard deviation of these observations is : **[2020, Main]**

(a) $\sqrt{\dfrac{3}{5}}$ **(b)** $\dfrac{7}{10}$

(c) $\dfrac{9}{10}$ **(d)** $\dfrac{4}{5}$

23. The mean and the standard deviation (s.d.) of 10 observations are 20 and 2 respectively. Each of these 10 observations is multiplied by p and then reduced by q, where $p \ne 0$ and $q \ne 0$. If the new mean and new s.d. become half of their original values, then q is equal to :

[2020, Main]

(a) -20 **(b)** 10

(c) -10 **(d)** -5

24. Let A and B be two independent events such that $P(A) = \dfrac{1}{3}$ and $P(B) = \dfrac{1}{6}$. Then, which of the following is TRUE ? **[2020, Main]**

(a) $P(A/B) = \dfrac{2}{3}$

(b) $P(A/(A \cup B)) = \dfrac{1}{4}$

(c) $P(A/B') = \dfrac{1}{3}$

(d) $P(A'/B') = \dfrac{1}{3}$

25. An unbiased coin is tossed 5 times. Suppose that a variable X is assigned the value k when k consecutive heads are obtained for $k = 3$, 4, 5 otherwise X takes the value -1. Then the expected value of X, is : **[2020, Main]**

(a) $\dfrac{3}{16}$

(b) $\dfrac{-3}{16}$

(c) $\dfrac{1}{8}$

(d) $-\dfrac{1}{8}$

26. If the variance of the first n natural numbers is 10 and the variance of the first m even natural Numbers is 16, then $m + n$ is equal to ....

27. A random variable X has the following probability distribution :

X : 1 2 3 4 5
P(X) : K^2 2K K 2 $5K^2$

Then $P(X > 2)$ is equal to : **[2020, Main]**

(a) $\dfrac{7}{12}$

(b) $\dfrac{23}{36}$

(c) $\dfrac{1}{36}$

(d) $\dfrac{1}{6}$

28. If 10 different balls are to be placed in 4 distinct boxes at random, then the probability that two of these boxes contain exactly 2 and 3 balls is : **[2020, Main]**

(a) $\dfrac{945}{2^{11}}$

(b) $\dfrac{965}{2^{11}}$

(c) $\dfrac{945}{2^{10}}$

(d) $\dfrac{965}{2^{10}}$

29. In a box there are 20 cards, out of which 10 are leabelled as A and the remaining 10 are labelled as B. Cards are drawn at random, one after the other and with replacement, till a second A-card is obtained. The probability that the second A-card appears before the third B-card is : **[2020, Main]**

(a) $\dfrac{11}{16}$

(b) $\dfrac{13}{16}$

(c) $\dfrac{9}{16}$

(d) $\dfrac{15}{16}$

30. Let the observations $x_i(1 \le i \le 10)$ satisfy the equations $\sum_{i=1}^{10}(x_i - 5) = 10$ and $\sum_{i=1}^{10}(x_i - 5)^2 = 40$. If μ and λ are the mean and the variance of the observations, $x_1 - 3, x_2 - 3, ..., x_{10} - 3$, then the ordered pair (μ, λ) is equal to : **[2020, Main]**

(a) $(6, 6)$

(b) $(3, 6)$

(c) $(6, 3)$

(d) $(3, 3)$

31. The mean and variance of 20 observations are found to be 10 and 4 respectively. On rechecking, it was found that an observation 9 was incorrect and the correct observation was 11. Then the correct variance is : **[2020, Main]**

(a) 3.99

(b) 3.98

(c) 4.02

(d) 4.01

32. Let A and B be two events such that the probability that exactly one of them occurs is $\dfrac{2}{5}$ and the probability that A or B occurs is $\dfrac{1}{2}$, then the probability of both of them occur together is : **[2020, Main]**

(a) 0.02

(b) 0.01

(c) 0.20

(d) 0.10

33. In a workshop, there are five machines and the probability of any one of them to be out of service on a day is $\dfrac{1}{4}$. If the probability that at most two machines will be out of service on the same day is $\left(\dfrac{3}{4}\right)^3 k$, then k is equal to : **[2020, Main]**

(a) $\dfrac{17}{2}$

(b) 4

(c) $\dfrac{17}{8}$

(d) $\dfrac{17}{4}$

34. If them mean and variance of eight numbers 3, 7, 9, 12, 13, 20, x and y be 10 and 25 respectively, then $x.y$ is equal to .... **[2020, Main]**

35. Two different families A and B are blessed with equal number of children. There are 3 tickets to be distributed amongst the childern of these families so that no child gets more than one ticket. If the probability that all the tickets to the children of the family B is $\dfrac{1}{12}$, then the number of children in each family is : **[2018, Main]**

(a) 3

(b) 4

(c) 5

(d) 6

36. A box 'A' contains 2 white, 3 red and 2 black balls. Another box 'B' contains 4 white, 2 red and 3 black balls. If two balls are drawn at random, without replacement, from a randomly selected box and one ball turns out to be white while the other ball turns out to be red, then the probability that both balls are drawn from box 'B' is ;

[2018, Main]

(a) $\dfrac{9}{16}$ (b) $\dfrac{7}{16}$

(c) $\dfrac{9}{32}$ (d) $\dfrac{7}{8}$

37. The mean and the standard deviation (s.d.) of five observations are 9 and 0, respectively. If one of the observations is changed such that the mean of the new set of five observations becomes 10, then their s.d. is : **[2018, Main]**

(a) 0 (b) 1

(c) 2 (d) 4

38. Let A, B and C be three events, which are pair-wise independent and $\overline{E}$ denotes the complement of an event E. If $P(A \cap B \cap C) = 0$ and $P(C) > 0$, then $P[(\overline{A} \cap \overline{B}) \mid C]$ is equal to :

[2018, Main]

(a) $P(\overline{A}) - P(B)$ (b) $P(A) + P(\overline{B})$

(c) $P(\overline{A}) - P(\overline{B})$ (d) $P(\overline{A}) + P(\overline{B})$

39. A bag contains 4 red and 6 black balls. A ball is drawn at random from the bag, its colour is observed and this ball along with two additional balls of the same colour are returned to the bag. If now a ball is drawn at random from the bag, then the probability that this drawn ball is red, is : **[2018, Main]**

(a) $\dfrac{3}{10}$ (b) $\dfrac{2}{5}$

(c) $\dfrac{1}{5}$ (d) $\dfrac{3}{4}$

40. If $\displaystyle\sum_{i=1}^{9}(x_i - 5) = 9$ and $\displaystyle\sum_{i=1}^{9}(x_i - 5)^2 = 45$, then the standard deviation of the 9 items $x_1, x_2, ..., x_9$ is : **[2018, Main]**

(a) 9 (b) 4

(c) 2 (d) 3

Paragraph 'A'

There are five students S_1, S_2, S_3, S_4 and S_5 in a music class and for then the five seats R_1, R_2, R_3, R_4 and R_5 arranged in a row, where initially the seat allotted to the students $Si, i = 1, 2, 3, 4, 5$. But, on the examination day, the students are randomly allotteed the given seats.

(There are two questions based on Paragrah 'A', the question given below is one of them)

41. The probability that, on the examination day, the student S_1 gets the previously allotted seat R_1, and **NONE** of the remaining students gets the seat previously allotted to him/her is :

[2018, Advanced]

(a) $\dfrac{3}{40}$ (b) $\dfrac{1}{8}$

(c) $\dfrac{7}{40}$ (d) $\dfrac{1}{5}$

42. For $i = 1, 2, 3, 4$, let T_i denote the event that the students S_i and S_{i+1} do **NOT** sit adjacent to each other on the day of the examination. Then, the probability of the event $T_1 \cap T_2 \cap T_3 \cap T_4$ is :

[2018, Advanced]

(a) $\dfrac{1}{15}$ (b) $\dfrac{1}{10}$

(c) $\dfrac{7}{60}$ (d) $\dfrac{1}{5}$

43. The sum of 100 observations and the sum of their squares are 400 and 2475, respectively. Later on, three observations, 3, 4 and 5, were found to be incorrect. If the incorrect observations are omitted, then the variance of the remaining observations is : **[2017, Main]**

(a) 8.25 (b) 8.50

(c) 8.00 (d) 9.00

44. Three persons P, Q and R independently try to hit a target. If the probabilities of their hitting the target are $\dfrac{3}{4}, \dfrac{1}{2}$ and $\dfrac{5}{8}$ respectively, then the probability that the target is hit by P or Q but not by R is : **[2017, Main]**

(a) $\dfrac{21}{64}$ (b) $\dfrac{9}{64}$

(c) $\dfrac{15}{64}$ (d) $\dfrac{39}{64}$

45. An unbiased coin is tossed eight times. The probability of obtaining at least one head and at least one tail is : **[2017, Main]**

(a) $\dfrac{255}{256}$ (b) $\dfrac{127}{128}$

(c) $\dfrac{63}{64}$ (d) $\dfrac{1}{2}$

46. A box contains 15 green and 10 yellow balls. If 10 balls are randomly drawn, one-by-one, with replacement, then the variance of the number of green balls drawn is : **[2017, Main]**

(a) 6   **(b)** 4

(c) $\dfrac{6}{25}$ **(d)** $\dfrac{12}{5}$

47. For three events A, B and C,

P(Exactly one of A or B occurs)

= P(Exactly one of B or C occurs)

= P(Exactly one of C or A occurs) = $\dfrac{1}{4}$ and P(All

the three events occur simultaneously) = $\dfrac{1}{16}$.

Then the probability that at least one of the event occurs, is : **[2017, Main]**

(a) $\dfrac{7}{16}$ **(b)** $\dfrac{7}{64}$

(c) $\dfrac{3}{16}$ **(d)** $\dfrac{7}{32}$

48. If two different numbers are taken from the set {0, 1, 2, 3, ..., 10}; then the probability that their sum as well as absolute difference are both multiple of 4, is : **[2017, Main]**

(a) $\dfrac{12}{55}$ **(b)** $\dfrac{14}{45}$

(c) $\dfrac{7}{55}$ **(d)** $\dfrac{6}{55}$

49. Let X and Y be two events such that $P(X) = \dfrac{1}{3}$,

$P(X / Y) = \dfrac{1}{2}$ and $P(Y / X) = \dfrac{2}{5}$. Then :

[2017, Advanced]

(a) $P(Y) = \dfrac{4}{15}$ **(b)** $P(X' / Y) = \dfrac{1}{2}$

(c) $P(X \cap Y) = \dfrac{1}{5}$ **(d)** $P(X \cup Y) = \dfrac{2}{5}$

50. Three randomly chosen non-negative integers x, y and z are found to satisfy the equation $x + y + z = 10$. Then the probability that z is even, is : **[2017, Advanced]**

(a) $\dfrac{36}{55}$ **(b)** $\dfrac{6}{11}$

(c) $\dfrac{1}{2}$ **(d)** $\dfrac{5}{11}$

51. The mean of 5 observations is 5 and their variance is 124. If three of the observations are 1, 2 and 6; then the mean deviation from the mean of the data is : **[2017, Main]**

(a) 2.4   **(b)** 2.8

(c) 2.5   **(d)** 2.6

52. If A and B are any two events such that $P(A) = \dfrac{2}{5}$ and $P(A \cap B) = \dfrac{3}{20}$, then the conditional probability, $P(A \mid (A' \cup B'))$, where A' denotes the complement of A, is equal to : **[2016, Main]**

(a) $\dfrac{1}{4}$ **(b)** $\dfrac{5}{17}$

(c) $\dfrac{8}{17}$ **(d)** $\dfrac{11}{20}$

53. A computer producing factory has only two plants T_1 and T_2. Plant T_1 produces 20% and plant T_2 produces 80% of the total computers produced. 7% of computers produced in the factory turn out to be defective. It is known that

P(computer turns out to be defective given that it is produced in plant T_1)

= 10 P(computer turns out to be defective given that it is produced in plant T_2),

where P(E) denotes the probability of an event E. A computer produced in the factory is randomly selected and it does not turn out to be defective. Then the probability that it is produced in plant T_2 is : **[2016, Advanced]**

(a) $\dfrac{36}{73}$ **(b)** $\dfrac{47}{79}$

(c) $\dfrac{78}{93}$ **(d)** $\dfrac{75}{83}$

54. Let two fair six-faced dice A and B be thrown simultaneously. If E_1 is the event that die A shows up four, E_2 is the event that die B shows up two and E_3 is the event that the sum of numbers on both dice is odd, then which of the following statements is **NOT true?** **[2016, Advanced]**

(a) E_1 and E_2 are independent.

(b) E_2 and E_3 are independent.

(c) E_1 and E_3 are independent.

(d) E_1, E_2 and E_3 are independent.

55. If the lengths of the sides of a triangle are decided by the three throws of a single fair die, then the probability that the triangle is of maximum area given that it is an isosceles triangle, is :

[2015, Main]

(a) $\dfrac{1}{26}$ **(b)** $\dfrac{1}{27}$

(c) $\dfrac{1}{21}$ **(d)** $\dfrac{1}{15}$

56. The minimum number of times a fair coin needs to be tossed, so that the probability of getting at least two heads is at least 0.96, is :

[2015, Advanced]

57. One of the two boxes, box I and box II, was selected at random and a ball was drawn randomly out of this box. The ball was found to be red. It the probability that this red ball was drawn from box II is $\frac{1}{3}$, then the correct options (s) with the possible values of n_1, n_2, n_3 and n_4 is (are) :

[2015, Advanced]

(a) $n_1 = 3$, $n_2 = 3$, $n_3 = 5$, $n_4 = 15$
(b) $n_1 = 3$, $n_2 = 6$, $n_3 = 10$, $n_4 = 50$
(c) $n_1 = 8$, $n_2 = 6$, $n_3 = 5$, $n_4 = 20$
(d) $n_1 = 6$, $n_2 = 12$, $n_3 = 5$, $n_4 = 20$

58. A ball is drawn at random from box I and transferred to box II. If the probability of drawing a red ball from box I, after this transfer, is $\frac{1}{3}$, then the correct option(s) with the possible value of n_1 and n_2 is (are) : **[2015, Advanced]**

(a) $n_1 = 4$ and $n_2 = 6$ **(b)** $n_1 = 2$ and $n_2 = 3$
(c) $n_1 = 10$ and $n_2 = 20$ **(d)** $n_1 = 3$ and $n_2 = 6$

59. If the mean and the variance of a binomial variate X are 2 and 1 respectively, then the probability that X takes a value greater than or equal to one is : **[2015, Main]**

(a) $\dfrac{1}{16}$ 　　　　　　**(b)** $\dfrac{9}{16}$

(c) $\dfrac{3}{4}$ 　　　　　　**(d)** $\dfrac{15}{16}$

60. If 12 identical balls are to be placed in 3 identical boxes, then the probability that one of the boxes contains exactly 3 balls is : **[2015, Main]**

(a) $\dfrac{55}{3}\left(\dfrac{2}{3}\right)^{11}$ 　　　**(b)** $55\left(\dfrac{2}{3}\right)^{10}$

(c) $220\left(\dfrac{1}{3}\right)^{12}$ 　　　**(d)** $22\left(\dfrac{1}{3}\right)^{11}$

61. Let x, M and σ^2 be respectively the mean, mode and variance of n observations x_1, x_2, ... x_n and $d_i = -x_i - a$, $i = 1, 2, ..., n$, where is any number.
Statement I : Variance of d_1, d_2, ..., d_n is σ^2
Statement II : Mean and mode of d_1, d_2, ..., dn are $-x-a$ and $-M-a$, respectively. **[2014 Main]**
(1) Statement I and Statement II are both false.
(2) Statement I and Statement II are both true.
(3) Statement I is true and Statement II is false.
(4) Statement I is false and Statement II is true.

62. A number x is chosen at random from the set {1, 2, 3, 4, ... , 1000}. Define the event : A = the chosen number x satisfies. $\dfrac{(x-10)(x-50)}{(x-30)} > 0$

Then P(A) is : **[2014, Main]**

(1) 0.71 　　　　　　(2) 0.70
(3) 0.51 　　　　　　(4) 0.20.

63. If X has a binomial distribution with parameter n and p such that $P(X = 2) = P(X = 3)$, then $E(X)$, then variable X, is : **[2014, Main]**

(a) $2 - p$ 　　　　　　**(b)** $3 - p$

(c) $\dfrac{p}{2}$ 　　　　　　**(d)** $\dfrac{p}{3}$

64. The variance of first 50 even natural numbers is :

(2014, Main)

(a) 437 　　　　　　**(b)** $\dfrac{437}{4}$

(c) $\dfrac{833}{4}$ 　　　　　　**(d)** 833

65. Box 1 contain three cards bearing number 1, 2, 3; box 2 contains five cards bearing numbers 1, 2, 3, 4, 5; and box3 contains seven cards bearing numbers 1, 2, 3, 4, 5, 6, 7. A card is drawn from each of the boxes. Let x_i be the number on the card drawn from the ith box, $i = 1, 2, 3$.

The probability that $x_1 + x_2 + x_3$ is odd, is **[2014, Advanced]**

(a) $\dfrac{29}{105}$ 　　　　　　**(b)** $\dfrac{53}{105}$

(c) $\dfrac{57}{105}$ 　　　　　　**(d)** $\dfrac{1}{2}$

66. Let A and B be two events such that $P(\overline{A \cup B}) = \dfrac{1}{6}$, $P(A \cap B) = \dfrac{1}{4}$ and $P(\overline{A}) = \dfrac{1}{4}$, where $\overline{A}$ stands for the complement of the event A. Then the events A and B are :

(a) independent but not equally likely.
(b) independent and equally likely.
(c) mutually exclusive and independent.
(d) equally likely but not independent.

67. If 1 ball is drawn from each of the boxes B_1, B_2 and B_3, the probability that all 3 drawn balls are of the same colour is : **[2014, Advanced]**

(a) $\dfrac{82}{648}$ 　　　　　　**(b)** $\dfrac{90}{648}$

(c) $\dfrac{558}{648}$ 　　　　　　**(d)** $\dfrac{566}{648}$

68. Four persons independently solve a certain problem correctly with probabilities $\dfrac{1}{2}, \dfrac{3}{4}, \dfrac{1}{4}, \dfrac{1}{8}$. Then the probability that the problem is solved correctly by at least one of them is :

[2013, Advanced]

(a) $\dfrac{235}{256}$ (b) $\dfrac{21}{256}$

(c) $\dfrac{3}{256}$ (d) $\dfrac{253}{256}$

69. If 2 balls are drawn (without replacement) from a randomly selected box and one of the balls is white and the other ball is red, the probability that these 2 balls are drawn from box B_2 is :

[2013, Advanced]

(a) $\dfrac{116}{181}$ (b) $\dfrac{126}{181}$

(c) $\dfrac{65}{181}$ (d) $\dfrac{55}{181}$

70. Four fair dice D_1, D_2, D_3 and D_4, each having six faces numbered 1, 2, 3, 4, 5 and 6 are rolled simultaneously. The probability that D_4 shows a number appearing on one of D_1, D_2 and D_3 is :

[2012, Advanced]

(a) $\dfrac{91}{216}$ (b) $\dfrac{108}{216}$

(c) $\dfrac{125}{216}$ (d) $\dfrac{127}{216}$

71. Let X and Y be two events such that $P(X \mid Y) = \dfrac{1}{2}$, $P(Y \mid X) = \dfrac{1}{3}$ and $P(X \cap Y) = \dfrac{1}{6}$. Which of the following is (are) correct ?

(a) $P(X \cup Y) = \dfrac{2}{3}$

(b) X and Y are independent

(c) X and Y are not independent

(d) $P(X^c \cap Y) = \dfrac{1}{3}$

72. The total number of ways in which 5 balls of different colours can be distributed among 3 persons so that each person gets at least one ball is :   **[2012, Advanced]**

(a) 75   (b) 150

(c) 210   (d) 243

73. A ship is fitted with three engines E_1, E_2 and E_3. The engines function independently of each other with respective probabilities $\dfrac{1}{2}, \dfrac{1}{4}$ and $\dfrac{1}{4}$. For the ship to be operational at least two of its engines must function. Let X denote the event that the ship is operational and let X_1, X_2 and X_3 denote respectively the events that the engines E_1, E_2 and E_3 are functioning. Which of the following is (are) true ?   **[2012, Advanced]**

(a) $P[X_1^c \mid X] = \dfrac{3}{16}$

(b) P[Exactly two engines of the ship are functioning $\mid X$] $= \dfrac{7}{8}$

(c) $P[X \mid X_2] = \dfrac{5}{16}$

(d) $P[X \mid X_1] = \dfrac{7}{16}$

74. The probability of the drawn ball from U_2 being white is :   **[2012, Advanced]**

(a) $\dfrac{13}{30}$ (b) $\dfrac{23}{30}$

(c) $\dfrac{19}{30}$ (d) $\dfrac{11}{30}$

75. An experiment has 10 equally likely outcomes. Let A and B be two non-empty events of the experiment. If A consiss of 4 outcomes, the number of outcomes that B must have so that A and B are independent, is :   **[2012, Advanced]**

(a) 2, 4 or 8   (b) 3, 6 or 9

(c) 4 or 8   (d) 5 or 10

76. Given that the drawn ball from U_2 is white, the probability that head appeared on the coin is :

[2011, Advanced]

(a) $\dfrac{17}{23}$ (b) $\dfrac{11}{23}$

(c) $\dfrac{15}{23}$ (d) $\dfrac{12}{23}$

77. Let E and F be two independent events. The probability that exactly one of them occurs is $\dfrac{11}{25}$ and the probability of none of them occurring is $\dfrac{2}{25}$. If $P(T)$ denotes the probability of occurrence of the event T, then :   **[2011, Advanced]**

(a) $P(E) = \dfrac{4}{5}, P(F) = \dfrac{3}{5}$ (b) $P(E) = \dfrac{1}{5}, P(F) = \dfrac{2}{5}$

(c) $P(E) = \dfrac{2}{5}, P(F) = \dfrac{1}{5}$ (d) $P(E) = \dfrac{3}{5}, P(F) = \dfrac{4}{5}$

78. A signal which can be green or red with probability $\dfrac{4}{5}$ and $\dfrac{1}{5}$ respectively, is received by station A and then transmitted to station B. The probability of each station receiving the signal correctly is $\dfrac{3}{4}$. If the signal received at station B is green, then .

the probability that the original signal was green is :   **[2010, Advanced]**

(a) $\dfrac{3}{5}$

(b) $\dfrac{6}{7}$

(c) $\dfrac{20}{23}$

(d) $\dfrac{9}{20}$

79. Consider the system of equations

$ax + by = 0$, $cx + dy = 0$, where $a, b, c, d \in \{0, 1\}$.

STATEMENT-1 : The probability that the system of equations has a unique solution is $\dfrac{3}{8}$.

[2008, Advanced]

and

STATEMENT-2 : The probability that the systerm of equations has a solution is 1.

(a) STATEMENT-1 is True, STATEMENT-2 is True; STATEMENT-2 is a correct explanation for STATEMENT-1

(b) STATEMENT-1 is True, STATEMENT-2 is True; STATEMENT-2 is **NOT** a correct explanation for STATEMENT-1

(c) STATEMENT-1 is True, STATEMENT-2 is False

(d) STATEMENT-1 is False, STATEMENT-2 is True

80. One Indian and four American men and their wives are to be seated randomly around a circular table. Then the conditional probability that the Indian man is seated adjacent to his wife given that each American man is seated adjacent to his wife is :   **[2007, Advanced]**

(a) $\dfrac{1}{2}$

(b) $\dfrac{1}{3}$

(c) $\dfrac{2}{5}$

(d) $\dfrac{1}{5}$

81. Let $H_1, H_2, ..., H_n$ be mutually exclusive and exhaustive events with $P(H_i) > 0$, $i = 1, 2, ..., n$. Let E be any other event with $0 < P(E) < 1$.

STATEMENT-1 : $P(H_i \mid E) > P(E \mid H_i) \cdot P(H_i)$ for $i = 1, 2, ..., n$.

because

STATEMENT-2 : $\displaystyle\sum_{i=1}^{n} P(H_i) = 1$. **[2007, Advanced]**

(a) Statement-1 is True, Statement-2 is True; Statement-2 is a correct explanation for Statement-1

(b) Statement-1 is True, Statement-2 is True; Statement-2 is **NOT** a correct explanation for Statement-1

(c) Statement-1 is True, Statement-2 is False

(d) Statement-1 is False, Statement-2 is True

82. Let E^c denote the complement of an event E. Let E, F, G be pairwise independent event with $P(G) > 0$ and $P(E \cap F \cap G) = 0$. Then $P(E^c \cap F^c / G)$ equals :   **[2007, Advanced]**

(a) $P(E^c) + P(F^c)$

(b) $P(E^c) - P(F^c)$

(c) $P(E^c) - P(F)$

(d) $P(E) - P(F^c)$

83. If $P(u_i) \propto i$, where $i = 1, 2, 3 ... , n$, then $\displaystyle\lim_{n \to \infty} P(\omega)$ is equal to :   **[2006.]**

(a) 1

(b) $\dfrac{2}{3}$

(c) $\dfrac{3}{4}$

(d) $\dfrac{1}{4}$

84. If $P(u_i) = c$, where c is a constant, then $P(u_n/w)$ is equal to :   **[2006, Main]**

(a) $\dfrac{2}{n+1}$

(b) $\dfrac{1}{n+1}$

(c) $\dfrac{n}{n+1}$

(d) $\dfrac{1}{2}$

85. A six faced fair dice is thrown until 1 comes, then the probability that 1 comes in even no. of trials is :   **[2005, Main]**

(a) 5/11

(b) 5/6

(c) 6/11

(d) 1/6

86. A person goes to office either by car, scooter, bus or train probability of which being $\dfrac{1}{7}, \dfrac{3}{7}, \dfrac{2}{7}$ and $\dfrac{1}{7}$ respectively. Probability that he reaches office late, if he takes car, scooter, bus or train is $\dfrac{2}{9}, \dfrac{1}{9}, \dfrac{4}{9}$ and $\dfrac{1}{9}$ respectively. Given that he reached office in time, then what is the probability that he travelled by a car.

[2005, Main]

87. If three distinct numbers are chosen randomly from the first 100 natural numbers, then the probability that all three of them are divisible by both 2 and 3 is :   **[2004 Main]**

(a) 4/25

(b) 4/35

(c) 4/33

(d) 4/1155

88. If A and B are two independent events, prove that $P(A \cup B) \cdot P(A' \cap B') \leq P(C)$, where C is an event defined that exactly one of A and B occurs.

[2004, Advanced]

89. A bag contains 12 red balls and 6 white balls. Six balls are drawn one by one without replacement of which at least 4 balls are white. Find the probability that in the next two draws exactly one white ball is drawn. (leave the answer in terms of ^nC_r). **[2004, Main]**

90. Two number are selected randomly from the set $S = \{1, 2, 3, 4, 5, 6,\}$ without replacement one by one. The probability that minimum of 2 numbers is less than 4 is : **[2006, Main]**

(a) $\dfrac{1}{15}$

(b) $\dfrac{14}{15}$

(c) $1/5$

(d) $\dfrac{4}{5}$

ANSWER KEY

1. (a)	**2.** (11)	**3.** (c)	**4.** (b)	**5.** (c)	**6.** (6)	**7.** (a)	**8.** (3)	**9.** (d)	**10.** (4)
11. (b)	**12.** (d)	**13.** (b)	**14.** (11)	**15.** (b)	**16.** (6)	**17.** (8)	**18.** (c)	**19.** (c)	**20.** (a)
21. (a)	**22.** (c)	**23.** (a)	**24.** (c)	**25.** (c)	**26.** (18)	**27.** (b)	**28.** (d)	**29.** (a)	**30.** (d)
31. (a)	**32.** (d)	**33.** (c)	**34.** (54)	**35.** (c)	**36.** (b)	**37.** (c)	**38.** (a)	**39.** (b)	**40.** (c)
41. (a)	**42.** (c)	**43.** (d)	**44.** (a)	**45.** (b)	**46.** (d)	**47.** (a)	**48.** (d)	**49.** (a,b)	**50.** (b)
51. (b)	**52.** (b)	**53.** (c)	**54.** (d)	**55.** (b)	**56.** (8)	**57.** (a,b)	**58.** (c,d)	**59.** (d)	**60.** (a)
61. (b)	**62.** (a)	**63.** (b)	**64.** (d)	**65.** (b)	**66.** (a)	**67.** (a)	**68.** (a)	**69.** (d)	**70.** (a)
71. (a,b)	**72.** (b)	**73.** (b,d)	**74.** (d)	**75.** (d)	**76.** (d)	**77.** (a,d)	**78.** (c)	**79.** (b)	**80.** (c)
81. (d)	**82.** (c)	**83.** (b)	**84.** (a)	**85.** (b)	**86.** ($\frac{1}{7}$)	**87.** (d)	**88.** (*)		

89. $\dfrac{^{12}C_2\,^6C_4\,^{10}C_1\,^2C_1 + {}^{12}C_1\,^6C_5\,^{11}C_1\,^1C_1\,^{12}C_1}{(^{12}C_2\,^6C_4\,^{12}C_1\,^6C_5 + {}^{12}C_0\,^6C_6)}$

90. (d)

ANSWERS WITH EXPLANATIONS

1. **Correct Respsonse :** (a)

Explanation :

$$\bar{x} = \frac{2+4+10+12+14+x+y}{7} = 8$$

$$x + y = 14 \qquad \text{...(i)}$$

$$(\sigma)^2 = \frac{\Sigma(x_i)^2}{n} - \left(\frac{\Sigma x_i}{n}\right)^2$$

$$16 = \frac{4+16+100+144+196+x^2+y^2}{7} - 8^2$$

$$16 + 64 = \frac{460+x^2+y^2}{7}$$

$$560 = 460 + x^2 + y^2$$

$$x^2 + y^2 = 100 \qquad \text{...(ii)}$$

$$(x+y)^2 = (x^2+y^2) + 2xy$$

$$(14)^2 = 100 + 2xy$$

$$xy = 48$$

$$(x-y)^2 = (x+y)^2 - 4xy$$

$$= (14)^2 - 4 \times 48$$

$$= 4$$

Clearly by (i) and (ii),

$$|\,x - y\,| = 2$$

2. **Correct Respsonse :** (11)

Explanation :

4 dice are independently thrown. Each die has probability to show 3 or 5 is

$$p = \frac{2}{6} = \frac{1}{3}$$

$$\therefore \quad q = 1 - \frac{1}{3} = \frac{2}{3} \text{ (not showing 3 or 5)}$$

Experiment is performed with 4 dices independently.

$\therefore$ Their binomial distribution is

$$(q+p)^4 = (q)^4 + {}^4C_1\,q^3p + {}^4C_2\,q^2p^2 + {}^4C_3\,qp^3 + {}^4C_4\,p^4$$

$\therefore$ In one throw of each dice probability of showing 3 or 5 at least twice is

$$= p^4 + {}^4C_3\,qp^3 + {}^4C_2\,q^2p^2$$

$$= \left(\frac{1}{3}\right)^4 + {}^4C_3\left(\frac{2}{3}\right)\left(\frac{1}{3}\right)^4 + {}^4C_2\left(\frac{2}{3}\right)^2\left(\frac{1}{3}\right)^2$$

$$= \frac{33}{81}$$

$\therefore$ Such experiment performed 27 times.

$\therefore$ So expected out comes $= np$

$$= \frac{33}{81} \times 27$$

$$= 11.$$

3. Correct Respsonse : (c)

Explanation :

Out of 11 consecutive natural numbers either 6 even and 5 odd numbers or 5 even and 6 odd numbers.

When 3 numbers are selected at random then total cases $= {}^{11}C_3$

Since these 3 numbers are in A.P. Let no's are a, b, c.

$$2b \Rightarrow \text{even number}$$

$$a + c \Rightarrow \begin{pmatrix} \text{even} + \text{even} \\ \text{odd} + \text{odd} \end{pmatrix}$$

so favourable cases $= {}^{6}C_2 + {}^{5}C_2$

$$= 15 + 10 = 25$$

$$P(3 \text{ numbers are in A.P.}) = \frac{25}{{}^{11}C_3} = \frac{25}{165} = \frac{5}{33}$$

4. Correct Respsonse : (b)

Explanation :

$$\text{S.D.} = \sqrt{\frac{\displaystyle\sum_{i=1}^{n}(x_i - a)^2}{n} - \left(\frac{\displaystyle\sum_{i=1}^{n}(x_i - a)}{n}\right)^2}$$

$$= \sqrt{\frac{na}{n} - \left(\frac{n}{n}\right)^2}$$

$$\left\{ \text{Given } \sum_{i=1}^{n}(x_i - a) = n \sum_{i=1}^{n}(x_i - a)^2 = na \right\}$$

$$= \sqrt{a - 1}.$$

5. Correct Respsonse : (c)

Explanation :

$$P(A \cup B) = P(A) + P(B) - P(A \cap B)$$

$$0.8 = 0.6 + 0.4 - P(A \cap B)$$

$$P(A \cap B) = 0.2$$

$$P(A \cup B \cup C) = \Sigma P(A) - \Sigma P(A \cap B) + P(A \cap B \cap C)$$

$$\alpha = 1.5 - (0.2 + 0.3 + \beta) + 0.2$$

$$\alpha = 1.2 - \beta \in [0.85, 0.95]$$

(where $\alpha \in [0.85, 0.95]$)

$$0.85 \leq \alpha \leq 0.95$$

$$0.85 \leq 1.2 - \beta \leq 0.95$$

$$\beta \in [0.25, 0.35].$$

6. Correct Respsonse : (6)

Explanation :

x	0	2	4	8	2^n
f	${}^{n}C_0$	${}^{n}C_1$	${}^{n}C_2$	${}^{n}C_3$	${}^{n}C_n$

$$\text{Mean} = \frac{\Sigma x_i f_i}{\Sigma f_i} = \frac{\displaystyle\sum_{r=1}^{n} 2^r \, {}^{n}C_r}{\displaystyle\sum_{r=0}^{n} {}^{n}C_r}$$

$$= \frac{0 \times {}^{n}C_0 + 2 \times {}^{n}C_1 + 2^2 \times {}^{n}C_2 + \ldots 2^n \times {}^{n}C_n}{{}^{n}C_0 + {}^{n}C_1 + {}^{n}C_2 + \ldots + {}^{n}C_n}$$

$$\text{Mean} = \frac{(1+2)^n - {}^{n}C_0}{2^n} = \frac{728}{2^n}$$

$$\Rightarrow \qquad \frac{3^n - 1}{2^n} = \frac{728}{2^n}$$

$$\Rightarrow \qquad 3^n = 729 \Rightarrow n = 6.$$

7. Correct Respsonse : (a)

Explanation :

Let remaining two observations are a and b.

$$\bar{x} = \frac{5 + 7 + 12 + 10 + 15 + 14 + a + b}{8}$$

$$= 10$$

$$63 + a + b = 80$$

$$a + b = 17 \qquad \ldots(i)$$

$$\sigma^2 = \frac{\Sigma x_i^2}{n} - \left(\frac{\Sigma x_i}{n}\right)^2$$

$$13.5 = \frac{25 + 49 + 144 + 100 + 225 + 196 + a^2 + b^2}{8} - 100$$

$$908 = a^2 + b^2 + 739$$

$$a^2 + b^2 = 169$$

$$(a + b)^2 - 2ab = 169$$

$$289 - 2ab = 169$$

$$ab = 60$$

$$|a - b|^2 = (a + b)^2 - 4ab$$

$$= 280 - 240$$

$$= 49$$

$$|a - b| = 7.$$

8. Correct Respsonse : (3)

Explanation :

$$p = \frac{1}{10}$$

$$q = \frac{9}{10} \qquad (\because q = 1 - p)$$

We have, $1 -$ (probability of all shots result in failure) $> \dfrac{1}{4}$

$$\Rightarrow \quad 1-\left(\frac{9}{10}\right)^n > \frac{1}{4}$$

$$\Rightarrow \quad \frac{3}{4} > \left(\frac{9}{10}\right)^n \Rightarrow n \geq 3$$

9. Correct Respsonse : (d)

Explanation :

Sum $6 \to (1, 5), (5, 1), (3, 3), (4, 2), (2, 4)$

Sum $7 \to (1, 6), (6, 1), (5, 2), (2, 5), (3, 4), (4, 3)$

$$P(6) = \frac{5}{36}$$

$$P(7) = \frac{6}{36} = \frac{1}{6}$$

$$P(A) = W + FFW + FFFFW + \dots$$

$$= \frac{5}{36} + \frac{31}{36} \times \frac{5}{6} \times \frac{5}{36} + \frac{31}{36} \times \frac{5}{6} \times \frac{31}{36} \times \frac{5}{6} \times \frac{5}{36} + \dots$$

$$= \frac{\frac{5}{36}}{1-\frac{155}{216}} = \frac{30}{61}.$$

10 Correct Respsonse : (4)

Explanation :

$\because$ Variance is independent of shifting of origin

$$x_i : \quad 15 \quad 25 \quad 35 \quad \text{or} \quad -10 \quad 0 \quad 10$$

$$\Rightarrow \quad f_i : \quad 2 \quad x \quad 2 \qquad\qquad 2 \quad x \quad 2$$

$$\Rightarrow \quad \text{Variance} (\sigma^2) = \frac{\Sigma x_i^2 f_i}{\Sigma f_i} - (\overrightarrow{x})^2$$

$$\Rightarrow \quad 50 = \frac{200+0+200}{x+4} - 0 \qquad \{\bar{x} = 0\}$$

$$\Rightarrow \quad 200 + 50x = 200 + 200$$

$$\Rightarrow \quad x = 4.$$

11. Correct Respsonse : (b)

Explanation :

A : Sum obtained is a multiple of 4.

$A = \{(1, 3), (2, 2), (3, 1), (2, 6), (3, 5), (4, 4), (5, 3), (6, 2), (6, 6)\}$

B : Score of 4 has appeared at least once.

$B = \{(1, 4), (2, 4), (3, 4), (4, 4), (5, 4), (6, 4), (4, 1), (4, 2), (4, 3), (4, 5), (4, 6)\}$

$$\text{Required probability} = P\left(\frac{B}{A}\right) = \frac{P(B \cap A)}{P(A)}$$

$$= \frac{1/36}{9/36} = \frac{1}{9}.$$

12. Correct Respsonse : (d)

Explanation :

$$\because \quad \sigma^2 \leq \frac{1}{4}(M-m)^2$$

where M and m are upper and lower bounds of values of any random variable.

$$\therefore \quad \sigma^2 < \frac{1}{4}(10-0)^2$$

$$\Rightarrow \quad 0 < \sigma < 5$$

$$\therefore \quad \sigma \neq 6.$$

13. Correct Respsonse : (b)

Explanation :

$$\text{Mean} = 5$$

$$\frac{3+5+7+a+b}{5} = 5$$

$$a + b = 10 \qquad\qquad \dots(i)$$

$$\text{S.D.} = 2 \Rightarrow \sqrt{\frac{\sum_{i=1}^{5}(x_i - \bar{x})^2}{5}} = 2$$

$(3-5)^2 + (5-5)^2 + (7-5)^2 + (a-5)^2 + (b-5)^2 = 20$

$$\Rightarrow \quad 4 + 0 + 4 + (a-5)^2 + (b-5)^2 = 20$$

$$a^2 + b^2 - 10(a+b) + 50 = 12$$

$$(a+b)^2 - 2ab - 100 + 50 = 12$$

$$ab = 19 \qquad \dots(ii)$$

Equation is $x^2 - 10x + 19 = 0$.

14. Correct Respsonse : (11)

Explanation :

$$P(H) = \frac{1}{2}$$

$$P(\overline{H}) = \frac{1}{2}$$

Let total 'n' bomb are required to destroy the target.

$$1 - {}^nC_n\left(\frac{1}{2}\right)^n - {}^nC_1\left(\frac{1}{2}\right)^n \geq \frac{99}{100}$$

$$1 - \frac{1}{2^n} - \frac{n}{2^n} \geq \frac{99}{100}$$

$$\frac{1}{100} \geq \frac{n+1}{2^n}$$

Now check for value of n.

$$n = 11$$

15. Correct Respsonse : (b)

Explanation :

$$P(H) = \frac{2}{3} \text{ for } C_1$$

$$P(H) = \frac{1}{3} \text{ for } C_2$$

for C_1

No. of Heads (α)	0	1	2
Probability	$\frac{1}{9}$	$\frac{4}{9}$	$\frac{4}{9}$

for C_2

No. of Heads (β)	0	1	2
Probability	$\dfrac{4}{9}$	$\dfrac{4}{9}$	$\dfrac{1}{9}$

for real and equal roots

$$\alpha^2 = 4\beta$$

$$(\alpha, \beta) = (0, 0), (2, 1)$$

So, probability $= \dfrac{1}{9} \times \dfrac{4}{9} + \dfrac{4}{9} \times \dfrac{4}{9} = \dfrac{20}{81}.$

16. Correct Respsonse : (6)

Explanation :

Let $P(r)$ = probability of r successes

$$= {}^nC_r \left(\dfrac{3}{4}\right)^r \left(\dfrac{1}{4}\right)^{n-r}$$

$$1 - [P(0 + P(1) + P(2)] \geq 0.95$$

$$\Rightarrow 1 - {}^nC_0 \left(\dfrac{1}{4}\right)^n - {}^nC_1 \left(\dfrac{3}{4}\right)\left(\dfrac{1}{4}\right)^{n-1}$$

$$- {}^nC_2 \left(\dfrac{3}{4}\right)^2 \left(\dfrac{1}{4}\right)^{n-2} \geq 0.95$$

$$\Rightarrow 1 - \left(\dfrac{1 + 3n + \dfrac{9n(n-1)}{2}}{4^n}\right) \geq 0.95$$

$$\Rightarrow 9n^2 - 3n + 2 \leq 0.05 \times 4^n \times 2 \leq \dfrac{4^n}{10}$$

for $n = 5$	$212 \leq 102.4$	(Not true)
for $n = 6$	$308 \leq 409.6$	(true)

$\therefore$ least value of $n = 6$.

17. Correct Respsonse : (8)

Explanation :

Square $\to$ 4 or 9 $\to$ (1, 3), (3, 1), (2, 2), (6, 3), (3, 6), (4, 5), (5, 4)

Prime $\to$ 2 or 3 or 5 or 7 or 11

(1, 1), (1, 2), (2, 1), (1, 4), (4, 1), (2, 3), (3, 2), (1, 6), (6, 1), (5, 2), (2, 5), (3, 4), (4, 3), (6, 5), (5, 6)

$$P(\text{square or prime}) = \dfrac{22}{36}$$

$$P(\text{prime}) = \dfrac{15}{36}$$

$$P(\text{perfect square}) = \dfrac{7}{36}$$

Required probability

$$= \dfrac{\dfrac{4}{36} + \dfrac{14}{36} \cdot \dfrac{4}{36} + \left(\dfrac{14}{36}\right)^2 \cdot \dfrac{4}{36} + \ldots}{\dfrac{7}{36} + \dfrac{14}{36} \cdot \dfrac{7}{36} + \left(\dfrac{14}{36}\right)^2 \cdot \dfrac{7}{37} + \ldots}$$

$$P = \dfrac{\dfrac{\dfrac{4}{36}}{\left(1 - \dfrac{14}{36}\right)}}{\dfrac{\dfrac{7}{36}}{\left(1 - \dfrac{14}{36}\right)}} = \dfrac{4}{7}$$

$$7P = 4$$

$$14P = 8.$$

18. Correct Respsonse : (c)

Explanation :

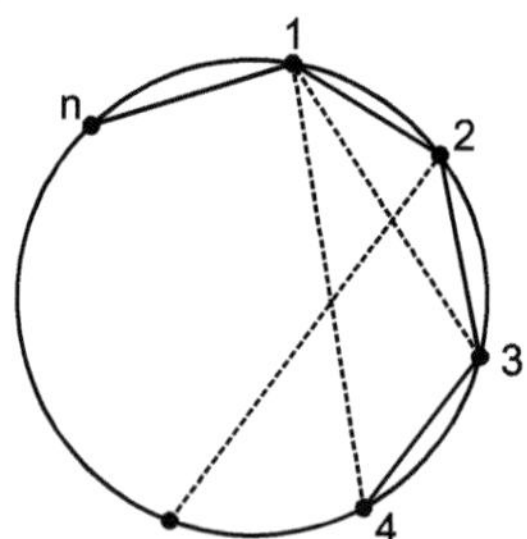

Number of blue lines = Number of sides = n

Number of red lines = number of diagonals

$$= {}^nC_2 - n$$

$${}^nC_2 - n = 99\,n \Rightarrow \dfrac{n(n-1)}{2} - n = 99n$$

$$\dfrac{n-1}{2} - 1 = 99 \Rightarrow n = 201$$

19. Correct Response : (c)

Explanation :

First Case : Choose two non-zero digits ${}^9C_2$.

Now, number of 5-digit numbers containing both digits $= 2^5 - 2$

Second Case : Choose one non-zero and one zero as digit ${}^9C_1$.

Number of 5-digit numbers containing one non-zero and one zero both $= (2^4 - 1)$

Required prob.

$$= \dfrac{\left({}^6C_2 \times (2^5 - 2) + {}^9C_1 \times (2^4 - 1)\right)}{9 \times 10^4}$$

$$= \dfrac{36 \times (32 - 2) + 9 \times (16 - 1)}{9 \times 10^4}$$

$$= \dfrac{4 \times 30 + 15}{10^4} = \dfrac{135}{10^4}$$

20. Correct Respsonse : (a)

Explanation :

Let B_1 be the event where Box-I is selected. & B_2 $\to$ where box-II selected

$$P(B_1) = P(B_2) = \dfrac{1}{2}$$

Let E be the event where selected card is non prime.

For B_1 : Prime numbers :
$$\{2, 3, 5, 7, 11, 13, 17, 19, 23, 29\}$$
For B_2 : Prime numbers :
$$\{31, 37, 41, 43, 47\}$$
$$P(E) = P(B_1)\, P(E/B_1) + P(B_2)\, P(E/B_2)$$
$$= \frac{1}{2} \times \frac{20}{30} + \frac{1}{2} \times \frac{15}{20}$$

Required probability :

$$P\left(\frac{B_1}{E}\right) = \frac{\dfrac{1}{2} \times \dfrac{20}{30}}{\dfrac{1}{2} \times \dfrac{20}{30} + \dfrac{1}{2} \times \dfrac{15}{20}} = \frac{\dfrac{2}{3}}{\dfrac{2}{3} + \dfrac{3}{4}} = \frac{8}{17}$$

21. Correct Respsonse : (a)

Explanation :

$$\sigma^2 = \text{variance}$$
$$\mu = \text{mean}$$
$$\sigma^2 = \frac{\sum\limits_{i=1}^{n} (x_i - \mu)^2}{n}$$
$$\mu = 17$$
$$\text{mean} = \frac{\sum\limits_{x=1}^{17} (ax + b)}{17}$$
$$\Rightarrow \quad \mu = \frac{a(1+2+3+4+5+......+17)}{17} + b$$
$$\Rightarrow \quad 17 = \frac{a \times 17 \times (17+1)}{2 \times 17} + b$$
$$\Rightarrow \quad 17 = 9a + b \qquad\qquad ...(1)$$
$$\Rightarrow \quad \frac{\sum\limits_{x=1}^{17} (ax + b - 17)^2}{17} = 216$$
$$\Rightarrow \quad \frac{\sum\limits_{x=1}^{17} a^2 (x - 9)^2}{17} = 216$$
$$\Rightarrow a^2 81 - 18 \times 9a^2 + a^2\, 3 \times (35) = 216$$
$$\Rightarrow \quad a^2 = \frac{216}{24} = 9 \Rightarrow a = 3 \ (a > 0)$$
$$\Rightarrow \text{From (1), } b = -10$$
So, $\quad a + b = -7$

22. Correct Respsonse : (c)

Explanation :

$$\text{Variance} = \frac{\Sigma(x_i - p)^2}{n} - \left(\frac{\Sigma(x_i - p)}{n}\right)^2$$
$$= \frac{9}{10} - \left(\frac{3}{10}\right)^2 = \frac{81}{100}$$

$$\text{S.D.} = \sqrt{\text{Variance}}$$
$$\text{S.D.} = \frac{9}{10}$$

23. Correct Response : (a)

Explanation :

$$20p - q = 10 \qquad\qquad ...(i)$$
$$\text{and} \qquad 2|p| = 1 \Rightarrow p = \pm\frac{1}{2} \qquad ...(ii)$$
$$\text{so,} \quad p = \frac{1}{2} \text{ and } q = -20$$

24. Correct Response : (c)

Explanation :

(a) $\qquad P(A/B) = P(A) = \dfrac{1}{3}$

(b) $P(A/(A \cup U)) = \dfrac{P(A \cap (A \cup B))}{P(A \cup B)}$

$$= \frac{\dfrac{1}{3}}{\dfrac{1}{3} + \dfrac{1}{6} - \dfrac{1}{18}} = \frac{3}{4}$$

(c) $\qquad P(A/B') = P(A) = \dfrac{1}{3}$

(d) $\qquad P(A'/B') = P(A') = \dfrac{2}{3}$

25. Correct Response : (c)

Explanation :

k	0	1	2	3	4	5
$P(k)$	$\dfrac{1}{32}$	$\dfrac{12}{32}$	$\dfrac{11}{32}$	$\dfrac{5}{32}$	$\dfrac{2}{32}$	$\dfrac{1}{32}$

$$\text{Expected value} = \sum XP(k)$$
$$= -\frac{1}{31} - \frac{12}{32} - \frac{11}{32} + \frac{15}{32} + \frac{8}{32} + \frac{5}{32}$$
$$= \frac{28 - 24}{32} = \frac{4}{32} = \frac{1}{8}$$

26. Correct Response : (18)

Explanation :

Variance of first 'n' natural numbers $= \dfrac{n^2 - 1}{12} = 10$

$$\Rightarrow \qquad n = 11$$

and variance of first 'm' even natural numbers

$$= 4\left(\frac{m^2 - 1}{12}\right)$$
$$\Rightarrow \qquad \frac{m^2 - 1}{3} = 16$$
$$\Rightarrow \qquad m = 7$$
$$m + n = 18$$

27. Correct Response : (b)

Explanation :

$$\sum P(X) = 1$$

$$\Rightarrow \ K^2 + 2K + K + 2K + 5K^2 = 1$$
$$\Rightarrow \quad\quad 6K^2 + 5K - 1 = 0$$
$$\Rightarrow \quad\quad (6K - 1)(K + 1) = 0$$
$$\Rightarrow \quad\quad\quad K = -1 \text{ (Rejected)}$$
$$\Rightarrow \quad\quad\quad K = \frac{1}{6}$$

$$P(X > 2) = K + 2K + 5K^2 = \frac{23}{36}$$

28. Correct Response : (d)

Explanation :

Total ways of distributing 10 different balls in 4 distinct boxes $= 4^{10}$

Required probability $= \dfrac{^4C_2 \times ^{10}C_2 \times ^8C_3 \times 2^5 \times 2!}{4^{10}}$

$$= \frac{\frac{4\times 3}{2} \times \frac{10\times 9}{2} \times \frac{8\times 7}{6} \times 12 \times 2}{2^{20}}$$

$$= \frac{6 \times 45 \times 56 \times 2}{2^{15}}$$

$$= \frac{2 \times 3 \times 45 \times 8 \times 7 \times 2}{2^{15}}$$

$$= \frac{3 \times 45 \times 7 \times 25}{2^{15}}$$

$$= \frac{945}{2^{10}}$$

29. Correct Response : (a)

Explanation :

A : Event when card A is drawn

B : Event when card B is drawn.

$$P(A) = P(B) = 1/2$$

Required probability = P(AA or (AB)A or (BA)A or (ABB)A or (BAB) A or (BBA)A)

$$= \frac{1}{2} \times \frac{1}{2} + \left(\frac{1}{2} \times \frac{1}{2} \times \frac{1}{2}\right) \times 2 + \left(\frac{1}{2} \times \frac{1}{2} \times \frac{1}{2} \times \frac{1}{2}\right) \times 3$$

$$= \frac{1}{4} + \frac{1}{4} + \frac{3}{16} = \frac{11}{16}$$

30. Correct Response : (d)

Explanation :

$$\sum_{i=1}^{10} (x_i - 5) = 10$$

$$\Rightarrow \text{Mean of observation } x_i - 5 = \frac{1}{10} \sum_{i=1}^{3} (x_i - 5) = 1$$

$$\Rightarrow \ \mu = \text{mean of observation } (x_i - 3)$$
$$= (\text{mean of observation } (x_i - 5)) + 2$$
$$= 1 + 2 = 3$$

Variance of observation

$$x_i - 5 = \frac{1}{10} \sum_{i=1}^{10} (x_i - 5)^2 - (\text{Mean of } (x_i - 5))^2 = 3$$

$$\Rightarrow \lambda = \text{variance of observation } (x_i - 3)$$
$$= \text{variance of observation } (x_i - 5) = 3$$
$$\therefore \quad\quad (\mu, \lambda) = (3, 3)$$

31. Correct Response : (a)

Explanation :

$$\frac{\sum x_i}{20} = 10$$

$$\Rightarrow \quad\quad \sum x_i = 200 \quad\quad\quad …(i)$$

$$\frac{\sum x_i^2}{20} - 100 = 4$$

$$\Rightarrow \quad\quad \sum x_i^2 = 2080 \quad\quad\quad …(ii)$$

$$\text{Actual mean} = \frac{200 - 9 + 11}{20} = \frac{202}{20}$$

$$\text{Variance} = \frac{2080 - 81 + 121}{20} - \left(\frac{202}{20}\right)^2 = 3.99$$

32. Correct Response : (d)

Explanation :

$$P(A) + P(B) - 2P(A \cap B) = \frac{2}{5}$$

$$P(A) + P(B) - (P \cap B) = \frac{1}{2}$$

$$P(A \cap B) = \frac{1}{10}$$

33. Correct Response : (c)

Explanation :

Probability that at most 2 machines are out of service

$$= \ ^5C_0 \left(\frac{3}{4}\right)^5 + \ ^5C_1 \left(\frac{3}{4}\right)^4 \left(\frac{1}{4}\right) + \ ^5C_2 \left(\frac{3}{4}\right)^3 \left(\frac{1}{4}\right)^2$$

$$= \left(\frac{3}{4}\right)^4 \times \frac{17}{8}$$

$$\Rightarrow k = \frac{17}{8}$$

34. Correct Response : (54)

Explanation :

$$\frac{3 + 7 + 9 + 12 + 13 + 20 + x + y}{8} = 10$$

$$x + y = 16$$

$$\frac{\sum x^2}{n} - \left(\frac{\sum x}{n}\right)^2 = 25$$

$$3^2 + 7^2 + 9^2 + 12^2 + 13^2 + 20^2 + x^2 + y^2 = 1000$$

$$x^2 + y^2 = 148$$

$$xy = 54$$

35. Correct Respsonse : (c)

Explanation :

Let n be the number of children in each family,

$$\frac{1}{12} = \frac{{}^nC_3 \cdot 3!}{{}^{2n}C_3 \cdot 3!}$$

$$\frac{{}^nC_3}{{}^{2n}C_3} = \frac{1}{12}$$

$$\frac{\left(\dfrac{n!}{3!\,(n-3)!}\right)}{\dfrac{2n!}{3!\,(2n-3)!}} = \frac{1}{12}$$

$$n = 5$$

36. Correct Response : (b)

Explanation :

Probability that a box A to be selected is,

$$P(A) = \frac{1}{2}$$

Probability that a box B to be selected is,

$$P(B) = \frac{1}{2}$$

Let, E is the event such that one ball is white while the other ball is red then,

$$P(E) = P(A) \cdot P\left(\frac{E}{A}\right) + P(B) \cdot P\left(\frac{E}{B}\right)$$

$$= \left(\frac{1}{2}\right)\left(\frac{2 \cdot 3}{{}^7C_2}\right) + \left(\frac{1}{2}\right)\left(\frac{4 \cdot 2}{{}^9C_2}\right)$$

$$= \frac{1}{2}\left(\frac{6}{21} + \frac{8}{36}\right)$$

$$= \frac{16}{63}$$

The probability that both balls are drawn from the box B is,

$$P\left(\frac{B}{E}\right) = \frac{P(B)P\left(\dfrac{E}{B}\right)}{P(E)}$$

$$= \frac{\left(\dfrac{1}{2}\right)\left(\dfrac{4 \cdot 2}{{}^9C_2}\right)}{\left(\dfrac{16}{63}\right)}$$

$$= \frac{\left(\dfrac{8}{36}\right)}{2}\left(\dfrac{63}{16}\right)$$

$$= \frac{7}{16}$$

Therefore, the probability that both balls are drawn from the box B is $\dfrac{7}{16}$.

37. Correct Response : (c)

Explanation :

If the standard deviation is zero, all five observations are exactly nine. Consider one of the observation that change by x. To find x just use the formula for the mean to solve :

$$\frac{(4 \times 9) + x}{5} = 10$$

$$x = 14$$

The standard deviation is,

$$\sqrt{\frac{(14-10)^2 + 4(9-10)^2}{5}} = 10$$

$$\sqrt{\frac{4^2 + 4}{5}} = 2$$

The difference between odd observation and new set of observation is zero. So, the standard deviation will remain same.

38. Correct Response : (a)

Explanation :

Write the given probability and apply the substitution,

$$P\left(\frac{(\bar{A} \cap \bar{B})}{C}\right) = \frac{P\big((\bar{A} \cup \bar{B}) \cap C\big)}{P(C)}$$

$$= \frac{P(C) - P(A \cap B) - P(A \cap B \cap C)}{P(C)}$$

$$= \frac{P(C)[P(A)P(C) + P(B)P(C)]}{P(C)}$$

$$= 1 - P(A) - P(B)$$

Further, solve the above expression.

$$P\left(\frac{(\bar{A} \cap \bar{B})}{C}\right) = P(\bar{A}) - P(B)$$

39. Correct Response : (b)

Explanation :

E_1 : Event that first ball drawn is black.

E_2 : Event that first ball drawn is red.

E : Event that again ball drawn is red.

The total probability will be,

$$P(E) = P(E_1) \cdot P\left(\frac{E}{E_1}\right) + P(E_2) \cdot P\left(\frac{E}{E_2}\right)$$

$$= \frac{6}{10} \times \frac{4}{12} + \frac{4}{10} \times \frac{6}{12}$$

$$= \frac{2}{5}$$

40. Correct Response : (c)

Explanation :

Here 5 is the radius of convergence of the series. As it common for all so that it can be neglected.

Let $x_j = (x_i - 5)$

Then the standard deviation is,

$$\sigma = \sqrt{\sum \frac{x_j^2}{n} - \left(\frac{\sum x_j}{n}\right)^2}$$

$$= \sqrt{\frac{45}{9} - \left(\frac{9}{9}\right)^2}$$

$$= \sqrt{5 - 1}$$

$$= 2$$

41. Correct Response : (a)

Explanation :

The event happening is,

$$n(A) = 4!\left(1 - \frac{1}{1!} + \frac{1}{2!} - \frac{1}{3!} + \frac{1}{4!}\right)$$

The event already occurred is,

$$n(S) = 5!$$

The probability that the student S_1 gets the previously allotted seat R_1 is,

$$P = \frac{n(A)}{n(S)}$$

$$P = \frac{4!\left(1 - \frac{1}{1!} + \frac{1}{2!} - \frac{1}{3!} + \frac{1}{4!}\right)}{5!}$$

$$= \frac{1 - \frac{1}{1} + \frac{1}{2} - \frac{1}{6} + \frac{1}{24}}{5}$$

$$= \frac{3}{40}$$

42. Correct Response : (c)

Explanation :

The total number of ways in which seat can be allotted are,

$$T = 5!$$

$$= 120$$

The number of ways in which student S_1, S_2, S_3 and S_4 do not sit together is,

$n(S_1 \cap S_2 \cap S_3 \cap S_4)$

$$= T - n(S_1 \cup S_2 \cup S_3 \cup S_4)$$

$$= 5! - \left(\begin{array}{l} {}^4C_1 4! 2! - ({}^3C_1 3! 2! + {}^3C_1 3! 2! 2!) \\ + ({}^2C_1 2! 2! + {}^4C_1(2)2!) - 2 \end{array}\right)$$

$$= 14$$

The probability that the student S_1 and student S_{i+1} do not sit together is,

$$P = \frac{n(S_1 \cap S_2 \cap S_3 \cap S_4)}{T}$$

$$= \frac{14}{120}$$

$$= \frac{7}{60}$$

43. Correct Response : (d)

Explanation :

The sum of 100 observations is,

$$\sum x_i = 400$$

The sum of square of 100 observations is,

$$\sum x_i^2 = 2475$$

Variance is calculated as,

$$\sigma^2 = \left[\frac{\sum x_i^2}{N} - \left(\frac{\sum x_i}{N}\right)^2\right]$$

$$= \left[\frac{2475}{100} - \left(\frac{400}{100}\right)^2\right]$$

When 3, 4, 5 are omitted, the new variance is,

$$\sigma^2 = \left[\frac{\sum x_i^2 - (3^2 + 4^2 + 5^2)}{N} - \left(\frac{\sum x_i - (3 + 4 + 5)}{N}\right)^2\right]$$

$$= \left[\frac{2475 - 50}{97} - \left(\frac{400 - 12}{97}\right)^2\right]$$

$$= \left[\frac{2425}{97} - 16\right]$$

$$= 9$$

44. Correct Response : (a)

Explanation :

The probability that the target hit by P, Q and R is,

$$P = (\text{P hits}) \cup (\text{Q hits}) \cup (\text{P and Q hit})$$

$$= \left(\frac{3}{4}\right)\left(\frac{1}{2}\right)\left(\frac{3}{8}\right) + \left(\frac{1}{4}\right)\left(\frac{1}{2}\right)\left(\frac{3}{8}\right) + \left(\frac{3}{4}\right)\left(\frac{1}{2}\right)\left(\frac{3}{8}\right)$$

$$= \frac{21}{64}$$

45. Correct Response : (b)

Explanation :

Probability to obtain at least one head and at least one tail is given as,

$$P = 1 - (P \text{ (all heads)} + P(\text{all tails}))$$

$$= 1 - \left(\frac{1}{2^8} + \frac{1}{2^8} \right)$$

$$= 1 - \frac{1}{2^7}$$

$$= \frac{127}{128}$$

46. Correct Response : (d)

Explanation :

The probability of drawing green ball is,

$$p = \frac{15}{15 + 10 + 10}$$

$$p = \frac{3}{5}$$

$$q = 1 - p$$

$$= \frac{2}{5}$$

The variance of the number of the green balls drawn is,

$$\text{var }(X) = n \cdot p \cdot q$$

$$= 10 \left(\frac{3}{5} \right) \left(\frac{2}{5} \right)$$

$$= \frac{12}{5}$$

47. Correct Response : (a)

Explanation :

The probability of exactly one of A or B occur is,

$$P(A) + P(B) - 2P(A \cap B) = \frac{1}{4} \qquad \ldots(1)$$

The probability of exactly one of C or B occur is,

$$P(B) + P(C) - 2P(C \cap B) = \frac{1}{4} \qquad \ldots(2)$$

The probability of exactly one of A or C occur is,

$$P(A) + P(C) - 2P(A \cap C) = \frac{1}{4} \qquad \ldots(3)$$

The probability of occurring of at least one of the events is the submission of equation (1), equation (2) and equation (3).

$$P(A \cup B \cup C)$$

$$= \left[\begin{array}{l} P(A) + P(B) + P(C) - P(A \cap B) - P(C \cap B) - P(A \cap C) \\ \qquad\qquad\qquad\qquad\qquad\qquad + P(A \cap B \cap C) \end{array} \right]$$

$$= \frac{3}{8} + \frac{1}{16}$$

$$= \frac{7}{16}$$

48. Correct Response : (d)

Explanation :

The total number of ways in which the number can be chosen is,

$$T_n = {}^{11}C_2$$

$$= \frac{11 \times 10}{2}$$

$$= 55$$

Total number of favourable events is,

$$T_f = (0, 4), (0, 8), (4, 8), (2, 6),$$
$$(2, 10), (6, 10)$$

$$= 6$$

The probability is.

$$P = \frac{T_f}{T_n}$$

$$= \frac{6}{55}$$

49. Correct Response : (a, b)

Explanation :

The expression to calculate $P\left(\dfrac{Y}{X} \right)$ is,

$$P\left(\frac{Y}{X} \right) = \frac{P(X \cap Y)}{P(X)}$$

Substitute the values.

$$\frac{2}{5} = \frac{P(X \cap Y)}{\dfrac{1}{3}}$$

$$P(X \cap Y) = \frac{2}{15}$$

The expression to calculate $P\left(\dfrac{X}{Y} \right)$ is,

$$P\left(\frac{X}{Y} \right) = \frac{P(X \cap Y)}{P(Y)}$$

Substitute the values.

$$\frac{1}{2} = \frac{\dfrac{2}{15}}{P(Y)}$$

$$P(Y) = \frac{4}{15}$$

The expression to calculate $P\left(\dfrac{X'}{Y} \right)$ is,

$$P\left(\frac{X'}{Y} \right) = \frac{P(X' \cap Y)}{P(Y)}$$

$$= \frac{P(Y) - P(X \cap Y)}{P(Y)}$$

$$= \frac{\dfrac{4}{15} - \dfrac{2}{15}}{\dfrac{4}{15}}$$

$$= \frac{1}{2}$$

The expression to calculate $P(X \cup Y)$ is,

$$P(X \cup Y) = P(X) + P(Y) - P(X \cap Y)$$

$$= \frac{1}{3} + \frac{4}{15} - \frac{2}{15}$$

$$= \frac{7}{15}$$

50. Correct Response : (b)

Explanation :

The total number of outcomes is given by :

$$n(s) = {}^{3+10-1}C_{10}$$

$$= {}^{12}C_{10}$$

$$= 66$$

Let $z = 2n$ where $n = 1, 2, 3, 4, 5$

The given equation becomes :

$$x + y + 2n = 10$$

$$x + y = 10 - 2n$$

The number of favourable outcomes is given by :

$$n(0) = \sum_{n=0}^{5} {}^{10-2n+2-1}C_{2-1}$$

$$= \sum_{n=0}^{5} {}^{11-2n}C_{1}$$

$$= \sum_{n=0}^{5} (11 - 2n)$$

$$= 11 + 9 + 7 + 5 + 3 + 1$$

$$= 36$$

The probability is given by :

$$P = \frac{n(0)}{n(s)}$$

$$= \frac{36}{66}$$

$$= \frac{6}{11}$$

51. Correct Response : (b)

Explanation :

The mean of 5 observations is 5 so,

$$\bar{x} = \frac{x_1 + x_2 + x_3 + x_4 + x_5}{5}$$

$$5 = \frac{x_1 + x_2 + x_3 + x_4 + x_5}{5}$$

$$x_1 + x_2 + x_3 + x_4 + x_5 = 25$$

$$\sum_{i=1}^{5} x_i = 25 \qquad \ldots(1)$$

The variance of these observations is,

$$\sigma^2 = 124$$

$$\frac{\sum x_i^2}{5} - (\bar{x})^2 = 124$$

$$\sum x_i^2 = 745$$

$$x_1^2 + x_2^2 + x_3^2 + x_4^2 + x_5^2 = 745$$

Substitute the given three observations,

Consider as the three observations x_3, x_4 and x_5 are 1, 2, and 6 respectively.

Therefore, from the above equation,

$$x_1^2 + x_2^2 + (1^2) + 2^2 + 6^2 = 745$$

$$x_1^2 + x_2^2 = 704 \qquad \ldots(2)$$

Similarly,

From equation (1),

$$x_1 + x_2 + 1 + 2 + 6 = 25$$

$$x_1 + x_2 = 16 \qquad \ldots(3)$$

From equation (2) and equation (3) is,

$$(x_1 + x_2)^2 = (16)^2$$

$$2x_1x_2 + 704 = 256$$

$$x_1x_2 = \frac{256 - 704}{2}$$

$$x_1x_2 = -224$$

Now, mean deiation is,

$$\frac{\sum |x_1 - 5|}{5}$$

$$= \frac{|x_1 - 5| + |x_2 - 5| + |1 - 5| + |2 - 5| + |6 - 5|}{5}$$

$$= \frac{8 + |x_1 - 5| + |16 - x_1 - 5|}{5}$$

$$= \frac{8 + 6}{5}$$

$$= 2.8$$

52. Correct Response : (b)

Explanation :

Given :

$$P(A) = \frac{2}{5}$$

$$P(A \cap B) = \frac{3}{20}$$

Hence,

$$P(A \mid (A' \cup B')) = \frac{P(A \cap A' \cup B')}{P(A' \cap B')}$$

$$= \frac{P((A \cap A') \cup (A \cap B'))}{P(A \cap B)'}$$

$$= \frac{P(\phi \cup (A \cap B'))}{1 - P(A \cap B)}$$

$$= \frac{P(A \cap B')}{1 - \dfrac{3}{20}}$$

Further simplify the above equation :

$$P(A \mid (A' \cup B')) = \frac{P(A) - P(A \cap B)}{\dfrac{17}{20}}$$

$$= \frac{\dfrac{2}{5} - \dfrac{3}{20}}{\dfrac{17}{20}}$$

$$= \frac{5}{17}$$

53. **Correct Response :** (c)

Explanation :

The computer produced in a company turn out to be defective is,

$$P[\text{Defective}] = 7\%$$
$$= 0.07$$

Therefore,

$$P[\text{Non-defective}] = 1 - 0.07$$
$$= 0.93$$

Consider that P is defective from the plant T_1 is,

$$P[\text{Defective from } T_1] = x$$

Therefore,

$$P[\text{Defective from } T_2] = \frac{x}{10}$$

The cycle related to production factory is,

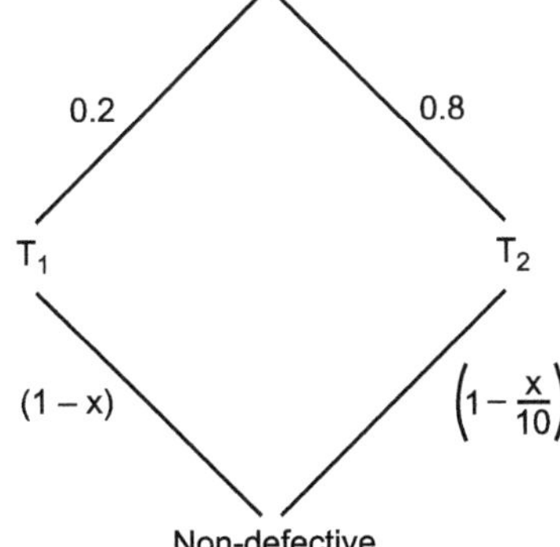

The equation for the total non-defective items from the above figure,

$$0.2(1-x) + 0.8\left(1 - \frac{x}{10}\right) = 0.93$$

$$x = \frac{1}{4}$$

Hence,

$$P[\text{Non-defective from } T_2] = \frac{0.8 \times \left(1 - \dfrac{x}{10}\right)}{0.93}$$

$$= \frac{\dfrac{8}{10} \times \dfrac{39}{40}}{\dfrac{93}{100}}$$

$$= \frac{78}{93}$$

54. **Correct Response :** (d)

Explanation :

The probability of the event are given as,

$$P(E_1) = \frac{1}{6}$$

$$P(E_2) = \frac{1}{6}$$

And,

$$P(E_3) = \frac{1}{2}$$

From the above value,

$$P(E_1 \cap E_2) = P(E_1)\, P(E_2)$$

$$= \frac{1}{6} \times \frac{1}{6}$$

$$= \frac{1}{36}$$

$$P(E_2 \cap E_3) = \frac{1}{12}$$

And,

$$P(E_1 \cap E_3) = \frac{1}{12}$$

Now the probability for the events E_1, E_2 and E_3 is,

$$P(E_1 \cap E_2 \cap E_3) = 0$$
$$\neq P(E_1).\, P(E_2).\, P(E_3)$$

Hence, E_1, E_2, E_3 are not independent.

Hence, the correct option is (d).

55. **Correct Response :** (b)

Explanation :

Probability of occurrence of an event,

Let S be the sample space then probability of occurrence of an event E is,

$$P(E) = \frac{n(E)}{n(S)}$$

$$P(E) \leq 1$$

$$P(E) = \lim_{x \to \infty}\left(\frac{r}{n}\right)$$

Here, n repeated experiment and E occurs r times. Consider 21 cases of isosceles triangle each case occurring thrice,

Total cases for $a + b > c$

$$\begin{cases}(1,1,1),(2,2,1),(2,\ 2,\ 2),(2,\ 2,\ 3),(3,\ 3,\ 1)\\(4,\ 4,\ 1),....,(4,\ 4,\ 6),(5,\ 5,\ 1)\ ...(5,\ 5,\ 6),\end{cases}$$

$$\left.\begin{matrix},...,(3,\ 3,\ 5),\\(6,\ 6,\ 1),....,(6,\ 6,\ 6)\end{matrix}\right\}$$

Hence, required probability is,

$$P = \frac{1}{21}$$

If consider equilateral triangle, there are 63 occurrences of non-equilateral triangle and 6 occurrences of the equilateral triangle.

Hence, the required probability is,

$$P = \frac{1}{27}$$

56. Correct Response : (8)

Explanation :

Let n is the minimum number of times of a fair coin is tossed.

Given that P (getting at least two heads) is equal to 0.96.

Therefore, from the probability of getting at least two heads is,

$${}^nC_2\left(\frac{1}{2}\right)^2\left(\frac{1}{2}\right)^{n-2} + {}^nC_3\left(\frac{1}{2}\right)^3\left(\frac{1}{2}\right)^{n-3}$$

$$+ {}^nC_4\left(\frac{1}{2}\right)^4\left(\frac{1}{2}\right)^{n-4} +....+ {}^nC_n\left(\frac{1}{2}\right)^n\left(\frac{1}{2}\right)^0$$

$$\geq 0.96 + {}^nC_0\left(\frac{1}{2}\right)^0\left(\frac{1}{2}\right)^n + {}^nC_1\left(\frac{1}{2}\right)^1\left(\frac{1}{2}\right)^{n-1}$$

Simplify the above equation :

$${}^nC_2\left(\frac{1}{2}\right)^2\left(\frac{1}{2}\right)^{n-2} + {}^nC_3\left(\frac{1}{2}\right)^3\left(\frac{1}{2}\right)^{n-3}$$

$$+ {}^nC_4\left(\frac{1}{2}\right)^4\left(\frac{1}{2}\right)^{n-4} +....+ {}^nC_n\left(\frac{1}{2}\right)^n\left(\frac{1}{2}\right)^0$$

$$\geq 0.96 + {}^nC_0\left(\frac{1}{2}\right)^0\left(\frac{1}{2}\right)^n + {}^nC_1\left(\frac{1}{2}\right)^1\left(\frac{1}{2}\right)^{n-1}$$

$$\left\{\left(\frac{1}{2}+\frac{1}{2}\right)^n\right\} \geq \left\{\left(\frac{1}{2}\right)^n + n\left(\frac{1}{2}\right)^{n-1} + 0.96\right\}$$

Further, simplify the given expression,

$$1 \geq \left\{\left(\frac{1}{2}\right)^n + n\left(\frac{1}{2}\right)^{n-1} + 0.96\right\}$$

$$\left\{1 - \left(\frac{1}{2}\right)^n - n\left(\frac{1}{2}\right)^{n-1}\right\} \geq 0.96$$

$$n = 8$$

57. Correct Response : (a, b)

Explanation :

The given possibility of the ball drawn from the box I and II is,

Box I	Box II
$Red \to n_1$	$Red \to n_3$
$Black \to n_2$	$Black \to n_4$

Event A is red ball drawn.

E_1 : Box I selected

E_2 : Box II selected

Apply the formula for the probability that the ball is drawn from the box II and it is a red ball that is $P\left(\dfrac{E_2}{A}\right)$,

$$P\left(\frac{E_2}{A}\right) = \frac{P(E_2)P\left(\dfrac{A}{E_2}\right)}{P(E_1)P\left(\dfrac{A}{E_1}\right) + P(E_2)P\left(\dfrac{A}{E_2}\right)}$$

$$\frac{1}{3} = \frac{\dfrac{1}{2}\dfrac{n_3}{n_3+n_4}}{\dfrac{1}{2}\dfrac{n_1}{n_1+n_2} + \dfrac{1}{2}\dfrac{n_3}{n_3+n_4}}$$

$$\frac{n_1}{n_1+n_2} + \frac{n_3}{n_3+n_4} = \frac{3n_3}{n_3+n_4}$$

Now, check option one by one,

(a). $\dfrac{3}{6} + \dfrac{5}{20} = \dfrac{3\times5}{20} \Rightarrow \dfrac{1}{2} + \dfrac{1}{4} = \dfrac{3}{4}$ (correct)

(b). $\dfrac{3}{9} + \dfrac{10}{60} = \dfrac{3(10)}{60} \Rightarrow \dfrac{1}{3} + \dfrac{1}{6} = \dfrac{1}{2} \Rightarrow \dfrac{1}{2} = \dfrac{1}{2}$

(correct)

(c). $\dfrac{8}{14} + \dfrac{5}{25} = \dfrac{3\times5}{25} \Rightarrow \dfrac{4}{7} + \dfrac{1}{5} \neq \dfrac{3}{5}$ (incorrect)

(d). $\dfrac{6}{18} + \dfrac{5}{25} = \dfrac{3\times5}{25} \Rightarrow \dfrac{1}{3} + \dfrac{1}{5} \neq \dfrac{3}{5}$ (incorrect)

58. Correct Response : (c, d)

Explanation :

Case (I) :

Red ball is transferred from the box I to box II is,

Red $\to n_1 - 1$

Black $\to n_2$

Case (II) :

Black ball is transferred from the box II to box I is

Red $\to n_1$

Black $\to n_2 - 1$

Now, the probability of drawing a red ball from box I is,

$$P = \underbrace{\left(\frac{n_1 - 1}{n_1 + n_2 - 1}\right)}_{\substack{\text{Probability of} \\ \text{red ball transferred}}} + \underbrace{\left(\frac{n_1}{n_1 + n_2}\right)}_{\substack{\text{Probability of} \\ \text{selecting red ball}}}$$

$$+ \underbrace{\left(\frac{n_2}{n_1 + n_2}\right)}_{\substack{\text{Probability of} \\ \text{black ball transferred}}} + \underbrace{\left(\frac{n_1}{n_1 + n_2 - 1}\right)}_{\substack{\text{Probability of} \\ \text{selecting red ball}}}$$

$$P = \frac{n_1^2 - n_1 + n_1 n_2}{(n_1 + n_2)(n_1 + n_2 - 1)}$$

$$= \frac{n_1(n_1 + n_2 - 1)}{(n_1 + n_2)(n_1 + n_2 - 1)}$$

$$= \frac{n_1}{(n_1 + n_2)}$$

The given value of the probability is,

$$P = \frac{1}{3}$$

Therefore, check the option one by one.

(a). $\frac{4}{10} \neq \frac{1}{3}$ (incorrect)

(b). $\frac{2}{5} \neq \frac{1}{3}$ (incorrect)

(c). $\frac{10}{30} = \frac{1}{3}$ (correct)

(d). $\frac{3}{9} = \frac{1}{3}$ (correct).

59. Correct Response : (d)

Explanation :

The given value of the mean and variance is,

Mean,

$$np = 2$$

Variance

$$npq = 1$$

Divide variance by mean,

$$p = \frac{1}{2}$$

Then,

$$q = \frac{1}{2}$$

And,

$$n = 4$$

Hence, the required probability is,

$$P(x \geq 1) = {}^4C_1 p^1 q^3 + {}^4C_2 p^2 q^2 + {}^4C_3 p^3 q^1 + {}^4C_1 p^4 q^0$$

$$= 1 - {}^4C_1 p^0 q^4$$

$$= 1 - \left(\frac{1}{2}\right)^4$$

$$= \frac{15}{16}$$

60. Correct Response : (a)

Explanation :

It is assumed that balls are different and each box contains three balls.

Number of ways,

$$n(S) = 3^{12}$$

The number of event is,

$$n(E) = {}^{12}C_3 \cdot 2^9$$

The probability is,

$$P(E) = \frac{n(E)}{n(S)}$$

$$= \frac{{}^{12}C_3 \cdot 2^9}{3^{12}}$$

$$= \frac{55}{3}\left(\frac{2}{3}\right)^{11}$$

61. Correct Response : (b)

Explanation :

Mean and mode depends upon change in origin and scale. So mean and mode of $-\bar{x} - a$ is $-x - a$ and $-M - a$ respectively.

Variance never depends upon the change in origin and it is always positive. So variance of $-x - a$ is same *i.e.*, σ^2.

Hence, both the statements are true.

62. Correct Response : (a)

Explanation :

The given expression is,

$$\frac{(x - 10)(x - 50)}{(x - 30)} \geq 0$$

Here, the range of x lies $x \in \{10, 11, 12, 13 \ldots 29\} \cup \{50, 51, 52 \ldots 100\}$.

The total value of x is 71.

So, the value of $P(A)$ is,

$$P(A) = \frac{71}{100}$$

$$= 0.71$$

63. Correct Response : (b)

Explanation :

The given relation of the binomial distribution,

$$p(X = 2) = p(X = 3)$$

$$^nC_2 p^2 (1-p)^{n-2} = {}^nC_3 p^3 (1-p)^{n-3}$$

$$\frac{1-p}{n-2} = \frac{p}{3}$$

$$np = 3 - p$$

Hence, the mean of variable X is $3 - p$.

64. Correct Response : (d)

Explanation :

The expression for the variance is,

$$\sigma^2 = \frac{\Sigma x_i^2}{N} - (\bar{x})^2$$

Substitute the value of the variance of first 50 even natural numbers is,

$$\sigma^2 = \frac{2^2 + 4^2 + \dots 100^2}{50} - \left(\frac{2 + 4 + \dots 100}{50}\right)^2$$

$$= \frac{4(1^2 + 2^2 + 3^2 + \dots + 50^2)}{50} - (51)^2$$

$$= 4\left(\frac{50 \times 51 \times 101}{50 \times 6}\right) - (51)^2$$

$$= 3434 - 2601$$

Further, simplify the above expression,

$$\sigma^2 = 833$$

65. Correct Response : (b)

Explanation :

The probability that $x_1 + x_2 + x_3$ is odd.

All three are odd or 2 are even and one is odd,

$$P = \frac{2}{3} \times \frac{3}{5} \times \frac{4}{7} + \frac{2}{3} \times \frac{2}{5} \times \frac{3}{7} + \frac{1}{3} \times \frac{3}{5} \times \frac{3}{7} + \frac{1}{3} \times \frac{2}{5} \times \frac{4}{7}$$

$$= \frac{24 + 12 + 9 + 8}{105}$$

$$= \frac{53}{105}$$

66. Correct Response : (a)

Explanation :

The given values are,

$$P(A \cap B) = \frac{1}{4}$$

$$P(\overline{A \cup B}) = \frac{1}{6}$$

$$P(A \cup B) = 1 - P(\overline{A \cup B})$$

$$= \frac{5}{6}$$

And,

$$P(\overline{A}) = \frac{1}{4}$$

$$P(A) = 1 - \frac{1}{4}$$

$$= \frac{3}{4}$$

Now,

$$P(A \cup B) = P(A) + P(B) - P(A \cap B)$$

$$P(B) = \frac{1}{3}$$

$$P(A) \neq P(B)$$

They are not equally likely.

Also,

$$P(A \cap B) = P(A) \cdot P(B)$$

So, A and B are independent also.

67. Correct Response : (a)

Explanation :

The probability that all 3 drawn balls are of same colour is calculated as,

$$P(\text{required}) = P(\text{all white balls}) + P(\text{all red balls}) + P(\text{all black balls})$$

$$= \left(\frac{1}{2} \times \frac{2}{9} \times \frac{3}{12}\right) + \left(\frac{3}{6} \times \frac{3}{9} \times \frac{4}{12}\right) + \left(\frac{2}{6} \times \frac{4}{9} \times \frac{5}{12}\right)$$

$$= \frac{6}{648} + \frac{36}{648} + \frac{40}{648}$$

$$= \frac{82}{648}$$

68. Correct Response : (a)

Explanation :

The probability that first person solve a certain problem correctly is,

$$P(A) = \frac{1}{2}$$

The probability that second person solve a certain problem correctly is,

$$P(B) = \frac{3}{4}$$

The probability that third person solve a certain problem correctly is,

$$P(C) = \frac{1}{4}$$

The probability that fourth person solve a certain problem correctly is,

$$P(D) = \frac{1}{8}$$

The probability that the problem is solved correctly by at least one of them is,

$$P(A \cup B \cup C \cup D) = 1 - \overline{P(A \cup B \cup C \cup D)}$$

$$= 1 - P(\bar{A} \cap \bar{B} \cap \bar{C} \cap \bar{D})$$

$$= 1 - P(\bar{A})P(\bar{B})P(\bar{C})P(\bar{D})$$

$$= 1 - \left(\frac{1}{2} \cdot \frac{1}{4} \cdot \frac{3}{4} \cdot \frac{7}{8}\right)$$

$$P(A \cup B \cup C \cup D) = 1 - \frac{21}{256}$$

$$= \frac{235}{256}$$

69. Correct Response : (d)

Explanation :

Let, A be the event for one ball drawn is white and other is red, E_1 be the event drawn from box B_1, E_2 be the event drawn from box B_2 and E_3 be the event drawn from box B_3.

The porbability that 2 balls drawn from bag B_2 is,

$$P\left(\frac{E_2}{A}\right)$$

$$= \frac{P\left(\dfrac{A}{E_2}\right) \cdot P(E_2)}{P\left(\dfrac{A}{E_1}\right) \cdot P(E_1) + P\left(\dfrac{A}{E_2}\right) \cdot P(E_2) + P\left(\dfrac{A}{E_3}\right) \cdot P(E_3)}$$

$$= \frac{\dfrac{{}^2C_1 \times {}^3C_2}{{}^9C_2} \times \dfrac{1}{3}}{\dfrac{{}^2C_1 \times {}^3C_1}{{}^6C_2} \times \dfrac{1}{3} + \dfrac{{}^2C_2 \times {}^3C_1}{{}^9C_2} \times \dfrac{1}{3} + \dfrac{{}^3C_1 \times {}^4C_1}{{}^{12}C_2} \times \dfrac{1}{3}}$$

$$= \frac{\dfrac{1}{6}}{\dfrac{1}{5} + \dfrac{1}{6} + \dfrac{2}{11}}$$

$$= \frac{55}{181}$$

70. Correct Response : (a)

Explanation :

There are several possibilities. The probability that the dice D_4 shows a number which also appears on one of the dices D_1, D_2, D_3.

Only one from dices D_1, D_2, D_3 shows the same number.

Only two from dices D_1, D_2, D_3 shows the same number.

Only three from dices D_1, D_2, D_3 shows the same number.

The probability is,

$$P = \frac{{}^6C_1\left({}^3C_1 \times 5 \times 5 + {}^3C_2 \times 5 + {}^3C_3\right)}{6 \times 216}$$

$$= \frac{6(3 \times 25 + 3 \times 5 + 1)}{6 \times 216}$$

$$= \frac{91}{216}$$

71. Correct Response : (a, b)

Explanation :

The value of P(X | Y) is,

$$P(X \mid Y) = \frac{1}{2}$$

$$\frac{P(X \cap Y)}{P(Y)} = \frac{1}{2}$$

$$\frac{\left(\dfrac{1}{6}\right)}{P(Y)} = \frac{1}{2}$$

$$P(Y) = \frac{1}{3}$$

The value of P(Y | X) is,

$$P(Y \mid X) = \frac{1}{3}$$

$$\frac{P(X \cap Y)}{P(X)} = \frac{1}{3}$$

$$\frac{\left(\dfrac{1}{6}\right)}{P(X)} = \frac{1}{3}$$

$$P(X) = \frac{1}{2}$$

(a)

$$P(X \cup Y) = P(X) + P(Y) - P(X \cap Y)$$

$$= \frac{1}{2} + \frac{1}{3} - \frac{1}{6}$$

$$= \frac{2}{3}$$

Option (a) is correct.

(b)

$$P(X \cap Y) = P(X) \cdot P(Y)$$

Thus, X and Y are independent

Option (b) is correct.

(d)

$$P(X^C \cap Y) = P(Y) - P(X \cap Y)$$

$$= \frac{1}{3} - \frac{1}{6}$$

$$= \frac{1}{6}$$

72. Correct Response : (b)

Explanation :

The total number of ways such that 5 balls of different colors can be distributed among three people. Each person must get at least one ball.

	A	B	C
Case 1	1	1	3
Case 2	2	2	1

The total number of ways of distribution is,

$$n = \frac{(5!)}{(3!)(2!)(1!)(1!)}(3!) + \frac{(5!)}{(2!)(2!)(2!)}(3!)$$

$$= \frac{5 \cdot 4 \cdot 3 \cdot 2}{2} + \frac{5 \cdot 4 \cdot 3 \cdot 2}{8} \cdot (3 \cdot 2)$$

$$= 60 + 90$$

$$= 150$$

Therefore, the total number of ways of distribution is 150.

73. Correct Response : (b, d)

Explanation :

The probabilities that the engine E_1 to be operational is,

$$P(X_1) = \frac{1}{2}$$

The probabilities that the engine E_2 to be operational is,

$$P(X_2) = \frac{1}{4}$$

The probabilites that the engine E_3 to be operational is,

$$P(X_3) = \frac{1}{4}$$

The probability that the ship is operational is,

$$P(X) = P(E_1 E_2 E_3) + P(\bar{E}_1 E_2 E_3) + P(E_1 \bar{E}_2 E_3)$$

$$+ P(E_1 E_2 \bar{E}_3)$$

$$= \frac{1}{2} \cdot \frac{1}{4} \cdot \frac{1}{4} + \left(1 - \frac{1}{2}\right)\frac{1}{4} \cdot \frac{1}{4} + \frac{1}{2}\left(1 - \frac{1}{4}\right) \cdot \frac{1}{4}$$

$$+ \frac{1}{2} \cdot \frac{1}{4}\left(1 - \frac{1}{4}\right)$$

$$= \frac{1}{32} + \frac{1}{32} + \frac{3}{32} + \frac{3}{32}$$

$$= \frac{1}{4}$$

(a)

$$P\left[X_1^c | X\right] = P\left(\frac{X_1^c}{X}\right)$$

$$= \frac{P(X_1^c X_2 X_3)}{P(X)}$$

$$= \frac{\frac{1}{2} \cdot \frac{1}{4} \cdot \frac{1}{4}}{\frac{1}{4}}$$

$$= \frac{1}{8}$$

Option (a) is incorrect.

(b)

$$P\left[\begin{array}{l}\text{Exactly two engines of} \\ \text{the ship are functioning} | X\end{array}\right]$$

$$= \frac{P\left[\begin{array}{l}\text{Exactly two engines of} \\ \text{the ship are functioning} \cap X\end{array}\right]}{P(X)}$$

$$= \frac{\frac{1}{2} \cdot \frac{1}{4} \cdot \frac{1}{4} + \frac{1}{2}\left(1 - \frac{1}{4}\right)\frac{1}{4} + \frac{1}{2} \cdot \frac{1}{4}\left(1 - \frac{1}{4}\right)}{\frac{1}{4}}$$

$$= \frac{7}{8}$$

Option (b) is correct.

(c)

$$P[X \mid X_2] = \frac{P(X \cap X_2)}{P(X_2)}$$

$$= \frac{\frac{1}{2} \cdot \frac{1}{4} \cdot \frac{1}{4} + \frac{1}{2} \cdot \frac{1}{4} \cdot \frac{1}{4} + \frac{1}{2} \cdot \frac{1}{4} \cdot \frac{3}{4}}{\frac{1}{4}}$$

$$= \frac{5}{8}$$

Option (c) is incorrect.

(d)

$$P[X \mid X_1] = \frac{P(X \cap X_1)}{P(X_1)}$$

$$= \frac{\frac{1}{2} \cdot \frac{1}{4} \cdot \frac{1}{4} + \frac{1}{2} \cdot \frac{3}{4} \cdot \frac{1}{4} + \frac{1}{2} \cdot \frac{1}{4} \cdot \frac{3}{4}}{\frac{1}{2}}$$

$$= \frac{7}{16}$$

Option (d) is incorrect.

74. Correct Response : (b)

Explanation :

Total number of balls in U_1 is 5 and total number of balls in U_2 is 1.

The probability that the ball drawn from U_2 is white can be calculated as,

$$\text{Probability} = \frac{1}{2}\left[\frac{^3C_1}{^3C_1}\times 1 + \frac{^2C_1}{^5C_1}\times\frac{1}{2}\right]$$

$$+\frac{1}{2}\left[\frac{^2C_2}{^5C_2}\times\frac{1}{3}+\frac{^3C_2}{^5C_2}\times 1+\frac{^3C_1\times^2C_1}{^5C_2}\right]$$

$$=\frac{1}{2}\times\frac{12}{15}+\frac{1}{2}\times\frac{11}{15}$$

$$=\frac{23}{30}$$

75. Correct Response : (d)

Explanation :

The condition for independent event is,

$$P(A\cap B) = P(A)\cdot P(B)$$

$$=\frac{4}{10}\times\frac{p}{10}$$

$$=\frac{(2p/5)}{10}$$

Since, $\dfrac{2p}{5}$ is an integer. So, possible values of p are 5 or 10.

76. Correct Response : (d)

Explanation :

It is given that ball drawn from U_2 is white, the probability that head appeared on the coin is,

$$\text{Probability} = \frac{\dfrac{1}{3}\left[\dfrac{3}{5}\times\dfrac{2}{2}+\dfrac{2}{5}\times\dfrac{1}{2}\right]}{\dfrac{23}{30}}$$

$$=\frac{\dfrac{12}{30}}{\dfrac{23}{30}}$$

$$=\frac{12}{23}$$

option (d) is correct.

77. Correct Response : (a, d)

Explanation :

Let, E and F be two independent events. The probability that exactly of them occurs is,

$$P(E\bar{F})+P(F\bar{E}) = \frac{11}{25}$$

$$P(E)P(\bar{F})+P(F)P(\bar{E}) = \frac{11}{25}$$

$$P(E)\,(1-P(F)) + P(F)\,(1-P(E)) = \frac{11}{25}$$

$$P(E)+P(F)-2P(E)\,P(F) = \frac{11}{25} \quad ...(1)$$

The probability that none of them occurs is,

$$P(\bar{E}\bar{F}) = \frac{2}{25}$$

$$(1-P(E))\,(1-P(F)) = \frac{12}{25}$$

$$1-P(E)-P(F)+P(E)\,P(F) = \frac{2}{25}$$

$$P(E)+P(F)-P(E)\,P(E)\,P(F) = \frac{23}{25} \quad ...(2)$$

Solve the equation (1) and (2).

$$P(E)\,P(F) =\frac{12}{25}\text{ and } P(E)+P(F) = \frac{7}{25}$$

Therefore, $P(E) = \dfrac{4}{5}$, $P(F) = \dfrac{3}{5}$ or $P(E) = \dfrac{3}{5}$,

$$P(F) = \frac{4}{5}.$$

78. Correct Response : (c)

Explanation :

The tree diagram of given conditions is shown below.

From the above diagram,

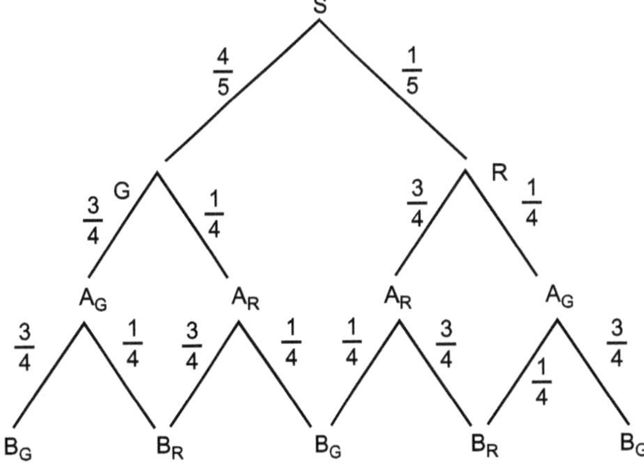

Here,

$$P(B_G) = P(S)\times P(G)\times P(A_G)$$

$$=\frac{4}{5}\times\frac{3}{4}\times\frac{3}{4}$$

$$=\frac{36}{80}$$

$$=\frac{9}{20}$$

The probability of green signal at station B is,

$$P(B_G\mid G) = \frac{P(B_G).P\left(\dfrac{G}{B_G}\right)}{P(B_G).P\left(\dfrac{G}{B_G}\right)+P(G).P\left(\dfrac{B_G}{G}\right)}$$

$$= \frac{10}{16}$$

$$= \frac{5}{8}$$

The probability of green signal is,

$$P(B_G \cap G) = \frac{5}{8} \times \frac{4}{5}$$

$$= \frac{1}{2}$$

Thus, the probability of original green signal is,

$$P(G/B_G) = \frac{P(B_G \cap G)}{P(B_G)}$$

$$= \frac{1}{2} \times \frac{80}{46}$$

$$= \frac{20}{23}$$

79. Correct Response : (b)

Explanation :

The given equations are $ax + by = 0$ and $cx + dy = 0$.

The total number of outcomes is $2^4 = 16$ as, $a, b, c, d \in \{0, 1\}$.

The condition for unique solutions of equation is,

$$\frac{a}{c} \neq \frac{b}{d}$$

$$ad \neq cb$$

For unique solution either $ad = 0$ and $bc = 1$ or $ad = 1$ and $bc = 0$. Total number of favourable outcomes is 6.

The probability that system of equations has unique solution is,

$$\frac{6}{16} = \frac{3}{8}$$

The probability that system of equations has one solution is 1. Therefore, both statements are correct but statement-2 is not correct explanation for statement-1.

80. Correct Response : (c)

Explanation :

Let A be the event that Indian man is seated adjacent to his wife and B be the event that each American man is seated adjacent to his wife.

$$P\left(\frac{A}{B}\right) = \frac{n(A \cap B)}{n(B)}$$

$$= \frac{(4!) \times (2!)^5}{(5!) \times (2!)^4}$$

$$= \frac{2}{5}$$

81. Correct Response : (d)

Explanation :

Statement-1 :

For some value of i. If $P(H_i \cap E) = 0$, then

$$P\left(\frac{H_i}{E}\right) = P\left(\frac{E}{H_i}\right) = 0.$$

For $i = 1, 2, ..., n$. If $P(H_i \cap E) \neq 0$, then

$$P\left(\frac{H_i}{E}\right) = \frac{P(H_i \cap E)}{P(H_i)} \times \frac{P(H_i)}{P(E)}$$

$$= \frac{P\left(\frac{E}{H_i}\right) \cdot P(H_i)}{P(E)}$$

$$> P\left(\frac{E}{H_i}\right) \cdot P(H_i)$$

Therefore, statement 1 always may not be true.

Statement-1 :

Let, $H_1, H_2, ... H_n$ be mutually exclusive and exhaustive event. So,

$$H_1 \cup H_2 \cup .... H_n = S$$

The sum of probabilities is 1. So,

$$P(H_1) + (H_2) + ... + (H_n) = 1$$

$$\sum_{i=1}^{n} H_i = 1$$

Therefore, statement-2 is true and statement-1 is false.

82. Correct Response : (c)

Explanation :

The given probability is calculated as,

$$P(E^c \cap F^c \mid G) = \frac{P\left(E^c \cap F^c \cap G\right)}{P(G)}$$

$$= \frac{P(G) - P(E \cap G) - P(G \cap F)}{P(G)}$$

$$= \frac{P(G)\left[1 - P(E) - P(F)\right]}{P(G)}$$

$$= 1 - P(E) - P(F)$$

Further simplify.

$$P(E^c \cap F^c \mid G) = P(E)^c - P(F)$$

83. Correct Response : (b)

Explanation :

The probability of u_i is,

$$P(u_i) = ki$$

$$\sum P(u_i) = 1$$

The value of k is,

$$k = \frac{2}{n(n+1)}$$

Now, the value of limit is calculated as,

$$\lim_{n \to \infty} P(w) = \lim_{n \to \infty} \sum_{i=1}^{n} \frac{2i^2}{n(n+1)^2}$$

$$= \lim_{n \to \infty} \frac{2n(n+1)(2n+1)}{n(n+1)^2 \, 6}$$

$$= \frac{2}{3}$$

84. **Correct Response :** (a)

Explanation :

The required probability is calculated as,

$$P\left(\frac{u_n}{w}\right) = \frac{c\left(\dfrac{n}{n+1}\right)}{c\left(\dfrac{\sum i}{(n+1)}\right)}$$

$$= \frac{2}{n+1}$$

85. **Correct Response :** (b)

Explanation :

The required probability is calculated as,

$$P = \frac{1}{6}\left(\frac{5}{6}\right) + \frac{1}{6}\left(\frac{5}{6}\right)^3 + \ldots$$

$$= \frac{1}{6}\left(\frac{5}{6}\right)\left[1 + \left(\frac{5}{6}\right)^2 + \ldots\right]$$

$$= \frac{1}{6}\left(\frac{5}{6}\right)\left[\frac{1}{1 - \dfrac{5}{6}}\right]$$

$$= \frac{5}{36}\left[\frac{6}{1}\right]$$

Solve further.

$$P = \frac{5}{6}$$

86. **Correct Response :** $\left(\dfrac{1}{7}\right)$

Explanation :

Let, A, B, C, D be the events that the person goes by car, scooter, bus and train respectively.

$$P(A) = \frac{1}{7}, \ P(B) = \frac{3}{7}, \ P(C) = \frac{2}{7}, \ P(D) = \frac{1}{7}$$

Let $\bar{E}$ be the event that person reach the office in time.

$$P\left(\frac{\bar{E}}{A}\right) = \frac{7}{9}, \ P\left(\frac{\bar{E}}{B}\right) = \frac{8}{9}, \ P\left(\frac{\bar{E}}{C}\right) = \frac{5}{9}, \ P\left(\frac{\bar{E}}{D}\right) = \frac{8}{9}$$

The probability that person travelled by car given that he reached office in time is,

$$P\left(\frac{C}{\bar{E}}\right) = \frac{P\left(\dfrac{\bar{E}}{C}\right)P(C)}{P(\bar{E})}$$

$$= \frac{\dfrac{1}{7} \times \dfrac{7}{9}}{\dfrac{1}{7} \times \dfrac{7}{9} + \dfrac{3}{7} \times \dfrac{8}{9} + \dfrac{2}{7} \times \dfrac{5}{9} + \dfrac{8}{9} \times \dfrac{1}{7}}$$

$$= \frac{1}{7}$$

Therefore, the required probability is $\dfrac{1}{7}$.

87. **Correct Response :** (d)

Explanation :

There are 16 numbers between 1 and 100 that are divisible by both 2 and 3.

The required probability is,

$$\frac{^{16}C_3}{^{100}C_3} = \frac{\dfrac{16!}{3!\,13!}}{\dfrac{100!}{3!\,97!}}$$

$$= \frac{4}{1155}$$

88. **Explanation :**

It is given that A and B are two independent events.

$$P(A \cup B) \cdot P(A')\,P(B') \le (P(A) + P(B)) \cdot P(A')\,P(B')$$

$$\le P(A) \cdot P(A')\,P(B') + P(B) \cdot P(A')\,P(B')$$

$$\le P(A)\,P(B')\,(1 - P(A)) + P(B) \cdot P(A')\,(1 - P(B))$$

Solve further.

$$P(A \cup B) \cdot P(A')\,P(B') \le P(A)\,P(B') + P(A')\,P(B)$$

$$\le P(C)$$

89. **Explanation :**

Let, $P(E)$ be the probability that at least 4 white ball drawn, $P(E_1)$ be the probability that exactly 4 white ball drawn, $P(E_2)$ be the probability that exactly 5 white balls drawn, $P(E_3)$ be the probability that exactly 6 white balls drawn and $P(B)$ be the probability that exactly 1 white ball is drawn from two draws.

$$P(B/E) = \dfrac{\displaystyle\sum_{i=1}^{3} P(E_i)\,P(B/E_i)}{\displaystyle\sum_{i=1}^{3} P(E_i)}$$

$$= \dfrac{\dfrac{{}^{12}C_2\,{}^{6}C_4}{{}^{18}C_6}\cdot\dfrac{{}^{10}C_1\,{}^{2}C_1}{{}^{12}C_2} + \dfrac{{}^{12}C_1\,{}^{6}C_5}{{}^{18}C_6}\cdot\dfrac{{}^{11}C_1\,{}^{1}C_1}{{}^{12}C_2}}{\dfrac{{}^{12}C_2\,{}^{6}C_4}{{}^{18}C_6} + \dfrac{{}^{12}C_1\,{}^{6}C_5}{{}^{18}C_6} + \dfrac{{}^{12}C_0\,{}^{6}C_6}{{}^{18}C_6}}$$

$$= \dfrac{{}^{12}C_2\,{}^{6}C_4\,{}^{10}C_1\,{}^{2}C_1 + {}^{12}C_1\,{}^{6}C_5\,{}^{11}C_1\,{}^{1}C_1}{{}^{12}C_2\left({}^{12}C_2\,{}^{6}C_4 + {}^{12}C_1\,{}^{6}C_5 + {}^{12}C_0\,{}^{6}C_6\right)}$$

90. Correct Response : (d)

Explanation :

The probability that minimum of the two numbers chosen is less than 4 is calculated as,

$$P = 1 - P \text{ (both numbers are more than or equal to 4)}$$

$$= 1 - \left(\dfrac{3}{6}\times\dfrac{2}{5}\right)$$

$$= \dfrac{4}{5}$$

●●

❓ QUESTIONS

1. If S is the sum of the first 10 terms of the series

$$\tan^{-1}\left(\frac{1}{3}\right)+\tan^{-1}\left(\frac{1}{7}\right)+\tan^{-1}\left(\frac{1}{13}\right)$$

$$+\tan^{-1}\left(\frac{1}{21}\right)+\cdots,$$

then tan (S) is equal to : **[2020, Main]**

(a) $\dfrac{5}{11}$ (b) $-\dfrac{6}{5}$

(c) $\dfrac{10}{11}$ (d) $\dfrac{5}{6}$

2. A ray of light coming from the point $(2, 2\sqrt{3})$ is incident at an angle $30°$ on the line $x = 1$ at the point A. The ray gets reflected on the line $x = 1$ and meets x-axis at the point B. Then, the line AB passes through the point : **[2020, Main]**

(a) $\left(3, -\dfrac{1}{\sqrt{3}}\right)$ (b) $(3, -\sqrt{3})$

(c) $\left(4, -\dfrac{\sqrt{3}}{2}\right)$ (d) $(4, -\sqrt{3})$

3. The angle of elevation of the top of a hill from a point on the horizontal plane passing through the foot of the hill is found to be $45°$. After walking a distance of 80 meters towards the top, up a slope inclined at an angle of $30°$ to the horizontal plane, the angle of elevation of the top of the hill becomes $75°$. Then the height of the hill (in meters) is .... **[2020, Main]**

4. The angle of elevation of the summit of a mountain from a point on the ground is $45°$. After climbing up one km towards the summit at an inclination of $30°$ from the ground, the angle of elevation of the summit is found to be $60°$. Then the height (in km) of the summit from the ground is : **[2020, Main]**

(a) $\dfrac{1}{\sqrt{3}-1}$ (b) $\dfrac{1}{\sqrt{3}+1}$

(c) $\dfrac{\sqrt{3}-1}{\sqrt{3}+1}$ (d) $\dfrac{\sqrt{3}+1}{\sqrt{3}-1}$

5. Two vertical poles AB = 15 m and CD = 10 m are standing apart on a horizontal ground with points A and C on the ground. IF P is the point of intersection of BC and AD, then the height of P (in m) above the line AC is : **[2020, Main]**

(a) 20/3   (b) 5

(c) 10/3   (d) 6

6. The angle of elevation of a cloud C from a point P, 200 m above a still lake is $30°$. If the angle of depression of the image of C in the lake from the point P is $60°$, then PC (in m) is equal to : **[2020, Main]**

(a) 400   (b) $400\sqrt{3}$

(c) 100   (d) $200\sqrt{3}$

7. $2\pi-\left(\sin^{-1}\dfrac{4}{5}+\sin^{-1}\dfrac{5}{13}+\sin^{-1}\dfrac{16}{65}\right)$ is equal to : **[2020, Main]**

(a) $\dfrac{7\pi}{4}$ (b) $\dfrac{5\pi}{4}$

(c) $\dfrac{3\pi}{2}$ (d) $\dfrac{\pi}{2}$

8. If $L = \sin^2\left(\dfrac{\pi}{16}\right)-\sin^2\left(\dfrac{\pi}{8}\right)$ and

$$M = \cos^2\left(\dfrac{\pi}{16}\right)-\sin^2\left(\dfrac{\pi}{8}\right),$$ then : **[2020, Main]**

(a) $M = \dfrac{1}{2\sqrt{2}}+\dfrac{1}{2}\cos\dfrac{\pi}{8}$

(b) $L = \dfrac{1}{4\sqrt{2}}-\dfrac{1}{4}\cos\dfrac{\pi}{8}$

(c) $M = \dfrac{1}{4\sqrt{2}}+\dfrac{1}{4}\cos\dfrac{\pi}{8}$

(d) $L = -\dfrac{1}{2\sqrt{2}}+\dfrac{1}{2}\cos\dfrac{\pi}{8}$

9. Let x, y and z be positive real numbers. Suppose x, y and z are lengths of the sides of a triangle opposite to its angles X, Y and Z, respectively. If

$$\tan\frac{X}{2}+\tan\frac{Z}{2}=\frac{2y}{x+y+z},$$

then which of the following statements is/are TRUE ? **[2020, Advanced]**

(a) $2Y = X + Z$

(b) $Y = X + Z$

(c) $\tan \dfrac{X}{2} = \dfrac{x}{y+z}$

(d) $x^2 + z^2 - y^2 = xz$

10. If the equation $\cos^4\theta + \sin^4\theta + \lambda = 0$ has real solutions for θ, then λ lies in the interval : **[2020, Main]**

(a) $\left[-\dfrac{3}{2}, -\dfrac{5}{4}\right]$

(b) $\left(-\dfrac{1}{2}, -\dfrac{1}{4}\right]$

(c) $\left(-\dfrac{5}{4}, -1\right)$

(d) $\left[-1, -\dfrac{1}{2}\right]$

11. The value of

$$\cos^3\left(\dfrac{\pi}{8}\right)\cdot\cos\left(\dfrac{3\pi}{8}\right)+\sin^3\left(\dfrac{\pi}{8}\right)\cdot\sin\left(\dfrac{3\pi}{8}\right)$$

is : **[2020, Main]**

(a) $\dfrac{1}{4}$

(b) $\dfrac{1}{\sqrt{2}}$

(c) $\dfrac{1}{2\sqrt{2}}$

(d) $\dfrac{1}{2}$

12. The number of distinct solutions of the equation $\log_{\frac{1}{2}}|\sin x| = 2 - \log_{\frac{1}{2}}|\cos x|$ in the interval $[0, 2\pi]$, is .... **[2020, Main]**

13. If $\dfrac{\sqrt{2}\sin\alpha}{\sqrt{1+\cos 2\alpha}} = \dfrac{1}{7}$ and $\sqrt{\dfrac{1-\cos 2\beta}{2}} = \dfrac{1}{\sqrt{10}}$, $\alpha, \beta \in \left(0, \dfrac{\pi}{2}\right)$, then $\tan(\alpha + 2\beta)$ is equal to ....

[2020, Main]

14. If $x = \displaystyle\sum_{n=0}^{\infty} (-1)^n \tan^{2n}\theta$ and $y = \displaystyle\sum_{n=0}^{\infty} \cos^{2n}\theta$, for $0 < \theta < \dfrac{\pi}{4}$, then : **[2020, Main]**

(a) $y(1 + x) = 1$

(b) $x(1 + y) = 1$

(c) $y(1 - x) = 1$

(d) $x(1 - y) = 1$

15. ABC is a triangular park with AB = AC = 100 meters. A vertical tower is situated at mid-point of BC. If the angles of elevation of the top of the tower at A and B are $\cot^{-1}(3\sqrt{2})$ and $\operatorname{cosec}^{-1}(2\sqrt{2})$ respectively, then the height of the tower (in metres) is : **[2019, Main]**

(a) $\dfrac{100}{3\sqrt{3}}$

(b) $10\sqrt{5}$

(c) 20

(d) 25

16. All the pairs (x, y) that satisfy the inequality $2\sqrt{\sin^2 x - 2\sin x + 5}\cdot\dfrac{1}{4^{\sin^2 y}}$ also satisfy the equation : **[2019, Main]**

(a) $2|\sin x| = 3 \sin y$

(b) $2 \sin x = \sin y$

(c) $\sin x = 2 \sin y$

(d) $\sin x = |\sin y|$

17. If $\cos^{-1} x - \cos^{-1}\dfrac{y}{2} = \alpha$, where $-1 \leq x \leq 1, -2 \leq y \leq x \leq \dfrac{y}{2}$, then for all x, y, $4x^2 - 4xy \cos\alpha + y^2$ is equal to : **[2019, Main]**

(a) $4 \sin^2 \alpha$

(b) $2 \sin^2 \alpha$

(c) $4 \sin^2 \alpha - 2x^2 y^2$

(d) $4 \cos^2 \alpha + 2x^2 y^2$

18. The angles A, B and C of a triangle ABC are in A.P. and $a : b = 1 : \sqrt{3}$. If $c = 4$ cm, then the area (in sq. cm) of this triangle is : **[2019, Main]**

(a) $\dfrac{2}{\sqrt{3}}$

(b) $4\sqrt{3}$

(c) $2\sqrt{3}$

(d) $\dfrac{4}{\sqrt{3}}$

19. Two poles standing on a horizontal ground are of heights 5 m and 10 m respectively. The line joining their tops makes an angle of 15° with the ground. Then the distance (in m) between the poles, is : **[2019, Main]**

(a) $5(2+\sqrt{3})$

(b) $5(\sqrt{3}+1)$

(c) $\dfrac{5}{2}(2+\sqrt{3})$

(d) $10(\sqrt{3}-1)$

20. The value of $\sin 10° \sin 30° \sin 50° \sin 70°$ is :

(a) $\dfrac{1}{16}$

(b) $\dfrac{1}{32}$

(c) $\dfrac{1}{18}$

(d) $\dfrac{1}{36}$

21. The value of $\cos^2 10° - \cos 10° \cos 50° + \cos^2 50°$ is : **[2019, Main]**

(a) $\dfrac{3}{4}+\cos 20°$

(b) $\dfrac{3}{4}$

(c) $\dfrac{3}{2}(1+\cos 20°)$

(d) $\dfrac{3}{2}$

22. Let $S = \{\theta \in [-2\pi, 2\pi] : 2\cos^2\theta + 3\sin\theta = 0\}$. Then the sum of the elements of S is : **[2019, Main]**

(a) $\dfrac{13\pi}{6}$

(b) $\dfrac{5\pi}{3}$

(c) 2π

(d) π

23. If $\cos(\alpha + \beta) = \dfrac{3}{5}$, $\sin(\alpha - \beta) = \dfrac{5}{13}$ and $0 < \alpha, \beta < \dfrac{\pi}{4}$, then $\tan(2\alpha)$ is equal to : **[2019, Main]**

(a) $\dfrac{63}{52}$ (b) $\dfrac{63}{16}$

(c) $\dfrac{21}{16}$ (d) $\dfrac{33}{52}$

24. If $\alpha = \cos^{-1}\left(\dfrac{3}{5}\right)$, $\beta = \tan^{-1}\left(\dfrac{1}{3}\right)$, where $0 < \alpha, \beta < \dfrac{\pi}{2}$, then $\alpha - \beta$ is equal to : **[2019, Main]**

(a) $\tan^{-1}\left(\dfrac{9}{5\sqrt{10}}\right)$ (b) $\cos^{-1}\left(\dfrac{9}{5\sqrt{10}}\right)$

(c) $\tan^{-1}\left(\dfrac{9}{14}\right)$ (d) $\sin^{-1}\left(\dfrac{9}{5\sqrt{10}}\right)$

25. $2y = \left(\cot^{-1}\left(\dfrac{\sqrt{3}\cos x + \sin x}{\cos x - \sqrt{3}\sin x}\right)\right)^2$, $x \in \left(0, \dfrac{\pi}{2}\right)$ then $\dfrac{dy}{dx}$ is equal to : **[2019, Main]**

(a) $\dfrac{\pi}{6} - x$ (b) $x - \dfrac{\pi}{6}$

(c) $\dfrac{\pi}{3} - x$ (d) $2x - \dfrac{\pi}{3}$

26. Two vertical poles of heights, 20 m and 80 m stand apart on a horizontal plane. The height (in meters) of the point of intersection of the lines joining the top of each pole to the foot of the other, from this horizontal plane is : **[2019, Main]**

(a) 15   (b) 18

(c) 12   (d) 16

27. If the lengths of the sides of a triangle are in A.P. and the greatest angle is double the smallest, then a ratio of lengths of the sides of this triangle is : **[2019, Main]**

(a) $5 : 9 : 13$ (b) $4 : 5 : 6$

(c) $3 : 4 : 5$ (d) $5 : 6 : 7$

28. The value of $\sin^{-1}\left(\dfrac{12}{13}\right) - \sin^{-1}\dfrac{3}{5}$ is equal to : **[2019, Main]**

(a) $\pi - \sin^{-1}\left(\dfrac{63}{65}\right)$ (b) $\dfrac{\pi}{2} - \sin^{-1}\left(\dfrac{56}{65}\right)$

(c) $\dfrac{\pi}{2} - \cos^{-1}\left(\dfrac{9}{65}\right)$ (d) $\pi - \cos^{-1}\left(\dfrac{33}{65}\right)$

29. The angle of elevation of the top of a vertical tower standing on a horizontal plane is observed to be 45° from a point A on the plane. Let B be the point 30 m vertically above the point A. If the angle of elevation of the top of the tower from B be 30°, then the distance (in m) of the foot of the tower from the point A is : **[2019, Main]**

(a) $15(3 + \sqrt{3})$ (b) $15(5 - \sqrt{3})$

(c) $15(3 - \sqrt{3})$ (d) $15(1 + \sqrt{3})$

30. If $[x]$ denotes the greatest integer $\leq x$, then the system of linear equation $[\sin \theta]\, x + [-\cos \theta]\, y = 0$, $[\cot \theta]\, x + y = 0$ **[2019, Main]**

(a) have infinitely many solutions if $\theta \in \left(\dfrac{\pi}{2}, \dfrac{2\pi}{3}\right)$ and has a unique solution of $\theta \in \left(\pi, \dfrac{7\pi}{6}\right)$.

(b) has a unique solution if $\theta \in \left(\dfrac{\pi}{2}, \dfrac{2\pi}{3}\right) \cup \left(\pi, \dfrac{7\pi}{6}\right)$.

(c) has a unique solution if $\theta \in \left(\dfrac{\pi}{2}, \dfrac{2\pi}{3}\right)$ and have infinitely many solutions if $\theta \in \left(\pi, \dfrac{7\pi}{6}\right)$.

(d) have infinitely many solutions if $\theta \in \left(\dfrac{\pi}{2}, \dfrac{2\pi}{3}\right) \cup \left(\pi, \dfrac{7\pi}{6}\right)$.

31. The value of

$$\sec^{-1}\left(\dfrac{1}{4}\sum_{k=0}^{10}\sec\left(\dfrac{7\pi}{12} + \dfrac{k\pi}{2}\right)\sec\left(\dfrac{7\pi}{12} + \dfrac{(k+1)\pi}{2}\right)\right)$$

in the interval $\left[-\dfrac{\pi}{4}, \dfrac{3\pi}{4}\right]$ equals ....

[2019, Advanced]

32. An aeroplane flying at a constant speed, parallel to the horizontal ground, $\sqrt{3}$ km above it, is observed that an elevation of 60° from a point on the ground. If, after five seconds, its elevation from the same point, is 30°, then the speed (in km/ hr) of the aeroplane is : **[2018, Main]**

(a) 1500   (b) 1440

(c) 750   (d) 720

33. If an angle A of a $\triangle ABC$ satisfies $5 \cos A + 3 = 0$, then the roots of the quadratic equation, $9x^2 + 27x + 20 = 0$ are : **[2018, Main]**

   (a) sec A, cot A   (b) sin A, sec A

   (c) sec A, tanA   (d) tan A, cos A

34. A man on the top of a vertical tower observes a car moving at a uniform speed towards the tower on a horizontal road. If it takes 18 min. for the angle of depression of the car to change from $30°$ to $45°$, then after this, the time taken (in min.) by the car to reach the foot of the tower, is :

   [2018, Main]

   (a) $9\,(1+\sqrt{3})$ (b) $18\,(1+\sqrt{3})$

   (c) $18\,(\sqrt{3}-1)$ (d) $\dfrac{9}{2}\,(\sqrt{3}-1)$

35. PQR is a triangular park with PQ = PR = 200 m. A T.V. tower stands at the mid-point of QR. If the angles of elevation of the top of the tower at P, Q and R are respectively $45°$, $30°$ and $30°$, then the height of the tower (in m) is : **[2018, Main]**

   (a) 100   (b) 50

   (c) $100\sqrt{3}$ (d) $50\sqrt{2}$

36. If sum of all the solutions of the equation

   $$8\cos x \cdot \left(\cos\left(\frac{\pi}{6}+x\right) \cdot \cos\left(\frac{\pi}{6}-x\right) - \frac{1}{2}\right) = 1$$

   in $[0, \pi]$ is $k\pi$, then k is equal to : **[2018, Main]**

   (a) $\dfrac{2}{3}$ (b) $\dfrac{13}{9}$

   (c) $\dfrac{8}{9}$ (d) $\dfrac{20}{9}$

37. Let a, b, c be three non-zero real numbers such that the equation **[2018, Main]**

   $$\sqrt{3}\,a\cos x + 2\,b\sin x = c, \; x \in \left[-\frac{\pi}{2}, \frac{\pi}{2}\right],$$

   has two distinct real roots α and β with $\alpha + \beta = \dfrac{\pi}{3}$.

   Then, the value of $\dfrac{b}{a}$ is ....

38. A value of x satisfying the equation $\sin [\cot^{-1}(1 + x)] = \cos [\tan^{-1} x]$ is : **[2018, Main]**

   (a) $-\dfrac{1}{2}$ (b) -1

   (c) 0   (d) $\dfrac{1}{2}$

39. If $5\,(\tan^2 x - \cos^2 x) = 2\cos 2x + 9$, then the value of $\cos 4x$ is : **[2017, Main]**

   (a) $\dfrac{1}{3}$ (b) $\dfrac{2}{9}$

   (c) $-\dfrac{7}{9}$ (d) $-\dfrac{3}{5}$

40. Let a vertical tower AB have its end A on the level ground. Let C be the mid-point of AB and P be a point on the ground such that $AP = 2AB$. If $\angle BPC = \beta$, then $\tan \beta$ is equal to : **[2017, Main]**

   (a) $\dfrac{1}{4}$ (b) $\dfrac{2}{9}$

   (c) $\dfrac{4}{9}$ (d) $\dfrac{6}{7}$

41. Let α and β be nonzero real numbers such that $2(\cos \beta - \cos \alpha) + \cos \alpha \cos \beta = 1$. Then which of the following is, are true? **[2017, Advanced]**

   (a) $\tan\left(\dfrac{\alpha}{2}\right) + \sqrt{3}\tan\left(\dfrac{\beta}{2}\right) = 0$

   (b) $\sqrt{3}\tan\left(\dfrac{\alpha}{2}\right) + \tan\left(\dfrac{\beta}{2}\right) = 0$

   (c) $\tan\left(\dfrac{\alpha}{2}\right) - \sqrt{3}\tan\left(\dfrac{\beta}{2}\right) = 0$

   (d) $\sqrt{3}\tan\left(\dfrac{\alpha}{2}\right) - \tan\left(\dfrac{\beta}{2}\right) = 0$

42. The value of $\tan^{-1}\left[\dfrac{\sqrt{1+x^2}+\sqrt{1-x^2}}{\sqrt{1+x^2}-\sqrt{1-x^2}}\right], |x| < \dfrac{1}{2},$ $x \neq 0$, is equal to : **[2017, Main]**

   (a) $\dfrac{\pi}{4} + \dfrac{1}{2}\cos^{-1}x^2$ (b) $\dfrac{\pi}{4} + \cos^{-1}x^2$

   (c) $\dfrac{\pi}{4} - \dfrac{1}{2}\cos^{-1}x^2$ (d) $\dfrac{\pi}{4} - \cos^{-1}x^2$

43. Let $P = \{\theta : \sin \theta - \cos \theta = \sqrt{2}\cos \theta\}$ and $Q = \{\theta : \sin \theta + \cos \theta = \sqrt{2}\sin \theta\}$ be two sets. Then :

   [2017, Main]

   (a) $P \subset Q$ and $Q - P \neq 0$ (b) $Q \not\subset P$

   (c) $P \not\subset Q$ (d) $P = Q$

44. The number of $x \in [0, 2\pi]$ for which $\left| \sqrt{2\sin^4 x + 18\cos^2 x} - \sqrt{2\cos^4 x + 18\sin^2 x} \right| = 1$ is : **[2016, Main]**

   (a) 2   (b) 4

   (c) 6   (d) 8

45. If $0 \leq x \leq 2\pi$, then the number of real values of x, which satisfy the equation **[2016, Advanced]**

   $\cos x + \cos 2x + \cos 3x + \cos 4x = 0$, is :

   (a) 3   (b) 5

   (c) 7   (d) 9

46. Let $S = \left\{ x \in (-\pi, \pi) : x \neq 0, \pm \dfrac{\pi}{2} \right\}$. The sum of all distinct solutions of the equation

$\sqrt{3} \sec x + \operatorname{cosec} x + 2 (\tan x - \cot x) = 0$ in the set S is equal to : **[2016, Advanced]**

(a) $-\dfrac{7\pi}{9}$

(b) $-\dfrac{2\pi}{9}$

(c) 0

(d) $\dfrac{5\pi}{9}$

47. A man is walking towards a vertical pillar in a straight path, at a uniform speed. At a certain point A on the path, he observes that the angle of elevation of the top of the pillar is $30°$. After walking for 10 minutes from A in the same direction, at a point B, he observes that the angle of elevation of the top of the pillar is $60°$. Then the time taken (in minutes) by him, from B to reach the pillar, is : **[2016, Advanced]**

(a) 6

(b) 10

(c) 20

(d) 5

48. If $\alpha = 3 \sin^{-1}\left(\dfrac{6}{11}\right)$ and $\beta = 3 \cos^{-1}\left(\dfrac{4}{9}\right)$, where the inverse trigonometric functions take only the principal values, then the correct option(s) is (are) : **[2015, Advanced]**

(a) $\cos \beta > 0$

(b) $\sin \beta < 0$

(c) $\cos (\alpha + \beta) > 0$

(d) $\cos \alpha < 0$

49. If the angles of elevation of the top of a tower from three collinear points A, B and C, on a line leading to the foot of the tower, are $30°$, $45°$ and $60°$ respectively, then the ratio, AB : BC, is : **[2015, Main]**

(a) $\sqrt{3} : 1$

(b) $\sqrt{3} : \sqrt{2}$

(c) $1 : \sqrt{3}$

(d) $2 : 3$

50. The number of distinct solutions of the equation

$\dfrac{5}{4} \cos^2 2x + \cos^4 x + \sin^4 x + \cos^6 x + \sin^6 x = 2$

in the interval $[0, 2\pi]$ is **[2015, Advanced]**

51. Column I   **Column II**

[2015, Advanced]

(a) In a triangle ΔXYZ, let a, b and c **(P) 1**
be the lengths of the sides opposite to the angles X, Y and Z respectively. If $2(a^2 - b^2) = c^2$ and $\lambda = \dfrac{\sin(X - Y)}{\sin Z}$, then possible values of n for which $\cos(n\pi\lambda) = 0$ is (are)

(b) In a triangle ΔXYZ, let a, b and c be   **(Q) 2**
the lengths of the sides opposite to the angles X, Y and Z, respectively. If $1 + \cos 2X - 2 \cos 2Y = 2 \sin X \sin Y$, then possible value(s) of $\dfrac{a}{b}$ is (are)

(c) In R^2, let $\sqrt{3}\,\hat{i} + \hat{j}, \hat{i} + \sqrt{3}\,\hat{j}$ and   **(R) 3**
$\beta\,\hat{i} + (1-\beta)\,\hat{j}$ be the position vectors of X, Y and Z with respect to the origin O, respectivley. If the distance of Z from the bisector of the acute angle of $\overrightarrow{OX}$ with $\overrightarrow{OY}$ is $\dfrac{3}{\sqrt{2}}$, then possible value(s) of $|\beta|$ is (are)

(d) Suppose that $F(\alpha)$ denotes the area   **(S) 5**
of the region bounded by $x = 0$, $x = 2$, $y^2 = 4x$ and $y\,|\alpha x - 1| + |\alpha x - 2| + \alpha x$, where $\alpha \in \{0, 1\}$. Then the value(s) of $F(\alpha) + \dfrac{8}{3}\sqrt{2}$, when $\alpha = 0$ and $\alpha = 1$, is (are)

(T) 6

52. Statement I : The equation $(\sin^{-1} x)^3 + (\cos^{-1} x)^3 - a\pi^3 = 0$ has a solution for all $a \geq \dfrac{1}{32}$.

Statement II : For any $x \in$ R,

$\sin^{-1} x + \cos^{-1} x = \dfrac{\pi}{2}$ and

$0 \leq \left(\sin^{-1} x - \dfrac{\pi}{4}\right)^2 \leq \dfrac{9\pi^2}{16}$. **[2014, Main]**

(a) Both statements I and II are true.

(b) Both statement I and II are false.

(c) Statement I is true and statement II is false.

(d) Statement I is false and statement II is true.

53. If $\operatorname{cosec} \theta = \dfrac{p+q}{p-q}$ $(p \neq q \neq 0)$, then $\left| \cot\left(\dfrac{\pi}{4} + \dfrac{\theta}{2}\right) \right|$ is equal to : **[2014, Main]**

(a) $\sqrt{\dfrac{p}{q}}$

(b) $\sqrt{\dfrac{q}{p}}$

(c) $\sqrt{pq}$

(d) pq

54. The function $f(x) = |\sin 4x| + |\cos 2x|$, is a periodic function with period : **[2014, Main]**

(a) 2π

(b) π

(c) $\dfrac{\pi}{2}$

(d) $\dfrac{\pi}{4}$

55. The principal value of $\tan^{-1}\left(\cot\dfrac{43\pi}{4}\right)$ is :

[2014, Main]

(a) $-\dfrac{3\pi}{4}$

(b) $\dfrac{3\pi}{4}$

(c) $-\dfrac{\pi}{4}$

(d) $\dfrac{\pi}{4}$

56. If $2\cos\theta + \sin\theta = 1$ $\left(\theta \neq \dfrac{\pi}{2}\right)$, then $7\cos\theta + 6\sin\theta$ is equal to :

[2014, Main]

(a) $\dfrac{1}{2}$

(b) 2

(c) $\dfrac{11}{2}$

(d) $\dfrac{46}{5}$

57. The angle of elevation of the top of a vertical tower from a point P on the horizontal ground was observed to be α. After moving a distance 2 metres from P towards the foot of the tower, the angle of elevation changes to β. Then the height (in metres) of the tower is :   [2014, Main]

(a) $\dfrac{2\sin\alpha \sin\beta}{\sin(\beta-\alpha)}$

(b) $\dfrac{\sin\alpha \sin\beta}{\cos(\beta-\alpha)}$

(c) $\dfrac{2\sin(\beta-\alpha)}{\sin\alpha \sin\beta}$

(d) $\dfrac{\cos(\beta-\alpha)}{\sin\alpha \sin\beta}$

58. For $x \in (0,\pi)$ the equation $\sin x + 2\sin 2x - \sin 3x = 3$ has   [2014, Advanced]

(a) infinitely many solutions

(b) three solutions

(c) one solution

(d) no solution

59. A bird is sitting on the top of a vertical pole 20 m high and its elevation from a point O on the ground is 45°. If flies off horizontally straight away from the point O. After one second, the elevation of the bird from O is reduced to 30°. Then the speed (in m/s) of the bird is :

[2014, Main]

(a) $20\sqrt{2}$

(b) $20(\sqrt{3}-1)$

(c) $40(\sqrt{2}-1)$

(d) $40(\sqrt{3}-\sqrt{2})$

60. In a triangle the sum of two sides is x and the product of the same two sides is y. If $x^2 - c^2 = y$, where c is the third side of the triangle, then the ratio of the in-radius to the circum-radius of the triangle is :   [2014, Advanced]

(a) $\dfrac{3y}{2x(x+c)}$

(b) $\dfrac{3y}{2c(x+c)}$

(c) $\dfrac{3y}{4x(x+c)}$

(d) $\dfrac{3y}{4c(x+c)}$

61. The number of values of α in $[0, 2\pi]$ for which $2\sin^3\alpha - 7\sin^2\alpha + 7\sin\alpha = 2$, is :   [2014, Main]

(a) 6

(b) 4

(c) 3

(d) 1

62. The value of $\cot\left(\displaystyle\sum_{n=1}^{23}\cot^{-1}\left(1+\sum_{k=1}^{n}2k\right)\right)$ is :

[2013, Advanced]

(a) $\dfrac{23}{25}$

(b) $\dfrac{25}{23}$

(c) $\dfrac{23}{24}$

(d) $\dfrac{24}{23}$

63. Match List I with List II and select the correct answer using the code given below the lists :

[2013, Advanced]

List – I

P. $\left(\dfrac{1}{y^2}\left(\dfrac{\cos(\tan^{-1}y)+y\sin(\tan^{-1}y)^2}{\cot(\sin^{-1}y)+\tan(\sin^{-1}y)}\right)+y^4\right)^{1/2}$

Q. If $\cos x + \cos y + \cos z = 0 = \sin x + \sin y + \sin x$ then possible value of $\cos\dfrac{x-y}{2}$ is

R. If $\cos\left(\dfrac{\pi}{4}-x\right)\cos 2x + \sin x \sin 2x \sec x$
$= \cos x \sin 2x \sec x + \cos\left(\dfrac{\pi}{4}-x\right)\cos 2x$
then possible value of $\sec x$ is

S. If $\cot(\sin^{-1}\sqrt{1-x^2}) = \sin(\tan^{-1}(x\sqrt{6}))$, $x \neq 0$, then possible value of x is

List – II

1. $\dfrac{1}{2}\sqrt{\dfrac{5}{3}}$

2. $\sqrt{2}$

3. $\dfrac{1}{2}$

4. 1

64. Let $f:(-1,1)\to \mathrm{IR}$ be such that $f(\cos 4\theta) = \dfrac{2}{2-\sec^2\theta}$ for $\theta \in \left(0,\dfrac{\pi}{4}\right)\cup\left(\dfrac{\pi}{4},\dfrac{\pi}{2}\right)$. Then the value(s) of $f\left(\dfrac{1}{3}\right)$ is (are)   [2012, Advanced]

(a) $1-\sqrt{\dfrac{3}{2}}$

(b) $1+\sqrt{\dfrac{3}{2}}$

(c) $1-\sqrt{\dfrac{2}{3}}$

(d) $1+\sqrt{\dfrac{2}{3}}$

65. Let PQR be a triangle of area Δ with $a = 2$, $b = \dfrac{7}{2}$ and $c = \dfrac{5}{2}$, where a, b and c are the lengths of the sides of the triangle opposite to the angles at P, Q and R respectively.

Then $\dfrac{2\sin P - \sin 2P}{2\sin P + \sin 2P}$ equals **[2012, Advanced]**

(a) $\dfrac{3}{4\Delta}$

(b) $\dfrac{45}{4\Delta}$

(c) $\left(\dfrac{3}{4\Delta}\right)^2$

(d) $\left(\dfrac{45}{4\Delta}\right)^2$

66. Consider the statements :

P : There exists some $x \in R$ such that $f(x) + 2x = 2(1 + x^2)$

Q : There exists some $x \in R$ such that $2 f(x) + 1 = 2x(1 + x)$

then

(a) both P and Q are true

(b) P is true and Q is false

(c) P is false and Q is true

(d) both P and Q are false

67. Let $P = \{\theta : \sin\theta - \cos\theta = \sqrt{2}\cos\theta\}$ and $Q = \{\theta : \sin\theta + \cos\theta = \sqrt{2}\sin\theta\}$ be two sets. Then

[2011, Advanced]

(a) $P \subset Q$ and $Q - P \neq \varnothing$

(b) $Q \not\subset P$

(c) $P \not\subset Q$

(d) $P = Q$

68. The positive integer value of $n > 3$ satisfying the equation **[2011, Advanced]**

$$\dfrac{1}{\sin\left(\dfrac{\pi}{n}\right)} = \dfrac{1}{\sin\left(\dfrac{2\pi}{n}\right)} + \dfrac{1}{\sin\left(\dfrac{3\pi}{n}\right)}$$

69. Let $f(\theta) = \sin\left(\tan^{-1}\left(\dfrac{\sin\theta}{\sqrt{\cos 2\theta}}\right)\right)$, where $-\dfrac{\pi}{4} < \theta < \dfrac{\pi}{4}$. Then the value of **[2011, Advanced]**

$$\dfrac{d}{d(\tan\theta)}(f(\theta)) \text{ is :}$$

70. For $0 < \theta < \dfrac{\pi}{2}$, the solution(s) of

$$\sum_{m=1}^{6} \operatorname{cosec}\left(\theta + \dfrac{(m-1)\pi}{4}\right)\operatorname{cosec}\left(\theta + \dfrac{m\pi}{4}\right) = 4\sqrt{2}$$

is (are) : **[2009, Advanced]**

(a) $\dfrac{\pi}{4}$

(b) $\dfrac{\pi}{6}$

(c) $\dfrac{\pi}{12}$

(d) $\dfrac{5\pi}{12}$

71. Let ABC and ABC′ be two non-congruent triangles with sides AB = 4, AC = AC′ = $2\sqrt{2}$ and angle B = 30°. The absolute value of the difference between the areas of these triangles is :

[2009, Advanced]

72. If $0 < x < 1$, then

$$\sqrt{1+x^2}\,[\{x\cos(\cot^{-1}x) + \sin(\cot^{-1}x)\}^2 - 1]^{\tfrac{1}{2}} =$$

[2008, Advanced]

(a) $\dfrac{x}{\sqrt{1+x^2}}$

(b) x

(c) $x\sqrt{1+x^2}$

(d) $\sqrt{1+x^2}$

73. The number of solutions of the pair of equations

$$2\sin^2\theta - \cos 2\theta = 0 \quad \textbf{[2007, Advanced]}$$
$$2\cos^2\theta - 3\sin\theta = 0$$

in the interval $[0, 2\pi]$ is :

(a) zero

(b) one

(c) two

(d) four

74. If $0 < \theta < 2\pi$, then the intervals of values of θ for which $2\sin^2\theta - 5\sin\theta + 2 > 0$, is.

[2007, Advanced]

(a) $\left(0, \dfrac{\pi}{6}\right) \cup \left(\dfrac{5\pi}{6}, 2\pi\right)$

(b) $\left(\dfrac{\pi}{8}, \dfrac{5\pi}{6}\right)$

(c) $\left(0, \dfrac{\pi}{8}\right) \cup \left(\dfrac{\pi}{6}, \dfrac{5\pi}{6}\right)$

(d) $\left(\dfrac{41\pi}{48}, \pi\right)$

75. Internal bisector of $\angle A$ of triangle ABC meets side BC at D. A line drawn through D perpendicular to AD intersects the side AC at E and the side AB at F. If a, b, c represent sides of $\triangle ABC$ then

(a) AE is HM of b and c

(b) AD = $\dfrac{2bc}{b+c}\cos\dfrac{A}{2}$

(c) EF = $\dfrac{4bc}{b+c}\sin\dfrac{A}{2}$

(d) the triangle AEF is isosceles

76. Let (x, y) be such that

$$\sin^{-1}(ax) + \cos^{-1}(y) + \cos^{-1}(bxy) = \dfrac{\pi}{2}.$$

Match the statements in **Column I** with statement in **Column II** ORS. **(2007, Advanced)**

Column I	Column II
(a) If $a = 1$ and $b = 0$, then (x, y)	(p) lies on the circle $x^2 + y^2 = 1$
(b) If $a = 1$ and $b = 1$, then (x, y)	(q) lies on $(x^2 - 1)(y^2 - 1) = 0$
(c) If $a = 1$ and $b = 2$, then (x, y)	(r) lies on $y = x$
(d) If $a = 2$ and $b = 2$, then (x, y)	(s) lies on $(4x^2 - 1)(y^2 - 1) = 0$

77. Match the following : **(2006, Main)**

(a) $\sum_{i=1}^{\infty} \tan^{-1}\left(\dfrac{1}{2i^2}\right) = t$, then $\tan t =$ (i) 0

(b) Sides a, b, c of a triangle ABC are in AP and $\cos \theta_1 = \dfrac{a}{b+c}$,   (ii) 1

$\cos \theta_2 = \dfrac{b}{a+c}$, $\cos \theta_3 = \dfrac{c}{a+b}$, then

$$\tan^2\left(\dfrac{\theta_1}{2}\right) + \tan^2\left(\dfrac{\theta_3}{2}\right) =$$

(c) A line is perpendicular to $x + 2y$ (iii) $\dfrac{\sqrt{5}}{3}$

$+ 2z = 0$ and passes through $(0, 1, 0)$. The perpendicular distance of this line from the origin is   (iv) 2/3

78. Given an isosceles triangle, whose one angle is $120°$ and radius of its incircle $= \sqrt{3}$. Then the area of the triangle in sq. units is : **[2006, Advanced]**

(a) $7 + 12\sqrt{3}$ (b) $12 - 7\sqrt{3}$

(c) $12 + 7\sqrt{3}$ (d) 4π

79. Let $\theta \in \left(0, \dfrac{\pi}{4}\right)$ and $t_1 = (\tan\theta)^{\tan\theta}$, $t_2 = (\tan\theta)^{\cot\theta}$,

$t_3 = (\cot\theta)^{\tan\theta}$ and $t_4 = (\cot\theta)^{\cot\theta}$, then

[2006, Advanced]

(a) $t_1 > t_2 > t_3 > t_4$ (b) $t_4 > t_3 > t_1 > t_2$

(c) $t_3 > t_1 > t_2 > t_4$ (d) $t_2 > t_3 > t_1 > t_4$

80. In ΔABC, a, b, c are the lengths of its sides and A, B, C are the angles of triangle ABC. The correct relation is given by   **[2005, Main]**

(a) $(b - c)\sin\left(\dfrac{B-C}{2}\right) = a\cos\dfrac{A}{2}$

(b) $(b - c)\cos\dfrac{A}{2} = a\sin\left(\dfrac{B-C}{2}\right)$

(c) $(b + c)\sin\left(\dfrac{B+C}{2}\right) = a\cos\dfrac{A}{2}$

(d) $(b - c)\cos\left(\dfrac{A}{2}\right) = 2a\sin\left(\dfrac{B+C}{2}\right)$

81. The sides of a triangle are in the ratio $1 : \sqrt{3} : 2$, then the angles of the triangle are in the ratio :

[2004, Main]

(a) $1 : 3 : 5$ (b) $2 : 3 : 4$

(c) $3 : 2 : 1$ (d) $1 : 2 : 3$

82. Given both θ and ϕ are acute angles and $\sin\theta = \dfrac{1}{2}$, $\cos\phi = \dfrac{1}{3}$, then the value of $\theta + \phi$ belongs to :

[2004, Main]

(a) $\left(\dfrac{\pi}{3}, \dfrac{\pi}{2}\right]$ (b) $\left(\dfrac{\pi}{2}, \dfrac{2\pi}{3}\right]$

(c) $\left(\dfrac{2\pi}{3}, \dfrac{5\pi}{6}\right]$ (d) $\left(\dfrac{5\pi}{6}, \pi\right]$

83. The value of x for which $\sin(\cot^{-1}(1 + x)) = \cos(\tan^{-1} x)$ is :   **[2004, Main]**

(a) $1/2$ (b) 1

(c) 0 (d) $-1/2$

84. Which of the following pieces of data does **NOT** uniquely determinede an acute-angled triangle ABC (R being the radius of the circumcircle)?

[2003, Screening]

(a) $a, \sin A, \sin B$ (b) a, b, c

(c) $a, \sin B, R$ (d) a, sin A, R

ANSWER KEY

1. (d)	**2.** (b)	**3.** (80)	**4.** (a)	**5.** (d)	**6.** (a)	**7.** (c)	**8.** (a)	**9.** (c)	**10.** (d)
11. (c)	**12.** (8.00)	**13.** (1.00)	**14.** (c)	**15.** (c)	**16.** (d)	**17.** (a)	**18.** (c)	**19.** (a)	**20.** (a)
21. (b)	**22.** (c)	**23.** (b)	**24.** (d)	**25.** (b)	**26.** (d)	**27.** (b)	**28.** (b)	**29.** (a)	**30.** (a)
31. (0.00)	**32.** (b)	**33.** (c)	**34.** (a)	**35.** (a)	**36.** (b)	**37.** (0.5)	**38.** (a)	**39.** (c)	**40.** (b)
41. (a,c)	**42.** (a)	**43.** (d)	**44.** (d)	**45.** (c)	**46.** (c)	**47.** (d)	**48.** (b,c,d)	**49.** (a)	**50.** (8)

51. (a) – (P,R,S), (b) – (P), (c) – (P,&), (d) – (S,T)   **52.** (b)   **53.** (b)   **54.** (c)   **55.** (c)   **56.** (b)

57. (a)   **58.** (d)   **59.** (b)   **60.** (b)   **61.** (c)   **62.** (b)   **63.** (b)   **64.** (a or b)   **65.** (c)   **66.** (c)

67. (d)   **68.** (7)   **69.** (1)   **70.** (c,d)   **71.** (4)   **72.** (c)   **73.** (c)   **74.** (a)   **75.** (a,b,c,d)

76. (a) – (p), (b) – (q), (c) – (p), (d) – (s)   **77.** (a) – (ii), (b) – (iv), (c) – (iii)   **78.** (c)   **79.** (b)   **80.** (b)

81. (d)   **82.** (b)   **83.** (d)   **84.** (d)

ANSWERS WITH EXPLANATIONS

1. Correct Response : (d)

Explanation :

$$S = \tan^{-1}\left(\frac{1}{3}\right) + \tan^{-1}\left(\frac{1}{7}\right) + \tan^{-1}\left(\frac{1}{13}\right) + \dots$$

$$S = \tan^{-1}\left(\frac{2-1}{1+1.2}\right) + \tan^{-1}\left(\frac{3-2}{1+2\times3}\right)$$

$$+ \tan^{-1}\left(\frac{4-3}{1+3\times4}\right) + \dots + \tan^{-1}\left(\frac{11-10}{1+10\times11}\right)$$

$$S = (\tan^{-1}2 - \tan^{-1}1) + (\tan^{-1}3 - \tan^{-1}2)$$
$$+ (\tan^{-1}4 - \tan^{-1}3) + \dots$$
$$+ [\tan^{-1}(11) - \tan^{-1}(10)]$$

$$S = \tan^{-1}11 - \tan^{-1}1 = \tan^{-1}\left(\frac{11-1}{1+11}\right)$$

$$\tan(S) = \frac{11-1}{1+11\times1} = \frac{10}{12} = \frac{5}{6}$$

2. Correct Response : (b)

Explanation :

For point A

$$\tan 60° = \frac{2\sqrt{3}-k}{2-1}$$

$$\sqrt{3} = 2\sqrt{3}-k$$

$$\therefore \qquad k = \sqrt{3}$$

so point $A(1, \sqrt{3})$

Now slope of line AB in $m_{AB} = \tan 120°$

$$m_{AB} = -\sqrt{3}$$

Now equation of line AB is

$$y - \sqrt{3} = -\sqrt{3}\,(x-1)$$

$$\sqrt{3}x + y = 2\sqrt{3}$$

Now satisfy options is (b)

3. Correct Response : (80)

Explanation :

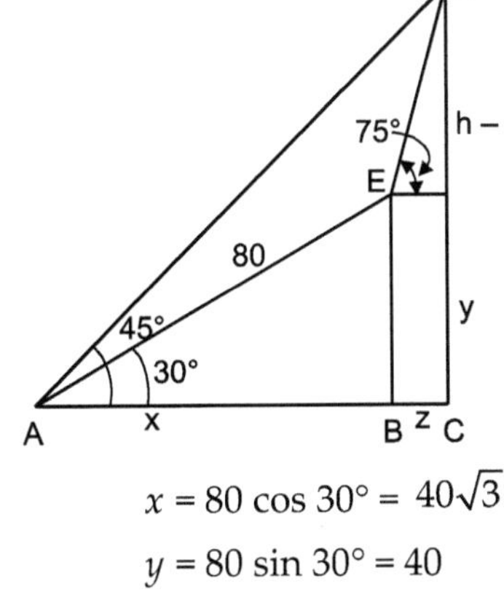

$$x = 80 \cos 30° = 40\sqrt{3}$$

$$y = 80 \sin 30° = 40$$

$$\tan 45° = 1$$

$$x + 2 = h$$

$$40\sqrt{3} + z = h$$

$$\tan 75° = \frac{h-y}{z}$$

$$2 + \sqrt{3} = \frac{h-40}{z}$$

$$z = \frac{h-40}{2+\sqrt{3}}$$

$$h - 40\sqrt{3} = \frac{h-40}{2+\sqrt{3}}$$

$$(1+\sqrt{3})h = 80(1+\sqrt{3})$$

$$h = 80.$$

4. Correct Response : (a)

Explanation :

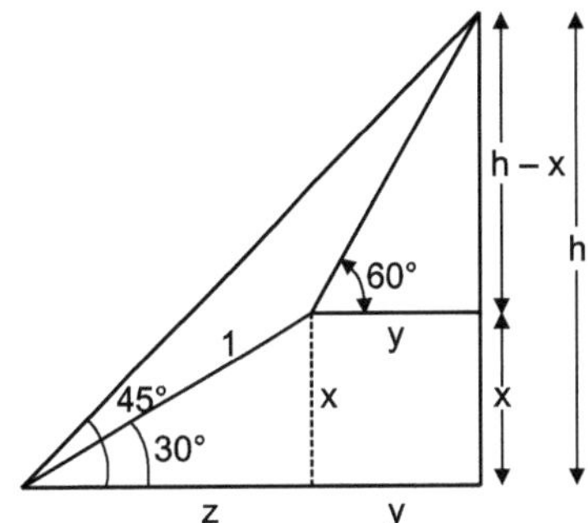

$$\sin 30° = x \Rightarrow x = \frac{1}{2}$$

$$\cos 30° = z \Rightarrow z = \frac{\sqrt{3}}{2}$$

$$\tan 45° = \frac{h}{y+z} \Rightarrow h = y+z$$

$$\tan 60° = \frac{h-x}{y} \Rightarrow \tan 60° = \frac{h-x}{h-z}$$

$$\sqrt{3}(h-z) = h-x$$

$$(\sqrt{3}-1)h = \sqrt{3}z - x$$

Put value of z and x

$$\Rightarrow \qquad (\sqrt{3}-1)h = \frac{3}{2} - \frac{1}{2}$$

$$\Rightarrow \qquad (\sqrt{3}-1)h = 1$$

$$h = \frac{1}{\sqrt{3}-1}$$

5. Correct Response : (d)

Explanation :

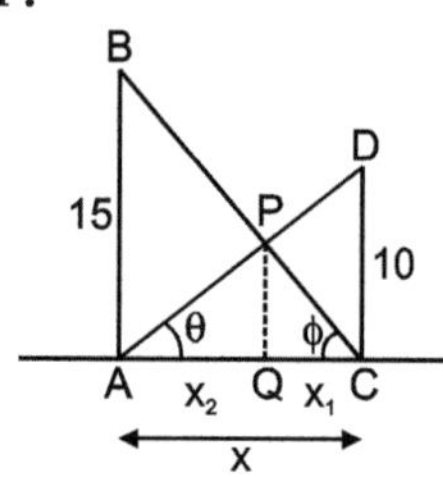

$$\Delta ACD \sim \Delta AQP$$

$$\tan \theta = \frac{10}{x} = \frac{h}{x_2} \Rightarrow x_2 = \frac{hx}{10}$$

$$\Delta CAB \sim \Delta CQP$$

$$\tan \phi = \frac{15}{x} = \frac{h}{x_1} \Rightarrow x_1 = \frac{hx}{15}$$

Now, $\quad x_1 + x_2 = x = \dfrac{hx}{15} + \dfrac{hx}{10}$

$$\Rightarrow \qquad 1 = \frac{h}{10} + \frac{h}{15} \Rightarrow h = 6.$$

6. Correct Response : (a)

Explanation :

$\Delta EPC \qquad \tan 30° = \dfrac{x}{y} = \dfrac{1}{\sqrt{3}}$

$$\Rightarrow \qquad y = \sqrt{3}x$$

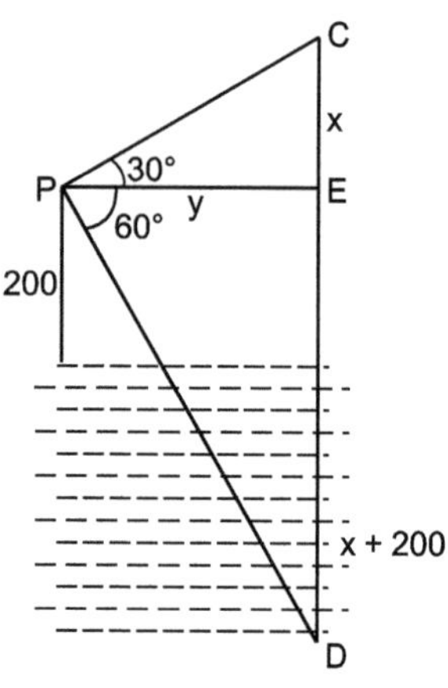

$\Delta EPD \qquad \tan 60° = \dfrac{x+400}{y} = \sqrt{3}$

$$x + 400 = y\sqrt{3}$$

$$x + 400 = \sqrt{3}x \times \sqrt{3}$$

$$x + 400 = 3x$$

$$x = 200$$

$\Delta EPC \qquad \sin 30° = \dfrac{200}{PC}$

$$PC = 400 \text{ m.}$$

7. Correct Response : (c)

Explanation :

$$2\pi - \left(\sin^{-1}\left(\frac{4}{5}\right) + \sin^{-1}\left(\frac{5}{13}\right) + \sin^{-1}\left(\frac{16}{65}\right) \right)$$

$$= 2\pi - \left(\tan^{-1}\left(\frac{4}{3}\right) + \tan^{-1}\left(\frac{5}{12}\right) + \tan^{-1}\left(\frac{16}{63}\right) \right)$$

$$= 2\pi - \left(\tan^{-1}\left(\frac{63}{16}\right) + \tan^{-1}\left(\frac{16}{63}\right) \right)$$

$$= 2\pi - \frac{\pi}{2} = \frac{3\pi}{2}.$$

8. Correct Response : (a)

Explanation :

$$L = \sin^2\left(\frac{\pi}{16}\right) - \sin^2\left(\frac{\pi}{8}\right)$$

$$\left(\because \sin^2\theta = \frac{1-\cos 2\theta}{2} \right) \& \left(\cos^2\theta = \frac{1+\cos 2\theta}{2} \right)$$

$$\Rightarrow \quad L = \left(\frac{1-\cos(\pi/8)}{2} \right) - \left(\frac{1-\cos(\pi/4)}{2} \right)$$

$$= \frac{1}{2}\left[\cos\left(\frac{\pi}{4}\right) - \cos\left(\frac{\pi}{8}\right) \right]$$

$$L = \frac{1}{2\sqrt{2}} - \frac{1}{2}\cos\left(\frac{\pi}{8}\right)$$

$$M = \cos^2\left(\frac{\pi}{16}\right) - \sin^2\left(\frac{\pi}{8}\right)$$

$$M = \frac{1+\cos(\pi/8)}{2} - \frac{1-\cos(\pi/4)}{2}$$

$$M = \frac{1}{2}\cos\left(\frac{\pi}{8}\right) + \frac{1}{2\sqrt{2}}.$$

9. Correct Response : (c)

Explanation :

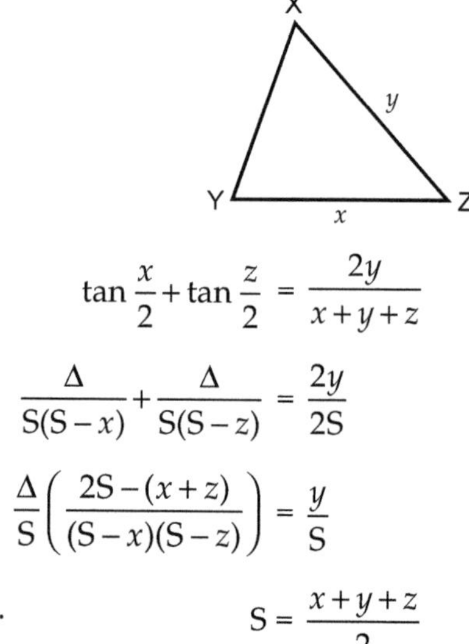

$$\tan\frac{x}{2} + \tan\frac{z}{2} = \frac{2y}{x+y+z}$$

$$\frac{\Delta}{S(S-x)} + \frac{\Delta}{S(S-z)} = \frac{2y}{2S}$$

$$\frac{\Delta}{S}\left(\frac{2S-(x+z)}{(S-x)(S-z)} \right) = \frac{y}{S}$$

$$\because \qquad S = \frac{x+y+z}{2}$$

$$\Rightarrow \quad \frac{\Delta y}{S(S-x)(S-z)} = \frac{y}{S}$$

$$\Rightarrow \quad \Delta^2 = (S-x)^2 (S-z)^2$$

$$\Rightarrow \quad S(S-y) = (S-x)(S-z)$$

$$\Rightarrow (x+y+z)(x+z-y) = (y+z-x)(x+y-z)$$

$$\Rightarrow \quad (x+z)^2 - y^2 = y^2 - (z-x)^2$$

$$\Rightarrow \quad (x+z)^2 + (x-z)^2 = 2y^2$$

$$\Rightarrow \quad x^2 + z^2 = y^2$$

$$\Rightarrow \quad \angle Y = \frac{\pi}{2}$$

$$\Rightarrow \quad \angle Y = \angle X + \angle Z$$

$$\tan\frac{x}{2} = \frac{\Delta}{S(S-x)}$$

$$\tan\frac{x}{2} = \frac{\frac{1}{2}xz}{\dfrac{(y+z)^2 - x^2}{4}}$$

$$\tan\frac{x}{2} = \frac{2xz}{y^2 + z^2 + 2yz - x^2}$$

$$\tan\frac{x}{2} = \frac{2xz}{2z^2 + 2yz}$$

$$(\text{using } y^2 = x^2 + z^2)$$

$$\tan\frac{x}{2} = \frac{x}{y+z}.$$

10. Correct Response : (d)

Explanation :

$$\lambda = -(\sin^4\theta + \cos^4\theta)$$
$$\lambda = -(\sin^2\theta + \cos^2\theta)^2 + 2\sin^2\theta\,\cos^2\theta$$
$$\lambda = \frac{\sin^2 2\theta}{2} - 1$$
$$\frac{\sin^2 2\theta}{2} \in \left[0, \frac{1}{2}\right]$$
$$\lambda \in \left[-1, -\frac{1}{2}\right]$$

11. Correct Response : (c)

Explanation :

$$\cos^3\frac{\pi}{8} \cdot \sin\frac{\pi}{8} + \sin^3\frac{\pi}{8} \cdot \cos\frac{\pi}{8}$$
$$= \sin\frac{\pi}{8} \cdot \cos\frac{\pi}{8} = \frac{1}{2}\sin\frac{\pi}{4} = \frac{1}{2\sqrt2}$$

12. Correct Response : (8.00)

Explanation :

$$\log_{1/2}|\sin x| = 2 - \log_{1/2}|\cos x| : x \in [0, 2\pi]$$
$$\Rightarrow \log_{1/2}|\sin x| + \log_{1/2}|\cos x| = 2$$
$$\Rightarrow \log_{1/2}(|\sin x \cos x|) = 2$$

$$\Rightarrow \quad |\sin x \cos x| = \frac{1}{4} \Rightarrow |\sin 2x| = \frac{\sqrt2\sin\alpha}{\sqrt2\cos\alpha}$$

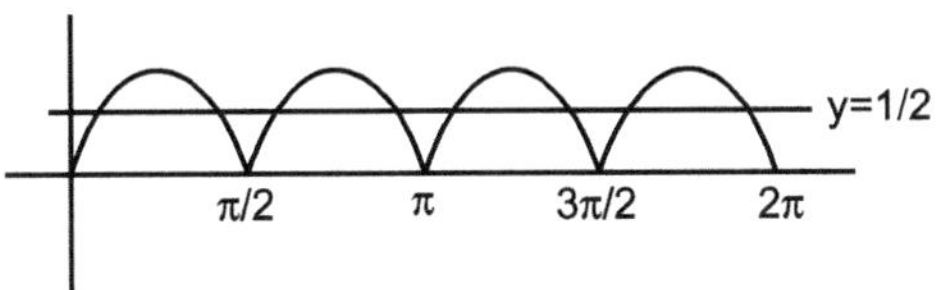

$$\Rightarrow 8 \text{ solutions}$$

13. Correct Response : (1.00)

Explanation :

$$\frac{\sqrt2\sin\alpha}{\sqrt2\cos\alpha} = \frac{1}{7} \Rightarrow \tan\alpha = \frac{1}{7}$$

$$\sin\beta = \frac{1}{\sqrt{10}} \Rightarrow \tan\beta = \frac{1}{3} \Rightarrow \tan 2\beta = \frac{3}{4}$$

$$\tan(\alpha + 2\beta) = \frac{\tan\alpha + \tan 2\beta}{1 - \tan\alpha \tan 2\beta} = 1$$

14. Correct Response : (c)

Explanation :

$$x = \sum_{n=0}^{\infty} (-1)^n \, \tan^{2n}\theta = 1 - \tan^2\theta + \tan^4\theta + \;\ldots$$

$$\Rightarrow \quad x = \cos^2\theta$$

$$y = \sum_{n=0}^{\infty} \cos^{2n}\theta \Rightarrow y = 1 + \cos^2\theta + \cos^4\theta + \ldots$$

$$\Rightarrow \quad y = \frac{1}{\sin^2\theta} \Rightarrow y = \frac{1}{1-x}$$

$$\Rightarrow \quad y(1-x) = 1$$

15. Correct Response : (c)

Explanation :

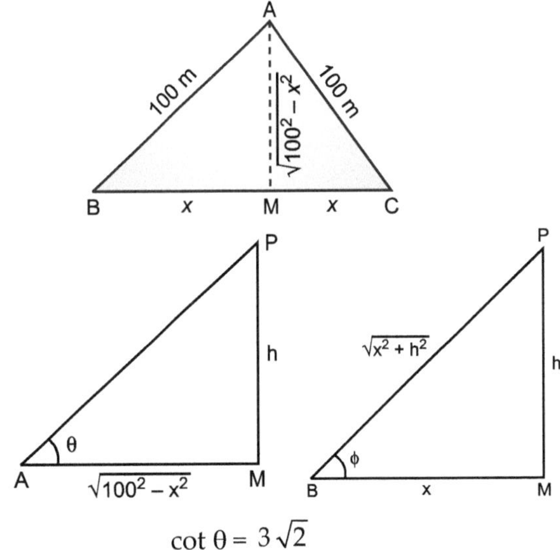

$$\cot\theta = 3\sqrt2$$

$$\Rightarrow \quad \frac{\sqrt{100^2 - x^2}}{h} = 3\sqrt2 \qquad \ldots(1)$$

$$\Rightarrow \quad 100^2 - x^2 = 18h^2$$

and
$$\operatorname{cosec} \phi = 2\sqrt{2}$$

$$\Rightarrow \quad \frac{\sqrt{x^2+h^2}}{h} = 2\sqrt{2}$$

$$\Rightarrow \quad x^2 + h^2 = 8h^2$$

$$\Rightarrow \quad x^2 = 7h^2 \qquad \ldots(2)$$

Equations (1) and (2) implies
$$100^2 - 7h^2 = 18h^2$$

This gives
$$h^2 = \frac{100 \times 100}{25}$$
$$= 400$$
$$\Rightarrow \quad h = 20$$

16. Correct Response : (d)

Explanation :

$$2^{\sqrt{(\sin x-1)^2+4}} \le 4\sin^2 y$$

Compare powers on both sides
$$2\sin^2 y \ge \sqrt{(\sin x-1)^2+4}$$

As $2\sin^2 y \in [0, 2]$

$$\sqrt{(\sin x-1)^2+4} \in \left[2, 2\sqrt{2}\right]$$

Thus, $2\sin^2 y = \sqrt{(\sin x-1)^2+4}$, for $|\sin y| = 1$
and $\sin x = 1$.

$$\Rightarrow \quad |\sin y| = \sin x.$$

17. Correct Response : (a)

Explanation :

$$\cos^{-1} x - \cos^{-1}\frac{y}{2} = \alpha$$

$$\Rightarrow \cos^{-1}\left(\frac{xy}{2} + \sqrt{1-x^2}\sqrt{1-\frac{y^2}{4}}\right) = \alpha$$

$$\Rightarrow \quad \frac{xy}{2} + \frac{\sqrt{1-x^2}\sqrt{4-y^2}}{2} = \cos\alpha$$

$$\Rightarrow \quad xy + \sqrt{1-x^2}\sqrt{4-y^2} = 2\cos\alpha$$

$$\Rightarrow \quad \sqrt{1-x^2}\sqrt{4-y^2} = 2\cos\alpha - xy$$

$$\Rightarrow \quad (1-x^2)(4-y^2) = 4\cos^2\alpha + x^2y^2$$
$$- 4xy\cos\alpha$$

$$\Rightarrow \quad 4 - y^2 - 4x^2 + x^2y^2 = 4\cos^2\alpha + x^2y^2$$
$$- 4xy\cos\alpha$$

$$\Rightarrow \quad 4x^2 + y^2 - 4xy\cos\alpha = 4 - 4\cos^2\alpha$$

$$\Rightarrow \quad 4x^2 + y^2 - 4xy\cos\alpha = 4\sin^2\alpha$$

18. Correct Response : (c)

Explanation :

From the above figure, $2B = A + C$.

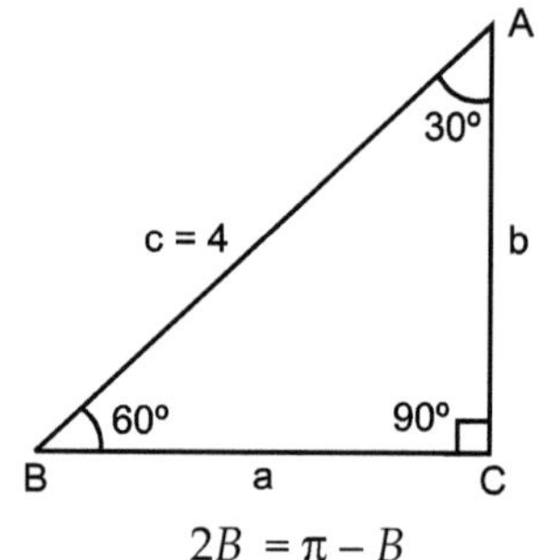

$$\Rightarrow \quad 2B = \pi - B$$
$$\Rightarrow \quad 3B = \pi$$
$$\Rightarrow \quad B = \frac{\pi}{3}$$

Now, $\quad \dfrac{a}{b} = \dfrac{1}{\sqrt{3}} \Rightarrow \dfrac{\sin A}{\sin B} = \dfrac{1}{\sqrt{3}}$

$$\Rightarrow \quad \frac{2\times\sin A}{\sqrt{3}} = \frac{1}{\sqrt{3}}$$

$$\Rightarrow \quad \sin A = \frac{1}{2}$$

$$\Rightarrow \quad A = 30°$$

Now,
$$\frac{a}{\sin 30°} = \frac{b}{\sin 60°} = \frac{c}{\sin 90°} = 4$$

$$\therefore \quad a = 4\times\frac{1}{2}$$
$$= 2$$

and
$$b = 4\times\frac{\sqrt{3}}{2}$$
$$= 2\sqrt{3}$$

Area of triangle is
$$\frac{1}{2}ab = \frac{1}{2}\times 2\times 2\sqrt{3}$$
$$= 2\sqrt{3}$$

19. Correct Response : (a)

Explanation :

From the figure

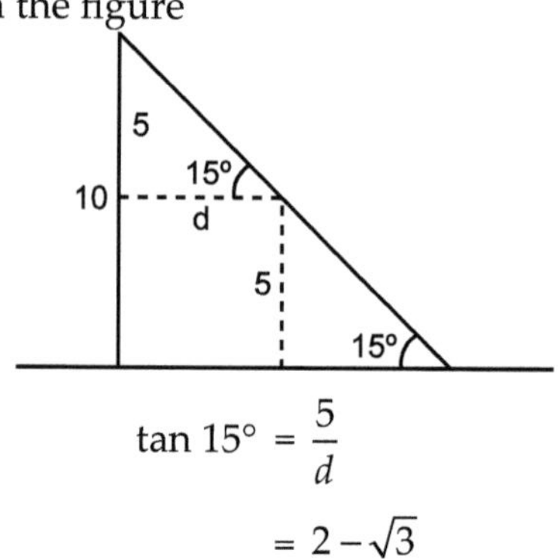

$$\tan 15° = \frac{5}{d}$$
$$= 2 - \sqrt{3}$$

The required distance is
$$d = \frac{5}{2-\sqrt{3}}$$
$$= 5\,(2+\sqrt{3})$$

20. Correct Response : (a)

Explanation :

$\sin 10° \sin 30° \sin 50° \sin 70°$

$= (\sin 30°)(\sin 10°)(\sin(60° - 10°))$

$\qquad\qquad\qquad (\sin(60° + 10°))$

$= \dfrac{1}{2}\left(\dfrac{1}{4}\sin 30°\right) = \dfrac{1}{16}$

21. Correct Response : (b)

Explanation :

$\cos^2 10° + \cos^2 50° - \cos 10° \cos 50°$

$= \dfrac{1}{2}(1 + \cos 20° + 1 + \cos 100° - \cos 60° - \cos 40°)$

$= \dfrac{1}{2}\left(\dfrac{3}{2} + \cos 20° + \cos 100° - \cos 40°\right)$

$= \dfrac{3}{2} + \dfrac{1}{2}[2\cos 60° \cos 40° - \cos 40°]$

$= \dfrac{3}{4}$

22. Correct Response : (c)

Explanation :

$2\cos^2\theta + 3\sin\theta = 0$

$\Rightarrow \quad 2\sin^2\theta - 3\sin\theta - 2 = 0$

$\Rightarrow \quad (\sin\theta - 2)(2\sin\theta + 1) = 0$

$\Rightarrow \quad \sin\theta = -\dfrac{1}{2}$

$\Rightarrow \quad \theta = -\dfrac{\pi}{6}, -\dfrac{5\pi}{6}, \dfrac{7\pi}{6}, \dfrac{11\pi}{6}$

Hence, the sum is 2π.

23. Correct Response : (b)

Explanation :

$0 < \alpha < \dfrac{\pi}{4}, \ 0 < \beta < \dfrac{\pi}{4} \Rightarrow 0 < \alpha + \beta < \dfrac{\pi}{2}$ and

$-\dfrac{\pi}{4} < \alpha - \beta < \dfrac{\pi}{4}$

Now, $\sin(\alpha - \beta) = \dfrac{5}{13} \Rightarrow \cos(\alpha - \beta) = \dfrac{12}{13}$

and $\cos(\alpha + \beta) = \dfrac{3}{5} \Rightarrow \sin(\alpha + \beta) = \dfrac{4}{5}$

Now,

$\tan 2\alpha = \tan[(\alpha + \beta) + (\alpha - \beta)]$

$= -\dfrac{\tan(\alpha + \beta) + \tan(\alpha - \beta)}{1 - \tan(\alpha + \beta)\tan(\alpha - \beta)}$

$= \dfrac{\dfrac{4}{3} + \dfrac{5}{12}}{1 - \dfrac{4}{3} \times \dfrac{5}{12}}$

$= \dfrac{63}{16}$

24. Correct Response : (d)

Explanation :

$\cos\alpha = \dfrac{3}{5} \Rightarrow \tan\alpha = \dfrac{4}{3}$

$\tan\beta = \dfrac{1}{3}$

$\tan(\alpha - \beta) = \dfrac{\dfrac{4}{3} - \dfrac{1}{3}}{1 + \dfrac{4}{3} \times \dfrac{1}{3}}$

$= \dfrac{9}{13}$

$\Rightarrow \quad \sin(\alpha - \beta) = \dfrac{9}{5\sqrt{10}}$

$\Rightarrow \quad \alpha - \beta = \sin^{-1}\left(\dfrac{9}{5\sqrt{10}}\right)$

25. Correct Response : (b)

Explanation :

$2y = \left(\cot^{-1}\left(\dfrac{\sqrt{3}\cos x + \sin x}{\cos x - \sqrt{3}\sin x}\right)\right)^2$

$2y = \left(\cot^{-1}\left(\dfrac{\sqrt{3} + \tan x}{1 - \sqrt{3}\tan x}\right)\right)^2$

$2y = \left(\cot^{-1}\left(\tan\left(\dfrac{\pi}{3} + x\right)\right)\right)^2$

$2y = \left(\dfrac{\pi}{2} - \tan^{-1}\left(\tan\left(\dfrac{\pi}{3} + x\right)\right)\right)^2$

$= \left(\dfrac{\pi}{2} - \left(\dfrac{\pi}{3} + x\right)\right)^2$

$2y = \left(\dfrac{\pi}{6} - x\right)^2$

$2y = x^2 - \dfrac{\pi}{3}x + \dfrac{\pi^2}{36}$

$y = \dfrac{\pi x^2}{2} - \dfrac{\pi}{6}x + \dfrac{\pi^2}{72}$

$y' = x - \dfrac{\pi}{6}$

26. Correct Response : (d)

Explanation :

Height of two poles are 20 m and 80 m

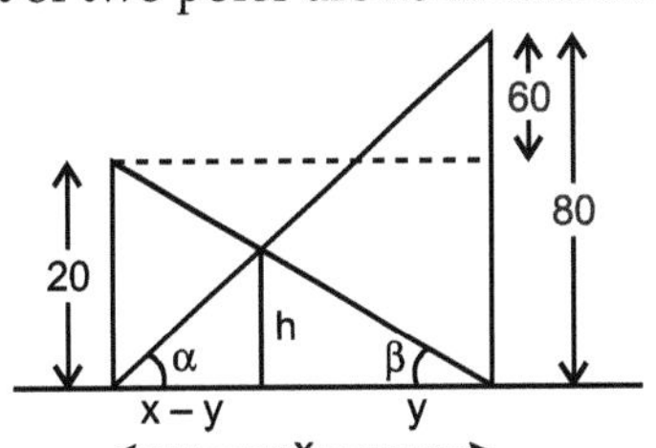

$$\therefore \qquad y = \frac{hx}{20}$$

$$\tan \alpha = \frac{h}{x-y} = \frac{80}{x}$$

$$\Rightarrow \qquad x - y = \frac{hx}{80}$$

$$\frac{hx}{20} + \frac{hx}{80} = x \quad \Rightarrow \left(\frac{h}{20} + \frac{h}{80}\right)x = x$$

$$\Rightarrow \qquad \frac{h}{20} + \frac{h}{80} = 1$$

$$\Rightarrow \qquad 5h = 80$$

$$\Rightarrow \qquad h = 16$$

27. Correct Response : (b)

Explanation :

Let a, b, c are the sides in increasing order
$2b = a + c$
$A = \theta$, $B = \pi - 3\theta$, and $C = 2\theta$
Now,

$$2 \sin B = \sin A + \sin C$$
$$2 \sin (\pi - 3\theta) = \sin \theta + \sin 2\theta$$
$$2 (3 - 4 \sin^2 \theta) = 1 + 2 \cos \theta$$
$$6 - 8 (1 - \cos^2 \theta) = 1 + 2 \cos \theta$$
$$8 \cos^2 \theta - 2 \cos \theta - 3 = 0$$
$$(2 \cos \theta + 1)(4 \cos \theta - 3) = 0$$
$$\cos \theta = \frac{3}{4}, \ \cos \theta = -\frac{1}{2} \ \text{(rejected)}$$

The ratio of sides $a : b : c$

$$\sin A : \sin B : \sin C$$
$$\sin \theta : \sin 3\theta : \sin 2\theta$$
$$1 : 3 - 4 \sin^2 \theta : 2 \cos \theta$$
$$1 : \frac{5}{4} : \frac{6}{4} = 4 : 5 : 6$$

28. Correct Response : (b)

Explanation :

The expression for $\sin^{-1}$ identity is given by,

$$\sin^{-1}(x) - \sin^{-1}(y) = \sin^{-1}(x\sqrt{1-y^2} - y\sqrt{1-x^2})$$

Substitute the values,

$$\sin^{-1}\left(\frac{12}{13}\right) - \sin^{-1}\left(\frac{3}{5}\right)$$

$$= \sin^{-1}\left(\left(\frac{12}{13}\right)\sqrt{1 - \left(\frac{3}{5}\right)^2} - \left(\frac{3}{5}\right)\sqrt{1 - \left(\frac{12}{13}\right)^2}\right)$$

$$= \sin^{-1}\left(\frac{33}{65}\right)$$

$$= \cos^{-1}\left(\frac{56}{65}\right)$$

$$= \frac{\pi}{2} - \sin^{-1}\left(\frac{56}{65}\right)$$

29. Correct Response : (a)

Explanation :

The required diagram is shown in the following figure.

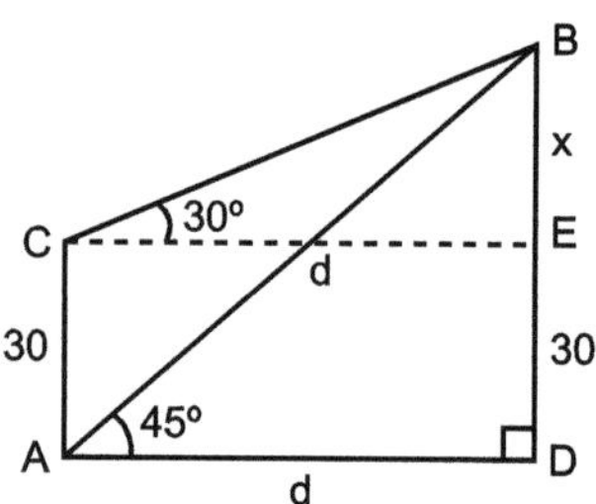

For ΔBCD,

$$\frac{x}{d} = \tan 30°$$

$$d = \sqrt{3}x$$

or $\qquad x = \dfrac{d}{\sqrt{3}}$ ...(1)

For Δ, ABD,

$$\frac{x + 30}{d} = \tan 45°$$

$$d = x + 30$$

$$x = d - 30 \qquad ...(ii)$$

Equate the equations (1) and (2).

$$d = \frac{d}{\sqrt{3}} + 30$$

$$\left(1 - \frac{1}{\sqrt{3}}\right)d = 30$$

$$d = \frac{30\sqrt{3}}{\sqrt{3} - 1}$$

$$= \frac{30\sqrt{3}(\sqrt{3} + 1)}{2}$$

On solving further,

$$d = 15\sqrt{3}(\sqrt{3} + 1)$$

$$= 15(3 + \sqrt{3})$$

30. Correct Response : (a)

Explanation :

For the value of θ between $\dfrac{\pi}{3}$ and $\dfrac{2\pi}{3}$, the value of $\cos \theta$ lies between $-\dfrac{1}{2}$ and 0. The value of $\sin \theta$ lies between $\dfrac{\sqrt{3}}{2}$ and 1. The value of $\cot \theta$ lies between $-\dfrac{1}{\sqrt{3}}$ and 0.

For the value of θ between π and $\dfrac{7\pi}{6}$, the value of $\cos \theta$ is between $\sqrt{3}/2$ and 1; value of $\sin \theta$

between $-\dfrac{1}{2}$ and 0; value of cot θ 1 between $\sqrt{3}$ and infinity.

Hence, for $\theta \in \left(\dfrac{\pi}{2}, \dfrac{2\pi}{3}\right)$, $[\sin \theta] = 0$, $[-\cos \theta] = 0$ and $[\cot \theta] = -1$.

Hence, θ = 0, $-x + y = 0$ and there are infinite solutions.

For $\theta \in \left(\pi, \dfrac{7\pi}{6}\right)$, $[\sin \theta] = -1$, $[-\cos \theta] = 0$ and

$[\cot \theta] = 1, 2, 3 \ldots\ldots\ldots$

The line $[\cot \theta]\, x + y = 0$ cuts $x = 0$ at exactly one point. Hence, there is a unique solution.

31. Correct Response : 0.00

Explanation :

The given function is,

$$f(k) = \sec^{-1}\left(\dfrac{1}{4}\sum_{k=0}^{10} \sec\left(\dfrac{7\pi}{12} + \dfrac{k\pi}{2}\right)\right.$$

$$\left.\sec\left(\dfrac{7\pi}{12} + \dfrac{(k+1)\pi}{2}\right)\right)$$

$$= \sec^{-1}\left(-\dfrac{1}{4}\sum_{k=0}^{10} \sec\left(\dfrac{7\pi}{12} + \dfrac{k\pi}{2}\right)\right.$$

$$\left.\mathrm{cosec}\left(\dfrac{7\pi}{12} + \dfrac{k\pi}{2}\right)\right)$$

$$= \sec^{-1}\left(-\dfrac{1}{4}\sum_{k=0}^{10} \dfrac{2}{\sin\left(\dfrac{7\pi}{6} + k\pi\right)}\right)$$

$$= \sec^{-1}\left(-\dfrac{1}{2}\sum_{k=0}^{10} \dfrac{1}{(-1)^{k+1}\sin\left(\dfrac{\pi}{6}\right)}\right)$$

$$= \sec^{-1}\left(-\sum_{k=0}^{10} \dfrac{1}{(-1)^{k+1}}\right)$$

$$= \sec^{-1}(1)$$

$$= 0.$$

32. Correct Response : (b)

Explanation :

The figure shows the position of the aeroplane as,

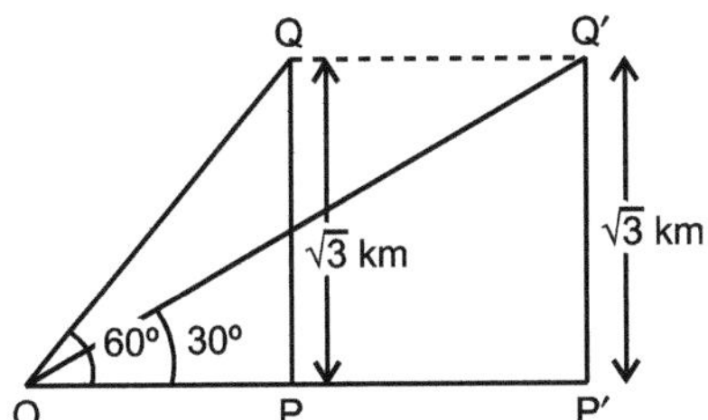

In ΔPOQ,

$$\tan 60° = \dfrac{\sqrt{3}}{PO}$$

$$\sqrt{3} = \dfrac{\sqrt{3}}{PO}$$

$$PO = 1 \text{ km}$$

In $\Delta P'OQ'$,

$$\tan 30° = \dfrac{\sqrt{3}}{P'O}$$

$$\dfrac{1}{\sqrt{3}} = \dfrac{\sqrt{3}}{P'O}$$

$$P'O = 3 \text{ km}$$

The distance PP' is,

$$PP' = P'O - PO$$

$$= 3 - 1$$

$$= 2 \text{ km}$$

The speed of the aeroplane is,

$$s = \dfrac{d}{t}$$

$$= \dfrac{2 \text{ km}}{\left(\dfrac{5}{3600} \text{ hr}\right)}$$

$$= 1440 \text{ km/hr}$$

Therefore, the speed of the aeroplane is 1440 km/hr.

33. Correct Response : (c)

Explanation :

The given relation,

$$5\cos A + 3 = 0$$

$$\cos A = -\dfrac{3}{5}$$

Since, cos θ is negative only in 2nd and 3rd quadrant.

Clearly A ∈ (90°, 180°)

$$\tan A = -\dfrac{\sqrt{25-9}}{3}$$

$$= -\dfrac{4}{3}$$

(Negative sign shows that it is in 2nd quadrant)

Now roots of equation,

$$9x^2 + 27x + 20 = 0$$

$$x = \dfrac{-5}{3}, \dfrac{-4}{3}$$

Thus, the trigonometric roots match with the equation roots is,

$$\dfrac{1}{\cos A} = \dfrac{1}{\left(-\dfrac{3}{5}\right)}$$

$$\sec A = -\frac{5}{3}$$

And,

$$\tan A = \frac{-4}{3}$$

Hence, roots are sec A and tan A.

34. Correct Response : (a)

Explanation :

The required diagram is,

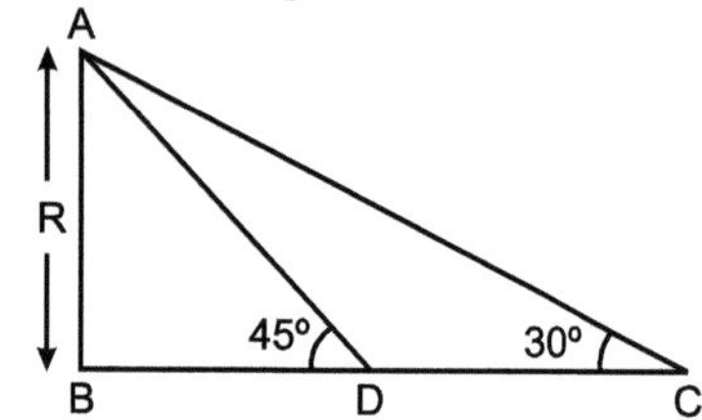

Let length of tower be h.

$$\tan 45° = \frac{AB}{BD}$$

$$BD = AB = h$$

And,

$$BC = AB \cot 30°$$

$$\therefore \qquad BC = \sqrt{3}\, h$$

$$CD = BC - BD = (\sqrt{3} - 1)h$$

Time taken by car to more from C to D = 18 min

Time taken by car to reach the foot of the tower,

$$\frac{18}{\sqrt{3} - 1} = 9(\sqrt{3} + 1) \text{ min}$$

35. Correct Response : (a)

Explanation :

Consider the diagram :

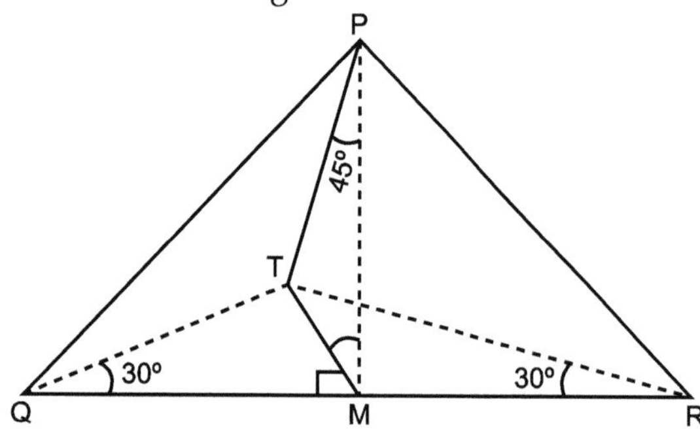

Let height of the tower TM is h so PM is also h.

In ΔTQM,

$$\tan 30° = \frac{h}{QM}$$

$$QM = \sqrt{3}\, h$$

In ΔPMQ,

$$PM^2 + QM^2 = PQ^2$$

$$h^2 + (\sqrt{3}h)^2 = 200^2$$

$$4h^2 = 200^2$$

$$h = 100 \text{ m}$$

36. Correct Response : (b)

Explanation :

Simplify the given equation :

$$8\cos x \cdot \left(\cos\left(\frac{\pi}{6} + x\right) \cdot \cos\left(\frac{\pi}{6} - x\right) - \frac{1}{2} \right) = 1$$

$$8\cos x \cdot \left(\cos^2\frac{\pi}{6} - \sin^2 x - \frac{1}{2} \right) = 1$$

$$8\cos x \cdot \left(\frac{3}{4} - \frac{1}{2} - 1 + \cos^2 x \right) = 1$$

$$8\cos x \cdot \left(-\frac{3}{4} + \frac{4\cos^2 x}{4} \right) = 1$$

Further simplify :

$$8\left(\frac{-3\cos x + 4\cos^3 x}{4} \right) = 1$$

$$\cos 3x = \frac{1}{2}$$

$$3x = \frac{\pi}{3}, \frac{5\pi}{3}, \frac{7\pi}{3}$$

$$x = \frac{\pi}{9}, \frac{5\pi}{9}, \frac{7\pi}{9}$$

The sum is calculated as,

$$\text{sum} = \frac{13\pi}{9}$$

$$k = \frac{13}{9}$$

37. Correct Response : 0.5

Explanation :

$$\sqrt{3}\cos\alpha + \frac{2b}{a}\sin\alpha = \frac{c}{a}$$

$$\sqrt{3}\cos\beta + \frac{2b}{a}\sin\beta = \frac{c}{a}$$

Subtract the above equations,

$$\Rightarrow \quad \sqrt{3}(\cos\alpha - \cos\beta) + \frac{2b}{a}(\sin\alpha - \sin\beta) = 0$$

$$\Rightarrow \quad \sqrt{3}\left(-2\sin\left(\frac{\alpha+\beta}{2}\right)\sin\left(\frac{\alpha-\beta}{2}\right) \right)$$

$$+ \frac{2b}{a}\left(2\cos\left(\frac{\alpha+\beta}{2}\right)\sin\left(\frac{\alpha-\beta}{2}\right) \right) = 0$$

$$\Rightarrow \qquad -\sqrt{3} + 2\sqrt{3}\,\frac{b}{a} = 0$$

$$\Rightarrow \qquad \frac{b}{a} = 0.5$$

38. Correct Response : (a)

Explanation :

Consider the given figure :

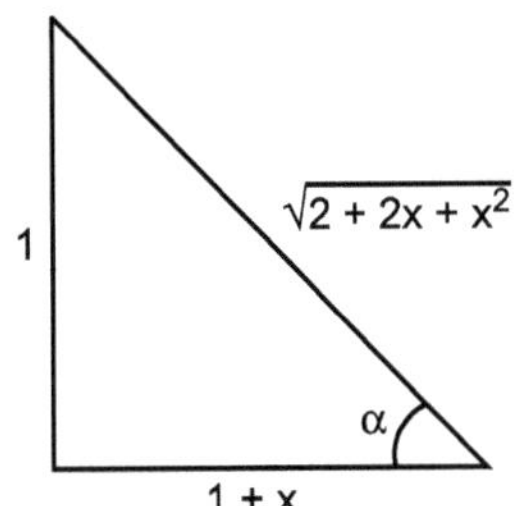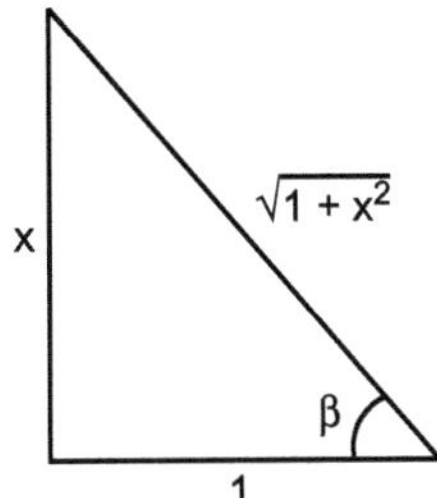

The given equation is,

$$\sin [\cot^{-1} (1 + x)] = \cos [\tan^{-1} x]$$

Simplify the above equation.

$$\sin \alpha = \cos \beta$$

$$\sin\left(\sin^{-1}\left(\frac{1}{\sqrt{(1+x)^2 + 1^2}} \right) \right) = \cos\left[\cos^{-1}\left(\frac{1}{\sqrt{1+x^2}} \right) \right]$$

$$\frac{1}{\sqrt{2 + 2x + x^2}} = \frac{1}{\sqrt{1 + x^2}}$$

Further simplify the above equation.

$$2 + 2x + x^2 = 1 + x^2$$

$$x = -\frac{1}{2}$$

39. Correct Response : (c)

Explanation :

The given equation is,

$$5 \tan^2 x = 9 \cos^2 x + 7$$

$$5 \sec^2 x - 5 = 9 \cos^2 x + 7$$

Let $\cos^2 x$ be taken as t.

$$\frac{5}{t} = 9t + 12$$

$$9t^2 + 12t - 5 = 0$$

$$t = \frac{1}{3}$$

$$\cos^2 x = \frac{1}{3}$$

The value of the consideration is,

$$\cos 4x = 2 \cos^2 2x - 1$$

$$= 2 (2 \cos^2 x - 1)^2 - 1$$

$$= \frac{2}{9} - 1$$

$$= -\frac{7}{9}$$

40. Correct Response : (b)

Explanation :

Consider the diagram.

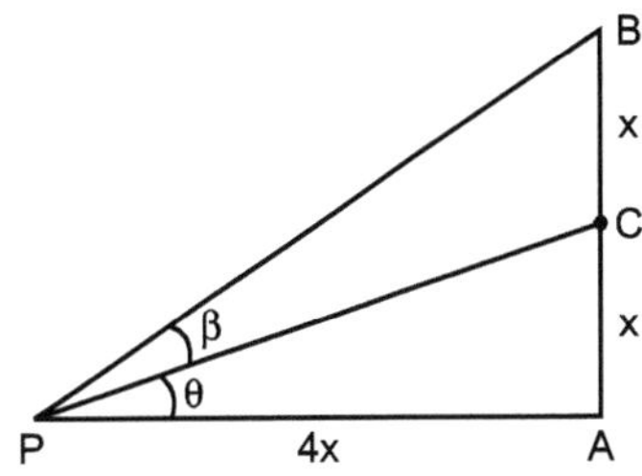

The total angle of view from the level is,

$$\tan (\theta + \beta) = \frac{1}{2}$$

$$\frac{\tan \theta + \tan \beta}{1 - \tan \theta \tan \beta} = \frac{1}{2}$$

$$\frac{\dfrac{1}{4} + \tan \beta}{1 - \left(\dfrac{1}{4}\right) \tan \beta} = \frac{1}{2}$$

$$\tan \beta = \frac{2}{9}$$

41. Correct Response : (a, c)

Explanation :

The given function is :

$$2 (\cos \beta - \cos \alpha) + \cos \alpha \cos \beta = 1$$

$$\cos \beta (2 + \cos \alpha) = 1 + 2 \cos \alpha$$

$$\frac{\cos \beta}{1} = \frac{1 + 2 \cos \alpha}{(2 + \cos \alpha)}$$

$$\frac{\cos \beta + 1}{\cos \beta - 1} = \frac{3(1 + \cos \alpha)}{\cos \alpha - 1}$$

Simplify the above expression.

$$\frac{2 \cos^2\left(\dfrac{\beta}{2}\right)}{-2 \sin^2\left(\dfrac{\beta}{2}\right)} = \frac{3 \times 2 \cos^2\left(\dfrac{\alpha}{2}\right)}{-2 \sin^2\left(\dfrac{\alpha}{2}\right)}$$

$$\tan^2\left(\frac{\alpha}{2}\right) = 3 \tan^2\left(\frac{\beta}{2}\right)$$

$$\tan\left(\frac{\alpha}{2}\right) = \pm \sqrt{3} \tan\left(\frac{\beta}{2}\right)$$

42. Correct Response : (a)

Explanation :

Consider $\quad x^2 = \cos 2A,$

$$A = \frac{1}{2} \cos^{-1} x^2$$

According to question;

$$\tan^{-1}\left[\frac{\sqrt{1+x^2} + \sqrt{1-x^2}}{\sqrt{1+x^2} - \sqrt{1-x^2}} \right]$$

$$= \tan^{-1}\left[\frac{\sqrt{1+\cos 2A}+\sqrt{1-\cos 2A}}{\sqrt{1+\cos 2A}-\sqrt{1-\cos 2A}}\right]$$

$$= \tan^{-1}\left[\frac{\sqrt{1+(2\cos^2 A-1)}+\sqrt{1-(1-2\sin^2 A)}}{\sqrt{1+(2\cos^2 A-1)}-\sqrt{1-(1-2\sin^2 A)}}\right]$$

$$= \tan^{-1}\left[\frac{1+\tan A}{1-\tan A}\right]$$

$$= \tan^{-1}\left\{\tan\left(\frac{\pi}{4}+A\right)\right\}$$

Further simplify the above equation.

$$\tan^{-1}\left[\frac{\sqrt{1+x^2}+\sqrt{1-x^2}}{\sqrt{1+x^2}-\sqrt{1-x^2}}\right] = \frac{\pi}{4}+\frac{1}{2}\cos^{-1}x^2$$

43. Correct Response : (d)

Explanation :

Solve the set P,

$$\sin\theta - \cos\theta = \sqrt{2}\cos\theta$$

$$\sin\theta = \cos\theta\,(\sqrt{2}+1)$$

$$= \cos\theta\left\{(\sqrt{2}+1)\times\frac{(\sqrt{2}-1)}{(\sqrt{2}-1)}\right\}$$

$$(\sqrt{2}-1)\sin\theta = \cos\theta$$

Now, solve the set Q as,

$$\sin\theta + \cos\theta = \sqrt{2}\sin\theta$$

$$\cos\theta = (\sqrt{2}-1)\sin\theta$$

It is clear that both the sets are equal to each other.

44. Correct Response : (d)

Explanation :

The given expression is,

$$\left|\sqrt{2\sin^4 x+18\cos^2 x}-\sqrt{2\cos^4 x+18\sin^2 x}\right| = 1$$

Simplify the above expression,

$$\left|\sqrt{2\sin^4 x+18\cos^2 x}\right| = 1+\left|\sqrt{2\cos^4 x+18\sin^2 x}\right|$$

Squaring both sides of the given equation

$$2\sin^4 x+18\cos^2 x = 1+2\cos^4 x+18\sin^2 x$$

$$+ 2\sqrt{2\cos^4 x+18\sin^2 x}$$

$$2(\sin^4 x-\cos^4 x)+18(\cos^2 x-\sin^2 x)$$

$$= 1+2\sqrt{2\cos^4 x+18\sin^2 x}$$

$$2(\sin^4 x-\cos^4 x)+18(\cos^2 x-\sin^2 x)$$

$$= \sin^2 x+\cos^2 x+2\sqrt{2\cos^4 x+18\sin^2 x}$$

$$2\left(\frac{1-\cos 2x}{2}\right)^2-2\left(\frac{1+\cos 2x}{2}\right)^2+18\cos 2x-1$$

$$= 2\sqrt{2\left(\frac{1+\cos 2x}{2}\right)^2+9(1-\cos 2x)}$$

Further simplify the above equation :

$$\left(\frac{1+\cos^2 2x-2\cos 2x}{-1-\cos^2 2x-2\cos 2x}\right)+36\cos 2x-2$$

$$= 4\sqrt{2\left(\frac{1+\cos 2x}{2}\right)^2+9(1-\cos 2x)}$$

$$-4\cos 2x+36\cos 2x$$

$$= 4\sqrt{2\left(\frac{1+\cos 2x}{2}\right)^2+9(1-\cos 2x)}$$

$$8\cos 2x = \sqrt{2\left(\frac{1+\cos 2x}{2}\right)^2+9(1-\cos 2x)}$$

$$64\cos^2 2x = 2\left(\frac{1+\cos 2x}{2}\right)^2+9(1-\cos 2x)$$

Further simplify the equation :

$$64\cos^2 2x-9+9\cos 2x-\frac{1}{2}\left(1+\cos^2 2x+2\cos 2x\right)$$

$$= 0$$

$$-127\cos^2 2x-19+16\cos 2x = 0$$

$$\cos 2x = \pm\sqrt{\frac{37}{254}} \in[-1,1]$$

Hence, clearly 8 solutions.

45. Correct Response : (c)

Explanation :

The given equation is,

$$\cos x + \cos 2x + \cos 3x + \cos 4x = 0$$

Simplify the given equation,

$$(\cos x + \cos 4x) + (\cos 2x + \cos 3x) = 0$$

$$2\cos\frac{5x}{2}\cos\frac{3x}{2}+2\cos\frac{5x}{2}\cos\frac{x}{2} = 0$$

$$2\cos\frac{5x}{2}\left(\cos\frac{3x}{2}+\cos\frac{x}{2}\right) = 0$$

$$\cos\frac{5x}{2}\cdot\cos x\cdot\cos\frac{x}{2} = 0$$

Further, simplify the above expression,

$$\frac{x}{2} = (2n+1)\frac{\pi}{2}$$

$$x = (2m+1)\frac{\pi}{2}$$

$$\frac{5x}{2} = (2k+1)\frac{\pi}{2}$$

Where $n, m, k \in Z$

$$x = (2n+1)\pi$$

$$x = (2m+1)\frac{\pi}{2}$$

$$x = (2k+1)\frac{\pi}{5}$$

Now the real values of the x within the range $0 \le x \le 2\pi$ for the different value :

$$x = \pi, \frac{\pi}{2}, \frac{3\pi}{2}, \frac{\pi}{5}, \frac{3\pi}{5}, \frac{7\pi}{5}, \frac{9\pi}{5}$$

So, the number of real values of x is 7.

46. Correct Response : (c)

Explanation :

The given equation is,

$$\sqrt{3}\sec x + \cos ec\, x + 2(\tan x - \cot x) = 0$$

Simplify the above equation,

$$\frac{\sqrt{3}}{2}\left(\frac{1}{\cos x}\right) + \frac{1}{2}\left(\frac{1}{\sin x}\right) = -\left(\frac{\sin x}{\cos x} - \frac{\cos x}{\sin x}\right)$$

$$\frac{\sqrt{3}}{2}\sin x + \frac{\cos x}{2} = \cos^2 x - \sin^2 x$$

$$\cos x \cos \frac{\pi}{3} + \sin \frac{\pi}{3}\sin x = \cos 2x$$

$$\cos\left(x - \frac{\pi}{3}\right) = \cos 2x$$

Further, simplify the above equation,
Apply the formula

$$\left[\cos a - \cos b = -2\sin\left(\frac{a+b}{2}\right)\sin\left(\frac{a-b}{2}\right)\right],$$

$$\cos 2x - \cos\left(x - \frac{\pi}{3}\right) = 0$$

$$-2\sin\left(\frac{2x + x - \frac{\pi}{3}}{2}\right)\sin\left(\frac{2x - x + \frac{\pi}{3}}{2}\right) = 0$$

$$\sin\left(\frac{2x + x - \frac{\pi}{3}}{2}\right)\sin\left(\frac{2x - x + \frac{\pi}{3}}{2}\right) = 0$$

Case I

From the above equation,

$$\sin\left(\frac{2x + x - \frac{\pi}{3}}{2}\right) = \sin(n\pi)$$

$$\frac{3x - \frac{\pi}{3}}{2} = n\pi$$

$$3x = 2n\pi + \frac{\pi}{3}$$

$$x = \frac{\pi}{9}, \frac{7\pi}{9}, \frac{-5\pi}{9}$$

Case II

Consider,

$$\sin\left(\frac{2x - x + \frac{\pi}{3}}{2}\right) = \sin(n\pi)$$

$$\frac{x + \frac{\pi}{3}}{2} = n\pi$$

$$x = 2n\pi - \frac{\pi}{3}$$

$$x = -\frac{\pi}{3}$$

Hence, the sum of the distinct roots form A and B is,

$$\frac{-3\pi + \pi + 7\pi - 5\pi}{9} = 0$$

47. Correct Response : (d)

Explanation :

The diagram for the given statements is,

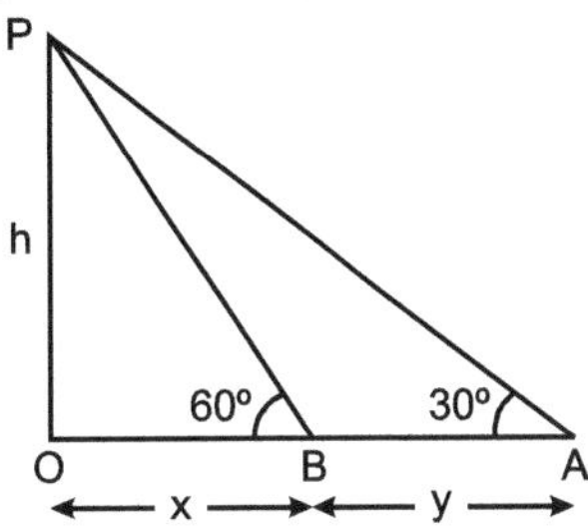

Now,
In $\triangle BOP$,

$$\tan 60° = \frac{h}{x}$$

$$h = \sqrt{3}\,x \qquad \ldots(1)$$

For the $\triangle AOP$,

$$\tan 30° = \frac{h}{x+y}$$

$$\sqrt{3}\,h = x + y \qquad \ldots(2)$$

From the equation (1) and (2),

$$3x = x + y$$

$$2x = y$$

Since speed is uniform and it is given that the time taken from A to B is 10 min.

Hence, time taken from B to pillar is 5 min.

48. Correct Response : (b, c, d)

Explanation :

Draw a right angle triangle by using the given value $\alpha = 3\sin^{-1}\left(\frac{6}{11}\right)$,

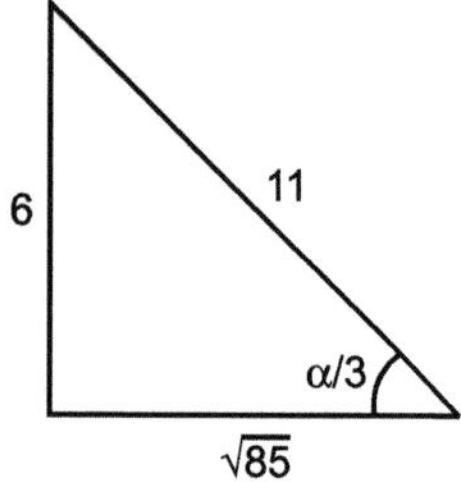

From the above diagram,

$$\frac{\alpha}{3} = \tan^{-1}\frac{6}{\sqrt{85}}$$

Consider a relation,

$$\frac{1}{\sqrt{3}} < \frac{6}{\sqrt{85}} < 1$$

Take $(\tan^{-1})$ of the above relation,

$$\tan^{-1}\left(\frac{1}{\sqrt{3}}\right) < \tan^{-1}\left(\frac{6}{\sqrt{85}}\right) < \tan^{-1}(1)$$

$$30° < \frac{\alpha}{3} < 45°$$

$$90° < \alpha < 135°$$

Hence, $\cos\alpha < 0$ (option (d) is correct).

Draw the right angle triangle for $\beta = 3\cos^{-1}\left(\frac{4}{9}\right)$,

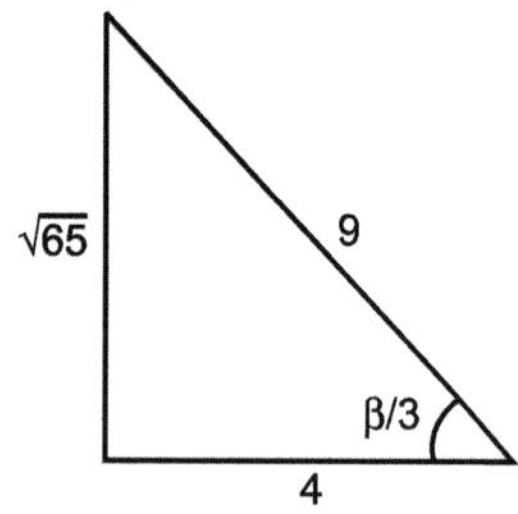

From the above triangle,

$$\frac{\beta}{3} = \tan^{-1}\frac{\sqrt{65}}{4}$$

Consider a relation,

$$\sqrt{3} > \frac{\sqrt{65}}{4} < 1$$

Therefore,

$$60° < \frac{\beta}{3} < 90°$$

$$\therefore\ 180° < \beta < 270°$$

$$\therefore\ \cos\beta < 0,\ \sin\beta < 0$$

So, option (a) is incorrect and option (b) is correct.

$$(30° + 60°) < \frac{\alpha+\beta}{3} < (45° + 90°)$$

$$270° < (\alpha + \beta) < 405°$$

Here, $(\alpha + \beta)$ will be lie in 4th quadrant.

So, $\cos(\alpha + \beta) > 0$

Hence, option (c) is correct.

49. Correct Respose : (a)

Explanation :

Consider the following figure.

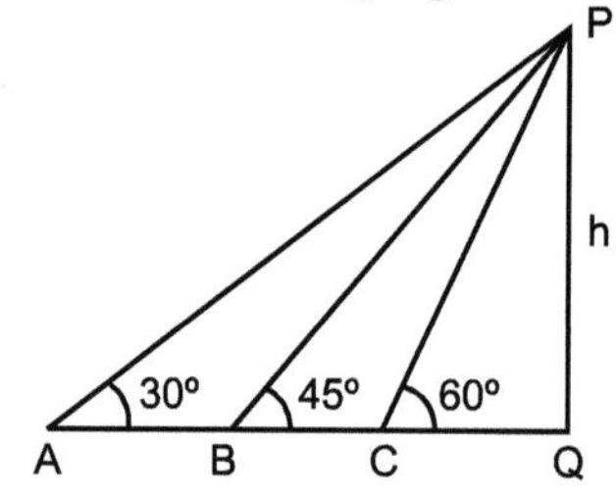

From $\triangle APQ$,

$$\tan 30° = \frac{h}{AQ}$$

$$\frac{1}{\sqrt{3}} = \frac{h}{AQ}$$

$$AQ = \sqrt{3}\,h$$

Similarly, in $\triangle BPQ$

$$\tan 45° = \frac{h}{BQ}$$

$$BQ = h$$

In $\triangle PCQ$,

$$CQ = \frac{h}{\sqrt{3}}$$

The ratio of AB and BC is,

$$\frac{AB}{BC} = \frac{AQ - BQ}{BQ - CQ}$$

$$= \frac{(\sqrt{3}-1)h}{\left(1 - \frac{1}{\sqrt{3}}\right)h}$$

$$= \sqrt{3}$$

50. Correct Response : 8

Explanation :

The given equation is,

$$\frac{5}{4}\cos^2 2x + \cos^4 x + \sin^4 x + \cos^6 x + \sin^6 x = 2$$

Simplify the given equation,

$$\Rightarrow \frac{5}{4}\cos^2 2x + \{\cos^4 x + \sin^4 x\} + \cos^6 x + \sin^6 x = 2$$

$$\Rightarrow \frac{5}{4}\cos^2 2x + \{(\cos^2 x + \sin^2 x)^2 - 2\cos^2 x \sin^2 x\}$$

$$+ (\cos^6 x + \sin^6 x) = 2$$

$$\Rightarrow \frac{5}{4}\cos^2 2x + \left(1 - \frac{\sin^2 2x}{2}\right) + \left(1 - \frac{3}{4}\sin^2 2x\right) = 2$$

$$\frac{5}{4}\cos^2 2x - \frac{5}{4}\sin^2 2x = 0$$

Further, simplify the above relation,

$$\frac{5}{4}\cos 4x = 0$$

$$\cos 4x = 0$$

Hence, the number of solution is 8.

51. Correct Response : (a)-(P, R, S), (b)-(P); (c)-(P, Q), (d)- (S, T)

Explanation :

(a)-(P, R, S)

The given relation is,

$$2(a^2 - b^2) = c^2$$

$$2(\sin^2 X - \sin^2 Y) = \sin^2 (Z)$$

$$2 \sin (X - Y) \sin (X + Y) = \sin^2 (Z)$$

$$\frac{\sin(X-Y)}{\sin(Z)} = \frac{1}{2} \quad [\because \sin (X+Y) = \sin Z]$$

Given that,

$$\frac{\sin(X-Y)}{\sin(Z)} = \lambda$$

$$\lambda = \frac{1}{2}$$

$$\therefore \cos\left(\frac{n\pi}{2}\right) = 0 \text{ for } n = 1, 3 \text{ and } 5$$

(b) - (P)

The given expression is,

$$1 + \cos (2X) - 2 \cos (2Y) = 2 \sin (X) \sin (Y)$$

$$1 + 1 - 2\sin^2 (X) - 2 (1 - 2 \sin^2 (Y)) = 2 \sin (X) \sin (Y)$$

$$2 - \frac{\sin^2 (X)}{\sin^2 (Y)} = \frac{\sin(X)}{\sin(Y)}$$

Let,

$$\frac{\sin(X)}{\sin(Y)} = \frac{a}{b} = k$$

Then the value of the k is,

$$2 - k^2 = k$$

$$k = 1, -2$$

(c) - (P, Q)

Draw the point on the XY plane is,

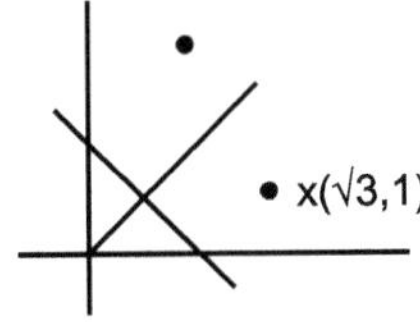

Here, Z lies on the line $x + y = 1$.

Angle bisector is $x - y = 0$.

Let $Z \equiv (\beta, 1 - \beta)$

Then,

$$\left|\frac{\beta - (1-\beta)}{\sqrt{2}}\right| = \frac{3}{\sqrt{2}}$$

$$|\beta| = 1, 2$$

(d) - (S, T)

Draw the bounded curve as per given equations,

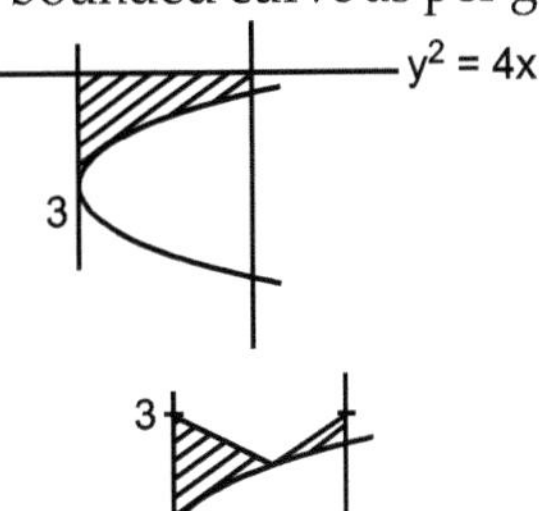

For $\alpha = 0$, $y = 3$,

$$f(0) = \int_0^2 3 - 2\sqrt{x}\, dx$$

$$= 6 - \frac{8\sqrt{2}}{3}$$

$$f(0) + \frac{8\sqrt{2}}{3} = 6$$

For $\alpha = 1$,

$$y = |x - 1| + |x - 2| + x$$

$$f(1) = \int_0^1 3 - x - 2\sqrt{x}\, dx + \int_1^2 x - 1 - 2\sqrt{x}\, dx$$

$$5 - \frac{8\sqrt{2}}{3} = f(1) + \frac{8\sqrt{2}}{3}$$

52. Correct Response : (b)

Explanation :

The given equation is,

$$(\sin^{-1} x)^3 + (\cos^{-1} x)^3 - a\pi^3 = 0$$

$$(\sin^{-1} x)^3 + (\cos^{-1} x)^3 = a\pi^3$$

$$(\sin^{-1} x + \cos^{-1} x)^3 - 3 \sin^{-1} x \cos^{-1} x$$

$$(\sin^{-1} x + \cos^{-1} x) = a\pi^3$$

$$\left(\frac{\pi}{2}\right)^3 - 3\left(\frac{\pi}{2} - \cos^{-1} x\right)\cos^{-1} x\left(\frac{\pi}{2}\right) = a\pi^3$$

Further solve the above equation.

$$\frac{\pi^3}{8} - \frac{3\pi^2}{4}\cos^{-1} x + \frac{3\pi}{2}(\cos^{-1} x)^2 = a\pi^3$$

$$\frac{3\pi}{2}\left[(\cos^{-1} x)^2 - \frac{\pi}{2}\cos^{-1} x\right] + \frac{\pi^3}{8} = a\pi^3$$

$$\frac{3\pi}{2}\left[\left(\cos^{-1} x - \frac{\pi}{4}\right)^2 - \frac{\pi^2}{16}\right] + \frac{\pi^3}{8} = a\pi^3$$

$$\left(\cos^{-1} x - \frac{\pi}{4}\right)^2 = \left(\frac{2a}{3} - \frac{1}{48}\right)\pi^2$$

Since, the value of $\cos^{-1} x$ lies,

$$0 \le \cos^{-1} x \le \pi$$

$$-\frac{\pi}{4} \le \left(\cos^{-1} x - \frac{\pi}{4}\right) \le \frac{3\pi}{4}$$

$$0 \le \left(\cos^{-1} x - \frac{\pi}{4}\right)^2 \le \frac{9\pi^2}{16}$$

So, statement I is false.

For statement II, the given equation is not applicable for any $x \in$ R. So, statement II is false.

53. Correct Response : (b)

Explanation :

The given expression is,

$$\left|\cot\left(\frac{\pi}{4}+\frac{\theta}{2}\right)\right|$$

Simplify the given expression,

$$\left|\cot\left(\frac{\pi}{4}+\frac{\theta}{2}\right)\right| = \left|\frac{1-\tan\frac{\theta}{2}}{1+\tan\frac{\theta}{2}}\right|$$

$$= \frac{\cos\frac{\theta}{2}-\sin\frac{\theta}{2}}{\cos\frac{\theta}{2}+\sin\frac{\theta}{2}} \times \frac{\cos\frac{\theta}{2}-\sin\frac{\theta}{2}}{\cos\frac{\theta}{2}-\sin\frac{\theta}{2}}$$

$$= \frac{\cos^2\frac{\theta}{2}+\sin^2\frac{\theta}{2}-2\cos\frac{\theta}{2}\sin\frac{\theta}{2}}{\cos\theta}$$

$$= \frac{1-\sin\theta}{\cos\theta}$$

Further, simplify the expression,

$$\frac{1-\sin\theta}{\cos\theta} = \frac{1-\dfrac{p-q}{p+q}}{\sqrt{1-\left(\dfrac{p-q}{p+q}\right)^2}}$$

$$= \frac{\sqrt{q}}{\sqrt{p}}$$

54. Correct Response : (c)

Explanation :

The given function is,

$$f(x) = |\sin 4x| + |\cos 2x|$$

Period of $\sin 4x$ is $\dfrac{\pi}{4}$ and $\cos 2x$ is $\dfrac{\pi}{2}$.

Hence, the period of the function is $\dfrac{\pi}{2}$.

55. Correct Response : (c)

Explanation :

Simplify the given function :

$$\tan^{-1}\left(\cot\frac{43\pi}{4}\right) = \tan^{-1}\left(\cot\left(11\pi-\frac{\pi}{4}\right)\right)$$

$$= \tan^{-1}\left(-\cot\frac{\pi}{4}\right)$$

$$= -\tan^{-1}\left(\cot\frac{\pi}{4}\right)$$

$$= -\tan^{-1} 1$$

$$= -\frac{\pi}{4}$$

56. Correct Response : (b)

Explanation :

The given trigonometric relation is,

$$2\cos\theta + \sin\theta = 1 \qquad \text{...(1)}$$

Consider the value of relation as k,

$$7\cos\theta + 6\sin\theta = k \qquad \text{...(2)}$$

From the equation (1) and (2),

$$\cos\theta = \frac{6-k}{5},$$

$$\sin\theta = \frac{2k-7}{5}$$

From the result of the above expression,

$$\cos^2\theta + \sin^2\theta = 1$$

$$\frac{(6-k)^2}{25} + \frac{(2k-7)^2}{25} = 1$$

$$(6-k)^2 + (2k-7)^2 = 25$$

$$36 + k^2 - 12k + 4k^2 + 49 - 28k = 25$$

Further simplify the above expression,

$$5k^2 - 40k + 60 = 0$$

$$k = 2, 6$$

57. Correct Response : (a)

Explanation :

The diagram of the tower as shown below,

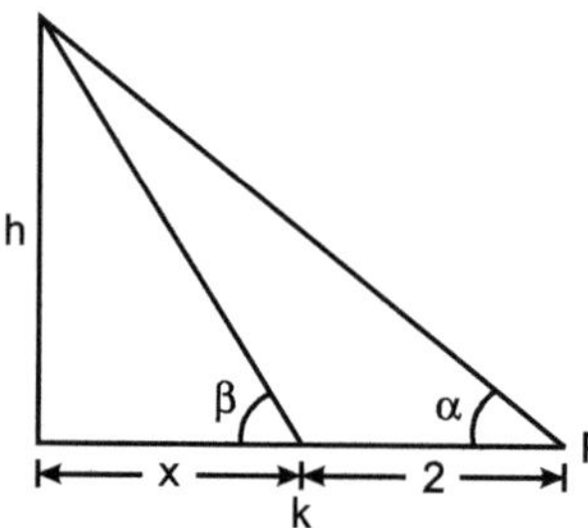

The relation of angle from diagram of figure (1),

$$\therefore \qquad \tan\alpha = \frac{h}{x+2}$$

$$\tan\beta = \frac{h}{x}$$

Further solve the above expression,

$$x\tan\alpha + 2\tan\alpha = h$$

$$h\frac{\tan\alpha}{\tan\beta} + 2\tan\alpha = h$$

$$h = \frac{2\sin\alpha\sin\beta}{\sin(\beta-\alpha)}$$

58. Correct Response : (d)

Explanation :

The given equation is,

$$\sin x + \sin 2x - \sin 3x = 3$$

Simplify the above equation.

$$\sin x\,(1 + 2\cos x - 3 + 4\sin^2 x) = 3$$

$$2 - 4\cos^2 x + 2\cos x = \frac{3}{\sin x}$$

$$\frac{9}{4} - \left(2\cos x - \frac{1}{2}\right)^2 = \frac{3}{\sin x}$$

From the result of the above expression,

$$\text{L.H.S.} \le \frac{9}{4}$$

$$\text{R.H.S.} \ge 3$$

Hence, the equation has no solution.

59. Correct Response : (b)

Explanation :

The diagram is represented as,

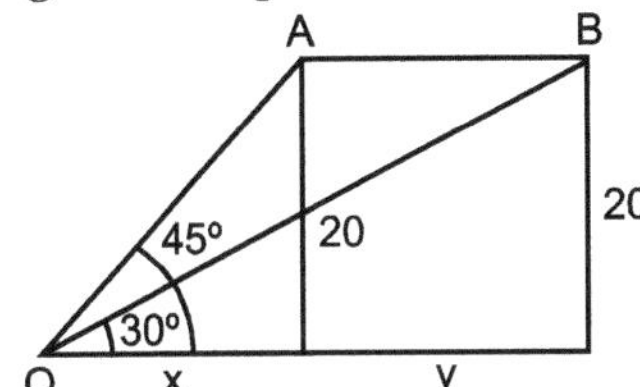

From the figure,

$$\tan 45° = \frac{20}{x}$$

$$x = 20$$

And,

$$\tan 30° = \frac{20}{x+y}$$

$$20 + y = 20\sqrt{3} \qquad [x = 20]$$

$$y = 20\,(\sqrt{3} - 1)$$

So, the speed will be,

$$\text{Speed} = \frac{\text{Distance}}{\text{Time}}$$

$$S = \frac{y}{t}$$

$$= \frac{20\,(\sqrt{3} - 1)}{1}$$

$$= 20\,(\sqrt{3} - 1)\ \text{m/s}$$

60. Correct Response : (b)

Explanation :

Consider the diagram :

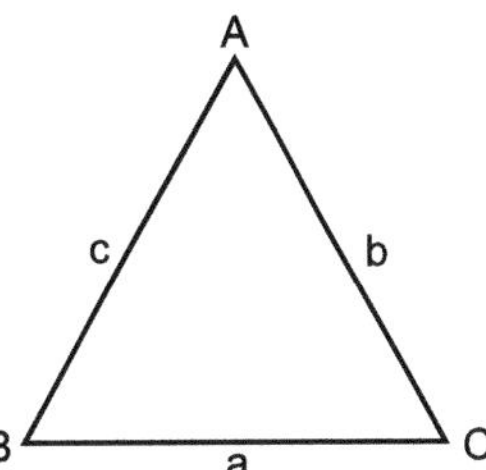

Consider the two sides of the triangle is a and b respectively.

The sum of two sides of the triangle is given by,

$$a + b = x$$

The product of the two sides of the triangle is given by,

$$ab = y$$

The relation of the third side of the triangle is given by,

$$x^2 - c^2 = y$$

Substitute the value of $a + b$ for x and ab for y in the above equation,

$$(a + b)^2 - c^2 = ab$$

$$a^2 + b^2 - c^2 = -ab$$

$$\frac{a^2 + b^2 - c^2}{2ab} = -\frac{1}{2}$$

$$\cos C = -\frac{1}{2}$$

Further solve the above expression for the value of the angle C,

$$C = \frac{2\pi}{3}$$

The ratio of the in-radius to the circum radius of the circle is given by,

$$\frac{r}{R} = \frac{\Delta \times 4\Delta}{s \times abc}$$

$$= \frac{4 \times \dfrac{1}{4} a^2 b^2 c^2 \sin^2 C}{(a+b+c)\,abc}$$

$$= \frac{3ab}{4c\,(x+c)}$$

$$= \frac{3y}{4c\,(x+c)}$$

61. Correct Response : (c)

Explanation :

The given expression is,

$$2\sin^3 \alpha - 7\sin^2 \alpha + 7\sin \alpha = 2$$

Simplify the given expression,

$$2\sin^3 \alpha - 7\sin^2 \alpha + 7\sin \alpha = 2$$

$$\Rightarrow \qquad 2\sin^3 \alpha - 2 = 7\sin^2 \alpha - 7\sin \alpha$$

$$\Rightarrow 2\,(\sin \alpha - 1)(\sin^2 \alpha + 1 + \sin \alpha)$$

$$= 7\sin \alpha\,(\sin \alpha - 1)$$

$$\Rightarrow (\sin\alpha - 1)\left(\sin^2\alpha + 1 + \sin\alpha - \frac{7}{2}\sin\alpha\right) = 0$$

Further, simplify the given expression,

$$\sin\alpha = 1 \text{ or } \sin\alpha = \frac{1}{2}, -2 \ (\sin\alpha \neq -2)$$

Draw the sine curve :

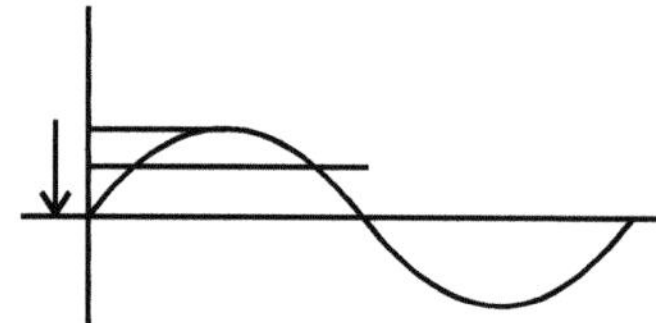

Hence, the number of solutions is 3.

62. **Correct Response :** (b)
Explanation :
The given expression is,

$$\cot\left(\sum_{n=1}^{23}\cot^{-1}\left(1+\sum_{k=1}^{n}2k\right)\right)$$

$$= \cot\left(\sum_{n=1}^{23}\cot^{-1}\left(1+k(k+1)\right)\right)$$

$$= \cot\left(\sum_{n=1}^{23}\tan^{-1}(k+1)-\tan^{-1}k\right)$$

$$= \cot(\tan^{-1}24 - \tan^{-1}1)$$

Simplify above value.

$$\cot(\tan^{-1}24 - \tan^{-1}1)$$

$$= \cot\left(\tan^{-1}\left(\frac{24-1}{1+24(1)}\right)\right)$$

$$= \cot\left(\tan^{-1}\left(\frac{23}{25}\right)\right)$$

$$= \frac{25}{23}$$

63. **Correct Response :** (b)
Explanation :
P.
Simplify the given expression.

$$\left[\frac{1}{y^2}\left(\frac{\cos\left(\tan^{-1}y\right)+y\sin\left(\tan^{-1}y\right)}{\cot\left(\sin^{-1}y\right)+\tan\left(\sin^{-1}y\right)}\right)+y^4\right]^{1/2}$$

$$= \left[\frac{1}{y^2}\left(\frac{\dfrac{1}{\sqrt{1+y^2}}+\dfrac{y^2}{\sqrt{1+y^2}}}{\dfrac{\sqrt{1-y^2}}{y}+\dfrac{y}{\sqrt{1-y^2}}}\right)+y^4\right]^{1/2}$$

$$= \left[\frac{1}{y^2}\left(\frac{y\sqrt{1+y^2}\sqrt{1-y^2}}{1}\right)^2+y^4\right]^{1/2}$$

$$= [\,1 - y^4 + y^4\,]^{1/2}$$
$$= 1$$

Q.
It is given that $\cos x + \cos y + \cos z = 0$.

$$\cos x + \cos y = -\cos z \qquad \text{...(1)}$$

Also, it is given that $\sin x + \sin y + \sin z = 0$.

$$\sin x + \sin y = -\sin z \qquad \text{...(2)}$$

Square and add equation (1) with equation (2).

$$1 + 1 + 2(\cos x \cos y + \sin x \sin y) = 1$$

$$2 + 2\cos(x-y) = 1$$

$$\cos(x-y) = -\frac{1}{2}$$

Further solve,

$$2\cos^2\left(\frac{x-y}{2}\right) - 1 = -\frac{1}{2}$$

$$2\cos^2\left(\frac{x-y}{2}\right) = \frac{1}{2}$$

R.
Solve the given equation.

$$\cos\left(\frac{\pi}{4}-x\right)\cos 2x + \sin x \sin 2x \sec x$$

$$= \cos x \sin 2x \sec x + \cos\left(\frac{\pi}{4}+x\right)\cos 2x$$

$$\cos 2x\left[\cos\left(\frac{\pi}{4}-x\right)-\cos\left(\frac{\pi}{4}+x\right)\right]$$

$$= \sin 2x(1-\tan x)$$

$$\cos 2x \cdot 2\sin\frac{\pi}{4}\cdot\sin x = \sin 2x(1-\tan x)$$

$$\frac{1}{\sqrt{2}}\cos 2x = \cos x - \sin x$$

Further solve above equation.

$$\frac{1}{\sqrt{2}}(\cos x + \sin x) = 1$$

$$x = \frac{\pi}{4}$$

Now, the value of $\sec x$ is,

$$\sec x = \sec\frac{\pi}{4}$$

$$= \sqrt{2}$$

S.
Solve the given equation.

$$\cot(\sin^{-1}\sqrt{1-x^2}) = \sin(\tan^{-1}(x\sqrt{6}))$$

$$\frac{x}{\sqrt{1-x^2}} = \frac{\sqrt{6}x}{\sqrt{1+6x^2}}$$

$$1 + 6x^2 = 6 - 6x^2$$

$$x = \pm\frac{1}{2}\sqrt{\frac{5}{3}}$$

64. Correct Response : (a or b)

Explanation :

The given function is,

$$f(\cos 4\theta) = \frac{2}{2 - \sec^2 \theta}$$

$$= \frac{1 + \cos 2\theta}{\cos 2\theta}$$

$$= \frac{1}{\cos 2\theta} + 1 \qquad ...(1)$$

Let,

$$\cos 4\theta = \frac{1}{3}$$

$$2\cos^2 2\theta - 1 = \frac{1}{3}$$

$$\cos 2\theta = \pm \sqrt{\frac{2}{3}}$$

From equation (1), the value of $f\left(\dfrac{1}{3}\right)$ is,

$$f\left(\frac{1}{3}\right) = \frac{1}{\pm \sqrt{\dfrac{2}{3}}} + 1$$

$$= 1 \pm \sqrt{\frac{3}{2}}$$

Function must have only one value. Two values are not possible.

65. Correct Response : (c)

Explanation :

Let, Δ be the area of the triangle

The figure shows the triangle PQR.

The perimeter of the triangle is,

$$s = \frac{a + b + c}{2}$$

$$= \frac{2 + \dfrac{7}{2} + \dfrac{5}{2}}{2}$$

$$= 4$$

The value of term is,

$$\frac{2\sin P - \sin 2P}{2\sin P + \sin 2P} = \frac{2\sin P - 2\sin P \cos P}{2\sin P + 2\sin P \cos P}$$

$$= \frac{1 - \cos P}{1 + \cos P}$$

$$= \tan^2\left(\frac{P}{2}\right)$$

$$= \left\{ \sqrt{\frac{(s-b)(s-c)}{s(s-a)}} \right\}^2$$

Further solve the above expression.

$$\frac{2\sin P - \sin 2P}{2\sin P + \sin 2P} = \frac{(s-b)(s-c)}{s(s-a)}$$

$$= \frac{(s-b)^2 (s-c)^2}{\Delta^2}$$

$$= \frac{\left(4 - \dfrac{7}{2}\right)^2 \left(4 - \dfrac{5}{2}\right)^2}{\Delta^2}$$

$$= \left(\frac{3}{4\Delta}\right)^2$$

66. Correct Response : (c)

Explanation :

The given function is,

$$f(x) = (1 - x)^2 \sin^2 x + x^2$$

$$f(x) + 2x = \{(1 - x)^2 \sin^2 x + x^2\} + 2x$$

$$(1 - x)^2 \sin^2 x + x^2 + 2x = 2 + 2x^2$$

$$(1 - x)^2 \sin^2 x = x^2 - 2x + 1 + 1$$

Further solve the above expression.

$$(1 - x)^2 \sin^2 x = (1 - x)^2 + 1$$

$$(1 - x)^2 (1 - \cos^2 x) = (1 - x)^2 + 1$$

$$(1 - x)^2 \cos^2 x = -1$$

It is not possible.

Statement **P** is false.

Let,

$$g(x) = 2f(x) + 1 - 2x(1 + x).$$

At $x = 0$,

$$g(0) = 2f(0) + 1 - 2(0)(1 + 0)$$

$$= 1$$

At $x = 1$,

$$g(1) = 2f(1) + 1 - 2(1)(1 + 1)$$

$$= 1 - 4$$

$$= -3$$

The function $g(x)$ exists. Statement **Q** is true.

Therefore, the statement **P** is false and **Q** is true.

67. Correct Response : (d)

Explanation :

For given set P.

$$\sin\theta - \cos\theta = \sqrt{2}\cos\theta$$

$$\sin\theta = \sqrt{2}\cos\theta + \cos\theta$$

$$\sin\theta = (\sqrt{2} + 1)\cos\theta$$

For given set Q.

$$\sin\theta + \cos\theta = \sqrt{2}\sin\theta$$

$$\sqrt{2}\sin\theta - \sin\theta = \cos\theta$$

$$(\sqrt{2} - 1)\sin\theta = \cos\theta$$

Multiply both sides by $(\sqrt{2}+1)$.

$$(\sqrt{2}+1)(\sqrt{2}-1)\sin\theta = (\sqrt{2}+1)\cos\theta$$

$$(2-1)\sin\theta = (\sqrt{2}+1)\cos\theta$$

$$\sin\theta = (\sqrt{2}+1)\cos\theta$$

Therefore, $P = Q$.

68. Correct Response : (7)

Explanation :

Solve the given equation.

$$\frac{1}{\sin\left(\dfrac{\pi}{n}\right)} = \frac{1}{\sin\left(\dfrac{2\pi}{n}\right)} + \frac{1}{\sin\left(\dfrac{3\pi}{n}\right)}$$

$$\sin\left(\frac{2\pi}{n}\right)\sin\left(\frac{3\pi}{n}\right) = \sin\left(\frac{\pi}{n}\right)\sin\left(\frac{3\pi}{n}\right)$$

$$+\sin\left(\frac{\pi}{n}\right)\sin\left(\frac{2\pi}{n}\right)$$

$$\sin\left(\frac{2\pi}{n}\right)\left[\sin\left(\frac{3\pi}{n}\right)-\sin\left(\frac{\pi}{n}\right)\right] = \sin\left(\frac{\pi}{n}\right)\sin\left(\frac{3\pi}{n}\right)$$

$$\sin\left(\frac{2\pi}{n}\right)\times 2\cos\left(\frac{2\pi}{n}\right)\sin\left(\frac{\pi}{n}\right) = \sin\left(\frac{\pi}{n}\right)\sin\left(\frac{3\pi}{n}\right)$$

Further simplify above equation.

$$\sin\left(\frac{4\pi}{n}\right)\sin\left(\frac{\pi}{n}\right) = \sin\left(\frac{\pi}{n}\right)\sin\left(\frac{3\pi}{n}\right)$$

$$\sin\left(\frac{4\pi}{n}\right) = \sin\left(\frac{3\pi}{n}\right)$$

For integer $n = 7$ above equation is true.

69. Explanation :

Correct Response : 1

The given function is,

$$f(\theta) = \sin\left(\tan^{-1}\left(\frac{\sin\theta}{\sqrt{\cos 2\theta}}\right)\right)$$

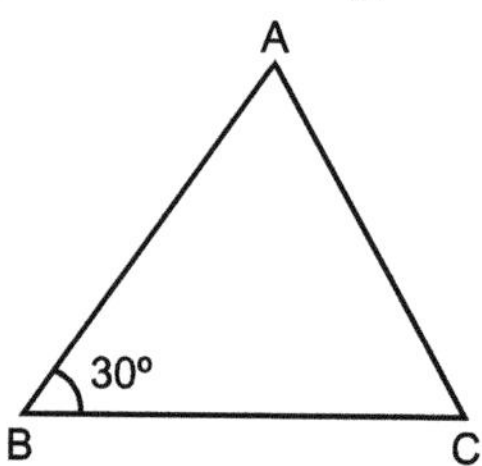

Now, the function can be

$$f(\theta) = \sin\left(\sin^{-1}\left(\frac{\sin\theta}{|\cos\theta|}\right)\right)$$

$$= \sin\left(\sin^{-1}\left(\tan\theta\right)\right)$$

$$= \tan\theta$$

Therefore,

$$\frac{d}{d(\tan\theta)}f(\theta) = \frac{d}{d(\tan\theta)}\tan\theta$$

$$= 1$$

70. Correct Response : (c, d)

Explanation :

The given expression is,

$$\sum_{m=1}^{6}\operatorname{cosec}\left(\theta+\frac{(m-1)\pi}{4}\right)\operatorname{cosec}\left(\theta+\frac{(m)\pi}{4}\right) = 4\sqrt{2}$$

Simplify the above equation.

$$\sum_{m=1}^{6}\frac{1}{\sin\left(\theta+\dfrac{(m-1)\pi}{4}\right)\sin\left(\theta+\dfrac{(m)\pi}{4}\right)} = 4\sqrt{2}$$

$$\sum_{m=1}^{6}\frac{\sin\left[\theta+\dfrac{m\pi}{4}-\left(\theta+\dfrac{(m-1)\pi}{4}\right)\right]}{\sin\dfrac{\pi}{4}\left(\sin\left(\theta+\dfrac{(m-1)\pi}{4}\right)\right)\sin\left(\theta+\dfrac{(m)\pi}{4}\right)}$$

$$= 4\sqrt{2}$$

$$\sum_{m=1}^{6}\frac{\left[\cot\left(\theta+\dfrac{(m-1)\pi}{4}\right)-\cot\left(\theta+\dfrac{(m)\pi}{4}\right)\right]}{1\sqrt{2}} = 4\sqrt{2}$$

Simplify the above equation.

$$\sum_{m=1}^{6}\cot\left(\theta+\frac{(m-1)\pi}{4}\right)-\cot\left(\theta+\frac{(m)\pi}{4}\right) = 4$$

Expand the above equation.

$$\left[\cot\theta-\cot\left(\theta+\frac{\pi}{4}\right)+\cot\left(\theta+\frac{\pi}{4}\right)-\cot\left(\theta+\frac{\pi}{2}\right)\right.$$

$$\left.+...+\cot\left(\theta+\frac{5\pi}{4}\right)-\cot\left(\theta+\frac{3\pi}{2}\right)\right] = 4$$

$$\tan^2\theta - 4\tan\theta + 1 = 0$$

The roots of $\tan\theta$ is,

$$\tan\theta = 2\pm\sqrt{3}$$

$$\theta = \frac{\pi}{12}\ \text{or}\ \frac{5\pi}{12}$$

71. Correct Answer : (4)

Explanation :

The triangle ABC with angle $B = 30°$ is,

Use cosine rule,

$$b^2 = a^2 + c^2 - 2ac \cos B.$$

Hence,

$$\cos B = \frac{a^2 + 16 - 8}{2 \times a \times 4}$$

Substitute $B = 30°$ in the above equation.

$$\frac{\sqrt{3}}{2} = \frac{a^2 + 8}{8a}$$

$$a^2 - 4\sqrt{3}a + 8 = 0$$

In the above quadratic equation,

$$a_1 + a_2 = 4\sqrt{3}$$

And,

$$a_1 a_2 = 8.$$

The value of $|a_1 - a_2| = 4$.

The absolute value of the difference between the areas of given triangle is,

$$|\Delta_1 - \Delta_2| = \frac{1}{2} \times 4 \sin 30° \times 4$$

$$= 4$$

72. **Correct Response :** (c)

Explanation :

Simplify given expression.

$$\sqrt{1+x^2}\left[\left\{\begin{matrix} x\cos\left(\cot^{-1}x\right) \\ +\sin\left(\cot^{-1}x\right) \end{matrix}\right\}^2 - 1\right]^{1/2}$$

$$= \sqrt{1+x^2}\left[\left\{\begin{matrix} x\cos\left(\cos^{-1}\dfrac{x}{\sqrt{1+x^2}}\right) \\ +\sin\left(\sin^{-1}\dfrac{1}{\sqrt{1+x^2}}\right) \end{matrix}\right\}^2 - 1\right]^{1/2}$$

$$= \sqrt{1+x^2}\left[\left(\frac{x^2}{\sqrt{1+x^2}} + \frac{1}{\sqrt{1+x^2}}\right)^2 - 1\right]^{1/2}$$

$$= \sqrt{1+x^2}\,(x^2 + 1 - 1)^{1/2}$$

$$= x\sqrt{1+x^2}$$

73. **Correct Response :** (c)

Explanation :

Solve the first equation.

$$2\sin^2\theta - \cos 2\theta = 0$$

$$2\sin^2\theta - 1 + 2\sin^2\theta = 0$$

$$\sin^2\theta = \frac{1}{4}$$

$$\sin\theta = \pm\frac{1}{2}$$

Solve the second equation.

$$2\cos^2\theta - 3\sin\theta = 0$$

$$2 - 2\sin^2 - 3\sin\theta = 0$$

$$\sin\theta = \frac{1}{2}$$

The number of solutions of given pair of equations in the interval $[0, 2\pi]$ is two.

74. **Correct Response :** (a)

Explanation :

Solve the given inequality for interval.

$$2\sin^2\theta - 5\sin\theta + 2 > 0$$

$$(\sin\theta - 2)(2\sin\theta - 1) > 0$$

$$\sin\theta < \frac{1}{2}$$

Therefore, the interval for values of θ is

$$\left(0, \frac{\pi}{6}\right) \cup \left(\frac{5\pi}{6}, 2\pi\right).$$

75. **Correct Response :** (a), (b), (c), (d))

Explanation :

According to the given condition,

$$\Delta ABC = \Delta ABD + \Delta ACD$$

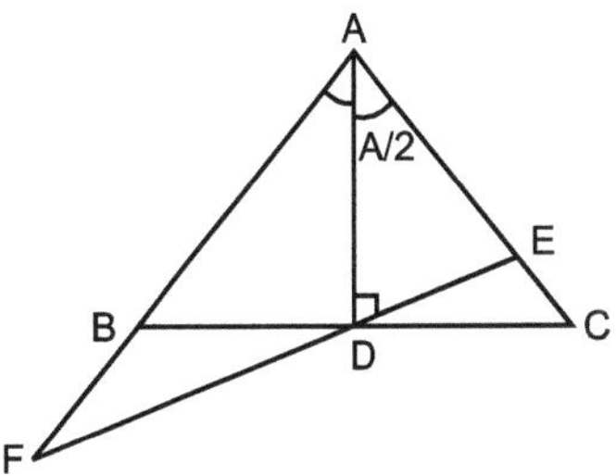

Now,

$$\frac{1}{2}bc\sin A = \frac{1}{2}c\,(AD)\sin\frac{A}{2} + \frac{1}{2}b\,(AD)\sin\frac{A}{2}$$

$$AD = \frac{2bc}{b+c}\cos\frac{A}{2}$$

Also,

$$AE = AD\sec\frac{A}{2}.$$

$$AE = \frac{2bc}{b+c}\cos\frac{A}{2}\sec\frac{A}{2}$$

$$= \frac{2bc}{b+c}$$

So, AE is harmonic mean of b and c.

From triangle,

$$EF = ED + DF.$$

$$EF = 2DE$$

$$= 2 \times AD\tan\frac{A}{2}$$

$$= \frac{2 \times 2bc}{b+c} \times \cos \frac{A}{2} \times \tan \frac{A}{2}$$

$$= \frac{4bc}{b+c} \sin \frac{A}{2}$$

It is known that AD is perpendicular to EF, DE = DF and AD is bisector. Thus, triangle AEF is isosceles.

Therefore, all options (a), (b), (c), (d) are correct.

76. Correct Response : (a)-(p), (b)-(q), (c)-(p), (d)-(s)

Explanation :

The given equation is,

$$\sin^{-1}(ax) + \cos^{-1}(y) + \cos^{-1}(bxy) = \frac{\pi}{2}$$

(a) If $a = 1$ and $b = 0$, then

$$\sin^{-1} x + \cos^{-1} y = 0$$
$$\sin^{-1} x = -\cos^{-1} y$$
$$x^2 + y^2 = 1$$

Thus, (x, y) lies on the circle.

(b) If $a = 1$ and $b = 1$, then

$$\sin^{-1} x + \cos^{-1} y + \cos^{-1} xy = \frac{\pi}{2}$$

$$\cos^{-1} x - \cos^{-1} y = \cos^{-1} xy$$

$$xy + \sqrt{1-x^2}\,\sqrt{1-y^2} = xy$$

$$(x^2 - 1)(y^2 - 1) = 0$$

Thus, (x, y) lies on $(x^2 - 1)(y^2 - 1) = 0$.

(c) If $a = 1$ and $b = 2$, then

$$\sin^{-1} x + \cos^{-1} y + \cos^{-1} 2xy = \frac{\pi}{2}$$

$$\cos^{-1} x - \cos^{-1} y = \sin^{-1}(2xy)$$

$$xy + \sqrt{1-x^2}\,\sqrt{1-y^2} = 2xy$$

$$x^2 + y^2 = 1$$

Thus, (x, y) lies on circle.

(d) If $a = 2$ and $b = 2$, then

$$\sin^{-1}(2x) + \cos^{-1}(y) + \cos^{-1}(2xy) = \frac{\pi}{2}$$

$$2xy + \sqrt{1-4x^2}\,\sqrt{1-y^2} = 2xy$$

$$(4x^2 - 1)(y^2 - 1) = 0$$

Thus, (x, y) lies on $(4x^2 - 1)(y^2 - 1) = 0$.

77. Correct Response : (a)-(ii), (b)-(iv), (c)-(iii)

Explanation :

(a) Solve given equation,

$$t = \sum_{i=1}^{\infty} \tan^{-1}\left(\frac{1}{2i^2}\right)$$

$$= \sum_{i=1}^{\infty} \tan^{-1}\left(\frac{2}{4i^2 - 1 + 1}\right)$$

$$= \sum_{i=1}^{\infty}\left[\tan^{-1}(2i+1) - \tan^{-1}(2i-1)\right]$$

$$= [(\tan^{-1} 3 - \tan^{-1} 1) + (\tan^{-1} 5 - \tan^{-1} 3) + ... $$
$$+ (\tan^{-1}(2n+1) - \tan^{-1}(2n-1))]$$

Further simplify :

$$t = \tan^{-1}(2n+1) - \tan^{-1} 1$$

$$= \lim_{n \to \infty} \tan^{-1} \frac{2n}{1 + (2n+1)}$$

$$= \frac{\pi}{4}$$

Therefore, $\tan \frac{\pi}{4} = 1$.

(b) It is given that $\cos \theta_1 = \frac{a}{b+c}$.

$$\frac{1 - \tan^2 \frac{\theta_1}{2}}{1 + \tan^2 \frac{\theta_1}{2}} = \frac{a}{b+c}$$

$$\tan^2 \frac{\theta_1}{2} = \frac{b+c-a}{b+c+a}$$

It is also given that $\cos \theta_3 = \frac{c}{a+b}$.

$$\frac{1 - \tan^2 \frac{\theta_3}{2}}{1 + \tan^2 \frac{\theta_3}{2}} = \frac{c}{a+b}$$

$$\tan^2 \frac{\theta_3}{2} = \frac{b+c-a}{b+c+a}$$

Therefore, the required value is,

$$\tan^2 \frac{\theta_1}{2} + \tan^2 \frac{\theta_3}{2} = \frac{b+c-a}{b+c+a} + \frac{a+b-c}{a+b+c}$$

$$= \frac{2b}{3b}$$

$$= \frac{2}{3}$$

(c) A line through point $(0, 1, 0)$ and perpendicular to plane $x + 2y + 2z = 0$ is,

$$\frac{x-0}{1} = \frac{y-1}{2} = \frac{z-1}{2} = r$$

If foot of perpendicular of straight line $P(r, 2r + 1, 2r)$, then

$$r \times 1 + (2r + 1)2 + 2 \times 2r = 0$$
$$r + 4r + 2 + 4r = 0$$
$$r = -\frac{2}{9}$$

So, $P\left(-\frac{2}{9}, \frac{5}{9}, -\frac{4}{9}\right)$.

The required perpendicular distance is,

$$\sqrt{\frac{4 + 25 + 16}{81}} = \frac{\sqrt{5}}{3} \text{ units}$$

78. Correct Response : (c)

Explanation :

The area of isosceles triangle is,

$$\Delta = \frac{\sqrt{3}}{4} b^2 \qquad \text{...(i)}$$

According to sine rule in a triangle,

$$\frac{\sin 120^\circ}{a} = \frac{\sin 30^\circ}{b}$$
$$a = \sqrt{3}\, b$$

The semi-perimeter of triangle is $s = \frac{1}{2}(a + 2b)$

and also the area is,

$$\Delta = \sqrt{3}\, s$$
$$\Delta = \frac{\sqrt{3}}{2}(a + 2b) \qquad \text{...(ii)}$$

Solve equation (i) and (ii) to find the area of triangle.

$$\Delta = (12 + 7\sqrt{3}) \text{ sq. units}$$

79. Correct Response : (b)

Explanation :

It is given that θ lies in the interval $\left(0, \frac{\pi}{4}\right)$. So,

$\tan \theta < 1$ and $\cot \theta > 1$.

If λ_1 and λ_2 are small and positive, then assume $\tan \theta = 1 - \lambda_1$ and $\cot \theta = 1 + \lambda_2$.

$$t_1 = (1 - \lambda_1)^{1 - \lambda_1}$$
$$t_2 = (1 - \lambda_1)^{1 + \lambda_2}$$
$$t_3 = (1 + \lambda_2)^{1 - \lambda_1}$$
$$t_4 = (1 + \lambda_2)^{1 + \lambda_2}$$

Therefore, $t_4 > t_3 > t_1 > t_2$.

80. Correct Response : (b)

Explanation :

In ΔABC, a, b, c are lengths of its sides and A, B, C are angles.

$$\Rightarrow \qquad \frac{b - c}{a} = \frac{\sin B - \sin C}{\sin A}$$

$$= \frac{2 \sin \dfrac{B - C}{2} \cos \dfrac{B + C}{2}}{2 \sin \dfrac{A}{2} \cos \dfrac{A}{2}}$$

$$= \frac{\sin \dfrac{B - C}{2}}{\cos \dfrac{A}{2}}$$

$$(b - c) \cos \frac{A}{2} = a \sin\left(\frac{B - C}{2}\right)$$

81. Correct Response : (d)

Explanation :

Let, sides of triangle be x, $\sqrt{3}\, x$ and $2x$.

$$a^2 + b^2 = x^2 + (\sqrt{3}\, x)^2$$
$$= x^2 + 3x^2$$
$$= 4x^2$$
$$= c^2$$

So, $\angle C = 90^\circ$.

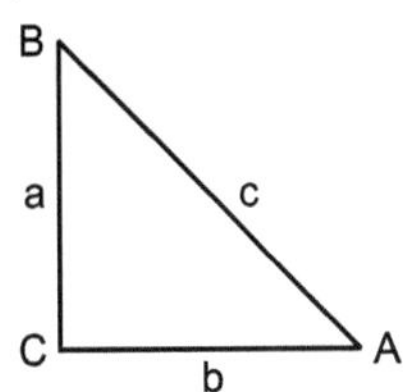

In ΔABC,

$$\tan A = \frac{1}{\sqrt{3}}$$
$$A = 30^\circ$$

So, $\angle B = 60^\circ$. The ratio of angles is,

$$A : B : C = 1 : 2 : 3$$

82. Correct Response : (b)

Explanation :

Solve for θ.

$$\sin \theta = \frac{1}{2}$$
$$\theta = \frac{\pi}{6}$$

Solve for ϕ.

$$\cos \phi = \frac{1}{3}$$
$$\frac{\pi}{3} < \phi < \frac{\pi}{2}$$

Therefore, $\theta + \phi \in \left(\dfrac{\pi}{2}, \dfrac{2\pi}{3}\right]$.

83. Correct Response : (d)

Explanation :

Solve the given equation.

$$\sin(\cot^{-1}(1+x)) = \cos(\tan^{-1} x)$$

$$\sin\left(\sin^{-1}\frac{1}{\sqrt{1+(1+x)^2}}\right) = \cos\left(\cos^{-1}\frac{1}{\sqrt{1+x^2}}\right)$$

$$\frac{1}{\sqrt{1+(1+x)^2}} = \frac{1}{\sqrt{1+x^2}}$$

Square both sides of above equation and solve.

$$1 + x^2 = 1 + x^2 + 2x + 1$$

$$x = -\frac{1}{2}.$$

84. Correct Response : (d)

Explanation :

Sine rule for a triangle is,

$$\frac{a}{\sin A} = \frac{b}{\sin B} = \frac{c}{\sin C} = 2R$$

An acutlangle triangle is possible with conditions given in A, B and C.

Therefore, a triangle is not possible with a, sin A and R.

●●

Mathematical Reasoning

QUESTIONS

1. Let A, B, C and D be four non-empty sets. The contrapositive statement of 'If $A \subseteq B$ and $B \subseteq D$, then $A \subseteq C$' is : **[2020, Main]**
   (a) If $A \subseteq C$, then $B \subset A$ or $D \subset B$
   (b) If $A \nsubseteq C$, then $A \nsubseteq B$ or $B \nsubseteq D$
   (c) If $A \nsubseteq C$, then $A \subseteq B$ and $B \subseteq D$
   (d) If $A \nsubseteq C$, then $A \nsubseteq B$ and $B \subseteq D$

2. Which of the following statements is a tautology ? **[2020, Main]**
   (a) $\sim p(\vee \sim q) \to p \vee q$
   (b) $\sim p(\wedge \sim q) \to p \vee q$
   (c) $\sim p(\vee \sim q) \to p \wedge q$
   (d) $p(\vee \sim q) \to p \wedge q$ **[2020, Mains]**

3. Negation of the statement : **[2020, Main]**
   $\sqrt{5}$ is an integer or 5 is irrational is :

   (a) $\sqrt{5}$ is irrational or 5 is an integer.

   (b) $\sqrt{5}$ is not an integer and 5 is not irrational.

   (c) $\sqrt{5}$ is an integer and 5 is irrational.

   (d) $\sqrt{5}$ is not an integer or 5 is not irrational.

4. If $p \to (p \wedge \sim q)$ is false, then the truth values of p and q are respectively : **[2020, Main]**
   (a) F, T   (b) T, T
   (c) F, F   (d) T, F

5. Which one of the following is a tautology ? **[2020, Main]**
   (a) $P \wedge (P \vee Q)$
   (b) $P \vee (P \wedge Q)$
   (c) $Q \to (P \wedge (P \to Q))$
   (d) $(P \wedge (P \to Q)) \to Q$

6. The logical statement $(p \Rightarrow q) \wedge q (\Rightarrow \sim p)$ is equivalent to : **[2020, Main]**
   (a) p   (b) q
   (c) ~p   (d) ~q

7. Which one of the following Boolean expressions is a tautology ? **[2019, Mains]**
   (a) $(p \wedge q) \vee (p \wedge \sim q)$ (b) $(p \vee q) \vee (p \vee \sim q)$
   (c) $(p \vee q) \wedge (p \vee \sim q)$ (d) $(p \vee q) \wedge (\sim p \vee \sim q)$

8. The negation of the Boolean expression $\sim s \vee (\sim r \vee s)$ is equivalent to : **[2019, Mains]**
   (a) $\sim s \wedge \sim r$ (b) r
   (c) $s \vee r$ (d) $s \wedge r$

9. If $p \Rightarrow (q \vee r)$ is false, then the truth values of p, q, r are respectively : **[2019, Mains]**
   (a) F, T, T   (b) T, F, F
   (c) T, T, F   (d) F, F, F

10. For any two statements p and q, the negation of the expression $p \vee (\sim p \wedge q)$ is : **[2019, Mains]**
    (a) $\sim p \wedge \sim q$ (b) $p \wedge q$
    (c) $p \leftrightarrow q$ (d) $\sim p \vee \sim q$

11. The contrapositive of the statement "If you are born in India, then you are a citizen of India", is : **[2019, Mains]**
    (a) If you are not a citizen of India, then you are not born in India.
    (b) If you are a citizen of India, then you are born in India.
    (c) If you are born in India, then you are not a citizen of India.
    (d) If you are not born in India, then you are not a citizen of India.

12. Which one of the following statements is not a tautology ? **[2019, Mains]**
    (a) $(p \vee q) \to (p \vee (\sim q))$ (b) $(p \wedge q) \to (\sim p) \vee q$
    (c) $p \to (p \vee q)$ (d) $(p \wedge q) \to p$

13. if the truth value of the statement $p \to (\sim q \vee r)$ is false (F), then the truth values of the statements p, q, r are respectively : **[2019, Mains]**
    (a) T, T, F   (b) T, F, F
    (c) T, F, T   (d) F, T, T

14. The Boolean expression $\sim (p \Rightarrow (\sim q))$ is equivalent to : **[2019, Mains]**
    (a) $p \wedge q$ (b) $q \Rightarrow \sim p$
    (c) $p \vee q$ (d) $(\sim p) \Rightarrow q$

15. Five persons A, B, C, D and E are seated in a circular arrangement. If each of them is given a hat of one of the three colours, red blue and green, then the number, of ways of distributing the hats such that the persons seated in adjacent seats get different coloured hats is
    [2019, Advanced]

16. Consider the following two statements :
    P : If 7 is an odd number, then 7 is divisible by 2.

Q : If 7 is a prime number, then 7 is an odd number.

If V_1 is the truth value of the contrapositive of P and V_2 is the truth value of contrapositive of Q, then the ordered pair (V_1, V_2) equals :

[2019, Mains]

(a) (T, T) (b) (T, F)

(c) (F, T) (d) (F, F)

17. Let p, q, r denote arbitrary statements. Then the logically equivalent of the statement $p \Rightarrow (q \vee r)$ is : **[2019, Mains]**

(a) $(p \vee q) \Rightarrow r$ (b) $(p \Rightarrow q) \vee (p \Rightarrow r)$

(c) $(p \Rightarrow \sim q) \wedge (p \Rightarrow r)$ (d) $(p \Rightarrow q) \wedge (p \Rightarrow \sim r)$

18. If $p \rightarrow (\sim p \vee \sim q)$ is false, then the truth values of p and q are respectively : **[2018, Mains]**

(a) F, F (b) T, F

(c) F, T (d) T, T

19. If $(p \wedge \sim q) \wedge (p \wedge r) \rightarrow \sim p \vee q$ is false, then the truth values of p, q and r are, respectively :

[2018, Mains]

(a) F, T, F (b) T, F, T

(c) T, T, T (d) F, F, F

20. The Boolean expression $\sim (p \vee q) \vee (\sim p \wedge q)$ is equivalent to : **[2018, Mains]**

(a) $\sim p$ (b) p

(c) q (d) $\sim q$

21. Contrapositive of the statement, "If two numbers are not equal, then their squares are not equal", is : **[2018, Mains]**

(a) If the squares of two numbers are equal, then the numbers are equal.

(b) If the squares of two numbers are equal, then the numbers are not equal.

(c) If the squares of two numbers are not equal, then the number are not equal.

(d) If the squares of two numbers are not equal, then the numbers are equal.

22. The contrapositive of the following statement, "If the side of a square doubles, then its area increases four times", is : **[2018, Mains]**

(a) If the side of a square is not doubled, then its area does not increase four times.

(b) If the area of a square increases four times, then its side is doubled.

(c) If the area of a square increases four times, then its side is not doubled.

(d) If the area of a square does not increase four times, then its side is not doubled.

23. The following statement $(p \rightarrow q) \rightarrow p[(\sim p \rightarrow q) \rightarrow q]$ is : **[2017, Mains]**

(a) equivalent to $\sim p \rightarrow q$

(b) equivalent to $p \rightarrow \sim q$

(c) a fallacy

(d) a tautolgy

24. The Boolean Expression $(p \wedge \sim q) \vee q \vee (\sim p \wedge q)$ is equivalent to : **[2015, Mains]**

(a) $\sim p \wedge q$ (b) $p \wedge q$

(c) $p \vee q$ (d) $p \vee \sim q$

25. Consider the following statements :

P : Suman is brilliant.

Q : Suman is rich.

R : Suman is honest.

The negation of the statement. **[2015, Mains]**

"Suman is brilliant and dishonest if and only if Suman is rich", can be equivalently expressed as :

(a) $\sim Q \leftrightarrow \sim P \wedge R$ (b) $\sim Q \leftrightarrow \sim P \vee R$

(c) $\sim Q \leftrightarrow P \vee \sim R$ (d) $\sim Q \leftrightarrow P \wedge \sim R$

26. The negation of $\sim s \vee (\sim r \wedge s)$ is equivalent to : **[2014, Mains]**

(a) $s \wedge \sim r$ (b) $s \wedge (r \wedge \sim s)$

(c) $s \vee (r \vee \sim s)$ (d) $s \wedge r$

27. The contrapositive of the statement "I go to school if it does not rain" is : **[2014, Mains]**

(a) If it rains, I do not go the school

(b) If I do not to the school, it rains

(c) I it rains, I go to school

(d) If I go to school, it rains.

28. The contrapositive of the statement "if I am not feeling will, then I will go to the doctor" is : **[2014, Mains]**

(a) If I am feeling well, then I will not go to the doctor

(b) If I will to the doctor, then I am feeling well

(c) If I will not go to the doctor, then I am feeling well

(d) If I will go to the doctor, then I am not feeling well.

29. The proposition $\sim (p \vee \sim q) \vee \sim (p \vee q)$ is logically equivalent to : **[2014, Mains]**

(a) p (b) q

(c) $\sim p$ (d) $\sim q$

30. X and Y are two sets and $f : X \rightarrow Y$. If $\{f(c) = y ; c \subset X, y \subset Y\}$ and $\{f^{-1}(d) = x; d \subset Y, x \subset X\}$, then the true statement is : **[2005, Mains]**

(a) $f(f^{-1}(b)) = b$ (b) $f^{-1}(f(a)) = a$

(c) $f(f^{-1}(b)) = b, b \subset y$ (d) $f^{-1}(f(a)) = a, a \subset x$

ANSWER KEY

1. (b)	**2.** (a)	**3.** (b)	**4.** (b)	**5.** (d)	**6.** (c)	**7.** (b)	**8.** (b)	**9.** (b)	**10.** (a)
11. (a)	**12.** (a)	**13.** (a)	**14.** (a)	**15.** (30.00)	**16.** (c)	**17.** (b)	**18.** (d)	**19.** (b)	**20.** (a)
21. (a)	**22.** (d)	**23.** (d)	**24.** (c)	**25.** (d)	**26.** (d)	**27.** (b)	**28.** (c)	**29.** (c)	**30.** (d)

ANSWERS WITH EXPLANATIONS

1. Correct Response : (b)

Explanation :

Contrapositive of $p \to q$ is $\sim q \to \sim q$

$$\sim(A \subseteq B) \wedge (B \subseteq D) \to (A \subseteq C)$$

Contrapositive is

$$\sim (A \subseteq C) \to \sim (A \subseteq B) \vee \sim (B \subseteq D)$$
$$A \not\subseteq C \to (A \not\subseteq B) \vee (B \not\subseteq D)$$

2. Correct Response : (a)

Explanation :

$$\sim (p \vee \sim q) \to p \vee q$$
$$\sim (p \vee \sim q) \to p \vee q$$
$$\sim \{(\sim p \wedge q) \wedge (\sim p \wedge \sim q)\}$$
$$\sim (\sim p \wedge f)$$

3. Correct Response : (b)

Explanation :

$$p = \sqrt{5} \text{ is an integer.}$$
$$q \vee p : 5 \text{ is irrational}$$
$$\sim (p \vee q) \equiv \sim p \wedge \sim q$$
$$= \sqrt{5} \text{ is not an integer and } 5$$
$$\text{is not irrational}$$

4. Correct Response : (b)

Explanation :

$p \to (p \wedge \sim q)$ is F $\Rightarrow q$ is T and $p \wedge \sim q$ is F $\Rightarrow q$ is T'

$\therefore p$ is T, q is T

5. Correct Response : (d)

Explanation :

(1) $P \wedge (P \vee Q) \equiv P$

(2) $P \vee (P \wedge Q) \equiv P$

(3) $Q \to (P \wedge (P \to Q))$

$\equiv Q \to (P \wedge (\sim P \vee Q)) \equiv Q \to (P \wedge Q)$

$\equiv (\sim Q) \vee (P \wedge Q) \equiv (P \wedge (\sim Q))$

(4) $(P \wedge (P \to Q)) \to Q$

$\equiv (P \wedge (\sim P \vee Q)) \to Q \equiv (P \wedge Q) \to Q$

$\equiv ((\sim P) \vee (\sim Q)) \vee Q \equiv (\sim P) \wedge t \equiv t$

6. Correct Response : (c)

Explanation :

$$(p \to q) \wedge (q \to \sim p)$$
$$\equiv (\sim p \vee q) \wedge (\sim q \vee \sim p)$$
$$\equiv \sim p \vee (q \wedge \sim q)$$
$$\equiv \sim p \vee C \equiv \sim p$$

7. Correct Response : (b)

Explanation :

(a) $(p \vee q) \wedge (p \vee \sim q) = p \vee (q \wedge \sim q)$
$$= p \wedge t$$
$$= p$$

(b) $(p \vee q) \wedge (\sim p \vee \sim q)$

p	q	$\sim p$	$\sim q$	$p \vee q$	$\sim p \vee \sim q$	$(p \vee q) \vee (p \wedge \sim q)$
T	T	F	F	T	F	F
T	F	F	T	T	T	T
F	T	T	F	T	T	T
F	F	T	T	F	T	F

(c) $(p \wedge q) \vee (p \wedge \sim q) = p \wedge (q \vee \sim q)$
$$= p \wedge t$$
$$= p$$

(d) $(p \vee q) \vee (p \vee \sim q) = p \vee (q \vee \sim q)$
$$= p \vee t$$
$$= t$$

8. Correct Response : (b)

Explanation :

$- s \vee (- r \wedge s)$

$\equiv (\sim s \vee \sim r) \wedge (\sim s \vee s)$

$\equiv (\sim s \vee \sim r) \wedge t$

$\equiv \sim s \vee \sim r$

$\equiv \sim (s \wedge r)$

So, the negation of $\sim s \vee (\sim r \wedge s)$ is $s \wedge r$.

9. Correct Response : (b)

Explanation :

For $p \Rightarrow \vee r$ to

r should be F and $p \Rightarrow q$ should be F.

For $p \Rightarrow q$ to be F,
$$p \Rightarrow T$$

and
$$q \Rightarrow F$$
$$p, q, r \Rightarrow F$$

10. Correct Response : (a)

Explanation :

$$p \vee (\sim p \wedge q) = (p \vee \sim p) \wedge (p \vee q)$$
$$= p \vee q$$

Hence, $\sim (p \vee q) = (\sim p \wedge \sim q)$

11. Correct Response : (a)

Explanation :

Contrapositive of $p \Rightarrow q$ is $\sim q \Rightarrow \sim p$. Hence, the answer is "If you are not a citizen of India, then you are not born in India."

12. Correct Response : (b)

Explanation :

$(p \vee q) \to p$

$$= \sim (p \wedge q) \vee p$$
$$= (\sim p \vee \sim q) \vee p$$
$$= (\sim p \vee p) \vee \sim q$$
$$= t \vee \sim q$$
$$= t$$

$p \to (p \vee q)$

$$= \sim p \vee (p \vee q)$$
$$= t \vee q$$
$$= t$$

$(p \wedge q) \to (\sim p) \vee q$

$$= \sim (p \wedge q) \vee (\sim p \wedge q)$$
$$= \sim p \vee \sim q \vee \sim p \vee q$$
$$= \sim p \vee t$$
$$= t$$

$\therefore$ Option (b) is correct.

13. Correct Response : (a)

Explanation :

The value is given by,

$p \to (\sim q \vee r)$

$$\equiv \sim p \wedge (\sim q \vee r)$$
$$\equiv (\sim p \vee \sim q) \vee r$$
$$\equiv \sim (p \vee q) \vee r$$

The required table is,

p	q	r	$(p \wedge q) \vee r$
T	T	T	T
T	T	F	F
T	F	T	T
T	F	F	T
F	T	T	T
F	T	F	T
F	F	T	T
F	F	F	T

14. Correct Response : (a)

Explanation :

The given Boolean expression is given by,

$$\sim (p \Rightarrow (\sim q))$$
$$\Rightarrow \sim (p \to \sim q)$$
$$\Rightarrow \sim (p \vee \sim q)$$
$$\Rightarrow p \wedge q$$

15. Correct Response : 30.00

Explanation :

Maximum number of hats used of same colour are 2. They cannot be 3 otherwise atleast 2 hats of same colour are consecutive.

Consider red hats to be R, blue hats to be B and green hats to be G.

The hats can be selected in three different ways such as,

R, R, G, G, B or R, G, G, B, B or R, R, G, B, B.

Consider blue hat goes to person A.

The required diagram is shown in figure below.

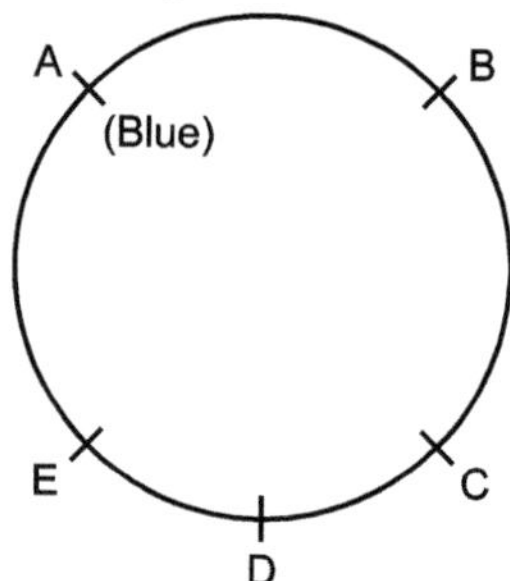

Now, either position B and D are filled by green hats and C and E are filled by red hats or B and D are filled by red hats and C and E are filled by green hats (2 ways are possible).

Hence, total number of ways are,

$$N = 3 \times 5 \times 2$$
$$= 30.$$

16. Correct Response : (c)

Explanation :

For the statement P,

Contrad positive of P is,

"If 7 is not divisible by 2, then it is not an odd number."

If is false.

For the statement Q,

Contrapositive of Q is,

"If 7 is not an odd number, then 7 is not a prime number".

It is true.

Hence, the ordered pair of the $(V_1, V_2) \equiv (F, T)$.

17. Correct Response : (b)

Explanation :

Solve the given statement as,

$$p \Rightarrow (q \vee r)$$
$$\sim p \vee (q \vee r)$$
$$(\sim p \vee q) \vee (\sim p \vee r)$$
$$(p \Rightarrow q) \vee (p \Rightarrow r)$$

18. Correct Response : (d)

Explanation :

The proposition of $(\sim p) \vee (p \wedge \sim q)$ is equivalent to :

p	q	$\sim$p	$\sim$q	p $\wedge \sim$ q	$(\sim$ p$) \vee (p \wedge \sim$ q$)$
T	T	F	F	F	F
T	F	F	T	T	T
F	T	T	F	F	F
F	F	T	T	F	F

Which is same as $p \to \sim q$.

19. Correct Response : (b)

The given condition is false,

$$(p \wedge \sim q) \wedge (p \wedge r) \to \sim p \vee q$$

(1)

$$(T \wedge F) \wedge (T \wedge T) \to (F \vee T)$$
$$\equiv (F \wedge T) \to T$$
$$\equiv F \to T \equiv T$$

(2)

$$(T \wedge T) \wedge (T \wedge T) \to (F \vee F)$$
$$T \to F \equiv F$$

(3)

$$(F \wedge T) \wedge (F \wedge F) \to (T \vee F)$$
$$(F \wedge F) \to T$$
$$F \to T \equiv T$$

20. Correct Response : (a)

Explanation :

Apply the truth table method for the simplify the Boolean expression,

p	q	$\sim p$	$(p \vee q)$	$\sim (p \vee q)$	$(\sim p \wedge q)$	$\sim (p \vee q) \vee (\sim p \wedge q)$
T	F	F	T	F	F	F
T	T	F	T	F	F	F
F	T	T	T	F	T	T
F	F	T	F	T	F	T

Thus, the Boolean expression is,

$$\sim (p \vee q) \vee (\sim p \wedge q) = \sim p.$$

21. Correct Response : (a)

Explanation :

It the statement p implies q,

$$p \to q$$

Then, the contrapositive statement is,

$$\sim q \to p$$

The contrapositive of the statement "If two numbers are not equal, then their squares are not equal" is "If the squares of two numbers are equal, then the numbers are equal."

Hence, the statement (a) from the options is correct.

23. Correct Response : (d)

Explanation :

Let the side of a square doubles is represents as p and area of square increases four time is represents as q. Then the contrapositive of $p \to q$ is $\sim q \to \sim p$.

Thus, the correct option is (d).

22. Correct Response : (d)

Explanation :

The truth table of the given expression is given below,

p	q	$p \to p$	$(\sim p \to q)$	$(\sim p \to q) \to q$	$(p \to q) \to \left[(\sim p \to q) \to q \right]$
T	T	T	T	T	T
T	F	F	T	F	T
F	T	T	T	T	T
F	F	T	F	T	T

Hence it is a tautology.

24. Correct Response : (c)

Explanation :

The given Boolean expression is,

$$(p \wedge \sim q) \vee q \vee (\sim p \wedge q)$$

Simplify the expression,

$$= \{(p \vee q) \wedge (\sim q \vee p)\} \vee (\sim p \wedge q)$$
$$[\because (p \vee \sim q) = (p \vee q) \wedge (\sim q \vee p)]$$
$$= \{(p \vee q) \wedge T\} \vee (\sim p \wedge q) [\because (\sim q \vee p) = T]$$
$$= (p \vee q) \vee (\sim p \wedge q)$$
$$= \{(p \vee q) \vee \sim p\} \wedge (p \vee q \vee q)$$

Further, simplify the above expression,

$$\{(p \vee q) \vee \sim p\} \vee (p \vee q \vee q) = T \wedge (p \vee q)$$
$$= (p \vee q)$$

25. Correct Response : (d)

Explanation :

Given statement is equivalent to,

$$(P \wedge \sim R) \leftrightarrow Q$$

This is same as,

$$Q \leftrightarrow (P \wedge \sim R)$$

Negation of the above statement is,

$$\sim Q \leftrightarrow P \wedge \sim R$$

26. Correct Response : (d)

Explanation :

The negation is,

$$\sim s \vee (\sim r \wedge s) = \sim (\sim s) \wedge \sim (\sim r \wedge s)$$
$$= s \wedge (r \vee \sim s)$$
$$= (s \wedge r) \vee (s \wedge \sim s)$$
$$= s \wedge r$$

27. Correct Response : (b)

Explanation :

Consider, p is equal to the statement, "if it does not rain"

And, q is equal to the statment "I go to school"

According to the contrapositive law,

$$p \rightarrow q = \sim q \rightarrow \sim p$$

Thus, Negation of $p(\sim p)$ is "its rains".

And $\sim q$ is "if I do not go to school".

Hence, $\sim q \rightarrow \sim p$ is "If I do not go to school, it rains."

28. Correct Response : (c)

Explanation :

Let p is I am not felling well.

And q is I will go to doctor.

The given statement is,

$$p \rightarrow q$$

The contrapositive of the statement is

$$\sim q \rightarrow \sim p$$

That is, "If I will not go to doctor then I am feeling well."

29. Correct Response : (c)

Explanation :

The proposition table as shown below :

P	q	$\sim$ q	p $\vee$ ($\sim$ q)	p $\vee$ q	$\sim$ (p $\vee$ $\sim$ q)	$\sim$ (p $\vee$ q)	A $\vee$ B
T	T	F	T	T	F	F	F
F	F	T	T	F	F	T	T
T	F	T	T	T	F	F	F
F	T	F	F	T	T	F	T

From the table, it is clear that the proposition $\sim$ (p $\vee$ $\sim$ q) $\vee$ $\sim$ (p $\vee$ q) is logically equivalent to $\sim$ p.

30. Correct Response : (d)

Explanation :

According to given data figure is shown below.

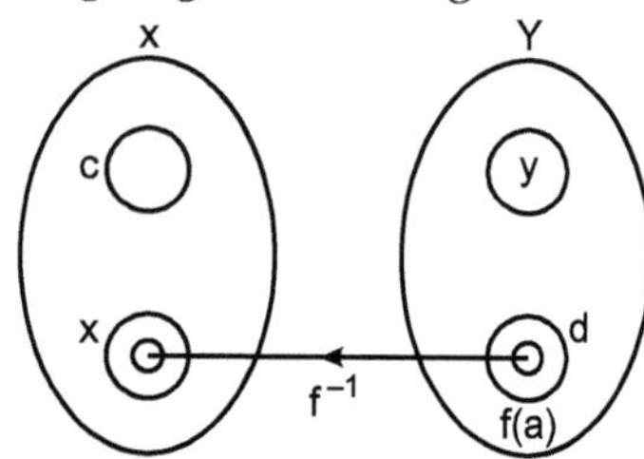

It is given that $f^{-1}(d) = x$.

$$f(x) = d$$

If $a \subset x, f(a) \subset d$, then

$$f^{-1}(f(a)) = a$$